Marketing

CONCEPTS AND STRATEGIES

SEVENTH EDITION

SALLY DIBB Open University Business School, The Open University

LYNDON SIMKIN Faculty of Business and Law, Coventry University

WILLIAM M. PRIDE Mays Business School, Texas A&M University

O.C. FERRELL Jack. C. Massey College of Business, Belmont University

CENGAGE
Learning

Australia • Brazil • ... • ... • United States

Marketing: Concepts and Strategies, 7th Edition
Sally Dibb, Lyndon Simkin, William M. Pride and O.C. Ferrell

Commissioning Editor: Jennifer Grene

Editorial Assistant: Lauren Cartridge

Marketing Manager: Amanda Cheung

Project Manager: Phillipa Davidson-Blake

Compositor: MPS Limited

For product information and technology assistance,
contact **emea.info@cengage.com.**

For permission to use material from this text or product,
and for permission queries,
email **emea.permissions@cengage.com.**

British Library Cataloguing-in-Publication Data
A catalogue record for this book is available from the British Library.

ISBN: 978-1-4737-2512-6

Cengage Learning EMEA
Cheriton House, North Way, Andover, Hampshire, SP10 5BE
United Kingdom

Cengage Learning products are represented in Canada by Nelson Education Ltd.
For your lifelong learning solutions, visit **www.cengage.co.uk**

Purchase your next print book, e-book or e-chapter at **www.cengagebrain.com**

Printed in China by RR Donnelley
Print Number: 01   Print Year: 2016

For Rosa, Samantha, Mae, Abby, James and Becky

Brief contents

Contents

NOTE Each chapter contains a Summary, Key links, a list of Important terms, Discussion and review questions, Recommended readings, an Internet exercise, Group tasks and an Applied mini-case.

Preface

The traditional view of marketing is of a team of managers inside an organization responsible for surveying customers, communicating the brand, managing advertising and developing campaigns. Perhaps this rather constrained remit was true many decades ago and certainly there are still organizations yet to recognize its full potential, but the reality is that marketing is responsible for so much more:

- Understanding markets, developing market insights and being the 'eyes and ears' for an organization, in terms of identifying threats and new business opportunities, tracking competition and staying on top of changing customer expectations.

- Shaping an organization's strategy in terms of the selection of which opportunities to pursue, product portfolios to sustain, target market decisions and competitive positioning.

- Managing brands and creating compelling product value propositions intended to excite customers, attract new ones, retain those already buying from the organization and to make life awkward for competitors.

- Managing customers' experience in order to maximise revenue, retain lucrative customers and combat competitors' actions.

Campaigns, advertising, brand strategy and marketing research are indeed part of the remit for Marketing, but there is so much more required for marketers to understand as they add value to their organizations.

The associated set of necessary capabilities is extensive, including market insight and analytics, strategic thinking and planning, creativity and programme development, project execution and performance evaluation. All occurring in hugely dynamic environments, in which market conditions are always evolving, strategies must be re-thought so as to remain pertinent, and marketing programmes kept fresh and relevant to these challenges. Here lies the excitement for most marketers, who relish this challenging and ever-changing life.

Marketing: Concepts and Strategies explores the scope and activities of marketing, providing the frameworks and toolkit required for marketers to deliver benefits for their organizations.

Whether for products or services; in consumer, business-to-business or public sector markets; for profit or non-profit making, the marketing function is a major part of an organization's overall resourcing and is responsible for a huge array of outputs. There is much more involved than merely surveying, developing a brand strapline and creating a new advertising campaign, as depicted in TV's 1960s-set *Mad Men*.

Marketing affects everyone. We are all consumers. Most businesses depend on marketing to provide an understanding of the marketplace, to identify opportunities, and to ensure that their products and services satisfy the needs of customers and that they are competing effectively. There is little doubt that marketing is an important part of today's society and commerce. Marketing matters! Therefore, it is important that marketers are well trained and are equipped with the skills required.

The first edition of *Marketing: Concepts and Strategies* appeared in 1991, just after Sally and Lyndon joined the fast-growing Warwick Business School and were introduced to American co-authors Bill Pride and 'OC' Ferrell. Since then, this text has become the leader in its market. Whether for undergraduates seeking a comprehensive introduction to marketing, MBAs requiring a grounding in marketing analysis or marketing management, or students in colleges wishing to pass degrees and CIM diplomas, *Marketing: Concepts and Strategies* is used by lecturers and teaching staff to provide an accessible, topical and enlightening insight into the world of marketing. *Marketing: Concepts and Strategies* is also recommended by the Chartered Institute of Marketing.

This edition has been totally revised to reflect the current core themes of marketing in terms of academic content, but also – given the authors' wide-ranging consultancy and research experience outside of the lecture theatre – from a practitioner's perspective. In particular, the world for marketers has gone digital, consumers communicate readily with each other via social media; marketing has become more aligned to ethical, responsible and sustainability issues; and Marketing as an academic discipline has become more critical and reflective – all of which are developments underpinning this new edition. These developments have steered this re-write of *Marketing: Concepts and Strategies*.

As ever, *Marketing: Concepts and Strategies* is supported by comprehensive indexing, a full glossary of important terms appearing in the margins of the relevant chapters and cross-referenced in the subject index, questions for discussion and full listing of the key terms and jargon detailed chapter-by-chapter.

The running order of *Marketing: Concepts and Strategies*, Seventh edition

PART ONE   **Marketing defined and marketing in context** – An introduction to the nature and scope of marketing and the marketing process, marketing strategy and competitive forces, the composition of the marketing environment and the importance of global marketing.

PART TWO   **Understanding and targeting customers** – Consumer and business-to-business buying behaviour, target marketing and brand positioning, customer relationship management and marketing research.

PART THREE   **Marketing programmes** – Products and services, brands, place and channels, promotion and marketing communications, digital and pricing in consumer, business and non-profit markets.

PART FOUR   **Marketing management** – Marketing planning and sales forecasting; implementing strategies, internal marketing relationships and measuring performance; ethics, and social responsibility in modern marketing, and social marketing applications.

Acknowledgements

This text would not have happened without the support and encouragement of American co-authors Bill Pride and O.C. Ferrell; the team at Cengage Learning; the comments and enthusiasm from fellow marketing lecturers at Warwick Business School, the Open University, Oxford Brookes, Henley Business School and Coventry University; colleagues in the Academy of Marketing; and, above all, the feedback from our students past and present.

Sally Dibb and Lyndon Simkin
Kenilworth, 2016

About the authors

Sally Dibb and Lyndon Simkin each spent around 20 years at the leading UK university management centre, Warwick Business School, teaching undergraduates, MBAs and executives the basics of marketing, advanced strategic marketing, marketing management, buyer behaviour, marketing communications and marketing research. Sally then moved to head up Marketing and Research at the innovative Open University Business School as Professor of Marketing, where she also established and co-directs the *Institute for Social Marketing*. Lyndon left Warwick to join fast-moving Oxford Brookes Business School as Professor of Strategic Marketing and Research Lead, before joining Henley Business School and recently Coventry University as Executive Director of the *Centre for Business in Society* and Professor of Strategic Marketing.

Sally and Lyndon's research focuses on market segmentation, marketing planning, social marketing applications, marketing strategy operationalization and teaching methods, in which areas they have published extensively in the academic journals in the UK and USA. They co-chair the Academy of Marketing's SIG in Market Segmentation and are both Associate Editors of the *Journal of Marketing Management*. Lyndon is a member of the Research Committee of the Academy, while Sally is a trustee of the research charity *Alcohol Research UK*.

In addition to being joint authors of *Marketing: Concepts and Strategies,* they produced the innovative *The Marketing Casebook: Cases and Concepts* (Thomson), mixing real-world cases with overviews of theory, and *The Market Segmentation Workbook* and *The Marketing Planning Workbook* (both published by Thomson), aimed at assisting marketing practitioners to reassess their target markets and understand the complexities of marketing planning. These workbooks were based on their consultancy experiences with organizations as diverse as ABB, Accenture, AstraZeneca, GalaCoral, Calor, EDF Energy, Eon, Ernst & Young, Fujitsu, Geocell, GfK, IKEA, JCB, Lockheed Martin, McDonald's, Nynas, QinetiQ, Raytheon, Royal SunAlliance, Tilda and Willis. Both *Workbooks* have been translated and published in China and Russia. Sally and Lyndon published the revision aid, *Marketing Briefs* (Elsevier Butterworth – Heinemann). While primarily targeted at students preparing for examinations in marketing, *Marketing Briefs* was also ideal for providing time-pressured managers with concise and topical insights into the core concepts and tools of strategic marketing. The acclaimed *Market Segmentation Success: Making It Happen!* was published by Routledge in America. Cengage published the very popular *Marketing Planning* title, aimed at practicing marketers. *Marketing Essentials* is the little sister to *Marketing: Concepts and Strategies*, targeting college courses introducing the subject of marketing. Sally and Lyndon have both also contributed chapters to many books of collected readings. Lyndon has just edited *The Dark Side of CRM* for Routledge and Sally has co-authored *The Private Security State?* for the CBS Press.

Bill Pride and O.C. Ferrell first teamed up to produce *Marketing* for Houghton Mifflin in 1977. Since then, the American sister of *Marketing: Concepts and Strategies,* now in its eighteenth edition, has been used by over two million students and has become one of the principal marketing texts in the USA. OC is the Distinguished Professor of Leadership and Business Ethics at the Jack C. Massey College of Business at Belmont University. He is a former President of the Academic Council for the prestigious American Marketing Association (AMA). He chaired committees that developed the AMA Code of Ethics and the AMA Code of Ethics for Marketing on the Internet. OC is the author of many texts, including *Marketing Strategy* (Dryden), *Business Ethics: Ethical Decision Making and Cases* (Cengage) and *Business: A Changing World* (Irwin/McGraw-Hill). Bill Pride is Professor of Marketing at Texas A&M University where he specializes in marketing communications, strategic marketing planning and business marketing education. Like OC, he has published a large number of journal papers and is widely recognized in the marketing field. Bill is also co-author of *Business* (Cengage).

Credits

PART ONE
Marketing defined and marketing in context

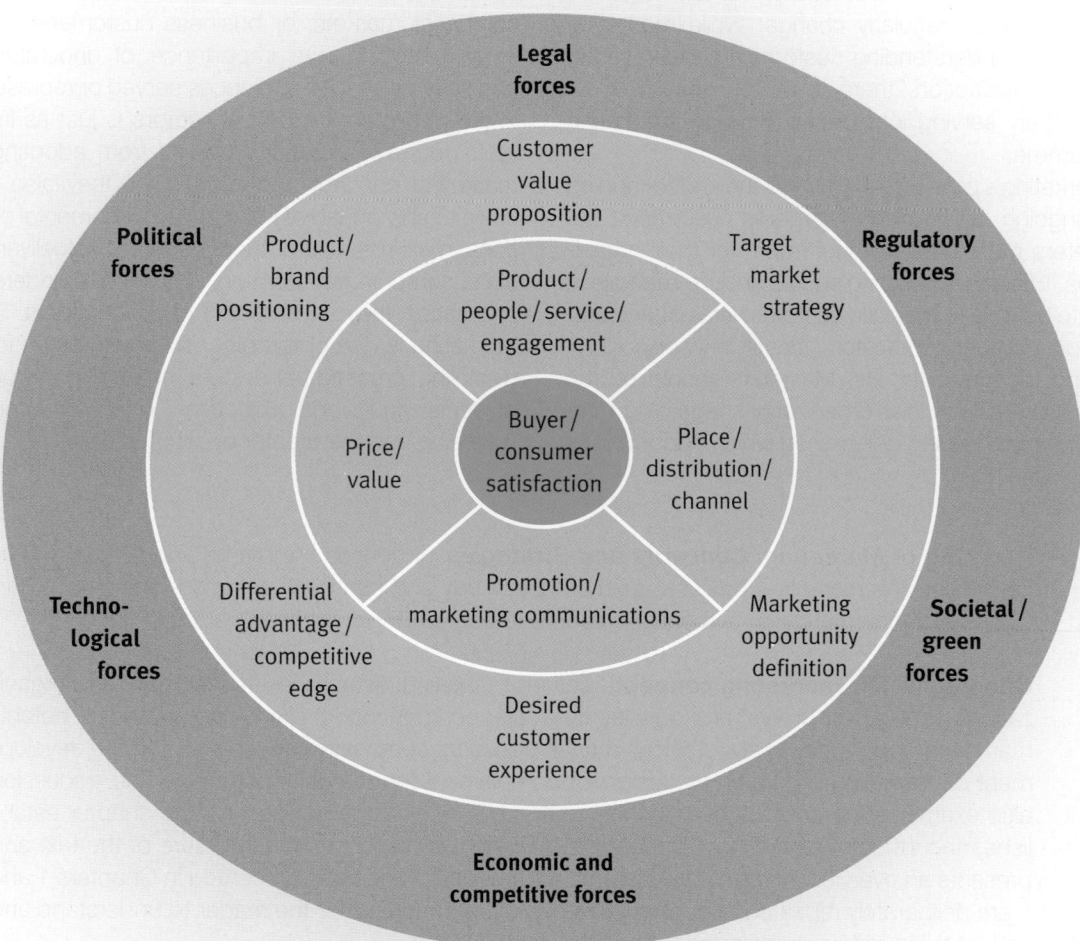

Legal forces

Customer value proposition

Political forces

Product/brand positioning

Product/people/service/engagement

Target market strategy

Regulatory forces

Price/value

Buyer/consumer satisfaction

Place/distribution/channel

Techno-logical forces

Differential advantage/competitive edge

Promotion/marketing communications

Marketing opportunity definition

Societal/green forces

Desired customer experience

Economic and competitive forces

Marketing centres on a set of processes for creating, communicating and delivering value to customers; for managing customer relationships; and for providing direction to an organization based on market insights. Marketing consists of individual and organizational activities that facilitate and expedite satisfying exchange relationships in a dynamic environment through the creation, distribution, promotion and pricing of goods, services and ideas.

The simple premise of marketing is that to be successful, any organization must understand its customers' requirements and satisfy them in a manner that gives the organization an edge over its competitors, and by staying abreast of changing market dynamics it will continue to offer compelling propositions to

Marketing mix
The tactical 'toolkit' of the marketing programme; product, place/distribution, promotion, price and people variables that an organization can control in order to appeal to the target market and facilitate satisfying exchange.

these targeted customers. This involves offering the 'right' **marketing mix** of product, people, service, pricing, promotion and distribution channel. Marketing depends, therefore, on constant updating of ideas and market knowledge. Customers are often surprisingly fickle and modify their needs and wants; rivals alter their strategies; and forces in the marketplace regularly change. While marketing focuses on understanding customers and delivering ongoing satisfaction, there is much more to marketing than serving customers through marketing programmes.

Marketing's core focus is indeed the understanding and ongoing satisfaction of targeted customers, but marketers must provide much more for their organizations. Effective marketing should analyze markets in order to be able to maintain customer interest and satisfaction, combat competitors, identify new opportunities and recognize threats. Marketers should be the 'eyes and ears' for their organizations regarding market dynamics. Having determined which opportunities

to pursue and having agreed the mix of target markets to prioritize, marketing should create target customer engagement strategies, establish the 'wow factor' and ensure there is a robust basis for competing. Marketing programmes should be developed which are appropriate for the successful execution of this strategy. Therefore, marketing as a process and in terms of its activities involves marketing analysis, marketing strategy and marketing management, as explored in *Marketing: Concepts and Strategies*.

The term 'customer' should be treated loosely. While in commercial settings, it means consumers in consumer markets, or business customers in business marketing, the importance of understanding and satisfying those audiences served or represented in the public and voluntary sectors is just as important. Such organizations benefit from adopting the marketing concept and process... they also must strive to stay ahead of changing environmental conditions, maximize use of their resources to deliver their aims, compete for attention, and seek to understand and satisfy their audiences and stakeholders. Social Marketing is one of the biggest growth areas for the discipline, creating behavioural change in the pursuit of social goals and objectives, often for improved wellbeing and the greater good of society.

Part One of *Marketing: Concepts and Strategies* introduces the nature and scope of marketing and the marketing process, marketing strategy and competitive forces. The aim of Part One is to define marketing and enable readers to appreciate its context.

Chapter 1, 'The marketing concept', defines marketing; establishes its importance to organizations and to consumers; and outlines the major components of marketing strategy – notably marketing opportunity analysis, target market selection, competitive advantage and the development of marketing programmes designed to implement the marketing strategy. The discussion also examines the concept of marketing orientation within an organization. The chapter establishes the ethos of *Marketing: Concepts and Strategies,* describes the structure of the text and presents an overview of the marketing process. Important concepts presented in Chapters 1 and 2 are deliberately repeated throughout this book. It is important for the reader to understand and accept them before progressing to the following chapters.

Chapter 2, 'Marketing strategy and understanding competitors', presents an overview of marketing strategy and the strategizing process. This chapter aims to highlight which strategic marketing considerations help to ensure that a product or service is marketed for the benefit of the organization as well as its targeted customers. The product or service should be marketed differently enough from competitors' marketing programmes to provide the organization's product or service with a perceived advantage over these competitors. The chapter first explores what is marketing strategy and the importance of organizational mission, goals and corporate strategy. The discussion next turns to assessing organizational opportunities, capabilities and SWOT (strengths, weaknesses, opportunities, threats) issues, as well as identifying strategic objectives. The chapter addresses the all-important role of identifying market segments, targeting and brand positioning in marketing strategy: the development of clear target market priorities. The chapter then focuses on competitive strategies for marketing: the role of competition, its ramifications for strategy, competitive positions and warfare strategies. The link between marketing objectives and marketing mix programmes is examined, along with implementation and performance monitoring.

Chapter 3, 'The marketing environment', explores the importance to marketers – and organizations – of staying informed by developments and changes around them. These forces of what is known as the 'macro marketing environment' include economic, political, legal, regulatory, societal and technological developments, which inevitably impact on markets, organizations operating in a particular sector, consumers and individual brands. They present opportunities (if observed and addressed) and threats (if unnoticed or ignored) to marketers. An organization's overall strategy must be informed by these forces of the marketing environment. The chapter also explores the concept of environmental scanning and the notion of strategic windows of opportunity. The 'micro marketing environment' consists of competitive forces and rivalry, which tend to have more specific impact on a particular organization or brand. These external competitive forces are also explored in this chapter. Without an appreciation of these forces and how they will impact, it is not possible for the Marketing team to be the eyes and ears for its company, identifying threats and emerging opportunities.

Chapter 4, 'Marketing in international markets', reflects the fact that many organizations and brands trade across national boundaries, requiring additional market insights and some flexibility in terms of marketing strategies and marketing programmes. The marketing environment forces, customer issues, competitor activities and an organization's capabilities differ from country to country and region to region. How marketers should address non-domestic markets is examined in this chapter, including available market entry strategies.

By the conclusion of Part One of *Marketing: Concepts and Strategies,* readers should understand what is meant by the terms *marketing, marketing orientation, marketing strategy* and the *marketing process*, the forces of the *macro and micro marketing environment*, *environmental scanning* and *strategic windows of opportunity*, as well as *international marketing*. The essential themes in Part One are developed further as the text continues.

CHAPTER 1
The marketing concept

"Satisfying and retaining customers better than rivals"

Objectives

To define marketing.

To appreciate the context of marketing and marketing orientation.

To explain the marketing process.

To understand the importance of marketing.

To gain insight into the basic elements of the marketing concept and its implementation.

To understand how the marketing concept has evolved and some of the current 'hot' themes.

To appreciate the major components of a marketing strategy and the marketing mix.

To gain a sense of general strategic marketing issues, such as market opportunity analysis, target market selection and marketing mix development.

To grasp the ethos and structure of this book.

INTRODUCTION

Marketing's primary aim is the identification of target markets and the satisfaction of these customers, now and in the future. In most organizations, marketing fulfils an analytical function, provides strategic direction and executes a set of tactical activities designed to attract and retain the targeted customers to the organization's products or services. Marketers should strive to be the 'radar' or 'eyes and ears' for their organizations in terms of assessing opportunities, identifying threats and preparing their colleagues for the evolving challenges in the marketplace. There is much more to marketing than creating an advertisement, producing an eye-catching price promotion, jazzing up a website or developing a brand.

Organizations with a marketing orientation have more than a few staff engaged in marketing activities. Such organizations have a sound awareness of customers' needs and buying behaviour, competitors' offerings and strategies, and of market trends. They take steps to ensure they know how these market conditions will evolve. In addition, they orientate their operational practices and coordinate the inter-functional thinking of their organization around these market conditions. Leadership teams have a desire for market insights and to align their thinking around developments in their markets.

Effective marketing involves an analytical process combining marketing analysis, strategizing and the creation of marketing programmes designed to implement a designated marketing strategy. Marketing opportunity analysis is a pivotal part of marketing, involving the determination of emerging and existing market opportunities and the choice of which to address. At the heart of a marketing strategy is the formation of a target market strategy and a basis for competing in order to focus on the opportunities prioritized by the organization.

Most members of the general public think of 'advertising', 'marketing research' or 'sales persuasion' when the term 'marketing' is mentioned. These brief introductory comments explain that there is in fact much more to marketing. This first chapter of *Marketing: Concepts and Strategies* is designed to define marketing and explain its role.

Attention-getting marketing for condoms

A major aim for marketers is to create awareness of their products among their targeted audiences, often through advertising and other forms of marketing communications. Not too long ago, advertisements were rarely seen for condoms. However, a mix of changing social attitudes, concerns about sexually transmitted diseases and campaigns to combat teenage pregnancies have led to a range of brands turning to mainstream TV and press advertising. Even so, this surge in marketing activity has not been without its critics.

Mates, launched by Richard Branson in 1987, is now part of Ansell Healthcare, the original manufacturers of Mates for the Virgin brand. Ansell produces products for the medical sector, such as rubber gloves, protective wear for occupational healthcare, and consumer products, including condoms. Ansell trades in France with the Manix brand, and the USA and Australia with its Lifestyles range. In two decades, Mates has become the No. 2 condom brand in the UK, challenging Durex. A recent ploy by Mates was to target women with a separate range of condoms, branded Pleasure. This brand launch was placed next to cosmetics and haircare products in supermarkets and pharmacies, rather than among other condom lines. Arguably this was smart marketing, placing condoms in unexpected parts of stores among products

sought by the same target consumers. In targeting women, Mates moved away from the traditional target audience, male purchasers. By persuading retailers to display the range among beauty products, the company strove to achieve an edge over its competitors in a way which demonstrated an affinity with the purchasing behaviour of its target customers. Mates' marketers were seeking to grow market share and to take advantage of changing attitudes to condoms. Mates has continually innovated in terms of designs, messages and added value, including a range incorporating a vibrating ring. Latex replacement sensoprene, used for Mates Skyn, is the latest innovation. Maintaining an emphasis on safety, reliability and health, Mates has a policy of constant product development supported by provocative advertising. Any new launch or campaign inevitably attracts critics for such a socially and culturally sensitive product category.

In the early days of permitted TV advertising, a storm of protest accompanied US brand Trojan broadcasting UK TV advertisements for its Shared Pleasure brand, showing a couple having sex. The first adverts ran in the commercial breaks of TV reality show *Big Brother*, which attracted a viewing profile similar to the target market profile for the brand. Trojan gained approval from the UK's Broadcast Advertising Clearance Centre for a post-9.00 p.m. watershed showing of the 20-second adverts. Trojan claimed that this marked the first time an orgasm had been shown in a UK television advert. The advert, made by agency Media Therapy, apparently showed people captured at the height of pleasure, linking to the Shared Pleasure brand name. Building on the back of a poster campaign, this advertising was bound to court controversy, receiving complaints to the Advertising Standards Authority that the campaign was offensive, demeaning to women, pornographic and not suitable for television audiences. While the brand-building creativity may have been clever, Trojan's marketers nevertheless caused uproar in certain circles and possibly misjudged its campaign's impact. Marketers must ensure their products are noticed, but not at any cost.

Sources: 'Trojan under fire for "her pleasure" ad', *Marketing Week*, 4 April 2004, p. 8; 'Trojan to screen first orgasm ad', *Marketing*, 26 April 2004, p. 6; 'Mates', *Marketing Week*, 3 June 2004, p. 10; wwwmates.co.uk, 10 March 2015; www.ansell.com, 10 March 2015.

This chapter first overviews the concept of marketing orientation before developing a definition of marketing. The focus then moves on to consider why people should study marketing and why marketing is important. The chapter proceeds to explore the marketing concept and examines several issues associated with successful implementation. The chapter explains the importance of an analytical process to effective marketing, from analysis to strategy formulation to the creation of marketing programmes. Mates – see 'Opener' box – analyzed the purchasing behaviour of its targeted consumers before developing the marketing strategy for its Pleasure range of condoms. How the marketing concept has evolved and topical themes are highlighted. The chapter concludes by discussing the organization and running order of this text.

The concepts and strategies discussed throughout this book are applicable to consumer goods and services, business-to-business products and services, public sector organizations, as well as to not-for-profit and many social sector organizations. As explained in the Part Opener, the term 'customer' in the definitions of marketing should be treated somewhat loosely. While, in commercial settings, it means consumers in consumer markets, or business customers in business marketing, the themes explored in *Marketing: Concepts and Strategies* extend beyond such parameters. The understanding and satisfying of audiences served or represented is just as important in the public and voluntary sectors. Such organizations benefit from adopting the marketing concept and process, as they also must strive to stay ahead of changing environmental conditions, maximize use of their resources to deliver their aims, compete for attention, and seek to understand and satisfy their audiences and stakeholders.

Like all the chapters in *Marketing: Concepts and Strategies*, this one contains detailed topical illustrative examples in highlighted boxes, presents cases for discussion, suggests Internet exercises at its conclusion, lists at the end all the key terms presented in the chapter, provides discussion and review questions to emphasize the key themes and offers suggested further reading choices. In addition, as the principal definitions are introduced in the text, they are repeated in the margins for ease of understanding, glossary-style. If you have not yet done so, before tackling the chapters you should read the 'Preface' to this book in order to understand the perspective, structure and chapter components of *Marketing: Concepts and Strategies*.

Marketing explained and defined

The traditional view of marketing is of a team of managers inside an organization responsible for surveying customers, communicating the brand, managing advertising and developing campaigns. Perhaps this rather constrained remit was true many decades ago and certainly there are still organizations yet to recognise its full potential, but the reality is that marketing is responsible for so much more:

- Understanding markets, developing market insights and being the 'eyes and ears' for an organization, in terms of identifying threats and new business opportunities, tracking competition and staying on top of changing customer expectations.

- Shaping an organization's strategy in terms of the selection of which opportunities to pursue, product portfolios to sustain, target market decisions and competitive positioning.

- Managing brands and creating compelling product value propositions intended to excite customers, attract new ones, retain those already buying from the organization and make life awkward for competitors.

- Managing customers' experience in order to maximize revenue, retain lucrative customers and combat competitors' actions.

Campaigns, advertising, brand strategy and marketing research – as depicted in TV's 1960s-set *Mad Men* – are indeed part of the remit for marketing, but there is so much more required for marketers to understand as they add value to their organizations.

The associated set of necessary capabilities is extensive, including market insight and analytics, strategic thinking and planning, creativity and programme development, project execution and performance evaluation. All occurring in hugely dynamic environments, in which market conditions are always evolving, strategies must be re-thought so as to remain pertinent and marketing programmes kept relevant to these challenges. Here lies the excitement for most marketers, who relish this challenging and ever-changing life.

Marketing orientation

Marketing orientation
A marketing-oriented organization devotes resources to understanding the needs and buying behaviour of customers, competitors' activities and strategies, and of market trends and external forces – now and as they may shape up in the future; inter-functional coordination ensures that the organization's activities and capabilities are aligned to this marketing intelligence.

An organization exhibiting a **marketing orientation** is said to have a sound understanding of customer needs, buying behaviour and the issues influencing the purchasing choices of customers. A marketing-oriented organization also has a shrewd appreciation of competitors and external marketing environment forces and trends.[1] In addition to comprehending these customer, competitor and marketing environment issues, a marketing-oriented organization ensures its operations, personnel and capabilities are aligned to reflect these external drivers. A truly marketing-oriented organization understands these current issues, but is also focused on identifying how they will evolve, so ensuring that the organization's strategy and capabilities are modified to reflect not just current market requirements but also future market conditions.

A marketing-oriented organization devotes resources to understanding the needs and buying behaviour of customers, competitors' activities and strategies and market trends and external forces (now and as they may shape up in the future). Inter-functional coordination ensures that the organization's activities and capabilities are aligned to this marketing intelligence.

Not all organizations can claim to have a marketing orientation. For example, some are purely sales-led, concentrating on short-term sales targets, whereas other organizations are production-oriented, choosing to emphasize product development and production efficiency in their business strategy. Few experts would argue against maximizing sales or seeking leading-edge production practices, or indeed the adoption of best-practice financial and human resource approaches. Similarly, the adoption of a marketing orientation is highly desirable. A marketing orientation is of significant benefit to an organization, as it facilitates a better understanding of customers and helps a business to prepare for external market developments, threats and opportunities. It is difficult to contemplate a scenario where a marketing orientation would not be beneficial to an organization.

An organization practising the concepts explained in *Marketing: Concepts and Strategies* is well on the way to having a marketing orientation, but it is important that inter-functional coordination aligns the activities within the organization and also the leadership team to the marketplace, and specifically to customer buying behaviour, competitive pressures and marketing environment forces, and to the evolving nature of these market conditions. The use of some of marketing's concepts and an understanding of the role of marketing in attracting and satisfying customers, are not enough on their own to establish a marketing orientation. However, failure to comprehend the core concepts of marketing will make a marketing orientation impossible to achieve. The focus of this text, therefore, is on explaining the core concepts of marketing which are the entry point requirements for going on to establish a marketing orientation.

It is possible for an organization lacking a full marketing orientation to nevertheless deploy and benefit from aspects of the marketing toolkit as described in the following chapters. For instance, many businesses have an adequate understanding of their customers, but not all have fully grasped their competitors' strategies or the challenges present in the external marketing environment. Obviously, it is better not to operate in ignorance of these external pressures, which may create threats or opportunities. The definition of marketing *per se* is not, therefore, the same as the definition of marketing orientation.

Marketing defined

Asking members of the public to define marketing is an illuminating experience. They will respond with a variety of descriptions, including 'advertising', 'selling', 'hype', 'conning people', 'targeting' and 'packaging'. In reality, marketing encompasses many more activities than most people realize and depends on a wealth of formal concepts, processes and models beyond the soundbites just listed. Since it is practised and studied for many different reasons, marketing has been defined in many different ways, whether for academic, research or applied business purposes. This chapter examines what is meant by the term **marketing**.

> Marketing consists of individual and organizational activities that facilitate and expedite satisfying exchange relationships in a dynamic environment through the creation, distribution, promotion and pricing of goods, services and ideas.
>
> *Dibb, Simkin, Pride and Ferrell in* Marketing: Concepts and Strategies

Marketing
Activities that facilitate and expedite satisfying exchange relationships in a dynamic environment, through the creation, distribution, promotion and pricing of goods, services and ideas. Marketing is a function and a set of processes for creating, communicating and delivering value to customers and for managing customer relationships in ways that benefit the organization and its stakeholders.

The basic rationale of marketing is that a successful organization requires satisfied and happy customers who return to the organization to provide additional custom. In exchange for something of value, typically payment or a donation, the customers receive a product or service that satisfies their needs. Such a product has an acceptable level of quality, reliability, customer service and support, is available at places convenient for the customer at the 'right' price and is promoted effectively by means of a clear message that is readily comprehended by the customers in question. For example, in return for quenching thirst at affordable prices with a reliable product that is widely available in easy-to-use containers, Coca-Cola receives a great deal of money from customers. Unfortunately for companies and their marketers, customers' requirements change as their needs alter, marketing messages infiltrate their thinking, friends and colleagues discuss purchases, and competing products are pushed by rival organizations. In the dynamic world of marketing, an effective solution to satisfying customer needs rarely has longevity. Newspapers are no longer adequate for most information-hungry people, who today turn to their smartphones and tablets for up-to-the-minute news and entertainment. Marketers must constantly assess their customers' requirements and competitors' propositions, being prepared to modify their marketing activity accordingly. An assessment of marketing opportunities is an ever-evolving process requiring regular revision and updating.

> Marketing is the management process responsible for identifying, anticipating and satisfying customer requirements profitably.
>
> *Chartered Institute of Marketing*

Understanding customers and anticipating their requirements is a core theme of effective marketing.[2] So, too, is understanding general market trends and developments that may affect both customers' views and the activities of organizations operating in a particular market. These factors may include social trends, technological enhancements, economic patterns and changes in the legal and regulatory arena, as well as political influences. These are often termed the forces of the **marketing environment**. Compared with five years ago, for example, look at how many companies now produce products in 'environmentally friendly' packaging in line with the social trend of the 'green consumer'. Or, owing to recession, consider how many companies now have value ranges. An organization does not have a marketplace to itself. There are direct competitors, new entrant rivals, and substitute products offering alternative solutions to a customer's specific need. Construction-equipment giant JCB markets trench-digging equipment to construction firms, utilities and local authorities. The growth of subterranean tunnelling robotic

Marketing environment
External changing forces within the trading environment: laws, regulations, political activities, societal pressures, economic conditions and technological advances.

'moles' for pipe laying, requiring no trench digging, is a substitute for the traditional JCB backhoe loader and is a major competitive threat, which JCB's marketers and product ranges must combat. The competitive context is of fundamental importance to marketers of any good or service. The internal resource base of the business which drives its strengths and weaknesses will determine which market opportunities are viable for the organization to pursue, so marketers must be aware of their capabilities. Marketers also must be aware of how the organization is succeeding and failing financially, and thereby which existing and new products and markets are worthwhile. Marketing, therefore, depends on the successful analysis of customers, the marketing environment, competition, internal capabilities and performance.

> The aim of marketing is to make selling superfluous. The aim is to know and to understand the customer so well that the product or service fits him/her and sells itself!
>
> *US management guru Peter Drucker*

With an understanding of these aspects of the marketplace, an organization must then develop a marketing strategy. Even the mighty global organizations such as GM, Apple, IBM, Vodafone or Unilever choose not to offer a product for every type of consumer or customer need. Instead, they attempt to identify groups of customers where each separate group – or 'market segment' – has 'similar' needs. Each group of customers may then be offered a specifically tailored product or service proposition and a 'marketing mix' programme. The Ford Kuga off-roader appeals to a separate group of customers than does the Ford Ka town car, and it is marketed totally differently. In developing unique marketing programmes for individual market segments – groups of customers – an organization must prioritize which particular groups of customers it has the ability to serve and which will provide satisfactory returns. Organizations have limited resources, which restricts the number of segments in a market which can be targeted. In deciding which segments to target, an organization must be clear about the image – or brand *positioning* – it intends to offer to each group of customers. The organization should endeavour to serve those customers it targets in a manner that gives it an edge over its competitors. Knowing how to group customers sensibly into homogeneous market segments; determining which to target; selecting a suitable positioning; and seeking superiority over rivals, are some of the core elements of marketing strategy.

> The marketing concept holds that the key to achieving organizational goals lies in determining the needs and wants of target markets and delivering the desired satisfaction more efficiently and effectively than the competition.
>
> *US marketer Philip Kotler*

Once a company has devised a marketing strategy, its attention must switch to marketing mix programmes.[3] As consumers of food brands, audio products or banking services, all readers of this text will have experienced the marketing mix programmes of major companies such as Cadbury's, Apple or Barclays. These are the tactical actions of marketing departments, which are designed to implement the desired marketing strategy by attracting, engaging and continuing to serve targeted customers. Companies strive to provide a good customer experience and to build an ongoing relationship with their most lucrative customers, with well-developed customer value propositions and carefully honed marketing programmes. The product or service must be aligned to target customer needs; service levels and guarantees must be determined; pricing and payment issues decided; channels of distribution established to make the product or service available; and promotional strategies devised and executed to communicate with the targeted customers. These tactical aspects of marketing programmes – often referred to as *the marketing mix* – must be well managed, monitored and controlled to ensure their successful execution and performance.

Marketers should understand their markets – customers, competitors, market trends – as well as their own capabilities and performance before developing marketing programmes. A marketing strategy must be determined that reflects the analyses, before the marketing programmes that will be used to action the recommended strategy are specified. **A**nalysis first, then **S**trategy decisions with, finally, the formulation of marketing **P**rogrammes: the *ASP* of the marketing process. The focus must be on providing customer satisfaction, but in a manner that leads to the organization's successful performance. For example, by addressing customers' needs and adopting a marketing culture incorporating clear controls, construction equipment manufacturer JCB has enjoyed the most successful financial returns in the company's history and has become a truly global leader in its field.

The intention of this introductory marketing text is to comprehensively explore these facets of marketing and thus provide a sound conceptual basis for understanding the nature and activities of marketing. There are many definitions of marketing, since it is not a pure science. However, certain core ingredients of the various definitions collectively indicate the basic priorities of marketing:

- satisfying customers
- identifying/maximizing marketing opportunities
- targeting the 'right' customers
- facilitating exchange relationships
- attracting and retaining rewarding customers
- staying ahead in dynamic environments
- endeavouring to beat and pre-empt competitors
- utilizing resources/assets effectively
- increasing market share
- enhancing profitability or income
- satisfying the organization's stakeholders.

These aims form the objectives for many marketing directors and marketing departments. They are featured throughout this book, which formally adopts two definitions of marketing by the American Marketing Association. As already stated, *marketing consists of individual and organizational activities that facilitate and expedite satisfying exchange relationships in a dynamic environment through the creation, distribution, promotion and pricing of goods, services and ideas.* Along with the Association's more recent explanation:

> *Marketing. Noun. An organizational function and a set of processes for creating, communicating and delivering value to customers and for managing customer relationships in ways that benefit the organization and its stakeholders.*

Marketing indeed must be viewed as a process... of analysis to gain market insights, strategy decisions to make choices, and the management of marketing programmes in order to implement the desired marketing strategy. Unless marketing is recognized to be this analytical process, most of the benefits of a strong market-led culture will not materialize. A definition of marketing must acknowledge that it relates to more than just tangible goods, that marketing activities occur in a dynamic environment and that such activities are performed by individuals as well as organizations.[4] The ultimate goal is to satisfy targeted customers and stakeholders, seeking their loyalty and consumption, in a way that adds value for the organization and its stakeholders. This should be achieved in a manner that is differentiated in the view of customers and stakeholders vis-à-vis competitors' marketing, that provides an organization with a competitive edge over rivals and that is updated regularly to reflect market forces and developments. To be in a position to satisfy targeted customers or stakeholders, much work is required by those tasked within the organization and their external partners to conduct the required marketing analyses, develop sensible marketing strategies and create appropriate marketing programmes to take to market . . . repeatedly and regularly.

The definitions of marketing explored

Marketing consists of individual and organizational activities that facilitate and expedite satisfying exchange relationships in a dynamic environment through the creation, distribution, promotion and pricing of goods, services and ideas.

Marketing consists of activities

The marketing of products or services effectively requires many activities. Some are performed by producers; some are accomplished by intermediaries, who purchase products from producers or from other intermediaries and resell them; and some are even performed by purchasers. Marketing does not include all human and organizational activities, only those aimed at facilitating and expediting exchanges. Table 1.1 lists several major categories and examples of marketing activities, as ultimately encountered by the consumer or business customer, who remains at the 'sharp end' of such decisions and marketing programmes. Note that this list is not all-inclusive. Each activity could be sub-divided into more specific activities.

Marketing is performed by individuals and organizations

All organizations perform marketing activities to facilitate exchanges. Businesses as well as not-for-profit and public-sector organizations – such as colleges and universities, charitable organizations, community theatres and hospitals – perform marketing activities. For example, colleges and universities and their students engage in exchanges. To receive instruction, knowledge, entertainment, a degree, the use of facilities and sometimes room and board, students give up time, money

TABLE 1.1 Possible decisions and activities associated with marketing mix variables

Marketing mix variables	Possible decisions and activities
Product	Develop and test market new products; modify existing products; eliminate products that do not satisfy customers' desires; formulate brand names and branding policies; create product guarantees and establish procedures for fulfilling guarantees; provide customer service; plan packaging, including materials, sizes, shapes, colours and designs
Place/distribution	Analyze various types of distribution channels; design appropriate distribution channels; select appropriate channel members and partners; design an effective programme for dealer relations; establish distribution centres; formulate and implement procedures for efficient product handling; set up inventory controls; analyze transportation methods; minimize total distribution costs; analyze possible locations for plants and wholesale or retail outlets; manage multiple channels to market; understand the role of digital channels
Promotion (marketing communications)	Set promotional objectives; determine major types of promotion to be used; select and schedule advertising media; develop advertising messages; measure the effectiveness of advertisements; recruit and train salespeople; formulate payment programmes for sales personnel; establish sales territories; plan and implement sales promotion efforts such as free samples, coupons, displays, competitions, sales contests and cooperative advertising programmes; prepare and disseminate publicity releases; evaluate sponsorships; provide direct mail; maintain active websites and a digital presence; address social media and seek to manage reputation
Price	Analyze competitors' prices; formulate pricing policies; determine method(s) used to set prices; set prices; determine discounts for various types of buyer; understand comparison pricing; establish conditions and terms of sales; determine credit and payment terms; understand the consumers' notion of value
People	Manipulate the marketing mix and establish service levels, guarantees, warranties, expertise, sales support, after sales back-up, customer handling requirements, personnel skills, training and motivation; make products and services available; manage intermediaries; deliver customer experience; handle customer distress; and execute customer retention plans

and perhaps services in the form of labour; they may also give up opportunities to do other things! Many organizations engage in marketing activities. Various police forces have surveyed their communities in order to prioritize services and reassure the general public that people's concerns will be addressed. Politicians now conduct analyses before determining strategies; they think of target markets rather than just the electorate. Even the sole owner of, and worker in, a small corner shop decides which products will sell, arranges deliveries to the shop, prices and displays products, advertises and serves customers.

Marketing facilitates satisfying exchange relationships

For an **exchange** to take place, four conditions must exist.

Exchange
The provision or transfer of goods, services and ideas in return for something of value.

1. Two or more individuals, groups or organizations must participate.

2. Each party must possess something of value that the other party desires (for example, cash for a product or a donation for a charitable cause).

3. Each party must be willing to give up its 'something of value' to receive the 'something of value' held by the other party. The objective of a marketing exchange is to receive something that is desired more than that which is given up to get it – that is, a reward in excess of costs.

4. The parties to the exchange must be able to communicate with each other to make their 'something of value' available.[5]

Figure 1.1 illustrates the process of exchange. The arrows indicate that the parties communicate and that each has something of value available to exchange. Note, though, that an exchange will not necessarily take place just because these four conditions exist. Nevertheless, even if there is no exchange, marketing activities have still occurred. The 'somethings of value' held by the two parties are most often products and/or financial resources, such as money or credit. When an exchange occurs, products are traded for other products or for financial resources.

Customer satisfaction
A state that results when an exchange meets the needs and expectations of the buyer.

An exchange should be *satisfying* to both the buyer and the seller. In fact, in a study of marketing managers, 32 per cent indicated that creating **customer satisfaction** was the most important concept in a definition of marketing.[6] Without satisfaction, customers are unlikely to return. Marketing activities should be oriented towards creating and maintaining satisfying exchange relationships. To maintain an exchange relationship, the buyer must be satisfied with the goods, service or idea obtained in the exchange; the seller must be satisfied with the financial reward or the 'something else of value' received in the exchange.

Maintaining a positive relationship with buyers is an important goal for a seller, regardless of whether the seller is marketing cereal, financial services or construction plant. Through buyer–seller interaction, the buyer develops expectations about the seller's future behaviour. To fulfil these expectations, the seller must deliver on promises made. Over time, a healthy buyer–seller relationship results in interdependencies between the two parties. The buyer depends on the seller to furnish information, parts and service; to be available; and to provide satisfying products in the future.

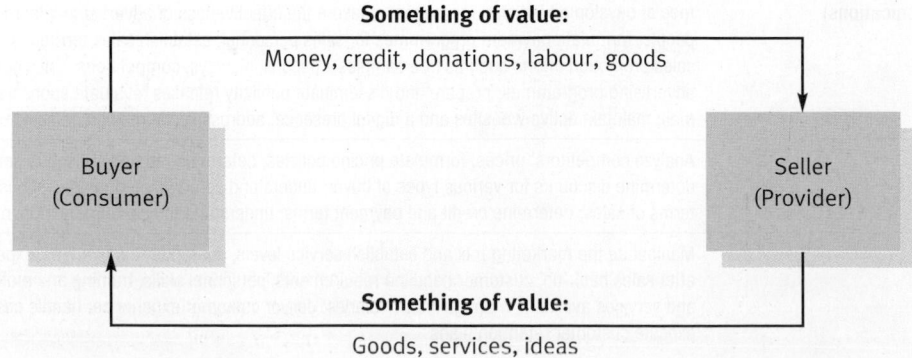

Something of value:

Money, credit, donations, labour, goods

Buyer
(Consumer)

Seller
(Provider)

FIGURE 1.1
Exchange between
buyer and seller

Something of value:

Goods, services, ideas

Marketing occurs in a dynamic environment

The marketing environment consists of many external changing forces within the trading environment: laws, regulations, political activities, societal pressures, changing economic conditions and technological advances. Each of these dynamic forces has an impact on how effectively marketing activities can facilitate and expedite exchanges. For example, the development and acceptance of the web has given organizations another vehicle through which to promote and distribute their products, engage with customers and develop ongoing relationships. Another example is the growth of the sustainability agenda and how it impacts on product development, packaging and marketing.

Marketing involves products, distribution, promotion, pricing and people

Marketing means more than simply advertising or selling a product; it involves developing and managing a product that will satisfy certain needs. It focuses on making the product available at the right place, at the right time, at a price that is acceptable to customers and with appropriate people and service support. It also requires transmitting through marketing communications the kind of promotional information that will help customers determine whether the product will in fact be able to satisfy their needs.

Product
A good, service or idea.

Good
A physical entity that can be touched.

Service
The application of human and mechanical efforts to people or objects in order to provide intangible benefits to customers.

Idea
A concept, philosophy, image or issue.

Marketing focuses on goods, services and ideas

The word 'product' has been used a number of times in this chapter. For purposes of discussion in this text, a **product** is viewed as being a good, a service or an idea. A **good** is a physical entity that can be touched. A Ford Focus, a Sony MP3 player, Kellogg's Cornflakes, a bar of Lux soap and a kitten in a pet shop are examples of goods. A **service** is the application of human and mechanical efforts to people or objects in order to provide intangible benefits to customers. Services such as air travel, dry cleaning, hairdressing, banking, medical care and childcare are just as real as goods, but an individual cannot actually touch or stockpile them. Marketing is utilized for services but requires certain enhancements in order to be effective (see Part Three). **Ideas** include concepts, philosophies, images and issues. For instance, a marriage counsellor gives couples ideas and advice to help improve their relationships. Other marketers of ideas include political parties, charities, religious groups, schools and marketing lecturers.

An organizational function and a set of processes for creating, communicating and delivering value to customers and for managing customer relationships in ways that benefit the organization and its stakeholders

This more recent definition suggested by the American Marketing Association came as a welcome addition, as for over two decades these authors have presented marketing to our students as an analytical process of analysis, strategizing and then programmes for implementation in our *marketing process*. This process is relevant to not only those organizations with consumers or business customers. Given that all organizations have stakeholders which must be influenced and satisfied, this process is suitable for any organization, including those in the third sector.

The marketing process

Marketers spend much of their time managing existing products, target markets and marketing programmes. Even with such so-called 'steady-state' operations, the dynamic nature of marketing leads to continual changes in the marketing environment, competitors and their activities, as well as in customers' needs, expectations, perceptions and buying behaviour. Without a sound understanding of these issues, marketing strategies and their associated marketing programmes cannot be truly effective. Marketers must, therefore, undertake analyses of these market conditions. As changes in the marketplace occur, marketers should revise their marketing strategies accordingly. Any strategy modifications will necessitate changes to the organization's marketing programmes.

This analytical process of marketing analyses, strategy formulation and the creation or modification of marketing programmes is necessary for existing activities and target markets. This marketing process is also required when an organization contemplates entering new markets, launching new or replacement products, modifying the brand strategy, changing customer service practices, rethinking advertising and promotional plans, altering pricing or evaluating distribution policies, developing digital marketing and managing multiple channels. Unexpected sales patterns also require such a process of understanding, thinking and action. This is the **marketing process**: the analysis of market conditions, the creation of an appropriate marketing strategy and the development of marketing programmes designed to execute the agreed strategy, as depicted in Figure 1.2. Finally, as part of this process, the implementation of the marketing strategy and its associated marketing programmes must be managed and controlled.

With an understanding of customers' needs, buying behaviour, expectations and product or brand perceptions, marketers are able to create marketing programmes likely to attract, satisfy and retain customers. With an appreciation of competitors' activities and plans, the marketing programmes are more likely to combat rivals' marketing

Marketing process
Analysis of market conditions, the creation of an appropriate marketing strategy, the development of marketing programmes designed to action the agreed strategy and, finally, the implementation and control of the marketing strategy and its associated marketing programmes.

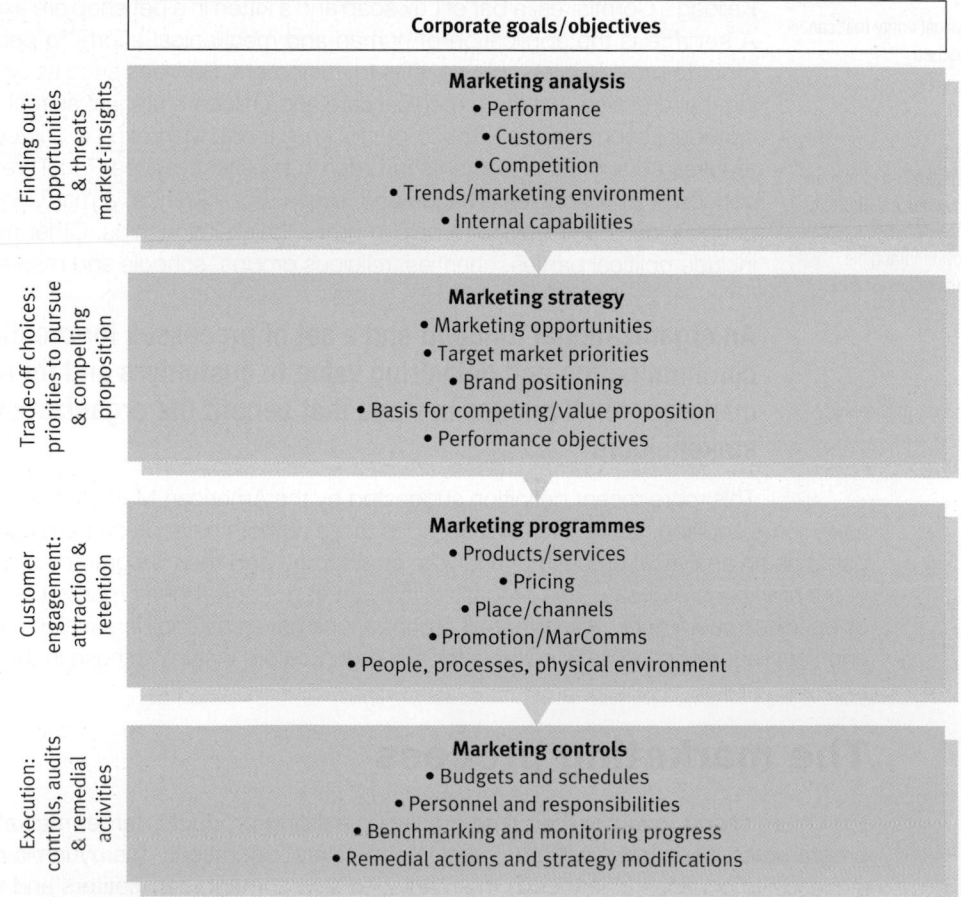

FIGURE 1.2
The marketing process

programmes and to differentiate an organization's product. Without an awareness of changes in the marketing environment, it is unlikely that the specified marketing programme will be sustainable in the longer term. As trading environment changes occur, it is important that an organization's capabilities are modified in order to reflect market conditions and likely demands. Marketers must be aware of where they make good financial returns and which products or markets are not performing well. The marketing analysis stage of the marketing process is, therefore, of fundamental importance.

Equipped with an awareness of the marketplace made possible through marketing analyses, a marketing strategy may be derived. This involves selecting the opportunities to be pursued and devising an associated target market strategy. Few organizations have adequate financial, managerial and employee resources to address all of the possible marketing opportunities that exist: there must be some trade-offs. This generally involves selecting only some of the opportunities to pursue and focusing on specific target markets. Having made these decisions, marketers must ensure that they develop a compelling value proposition and clear brand positioning, with a strong basis for competing versus their rivals, aimed specifically at attracting customers in the prioritized target markets. These strategic recommendations should then translate into specific marketing objectives, designed to steer the creation of marketing programmes.

In most organizations the majority of the budget, time and effort within the marketing function is devoted to creating and managing marketing programmes. These programmes revolve around specifying product, people, promotion (communication), pricing and place (distribution channel) attributes and policies, designed to appeal to and serve those customers identified as being in the priority target market(s). In addition to these ingredients of the marketing mix, marketers of services include other ingredients, as detailed in Chapter 13. Finally, the marketing programmes must be rolled out, monitored and controlled.

Part Three of *Marketing: Concepts and Strategies* addresses the creation of marketing programmes. Chapters 10 to 21 examine extensively each of the ingredients of the marketing mix, which are the essentials for a marketing programme. However, the marketing programmes should not be created before marketers have fully analyzed the market and then devised a marketing strategy. These aspects of marketing analysis and marketing strategy are, therefore, explored in the early stages of *Marketing: Concepts and Strategies*, in Parts One and Two. The chapter running order is also structured to reflect the syllabus content popular on most mainstream marketing modules and courses at diploma and degree level.

The importance of marketing

Marketing activities are carried out in many organizations

The commercial importance of marketing and its relevance as a topic worth studying are apparent from the definitions of marketing just presented. The use of marketing techniques and the development of a marketing orientation should enable an organization to understand its customers and stakeholders better, address competitors' activities and market developments, and effectively harness its capabilities. The results should be enhanced customer satisfaction and retention, improved market share in key target markets and stronger financial performance. This section discusses several less obvious reasons why marketing should be studied.

In Europe and the USA between 25 per cent and 33 per cent of all civilian workers perform marketing activities. The marketing field offers a variety of interesting and challenging career opportunities, such as strategic planning, personal selling, advertising, packaging, transport, storage, marketing research, product development, creative design, digital marketing, wholesaling, retailing, marketing planning and consultancy. In addition, many individuals who work for not-for-profit organizations – such as charities or health agencies – engage in marketing activities.

Marketing skills are used to promote political, cultural, religious, civic and charitable activities. The advertisement in Figure 1.3 encourages support of the Jeans for Genes campaign, a non-profit organization. Whether a person earns a living through marketing activities or performs them without reward in non-business settings, marketing knowledge and skills are valuable assets. For both commercial and non-profit organizations there are needs to satisfy, exchanges to expedite, changing circumstances to monitor and decisions to make. Even a country benefits from marketing, as described in the Topical Insight box below.

Marketing activities are important to organizations and the economy

An organization must sell products in order to survive and grow. Directly or indirectly, marketing activities help to sell an organization's products. By doing so, they generate financial resources that can be used to develop innovative products. New products allow a company to satisfy customers' changing needs more efficiently, which in turn enables the company to generate more profits. Charities and other not-for-profit organizations use marketing to generate revenues and funds.

FIGURE 1.3
Promotion of a non-profit organization. Jeans for Genes uses marketing to communicate its message

Source: Jeans for Genes advert, www.jeansforgenesday .com, copyright © Jeans for Genes.

Ireland: marketing a country

Topical insight

Not only products benefit from marketing. How do you develop a marketing strategy for a country? This was a question faced by the Irish government during difficult times in the 1960s and 1970s; and following the recent global economic meltdown is the task facing the country once more. The original challenge was to build the Irish economy to match the affluence enjoyed by some of its European neighbours. At the time, Ireland was viewed as being backward and unattractive for investment by international corporations. The Industrial Development Authority (IDA) played an important role in developing the country's economy, moving it away from its traditional over-reliance on agriculture, by attracting significant foreign direct investment. Today, with well over a third of the country's GDP coming from industry, and services also accounting for approaching a third, agriculture's contribution has fallen to just 10 per cent.

Marketing and good promotion alone were not responsible for this turnaround. The Irish government realized that to attract investment from overseas it had to provide a stable economy, desirable residential suburbs, modern road and air infrastructure, state-of-the-art telecommunications and, crucially, a well-qualified, dynamic and motivated workforce. These improvements took some time to achieve, but today the companies located in Dublin and around Ireland's airports testify readily to the excellent infrastructure, communications, workforce and tax breaks. The Irish workforce is one of the best educated and most highly prized in Europe.

Having improved the amenities, infrastructure and the workforce, the perceptions of investors overseas had to be addressed. In order to instigate this change, the IDA established a clear strategy by pinpointing attractive sectors for growth and actively encouraging growth businesses in those areas. Consumer products, electronics, healthcare and financial services were some of the key targets. Once decisions about growth priorities had been made, the aim was to develop a marketing programme based around the particular assets that Ireland was able to offer. For example, promotional material focused on – among other things – the young, highly educated workforce, the low rates of corporate taxation, excellent digital and satellite telecommunications systems and a stable currency with low inflation. The attractive countryside and vibrant cultural scene also featured prominently in the IDA's branding of Ireland.

Considerable care was taken to ensure that the propositions developed matched the requirements of the businesses targeted. This provided many overseas businesses with substantial, tangible reasons for establishing a European base in Ireland, bringing with them the investment the country so badly craved. Leading computer manufacturers, pharmaceutical businesses, financial corporations and telecommunications businesses are just some of those who have located facilities in the country: over 1000 well-known organizations have chosen Ireland ahead of other locations for their European operations.

After the recent meltdown of the Irish economy following the global financial crisis, there is once more the need to develop a marketing strategy for Ireland. Most of the work of the past 20 years must be repeated and reinforced, in order to ensure continued inward investment. The Irish economy has been one of the first bail-out economies to recover and to demonstrate an end to recession, providing a sound base for the IDA's marketing.

The marketing toolkit is once again playing a significant part in the overhaul of Ireland's target market strategy, positioning and new-look measures to attract global businesses to locate in the country. London, Germany, the USA and South East Asia have been targeted by the IDA's marketing team. In order to regain its former glory, the IDA is focusing on high value inward investment for research and development, European headquarters, advanced manufacturing and supply chain activities. The *Winning Abroad* marketing programme aims to attract 10 000 new jobs on the back of foreign investments in Ireland over the next few years.

Sources: Irish Embassy, London; Industrial Development Authority (IDA); 'Facts about Ireland', IDA, 1995, 1996, 1999, 2003, 2008, 2011, 2015; www.idaireland.com, 2 February 2011 and 10 March 2015.

Europe's highly complex economy depends heavily on marketing activities. These help produce the profits that are essential not only to the survival of individual organizations but also to the health and ultimate survival of the economy as a whole. Profits are essential to economic growth because without them organizations find it difficult, if not impossible, to buy more raw materials, recruit more employees, attract more capital and create the additional products that in turn lead to more profits.

TABLE 1.2 Popular marketing myths

Myths	Strongly agree	Somewhat agree	Neither agree nor disagree	Somewhat disagree	Strongly disagree
Marketing is selling	34%	14%	26%	18%	8%
Marketers persuade	21%	25%	20%	11%	23%
Dealers' profits significantly increase prices consumers pay	21%	32%	12%	8%	27%
Marketing depends on advertising	44%	17%	12%	9%	18%
Strategic planning has nothing to do with marketing	19%	19%	21%	17%	24%

Marketing knowledge enhances consumer awareness

Besides contributing to a country's economic well-being, marketing activities permeate everyone's lives. In fact, they help to improve quality of life. Studying marketing activities enables the costs, benefits and downsides of marketing to be evaluated. The need for improvement and ways to accomplish changes can be determined. For example, an unsatisfactory experience with a guarantee may lead consumers to demand that laws be enforced more strictly to make sellers fulfil their promises. Similarly, there may be the desire for more information about a product – or more accurate information – before purchase. Understanding marketing leads to the evaluation of the corrective measures – such as laws, regulations and industry guidelines – that may be required to stop unfair, misleading or unethical marketing practices. The results of the survey presented in Table 1.2 indicate that there is a considerable lack of knowledge about marketing activities, as reflected by the sizeable proportion of respondents who agree with the myths in the table.

Marketing costs consume a sizeable proportion of buyers' incomes

The study of the marketing discipline emphasizes that many marketing activities are necessary to provide people with satisfying goods and services. Obviously, these marketing activities cost money. A family with a monthly income of £2000, of which £600 goes towards taxes and savings, spends about £1400 on goods and services. Of this amount, typically £700 goes towards marketing activities. Clearly, if marketing expenses consume that much income, it is necessary to know how this money is used.

Business performance

Marketing puts an emphasis on satisfying customers. Marketing analyses should lead an organization to develop a marketing strategy that takes account of market trends, aims to satisfy customers, is aware of competitive activity and targets the right customers with a clear positioning message. In so doing, an organization should benefit from customer loyalty and advantages over its rivals, while making the most efficient use of resources to effectively address the specific requirements of those markets it chooses to target. Hence, marketing should provide both a financial benefit and a greater sense of well-being for the organization.

The marketing concept and its evolution

Some organizations have tried to be successful by buying land, building a factory, equipping it with people and machines, and then making a product that they believe consumers need. However, these organizations frequently fail to attract buyers with what they have to offer because they defined their business as 'making a product' rather than as 'helping potential customers satisfy their needs and wants'. Such organizations have failed to implement the marketing concept. It is not enough to be product-led, no matter how good the product. An organization must be in tune with consumer or business customer requirements.

Marketing concept
The philosophy that an organization should try to provide products that satisfy customers' needs through a coordinated set of activities that also allows the organization to achieve its goals.

According to the **marketing concept**, an organization should try to provide products that satisfy customers' needs through a coordinated set of activities that also allows the organization to achieve its goals. Customer satisfaction is the major aim of the marketing concept. First, an organization must find out what will satisfy customers. With this information, it then attempts to create satisfying products. But the process does not end there. The organization must continue to alter, adapt and develop products to keep pace with customers' changing desires and preferences. The marketing concept stresses the importance of customers, and emphasizes that marketing activities begin and end with them.[7]

In attempting to satisfy customers, organizations must consider not only short-term, immediate needs but also broad, long-term desires. Trying to satisfy customers' current needs by sacrificing their long-term desires will only create future dissatisfaction. For instance, people want efficient, low-cost energy to power their homes and cars, yet they react adversely to energy producers that pollute the air and water, kill wildlife or cause disease or birth defects. To meet these short- and long-term needs and desires, a company must coordinate all its activities. Production, finance, accounting, personnel, sales and marketing departments must work together.

Production era
The period of mass production following industrialization.

The marketing concept is not another definition of marketing. It is a way of thinking: a management philosophy guiding an organization's overall activities. This philosophy affects all the efforts of the organization, not just marketing activities, and is strongly linked to the notion of marketing orientation. However, the marketing concept is by no means a philanthropic philosophy aimed at helping customers at the expense of the organization. A company that adopts the marketing concept must not only satisfy its customers' objectives but also achieve its own goals, or it will not stay in business long. The overall goals of an organization may be directed towards increasing profits, market share, sales or a combination of all three. The marketing concept stresses that an organization can best achieve its goals by providing customer satisfaction. Thus, implementing the marketing concept should benefit the organization as well as its customers.

Sales era
The period from the mid-1920s to the early 1950s when competitive forces and the desire for high sales volume led a company to emphasize selling and the sales person in its business strategy.

The evolution of the marketing concept

The marketing concept may seem an obvious and sensible approach to running a business. However, business people have not always believed that the best way to make sales and profits is to satisfy customers. A famous example is the marketing philosophy for cars widely attributed to Henry Ford in the early 1900s: 'The customers can have any colour car they want as long as it's black.' The philosophy of the marketing concept emerged in the third major era in the history of business, preceded by the **production era** and the **sales era**. Surprisingly, it took nearly 40 years after the **marketing era** began before many organizations started to adopt the marketing concept. The more advanced marketing-led companies have now entered a spin-off from the marketing era: the **relationship marketing era**. More recently, there have been several significant developments for marketers, most notable of which are value-based marketing, digital marketing and the associated surge in consumer-to-consumer communication, the growth of social marketing applications, and the emergence of so-called critical marketing.

Marketing era
The period in which product and aggressive selling were no longer seen to suffice if customers either did not desire a product or preferred a rival brand, and in which customer needs were identified and satisfied.

Relationship marketing era
In which the focus is not only on expediting the single transaction but on developing ongoing relationships with customers to maintain lifetime share of wallet.

The production era   During the second half of the nineteenth century, the Industrial Revolution was in full swing in Europe and the United States. Electricity, railways, the division of labour, the assembly line and mass production made it possible to manufacture products more efficiently. With new technology and new ways of using labour, products poured into the marketplace, where consumer demand for manufactured goods was strong. This production orientation continued into the early part of the last century, encouraged by the scientific management movement that championed rigidly structured jobs and pay based on output.

The sales era   In the 1920s, the strong consumer demand for products subsided. Companies realized that products, which by this time could be made quite efficiently, would have to be 'sold' to consumers. From the mid-1920s to the early 1950s, companies viewed sales as the major means of increasing profits. As a result, this period came to have a sales orientation. Business people believed that the most important marketing activities were personal selling and advertising.

The marketing era   By the early 1950s, some business people began to recognize that efficient production and extensive promotion of products did not guarantee that customers would buy them. Companies found that they first had to determine what customers wanted and then produce it, rather than simply making products first and then trying to change customers' needs to correspond to what was being produced. As organizations realized the importance of knowing customers' needs, companies entered into the marketing era – the era of customer orientation.[8]

The relationship marketing era   By the 1990s, many organizations had grasped the basics of the marketing concept and had created marketing functions. However, their view of marketing was often largely transaction-based. The priority for marketing was to identify customer needs, determine priority target markets and achieve sales through marketing programmes. The focus was on the individual transaction or exchange. It should be recognized that long-term success and market share gains depend on such transactions, but also on maintaining a customer's loyalty and on repeatedly gaining sales from existing customers. This requires ongoing, committed, reassuring and tailored relationship-building marketing programmes.

Relationship marketing refers to 'long-term, mutually beneficial arrangements in which both the buyer and seller focus on value enhancement through the creation of more satisfying exchanges'.[9] Relationship marketing continually deepens the buyer's trust in the company and, as the customer's confidence grows, this in turn increases the company's understanding of the customer's needs. Successful marketers respond to customers' needs and strive to increase value to buyers over time. Eventually this interaction becomes a solid relationship that allows for cooperation and mutual dependency.

As the era of relationship orientation developed, it became clear that it is not only relationships with customers that are important. Suppliers, agents, distributors, recruiters, referral bodies (such as independent financial advisers recommending financial services companies' products), influencers (such as government departments, national banks or the European Union (EU)), all should be 'marketed to' in order to ensure their support, understanding and resources. The internal workforce must be motivated and provided with a clear understanding of a company's target market strategy, marketing mix activities and, indeed, of the corporate strategy and planned direction. Hence, there is a move away from transaction-based marketing and towards nurturing ongoing relationships.[10]

In the 1990s, lifetime value (of the customer) became a buzz term for marketers. This concept is linked to relationship marketing, said by many observers to be a step-change paradigm for marketing. This evolution of marketing, from focusing on individual transactions with customers to building ongoing relationships and repeat business, has been very important for the success of many organizations.

Until relatively recently, relationship marketing was the main significant change in how the discipline has been perceived. In the last few years, however, there have been several new trends for marketing, each of which has stretched the bounds for the discipline, adding complex new dimensions and further shaping the marketing paradigm.

The digital era   has had a significant impact on how businesses interact with their customers, presenting marketers with a whole raft of new opportunities, techniques and challenges. Digital media, the surge in internet usage and the uptake of personal mobile communications and information provision, have fostered changing consumer behaviours, greater consumer-to-consumer influence on brands and purchasing decisions, and business-to-business interaction. They have also led to 'big data', enhanced degrees of customer insight and a new breed of experts in analytics. These developments have created an entirely new domain for marketers, known as **digital marketing**.

Digital marketing is the use of the web, computers and smartphones, as well as radio, TV and any other forms of digital media, to attract, engage and build relationships with customers and other target audiences. It is the use of technology-led channels of communication and selling to manage customer interaction and provide customer experience in a digitally-connected environment. With the growth of mobile devices this presents marketers with the opportunity to engage with consumers anywhere and anytime. The immediacy, intimacy and customization of many internet and mobile digital communications and customer interactions have transformed the ability of marketers to target customer groups and individuals with bespoke propositions and nurture an ongoing relationship. Most marketers are excited by the potential of digital. However, the digital era has brought downsides, too.

The growth of consumer-to-consumer (C2C) communications in the digital era

This has significant consequences for brands and marketers, for consumers and for society in general. Previously, brand managers largely controlled what information was available to consumers and business customers. These customers based their decisions about brands and products on the marketing and sales information communicated to them by brand managers. Today, **consumer-to-consumer (C2C) communication** is routine, enabled by the digital era generally and social media in particular. Consumers readily and rapidly share views, experiences and information with one another. A positive or negative customer experience is tweeted instantly, blogged or shared on Facebook with many potential fellow consumers. Such messaging, whether positive or negative, has moved beyond the control of marketers. Many consumers trust and value the views of their peers far more than the views of brand managers, advertising messages or media reviews. The surge of C2C communication has redefined the boundaries and created huge new challenges for marketers. The role of C2C interaction and communication is picked up throughout this edition of *Marketing: Concepts and Strategies*.

Social marketing's adoption of marketing's toolkit in non-commercial settings

Social marketing: uses tools and techniques from commercial marketing to encourage positive behavioural changes, such as quitting smoking, reducing alcohol consumption, minimizing anti-social behaviours or reducing carbon footprint. The health and well-being of individuals, society and the planet are at the core of social marketing. The social marketing field now provides interesting career opportunities for marketing professionals interested in applying marketing analyses, notably in terms of monitoring external trends and opportunities (Chapter 3), understanding behaviours of a particular audience or social group (Chapter 5), developing targeting strategies (Chapter 7), establishing appropriate value propositions (Chapter 8) and in creating programmes to communicate with such audiences (Chapters 16 and 19). Rising interest in these applications reflects the increasing importance of the strategic marketing process to a growing set of audiences and stakeholders beyond those from traditional commercial markets. The growth of social marketing is also reflected throughout this edition of *Marketing: Concepts and Strategies*.

Most readers of this book will be students undertaking a business studies degree or marketing qualification. Some readers will be students on more general management degrees who do not inhabit the world of commercial marketing managers. For either audience, this text demonstrates how the marketing philosophy permeates many

---

Digital marketing
The use of the web, computers and smartphones, as well as radio, TV and any other forms of digital media, to attract, engage and build relationships with customers and other target audiences; the use of technology-led channels of communication and selling to manage customer interaction and provide customer experience in a digitally -connected environment.

Consumer-to-consumer (C2C) communication
Consumer-to-consumer (C2C) communication is now routine, enabled by the digital era and social media in particular. Consumers readily and rapidly share views, experiences and information with each other. A positive or negative customer experience is tweeted instantly, blogged or shared on Facebook with potentially very many fellow consumers.

Social marketing
Social marketing uses tools and techniques from commercial marketing to make interventions which encourage positive behavioural changes, such as quitting smoking, reducing alcohol consumption, minimizing anti-social behaviours or reducing carbon footprint, to enhance the health and well-being of individuals, society and the planet.

An alternative view of the scope for marketing: social marketing

Topical insight

The Institute for Social Marketing (ISM) was established 30 years ago with the aim of improving the health and well-being of individuals and society through social marketing research. Now based at the University of Stirling and the Open University, ISM is interested in social marketing's use of tools and techniques from commercial marketing to encourage positive behaviour changes, such as quitting smoking, responsible management of personal debt, or reducing carbon footprint.

Key priority research areas for ISM include alcohol and alcohol marketing, tobacco control, sustainability and sustainable consumption, faith and community partnerships, problem gambling, personal debt, health, well-being and quality of life, ageing, food and nutrition.

This agenda differs from the common perception of marketing that is widely held by the general public. This implies there is more scope for applying marketing principles than only for the marketing of FMCG supermarket products, financial services, holiday packages or – as illustrated in the chapter's opener – condoms!

ISM explains the purpose of social marketing and about its use of commercial marketing ideas:

Social marketers are interested in human behaviour. They seek to understand why we live our lives as we do, sometimes healthily as when we eat a good diet or take regular exercise and at other times unhealthily as when we smoke or binge drink. Given that more than fifty percent of premature deaths are attributable to such individual lifestyle decisions, there is enormous potential for any discipline that can progress thinking in this area. Social marketing brings a unique perspective to the issue.

Marketing is typically concerned with behaviour in the limited area of consumption and the marketplace. However, from the discipline's beginnings, marketers have argued that their behaviour change thinking can also be applied to other contexts; as Wiebe famously argued, you can sell brotherhood like soap.

So, just as Big Tobacco can use marketing to encourage smoking, so 'social marketing' can do the reverse. The same principles – of understanding the consumer, strategic thinking and building satisfying relationships based on emotional as well as rational benefits – can be brought to bear. Social marketing also recognizes that, although commerce brings many benefits, it can also cause harm to both the individual and society. Tobacco, which kills half of its long term users, provides an extreme example of this, but other industries like alcohol and food are also coming under scrutiny. Social marketing's understanding of both the commercial and social sectors puts it in a unique position to provide realistic critiques, and identify intelligent solutions. This forms an important part of the growing field of critical marketing.

These realities informed Lazer and Kelly's original definition of social marketing: Social marketing is concerned with the application of marketing knowledge, concepts and techniques to enhance social as well as economic ends. It is also concerned with the analysis of the social consequences of marketing policies, decisions and activities.

www.open.ac.uk/oubs/ism, March 2015.

Readers may be surprised to learn that those fighting obesity, smoking, alcohol abuse, energy wastage, problem gambling or personal debt, are using ideas from commercial marketing in their efforts. Just as in commercial settings, social marketers must understand the attitudes, perceptions and behaviour of those they are targeting, before creating strategies and interventions to tackle these problems areas. Once decisions about who to target have been made, well-articulated and carefully communicated propositions are needed to engage with these audiences. In these respects, the development and execution of a social marketing strategy has many similarities with commercial marketing practice.

Sources: www.open.ac.uk/oubs/ism; www.management.stir.ac.uk/about-us/institute-of-social-marketing; Philip Kotler and Nancy Lee (eds), *Social Marketing: Influencing Behaviors for Good*, Thousands Oaks, CA: Sage Publications Inc., 2008; Gerard Hastings, *Social Marketing*, Abingdon: Routledge, 2013; Sally Dibb, 'Up, Up and Away: Social Marketing Breaks Free', *Journal of Marketing Management*, 30 (11–12), 2014, pp. 1159–1185.

aspects of our lives and society, including in the overtly non-commercial realms of social marketing. As the second Topical Insight reveals, marketing principles extend much further than promoting Red Bull energy drinks, the iPhone, McDonald's burgers or JCB diggers.

The emergence of critical marketing   Although this cannot really be described as a paradigm shift in the sense of relationship marketing or digital marketing, critical marketing nevertheless warrants consideration. Those interested in this field agree that critical marketing is difficult to define.

Critical marketing
Critical marketing involves challenging orthodox views that are central to the core principles of the discipline. Sometimes this involves promoting radical philosophies and theories in relation to the understanding of economies, society, markets and consumers, which may have implications for the practice of marketing. Critical marketing is connected with the growing area of critical management.

Critical marketing: is espoused by individuals who challenge orthodox views that are central to the core principles of the discipline. Sometimes this involves promoting radical philosophies and theories in relation to the understanding of economies, society, markets and consumers, which may have implications for the practice of marketing. In some instances, the assumptions at the heart of many of the core principles of the discipline are challenged. Critical marketing is connected with the growing area of critical management.

While a detailed exploration of critical marketing is beyond the scope of this text, it is right to highlight the alternative views that exist about the domain and the activities associated with it. Once readers are familiar with the core concepts associated with effective marketing, they might also wish to explore the views of critical marketers.[11] This group is interested in issues such as postmodernism; the biological base for consumer behaviour; the connections between marketing activities and society (including social marketing), such as sustainable marketing; anti-globalization challenges to marketing; ecofeminism; and the inter-connection of cultural studies and consumer research. Although many of these themes are not explored in detail here, a more detailed examination of aspects of social marketing is included. In addition, reflections on marketing in practice are incorporated throughout this book, contributing to the critical marketing debate around the distinction between theory and practice.

A further aspect of critical marketing that warrants consideration relates to concerns that marketing sometimes has damaging consequences and that marketers are not always aware of these outcomes.[12] For example, some critics argue that marketing is responsible for heightening consumerism and generating 'must have' attitudes among consumers. This has resulted in negative consequences for society in relation to carbon footprint, the use of scarce resources, landfill, state spending priorities and even on changing societal values. Although there are divergent opinions on these matters, there can be little doubt that marketing influences consumption and that these patterns have significant impacts for the environment, for society and for consumers. These and other impacts of marketing, including a discussion of some of the ethical issues facing marketers, are considered later in this edition.

The essentials of marketing

Marketing analyses

From these brief introductory comments, it should be evident that marketing can enhance an organization's understanding of its customers, competitors, market trends, threats and opportunities. Marketing should direct an organization's target market strategy, product development and communication with its distribution channels and customers. In order to carry out these activities, marketing personnel need access to good quality marketing intelligence about the following issues:

- customers
- competitors
- marketing environment forces
- the organization's capabilities, marketing assets and performance.

As will be seen later in this book, there are other marketing analyses which can be carried out, but these just mentioned are the essential building blocks for the development of marketing strategies and the creation of marketing programmes. The majority of the chapters in Parts One and Two of *Marketing: Concepts and Strategies* address these marketing analyses, which are the foundation of the marketing process.

Marketing strategy

To achieve the broad goal of expediting desirable exchanges, an organization's marketing managers are responsible for developing and managing marketing strategies. A **marketing strategy** involves the selection of new opportunities to pursue and current activities to support, identification of associated target markets and competitive positioning, and the creation of appropriate value propositions and customer engagement plans, in order to deliver the specified performance goals in the corporate strategy. A marketing strategy articulates a plan for the best use of the organization's resources and directs the required tactics to meet its objectives.

When marketing managers attempt to develop and manage marketing activities, they must deal with three broad sets of variables:

1. those relating to the marketing mix
2. those inherent in the accompanying target market strategy
3. those that make up the marketing environment.

The marketing mix decision variables – product, place/distribution, promotion, price and people – and the target market strategy variables are factors over which an organization has control. As Figure 1.4 shows, these variables are constructed around the

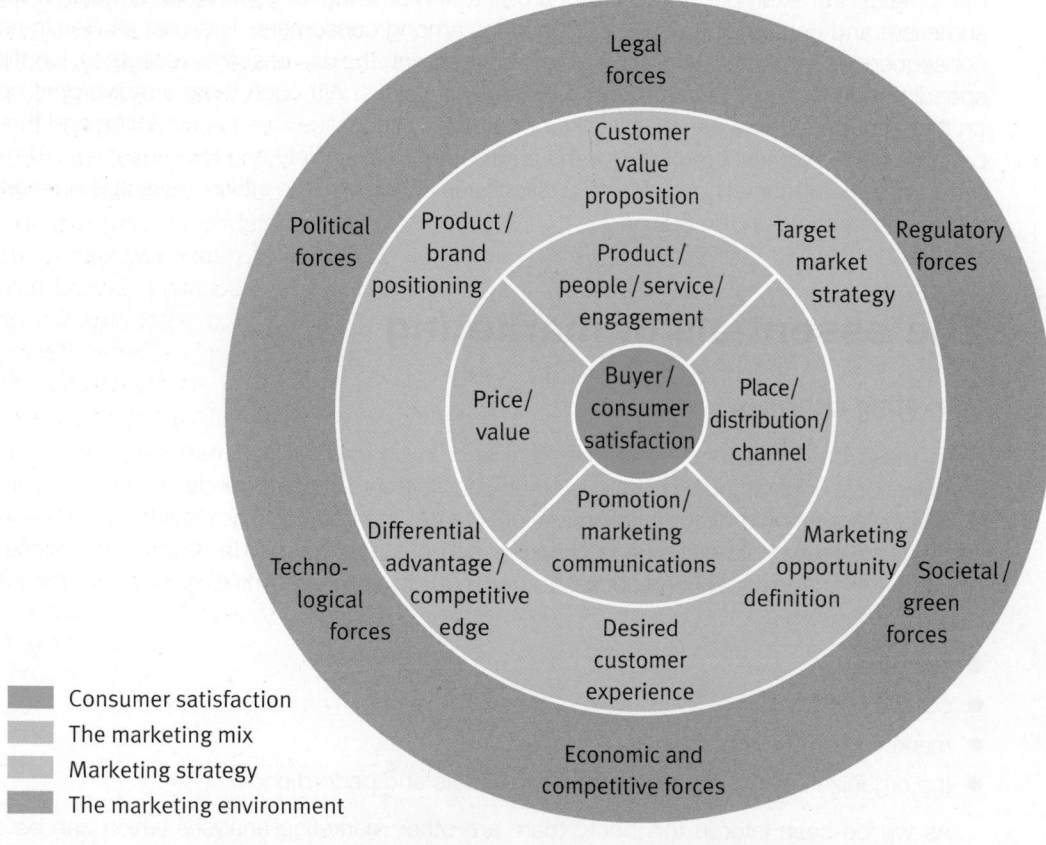

FIGURE 1.4

Marketing environment, marketing strategy, marketing mix and customer satisfaction; consumers and organizations are affected by the forces of the marketing environment; organizations must determine a marketing strategy, implemented through the ingredients of the marketing mix, which aims to satisfy targeted customers

buyer or consumer. The marketing environment variables are political, legal, regulatory, societal, technological and economic and competitive forces. These factors are subject to less control by an organization, but they affect buyers' needs as well as marketing managers' decisions regarding marketing mix variables.

To develop and manage marketing strategies, marketers must focus on several marketing tasks: marketing opportunity analysis and marketing analyses, the determination of a marketing strategy and target market selection, marketing mix development and management of the programmes that facilitate implementation of the marketing strategy.

Marketing opportunity
One that exists when circumstances allow an organization to take action towards reaching a particular group of consumer or business customers in order to develop relationships and achieve commercial goals.

Marketing opportunity analysis A **marketing opportunity** exists when circumstances allow an organization to take action towards reaching a particular group of customers. An opportunity provides a favourable chance or opening for a company to generate sales from identifiable markets for specific products or services. For example, during a heatwave, marketers of electric fans have a marketing opportunity – an opportunity to reach customers who need electric fans. Various 'no frills' airlines have entered the rapidly growing market for low-priced scheduled air travel, as consumers have demonstrated their liking for this alternative to high-priced full-service airlines or charters. Bluetooth and wireless connectivity are creating numerous opportunities for brands, as mobile apps engage with consumers anytime and anywhere. Most new products or services exist because marketers identified a marketing opportunity.

Marketers should be capable of recognizing and analyzing marketing opportunities. An organization's long-term survival depends on developing products that satisfy its customers. Few organizations can assume that products popular today will interest buyers ten years from now. A marketing-led organization can choose among several alternatives for continued product development through which it can achieve its objectives and satisfy buyers. It can modify existing products (for example, by reducing salt content and additives in foods to address increasing health consciousness among customers), introduce new products (such as smart watches, hybrid cars, cold water washing machines, or longer-life nappies) and delete some that customers no longer want (such as compact cameras or upright vacuum cleaners). A company may also try to market its products to a greater number of customers, persuade current customers to use more of a product, or perhaps expand marketing activities into additional countries. Diversification into new product offerings through internal efforts or through acquisitions of other organizations may be viable options for a company. For example, Virgin has entered financial services. An organization's ability to pursue any of these alternatives successfully depends on its internal characteristics and the forces within the marketing environment. These strategic options are discussed further in Chapter 2 of *Marketing: Concepts and Strategies*.

Internal organizational factors The primary factors inside an organization to be considered when analyzing marketing opportunities and devising target market strategies are organizational objectives, financial resources, managerial skills, organizational strengths and weaknesses, and cost structures. Most organizations have overall organizational objectives. Some marketing opportunities may be consistent with these objectives; others may not, and to pursue them is hazardous. Frequently, the pursuit of such opportunities ends in failure, or forces the company to alter its long-term objectives. The links with corporate strategy and an organization's mission are discussed in Chapter 2.

An organization's financial resources constrain the type of marketing opportunities it can pursue. Typically, an organization avoids projects that might bring economic catastrophe. In some situations, however, a company must invest in a high-risk opportunity, because the costs of not pursuing the project are so great. Thus, despite an economic recession and reduced consumer spending, companies such as BMW have continued to launch new products and enter more markets.

The skills and experience of management also limit the types of opportunity that an organization can pursue. A company must be particularly cautious when exploring the possibility of entering unfamiliar markets with new products. If it lacks appropriate managerial skills and experience, the business can sometimes acquire them by recruiting additional managerial personnel. Most organizations at some time are limited in their growth plans by a lack of sufficient managers with suitable skills and market insights.

Like people, most organizations have strengths and weaknesses. Due to the types of operation in which a company is engaged, it will normally have employees with specialist skills and technological information. Such characteristics are a strength when launching marketing strategies that require them. However, lack of them may be a weakness if the company tries to compete in new, unrelated product areas. A major IT services company altered its strategy to focus on winning more business for IT infrastructure management from existing clients rather than from attracting new clients. This required a different set of selling skills, and managers with the ability to nurture relationships and exploit emerging sales opportunities within a client company. The revised target market strategy resulted in redundancies among the existing salesforce, and the recruitment of account managers with the necessary skills and interpersonal abilities.

An organization's cost structure may be an advantage if the company pursues certain marketing opportunities, and a disadvantage if it pursues others. Such factors as geographic location, employee skills, access to raw materials and type of equipment and facilities can all affect cost structure. Previous investment levels and priorities will have ramifications for the current cost structure. As discussed in Chapter 2, the cost structure of an organization may provide a competitive advantage over rivals, or may place a business at a competitive disadvantage.

Marketing environment forces   The marketing environment, which consists of political, legal, regulatory, societal, technological and economic/competitive forces, surrounds the buyer (consumer) and the organization's marketing mix (see Figure 1.4), impacting on both. Each major environmental force is explored in considerable depth in Chapter 3. Marketers know that they cannot predict changes in the marketing environment with certainty. Even so, over the years marketers have become more systematic in taking these forces into account when planning their competitive actions.[13] An organization that fails to monitor the forces of the marketing environment is likely to miss out on emerging opportunities at the expense of rivals with the foresight to examine these market drivers.

Marketing environment forces affect a marketer's ability to facilitate and expedite exchanges, in four general ways:

1. They influence customers by affecting or regulating their lifestyles, standards of living, preferences and needs for products. As a marketing manager tries to develop and adjust the marketing mix to satisfy consumers or business customers, the effects of environmental forces on customers also have an indirect impact on the marketing mix components.

2. Marketing environment forces help determine whether and how a marketing manager can perform certain marketing activities. They may force marketers to cease certain practices or to adopt new strategies.

3. Environmental forces may affect a marketing manager's decisions and actions by influencing buyers' reactions to the company's marketing mix.

4. Marketing environment forces may provide an organization with a window of opportunity over rivals that fail to notice the market development or that take no action themselves.

Equally, market drivers may provide competitors with such an opportunity ahead of a marketer's own organization.

Although forces in the marketing environment are sometimes viewed as 'uncontrollables', a marketing manager may be able to influence one or more of them. However, marketing environment forces fluctuate quickly and dramatically, which is one reason why marketing is so interesting and challenging. As these forces are highly interrelated, a change in one may cause others to change. For example, from Freons in fridges to additives in foods, most consumers have become increasingly aware of health and environmental issues. Manufacturers have altered product specifications and production methods to reflect this awareness. Legislators and regulatory bodies have also responded to expert and consumer opinions with new regulations and informal agreements, forcing companies to rethink their manufacturing and marketing policies.

Even though changes in the marketing environment produce uncertainty for marketers and at times impede marketing efforts, they can also create opportunities. After the 1989 oil spills, for example, more companies began developing and marketing products designed to contain or dissipate spilled oil. The BSE beef crisis gave producers of other meats significant opportunities. Environmental concerns have encouraged car manufacturers to develop emission-free engines. Rising mobile phone usage and improvements to network technologies have enabled various information providers to tailor their services for sports fans or stock-market investors. Recession has led to a growth in demand for domestic vacations, at the expense of more expensive flight-based holidays. Thus, marketers must be aware of changes in environmental forces so that they can capitalize on the opportunities they provide. The marketing environment is discussed more fully in Chapters 2 and 3 of *Marketing: Concepts and Strategies*.

Target market selection   A **target market** is a group of people for whom a company creates and maintains a marketing mix that specifically fits the needs and preferences of that group.[14] When choosing a target market, marketing managers try to evaluate possible markets to see how entering them would affect the company's sales, costs and profits. Marketers also attempt to determine whether the organization has the resources to produce a marketing mix that meets the needs of a particular target market, and whether satisfying those needs is consistent with the company's overall objectives and mission. The size and number of competitors already marketing products in possible target markets are also of concern.

Target market
A group of people or organizations for whom a company creates and maintains a marketing mix that specifically fits the needs and preferences of that group.

Marketing managers may define a target market as a vast number of people or as a relatively small group. For example, Ford produces cars suitable for much of the population – although specific models are quite narrowly targeted, such as the family runaround Focus or the executive Mondeo. Porsche focuses its marketing effort on a small proportion of the population, believing that it can compete more effectively by concentrating on an affluent target market desiring sports coupés. Although a business may concentrate its efforts on one target market through a single marketing mix, organizations often focus on several target markets by developing and deploying multiple marketing mixes. Reebok, for example, markets different types of shoes to meet the specific needs of joggers, walkers, aerobics enthusiasts and other groups.

Target market selection is crucial to generating productive marketing efforts. At times, products and organizations fail because marketers do not identify the appropriate customer groups at which to aim their efforts. Organizations that try to be all things to all people typically end up not satisfying the needs of any customer group very well. It is important for an organization's management to designate which customer groups the company is trying to serve and to have adequate information about these customers. The identification and analysis of a target market provide a foundation on which a marketing mix can be developed. Marketers must strive to develop attractive and compelling value propositions for these targeted consumers or business customers and to provide a rewarding and satisfying customer experience. As will be explored in the next chapter, it is important to strive to develop an advantage over competitors in the markets targeted.

Marketing programmes

In order to make the devised marketing strategy become a reality, marketers must specify the set of marketing mix ingredients forming the marketing programme for implementing the agreed marketing strategy. These marketing mix decisions occupy the majority of marketers' time and account for the bulk of a marketing department's budget. However, as previously explained, before the marketing mix is specified, marketers should undertake sufficient marketing analyses and reflect the findings of these analyses in their marketing strategy.

Marketing mix development   Traditionally, the marketing mix was deemed to consist of four major components: product, place (distribution), promotion and price. Increasingly, a fifth component is viewed as 'people', who provide customer service and interact with customers and organizations within the supply chain. These components are called 'marketing mix decision variables' because a marketing manager decides which type of each component to use and in what amounts. A primary goal of a marketing manager is to create and maintain a marketing mix that satisfies consumers' needs for a general product type. Note that in Figure 1.4, the marketing mix is built around the buyer – as is stressed by the marketing concept and definition of marketing. Bear in mind, too, that the forces of the marketing environment affect the marketing mix variables in many ways.

Marketing mix variables are often viewed as controllable variables because they can be changed. However, there are limits to how much these variables can be altered. For example, because of economic conditions or government regulations, a manager may not be free to adjust prices daily. Changes in sizes, colours, shapes and designs of most tangible goods are expensive; therefore such product features cannot be altered very often. In addition, promotional campaigns and the methods used to distribute products ordinarily cannot be changed overnight. People, too, require training and motivating, and cannot be recruited or sacked overnight, so customer service is not always flexible.

Marketing managers must develop a marketing mix that precisely matches the needs of the people – or organizations in business-to-business marketing – in the target market. Before they can do so, they have to collect in-depth, up-to-date information about those needs. The information might include data about the age, income, ethnic origin, sex and educational level of people in the target market; their preferences for product features; their attitudes towards competitors' products; and the frequency and intensity with which they use the product. Armed with these kinds of data, marketing managers are better able to develop a product, service package, distribution system, promotion programme and price that will satisfy the people in the target market.

This section looks more closely at the decisions and activities related to each marketing mix variable (product, place/distribution, promotion, price and people – the '5Ps' of the marketing mix). Table 1.1 contains a list of the decisions and activities associated with each marketing mix variable.

Marketing mix
The tactical 'toolkit' of the marketing programme; product, place/distribution, promotion, price and people variables that an organization can control in order to appeal to the target market and facilitate satisfying exchange.

The product variable   A product can be a good, a service or an idea. The product variable is the aspect of the marketing mix that deals with researching consumers' product wants and designing a product with the desired characteristics. It also involves the creation or alteration of packaging and brand names, and may include decisions about guarantees, repair services and customer support. The actual manufacturing of products is not a marketing activity, but marketing-oriented businesses look to marketers to specify product development requirements that reflect customer needs and evolving expectations.

Product-variable decisions and related activities are important because they directly involve creating products and services that satisfy consumers' needs and wants. To maintain a satisfying set of products that will help an organization achieve its goals, a marketer must be able to develop new products, modify existing ones and eliminate those that no longer satisfy buyers or yield acceptable profits. For example, after realizing that competitors were capturing large shares of the low-calorie market, Heinz introduced new product items under its Weight Watchers name. To reflect greater use of microwave ovens, rice company Tilda introduced its steam-in-a-pouch range of quickcook microwavable sachets.

Product variable
The aspect of the marketing mix that deals with researching consumers' product wants and designing a product with the desired characteristics.

The place/distribution variable   To satisfy consumers, products must be available at the right time and in a convenient location. In dealing with the place/distribution variable, a marketing manager seeks to make products available in the quantities

Place/distribution variable
The aspect of the marketing mix that deals with making products available, perhaps through multiple channels, in the quantities desired, to as many customers as possible, while keeping the total inventory, transport and storage costs as low as possible.

desired to as many intended customers as possible, and to keep the total inventory, transport and storage costs as low as possible. A marketing manager may become involved in selecting and motivating intermediaries (wholesalers, retailers and dealers), establishing and maintaining inventory control procedures, and developing and managing transport and storage systems. Many organizations distribute their products through multiple channels, now typically including the web, adding to the complexity of marketing management but providing exciting opportunities. As more than one channel is often deployed, a challenge for marketers is to manage the customer's experience across these multiple channels, providing a consistent experience of the brand.

Promotion variable
The aspect of the marketing mix that relates to marketing communications used to inform one or more groups of people about an organization and its products and to maintain an ongoing relationship.

The promotion variable   The **promotion variable** relates to communication activities that are used to inform one or more groups of people about an organization and its products. Promotion can be aimed at increasing public awareness of an organization and of new or existing products. In addition, promotion can serve to educate consumers about product features or to urge people to take a particular stance on a political or social issue. It may also be used to keep interest strong in an established product that has been available for decades. The advertisement in Figure 1.5 is an example. Marketers increasingly refer to the promotion variable in the marketing mix as 'marketing communications'. Recently, this has become even more important for marketers, as they struggle to understand the power of growing consumer-to-consumer communications about their brands, made possible by social media and the web.

Price variable
The aspect of the marketing mix that relates to activities associated with establishing pricing policies and determining product prices.

The price variable   The **price variable** relates to activities associated with establishing pricing policies and determining product prices. Price is a critical component of the marketing mix because consumers and business customers are concerned about the value obtained in an exchange. Price is often used as a competitive tool; in fact, extremely intense price competition sometimes leads to price wars. For example,

FIGURE 1.5
Promotion of an established brand. Champagne house Moët & Chandon uses its heritage in its advertising to reinforce its brand appeal

airlines like Aer Lingus, British Airways and Virgin Atlantic are engaged in ruthless price cutting in the battle for transatlantic routes. Price can also help to establish a product's image. For instance, if Chanel tried to sell Chanel No. 5 in a two-litre bottle for £3 or €4, consumers would probably not buy it because the low price would destroy the prestigious image of this deluxe brand. Linked to the notion of perceived value, recent recession has placed even greater emphasis on the pricing ingredient of many organizations' marketing programmes.

The people variable Product, place/distribution, promotion and price are traditionally the principal elements of the marketing mix: the '4Ps'. Marketers of services include people as a core element, along with other ingredients (see Chapter 13). Whether part of the product element or a separate element of the marketing mix, there is no doubt that people are important, and are integral to providing customer service. As marketers, they manipulate the rest of the marketing mix. As intermediaries in the marketing channel, they help make products and services available to the marketplace. As consumers or organizational purchasers, they create the need for the field of marketing. In the marketing mix, the **people variable** reflects the level of customer service, advice, sales support and after-sales back-up required, involving recruitment policies, training, retention and motivation of key personnel. For many products and most services, personnel interface directly with the intended purchaser and are often perceived by such consumers as being part and parcel of the product offering.

People variable
The aspect of the marketing mix that reflects the level of customer service, advice, sales support and after-sales back-up required, involving recruitment policies, training, retention and motivation of key personnel.

Developing and maintaining an effective marketing mix is a major requirement for a strong marketing strategy. Thus, as indicated in Figure 1.5, a large proportion of this book (Chapters 10 to 21) focuses on the concepts, decisions and activities associated with the components of the marketing mix. It is the marketing mix that readers, as consumers, will most frequently have experienced for products and services purchased. It is important to remember, however, that analysis must precede the development of a marketing strategy, which in turn must be formulated before the marketing mix is determined for a product or a service.

Marketing management

Marketing management
A process of planning, organizing, implementing and controlling marketing activities to facilitate and expedite exchanges effectively and efficiently.

Marketing management is the process of planning, organizing, implementing and controlling marketing activities to facilitate and expedite exchanges effectively and efficiently. Effectiveness and efficiency are important dimensions of this definition. *Effectiveness* is the degree to which an exchange helps achieve an organization's objectives. *Efficiency* is the minimization of resources an organization must spend to achieve a specific level of desired exchanges. Thus, the overall goal of marketing management is to facilitate highly desirable exchanges and to minimize as much as possible the costs of doing so.

Marketing planning
A systematic process of assessing marketing opportunities and resources, determining marketing objectives and developing a thorough plan for implementation and control.

Marketing planning is a systematic process of assessing opportunities and resources, determining marketing objectives, developing a marketing strategy and constructing plans for implementation and control. Planning determines when and how marketing activities will be performed and who is to perform them. It forces marketing managers to think ahead, to establish objectives and to consider future marketing activities. Effective marketing planning also reduces or eliminates daily crises. Marketing planning and the management of the execution of the resulting marketing plan are intrinsic aspects of marketing management.

Organizing marketing activities refers to developing the internal structure of the marketing unit. The structure is the key to directing marketing activities. The marketing unit can be organized by function, product, region, type of customer or a combination of all four.

Proper implementation of marketing plans hinges on the coordination of marketing activities, motivation of marketing personnel and effective communication within the unit. Marketing managers must motivate marketing personnel, coordinate their activities and integrate their activities, both with those in other areas of the company and with the marketing efforts of personnel in external organizations, such as advertising agencies and marketing research businesses. An organization's communication system must allow the marketing manager to stay in contact with high-level management, with managers of other functional areas within the company and with personnel involved in marketing activities both inside and outside the organization.

The marketing control process consists of establishing performance standards, evaluating actual performance by comparing it with established standards and reducing the difference between desired and actual performance. An effective control process has the following four requirements:

1. The control process should ensure a rate of information flow that allows the marketing manager to quickly detect differences between actual and planned levels of performance.

2. The control process must accurately monitor different kinds of activities and be flexible enough to accommodate changes.

3. The control process must be economical so that its costs are low, relative to the costs that would arise if there were no controls.

4. Finally, the control process should be designed so that both managers and subordinates can understand it. To maintain effective marketing control, an organization needs to develop a comprehensive control process that evaluates marketing operations at regular intervals. The authors' other titles, including *Marketing Planning* (Cengage), *Market Segmentation Success: Making It Happen!* (The Howarth Press/Routledge) and *Marketing Essentials* (Cengage) explore the operationalization of marketing strategies and marketing control processes in more detail.

The organization of this book

The structure of this book adheres to the principle that it is important to analyze markets and marketing opportunities, then develop marketing strategies and construct marketing programmes that implement the desired marketing strategy, before ensuring suitable controls are in place to manage the roll-out of the strategy and programmes: the marketing process. Marketing analyses develop a thorough understanding of the marketplace, focusing particularly on customers, competitors and market trends. This knowledge of the marketplace provides a sound basis from which to devise marketing strategies. These strategies should determine marketing opportunities to pursue, identify attractive target markets, and develop a clear brand positioning and basis for competing. In order to implement the recommended target market strategy, marketing programmes must be designed with marketing mix combinations and control processes to ensure effective implementation. This marketing process, as presented in Figure 1.2, is fundamental to sound marketing practice.

What does each part of this book cover?

The first part of *Marketing: Concepts and Strategies* provides an explanation of the marketing concept, presents the marketing process and overviews the principles of marketing strategy. Part One also examines the concept of the marketing environment and the nuances of marketing in international markets:

● Part One: Marketing Defined and Marketing in Context

The second part explores the essential marketing analyses for developing an understanding of consumers and business customers, while producing a target market strategy:

● Part Two: Understanding and Targeting Customers

Having explored the core marketing analyses and requisites for developing a marketing strategy, Part Three provides an examination of the ingredients of the marketing mix, starting with product, branding and service issues; then exploring place and channels; promotion and marketing communications; digital marketing; pricing decisions; and concluding with modifying the marketing mix in international markets and for the marketing of services and business-to-business markets:

- Part Three: Marketing Mix Decisions

The focus switches in Part Four to the execution of marketing strategies and operationalization of marketing programmes:

- Part Four: Marketing Management

Marketing: Concepts and Strategies also offers:

- an indexed margin/glossary of key terms
- full subject and name indexing
- extended cases to enhance readers' understanding of key topics
- internet-based exercises
- questions for discussion
- recommended further reading on each topic
- detailed illustrative examples in every chapter
- up-to-date statistics for the marketing industry
- support material on its own website
- various auxiliaries are also available to tutors on the companion website.

Summary

Organizations that practise marketing do not necessarily have a *marketing orientation*. Organizations with a marketing orientation have a sound awareness of customers' needs and buying behaviour, of competitors' offerings and strategies, and of market trends. They also take steps to ensure they know how these market conditions will evolve. Crucially, they orientate their operational practices and coordinate their inter-functional thinking around these market conditions. In order to have a marketing orientation, it is necessary to adopt a range of marketing concepts and techniques. To practise marketing and to benefit from the activities of marketing, however, it is not necessary for an organization to have a fully developed marketing orientation. A few managers, whether or not in an organization's marketing function, utilizing the concepts described in this book, will make a significant contribution to the organization's fortunes and its understanding of its marketplace.

Marketing consists of individual and organizational activities that facilitate and expedite satisfying exchange relationships in a dynamic environment through the creation, distribution, promotion and pricing of goods, services and ideas. Marketing is an organizational function and a set of processes for creating, communicating and delivering value to customers and for managing customer relationships in ways that benefit the organization and its stakeholders.

Marketing opportunity analysis involves reviewing both internal factors (organizational objectives and mission, financial resources, managerial skills, organizational strengths, organizational weaknesses and cost structures) and external ones in the *marketing environment* (the political, legal, regulatory, societal, technological and economic/competitive forces).

An *exchange* is the provision or transfer of goods, services and ideas in return for something of value. Four conditions must exist for an exchange to occur: (1) two or more individuals, groups or organizations must participate; (2) each party must have something of value desired by the other; (3) each party must be willing to give up what it has in order to receive the value held by the other; and (4) the parties to the exchange must be able to communicate with each other to make their 'somethings of value' available. In an exchange, products are traded either for other products or for financial resources, such as cash or credit. Through the exchange, the recipient (the customer) and the provider (the organization) must be satisfied (leading to *customer satisfaction*). *Products* can be *goods, services or ideas*.

The *marketing process* is the analysis of market conditions, the creation of an appropriate marketing strategy, the development of marketing programmes designed to action the agreed strategy and, finally, the implementation and control of the marketing strategy and its associated marketing programme(s). Organizations contemplating entering new markets or territories, launching new products or brands, modifying their strategies or manipulating their marketing programmes, should use this sequential analytical process. Even steady-state markets and products encounter changing market conditions, and marketers should continually analyze and then modify their marketing strategies and marketing programmes accordingly.

It is important to study marketing because it permeates society. Marketing activities are performed in both business and non-business organizations. Moreover, marketing activities help business organizations generate profits and income, the lifeblood of an economy. Even organizations without 'customers' have to maximize the deployment of their resources, address trends, identify stakeholders and develop compelling propositions to satisfy these stakeholders. The study of marketing enhances consumer awareness. Marketing costs absorb about half of what the consumer spends. Marketing, practised well, improves business performance.

The *marketing concept* is a management philosophy that prompts an organization to try to satisfy customers' needs through a coordinated set of activities that also allows the organization to achieve its goals. Customer satisfaction is the major objective of the marketing concept. The philosophy of the marketing concept emerged during the 1950s, as the *marketing era* succeeded the *production era* and the *sales era*. As the 1990s progressed into the *relationship marketing era*, a focus on transaction-based marketing was replaced by relationship marketing. Recent significant advances in the field of marketing relate to demands for *value-based marketing*, growing *consumer-to-consumer communication* and *digital marketing*, the growth of *social marketing* applications, and the challenges posed to the discipline by critical management scholars and theorists in the form of *critical marketing*. Today, we are in the digital era. To make the marketing concept work, top management must accept it as an overall management philosophy.

The essentials of marketing are that there are marketing analyses, a marketing strategy, marketing programmes centred around well-specified marketing mixes, plus marketing management controls and implementation practices. *Marketing strategy* involves selecting which marketing opportunities to pursue, analyzing a target market (the group of people the organization wants to reach), and creating and maintaining an appropriate *marketing mix* (product, place/distribution, promotion, price and people) to satisfy this target market. Effective marketing requires that managers focus on four tasks to achieve set objectives: (1) marketing opportunity analysis, (2) target market selection, (3) marketing mix development and (4) marketing management.

Marketers should be able to recognize and analyze *marketing opportunities*, which are circumstances that allow an organization to take action towards reaching a particular group of customers.

A *target market* is a group of people or organizations for whom a company creates and maintains a marketing mix that specifically fits the needs and preferences of that group. It is important for an organization's management to designate which customer groups the company is trying to serve and to have some information about these customers. The identification and analysis of a target market provide a foundation on which a marketing mix can be developed.

The five principal variables that make up the marketing mix are product, place/distribution, promotion, price and people: the '5Ps'. The *product variable* is the aspect of the marketing mix that deals with researching consumers' or business customers' wants and designing a product with the desired characteristics. A marketing manager tries to make products available in the quantities desired to as many customers as possible, and to keep the total inventory, transport and storage costs as low as possible – the *place/distribution variable*. The *promotion variable* relates to marketing communications used to inform one or more groups of people about an organization and its products. The *price variable* refers to establishing pricing policies and determining product prices. The *people variable* controls the marketing mix; provides customer service and often the interface with customers, facilitates the product's distribution, sale and service; and – as consumers or buyers – gives marketing its rationale. Marketing exists to encourage consumer satisfaction.

Marketing management is a process of planning, organizing, implementing and controlling marketing activities to facilitate and expedite exchanges effectively and efficiently. Marketing planning is a systematic process of assessing opportunities and resources, developing a marketing strategy, determining marketing objectives and developing plans for implementation and control. The operationalization of the marketing plan is a core element of marketing management. Organizing marketing activities refers to developing the internal structure of the marketing unit. Properly implementing marketing plans depends on coordinating marketing activities, motivating marketing personnel and communicating effectively within the unit. The marketing control process consists of establishing performance standards, evaluating actual performance by comparing it with established standards, and reducing the difference between desired and actual performance.

Key links

At the end of each chapter summary, a 'Key links' box will steer readers to any chapters that are directly related.

Given that this is an introductory chapter, the other chapters of *Marketing: Concepts and Strategies* are all relevant links.

Specifically, Chapters 2 and 3 are required reading associated to this introductory chapter.

Important terms

Consumer-to-consumer (C2C) communication
Critical marketing
Customer satisfaction
Digital era
Digital marketing
Exchange
Good
Idea
Marketing
Marketing concept
Marketing environment
Marketing era
Marketing management
Marketing mix
Marketing opportunity
Marketing orientation
Marketing planning
Marketing process
Marketing strategy
People variable
Place/distribution variable
Price variable

Product
Product variable
Production era
Promotion variable
Relationship marketing era
Sales era
Service
Social marketing
Target market

Discussion and review questions

1. What is meant by marketing orientation?
2. What is marketing? How did you define marketing before you read this chapter?
3. Why should someone study marketing?
4. What is the marketing process? Why should the process be so sequenced?
5. Discuss the basic elements of the marketing concept. Which organizations use this concept? Have these organizations adopted the marketing concept? Explain your views.
6. Identify several organizations that obviously have not adopted the marketing concept. What characteristics of these organizations indicate non-acceptance of the marketing concept?
7. What is digital marketing and why is it now so important to marketers?
8. Give an overview of what is meant by social marketing.
9. Briefly outline some issues of importance to critical marketers.
10. Describe the major components of a marketing strategy. How are these major components related?
11. Identify the tasks involved in developing a marketing strategy.
12. What are the primary issues that marketing managers consider when conducting a market opportunity analysis?

13. What are the variables in the marketing environment? How much control does a marketing manager have over environmental variables?

14. Why is the selection of a target market such an important issue?

15. Why are the elements of the marketing mix known as variables? What are these variables?

16. What type of management activities are involved in marketing management?

17. Why is it important to adhere to the principle of analyses first, then marketing strategy development, followed ultimately by programmes for implementing the recommended marketing strategy?

Further readings

In addition to the general marketing introductory texts recommended at the end of this chapter, readers studying for marketing examinations or wishing to put into practice these concepts of marketing may find the following books useful:

● *Marketing Briefs: A Study and Revision Guide,* Sally Dibb and Lyndon Simkin (Oxford: Elsevier Butterworth-Heinemann), 2004. As implied in the title, this is a revision aid, complete with brief overviews of concepts, illustrative examples and cases, trial questions and revision guidance.

● *Marketing Essentials*, Sally Dibb and Lyndon Simkin (London: Cengage), 2013. An abbreviated version of this text, useful for revision purposes.

● *Marketing Planning,* Sally Dibb and Lyndon Simkin (London: Cengage), 2008. Aimed at marketing practitioners and offering a step-by-step guide to undertaking planning.

Internet exercise

Seat cars used to be cheap and cheerful. Under VW's ownership the marque has been repositioned as better built, sporty but still good value. The range of cars is well specified, produced to VW's high standards, reasonably quick, but keenly priced. Take a look at Seat's website at: www.seat.co.uk or www.seat.com

1. How user-friendly is the site?

2. To what extent does the site provide the information required by someone seeking additional product information in order to construct a shortlist of possible car models to purchase?

3. Consider the decision-making process of a car buyer: to what extent is this website reflecting the issues considered by car buyers?

● *Market Segmentation Success: Making It Happen!,* Sally Dibb and Lyndon Simkin (New York: The Haworth Press/Routledge), 2008. Aimed at marketing practitioners undertaking market segmentation and devising a target market strategy.

Recommended readings

Baker, M., *Marketing Strategy and Management* (Palgrave Macmillan, 2014).

Baker, M. and Saren, M., *Marketing Theory: A Student Text* (Sage, 2015).

Boone, L. and Kurtz, D., *Contemporary Marketing* (Cengage, 2015).

Day, G.S., *The Market Driven Organization: Attracting and Keeping Valuable Customers* (Free Press, 1999).

Fahy, J. and Jobber, D., *Foundations of Marketing* (McGraw-Hill, 2012).

Kotler, P. and Armstrong, G., *Principles of Marketing* (Pearson, 2013).

Group tasks

1. Consider the importance of marketing to the major smartphone producers, such as Apple and Samsung. What does marketing do for these companies?

2. As a group, brainstorm what marketers do … their remit, principal tasks and the activities they undertake in order to fulfil their remit.

Applied mini-case

The market for crisps (potato chips) is dominated by global giants such as Kellogg's and PepsiCo. Brands including Pringles, Walkers and KP are household names. So what of Salty Dog? Never heard of these hand-cooked crisps that bite back? Salty Dog has been voted one of the coolest brands in the UK for four years (www.saltydog-grrr.com). They are produced by a very small-scale operation, run from a barn deep in the Chiltern hills in the UK. Since their launch in 2002, sales have been way ahead of forecasts and exports are heading to France, Germany, Norway, Belgium and even China. So far so good, but, in order to grow, the company has to attract major retailers and pub/bar chains, and broaden the brand's appeal among consumers – not easy tasks. Worse, the company is now attracting the attention of the major players in this market, which are unlikely to stand back and permit Salty Dog to steal their market shares.

Question

As a newly recruited marketing manager for Salty Dog, what would be your priorities? How would you explain these to the owners of Salty Dog?

Sweden's IKEA marches on

Welcome to IKEA. We believe everyone deserves to have a beautiful home filled with well-designed furniture. And still have money left over for other things to enjoy in life. That's why we offer our home furniture at prices so low, that as many people as possible will be able to afford them. Here you can find inspiration for your home, and shop our range of home furnishings – including beds, sofas, sofa beds, curtains, oak furniture, rugs, bedding and blinds.

When Swedish home furnishings retailer IKEA opened its first store in the UK, a retail shed near the M6 at Warrington, curious shoppers found queues jamming nearby roads, parking spaces at a premium and retailing analysts by the score. With just one store, IKEA had the UK furniture industry on its toes: large retail groups and manufacturers alike feared large market share losses. With the opening of a national network of 18 IKEA-branded stores, IKEA has conquered yet another territory. Such an impact is not confined to the UK market. The leading five countries for IKEA are Germany, the UK, the USA, France and Sweden, but global expansion is extensive … just check out details of store openings on www.ikea.com.

IKEA has grown from one store in 1958 to 315 stores in 27 countries belonging to the IKEA Group; with sales of 29.3 billion euros, 716 000 000 customer visitors to stores each year and 1.5 billion web visits. Annually, 217 000 000 copies of the famous IKEA catalogue are distributed. Close to 70 per cent of sales are from within Europe, but expansion in North America, South-East Asia and Australasia is now increasing sales in the rest of the world – despite some initial franchising difficulties in certain territories. IKEA's distinctive catalogue is produced in-house and now printed in 30 languages. IKEA is perhaps one of the world's most successful retailers, with a brand name that is known, recognized and discussed; a retail concept that stands for value, style and quality; everything for the home under one roof, with easy parking, children's play areas and cafés – in fact, 'a day out'!

As the company succinctly stated in its advertising:

IKEA: the furnishings store from Sweden
   More for your money
   IKEA is more than just furnishing ideas. It's a day out for all the family.
   Most of the time, beautifully designed home furnishings are created for a small part of the population – the few who can afford them. From the beginning, IKEA has taken a different path. We have decided to side with the many.

That means responding to the home furnishing needs of people throughout the world. People with many different needs, tastes, dreams, aspirations… and wallets. People who want to improve their home and create a better everyday life.

For IKEA, helping create a better everyday life means offering a wide range of home furnishings in IKEA stores. Home furnishings that combine good design, good function and good quality with prices so low that as many people as possible can afford them.

Source: IKEA

IKEA's huge volumes – 9500 items in a typical store – cheap out-of-town sites and dedication to keeping costs low through self-assembly packs mean that, unlike many competitors, the company can cope with any troughs in consumer spending. Low prices have been the key to IKEA's success, but price alone cannot create an international long-term marketing success story. Products are updated consistently to match consumers' expectations and lifestyles. In-store service and staff training are integral to the IKEA shopping experience. Store sites are chosen to maximize catchment areas, to make access easy for shoppers and to bring the brand name to the attention of the whole community. Logistics give IKEA an edge, with carefully managed ordering and delivery reducing both stock holdings and stock-outs. Promotion emphasizes the 'style without expense' philosophy and the IKEA name. The result has been a country-by-country revolution as staid furniture markets have been rejuvenated with the entry of IKEA. Shoppers intending to buy just a sofa return home with a sofa, a chair, some lamps and a general excitement about a new store where they can buy home furnishings at unbelievable prices. The IKEA vision is simple: 'Good design and function at low prices.'

The latest strategic developments for IKEA include entering eastern European markets, developing new IKEA formats and expanding its mail-order/electronic ordering. For a long time, IKEA resisted e-shopping, wanting customers instead to visit stores to appreciate the full IKEA range and brand experience. Now there are over 1.5 billion web visits per annum and rising. Eastern Europe has been a recent target for expansion, with IKEA stores opening in Poland, the Czech Republic and Hungary. Russia, Greece and Turkey have witnessed recent expansion. The company is also sourcing furniture from eastern European manufacturers, which now supply 15 per cent of its range. As an experiment, the standard 'big box' IKEA concept was brought to a smaller stage with the New York opening in Manhattan of the first IKEA Marketing Outpost, a 720-square-metre (7500-square-foot) 'boutique', significantly smaller than the normal 19 000-square-metre (200 000-square-foot) IKEA superstore. Even more unusual was the decision – in this test concept – to offer only a selected, themed, reduced range at any point in time. For example, IKEA Cook showcased the company's kitchen-related merchandise. In 2008, Coventry in the UK saw the opening of IKEA's first ever 'vertical store': built on the city centre site of a former grocery superstore, the constrained site led IKEA to develop a new-look format that retails on three levels, with parking on three others. Its city-centre location enabled more scope for IKEA's well known catering outlets, including an on-street pavement café.

IKEA has its ideals and operating philosophies: standards matter. IKEA has a forceful, well-directed marketing strategy actioned through primarily one tightly developed marketing mix for the core superstore operation. The result is a successful, expanding company, satisfied target customers, highly motivated personnel and unhappy competitors. Despite global economic problems, the company is going from strength-to-strength.

Questions for discussion

1. Explain why IKEA is successful.

2. Why has IKEA developed new formats?

3. In what ways does IKEA deploy the marketing concept?

Sources: www.ikea.com, 1 February, 2011; www.ikea.co.uk, 2004; Helen Jones, 'IKEA's global strategy is a winning formula', *Marketing Week*, 15 March 1996, p. 22; Jennifer Pellet, 'IKEA takes Manhattan!', *Discount Merchandiser*, October 1995, pp. 22–23; 'IKEA', *Retail Business*, March 1995, pp. 78–81; Jonathan Pell, 'IKEA successfully penetrates east European consumer markets', *Central European*, June 1994, pp. 13–14; www.ikea.com, 2007; IKEA Coventry store, 2008 and 2011; IKEA Delft (strategy HQ), 2009/10; Eli Greenblat, 'IKEA ups sales and profit despite tight market', *The Sydney Morning Herald*, 15 January 2014; Claire Reilly, 'The sleeping giant: IKEA appliances and electrical', *Appliance Retailer*, 18 February 2013; Ikea.com, April 2015.

CHAPTER 2

Marketing strategy and understanding competitors

"Identifying where are the opportunities and which to pursue is fundamental to effective marketing"

Objectives

- To define marketing strategy and explore the relationship with a company's organizational mission, goals and corporate strategy.

- To assess organizational opportunities, capabilities and the SWOT analysis.

- To consider strategic objectives.

- To appreciate the role of target market strategy, customer value and brand positioning in marketing strategy.

- To examine competitive advantage, competitive positions and differential advantage.

- To explore marketing objectives and understand the role of marketing mix programmes in marketing strategy.

- To understand the importance of implementation and performance monitoring in marketing strategy.

INTRODUCTION

Marketing strategy involves planning and decision-making, with the aim of selecting and pursuing marketing opportunities, identifying appropriate target markets, and establishing a competitive advantage. This requires an awareness of the external trading environment and market trends, an appreciation of the organization's capabilities and resource base, an understanding of changing customer behaviours and expectations, knowledge of competitors' intentions and propositions, and understanding of how an organization is performing. Marketing mix programmes must be developed to reflect these market conditions, organizational characteristics, agreed pursuit priorities and target market strategies. The marketing strategy needs careful consideration before marketing programmes are created or executed.

Marketing-oriented organizations have a marketing strategy that clearly articulates to a broad set of internal audiences the opportunities the organization has decided to address, and aligns the organization to a specific set of target markets, while reflecting external drivers in the marketplace. Decisions will have been made with the knowledge of market drivers and marketing environment forces; an understanding of customer needs, expectations and buying behaviour; and with full knowledge of competitors' activities and their likely impact in target markets. The strategy will reflect the marketing assets and capabilities of the organization. This mix of external and internal awareness is pivotal to effective marketing strategy development. An organization's marketing plan will then specify marketing programmes and a roadmap designed to execute this marketing strategy.

Diversification of a brand: Coca-Cola's move into clothing

Sassi Sam Girlie Gossip Files focuses on fashion, beauty, lifestyle and pop culture. According to its creator, 'Sassi is a self-proclaimed shopaholic who loves all things fun and girlie and I have created a website and blog that embodies this ideal. Everything is from Sassi's perspective, she's your online virtual friend.' This is what Sassi had to say about a well-known brand in a blog:

I know this is a completely random ad campaign to post and you may not even know that Coca-Cola have a fashion collection, but they do in Brazil and this is their ad campaign.

The reason why I'm posting this campaign is from a branding perspective. As you know I'm obsessed with branding, and you seriously couldn't get a more perfect on-brand campaign than this one for Coca-Cola. It is exactly what you would imagine a Coca-Cola Fashion campaign to look like. It's so on-brand it just doesn't seem real!

Featuring Brazilian models Ana Paula Scopel, Iuri Jasper, Leonardo Alberici, Reinaldo Berthoti and Renata Sozzi at the beach, where else, having fun in the sun which is the Coca-Cola brand message from the beginning of time!

www.sassisamblog.com
/coca-cola-clothing-springsummer-campaign/

So why has Coca-Cola extended the well-known brand for soft drinks into new territory? In general, Coca-Cola has enjoyed the effects of massive growth in global soft drinks sales. However, in recent times growth has been more erratic. Senior managers were quick to deny that the core soft drinks business had reached maturity, instead blaming economic problems in key markets for the difficulties. The launch of clothing - Coca-Cola Ware — was not, they stated, because of difficulties with the core business. Instead, the company sees the clothing as a promotional activity and extension of Coca-Cola's licencing programme, which raises the profile of the brand around the world and is a core ingredient of the brand's strategy. It is also a growing revenue stream in its own right. Sassi's blog indicates that Coca-Cola's strategy is working. It also illustrates the power of websites and social media in today's marketplace. The clothing range certainly added an extra dimension to the company's existing licencing activities.

The clothing range, which comprises casual clothing and accessories, was test marketed prior to being launched globally. The target market for the jeans, woven clothing and knitwear is teenagers and young adults. According to Coca Cola, 'This is an integrated approach to create a fashion line with a cohesive feel and a sense of lifestyle.' Coca-Cola Ware is sold through department stores, fashion boutiques, specialist 'active' wear shops and by Coke on line (www.coca-colastore.com). The company was quick to stress that the range is used to support and communicate Coca-Cola brand values, rather than to detract from the company's core products of soft drinks. This is a similar brand-building approach to that adopted by construction equipment giants CAT and JCB, whose footwear, clothing and children's toy ranges have done much to raise the profile of their brands. Jaguar also entered the fray, with a range of men's clothing competing with the likes of Boss and Armani.

The extension of familiar brands into clothing is not a new trend. However, in a highly competitive market, already saturated with well-known fashion house labels, success is difficult to achieve. One brand extension expert believes that brands seeking such a move must exhibit three crucial strengths: expertise, image and reputation. Few would deny that the classic and timeless brand of Coca-Cola possesses these qualities. Certainly, Sassi's Brazilian endorsement implies that Coca-Cola Ware is creating the right impression.

All marketers strive to promote their brands. Coca-Cola's marketers hope Coca-Cola Ware will lead to thousands of walking 'adverts', raising the profile of this already ubiquitous and successful brand. Nevertheless, the move into clothing was a significant diversification from the company's soft drinks business.

A model presents a creation by Coca-Cola

Sources: www.Coca-Cola.com, 2004, 2007, 2011, 2015; Julia Day, 'Coke plans global clothing brands', *Marketing Week*, 21 January 1999, pp. 37–42; www .colacorner.com/vintageitems.html, 12 February 2011; www.coca-colastore .com, 12 February 2011 and 15 April 2015; www.sassisamblog.com/2010/08/08/coca-cola-clothing-springsummer-campaign, 12 February 2011.

his chapter aims to highlight which strategic marketing considerations help to ensure that a product or service is marketed for the benefit of the organization as well as its targeted customers. The product or service should be marketed differently enough from competitors' marketing programmes and customer value propositions to provide the organization's product or service with a perceived advantage over these competitors in shrewdly selected target markets. These core components of marketing strategy are illustrated in Figure 2.1 and are clearly of great concern to the business described in this chapter's opener, Coca-Cola, as it chose to diversify into clothing.

The chapter first scopes what is meant by marketing strategy, before exploring linkages with corporate strategy and strategic market planning, stressing the importance of organizational mission and goals. The discussion next turns to assessing organizational opportunities and resources, as well as identifying strategic objectives and strategic focus. The chapter addresses the all-important role of identifying market segments, targeting and brand positioning in marketing strategy: the development of clear target market priorities. The importance of customer value propositions is also established. The chapter then focuses on competitive strategies for marketing: the role of competition, its ramifications for strategy, competitive positions and warfare strategies. The link between marketing objectives and marketing mix programmes is examined, along with implementation and performance monitoring.

Marketing strategy defined

Marketing strategy
The selection of new opportunities to pursue and current activities to support, identification of associated target markets and competitive positioning, and the creation of appropriate value propositions and customer engagement plans, in order to deliver the specified performance goals in the corporate strategy.

Marketing strategy is often described as the vision and the required planning for how to increase sales in priority target markets, achieve a sustainable competitive advantage and continue to satisfy customers,[1] combining all of the organization's marketing goals in a comprehensive plan.[2] *Marketing strategy* is defined here as the selection of new opportunities to pursue and current activities to support, identification of associated target markets and competitive positioning, and the creation of appropriate value propositions and customer engagement plans, in order to deliver the specified performance goals in the corporate strategy.

This is because marketing strategy involves a set of very important activities:

- An awareness of performance regarding where the organization currently succeeds and loses in terms of net revenues, market shares, customer satisfaction and the ability to compete effectively.

- The identification and assessment of new opportunities to pursue and the selection of the overall mix of existing and new activities to support.

- The creation of an associated target market strategy and decisions regarding which potential customers in a market to focus on and which to ignore.

- Development of a competitive advantage and basis for competing.

- The communication of a compelling value proposition and brand positioning.

- Effective consumer or business customer engagement and retention.

- The execution of appropriate marketing programmes for initial engagement on ongoing customer experience management.

- The management of this implementation with appropriate resources, controls and benchmarks.

In developing and managing a marketing strategy, marketers should be the 'eyes and ears' or the 'radar' for their organizations, identifying threats and opportunities, devising smart target market strategies, understanding competitors' moves, while satisfying ever-changing customer buying behaviour with value-enhancing propositions. The other functions in a business, such as HR (human resources), IT, Production, R&D (research and development), Finance, Sales,

Logistics and Supply Chain do not have any desire to look out into a market, assess its dynamics, report the implications and seek to align the organization's strategy to these market conditions. It is the marketing or business development function which has this strategically hugely important responsibility.

Therefore, it is important to acknowledge that there are strong linkages between the creation of an effective marketing strategy and the organization's over-arching corporate strategy. **Strategy** is defined[3] as:

> *Strategy* is the *direction* and *scope* of an organization over the *long term*, which achieves *advantage* for the organization through its configuration of *resources* within a challenging *environment*, to meet the needs of *markets* and to fulfil *stakeholder* expectations.

Strategy
The direction and scope of an organization over the longer-term, which achieves advantage for the organization through its configuration of resources within a challenging environment, to meet the needs of markets and to fulfil stakeholder expectations.

To expand on this definition of strategy:

- Direction: To where is the business trying to reach in the longer term?
- Scope: In which markets should a business compete and what kinds of activities are involved in such markets?
- Advantage: How can the business perform better than the competition in those markets?
- Resources: What resources (skills, assets, finance, relationships, technical competence, facilities) are required in order to be able to compete?
- Environment: What external environmental factors affect the business's ability to compete?
- Stakeholders: What are the values and expectations of those who have power in and around the business?

A decade or so ago, marketing strategy merely would have been part of the strategy's execution plan, articulating target market segments on which to focus in order to achieve the stated corporate strategy, identifying an appropriate competitive brand positioning and developing the required marketing programmes for pursuing these targeted customers. The rigour of robust marketing planning, greater prowess in the collection of market insight and analytics, and the desire to seek new business, today result in a marketing function providing so much of the market intelligence necessary for shaping an organization's overall strategy. The marketing function might not have responsibility for managing shareholder value, setting corporate financial goals or the big investment decisions handled by a company's leadership, but marketing is very much pivotal in the other aspects of formulating a corporate strategy.

In creating a corporate strategy, a company's leadership team generally finds that it must address these questions:

1. How best to improve performance, grow the business, provide shareholder value or survive?
2. Which opportunities to prioritize and which products or services to fund?
3. What to stop doing or where to limit resourcing as benefits will be limited?
4. Which target markets to prioritize and with what edge over rivals?
5. How best to engage and excite these markets and customers?
6. How to mobilize internally and ensure alignment to the evolving strategy?

The marketing or business development function has a role in all of these decisions, through insight and analysis, strategic marketing planning, customer engagement and management, as well as supporting communications. Therefore, there is much more to effective marketing than the creation, execution and management of marketing mix programmes. At the heart of this contribution is the strategic marketing process described in Chapter 1, involving marketing analysis, marketing strategy, marketing programmes and marketing controls.

A company's top-level *corporate strategy* sets the agenda for the business's over-arching aims, which is in many cases related to a *strategic market plan* or *business plan*. In order to achieve the objectives in the corporate strategy and to meet the needs of the strategic market plan, they also have a *marketing strategy*. This is operationalized through the *marketing plan*. A later chapter explores marketing planning in more detail.

Marketing strategy articulates the best uses of an organization's resources and tactics to achieve its objectives. It states which opportunities are to be pursued by an organization, indicates the specific markets towards which activities are to be targeted, identifies the types of competitive advantage that are to be developed and exploited, and provides direction for marketing programmes.[4] Implicitly, as described in Figure 2.1, the strategy requires clear objectives and a focus in line with an organization's corporate goals; the 'right' customers must be targeted more effectively than they are by competitors, and associated marketing programmes should be developed to implement the marketing strategy successfully.[5]

Strategic market plan
An outline of the methods and resources required to achieve an organization's goals within a specific target market.

A **strategic market plan** is an outline of the methods and resources required to achieve an organization's goals within a specific target market. It takes into account not only marketing but also all the functional aspects that must be coordinated, such as production, IT, logistics, finance and personnel. Environmental issues are an important consideration too. The concept of the strategic business unit is often used to define areas for consideration in a specific strategic market plan. Each **strategic business unit (SBU)** is a division, product line or other profit centre within a parent company. Each sells a distinct set of products to an identifiable group of customers, and each competes with a well-defined set of competitors. Each SBU's revenues, costs, investments and strategic plans can be separated from those of the parent company and evaluated. SBUs operate in a variety of markets, which have differing growth rates, opportunities, degrees of competition and profit-making potential. Vodafone, for example, has separate management teams for business units handling corporate and private users, pay-as-you-go and those customers on monthly contracts. Strategic planners must recognize the different performance capabilities of each SBU and allocate resources carefully. They must also ensure that the SBUs complement each other for the greater good of the overall business.

Strategic business unit (SBU)
A division, product line or other profit centre within a parent company.

Marketing plan
The written document or blueprint for specifying, implementing and controlling an organization's marketing activities and marketing mixes.

The strategic planning process should be guided by a marketing-oriented culture and processes in the organization.[6] A **marketing plan** includes the framework and entire set of marketing activities to be performed; it is the written document or blueprint for specifying, implementing and controlling an organization's marketing activities and marketing mixes. Thus, a strategic market plan is not the same as a marketing plan; it is a plan of all aspects of an organization's strategy in the marketplace.[7] A marketing plan, in contrast, deals primarily with implementing the marketing strategy as it relates to specific target markets and marketing programmes.[8] The marketing plan states which are priority target markets and details the marketing programmes, specifying also timeframes, budgets and responsibilities.

Marketing objectives must be designed so that their achievement will contribute to the overall corporate strategy and so that they can be accomplished through efficient use of the company's resources. For example, IT services company Fujitsu wants to be the dominant provider of IT solutions and outsourcing to government and the public sector, along with certain commercial sectors such as financial services. The marketing and business development functions in Fujitsu must identify opportunities to pursue in these sectors, specifying target market prospects, developing appropriate services and marketing messages, engaging with potential clients, building relationships and helping to win individual pieces of business within the organization's priority sectors. In some organizations, marketers steer the development of the strategic market plan because they are the holders of market knowledge.

Organizational mission, goals and corporate strategy

Organizational opportunities and capabilities
- Environmental scanning
- Customer and competitor analysis
- Marketing opportunities
- Capabilities and resources

Strategic objectives
- Intense growth
- Diversified growth
- Integrated growth
- Maintenance

Target market strategy and brand positioning
- Market segmentation
- Priority target markets value proposition
- Brand positioning
- Differential advantage

Marketing programme objectives
- Acquisition and retention
- Customer experience across channels

Marketing programmes for implementation
- Marketing mix tactics
- Operational controls

Performance assessment and benchmarking
- Remedial actions

FIGURE 2.1
The components of marketing strategy

Marketing programme
A marketer's marketing mix activities and implementation processes designed to operationalize the marketing strategy.

In other organizations, the board of directors develops the strategic market plan and marketers focus on devising marketing strategies capable of achieving the aims of the top-line strategic market plan.

To achieve its marketing objectives, an organization must develop a marketing strategy or a set of marketing strategies. To operationalize a marketing strategy, a marketing mix must be developed. Most marketers refer to their marketing mix activities as their **marketing programme**. Marketing programmes centre on a detailed marketing mix

FIGURE 2.2
British Gas strives to market the appeal of its range and services

specification and include internal controls and procedures to ensure that they are implemented effectively. Through the process of strategic market planning, an organization can develop marketing strategies that, when properly implemented and controlled, will contribute to the achievement of its marketing objectives and its overall goals. To formulate a marketing strategy, the marketer identifies and analyzes opportunities and the associated target market, and develops a marketing mix to satisfy individuals in that market. Marketing strategy is best formulated when it reflects the overall direction of the organization and is coordinated with all the company's functional areas.

The strategic market planning process is based on an analysis of the broader marketing environment. As detailed in Chapter 3, marketing environment forces can place constraints on an organization and possibly influence its overall goals; they also affect the amount and type of resources that a business can acquire. However, these forces can create favourable opportunities as well opportunities that can be translated into overall organizational goals and marketing objectives. For example, when oil prices increased a few years ago, there was greater opportunity for the emergence of hybrids and eco-friendly transport solutions.

Marketers differ in their viewpoints concerning the effect of marketing environment variables on planning and strategy development. Some take a deterministic perspective, believing that companies must react to external conditions and tailor their strategies and organizational structures to deal with these conditions. According to others, however, companies can influence their environments by choosing in which markets to compete, lobbying regulators and politicians, striving to modify social views, joining forces with trade bodies for campaigning purposes and so forth. They can also change the structures of their industries, engaging in activities such as mergers and acquisitions, demand creation or technological innovation.[9]

Regardless of which viewpoint is adopted, marketing environment variables play a part in the creation of a marketing strategy. When environment variables affect an organization's overall goals, resources, opportunities or target markets, they also affect its marketing strategies, which are based on these factors. Marketing environment forces more directly influence the development of a marketing strategy through their impact on consumers' needs and desires, as well as their effect on competitors' plans, and how they impact on other organizations in their supply chain. In addition, these forces have a bearing on marketing mix decisions. For instance, competition strongly influences marketing mix decisions. An organization must diagnose the marketing mix activities it performs, taking into account competitors' marketing mix decisions, and develop a differential advantage to support a strategy. Thus, as Honda and Toyota entered the luxury car market with the Acura and Lexus models, European car makers BMW, Mercedes and Jaguar had to change their marketing strategies to maintain their market shares. They did so by lowering prices, introducing new models and creating brand-building marketing communications campaigns to compete with the new Japanese models.

Organizational mission, goals and corporate strategy

Central to the strategic market plan is a clear view of the organizational mission, goals and corporate strategy. A company's organizational goals should be derived from its mission the broad, long-term tasks that the organization wants to accomplish. Computer producer Dell has three parts to its mission, co-created by its employees:

- CUSTOMER SATISFACTION: We are an established company striving to satisfy customers by meeting their demands of quality, responsiveness and competitive pricing. Each customer is #1.

- TEAM SATISFACTION: Management and employees are committed to cooperating as a team for the purpose of profitability and gratification of a job well done.

- COMMUNITY SATISFACTION: We will provide jobs in a clean, safe, environmentally sound atmosphere and be an active participant in community affairs.

When a company decides on its mission, it really answers three questions:

1. What is company's core business/areas of activity?
2. How should these evolve?
3. What behaviours are required and expected?[10]

Although these questions seem very simple, they are in fact three of the hardest, yet most important, for any organization to answer.

Creating or revising a mission statement is very difficult because of the many complex variables that must be examined. However, having a mission statement can greatly benefit the organization in at least five ways.[11] A mission statement:

1. Gives the organization a clear purpose and direction, keeping it on track and preventing it from drifting.

2. Describes the unique aim of the organization that helps to differentiate it from similar competing organizations.

3. Keeps the organization focused on customer needs rather than its own abilities. This ensures that the organization remains externally rather than internally focused.

4. Provides specific direction and guidelines to top managers for selecting alternative courses of action. It helps them decide which business opportunities to pursue, as well as which opportunities not to pursue.

5. Offers guidance to all employees and managers of an organization, even if they work in different parts of the world. As a result, the mission statement acts like 'glue' to hold the organization together.

A company's mission and overall organizational goals should guide all its planning efforts. Its goals should specify the ends, or results, that are sought. Examples of organizational goals include profit, return on investment, an increase in market share, an increase/decrease in the number of active markets, the desire to enter specific market sectors, to develop a particular reputation and track record, to contribute to society in specific ways, and to touch employees in a manner desired by them. Organizations can also have short-term and long-term goals. Companies experiencing financial difficulty may be forced to focus solely on the short-term results necessary to stay in business, such as increasing cash flow by lowering prices or selling off parts of the business. Other organizations may have more optimistic long-term goals. In many cases, companies that pursue long-term goals have to sacrifice short-term results to achieve them. Businesses that are successful over time tend to have a longer-term, market-share-driven strategy, rather than a short-term, 'profits only' sales-led emphasis.

An organization in serious financial trouble may be concerned solely with short-run results needed for remaining viable and fending off creditors. There is usually, for example, an airline or major retailer being forced by cash shortages to take drastic action to stay in business. Lowndes Queensway, once the UK's largest retailer of carpets and furniture, had to renegotiate its financing several times with city institutions, alter payment and credit lines and terms with its suppliers, and ultimately identify which of its 500 superstores should be closed to save costs. The company went into receivership despite all its efforts and ceased trading. Woolworths and Republic followed a similar path, while more recently HMV and Waterstones turned to a major store closure programme in order to remain trading. On the other hand, some companies have more optimistic goals. Often manufacturers, such as General Motors, have goals that relate to return on investment. A successful company may want to sacrifice the current year's profits for the long run and at the same time pursue other goals, such as increasing market share.

Corporate strategy
A strategy that determines the organization's vision and goals, and how they are to be addressed, in which markets, with what advantages over competitors, and so aligning resources in key functions accordingly across the business.

Corporate strategy determines the organization's vision and goals, and how best to utilize resources and capabilities in the areas of production, logistics, finance, research and development, human resources, IT, sales, business development and marketing to reach the organization's goals. A corporate strategy determines not only the scope of the business but also its resource deployment, differential advantages and overall coordination of its functional areas, people and their activities. The term 'corporate' in this context does not apply only to corporations: corporate strategy is used by all organizations, from the smallest sole proprietorship to the largest multinational corporation. Corporate strategy is that created centrally and at the top of the organization's decision-making, in order to satisfy the aims of owners, investors and directors.

Corporate strategy is concerned with issues such as diversification, internationalization, acquisitions and mergers, competition, differentiation, interrelationships among business units and environmental issues. Strategic planners attempt to match the resources of the organization with the various opportunities and risks in the external environment. Corporate strategy planners are also concerned with defining the scope and role of the strategic business units of the organization so that they are coordinated to reach the ultimate goals desired.

While not the focus of *Marketing: Concepts and Strategies*, it is important to recognize that the marketing strategy, marketing plan and marketing mix programmes actioned by an organization's marketers must reflect the aims and ethos of the overall corporate strategy. Unfortunately, in some instances those empowered to deliver marketing programmes are unaware of or are unconcerned about the nuances of the organization's overall corporate plan, and may even be pursuing a course of action that is at odds with the leadership team's sense of purpose. In some businesses, this reflects the paucity of analysis behind corporate planning, and the failure to involve senior marketers in such strategy development. In most organizations, the forces of the external marketing environment, competitors' strategies and evolving customer expectations are poorly assessed. In other cases, only an organization's marketers are aware of these issues and have the relevant marketing intelligence to be able to suggest likely scenarios. It is therefore essential that those responsible for establishing corporate plans tap into this expertise and knowledge within the marketing function, just as it is essential for marketers to devise target market strategies and marketing programmes that properly reflect the direction desired by the corporate strategy and their company's leadership team.

Organizational opportunities and resources

There are three major considerations in assessing opportunities and resources:

1. evaluating marketing opportunities
2. environmental scanning (discussed in Chapter 3)
3. understanding the organization's capabilities and assets.

An appreciation of these elements is essential if an organization is to build up a sustainable differential advantage or competitive edge.

Marketing opportunities

Marketing opportunities
Circumstances and timing that allow an organization to take action towards reaching a target market.

A **marketing opportunity** arises when the right combination of circumstances occurs at the right time to allow an organization to take action towards reaching a target market, achieve sales and perform successfully against competitors. Government concerns about energy supplies have provided the turbine makers for wind farms with an opportunity that a few years ago did not exist. An opportunity provides a favourable chance or opening for an organization to generate sales from identifiable markets. For example, in reaction to the overwhelming growth in cereals and other foods containing oat bran which some researchers believe helps lower cholesterol levels the Quaker Oats Company developed an advertising campaign to remind consumers that Quaker porridge oats have always contained oat bran. Increasing concerns about cancer and heart disease gave Quaker a marketing opportunity to reach consumers who are especially health-conscious by touting the health benefits of its oats.

Strategic window
A temporary period of optimum fit between the key requirements of a market and the particular capabilities of a company competing in that market.

The term **strategic window** has been used to describe what are often temporary periods of optimum fit between the key requirements of a market and the particular capabilities of a company competing in that market.[12] A few years ago, there was much interest in organically grown/produced foods, with retailers increasing shelf-space in response to growing consumer demand. Often more expensive than non-organic versions, economic meltdown and tightening consumer spending reduced consumer interest and retailers' displays accordingly … the window of opportunity had closed for certain organic lines.

The attractiveness of marketing opportunities is determined by market factors such as size and growth rate; by political, legal, regulatory, societal, economic and competitive, and technological marketing environment forces; by internal capital, plant, and human and financial resources; and, by expected financial performance.[13] Because each industry and each product is somewhat different, the factors that determine attractiveness tend to vary for different leadership teams, as illustrated in Table 2.1.

TABLE 2.1 Examples of dimensions for attractiveness

Mobile phone operator	Leisure industry company	Insurance business
• Disposable income	• Profitability	• Profit potential
• Willingness to spend on mobiles	• Market growth potential	• Sales level
• Interest in value-added services	• Market share	• Income potential
• ARPU/revenue/profitability the financial worth of the opportunity	• Differentiator possible	• Longevity of opportunity
• Customer share likely in three years	• Competitive intensity	• Size of market
• Loyalty level	• Certainty of customer demand	• Market growth prospects
• Size of the market	• Barriers to entry as blockers to rivals	• Differential advantage possible
• Competitive intensity degree of competition	• Expanding the company's footprint within the market	• Exclusivity possible
• Potential growth		• Competitive situation favourable
• Market share now		• Insurer support
		• Supplier partnership/resource
		• Endorsements
		• Similar markets adaptable capabilities
		• Ease of entry
		• Quality of customers
		• Resources/expertise required

Market requirements
Requirements that relate to customers' needs or desired benefits.

Market requirements relate to customers' needs or desired benefits. Market requirements are satisfied by components of the marketing mix that provide buyers with these benefits. Of course, buyers' perceptions of what requirements fulfil their needs and provide the desired benefits determine the success of any marketing effort. Marketers must devise strategies to out-perform competitors by finding out what product attributes buyers use to select products. An attribute must be important and differentiating if it is to be useful in strategy development. When marketers fail to understand buyers' perceptions and market requirements, the result may be failure. Toyota had failed to attract prestige-led car purchasers, even though it produced well-specified executive cars. The brand image was not attractive enough to these target customers. As a result, Toyota created its highly successful Lexus marque, focusing on the brand values desired by these customers.

Environmental scanning

Environmental scanning
The process of collecting information about the marketing environment to help marketers identify opportunities and threats, and assist in planning.

Environmental scanning is the process of collecting information about the marketing environment to help marketers identify opportunities, prepare for impending threats and assist in planning. Some companies have derived substantial benefits from establishing an environmental scanning (or monitoring) unit within the strategic planning group, as part of their marketing planning activity, or by including line management in teams or committees to conduct environmental analysis. This approach engages management in the process of environmental forecasting and enhances the likelihood of successfully integrating forecasting efforts into strategic market planning.[14] Results of forecasting research show that even simple quantitative forecasting techniques out-perform the unstructured intuitive assessments of experts.[15]

Environmental scanning to detect changes in the environment is extremely important if an organization is to avoid crisis management. A change in the external marketing environment, as explored in the next chapter, can suddenly alter an organization's opportunities or resources. Reformulated strategies may then be needed to guide marketing efforts. For example, after the global banking crisis led to tighter consumer spending and less disposable income, many brands had to re-think their propositions and seek ways for demonstrating value-for-money. Environmental scanning should identify new developments and determine the nature and rate of change.

Capabilities and assets

Capabilities
A company's distinctive competencies to do something well and efficiently.

A company's **capabilities** relate to *distinctive competencies* that it has developed to do something well and efficiently. A company is likely to enjoy a differential advantage over its rivals in an area where its competencies out-do those of its potential competitors.[16] Often a company may possess manufacturing or technical skills that are valuable in areas outside its traditional industry. For example, defence giant Lockheed Martin provided military customers with sensors and data analytics relevant also to the owners of fleets of commercial vehicles interested in optimizing fuel performance and carbon footprints. Capabilities can be classified in terms of **marketing assets**, highlighting capabilities that managers and the marketplace view as beneficially strong. These capabilities can then be stressed to the company's advantage. Marketing assets are commonly classified as either customer-based, distribution-based or internal. *Customer-based* assets include capabilities that are customer-facing, such as brand image and reputation, product quality and customer service expertise; *distribution-based* assets relate to marketing channel issues and may involve density of dealers and geographic coverage, the responsiveness of distributors, after-sales support and logistical capabilities; *internal marketing* assets are operational, process and resource capabilities, including skills, experience, economies of scale, technology, working practices and people resources.[17] It is essential for a business to take time to assess its capabilities and assets, and to map these alongside identified opportunities. Research findings suggest that the mix of these capabilities and assets affects the types of strategy that should be pursued.[18] Table 2.2 depicts the capabilities that certain companies believe are the most important in their respective sectors. The capabilities and

Marketing assets
Customer, distribution and internal capabilities that managers and the marketplace view as beneficially strong.

TABLE 2.2   Examples of capabilities

Mobile phone operator	Leisure industry company	Insurance business
• Network coverage	• IT capability	• Expertise/skills
• Network quality	• Expertise and skills of the company's people	• Brand awareness/presence
• Voice/data roaming	• Marketing skills and effectiveness	• Reputation
• Attractive tariffs	• Market insights/business information	• Relationship with key supplier
• Fair billing	• Management bandwidth/focus	• Creation of differentiators
• Products/services/value added services	• Ability to fund	• Access to distribution channel
• Distribution (sales) network	• Ability to serve/provide customer service	• Quality of service
• Brand awareness (strong image)	• Long-term commitment	• Link to trade associations
• Innovativeness	• Suitable track record	• Sales process and skills
• Quality of marketing staff and their outputs		• Marketing/communication
• Customer orientation		• Service ability (spread of base)
		• Resources: IT
		• Resources: financial
		• Resources: people
		• Customer empathy/partnership
		• Long-term commitment
		• Resources: adaptability
		• Delivery/process cost effective solution
		• Experience/credibility
		• Existing customers

SWOT analysis
The examination of an organization's strengths and weaknesses, opportunities and threats, usually depicted on a four-cell chart.

marketing assets that are viewed as being essential for success vary dramatically between industries and sectors, reflecting the nuances of their operations and characteristics.

SWOT analysis (strengths, weaknesses, opportunities, threats) is one of the most simplistic used by marketers; fundamentally it is little more than a set of checklists. However, it cannot be ignored in a book such as this owing to its popularity and widespread use. The strengths it refers to relate to those internal operational, managerial, resource and marketing factors that managers believe provide a strong foundation for their organization's activities and for their ability to compete effectively in the marketplace. Many marketers treat the notion of marketing assets as a means for classifying strengths. Weaknesses are those aspects of the organization, its products and activities in the marketplace that place the organization at a disadvantage vis-à-vis competitors and in the view of targeted customers. Best practice indicates that an organization should strive to remedy such faults, particularly those that may be exploited by rivals. An analysis of strengths and weaknesses is a fundamental aspect for developing a marketing strategy, as an organization must have an awareness of its capabilities and how these map out against competitors' strengths and weaknesses.

The other elements of the SWOT analysis are opportunities and threats, which are external issues in the trading environment. As explained in Chapter 1, at the forefront of the marketing concept is marketing opportunity analysis. A sound appreciation of marketing environment forces and evolving market trends is essential for a marketing-oriented organization. It is difficult to contemplate a scenario in which an organization lacking such an external awareness is able to develop a truly meaningful marketing strategy. As described above, marketing environmental scanning identifies numerous issues that marketers must consider when developing marketing strategies. These market developments may offer opportunities for marketers to exploit or they may be the cause of threats to the fortunes of an organization. As explained in more detail in the next chapter, an awareness of the marketing environment may lead to strategic windows of opportunity. The SWOT analysis, in its simplistic way, has the benefit of placing an organization's strengths and weaknesses in the context of the identified opportunities and threats, so implying the extent to which an organization is capable of leveraging an opportunity or fending off an apparent threat. The SWOT analysis can be an effective scene-setting tool, but *only* if the guidelines detailed in the Marketing Tools and Techniques box below are followed.

Strategic objectives and strategic focus

Ansoff matrix
Ansoff's product–market matrix for determining competitive strategies: market penetration, market development, product development or diversification.

Having evaluated the overall corporate vision, those responsible for devising the marketing strategy must build on their analysis of opportunities and internal capabilities by analytically assessing the most promising directions for their organization and marketing activity. Ansoff developed a well-known tool, the product–market matrix, popularly known as the **Ansoff matrix**, to assist in this decision-making, as depicted in Figure 2.3. A business may choose one or more competitive strategies as the basis for its **strategic objectives**, including intense growth, diversified growth and integrated growth. This matrix can help in determining growth that can be implemented through marketing strategies. Its underlying principles often assist marketers in identifying sources for growth by addressing whether there are the following types of opportunities:

Strategic objectives
Includes intense growth, diversified growth or integrated growth.

- Existing customers – existing products/programmes.
- Existing customers – new products/programmes.
- New customers – existing or new products/programmes.
- Adjacent/new markets – existing or new products/programmes.

Intense growth
Growth that occurs when current products and current markets have the potential for increasing sales.

These are the categories of growth most often discussed by leadership teams, who traditionally shy away from the diversification option included in Ansoff's work. This is a pity, as there are examples of very successful corporations targeting unrelated markets with great success, such as Samsung's belated move into mobile phones, Apple's diversification from computers to audio and then media players, or Fujitsu's manufacturing (under many other brands) of flatscreen televisions.

Ansoff's original work identified categories for growth:

Market penetration
A strategy of increasing sales of current products in current markets.

Intense growth

Intense growth can take place when current products and current markets have the potential for increasing sales. There are three main strategies for intense growth, market penetration, market development and product development.

Market penetration is a strategy of increasing sales in current markets with current products. For example, Coca-Cola and PepsiCo try to achieve increased market share through aggressive advertising and brand building.

Market development
A strategy of increasing sales of current products in new markets.

Market development is a strategy of increasing sales of current products in new markets. For example, a European aircraft manufacturer was able to enter the

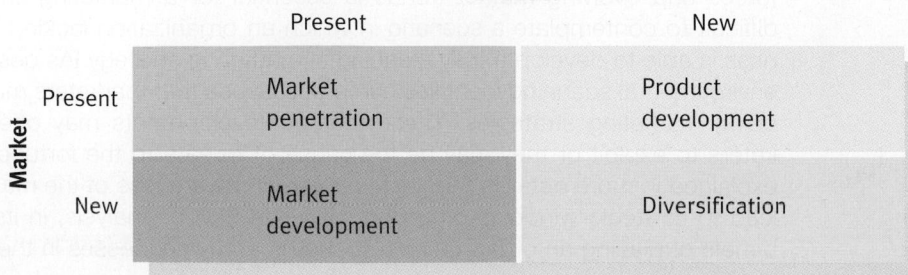

FIGURE 2.3
Ansoff's competitive strategies

Source: 'Ansoff's competitive strategies' from *The New Corporate Strategy* by H. I. Ansoff, John Wiley & Sons, 1988, p. 83. Granted by permission of the Ansoff Family Trust

Practitioners' use of SWOT analysis

The SWOT analysis is a very simplistic tool, yet it appears in most marketing plans and is popular with boards of directors because it conveys so much information: strengths (S)

Marketing tools and techniques

on which to build, weaknesses (W) to rectify, opportunities (O) to consider and threats (T) to address.

The first SWOT depicted (this page) is typical. This was produced by a brainstorming workshop involving 25 sales and marketing personnel. Workshops are often

Strengths	Weaknesses
• Experience and quality of people	• Multiple image
• Safety/environmental standards	• Inconsistent site presentation
• Brand heritage low price perception	• Brand equity value
• Co-op mode of operation	• Inflexible logistics
• Teamwork/alignment	• Lack of maintaining business investment
• New concept	• High break-even cost
• Merchandizing	• Lack of flexible resources
• Category management structure	• Inflexible technology
• Store locations	• Inconsistent focus on retailing/lack of selling structure
• Streamlined organization	• Staff turnover
• Fully integrated company	• Quality of data and analysis
• Ability to change quickly	• Inadequate benchmarking
• Dealer loyalty	• Consumer research
	• Reactive rather than proactive
	• Communication quality/mode
	• Poor succession planning
	• Cost control
	• Total overheads too high
	• Too many non-performing sites

Opportunities	Threats
• Dealer buying group	• Industry restructuring
• Customer loyalty promotion	• By store categories
• Optimizing distribution e.g. push/pull	• By supplier/retailer alliances/JVs
• Market growth of forecourt convenience	• Lack of loyalty programme
• Synergies for services with other brands	• Government transport policy
• Green products	• Lack of shop image and investment
• European purchasing agreements	• Majors targeting smaller dealers
• Joint venture on payment card	• Cost of environmental legislation
• Detailed economic analysis for sites	• Control of costs
• Concessions/rebranding	• Continued low margins
• Alcohol/fast food/bakeries	• Failure to capture convenience market growth
• Technology	
• Small profitable dealers (brand standards)	
• Cost effective store and design	
• More and better use of consumer/customer research industry data	
• Active selling by sales attendants	
• Optimization of site opening hours	
• Promoting underperforming sites/micro marketing	
• Margin enhancement through loyalty scheme	
• Alliance with shop retailers	
• Market attrition	
• Linking site to local community	
• Co-op portfolio management	
• Differentiation through customer service excellence	
• Closer supplier relations	
• Telesales	

used to generate SWOTs; alternatively, individual managers may spend a few minutes producing them, for example, while killing time at an airport. The problems in the example are that:

- the lists were not ranked in order of importance, only listed in the order they were suggested
- many of the bulleted points are vague or ambiguous
- there is no validation or evidence to support these points being included, only the personal judgement of the managers present at the meeting
- the implications are not detailed
- there are far too many non-prioritized points listed to act upon.

By contrast, the following SWOT grid for a major insurance company has a more manageable set of issues, although the points are still horrendously ambiguous. Such ambiguity in practice would need rectifying. For example, what 'network' is a strength: IT, branch, broker, distribution geographically; and in what way?

SWOT grid for an insurance business

	STRENGTHS	WEAKNESSES
Internal issues	Brand recognition Expertise in underwriting Network British, leading UK market Wide product range	Share price Press reports Media targeting Uncertainty redirection/ market segments Poor product differentiation Cost base Wide network
External issues	Profitable markets still far from mature Broker loyalty Business unit focus strategy Technology Joint ventures with 3rd parties, such as major retailers entering fin/servs	Regulation Solvency Share price and ownership Negative press Losing customers Competitors – many mergers taking place Our markets are desirable to Euro-rivals Changing weather patterns
	OPPORTUNITIES	THREATS

Effective SWOTs should adhere to the following essential guidelines:

- Be as focused as possible – no huge lists.
- Use teamwork to generate a range of opinions, then verify with external stakeholders (e.g. channel members, suppliers, customers) and benchmark against any available marketing research or customer satisfaction audit data.
- Concentrate on a customer orientation in allocating priorities: deal first with issues of importance to customers, particularly weaknesses that rivals could exploit.
- Strengths and weaknesses are more revealing when benchmarked against key rivals.
- Use an analysis of the macro marketing environment (see Chapter 3) as input to the opportunities and threats.
- Rank the points listed in order of importance: senior managers assume lists presented to them to be prioritized.
- Have supporting evidence, otherwise exclude the issue from the list.
- Be honest! Include bad news too, such as major weaknesses to rectify and nasty threats to now combat. All too often, managers only wish to communicate opportunities and supporting strengths to their superiors, yet it is unfixed weaknesses which will ruin a strategy and ignored threats which will damage the organization's performance.

Having produced the top-line SWOT depicted here the insurance company team then debated in detail each point in order to clarify the issues, verify their importance and discuss the implication of each issue to the business. This discussion led to a prioritization of tasks to action. This phase is crucial if the SWOT is to help direct a business's thinking.

By following these guidelines, this insurance business eventually produced a meaningful, objective SWOT that led to specific action programmes, notably to address the stated weaknesses and steer the board's thinking about possible opportunities to consider.

Source: © Dibb/Simkin.

Note: a more extensive explanation of this technique is offered in either *The Market Segmentation Workbook* (Dibb and Simkin) *or The Marketing Planning Workbook* (Dibb, Simkin and Bradley), both originally published in 1996 by Thomson, and in *Marketing Planning* (Dibb and Simkin), published by Cengage in 2008.

Product development
A strategy of increasing sales by improving present products or developing new products for current markets.

US market by offering Eastern Airlines financing that Boeing could not match. Evian devised a new use for its mineral water by developing its Brumisateur, an atomiser spray for the skin.

Product development is a strategy of increasing sales by improving present products or developing new products for current markets. PepsiCo and Coca-Cola both have new container sizes, low-calorie/low-sugar/low-carb versions and vending machine services.

Diversified growth

Diversified growth
Growth that occurs when new products are developed to be sold in new markets.

Diversified growth occurs when new products are developed to be sold in new markets. Companies have become increasingly diversified since the 1960s, although many European businesses are reluctant to 'gamble' in what are for them uncharted markets. Diversification offers some advantages over single-business companies, because it allows businesses to spread their risk across a number of markets. More important, it allows them to make better and wider use of their management, technical and financial resources. For example, marketing expertise can be used across businesses, which may also share advertising themes, distribution channels, warehouse facilities or even salesforces.[19] The three forms of diversification are horizontal, concentric and conglomerate.

Horizontal diversification
A process that occurs when new products not technologically related to current products are introduced into current markets.

Horizontal Diversification **Horizontal diversification** results when new products that are not technologically related to current products are introduced to current markets. Sony, for example, diversified from electronics to movie production through its purchase of Columbia Pictures. The purchase gave Sony a library of 2700 films, including *Ghostbusters* and *When Harry Met Sally*, as well as 23 000 television episodes, which it has used to establish its line of video tapes and DVDs.[20]

Concentric diversification
A process that occurs when new products related to current products are introduced into new markets.

Concentric diversification In **concentric diversification**, the marketing and technology of new products are related to current products, but the new ones are introduced into new markets. Apple's now famous and hugely successful move into consumer media players and smartphones leveraged capabilities from its business computing heritage.

Conglomerate diversification
A process that occurs when new products unrelated to current technology, products or markets are introduced into new markets.

Conglomerate diversification **Conglomerate diversification** occurs when new products are unrelated to current technology, products or markets, and are introduced into markets new to the company. For example, Bass, the British brewer and pubs business, acquired the American Holiday Inn hotel chain. Laura Ashley, the UK clothing and furnishings company, moved into the fragrance market with Laura Ashley No. 1. Samsung diversified into everything from air conditioning and construction equipment to shipbuilding, home entertainment centres and mobile phones.

Integrated growth

Integrated growth
Growth that occurs in three possible directions: forwards, backwards or horizontally.

Integrated growth can occur in the same industry that the company is in and in three possible directions: forwards, backwards or horizontally.

1. A company growing through forward integration takes ownership or increased control of its distribution system. For example, a shoe manufacturer might start selling its products through wholly-owned retail outlets.

2. In backward integration, a company takes ownership or increased control of its supply systems. A newspaper company that buys a paper mill is integrating backwards.

3. Horizontal integration occurs when a company takes ownership or control of some of its competitors, such as BMW's acquisition of Mini.

An absolutely crucial part of developing both a corporate strategy and a marketing strategy is the need to seek competitive advantage over rivals and the associated importance of gaining competitor intelligence. In developing strategies, an organization must consider the competitive positions in the marketplace and formulate marketing strategies and tactics accordingly. Some authors have adopted warfare analogies to describe the strategic options for competing in a market.[21] This chapter later examines the concept of competitive positions.

Target market strategy and brand positioning

Central to achieving a company's corporate vision is the need to build up a loyal customer base of satisfied customers. Tesco did not overtake Sainsbury's by chance; it developed a clear marketing strategy based on a desire to fully satisfy a carefully targeted set of market segments. More recently, Tesco lost its way with a poorly defined marketing strategy, enabling discounters Lidl and Aldi to take on some of Tesco's value customers and Waitrose to acquire many of its upper-end consumers.

Market segmentation is at the core of robust marketing strategy development. As explained in Chapter 7, this involves identifying customer needs, expectations, perceptions, decision-making and buying behaviours, so as to group those customers with similar needs and behaviours and who will be marketed to in a similar manner together in homogeneous groups or market segments. One segment will differ from another in terms of customer profile and buying behaviour, and also with regard to the sales and marketing activity likely to satisfy these customers; but within a particular segment customers will share similar needs, buying behaviour and expectations. Without a thorough understanding of customers, therefore, it is difficult to produce a marketing strategy. Developing an understanding of customers is explored in Chapters 5 and 6.

Taking the time to objectively and sensibly group a market's customers into meaningful market segments is a discipline many organizations are only now discovering, particularly in business-to-business markets. Most of the fast movers, market leaders and successful brands in a marketplace base their marketing strategies on carefully honed market segmentation analyses. It is important to remember that the process of market segmentation involves more than simply grouping customers into segments or groups. Shrewd targeting of certain segments and the development of a clear brand positioning are part of the market segmentation process. **Brand positioning** is the creation of a desirable, distinctive and plausible image for a brand that will have strong appeal for the customers in a target market segment. The basis of Chapters 7 and 8 – identifying segments, deciding which to target, developing desirable positionings and establishing strong customer value propositions – is one of the foundations of a marketing strategy.

Brand positioning
The creation of a desirable, distinctive and plausible image for a brand in the minds of targeted customers.

A **target market strategy** is the choice of which market segment(s) an organization decides to prioritize and for which to develop marketing programmes. An organization must first have agreed an over-riding corporate strategy and decided on which opportunities to focus, as described above. The selected target markets should be appropriate for this selection of opportunities, within the stated corporate strategy. Organizations must identify priority target markets that are worthwhile targeting with bespoke marketing mix programmes: product, price, place (distribution), promotion and people. Even the mighty Ford or General Motors has to decide which segments in the car and van markets to pursue, opting not to have models aimed at all buyers in the market. It is important to balance current core target markets with those offering future viability.

Target market strategy
The choice for which market segment(s) an organization decides to develop marketing programmes.

Once determined, in each target market an organization must strive to emphasize to those targeted customers the relevance and applicability of its product and marketing mix proposition. This is achieved through all ingredients of the marketing mix, but specifically through developing a distinctive, plausible and memorable brand positioning, such as BMW's 'The Ultimate Driving Machine'. This positioning imagery is communicated to targeted customers primarily through the promotional mix, packaging and design, but product attributes, pricing, choice of distribution and customer service provision must also support the positioning strategy. An upmarket restaurant, for example, requires a suitably lavish ambience, slick service, quality food, appropriate location and a suitable price to match its branding and promotional campaigns. Associated with brand positioning is the development of customer value propositions, which reflect customers' needs and wants and how they trade-off their options. It is important to agree on the target market strategy, required brand positioning and the **customer value proposition** before developing the marketing programmes destined to implement this strategy. These marketing mix activities must reflect the marketing analyses and target market strategy requirements rather than being merely a continuation of previous marketing mix activities.

Customer value proposition
Based on understanding the perceived customer values and psychological, functional and economic factors traded-off when customers select a particular product or brand to purchase.

Competitive advantage

Competitors
Organizations viewed as marketing products similar to, or substitutable for, a company's products, when targeted at the same customers.

Competitive advantage
The achievement of superior performance vis-à-vis rivals, through differentiation to create distinctive product appeal or brand identity; through providing customer value and achieving the lowest delivered cost; or by focusing on narrowly scoped product categories or market niches so as to be viewed as a leading specialist.

Generic routes to competitive advantage
Cost leadership, differentiation and focus; not mutually exclusive.

Competitors are generally viewed by an organization as those businesses marketing products similar to, or substitutable for, its products when targeted at the same customers. In order to persuade customers to purchase an organization's products in preference to those products marketed by its **competitors**, leading strategists argue that it is necessary to develop a **competitive advantage**. Competitive advantage is the achievement of superior performance vis-à-vis rivals, through differentiation, to create distinctive product appeal or brand identity; through offering customer value and achieving the lowest delivered cost; or by focusing on narrowly scoped product categories or market niches so as to be viewed as a leading specialist. The creation of a competitive advantage is a core component of the development of a marketing strategy. It is not easy to achieve, as rivals often have sensible strategies, good products and customer service and smart marketing programmes.

Marketing strategist Michael Porter identified the so-called **generic routes to competitive advantage**, claiming them to result in success for companies competing for position in any particular market. Although created over 40 years ago, this framework is still appropriate and highly directional for companies seeking to examine thoroughly their likely basis for competing. As depicted in Figure 2.4, these three generic strategies are as follows:

1. *Cost leadership.* This involves developing a low cost base, often through economies of scale associated with high market share and economies of experience, to give high contribution. This high financial contribution can then be used to further develop the low cost base. Very tight cost controls are essential to the success of this strategy. Generally, within a single market, only one competitor is secure in adopting this strategy for creating a competitive advantage: the organization with the lowest cost base and best experience curve.

2. *Differentiation.* Companies adopting a differentiation strategy strive to offer product and marketing programmes that have a distinct advantage or are different to those offered by competitors. Differentiation can be achieved on a number of fronts, including creative and innovative product or brand designs, or novel distribution channel, pricing and customer service policies. This theme is taken further when marketers seek a *differential advantage*, as discussed later in this chapter.

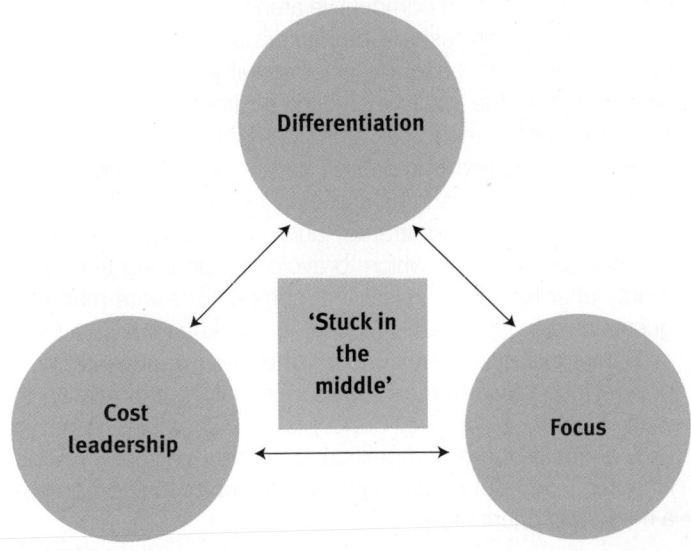

FIGURE 2.4
Porter's generic routes to competitive advantage

3. *Focus.* Companies must maintain close links with the market so that product and marketing effort are designed with a particular target group in mind. Typically of small size, unable to achieve cost leadership or maintain significant differentiation, such companies succeed by effectively meeting customer needs that may be being missed by larger players in the market and by gaining a reputation for being experts or specialists in their narrowly defined area of activity.

Failure to achieve any of these strategies can result in companies becoming 'stuck in the middle', with no real competitive advantage. It is not usually possible to simultaneously follow all three generic strategies for competitive advantage, but it is common for businesses to gain cost leadership while also differentiating their proposition, and also for organizations to seek both a focused and a differentiated approach. Discounter Aldi adopts a cost leadership and a differentiated approach for developing a competitive advantage, as does no-frills airline easyJet. Sports coupé manufacturer Porsche adopts a focused and differentiated approach to defining a competitive advantage. It is sometimes more difficult to create a focused and cost leadership approach, as niche players rarely have the necessary scale economies, but it is not impossible. Companies or brands failing to master at least one of Porter's dimensions invariably struggle to compete or indeed to survive in the medium-term.

Competitive positions and differential advantage

In order to compete effectively, marketers should seek to develop a differential advantage. In order to ensure this will be effective, marketers must understand the nature of the

Competitive set
All competing organizations and brands, irrespective of size and history, including substitutable solutions to customers' needs, as defined by the target market customers.

competitive set and also identify those rivals with which to do battle. The competitive set includes all competing organizations and brands, irrespective of size and history, including substitutable solutions to customers' needs, as defined by target market customers. Leading marketing strategists David Aaker and Michael Porter both argue that the scoping of the competitive set in many organizations is too limited. Ask most management teams who are their competitors and they will simply name the leading few organizations and brands in the market, ignoring smaller fast-moving rivals, probable new entrants to the market or substitutable solutions to their customers' needs offered by dissimilar organizations. It is often the case that when a company's customers are asked to name the competing companies or brands, they list a few names not routinely considered by the company's marketers. The customer's view of his or her options is of paramount importance and marketers should ensure that their interpretation of the competitive set is shared by their target market customers.

The scoping of the competitive arena and the identification of the competitive set are important marketing analysis tasks. Competitors are outside the control of an organization, so the forces of competition are generally included within the forces of the *marketing environment*, as part of what is termed the 'micro marketing environment'. This concept is described in Chapter 3, which discusses further the forces of the competitive environment.

For the identified competitive set, marketers should assess the objectives and strategies of these rivals, their strengths and weaknesses, and determine how competitors are likely to react to their own marketing strategy and programmes. In effect, this leads to a decision about which competitors to 'fight', which to avoid antagonizing and which to treat as unimportant. Veronica Wong (after Kotler) suggests that competitor-aware marketers should be able to answer six key questions, as described in Figure 2.5. Marketers require these insights into competitors.

Before examining the concept of differential advantage, this chapter looks at the increasingly popular use of warfare analogies in identifying the relative threat posed by the competitors in a market. While *Marketing: Concepts and Strategies* is not intended to be a marketing strategy text, analysis of the competition is a core principle for effective marketing and, as explained in Chapter 1, without a thorough appreciation of the competitive arena an organization cannot have a marketing orientation.

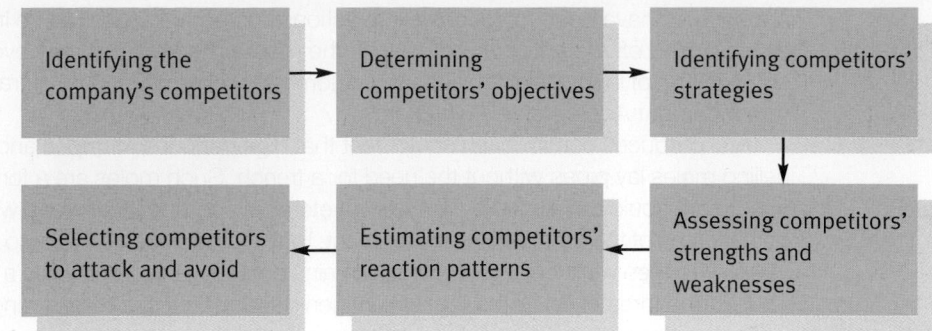

Competitive positions

Evidently it is important to understand the nature of competition. This involves more than a cursory examination of like-for-like major rivals. Most organizations consider only similar companies or brands to be their competitors. As shown in Figure 2.6, there are other facets of competition that must be evaluated. What of the smaller players that may one day emerge as dominant in a market or specific segment? Why not pre-empt such an outcome by developing a strategy to destroy them while still only a small rival? What about the new entrant into the marketplace? Could its

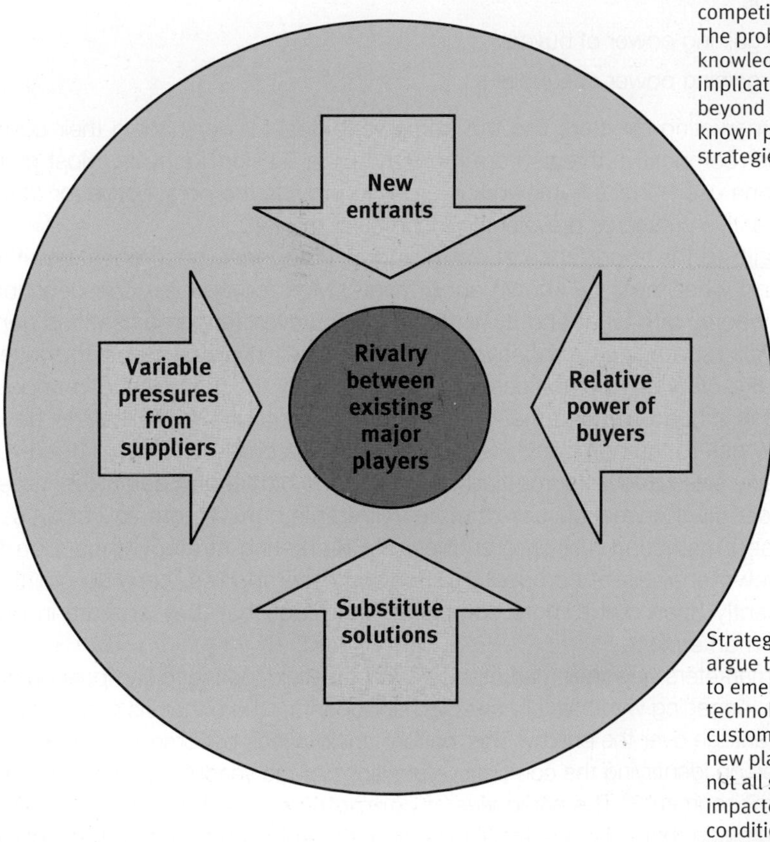

Research reveals that most companies merely monitor like-for-like major competitors, often less than effectively. The problems associated with poor knowledge of competitors and the implications of their activities reach beyond failing to adequately assess known players and their likely strategies and activities.

New entrants

Variable pressures from suppliers

Rivalry between existing major players

Relative power of buyers

Substitute solutions

Strategists such as Michael Porter argue that organizations should look to emerging threats from substitute technologies and solutions to a customer's need, the appearance of new players, as well as recognize that not all suppliers or customers will be impacted in the same way by market conditions and the activities of an individual competitor or market issue.

FIGURE 2.6
Forecasting market potential and sales

appearance have been foreseen? What actions are required to minimize its threat? How did Nokia or Moto fend off the entry of Samsung in the mobile market? Did they even anticipate Samsung's entry? What of innovative solutions to customers' problems? How will traditional watch manufacturers combat Apple's smart watches?

JCB produces construction equipment that digs trenches for pipes and cables. Micro-bore tunnelling moles lay pipes without the need for a trench. Such moles are a form of substitute competition, which could be missed by JCB's marketers as a competitive threat, without a rigorous analysis of the forces of the competitive environment. Web-coms posed a threat to traditional BT phone services, who then went online in order to remain competitive and ended as a major broadband player. The iPhone threatened Samsung, which then developed a successful range of rival smartphones.

The power of suppliers and of consumers can also vary per company and act as a competitive force, particularly if one organization encounters greater supply problems or more severe customer bargaining than its rivals face from their suppliers and customers. These competitor categories are in addition to the like-for-like rivals considered by most organizations to be their competitors.

Figure 2.6 is particularly useful for scoping the nature of a market place. This framework still offers management teams a very smart approach for assessing their competitive arenas. Porter defined **five competitive forces** that together determine competition in an industry or market:

Five competitive forces
Together these determine competition in an industry or market: rivalry amongst existing like-for-like players; the threat of new entrants; the threat of substitute solutions; the bargaining power of buyers; and the bargaining power of suppliers.

1. rivalry among existing like-for-like players
2. the threat of new entrants
3. the threat of substitute products or services as a solution to customers' problems or needs
4. the bargaining power of buyers
5. the bargaining power of suppliers.

Many marketing directors find this framework ideal for persuading their colleagues to consider competitive threats from more than just like-for-like rivals. Most marketing dissertations use Porter's framework in order to provide the perspective for describing the competitive pressures prevalent in a particular market.

In addition to realizing the importance of examining all categories of competitors, it is necessary to understand what must be known about rivals. Most companies can describe their competitors: who, where, with what and at what price. However, few organizations genuinely understand their rivals' strategies or endeavour to predict their rivals' reaction to moves they themselves may make. Very few companies attempt to identify those individual competitors it is sensible to avoid in a head-to-head marketing campaign or those most likely to be vulnerable to attack at low risk to the company's resource base. It is prudent to avoid head-to-head conflict with a similarly sized and resourced adversary, or one bigger and better resourced. It is more desirable to identify the weaknesses of more vulnerable competitors and address these through the proposed marketing mix programmes. No marketing strategy should be formulated without a shrewd analysis of competitors. For some companies, carrying out this kind of analysis has recently been made more complex by the fact that they operate in both the physical and digital marketplace.[22]

Competitive positions
Competitors' roles in the marketplace, which influence their marketing strategies and programmes.

Many marketers view their marketplace as a battlefield, opting to compete on only certain fronts, engaging with carefully selected opponents, where there is a perceived differential advantage over the enemy. This warfare analogy has become increasingly popular and hinges on identifying the competitive positions of the various businesses competing in a market segment.[23] The categories of **competitive positions** competitors' roles in the marketplace that influence their marketing strategies and programmes include the market leader, market challengers, fast movers, market followers and market nichers. These should be identified within each target market segment: a market challenger in one market segment may be a follower or even absent in a second market segment.

Market leader
The single player enjoying the largest individual share in the market.

In the ranking of market shares, there is one and only one **market leader**: the player enjoying individually the largest slice of the market. In some business-to-business markets, a market leader can have a majority of industry sales, particularly when patent protection or technical innovation gives it an advantage over competitors. In most markets, however, the market leader may have only 10 to 20 per cent of the market's sales. The market leader has the highest market share and retains its competitive position by expanding the total market or expanding market share at the expense of its rivals, while protecting or defending current market share by retaining its customer base. In this context, the market leader, although successful, has the most difficult task: it must find strategies to increase market size and market share, as well as maintaining strategies to defend its current share. The marketing programmes necessary for maintaining ongoing relationships with existing customers are quite different to the marketing programmes used to attract and entice potential customers.

Market challengers
Non-market leaders that aggressively try to capture market share from their rivals.

Behind the market leader are competing companies, which are market challengers, fast movers, market followers or market nichers. **Market challengers** are non-market leaders that aggressively attack rivals, including the market leader, to take more market share, as they strive for leadership. In most instances, these players are number two, three and perhaps four in a market, aspiring to market leadership. When Virgin entered the transatlantic market, its intention was to steal BA's market leadership. Apple wants leadership of the smartphone market, while Samsung wants to dominate in tablets. It is important to remember that to qualify as challengers, these companies must be proactive and aggressive in their sales and marketing rather than passively reinforcing the existing hierarchy. **Fast movers** are smaller rival companies not yet destined to be major challengers, but growing rapidly on a smaller scale. A new entrant may have only 2 per cent of the market but what is to stop it from increasing its share to 8 per cent within two years? A business may only have 4 per cent of the market, but three years ago it only had 1 per cent. What is to prevent it from having 8 per cent or 19 per cent in three years' time? The market leader and key challengers should take steps to prevent such continued growth.

Fast movers
Smaller rival companies not yet destined to be major challengers, but growing rapidly on a smaller scale.

Market followers are low-share competitors without the resources, market position, research and development, or commitment to challenge for extra sales and market share. These companies tend to be the 'me-too, also-rans' in a market, whose raison d'être is to do as before and simply survive. In boom times these players can latch on to the success of their larger rivals, but in recession or when faced with larger rivals' product innovations they often struggle to achieve sales. Most markets also contain **market nichers**: companies that specialize by focusing on only a very narrow range of products, or on a select band of consumers, such as The Body Shop or Porsche. Nichers survive by finding a safe, small, profitable market segment often apparently too small to attract the market leaders and challengers. Nichers specialize and can genuinely prepare a marketing mix that exactly matches their target customers' needs. They are vulnerable to market downturns, the entry of rival nichers and the sudden attention of the major players in the marketplace, as happened to Sock Shop, Tie Rack and Saab.

Market followers
Low-share competitors without the resources, market position, research and development, or the commitment to challenge for extra sales and market share.

Market nichers
Companies that specialize by focusing on only a very narrow range of products or on a select band of consumers.

A market leader must defend its position, while simultaneously seeking more market share. Only a market leader should consider **defensive warfare** as a strategic foundation. Strong defence involves striking a balance between waiting for market developments or competitor activity and proactively parrying competitors' actions. As market leader, the company must remember that a false sense of security and passive inactivity lead to disaster: the best defensive strategy is the courage to attack; and strong moves by competitors should always be blocked, never ignored. To defend its market share, a market leader must treat existing customers well and attentively, and never take them for granted. The marketing mix must be updated continually and target customers' needs must regularly be considered. New markets, products and opportunities should always be sought and evaluated. Occasionally, if faced by a strong challenger in a small or declining market, a market leader should consider divesting and concentrating resources in its other markets.

Defensive warfare
A policy of striking a balance between waiting for market developments or competitor activity and proactively parrying competitors' actions.

Others may have to turn to defensive warfare when attacked by the market leader or challengers, but only the market leader should build a strategy around the desire to defend its current position. A challenger has to attack for market share, but on what basis? The leader, and perhaps other challengers, will be strong and rich in resources. A challenger's attack must be well thought out and not suicidal in terms of the company's medium-term future. Lidl and Aldi have very effectively challenged Tesco and Sainsbury's in certain key market segments in the grocery wars.

Offensive warfare
A policy whereby challengers aggressively seek market share by identifying any weaknesses in the leader's and other challengers' marketing mixes and developing a genuine corresponding strength.

In **offensive warfare**, the main consideration is the market leader's strength: where are there any chinks in the leader's armour? A challenger seeking market share must identify a weakness in the leader's marketing mix and in other challengers' marketing programmes, and develop a genuine corresponding strength. With such a differential advantage or competitive edge, the challenger's resources may well be sufficient to steal ground successfully from the leader and the other challengers. Any attack should be on a narrow front, where the challenger is perceived by the target customers to have an advantage and where resources can be focused. If no real weakness in the market leader exists, a challenger may attack head-on. Such an attack can be successful only if there are numerous, very weak market followers, if the leader is slow to react and if a price-cutting war does not result. In the last situation, the leader's resource base may fend off the challenger's attack.

Followers are vulnerable, but careful monitoring of market segments, marketing environment forces and competitive trends can help ensure their survival. They must serve exactly only a few market segments, specializing rather than diversifying in terms of products and markets, and making prudent use of what research and development resources are available. Nichers must watch for signs of competitor threats and possible changes in target segment customers' needs, and they may need to consider product development and, ultimately, diversification. Their marketing mixes must be tailored exactly to meet the expectations of their target segment.

Competitor scanning
The monitoring of competitive positions and competitors' strategies.

All organizations should know, for all their markets and target segments, which companies occupy these competitive positions. They must alter their strategies and marketing programmes accordingly. Organizations should also review their rivals' marketing strategies and marketing programmes: many companies are surprisingly predictable. Response to rivals' pricing policies, frequency of new product launches, entry into new markets and timing of promotional campaigns, for example, can often be accurately anticipated. In this way, **competitor scanning**, the monitoring of competitive positions and competitors' strategies, helps to establish more realistic marketing goals, develop successful strategies and programmes, and pre-empt nasty shocks caused by competitors' actions.[24] The leading marketing strategists agree that it is essential to understand competitors' strategies, their strengths and weaknesses in satisfying customers, and any differential advantages they hold that must be combated.[25] The **competitive positions proforma** has been developed by the authors of *Marketing: Concepts and Strategies*, in conjunction with many organizations such as JCB, HSBC, Fujitsu, EDF and IBM, as a way of scoping the competitive set, helping a company in understanding the competitive positions in its target markets and diagnosing the effectiveness of a marketing strategy. This particular tool for practitioners is described in the Marketing Tools and Techniques box on page 61.

Competitive positions proforma
A tool for scoping the competitive set, helping a company to understand the competitive positions in its target markets and diagnosing the effectiveness of a marketing strategy.

Differential advantage

If a marketing mix is developed that matches target market needs and expectations and is superior to those offered by competitors, there is a real or perceived differential advantage.

Differential advantage
An attribute of a brand, product, service or marketing mix that is desired by the targeted customer and provided by only one supplier.

A **differential advantage** is an attribute of a brand, product, service or marketing mix that is desired by the targeted customer and provided by only one supplier: it is a unique edge over rivals in satisfying this customer. If successful in developing a differential advantage, an organization is likely to have its differential advantage copied by rivals. Direct Line innovated in selling car insurance over the telephone, cutting out the broker. This more convenient and cheaper service was very popular with customers, gaining market leadership for Direct Line. Very high profits followed. Rivals caught up, offering their own telephone-based direct selling of car insurance. Nevertheless, Direct Line developed a sizeable and successful customer base, which is still proving difficult for competitors to win back.

Achieving a differential advantage or competitive edge requires an organization to make the most of its opportunities and resources while offering customers a satisfactory mix of tangible and intangible benefits.[26] When striking a balance between customer requirements on the one hand and company resources on the other, competitor activity must also be monitored. For example, there is little sense in promoting speedy distribution to customers if several large competing organizations offer a faster service. An understanding of competitors and customers' perceptions of companies' propositions is an essential part of identifying a differential advantage. Once determined, it is sensible to maximize the use of any differential advantage in the marketing mix, particularly in the promotional mix and all marketing communications.

There are many different sources of differential advantage that companies can pursue. It is important to ensure that the promoted differential advantage is:

- unique to the one organization, otherwise it is not a differential advantage, only a strength or capability
- desirable to the targeted customer
- not simply the expected marketing mix taken for granted by the target market
- not simply an internal perception by a team of marketers.

For example, a new range may be superior to the company's former product range, but compared to competitors' products may offer few benefits to the customer. The marketers could be guilty of identifying the new range's advantages over the former range, wrongly, as offering a differential advantage.

Marketing tools and techniques

Practitioners' use of competitor intelligence: the Dibb/Simkin competitive positions proforma

The understanding of competition is not generally strong in most organizations. Managers may be able to name their rivals, and these businesses' products, price points and outline promotional activity, but rarely are managers able to suggest rivals' next moves or to identify an individual competitor's strengths or weaknesses. Therefore, managers cannot be taking into account the capabilities and market standing of such rivals when they construct their own target market strategies. The result could be a significant waste, as a company's marketing programme may fail to enable the company to set itself apart from its principal rivals. Worse, the company may be incapable of combating its rivals' marketing strategies.

The ultimate goal in marketing is to produce a differential advantage: something desired by targeted customers and only offered by a single supplier. Failure to analyze rivals means that the creation of a differential advantage is going to occur only by chance, rather than due to knowledge of competitors' strengths and weaknesses.

The strategists also point to the need to address an organization's own weaknesses. In particular, a management team should be aware of which rivals are best placed to exploit any weaknesses in the organization or in its marketing mix. Over time, the competitive set will change, as new entrants and substitution solutions to customers' requirements emerge. The relative strengths and weaknesses of competitors will alter too, often rapidly. The competitive set must be monitored closely and not just occasionally.

Chapter 9 identifies methods for collecting competitor intelligence. Once the competitive set has been defined through the customer's eyes and some knowledge has been built up about these brands, a useful tool to deploy is the competitive positions proforma.

This technique is based on warfare analogies and assumes that the analysis is replicated for each individual target market segment. Within each segment, it is necessary

The Dibb/Simkin competitive positions proforma

		Grocery superstores (out-of-town)	Supermarkets (town centres)
Market leader	ID: Market share: KCVs: Weaknesses: Differential adv.:	Doing Well plc 28%++ (growing) Range, fresh produce, store amenities, deals Board's focus overseas, comp commission Loyalty card scheme	Still Trying plc 24% +/– (static) Locations, fresh produce No compelling wow factor, poor PR —
Challenger 1	ID: Market share: KCVs: Weaknesses: Differential adv.:	Going For It Ltd 21%+ (growing) Range, non-food mix, clothing, amenities, value Some tired stores, no town centre stores US owner = greater resources, buying power	Doing Well plc 16++ (growing) Brand reputation, e-service, fresh produce Pulled out, now re-establishing —
Challenger 2	ID: Market share: KCVs: Weaknesses: Differential adv.:	Still Trying plc 19% (declining) Store ambience, range, reputation, amenities Poor analysis and PR, limited non-food —	New Kid on the Block (merger) 9%++ (growing) Many good locations, fresh produce, value Had lost its way, now catching up —
Challenger 3	ID: Market share: KCVs: Weaknesses: Differential adv.:	New Kid on the Block (merger) 18%++ (growing) Value, fresh produce In-store amenities, no national coverage —	Still Just About Here plc 9%+ (growing) Value-for-money, brands stocked Poor brand reputation, few strengths —
Follower 'me too'	ID: Market share: KCVs: Weaknesses: Differential adv.:	Still Just About Here plc 5% (declining) Store ambience No brand strengths, no buying power —	Also Just Surviving Ltd 7% +/– (static) — Mix of merchandise —
Fast mover	ID: Market share: KCVs: Weaknesses: Differential adv.:		SavaLot Ltd 6%++ (rapid expansion) Value-for-money, merchandise mix Low brand awareness, poor buying power
Nicher	ID: Market share: KCVs: Weaknesses: Differential adv.:	HyperLand plc (JV) 3% Range, value, store amenities, one-stop Few outlets, few scale benefits —	Deluxe Deli Ltd 2%+ (growing, SE only) Service, staff attitude, opening hours, locations Poor buying power, limited network, branding Upscale appeal and target marketing

to allocate the competitive set which may include substitutes and possible new entrants into the following categories:

- *Market leader*. Only ever one in a segment: the player or brand with the biggest market share. The market leader should (1) expand the total market, (2) expand its own market share, and (3) protect existing market share. The market leader has to defend and attack.

- *Market challenger(s)*. Non-market leaders that want to be the leader! Aggressively attacking for market share gains by investing in new product development, establishing distribution, promotional activity, field force increases, customer experience or price incentives.

- *Market follower(s)*. Low-share rivals without resources, market position, R&D or commitment to challenge. The 'me-too' smaller players in a market segment.

- *Market nicher(s)*. Companies that specialize in terms of market/product/customers, by finding a safe, profitable niche or narrowly defined segment.

- *Market fast mover(s)*. Smaller players with intentions to be much bigger. A rival not yet large enough to be classed as a challenger, but one worth watching or 'knocking out' before it is too late.

One column of the proforma is completed for each market segment. A company should include itself within the columns. In this way, a management team may assess the business's relative performance across market segments and identify rivals making gains in more than one segment. In this context, the technique is of great value to the board of a company and not only to marketing managers.

Marketing-oriented businesses repeat this analysis every few months, in order to reveal movements within the columns and to identify fast movers, new entrants or emerging substitute competition. The changing strengths and weaknesses

of rivals also become apparent. If a company is not moving up the column or 'league table' it is likely that its marketing strategy and/or marketing programme are inappropriately specified. Remedial action should be taken.

The competitive positions

For reasons of commercial confidentiality, the identities of the cited retailers have been disguised.
The competitive positions proforma identifies:

- the key players and their relative positions
- current successes and probable reasons
- the KCVs (key customer values or needs) each rival is good at serving rivals' customer-facing strengths that must be addressed
- any differential advantages (DAs) to fear these must be combated
- the company's own standing, which should improve over time
- emerging and fast-moving rivals, including substitute solutions to customers' needs
- the evolving competitive set with which to do battle, and how!

The proforma, therefore, is a 'call to action' to a company's marketers and leadership teams. In addition, the technique acts as a diagnostic over time of a business's successes or failures in terms of its marketing strategy and programmes.

Note: The Dibb/Simkin competitive positions proforma is copyright Sally Dibb and Lyndon Simkin. A more extensive explanation of this technique is offered in *The Market Segmentation Workbook* (Dibb and Simkin) and *The Marketing Planning Workbook* (Dibb, Simkin and Bradley), both originally published in 1996 by Thomson (London), or in *Marketing Planning* (Cengage, 2008).

Basis for competing
A company's combined strengths as identified in a SWOT analysis and any differential advantage, which should form the leading edge of the company's marketing strategy.

Low price should also be avoided as a differential advantage at the centre of a marketing programme unless a company genuinely has the scale economies to maintain a low cost base and offer cost leadership. Only one company in any market can occupy this platform, as explained by Porter's generic routes to achieving a competitive advantage. Others are vulnerable to being undercut and losing their apparent differential advantage. Jet's lowest price proposition was undermined by Esso's highly effective Tigerwatch lowest price guarantee, and then further under-mined by the low price fuel sold by the supermarket brands. Low price can be utilized as a short-term tactic to off-load excessive stocks, for example, but should not form a basis for competing unless it can be defended against all challenges.

If there is no observable differential advantage, an organization must look to its strengths over its rivals. While not unique, these will still form the foundation for its ability to compete effectively. The SWOT analysis assists marketers in identifying their strengths and capabilities. The composite of any differential advantage with any strengths is a company's **basis for competing**, which should form the leading edge of the organization's marketing strategy. For some companies, such as 3M, innovativeness is the basis for competing, while for others, like Vidal Sassoon hair salons, image plays an important part. The Body Shop concentrates on environmentally friendly cosmetics, whereas for multiplex cinemas the basis for competing is the choice of multiple screens at one location. Some of these ways of gaining an edge are easier to sustain than others. For example, many UK companies that have traditionally focused on low price have found this advantage difficult to maintain in the long term.[27] The airline industry is just one to be plagued by periodic price wars, with many companies turning instead to flexibility and customer service as the basis for competing, while others have adopted a value-based strategy.

Identifying differential advantage   There is a straightforward sequence that marketers follow when attempting to identify a differential advantage:

1. Identify the market's segments.
2. Establish what product and service attributes are desired and demanded by customers in each segment.
3. Decide which of these attributes the company in question offers.
4. Determine which attributes the company's competitors offer.
5. Consider what the marketplace perceives the competitors' genuine strengths to be.
6. Identify whether any gaps exist between customer expectations of the product/service on offer and perceptions of the competitors' marketing programmes.
7. Consider whether any gaps identified in step 6 are matched by the company and its own offerings. If the company is able to match one or more of these gaps, the potential exists for a differential advantage to be developed.
8. Question whether any of these potential advantages for the company can be emphasized through sales and marketing programmes.
9. Consider the sustainability of these advantages for the company. How easily and quickly can competitors catch up? Is it possible for the company to defend these advantages?
10. If there are no current advantages for the company, given the gaps identified between competitors' propositions and customer expectations, consider which areas offer potential for developing a future differential advantage.
11. In order to maximize any existing or potential differential advantages, detail the changes the company must make to its research and development, engineering, sales and marketing activities.

It is important to remember that companies frequently examine their relative strengths and weaknesses in relation to their rivals. A strength is not the same as a differential advantage. For example, many rivals may also have strong brand awareness, products that perform well, loyal distributors or high profitability. A differential advantage is something that targeted customers want and value, and that only one supplier is able to provide.

Marketing objectives

Once a company has agreed which marketing opportunities are worth pursuing, on which target markets to focus marketing and sales activities, and how best to compete, the organization must ensure that its marketing strategy specifies its core marketing objectives. These marketing objectives are typically defined in terms of which are the most desirable market segments to target and, for each of these priority market segments, what market share is being sought and thereby what sales volumes or levels are expected to be achieved. They will definitely include financial performance measures.

Marketers must specify a raft of performance metrics, including customer satisfaction or brand awareness measures, profitability and financial contribution, or in retailing sales per square metre of selling space. Marketing objectives may include various product and market developments that marketers expect to achieve. These developments may include new product launches, new territory or market segment entry, the creation of innovative distribution channels or partnerships with marketing channel members. Without specification of these expectations it is difficult to ensure a fit with the organization's overall corporate strategy. It is impossible, too, to monitor ongoing performance or benchmark the effectiveness of the recommended marketing strategy against competitors' strategies.

Marketing mix decisions

As mentioned in Chapter 1, marketers must decide which products or services to offer to selected target markets, the attributes, specifications, performance characteristics and designs of these products, and the levels of customer service required to support them and to encourage customer satisfaction. In addition, prices must be set, payment terms and mechanisms agreed; distribution channels have to be chosen and distribution channel members orchestrated, in order to ensure product availability at places appropriate for the targeted customers. These customers must be made aware of the product through promotional activity marketing communications and their interest in the product maintained through promotional campaigns. These product, people, price, place and promotion decisions are what are termed the marketing mix decisions. They occupy the majority of marketers' time and account for most of a marketing department's budget.

Part Three of *Marketing: Concepts and Strategies* explores in detail the ingredients of the marketing mix, and the tactical toolkit utilized by marketers in developing marketing programmes designed to implement their recommended marketing strategy and target market strategy.

These product, people, price, place/distribution and promotion issues should be determined only after the marketing strategy has been agreed. The marketing strategy itself should be developed only after the core marketing analyses have been undertaken addressing market trends, marketing environment forces, customer buying behaviour, competition, opportunities, capabilities and performance. The marketing process outlined in Chapter 1 requires analysis, strategy formulation and then the specification of a marketing mix to facilitate the implementation of the desired target market strategy. Marketing programmes created from the ingredients of the marketing mix are part of the creation of an effective marketing strategy. Without the specification of marketing mixes, marketing strategies will not be effectively operationalized.

Implementation and performance monitoring

Marketing programmes depend on a detailed marketing mix specification: product, place/distribution, promotion, price and people issues. In addition, marketing programmes require the specification of budgets for actioning the desired marketing mix recommendations. These budgets must reflect the anticipated sales from the sales forecast and the trends inherent in the targeted market segments. Sales and marketing personnel must know of their responsibilities in implementing the recommended marketing programmes. There may be a requirement on colleagues outside the sales and marketing functions or on senior executives. Schedules must be determined so that it is clear when specific marketing mix activities are expected to occur.

It is essential that the implementation of a marketing strategy is managed and facilitated. This involves specifying by whom, when, how and at what cost the desired marketing mix programmes will be actioned. There may be internal marketing issues to address, such as those connected with the sharing of marketing intelligence and strategies; communication channels within the business; hierarchical support and resources. Finally, marketing must demonstrate its worth. Marketing programmes should be evaluated against predetermined performance measures to ensure their effective implementation and success in terms of the desired marketing objectives detailed within the marketing strategy.

Summary

Companies typically have a top-level over-arching corporate strategy and an associated strategic market or business plan. A marketing strategy, generally operationalized via the annual marketing plan, is developed in order to deliver the corporate strategy. *Marketing strategy* identifies which opportunities are to be pursued, indicates the specific markets towards which activities are to be targeted, defines the types of competitive advantage that are to be developed and exploited, and provides direction for marketing programmes. A marketing strategy aims to target customer segments of most benefit to an organization in a manner that best utilizes the organization's capabilities, provides a differential advantage over competitors and matches the organization's corporate goals. The marketing strategy is an integral part of an organization's over-arching *strategy*.

A company's *strategic market plan* is an outline of the methods and resources required to achieve an organization's overall goals within specific target markets; it takes into account all the functional areas of a business unit that must be coordinated. A *strategic business unit (SBU)* is a division, product line or other profit centre within a parent company, and is used to define areas for consideration in a specific strategic market plan. The process of *strategic market planning* yields a marketing strategy that is the framework for a marketing plan. A *marketing plan* includes the framework and entire set of activities to be performed; it is the written document or blueprint for specifying, implementing and controlling an organization's marketing activities and marketing mixes. The marketing plan executes the marketing strategy, which in turn should help to deliver the over-arching corporate strategy.

Through the process of strategic market planning, an organization can develop marketing strategies that, when properly implemented and controlled, will contribute to achieving the organization's overall goals. The marketing mix and associated implementation processes designed to operationalize the marketing strategy are the organization's *marketing programme*. Most marketing programmes centre around a detailed marketing mix specification and include internal controls and procedures to ensure that they are implemented effectively. Marketing environment forces are important in and profoundly affect the strategic market planning process. These forces imply opportunities and threats that influence an organization's overall goals.

Central to the marketing strategy is a clear view of the corporate mission and goals. These may well be developed separately to the marketing strategy but the marketing strategy must aim to reflect the overall corporate vision. A company's organizational goals should be derived from its *mission,* that is, the broad, long-term tasks that the organization wants to achieve. These goals should guide planning efforts and specify the ends, or results, that are sought. *Corporate strategy* determines the means for utilizing resources in the areas of production, logistics, finance, research and development, human resources, IT and marketing to reach the organization's goals.

There are three major considerations in assessing opportunities and resources: (1) evaluating marketing opportunities, (2) environmental scanning, and (3) understanding the company's capabilities and assets. A *marketing opportunity* arises when the right combination of circumstances occurs at the correct time, allowing an organization to take action towards reaching a target market. An opportunity offers a favourable chance for the company to generate sales from identifiable markets. A *strategic window* is a temporary period of optimum fit between the key requirements of a market and the particular capabilities of a company competing in that market. Market requirements relate to customers' needs or desired benefits. *Market requirements* are satisfied by components of the marketing mix that provide buyers with these benefits. *Environmental scanning* is the process of collecting information about the marketing environment to help marketers identify opportunities and threats, and assist in planning. A company's *capabilities* relate to distinctive competencies that it has developed to do something well and efficiently. A company is likely to enjoy a differential advantage in an area in which its competencies and *marketing assets* out-do those of its potential competition. Marketing assets are a categorization of an organization's strengths or capabilities in terms of customer-facing assets; distribution-based assets; and internal, operational or resource assets.

The *SWOT analysis* is little more than a set of checklists, but it is a popular tool for analyzing the capabilities of an organization in terms of strengths and weaknesses, and for linking identified opportunities and threats to these capabilities. As long as the analysis identifies the most important issues supported with validation and managers consider appropriate actions to address the emerging priorities, the SWOT analysis is useful for identifying necessary actions. It is important that any weaknesses that could be leveraged by competitors are rectified, and that managers strive to pre-empt any threats identified.

Having evaluated the overall corporate vision, those responsible for devising the marketing strategy must build on their analysis of opportunities and internal capabilities by analytically assessing the most promising directions for their business and its marketing activity. *Ansoff's matrix* for determining competitive strategies is a suitable tool, offering four options: market penetration, market development, product development or diversification. Strategic objectives that can be implemented through marketing include intense growth, diversified growth and integrated growth. *Intense growth* includes *market penetration, market development or product development. Diversified growth* includes *horizontal, concentric and conglomerate diversification. Integrated growth* includes forwards, backwards and horizontal integration.

Integral to achieving a company's corporate vision is the need to develop a loyal customer base of satisfied customers. It is essential to continuously improve the company's marketing programmes so as to address evolving target market customer needs and expectations. The market segmentation process of segmentation, targeting and positioning is a core element of a recommended marketing strategy. *Brand positioning* is the creation of a desirable, distinctive and plausible image for a brand that will have strong appeal for the customers in a target market segment. *Customer value propositions* should be defined in order to cement the brand positioning and satisfy targeted customers. A *target market strategy* is the choice of which market segment(s) an organization decides to prioritize and for which to develop marketing programmes.

The *competition* faced by a company are those organizations viewed as marketing products similar to, or substitutable for, a company's products, when targeted at the same customers. Strategists argue that organizations should work to attain a *competitive advantage*. While not always possible to achieve, success without a competitive advantage is unlikely in most markets. Competitive advantage is the achievement of superior performance vis-à-vis rivals: through differentiation to create distinctive product appeal or brand identity; through providing customer value and achieving the lowest delivered cost; or by focusing on narrowly scoped product categories or market niches so as to be viewed as a leading specialist. The so-called *generic routes to competitive advantage* are cost leadership, differentiation and focus, and are not mutually exclusive: while it is not possible to pursue all three routes to creating a competitive advantage, many businesses successfully pursue two of these routes.

It is important to understand the nature of competition and to utilize this knowledge in determining a marketing strategy. Aspects of the marketing strategy should be purposively designed to maximize any weaknesses in competitors' activities and pre-empt any impending moves from rivals. As defined by Porter's *five competitive forces*, competitors should not be viewed only as like-for-like rivals: new entrants, substitute products or services, and the bargaining power of suppliers and of buyers can all form competitive threats or opportunities. The competitive set must be defined by marketers, ensuring it reflects customers' views of direct alternatives and substitute options.

In developing strategies, an organization should consider the *competitive positions* in the marketplace. The *market leader* must both defend its position and seek new sales opportunities. Attack may prove the best form of defence. *Market challengers* must aggressively seek market share gains but carefully select the basis on which to attack: a chink in the leader's armour, for example, or a quick response to changing consumer needs. *Fast movers* may be small but they have the potential to win market share from rivals and should be combated. *Market followers* are the 'me-too, also-rans', prone to be squeezed in times of recession or in response to challengers' aggression. *Market nichers* specialize in terms of product and customer segment: they can very successfully tailor their marketing to their customers' needs but are vulnerable to competitors' entry into their target segments. To compete successfully, any organization needs to consider the principles of *defensive* and *offensive warfare* and to understand its competitors' strategies through *competitor scanning.* The competitive positions proforma is an increasingly popular tool for evaluating competition across a company's segments or markets.

An organization should strive for a *differential advantage* or competitive edge in its markets. A differential advantage is an attribute of a brand, product, service or marketing mix that is desirable to targeted customers and provided by only one supplier. Marketers should emphasize the desirable attributes of a company's marketing mix that their target customers consider unmatched by competitors. The combined strengths, as identified in a SWOT analysis, and any differential advantages make up the *basis for competing*, which should form the leading edge of a company's marketing strategy.

A marketing strategy must specify its core marketing objectives, typically defined in terms of market segments, to address desired market shares, customer satisfaction or brand awareness measures, profitability and financial contribution, plus any planned product and market developments. Without specification of objectives it is difficult to assess the performance of the marketing strategy or to ensure its fit with the overall corporate strategy.

The ingredients of the marketing mix — product, place/distribution, promotion, price and people — issues should be determined only after a marketing strategy has been specified. The marketing strategy must be decided only after the essential analyses of marketing market trends, the marketing environment forces, customer buying behaviour, competition, opportunities and capabilities have been undertaken. Analysis should come first, then strategic thinking and, finally, determination of implementation programmes, as explained in Chapter 1's examination of the marketing process.

Marketing programmes depend on detailed marketing mix specifications, but also on the determination of budgets for implementing these marketing mix requirements. These budgets must reflect the sales forecast and trends in the targeted market segments. Sales and marketing personnel should take responsibility for implementing the marketing plan's recommendations, and schedules for marketing mix activity must be established. Implementation of a marketing strategy has to be facilitated, which involves specifying by whom, when, how and at what cost the desired marketing programmes will be implemented. These programmes must be evaluated against predetermined performance measures.

Key links

The content of this chapter examining marketing strategy must be read after having understood the scope of marketing and the marketing process as outlined in Chapter 1. Other links include:

- Chapter 3's explanation of the forces of the macro and micro marketing environment and the importance of environmental scanning.
- Chapter 7's discussion of the market segmentation process, central to developing a target market strategy.
- Chapter 8's examination of targeting strategy, brand positioning and customer value propositions.

Important terms

Ansoff matrix
Basis for competing
Brand positioning
Capabilities
Competitive advantage
Competitive positions
Competitive positions proforma

Competitive set
Competitor scanning
Competitors
Concentric diversification
Conglomerate diversification
Corporate strategy
Customer value proposition
Defensive warfare
Differential advantage
Diversified growth
Environmental scanning
Fast movers
Five competitive forces
Generic routes to competitive advantage
Horizontal diversification
Integrated growth
Intense growth
Market challengers
Market development
Market followers
Market leader
Market nichers
Market penetration
Market requirements
Marketing assets

Marketing opportunities
Marketing plan
Marketing programme
Marketing strategy
Offensive warfare
Product development
Strategic business unit (SBU)
Strategic market plan
Strategic objectives
Strategic window
Strategy
SWOT analysis
Target market strategy

Discussion and review questions

1. What is a marketing strategy?

2. Why should an organization develop a marketing strategy?

3. Identify the major components of corporate strategy, strategic market planning and marketing strategy. Explain how they are interrelated.

4. In what ways do marketing environment forces affect strategic market planning? Give some specific examples.

5. What is a mission statement? Why must marketing strategists understand their organization's corporate strategy?

6. What are some of the issues that must be considered in analyzing an organization's opportunities and resources? How do these issues affect marketing objectives and marketing strategy?

7. Why is marketing opportunity analysis necessary? What are the determinants of marketing opportunity?

8. What are the components of a SWOT analysis?

9. In relation to resource constraints, how can environmental scanning affect a company's long-term strategic market planning? Consider product costs and benefits affected by the environment.

10. What is the difference between market penetration, market development and product development?

11. Why do you think more companies are diversifying? Give some examples of diversified businesses.

12. The market segmentation process is at the heart of a marketing strategy. Why must this be so?

13. What is competitive advantage?

14. Why should companies attempt to understand the strategies of their competitors? Explain your views.

15. How can a market leader best defend its competitive position?

16. What are the strengths of a market nicher? In what way is a nicher vulnerable?

17. What is meant by the term differential advantage? How does this relate to the concept of competitive advantage?

18. Why must a marketing strategy include detailed marketing objectives?

19. In what ways should implementation of a marketing strategy be managed and facilitated?

Recommended readings

Aaker, D. and McLoughlin, D., *Strategic Marketing Management* (Wiley, 2010).

Chernev, A., *Strategic Marketing Management* (Cerebellum Press, 2012).

Dibb, S. and Simkin, L., *Market Segmentation Success* (The Haworth Press/Routledge, 2008).

Hooley, G., Piercy, N. and Nicoulaud, B., *Marketing Strategy and Competitive Positioning* (FT/Prentice Hall, 2011).

Moutinho, L. and Southern, G., *Strategic Marketing Management: A Process-Based Approach* (Cengage, 2009).

Porter, M.E., *Competitive Strategy: Techniques for Analyzing Industries and Competitors* (The Free Press, 1980 and 2004).

West, D., Ford, J. and Ibrahim, E., *Strategic Marketing: Creating Competitive Advantage* (OUP, 2015).

Internet exercise

Consider a large, well-known company with which you have regular dealings, such as a major retailer, financial institution or hotel group. Or select a supplier whose products you purchase frequently, such as Innocent, Boots, Samsung or Vodafone. Log on to the selected organization's website.

Ignore the investors' pages, corporate information pages, PR releases and so forth. Look at the site from the perspective of a customer and access only the customer-relevant pages (those to do with products, services, offers, customer services, stockist location and so on).

1. What customer-relevant information is offered by the website you have chosen?

2. In what ways is the website striving to make the organization appear 'special' or particularly good?

3. Given the website material, how would you interpret the selected strategy for this organization? What is its apparent sense of purpose and what seem to be its leading priorities?

Group tasks

1. Red Bull has identified a varied set of target segments, ranging from students revising, young adults clubbing, sporty types requiring energy, jaded business executives in long meetings or flagging motorists on the move. Consider the nature of competition Red Bull faces in *each* of these usage situations.

2. Consider the principal target markets (customer types) pursued by each of the major mobile phone networks. To what extent do their target market priorities vary?

Applied mini-case

Since the 1980s, Korean-based Kia, part owned by Hyundai, has been a global player in the car market, now producing around 3 000 000 cars per annum. Its European business, run from Frankfurt, has become a key focus for growth and has been at the heart of the company's strategy since 2005. By 2009, the Kia brand had become a significant player in the UK market, notably in the small, medium and SUV sectors, achieving sales of over 50 000 for the first time and a market share of 2 per cent. Its Picanto city car sold 17 000. More recently, its Cee'd range has competed very effectively against the likes of the VW Polo and Golf, Vauxhall Astra and Ford Focus and Mondeo, while Kia's SUV Sportage and Sorento ranges continue to make strong in-roads. Kia does not have as complete a range as Ford or VW, or compete in the areas dominated by Audi, BMW or Mercedes. Should Kia focus on its current core areas of strength or seek to expand its range and target additional market segments? As a successful and growing brand, these are the dilemmas facing the company's marketing strategists.

Question

As the senior marketer tasked to assess the market's potential for the growth of sales under the Kia brand, what steps would you take?

St Andrew's Healthcare: a charity's marketing strategy

Case study

St Andrew's Healthcare in Northampton is the market leader in many types of mental healthcare in the UK. In addition to its large site in Northampton, St Andrew's has also created satellite facilities. As a leading specialist provider, the organization's patients are referred to its hospitals from throughout the UK and beyond. In its own words:

> We are a unique and influential pioneer in mental health, with a reputation grown over 175 years and a unique independent national teaching hospital. We train clinical leaders for the future, share our knowledge widely and have a research centre, partnered with King's College London.
>
> We have sites in Northampton, Birmingham, Essex and Nottinghamshire where we provide specialist and secure care pathways in mental health and neuropsychiatry. We have national services for young people, women, men and older adults.
>
> Our in-depth expertise includes trauma, personality disorder, psychosis, autism, learning disability, brain injury and progressive neurological conditions such as Huntington's disease and dementia.
>
> We are a mindful employer of over 4000 valued people. Our comprehensive clinical teams deliver effective treatment, therapies and recovery and work with the criminal justice system and the courts as well as offering clinical consultancy, vocational rehabilitation and outpatient care.

www.standrewshealthcare.co.uk/who-we-are, 21 April 2015

As a charity, its focus is not on helping mental health sufferers in the community, or charity shop-style fundraising, or increasing the general public's awareness of mental health

issues – other charities and bodies address these important tasks. St Andrew's Healthcare is a fully specified hospital with leading experts, state-of-the-art care pathways and an eminent reputation within the mental healthcare profession. St Andrew's divisions address everything from adolescent learning difficulties through to major behavioural problems, with patients requiring secure accommodation and lengthy treatment programmes. It has a specialist unit dealing with brain injuries and, through an on-site partner, also offers clinic facilities for patients needing to 'dry out'. Its staff are recognized as being leading-edge health professionals.

The St Andrew's brand reputation is based on the quality of its care, its multiple care pathways and its ability to relate to patients, their families, and to the medical staff or personnel in social services who refer patients to the hospital. St Andrew's has charitable status, but strives to set its fees sufficiently high to permit it to provide the high-quality care that is at the core of its ethos, and to continually reinvest in its facilities and treatment programmes.

Despite its success, its diversity of operations places significant demands on its capital spending: wards and facilities require modernizing, newly devised care programmes may require remodelled facilities, the expansion of demand led by reduced state provision of mental health facilities pressurizes the organization's caring professionals to provide expanded facilities. Private-sector commercial businesses have entered the more financially lucrative parts of the market. St Andrew's must defend its position in these segments, as fee income from these activities is required to support the hospital as a whole and to cross-subsidize other segments of the market deemed less financially attractive by new-entrant competitors. In order to defend its market share in these segments, the hospital has to develop marketing strategies and devote resources to marketing programmes designed to maintain the loyalty of referring GPs, medical consultants and social workers. The requirement is growing to tailor marketing messages to a growing mix of audiences. Commercially minded competitors

are developing 'glitzy' marketing programmes and St Andrew's has to maintain its visibility to key stakeholders in this quickly evolving marketplace.

While some patients deal directly with the charity, the vast majority are referred from the National Health Service (NHS). St Andrew's has a reputation for being able to deal with difficult patients suffering from complex problems. However, the NHS is moving towards fragmented buying, with numerous regionalized buying consortia of medics able to purchase services – such as those offered by St Andrew's – from a variety of providers. In addition to the medical staff diagnosing the patients' problems and recommending appropriate courses of treatment, the NHS has risk assessors, financial managers and professional purchasing executives, who all are involved in the decisions concerning which treatment programme to purchase and from which provider. For St Andrew's and other suppliers to the NHS, such formalized purchasing and group buying centre dynamics complicate the marketing activity and the engagement programmes the charity runs with its 'customers'. For the patient, to his/her family, to the referring medical staff and the numerous administrators involved, St Andrew's must develop bespoke messages, marketing communications and client-handling programmes. This complex buying centre must be addressed for St Andrew's to operate with full bed occupancy, in order to fulfil its mission to truly help those suffering with mental health problems.

The organization has responded to these market forces by developing a corporate strategy and a marketing strategy, by allocating resources to producing and implementing marketing programmes, and by recruiting a set of marketing managers to support the various divisions' marketing activities.

Questions for discussion

1. For a non-profit organization such as St Andrew's Healthcare, what aspects of a marketing strategy will be the most important?

2. Why are organizations such as St Andrew's Healthcare turning to marketing and the development of marketing strategies?

3. In what ways would a marketing strategy benefit St Andrew's Healthcare?

Sources: St Andrew's Healthcare, 2004–15; James Watkins, director of marketing and strategy, St Andrew's Healthcare, 2003–15; *Marketing Briefs*, Sally Dibb and Lyndon Simkin (Elsevier Butterworth-Heinemann, 2004); www .stah.org, February 2011 and April 2015.

CHAPTER 3

The marketing environment

"Marketers must have insights into their emerging market challenges, many of which will not be of their making, but which will impact hugely on their practices"

Objectives

To understand the concept of the marketing environment and the importance of environmental scanning and analysis.

To explore the broad forces of the macro marketing environment: political forces relevant to marketers, the influence of laws on marketing practices, the impact of government regulations and regulatory agencies, societal issues important to marketers, the effects of new technology on society and marketing activities, economic and competitive factors and their impact on organizations, and customers' willingness and ability to buy.

To examine the company-specific micro marketing environment forces: the competitive pressures facing an organization in terms of the supply chain, marketing intermediaries, competitors and from other publics.

To understand the role of the marketing environment in marketing opportunity analysis and the importance of strategic windows in marketing strategy.

INTRODUCTION

This chapter explores the external forces that impact on an organization's trading and ability to satisfy its customers. These forces, over which organizations rarely have any direct control, are termed the *marketing environment* and fall into two categories: the macro and the micro forces of the marketing environment. Most senior marketers believe that the marketing function should provide market insights to an organization, framing opportunities and threats, and acting as the 'radar' for colleagues in other functions so that they can align strategies and plans to developments in the market. A fundamental part of such a remit is to develop an understanding of the forces of the marketing environment. This is a core concept in both corporate strategy and for marketers with their marketing strategy.

The very broad forces are the *macro marketing environment*: the political, legal, regulatory, societal, technological and economic/competitive forces that impact on all organizations operating in a market and on their ability to carry out their affairs. Authors have increasingly distinguished these broad forces from an additional set of more company-specific external forces termed the *micro marketing environment* forces. These micro marketing environment forces are largely aspects of the competitive arena.

After defining the marketing environment and considering why it is necessary for marketers to *scan* and analyze these forces, each of these macro and micro forces is discussed. Awareness of these issues and trends may create *strategic windows* of opportunity. Ignorance of such forces jeopardizes an organization's ability to perform well and may leave the organization more vulnerable to the actions of more aware competitors.

Regulatory influence: the EU single market

In 1947 the launching of the Marshall Plan presented a blueprint for the economic reconstruction of a Europe devastated by the Second World War. This led in 1948 to the creation of the Organization for European Economic Cooperation (OEEC), the precursor of today's economic union. In March 1957 the Treaty of Rome was signed to establish the European Economic Community (EEC). By 1973, with the arrival of Denmark, Ireland and the UK, the EEC had grown to nine member states. Greece joined in 1981 and Portugal and Spain in 1986 to create the 'Euro 12'. The momentous signing of the Maastricht Treaty in 1992 established the European Union (EU) and by 1 January 1993 the European single market was at last a reality. The single market is defined by the EU as 'an economic area within which persons, goods, services and capital have unrestricted freedom of movement, which entails not only the elimination of customs barriers, but also of technical, tax and legislative obstacles'. By 2013, membership had swelled to 28 countries, including many eastern European countries, such as the Czech Republic, Estonia, Hungary, Latvia, Lithuania, Poland, Slovakia and Slovenia, plus Mediterranean countries Cyprus and Malta. Bulgaria and Romania joined in 2007 and Croatia in 2013. Candidate countries include Turkey, Serbia, Montenegro, Albania and Iceland, with Bosnia and Kosovo as potential candidates. Iceland, Norway and Liechtenstein are part of the European Economic Area (EEA), which permits them to be part of the EU's single market.

The single market has had a significant impact on the populations of member and non-member trading states, as well as on marketers representing their companies. With the removal of so many bureaucratic barriers on 1 January 1993, professionally qualified personnel could seek employment without retraining in other member states; companies could tender for government contracts throughout the EU; imports and exports became subject to far fewer restrictions, less 'red tape', reduced customs controls and allowed much freer movement within and between EU states. Immigration and travel have become much quicker and simpler than before. Health and safety working regulations have been harmonized, as have air travel regulations and even standards for mobile phone networks and VAT collection. The creation of the euro currency – to which most member states are now signed up – further simplified cross-border business transactions and travel arrangements.

The EU has many critics, not least due to (a) its Common Agricultural Policy (CAP), which takes more than half of the entire EU budget, is a significant drain on the resources of the richer member states and is currently being renegotiated; (b) national governments' reaction to the free-movement of migrants within the EU, impacting on planning, social provision, housing and employment patterns; (c) moans about the often top-heavy bureaucracy of European government in Brussels; (d) the inevitable formalization of a great number of working practices when so many countries' rules and regulations are combined to form a single and cohesive approach; (e) the financial conditions that must be met in order to participate in the euro, and the apparent flouting of these conditions by certain 'major league' member states and recent member states, which has added to the criticisms; and (f) the inclusion of seemingly 'weaker' eastern European economies, which has concerned people in the western European economies, which may well be cross-subsidizing these newer member economies.

However, there are few marketers who would claim that in the years since the harmonization of Europe in 1993, doing business across Europe has not been simplified, opening up significant marketing opportunities for many businesses and presenting new competitive threats. The recent expansion of EU membership – doubling the number of consumers inside the single market – is of great interest to marketers. The EU continues to present new challenges and a reason to rethink marketing strategies. There is little doubt that the EU is an external factor in the marketing environment of most businesses and consumers that cannot be ignored, providing trading opportunities, presenting European products to a global market, while increasing competitive threats and creating significant bureaucracy and regulation with which to deal.

For a list of Member States of the EU please go to page 105.

Sources: EU policy documents, 1990–2007; *Europe in Figures*, Eurostat, Luxembourg, 1995; *Europe on the Move, From Single Market to European Union, Internal Market* all EU, Brussels, publications; www.gov.uk/eu-eea, March 2015; http://europa.eu/about-eu/, March 2015.

The EU has a tremendous impact on the decisions and activities of marketers. The regulations and legal directives produced by the EU, plus the financial implications of many of its policies – such as the CAP and the criteria for participating in the euro – are aspects of the macro marketing environment. Greece's response to the Euro-crisis and its EU rescue conditions are good examples of the impact of the marketing environment. This chapter discusses both macro and micro forces, commencing with the broader macro issues. It includes a discussion of why and how marketers scan the forces of the marketing environment. The chapter concludes with an examination of how an understanding of these marketing environment forces assists a company in identifying strategic windows, maximizing marketing opportunities and recognizing impending threats.

Examining and responding to the marketing environment

Marketing environment
The external forces that directly or indirectly influence an organization's acquisition of inputs and generation of outputs, comprising six categories of forces: political, legal, regulatory, societal, technological and economic/competitive.

The **marketing environment** consists of external forces that directly or indirectly influence an organization's acquisition of inputs and generation of outputs. Inputs might include personnel, financial resources, raw materials and information. Outputs could be information such as advertisements or packages, goods, services and ideas. As indicated in Chapter 1 and as shown in Figure 1.4, the broad marketing environment consists of six categories of forces: political, legal, regulatory, societal, technological and economic/competitive. Although there are numerous environmental factors, most fall into one of these six categories. These are termed the 'macro forces' of the marketing environment as they affect all organizations operating in a particular market. In addition, many authors have identified a set of issues termed the 'micro forces' of the marketing environment. These micro forces are more situation- and organization-specific, including the organization's internal environment, suppliers, marketing intermediaries, buyers, competitors and the organization's publics … they tend to be centred on competitor issues directly impacting on a specific organization.

Whether they fluctuate rapidly or slowly, environmental forces are always dynamic. Changes in the marketing environment can create uncertainty, threats and opportunities for marketers. Although the future is not very predictable, marketers can estimate what will happen, although some fail to do so, thus negatively affecting the performance of their businesses. Astute marketers continually modify their marketing strategies in response to the dynamic environment. Marketing managers who fail to recognize changes in environmental forces leave their companies unprepared to capitalize on marketing opportunities or to cope with threats created by changes in the environment.

Organizations that cannot deal with an unfavourable environment are at risk of going under.[1] The 1990 Persian Gulf Crisis caused huge increases in the price of petrol, repeated in 2004 following the start of the last Gulf War. Civil war in the former Yugoslavia had tragic implications for the peoples of that region and an economic impact on the tour operators who specialized in holidays to the Yugoslav coast. The BSE beef crisis affected farmers, meat producers and supermarkets. Genetically modified (GM) foods caused a storm with implications for food manufacturers and supermarkets. The activities of terrorists have had a significant impact on companies and the general public in many countries, with tourism and airline operators being particularly badly affected. Sub-prime mortgages led to huge economic troubles, impacting on consumers' spending potential and their priorities. Recent political upheaval in Egypt has disrupted the tourism industry there, tour operators marketing holidays to the country, and consumers planning to holiday there. The ebola pandemic has impacted on tourism and economic trade to parts of Africa. It is not just such big crises that impact on marketers. Monitoring the marketing environment is crucial to an organization's survival and to the long-term achievement of its goals.

Environmental scanning and analysis

Environmental scanning
The process of collecting information about the forces in the marketing environment.

Environmental analysis
The process of assessing and interpreting the information gathered through environmental scanning.

To monitor changes in the marketing environment effectively, marketers must engage in environmental scanning and analysis. **Environmental scanning** is the process of collecting information about the forces in the marketing environment. Scanning involves: observation; keeping 'an ear to the ground'; perusal of secondary sources, such as the web, business, trade, government and general interest publications; and marketing research. However, managers must be careful not to gather so much information that sheer volume makes analysis impossible. **Environmental analysis** is the process of assessing and interpreting the information gathered through environmental scanning. A manager evaluates the information for accuracy, tries to resolve inconsistencies in the data and, if warranted, assigns significance to the findings. Through analysis, a marketing manager seeks to describe current environmental changes and to predict future changes. By evaluating these changes, the manager should be able to determine possible threats and opportunities linked to environmental fluctuations. Understanding the current state of the marketing environment and recognizing the threats and opportunities arising from changes within it, help marketing managers assess the performance of current marketing efforts and develop marketing strategies for the future. The Marketing Tools and Techniques box below describes how organizations often conduct an analysis of the marketing environment.

Marketing tools and techniques

Practitioners' assessment of the macro marketing environment

The marketing environment forces are not obviously part of an individual manager's routine job specification, particularly within the marketing function. However, businesses must monitor these forces through environmental scanning not only to pre-empt possible problems caused by unfavourable market developments, but also in order to leverage any emerging opportunities ahead of competitors. The identification of strategic windows and the chance to take first mover advantage are desires among senior managers and marketers.

The forces of the micro marketing environment and competitive pressures are usually evaluated within a marketing team's analysis of competition (see Chapter 2). Companies must examine the macro forces, too, however. Many managers refer to this macro marketing environmental analysis as a PESTLE analysis: political, economic, societal, technological, legal and environmental. While research indicates that many fail to examine the opportunities and threats from the marketing environment, 'best practice' companies typically adopt one of three approaches to assessing their marketing environments.

1. Individual managers or small work groups are allocated to each of the macro forces: social, economic, legal, regulatory, political and technological. As 'champions' for their allocated topic, such managers collate intelligence from stakeholders, employees and external sources in order to build up a picture of the key trends and developments. These managers either suggest the emerging implications for their business and make recommendations, or they present their findings at a sales and marketing meeting or to senior managers for their debate and consideration. The development of company intranets has significantly assisted the networking so important for the collation of topical and relevant information.

2. The task of assessing the marketing environment may be handed to external consultants. This is not common, as few consultancies know enough about all of the forces of the macro marketing environment, or about the organization in question, to judge likely implications. However, in certain industries, such as automotive, IT and pharmaceuticals, such is commonplace.

3. An organization may intermittently stage workshops to which cross-functional and multi-hierarchical personnel are invited. For example, R&D personnel may be aware of technological trends, the company secretary of legal or regulatory issues, the salesforce of economic or social

on. Typically, each of the macro marketing ...rces is discussed in turn, in a 'brainstorm-...g exercise. Certain themes or 'hot topics' then emerge to be debated further within the workshop. The company then allocates an individual manager or creates a small taskforce to examine a particular issue in more detail, in order to subsequently develop an action plan based on more information.

Some companies invite external experts, suppliers, partners or even customers to such a workshop. If these external opinions are not sought as part of the workshop, any planned activity by the business resulting from this workshop-based analysis must await some external validation after the workshop.

Such sessions are an excellent way in which a business can harness the expertise across its functions and within its marketing channel in order to prioritize actions that should minimize the impact of a negative external development or maximize an emerging opportunity.

In this type of forum, the senior management team supported by functional experts and channel partner personnel brainstormed the key issues from the macro marketing environment for a leading insurance business. The priorities emerged as shown in the boxed list (right).

While some of these forces, such as the weather, were outside the influence of the business, many of them could be addressed. Indeed, while the weather could not be altered, the company did decide to re-examine its exposure to flood plain customers and modified its policy cover accordingly.

Within each of these rather broad-brush summary bullets lay much detail to explore and discuss. An example of a resulting action was to more closely manage the activities of the field salesforce, harnessing the latest mobile office technology solutions and customer relationship management field systems. As a result, the already low level of client complaints for inappropriate selling approaches virtually disappeared, and the highly ethical stance in controlling the salesforce bolstered the company's brand reputation and thereby its ability to recruit high-calibre personnel. This strategy also reflected the growing litigious culture among consumers, and thereby addressed another of the trends identified during the workshop.

It is important to have a good mix of inputs, from market information and personnel to any assessment of the macro forces of the marketing environment, and to solicit the views of stakeholders other than those participating in the session.

For example, partners, channel members, market analysts, industry experts or consultants and even customers, are all useful sources both for marketing intelligence and for checking out suggested action plans. It is better not to involve only marketers.

Having identified the key issues of the macro marketing environment forces currently of relevance, the business must consider the implications. The 'So what does this mean to us and to our business?' question has to be answered. Is the issue a threat or an opportunity? What resulting actions must be taken? Certain trends and developments may pose a threat, while other forces may create an opportunity. Sometimes, the same issue is both an opportunity and a threat. In the above example, had this company failed to implement changes to its field force's working practices, it would not have bolstered its reputation or improved the completion rate of its sales representatives. Worse, rivals may have been able to steal a march and measures designed to minimize the likelihood of client litigation would not now be in place.

The macro marketing environment for a leading insurance company

- Stock market (worthless investments, own share price/company value)
- New/more regulations (FCA, Gov, EU, within client sectors, accountancy)
- Over/under capacity in the industry/key sectors
- Many mergers and changes to the competitive set
- Structural changes in the sector and for clients
- Emerging compensation culture among clients and brokers
- Customers' expectation of better advice
- Greater role for technology CRM (customer relationship management), online quotes/claims, e-business
- Distribution channel developments (role of brokers, e-commerce, tele-business, retailer new entrants)
- Recruitment problems/inability to make the sector attractive
- Global warming/changes to weather: greater claims

© Dibb/Simkin

Note: a more extensive explanation of this technique is offered in either *The Market Segmentation Workbook* (Dibb and Simkin) or *The Marketing Planning Workbook* (Dibb, Simkin and Bradley), both originally published in 1996 by Thomson, London, or in the authors' newer titles *Market Segmentation Success: Making It Happen!* (The Haworth Press/Routledge, 2008) and *Marketing Planning* (Cengage Learning, 2008).

JCB, the construction equipment producer, allocated to individual managers the task of monitoring aspects of the macro marketing environment: political, legal, regulatory, societal (particularly the Green movement), technological, economic and competitive. A small committee met to prepare short papers and presentations to interested colleagues. When the laws relating to roadworks were amended, making contractors responsible for the safety of their sites and the long-term quality of the relaid road surface, JCB recognized that many of its customers would have to alter their working practices as a result. So the company produced guides to assist these contractors in responding to the new legislation. In so doing, JCB was able to enhance its image and reputation as a leading player in the industry, and at the same time promote its products.

Responding to environmental forces

In responding to environmental forces, marketing managers can take two general approaches: accept environmental forces as uncontrollable or confront and mould them. If environmental forces are viewed as uncontrollable, the organization remains passive and reactive towards the environment. Instead of trying to influence forces in the environment, its marketing managers tend to adjust current marketing strategies to environmental changes. They approach marketing opportunities discovered through environmental scanning and analysis with caution. On the other hand, marketing managers who believe that environmental forces can be shaped adopt a proactive approach. For example, if a market is blocked by traditional environmental constraints, marketing managers may apply economic, psychological, political and promotional skills to gain access to it or operate within it. Once they identify what blocks a marketing opportunity, marketers can assess the power of the various parties involved and develop strategies to try to overcome environmental forces.[2]

In trying to influence environmental forces, marketers may seek to either create new marketing opportunities or extract greater benefits relative to costs from existing marketing opportunities. For instance, a company losing sales to competitors with lower-priced products may strive to develop technology that would make its production processes more efficient; greater efficiency would allow it to lower the prices of its own products. Political action is another way of affecting

FIGURE 3.1
Growing social awareness of healthy eating and the problems of obesity have created opportunities for many products, including Innocent smoothies and other products promising to help have 'five a day' of fresh fruit and veg

Source: Image courtesy of Innocent Drinks

environmental forces. UK retailers, for example, successfully lobbied government to permit longer Sunday trading and legal opening of retail outlets all day. Recently, bodies representing the alcoholic drinks industry and the tobacco manufacturers have successfully limited proposed legislation that would have altered the sales of these products. A proactive approach can be constructive and bring desired results. However, managers must recognize that there are limits on how much an environmental force can be shaped and that these limits vary across environmental forces. Although an organization may be able to influence the enactment of laws through lobbying, it is unlikely that a single organization can significantly increase the national birth rate or move the economy from recession to prosperity!

Generalizations are not possible. It cannot be stated that one of these approaches to environmental response is better than the other. For some organizations, the passive, reactive approach is more appropriate, but for other companies, the aggressive approach leads to better performance. What is certain is that ignorance of the forces of the marketing environment leads to problems and creates opportunities for rivals. The selection of a particular approach depends on an organization's managerial philosophies, objectives, financial resources, customers and human skills and on the specific composition of the set of environmental forces within which the organization operates.

The rest of this chapter explores in detail the macro and micro marketing environment forces, and then examines the link between an understanding of these issues and marketing opportunity analysis. Identifying opportunities and mitigating threats are core to developing effective marketing strategies.

Political forces

The political, legal and regulatory forces of the marketing environment are closely interrelated. Legislation is enacted, legal decisions are interpreted by the courts, and regulatory agencies are created and operated, for the most part, by people elected or appointed to political offices or by civil servants. Legislation and regulations (or the lack of them) reflect the current political outlook. Consequently, the political force of the marketing environment has the potential to influence marketing decisions and strategies.

Marketers need to maintain good relations with elected political officials for several reasons. When political officials are well disposed towards particular companies or industries, they are less likely to create or enforce laws and regulations unfavourable to these companies. For example, political officials who believe that oil companies are making honest efforts to control pollution are unlikely to create and enforce highly restrictive pollution control laws. In addition, governments are big buyers, and political officials can influence how much a government agency purchases and from whom. The UK government's liking of public–private partnerships for financing capital projects such as schools and hospitals has created significant opportunities for construction companies Carillion and Laing O'Rourke or outsourcing specialists such as Capita and Fujitsu. Finally, political officials can play key roles in helping organizations to secure foreign markets.

Many marketers view political forces as beyond their control; they simply try to adjust to conditions that arise from those forces. Some organizations, however, seek to influence political events by helping to elect to political office individuals who regard them positively. Much of this help is in the form of contributions to political parties. A sizeable contribution to a campaign fund may carry with it an implicit understanding that the party, if elected, will perform political favours for the contributing company. There are, though, strict laws governing donations and lobbying in most countries and, increasingly, ethical considerations for donor marketers.

Legal forces

A number of laws influence marketing decisions and activities. This discussion focuses on pro-competitive and consumer protection laws and their interpretation.

Procompetitive legislation

Procompetitive legislation
Laws enacted to preserve competition and to end various practices deemed unacceptable by society.

Procompetitive legislation is enacted to preserve competition and to end various practices deemed unacceptable by society, for example monopolies and mergers. In the UK, the Department for Business, Innovation and Skills (BIS) can refer monopolies for investigation by the **Competition and Markets Authority**, an independent body whose members are drawn from a variety of backgrounds, including lawyers, economists, industrialists and trades unionists. The legislation defines a monopoly as a situation in which at least a quarter of a particular kind of good or service is supplied by a single person or a group of connected companies, or by two or more people acting in a way that prevents, restricts or distorts competition. Local monopolies can also be referred to the Authority. If the CMA finds that a monopoly operates against the public interest, BIS has power to take action to remedy or prevent the harm that the CMA considers may exist. The government believes that the market is a better judge than itself of the advantages and disadvantages of mergers, so most take-overs and proposed mergers are allowed to be decided by the companies' shareholders. However, when too much power would be placed in the hands of one organization, company or person, the government will insist on a Competition and Markets Authority appraisal. If the CMA believes it is against the public interest for a take-over or merger to proceed, then it will prohibit or limit any agreement between the companies or organizations involved.[3] For example, when Morrisons acquired rival supermarket chain Safeway, the deal was permitted only on the basis that a number of Safeway stores were sold to a third party, ultimately Waitrose. BAA was forced to sell on three UK airports if it wanted to maintain control over Heathrow, as owning seven major hubs was deemed not to be in the consumers' or airlines' interests. The EU has a commissioner responsible for competition. In recent years, the commissioner has ruled on anticompetitive practices in many industries, from airlines to financial services, forcing companies to alter their trading practices and encouraging competition from a broader base of organizations. Under anti-competitive practices legislation, the Competition and Markets Authority can investigate any business practice, whether in the public or private sector, that may restrict, distort or prevent competition in the production, supply or acquisition of goods or services. The Secretary of State has power to take remedial action.

Competition and Markets Authority
An independent body in the UK that investigates monopolies to determine whether they operate against the public interest.

Within the European Union (EU), the objective of the competition policy is to ensure that there is free and fair competition in trade among member states and that the government trade barriers, which the Treaty of Rome seeks to dismantle, are not replaced by private barriers that fragment the Common Market. The EU has powers to investigate and terminate alleged infringements and to impose fines. The Treaty of Rome prohibits agreements or practices that may affect trade among member states, and aims to prevent restriction or distortion of competition within the Common Market.[4] Most countries have similar procompetitive legislation.

Consumer protection legislation

The second category of regulatory laws, consumer protection legislation, is not a recent development. However, consumer protection laws mushroomed in the mid-1960s and early 1970s. A number of them deal with consumer safety, while others relate to the sale of various hazardous products such as flammable fabrics and toys that might injure children. With the abolition of the Office of Fair Trading, such responsibilities passed to the Competition and Markets Authority and the **Financial Conduct Authority**, supported by local Trading Standards agencies. Consumers' interests with regard to the purity of food, the description and performance of goods and services, and pricing information are safeguarded by many Acts of parliament. Legislation more recently has established frameworks for food labelling concerning the production, packaging, supply and use of food. Branded packaging for cigarettes has recently been banned in the UK, much to the annoyance of the cigarette manufacturers.

Financial Conduct Authority
The regulatory authority for financial services in the UK.

In addition, consumer advice and information are provided to the general public at the local level by the Citizens Advice Bureau, and the Trading Standards or Consumer Protection departments of local authorities, and in some areas by specialist consumer advice centres. The independent, non-statutory Consumer Futures (formerly the National Consumer Council), which receives government finance, ensured that consumers' views are made known to those in government and industry. Nationalized industries and utilities have consumer councils whose members investigate questions of concern to the consumer, and many trade associations in industry and commerce have established codes of practice. In addition, several private organizations work to further consumer interests, the largest of which is the **Consumers' Association** funded by the subscriptions of its membership of over one million people. The association conducts an extensive programme of comparative testing of goods and investigation of services; its views and test reports are published in its monthly magazine *Which?* and other publications.

> **Consumers' Association**
> A private organization, funded by members' subscriptions, that works to further consumer interests.

Interpreting laws

Laws certainly have the potential to influence marketing activities, but the actual effects of the laws are determined by how marketers and the courts interpret them. Laws seem to be quite specific because they contain many complex clauses and sub-clauses. In reality, however, many laws and regulations are stated in vague terms that force marketers to rely on legal advice rather than their own understanding and common sense. As a result of this vagueness, some organizations attempt to gauge the limits of certain laws by operating in a legally questionable way to see how far they can go with certain practices before being prosecuted. Other marketers, however, interpret regulations and statutes very conservatively and strictly to avoid violating a vague law. Although court rulings directly affect businesses accused of specific violations, they also have a broader, less direct impact on other businesses. When marketers try to interpret laws in relation to specific marketing practices, they often analyze recent court decisions, both to understand better what the law is intended to do and to gain a clearer sense of how the courts are likely to interpret it in the future.

Regulatory forces

Interpretation alone does not determine the effectiveness of laws and regulations; the level of enforcement by regulatory agencies is also significant. Some regulatory agencies are created and administered by government units; others are sponsored by non-governmental sources.

Government

In the UK, the Department for Environment, Food and Rural Affairs (DEFRA) develops and controls policies for agriculture, horticulture, fisheries and food; it also has responsibilities for environmental and rural issues and food policies. The Department for Employment and Learning controls the Employment Service, employment policy and legislation, training policy and legislation, health and safety at work, industrial relations, wages councils, equal opportunities, small businesses and tourism, statistics on labour and industrial matters for the UK, the Careers Service, and international representation on employment matters and educational policy. DEFRA controls policies for planning and regional development, local government, new towns, housing, construction, inner-city matters, environmental protection, water, the countryside, sports and recreation, conservation, historic buildings and ancient monuments. The Export Credit Guarantee Department is responsible for the provision of insurance for exporters against the risk of not being paid for goods and services, access to bank finance for exports and insurance cover for new investment overseas.

The Office for National Statistics (ONS) prepares and interprets statistics needed for central economic and social policies and management; it coordinates the statistical work of other departments. The Department for Business, Innovation and Skills (BIS) controls industrial and commercial policy, promotion of enterprise and competition in the UK and abroad, and investor and consumer protection. The Department of Transport is responsible for: land, sea and air transport; rail network regulation; domestic and international civil aviation; international transport agreements; shipping and ports industries; navigation issues, HM Coastguard and marine pollution; motorways and trunk roads; road safety; and overseeing local authority transport.

These examples of British government departments are not unusual. Similar administrative bodies exist in most countries. Increasingly in the EU, political, legal and regulatory forces are being harmonized to reflect common standards and enforcement.

Local authorities

The functions of UK local authorities are far-reaching; some are primary duties, whereas others are purely discretionary. Broadly speaking, functions are divided between county and district councils on the basis that the county council is responsible for matters requiring planning and administration over wide areas or requiring the support of substantial resources, whereas district councils on the whole administer functions of a more local significance. English county councils are generally responsible for strategic planning, transport planning, highways, traffic regulations, local education, consumer protection, refuse disposal, police, the fire service, libraries and personal social services. District councils are responsible for environmental health, housing decisions, most planning applications and refuse collection. They may also provide some museums, art galleries and parks. At both county and district council level, arrangements depend on local agreements.

Most countries in Europe have a similar structure: resource-hungry issues with wide-ranging social and political consequences are controlled centrally. Planning and service provision within the community are viewed as being better controlled at the local level by the actual communities that will experience the advantages or problems resulting from such decision-making. The EU aims to establish commonly accepted parameters for planning, service provision and regulation and a framework to assist in inter- and intra-country disputes.

Non-governmental regulatory forces

In the absence of governmental regulatory forces and in an attempt to prevent government intervention, some organizations try to regulate themselves. For example, many newspapers have voluntarily banned advertisements for telephone chat services used for undesirable activities, even though such services are technically not illegal. Trade associations in a number of industries have developed self-regulatory programmes. Even though these programmes are not a direct outcome of laws, many were established to stop or stall the development of laws and governmental regulatory groups that would regulate the associations' marketing practices. Sometimes trade associations establish codes of ethics by which their members must abide, or risk censure by other members or even exclusion from the programme. For example, many cigarette manufacturers agreed, through a code of ethics, not to promote their products to children and teenagers. The Ofcom Code of Advertising Standards and Practice aims to keep broadcast advertising 'legal, decent, honest and truthful'.[5]

Self-regulatory programmes have several advantages over governmental laws and regulatory agencies. They are usually less expensive to establish and implement, and their guidelines are generally more realistic and operational. In addition, effective industry self-regulatory programmes reduce the need to expand government bureaucracy. However, these programmes also have several limitations. When a trade association creates a set of industry guidelines for its members, non-member organizations do not have to abide by them. In addition, many self-regulatory programmes lack the tools or the authority to enforce guidelines. Finally, guidelines in self-regulatory programmes are often less strict than those established by government agencies.

Deregulation

Governments can drastically alter the environment for businesses. In the UK, the privatization of the public utilities created new terms and conditions for their suppliers and sub-contractors. The state's sales of Jaguar and Land Rover in the car industry and of British Airways created commercially lean companies that suddenly had new impetus to become major competitors in their industries. In the EU, deregulation has created opportunities across borders and also new threats. Car manufacturers were previously able to restrict certain models to specific countries. They placed rigorous controls on their dealers, forbidding them to retail cars produced by rival manufacturers in the same showroom or on the same site. Many of these controls have since been swept aside.

Societal forces

Societal forces
Individuals and groups, and the issues engaging them, that pressure marketers to provide high living standards and enjoyable lifestyles through socially responsible decisions and activities.

Societal forces comprise the structure and dynamics of individuals and groups and the issues that engage them. Society becomes concerned about marketers' activities when those activities have questionable or negative consequences. For example, in recent times, well-publicized incidents of unethical behaviour by marketers and others have perturbed and even angered consumers, notably in connection with banks' policies and the resulting economic meltdown. When marketers do a good job of satisfying society, praise or positive evaluation rarely follows. Society expects marketers to provide a high standard of living and protect the general quality of life. This section examines some of society's expectations, the means used to express those expectations, and the problems and opportunities that marketers experience as they try to deal with society's often contradictory wishes.

Living standards and quality of life

Most people want more than just the bare necessities; they want to achieve the highest standard of living possible. For example, there is a desire for homes that offer not only protection from the elements but also comfort and a satisfactory lifestyle. People want many varieties of safe and readily available food that is also easily prepared. Clothing protects bodies, but many consumers want a variety of clothing for adornment and to project a certain image to others. Consumers want vehicles that provide rapid, safe and efficient travel. They want communications systems that give information from around the globe, 24/7; a desire apparent in the popularity of products such as smartphones, social media, mobile devices and the 24-hour news coverage provided by cable and satellite television networks and by the internet. In addition, there is a demand for sophisticated medical services that prolong life expectancy and improve physical appearance. Education is expected to help consumers acquire and enjoy a higher standard of living.

Society's high material standard of living is often not enough. Many desire a high degree of quality in their lives. People do not want to spend all their waking hours working: they seek leisure time for hobbies, voluntary work, recreation and relaxation. Quality of life is enhanced by leisure time, clean air and water, unlittered beaches, conservation of wildlife and natural resources and security from radiation and poisonous substances. A number of companies are expressing concerns about quality of life. Consumers, too, are expressing concern over 'Green' issues such as pollution, waste disposal and the so-called greenhouse effect … sustainability and issues around carbon footprint are now centre stage. Society's concerns have created both threats and opportunities for marketers. For example, one of society's biggest environmental problems is lack of space for refuse disposal, especially of plastic materials such as disposable nappies and Styrofoam packaging, which are not biodegradable. In the US, several cities have passed laws banning the use of all plastic packaging in stores and restaurants, and governments around the world are considering similar legislation. This trend has created problems for McDonald's and other fast-food restaurants, which have now developed packaging alternatives. Other companies, however, see such environmental problems as opportunities. Procter & Gamble, for example, markets cleaners in bottles visibly made of recycled plastic.[6] Environmentally responsible or green marketing is increasingly extensive. For example, the German companies Audi, Volkswagen and BMW are manufacturing 'cleaner' cars that do not pollute the atmosphere as much as traditional ones. BP launched a 'green' diesel fuel with hardly any noxious emissions. Italian chemical companies are investing billions to reduce toxic wastes from their plants, and British industry is investing equally large sums to scrub acid emissions from power stations and to treat sewage more effectively.[7]

Green movement
The trend arising from society's concern about pollution, waste disposal, manufacturing processes and the greenhouse effect.

The **Green movement** is concerned with these environmental issues. Several years ago few consumers were concerned about the well-being of their natural environment on their planet. Resources were not seen as scarce, pollution was barely acknowledged and people had a short-term, perhaps selfish, perspective. Now there is a growing awareness that is affecting everyone: consumers, manufacturers and legislators. Supermarket shelves are rapidly filling with packaging that can be recycled or reused and products for which manufacturing processes have altered. Children are now taught in the classroom to 're-educate' their parents to take a more responsible view of the Earth's environment. The changes are not just in the supermarkets and schools, with ever more households sorting their rubbish into various containers for collection by local authorities striving to recycle growing amounts of rubbish.

The rising importance and role of the green aspect – sustainability – of the societal forces must not be underestimated. Changes in the forces of the marketing environment require careful monitoring, and often demand a clear and effective response. Since marketing activities are a vital part of the total business structure, marketers have a responsibility to help provide what members of society want and to minimize what they do not want.

Consumer movement forces

Consumer movement
A diverse collection of independent individuals, groups and organizations seeking to protect the rights of consumers.

The **consumer movement** is a diverse collection of independent individuals, groups and organizations seeking to protect the rights of consumers. The main issues pursued by the consumer movement fall into three categories: environmental protection, product performance and safety, and information disclosure. The movement's major forces are individual consumer advocates, consumer organizations and other interest groups, consumer education and consumer laws.

Consumer advocates take it upon themselves to protect the rights of consumers. They band together into consumer organizations, either voluntarily or under government sponsorship. Some organizations, such as the Consumers' Association, operate nationally, whereas others are active at local levels. They inform and organize other consumers, raise issues, help businesses develop consumer-oriented programmes and pressure legislators to enact consumer protection laws. Some consumer advocates and organizations encourage consumers to boycott products and businesses to which they have objections. For marketers, it is better to work with such activists than to incur their displeasure.

Educating consumers to make wiser purchasing decisions is perhaps one of the most far-reaching aspects of the consumer movement, which is now impacting on a growing number of organizations (see Figure 3.2). This is a motive of the Fairtrade Foundation, as detailed in the Topical Insight box (see page 85). Increasingly, consumer education is becoming a part of school curricula and adult education courses. These courses cover many topics; for instance, what major factors should be considered when buying specific products, such as insurance, housing, cars, appliances and furniture, clothes and food? The courses also cover the provisions of certain consumer protection laws and provide the sources of information that can help individuals become knowledgeable consumers.

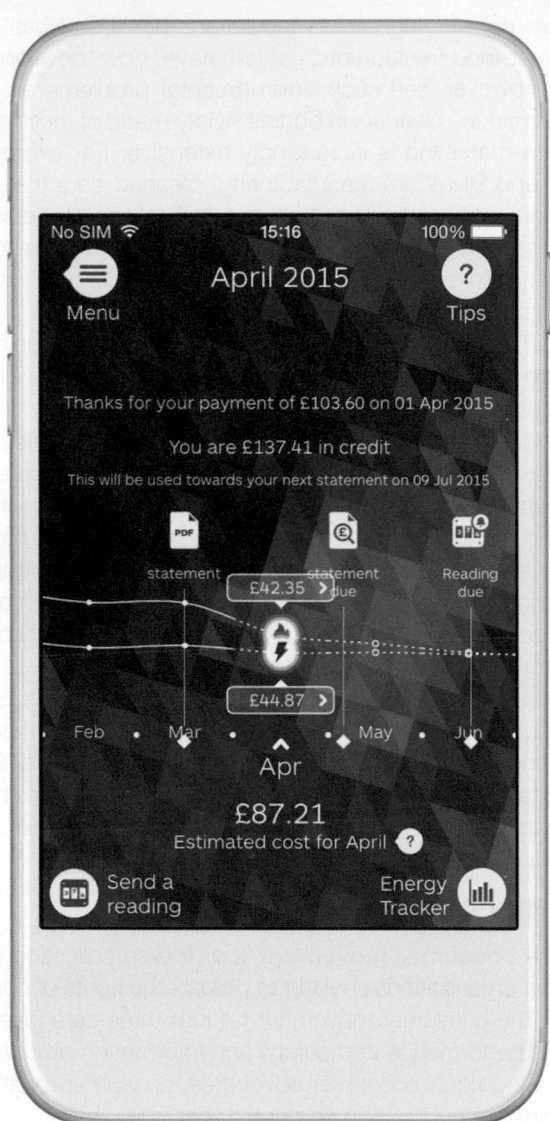

FIGURE 3.2
'Npower's 'energy smart' campaign
capitalises on a growth in concern for
natural resources and technological
advancements in monitoring energy
consumption

Source: Image courtesy of Npower.

Technological forces

The word technology brings to mind creations of progress such as mobile phones, tablets, computers, the web, superconductors, lasers, hybrid cars, GM foods, wind farms, cloning and organ transplants. Even though such items are outgrowths of technology, none of them are technology. **Technology** has been defined as the application of knowledge and tools to solve problems and perform tasks more efficiently.[8] Often this knowledge comes from scientific research. The effects of technology are broad in scope and today exert a tremendous influence on everyone's lives. Technology grows out of research performed by businesses, universities and not-for-profit organizations. Much of this research is paid for by governments, which support investigations in a variety of areas, including health, defence, agriculture, energy and pollution. Because much centrally funded research requires the use of specialized machinery, personnel and facilities, a sizeable proportion of this research is conducted by large commercial organizations or research institutions that already possess the necessary specialized equipment and people.

Technology
The application of knowledge and tools to solve problems and perform tasks more efficiently.

The rapid technological growth of recent decades is expected to continue. Areas that hold great technological promise include digital electronics, artificial intelligence, superconductors, materials research and biotechnology. Current research is investigating new forms of memory chips and computers that will think for themselves or be more responsive to their specific users' characteristics. Because these and other technological developments will clearly have an impact on buyers' and marketers' decisions, it is important to discuss here the effects of technology on society and marketers, and to consider several factors that influence the adoption and use of technology.

The impact of technology

Marketers must be aware of new developments in technology and their possible effects because technology does affect marketing activities in many different ways. Consumers' technological knowledge influences their desire for goods and services. To provide marketing mixes that satisfy consumers, marketers must be aware of these influences. For example, the web has led to easy access for consumers to comparative information about products and brands, while providing marketers with an important channel for communications and selling. The massive growth of digital media and social networking is impacting on all markets and marketers' practices, as they battle to keep pace with the associated changing consumer behaviours and societal implications. Within marketing departments, technology has enabled far more sophisticated customer profiling and engagement through increasingly sophisticated CRM (customer relationship management) systems. These are three of the most dramatic illustrations in recent years of how markets and marketing have changed as a result of new technology and associated consumer behaviours. The various ways in which technology affects marketing activities fall into two broad categories:

1. effects on consumers and society in general
2. influences on what, how, when and where products are marketed.

Brands and consumers embrace Fairtrade

Topical insight

Fairtrade labelling was created in the Netherlands in the 1980s, with coffee from Mexico being the first recipient of the eco-label.

Fairtrade exists to guarantee that the suppliers of products consumed in the developed world, based in the developing regions, benefit from a fair price. By negotiating better deals, improving the negotiating power and marketing expertise of farmers and producers, and seeking a greater proportion of the retail price, the movement helps sustain development and is largely welcomed by the leading development agencies. A core aim is to minimize dramatically fluctuating prices that, when low, force farmers into crippling debt or out of production. More information is available at www.fairtrade.org.uk.

By putting the FAIRTRADE Mark on your products, stocking Fairtrade goods or serving them to your customers you can demonstrate your ethical commitment to your customers, have a positive impact on the producers of the commodities with which you work and get closer to your supply chain.

Fairtrade Foundation, April 2015

Now there are about 20 organizations around the world, including the Fairtrade Foundation, overseeing the labelling of Fairtrade products. Over 1140 Fairtrade-certified producer groups and 1 400 000 farmers in 74 countries have helped many impoverished and vulnerable regions. In order to achieve this, the movement must lobby retailers, the media and consumers to purchase or support Fairtrade products, which are now sold in 125 countries. In the UK there are now over 4500 Fairtrade retail and catering products (up from 1500 in 2006), from tea to fruit, roses to footballs, snacks to wines. These are now worth £1.6 billion in UK retail sales. One key product receiving such high-profile attention is coffee.

Leading coffee houses Costa Coffee, Prêt à Manger and Starbucks have retailed Fairtrade coffees for a while, but now it is the turn of the major manufacturers. Until relatively recently, most Fairtrade products were niche brands produced by marginal manufacturers. Now, even the giants of the global food industry have embraced the movement, reflecting the growing interest in ethical trading by consumers and major retail chains.

First, Nestlé announced a Fairtrade addition to its Nescafé brand. Today there is a full range of Nescafé Partners Blend Coffee lines, supported with some innovative branding (www.growmorethancoffee.co.uk). However, before its launch, rival Kraft stole a march by introducing a Fairtrade coffee range under its well-known Kenco brand. Kenco Sustainable Development comprised two lines: a filter pack and an espresso bean pack. First available to consumers in restaurants, hotels, coffee shops and vending machines, then through supermarkets, both Kenco lines carry an eco-label from sustainable agriculture organization the Rainforest Alliance, which guarantees that the beans are from certified farms. Kraft also reformulated its flagship brands Maxwell House and Kenco Really Smooth so that they contain at least 5 per cent certified beans, but they do not carry the eco-label. Now all of the major supermarket groups, many buying groups and even the discounters, stock Fairtrade or ethically-sourced coffee lines.

Did growing consumer interest in Fairtrade encourage these manufacturers to launch the new lines? Were moves by the more socially aware retailers responsible? Had lobbying by organizations such as the Rainforest Alliance or Fairtrade Foundation created the necessary swell of positive public opinion? Were Kraft and Nestlé simply reaping the rewards of their environmental scanning of market trends? In reality, a mix of these drivers combined to create the impetus for these products and the growth of other companies' Fairtrade products.

Sources: www.growmorethancoffee.co.uk, 28 February 2011; Kraft, 2004; www.fairtrade.org.uk, 28 February 2011; Mark Sweeney, 'Kraft beats Nestlé to launch of fair trade coffee', *Marketing*, 7 July 2004, p. 1; www.nescafé.co.uk /CoffeeCupboard, 2011; 'Starbucks and Fairtrade' at www.starbucks.co.uk, 28 February 2011; www.fairtrade.org.uk/en/what-is-fairtrade/faqs, April 2015; www.nestleprofessional.com, April 2015; www.coffeebeansblog.co.uk/tag/kenco -sustainable-development-coffee-2, April 2015.

Effects of technology on society

Technology determines how consumers as members of society satisfy their physiological needs. In various ways and to varying degrees, eating and drinking habits, sleeping patterns, sexual activities and healthcare are all influenced both by existing technology and by changes in technology. Right now, many consumers seek technology solutions for the planet's sustainability needs and carbon problems. Technological developments have improved standards of living, thus creating more leisure time; they have also enhanced information, entertainment and education. Nevertheless, technology can detract from the quality of life through undesirable side-effects, such as unemployment, 'couch potato' lazing around, cyber-bullying, polluted air and water and other health hazards. Some people believe that further applications of technology can soften or eliminate these undesirable side-effects. Others argue, however, that the best way to improve the quality of our lives is to decrease the use of technology.

Effects of technology on marketing

Technology also affects the types of product that marketers can offer. The introduction and general acceptance of cassette tapes and compact discs drove most manufacturers of vinyl long-playing (LP) albums out of business or forced them to invest in new technology. Yet this technology provided new marketing opportunities for recording artists and producers, record companies, retailers and those in related industries. More recently, music downloads and streaming from the web have created a new set of opportunities and challenges for marketers in the music industry, while giving greater flexibility and immediacy to consumers. The following items are just a few of the many thousands of existing products that were not available to consumers 20 years ago: webcams, digital cameras, smartphones, sat nav, tablets, high-resolution televisions, mobile video cameras, the internet, mobile media applications, e-readers, Skype and social networks. All of these are products that have transformed lifestyles and people's access to information.

Computer technology helps make warehouse storage and keeping track of stored products more efficient and, therefore, less expensive. Often, these savings can be passed on to consumers in the form of lower prices. Because of technological changes in communications, marketers can now use a variety of media to reach large masses of people more efficiently. The development and widespread use of fax, email and text messaging, for example, allowed marketers to send their advertisements or sales specifications directly to selected groups of customers who want their products. In recent years the internet has permeated the lives of many, bringing a world of information into the home and allowing consumers to shop for products on-line. Facebook, LinkedIn and other digital social media networks have revolutionized how consumers find out about events, products, services, brands and how they share their views (see Chapter 19). Technological advances in transport enable consumers to travel further and more often, to shop at a larger number of stores, or to broaden their options. Changes in transport have also affected producers' ability to get products to retailers and wholesalers. The ability of present-day manufacturers of relatively lightweight products to reach any of their dealers within hours via express delivery services would astound their counterparts of 50 years ago. Geographical boundaries for markets have been revolutionized thanks to transport, digital, communication and customer engagement technological changes.

The adoption and use of technology

Technology assessment
A procedure by which managers try to foresee the effects of new products and processes on their company's operation, on other commercial organizations and on society in general.

Through a procedure known as **technology assessment**, some managers try to foresee the effects of new products and processes on their company's operation, on other organizations and on society in general. With the information gained through a technology assessment, management tries to estimate whether the benefits of using a specific kind of technology outweigh the costs to the business and to society at large. Increasing numbers of companies are encouraged to proceed in this direction as carbon footprint pressures and corporate social responsibility (CSR) policies drive change. Although available technology could radically improve their products or other parts of the marketing mix, some companies may put off applying this technology as long as their competitors do not try to use it. The extent to which an organization can protect inventions stemming from research also influences its use of technology. The extent to which a product is secure from imitation depends on how easily others can copy it without violating its patent. If new products and processes cannot be protected through patents, a company is less likely to market them and make the benefits of its research available to competitors. How a company uses or does not use technology is important for its long-term survival. An organization that makes the wrong decisions may well lose out to the competition. Poor decisions may also affect its profits by requiring expensive corrective action. Poor decisions about technological forces may even drive a company out of business.

When a company's marketers undertake an assessment of the marketing environment they will identify many aspects of technology pertinent to their own industry, markets and products, presenting both opportunities and threats. To illustrate just some of the ramifications of technological change, five aspects of technology ahead of all others warrant further discussion in terms of their implications for how marketing has itself altered: customer relationship management (CRM), internet marketing, mobile marketing, social media and 'big data'; all of which relate to digital marketing. Digital marketing is explored in Part Three of *Marketing: Concepts and Strategies* and CRM is examined in more detail in Chapter 7.

CRM

There is nothing more important for marketers than identifying prospective customers, engaging effectively with them, building ongoing relationships and managing the varied personnel across the many functions in a typical company who interact with customers. In today's multi-media and multi-channel environment, managing a relationship with a customer across the many ways in which he or she can interact with the brand or the company is very challenging, but also presents numerous opportunities for achieving more business. CRM illustrates well how technology has impacted on marketers. Not too long ago it was an arduous and manual paper-driven task to keep track of contacts with customers and to build up profiles of a company's customers or customer segments. Now CRM packages and suppliers provide off-the-shelf or bespoke approaches to managing customer contacts and relationships.

In essence, CRM helps a business to recognize the value of its customers and to capitalize on improved customer relations, in order to extend relationships and extract maximum returns from individual customers. CRM can be achieved by:

● Finding out about customers' purchasing habits, opinions and preferences.

● Profiling individuals and groups so as to market more effectively and increase sales.

● Changing the way a company operates, to improve customer service and marketing.

Therefore using technology to improve CRM makes good business sense. There are many IT solutions to CRM available.

Many software companies offer CRM applications that integrate with existing customer data and sales management packages. Cut-down versions of such software may be suitable for smaller businesses. While not tailored to a company's unique customer base, product portfolio and marketing environment, such solutions are readily available and popular. Some users want to have a more customized and bespoke software solution, and are prepared to pay more for such benefits. If a company does not wish to fully outsource its operation, it may opt to select a managed solution, in effect renting a customized suite of CRM applications as a bespoke package. Some companies opt to fully outsource their CRM requirements to IT services businesses. Application service providers, such as Accenture Interactive, can provide web-based CRM solutions, increasingly harnessing the benefits of cloud computing, which frees up an organization from having to provide its own IT infrastructure. Such providers host their clients' CRM operations for them. Outsourcing is a significant commitment and tends to be an option for larger corporate clients.

CRM involves data capture about customers and their buying habits, analysis and profiling of such behaviours, so that tailored propositions and communications may be created in order to maintain an ongoing relationship and continue to interest customers in the company's brand, products and activities. IT and software have routinized this aspect of customer handling in many organizations. There are even CRM apps for smartphone users and most businesses now utilize such ready-made packages. CRM will be explored in more detail in Chapter 7.

CRM
Data capture about customers and their buying habits, analysis and profiling of such behaviours, so that tailored propositions and communications may be created in order to maintain an ongoing relationship and continue to interest customers in the company's brand, products and activities.

The internet and digital marketing

Fifteen years ago, the internet was big news for marketers and e-marketing was a buzzword. This was the process of creating, distributing, promoting and pricing products for targeted customers in the digital environment of the internet. The internet impacted largely in three ways: (a) for distributing products, as an alternative marketing channel to retail stores or trade depots; (b) for marketing communications, as an additional option to sales promotion, traditional advertising, public relations or personal selling; and (c) as a means for finding out information about markets, competitors, market trends and customers. Internet marketing was deemed to be a part of what was termed direct marketing (see Chapter 18). In recent years, the speed of technological innovation, social acceptance of such advances and their deployment by marketers, have rapidly taken this aspect of marketing to new heights. Now more generally termed digital marketing, this also encompasses mobile marketing and social media. There is no doubt about the extent to which the internet has altered the bounds for consumers, business customers, marketers and brands, as described later in this book.

Digital marketing
The use of technology-led channels of communication and selling to manage customer interaction and provide customer experience in a digitally-connected environment.

Digital marketing tools and techniques are used by marketers to improve their proposition to customers and overall competitiveness, with a value-adding website and interrelated digital marketing techniques to drive traffic, conversion, positive experience and referrals. These techniques include website, online public relations, email, blogs/microblogs, social networks, podcasts, wikis and search engine management to ensure preferential web search. There is a bewildering and fast-evolving landscape of digital marketing touch points for marketers to understand ... consumers have a growing selection of web and mobile options for learning about products, services and brands, and sharing opinions and views directly with fellow consumers. The digital era has also enabled the capture of far more market information and customer insight, providing what has come to be known as 'big data'. This theme is explored further in Chapter 19.

Two very important aspects of digital marketing are mobile marketing and social media.

Mobile marketing

Mobile marketing
Encourages consumer engagement anywhere or anytime while on or using a mobile device, such as a smartphone or tablet, and heavily dependent on mobile apps which provide users with information, entertainment and location-based services.

A traditional definition of **mobile marketing** is marketing activity in a moving manner or encountered by consumers on the move, such as moving advertising boards at sports events or stations, but increasingly the term stands for marketing via a mobile device such as a smartphone, to provide customers with time and location-sensitive, personalized information, anytime and anywhere, that promotes goods, services and ideas. Mobile marketing encourages consumer engagement anywhere or anytime while on or using a mobile device, such as a smartphone or tablet, and is heavily dependent on mobile apps which provide users with information, entertainment and location-based services.

Brand managers have launched apps and developed interactive websites suitable for smartphones, tablets, laptops on the move and interactive points at a host of locations. Technology now permits ready and immediate access to customers wherever they are, whenever and irrespective of whatever they are doing. Whether searching for flight information whilst in a meeting or taxi, paying a utility bill when watching TV, betting on a sports result over dinner or Googling for the answer to a pub quiz question, instant hooking up whenever and wherever to the digital community is now routine, providing marketers with a selection of mobile possibilities.

Social media and networks

Facebook, LinkedIn, Twitter and Instagram are familiar to most readers of this text and to most marketers. Insight consultants Gartner examined 400 social media cases, concluding that, '... social-media technologies, such as social networking, wikis and blogs, enable collaboration on a much grander scale and support tapping the power of the collective in ways previously unachievable'.[9] As explained in Chapter 1, the emergence of social media and networking has radically shifted the boundaries for marketers and consumers, not least because they have taken a great deal of communication about brands and products out of the hands of marketers and into the hands of consumers, who easily may share their experiences and views with each other.

Social media
Social media incorporate the online technology and methods through which people can share content, personal opinions, different perspectives and insights, using text, images, audio and video, via social networks, video and photo sharing, microblogs, wikis and news aggregators.

Social media offer a way to more effectively reach audiences and engage them in commercial transactions, but also the social/third sector is able develop low-cost conversational communication strategies. **Social media** incorporate the online technology and methods through which people can share content, personal opinions, and swap different perspectives and insights, using text, images, audio and video. Social networking sites such as Facebook are one form of social media; others include wikis, video sharing such as YouTube, photo sharing on sites like Flickr, news aggregators typified by Digg, social bookmarking, online gaming and micro-blogging on presence apps such as Twitter.

Economic and competitive forces

Economic and competitive forces
Factors in the marketing environment such as the effects of general economic conditions; buying power; willingness to spend; spending patterns; types of competitive structure, competitive tools and competitive behaviour that influence both marketers' and consumers' decisions and activities.

The **economic and competitive forces** in the marketing environment influence both marketers' and customers' decisions and activities. This section first examines the effects of general economic conditions, also focusing on buying power, willingness to spend and spending patterns. Then the discussion moves to the broad competitive forces, including types of competitive structure, competitive tools and some methods for monitoring competitive behaviour. The strategic importance of understanding and evaluating the competitive arena has been discussed in Chapter 2.

General economic conditions

The overall state of the economy fluctuates in all countries. Table 3.1 illustrates demographic data linked to economic performance. These changes in general economic conditions affect and are affected by the forces of supply and demand, buying power, willingness to spend, consumer expenditure levels and the intensity of competitive behaviour. Therefore, current economic conditions and changes in the economy have a broad impact on the success of organizations' marketing strategies.

TABLE 3.1   EU population data

	Population, 1 January 2012	Live births	Deaths	Natural change (^{1})	Net migration and statistical adjustment (^{2})	Total change between 1 January 2012 and 2013	Population, 1 January 2013
EU-28	504 582.5	5 231.2	5 010.0	221.1	899.5	1 120.6	505 665.7
Belgium	11 094.9	128.1	109.1	19.0	47.8	66.8	11 161.6
Bulgaria	7 327.2	69.1	109.3	−40.2	−2.5	−42.7	7 284.6
Czech Republic	10 505.4	108.6	108.2	0.4	10.3	10.7	10 516.1
Denmark	5 580.5	57.9	52.3	5.6	16.5	22.1	5 602.6
Germany	80 327.9	673.5	869.6	−196.0	391.9	195.8	80 523.7
Estonia	1 325.2	14.1	15.5	−1.4	−3.6	−5.0	1 320.2
Ireland	4 582.7	72.2	28.8	43.4	−35.0	8.4	4 591.1
Greece	11 123.0	100.4	116.7	−16.3	−44.2	−60.5	11 062.5
Spain	46 818.2	453.3	401.1	52.2	−142.6	−90.3	46 727.9
France	65 287.9	821.8	570.0	251.9	39.1	291.0	65 578.8
Croatia	4 276.0	41.8	51.7	−9.9	−3.9	−13.8	4 262.1
Italy	59 394.2	534.2	612.9	−78.7	369.7	291.0	59 685.2
Cyprus	862.0	10.2	5.7	4.5	−0.6	3.9	865.9
Latvia	2 044.8	19.9	29.0	−9.1	−11.9	−21.0	2 023.8
Lithuania	3 003.6	30.5	40.9	−10.5	−21.3	−31.7	2 971.9
Luxembourg	524.9	6.0	3.9	2.2	10.0	12.2	537.0
Hungary	9 931.9	90.3	129.4	−39.2	16.0	−23.1	9 908.8
Malta	417.5	4.1	3.4	0.7	3.1	3.8	421.4
Netherlands	16 730.3	176.0	140.8	35.1	14.1	49.2	16 779.6

(Continued)

TABLE 3.1 Continued

	Population, 1 January 2012	Live births	Deaths	Natural change (¹)	Net migration and statistical adjustment (²)	Total change between 1 January 2012 and 2013	Population, 1 January 2013
Austria	8 408.1	79.0	79.4	−0.5	44.2	43.7	8 451.9
Poland	38 538.4	386.3	384.8	1.5	−6.6	−5.1	38 533.3
Portugal	10 542.4	89.8	107.6	−17.8	−37.3	−55.1	10 487.3
Romania	20 096.0	201.1	255.5	−54.4	15.9	−38.5	20 020.1
Slovenia	2 055.5	21.9	19.3	2.7	0.6	3.3	2 058.8
Slovakia	5 404.3	55.5	52.4	3.1	3.4	6.5	5 410.8
Finland	5 401.3	59.5	51.7	7.8	17.6	25.4	5 426.7
Sweden	9 482.9	113.2	91.9	21.2	51.8	73.0	9 555.9
United Kingdom	63 495.3	813.0	569.0	243.9	156.8	400.8	63 896.1
Iceland	319.6	4.5	2.0	2.6	−0.3	2.3	321.9
Liechtenstein	36.5	0.4	0.2	0.1	0.2	0.4	36.8
Norway	4 985.9	60.3	42.0	18.3	47.1	65.4	5 051.3
Switzerland	7 954.7	82.2	64.2	18.0	66.4	84.4	8 039.1
Montenegro	621.2	7.5	5.9	1.5	0.0	1.5	622.8
FYR of Macedonia	2 059.8	23.6	20.1	3.4	−0.9	2.5	2 062.3
Serbia	7 216.6	67.3	102.4	−35.1	0.0	−35.1	7 181.5
Turkey	74 724.3	1 279.9	374.9	905.0	−1.9	903.1	75 627.4

(¹) Live births minus deaths.
(²) Total change minus natural change.
Source: Europe in Figures, *Eurostat Yearbook*, Luxembourg: Eurostat, accessed 30 April 2015.

Business cycle
Fluctuations in the economy that follow the general pattern of prosperity, recession, depression and recovery.

Fluctuations in the economy follow a general pattern often referred to as the **business cycle**. In the traditional view, the business cycle consists of four stages: prosperity, recession, depression and recovery.

Prosperity During **prosperity**, unemployment is low and total income is relatively high. Assuming a low inflation rate, this combination causes buying power to be high. To the extent that the economic outlook remains prosperous, consumers are generally willing to buy. In the prosperity stage, marketers often expand their marketing mixes (product, place/distribution, promotion, price and people) to take advantage of the increased buying power. They sometimes capture a larger market share by intensifying distribution and promotion efforts.

Prosperity
A period during which unemployment is low and total income is relatively high.

Recession Unemployment rises during a **recession**, so total buying power declines. The pessimism that accompanies a recession often stifles both consumer and business spending, as is the case as this edition of *Marketing: Concepts and Strategies* is produced. As buying power decreases, many consumers become more price- and value-conscious; they look for products that are basic and functional. For instance, people ordinarily reduce their consumption of more expensive convenience foods and strive to save money by growing and preparing more of their own food. Individuals buy fewer durable goods and more repair and do-it-yourself products. During a recession, some

Recession
A period during which unemployment rises and total buying power declines.

companies make the mistake of drastically reducing their marketing efforts and thus damage their ability to survive. Obviously, marketers should consider some revision of their marketing activities during a recessionary period. Because consumers are more concerned about the functional value of products, a company must focus its marketing research on determining what product functions buyers want and then make sure that these functions become part of its products. Promotional efforts should emphasize value and utility.

Depression
A period during which unemployment is extremely high, wages are very low, total disposable income is at a minimum and consumers lack confidence in the economy.

Depression   A **depression** is a period in which unemployment is extremely high, wages are very low, total disposable income is at a minimum and consumers lack confidence in the economy. Governments have used both monetary and fiscal policies to offset the effects of recession and depression. Monetary policies are employed to control the money supply, which in turn affects spending, saving and investment by both individuals and businesses. Through the establishment of fiscal policies, the government is able to influence the amount of saving and expenditure by adjusting the tax structure and by changing the levels of government spending. Some economic experts believe that the effective use of monetary and fiscal policies can completely eliminate depressions from the business cycle, although the credit crunch at the end of the decade posed some challenge to this view.

Recovery
The stage of the business cycle in which the economy moves from depression or recession to prosperity.

Recovery   **Recovery** is the stage of the business cycle in which the economy moves from depression or recession to prosperity. During this period, the high unemployment rate begins to decline, total disposable income increases and the economic gloom that lessened consumers' willingness to buy subsides. Both the ability and the willingness to buy rise. Marketers face some problems during recovery; for example, the difficulty of ascertaining how quickly prosperity will return and of forecasting the level of prosperity that will be attained. During this stage, marketers should maintain as much flexibility in their marketing strategies as possible to be able to make the required adjustments as the economy moves from recession to prosperity. Fluctuations in economic conditions have a significant impact on marketers' activities and fortunes.

Consumer demand and spending behaviour

Buying power
Resources such as goods, services and financial holdings that can be traded in an exchange situation.

Marketers must understand the factors that determine whether, what, where and when people buy. Chapters 5 and 6 look at the behavioural factors underlying these choices, but here the focus is on the economic components: buying power, willingness to purchase and spending patterns.

Income
The amount of money received through wages, rents, investments, pensions and subsidy payments for a given period.

Buying power   The strength of a person's **buying power** depends on the size of the resources that enable the individual to purchase, as well as on the state of the economy. The resources that make up buying power are goods, services and financial holdings. Fluctuations of the business cycle affect buying power because they influence price levels and interest rates. For example, during inflationary periods, when prices are rising, buying power decreases because more pounds or euros are required to buy products. The major financial sources of buying power are income, credit and wealth. From an individual's viewpoint, **income** is the amount of money received through wages, rents, investments, pensions and subsidy payments for a given period, such as a month or a year. Normally, this money is allocated among taxes, spending for goods and services, and savings. However, because of the differences in people's educational levels, abilities, occupations and wealth, income is not distributed equally in any country.

Disposable income
After-tax income, which is used for spending or saving.

Marketers are most interested in the amount of money that is left after payment of taxes. After-tax income is called **disposable income** and is used for spending or saving. Because disposable income is a ready source of buying power, the total amount available in a country is important to marketers. Several factors affect the size of total disposable income. One, of course, is the total amount of income. Total national income is affected by wage levels, rate of unemployment, interest rates and dividend rates. These factors in turn affect the size of disposable income. Because disposable income is the income left after taxes are paid, the number of taxes and their amount directly affect the size of total disposable income. When taxes rise, disposable income declines; when taxes fall, disposable income increases. Disposable income that is available for spending and saving after an individual has purchased the basic necessities of food, clothing and shelter is called **discretionary income**. People use discretionary income to purchase entertainment, holidays, cars, education, pets and pet supplies, furniture, appliances and so on. Changes in total discretionary income affect the sales of these products, especially cars, furniture, large appliances and other costly durable goods. The marketers of such products must monitor factors likely to alter their target customers' discretionary income.

Discretionary income
Disposable income that is available for spending and saving after an individual has purchased the basic necessities of food, clothing and shelter.

Credit enables people to spend future income now or in the near future. However, credit increases current buying power at the expense of future buying power. Several factors determine whether consumers use or forgo credit. First, credit must be available to them. Interest rates, too, affect consumers' decisions to use credit, especially for expensive purchases such as homes, appliances and cars. When credit charges are high, consumers are more likely to delay buying expensive items. Use of credit is also affected by credit terms, such as the size of the down payment and the amount and number of monthly payments. Many marketers offer 'interest-free credit' or low interest rates as part of the marketing proposition for their products.

Wealth
The accumulation of past income, natural resources and financial resources.

A person can have a high income and very little wealth. It is also possible, but not likely, for a person to have great wealth but not much income. **Wealth** is the accumulation of past income, natural resources and financial resources. It may exist in many forms, including cash, securities, savings accounts, jewellery, antiques and property. Like income, wealth is distributed unevenly. The significance of wealth to marketers is that as people become wealthier they gain buying power in three ways: they can use their wealth to make current purchases, to generate income and to acquire large amounts of credit. Buying power information is available from government sources, trade associations and research agencies. One of the most current and comprehensive sources of buying power data is the Office for National Statistics (www.statistics.gov.uk) and the *National Income, Expenditure and Output Surveys*. The EU's Eurostat (epp.eurostat.ec.europa.eu) provides similar data across member states of the EU. Income, wealth and credit equip consumers to purchase goods and services. Marketing managers should be aware of current levels and expected changes in buying power in their own markets because buying power directly affects the types and quantities of goods and services that consumers purchase, as explained later in the discussion of spending patterns. Just because consumers have buying power, however, does not necessarily mean that they will buy. Consumers must also be willing to use their buying power. Marketers must encourage them to do so.

Willingness to spend
A disposition towards using buying power, influenced by the ability to buy, expected satisfaction from a product and numerous psychological and social forces.

Consumers' willingness to spend   People's **willingness to spend** is, to some degree, related to their ability to buy; that is, people are sometimes more willing to buy if they have the buying power. However, a number of other elements also influence willingness to spend. Some elements affect specific products; others influence spending in general. A product's absolute price and its price relative to the price of substitute products influences almost everyone. The amount of satisfaction currently received or expected in the future from a product already owned may also influence consumers' desire to buy other products. Satisfaction depends not only on the quality of the functional performance of the currently owned product, but also on numerous psychological and social forces.

Factors that affect consumers' general willingness to spend include expectations about future employment, income levels, prices, family size and general economic conditions. If people are unsure whether or how long they will be employed, willingness to buy usually declines.

Current realignment following the global banking crisis and the credit crunch has caused high levels of uncertainty for many consumers and businesses, altering spending patterns and willingness to buy. Willingness to spend may increase if people are reasonably certain of higher incomes in the future. Expectations of rising prices in the near future may also increase willingness to spend in the present. For a given level of buying power, the larger the family, the greater the willingness to buy. One of the reasons for this relationship is that as the size of a family increases, a larger amount of money must be spent to provide the basic necessities of life to sustain the family members. Finally, perceptions of future economic conditions influence willingness to buy. For example, rising short-term interest rates cool consumers' willingness to spend.

Consumer spending patterns   Marketers must be aware of the factors that influence consumers' ability and willingness to spend, but they should also analyze how consumers actually spend their disposable incomes. Marketers obtain this information by studying consumer spending patterns. **Consumer spending patterns** indicate the relative proportions of annual family expenditures or the actual amount of money spent on certain kinds of goods and services. Families are usually categorized by one of several characteristics, including family income, age of the head of household, geographic area and family life cycle. There are two types of spending pattern: comprehensive and product-specific.

The percentages of family income allotted to annual expenditures for general classes of goods and services constitute **comprehensive spending patterns**. Comprehensive spending patterns or the data to develop them are available in government publications and in reports produced by the major marketing research companies and by trade associations. **Product-specific spending patterns** indicate the annual monetary amounts families spend for specific products within a general product class. Information sources used to construct product-specific spending patterns include government publications, trade publications and consumer surveys. A marketer uses spending patterns to analyze general trends in the ways that families spend their incomes for various kinds of product. Analyses of spending patterns yield information that a marketer can use to gain perspective and background for decision-making. However, spending patterns reflect only general trends and thus should not be used as the sole basis for making specific decisions.

Assessment of competitive forces

Few organizations, if any, operate free of competition. Broadly speaking, all companies compete with each other for consumers' money. In other walks of life, such as the public sector or third sector, organizations may compete for attention, people's time or involvement, goodwill, donations or payment. In commercial settings, a business generally defines **competition** as those organizations marketing products that are similar to, or can be substituted for, its own products in the same geographic area or marketing channel. For example, a local Tesco or Aldi supermarket manager views all grocery stores in a town as competitors, but almost never thinks of other types of local or out-of-town stores (DIY or electrical, for example) as competitors. This section considers the types of competitive structure and the importance of monitoring competitors.

Types of competitive structure   The number of organizations that control the supply of a product may affect the strength of competition. When only one or a few companies control supply, competitive factors will exert a different sort of influence on marketing activities than when there are many competitors. Table 3.2 presents four general types of competitive structure: monopoly, oligopoly, monopolistic competition and perfect competition.

Consumer spending patterns
Information indicating the relative proportions of annual family expenditures or the actual amount of money spent on certain kinds of goods and services.

Comprehensive spending patterns
The percentages of family income allotted to annual expenditures for general classes of goods and services.

Product-specific spending patterns
The annual monetary amounts families spend for specific products within a general product class.

Competition
Those companies marketing products that are similar to, or can be substituted for, a given business's products in the same geographic area or marketing channel.

TABLE 3.2 Selected characteristics of competitive structures

Type of structure	Number of competitors	Ease of entry into market	Product	Knowledge of market	Examples
Monopoly	One	Many barriers	Almost no substitutes	Perfect	Non-privatized railways, many government departments
Oligopoly	Few	Some barriers	Homogeneous or differentiated (real or perceived differences)	Imperfect	Airlines, petroleum retailers, some utility providers
Monopolistic competition	Many	Few barriers	Product differentiation with many substitutes	More knowledge than oligopoly; less than monopoly	Jeans, fast food, audio-visual
Perfect competition	Unlimited	No barriers	Homogeneous products	Perfect	The London commodity markets, vegetable farms

Monopoly
A market structure that exists when a company turns out a product that has no close substitutes or rivals.

Oligopoly
A market structure that exists when a few sellers control the supply of a large proportion of a product.

Monopolistic competition
A market structure that exists when a business with many potential competitors attempts to develop a differential marketing strategy to establish its own market share.

Perfect competition
A market structure that entails a large number of sellers, not one of which could significantly influence price or supply.

A **monopoly** exists when a company turns out a product that has no close substitutes or rivals. As the organization has no competitors, it completely controls the supply of the product and, as a single seller, can erect barriers to potential competitors. In reality, the monopolies that survive today are some utilities, such as telephone, electricity and some railways (in many countries), and cable companies, which are heavily regulated. These monopolies are tolerated because of the tremendous financial resources needed to develop and operate them; few organizations can obtain the resources to mount any competition against a local electricity producer, for example. An **oligopoly** exists when a few sellers control the supply of a large proportion of a product. In this case, each seller must consider the reactions of other sellers to changes in marketing activities. Products facing oligopolistic competition may be homogeneous, such as aluminum, or differentiated, such as cigarettes and cars. Usually, barriers of some sort make it difficult to enter the market and compete with oligopolies. For example, because of the enormous financial outlay required, few companies or individuals could afford to enter the oil-refining or steel-producing industries. Moreover, some industries demand special technical or marketing skills that block the entry of many potential competitors.

Monopolistic competition exists when an organization with many potential competitors attempts to develop a differential marketing strategy to establish its own market share. For example, Levi's has established a differential advantage for its blue jeans through a well-known trademark, design, advertising and a quality image. Although many competing brands of blue jeans are available, this company has carved out its market share through use of a differential marketing strategy. **Perfect competition**, if it existed at all, would entail a large number of sellers, not one of which could significantly influence price or supply. Products would be homogeneous, and there would be full knowledge of the market and easy entry. The closest thing to an example of perfect competition would be an unregulated agricultural market. Few, if any, marketers operate in a structure of perfect competition. Perfect competition is an ideal at one end of the continuum, with monopoly at the other end. Most marketers function in a competitive environment that falls somewhere between these two extremes.

Competitive tools   Another set of factors that influences the level of competition is the number and types of competitive tools used by competitors. To survive, an organization uses one or several available competitive tools to deal with competitive economic forces. Once a company has analyzed its particular competitive environment and decided which factors in that environment it can or must adapt to or influence, it can choose among the variables that it can control to strengthen its competitive position in the overall marketplace. Probably the competitive tool that most organizations grasp is price. Bic, for example, markets disposable pens and lighters that are similar to competing products but less expensive. However, there is one major problem with using price as a competitive tool: competitors will often match or beat the price. This threat is one of the primary reasons for employing non-price competitive tools that are based on the differentiation of market segments, product offering, service, promotion, distribution or enterprise.[10] By focusing on a specific market segment, a marketer sometimes gains a competitive advantage.

For instance, Bentley cars and Porsche sports coupés are narrowly targeted at specific groups of consumers. Most manufacturers try to gain a competitive edge by incorporating product features that make their brands distinctive to some extent. Companies use distinguishing promotional methods to compete, such as advertising and personal selling. Competing producers sometimes use different distribution channels to prevail over one another. Retailers may compete by placing their outlets in locations that are convenient for a large number of shoppers. Dealers and distributors offer wide ranges, advice and service.

Monitoring competition   Marketers in an organization need to be aware of the actions of major competitors. They should monitor what competitors are currently doing and assess the changes occurring in the competitive environment, as explained in Chapter 2. **Competitor monitoring** allows organizations to determine what specific strategies competitors are following and how those strategies affect their own. It can also guide marketers as they try to develop competitive advantages and can aid them in adjusting current marketing strategies, as well as in planning new ones. Information may come from direct observation and product testing of competing products, or from sources such as the web, sales people, customers' feedback and marketing research, trade publications, media comments, online postings, syndicated marketing research services, distributors, supply chain feedback and marketing studies. Unfortunately, less ethical information sources for competitor insights sometimes are utilized. An organization needs information about competitors that will allow its marketing managers to assess the performance of its own marketing efforts. Comparing their company's performance with that of competitors helps marketing managers recognize strengths and weaknesses in their own marketing strategies. Data about market shares, product movement, sales volume and expenditure levels can be useful. However, accurate information on these matters is often difficult to obtain.

Competition exists in most markets and situations. Even charities compete with one another and with manufacturers for consumers' attention and financial commitment. Marketing places an emphasis on meeting consumers' needs and offering satisfaction. To be successful, however, competing organizations need to identify unique marketing programmes; otherwise all rival products and services will merely replicate each other. The search for a competitive edge over competitors is central to effective marketing strategy. As well as monitoring direct competitors, marketers should be aware of new entrants coming into a market with competing propositions, and of the danger of substitute products or services being developed. Marketers' strategic understanding of competition was addressed in Chapter 2.

Competitor monitoring
The process by which a company studies the actions of its major competitors in order to determine what specific strategies they are following and how those strategies affect its own; also used by marketers as they try to develop competitive advantages, adjust current marketing strategies and plan new ones.

Macro marketing environment
The broader forces affecting all organizations in a market: political, legal, regulatory, societal/green, technological and economic/competitive.

The micro marketing environment

Many authors, notably Michael Porter,[11] have made a distinction between the very broad forces of the **macro marketing environment**, discussed up to now in this chapter – political, legal, regulatory, societal, technological, economic/competitive – and a set

Micro marketing environment
The more company-specific forces reflecting the nature of the business, its suppliers, marketing intermediaries, buyers, all types of competitors: direct, substitute and new entrant and its publics.

of more company-specific forces often termed the micro marketing environment forces. The distinction, put simply, is that the broad macro forces have an impact on every organization operating in a particular market, from manufacturers to distributors to customers, and such an impact is largely universally felt by such organizations. The micro forces, on the other hand, are still forces external to the organization and not directly controllable, but often have an organization-specific impact subject to the characteristics and status of the individual business. For example, a new entrant competitor might only target customer segments currently served by certain existing rivals and not impinge on the activities of other competitors.

The core aspects of the micro marketing environment

Although categorizations vary among authors, the core aspects of the micro marketing environment worthy of note include the organization itself, suppliers, marketing intermediaries, buyers, competitors and publics (see Figure 3.3).

The organization It is necessary when creating and implementing marketing strategies and marketing mix programmes to consider the reaction, attitudes and abilities of the internal environment: top management, finance, research and development, purchasing, manufacturing, sales and marketing, and logistics. The marketing function's recommendations must be consistent with senior management's corporate goals; be conveyed to other functions within the organization;

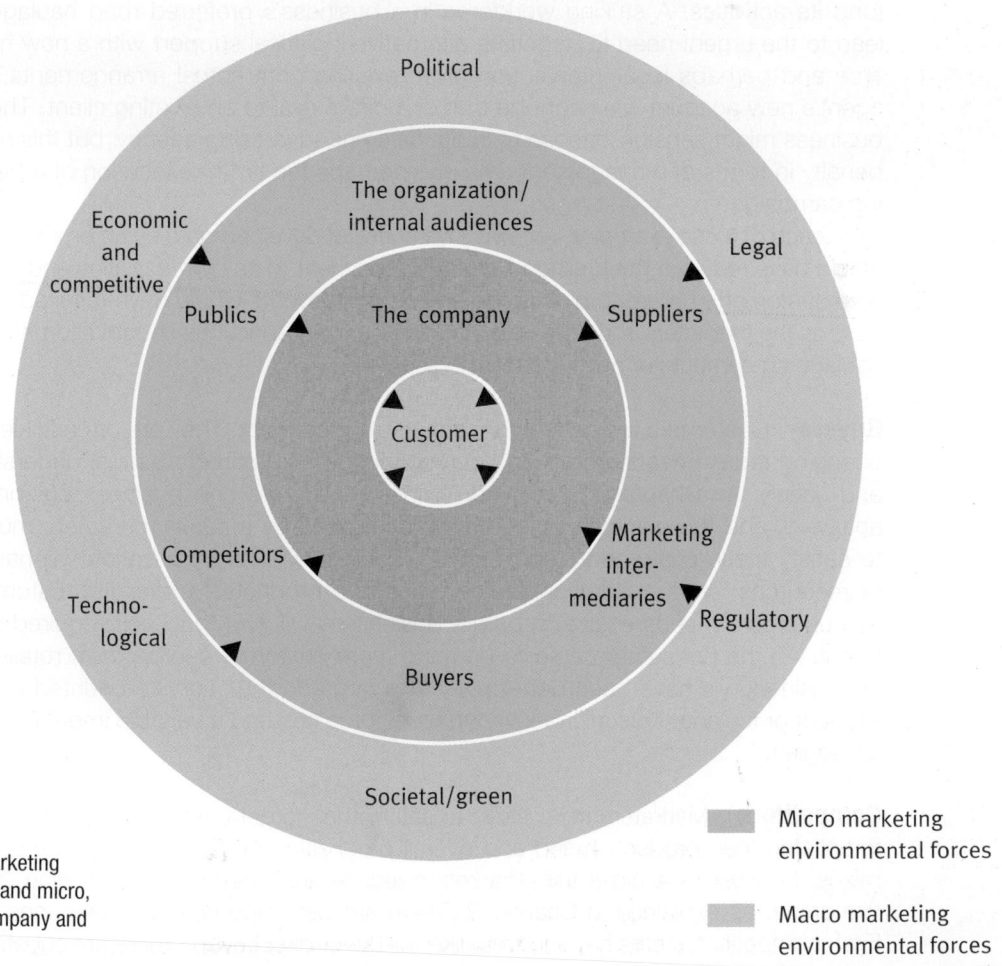

FIGURE 3.3
The forces of the marketing environment: macro and micro, impacting on the company and its customers

Micro marketing environmental forces

Macro marketing environmental forces

and reflect colleagues' views, input, concerns and abilities to implement the desired marketing plan. Marketers must be aware of these organizational factors, monitor them, and modify their actions accordingly to ensure internal take-up of their ideas and plans.

Suppliers   Most organizations source raw materials, components or supplies from third parties. Without the understanding and cooperation of these other organizations, a business would fail to deliver a quality product or service that satisfies its customers' needs. Marketers must be aware of aspects of supply that might affect the way in which their organization functions in satisfying its customers. These forces could include supplier innovations; deals with rivals; supply shortages, delays or quality concerns; strikes or recruitment difficulties; legal actions or warranty disputes; supply costs and price trends; new entrants into the supply chain; or anything prone to altering the business's receipt of its required supplies.

Marketing intermediaries   Some businesses sell directly to their targeted customers. Most, though, utilize the skills, network and resources of intermediaries to make their products available to the end-user customer. Intermediaries are discussed later (see Chapters 14 and 15) and include resellers such as retailers, wholesalers, agents, brokers, dealers; as well as physical distribution companies responsible for logistical needs; providers of marketing services such as advertising agencies or packaging design consultancies; and financial facilitators of credit lines and export guarantees. Without the smooth cooperation of such intermediaries, an organization is unlikely to be able to deliver its products as required by its customers. For example, the collapse of a credit company or bank severely reduces the ability of a client business to fund its activities. A striking workforce in a business's preferred road haulage company will lead to the urgent need to negotiate alternative logistical support with a new haulier, requiring time and perhaps legal intervention given existing contractual arrangements. An advertising agent's new account win might be that of a direct rival to an existing client. The existing client business might sensibly choose to find a different advertising agency, but this move will have a penalty in terms of management time and perhaps the timely execution of a planned advertising campaign.

   In each of these examples, shrewd awareness of developments by an organization's marketers would have reduced the likelihood of any impediment to its own activities and ability to serve its own customers. Failure to pick up on any of these events would have resulted in a loss of business as the marketers and colleagues in other business functions sought alternative lines of credit, haulage agreements or advertising expertise.

Buyers   Customers are central to the marketing concept. They are often fickle and have ever-changing requirements, needs and perceptions, which marketers must understand, anticipate and satisfy. As Chapters 5 and 6 describe, consumers and business customers should be analyzed, and the marketing programme developed by a set of marketers must be designed to satisfy these customers' requirements. Each individual organization will have a unique set of resources, skills, marketing programmes and products to offer its customers. Therefore, as customers' needs evolve, separate businesses will find that their required response is different. As the consumer came to demand more customer service from retailers, John Lewis and Sainsbury's have been better placed to upgrade their service-oriented propositions than Primark or Iceland. This micro environmental force has had a variable impact on these retailers' strategies.

Competitors   Marketers must strive to satisfy their target customers, but in a manner that differentiates their product, brand and overall proposition from competing companies' marketing mixes. In order to achieve this, marketers require an in-depth understanding of their competitive arena, as explained in Chapter 2. There are two important considerations in this analysis. First, competition stems not only from like-for-like or direct rivals. There are substitute solutions to monitor and new entrants to anticipate. For example, construction equipment manufacturer JCB competes with a plethora of big businesses such as Caterpillar or Case. Iseki manufactures none of the same equipment, but it produces a micro-bore tunnelling 'mole' that lays pipes without the need to dig trenches, thus rendering the need for a JCB backhoe loader digger redundant. Such substitute competition can seriously erode an organization's market position if not observed and combated. Kindle e-readers have been a non-store competitor for book shop chains such as Waterstones. Skype has become a rival to long landline-based phone conversations or sometimes meeting face-to-face.

The second consideration is the organization's own position: resources, market standing, capabilities, strengths and any competitive edge held over rivals. These characteristics are different for each organization, so the impact of any competitive activity will vary between businesses. Marketers must be aware of direct, substitute and new entrant competitor activity but should also gauge the likely impact of competition on their own business in the context of a sound understanding of their capabilities and standing, as explained in Chapter 2.

In terms of the micro marketing environment, competitors are external forces beyond the direct control of marketers. The impact of a particular competitor will vary for one organization to the next or for one brand to the next in the same market. These are the reasons why competition is included in Porter's view of the micro marketing environment.

Publics   The micro marketing environment also includes any group public that does or could impact on an organization's ability to satisfy its target customers and achieve its corporate objectives.[12] These include: financial bodies such as banks, investment houses, financial analysts or shareholders; newspaper, magazine, radio, television, or web media that carry features about a business, its products and activities; government bodies that may intervene over operating or consumer issues; consumer and pressure groups; neighbourhood publics such as residents adjacent to a large manufacturing plant; the general public, whose view of an organization must be assessed and taken into account when developing marketing programmes; and internal publics such as the workforce. Most businesses are increasingly recognizing the importance of communicating effectively with these audiences. The growth of social media and networks such as Facebook or LinkedIn has made communication with publics more straightforward, but has also significantly increased the risk of groups of consumers or other parties instigating discussions about a company's products, services or practices, and not necessarily constructively or positively.

The notion of relationship marketing outlined in Chapter 1 is designed to emphasize the need to address more publics than solely customers through marketing programmes and communications (see Chapter 23). In order to achieve this effectively, however, it is necessary for an organization to understand these micro marketing environment forces.

The marketing environment and strategic opportunities

Strategic windows
Major developments or opportunities triggered by changes in the marketing environment.

When changes occur in the marketing environment they can trigger major developments. If large enough, such changes are called **strategic windows** or paradigm shifts.[13] If market leaders have failed to spot the underlying development or evolutionary change, rivals may have an opportunity to gain an advantage over established companies and brands by 'stepping through the open window'. The established company must strive to 'close the window' with its own proposition speedily enough to pre-empt competitors' inroads. For example, global recession created opportunities for value brands at the expense of premium brands, many of which had to work hard to re-engineer their propositions in order to maintain relevance for their customers and to 'close the window' on their upstart rivals. Tesco failed to close the window on Aldi and Lidl. Failure to monitor the marketing environment and take appropriate action invariably results in an organization being unable to react to the change quickly enough to keep out competitors.

Opening strategic windows

Marketing strategists believe there are six broad causes of strategic windows opening, as described below.[14]

New technology   Duracell overtook market leader EverReady because it took advantage of new lithium technology before EverReady modified its product range. Now rechargeable lithium batteries are impacting on Duracell. Direct Line gained leadership in the car insurance market because it turned to direct selling via telephone call centres before any of the major insurance companies recognized this evolving use of technology. However, more recently, other brands were quicker to harness the web and comparison sites, helping them to compete with Direct Line. Motorola and Nokia, once dominant in mobile phones, were overtaken by smartphone technologies such as Android and the iPhone. Digital media have taken over from old media such as newspapers.

New markets   Many businesses have been quick to recognize how digital channels, mobile communications and changing consumer behaviours combine to open up new markets, with companies being newly established to provide online and mobile gaming and gambling services.

New distribution channels   Ocado, the online grocery retailer, has no supermarkets. Unlike established players such as Tesco or Sainsbury's, it entered the grocery market directly on an e-commerce platform, negating the need to create a store network in order to serve consumers across much of England. Amazon similarly sidestepped the need for a network of retail stores by turning to the web.

Market redefinition   NCR – National Cash Registers – used to dominate the market for providing electronic cash tills in retailers' stores. As retailers discovered the convenience of stock management through barcodes and EPoS (electronic point-of-sale) systems, they turned to more sophisticated systems. Retail management's desire to monitor and record detailed sales data altered the buyer's requirement for in-store technology. Fujitsu and Nixdorf were quick to spot this change and build on their computer industry resources to develop all-in retail systems that incorporated the cash till with much more. This redefinition of the market eroded NCR's once dominant position while giving rivals a marketing opportunity.

New legislation and regulation   Laws, regulations and international agreements create strategic windows. The 'open skies' policy of the EU has created route opportunities for smaller airlines once precluded from hubs by state-protected national airlines. Privatization of the UK rail network enabled Stagecoach and Virgin to diversify their businesses into rail services. Growth of the EU presented new trading opportunities in eastern Europe for EU member states, but not all companies were quick to recognize the opportunities for business growth in this region.

Financial and political 'shocks'   Sudden changes in currency prices, interest rates, trade agreements, inflation, unemployment levels, protectionist policies or political leadership can have a major impact on business. A new government might decide to privatize state-owned assets or regulate an industry's activities more tightly. A trade war between states will impact on organizations operating in such markets. The UK's approach to addressing the global financial crisis was very different under the Conservative/LibDem Coalition than had there been a Labour Government, with implications for many companies serving the public sector which faced large budget cuts, reduced spending and job losses.

The importance of keeping a lookout for the strategic window

Often managers only notice sales dips months after a marketing environment force has created a problem. In the meantime, this has created a window for competitors to enter. While there are many psychological factors that can hinder managerial activity, such as a preference for retrenchment and an aversion to change,[15] a common problem is simply the failure to formally and routinely monitor the forces of the marketing environment through environmental scanning, the process of collecting and analyzing information about the forces of the marketing environment. An organization must determine which aspects of the marketing environment – macro and micro – to monitor and how. Strategists believe a regular and routinized system enables identification of strongly-signalled issues, which senior management or a marketing function can then prioritize for more detailed investigation. Clearly, given the vast array of issues examined in this chapter, it is not feasible or desirable for a set of managers to address every conceivably pertinent facet of the trading environment. However, failure to examine the marketing environment is a major problem for many poorly run organizations lacking a marketing orientation.

As described in the Marketing Tools and Techniques box (see page 75), companies opt for different solutions.[16] Some require line managers to undertake environmental scanning in addition to their other responsibilities. Occasionally, a strategic planner undertakes such monitoring, although this head office position is often too divorced from the organization's operations to identify which crucial core forces to investigate. Consultancies may be handed the task. A few large companies have created a bespoke marketing environment unit of cross-functional managers responsible for researching, analyzing, disseminating and recommending. This ensures scanning occurs but is costly and, again, can be too removed from a company's operations. More frequently, marketing planning identifies core trends and evolving forces to monitor.[17]

Marketing planning is practiced in most medium-sized and large companies, and part of the cross-functional, multi-hierarchical team's remit is to report annually on marketing environment forces likely to have implications for the organization.

Some companies have no more than a box in the centre of an open-plan office in which any manager can deposit marketing environment information stemming from press comments, customer feedback, dealer observations, trade show intelligence, analysts' reports or any other inputs. This material is sifted regularly, summarized and circulated, with individual issues followed up as determined necessary by managerial judgement. Other organizations have formalized this approach using email newsletters, intranet boards or a wiki for personnel and sites within the organization, often globally, with interactive dialogue aiding the understanding of the environmental forces noted.

PEST analysis/PESTLE analysis
PEST is a popular name for an evaluation of the marketing environment, looking at political, including legal and regulatory issues, economic, social and technological developments, and assessing the implications of such issues. Another term used by marketers is PESTLE: political, economic, societal, technological, legal and environmental forces.

No matter how it is orchestrated, it is essential that the marketing environment is monitored thoroughly and regularly.[18] This must translate into managerial recommendations when necessary, with target market strategies and marketing programmes reflecting the issues identified. Such an analysis is often termed by marketing managers as a **PEST analysis**, looking at political (P) including legal and regulatory issues, economic (E), social (S) and technological (T) developments, and assessing the implications of such issues, or it is referred to as a **PESTLE analysis** (political, economic, societal, technological, legal and environmental issues). An understanding of the marketing environment macro and micro forces is essential for a rigorous and meaningful assessment of marketing opportunities.

Without such an analysis, any recommended marketing strategy is unlikely to take account of newly opening strategic windows. Competitors may be offered the chance to make inroads and the organization may fail to benefit from potential marketing opportunities. Threats will go unnoticed until they are damaging a company's revenues.

Summary

The *marketing environment* consists of external forces that directly or indirectly influence an organization's acquisition of inputs (personnel, financial resources, raw materials, information) and generation of outputs (information, packages, goods, services, ideas). Generally, the forces of the marketing environment are divided into two categories: macro and micro. The macro marketing environment comprises political, legal and regulatory forces, societal forces, including concerns for the Earth's natural environment, and technological forces. Along with economic forces and trends, these macro, broader, aspects of the marketing environment have an impact on manufacturers and their customers. The forces of the micro marketing environment are more company-specific and include the organization's internal environment, suppliers, marketing intermediaries, buyers, specific competitors and publics.

To monitor changes in these forces, marketers should practice environmental scanning and analysis. *Environmental scanning* is the process of collecting information about the forces in the marketing environment; *environmental analysis* is the process of assessing and interpreting the information obtained in scanning. This information helps marketing managers predict opportunities and threats associated with environmental fluctuation. Marketing management may assume either a passive, reactive approach or an active, aggressive approach in responding to these environmental fluctuations. The choice depends on an organization's structure and needs, and on the composition of the environmental forces.

The political, legal and regulatory forces of the marketing environment are closely interrelated. The current political outlook is reflected in legislation and regulations, or the lack of them. The political environment may determine what laws and regulations affecting specific marketers are enacted, and how much the government purchases and from which suppliers; it can also be important in helping organizations secure foreign markets.

Legislation affecting marketing activities can be divided into *procompetitive legislation* laws designed to preserve competition and to end various practices deemed unacceptable by society and consumer protection laws. In the UK, Acts of Parliament sought to prevent monopolies and activities that limit competition; while much legislation has been enacted to protect consumers in terms of safety, pricing and descriptions of products. Consumer protection laws generally relate to product safety and information disclosure. The actual effects of legislation are determined by how marketers and the courts interpret the laws.

Regulatory agencies influence most marketing activities. For example, in the UK the *Competition and Markets Authority* and the *Financial Conduct Authority* usually have the power to enforce specific laws and some discretion in establishing operating rules and drawing up regulations to guide certain types of industry practice. Self-regulation by industry represents another regulatory force; marketers are more in favour of this type of regulation than government action, because they have more opportunity to take part in creating the guidelines. Self-regulation may be less expensive than government regulation, and its guidelines are often more realistic. However, such regulation generally cannot assure compliance as effectively as government agencies.

Societal forces refer to the structure and dynamics of individuals and groups, and the issues that concern them. Many members of society want a high standard of living and a high quality of life, and they expect business to help them achieve these goals. Of growing concern is the well-being of the Earth, its resources, climate and peoples. The *Green movement* is increasing general awareness of the natural environment and sustainability, and is altering product design, manufacture, packaging and use. The *consumer movement* is a diverse collection of independent individuals, groups and organizations that attempt to protect the rights of consumers. The major issues taken up by the consumer movement fall into three categories: environmental protection, product performance and safety, and information disclosure. Consumer rights organizations inform and organize other consumers, raise issues, help organizations develop consumer-oriented programmes and pressure legislators to enact consumer protection laws. Some are quite formally organized, such as the *Consumers' Association*.

Technology is the knowledge of how to accomplish tasks and goals. Product development, packaging, promotion, prices and distribution systems are all influenced directly by technology. Several factors determine how much and in what way a particular organization will make use of technology. These factors include the company's ability to use technology;

consumers' ability and willingness to buy technologically improved products; the business's perception of the long-term effects of applying technology; the extent to which the company is technologically based; the degree to which technology is used as a competitive tool; and the extent to which the business can protect technological applications through patents. Many organizations conduct a *technology assessment*. For marketers, technological forces of the marketing environment have provided significant consequences in recent years, particularly in terms of more sophisticated *customer relationship management* systems, eMarketing with web-based communications and selling, '*big data*', *mobile marketing* and *social media* fostering greater consumer-to-consumer communication about products, brands and companies' activities. The *digital marketing* era has radically impacted on marketing.

The *economic forces* that can strongly influence marketing decisions and activities are general economic conditions, buying power, willingness to spend, spending patterns and *competitive forces*. The overall state of the economy fluctuates in a general pattern known as the *business cycle*. The stages of the business cycle are *prosperity, recession, depression and recovery*.

Consumers' goods, services and financial holdings make up their *buying power* – their ability to purchase. The financial sources of *buying power* are *income*, credit and wealth. After-tax income used for spending or saving is called *disposable income*. Disposable income left after an individual has purchased the basic necessities of food, clothing and shelter is called discretionary income. It is important to identify levels of *wealth*. Two measures of buying power are: effective buying income (which includes salaries, wages, dividends, interest, profits and rents, less taxes); and the buying power index (a weighted index consisting of population, effective buying income and retail sales data). The factors that affect consumers' *willingness to spend* are product price, the level of satisfaction obtained from currently used products, and expectations about future employment, family size, income, prices and general economic conditions. *Consumer spending patterns* indicate the relative proportions of annual family expenditures, or the actual amount of money spent, on certain kinds of goods and services. *Comprehensive spending patterns* specify the percentages of family income allotted to annual expenditures for general classes of goods and services. *Product-specific spending patterns* indicate the annual amounts families spend for specific products within a general product class.

Competition is a fundamental concern for all marketers. Although all businesses compete for consumers' spending, a company's direct competitors are usually the organizations in its geographic area marketing products that resemble its own or which can be substituted for them. The number of businesses that control the supply of a product may affect the strength of competition. There are four general types of competitive structure: *monopoly, oligopoly, monopolistic competition* and *perfect competition*. Marketers use *competitor monitoring* to determine what competitors are currently doing and to assess the changes occurring in the competitive environment.

Increasingly, marketers make a distinction between the broader trading *macro marketing environment* forces: political, legal, regulatory, societal, technological, economic/competitive, and the more company-specific forces of the *micro marketing environment*. Micro forces include the organization in question, its suppliers, marketing intermediaries, buyers, business-specific competition, direct, substitute and new entrant rivals, and the various publics of an organization: financial bodies, media, government, consumer and pressure groups, neighbours, the general public and the internal workforce.

Changes in the marketing environment often create *strategic windows* that, if they are not quickly identified, can enable rivals to gain an edge. There are six key causes of the creation of strategic windows, all aspects of the macro or micro marketing environment: new technology, new markets, new distribution channels, market redefinition, new legislation and regulation, plus financial and political 'shocks'. Often, managers fail to notice sales dips until months after the impact of an aspect of the marketing environment. This may be because they are averse to change and prefer retrenchment, but often it stems from a lack of environmental scanning. Strategists believe a regular and routinized assessment of the marketing environment is essential prior to the formulation of any target market strategies or marketing mix programmes. Practitioners often term such an assessment a *PEST analysis* or *PESTLE analysis*. Companies adopt different solutions to monitoring the marketing environment, it can be carried out by: line managers, strategic planners, consultants, specialist units or be incorporated as an integral part of the annual marketing planning process. It is essential that the marketing environment macro and micro forces are monitored continually in order to maximize marketing opportunities and fend off competitors' actions.

Key links

Marketers must analyze the marketing environment in order to identify opportunities and minimize threats. This chapter should be read in conjunction with:

● Chapter 1, examining marketing opportunity analysis.

● Chapter 2, the overview of marketing strategy development.

Important terms

Business cycle
Buying power
Competition
Competition and Markets Authority
Competitor monitoring
Comprehensive spending patterns
Consumer movement
Consumer spending patterns
Consumers' Association
CRM
Depression
Digital marketing
Discretionary income
Disposable income
Economic and competitive forces
Environmental analysis
Environmental scanning
Financial Conduct Authority
Green movement
Income
Macro marketing environment
Marketing environment
Micro marketing environment
Mobile marketing
Monopolistic competition
Monopoly
Oligopoly
Perfect competition
PEST analysis/PESTLE analysis
Procompetitive legislation
Product-specific spending patterns
Prosperity
Recession
Recovery
Social media
Societal forces
Strategic windows
Technology
Technology assessment

Wealth
Willingness to spend

Discussion and review questions

1. Why are environmental scanning and analysis so important?

2. How are political forces related to legal and regulatory forces?

3. Describe marketers' attempts to influence political forces.

4. What types of procompetitive legislation directly affect marketing practices?

5. What is the major objective of most procompetitive laws? Do the laws generally accomplish this objective? Why or why not?

6. What types of problem do marketers experience as they interpret legislation?

7. What are the goals of the Competition and Markets Authority? How does the Authority affect marketing activities?

8. Name several non-governmental regulatory forces. Do you believe that self-regulation is more or less effective than governmental regulatory agencies? Why?

9. How is the so-called 'Green movement' altering the shape of business?

10. Describe the consumer movement. Analyze some active consumer forces in your area.

11. What does the term 'technology' mean to you?

12. How does technology affect you as a member of society? Do the benefits of technology outweigh its costs and dangers?

13. Discuss the impact of technology on marketing activities.

14. What factors determine whether an organization adopts and uses technology?

15. In what ways can each of the business cycle stages affect consumers' reactions to marketing strategies?

16. What is the current business cycle stage? How is this stage affecting businesses in your area?

17. Define income, disposable income and discretionary income. How does each type of income affect consumer buying power?

18. How is consumer buying power affected by wealth and consumer credit?

19. How is buying power measured? Why should it be evaluated?

20. What factors influence a consumer's willingness to spend?

21. What are the principal types of competition?

22. What differentiates the forces of the micro marketing environment from those of the macro marketing environment?

23. Why must marketers monitor changes in supplier and marketing intermediary practices?

24. Why should marketers not only track direct, like-for-like competitors? What other types of competitor are there?

25. Why should marketers be aware of their organization's publics?

26. How does an assessment of marketing environment forces assist in marketing opportunity analysis?

27. What are the main causes of the opening of strategic windows?

28. How can a business instigate environmental scanning?

Recommended readings

Blythe, J. and Megicks, P., *Marketing Planning: Strategy, Environment and Context* (FT Prentice-Hall, 2010).

Dibb, S. and Simkin, L., *Marketing Planning* (Cengage, 2008).

Drucker, P., *Management in Turbulent Times* (Butterworth-Heinemann/ Pan, 1994).

Palmer, A. and Hartley, B., *The Business Environment* (McGraw-Hill, 2011).

Porter, M.E., 'How competitive forces shape strategy', *Harvard Business Review*, March–April 1979, pp. 137–45.

Otter, D. and Wetherly, P., *The Business Environment: Themes and Issues in a Globalizing World* (OUP, 2014).

Worthington, I. and Britton, C., *The Business Environment* (FT Prentice-Hall, 2011).

Member states of the European Union

Full members

Austria (1995), Belgium (1958), Bulgaria (2007), Croatia (2013), Cyprus (2004), Czech Republic (2004), Denmark (1973), Estonia (2004), Finland (1995), France (1958), Germany (1958), Greece (1981), Hungary (2004), Ireland (1973), Italy (1958), Latvia (2004), Lithuania (2004), Luxembourg (1958), Malta (2004), Netherlands (1958), Poland (2004), Portugal (1986), Romania (2007), Slovakia (2004), Slovenia (2004), Spain (1986), Sweden (1995), United Kingdom (1973).

Candidate countries

Turkey is the next candidate country, along with Albania, Iceland, Montenegro, Serbia and the former Yugoslav Republic of Macedonia, as probable members to join the EU. Future possible candidates include Bosnia Herzegovina and Kosovo.

Internet exercise

Choose the websites of key government departments, EU departments or of leading regulatory bodies and learn more about the ways in which their activities and powers impact on marketers and consumers. For example, log on to the websites for the Competition and Markets Authority and the Financial Conduct Authority at: www.gov.uk/government/organisations /competition-and-markets-authority and www.fca.org.uk.

1. What are the implications of these organizations' powers and recommendations for marketers?

2. In what ways do the activities of these bodies impact on consumers?

Group tasks

1. For the marketers of theme park resorts such as Disneyland Paris, Universal Orlando Resort or PortAventura in Spain, what forces of the marketing environment currently present opportunities and threats?

2. If the UK were to leave the European Union, consider the implications for brands currently widely available across Europe and the UK.

Applied mini-case

Until recently, excepting the low-sugar variants, few observers would have included the producers of the leading colas as aiding healthy diets or encouraging greater awareness of obesity issues. A decade ago, the leading suppliers launched low-carb versions, and now they are proactively striving to educate consumers. Coca-Cola, for example, launched a major initiative to encourage people to exercise more. Coke launched an anti-obesity campaign under the title 'Active Lifestyle', engaging with young people through a variety of media. The initiative aimed to promote the route to a healthy lifestyle through a combination of effective hydration, a balanced diet and physical activity. Today, its website has a wide array of health-related messages and educational campaigns under *Health* and *Get Active*, as well as information about how the company is reducing sugar and calories (www.coca-cola.co.uk).

Sources: Ben Bold, 'Coca-Cola debuts healthy living initiative in UK', *Marketing*, 1 July 2004, p. 1; www.coca-cola.co.uk/?kid=sr3_43523989_go&WT.srch=1, 18 February 2011; www.coca-cola.co.uk, March 2015.

Question

As Coca-Cola's marketing manager, how would an understanding of the marketing environment have led to the *Health* and *Get Active* initiatives now promoted on its web pages? How might the company have monitored the forces of its marketing environment?

The world of rice: external challenges for Tilda's marketers

Case study

Known as the 'Prince of Rice', basmati can only be grown in one place on earth at the foothills of the Himalayas. It is here where the combination of unique climate and soil conditions allow basmati to truly flourish. We select the highest quality pure basmati from over 10,000 independent farmers, all of whom we know by name.

www.tilda.com

Tilda is rightly proud of basmati rice, which it is largely responsible for introducing to the UK and many other markets. Today, basmati accounts for 46 per cent of all UK rice sales, or around £72m, much of which comes from Tilda. Something of a 'supergrain', being gluten-free and low in fat, basmati is a delicate, light and fluffy grain with a wonderful aroma – literally translated it is 'the fragrant one'. However, with the need to help protect the single annual harvest, a fairplay buying policy with farmers, storing grains until they are suitably mature, and Tilda's long-held belief in providing consistency to the consumer's experience with extensive and fastidious milling techniques, there comes a high price. Compared with many other rices, basmati is far from cheap and Tilda's is premium-priced to reflect the quality of its famously blue-bagged basmati and the care of its milling processes.

A difficulty of premium-pricing is that if external factors force changes to supply costs or to the availability of quality rice, there are difficulties (a) persuading consumers to pay more if Tilda raises its retail prices or (b) in maintaining such prices, especially if the harvest leads to inferior grains in a particular season. In recent years, Tilda's marketers have faced a number of challenges, none of which has been in their control or a result of Tilda's decisions.

A few years ago, the world's rice harvest was poor, with basmati badly affected. Tilda has no control over the rains and climatic conditions necessary for a good harvest. The quality of the grain was poorer, but there was also much lower volume available to purchase from the farmers, so competing brands were chasing scarce supplies. Inevitably, raw material prices soared. Tilda had to almost double its retail prices in order to cover the costs of acquiring adequate tonnages and for the extra milling activities required to provide discerning consumers with an appropriate cooking and taste experience. Sales dropped, as many consumers were priced out of buying this 'Prince of Rice'. No-one could have predicted the poor harvest and huge rise in world rice prices.

Owing to rice shortages, largely caused by poor harvests, the Indian Government had to protect supplies of this staple food for its own population. As basmati in its purest form comes only from the foothills of the Himalayas, any ban on exports from India would catastrophically impact on the basmati part of Tilda's rice business. Tilda's stock pile of reserves was just adequate to cover the period of the ban, but the company's marketers and executives felt significant pressure from this regulatory impact within the marketing environment thousands of miles from its Essex milling base.

Tilda's sourcing of basmati, from farmers the company knows and who nurture their rice using traditional methods, precludes the use of GM rices. However, a leading competitor allowed GM grains to enter its supply chain, causing negative publicity for rice in the press and in Government circles, not only for its own brand but for rice in general. Although Tilda had no link with this adulterated rice, the company had to invest significant time and resources explaining this and to reassuring its retail stockists.

The global economic meltdown has caused many consumers to revaluate their consumption patterns and spending priorities. Tilda has many ranges and brands, catering for most rice-eating communities and consumer segments, but its flagship brand, Tilda blue bag basmati, is premium priced and branded to reflect its status amongst rices. Few observers predicted the credit crunch or its longer-term implications on global finances and consumer priorities. Most premium brands, such as BMW or John Lewis, have worked very hard to re-engineer their propositions to provide relevance and value for target consumers. Upmarket grocer Waitrose is now well-known for its *Essentials* range and competitive pricing comparison for 1000 brands versus Tesco. Tilda's marketers also had to come up with a value-based proposition, launching its *Everyday Rice* range.

The above examples are aspects of Tilda's macro marketing environment, but micro marketing environmental forces are also important for Tilda's marketers. The economic crisis has forced retailers to re-think their strategies and merchandising, putting pressure on suppliers such as Tilda to reduce prices and margins offered to trade customers such as the major supermarkets. Many retailers are seeking ways for reducing their carbon footprints to reflect social and regulatory pressures, in turn demanding lower delivery miles, environmentally responsible packaging and altered manufacturing processes from their suppliers, such as Tilda. Such buyer pressures are commonplace for marketers examining the micro environment. The rise of own label has been an issue for Tilda and its leading branded competitors such as Uncle Ben's, Veetee or Kohinoor, and is an example of the competitive forces within the micro marketing environment.

Readers should not think that the marketing environment brings little good news to a company's marketers. The increased attention by Government, nutritionists, medics, educationalists, the media and many food producers to healthier eating presents an opportunity for Tilda, as many health experts and nutritionists believe rice to be preferable to other carbs such as potatoes and pasta. Within the rice arena, basmati has specific health attributes, being gluten-free, low in fat, very low in sodium, with no cholesterol and containing all eight essential amino acids. Perfect for diabetic sufferers and very useful in many diets as an alternative to chips or butter-filled jacket potatoes, there is a window of opportunity for rice producers – such as Tilda – caused by obesity scares and healthier eating social marketing initiatives from various state bodies, medics and the media.

These are just a few examples of how external forces impact on one large food company, but Tilda is far from being alone in facing such a diverse and never-ending set of externally-derived challenges, many of which flair up unexpectedly. The demands on marketers in such companies are to identify such issues and raise awareness of their concerns, where possible in advance of any negative impact on customer demand, financial performance or brands; and, to provide suggestions for how best to navigate such market conditions. Inevitably, even the most tuned-in marketers on occasion are caught out by surprising events. In such circumstances, the expectation is that marketers will quickly evaluate and propose a plan for addressing the issue in question. All organizations face a myriad of challenges from their marketing environments. It should be the onus of marketers to be the 'eyes and ears' for their

organizations, so as to foster an understanding of the issues and their implications.

Questions for discussion

1. Which of the issues faced by Tilda's marketers would cause them the most concern and why?

2. What approaches could a company such as Tilda adopt in order to develop a sound appreciation of changes to its marketing environment?

3. Why might marketers struggle to gain appropriate insights into aspects of their marketing environments?

Sources: www.tilda.com, February 2011 and March 2015; www.waitrose .com/footer/corporateinformation, February, 2011 and March 2015; www .riceassociation.org.uk, 20 February 2011 and 15 March 2015.

CHAPTER 4

Marketing in international markets and globalization

"The world is seemingly smaller, while markets are feeling bigger"

Objectives

- To define international marketing and understand the nature of international involvement.

- To understand the importance of international marketing intelligence.

- To recognize the impact of environmental forces on international marketing efforts.

- To become aware of regional trade alliances and markets.

- To look at alternative market entry strategies for becoming involved in international marketing activities.

- To appreciate that international marketing strategies fit along a continuum from customization to globalization.

- To understand the growing importance of international cooperation.

INTRODUCTION

International marketing generally refers to marketing activities performed across national boundaries.[1] With international travel and trade now commonplace, digital communications creating access to new consumers, and many brands marketed globally, marketers often find themselves addressing a variety of markets in addition to their domestic market. Not only consumer goods such as those produced by Pepsi, Nike and Sony involve marketing in many parts of the world. Services, from healthcare to education, banking to management consultancy, theme parks to real estate, are marketed internationally, as are products in most business markets.

The fundamental concepts and practices of marketing as described so far in *Marketing: Concepts and Strategies* apply whether the product is a consumer good, service or business product, in local, national or international markets. Nevertheless, the marketer involved with international markets has a more complex task than colleagues only responsible for national markets. Market knowledge outside the domestic market may be less robust and complete; understanding of the forces of the marketing environment is essential for all marketers but is a more complex undertaking when scanning numerous countries, many of which may be relatively unfamiliar; there are market entry strategies to consider; and the operationalization of marketing programmes is far more challenging to control. Assuming that the marketing concept and marketing process are similar to the marketing activities described so far, this chapter examines the nuances of international marketing.

Global growth by acting locally

For several decades the world's beer industry has been driven by two trends: consolidation, as major companies merged or acquired competitors, and by a move to global brands. For example, Holland's Heineken brews numerous brands but its eponymous well-known Heineken lager is produced and distributed globally with a premium branding that unashamedly plays to the brand's international reach. Heineken is indeed the leading global beer brand, but actually commands only 1.5 per cent of the worldwide market. Rival Anheuser-Busch InBev adopts a fairly similar strategy for its key brands Becks and Stella Artois. SABMiller has chosen a different course, based on the premise that beer is intensely local, with consumers taking pride in their local beer. SABMiller's contention is that markets in which an overseas brand can out-perform a well-liked brand that has local origins are very limited.

Nick Fell, head of marketing at SABMiller, explains that the company has rejected the notion that beer is globalizing around a handful of brands. Instead, SABMiller is developing portfolios based on local markets, thanks to the company's *Pride in Local Origins* research. This approach reveals that some countries associate beer with socializing, in others beer is very masculine, while for some beer is perceived to be very down to earth. A global uniform brand strategy would struggle to reflect such nuances, argues Nick Fell, so SABMiller has adopted a much more flexible and localized approach. The company does own pillar brands but has over 200 regional beer brands. The company's roots are in South Africa with its Castle brand, so it had not the global reach or established international presence of Stella, Heineken, Budweiser, Becks or Guinness. This permitted far more localized branding than for their fellow global giants in the beer industry. This *growth locally* flexibility has led to Peroni leading the way in the UK, Kozel in its Czech market, Tyskie in Poland, Timisoara in Romania and Arequipena in Peru, rather than a single global brand such as Heineken or Budweiser rolling out in all markets. Peroni represents Italian style, a concept well suited it seems to the UK, Australia, Romania and the USA, but not to all parts of the world, illustrating the company's pragmatic international branding.

SABMiller is active in six continents; focusing on established markets in Europe alongside fast growing markets such as China and India. A truly international business, its leading performance indicators that it visibly measures and publicizes include the number of markets it dominates in terms of market share, but also the proportion of cash earned from developing and emerging economies. Currently this latter metric, reflecting the company's global ambitions, is around 78 per cent. SABMiller owns premium international beers such as Pilsner Urquell, Peroni Nastro Azzurro, Miller Genuine Draft and Grolsch, as well as leading local brands Aguila, Castle, Miller Lite, Snow and Tyskie. The company also is a major bottler for Coca-Cola products. So much of SABMiller's impressive performance and global expansion in the past decade stems from its desire to trade globally but in ways fully reflecting local consumer preferences and market conditions. Without extensive market insights in each of its local markets, SABMiller could not operate its stated strategy, which hinges on:

- creating a balanced and attractive global spread of business
- developing strong, relevant brand portfolios that win in the local market
- constantly raising the profitability of local businesses, sustainably
- leveraging the company's skills and global scale.

Sources: 'Premium beer brands need a local flavour', Mark Choueke, *Marketing Week*, 2 December 2010, pp. 20–21; www.sabmiller.com, March 2011 and March 2015; www.heinekeninternational.com, March 2011 and March 2015.

This chapter looks closely at the unique features of international marketing. It begins by examining companies' levels of commitment to and degrees of involvement in international marketing, and then considers the importance of international marketing intelligence when a company is moving beyond its domestic market. SABMiller's strategy would not be feasible without such market insights. Next the chapter focuses on the need to understand various environmental forces in international markets and discusses several regional trade alliances and markets. The concluding section describes alternative market entry strategies for becoming involved in international marketing and trading globally.

Involvement in international marketing

Domestic marketing
Marketing activities directed exclusively to business's home market.

In order to practice international marketing, companies with the necessary resources and skills have to develop an interest in expanding their businesses beyond national boundaries. Once interested, marketers engage in international marketing activities at several levels of involvement. Regardless of the level of involvement, they must decide on the degree to which it is possible to standardize their marketing strategies for different markets.

Export marketing
Marketing activities through which a business takes advantage of opportunities outside its home market but continues production in the home country.

Levels of international involvement

The level of involvement in international marketing covers a wide spectrum, as shown in Figure 4.1. A business that undertakes marketing activities exclusively in its home market is involved in **domestic marketing**. Such organizations may have deliberately chosen to restrict their business to domestic customers or may simply not have considered the possibility of international marketing. **Export marketing** takes place when a business takes advantage of opportunities outside its home market.

Domestic marketing	Export marketing	International marketing	Multinational marketing	Global marketing
Home market involvement only.	This is an attempt to create sales without significant changes in the company's products and overall operations. An active effort to find foreign markets for existing products is most typical.	Greater commitment to international markets. International marketing activities are seen as part of overall planning. Direct investment in non-domestic markets is likely and products may also be sourced away from the home market.	Further steps are taken to adapt to local tastes. Modifications may be made to aspects of the marketing mix to make them more appealing to local markets.	Total commitment to international marketing which involves applying the organization's assets, experience and products to develop and maintain marketing strategies on a global scale. Although a single global marketing strategy is required, some adaptation to local needs is still needed.

Domestic orientation ←——————————————————→ **Global orientation**

FIGURE 4.1
Levels of involvement in international marketing

In some cases, exporting activity begins almost by accident. For example, the products of a small medical supplies manufacturer may occasionally be purchased by hospitals or clinics in nearby countries, or its products may be purchased by other countries through an export agent. Whatever the reasons behind the initial export activity, production in the home country will be used to supply these new markets; for most companies the domestic market will remain the key area of business. Companies that go beyond simple exporting become involved in **international marketing**, reducing their reliance on intermediaries and establishing direct links and relationships in the countries in which trading takes place. At this stage a foreign subsidiary may be set up or a joint venture, and products may be sourced away from the domestic market.

Multinational marketing takes marketing for non-domestic markets one step further by adapting some of the company's marketing activities, such as marketing communications, to appeal to local culture and differences in tastes. **Multinational companies** are those that behave in their foreign markets as if they were local companies. Full-scale **global marketing** requires total commitment to international marketing and involves applying the organization's assets, experience and products to develop, resource and maintain marketing strategies on a global scale. **Global marketing** occurs when marketing strategies are developed for major regions or the entire world to enable organizations to compete globally.

International marketing
Marketing activities in which a business reduces reliance on intermediaries and establishes direct involvement in the countries in which trade takes place.

Multinational marketing
Adaptation of some of a company's marketing activities to appeal to local culture and differences in taste.

Multinational companies
Companies that behave in their foreign markets as if they were local companies.

Global marketing
A total commitment to international marketing, in which a company applies its assets, experience and products to develop and maintain marketing strategies on a global scale.

Understanding global marketing

Global marketing is the most extreme case of international involvement, representing the full integration of international marketing into strategic planning.[2] The underlying principle is to identify products or services for which similarities across many markets allow a single global strategy to be pursued. This approach is attractive to managers because one marketing strategy can be used across a number of markets; a business can spread the costs of its research and development, technology and distribution, taking advantage of economies of scale in the process. True globalization goes further.

Economist Daniel Park summed up globalization well:

> Globalization is, in my view, about creating a new set of competencies that enable a company to utilize resources on an optimal basis to meet differentiated customer demand profitably and cost-competitively without regard for geography. Put more simply, globalization is about getting an organization into a position of doing business in any market it chooses, and doing business is not just about marketing and selling. Looking at globalization as a process of acquiring and renewing competencies helps us understand how and why new forms of organization are emerging to take on and defeat established high-profile companies.

www.b2binternational.com/publications/white-papers
/globalization-and-marketing

Despite the fact that global marketing strives for a single over-arching global strategy,[3] it is a mistake to assume that local differences can be ignored. During the 1980s, marketers sought to globalize the marketing mix as much as possible by employing standardized products, promotion campaigns, prices and distribution channels for all markets. The potential economic and competitive pay-offs for such an approach were certainly great. More recently, marketers have realized that, while it may be feasible to standardize a company's offerings in different markets, a degree of adaptation to local differences is also required. Many companies design and manufacture in their home territory, but customer engagement, interaction and management are tailored to fit with local cultures, customs, expectations and behaviours. Honda, IBM, HSBC and Tesco are just some large global players operating in this way. Even IKEA – famous for its 'one approach globally' stance – has recognized it has to modify its strategy, merchandizing and engagement region by region, creating a whole new marketing planning approach to provide regional teams with the necessary skills for creating their own plans.

While brand name, product characteristics, packaging and labelling may be relatively straightforward to standardize, media allocation, retail outlets, customer service and price may be more difficult. For example, a supplier of animal feeds may decide to send promotional material about a new product range to farmers and producers in a variety of different markets. Although the business may have decided on a suitable platform for the promotion, help may be needed from each country's marketing team to devise an appropriate mailing list and tone of voice to adopt. In many business markets, interaction between customer personnel and an organization's own staff is integral to the marketing and sales processes: cultural differences vary significantly between countries, and a standardized marketing approach is unlikely to succeed. This is particularly so in global banking, management consultancy and corporate legal affairs, where marketers must take account of local practices, cultures and behaviours.

Some companies have moved from customizing or standardizing products for a particular region of the world to offering globally standardized products that are advanced, functional, reliable and low in price.[4] Reebok, for example, provides a standardized product worldwide. Examples of globalized products are electrical equipment, DVDs, films, soft drinks, rock music, cosmetics and toothpaste. Sony televisions, Levi's jeans and UK confectionery brands seem to make annual gains in the world market. Even McDonald's restaurants seem to be widely accepted in markets throughout the world. Yet, even here, there is some adaptation to local tastes, with small variations in McDonald's menus in certain countries. For example, in Portugal there is more emphasis on ice creams and in Switzerland more beer and wine than in the UK. Some products that are regarded by many as globally standard, such as Coca-Cola, are in fact adapted for certain markets. Coke's flavouring, packaging, promotion and range are often modified between countries.

Debate about the feasibility of globalized marketing strategies has continued for nearly 50 years. Questions about standardized advertising have been a primary concern. The debate about customization versus globalization will doubtless continue, although neither is implemented in its pure form.[5] Consumers' access to global insights via the web is altering the parameters for marketers and changing expectations in many non-domestic markets. In the end, the feasibility

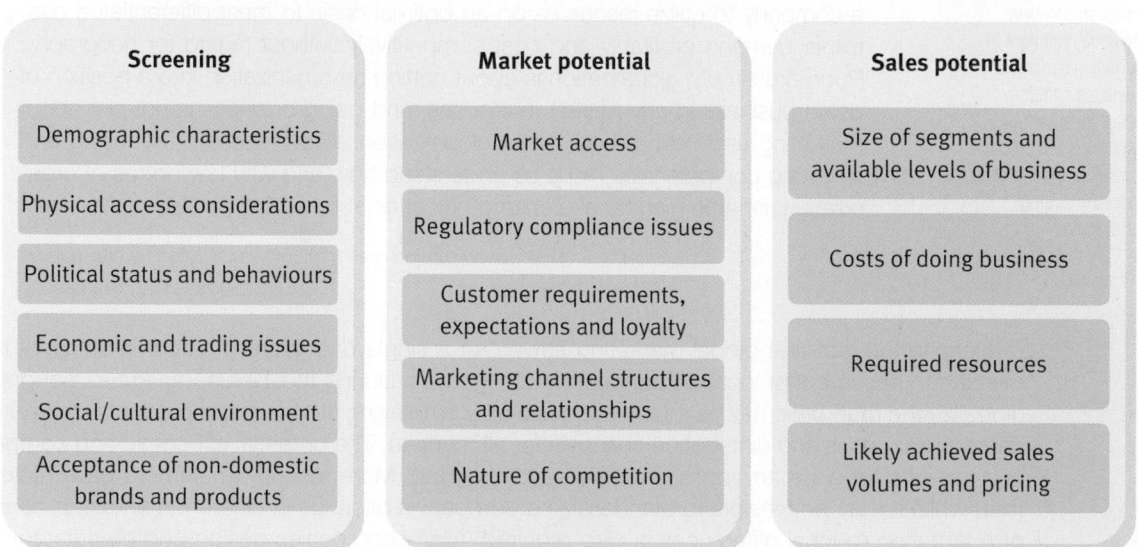

FIGURE 4.2
Information needed for international marketing analyses

Screening	Market potential	Sales potential
Demographic characteristics	Market access	Size of segments and available levels of business
Physical access considerations	Regulatory compliance issues	Costs of doing business
Political status and behaviours	Customer requirements, expectations and loyalty	Required resources
Economic and trading issues	Marketing channel structures and relationships	Likely achieved sales volumes and pricing
Social/cultural environment	Nature of competition	
Acceptance of non-domestic brands and products		

of globalization is determined by the degree of similarity between the various environmental and market conditions. Some marketers now believe that some of the best global opportunities are presented by 'global market segments', as long as similar product needs, buying behaviour and brand perceptions are evident across national borders. Even if such global market segments are identified – and there is no doubt they exist for many consumer goods, services and business products – the marketing programmes may require modification to reflect local market conditions, culture and customer purchasing. It should be remembered that failure to reflect properly local consumer needs and buying behaviours will create a window of opportunity for more attuned competitors. Marketers must understand the detail of the markets being considered, and this requires international marketing intelligence.

International marketing intelligence

Despite the ongoing debate over globalization, most businesses perceive international markets as differing in some ways from domestic markets, which is often true. Analyses of international markets and possible marketing efforts can be based on many dimensions. Chapter 9 contains a more detailed discussion of marketing research and data collection.[6]

Gathering secondary data (see Chapter 9) should be the first step in analyzing a foreign market. Sources of information include government publications, financial services companies, international organizations such as the United Nations, foreign governments and international trade organizations. UK companies seeking to market their products in Russia, for example, can obtain information about Russian markets and regulations from government departments, embassies, the Chamber of Commerce and the Industry of the Russian Federation and various international analysts. Marketers must be vigilant in assuring the reliability, validity and comparability of data, as information from some sources may be misleading.

In some circumstances, marketers may need primary data to understand consumers' buying behaviour in the country under investigation. Buying behaviour is discussed in detail in Chapters 5 and 6. Marketers may have to adjust their techniques of collecting primary data for foreign markets.[7] Attitudes towards privacy, unwillingness to be interviewed, language differences, low literacy rates and erratic web access can be serious research obstacles. In a bi-cultural country such as Canada, a uniform national questionnaire cannot be used because of the cultural and language differences. In China, certain restrictions on free speech mean that many businesses or consumers are reluctant or not permitted to respond to questionnaires.

Primary research should uncover significant cultural characteristics before a product is launched so that the marketing strategy is appropriate for the target market. It may be necessary

FIGURE 4.3
McDonald's practises global marketing

to investigate basic patterns of social behaviour, values and attitudes to plan a final marketing strategy. Overall, the cost of obtaining such information may be higher than the cost of domestic research; the reasons include the large number of foreign markets to be investigated, the distance between the marketer and the foreign market, unfamiliar cultural and marketing practices, language differences, and the scarcity or unreliability of published statistics.[8]

After analyzing secondary and primary data, marketers should plan a marketing strategy, as explained in Chapter 2. An organization must be clear about which consumers or business customers are being targeted, with what proposition, through which marketing programme, against which rivals, and with the involvement of which partners and marketing channel members. A full appreciation of the forces of the marketing environment (as described in Chapter 3) is critical to ensuring markets with growing potential are prioritized as part of the marketing strategy. A full assessment of the market situation will enable decisions to be made about whether to withdraw from the foreign market, to continue to expand operations or to consider additional foreign markets. Marketers must ensure they acquire the necessary marketing intelligence in order to provide a full understanding of trading conditions in all of the non-domestic markets.

Environmental forces in international markets

A detailed analysis of the marketing environment is essential for any business considering entry into a foreign market. If a marketing strategy is to be effective across national borders, the complexities of all the environments involved must be understood. This section examines how the cultural/social, economic, political, legal and technological forces of the marketing environment in different countries vary. The process for examining the forces of the marketing environment as described in Chapter 3 also apply in this context.

Cultural forces

Culture can be defined as the concepts, values and tangible items (such as tools, buildings and foods) that make up a particular society. Culture is passed on from one generation to another and is a kind of blueprint for acceptable behaviour in a particular society. When products are introduced into one nation from another, acceptance is far more likely if there are similarities between the two cultures.

The connotations associated with body motions, greetings, colours, numbers and shapes, sizes and symbols vary considerably across cultures. In many parts of Europe black has negative overtones, whereas in the Middle East it has positive connotations. The Topical Insight box on page 126 explains how knowledge of cultures and behaviours for a marketer's colleagues and supply chain contacts is also of paramount importance, if applicable business practices are to be adopted to support a company's global ambitions.

The Building Customer Relationships box on page 115 details more examples of the role of colour in marketing. Yet even here it is important to watch out for more subtle cultural differences. This is important because multinational marketers know that cultural differences have implications for product development, personal selling, advertising, packaging and pricing. For example, the illustration of feet is regarded as despicable in Thailand. An international marketer must also know a country's customs regarding male–female social interaction. In Italy it is unacceptable for a salesman to call on a woman if her husband is not at home.

It is also important for marketers to tune in to changes in culture. For example, in Japan the government expressed concern about its citizens' emphasis on work and has declared that people should start enjoying life. With an official reduction of the working week to 40 hours, many new leisure industry opportunities were created. In one year alone, 200 companies applied for permits to develop new theme parks. Meanwhile, to help people deal with these new leisure opportunities, the National Recreation Association offered a one-year course on how to enjoy life.[9]

Product adoption and use are also influenced by consumers' perceptions of other countries.[10] When consumers are generally unfamiliar with products from another country, their perceptions of the country itself affect their attitude towards and adoption of its products. The digital economy and access to the web are shrinking the world and introducing populations to the behaviours of others, but still awareness of consumers in non-domestic markets tends to be questionable.

If a country has a reputation for producing quality products, marketers will want to make the country of origin well-known. For example, a generally positive image of Western computer technology has fuelled sales of HP personal computers and Microsoft software in Japan.[11] Consumers' perceptions of a country are influenced by more than its products, however. Recently, America's 'war on terrorism' created a problem for the marketers of many US companies, as consumers in parts of the world and particularly those adhering to specific religions boycotted US brands. Even US pop and rock stars found it difficult to tour safely in parts of the world previously visited routinely.

Culture may also affect the marketing negotiations and decision-making behaviour of marketers, business buyers and other executives. Research has shown that when marketers use a problem-solving approach, that is to gain information about a particular client's needs and tailor products or services to meet those needs, it leads to increased customer satisfaction in marketing negotiations in France, Germany, the UK and the US. Furthermore, the role and status of the seller are particularly important in both the UK and France.[12] However, the attractiveness of the sales person and his or her similarity to the customer increase the levels of satisfaction only for Americans.

Building customer relationships

A cross-cultural comparison of colour and international branding

Anthony Grimes and Isobel Doole explored the relationship between colour and international branding. Their cross-cultural comparison, which focused on consumers in the UK and Taiwan, used a series of semi-structured focus groups to examine perceptions of colour and international branding. The findings of their research appear to suggest that associations of colour are surprisingly similar across national boundaries, and apparently support the notion that standardization of brand colours across international markets may be possible. However, the research also highlights that colour is only one aspect of the make-up of an international brand and as such may have a relatively small role to play in developing brand image. This is demonstrated clearly by the fact that while perceptions of colour across cultures may fluctuate relatively little, impressions of international brands may vary widely.

Colour association in the UK and Taiwan

Colour	UK associations	Taiwan associations
Green	Inexpensive, reliable, light and good-tasting. Old, quiet, traditional, trustworthy and safe. Life, calm, tenderness, health and happiness. Environment, natural, pure and fresh. Ireland and to some extent Italy.	Inexpensive, reliable, light and good-tasting. Quiet, calm, male and old. Safe, trustworthy, unadventurous and stable. Environment, life, tender, pure, fresh, natural. Ireland and to some extent the UK.
Red	Expensive, premium, high quality and good-tasting. Young, warm, fun, loud, playful and happy. Dangerous, adventurous, luxurious and exciting. Life, love, passion, power and aggression. China and to some extent the US.	High quality, expensive and good-tasting. Warm, female, loud, playful and adventurous. Love, passion, danger and aggression. Life, excitement and happiness. US and to some extent Italy.

Colour	UK associations	Taiwan associations
Blue	Heavy, reliable, high quality and expensive. Male, mature, quiet, subdued, calm and thoughtful. Serious, trustworthy, dependable, dignified and sad. US, and the UK to a limited extent.	Heavy, reliable, high quality and expensive. Calm, dignified, trustworthy. Sadness, depression and to some extent power.
Black	Expensive, high quality, high tech and premium. Old, heavy and reliable. Male, old, quiet and serious. Mysterious, luxurious, sophisticated and dangerous. Death, dignity, power and aggression.	High quality, high tech, premium and expensive. Old, male, quiet and heavy. Mysterious, sophisticated and serious. Death, sadness, depression, power, fear and aggression. Strongly associated with China.
Yellow	High quality, expensive, reliable, light and good-tasting. Pert, fresh and playful. Luxury, sophistication and to some extent safety. Life, happiness, tenderness and warmth.	New, expensive, light and good-tasting. Young, warm, loud, playful and adventurous. Life, love, happiness and power. Strongly associated with China.
Purple	Expensive, luxurious and good-tasting. Warm, and to some extent female. Sophisticated and mysterious. Death, dignity, passion and power. France and to some extent Japan.	High quality, premium and expensive. Warm, female, old and quiet. Love, passion, luxury, sophisticated and mystery. Serious, sadness, dignity, power and aggression. France and to some extent Japan.

Perceptions of key brands in the UK and Taiwan

Brand	UK	Taiwan
Pepsi	Male, muscular, young, sexy and energetic. Wild, fun and sporty. Associated with beach settings. Not very healthy—sugar and caffeine. Challenger to Coca-Cola and the status quo.	Male, muscular, young, energetic, sporty and attractive. Fun, sexy, loud, wild and a little crazy. Associated with the beach, the sun and the Spice Girls. Good-tasting and refreshing. Intensely competitive with regard to Coca-Cola.
Marlboro	Original brand is masculine, American and red. Cool, sexy, wild, adventurous and strong. Rough but with a lot of style. Associated with cowboys, the desert and music. Unhealthy and anti-social—cancer, smoke and smells. Marlboro Lights are less damaging and more popular. Associated with pubs, music, youth and the colour gold.	Masculine, American and red. Cool, strong, young, adventurous and exciting. Powerful and stylish. Associated with cowboys, the desert and music.
Kodak	Masculine, mature, intelligent, creative and well-respected. Warm, friendly and colourful. High quality, high tech and very professional. Associated with happy times, sunshine, happiness, fun, colourfulness and the colour yellow. Safe, reliable, trustworthy, affordable and popular.	Masculine, intelligent, innovative and creative. High quality, expensive and professional. Modern, colourful and hugely popular. Associated with high tech.
Cadbury	Feminine, smooth, silky, sexy and sultry. Beautiful, luxurious, stylish and expensive. High in quality, reliability and class. Associated with velvet, satin and silk. Old, friendly, aristocratic and eccentric. Very young, sweet and cute.	Masculine, old, friendly, warm, loving but poor brand. Feminine, young, sweet, sensual and cute. Overall: low quality, cheap, no class and largely unpopular. A sticky, sickly, lazy brand, predominantly for children.

Brand	UK	Taiwan
BP	Masculine, big, old, greedy, rich, powerful and British. Grey, faceless, boring, uncaring, mysterious, even sinister and to some extent arrogant. Associated with intelligence, power, wealth, technology, heavy production and pollution.	Masculine, rich, powerful, distinguished and serious. High in class and style, intelligent and authoritative. A leader.
Guinness	Masculine, modern, young, cool, streetwise, sociable, attractive, quiet, secretive and mysterious. Old, traditional, simple and genuine. Associated with goodness, honesty and hard work. Overall: smooth, creamy, bitter, heavy and good quality.	Male, powerful, intelligent, attractive and mysterious. Calm, quiet and distant on the surface, but crazy inside. Independent, unique, stylish and dangerous.

Source: Reprinted with permission from the *Journal of Marketing Management*, 15(6), pp. 449–62. Copyright © Westburn Publishers Ltd, 1995.

Social forces

Marketing activities are primarily social in purpose; therefore, they are structured by the institutions of family, religion, education, health and recreation. For example, in the UK, where listening to music on hi-fi systems or personal stereos is a common form of relaxation, Japanese products have a large target market. In all countries, these social institutions can be identified. By finding major deviations in institutions among countries, marketers can gain insights into the adaptation of a marketing strategy. Although American football is a popular sport in the US and a major opportunity for many television advertisers, football is the most popular television sport in Europe. The role of children in the family and a society's overall view of children also influence marketing activities. For example, in the Netherlands, children are banned from appearing in advertisements for sweets, and confectionery manufacturers are required to place a little toothbrush symbol at the end of each confectionery advertisement.[13]

Economic forces

Economic differences dictate many of the adjustments that must be made in marketing abroad. The most prominent adjustments are caused by differences in standards of living, availability of credit, discretionary buying power, income distribution, national resources and conditions that affect transport. Exchange rate fluctuations and differences in interest rates can also have a major impact. The strength of a country's currency and high interest rates may make it difficult for companies to succeed in exporting their goods and services. Consumers place different values on

FIGURE 4.4
Even global brands adapt to reflect local cultural and social considerations

specific product categories or brands in different countries, reflecting social mores, standards of living, religion, culture and so forth.

Gross domestic product (GDP) is the total value of all goods and services produced by a country in one year. A comparison of GDP for Europe, the US and Japan shows that the US has the largest gross domestic product. By dividing this figure by the size of the population, an understanding of the standard of living can be achieved. In this way it is possible to gain insight into the level of discretionary income or buying power of individual consumers. Knowledge about aggregate GDP, credit and the distribution of income provides general insights into market potential. For example, China has overtaken Japan as the world's second biggest economy, reflecting the significant growth of China's industry and consumerism. This creates opportunities for Western brands inside China, but presents Chinese-sourced products and brands as emerging rivals on the international stage.

Opportunities for international marketers are certainly not limited to those countries with the highest incomes. Indeed, as recent events in the Asia-Pacific region and parts of the Middle East have shown, high income is no guarantee of an attractive market. Some countries are progressing faster than they were even a few years ago; and these countries, especially in eastern Europe, Latin America, Africa and parts of Asia, have great market potential for specific products. However, marketers must first understand the political and legal environment before they can convert buying power into actual demand for specific products.

Political, regulatory and legal forces

A country's political system, national laws, regulatory bodies, national pressure groups and courts each have a great impact on global marketing. A government's policies towards public and private enterprise, consumers and foreign companies, influence marketing across national boundaries. The types of measures a government can take to govern cross-border trade include the use of tariffs, quotas and non-tariff barriers. For example, the Japanese have established many barriers to imports into their country. Even though they are reducing the tariffs on certain items, many non-tariff barriers still make it difficult for other companies to export their products to Japan.[14] **Tariffs** are taxes that affect the movement of goods across economic or political boundaries, and can affect imports, exports or goods in transit.[15] These taxes provide governments with revenue and can give domestic companies an important advantage. For example, import tariffs in the form of import duties effectively increase the price of imported products, giving local companies an automatic advantage. **Quotas** involve physical restrictions on the amount of goods that can be imported into a particular country or region. The imposition of quotas is not always in the best interest of consumers, as choice is limited and allocations tend to be used up on imports of goods carrying the greatest profit margin. **Non-tariff barriers** are much more difficult to define: they include a wide range of rules, regulations and taxes that have an impact on trade. As shown in Table 4.1, these barriers can include anything from port and border taxes to trademark and health and safety regulations. For example, not too many years ago, companies exporting electronic equipment to Japan had to wait for the Japanese government to inspect each item. A government's attitude towards cooperation with importers has a direct impact on the economic feasibility of their exporting to that country. As barriers to trade decline, opportunities are presented. Attempts to bring trade barriers down and improve the flow of goods between countries have come to the forefront in recent decades, notably in the practices adopted between 'partner' countries within the EU. The rules and frameworks for world trade are partly determined by the General Agreement on Tariffs and Trade (GATT). From a marketing standpoint, principles such as those defended by GATT increase competition.

Gross domestic product (GDP)
The total value of all goods and services produced by a country in one year.

Tariffs
Taxes that affect the movement of goods across economic or political boundaries, and that can also affect imports, exports or goods in transit.

Quotas
Physical restrictions on the amount of goods that can be imported into a particular country or region.

Non-tariff barriers
A wide range of rules, regulations and taxes that have an impact on trade.

TABLE 4.1 Non-tariff trade barriers

Non-tariff price-related import restrictions

- Discriminatory and non-discriminatory excise duties, registration charges and state insurance requirements
- Discriminatory and non-discriminatory turnover/sales taxes
- At-border surcharges
- Port handling levies
- Import levies
- Variable levies
- Consular fees
- Stamp taxes
- Sales surcharges

Trade limitations and quantity-related restrictions

- Embargoes and export restrictions
- Quotas and ceiling limits
- Licencing regulations and stipulations
- Foreign exchange and currency restrictions
- Government price-setting
- Purchase stipulations
- Specified performance standards
- Restrictive business practices
- Regulated preference for domestic producers
- Discriminatory bi-lateral trading agreements and partnerships
- Discrimination regarding permitted countries of origin and trading partners

Discriminatory freight rates

- Preferential treatment of certain countries of origin
- Insistence on haulage providers/channel players
- Bureaucratic at-border levies and delays

State's participation in trading

- State-controlled competitors
- Subsidies and government payments
- Preferential loan rates
- Government monopolies
- Government domestic R&D resourcing and investment
- Granting of licences or concessions

- Laws and regulations hindering imports
- Government's own procurement practices and preferred suppliers
- Discriminatory tax relief
- Credits and state-provided guarantees
- State-sponsored boycotts
- State-controlled consortia and trading partnerships
- Golden shareholdings in domestic companies/sectors
- Political global trading blocs and arrangements
- Sector-specific regulatory regime

Consumer protection and product specifications

- R&D control regulations
- Intellectual property rights
- Trademark and patent provision and guarantees
- Pharmaceutical controls
- Health and safety regulations
- Shipment regulations
- Product design and safety regulations
- Size and weight regulations
- Packaging and labelling regulations and standards
- Usage regulations
- Consumer guarantees and safeguards
- Complaint procedures and adjudication
- Consumer redress practices and penalties

Customs processing and administration

- Anti-dumping regulations
- Customs processing and costs
- Consular arrangements and fees
- Certification and labelling regulations
- Merchandise classification
- Usage classification
- Regulations for samples and trials
- Re-export regulations
- Appeal law
- Transparency of practices

Differences in political and government ethical standards are enormous. The use of payoffs and bribes is deeply entrenched in many governments and trade authorities, while in others such involvement is prohibited. European companies that do not engage in such practices may have a hard time competing with foreign businesses that do. Some businesses that refuse to make pay-offs are forced to hire local consultants, public relations businesses or advertising agencies, resulting in indirect pay-offs. The ultimate decision about whether to give small tips or gifts where they are customary must be based on a company's code of ethics and their scrutiny panels. It is a difficult challenge in many markets for international marketers striving to compete effectively in a country exhibiting markedly different 'worse' ethics than in the domestic market, while adhering to the laws governing the company's head office and the codes stipulated by the company's domestic stakeholders. Arms business BAE discovered this to its cost in terms of US and UK fines for dubious business practices[16] in various overseas markets.

Technological forces

Much of the marketing technology used in Europe and other industrialized regions of the world may be inappropriate for developing countries. For example, promoting products via the internet will be difficult in countries where computer ownership is low or state-controlled. Nonetheless, many countries, particularly China, South Korea, Mexico and the countries of the former Soviet Union, want to engage in international trade, often through partnerships with American, European and Japanese businesses, so that they can gain valuable industrial and agricultural technology. However, there may be export restrictions that limit trade in certain goods. For example, the export of defence equipment is tightly controlled by many European governments. Distribution channels, logistics, the tracking of goods in transit, automatic reordering using IT, CRM systems, customer interaction and internal company communications, may be severely impeded in certain countries owing to their infancy in terms of the life cycles of technology used routinely in North America, the EU or Asia-Pacific to manage such marketing activities. Over a decade since its UK introduction, Tesco's Clubcard loyalty scheme appeared in its stores in Asia, becoming the first loyalty card to embrace the opportunities provided by current CRM technology in those markets. In other instances, the non-domestic market may be more advanced than the domestic market, providing marketers with a different set of challenges.

Regional trade alliances and markets

While some businesses are beginning to view the world as one huge marketplace, opportunities for companies are affected by a range of regional trade alliances. This section examines several regional trade alliances and changing markets, including NAFTA, the European Union, the Pacific Rim markets, changing conditions in central and eastern Europe, GATT and the World Trade Organization.

The North American Free Trade Agreement (NAFTA)

North American Free Trade Agreement (NAFTA) Implemented in 1994, and designed to eliminate all tariffs on goods produced and traded between Canada, Mexico and the US, providing for a totally free trade area by 2009.

The **North American Free Trade Agreement (NAFTA)**, implemented in 1994, effectively merged Canada, Mexico and the US into one market of more than 575 million consumers. NAFTA has eliminated virtually all tariffs on goods produced and traded between Canada, Mexico and the US.

NAFTA makes it easier for businesses to invest in the participating countries; provides protection for intellectual property of special interest to high-tech and entertainment industries; expands trade by requiring equal treatment of companies in all countries; and simplifies country-of-origin rules, hindering Japan's use of Mexico as a staging ground for further penetration into US markets. NAFTA also links the US with other Latin American countries, providing additional opportunities to integrate trade among all the nations in the Western hemisphere. Although NAFTA has been controversial, it has become a positive factor for US companies wishing to engage in international marketing. Since licencing requirements have been relaxed under the pact, smaller businesses that previously could not afford to invest in Mexico and Canada are able to do business in those markets without having to locate there.

The European Union (EU)

European Union (EU) The major grouping in western Europe, the EU has 27 members: Austria, Belgium, Denmark, Finland, France, Germany, Greece, Ireland, Italy, Luxembourg, the Netherlands, Portugal, Spain, Sweden and the UK have been joined by Bulgaria, Cyprus, the Czech Republic, Estonia, Hungary, Latvia, Lithuania, Malta, Poland, Romania, Slovakia and Slovenia.

The **European Union (EU)** is one of three major market groups in western Europe.[17] Formed by the Treaty of European Union, the EU has its origins in the European Common Market, set up in 1958, which later became known as the European Community (EC).

Following the signing of the **Maastricht Treaty** in 1992 and the creation of the single European market in 1993, the group became known as the European Union (EU). Today the EU has 28 members, including many eastern European countries, such as the Czech Republic, Estonia, Hungary, Latvia, Lithuania, Poland, Slovakia and Slovenia, plus Mediterranean countries Cyprus, Greece and Malta. Bulgaria and Romania joined in 2007 and Croatia in 2013. The objectives of the Union are set out in the following extract from Article B of the Treaty on European Union.[18]

- to promote economic and social progress which is balanced and sustainable, in particular through the creation of an area without internal frontiers, through the strengthening of economic and social cohesion and through the establishment of economic and monetary union, ultimately including a single currency in accordance with the provisions of this Treaty;

- to assert its identity on the international scene, in particular through the implementation of a common foreign and security policy including the eventual framing of a common defence policy, which might in time lead to a common defence;

- to strengthen the protection of the rights and interests of the nationals of its Member States through the introduction of a citizenship of the Union;

- to develop close cooperation on justice and home affairs.

On 1 January 1999 the EU moved closer to economic and monetary union with the launch of the euro, the unit of European currency;[19] 11 of the then 15 EU members became committed to the new currency. Only Sweden, Denmark and Britain postponed participation in the single currency, while Greece initially failed to meet the economic criteria!

Although the 28 countries of the EU essentially function as one large market, and consumers in the EU are likely to become more homogeneous in their needs and wants, marketers know that cultural and social differences among the member states will require modifications in the marketing mix for consumers in many countries. Some researchers believe that eventually it will be possible to segment the EU into six markets on the basis of cultural, geographic, demographic and economic variables. For example, the UK and Ireland would form one market, while Greece and southern Italy would form another.[20] Differences in taste and preferences among these markets are significant for international marketers. For example, the British consume far more instant coffee than their European neighbours. Consumers in Spain eat far more poultry products than Germans do.[21] In some geographic regions, preferences even vary within the same country. Thus, international marketing intelligence efforts remain very important in determining European consumers' needs and in developing marketing strategies that will satisfy those needs. It is also clear that EU organizations will have to face up to considerable changes in the way they operate and, for some, such as pharmaceutical companies, the prospects include harmonization of prices and formulations and likely job losses.

Pacific Rim nations

Countries in the Pacific Rim represent an enormous part of the world market, with 60 per cent of the world's population living there. Although the region is characterized by considerable diversity, in general companies of the Pacific Rim nations: Japan, China, South Korea, Taiwan, Singapore, Hong Kong, the Philippines, Malaysia, Indonesia, Australia and Indochina, have become increasingly competitive and sophisticated in their marketing efforts in the last three decades. Throughout the early to mid-1990s the performances of Japan and the four so-called Tiger economies of the region: South Korea, Singapore, Taiwan and Hong Kong, were particularly impressive.[22] The Japanese, in particular, made considerable inroads into the world consumer markets for cars, motorcycles, watches, cameras and audio-visual equipment. Products made by Sony, Sanyo, Toyota, Honda, Canon, Suzuki and others are sold all over the world and have set quality standards by which other products are often judged. Through direct investment in Europe, the Japanese built strong distribution and developed a keen understanding of the market. However, Japan's marketing muscle attracted criticism in certain quarters, fuelled partly by fears that Japanese products might swamp the market. These concerns are compounded by Japan's reluctance to accept imports from other countries.[23]

South Korea also became very successful in world markets with familiar brands such as Samsung and Hyundai. South Korean companies even took market share away from Japanese companies in the world markets for VCRs, televisions and computers, despite the fact that the South Korean market for these products is limited. In Canada, the Hyundai Excel overtook Japan's Honda in just 18 months.[24]

Less visible Pacific Rim regions, such as Singapore, Taiwan and Hong Kong, are major manufacturing and financial centres. Singapore also has large world markets for pharmaceutical and rubber goods. Taiwan may have the most promising future of all the Pacific Rim nations. It has a strong local economy and has lowered many import barriers, sending imports up. Taiwan has privatized state-run banks and is also opening its markets to foreign businesses. Some analysts believe that it may replace Hong Kong as a regional financial power centre.[25]

Much attention is now being given to the Pacific Rim nations that have reached the point of massive industrial growth. Thailand, Malaysia, Indonesia and of course China all offer considerable marketing potential.[26] For example, China has great market potential and opportunities for joint venture projects. Analysts are keeping a close watch on how these countries are affected by economic uncertainty in the region. The emergence of China presents marketers with considerable opportunities for exporting via joint ventures or trading alliances aided by China's 'open door' policy. There is also a huge threat to Western companies, as Chinese enterprises strive to emulate Japan and enter global markets with their own products and services, and acquire Western businesses.

In general, attempts to form groups promoting trade and other links between Pacific Rim countries have not been particularly successful. Perhaps the best known is the **Association of South East Asian Nations (ASEAN)**, formed in 1967, which aims to build trade and other links between its members: Indonesia, Malaysia, the Philippines, Singapore, Thailand, Brunei, Cambodia, Laos, Myanmar and Vietnam. More recently, the **Asia-Pacific Economic Cooperative (APEC)** has been set up to for 21 Pacific Rim states, including Indonesia, Malaysia, the Philippines, Singapore, Thailand, Brunei, the US, Australia, Canada, New Zealand, Japan, China, South Korea, Hong Kong and Taiwan.[27]

Central and Eastern Europe (CEE)

Central and Eastern Europe (CEE) encompasses the Commonwealth of Independent States (CIS, formerly the Soviet Union), the Czech and Slovak Republics, Hungary, Poland, Slovenia, Croatia, Bosnia Herzegovina, Serbia, Montenegro, Bulgaria, FYR Macedonia and Albania. The decline of communism in central and eastern Europe, the fall of the Berlin Wall in 1989 and the break-up of the former Soviet Union in 1990 resulted in a host of new marketing opportunities in the region.

Following a policy of *perestroika,* encompassing considerable political and economic change, the CEE countries replaced the Communist Party's centrally planned economies with marketing-oriented democratic institutions. This process of market reforms, designed to lead to greater imports and exports, was not without difficulty. The challenge for many of the eastern European countries has been to move forward from the inefficiencies of state-owned industry and to develop the marketing expertise, business culture, infrastructures and legal frameworks required to trade with capitalist countries.[28] For example, the poorly developed distribution infrastructure in many parts of central and eastern Europe has restricted the outlets where Western products can be sold and limits the opportunities domestic companies can pursue.[29] However, the move towards

Association of South East Asian Nations (ASEAN)
Formed in 1967 with the intention of building trade and other links among its six members: Brunei, Indonesia, Malaysia, the Philippines, Singapore and Thailand.

Asia-Pacific Economic Cooperative (APEC)
Aims to promote trade between its members: the six ASEAN members plus the United States, Australia, Canada, New Zealand, Japan, China, South Korea, Hong Kong and Taiwan.

Central and Eastern Europe (CEE)
Encompasses the Commonwealth of Independent States (formerly the Soviet Union), the Czech and Slovak Republics, Hungary, Poland, Slovenia, Croatia, Bosnia Herzegovina, Serbia, Montenegro, Bulgaria, FYR Macedonia and Albania.

market change has resulted in considerable social upheaval and, in some cases, unrest in countries going through this transition.

The **Commonwealth of Independent States (CIS)** emerged in 1996 as a loosely connected group of former Soviet Union states. The CIS unites Azerbaijan, Armenia, Belarus, Georgia, Kazakhstan, Kyrgyzstan, Moldova, Russia, Tajikistan, Turkmenistan, Ukraine and Uzbekistan.[30] But key economic data show these countries to be relatively weak compared with western EU states.

Although after it was set up there were potential opportunities for the CIS to trade as a market group, in practice this idea has been severely restricted by the lack of cooperation between member states and in particular by economic and political problems in Russia and political rivalries, such as tensions between Ukraine and Russia.[31] The importance of Russia, the largest market, cannot be overlooked in the region's development.[32] For Western companies, the potential is considerable. Hewlett Packard enjoyed a fourfold increase in sales in one year alone, and others such as Coca-Cola and McDonald's have also taken advantage of the new opportunities.

General Agreement on Tariffs and Trade (GATT) and the World Trade Organization (WTO)

Like NAFTA and the EU, the **General Agreement on Tariffs and Trade (GATT)** was based on negotiations among member countries to reduce worldwide tariffs and increase international trade. Originally signed by 23 countries in 1947, GATT provided a forum for tariff negotiations, and a place where international trade problems could be discussed and resolved. Eventually, GATT involved some 124 countries before giving way to the World Trade Organization in the mid-90s. The Uruguay Round of negotiations reduced trade barriers for most products and provided new rules to prevent **dumping** – the selling of products at unfairly low prices.

The most significant outcome of the Uruguay Round was the establishment of the **World Trade Organization (WTO)** to promote free trade among member countries. Fulfilling this purpose requires eliminating trade barriers; educating individuals, companies and governments about trade rules around the world, and assuring global markets that no sudden changes of policy will occur. The WTO also serves as a forum for trade negotiations and dispute resolution. At the heart of the WTO are agreements that provide legal ground rules for international commerce and trade policy.

Alternative market entry strategies

The level of commitment to international marketing is a major variable in deciding what kind of involvement is appropriate. A company's market entry options range from occasional exporting to expanding overall operations (production and marketing) into other countries. This section examines exporting, licencing, franchising, contract manufacturing, joint ventures, trading companies, foreign direct investment, cooperation and other approaches to international involvement.[33]

Exporting

Exporting is the lowest and most flexible level of commitment to international marketing. A business may find an exporting intermediary that can perform most marketing functions associated with selling to other countries. This approach entails minimum effort and cost. Modifications in packaging, labelling, style or colour may be the major expenses in adapting a product. There is limited risk in using export agents and merchants because there is no direct investment in the foreign country.

Commonwealth of Independent States (CIS)
The CIS unites Azerbaijan, Armenia, Belarus, Georgia, Kazakhstan, Kyrgyzstan, Moldova, Russia, Tajikistan, Turkmenistan, Ukraine and Uzbekistan in a trading bloc.

General Agreement on Tariffs and Trade (GATT)
An agreement between countries to reduce worldwide tariffs and increase international trade.

Dumping
Selling products at unfairly low prices outside domestic markets.

World Trade Organization (WTO)
An entity that promotes and facilitates free trade between member states.

Exporting
Use of an intermediary that performs most marketing functions associated with selling to other countries; entails the minimum effort, cost and risk involved in international marketing.

Export agents bring together buyers and sellers from different countries; they collect a commission for arranging sales. Export houses and export merchants purchase products from different companies and then sell them to foreign countries. They specialize in understanding customers' needs in foreign countries.

Foreign buyers from companies and governments provide a direct method of exporting and eliminate the need for an intermediary. Foreign buyers encourage international exchange by contacting domestic businesses about their needs and the opportunities available in exporting. Domestic companies that want to export with a minimum of effort and investment seek out foreign importers and buyers.

Licencing

Licencing
System in which a licensee pays commissions or royalties on sales or supplies used in manufacturing.

When potential markets are found across national boundaries and when production, technical assistance or marketing know-how is required, **licencing** is an alternative to direct investment. The licensee (the owner of the foreign operation) pays commissions or royalties on sales or supplies used in manufacturing. An initial fee may be charged when the licencing agreement is signed. Exchanges of management techniques or technical assistance are primary reasons for licencing agreements. Yoplait is a French yoghurt that is licenced for production in the US and numerous other countries, but the Yoplait brand tries to maintain a French image.

Licencing is an attractive alternative to direct investment when the political stability of a foreign country is in doubt or when resources are unavailable for direct investment. This approach is especially advantageous for small manufacturers wanting to launch a well-known brand internationally. For example, Pierre Cardin has issued 500 and Yves St Laurent 200 licences to make their products.[34] Löwenbrau has used licencing agreements to increase sales worldwide without committing capital to build breweries.

Franchising

Franchising
A form of licencing granting the right to use certain intellectual property rights, such as trade names, brand names, designs, patents and copyrights.

Another alternative to direct investment in non-domestic markets is **franchising**. This form of licencing, which grants the right to use certain intellectual property rights, such as trade names, brand names, designs, patents and copyrights, is becoming increasingly popular in Europe.[35] Under this arrangement the franchiser grants a licence to the franchisee, who pays to be allowed to carry out business under the name owned by the franchiser. The franchiser retains control over the manner in which the business is conducted and assists the franchisee in running the business. The franchisee retains ownership of his or her own business, which remains separate from that of the franchiser.[36] Franchising has recently experienced a period of rapid growth. Companies such as Benetton, Burger King, Holiday Inn and IKEA are particularly well-known for their commitment to growing global business in this way. There are various reasons why the popularity of franchising has increased so rapidly.[37] First, the general world decline in manufacturing and shift to service industries has increased the relevance of franchising. This is significant, because franchising is a very common internationalization process for service organizations. Second, franchising has been relatively free of restrictions from legislation, especially in the EU. Third, an increase in self-employment has provided a pool of individuals willing to become involved in franchising, and this activity has generally been supported by the major clearing banks.

Contract manufacturing

Contract manufacturing
The practice of hiring a foreign company to produce a designated volume of product to a set specification.

Contract manufacturing is the practice of hiring a foreign company to produce a designated volume of the domestic company's product to a set specification. The final product carries the domestic company's name. Gap, for example, relies on contract manufacturing for some of its clothing, and Reebok uses Korean contract manufacturers to produce many of its sports shoes. Marketing activity may be handled by the contract manufacturer or by the contracting company.

Joint ventures and strategic alliances

Joint venture
A partnership between a domestic company and a foreign company or government.

In international marketing, a **joint venture** is a partnership between a domestic company and a foreign company or government. Joint ventures are especially popular in industries that call for large investments, such as natural resources extraction or car manufacturing. Control of the joint venture can be split equally or can be retained by one party. Joint ventures are often a political necessity because of nationalism and governmental restrictions on foreign ownership. They also provide legitimacy in the eyes of the host country's people. Local partners have first-hand knowledge of the economic and socio-political environment, access to distribution networks or privileged access to local resources (raw material, labour management, contacts and so on). Moreover, entrepreneurs in many less-developed countries actively seek associations with an overseas partner as a ready means of implementing their own corporate strategy.[38]

Joint ventures are assuming greater global importance because of cost advantages and the number of inexperienced businesses entering foreign markets. They may be the result of a trade-off between a company's desire for completely unambiguous control of an enterprise and its quest for additional resources. They may occur when internal development or acquisition is not feasible or unavailable, or when the risks and constraints leave no other alternative. As project sizes increase in the face of global competition, and businesses attempt to spread the huge costs of technological innovation, there is increased impetus to form joint ventures.[39] Joint ventures are also possible between partners from different continents. The leading IT consultancies frequently form joint ventures or alliances with partners in order to exploit domestic and non-domestic opportunities.

Joint ventures are sometimes criticized as being inherently unstable,[40] or because they might result in a takeover attempt. For businesses trying to build longer-term joint ventures, there is also the danger that the relationship stifles flexibility. Of course, for many companies that become involved in joint ventures this may be their only feasible mode of entry at the time and may in any case be regarded purely as a transitional arrangement.[41] For example, European construction companies bidding for business in the Middle East found that joint ventures with Arab construction companies gain local support among the handful of people who make the contracting decisions.

Strategic alliances
Partnerships formed to create a competitive advantage on a world-wide basis.

Strategic alliances are partnerships formed to create a competitive advantage on a worldwide basis. They are very similar to joint ventures. Strategic alliances have been defined as 'cooperation between two or more industrial corporations, belonging to different countries, whereby each partner seeks to add to its competencies by combining its resources with those of its partner'.[42] The number of strategic alliances is growing at an estimated rate of about 20 per cent per year.[43] In fact, in some industries, such as cars and high technology, strategic alliances are becoming the predominant means of competing. International competition is so fierce and the costs of competing globally so high that few businesses have the required individual resources, and it makes sense to collaborate with other companies. Many car brands are co-created by apparently rival manufacturers acting in a strategic alliance.[44]

The partners forming international strategic alliances share common goals, yet often retain their distinct identities, each bringing a distinctive competence to the union. What distinguishes international strategic alliances from other business structures is that member companies in the alliance may have been traditional rivals competing for market share in the same product class.[45] This situation is common in the aerospace industry. Raytheon may partner certain companies in bidding for work from Boeing, while competing with the same suppliers when seeking work with Lockheed or Airbus.

Global strategic partnerships
Link-ups between companies from two or more regions which jointly decide to pursue a marketing opportunity, share resources and combine ideas, retaining independence, but pooling many activities and sharing rewards.

Global strategic partnerships are increasingly prevalent. They are link-ups between companies from two or more regions which jointly decide to pursue a marketing opportunity, share resources and combine ideas. The participants retain independence, but pool many activities and share the rewards. Many high technology, automotive designs and power technologies are collaboratively developed and marketed. Sometimes, the partners allocate markets between themselves or they might all seek to commercialize an opportunity under separate brands, each harnessing the same underlying design or technology. **Virtual corporations** are a spin on this concept.

Trading companies

A **trading company** provides a link between buyers and sellers in different countries. As its name implies, a trading company is not involved in manufacturing or owning assets related to manufacturing. The trading company buys in one country at the lowest price consistent with quality and sells to buyers in another country. An important function of trading companies is taking title to products and undertaking all the activities necessary to move the products from the domestic country to a foreign country. Large grain trading companies, for example, control a major portion of the world's trade in basic food commodities. These trading companies sell agricultural commodities that are homogeneous, and can be stored and moved rapidly in response to market conditions.

Trading companies reduce risk for companies interested in becoming involved in international marketing, assisting producers with information about products that meet quality and price expectations in domestic or international markets. Additional services a trading company may provide

Much more than understanding customers' behaviours and culture

Topical insight

In order to be actively involved in an overseas market, marketers must have the required insights into the market's trends, competitive set, supply considerations, business practices and, of course, customers' behaviours. However, the required skills and understanding go much deeper, particularly as most globally engaged companies will have executives in control who do not originate from the part of the world they now must manage.

In order to operate their brands effectively, such personnel must have capabilities beyond an understanding of the marketing toolkit and how to operationalize a marketing plan … they must also be able to quickly deduce how to do business in the markets for which they have responsibility. In reality, this involves re-learning how to be a manager and what must take place in order to be able to practice marketing.

In order to be successful in non-domestic markets it is important to understand not only the culture and behaviours of potential consumers, but also how to engage with business partners, suppliers, distributors, agencies and all parties necessary for doing business. Business-to-business marketers face particularly complicated interactions with their customers, with whom they must have direct contact. To illustrate these challenges, consider these scenarios as posed by *Marketing Week* magazine, a weekly publication targeted at marketers:

● *Any meeting with Chinese business people is always relaxed and informal, so it is good to be the first to break the ice with good-humoured anecdotes.* In reality, this is far from the truth.

● *In Japan it is common to celebrate agreeing a contract with a Japanese client by going to a karaoke club or sushi bar, but visiting businesspeople are not expected to join in or stay as late as the Japanese hosts.* True in terms of the expectation to go to the bar or club, but the hosts would want visitors to join in and stay as late as them.

● *An Egyptian colleague will stand much closer and display more physical contact than might be the norm in another country.* This is generally the case.

● *In Russia respect must be shown to the bosses of a company and to the hierarchy.* Very much the expectation.

● *Appearances matter little in Brazil, so wearing jeans, flip-flops and other similar casual dress signals success and being at ease.* In practice this is not true, but were you certain?

● *Appointments with Saudi Arabian business contacts are often interrupted by phone calls and family visits, and visitors must remain cool and not exhibit signs of frustration.* Often this is the case.

Source: 'Beware the culture gap on global growth trail', Marylou Costa, *Marketing Week*, 7 October 2010, pp. 20–4.

include consulting, marketing research, advertising, insurance, research and development, legal assistance, warehousing and foreign exchange.

Foreign direct investment

Foreign direct investment (FDI)
A long-term commitment to marketing in a foreign nation through direct ownership of a foreign subsidiary or division.

Once a company makes a long-term commitment to foreign marketing, direct owner-ship of a foreign subsidiary or division is a possibility. **Foreign direct investment (FDI)** involves making a long-term commitment to marketing in a foreign nation through direct ownership of a foreign subsidiary or division. The expense of developing a separate foreign distribution system, in particular, can be tremendous. For example, as French hypermarket chain Carrefour discovered, the opening of retail stores in neighbouring countries can require a large financial investment in facilities, research and management.

Multinational enterprise
A company with opera-tions or subsidiaries in many countries.

The term **multinational enterprise** refers to companies that have operations or subsidiaries located in many countries. Often the parent company is based in one country and cultivates production, management and marketing activities in other coun-tries. The company's subsidiaries may be quite autonomous in order to respond to the needs of individual international markets. Companies such as Dell, Unilever and General Motors are multinational companies with worldwide operations.

A wholly-owned foreign subsidiary may be allowed to operate independently of the parent company so that its management can have more freedom to adjust to the local environment. Cooperative arrangements are developed to assist in marketing efforts, production and management. A wholly-owned foreign subsidiary may export products to the home country. Some car manufacturers, such as Ford and General Motors, for example, import cars built by their foreign subsidiaries. A foreign subsidiary offers important tax, tariff and other operating advantages. The greatest advantages of direct foreign investment are greater strategy control and enhanced market capacity. To maximize these, a subsidiary may operate under for-eign management, so that a genuinely local identity can be developed. A company's success in achieving these advantages will tend to depend on whether the business has a competitive advantage allowing it to recover the costs of its investment.

Customization versus the globalization of international marketing strategies

As for domestic marketers, international marketers develop marketing strategies to serve specific tar-get markets. Traditionally, international marketing strategies have customized marketing mixes accord-ing to cultural, regional and national differences. Detergent producers such as Procter & Gamble or Unilever customize their products to local water conditions, weather, equipment and washing habits. Colgate-Palmolive even developed a cheap hand-powered washing machine for households lacking electricity in developing regions. Such customization of the product or service, to reflect local nuances, attitudes and behaviours, can bring significant rewards to marketers. Failure to reflect such localized market conditions may leave marketers with an unattractive customer-facing proposition.

Globalization
The development of marketing strategies that treat the entire world, or its major regions, as a single entity.

Along the continuum, away from customization, is the globalization of marketing. **Globalization** involves developing marketing strategies as though the world's consumers or business customers share homogeneous product needs and purchasing behaviour. Nike and adidas footwear, for example, are standardized globally and the same advertis-ing campaigns are run across the globe. Mobile phones, televisions, clothing, movies, soft drinks, cosmetics, toothpaste, batteries and cigarette brands are examples of globalized products: the same product attributes and specifications are marketed around the world.

Throughout the 1980s and 1990s, the trend was for large corporations to globalize their products and, wherever possible, the remaining ingredients of their marketing programmes, notably marketing communications, pricing and distribution channels. The goals were to reduce

TABLE 4.2 Most valuable global brands – $m value, 2014

Brand	Country of origin	Brand value ($m)	Brand	Country of origin	Brand value ($m)
Apple	USA	118 863	Oracle	USA	25 980
Google	USA	107 439	HP	USA	23 758
Coca-Cola	USA	81 563	Gillette	USA	22 845
IBM	USA	72 244	Louis Vuitton	France	22 552
Microsoft	USA	61 154	Honda	Japan	21 673
General Electric	USA	45 480	H&M	Finland	21 083
Samsung	S Korea	45 462	Nike	USA	19 875
Toyota	Japan	42 392	Amex	USA	19 510
McDonald's	USA	42 254	Pepsi	USA	19 119
Mercedes	Germany	34 338	SAP	Germany	17 340
BMW	Germany	34 214	IKEA	Sweden	15 885
Intel	USA	34 153	UPS	USA	14 470
Disney	USA	32 223	ebay	USA	14 358
Cisco	USA	30 936	Facebook	USA	14 349
Amazon	USA	29 478	Pampers	USA	14 078

Source: Interbrand's Best Global Brands 2014 report is a look at financial performance of the brand, role of brand in the purchase decision process and the brand strength. Go to www.bestglobalbrands.com for more information.

costs by harmonizing product mixes, branding, packaging and labelling and to create a more cohesive and recognizable brand identity. The choice of marketing channels, media options for advertising, pricing and particularly customer service often proved more challenging to harmonize: different practices and cultures from region to region or country to country proved difficult to address through a single marketing mix.

Over time, the champions of globalized marketing recognized that a 'think globally, act locally' compromise was sensible. Economies of effort and scale in a single product and brand identity were worthwhile, but the route to market, the way in which the brand and product were communicated to the intended target audiences, the pricing and service required, often had to be manipulated at a local level to reflect the pertinent localized market conditions. Even such ubiquitous brands as McDonald's and Coca-Cola modify their marketing mixes to reflect local tastes, customs, buying behaviour and social values. This requirement by international marketers to manipulate the ingredients of the marketing mix in order to reflect local needs is developed further in Chapter 21.

International marketing and globalization require strategic planning if a company is to incorporate non-domestic sales into its overall marketing strategy. International marketing activities often require customized marketing mixes to achieve an organization's goals. Globalization requires a total commitment to the world, regions or multinational areas as an integral part of the company's markets. Regardless of the extent to which a company chooses to globalize its marketing strategy, extensive analysis of the marketing environment, marketing intelligence and often marketing research, are required in order to understand the needs and desires of the target market(s) and to implement the selected marketing strategy successfully. While a global presence does not guarantee a global competitive advantage (see Chapter 2) a global presence does generate five opportunities for creating value:

1. to adapt to local market differences
2. to exploit economies of global scale
3. to exploit economies of global scope
4. to seek optimal locations for activities and resources
5. to maximize the transfer of knowledge across locations.

However, without a sound appreciation of the forces of the marketing environment internationally, an organization's ability to seek suitable opportunities will be limited. A marketing strategy, as described in Chapter 2, must be developed in order to specify the opportunities to be pursued internationally, select an appropriate target market strategy and basis for competing, and specify applicable marketing programmes to operationalize the agreed international marketing strategy. This use of the marketing process may suggest customization, full globalization or some hybrid part-way between these two extremes.

Summary

Marketing activities performed across national boundaries are usually significantly different from domestic marketing activities. International marketers must have a profound awareness of the foreign environment. The marketing strategy is ordinarily adjusted to meet the needs and desires of markets across national boundaries.

The level of involvement in international marketing covers a wide spectrum from *domestic marketing* to *export marketing*, *international marketing*, *multinational marketing* and *global marketing*. Although all companies involved in international marketing must make some modifications to their marketing activities, full-scale global marketing requires total commitment to international marketing and involves applying the company's assets, experience and products to develop and maintain marketing strategies on a global scale. *Globalized marketing* occurs when marketing strategies are developed for major regions or the entire world to enable organizations to compete globally. *Multinational companies* are those that operate in overseas markets as if they were local companies.

Marketers must rely on international marketing intelligence to understand the complexities of the international marketing environment before they can formulate a marketing strategy and develop a marketing mix. That is why they collect and analyze secondary data and primary data about international markets.

Environmental aspects of special importance include cultural, social, economic, political, regulatory, legal and technological forces. Cultural aspects of the environment that are most important to international marketers include customs, concepts, values, attitudes, morals and knowledge. Marketing activities are primarily social in purpose; they are structured by the institutions of family, religion, education, health and recreation. The most prominent economic forces that affect international marketing are those that can be measured by income and resources. *Gross domestic product (GDP)* is the total value of all goods and services produced by a country in a year. Credit, buying power and income distribution are aggregate measures of market potential. Political and legal forces include the political system, national laws, regulatory bodies, national pressure groups and courts.

Measures that governments can take to govern cross-border trade include the use of tariffs, quotas and non-tariff barriers. *Tariffs* are taxes that affect the movement of goods across economic or political boundaries. *Quotas* involve physical restrictions on the amount of goods that can be imported. *Non-tariff barriers* include a wide range of rules, regulations and taxes that have an impact on trade. The foreign policies of all nations involved in trade determine how marketing can be conducted. The level of technology helps define economic development within a nation and indicates the existence of methods to facilitate marketing.

Various regional trade alliances and specific markets are creating both difficulties and opportunities for organizations. The *North American Free Trade Agreement (NAFTA)*, set up in 1994, aims to eliminate all tariffs on goods produced and traded between Canada, Mexico and the US. The creation of the single European market in 1993, following the signing of the *Maastricht Treaty* in 1992, led to the formation of the *European Union (EU)*, which was enlarged in 2013 to include 28 countries, most of which adopted the euro as their currency. More recently, the *Asia-Pacific Economic Cooperative (APEC)* has been set up to promote trade in the region. The group includes the US, Australia, Canada, New Zealand, Japan, China, South Korea, Hong Kong, Taiwan and ASEAN members. The best-known trading group in the Pacific Rim is the *Association of South East Asian Nations (ASEAN)*. *Central and Eastern Europe (CEE)* encompasses the *Commonwealth of Independent States (CIS)*, the Czech and Slovak Republics, Hungary, Poland, Slovenia, Croatia, Bosnia Herzegovina, Serbia, Montenegro, Bulgaria, FYR Macedonia and Albania. The CIS unites Azerbaijan, Armenia, Belarus, Georgia, Kazakhstan, Kyrgyzstan, Moldova, Russia, Tajikistan, Turkmenistan, Ukraine and Uzbekistan.

The *General Agreement on Tariffs and Trade,* known as GATT, was an agreement between countries to reduce worldwide tariffs and increase international trade. There was a particular focus on preventing *dumping,* the selling of products at unfairly low prices outside domestic markets. An important development out of GATT has been the *World Trade Organization (WTO),* an entity that promotes and facilitates free trade between member states.

There are several ways of becoming involved in international marketing. *Exporting* is the easiest and most flexible method. *Licencing* is an alternative to direct investment; it may be necessitated by political and economic conditions. *Franchising* is a form of licencing granting the right to use certain intellectual property rights such as trade names, brand names, designs, patents and copyrights. *Contract manufacturing* is the practice of hiring a foreign company to produce a designated volume of product to a specification. *Joint ventures* and *strategic alliances* are often appropriate when outside resources are needed, when there are governmental restrictions on foreign ownership or when changes in global markets encourage competitive consolidation. *Global strategic partnerships* are increasingly prevalent; link-ups between companies from two or more regions who jointly decide to pursue a marketing opportunity, share resources and combine ideas. *Virtual corporations* are a spin on this concept. *Trading companies* are experts at buying products in the domestic market and selling to foreign markets, thereby taking most of the risk in international involvement. *Foreign direct investment (FDI)* in divisions or subsidiaries is the strongest commitment to international marketing and involves the greatest risk. When a company has operations or subsidiaries located in many countries, it is termed a *multinational enterprise*.

Most organizations adjust their marketing programmes to reflect differences in target markets and marketing environments. Some companies standardize their marketing activity worldwide. Traditionally, international marketing has involved customizing products according to cultural, regional or national differences. *Globalization,* on the other hand, involves developing marketing strategies for the whole world, or major regions, ignoring localized market dynamics. A globalized company standardizes products in the same way, everywhere.

International marketing demands strategic planning, the assessment of the international marketing environment and the development of a marketing strategy in order to specify the opportunities to be pursued internationally, select an appropriate target market strategy and basis for competing, and specify applicable marketing programmes to operationalize the agreed international marketing strategy. This use of the marketing process may suggest customization, full globalization, or some hybrid part-way between these two extremes. Most organizations practicing globalization in fact tailor aspects of their customer engagement and interaction to reflect local expectations, conditions and behaviours.

Key links

This chapter should be read in conjunction with:

● Chapter 2's explanation of marketing strategy.

● Chapter 3's examination of the forces of the marketing environment and environmental scanning.

● Chapter 21's exploration of the manipulation of the marketing mix to reflect localized market conditions.

Important terms

Asia-Pacific Economic Cooperative (APEC)
Association of South East Asian Nations (ASEAN)
Central and Eastern Europe (CEE)
Commonwealth of Independent States (CIS)
Contract manufacturing

Domestic marketing
Dumping
European Union (EU)
Export marketing
Exporting
Foreign direct investment (FDI)
Franchising
General Agreement on Tariffs and Trade (GATT)
Global marketing
Global strategic partnerships
Globalization
Gross domestic product (GDP)
International marketing
Joint venture
Licencing
Maastricht Treaty
Multinational companies
Multinational enterprise
Multinational marketing

Non-tariff barriers
North American Free Trade Agreement (NAFTA)
Quotas
Strategic alliances
Tariffs
Trading company
Virtual corporation
World Trade Organization (WTO)

Discussion and review questions

1. How does international marketing differ from domestic marketing?

2. What must marketers consider before deciding whether to become involved in international marketing?

3. Are the largest industrial companies in Europe committed to international marketing? Why or why not?

4. Why do you think so much of this chapter is devoted to an analysis of the international marketing environment?

5. A manufacturer exported peanut butter with a green label to a nation in the Far East. The product failed because it was associated with jungle sickness. How could this mistake have been avoided?

6. How do religious systems influence marketing activities in foreign countries?

7. Recent recession has affected trade opportunities for many businesses. How could businesses minimize the impact of such problems?

8. If you were asked to provide a small tip or bribe to have a document approved in a foreign nation where this practice was customary, what would you do?

9. What should marketers consider as they decide whether to licence or to enter into a joint venture in a foreign nation?

10. Discuss the impact of strategic alliances on marketing strategies.

11. What is meant by globalization?

12. What are the differences between customization and globalization?

Recommended readings

Doole, I. and Lowe, R., *International Marketing Strategy* (Cengage, 2012).

Ghauri, P. and Cateora, P., *International Marketing* (McGraw-Hill, 2014).

Hollensen, S., *Global Marketing* (Pearson, 2013).

Keegan, W.J., *Global Marketing Management* (Pearson, 2013).

Kotabe, M., *International Marketing Management* (John Wiley, 2010).

Terpstra, V. and Sarathy, R., *International Marketing* (South Western, 2000).

Internet exercise

There are many organizations with global aspirations. Examine a selection by logging on to the following websites:
www.jcb.com
www.ikea.com
www.samsung.com
www.ford.com
www.carrefour.com

1. To what extent have these organizations tailored their messages to specific geographic regions?

2. To what extent are these organizations practising globalized marketing?

3. To what extent do these organizations' websites infer a knowledge of their international marketing environments?

Group tasks

1. Your group's business has established a strong presence in its domestic market, but to achieve significant growth it now must consider international markets. What process of investigation is required in order to identify non-domestic target markets?

2. Your group's business has identified some attractive markets to enter outside of your home territory. Explore your entry options and their respective merits.

Applied mini-case

What is your favourite flavour of lollipop? Cherry? Root beer? Blue raspberry? These are options in the US, but the choice may have been liquorice in the Netherlands, lychee nut in China or tarte-tatin in France. Barcelona-based Chupa Chups, owned by Italy's Perfetti Van Melle, produces over four billion lollipops each year, distributed to more than 270 countries. The sixth largest seller of hard candy in the world now achieves more than 90 per cent of sales from outside Spain. The lollies, distributed across the globe, vary in flavour from country to country. Throughout its 55-year history, Chupa Chups has opted to tailor its products to suit tastes in specific target market territories.

Source: Chupa Chups, 2015.

Question

As the marketing director of Chupa Chups, when considering an additional country in which to operate, what information about the territory would be required before the country in question received Chupa Chups lollipops?

Carrefour's 'G4' and international growth strategy

Carrefour has been in the business of managing hypermarkets for more than 50 years. The original business idea was generated in the early 1960s, when Marcel Fournier and Denis and Jacques Defforey visited a retailing conference in the US. The hypermarket concept they developed is based on choice, low prices, self-service and free car parking, allowing consumers to do all their shopping under one roof. The first outlets were opened in the Paris suburbs, followed in 1966 by Europe's largest self-service hypermarket outside Lyon. The main features of the Carrefour concept are:

- large, spacious stores with wide aisles and free car parks
- store size of around 10 000 square metres, serving three million shoppers each year
- flexibility in product and service offerings to reflect local tastes
- food representing about 45 per cent of sales, gross margins of about 18 per cent
- narrow profit margins and high-volume purchases, allowing discount prices to be offered on a daily basis
- a choice of branded, private and generic labels, usually arranged on the shelves vertically in that order.

The Carrefour Group: one of the world's leading retailers

The Carrefour Group is the leading retailer in Europe and the second-largest retailer in the world, employing more than 380 000 people. With more than 10 800 stores in 34 countries, it generated revenues of €100.5 billion under banners in 2014. As a multi-local, multi-format and multi-channel retailer, Carrefour is a partner for daily life. Every day, it welcomes more than 10 million customers around the world, offering them a wide range of products and services at fair prices.

An international retailer

A pioneer in countries such as Brazil in 1975 and China in 1995, the Group now operates in three major markets: Europe, Latin America and Asia.

With a presence in more than 30 countries, it generates more than 53 per cent of its sales outside France.

A force in local economic development

Everywhere it operates, the Carrefour Group demonstrates its commitment to local economic growth. As retail involves people, it always gives priority to recruiting people who live locally, and to training its managers and staff on site.

Very often, the Carrefour Group is the premier private employer in the countries in which it operates. This is obviously the case in France – where the group was founded – but it also holds true in countries such as Brazil, Argentina and Italy. At the same time, the Group gives priority to local supply chains. So 73 per cent of all its food products come from local suppliers in the countries in which it operates.

www.carrefour.com/content/presentation-group-0

An early foray into international expansion, with new stores in Belgium, Italy, Switzerland and the UK, was not particularly successful and the group quickly abandoned this activity to concentrate on its home operations. However, in the mid-1970s a period of organic growth began, with new openings in France, Spain and Brazil. This continued until the early 1980s, with Carrefour opening its first Argentinian and Taiwanese outlets. During this same time period, Carrefour France concentrated on developing new retail concepts and formats that might be adopted in overseas markets. Once such initiative was the change of name in Spain from Carrefour to Pryca. Carrefour was one of the first large retail groups to truly exhibit global ambition.

At the beginning of the 1990s, Carrefour decided to concentrate on growth by acquisition, buying the French chains Montlaur and Euromarché. But Carrefour was not confining its growth to the hypermarket sector. By acquiring Picard Sugelés, a French frozen-food business, Carrefour was signalling its expansion into other retail sectors, such as eyewear, frozen food, discounting, cash and carry, and office supply stores in 15 different countries.

Carrefour's commitment to an international strategy was initially encouraged by problems in developing its domestic business. These difficulties were caused partly by government regulations designed to protect small retailers. For example, tight controls were imposed on the opening of new stores and, in some cases, on the increase of selling space in existing outlets. For Carrefour, this restricted new domestic opportunities to those that could be gleaned through the acquisition of existing businesses. Once these opportunities had been exploited, the only other growth option for Carrefour was to expand overseas.

The international success the business has enjoyed can be attributed to a number of factors. First, the business has been a fast mover in many of the countries in which it has expanded. By carefully choosing the right time to enter new countries, Carrefour has been able to make the most of appropriate retail conditions. Second, Carrefour has consistently applied its proven and well-developed hypermarket and cash and carry concepts. In many cases, by maintaining the same basic operational and marketing characteristics, the business has been able simply to transplant its operation to a new market. However, Carrefour has also shown the flexibility to make appropriate modifications to local taste where required. Finally, the business has a deep-seated commitment to its international expansion strategy.

The 1999 acquisition of Promodes created the world's second largest retail group behind only Wal-Mart of the US. Current successes lie primarily outside France, although the domestic supermarket chain has staged something of a recovery. There has been significant success for Carrefour in Poland and Romania, Argentina, Brazil and now China. Carrefour has a three-pronged strategy: (i) leadership in its domestic French market, (ii) dominance in Spain, Italy and Belgium, which along with France form its so-termed 'G4 countries', and (iii) significant expansion in key fast growing international markets, such as Brazil, China and India.

The Carrefour commitment to expansion means that the business has often been prepared to forgo short-term profits in the interests of longer-term competitive advantage. However, as retail globalization continues, Carrefour will have to continue reacting with speed and flexibility if it is to maintain its position. In particular, as the growing use of the internet and home shopping begin to alter buying behaviour and recession encourages more value-driven consumers and discounting, the

company must address how the hypermarket concept will be able to adapt to changing consumer needs and profiles.

Sources: www.carrefour.com, 5 March 2015 and previous editions.

Questions for discussion

1. What drove Carrefour to expand its businesses internationally?

2. What new international opportunities might be open to Carrefour?

3. To what extent has Carrefour adopted a strategy of globalization?

Postscript

Effective marketing hinges on satisfying customers and establishing relationships. There are many forces at work, however, which affect how organizations endeavour to achieve these goals. Part One of *Marketing: Concepts and Strategies* has explored the nature and scope of the concepts of marketing, marketing orientation and marketing strategy, and gone on to describe the forces of the macro and micro marketing environment and the essential requirements for marketing in global markets.

The focus of *Marketing: Concepts and Strategies* now turns to the customer and the identification of target markets. As outlined in Figure 1.4, the customer must be at the centre of the marketing process. Organizations must target specific groups of customers, understand their needs, and endeavour through their marketing activities to satisfy those needs. It is essential to recognize that a business does not deal with its customers in a vacuum: there are many marketing environment forces at work, affecting the behaviour of customers and those organizations attempting to market to them. The role of technology, in particular, has created many opportunities for marketers to communicate with customers and build relationships. For businesses operating across national borders, involved with marketing in global markets, the impact of these forces and the trading decisions required are even more complex. These are the issues that have been examined in Part One.

Before progressing, readers should be confident that they are now able to do the following.

Define and explain the marketing concept

- Define marketing.
- Appreciate the context of marketing and marketing orientation.
- Explain the marketing process.
- Understand the importance of marketing.
- Gain insight into the basic elements of the marketing concept and its implementation.
- Understand how the marketing concept has evolved and some of the current 'hot' themes.
- Appreciate the major components of a marketing strategy and the marketing mix.
- Gain a sense of general strategic marketing issues, such as market opportunily analysis,

target market selection and marketing mix development.

- Grasp the ethos and structure of this book.

Define and explain the nature of marketing strategy

- Define marketing strategy and explore the relationship with a company's organizational mission, goals and corporate strategy.
- Assess organizational opportunities, capabilities and the SWOT analysis.
- Consider strategic objectives.
- Appreciate the role of target market strategy, customer value and brand positioning in marketing strategy.
- Examine competitive advantage, competitive positions and differential advantage.
- Explore marketing objectives and understand the role of marketing mix programmes in marketing strategy.
- Understand the importance of implementation and performance monitoring in marketing strategy.

Outline the forces at work in the marketing environment

- Understand the concept of the marketing environment and the importance of environmental scanning and analysis.
- Explore the broad forces of the macro marketing environment: political forces relevant to marketers, the influence of laws on marketing practices, the impact of government regulations and regulatory agencies, societal issues important to marketers, the effects of new technology on society and marketing activities, economic and competitive factors and their impact on organizations and customers' willingness and ability to buy.
- Examine the company-specific micro marketing environment forces: the competitive pressures facing an organization in terms of the supply chain, marketing intermediaries, competitors and from other publics.
- Understand the role of the marketing environment in marketing opportunity analysis and the importance of strategic windows in marketing strategy.

Describe the additional complexities facing marketers engaged in international markets

● Define international marketing and understand the nature of international involvement.

● Understand the importance of international marketing intelligence.

● Recognize the impact of environmental forces on international marketing efforts.

● Become aware of regional trade alliances and markets.

● Look at alternative market entry strategies for becoming involved in international marketing activities.

● Appreciate that international marketing strategies fall along a continuum from customization to globalization.

● Understand the growing importance of international cooperation.

McDonald's marketing serves up global and local profits

Strategic case

Serving 69 million customers in 36 000 locations worldwide may be a tall order, but it is just an ordinary day for McDonald's. Facing intense competition from traditional fast-food rivals like Burger King and KFC, and casual dining chains like Pizza Express or Pizza Hut, McDonald's never stops looking for new ways to reinforce customer loyalty and build profits. While not everyone is a fan, it is difficult to dispute the marketing success story that is McDonald's, a brand found today around the world and employing 1.8 million staff.

> McDonald's customer-focused Plan to Win provides a common framework that aligns our global business and allows for local adaptation. We continue to focus on our three global growth priorities of optimizing our menu, modernizing the customer experience, and broadening accessibility to Brand McDonald's within the framework of our Plan. Our initiatives support these priorities, and are executed with a focus on the Plan's five pillars – People, Products, Place, Price and Promotion – to enhance our customers' experience and build shareholder value over the long term. We believe these priorities align with our customers' evolving needs, and – combined with our competitive advantages of convenience, menu variety, geographic diversification and system alignment – will drive long-term sustainable growth.

> www.aboutmcdonalds.com/mcd/investors/company
> _profile.html, March 2015

What's in store?

One key to McDonald's success is its menu of core items that are inextricably linked to the McDonald's brand and other items that are adapted to regional tastes. In Moscow, consumers have made Fresh McMuffin sausage sandwiches a top-selling morning item. In Argentina, the Ranchero hamburger sandwich, with a special salsa sauce, is a particular customer favourite. In France, the Croque McDo is McDonald's version of the popular Croque Monsieur hot ham-and-cheese sandwich.

Although McDonald's built its reputation on burgers and fries, its marketers recognize that many consumers have become more health conscious. That's why McDonald's has developed lighter fast-food fare for adults and children alike, including new salads, wrap sandwiches and apple slices. The company now posts nutrition information online for consumers and has changed its cooking oil so that all fried items have zero grams of trans-fats per serving.

Ready for customers early, late, and on the go

Another way McDonald's has increased sales and profits is by opening stores early to serve the breakfast crowd and keeping selected stores open until midnight or later. Some of its units operate drive-through services 24 hours a day. In China, where McDonald's has more than 1 400 outlets, late-night hours are popular and have helped the company significantly increase revenues. Also, McDonald's sees drive-through lanes as an important competitive element in China, where car ownership is growing fast and competitors like KFC have few drive-through locations. Now half of the new stores McDonald's opens in China are equipped for drive-through operations. Under an agreement with state-owned Sinopec, McDonald's is adding drive-through outlets at Sinopec gas stations all around China.

Dealing with the dollar menu

In the US, to appeal to its customers who have very tight budgets, McDonald's offers a Dollar Menu. The idea is to 'bring in consumers who are looking for ways to stretch their wallets', explains the company's president. In fact, the Dollar Menu items account for more than 10 per cent of overall sales in US restaurants. However, with food prices rising and other costs inching upwards, some McDonald's franchisees complain that they are earning low profit margins on Dollar Menu items. Under the terms of their franchise agreements with McDonald's, franchisees are free to charge more (or less) than the corporation's official Dollar Menu price. Therefore, some stores in high-cost markets charge $1.29 or $1.39 for the Double Cheeseburger that in other areas sells for $1.

Rising costs are a problem for McDonald's international stores as well. In Russia, for example, McDonald's boosts menu prices multiple times in a year to cope with inflation that drives up the costs of food. The company increases the price of less-expensive menu items by about half the inflation rate but increases the price of premium menu items by more than the inflation rate because, according to one executive, 'We still have a huge amount of people who are price sensitive'. Despite the price hikes, the McDonald's in Moscow's Pushkin Square remains the busiest McDonald's on the planet (except when politics intervene and the Russian Government falls out with anything American), with 26 cash registers and seating for 900.

Social responsibility on the menu

Ronald McDonald is one of the world's most recognizable brand mascots. Not only does he appear in McDonald's marketing communications, but he also headlines the company's Ronald McDonald House Charities, which provide accommodation for families while their critically ill children are treated in hospitals far from home. The non-profit group, now more than three decades old, operates houses in 52 nations. Local McDonald's outlets support neighbourhood charities and community causes as well.

Prodded in part by animal activists, the company has established animal-handling standards for its meat suppliers. It's also going green by using paper and cardboard packaging made from recycled materials. To showcase its charitable and environmental activities, the company issues a yearly corporate responsibility report and publicizes achievements such as raising millions of dollars on World Children's Day.

Blogging about beef

McDonald's has a strong presence on the internet, with a corporate website, products and nutrition websites and individual websites geared to each country where it does business. To generate grassroots word-of-mouth communications about food and service quality, it has enlisted *Mom's Quality Correspondents* to go behind the scenes at headquarters, suppliers' facilities and individual McDonald's stores. The 'mums' consumers are free to look around, ask questions, videotape what they see and then blog about their experiences, including video snippets.

These bloggers can say whatever they like because, says a McDonald's marketing official, 'if mums were out there speaking to their communities and online communities unedited, it would get us far more credibility that just posting an article or doing website copy'. For example, after the 'mums' travelled to a McDonald's beef supplier in Oklahoma City, one wrote on the blog, 'Hey, moms across America it is really 100 per cent beef!'

McDonald's also maintains a corporate social responsibility blog where its managers post informal notes about issues such as environmental programmes, healthy lifestyles and responsible purchasing. When consumers post comments in response to these blogs, the resulting dialogue helps McDonald's to better understand public sentiment surrounding such issues and to plan appropriate actions and communications.

Our food. Your questions

A recent push to open up McDonald's to questions has encouraged operating companies to create Q&A websites and to provide interesting facts about the company's food. For example, its eggs at breakfast are not reconstituted as many consumers assumed, but are made from freshly cracked eggs cooked in round moulds to provide muffin-shaped eggs.

Selling the Arch Card

Although McDonald's has sold gift certificates for many years, it now has a corporate sales division that targets businesses that want to give small incentives to employees or customers. The incentive programme that McDonald's offers is its Arch Card, a prepaid gift card issued in the amount of $5, $10, $25 or $50. Businesses can buy up to 25 Arch Cards through local McDonald's outlets. The corporate sales division handles bulk purchases and gives business customers a discount if they buy $10 000 worth of Arch Cards. After recipients spend the initial gift amount they can pay to reload up to $110 on each card. The next time they visit a McDonald's restaurant, they'll be ready to grab and go with just a swipe of plastic.

Questions for discussion

1. How is McDonald's using marketing to spark learning and positive attitudes toward its brand and offerings?

2. Why would McDonald's select businesses rather than consumers as a target market for its Arch Cards?

3. What environmental forces have created challenges for McDonald's in global markets? What forces have created opportunities in global markets?

Sources: www.mcdonalds.com/us/en/your_questions/our_food.html; www.mcdonalds.com/us; www.mcdonalds.co.uk, March 2015.

PART TWO
Understanding and targeting customers

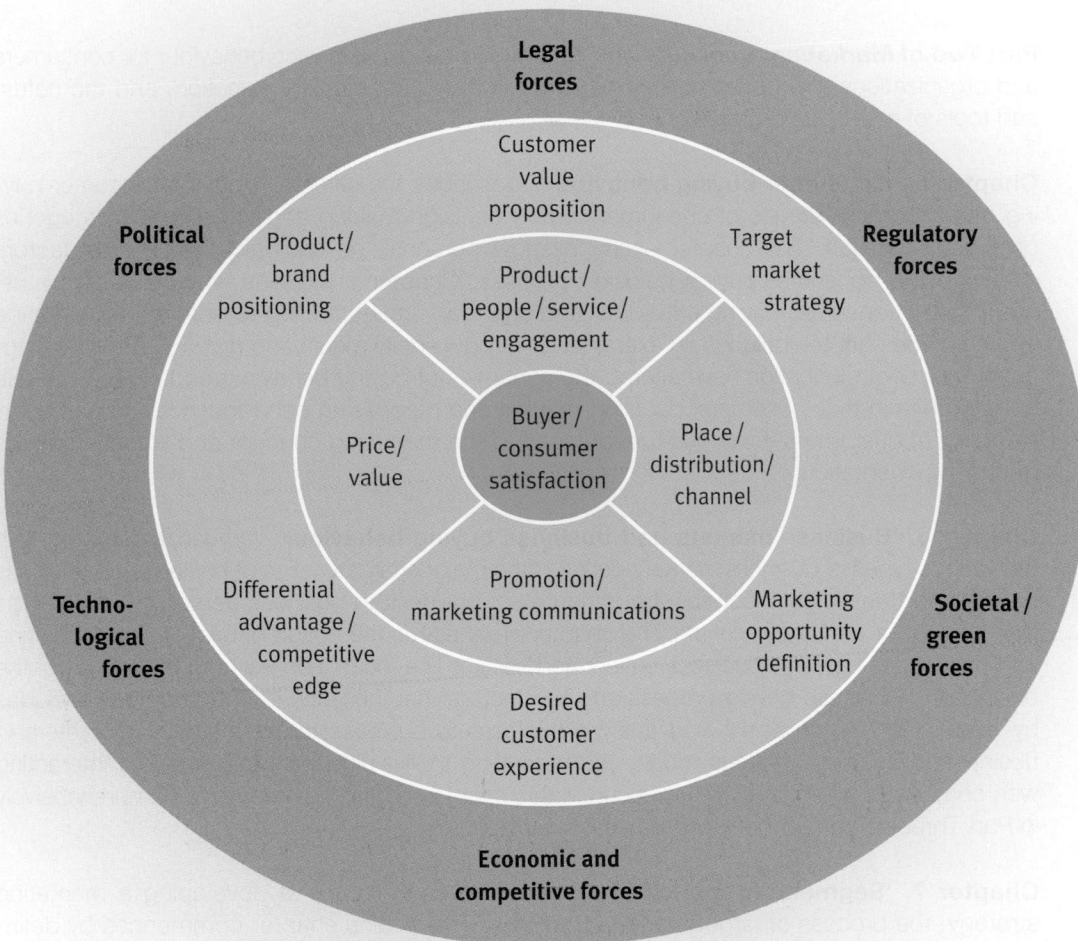

As outlined in the above figure, customers must be at the centre of the marketing process. Organizations – whether for-profit or not-for-profit – must target specific groups of customers, target audiences or stakeholders, understand their needs and endeavour through their marketing activities to satisfy these customer needs.

Part Two of *Marketing: Concepts and Strategies* commences with a thorough examination of the nature of consumer buying behaviour and buying processes, and continues to examine the nature of buying in business-to-business or organizational markets. Having developed an understanding of a marketplace and particularly the customers within it, marketers must then develop a target market strategy. This should identify which customers they wish to target, what positioning they intend to use and which approach will provide an advantage over competitors. Part Two includes, therefore, an examination of target market strategy selection and the all-important concept of market segmentation. The segmentation process embraces targeting decisions and brand positioning strategy. There are times when managers' existing knowledge of their customers is sufficient for marketing decision-making, or when they are content to trust their intuition. On many occasions, however, marketers may not feel confident with the level of marketing intelligence available and will instigate research into the market in order to fill any gaps in their understanding of customers, competitors or market trends. The nature, uses and types of marketing research are introduced in the final chapter of Part Two of *Marketing: Concepts and Strategies*.

Part Two of *Marketing: Concepts and Strategies* examines buying behaviour for consumers and organizations, the issues concerned with target market strategy selection, and the nature and tools of marketing research.

Chapter 5, 'Consumer buying behaviour', describes the different types of consumer buying behaviour, the stages of consumer buying decision-making and the different categories of buying decision. The chapter examines how personal, psychological and social factors influence the consumer buying decision process. Chapter 5 explains why marketers must understand consumer buying behaviour and use their understanding to determine marketing strategy. The chapter includes an examination of how social media and growing consumer-to-consumer communication have altered the dynamics of buying behaviour and indeed the role of marketers in their cusomers' decision-making and purchasing behaviour. Having an understanding of customers' buying is fundamental to the marketing concept and to developing a marketing orientation.

Chapter 6, 'Business markets and business buying behaviour', familiarizes readers with the various types of business market, identifies the major characteristics of business-to-business buyers and transactions, outlines the attributes of business-to-business demand and presents the concept of the buying centre. The chapter emphasizes the notion of relationship marketing and exchanges between business buyers and sellers. The focus then shifts to the stages of the business-to-business buying process and the factors that influence it. The chapter concludes by examining how to select and analyze business-to-business target markets. Marketers in business-to-business markets modify the marketing toolkit differently to marketers interacting with consumers: this theme is introduced in this chapter, but is explored more comprehensively in Part Three of *Marketing: Concepts and Strategies*.

Chapter 7, 'Segmenting markets', explains the core aspect of developing a marketing strategy: the process of target market strategy selection. The chapter commences by defining the concept of a market and outlining the various types of market. The focus then shifts to how organizations segment markets and identify target markets. Finally, the chapter discusses the importance of maintaining a strong relationship with those markets, segments and customers deemed to be priority targets, along with the related topic of customer relationship management (CRM).

Chapter 8, 'Targeting and positioning' builds from Chapter 7 to explore the rest of the segmentation process, namely targeting criteria and target market selection, and brand positioning strategy. It first explores the available strategies for addressing a market and the opportunities identified. Positioning strives to ensure targeted consumers or business customers empathize with the brand and customer value proposition that is offered to them, and that the brand has a compelling and differentiated image or appeal. The chapter also highlights the importance of understanding market and sales potential in target market selection.

Chapter 9, 'Marketing research', explains the importance of research in marketing decision-making, distinguishes between research and intuition in solving marketing problems, and outlines the five basic steps for conducting formal marketing research. The fundamental methods of gathering data for marketing research are examined. The chapter then introduces the wide variety of marketing research tools available and explains their relative pros and cons.

By the conclusion of Part Two of *Marketing: Concepts and Strategies*, readers should understand the concepts of buying behaviour in consumer and business-to-business markets, the fundamentals of target market strategy selection and brand positioning and the essentials of marketing research necessary to glean customer insight. Arguably many of the most important concepts for marketing are located in Chapters 5 to 8.

CHAPTER 5
Consumer buying behaviour

"Getting into the heads and hearts of consumers is the fundamental requirement of marketing"

Objectives

- To understand the different types of consumer buying behaviour.

- To recognize the stages of the consumer buying decision process and understand how this process relates to different types of buying decisions.

- To explore how personal factors may affect the consumer buying decision process.

- To learn about the psychological factors that may affect the consumer buying decision process.

- To examine the social factors that influence the consumer buying decision process.

- To understand why it is important for marketers to attempt to understand consumer buying behaviour and the role of this behaviour in marketing strategy.

- To appreciate the growing role of consumer-to-consumer communication, social media and the digital environment regarding buying behaviour.

- To also understand the growing impact of consumer-to-consumer communication on the buying choices that consumers make.

INTRODUCTION

The decision processes and actions of people involved in buying and using products are termed their **buying behaviour**.[1] **Consumer buying behaviour** is the buying behaviour of ultimate consumers – those who purchase products for personal or household family use. Consumer buying behaviour is not concerned with the purchase of items for business use. The next chapter of *Marketing: Concepts and Strategies* examines business or organizational buying behaviour.

Buying behaviour
The decision processes and actions of people involved in buying and using products.

Consumer buying behaviour
The buying behaviour of ultimate consumers – those who purchase products for personal or household use.

There are important reasons for marketers to analyze consumer buying behaviour. The success of a company's marketing strategy will depend on how buyers react to it. As Chapter 1 indicated, the marketing concept requires companies to develop a marketing mix that meets customers' needs. To find out what satisfies customers, marketers must examine the main influences on what, where, when and how consumers buy. Having a good understanding of all of these factors enables marketers to satisfy customers better because they are able to develop more suitable marketing strategies. Ultimately, this information helps companies compete more effectively in the marketplace.

Although marketers try to understand and influence consumer buying behaviour, they cannot control it. Some critics credit them with the ability to manipulate buyers, but marketers have neither the power nor the knowledge to do so. Their knowledge of behaviour comes from what psychologists, social psychologists and sociologists know about human behaviour in general.

Raleigh cycles to stay in touch with consumers

From its 19th century roots as a British bicycle company, Raleigh has developed a worldwide reputation for marketing sturdy, comfortable, steel-frame bicycles. The firm, named after the street in Nottingham, England, where it was originally located, was a trend-setter in designing and manufacturing bicycles. Despite being an iconic brand, the company has to keep a close eye on changing consumer tastes and behaviour. As a result of these insights and inspired by the European tradition of getting around by bike, Raleigh is developing new models for contemporary consumers that are lighter, faster and better.

Raleigh's marketers know how important it is for consumers to find out about and try out their products. In recent years they have stepped up the practice of bringing demonstration fleets to public places where potential buyers can hop on one of the company's bicycles and pedal for a few minutes. The idea is to allow consumers who enjoy bicycling to actually experience the fun feeling of riding a Raleigh. As Raleigh sought to increase its share of the US bike market, it sent representatives out to visit bicycle races and meet cyclists in cities and towns across America. The company wanted to encourage discussion about Raleigh and about cycling in general, so that it could gain feedback on Raleigh products and on the factors which influence purchase.

To stay in touch with current and potential customers, Raleigh has increased its social media activity. It has many thousands of visitors to its Facebook page to see the latest product concepts and post their own photos and comments about Raleigh bicycles. It also uses Twitter to keep customers informed and answer questions about its bicycles and upcoming demonstration events. The company's main blog communicates the latest news about everything from frame design and new bike colours under consideration to product awards and racing activities.

By listening to customers and showing that it understands the daily life of its target market, Raleigh is developing a better understanding of consumer buying in this marketplace, and wheeling toward higher sales.

Source: www.raleighusa.com/blog

When someone decides to buy a new bicycle, there are many factors directing their choices and numerous underlying motivations. Raleigh must understand these behaviours and influences. Any set of marketers has a responsibility to explore the buying behaviour of intended purchasers and those consumers expected to return for more. Chapter 5 begins by examining the types of decision-making in which consumers engage. The chapter then analyzes the major stages of the consumer buying decision process and the personal, psychological and social factors that influence it. How the growth of social media and consumer-to-consumer communication are changing how individuals buy is considered next. Finally, the chapter examines why marketers must develop a good understanding of consumer buying behaviour.

Types of consumer buying behaviour

Different consumers have a varied and wide range of needs and wants. The acquisition of products and services helps these consumers to satisfy their current and future needs. To achieve this objective, consumers make many purchasing decisions. For example, people make many decisions daily regarding food, clothing, shelter, medical care, education, recreation or transport. When making these decisions, they engage in decision-making behaviour. The amount of time and effort, both mental and physical, that buyers expend in decision-making varies considerably from situation to situation – and from consumer to consumer. Consumer decisions can thus be classified into one of three broad categories: routine response behaviour, limited decision-making and extensive decision-making.[2]

Routine response behaviour

Routine response behaviour
Behaviour that occurs when buying frequently purchased, low-cost, low-risk items that need little search and decision effort.

A consumer practises **routine response behaviour** when buying frequently purchased, low-cost, low-risk items that need very little search and decision effort. When buying such items, a consumer may prefer a particular brand, but will probably be familiar with several brands in the product class and view more than one as acceptable. The products a consumer buys through routine response behaviour are purchased almost automatically. For most buyers, the time and effort involved in selecting a bag of sugar or a bar of soap is minimal. If the supermarket has run out of the preferred brand, the buyers will probably choose an alternative brand instead.

Limited decision-making

Limited decision-making
Behaviour that occurs when buying products purchased only occasionally, for which a moderate amount of information gathering and deliberation is needed.

Buyers engage in **limited decision-making** when they buy products occasionally and when they need to obtain information about an unfamiliar brand in a familiar product category. This type of decision-making requires a moderate amount of time for information gathering and deliberation. For example, when a new Sony PlayStation game is launched aimed at teenagers, buyers may seek additional information about the new product, perhaps by asking a friend who has tried the game or seen it reviewed. Similarly, if a well-known brand appears in a new form, the consumer will take extra time to consider whether to buy it.

Extensive decision-making

Extensive decision-making
Behaviour that occurs when a purchase involves unfamiliar, expensive, high-risk or infrequently bought products for which the buyer spends much time seeking information and comparing brands before deciding on the purchase.

The most complex decision-making behaviour, **extensive decision-making**, comes into play when a purchase involves unfamiliar, expensive, high-risk or infrequently bought products – for instance, cars, homes, holidays or personal pensions. The buyer uses many criteria to evaluate alternative brands or choices, and takes time seeking information and comparing alternative brands before making the purchase decision.

Impulse buying
Behaviour that involves no conscious planning but results from a powerful, persistent urge to buy something immediately.

Impulse buying   By contrast, **impulse buying** involves no conscious planning but a powerful, persistent urge to buy something immediately. Self-control failure is one factor that appears to affect whether or not consumers indulge in this kind of buying.[3] As the Topical Insight box explains, consumers are increasingly engaging in impulse buying. Sophisticated point-of-sales (POS) displays are part of the reason. For some individuals, impulse buying may be the dominant buying behaviour. Impulse buying, however, often provokes emotional conflict. For example, a young woman buying a new outfit for clubbing, may later regret the expense because a friend has purchased the same item or she only uses the outfit once. Marketers often capitalize on the tendency towards impulse buying – for example, by placing magazines and confectionery next to supermarket checkout counters.

Variations in decision-making behaviour

The purchase of a particular product does not always elicit the same type of decision-making behaviour.[4] In some instances, buyers engage in extensive decision-making the first time they purchase a certain kind of product but find that limited decision-making suffices when they buy

Point-of-sale moves into the changing room

Topical insight

When did you last buy something that you spotted on promotion? Consumers who make such purchases are often responding to a point-of-sale (POS) promotion.

POS tools are an important element in this picture. In the past, POS tools were mostly used to offer one-off promotions, such as buy one, get one free. Now a new generation of POS is working much harder to educate consumers about product features, explain how they work, or to deliver messages about product fit with people's lifestyle. Asda promoted Johnson & Johnson baby bath products using a branded bath and rubber duck tray. The recent launch of Dr Dre Beat's 'Mini Pill' WiFi speaker was supported by a specially created POS display, incorporating an illuminated logo, special lighting and a bespoke mp3 player. Meanwhile, Burberry is attempting to inspire consumers about the brand by streaming live images of its fashion shows direct to video walls in its stores.

Technological advances, such as the development of digital signage, have revolutionized the possibilities for POS, which include 3D signage and augmented reality displays.

Fashion retailers are amongst those to benefit from these developments. New Look has added in-store screens that can promote new lines while entertaining store visitors at the same time. The real beauty is that messages can be tailored to suit the location and store catchment and can readily updated to reflect the latest offers.

New technology is even being incorporated into the way that we try on outfits when shopping for clothes with the potential to increase sales.

John Lewis is testing an interactive fitting room mirror which allows customers to view themselves in a variety of garments, so that they don't need to undress to try on different clothes. A range of options and outfits can quickly be viewed, so customers can judge which items fit together well, with the prospect of increasing their spend. The Burberry flagship store in London has incorporated RFID enabled mirrors into its fitting rooms which display content that is relevent to the items being tried on. Meanwhile, lingerie business Boux Avenue has incorporated a new lighting system into its changing rooms. Customers can choose from three different moods of lighting – day, dusk or night – each of which is design to flatter and help them look their best.

As a spokeperson from retail design consultants Dalziel & Pow explained: 'If handled well, both in terms of environment and service, they (changing rooms) can be a valuable asset in terms of tipping the balance of a decision to buy. Flattering lighting, a comfortable atmosphere, helpful staff and event details like the right temperature can add up to a big difference in the bottom line.'

Sources: Gemma Balmford, 'Changing Ways', *Retail Focus*, November 2012, at: www.retail-focus.co.uk/features/671-changing-ways-790; Kate Hilpern, 'POS persuasion', *The Marketer*, May 2011, pp. 28–32; Caroline Parry, 'Enthusiastic for listless shopping', *Marketing Week,* 4 March 2004, pp. 30–1; http://fastrakretail.co.uk/case-studies/dre-beats/.

the product again. If a routinely purchased brand no longer pleases the consumer, either limited or extensive decision processes may be used to switch to a new brand. For example, if the weed killer that a gardener buys to keep his or her allotment free of weeds is no longer effective, a different brand may be chosen in future.

The consumer buying decision process

A major part of buying behaviour is the decision process used in making purchases. The **consumer buying decision process**, shown in Figure 5.1, includes five stages:

Consumer buying decision process
A five-stage process that includes problem recognition, information search, evaluation of alternatives, purchase and post-purchase evaluation.

1. problem recognition
2. information search
3. evaluation of alternatives
4. purchase
5. post-purchase evaluation.

Although a detailed understanding of these stages is needed, a number of general observations are also pertinent. First, the actual act of purchasing is only one stage in

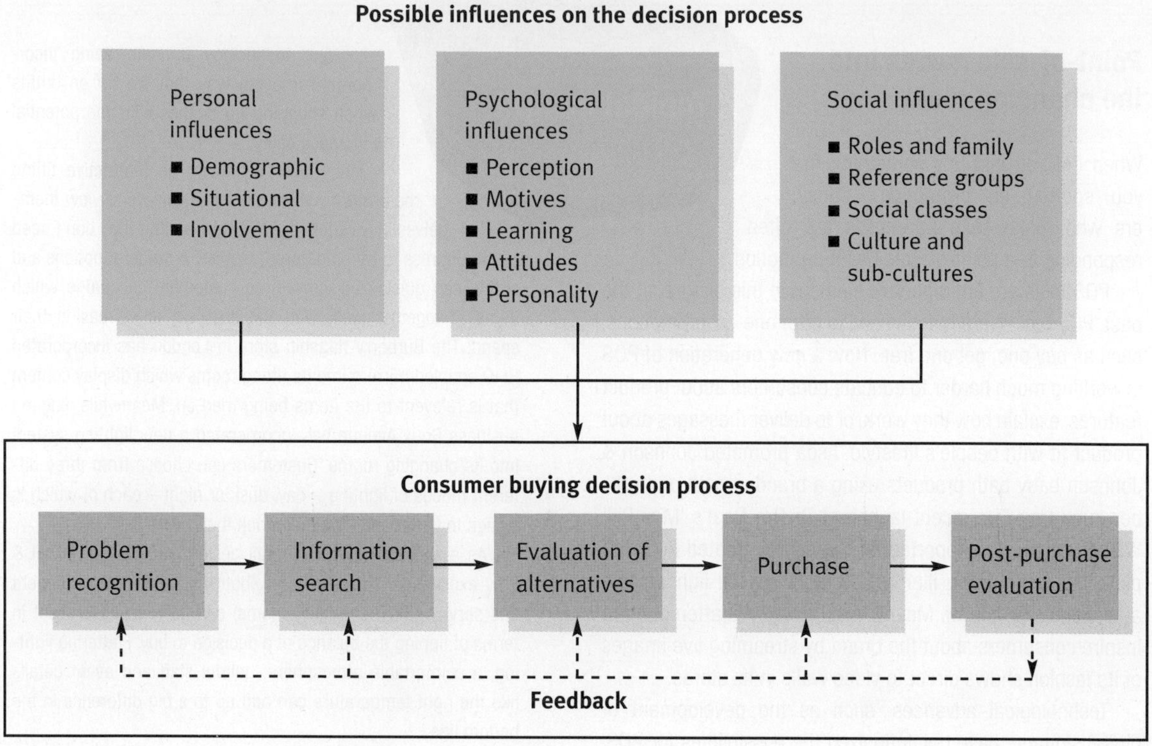

Possible influences on the decision process

FIGURE 5.1

The consumer buying decision process and possible influences on the process

the process; the process begins several stages before the purchase itself. Second, not all decision processes lead to a purchase, even though the diagram implies that they do. A consumer may stop the process at any time, follow a different sequence of stages, or revisit certain stages. Finally, consumer decisions do not always include all five stages. People engaged in extensive decision-making usually go through all stages of this decision process, whereas those engaged in limited decision-making and routine response behaviour may omit certain parts, leaping from problem recognition (need) to purchase.

Stage 1: Problem recognition

Problem recognition occurs when a buyer becomes aware that there is a difference between a desired state and an actual condition. For example, when a driver making deliveries for a florist runs low on fuel for her van, she recognizes that a difference exists between the desired state (sufficent fuel) and the actual condition (an empty tank). She therefore calls at a fuel station to replenish the tank.

Sometimes a person has a problem or need but is unaware of it. Some consumers may be concerned about their weight but may not be aware that low-calorie options exist for favourite products or that there are mobile apps available to help monitor their eating habits. Marketers use sales staff, advertising, sales promotion and packaging to help trigger such need recognition. This is why weightloss clubs such as Weight Watchers advertise their services after national holidays, a time when people might have over-indulged. Consumer problem recognition can be either slow or rapid, depending on the individual concerned and the way in which need recognition was triggered.

FIGURE 5.2
Along with the web, travel agents provide a valuable source of information for consumers selecting a holiday

Stage 2: Information search

After recognizing the problem or need, the buyer (if continuing the decision process) searches for information about products that will resolve the problem or satisfy the need. For example, consumers who have recognized they need to lose weight may search online for information about different weight loss clubs or peruse the supermarket for low calorie meals. Information is acquired over time from the consumers' surroundings. The impact the information has will depend on how the consumers interpret it.

Internal search
One in which the buyer searches his or her memory for information about products.

External search
One that focuses on information not available from the consumer's memory.

There are two aspects to information search. In the **internal search**, buyers search their memory for information about products that might solve the problem. If they cannot retrieve enough information from their memory to make a decision, they seek additional information in an **external search**. The external search may involve communicating with friends and colleagues, comparing available brands and prices, looking at online offers, reading reviews on social networking sites or reviewing press advertisements. An individual's personal contacts – friends, relatives, associates – are often viewed as credible sources of information because the consumer trusts and respects them. A consumer study has shown that word-of-mouth communication often impacts more strongly on consumer judgements of products than printed communications. Using marketer-dominated information sources, such as sales staff, advertising, packaging, corporate websites, in-store demonstrations and displays, typically does not require much effort on the consumers' part. Buyers can also obtain information from public sources – for instance, government reports, news stories, the internet, consumer publications and reports from product testing organizations. Many companies use public relations to try to capitalize on these sources because consumers often perceive them as factual and unbiased. The external search is also characterized by the extensiveness, manner and order in which brands, stores, attributes and sources are considered. For example, a man buying a new suit for work may look at or try on several styles at a number of clothing outlets before reaching a final decision.

Consumer groups are increasingly demanding access to greater quantities of relevant product information. However, research shows that buyers make poorer choices if overloaded with too much information.[5] Improving the quality of information and stressing features important to buyers in the decision process may help buyers make better purchase decisions.

How consumers use and process the information obtained in their search depends on features of the information itself, namely availability, quantity, quality, repetition and format. If all the necessary information for a decision is readily to hand, either in-store or online, consumers may have no need to conduct an internal information search and the decision process may be easier.[6] However, adequate information may not always be available, and consumers may have to make do with whatever data are to hand. For example, a motorist replacing a broken windscreen following a road accident may not have enough time to review all relevant sources of information because the car is needed again urgently.

Repetition　Repetition, a technique well known to advertisers, increases consumer learning of information. When seeing or hearing an advertisement for the first time, the recipient may not grasp all its important details but learns more as the message is repeated. Nevertheless, even when commercials are initially effective, repetition eventually causes 'wear-out': consumers pay less attention and respond less favourably to the advertisement than they did at first.[7] Consumers are more likely to be receptive to repetition when making a low-involvement purchase. **Involvement** refers to the level of interest, emotion and activity the consumer is prepared to expend on a particular purchase. For example, consumers who buy replacement lightbulbs may buy whatever brand is stocked at their local store.

Involvement
The level of interest, emotion and activity the consumer is prepared to expend on a particular purchase.

Format　The format in which information is transmitted to the buyer may also determine its effectiveness. Information can be presented verbally, numerically or visually. Consumers often remember pictures better than words, and the combination of pictures and words further enhances learning.[8] Consequently, marketers pay great attention to the visual components of their advertising materials.

A successful information search yields a group of possible brand alternatives. This group of products is sometimes called the buyer's **evoked set**. For example, an evoked set of hairdryers might be those manufactured by Babyliss, Braun and Remington.

Evoked set
The group of products that a buyer views as possible alternatives after conducting an information search.

Stage 3: Evaluation of alternatives

When evaluating the products in the evoked set, a buyer establishes criteria for comparing the products. These criteria are the characteristics or features that the buyer wants (or does not want). For example, one buyer may favour a compact hairdryer because they travel a lot, while another may prefer a high-powered model. The buyer also assigns a certain **salience**, or level of importance, to each criterion; some features carry more weight than others. The salience of criteria varies from buyer to buyer. For example, when choosing a newspaper one buyer may consider the political stance of the editorial to be crucial, while another may place greater importance on the quality and coverage of sports. The criteria and their salience are used by the buyer to rank the brands in the evoked set. This involves comparing the brands with each other as well as with the criteria. If the evaluation stage does not yield a brand that the buyer wishes to buy, further information search may be necessary.

Salience
The level of importance a buyer assigns to each criterion for comparing products.

Marketers can influence consumers' evaluation by *framing* the alternatives – that is, by the manner in which the alternative and its attributes are described. Framing can make a characteristic seem more important and can facilitate its recall from memory. For example, by emphasizing whitening ingredients in toothpaste, manufacturers can encourage the consumer to consider this particular aspect to be important. Framing affects the decision processes of inexperienced buyers more than those of experienced ones. If the evaluation of alternatives yields one or more brands that the consumer is willing to buy, the consumer is ready to move on to the purchase stage.

Stage 4: Purchase

The purchase stage, when the consumer chooses which product or brand to buy, is mainly the outcome of the consumer's evaluation of alternatives, but other factors have an impact too. The closeness of alternative stores and product availability can both influence which brand is purchased. For example, if the brand the buyer ranked highest is not available locally, an alternative may be selected.

During this stage, the buyer also picks the seller from whom the product will be purchased and finalizes the terms of the sale. Other issues such as price, delivery, guarantees, service agreements, installation and credit arrangements are discussed and settled. Finally, provided the consumer does not terminate the buying decision process before then, the purchase is made.

Stage 5: Post-purchase evaluation

After the purchase has taken place, the buyer begins evaluating the product to check whether its actual performance meets expected levels. Many of the criteria used in evaluating alternatives are revisited during this stage. The outcome will determine whether the consumer is satisfied or dissatisfied, and will influence future behaviour. The level of satisfaction a consumer experiences will determine whether they make a complaint, communicate with other possible buyers or purchase the product again.[9] Figure 5.3 illustrates the types of action that dissatisfied consumers may take. The likelihood that consumers will stop buying a particular product will depend on a range of factors, including how much knowledge they have about alternatives.[10] Some marketing experts believe that increasing consumer assertiveness is a positive move, which illustrates industry's willingness to respond to feedback about products and services.[11] As consumers routinely now share their product experiences via social media, marketers must increasingly be ready to respond.[12] The impact of post-purchase evaluation is illustrated by the feedback loop in Figure 5.1.

Cognitive dissonance
Doubts that occur as the buyer questions whether he or she made the right decision in purchasing the product or service.

The evaluation that follows the purchase of some products, particularly expensive or important items, may result in **cognitive dissonance** – doubts that occur because the buyer questions whether the best purchase decision was made. For example, after buying a branded football shirt from a market stall, a consumer may worry about whether the item is genuine. A buyer who experiences cognitive dissonance may attempt to return the product or may seek positive information about it to justify the choice. For example, motoring journalists often note with amusement that car shows and exhibitions are frequented by consumers who have recently purchased a new car.

As shown in Figure 5.1, three major categories of influence are believed to affect the consumer buying decision process: personal, psychological and social factors. These factors determine which particular coffee, shampoo, mobile apps, cleaning products, holiday, car or house a particular consumer will buy. Understanding these aspects helps marketers gain valuable insights into their customer base and can help ensure that a more suitable marketing mix is developed. The remainder of this chapter focuses on these factors. Although each major factor is discussed separately, it is a combination of their effects that influences the consumer buying decision process.

FIGURE 5.3
The nature of customer complaints

Source: A recent survey of customer dissatisfaction and complaint behaviours for a retailer of consumer electronics.

Personal factors influencing the buying decision process

Personal influencing factors are unique to a particular person. Many different personal factors can influence purchasing decisions. In this section, three types are considered: demographic factors, situational factors and level of involvement.

Demographic factors

Demographic factors are individual characteristics such as age, sex, race, ethnic origin, income, family life cycle and occupation. (These and other characteristics are discussed in Chapter 7 as possible segmentation variables.) Given the potential impact of such features on buying requirements and behaviour, marketing professionals must develop a clear understanding of them.

Demographic factors have a bearing on who is involved in family decision-making. For example, the UK, Germany and Turkey are some of the largest markets for children's toys and clothes in the EU, based on the number of children in the population. Children aged 6 to 17 are known to have growing influence in the buying decision process for breakfast cereals, ice cream, soft drinks, holidays and even the family car.[13] This influence is increasingly reflected in the way such products are designed and marketed. For example, the packaging of many breakfast cereals includes pictures and competitions designed to appeal to children and teenagers. Demographic factors may also shape behaviour during a specific stage of the decision process. For example, during information search, a young person may consult more information sources than an older, more experienced adult.

Demographic factors also affect the manner in which products in a specific product category are used. While consumers aged 20 to 30 may spend a lot of their disposable income on necessities for establishing their households, such as furniture, appliances and DIY products, those aged 45 to 54 whose children have left home spend more on luxury and leisure items.[14] Brand preferences, retailer choice and timing of purchases are also affected by demographic factors. Consider, for example, how differences in occupation result in variations in product needs. A teacher and a plumber may earn similar incomes, yet spend their earnings entirely differently. While both require work clothes, the plumber will buy heavy-duty boots and overalls, while the teacher opts for a smarter, more formal wear. Their choice of vehicle is also likely to differ. While the plumber selects a basic but robust van to carry tools and other equipment, the teacher only needs to transport books and papers to his or her place of work.

Situational factors

Situational factors are the external circumstances or conditions that exist when a consumer is making a purchase decision. These factors can influence the buyer at any stage of the consumer buying decision process and may cause the individual to shorten, lengthen or terminate the process. For example, a commuter who usually buys her take-out coffee from Starbucks may be forced to go elsewhere when her local branch is refurbished.

Similarly, a family trip to the movies may have to be postponed if one of the family members is ill. The effects of situational factors can be felt throughout the buying decision process. Uncertainty about employment may sway a consumer against making a purchase. On the other hand, a conviction that the supply of a particular product is sharply limited may impel an individual to buy it. Consumers have purchased and hoarded fuel, food products and even toilet tissue when these products were believed to be in short supply. These and other situational factors can change rapidly; their influence on purchase decisions can be sudden and short-lived.

The amount of time a consumer has available to make a decision strongly influences buying decisions. If there is little time for selecting and purchasing a product, an individual may quickly decide to buy a readily available brand. The time available also affects the way consumers process the information contained in advertisements[15] and the length of the stages within the decision process. For example, if a family is planning to redecorate its house, everyone may get together to collect and review a wide range of information from a variety of sources. They may read home and garden magazines, visit DIY outlets to collect paint charts and wallpaper samples, talk to friends and decorators, look at a number of advertisements and spend time comparing special offers in-store and online. However, if the family has just moved to a new house that urgently needs renovating, the extent of the information search, the number of alternatives considered and the amount of comparative shopping may be more restricted.

Levels of involvement

Level of involvement
The level of interest, emotional commitment and time spent searching for a product in a particular situation.

Many aspects of consumer buying decisions are affected by the individual's **level of involvement**. This term refers to the level of interest, emotional commitment and time spent searching for a product in a particular situation. The level of involvement determines the extent to which a buyer is motivated to spend time seeking information about a particular product or brand. The extensiveness of the buying decision process therefore varies greatly with the consumer's level of involvement. The sequence of the steps in the process may also be altered. Low-involvement buyers may form an attitude towards a product – perhaps as a result of an advertising campaign – and evaluate its features after purchasing it rather than before.[16] Conversely, high-involvement buyers often spend a great deal of time and effort researching their purchase beforehand. For example, the purchase of a car is a high involvement decision.

The level of consumer involvement is linked to a number of factors. Consumers tend to be more involved in the purchase of high-priced goods and products that are visible to others, such as fashion items, electronic goods or cars. As levels of perceived risk associated with a purchase increase, involvement levels are likely to rise.

Enduring involvement   Sometimes individuals experience enduring involvement with a product class. Enduring involvement is an ongoing interest in a product class because of personal relevance. For example, people often have enduring involvement with products associated with their leisure activities. These individuals engage in ongoing search and information gathering for these products over extensive periods of time, irrespective of whether or not a purchase is imminent. Football fans often watch the sport on television, attend their local club's games, read the football pages of the newspaper and may even buy their favourite team's football strip.

Situational involvement   Situational involvement is experienced by buyers as a result of the particular circumstance or environment in which they find themselves. This type of involvement, sometimes also called pre-purchase involvement, is temporary because the conditions that triggered this high involvement may change.[17] A man searching for an engagement ring for his prospective fiancée, for example, will probably experience a high level of involvement in the purchase decision. His information search and evaluation of alternatives may be lengthy. However, once the choice is made, an engagement ring is probably no longer personally relevant.

Low consumer involvement   Many purchase decisions do not generate much consumer involvement. When the involvement level is low, as with routine response purchases, the buying is almost automatic, and the information search and evaluation of alternatives are extremely limited. Thus the purchase of bottled water is low involvement for many consumers; the product is chosen out of habit and with minimal effort.

FIGURE 5.4

The purchase of a car is high involvement, particularly for those utilizing innovative energy solutions

Source: Toyota (GB) PLC for a Toyota Prius image. Reproduced with permission from Toyota (GB) PLC.

Psychological factors influencing the buying decision process

Psychological factors
Factors that influence consumer behaviour, including perception, motives, learning, attitudes and personality.

Psychological factors operating within individuals partly determine people's general behaviour and thus influence their behaviour as consumers. The primary psychological influences on consumer behaviour are:

- perception
- motives
- learning
- attitudes
- personality.

Even though these psychological factors operate internally, it will become apparent later in this chapter that they are highly affected by social forces external to the individual.

Perception

Are the fish in Figure 5.5 changing into birds or are the birds changing into fish? It could be either depending on how you perceive the birds. People's perception of the same thing varies.

FIGURE 5.5
Fish or birds? Do you see the fish changing into birds or the birds changing into fish?

Perception
The process of selecting, organizing and interpreting information inputs to produce meaning.

Information inputs
The sensations received through sight, taste, hearing, smell and touch.

Selective exposure
The selection of inputs that people expose to their awareness.

Selective distortion
The changing or twisting of currently received information.

Selective retention
The process of remembering information inputs that support personal feelings and beliefs, and of forgetting those that do not.

Similarly, the same individual at different times may perceive the same item in a number of ways. **Perception** involves a three-step process of selecting, organizing and interpreting information inputs to produce meaning.

Information inputs are the sensations received through sight, taste, hearing, smell and touch. Each time we see an advertisement, go online, visit shops or use a product, we receive information inputs.

The first step of the perceptual process is the selection of information. Individuals receive numerous pieces of information all the time, yet only a few of these reach awareness. Certain inputs are selected while others are ignored. **Selective exposure** occurs because consumers cannot be conscious of all inputs at the same time, and involves the selection of inputs that are to be exposed to awareness. A student typing a report may be unaware that the light is on, that the computer is making a humming sound, that there is background noise in the room or that other students are working at the same table. All of these inputs are being received, but the student will ignore them unless his or her attention is specifically drawn to them.

An input is more likely to reach awareness if it relates to an anticipated event or relates to current needs. A couple who are moving house are much more likely to notice a newspaper advertisement promoting removal services. Similarly, thirsty people are more likely to notice a billboard advertising a soft drink or a café that they pass than are those who are not thirsty.

Finally, an input is more likely to be noticed if its intensity changes significantly. Consumers are much more likely to notice if a gym or health club cuts its prices by half than if the same facility offers a much smaller reduction. The selective nature of perception leads to two other conditions: selective distortion and selective retention. **Selective distortion** is the changing or twisting of currently received information. This sometimes happens when someone receives information that is inconsistent with personal feelings or beliefs. For example, an individual who reads some favourable publicity about a company he or she dislikes is likely to distort the information to make it more consistent with personally held views. The publicity may therefore have greater impact on another consumer who views the same brand more positively. **Selective retention** means that an individual remembers information inputs that support personal feelings and beliefs, and forgets inputs that do not. After hearing a sales presentation and leaving the shop, a customer may forget many of the selling points if they contradict pre-existing beliefs. The information inputs that do reach awareness are not received in an organized form. For them to be meaningful, an individual must enter the second step of the perceptual process – organizing and integrating the new information with that already stored in the memory. Although this step is usually carried out quickly, it may take longer when the individual is considering an unfamiliar product area.

Interpretation – the third step in the perceptual process – is the assignment of meaning to what has been organized. All consumers base their interpretation on what is familiar, on knowledge already stored in memory. For this reason, a company that changes a package design or logo can face major problems. Since people look for the product in the old, familiar package, they may not recognize it in the new one. Companies often try to get around this difficulty by making only small changes to their logo or brand identity. Unless a package or logo change is accompanied by a promotional programme making people aware of the change, sales may be lost. Even when such a programme is conducted, positive consumer reaction cannot be guaranteed. When Gap gave its logo a makeover, consumers were quick to insist that the old logo be reinstated. An online social media backlash quickly showed that the company had got it wrong. Initially, Gap decided to use crowdsourcing to help solve its branding crisis, by seeking the consumers' views. In practice, Gap quickly made the decision to return to the original logo only a week later.

Although marketers cannot control people's perceptions, they often try to influence them. This may be difficult to achieve for a number of reasons. First, a consumer's perceptual process may prevent the information from being received. Second, a buyer may receive the information but perceive it differently from the way that was intended. For example, when an anti-wrinkle face cream manufacturer advertises that '80 per cent of consumers using this product notice a reduction in wrinkles', a customer might infer that 20 per cent of the people who use the product have more wrinkles. Third, buyers who perceive information inputs to be inconsistent with their personally held beliefs tend to forget the information quickly. Sometimes consumers can be over-whelmed by the large number of information inputs they encounter, making it difficult to interpret the information.[18] For example, a lifestyle magazine may contain dozens of different advertisements, but a consumer reading it may notice only one or two. In addition to perceptions about packages, products, brands and organizations, individuals also have self-perceptions. These perceptions are known as the **self-concept** or self-image.

Self-concept
A person's perception of him or her-self; self-image.

The results of some studies suggest that buyers purchase products that reflect and enhance their self-concepts. For instance, one man might buy a Boss suit to project a sophisticated and businesslike image, while another might buy an outfit from Hollister to enhance acceptability within his peer group.

Motives

Motive
An internal, energy-giving force that directs a person's activities towards satisfying a need or achieving a goal.

A **motive** is an internal, energy-giving force that directs an individual's activities towards satisfying a need or achieving a goal. Motivation is the set of mechanisms for controlling movement towards goals.[19] At any time a buyer's actions are affected by a set of motives rather than by just one. These motives are unique to the individual and to the situation. At any point in time some motives in the set will have priority. For example, someone's motives for stocking up on food may be particularly strong if a prolonged period of bad weather is forecast. Motivation affects the direction and intensity of behaviour, as individuals must choose which goals to pursue at a particular time. Motives influencing where a person regularly purchases products are called patronage motives. A buyer may use a particular shop because of **patronage motives** such as price, service, location, honesty, product variety or friendliness of sales staff. Marketers seeking to capitalize on these motives should determine why regular customers patronize a store and then emphasize these characteristics in the store's marketing mix. Motivation research can be used to analyze the major motives that influence whether consumers buy particular products. However, some of these motives are sub-conscious and people are

Patronage motives
Those motives that influence where a person purchases products on a regular basis.

FIGURE 5.6
Discussing the customers' buying decision-making process, perceptions and attitudes is an important aspect of the marketer's role

therefore unaware of them. As a consequence, marketers cannot always elicit these motives through direct questioning. Most motivation research therefore relies on interviews or projective techniques (see Figure 5.6).

In-depth interview
The collection of data from an individual by interview.

Researchers using interviews to study motives may use individual **in-depth interviews**, focus groups or a combination of the two. In an in-depth interview, the researcher encourages the subject to talk freely about general topics before focusing the discussion on the areas of interest. In a process that may last for several hours, the interviewer can then probe the subject's answers for clarification. In a **focus group**, the moderator – through leadership that appears to be not highly structured – tries to generate discussion about one or several topics in a group of six to 12 people. Through the discussion, the moderator attempts to discover people's motives relating to some issue such as the use of a product. The researcher usually cannot probe as far in a focus group as in an in-depth interview, and some products may not be suitable for such group discussion. To determine successfully the sub-conscious motives reflected in the interviews, motivation researchers must have certain qualities: they must be perceived as non-threatening by members of the group, must be able to adopt a demeanour appropriate to the characteristics of those in the group and must be well trained in clinical psychology. The use of sound and video recordings can simplify the process of analysis. Both in-depth and focus group techniques can yield a variety of information. For example, they may help marketers discover why customers continue to buy and smoke cigarettes despite being aware of the profound health risks.

Focus group
A semi-structured discussion involving six to 12 people, led by a moderator.

Projective techniques
Tests in which subjects are asked to perform specific tasks for particular reasons, while actually being evaluated for other purposes.

Projective techniques are tests in which subjects are asked to perform specific tasks for particular reasons, while actually being evaluated for other purposes. Such tests are based on the assumption that subjects will unconsciously 'project' their motives through the tasks they perform. Researchers trained in projective techniques can analyze the results and make predictions about the subject's sub-conscious motives. Common types of projective technique include word association tests, sentence completion tests and bubble drawings. These are illustrated in Figure 5.7. Such tests can be useful to marketers in a number of ways, such as helping to make advertising more effective.[20] The complexity of motivation research means that marketers wishing to research people's motives should employ the services of professional psychologists with specific skills in the area.[21]

Learning

Learning
Changes in a person's behaviour caused by information and experience.

Learning refers to changes in behaviour caused by information and experience. The consequences of behaviour strongly influence the learning process. Thus, behaviour resulting in satisfying outcomes tends to be repeated. For example, if a consumer buys a hair gel that he believes makes him appear trendy, he is more likely to buy the same brand next time. If the consumer's hair subsequently starts to look out of condition, he may switch allegiance to an alternative brand.

Word association tests

Subjects are asked to say what words come into their minds when a particular topic/product is mentioned.

Fresh foods are . . .	Frozen foods are . . .
Natural	Processed
Fresh	Quick
Healthy	Simple
Expensive	Convenient
Good for you	Preservatives
Real	Manufactured

Sentence completion tests

Subjects are asked to complete the sentences.

'People who use recycled toilet tissue . . .'
'People who look for the ingredients on packets before they buy them are . . .'
'People who buy Swatch watches . . .'

Bubble drawings

Subjects are asked to say what the man is thinking.

FIGURE 5.7
Common types of projective technique

The ability of buyers to process information when making purchasing decisions varies. For example, when purchasing a tablet computer, a well-educated potential buyer who has experience with tablets may be able to read, comprehend and synthesize the considerable quantities of information found in the technical brochures for competing brands. On the other hand, a buyer with more limited abilities may be incapable of performing this task and will have to rely instead on information obtained from advertisements, sales staff or acqaintances.

A critical aspect of an individual's ability to process information is knowledge. **Knowledge**, in this context, has two components: familiarity with the product, and

Knowledge
Familiarity with the product and expertise – the ability to apply the product.

expertise or the ability to apply the product.[22] The duration and intensity of the buying decision process depends on the buyer's familiarity with or prior experience in purchasing and using the product. The individual's knowledge influences his or her search for, recall and use of information.[23] Inexperienced buyers may use different types of information from more experienced shoppers when making purchasing decisions. Inexperienced buyers use price as an indicator of quality more frequently than buyers who are knowledgeable about a particular product category.[24] Thus, two potential buyers of climbing equipment may use quite different types of information in making their purchase decision. The more experienced climber, who has scaled several of the world's most challenging mountains, will seek detailed information about the performance of the equipment in extreme conditions; while the novice climber, may judge the kit on the basis of its affordability.

Consumers who lack expertise are more likely to seek advice from others when making a purchase. More experienced buyers have greater confidence, are more knowledgeable about the options, and can tell which features are reliable indicators of product quality. For example, consider two families choosing a long-haul holiday. Members of one family are unused to overseas travel, are unsure of the suitability of locations offered on online websites, and do not understand how to investigate flight options or insurance requirements. Members of the other family have regularly holidayed abroad. Even if they intend to visit a country that is new to them, they are sufficiently conversant with this type of travel to make their purchase without assistance and with confidence.

Consumers can gain the knowledge they need to make decisions from marketers or from other sources. Marketers sometimes help customers to learn about and gain experience of their products. Free samples encourage consumer trial and reduce purchase risk. In-store demonstrations help people acquire knowledge of product uses. Innovative technology company Dyson, well known for its bagless vacuum cleaners and Airblade hand dryers, has videos on its website which explain how its Air Multiplier range of bladeless fans work.

However, consumers are increasingly turning to other consumers for information about different product offerings. As discussed later in this chapter, sharing of information on the internet through social networking sites and other digital sources has provided a host of new opportunities for consumers gathering insights into product and services. The website, Gransnet, provides social networking and advice forums for older people, as well as featuring information about brands targeting this group.

In view of these trends, it is no surprise that marketers encounter problems in attracting and holding consumers' attention, providing the kinds of information that are important for making purchase decisions, and convincing consumers to try the product. These attempts are most likely to be successful when designed to appeal to a well-defined target market. In Figure 5.8, Walkers is striving for attention through strong and evocative images for its 'posh crisps'.

Attitudes

Attitude
An individual's enduring evaluation, feelings and behavioural tendencies towards an object or activity.

An **attitude** is an individual's enduring evaluation, feelings and behavioural tendencies towards an object or activity. These objects or activities may be tangible or intangible, living or non-living. Some attitudes relate to things that have a major impact on our lives, while others are less important. For example, we have attitudes towards relationships, culture and politics, just as we do towards pop music, football and sushi. An individual learns attitudes through experience and interaction with others. Just as attitudes are learned, they can also be changed. Nevertheless, an individual's attitudes are generally quite stable and do not change from moment to moment. Likewise, at a particular point in time, some attitudes may be stronger than others. For example, a consumer who recently lost money to an internet scam, may have strong views about the need for consumer protection legislation in this area. An attitude consists of three major components: cognitive, affective and behavioural. The cognitive (or thinking) component is a person's knowledge and information about the object or idea, whereas the affective (or feeling) component comprises feelings and emotions towards the object or idea. The behavioural (or action) component consists of the action tendencies

FIGURE 5.8

These advertisements for 'posh' crisps evidently play on consumers' aspirations to portray a certain image through the brands and products they select

Source: Courtesy of Kate Plumb, Abbot Mead Vickers. BBDO.

exhibited towards the object or idea. Changes in one of these components may or may not alter the other components. Thus, consumers may become more knowledgeable about a specific brand without changing the affective or behavioural components of their attitude towards that brand.

Consumer attitudes towards a company and its products greatly influence the products individuals will buy, and therefore impact on the success or failure of the company's marketing strategy. When consumers are strongly negative towards aspects of a business's practices, they may stop using the business's product, and may urge relatives and friends to do the same. When Apple made U2's latest album automatically available free to iTunes customers, there was an indignant reaction from those who did not like the band. Apple quickly had to develop a way for subscribers to remove the album from their libraries. In this case, however, the effects were not long-lived.[25]

Since attitudes can play such an important part in determining consumer behaviour, marketers should measure consumer attitudes towards prices, package designs, company logos and brand names, advertisements, warranties, store design and location, features of existing or proposed products, and social responsibility issues. Marketers can use a range of techniques to gauge these attitudes. One of the simplest ways is to question people directly. A marketing research agency carrying out attitude research for Rayban, for example, might question consumers about their opinions on the latest trends in eye wear. Sometimes marketers evaluate attitudes through attitude scales. An **attitude scale** usually consists of a series of adjectives, phrases or sentences about an object. Subjects are asked to indicate the intensity of their feelings towards the object. For example, attitudes towards flexible mortgages might be measured by asking respondents to state the degree to which they agree or disagree with a number of statements, such as 'When I have spare money I would like the opportunity to pay more than my usual monthly repayment amount.'

Attitude scale
A series of adjectives, phrases or sentences about an object used by a subject to indicate his or her feelings towards that object.

If marketers identify particularly negative attitudes towards an aspect of a marketing mix, they may try to make consumer attitudes more favourable. This task is generally long, expensive, difficult and may require extensive promotional efforts. For example, in the UK, the Post Office embarked on a prolonged advertising campaign to draw customers' attention to the fact that local post offices offer a wide range of services. This publicity aimed to alter customers' attitude that the Post Office exists purely for mailing letters and parcels.

Personality

Personality
All the internal traits and behaviours that make a person unique.

Personality includes all the internal traits and behaviours that make a person unique. Each person's unique personality is both inherited and the result of personal experiences. Personalities are typically described as having one or more characteristics, such as compulsiveness, ambitiousness, gregariousness, dogmatism, authoritarianism, introversion, extroversion, aggressiveness and competitiveness. Many marketers believe that a consumer's personality does influence the types and brands of products purchased, and there has been a drive to increase research in this area.[26] For example, the type of make-up or clothing that people buy, as well as the social activities in which they engage, may reflect one or more personality characteristics. Perhaps surprisingly, marketing researchers who have tried to find relationships among such characteristics and buying behaviour have reported inconclusive results. However, some of these researchers see this apparently weak association between personality and buying behaviour as due to unreliable measures rather than because no such relationship exists.[27]

At times, marketers aim advertising campaigns at general types of personality. In doing so, they use positively valued personality characteristics, such as gregariousness, independence or competitiveness. Products promoted in this way include drinks, cars, e-cigarettes, clothing and computer games. For example, television advertising promoting the alcoholic beverage Lambrini is designed to appeal to young, outgoing women.

Social factors influencing the buying decision process

Social factors
The forces that other people exert on buying behaviour.

The forces that other people exert on buying behaviour are called **social factors**. As shown in Figure 5.1, they can be grouped into four major areas:

1. roles and family
2. reference groups
3. social classes
4. culture and sub-cultures.

Roles and family

Role
A set of actions and activities that a person in a particular position is supposed to perform, based on the expectations of both the individual and surrounding people.

All of us occupy positions within our family, social setting, organizations and institutions. Associated with each position is a **role** – a set of actions and activities that a person is supposed to perform, based on their own expectations and those of others around them. As people occupy numerous positions, they also have many roles. For example, one woman may perform the roles of mother, wife, grandmother, daughter, sister, teacher, part-time youth club organizer and member of the local music society. Thus, there are several sets of expectations for each person's behaviour.

An individual's roles influence both general behaviour and buying behaviour. The demands of different roles may be inconsistent and confusing. For example, assume that a man is thinking about buying a boat. While he wants a boat for fishing, his children want one suitable for water skiing. His wife wants him to delay the boat purchase until next year. A colleague at work suggests that he should buy a particular brand, known for high performance. Thus an individual's buying behaviour may be partially affected by the opinions of family and friends.

Family roles relate directly to purchase decisions. One partner in a household may be heavily involved in the purchase of products such as household insurance, DIY products or arranging the servicing of the household car. The other may make buying decisions relating to food and other household items. Both may share these roles or be jointly involved in buying durable goods, such as a washing machine or DVD player. Children are also increasingly involved in household purchase decisions that were traditionally made only by their parents. Some buying decisions, such as the purchase of a family holiday, are made by the whole family, with different family members playing different roles in the process. When two or more individuals participate in a purchase, their roles may dictate that each is responsible for performing certain tasks: initiating the idea, gathering information, deciding whether to buy the product or selecting the specific brand. The particular tasks performed depend on the types of product being considered. Marketers need to be aware of how roles affect buying behaviour. To develop a marketing mix that precisely meets the target market's needs, marketers must know not only who does the actual buying but also what other roles influence the purchase.

Reference groups

Reference group
A group with which an individual identifies so much that he or she takes on many of the values, attitudes or behaviour of group members.

A group is referred to as a **reference group** when an individual identifies with it so much that he or she takes on many of the values, attitudes or behaviour of group members. Most people have several reference groups, such as families, friends, work colleagues and social, religious and professional organizations. Social media networks have added a new dimension to the notion of reference groups, with consumers sharing opinions and experiences about products, services and brands in contexts deemed relevant by many consumers. Sometimes such digital networks are created or encouraged by brands themselves, otherwise they are within people's Twitter or Facebook networks.

A group can be a negative reference group for an individual. Someone may have been a part of a specific group at one time but later have rejected its values and members, even taking specific action to avoid it.[28] However, in this discussion reference groups mean those that the individual involved views positively.

An individual may use a reference group as a point of comparison and a source of information, and may change his or her behaviour to be more in line with other group members. For example, a young couple may decide not to eat at a new restaurant on the advice of a close friend. An individual may seek information from a reference group about the best brand to buy or about where to buy a certain product. The degree to which a reference group will affect a purchase decision depends on an individual's susceptibility to its influence, and the strength of his or her involvement with the group. Young people are often especially susceptible to this kind of influence. In general, the more conspicuous a product, the more likely the brand decision will be influenced by reference groups. A marketer sometimes tries to use reference group influence in marketing communications by suggesting that people in a specific group buy and are highly satisfied with a product. The marketer is hoping that people will accept the suggested group as a reference group and buy (or react more favourably to) the product as a result. Whether this kind of marketing communication succeeds depends on three factors:

1. how effectively the message is communicated
2. the type of product
3. the individual's susceptibility to reference group influence.

For example, as the Building Customer Relationships box on page 163 demonstrates, teenagers are heavily influenced by their peers, with the result that they often follow the same trends.

In most reference groups, one or more members stand out as opinion leaders. An **opinion leader** provides information about a specific sphere of interest to reference group participants who seek such information. Opinion leaders are viewed by other group members as being well informed about a particular area, and easily accessible. Such individuals often feel a responsibility to remain informed about the sphere of interest, and thus seek out websites, discussion groups, advertisements, manufacturers' brochures, sales people and other sources of information.

Opinion leader
The member of a reference group who provides information about a specific sphere of interest to reference group participants seeking information.

Social classes

Social class
An open group of individuals who have similar social rank.

Within all societies, people rank others into higher or lower positions of respect. This ranking results in social classes. A **social class** is an open group of individuals who have similar social rank. A class is referred to as 'open' because people can move into and out of it. The criteria for grouping people into classes vary from one society to another. In the UK, as in other Western countries, many factors are taken into account, including occupation, education, income, wealth, race, ethnic group and possessions.

In Russia, wealth and income are less important in determining social class than education and occupation: although Russian doctors and scientists do not make a great deal of money, they are highly valued in Russian society. A person who is ranking someone does not necessarily apply all of a society's criteria. The number and importance of the factors chosen depend on the characteristics of the individual being ranked and the values of the person who is doing the ranking. For example, one individual may particularly respect status within a church or religious sect, while another may regard it as having little relevance.

To some degree, people within social classes develop and assume common patterns of behaviour. They may have similar attitudes, values, language patterns and possessions. Social class influences many aspects of people's lives. For example, it affects whom they marry, their likelihood of having children and the children's chances of surviving infancy. It influences childhood training, choice of religion, selection of occupation and the way in which people spend their time. As social class has a bearing on so many aspects of a person's life, it also affects buying decisions. For example, upmarket fashion labels Fendi and Versace are popular among upper-class Europeans because they believe these brands symbolize their status, income and aspirations.

Social class affects the type, quality and quantity of products that a person buys and uses. Social class also affects an individual's shopping patterns and the types of store patronized. Advertisements are sometimes based on an appeal to a specific social class. Different countries often collate data about their populations based on social or socio-economic factors. For example, for many years the UK, like some other countries, used a relatively simple classification based on social status and occupation (see Table 5.1). However, in 2001, the UK's

TABLE 5.1 Socio-economic classification

Social grade	Social status	Head of household's occupation
A	Upper middle class	Higher managerial, professional or administrative positions; often living in expensive accommodation in the best residential areas
B	Middle class	Middle managerial, professional or administrative jobs; good living standards, usually in good accommodation in reasonable areas
C1	Lower middle class	Junior managerial, professional or administrative, supervisory or clerical jobs; sometimes referred to as 'white collar' workers
C2	Skilled working class	Skilled manual workers, perhaps who have served some kind of apprenticeship to train
D	Working class	Semi-skilled and unskilled manual workers
E	Those at lowest levels of subsistence	Old age pensioners, widows, casual workers, the unemployed or those who are dependent on social security or have little in the way of independent means

See www.abc1demographic.co.uk/

TABLE 5.2 NS SEC eight-class socio-economic classification

Class	Occupation groups
1	Higher managerial and professional occupations (ABs): e.g. business executives, doctors, vets, teachers
2	Lower managerial and professional occupations (C1s): e.g. nurses, police sergeants and constables, market researchers, junior managers
3	Intermediate occupations (C2s): e.g. secretaries, clerical staff, technicians and telephone engineers
4	Small employers and own-account workers: e.g. the self-employed and those employing fewer than 25 people
5	Lower supervisory and technical occupations: e.g. supervisors in factories
6	Semi-routine occupations: e.g. drivers, assembly-line workers, shop staff
7	Routine occupations: e.g. porters, labourers, domestic staff
8	Never worked or long-term unemployed

Source: Adapted from Angela Donkin, Yuan Huang Lee and Barbara Toson, 'Implications of change in the UK social and occupational classifications in 2001 for vital statistics', *Population Trends*, 107, *National Statistics*, Spring 2002, pp. 23–9.

Office for National Statistics introduced a modified system known as NS SEC (National Statistics Socio-Economic Classification). This approach is still based on occupation, but aims to more closely reflect consumers' purchasing power on the basis of their position in the labour market.[29] Table 5.2 describes the NS SEC social class categories. You can find your NS SEC category online.

Culture and sub-cultures

Culture
All the things around us that are made by human beings: tangible items, such as food, furniture, buildings, clothing and tools; and intangible concepts, such as education, the legal system, healthcare and religion; plus values and behaviours.

Culture consists of everything in our surroundings that is made by human beings. It includes tangible items, such as food, furniture, buildings, clothing and tools and intangible concepts, such as education, the legal system, healthcare and religion. Culture also includes the values and wide range of behaviours that are acceptable within a specific society. The concepts, values and behaviours that make up a culture are learned and passed on from one generation to the next.

Culture influences buying behaviour, determining what people wear and eat, how they socialize, where they live and travel. Society's interest in the health-related aspects of food has affected companies' approaches to developing and promoting their products. Recent concern about increasing levels of obesity and its impact on health has caused the food industry to question how it markets high-fat and high-sugar products.[30] Culture also influences how consumers buy and use products, and the satisfaction gained from them. For example, the consumption of packaged goods, and the usage and ownership of durable goods varies across cultures.[31] In many Western cultures, shortage of time is a growing problem because of the increasing number of women who work and the current emphasis placed on physical and mental self-development. Many people buy convenience and labour-saving products to cope with this problem.[32]

As culture partly determines how products are purchased and used, it also affects the development, promotion, distribution and pricing of products. Food marketers have needed to radically overhaul their marketing efforts to reflect day-to-day changes in how consumers live their lives. Some 45 years ago, most families ate at least two meals a day together, and the mother devoted four to six hours a day to preparing those meals. Over the same time period, the number of women in the UK employed outside the home has risen from a little over 50 per cent to 65 per cent, while male employment has dropped from just over 90 per cent to 76 per cent. Average family incomes have also risen considerably. These shifts, along with lack of time, have resulted in dramatic increases in per capita consumption of refrigerated and frozen ready meals and shelf-stable foods such as microwavable rice and pre-prepared sauces. As a result of increasing demands from those wishing to shop on the way to and from work, retailers such as Sainsbury's and Marks & Spencer have opened up convenience stores at fuel stations.

An increase in ethnic diversity in many societies has important implications for the way in which new products and services are developed and marketed. A key part of this process is ensuring the availability of good-quality data, so that the attitudes and behaviour of minority groups are properly understood. When marketers sell products overseas, they often see the tremendous impact that culture has on the purchase and use of products. International marketers find that people in other regions of the world have different attitudes, values and needs, which call for different methods of doing business. Some international marketers fail because they do not adjust to cultural differences. A culture can be divided into **sub-cultures** according to geographic regions or human characteristics, such as age or ethnic background. In any country, there are a number of different sub-cultures. Within these, there are even greater similarities in people's attitudes, values and actions than within the broader culture, resulting in stronger preferences for specific types of clothing, furniture or leisure activity. For example, the wearing of kilts tends to be confined to Scotland rather than England or Wales. Marketers must recognize that, even though their operations are confined to one country, state or city, sub-cultural differences may dictate considerable variations in what products people buy and how they make their purchases. To deal effectively with these differences, marketers may have to alter their product, promotion, distribution systems, price or people to satisfy members of particular sub-cultures.

> **Sub-cultures**
> Sub-divisions of culture according to geographic regions or human characteristics, such as age or ethnic background.

The impact of new thinking and new technologies

Marketers must continually endeavour to understand consumer buying behaviour and the factors which influence it, in order to offer consumers greater satisfaction. In doing so, they need to be aware of changes in thinking about how purchase decisions are made. The model of consumer decision-making presented in this chapter is often described as rational, because it depicts the stages that consumers progress through in making choices. However, marketers now recognize that there is also a sub-conscious element to consumer choice. Techniques from neuroscience are increasingly being used to uncover these less tangible aspects of choice.

New technologies and the increased time that consumers spend online are also affecting their shopping habits and purchase decisions. Companies are extending their efforts to understand how these developments are changing product and service choices, and modifying their marketing efforts accordingly.

Neuromarketing

Marketers now recognise that in addition to the rational model of consumer decision-making depicted in this chapter, there is a sub-conscious element to consumer choice. Daniel Kahneman developed a framework of decisions and behaviour which distinguishes between two systems of processing: System 1 is implicit, quick, effortless, and automatic, while System 2 is explicit, methodical and thinking-based. Experts believe that both systems work in conjunction in order to reach a decision.[33] The Stroop test, illustrated in Figure 5.9, illustrates the combined effects of these

Green	Yellow	Blue	Red	Red
Blue	Green	Blue	Yellow	Green
Yellow	Yellow	Red	Blue	Green
Blue	Red	Yellow	Green	Red

FIGURE 5.9
The Stroop effect colour test

systems. Both the colour and meaning of these words can readily be processed under System 1; however, because of the mismatch between them, consideration needs to be given to the answer through processing under System 2.[34]

Neuromarketing, which is the study of consumers' brain patterns to reveal responses to marketing stimuli, uses brain scanning approaches from neuroscience to shed light on these sub-conscious elements. Techniques such as functional magnetic resonance imaging (fMRI), allow researchers to assess responses to particular stimuli by monitoring changes in brain activity. Another approach, electroencephalography (EEG), monitors electrical activity in the brain via electrodes attached to the head. As these approaches do not require conscious input from the consumer, the responses can be judged in the absence of other interference.

> **Neuromarketing**
> is the study of consumers' brain patterns to reveal responses to marketing stimuli.

The value of these approaches is shown in experiments that assess consumer preferences for products. Tests examining neural responses to tasting identical wines, showed that these responses were greater when consumers were informed that they were testing an expensive wine. Those participating in the experiment also expressed a preference for the wine they believed to be more costly. These findings demonstrate that the judgements we make about products extend beyond their physical characteristics.[35]

Social media and consumer-to-consumer (C2C) communication

The amount of time that consumers spend online is influencing how they share product information and experiences. As a consequence, the influence of social media, online forums and price comparison websites on the purchase decisions that they make is also increasing. For example, when searching for a restaurant in an unfamiliar town, many consumers now routinely study reviews on TripAdvisor. A growing body of scientific evidence demonstrates the impact of such behaviour on the choices we make. For example, research carried out in the hotel sector shows that how consumers rate their stay is affected by what others say online as well as by their own experience. As one expert explains: '... these findings suggest that social influence effects make positive online product ratings a double-edged sword, exacerbating the negative effect of failure and strengthening the benefit of failure recovery'.[36]

Increasingly this sharing of views takes place without company interferences, allowing individuals to get the 'real story' about a brand or company. In many ways the power of marketing practitioners to control and disperse information is being placed in the hands of the consumers. **Consumer-to-consumer communication (C2C)** refers to communication taking place between consumers through face-to-face, online or other electronic media. Today, blogs, wikis, podcasts and rating sites and the like have the capability to publicize, praise or challenge the company.

> **Consumer-to-consumer communication (C2C)**
> refers to communication taking place between consumers through face-to-face, online or other electronic media.

Forrester Research, a technology and market research company, emphasizes the importance of understanding these changing relationships between corporates and consumers. By grouping online customers into different segments based on how they use digital online media, marketers can gain a better understanding of the online influences on consumers. As well as learning about how C2C is likely to affect their products, they can use these insights to influence consumers through their own marketing strategies. The Social Technographics Profile developed by Forrester Research, groups the online community into six segments according to how they interact with new digital media. It is important to note that in this particular analysis some

Building customer relationships

Teenage trends, Twilight and the power of reference groups

Ever since Elvis Presley and The Beatles, teenagers have followed their favourite music bands, films, actors and books, sometimes affording cult-like status upon them. Such trends are common among this age group, because of a desire to find ways to 'fit in' and connect with their peers.

The power of mobile technology has accelerated these trends, as teenagers enjoy 24/7 smartphone access to fanzine sites, blogs and social media through which they can share their interest. Books have often been at the heart of these obsessions. Who can forget the impact of a young wizard called Harry Potter on teens and tweens alike? In recent years, books series *Twilight*, *The Hunger Games* and *Divergent* have all achieved cult status among this group. In each of these cases, the initial success of the books has been the impetus for Hollywood movies and memorabilia, which have reinforced and caused the phenomenon to grow.

Huge merchandise sales occur alongside this media activity. An avalanche of such products has accompanied the success of the Disney film *Frozen*; while 2013 figures put sales of boy band One Direction's merchandise at around £50m. As well as dressing to match characters in the *Twilight* films, some fans – known as Twi-Hards – have even splashed out hundreds of pounds in having vampire fangs fitted. Meanwhile magazine *Marie-Claire* reported a huge growth in the sale of pale foundations following the launch of the second *Twilight* film.

Social media sites, such as Facebook and Twitter, provide momentum for these trends, enabling enthusiasts from across the globe to come together and build communities, through which they can share their views and become identified as 'fans'. Fanzine websites are part of this picture, enabling these enthusiastic followers to co-create the trends, as they share anecdotes, observations and images. According to Danny Weitzkorn from content marketing agency Kameleon, 'Teenagers are brought into a digital world in which everyone is going along the same journey. The trends have enabled brands to develop definitive identities and sell a lifestyle for teenagers to buy into.'

This process of co-creation via digital media is reinforced by the artists, who use the same sites to connect with and reinforce their bonds with fans, one day by posting a photograph and another by offering insights into how they are spending their time. As Zoe Jones, Digital Cinema Media marketing director explains, 'Social media enables artists to have a powerful direct relationship with fans internationally, something that wasn't possible with traditional media.'

Sources: Leonie Roderick, Cult creation, *The Marketer*, March/April 2015, 30–3; Steven Eggermont, Youth culture, media, and the vampire franchise, *Journal of Children and Media*, 5(4) 2011, 474–7; Melissa Click, Jennifer Stevens Aubrey and Elizabeth Behm-Morawitz, *Bitten by Twilight: Youth Culture, Media, & the Vampire Franchise*, 2010, Peter Lang Publishing, New York.

consumers can belong to multiple segments at the same time. Table 5.3 describes the six groups. Creators are consumers who create their own media outlets, such as blogs, podcasts, consumer-generated videos and wikis. Online marketers are recognizing the power of this C2C communication and are harnessing it as a conduit for addressing consumers directly. For instance, many marketers are now pitching public relationship products or stories to professional reporters and bloggers.

The second group of internet users are the *Critics*. These are people who comment on blogs or post ratings or reviews. Anyone who has ever posted a product review or rated a bar or movie, has engaged in this activity. Critics need to be an important component in a company's digital marketing strategy, because the majority of online shoppers read ratings and reviews to aid in their purchasing decisions. Consumer-generated content like ratings and reviews tends to be viewed as more credible than corporate messages. Hence marketers must carefully monitor what consumers are saying about their products and address consumers' concerns that may affect their corporate reputation.

Collectors are the most newly recognized group of the six. They gather information and organize content generated by Critics and Creators. The growing popularity of this segment is leading to the creation of social networking sites like Digg, del.icio.us, and RSS feeds. Such sites allow users to vote on the sites or stories that they like the best; collectors are active members in the online community, a company story or site that catches the eye of a collector is likely to be posted and discussed on collector sites.

TABLE 5.3 Social technographics

Creators	• Publish a blog
	• Publish personal web pages
	• Upload original videos
	• Write articles or stories and post them
Critics	• Post ratings/reviews of products or services
	• Comment on someone else's blog
	• Contribute to online forums
	• Contribute to/edit articles in a wiki
Collectors	• Use RSS feeds
	• Add tags to web pages or photos
	• 'Vote' for websites online
Joiners	• Maintain profile on a social networking site
	• Visit social networking sites
Spectators	• Read blogs
	• Watch video from other users
	• Listen to podcasts
	• Read online forums
	• Read customer ratings/reviews
Inactives	• None of the activities

Source: Charlene Li and Josh Bernoff, *Groundswell* (Boston, MA: Harvard Business Review) 2008, p. 43.

Another technographic segment known as *Joiners* is growing dramatically. Anyone who becomes a member of Snapchat, Twitter, Facebook, or other social networking sites is a Joiner. These consumers are often members of more than one such site. Joiners join these sites to connect and network with other users. Marketers can also take significant advantage of these sites to connect with consumers and form customer relationships.

The last two segments are the *Spectators* and *Inactives*. Online users who are Inactives do not participate in any digital online media, but as more and more people use computers as a resource, this number is dwindling. Spectators are the largest group in most countries. They are those consumers who read what other consumers produce but do not post any comment themselves.

Understanding consumer behaviour

Marketers try to understand consumer buying behaviour so that they can satisfy consumers more effectively. For example, consumer concerns about the exploitation of clothing workers in less developed countries following disasters such as Rana Plaza in Bangladesh have raised the profile of workers' rights and encouraged retailers to stock more ethical products. Shoppers now have a greater awarness of these issues, An appreciation of how and why individuals buy products and services helps marketers design more appropriate and relevant marketing programmes.[37]

At a time when consumers are increasingly focused on maximizing the value of what they buy, it is more important than ever to keep abreast of trends in consumer behaviour. If marketers are to keep consumers satisfied, they must focus carefully on the marketing concept and on being consumer oriented. They must be equipped with a clear understanding of the process and motivations of consumer buying, and also of how changing use of media is altering how that process takes place.

The fact that it may be difficult to analyze consumer behaviour precisely, does not detract from the importance of doing so. Even though research on consumer buying behaviour has not supplied all the knowledge that marketers need, considerable progress has been made in recent years. Advances in technology, changing shopping habits and the huge growth in big data are increasing the opportunities for capturing and managing information about consumers. For example, the increasing use of online banking has been made possible by the development of computer systems that can handle the full range of banking transactions in which consumers wish to engage. The same systems are enabling providers such as First Direct and Barclays to store and analyze a huge variety of information about customers' spending and savings patterns. When analyzed, this information provides vital insights into the needs and wants of different customer types. These insights can be used to develop and market new products and services. At a time when an increasingly competitive business environment is making it more difficult to develop an edge over rival organizations, the demands for such information are only likely to grow.

Summary

Buying behaviour comprises the decision processes and actions of people involved in buying and using products. *Consumer buying behaviour* refers to the buying behaviour of ultimate consumers – those who purchase products for personal or household use, not for business purposes. Analyzing consumer buying behaviour helps marketers to determine what satisfies customers, so that they can implement the marketing concept and better predict how consumers will respond to different marketing programmes.

Consumer decisions can be classified into three categories: routine response behaviour, limited decision-making and extensive decision-making. A consumer uses *routine response behaviour* when buying frequently purchased, low-cost, low-risk items that require very little search and decision effort. *Limited decision-making* is used for products purchased occasionally or when a buyer needs to acquire information about an unfamiliar brand in a familiar product category. *Extensive decision-making* is used when purchasing an unfamiliar, expensive, high-risk or infrequently bought product. *Impulse buying* is an unplanned buying behaviour involving a powerful, persistent urge to buy something immediately. The purchase of a certain product does not always elicit the same type of decision-making behaviour. Individuals differ in their response to purchase situations. Even the same individual may make a different decision in other circumstances.

The *consumer buying decision process* comprises five stages: problem recognition, information search, evaluation of alternatives, purchase and post-purchase evaluation. Decision processes do not always culminate in a purchase, and not all consumer decisions include all five stages. Problem recognition occurs when a buyer becomes aware that there is a difference between a desired state and an actual condition. After recognizing the problem, the buyer searches for product information that will help resolve the problem or satisfy the need. *Internal search* involves buyers searching their memory for information about products that might solve the problem. If insufficient information is retrieved in this way, additional information is sought through *external search*. A successful information search will yield a group of brands, called an *evoked set*, that are viewed as possible alternatives. The level of involvement, which is the amount of interest, emotion and activity expended on a purchase, affects the degree of the external search. To evaluate the products in the evoked set, a buyer establishes certain criteria and assigns each a certain *salience* – or level of importance – by which to compare, rate and rank the different products. During purchase, the consumer selects the product or brand on the basis of results from the evaluation stage and on other factors. The buyer also chooses the seller from whom to buy the product. After the purchase, the buyer evaluates the product's actual performance. Shortly after the purchase of an expensive product the post-purchase evaluation may provoke *cognitive dissonance* – dissatisfaction brought on by the consumer's doubts as to whether he or she should have bought the product in the first place. The results of the post-purchase evaluation will affect future buying behaviour.

Three major categories of influences are believed to affect the consumer buying decision process: personal, psychological and social factors. A *personal factor* is one that is unique to a particular person. Personal factors include demographic factors, situational factors and level of involvement. *Demographic factors* are individual characteristics such as age, sex, race, ethnic origin, income, family life cycle and occupation. *Situational factors* are the external circumstances or conditions that exist when a consumer is making a purchase decision, such as the time available. An individual's *level of involvement* – the level of interest, emotional commitment and time spent searching for a product in a particular situation – also affects the buying decision process. Enduring involvement is an ongoing interest in a product class because of personal relevance. Situational involvement is a temporary interest resulting from the particular circumstance or environment in which buyers find themselves.

Psychological factors partly determine people's general behaviour and thus influence their behaviour as consumers. The primary psychological influences on consumer behaviour are perception, motives, learning, attitudes and personality. *Perception* is the process of selecting, organizing and interpreting *information inputs* (the sensations received through sight, taste, hearing, smell and touch) to produce meaning. The first step in the perceptual process is the selection of information. *Selective exposure* is the phenomenon of people selecting the inputs that are to be exposed to their awareness; *selective distortion* is the changing or twisting of currently received information. *Selective retention* involves remembering information inputs that support personal feelings and beliefs, and forgetting those that do not. The second step of the perceptual process requires organizing and integrating the new information with that already stored in memory. Interpretation – the third step in the perceptual process – is the assignment of meaning to what has been organized. In addition to perceptions of packages, products, brands and organizations, individuals also have a *self-concept* or self-image.

A *motive* is an internal, energy-giving force directing a person's activities towards satisfying a need or achieving a goal. *Patronage motives* influence where a person purchases products on a regular basis. To analyze the major motives that influence consumers to buy or not buy products, marketers conduct motivation research, using *in-depth interviews, focus groups* or *projective techniques*. Common types of projective technique include word association tests, bubble drawings and sentence completion tests.

Learning refers to changes in a person's behaviour caused by information and experience. *Knowledge*, in this context, has two components: familiarity with the product and expertise – the ability to apply the product.

Attitude refers to an individual's enduring evaluation, feelings and behavioural tendencies towards an object or activity. Consumer attitudes towards a company and its products greatly influence the success or failure of its marketing strategy. Marketers measure consumers' attitudes using *attitude scales*.

Personality comprises all the internal traits and behaviours that make a person unique. Although the results of many studies have been inconclusive, some marketers believe that personality does influence the types and brands of products purchased.

Social factors are the forces that other people exert on buying behaviour. They include the influence of roles and family, reference groups, social classes and culture and sub-cultures. We all occupy positions within groups, organizations and institutions. Each position has a *role* – a set of actions and activities that a person in a particular position is supposed to perform. A group is a *reference group* when an individual identifies with the group so much that he or she takes on many of the values, attitudes or behaviours of group members. In most reference groups, one or more members stand out as *opinion leaders*. A *social class* is an open group of individuals who have similar social rank. *Culture* is everything in our surroundings that is made by human beings, plus values and behaviours. A culture can be divided into *sub-cultures* on the basis of geographic regions or human characteristics, such as age or ethnic background. The arrival of social networking sites and digital media like blogs is changing the way consumers learn about and evaluate products. Through these connections consumers can share information and experiences without company interferences. This is putting more power to control and disperse information in the hands of consumers.

Marketers try to understand consumer buying behaviour so that they can offer consumers greater satisfaction. In doing so they need to consider the impact of new thinking and new technologies on consumer behaviour. Marketers now recognise that in addition to the rational model of consumer decision-making depicted in this chapter, there is a sub-conscious element to consumer choice. Neuromarketing research using approaches from neuroscience, such as MRI and other brainscanning approaches, to shed light on these sub-conscious aspects.

Greater consumer access to digital and online technologies is also affecting the buying decisions that are made. Social media, online forums, and price comparison websites all have an influence on consumer perceptions of the products and services that they buy. Consumer-to-consumer communication (C2C) refers to communication taking place between consumers through face-to-face, online or other electronic media.

Improvements in technology, the increasing availability of digital data, and refinements in research methods are increasing opportunities to capture and manage data about consumers and their behaviour. The combination of the pressure of rising consumer expectations, and an increasingly competitive business environment, will spur marketers to seek a fuller understanding of consumer decision processes.

Key links

This chapter, about consumer buying behaviour, should be read in conjunction with Chapter 6, which examines buying behaviour in business markets.

● Without an understanding of customers' buying behaviour, it is difficult for marketers to develop effective marketing programmes, as discussed in Part Three.

● An understanding of customer buying behaviour is also essential for two core facets of marketing strategy: developing target market strategies (see Chapter 7); and creating powerful brand propositions (see Chapters 8 and 11).

Important terms

Attitude
Attitude scale
Buying behaviour
Cognitive dissonance
Consumer buying behaviour
Consumer buying decision process
Consumer-to-consumer (C2C) communication
Culture
Demographic factors
Evoked set
Extensive decision-making
External search
Focus group
Impulse buying
In-depth interview
Information inputs
Internal search
Involvement
Knowledge
Learning
Level of involvement
Limited decision-making
Motive
Neuromarketing
Opinion leader
Patronage motives
Perception
Personal influencing factors
Personality
Projective techniques
Psychological factors
Reference group
Role
Routine response behaviour
Salience
Selective distortion
Selective exposure
Selective retention
Self-concept
Situational factors
Social class
Social factors
Sub-cultures

Discussion and review questions

1. Name the types of buying behaviour consumers use. List some products that you have bought using each type of behaviour.

2. In what circumstances have you bought a product on impulse?

3. What are the five stages in the consumer buying decision process? Are all these stages used in all consumer purchase decisions?

4. What are the personal factors that affect the consumer buying decision process? How do they affect the process?

5. How does a consumer's level of involvement affect his or her purchase behaviour?

6. What is the function of time in a consumer's buying decision process?

7. What is selective exposure and what effect does it have on consumer buying?

8. How do marketers attempt to shape consumers' learning?

9. Why are marketers concerned about consumer attitudes?

10. Describe reference groups. How do they influence buying behaviour? Name some of your own reference groups.

11. In what ways does social class affect a person's purchase decisions?

12. What is culture? How does it affect a person's buying behaviour?

13. Describe the sub-cultures to which you belong. Identify buying behaviour that is unique to your sub-culture.

14. If consumers are dissatisfied with a particular purchase, what actions are open to them? What can marketers do to respond to these actions?

15. How is consumer-to-consumer communication changing the way consumers buy products?

Recommended readings

Evans, M.E., Foxall, G. and Jamal, A., *Consumer Behaviour* (John Wiley, 2009).
Foxall, G.R., *Understanding Consumer Choice* (Palgrave Macmillan, 2005).
Hanson, H., Schiffman, L.G. and Kanuk, L., *Consumer Behaviour* (FT/Prentice-Hall, 2011).
Jansson-Boyd, C.V., *Consumer Psychology* (Open University Press, 2010).
Solomon, M., Bamossy, G., Askegaard, S. and Hogg, M.K., *Consumer Behaviour* (FT/Prentice Hall, 2009).
Szmigin, I. and Piacentini, M., *Consumer Behaviour* (Oxford University Press, 2015).

Internet exercise

Some mass-market or mainstream eCommerce sites, such as Amazon.co.uk, have extended the concept of customization to their customer base. Amazon has analyzed its customer data, then used its understanding of certain users' likes and dislikes to make recommendations to other users. Take a look at this online retailer at: www.amazon.co.uk or www.amazon.com. Focusing on the organization's bookselling activities, answer the following:

1. What might motivate some consumers to read a 'best-selling' list?

2. Is the consumer's level of involvement with online book purchase likely to be high or low?

3. Discuss the consumer buying decision process as it relates to a decision to purchase from Amazon.co.uk.

Group tasks

1. Your team is made up of very similar people... all well-educated, studying the same course and with student-like lifestyles. But is this true? Are you all really similar? Select an item of clothing and a technology product that you all own. To what extent do you all have identical needs, preferences and buying behaviour when shopping for these items?

2. You need to acquire some new smart clothes for a round of job interviews. Where do you go for these purchases? What influences your choices? To what extent are you all voicing similar points and opinions or are there differences amongst you?

Applied mini-case

InterContinental Hotels Group is the world's largest hotel group, with 4800 hotels and 710 000 guest rooms in over 100 countries. The company has adopted a multi-segment strategy in order to address a variety of consumer requirements in the lodging industry. Its hotels include the upmarket InterContinental and Crown Plaza brands, boutique chain Hotel Indigo, Holiday Inn, budget brand Holiday Inn Express, as well as hotel suite operations Staybridge and Candlewood. In deriving its brand and target market strategies, InterContinental's marketers have considered a host of customer characteristics, requirements and behaviours, such as duration of stay, hotel location and proximity to other addresses, amenities and services sought or expected, desired luxury, value-for-money, hotel ambiance and feel, hotel usage, size of guest room, purpose of stay, booking/decision-making personnel and organizations, among other variables.

Sources: Sally Dibb and Lyndon Simkin, *Market Segmentation Success: Making It Happen!*, 2008, New York: The Haworth Press; www.ihgplc.com /files/pdf/factsheets/factsheet_worldstats.pdf

Question

A large company such as InterContinental Hotels Group is interested in finding out more about the factors that influence people buying hotel weekend breaks. Relating your answer to this example, review the different personal, psychological and social influences that might impact on someone seeking to make this kind of purchase.

Crayola: colouring in the 21st century

Case study

While Nintendo and Playstation games, music videos, satellite TV cartoon channels and web-based interactive gaming have captured children's attention, Crayola Crayons has maintained a role in children's play and remained on store shelves. Crayola LLC, formerly Binney & Smith, fought back with a new marketing strategy and marketing plan for the venerable crayon. The company launched a huge MTV-style campaign, targeted at children rather than parents.

Traditionally, Crayola Crayons were targeted at parents, using educational themes. But after recognizing that children's purchasing power and influence on family purchases have

increased in recent years, the company decided to change the crayon's image as an old-fashioned toy to an exciting way for kids and teens to express themselves. To this end, the company developed new advertisements featuring rock music, 'hip' kids and soaring colours for showing during television programmes seen by children. In-store videos provided to toy stores and retailers of children's clothing followed up the theme.

After marketing research indicated that children prefer brighter colours, the company decided to retire blue grey, green blue, lemon yellow, maize, orange red, orange yellow, raw umber and violet blue to the Crayola Hall of Fame and to replace them with the more vivid cerulean, dandelion, fuchsia, jungle green, royal purple, teal blue, vivid tangerine and wild strawberry. This decision was controversial, however. The company was inundated with phone calls, letters and petitions from people who missed the old colours. Protesters marched on the company, carrying placards with slogans like 'We hate the new 8!' and 'They call it a retirement, I call it a burial'. RUMPS, the Raw Umber and Maize Preservation Society, finally got its way. The company issued a commemorative tin containing the 64 crayon box and a special pack of the eight colours dropped one year earlier. Even though children liked the new colours, parents liked the old eight colours. The company issued a statement saying that the old colours were revived partly because the company is in the business of providing what the consumer wants.

Along with new advertisements and colours, the company introduced ColourWorks, a line of erasable crayon sticks and retractable coloured pencils and pens. The company brought out Silver Swirls, crayons that have twirls of silver mixed in with the wax colours. Pictures coloured with Silver Swirls can be buffed to a high sheen with tissue. The new line was not only tested

by children but also named by them. The company has also launched a range of Crayola clothing and other merchandise and has extended its range of toys. These include Beadola bead maker and other jewellery kits, a range of light designers, and interactive colouring software that encourages art and design featuring Barbie, mythical creatures and skylanders.

The familiar wax crayon remains the company's core line, though it now features as part of making kits – Badge Bonanza or Crayola Jewellery – and a whole host of design sets. Clearly, the Crayola brand is still very popular with children, parents and toy stores. More and more children are discovering the Crayola name, encouraged by Crayola's embracing of the internet. As well as providing a shop window for Crayola products, the website – www.crayola.com – offers free colouring pages, craft activities, educational resources and lesson plans. The company has very effectively created an online community around its wax crayon brand. Kids can also visit the Crayola's Playzone, where they can become the star of their own colouring book, transform digital photos into colouring pages, or get involved in a range of online games. For parents, the DIY Crafts & Activities, offers a wealth of make at home activities that can be filtered by age and colour. Step-by-step guidance helps kids to make their own circus out of recyclable items, create a neon flower bouquet, or construct a birds in the tree mobile.

Despite its focus on children, the company has not forgotten who actually holds the purse strings. The company continues to target parents with advertisements in women's and parents' magazines, while new products or services include educational and child development messages aimed at parents. However, the revised marketing strategy and accompanying marketing plan have led more children to reach for Crayola Crayons. Sales are up and shelf space in toy stores could not be better, despite stiff competition from a host of rival entertainment products and toys.

Sources: www.crayola.com, 2015; Ellen Neuborne, 'Crayola crayons have old colors back', *USA Today*, 2 October 1991, p. 2B; Ken Riddle, 'Crayola draws brighter lines in the market', *Marketing*, 21 January 1991, p. 4; Beefeater Restaurants, 1993; Toys 'R' Us, Leicester, 1996; Loretta Roach, 'Single use explosion', *Discount Merchandiser*, September 1995, pp. 28–30; Robyn Parets, 'Children's edutainment titles vie for shelf space', *Discount Store News*, 19 June 1995, pp. C6–C9; Binney & Smith UK, 1999; Toys 'R' Us, 1999, 2004, 2007, 2011.

Questions for discussion

1. Why did Crayola LLC have to update its marketing and change its strategy?

2. What are Crayola's target audiences? Why did the company need to approach them differently?

3. Why has the company embraced the internet?

CHAPTER 6

Business markets and business buying behaviour

"Business customers are complex, multi-faceted, highly demanding and require managing differently to consumers"

Objectives

To become familiar with the various types of business market.

To identify the major characteristics of business buyers and transactions.

To understand several attributes of business demand.

To become familiar with the major components of a buying centre or decision-making unit.

To understand relationship marketing and exchanges between business buyers and sellers.

To understand the stages of the business buying decision process and the factors that affect this process.

To learn how to select and analyze business target markets.

To appreciate some of the nuances of marketing business products.

INTRODUCTION

Most readers of this book will have related the material in the previous chapter to their own purchasing experiences as consumers. Many marketers, though, do not address consumers. Instead, their target customers are other businesses or organizations. Or, they must develop marketing strategies for consumers and engage with them, while also managing trade channel relationships in order to reach their final customers, so they must be able to engage with both business customers and consumers. Either way, many marketers are involved with B2B (business-to-business) rather than B2C (business-to-consumer) marketing. This chapter addresses the nature of business-to-business marketing, known here as business marketing. It needs to be read in conjunction with Chapter 21, which examines business marketing programmes.

A **business market** is one in which the customer is not a consumer, a private individual or household. In business markets, the target customers are other businesses and organizations that purchase a specific type of product or service for resale, for use in making or marketing other products, or for use in their daily operations. In older books, this used to be known as **industrial** or **organizational marketing**. More recently, the term **business-to-business marketing** has become popular. Now, this has been abbreviated to 'business marketing' or B2B. Whether known as industrial, organizational, business-to-business or simply business marketing, the emphasis is on other businesses and organizations as customers, rather than end-user consumers.

Business market
The customers are not consumers, private individuals or households: instead the target customers are other businesses and organizations that purchase a specific type of product or service for resale, for use in making other products, or for use in their daily operations.

Industrial, organizational or business-to-business marketing
See business market

Nectar Business

Many consumers have a purse or wallet full of loyalty cards, such as Tesco Clubcard, AirMiles or Nectar. How often when filling up with fuel at a BP service station are you asked whether you have a Nectar card? It is not only consumers who receive loyalty cards. Businesses also are persuaded to sign up in B2B deals with the major loyalty schemes. Nectar Business was launched in 2005 and now has around 600 000 SMEs as corporate members.

What is Nectar Business?

Since 2005 we've given back rewards to British businesses including team dinners, holidays and trips to the cinema.

Nectar Business makes it easy for you to collect points on your business purchases and personal shopping at a wide range of great names. It's up to you whether you spend your points on yourself or your business!

If you run a small business, join us and collect Nectar points on almost everything you buy for your business from stationery and trade supplies, to deliveries, travel and fuel. Nectar Business has partnered with a range of leading business suppliers, to reward the loyalty of small businesses like yours.

www.nectar.com/dynamic/business/about-nectar

Nectar Business customers can collect reward points when they hire Hertz vehicles, purchase from Dulux Decorator Centres, consume snacks from Brakes, use DHL couriers or acquire

stationery from Viking. 'It's easy to collect points on the things you already buy for your business every day, from stationery and insurance to specialist trade equipment or even food supplies', explains Nectar Business. Perhaps for some surprises, too ... 'Collect Nectar points when you purchase quality industrial and refrigerant gases, equipment and much more via BOC's nationwide network of retail stores or via the telephone'.

Just as for any consumer product, Nectar Business's marketers must work hard to reflect customer views, refresh the proposition and communicate effectively to both new account prospects and to the 600 000 business customers already signed up. In particular, the company wanted to increase redemption rates of its reward points so that more personnel in its 600 000 SME customers were actively using the service. A piece of marketing research found that many potential users were too 'time-poor' to spend their points on the items included in Nectar's official rewards portfolio.

As a result of the survey findings, the redemption process was re-thought and simplified. A group of highest value collectors was offered a one-to-one concierge service that identified, sourced, secured and shipped the items on which they wanted to spend their points. Certain call centre staff were dedicated to the Silver Service concierge proposition. In addition, the categorization of rewards on offer was streamlined and made easier to navigate. Two mailings were developed, one for email and one for direct mail. The email response rate was 28 per cent with an 80 per cent increase in redemptions, while the direct mail approach enjoyed a response rate of 13 per cent and an uplift in people redeeming of 192 per cent. Further campaigns have since been run to support the Silver Service concept, resulting in good improvements in redemption rates and a growing number of active users.

Sources: www.nectar.com/business/NectarHomeForward.nectar, 22 March 2011; www.nectar.com/dynamic/business/about-nectar, 22 March 2011; www.boconline.co.uk/how_to_buy/nectar_business.asp, 22 March 2011; Meg Carter, 'Silver service', *The Marketer*, March 2011, pp. 20–22; www.nectar.com/dynamic/business/about-nectar, 15 March 2015.

Nectar Business provides a loyalty card scheme for members and partners such as Hertz and Viking, targeting business users rather than consumers. This chapter explores what is meant by business marketing, before examining the characteristics of business buying and the nature of demand for business products. The chapter's focus is on the buying centre or decision-making unit and the buying decision process as applied to business-to-business marketing. The chapter concludes by examining how marketers select and analyze business markets, and the ways in which marketers in business markets modify their use of the marketing toolkit. For example, in terms of branding, addressing customer needs, determining market segments, understanding competitive forces, undertaking marketing research and in constructing marketing programmes. Read in conjunction with the previous chapter, users of *Marketing: Concepts and Strategies* will have a sound appreciation of buying behaviour and also how marketing must differ between business and consumer markets (a theme picked up in Chapter 21). An understanding of buying behaviour is central to market segmentation and target market strategy, as explained in the next two chapters, but additionally without such understanding of consumers or business customers it is difficult for marketers to successfully develop marketing programmes, engage with customers or provide satisfaction.

Types of business market

There are four broad kinds of business markets: producers, resellers (retailers, wholesalers, distributors), public sector and governments, plus institutions. Some would argue that aspects of the third sector warrant their own category. The following section describes the characteristics of the customers that make up these markets.

Producer markets

Producer markets
Buyers of raw materials and semi-finished and finished items used to produce other products or in their own operations.

Individuals and business organizations that purchase products to make a profit by using them to produce other products or by using them in their own operations are classified as **producer markets**. Producer markets include buyers of raw materials and semifinished and finished items used to produce other products. For example, a manufacturer such as BMW or Ford buys raw materials and component parts to use directly in the production of its products. Grocers and supermarkets are producer markets for numerous support products, such as paper and plastic bags, displays, scanners and floor-care products. Hotels are producer markets for food, cleaning equipment, laundry services and furniture. Figure 6.1 shows how easyJet will also advertise their services to business users rather than holiday-makers. Producer markets cover a broad array of industries, ranging from agriculture, forestry, fisheries and mining, to construction, transport, communications and public utilities.

Manufacturers tend to be geographically concentrated in certain industries, particularly if dependent on certain locally available raw materials, grants and financial inducements or skills. Heavy industry centred on the Ruhr valley in Germany, North Sea oil support around Aberdeen in Scotland, or technology along the M4 corridor in the UK, for example. Sometimes an industrial marketer may be able to serve customers more efficiently as a result. Within certain sectors, production in just a few regions may account for a sizeable proportion of total industrial output.

Reseller markets

Reseller markets
Intermediaries, such as wholesalers and retailers, who buy finished goods and resell them to make a profit.

Reseller markets consist of intermediaries, such as wholesalers and retailers, who buy finished goods and resell them to make a profit. These intermediaries are discussed in Chapter 15. Other than making minor alterations, resellers do not change the physical characteristics of the products they handle. Tesco stocks and sells Heinz or Tilda products without altering the branding, content or packaging. With the exception of items that producers sell directly to consumers, all products sold to consumer markets are first sold to reseller markets.

Wholesalers
Intermediaries who purchase products for resale to retailers, other wholesalers and producers, governments and institutions.

Wholesalers   **Wholesalers** or distributors purchase products for resale to retailers, other wholesalers and producers, governments and institutions. Although some highly technical products are sold directly to end users, many products are sold through wholesalers/intermediaries, who in turn sell products to other companies in

FIGURE 6.1
This easyJet advertisement is targeting business users rather than holiday-makers.

the distribution system. Thus wholesalers are very important in helping to get a producer's product to customers. Wholesalers often carry many products, perhaps as many as 250,000 items. From the reseller's point of view, having access to such an array of products from a single source makes it much simpler to buy a variety of items. When inventories are vast, the re-ordering of products is normally automated and the wholesaler's initial purchase decisions are made by professional buyers and buying committees.

Retailers
Intermediaries that purchase products and resell them to final consumers.

Retailers **Retailers** purchase products and resell them to final consumers. Some retailers carry a large number of items. Chemists, for example, may stock up to 12 000 items, and some supermarkets may handle in excess of 20 000 different products. In small, family-owned retail stores, the owner frequently makes purchasing decisions. Large department stores or supermarket retailers have one or more employees in each department or product category who are responsible for buying products for that department. As for chain stores, a buyer or buying committee in the central office frequently decides whether a product will be made available for selection by store managers. For smaller businesses, local managers or the owners make the actual buying decisions.

Factors considered by resellers When making purchase decisions, resellers consider several factors. They evaluate the level of demand for a product, to determine in what quantity and at what prices it can be resold. They assess the amount of space required to handle a product relative to its potential profit. Sometimes resellers will put a product on trial for a fixed period, allowing them to judge customers' reactions and to make better-informed decisions about shelf space and positions as a result. Retailers, for example, sometimes evaluate products on the basis of sales per square metre of selling area or contribution to overall gross margin. Since customers often depend on a reseller to have a product when they need it, a reseller typically evaluates a supplier's ability to provide adequate quantities when and where wanted. Resellers also take into account the ease of placing orders, and the availability of technical assistance and training programmes from the producer.

More broadly, when resellers consider buying a product not previously carried, they try to determine whether the product competes with or complements the products the company is currently handling. These types of concern distinguish reseller markets from other markets. Sometimes resellers will start stocking a new line of products in response to specific requests from customers. Marketers dealing with reseller markets must recognize these needs and be able to serve them.

Government and public sector markets

Government markets
Departments that buy goods and services to support their internal operations, and to provide the public with education, water, energy, national defence, road systems and healthcare.

National and local governments make up **government markets** and contribute to **public sector markets**. They spend huge amounts annually for a variety of goods and services to support their internal operations and to provide the public with education, utilities (in some countries), national defence, road systems and healthcare. In Europe, the amount spent by local governments varies from country to country, depending on the level and cost of services provided. The types and quantities of products bought by government markets reflect social demands on various government agencies. As the public's needs for government services change, so do the government markets' demands for products.

As government agencies spend public funds to buy the products they need to provide services, they are accountable to the public. This accountability is responsible for a relatively complex set of buying procedures. Some organizations, unwilling to deal with so much red tape, do not even try to sell to government buyers, while others have learned to deal efficiently with government procedures. For certain companies, such as BAE, and for certain products, such as defence-related items, the government may be one of only a few customers.

Public sector markets
Government and institutional not-for-profit customers and stakeholder groups.

Governments usually make their purchases through bids or negotiated contracts. To make a sale under the bid system, a company must apply and receive approval to be placed on a list of qualified bidders. When a government unit wants to buy, it sends out a detailed description of the products to these qualified bidders. Organizations that wish to sell such products then submit bids. The government unit is usually required to accept the lowest bid. When buying non-standard or highly complex products, a government unit often uses a negotiated contract. Under this procedure, the government unit selects only a few companies, negotiates specifications and terms, and eventually awards the contract to one of the negotiating companies. Most large defence contracts held by such companies as BAE or Thales are reached through negotiated contracts.

Although government markets have complicated requirements, they can also be very lucrative. When government departments modernize obsolete computer systems, for example, successful bidders can make high sales with attractive margins during the life of a contract, which may last for five years or more. Some companies have established separate departments to facilitate marketing to government units, while others specialize entirely in this area. The buying behaviour of governments is complex, though. A business such as Fujitsu sells IT services to banks, retailers, manufacturers and utility companies. Fujitsu is a leading supplier of IT services to central and local government and the health service: it has specialist management teams and sales and marketing specialists who focus purely on these public-sector clients owing to the specialized nature of their buying.

Institutional markets

Institutional markets
Organizations with charitable, educational, community or other non-business goals.

Organizations with charitable, educational, community or other non-business goals constitute **institutional markets**. Members of institutional markets include libraries, museums, universities, charitable organizations and some churches and hospitals. Some of these are also public-sector bodies, such as libraries and museums. Increasingly,

Third sector
Includes charities, the
voluntary sector, not-
for-profit organizations
and NGOs.

government and institutional markets are being grouped together and referred to as public sector markets, although the term **third sector** has emerged to cover charities, the voluntary sector, not-for-profit organizations and NGOs.

Institutions purchase large amounts of products annually to provide goods, services and ideas to members, congregations, students and other stakeholder groups. For example, a library must buy new books for its readers; pay rent, fuel and water bills; fund the staffing and cleaning of its buildings; invest in IT facilities; and pay to produce publicity material about its services. Although such institutions often have different goals and fewer resources than other types of organization, marketers may use special marketing activities to serve these markets. Public sector markets consist of government and institutional not-for-profit customers and stakeholder groups: public sector marketing is a significant growth area within the marketing discipline. Within some of these activities, notably government bodies promoting health and well-being for the population and the planet, there is a role for social marketing (see Chapter 1), which has further extended marketing's contribution in this domain.

Dimensions of business buying

Having clarified the different types of business customer, the next step is to consider the dimensions of business-to-business buying. After first examining several characteristics of business transactions, this section then discusses various attributes of business buyers and some of their primary concerns when making purchase decisions. Next it looks at methods of business buying and the major types of purchase that organizations make. The section concludes with a discussion of how the demand for business products and services differs from the demand for consumer products and services.

Characteristics of business transactions

Although the marketing concept is equally applicable to business and consumer markets, there are several fundamental differences between the transactions that occur in each. Business buyers tend to order in much larger quantities than individual consumers and often demand customized or tailored propositions. Suppliers must often sell their products in large quantities to make profits; consequently, they prefer not to sell to customers who place small orders.

Generally, business purchases are negotiated less frequently than consumer sales. Some purchases involve expensive items, such as machinery or office equipment, that are used for a number of years. Other products, such as raw materials and component items, are used continuously in production and may have to be supplied frequently. However, the contract regarding the terms of sale of these items is likely to be a long-term agreement, requiring periodic negotiations.

Negotiations in business sales may take much longer than those for consumer sales. Most consumers do not negotiate on prices paid, whereas many business customers never pay the list price. Purchasing decisions are often made by a committee; orders are frequently large, expensive and complex; and products may be custom built. There is a good chance that several people or departments in the purchasing organization will be involved. One department might express a need for a product; a second department might develop its specifications; a third might stipulate the maximum amount to be spent; and a fourth might actually place the order. This approach allows individuals with relevant expertise to be incorporated into the process when required. Sales personnel play an important role in negotiations with customers. The quality of the relationship that develops has been shown to impact on the outcome of such negotiations.

One practice unique to business-to-business sales is **reciprocity**, an arrangement in which two organizations agree to buy from each other. In some countries, reciprocal agreements that threaten competition are illegal, and action may be taken to stop anti-competitive reciprocal practices. Nonetheless, a certain amount of reciprocal dealing occurs among small businesses and, to a lesser extent, among larger companies as well. Such companies often find that developing long-term relationships of this kind can be an effective competitive tool.[1] Reciprocity can create a problem because coercive measures may be used to enforce it or because reciprocity influences purchasing agents to deal only with certain suppliers.

Attributes of business buyers

Business buyers are usually thought of as being different from consumer buyers in their purchasing behaviour because they are better informed about the products they purchase and often deliberate/negotiate for longer. The viability of their employer's business and thereby their own careers may well depend on their purchasing decisions, so they must be well informed. To make purchasing decisions that fulfil an organization's needs, business buyers demand detailed information about a product's functional features and technical specifications, as well as aftermarket support and back-up.

Business buyers, however, also have personal goals that may influence their buying behaviour. Most buyers seek the psychological satisfaction that comes with promotion and financial rewards. In general, managers are most likely to achieve these personal goals when they consistently exhibit rational buying behaviour and perform their jobs in ways that help their companies achieve their organizational objectives. Suppose, though, that a business buyer develops a close friendship with a certain supplier. If the buyer values the friendship more than organizational promotion or financial rewards, he or she may behave irrationally from the company's point of view. Dealing exclusively with that supplier regardless of better prices, quality or service from competitors may indicate an unhealthy or unethical alliance between the buyer and seller. Companies have different ways of dealing with such problems. Some require more than one person to be involved in buying products, while others periodically review their use of suppliers.

Primary concerns of business buyers

When they make purchasing decisions, business customers take into account a variety of factors. For example, in the business advertisement in Figure 6.2 the product choice, simplicity and cost effectiveness are emphasized. Among their chief considerations are quality, delivery, service and price. Product range, innovation, reliability and logistical support may also be significant considerations. Increasingly, business buyers are concerned with service support levels and ongoing commitment from their selected suppliers. There is a growing view, too, that a supplier's personnel in terms of knowledge, motivation, attitude and passion for assisting the customer, are an integral part of the product proposition being 'consumed' by the business customer (see Chapter 10).

Most business customers try to achieve and maintain a specific level of quality in the products they offer to their target markets. To accomplish this goal, they often buy their products on the basis of a set of expressed characteristics, commonly called specifications. These allow a business buyer to evaluate the quality of the products being considered according to particular features and thus to determine whether or not they meet the organization's needs.

Meeting specifications and deadlines is extremely important to business customers. If a product fails to meet specifications and malfunctions for the ultimate consumer, that product's supplier may be dropped and an alternative supplier sought. On the other hand, a business buyer is usually cautious about buying products that exceed specifications, because such products

Business catering doesn't
have to be complicated

Tiffin box

10 people - £35

www.jagscatering.co.uk

JAGS
CATERING

FIGURE 6.2

This business-to-business advertisement for
Jags Catering makes business catering simple

often cost more and thus increase production costs. Suppliers, therefore, need to design their products carefully to come as close as possible to their customers' specifications without incurring any unnecessary extras.

Business buyers also value service. The services offered by suppliers directly and indirectly influence their customers' costs, sales and profits. When tangible goods are the same or quite similar, as with most raw materials, they may have the same specifications and be sold at the same price in the same kind of containers. Under such conditions, the mix of services a business marketer provides to its customers represents its greatest opportunity to gain a competitive advantage. For example, bitumen supplier Nynas has a reputation for technical expertise, technical assistance and flexible logistics. Competitors may be able to offer a similar bitumen product, but few can emulate Nynas's ability to look after customers or offer bespoke solutions.

Among the most commonly expected services are market information, regulatory compliance support, inventory maintenance, on-time delivery, flexible ordering and logistical support, technical assistance, warranty back-up, repair services and credit facilities. Specific services vary in importance, however, and the mix of services that companies need is also affected by environmental conditions.

Market information   Business buyers in general are likely to need technical product information, data regarding demand, information about general economic conditions or supply and delivery information. For example, when technology is changing rapidly, forcing companies to change their production machinery, the demand for consultancy support services and warranty assurances will be especially high.

Regulatory compliance   In many markets, regulators and government agencies insist on certain product conformity, production and distribution practices, commercial practices and customer management, and customers may demand or welcome support in these regards from their suppliers.

Inventory maintenance   It is critical for suppliers to maintain an adequate inventory in order to keep products accessible for when a business buyer needs them and to reduce the buyer's inventory requirements and costs.

On-time delivery   Reliable, on-time delivery by suppliers also enables business customers to carry less inventory.

Warranty back-up   Purchasers of machinery and high-tech equipment are especially concerned about adequate warranties. They are also keen to obtain repair services and replacement parts quickly, because equipment that cannot be used is costly.

Credit facilities   Suppliers can also give extra value to business buyers by offering credit. Credit helps to improve a business customer's cash flow, reduces the peaks and troughs of capital requirements and thus lowers the company's cost of capital. Although no single supplier can provide every possible service to its customers, a marketing-oriented supplier will try to create a service mix that satisfies the target market.

The importance of service quality

Service quality has become a critical issue because customer expectations of service have broadened. Marketers also need to strive for uniformity of service, simplicity, truthfulness and accuracy; to develop customer service objectives; and to monitor or audit their customer service programmes. Companies can monitor the quality of their service by formally surveying customers or calling on them informally to ask questions about the service they have received. Marketers with a strong customer service programme reap a reward: their customers keep coming back long after the first sale.[2] With customer expectations increasing, it is becoming more difficult for companies to achieve a differential advantage in these areas, and companies must take care to ensure that complaints are handled properly.[3] This reduces the likelihood that dissatisfied customers will give negative feedback to others in the marketplace.[4] One study found that boosting customer retention by 5 per cent could double a small company's profitability.[5] As explored in Chapter 13, some experts argue that service quality delivery is the most important aspect of marketing.

The importance of price

Price matters greatly to a business customer because it influences operating costs and costs of goods sold, and these costs affect the customer's selling price and profit margin. When purchasing major equipment, an industrial buyer views the price as the amount of investment necessary to obtain a certain level of return or savings. Such a purchaser is likely to compare the price of a machine with the value of the benefits that the machine will yield. A while ago, Caterpillar lost market share to foreign competitors because its prices were too high, so it had to re-engineer its cost base and align pricing to customer expectations. A business buyer does not compare alternative products by price alone, though. Other factors, such as product quality and supplier services, are also major elements in the purchase decision. For example, one study found that in the buying decision process for mainframe computer software operating systems, intangible attributes, such as the seller's credibility and understanding of the buyer's needs, were very important in the buyer's decision process.[6]

Methods of business buying

Although no two business buyers go about their jobs in the same way, most use one or more of the following purchase methods: description, inspection, sampling and negotiation.

Description   When products being purchased are commonly standardized according to certain characteristics such as size, shape, weight and colour and graded using such standards, a business buyer may be able to purchase simply by describing or specifying quantity, grade and other attributes. Agricultural produce often falls into this category. In some cases a buyer may specify a particular brand or its equivalent when describing the desired product. Purchases on the basis of description are especially common between a buyer and seller who have established an ongoing relationship built on trust.

Inspection   Certain products, such as large industrial machinery, used vehicles and buildings, have unique characteristics and are likely to vary in condition. A clothing producer would want to see the latest automated pattern-cutting machine in action with another customer before committing to purchase. Consequently, buyers and sellers of such products must base their purchase decisions on inspection.

Sampling   In buying based on sampling, a sample of the product is taken from the lot and evaluated. It is assumed that the characteristics of this sample represent the entire lot. This method is appropriate when the product is homogeneous, for instance grain, and examination of the entire lot is not physically or economically feasible.

Negotiation   Some business purchasing relies on negotiated contracts. In certain instances, a business buyer describes exactly what is needed and then asks sellers to submit bids. The buyer may take the most attractive bids and negotiate with those suppliers. In other cases, the buyer may not be able to identify specifically what is to be purchased but can provide only a general description, as might be the case for a special piece of custom-made equipment. A buyer and seller may negotiate a contract that specifies a base price and contains provisions for the payment of additional costs and fees. These contracts are most likely to be used for one-off projects, such as buildings and capital equipment. For example, the prices that Orbital Sciences Corporation charges its customers for launching and placing satellites in orbit are determined through negotiated contracts.

Types of business purchase

Most business purchases are one of three types: new task purchase, modified re-buy purchase or straight re-buy purchase. The type of purchase affects the number of individuals involved, the length of the buying process and the nature of marketing appropriate.

New task purchase
An organization's initial purchase of an item to be used to perform a new job or to solve a new problem.

New task purchase   In a **new task purchase**, an organization makes an initial purchase of an item to be used to perform a new job or to solve a new problem. This may take a long time because it might require the development of product specifications, supplier specifications and procedures for future purchases. To make the initial purchase, the business buyer usually needs a good deal of information and may formally review a set of possible suppliers. A new task purchase is important to the supplier because it may lead to the sale of large quantities of the product over a period of years.

Modified re-buy purchase
A new task purchase that is changed when it is re-ordered or when the requirements associated with a straight re-buy purchase are modified.

Modified re-buy purchase   In a **modified re-buy purchase**, a new task purchase is changed the second or third time it is ordered, or the requirements associated with a straight re-buy purchase are modified. For example, an organization might seek faster delivery, lower prices or a different quality of product specifications. When modified re-buying occurs, regular suppliers may become more competitive to keep the account. Competing suppliers may have the opportunity to obtain the business.

Straight re-buy purchase   A **straight re-buy purchase** occurs when a buyer re-purchases the same products routinely under approximately the same terms of sale. For example, when re-ordering photocopying paper, a buyer requires little additional information and can usually place the order relatively quickly, often using familiar suppliers that have provided satisfactory service and products in the past. These suppliers try to set up automatic re-ordering systems to make re-ordering easy and convenient for business buyers, and may even monitor the organization's inventory to indicate to the buyer what needs to be ordered.

> **Straight re-buy purchase**
> A routine re-purchase of the same products under approximately the same terms of sale.

Demand for business products

Products sold to business customers are called business products and, consequently, the demand for these products is called business demand. Unlike consumer demand, business demand, formerly known as industrial demand, is:

- derived
- inelastic
- joint, and
- more fluctuating.

Derived demand   As business customers, especially producers, buy products to be used directly or indirectly in the production of goods and services to satisfy consumers' needs, the demand for business products arises from the demand for consumer products; it is, therefore, called **derived demand**. In fact, all business demand can in some way be traced to consumer demand. This occurs at a number of levels, with business sellers being affected in various ways. For instance, consumers today are more concerned with good health and nutrition than ever before, and as a result are purchasing food products containing less cholesterol, saturated fat, sugar and salt. When some consumers stopped buying high-cholesterol cooking fats and margarine, the demand for equipment used in manufacturing these products also dropped. Thus factors influencing consumer buying of various food products have ultimately affected food processors, equipment manufacturers, suppliers of raw materials and even fast-food restaurants, which have had to switch to lower-cholesterol oils for frying. Changes in derived demand result from a chain reaction. When consumer demand for a product changes, a wave is set in motion that affects demand for all of the items involved in the production of that consumer product.

> **Derived demand**
> Demand for business products that arises from the demand for consumer products.

Inelastic demand   The demand for many business products at the industry level is **inelastic demand**, that is, a price increase or decrease will not significantly alter demand for the item. The concept of price elasticity of demand is discussed further in Chapter 20. As many business products contain a number of parts, price increases that affect only one or two parts of the product may yield only a slightly higher per-unit production cost. Of course, when a sizeable price increase for a component represents a large proportion of the total product's cost, demand may become more elastic, because the component price increase will cause the price at the consumer level to rise sharply. For example, if manufacturers of aircraft engines substantially increase the price of these engines, forcing Boeing in turn to raise the prices of its aircraft, the demand for aircraft may become more elastic as airlines reconsider whether they can afford them. An increase in the price of windscreens, however, is unlikely to affect greatly the price of the aircraft or the demand for them.

> **Inelastic demand**
> Demand that is not significantly affected by a price increase or decrease.

The characteristic of inelasticity applies only to industry demand for the business product, not to the demand curve faced by an individual company. For example, suppose that a car component company increases the price of rubber seals sold to car manufacturers, while its competitors retain their lower prices. The car component company would probably experience reduced unit sales because most of its customers would switch to the lower-priced brands. A specific organization is vulnerable to elastic demand, even though industry demand for a particular product is inelastic.

Joint demand The demand for certain business products, especially raw materials and components, is subject to joint demand. Joint demand occurs when two or more items are used in combination to produce a product. For example, a company that manufactures cork noticeboards for schools and colleges needs supplies of cork and wood to produce the item; these two products are demanded jointly. A shortage of cork will cause a drop in the production of wooden surrounds for noticeboards or a lack of chips will hinder computer manufacture.

Joint demand
Demand that occurs when two or more products are used in combination to produce another product.

Marketers selling many jointly demanded items must realize that when a customer begins purchasing one of the jointly demanded items, a good opportunity exists for selling related products. Similarly, when customers purchase a number of jointly demanded products, the producer must take care to avoid shortages of any one of them, because such shortages jeopardize sales of all the jointly demanded products.

Fluctuating demand As the demand for business products fluctuates according to consumer demand, when particular consumer products are in high demand, their producers buy large quantities of raw materials and components to ensure that they can meet long-run production requirements. Such producers may also expand their production capacity, which entails the acquisition of new equipment and machinery, more workers, a greater need for business services, and more raw materials and component parts.

Conversely, a decline in the demand for certain consumer goods significantly reduces the demand for business products used to produce those goods. When consumer demand is low, business customers cut their purchases of raw materials and components, and stop buying equipment and machinery, even for replacement purposes. This trend is especially pronounced during periods of recession.

A marketer of business products may notice changes in demand when its customers change their inventory policies, perhaps because of expectations about future demand. For example, if several dishwasher manufacturers who buy timers from one producer increase their inventory of timers from a two-week to a one-month supply, the timer producer will experience a significant immediate increase in demand.

Sometimes price changes can lead to surprising temporary changes in demand. A price increase for a business item may initially cause business customers to buy more of the item because they expect the price to rise further. Similarly, demand for a business product may be significantly lower following a price cut as buyers wait for further price reductions. Such behaviour is often observed in companies purchasing information technology. Fluctuations in demand can be significant in industries in which price changes occur frequently.

Business buying decisions

Business (or business-to-business) buying behaviour
The purchase behaviour of producers, resellers, the public sector, government units and institutions.

Business (or business-to-business) buying behaviour refers to the purchase behaviour of producers, resellers, the public sector, government units and institutions. Although several of the same factors that affect consumer buying behaviour (discussed in Chapter 5) also influence business buying behaviour, a number of factors are unique to the latter. This section first analyzes the buying centre to learn who participates in making business purchase decisions and then focuses on the stages of the buying decision process and the factors that affect this process.

The buying centre

Most business-to-business purchase decisions are made by more than one person. The group of people within an organization, from various functions, who are involved in making business purchase decisions are usually referred to as the **buying centre** or decision-making unit. These individuals include users, influencers, buyers, deciders and gatekeepers, although one person may perform several of these roles.[7] Participants in the buying process share the goals and risks associated with their decisions. Effective marketers strive to understand the constituents of risk, as perceived by their target customer personnel, so that they may tailor their messages and marketing propositions to reassure members of the buying centre. In this way, marketers hope to gain an advantage over those rivals that fail to understand these customer concerns and issues.

> **Buying centre**
> The group of people within an organization who are involved in making business-to-business purchase decisions.

Users are those in the business who actually use the product being acquired. They frequently initiate the purchase process and/or generate the specifications for the purchase. After the purchase, they also evaluate the product's performance relative to the specifications. Although users do not ordinarily have sufficient power to make the final decision to buy, it is important that their views be considered. A user who is unhappy with a piece of equipment may not work efficiently. Influencers are often technical personnel, such as engineers, who help develop the specifications and evaluate alternative products. Technical personnel are especially important influencers when the products being considered involve new, advanced technology. For example, a chemicals manufacturer seeking to install new processing equipment may take advice from a wide range of technical experts.

Buyers are responsible for selecting suppliers and actually negotiating the terms of purchase. They may also become involved in developing specifications. Buyers are sometimes called purchasing agents or purchasing managers and, in retailers, merchandizers. Their choices of suppliers and products, especially for new task purchases, are heavily influenced by individuals occupying other roles in the buying centre. For straight re-buy purchases, the buyer plays a major role in the selection of suppliers and in negotiations with them. Deciders actually choose the products and suppliers. Although buyers may be the deciders, it is not unusual for different people to occupy these roles. For routinely purchased items, buyers are commonly the deciders. However, a buyer may not be authorized to make purchases that exceed a certain monetary value, in which case higher-level management personnel are the deciders. Gatekeepers, such as secretaries and technical personnel, control the flow of information to and among others in the buying centre. The flow of information from supplier sales representatives to users and influencers is often controlled by buyers or other personnel in the purchasing department. Unfortunately, relations between members of the buying centre can become strained at times.

The size and characteristics of an organization's buying centre are affected by the number of its employees and its market position, the volume and types of products being purchased and the company's overall managerial philosophy regarding exactly who should be involved in purchase decisions. A marketer attempting to sell to a business customer needs to know who is in the buying centre, the types of decisions each individual makes and which individuals are the most influential in the decision process. The marketer should also strive to understand the respective needs of these members and how each perceives risk in terms of the proposed purchase: the marketer should then tailor messages to reassure the various members of the buying centre. Then the marketer will be in a position to contact those in the buying centre who have the most influence. Such an approach is detailed in the Marketing Tools and Techniques box on page 183, which also explains how many organizations deploy the buying behaviour concepts presented in this chapter as they build up an understanding of their customers.

Practitioners' use of the buying behaviour theory: the Dibb/Simkin buying proforma

Marketing tools and techniques

Most practitioners do not want to read a 500-page textbook about understanding customers, but equally they recognize that in order to fully appreciate a business customer's requirements or consumers' buying behaviour, they must be able to:

● profile the targeted customers/consumers – be like them!

● understand the composition of the buying centre

● identify their key customer values (KCVs), customer/consumer needs and expectations

● determine how the customers/consumers buy – their buying process

● understand the influences at work on this process.

In order to devise effective marketing strategies and programmes, marketers must be able to answer three key questions:

1. What needs must be satisfied and for whom?

2. Where should marketers be active in the business customer (or consumer) buying process?

3. Which influencing factors can they in turn influence?

There are many approaches to addressing such an understanding of business customers or consumers, but one proposed by Dibb and Simkin has been widely adopted across consumer, business and service markets. Two examples are presented here in order to illustrate this approach.

Example 1

A leading supplier of herbicides, pesticides and seeds segmented the farmers, its customers in Latin America, identifying 22 market segments (see Chapter 7). As an example, one segment is profiled below, illustrating the types of farmer in this segment, the nature of the buying centre and the very specific, ego-led customer needs. In order to operate successfully in this market segment, a supplier has to satisfy these needs but also tailor marketing campaigns to the characteristics of these farmers and the varied mix of professionals within this buying centre. In developing a better understanding of the buying process, this agrichemicals business realized there were important influencing factors impacting on customer choice that it had previously ignored. Contact was made with organizers of the technical seminars and the trade association in order to gain an advantage over rivals.

Example 2

The example from the civilian aircraft market reveals the complexity of many business markets. The customer needs are extensive but do not provide the challenge. The mix of stakeholders identified within the buying centre or decision-making unit requires a variety of the plane manufacturer's personnel and involvement of some of its strategic partners. The types of sales approach and messaging likely to appeal to the airline's senior executives are not those which will attract the airline's inspection (purchasing) team or its shareholders, so different teams will be required along with tailored messaging and content in order to ensure all parties involved in the decision are adequately addressed. Many of the influencing factors impacting on the customer's decision also require such careful consideration. The customer value proposition required here goes well beyond establishing that the plane satisfies the list of customer needs. However, the analysis provides a very clear picture of what the producer must discuss, with whom and how, if its plane is to be selected by the airline.

The Dibb/Simkin buying proforma:

● forces managers to 'think customer'!

● provides much more than just a description of 'who to sell to'

● identifies exactly what a company must provide/offer

● reveals the influences the company in turn must strive to influence

● provides a framework against which to compare competitors' moves and marketing programmes.

The Dibb/Simkin buying proforma is copyright Sally Dibb and Lyndon Simkin. A more extensive explanation of this technique is offered in either *The Market Segmentation Workbook* (Dibb and Simkin) or *The Marketing Planning Workbook* (Dibb, Simkin and Bradley), both originally published in 1996 by Thomson, London; or in the authors' newer titles *Market Segmentation Success: Making It Happen!* (The Haworth Press/Routledge, 2008) and *Marketing Planning* (Cengage Learning, 2008).

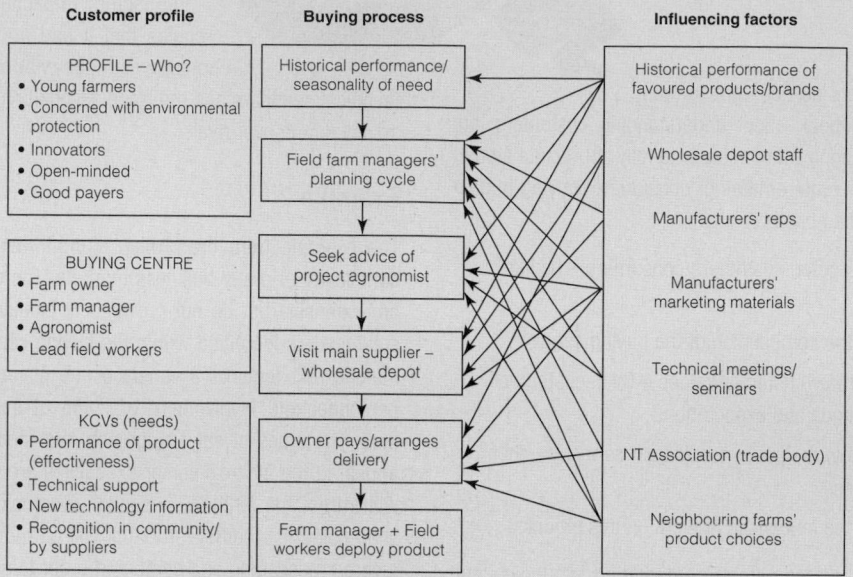

The Dibb/Simkin buying proforma: B2B
Example of an agrichemicals business selling to no-till soya farmers in Latin America

© Sally Dibb and Lyndon Simkin

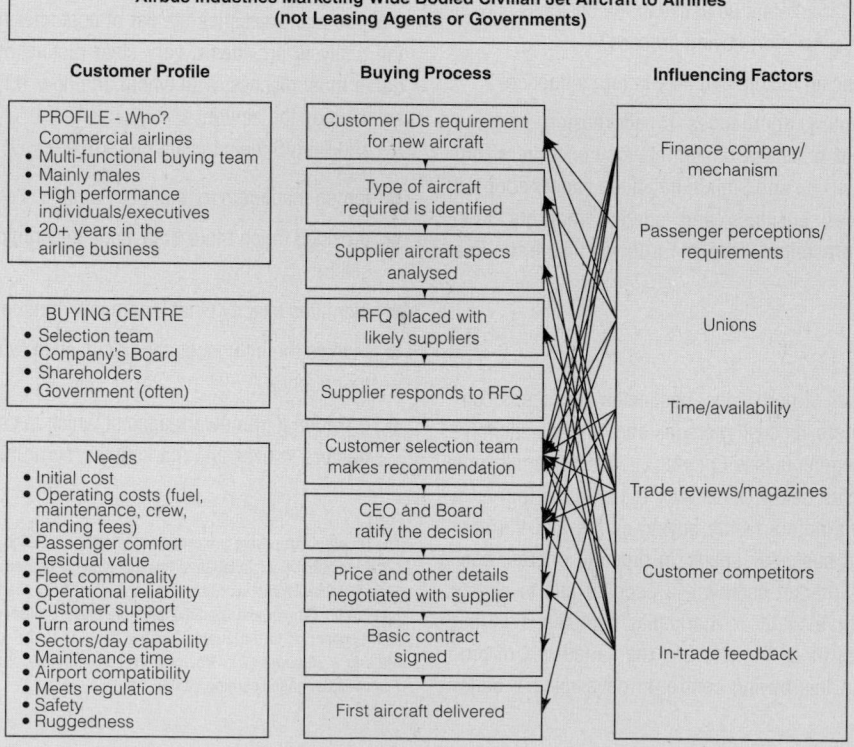

Relationship marketing and managing exchange relationships

The relationship that exists between a supplying organization and its customers is an important aspect of the buying process that deserves special consideration. In fact, marketing experts have become much more interested in marketing relationships in general.[8] The term **relationship marketing** has been used to express this particular development, as explained in Chapter 1. Instead of being concerned about individual transactions between suppliers and buyers, the relationship marketing approach emphasizes the importance of the whole relationship between the parties. Relationship marketing can, therefore, be regarded as all of the activities an organization uses to build, maintain and develop ongoing customer relations.[9] The intention is to nurture a mutually beneficial sustainable relationship and to maximize the 'share of wallet' from the customer over a period of time.

> **Relationship marketing**
> All of the activities an organization uses to build, maintain and develop ongoing customer relations.

Put simply, relationship marketing is concerned with acquiring and keeping customers by ensuring that an appropriate combination of marketing, customer service and quality is provided.[10] Underlying the relationship marketing concept is the idea that the relationship between a supplying organization and its buyers is essentially similar to the relationship between two individuals. For example, bitumen company Nynas, featured in the case at the end of this chapter, has achieved market leadership in many of its key markets through building ongoing relationships with a diversity of customers 24 hours a day and 365 days a year. Such relationships are conducted over a period of time through a series of meetings and interactions, which allow each party to get to know the other, to share information, to adapt to each other, and generally to build trust and cooperation.[11]

As explained in Chapter 1, the concept of relationship marketing is changing the way in which marketers for both consumer and business markets are looking at marketing. However, it is also particularly pertinent to this chapter's discussion of the exchange relationships that develop between buyers and sellers.[12] When a company buys a product or service from another company, both organizations become involved in an exchange process. During the transaction, both buyer and seller will exchange items of value in return for something else. For example, when a software company provides a printing company with a desktop publishing package, it will provide the buyer with a package of benefits that include the software, regular updates, a helpline, on-site support, detailed users' guide, warranty details, a variety of payment options and the opportunity to attend a training course. In exchange, the printer will agree to pay the price negotiated with the manufacturer. Figure 6.3 shows the range of factors that can be exchanged during the purchase process.

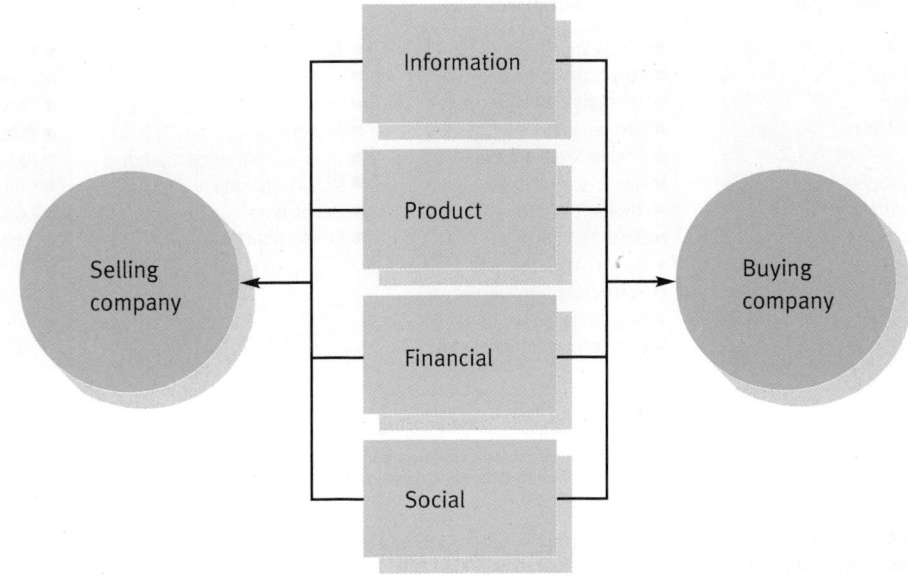

FIGURE 6.3
The exchange process in business buying

It is often in the interests of both parties to develop long-term relationships. If buying and selling companies are used to dealing with each other, they are more likely to be able to adapt to each other's needs and to reach an agreement quickly and easily. Some research suggests that adaptation by suppliers happens more often than adaptation by buyers. However, long-term relationships are often attractive to both companies because they reduce the level of financial and practical risk associated with the purchase. The trend towards long-term relationships has resulted in the development of what is called **relationship management**.[13] This process encourages a match between the seller's competitive advantage and the buyer's requirements over the life cycle of the item being purchased. Larger customer accounts warrant close attention and bespoke customer support, nurturing an ongoing relationship and protecting sales. **Key account management** is practiced by businesses with several very large and important customers, whose volume of business justifies one-to-one tailored handling.

Stages of the business buying decision process

Like consumers, businesses follow a buying decision process. This process is summarized at the top of Figure 6.4.

Stage 1 In the first stage, one or more individuals recognize that a problem or need exists. Problem recognition may arise under a variety of circumstances, either from inside or outside the company. For example, a machine might reach the end of its working

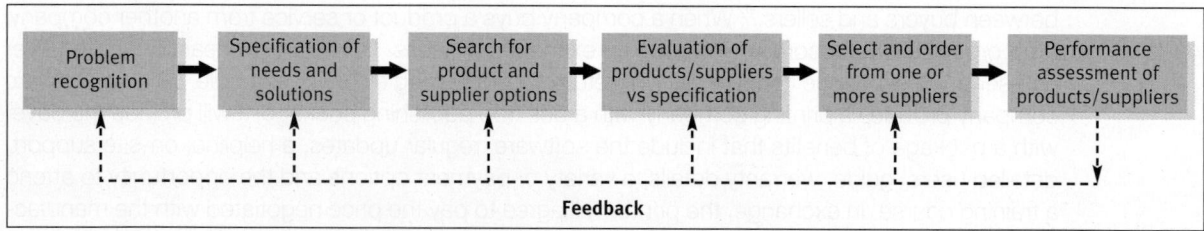

Buying decision-making process

Environmental	Organizational	Cultural	Individual
■ Political ■ Economic ■ Societal ■ Technological ■ Legal ■ Regulatory ■ Competitive ■ Supply chain and channel	■ Corporate strategy ■ Corporate policies ■ Strategic alliances ■ Partnerships ■ Commercial objectives ■ Financial directives ■ Resources ■ Purchasing policies ■ Codes of conduct ■ Purchasing transparency ■ Buying centre structure ■ Deciders and influencers	■ Cultural fit ■ Cooperation ■ Conflict ■ Power relationships ■ Strategic partnershipping ■ Relative positions ■ Behaviours ■ Ethical standards	■ Role and position ■ Level of experience ■ Perceptions of risk ■ Extent of empowerment ■ Age ■ Culture ■ Education/training ■ Pay and incentives ■ Personality ■ Relationship histories ■ Key performance indicators

Influencing factors

The B2B decision-making process is similar to that for consumer purchasing, but is more formal and is specified in greater detail. The set of probable influencing factors is significantly different to those explored in the previous chapter's examination of consumer buying.

FIGURE 6.4
The business buying decision process and factors that may influence it

life and need to be replaced, the CEO may dictate the desirability of finding a supplier for an IT outsourcing agreement, a key customer might demand a new material be sourced, or changes in fire regulations might dictate the need for a new approach to manufacturing. Often, the problem recognized is simply the need to replenish stocks of raw materials or components. Individuals in the buying centre, such as users, influencers or buyers, may be involved in problem recognition, but this may be stimulated by external sources, such as sales representatives or customers.

Stage 2   The second stage of the process, development of product specifications, requires those involved to assess the problem or need, and to determine what is necessary to resolve or satisfy it. During this stage, users and influencers, such as technical personnel, production managers and engineers, often provide information and advice for developing product specifications. By assessing and describing needs, the organization should be able to establish product specifications.

Stage 3   Searching for possible products and suppliers to solve the problem is the third stage in the decision process. Search activities may involve surfing the web, looking in company files and trade directories, contacting suppliers for information and networking, visiting trade shows, identifying suppliers used by rivals, soliciting proposals from known suppliers, and examining catalogues and trade publications. Suppliers may be viewed as unacceptable because they are too small to supply the quantities needed, or because they do not have the necessary information technology systems to keep appropriate delivery records. In some instances, the product may not be available from any existing supplier and the buyer must then find an innova-

Value analysis
An evaluation of each component of a potential purchase.

tive company that can design and build the product. During this search stage, some organizations engage in **value analysis**, which is an evaluation of each component of a potential purchase. Value analysis examines quality, designs, materials and possibly item reduction or deletion to acquire the product in the most cost-effective way. Usually suppliers are judged against several criteria and some will be ruled unsuitable. Some organizations practice **supplier analysis**, a formal and systematic appraisal of current and potential suppliers or vendors, focusing on factors such as price, product quality, delivery service, product availability, reliability, reputation, client profile and customer service.

Supplier analysis
A formal and systematic evaluation of current and potential suppliers.

If all goes well, the search stage will result in a list of several alternative products and suppliers.

Stage 4   The fourth stage is evaluating the products on the list to determine which options (if any) meet the product specifications developed in the second stage. The advertisement in Figure 6.5 stresses the particular product quality attributes that may help customers evaluate whether a particular offering meets their requirements. At this point, various suppliers are evaluated according to multiple criteria, such as price, service, technical support, ability to deliver, as well as brand reputation and track record.

Stage 5   The results of the deliberations and assessments in the fourth stage are used during the fifth stage, to select the most appropriate product and supplier. In some cases the buyer may

Sole sourcing
A buying process that involves the selection of only one supplier.

decide on several suppliers. In others, only one supplier is selected, which is a situation known as **sole sourcing**. Sole sourcing has traditionally been discouraged except when a product is available from only one company. In recent times sole sourcing has become more popular, partly because such an arrangement means better communications between buyer and supplier, stability and higher profits for the supplier and, often, lower prices for the buyer. The popular manufacturing approach of just-in-time often requires sole sourcing, in order to facilitate the logistical arrangements between buyer and supplier. However, many organizations prefer to purchase goods and services from several suppliers,

FIGURE 6.5
DHL promotes the quality and reliability of its courier services

Multiple sourcing
A business's decision to use several suppliers.

multiple sourcing to reduce the possibility of disruption caused by strikes, shortages, quality problems, delivery glitches or bankruptcy. The actual product is ordered in this fifth stage and specific details regarding terms, credit arrangements, delivery dates and methods, and technical assistance are worked out.

Stage 6 During the sixth stage, the performance of the supplier and the product or service is evaluated, by comparing outcomes with specifications and customer expectations of the relationship. Sometimes, even though the product meets the specifications, its performance does not adequately solve the problem or satisfy the need recognized in the first stage. In such cases, the product specifications must be adjusted. The supplier's performance is also evaluated during this stage, and if it is found wanting, the buyer seeks corrective action from the supplier or searches for a new supplier. Buyers are increasingly concerned with obtaining high-quality service from suppliers and may formally set performance targets for them. The results of such performance evaluations become feedback for the other stages and influence future purchase decisions. In many business relationships, particularly long-term relationships, suppliers formally audit their customers' satisfaction levels in order to minimize any problems that may eventually lose a customer to a competitor.

Uses of the business buying decision process This business buying decision process is used in its entirety primarily for new task purchases. Several of the stages, but not necessarily all, are used for modified re-buying and straight re-buying, and fewer individuals are likely to be involved in these decisions. If a buyer–supplier relationship is working well, there may be no consideration of alternative suppliers. Indeed, customers may work with such well-regarded suppliers when specifying their next product or purchasing needs. There is a desire in many business markets, particularly in supplier–manufacturer relationships, to create mutually beneficial ongoing partnerships, with customers and suppliers openly sharing market data, knowledge of product or competitor developments, and future plans.

Influences on business buying

Figure 6.4 also lists the four major categories of factors that influence business buying decisions: environmental, organizational, interpersonal and individual. In the Topical Insight box (see page 190), insurance broker Willis's SME clients reflect in their customer engagement the influencing factors that impact on their corporate customers' decision-making.

Environmental factors
Uncontrollable forces such as politics, competitive and economic factors, legal and regulatory issues, technological changes and socio-cultural issues.

Environmental factors   Chapter 3 explained that **environmental factors** are uncontrollable forces such as politics, laws, regulations and regulatory agencies, activities of interest groups, changes in the economy, competitors' actions and technological changes. These forces generate a considerable amount of uncertainty for an organization, which can make individuals in the buying centre apprehensive about certain types of purchase. Changes in one or more environmental forces can create new purchasing opportunities. For example, changes in competition and technology can make buying decisions difficult in the case of products such as computers, a field in which competition is increasingly affected by new cooperative strategies between companies. Compaq Computers, for instance, grew into a billion-dollar company by competing only against IBM and developing cooperative relationships with all other potential competitors, ultimately tying up with HP.[14]

Organizational factors
Include the buyer's objectives, purchasing policies and resources, as well as the size and composition of its buying centre.

Organizational factors   **Organizational factors** influencing the buying decision process include the buyer's objectives, purchasing policies and resources, as well as the size and composition of its buying centre. An organization may have certain buying policies to which buying centre participants must conform. For instance, a company's policies may require long-term contracts, perhaps longer than most sellers desire. The nature of an organization's financial resources may require special credit arrangements. Any of these conditions could affect purchase decision processes.

Interpersonal factors
The relationships among people in the buying centre and with suppliers' personnel.

Interpersonal factors   **Interpersonal factors** are the relationships among the people in the buying centre or decision-making unit, where the use of power and the level of conflict significantly influence organizational buying decisions. Certain managers in the buying centre may be better communicators than others and thus more persuasive. Often these interpersonal dynamics are hidden, making them difficult for business marketers and key account managers to appraise. There are also interpersonal factors to consider between supplier and customer personnel. While a customer may be purchasing a particular product, the supplier's personnel involved with placing the order, offering technical assistance or customer service, and in logistical arrangements, become a very important concern for the customer's managers. No matter how good the product may be, if the supplier's personnel are not regarded in a good light by the customer's managers, there is unlikely to be a high level of customer satisfaction. Suppliers must select, train, motivate and reward, control and orientate their customer-facing personnel very carefully. The individual factors pertinent to particular managers are, therefore, important.

Individual factors
The personal characteristics of individuals in the buying centre, such as age, education, personality, position in the organization and income level.

Individual factors   **Individual factors** are the personal characteristics of individuals in the buying centre, such as age, education, personality, position in the organization and income level. For example, a 60-year-old manager who left school at 16 and has been with the organization ever since may affect the decisions of the buying centre differently from a 30-year-old with a two-year employment history, who left university with a business studies degree and an MBA. How influential these factors will be depends on the buying situation, the type of product being purchased and whether the purchase is new task, modified re-buy or straight re-buy. The negotiating styles of individuals will undoubtedly vary within an organization and from one organization to another. To be effective, a marketer needs to know customers well enough to be aware of these individual factors and the effects they may have on purchase decisions.

Insurance brokers reflect influences on clients' decision-making

Topical insight

Willis is a global leading Anglo-American insurance broker serving many large commercial clients. In order to look after the SME Willis market, Willis established the innovative Willis Network and its sister N^2. Independent insurance brokers can sign up to become a member of the Willis Network and the support, market insight, products and negotiating power with the large insurers that would normally only be available to large-scale insurance firms. Members are guaranteed a regional monopoly within the Network.

> The Willis Networks offer independent regional insurance brokers The Best of Both Worlds through the Willis Commercial Network and Willis N^2. Our regional broker network members can access Willis' resources to help them to flourish and grow in a dynamic market.

Member broker firms in the network serve many private and commercial customers. One key market is the insurance cover provided to corporate SME clients to cover their commercial activities. For example, the insurance cover required by a manufacturing business with turnover of around £5m and employing 80 workers. The cover generally is provided by the major insurers, such as Allianz, AXA, RSA or Zurich, but is purchased via an intermediary, which is the local broker. The purchasing power and scale of Willis enables the company to negotiate preferential terms and customer service on behalf of network members, the local brokers, who in turn may deliver improved deals and service to their corporate clients.

Marketing research identified SME client needs for commercial combined insurance to be value, credibility of the package and supplier, well-specified products, incentives, customer service, supportive advice and peace of mind. The proposition offered and the way in which it is conveyed by the broker must reflect these B2B client requirements. While the product and service package is a key determining factor in gaining client interest, members of the Willis Network must reflect other research findings in their sales and marketing practices. For example, these corporate customers seek value for money, but also reassurance that the provided insurance cover will be fit for purpose and give them peace of mind. The personal relationship and degree of empathy between the boss of the SME client and the broker's staff are essential requisites for success and for giving such peace of mind.

One of the most important influences upon these companies' selection of preferred broker and the purchase of the specific insurance package relates as much to peer comments as to the overt activities of the broker's staff. If the bosses of other SMEs speak highly about Willis Networks' local broker, there is likely to be a sales opportunity for the broker. As a result, the broker must identify and then engage with clients' networks and business circles, ensuring positive reinforcement for its brand reputation, service and products from the trusted contacts of the prospective SME's owner. This networking and reputation building often involves many afternoons on the golf course, business lunches, sponsoring local business gatherings and gaining coverage in the business pages of the local press or on LinkedIn fora. The importance of understanding such influencing forces and the various roles within the purchase decision-making process is essential for marketers in this challenging and very competitive sector.

Sources: www.willisnetworks.co.uk/why-willis-networks/gatewayto-willis, 22 March 2011; www.willis.com/About_Willis, 22 March 2011; Willis, March 2015; IHN, December 2014.

Selection and analysis of business markets

Marketing research is becoming more important in business markets. Most of the marketing research techniques discussed in Chapter 9 can be applied to **business marketing**. This section focuses on important and unique approaches to selecting and analyzing business markets.

Many business marketers have easy access to a considerable amount of information about potential customers, particularly in industrial or manufacturing markets, for much of this information appears in government and industry publications. Even though

Business marketing
Activities directed towards facilitating and expediting exchanges between businesses.

marketers may use different procedures to isolate and analyze target markets, most follow a similar pattern:

1. determining who potential customers are and what they require
2. deciding how many and locating where they are
3. estimating their purchase potential and likelihood of ongoing loyalty
4. identifying how to engage with them.

Identifying potential customers

All marketers must determine who are potential customers.

Standard Industrial Classification (SIC) system
A system that provides information on different industries and products, and classifies economic characteristics of industrial, commercial, financial and service organizations.

The Standard Industrial Classification system Much information about business customers is based on the **Standard Industrial Classification (SIC) system**, which provides information on different industries and products, and was developed to classify selected economic characteristics of industrial, commercial, financial and service organizations. In the UK, this system is administered by the Office for National Statistics (www.gov.uk/government/publications/standard-industrial-classification-of-economic-activities-sic). Table 6.1 shows how the SIC system can be used to categorize products.

The most recent SIC manual contains 19 broad divisions, each broken into many sub-types, each denoted by a five-digit code. For example, one of the broader 19 categories is Accommodation and Food Service, which contains 13 sub-categories, such as Hotels, Trailer Parks and Licenced Restaurants. The Manufacturing category

TABLE 6.1 The Standard Industrial Classification (SIC) system for categorizing industrial customers

Agriculture, Forestry and Fishing
Mining and Quarrying
Manufacturing
Electricity, Gas, Steam and Air Conditioning Supply
Water Supply, Sewerage, Water Management and Remediation Activities
Construction
Transportation and Storage
Accommodation and Food Service Activities
Infrastructure and Communication
Financial and Insurance Activities
Real Estate Activities
Professional, Scientific and Technical activities
Administration and Support Service Activities
Public Administration and Defence
Education
Human Health and Social Work Activities
Arts, Entertainment and Recreation
Activities of Households as Employers and Own Use
Activities of Extraterritorial Organizations and Bodies

contains dozens and dozens of sub-types, such as Manufacturers of Men's Underwear, Manufacturers of Plaster, Copper Production and Manufacturers of Pumps. Other countries, including the USA, have their versions of SIC.

Data are available for each SIC category through various government publications and departments. Table 6.2 shows the types of information that can be obtained from government sources. Some data are available by town, county and metropolitan area. Business market data also appear in such non-government sources as Dun & Bradstreet's *Market Identifiers*.

The SIC system is a ready-made tool that allows business marketers to allocate industrial organizations to market segments based mainly on the type of product manufactured or handled. Although the SIC system is a vehicle for segmentation identifying groupings of customers (see Chapter 7) it must be used in conjunction with other types of data to enable a business marketer to determine exactly which customers he or she can reach and how many of them can be targeted. The SIC system is a convenient grouping categorization, but it does not negate the need to fully explore customer buying behaviour, as depicted in the Marketing Tools and Techniques box on pages 183–4, in order to properly consider target market priorities.

Input–output analysis   Input–output analysis works well in conjunction with the SIC system. This type of analysis is based on the assumption that the outputs or sales of one industry are the input or purchases of other industries. For example, component manufacturers provide products that form an input for manufacturers of white goods such as washing machines, dishwashers and fridges. **Input–output data** tell what types of industries purchase the products of a particular industry.

> **Input–output data**
> Information on what types of industries purchase the products of a particular industry.

After discovering which industries purchase the major portion of an industry's output, the next step is to find the SIC numbers for those industries. Although organizations are grouped differently in the input–output tables and the SIC system, ascertaining SIC numbers can be difficult. However, the Office for National Statistics does provide some limited conversion tables with the input–output data. These tables can assist business marketers in assigning SIC numbers to the industry categories used in the input–output analysis. Having determined the SIC numbers of the industries that buy the company's output, a business marketer is in a position to ascertain the number of establishments that are potential buyers nationally, by town and by county. Government publications report the number of establishments within SIC classifications, along with other types of data, such as those shown in Table 6.2.

Identifying and locating potential customers   Once business marketers have achieved this level of information, they can identify and locate potential customers using the internet or business directories such as Kompass. Sixty-six countries, over five million companies and 15 million contacts are included in Kompass's business database (http://gb.kompass.com). These sources contain information about a company such as its name, SIC number, address, phone number and annual sales, allowing organizations to develop lists of potential customers by area.

TABLE 6.2   Types of government information available about industrial markets (based on SIC categories)

Value of industry shipments
Number of establishments
Number of employees
Exports as a percentage of shipments
Imports as a percentage of apparent consumption
Compound annual average rate of growth
Major producing areas

A second approach, which is more expedient but also more expensive, is to use one of the many marketing services businesses. For example, Market Location (www.marketlocation.com) and Experian (www.experian.co.uk/business-services/b2bmarketing-overview.html) are able to provide lists of organizations that fall into particular SIC groups or any categorization created by clients. Information can include name, location, sales volume, number of employees, types of product handled and names of chief executives. Business marketers can then decide which companies on the list to pursue. This will usually involve an assessment of attractiveness and purchase potential. As described in Chapters 8 and 12, there are also many techniques that assist marketers in assessing the relative attractiveness of customers and market segments, such as the directional policy matrix and 'ABC sales: contribution' analysis, explained later in *Marketing: Concepts and Strategies*.

In business marketing, situation-specific variables may be more relevant in segmenting markets than general customer characteristics. Business customers concentrate on benefits sought; therefore, understanding the end use of the product is more important than the psychology of decisions or socio-economic characteristics. Segmenting by benefits rather than by customer characteristics can provide insight into the structure of the market and opportunities for new customers.[15]

To estimate the purchase potential of business customers or groups of customers, a marketer must find a relationship between the size of potential customers' purchases and a variable available in SIC data, such as the number of employees. For example, a fabric manufacturer might attempt to determine the average number of metres of different materials purchased by a specific type of potential clothing manufacturer relative to the number of people employed. If the marketer has no previous experience in this market segment, it will probably be necessary to survey a random sample of potential customers in order to establish a relationship between purchase sizes and numbers of people employed. Once this relationship has been established, it can be applied to potential customer segments to estimate their purchases. After deriving these estimates, the marketer selects the customers to be included in the target market.

More and more businesses are adopting segmentation schemes that are based on the needs, buying behaviour and characteristics of their customers, rather than on simple trade categories or SIC codes. Such segmentation demands a thorough understanding of the nature of purchasing, the buying decision-making process and influencing factors, as described in this chapter. The next chapter *of Marketing: Concepts and Strategies* explores the ways in which business marketers derive market segments and establish target market strategies.

FIGURE 6.6

Networking, discussing and engaging with prospective business customers is an important part of identifying likely sales leads and honing an appropriate marketing proposition

Marketing's variations in business markets

Business marketers often have to address the needs of business customers within a marketing channel and the needs of their intended business customers. Some business marketers must also serve the needs of consumers. Marketers of consumer goods often manage many products and deal with perhaps thousands of customers. Mostly, although not always, such consumer products pass through a marketing channel so that a manufacturer's marketing managers deal primarily with channel member business customers. So for example, the marketers handling Snickers or Mars bars are concerned with understanding and satisfying their retail customers, such as the large cash-and-carry groups and the supermarkets. However, these marketers are also developing the marketing programmes targeting the end-user consumers. Mars' marketers also handle the company's marketing activity aimed at the individual consumer. While a manufacturer's marketers often have to address dual audiences, channel member customers and consumers, it is more likely that their focus will be on the business (trade) customer.

Many business marketers handle a relatively small number of clients and the need to tailor marketing propositions to these customers' wishes is arguably more important than in consumer markets. While all marketers must properly understand buying behaviour and purchasers' characteristics, it is absolutely crucial in business marketing for marketers to develop such an understanding. Sales staff play a central role in building this understanding. Their relationships with customers can be leveraged to gain a particularly in-depth appreciation of customers' needs. Not surprisingly, the sales and marketing personnel in many business-to-business companies work together very closely.

There are other nuances worth mentioning. Most advertisements shown on television over the course of an evening are for consumer goods and services: they are eye-catching, emotive and highly persuasive. This style of advertising reflects the emotive brand positionings developed for many consumer goods, such as Nike or Guinness. While business marketers also strive to create strong brands[16] (see Chapter 11) that are distinctive and attractive, much business branding lacks the emotion of consumer branding and suffers from a relative paucity of investment in supportive marketing communications activity and spending. Business branding tends to be more simplistic, focusing on identification and product differentiation. There are, of course, exceptions, with some business-to-business brands such as IBM or JCB being just as powerful as consumer brands.

The role of competition is different, too. It is unlikely that arch-rivals Tesco, Sainsbury's and ASDA would ever cooperate and work together. Similarly, why would KP and Walkers ever unite? Many brands between which a consumer may choose are unlikely ever to cooperate and work in harmony with each other. Indeed, the Competition and Markets Authority and EU regulators would probably be unimpressed if they did. In many business situations, though, individual companies pool their expertise and resources in order to win contracts with customers. For example, to offer retailers a viable chip-and-pin payment service, IT services company Fujitsu joined forces with Barclaycard Merchant Services (payment transactions), Box (hardware) and Cybertill (installation and maintenance) as a partnership. However, partners in one market segment may in fact be arch-rivals in another. Fujitsu may compete with CapGemini, BT or IBM in one segment, but partner such companies in order to serve the needs of business customers in another. The implication is that the understanding of competitive forces is often more complex and intriguing in many business markets and rivals cannot always be treated as the enemy!

Target market strategies are important to all marketers, irrespective of product or market. In order to develop a target market strategy, marketers must be able to allocate a market's customers into groups or market segments. The consumer marketer may use lifestyles, socio-economic information or consumers' perceived benefits to create market segments or groups of like-minded consumers. The business marketer, however, may fall back on more simple criteria, such as SIC codes or the trade sectors of their customers, in order to determine market segments. This very important aspect of marketing strategy is explored in Chapter 7. Until an understanding of business customers' buying behaviour has been developed, as described in this chapter, it is not possible to produce a market segmentation scheme. Armed with customer insights as depicted in the Topical Insight (page 190), it is straightforward to develop market segments.

If consumer marketers feel they have an inadequate appreciation of consumers' issues and buying behaviour, it is relatively straightforward to embark on suitable marketing research activities in order to rectify this deficiency. As described in Chapter 9, undertaking observations or surveys of consumers is fairly routine. However, busy executives and decision-makers inside business customers rarely offer to attend focus groups, they discard questionnaires and are not easy to access for interviews. Apart from access problems, business customers may well use any surveying to lobby suppliers for a better deal. For example, they may feed back to the supplier's marketers behind the survey, the apparent importance of a better pricing option or improved customer service systems, rather than objectively and openly engage in the marketing research activity. Consumer products are readily visible on retailers' shelves; their prices, marketing communications campaigns, product features or attributes, and their channels to market are there to be seen by competitors' marketers. In most business markets, it is not easy to gain access to rivals' products or services, and the marketing programmes are not so readily visible.

The marketing mix is the set of tactical ingredients manipulated by marketers in marketing programmes designed to implement a target market strategy. As described in Part Three of *Marketing: Concepts and Strategies*, all marketers manipulate the marketing mix in order to reflect the nature of their market, customer buying behaviour, the activities of competitors, organizational capabilities and corporate objectives. Compared with consumer marketers, those tasked with marketing business products have to make certain adjustments to their marketing mix programmes.

The overall implication is that business marketers must modify their use of the marketing toolkit to reflect the nature of their markets and the characteristics of their business customers. The overall marketing process and the toolkit apply irrespective of the marketplace, but it is evident that business marketers, consumer goods marketers and the marketers of services need to make certain modifications. These themes are discussed in more detail in Chapter 21.

Business marketers often have to address the needs of customers within a marketing channel as well as the needs of their intended customers. Some business marketers must also serve the needs of consumers. Many business marketers handle a relatively small number of customers and must tailor marketing propositions to these customers' specific wishes. The sales and marketing personnel in many business-to-business companies work together very closely.

Summary

Business marketing or B2B marketing used to be known as *organizational, industrial* or *business-to-business marketing*. Business markets consist of individuals or groups that purchase a specific kind of product for resale, for direct use in producing other products, or for use in their day-to-day operations. *Producer markets* include those individuals and business organizations that purchase products for the purpose of making a profit by using them either to produce other products or in their own operations. Classified as reseller *markets* are intermediaries, such as *wholesalers*, distributors and *retailers*, who buy finished products and resell them for the purpose of making a profit. *Government markets* consist of national and local governments, which spend huge amounts annually on goods and services to support their internal operations and provide citizens with needed services. Many businesses refer to government, local government and institutions collectively as the public sector, and the *public sector market* is a growing area of activity within the marketing discipline. Organizations that seek to achieve charitable, educational, community or other non-business goals constitute *institutional markets*. Aspects of government and much of institutional marketing today are described as the third sector, with social marketing addressing their customers.

Business-to-business transactions differ from consumer transactions in several ways. The transactions tend to be larger, and negotiations occur less frequently, though they are often lengthy. Business transactions sometimes involve more than one person or one department in the purchasing organization. They may also involve *reciprocity*, an arrangement in which two organizations agree to buy from each other, although some countries have strict rules governing such agreements. Business customers are usually viewed as more rational and more likely to seek information about a product's features and technical specifications than are ultimate consumers.

When purchasing products, business customers must be particularly concerned about quality, delivery, service, price and reputation. Quality is important because it directly affects the quality of the organizational buyer's ultimate product. To achieve an exact standard, organizations often buy their products on the basis of a set of expressed characteristics, called specifications. Reliable and fast delivery is crucial to many organizations, whose production lines must be fed with a continuous supply of component parts and raw materials. Because services can have a direct influence on a company's costs, sales and profits, such matters as market information, on-time delivery and availability of parts can be crucial to a business buyer. Although a business customer does not decide which products to purchase solely by their price, cost is of prime concern because it directly influences a company's profitability. Product range, regulatory compliance, innovation, reliability and logistical support may also be significant considerations. Increasingly, business buyers are concerned with service support levels and the ongoing commitment from their selected suppliers. There is a view that a supplier's personnel in terms of knowledge, motivation, attitude and passion for assisting the customer, are an integral part of the product proposition being 'consumed' by the business customer.

Business buyers use several purchasing methods, including description, inspection, sampling and negotiation. Most business purchases are new task, modified re-buy or straight re-buy. In a *new task purchase*, an organization makes an initial purchase of an item to be used to perform a new job or to solve a new problem. In a *modified re-buy purchase,* a new task purchase is changed the second or third time it is ordered, or the requirements associated with a straight re-buy purchase are modified. A *straight re-buy purchase* occurs when a buyer repurchases the same products routinely under approximately the same terms of sale.

Business demand differs from consumer demand along several dimensions. *Derived demand* is the demand for business products that arises from the demand for consumer products. At the industry level, *inelastic demand* is a demand that is not significantly affected by a price increase or decrease. If the price of an industrial item changes, demand for the product will not change proportionally. Some business products are subject to *joint demand*, which occurs when two or more items are used in combination to make a product. Finally, because business demand ultimately derives from consumer demand, the demand for business products can fluctuate widely.

Business (or business-to-business) buying behaviour refers to the purchase behaviour of producers, resellers, government units and institutions. Business purchase decisions are made through a *buying centre* or decision-making unit; the group of people who are involved in making organizational purchase decisions. Users are those in the organization that actually use the product. Influencers help develop the specifications and evaluate alternative products for possible use. Buyers are responsible for selecting the suppliers and negotiating the terms of the purchases. Deciders choose the products and suppliers. Gatekeepers control the flow of information to and among people who occupy the other roles in the buying centre.

When a company buys a product or service from another company, both organizations enter into a process during which items of value are exchanged in return for something else. This exchange process may lead to a long-term relationship between buyer and seller. *Relationship marketing* is the term used to explain the special attention being given to this area and is defined as the activities an organization uses to build, maintain and develop customer relations (for both business and consumer markets). The trend towards long-term relationships has resulted in *relationship management,* increased *value analysis* and the more systematic evaluation of suppliers in *supplier analysis. Key account management* is an associated development.

The stages of the business buying decision process are (1) problem recognition, (2) development of product specifications to solve the problem, (3) search for products and suppliers, (4) evaluation of products relative to specifications, (5) selection and ordering of the most appropriate product, and (6) evaluation of the product's and the supplier's performance. The evaluation of product and suppliers will directly affect future purchasing decisions. *Sole sourcing*, the process of selecting only one supplier, is becoming more popular, particularly where manufacturers are practicing just-in-time production. Many organizations still opt to practice *multiple sourcing.*

Four categories of factors influence business buying decisions: environmental, organizational, interpersonal and individual. *Environmental factors* include politics, laws and regulations, economic conditions, competitive forces and technological changes. *Organizational factors* include the buyer's objectives, purchasing policies and resources, as well as the size and composition of its buying centre. *Interpersonal factors* refer to the relationships among the people in the buying centre or decision-making unit, and relationships between supplier and customer personnel. *Individual factors* refer to the personal characteristics of individuals in the buying centre, such as age, education, personality, position in the organization and income.

Business marketing is a set of activities directed at facilitating and expediting exchanges between organizations rather than with consumers.

Business marketers have a considerable amount of information available to them for use in planning their marketing strategies and for identifying sales potential. Much of this information is based on the *Standard Industrial Classification (SIC) system*, which classifies businesses into major industry divisions, classes, groups and activities. The SIC system provides business marketers with information needed to identify market leads. It can best be used for this purpose in conjunction with other information, such as *input–output data.* After identifying target industries, the marketer can locate potential customers by using the internet or directories, or by employing a marketing services business. The marketer must then estimate the potential purchases of business customers. Segmentation is now at the heart of most business-to-business marketing strategies, as explained in the next chapter.

Business-to-business branding tends to be more simplistic than is the case with consumer brands, focusing on identification and product differentiation. In many business situations, individual companies pool their expertise and resources in order to win contracts with customers. However, partners in one market segment may in fact be arch-rivals in another. The implication is that the understanding of competitive forces is often more complex and intriguing in business markets and rivals cannot always be treated as 'the enemy'.

Although SIC codes and industry trade categories are often used by business marketers, increasingly the approaches deployed by consumer marketers in creating market segments are being deployed in business markets. Undertaking marketing research in business markets is quite different from researching consumers. Compared with consumer markets, those tasked with marketing business products have to reflect certain market nuances when developing their marketing mix programmes.

Key links

● This chapter must be read in conjunction with Chapter 5, which details the buying behaviour of consumers. A popular examination question is to compare and contrast the buying behaviour models in consumer and business markets.

● In strategic marketing, a key use of an understanding of customer behaviour is the construction of market segments, as discussed in Chapter 7.

● The marketing mix should reflect the nuances of the market in question, as described in Chapter 21.

Important terms

Business (or business-to-business) buying behaviour
Business market
Business marketing
Buying centre
Derived demand
Environmental factors
Government markets
Individual factors
Industrial, organizational or business-to-business market
Inelastic demand
Input–output data
Institutional markets
Interpersonal factors
Joint demand
Key account management
Modified re-buy purchase
Multiple sourcing
New task purchase
Organizational factors
Producer markets
Public sector markets
Reciprocity
Relationship management
Relationship marketing
Reseller markets
Retailers
Sole sourcing
Standard Industrial Classification (SIC) system
Straight re-buy purchase
Supplier analysis
Third sector
Value analysis
Wholesalers

Discussion and review questions

1. Identify, describe and give examples of four major types of business market.

2. Why are business buyers generally considered more rational in regard to their purchasing behaviour than consumers?

3. What are the primary concerns of business customers?

4. List several characteristics that differentiate business transactions from consumer ones.

5. What are the commonly used methods of business buying?

6. Why do buyers involved in a straight re-buy purchase require less information than those making a new task purchase?

7. How does business demand differ from consumer demand?

8. What are the major components of a buying centre or decision-making unit?

9. What elements may be exchanged by a buyer and seller when a purchase transaction takes place?

10. Why has relationship management attracted so much interest in business markets?

11. Identify the stages of the business buying decision process. How is this decision process used when making straight re-buys?

12. What impact does the evaluation of a particular purchase have on future buying decisions?

13. How do environmental, organizational, interpersonal and individual factors affect business purchases?

14. What function does the SIC system help business marketers perform?

15. List some sources that a business marketer can use to determine the names and addresses of potential customers.

16. In what ways do business marketers have to reflect the nuances of business markets when deploying the marketing toolkit?

Recommended readings

Brennan, R., Canning, L. and McDowell, R., *Business-to-Business Marketing* (Sage, 2014).

Ellis, N., *Business-to-Business Marketing: Relationships, Networks and Strategies* (Oxford University Press, 2010).

Gillin, P. and Schwartzman, E., *Social Marketing to Business Customers: Listen To Your B2B Market, Generate Major Account Leads and Build Client Relationships* (Wiley, 2011).

Hakansson, H., Ford, D., Gadd, L.-E., Snehota, I. and Waluszewski, A., *Business in Networks* (Wiley, 2011).

Hutt, M.D. and Speh, T.W., *Business Marketing Management: B2B* (Cengage, 2013).

Webster, F.E., *Industrial Marketing Strategy* (Wiley, 1995).

Internet exercise

Log onto Dell's website. Ignore the sections aimed at consumers, such as *For Home*. Instead, go to *For Work*. This section details Dell's business-to-business products, services and upcoming events. There are sections offering solutions to small business, public sector and large enterprises, in many areas such as healthcare, education, manufacturing, energy, retailing, financial services, telecommunications, as well as government. Visit Dell's website at: www1.euro.dell.com or www.dell.com.

1. In what ways do Dell's web pages for business products reflect the requirements of business customers?

2. How have the messages been tailored to reflect the buying behaviour of Dell's business customers?

Group tasks

1. In seeking to persuade a business customer to sign a contract, a supplier must identify the composition of the buying centre or decision making unit, the influencers and deciders, and address a myriad of different stakeholders. Select a business product or service of your choice and map out the likely buying centre.

2. The days of PG Tips and Tetley dominating the tea aisle in the supermarket have long gone. Today there are many brands but also many types of infusions on offer. How does a retailer such as Waitrose or Tesco determine which brands and what tea types to stock?

Applied mini-case

Opportunities from social media are blossoming. American Express's B2B networking site *Openforum.com* is accessible to both new business customers and current Open Card members. It provides small and medium-sized enterprises (SMEs) access to a wealth of advice and insight, including the views of Barbara Corcoram, Guy Kawasaki, Richard Branson and Seth Godin. Visitors to the site are offered *Planning For Growth*, *Managing Money*, *Getting Customers* or *Building Your Team*. Intel's blog network allows readers to 'dig' or recommend its blogs on news sharing site Digg. Some Intel staff blogs have been recommended by over a thousand Digg users, providing a valuable platform for shaping opinion in Intel's markets, building reputation, and conveying a point of view favourable to supporting the company's marketing strategy. LinkedIn enables businesses or individuals to promote their views and join discussion groups across a range of specialist business topics and sector-specific expertise. Social media applications are no longer only of interest to marketers addressing consumers.

Question

As the marketing director of a business-to-business organization, why might you be excited by the potential of communicating on social networking sites?

Case study

Nynas: in the black and leading

For most people, oil is evident as a fuel for cars, heating and the generation of electricity, or as the basis for the plastics industry. What about the black surfaces of pavements, roads, driveways, car parks and school playgrounds? Bitumen is an oil-based product most of us take for granted, but it is a major part of the revenue for companies such as Shell, BP, Esso, Total, Colas or Lanfina. The leading bitumen player in the UK, Scandinavia and much of western Europe is Stockholm-based Nynas. In the UK, this relatively small player in the petrochemicals industry has overall market leadership in the bitumen market and is renowned for its innovative product development with polymer formulations.

Bitumen is one of the most ubiquitous materials made by industry, underfoot almost everywhere as a core ingredient of the macadams and asphalts in roads and pavements. There are numerous specialist applications too, such as the backing for carpet tiles, roofing felts, sealants for mighty dams and waterproofing for bridge decks. Inevitably this results in a diverse customer base for an organization such as Nynas. In a market with competitors as large as Esso or Shell, Nynas's leadership has not occurred by accident. Nynas has established its enviable position by astutely utilizing the resources required to develop innovative products, customer service schemes and flexible delivery capabilities in order to ensure customer satisfaction. At the heart of its business strategy is a desire to innovate, listen to customers and develop services that genuinely enable customers to be served properly.

Nynas believes it has several important edges over its rivals, as described below.

Customer dialogue

As a major producer with significant R&D technical support, Nynas's laboratories can determine a product formulation for most bitumen-based applications. Whether the customer is a local authority requiring a cost-effective thin surfacing for a housing estate's ageing pavements; a contractor such as Tarmac requiring 24-hour supply of high-quality, state-of-the-art bitumen for the construction of a new motorway; or a builder buying polymer-enhanced mastic asphalts to act as a waterproofing membrane for regency mews properties, Nynas can develop a quality bitumen-based product.

Consistent quality and innovative product development

Refineries in Belgium, Sweden and the UK, supported by a network of terminals and research laboratories across Europe, enable Nynas to continually improve its products and their performance. Customers do not want to have to resurface major roads or busy shopping centre pavements on a frequent basis. Specialist applications such as waterproofing dams or houses are time consuming, costly and inconvenient remedial activities that clients do not want to repeat in a hurry. Nynas has access to high-grade Venezuelan bitumen, not readily available to its major competitors, which gives it added flexibility in producing high-quality bitumen grades for specific applications. Whether it is for a routine commodity bulk job such as a school playground surface or an unusual requirement for waterproofing a royal building, Nynas has developed a reputation as being a leading supplier.

Logistical support

Users of bitumen often require deliveries at very short notice, in specific quantities and to guaranteed quality levels. These deliveries may be anywhere at any time. A contractor repairing a busy commuter route out of daylight hours needs on-time delivery of ready-to-use bitumen products. Repairs to a remote bridge still require guaranteed on-time delivery. Nynas's depots operate around the clock despatching computer-monitored deliveries by tanker to clients as and when the customer has specified. Twenty-four hours a day, 365 days a year, Nynas prides itself on its high levels of responsiveness and reliability of delivery.

Nynas's composition of customers is varied. A major new road-building scheme will involve formal tendering and guarantees with penalties for inferior product or missed deliveries. The buying process of such customers will be highly formal, involving numerous managers, and functions as diverse

as purchasing, technical support, construction, finance and logistical support. On both sides customer and Nynas cross-functional teams of scientists, engineers, managers and the field force will spend many months agreeing on the product requirements, contractual obligations, delivery requirements and application techniques. For other customers, the purchase is perhaps more of a routine re-buy, with only limited interaction and discussion between Nynas and the customer. On other occasions, the Nynas helpline may receive a midnight telephone call from a highways agency surveyor who has just discovered cracks in the surface of a major road and requires immediate assistance in both identifying the cause of the problem and rectifying the situation before commuters awake the next morning.

For a rather bland-looking substance such as bitumen, the market is diverse and challenging. Nynas has established its successful position in the European market for bitumen-based products by practicing the best principles of marketing. The company strives to understand its customers' needs and to offer reliable products supported with effective customer service, round the clock. Product innovation is at the forefront of the company's strategy and, coupled with constantly improving ways of offering peace of mind to customers, provides an edge over rivals. Shrewd marketing analysis constantly monitors product changes, customers' expectations, competitors' activities and those aspects of the marketing environment, notably technological and regulatory forces, that will impact on the business's fortunes. Resources are allocated to match this thorough assessment of market opportunities and marketing requirements.

Questions for discussion

1. Who are Nynas's customers?

2. What types of business markets as classified in this chapter purchase the products made by Nynas?

3. Would most purchases of Nynas's products be new task, modified re-buy or straight re-buy?

Sources: Siobhan McKelvey and Willie Hunter, Nynas UK; Network magazine; the Nynas Annual Review.

CHAPTER 7
Segmenting markets

The essence of successful segmentation lies not in fragmentation but in building an excellent understanding of the marketplace

Objectives

To understand the definition of a market.

To recognize different types of market.

To appreciate what is meant by market segmentation.

To grasp why so many marketers place segmentation at the heart of their marketing strategies.

To know the most commonly adopted bases for segmenting markets.

To learn how companies go about segmentation.

To understand the importance and role of customer relationship management.

INTRODUCTION

As explained in Chapter 2, marketing strategy revolves around the choice of which opportunities should be pursued and the specification of an appropriate target market strategy. Market segmentation is a fundamental part of marketing strategy, assisting organizations to deal with the fact that not all consumers or business customers share identical needs, buying behaviour or product requirements, yet companies do not have the resources or bandwidth to address each individual customer separately.

The market segmentation process has a number of stages: segmenting, targeting and positioning. Limited resources generally result in organizations being unable to serve all of the needs in the market, and marketers must make trade-off choices based on the relative merits of different market segments in determining which groups to prioritize or target. The consumers or business customers in those market segments deemed to be priorities for a company must be communicated with in a manner that emphasizes their importance to the company, which is the positioning task. Many marketers believe these aspects of marketing are the most important decisions made by marketers. Targeting and positioning are explored in the next chapter. The focus in this chapter is on scoping what is meant by market segmentation and understanding the approaches for creating market segments.

Rice ...not all grains seem the same

Do you enjoy rice? Which brand and variety do you buy? In the rice aisle of the supermarkets there are many brands, several of which offer similar varieties such as basmati or long grain, brown or white. However, most households have a preference and purchase their favourite brand each time they require more rice. This is partly because of the branding adopted by the leading players, sometimes owing to the promo price deal, but often it stems from the segmentation strategies adopted by the leading brands.

Market leader Uncle Ben's, part of the Mars family of companies within Masterfoods, has been producing good tasting rice since the 1940s, very much targeted at families or couples who are either in a hurry or needing the convenience of pre-prepared easy-to-cook rice in a variety of guises and cooking styles. Uncle Ben's brought rice to the attention of many consumers in the 1960s and 1970s, with generations now having grown up enjoying simple-cook long-grain rice out of the familiar orange packaging.

Recently, Indian business Veetee launched its Dine In range of innovative plastic trays packed to show off the ready-cooked range of enticing rices: basmati, pilau, long grain, Thai jasmine, basmati, wild, Thai lime and herb and wholegrain; all ready to eat in two-minutes. Not aimed at scratch cooks or those prepared to boil on the hob, this range is targeting 'food cheats' who want an easy-to-prepare good looking product in no time at all so as to get on with their evening. Re-branded as part of its Heat & Eat range of microwavable lines, Veetee now has pasta products in the range, too.

Further up the rice fixture will be found premium-priced Tilda. While Tilda also has a microwave range, the bulk of its business is from dry rice, predominantly top-end dry basmati. Priced way above competitors, Tilda enjoys a strong market share and has legions of loyal users who are convinced they can discern a taste premium from the perfect looking aromatic basmati grains. Although far from complicated to cook, Tilda's appeal is more to scratch cooks and those who enjoy both cooking and consuming great tasting food. Not that Uncle Ben's or Veetee do not taste good, but their appeal is to consumers in a hurry or who are less confident cooks, seeking a value for money reliable rice.

Each of these leading rice brands has managed to differentiate what in many parts of the world is a basic commodity ... grains of rice. Each company, through recipes, packaging, product formulations, cooking methods, pricing and branding, has managed to appeal to a distinctive set of consumers. While they compete with retailers' own label rice ranges and with each other for many of the same consumers, each rice company has adopted a segmented approach to guide its product innovation, proposition development, marketing messages and consumer engagement programmes.

The consumers for rice are varied. A small segment is most interested in food provenance, organic credentials and the ethics of the supplying company. Experienced scratch cooks are unlikely to favour the brands selected by the micro-waving 'food cheats'. Some consumers switch between being time-pressured in the week and focused on limiting time spent in the kitchen to enjoying trying out new scratch cook recipes at the weekend when entertaining friends and family. For others, the ever-changing pattern of commitments of family members suggest mealtimes with family or alone, dictating the recipe, style of cooking and brands purchased. Health and nutrition might drive the purchasing decisions of some; while some cooks simply are scared to cook rice in any form, anticipating disaster if they do. Understanding these varied behaviours, motives, lifestyles and attitudes is essential as marketers decide which consumers to pursue.

Even in an apparent commodity market such as rice, segmentation has become firmly entrenched to direct the major players' strategies for product development, retailer selection and marketing programmes. Tilda, Veetee, Uncle Ben's, retailer own label and the host of other brands, all have to decide on which consumers to focus their marketing.

This chapter begins by considering the nature of markets, first defining the term and then describing the different types. The market segmentation concept is then explained and the rationale for its use explored. Not only rice companies apply the concept of market segmentation. Management consultancies, manufacturers, healthcare providers, leisure operators and universities all practice market segmentation. The explanation of segmenting focuses on the variables used to segment consumer and business markets, which in the era of 'big data' have changed considerably in the last few years. An understanding of customer needs and buying behaviour, as described in Chapters 5 and 6, is essential for developing market segments. The importance of customer relationship management within key market segments concludes the chapter.

What are markets?

The word 'market' has various meanings. It used to refer primarily to the place where goods were bought and sold. It can also refer to a large geographic area. In some cases, the word is used to describe the relationship between the demand and supply of a specific product. For instance, 'What is the state of the market for IT outsourcing of call centres'? Sometimes, 'market' is used to mean the act of selling something. The dictionary defines 'market' as an occasion on which goods are publicly exposed for sale, a place in which goods are exposed for sale, or to offer for sale. In marketing terms, a market is defined in terms of customers, their need for a product, and their ability to purchase or consume.

Market
An aggregate of people who, as individuals or within organizations, have a need for certain products and the ability, willingness and authority to purchase such products.

In this book a **market** is defined as a group of people who, as consumers or as part of organizations, need and have the ability, willingness and authority to purchase products in a product class. The definition used here is specific, referring to individuals seeking products in a specific product category. For example, students are part of the market for textbooks, as well as being markets for laptops, smartphones, stationery, accommodation, food, transport, music and other products. Obviously, there are many different markets in any economy. In this section, the requirements for markets are considered in conjunction with these different types.

Requirements for a market

For a group of people to be a market, the members of the group must meet the following four requirements:

- They must need or want a particular product or service.
- They must have the ability to purchase the product or service. Ability to purchase is related to buying power, which consists of resources such as money, goods and services that can be traded in an exchange situation.
- They must be willing to use their buying power.
- They must have the authority to buy the specific products or services.

Consumer market
Purchasers or individuals in their households who personally consume or benefit from the purchased products and do not buy products primarily to make a profit.

Individuals sometimes have the desire, the buying power and the willingness to purchase certain products but may not be authorized to do so. For example, secondary school students may want, have the money for and be willing to buy alcoholic drinks, but a brewer does not consider them a market until they are legally old enough to buy alcohol. An aggregate of people that lacks any one of the four requirements does not constitute a market.

Types of market

Markets can be divided into two categories: consumer markets and business markets. A **consumer market** consists of purchasers and/or individuals in their households who personally consume or benefit from the purchased products and who do not buy products primarily to make a profit. Each of us belongs to numerous consumer markets for such products as housing, cars, appliances, furniture, clothing, food, financial services and leisure activities. Consumer markets are discussed in more detail in Chapter 5 of *Marketing: Concepts and Strategies*.

A **business market**, also referred to as an *organizational or business-to-business market*, consists of individuals or groups that purchase a specific kind of product for one of three purposes: resale, direct use in producing other products, or use in their general daily operations. The four categories of business market – producer, reseller, government and institutional – are discussed in Chapter 6. The so-termed Third Sector of non-profit markets generally feature within this category, although some authors now believe they warrant separate classification.

Business market
Individuals or groups that purchase a specific kind of product to resell, use directly in producing other products or use in general daily operations.

What is market segmentation?

Chapter 1 explained that at the heart of marketing strategy are the decisions about which opportunities to pursue and which markets to target. Segmentation is a popular approach to identifying target markets. As will be explained later in this chapter, organizations sometimes decide to target the total market, using an **undifferentiated (or total market) approach**. However, it is much more usual for a differentiated approach using market segmentation to be followed, identifying only certain groups of consumers or business customers as the ones to pursue and look after.

Undifferentiated (or total market) approach
An approach which assumes that all customers have similar needs and wants, and can be served with a single marketing mix.

Defining market segmentation

The varying characteristics, needs, wants and interests of customers mean that there are few markets where a single product or service is satisfactory for all. The extensive array of goods on supermarket shelves reflects basic differences in customers' requirements. The trend is away from a mass-marketing approach. Even markets that were traditionally undifferentiated have undergone change, with an ever increasing number of products on offer. For instance, the market for food seasoning used to be dominated by salt. Now, low-sodium substitutes are being offered as alternatives for the increasingly health-conscious consumer. Armed with digital marketing options, few marketers today consider a mass-marketing approach as worthwhile.

Heterogeneous markets
Markets in which all customers have different requirements.

Markets in which all customers have different requirements are termed **heterogeneous markets**. For example, the market for wrist watches is quite diverse. Swatch designs relatively low-priced watches for the fashion-conscious customer; Rotary markets much more conservative and expensive designs for an older customer group; Apple now provides high-tech smart watches. In completely heterogeneous markets the only way to satisfy everyone is by offering tailor-made or bespoke products. This situation is more prevalent in business-to-business markets, where, for example, plant machinery is designed for a specific task and situation. While it may not be feasible to offer every customer a tailor-made product, it is often possible to aggregate customers into groups with similar product needs and wants.

Market segmentation
The process of grouping customers in markets with some heterogeneity into smaller, more similar or homogeneous segments. The identification of target customer groups in which customers are aggregated into groups with similar requirements and buying characteristics.

Market segmentation is the process by which customers in markets with some heterogeneity can be grouped into smaller, more similar or homogeneous segments. A **market segment** is therefore a group of individuals, groups or organizations sharing one or more similar characteristics that cause them to have relatively similar product needs and buying characteristics. Market segmentation involves identifying such groups, so that marketers are better able to develop product or service benefits that are appropriate for them (see Figure 7.1). They do this by designing products and brands

Market segment
A group of individuals, groups or organizations sharing one or more similar characteristics that cause them to have relatively similar product needs and buying characteristics.

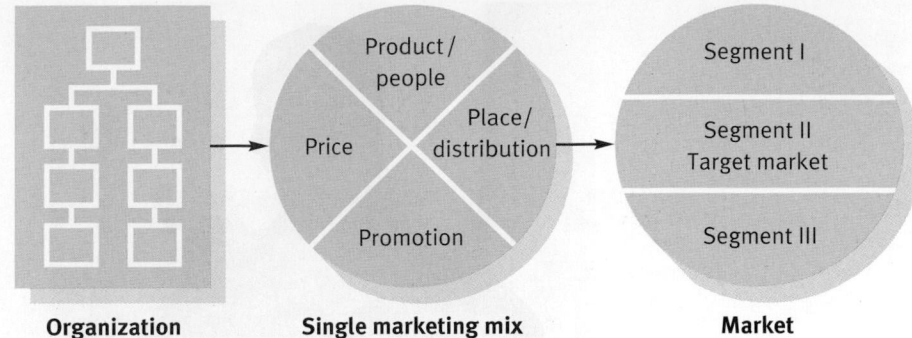

FIGURE 7.1
The market segmentation approach

Organization   Single marketing mix   Market

to appeal to particular target segments and to be supported by an appropriate promotional campaign, relevant customer service, and suitable pricing and place/distribution strategies.[1,2] For example, clothing sold through Top Shop or New Look is manufactured for youthful female consumers; this is reflected in the product styling, promotional campaigns, store design and branding.

Once market segments have been identified, marketers decide which they intend to enter. A marketing programme covering all elements of the marketing mix can then be designed to suit the particular requirements of each segment targeted. German-owned BMW previously concentrated on selling premium-priced luxury vehicles aimed at the luxury and executive segments of the car market. In order to appeal to a younger age group, during the 1990s BMW introduced the Compact version of its popular 3 Series. This had the desired effect of attracting buyers who previously could not afford this aspirational marque. Now BMW has gone further, with the launch of the 1 Series, aiming to further broaden the appeal of its brand to young professionals. The 4 × 4 X3 and X5 appeal to other customers. As BMW launches new models it has very clear target market segments in mind.

Reasons for using market segmentation

Companies have turned to market segmentation with good reason.[3] Careful segmentation, and the customer understanding underlying it, can make it easier for companies to identify and exploit different market opportunities. For example, segmentation can help minor players in the market achieve a foothold in a particular niche, perhaps by identifying an opportunity not directly exploited by market leaders. Larger and more mature companies turn to segmentation in order to more closely pursue groups of customers with well-honed messages and marketing programmes, seeking to differentiate themselves in highly competitive markets. It is no longer adequate for a mobile phone brand to think of its market as corporate users, private pay-monthly and private pay-as-you-go subscribers; instead the major brands all have created detailed and well-researched market segmentations based on users' lifestyles, behaviours, demographics and needs. Figure 7.2 shows how the motorbike producer Harley Davidson supports its branding with a diverse range of merchandizing for its brand community.

Segmentation is seen to offer businesses a number of advantages that make it easier to develop and capitalize on opportunities available to them. These advantages can be considered at the customer level, in relation to the competition or in terms of the effectiveness of resource allocation and strategic planning.[4]

Customer analysis Segmenting markets facilitates a better understanding of customers' needs, wants and other characteristics. The sharper focus that segmentation offers, allows those personal, situational and behavioural factors that characterize customers in a particular segment to be considered. In short, questions about how, why and what customers buy can be addressed. By being closely in touch with segments, marketers can respond quickly to even slight changes in what target customers want. For example, by monitoring the trends towards healthier eating and lifestyles, McDonald's was able to respond by introducing a wider range of salads and healthy eating options, including grilled chicken, fruit and yoghurt on to its menus.

FIGURE 7.2
Motorbike producer Harley Davidson supports its branding with a diverse range of merchandizing, events and club for its brand community, all intended to cement its reputation with key target audiences

Competitor analysis Most markets are characterized by intense competition. Within this environment, companies need to understand the nature of the competition they face. Who are their main competitors? At which segments are they targeting their products? Answering these questions allows marketers to make decisions about the most appropriate segments to target and the kind of competitive advantage to seek. For example, before opening a new restaurant outlet, Pizza Express needs to build a picture of the existing café, restaurant and other outlets offering a comparable proposition in the location. The company must also appraise the extent to which the needs of the consumers it aims to target are already served by what is currently available and how strong are such rival restaurants. Companies that do not understand their competitive environment risk encountering competition they had not envisaged or putting resources into unattractive areas of the market.

Effective resource allocation All companies have limited resources. To target the whole of the market is usually unrealistic. The effectiveness of personnel and material resources can be greatly improved when they are more narrowly focused on a particular segment of customers. With limited resources, Kia and Hyundai target only a few market segments compared with Ford or Toyota, maximizing their use of resources and marketing mix activities. Often the sponsor of a segmentation strategy is the Chief Finance Officer rather than the Chief Marketing Officer. The latter reaps the benefits, but the former seeks prudent allocation of the company's resources, budgets and investments, and values the fact that a market segmentation study identifies customers not of importance, so directing spends on those customers who really matter.

Strategic marketing planning Companies operating in a number of segments are unlikely to follow the same strategic plans in them all. Dividing up markets allows marketers to develop plans that give special consideration to the particular needs and requirements of customers in different segments. The timescale covered by the strategic plan can also be structured accordingly, because some segments change more rapidly than others. The market for recorded music is a typical example. While tastes in classical music remain fairly steady, tastes in pop music change very rapidly. Music publishers, distributors and labels clearly need to consider this factor when developing corporate plans.

Segmenting, targeting and positioning

There are three stages to carrying out market segmentation: segmentation, targeting and positioning. Figure 7.3 gives an overview of these stages.

Segmenting the market

There are many ways in which customers can be grouped and markets segmented. In different markets, the variables that are appropriate change. The key is to understand which are the most suitable for distinguishing between different product requirements. Understanding as much as possible about the customers in the segments is also important, as marketers who 'know' their targets are more likely to design an appropriate marketing mix for them. Betting businesses such as Ladbrokes or Paddy Power evidently have very clearly defined target market segments when they develop their gambling products, advertising and sponsorships.

Targeting strategy

Once segments have been identified, decisions about which and how many customer groups to target can be made. There are several options:

- adopt an undifferentiated approach, focusing on the total market
- concentrate on a single segment with one product and marketing programme
- offer one product and marketing programme to a number of segments
- target a different product and marketing programme at each of a number of segments.

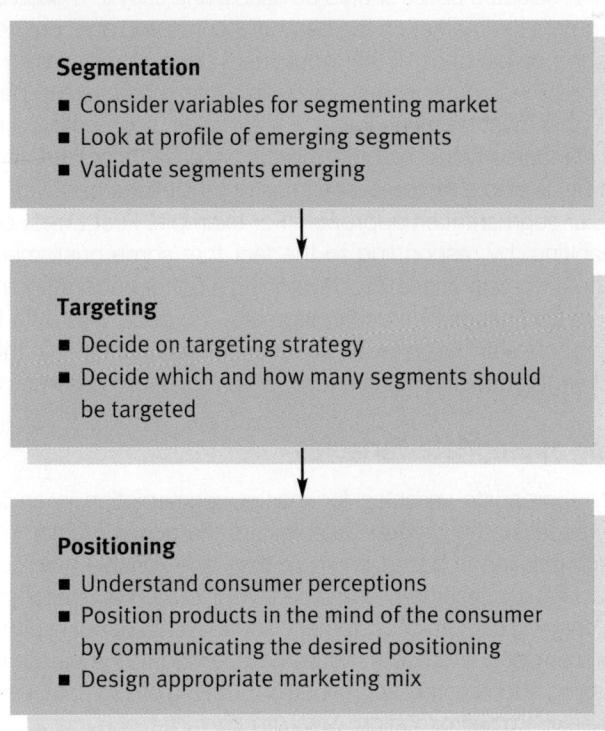

FIGURE 7.3
Basic elements of segmentation

These options are explored in more detail in the next chapter. The choices companies make should take resource implications into consideration.

Positioning the product

Companies must decide precisely how and where, for the targeted segments, to aim a product or products, brand or brands. The needs and wants of targeted customers must be translated into a tangible mix of product/service, personnel, price, promotion and place/distribution activities, messaging and tone of voice. Consumers' views of the product and where it is positioned relative to the competition are particularly critical. After all, the paying public does not always perceive a product or brand in the way the manufacturer or marketing team would like. For example, to the dismay of those who developed it, Blackberry's attempt to position a smartphone against Apple for teenagers failed. Whereas the marketers in discounters Aldi and Lidl identified certain Tesco and Sainsbury's segments, when faced with economic recession, as being susceptible to their charms, achieving significant market share gains from the established large supermarket operators.

Each of the three market segmentation stages will now be considered.

Segmentation variables

Segmentation variables or bases
The dimensions or characteristics of individuals, groups or businesses that are used for dividing a total market into segments.

Segmentation variables or bases are the dimensions or characteristics of individuals, groups or businesses that are used for dividing a total market into segments.[5] There is rarely one best way to segment a market. Companies must make choices about the most appropriate variables to use but they must consider the needs and buying behaviour of their intended customers, as discussed in Chapters 5 and 6. In consumer markets, background characteristics like age, sex and occupation are widely used. In business-to-business markets, customer size, location and product use are often the focus.

The choice of segmentation variables is based on several factors. The variables chosen should relate to customers' needs for, uses of, or behaviour towards the product or service. The selected bases should be usable and easy to measure. Laptop computer manufacturers might segment the market on the basis of income and age, but not on the basis of religion, because one person's usage of computer equipment does not differ from those of people of other religions. Furthermore, if individuals or businesses in a total market are to be classified accurately, the segmentation variable must be measurable. For example, segmenting a market on the basis of intelligence or moral standards would be quite difficult because these attributes are hard to measure accurately.

Creativity is also a factor; sometimes organizations benefit from moving away from a traditionally popular segmentation approach. For example, First Direct bank led the way in telephone and online banking, by responding to the fact that some customers' needs were not being met by existing banking operations. By developing a better understanding of the demographics, lifestyles, behaviours and needs of these customers, the bank was able to develop a new kind of service, with no branches and high levels of customer service. Later in this chapter there is a more detailed review of segmentation effectiveness, which focuses on some of these issues.

Selecting appropriate variables

Selecting appropriate variables for market segmentation is an important marketing management decision, because the chosen variables are the primary factor in defining the target market.[6] Generally, segmentation is based on more than one variable, particularly in today's 'big data' environment. Tracking of consumers' online behaviour, customer relationship management systems and data analysis, ongoing capture of customers' subsequent spending behaviour, and the dialogues permitted by digital marketing and social media, have added to the wealth of customer insight readily to hand when thinking about market segmentation. The era of 'big data' in the digital age has transformed how marketers explore segmentation, which is now faster, cheaper and more data-driven than ever before.

In general, as developments in information technology make it easier to capture and manage customer information, the move is towards more complex segmentation schemes. Many organizations now have databases providing a wider range of segmentation variables than was previously possible.[7] One outcome is that there is, increasingly, a tendency to use multivariable segmentation rather than single-variable segmentation.[8] Indeed, technological advance means that it is now technically feasible to capture information about and respond to the needs and wants of smaller and smaller segments.[9] Many companies now further sub-divide their market segments into micro-segments. Previously, the required insights to achieve this would have been too costly and marketers subsequently would have struggled to address the emerging micro-segments. Digital marketing, as explained in Chapter 19, permits much more focused marketing than ever before. Taken to its extreme, this means that instead of dealing at the mass-market or segment level, it is even possible to develop relationships with *individual* customers. This principle has been variously referred to as 'customer-centric marketing'[10] or 'one-to-one marketing'.[11] **One-to-one marketing** involves developing long-term relationships with individual customers in order to understand and satisfy their needs.[12] However, despite the attention these new ideas have attracted, it is widely recognized that one-to-one involves a substantial injection of resources, raising concerns about whether the returns are sufficiently high to justify the required investment. Most companies now identify the segments in the market, select which of these are most worthwhile to address, and then within these priority segments they engage one-to-one with the most rewarding and important individual customers.

One-to-one marketing
Customized marketing engaging individual customers for the development of longer-term relationships.

Single variable segmentation
Segmentation achieved by using only one variable, the simplest type of segmentation to perform.

Multivariable segmentation
Segmentation using more than one characteristic to divide a total market.

Single variable segmentation
Single variable segmentation, which is the simplest to perform, is achieved by using only one variable, for example, country. However, the sales of one product in different countries will differ and the numbers of relevant consumers in each country will vary. A single characteristic gives marketers only moderate precision in designing a marketing mix to satisfy individuals in a specific segment. It is rarely used today.

Multivariable segmentation
To achieve **multivariable segmentation**, more than one characteristic is used to divide a total market (see Figure 7.4). Notice in the figure

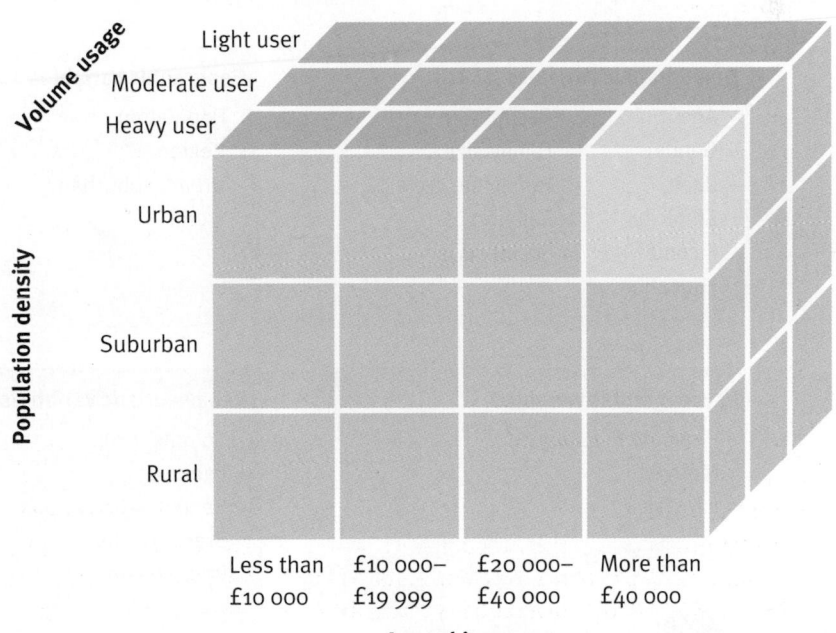

FIGURE 7.4
Multivariable segmentation

that the market is segmented by three variables: annual income, population density and volume usage. The people in the highlighted segment earn more than £40 000, are urban dwellers and heavy users. Multivariable segmentation provides more information about the individuals in each segment, which may enable a company to develop a marketing mix that will satisfy customers in a given segment more precisely. A recent segmentation of the mobile phone sector explored consumers' demographics, lifestyles, usage and attitudes to mobile phones, revenue generation patterns, but also the role of the phone in the individual's life. One major operator identified 15 very contrasting sets of behaviours, recognizing that the requirements of all 15 segments contrasted significantly.

In the last few years, so-termed 'big data' and a step-change in analytical expertise (see Chapter 19) have brought a wealth of information very quickly to hand to assist with multi-faceted understanding of customers and their behaviours, assisting segmentation significantly and reducing the cost and duration of segmentation projects.

Variables for segmenting consumer markets

Companies developing their strategy for segmentation can choose one or several variables or bases from a wide range of choices. As Figure 7.5 shows, segmentation variables can be grouped into four categories: demographic, geographic, psychographic and behaviouristic. Most marketers no longer focus on only one or two of these categories, instead preferring to immerse themselves in all of their customers' characteristics and behaviours. Improvements in data capture, 'big data', analytics, heuristics and computing power now make this relatively quick and easy to achieve. Segmentation projects are now much shorter and cheaper to complete than ever before. In fact, many marketing projects undertaken for other purposes – multi-channel strategic planning, mobile marketing, brand strategy, product development planning, customer experience and customer relationship management – typically start with a segmentation study incorporated as an initial building block. Previously, the cost, complexity and time to undertake segmentation would have precluded such an approach. When perusing the categories of variables below, please bear in mind that marketers increasingly utilize most of these criteria and characteristics, developing very detailed understanding of customers and their behaviours.

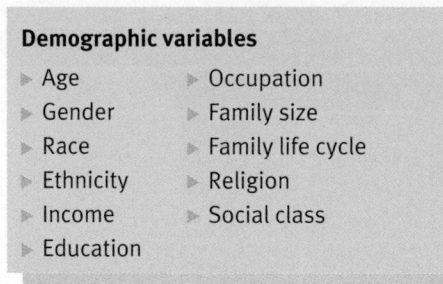

Demographic variables

▸ Age	▸ Occupation
▸ Gender	▸ Family size
▸ Race	▸ Family life cycle
▸ Ethnicity	▸ Religion
▸ Income	▸ Social class
▸ Education	

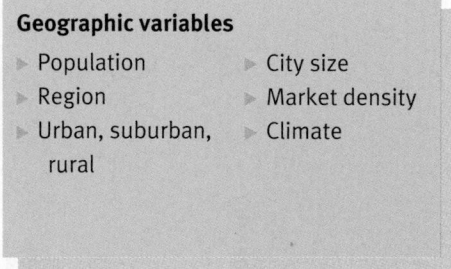

Geographic variables

▸ Population	▸ City size
▸ Region	▸ Market density
▸ Urban, suburban, rural	▸ Climate

Psychographic variables

- ▸ Personality attributes
- ▸ Motives
- ▸ Lifestyles

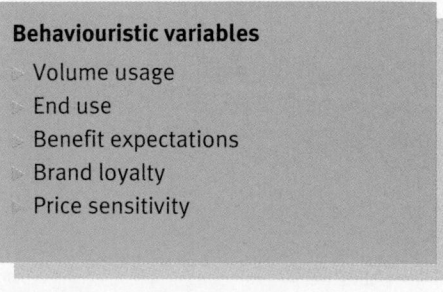

Behaviouristic variables

- Volume usage
- End use
- Benefit expectations
- Brand loyalty
- Price sensitivity

FIGURE 7.5
Segmentation variables for consumer markets

Marketing insight

Targeting fashion

Venture into a branch of White Stuff and the consumers tend to be between 30 and 50, seeking well-produced and stylish casual clothing for home or office. They will often be from the leafy suburbs and professional families, educated to degree level and with children. The ambience in-store is quiet but visually stimulating, the stores packed with vibrant designs and helpful sales assistants. While not retailing the latest catwalk fashions with four-figure pricing, White Stuff targets an upmarket and discerning independent consumer.

By contrast, a New Look store will be packed to the rafters with the latest look sought by sixth formers and ladies in their twenties. Little customer service is desired or offered. The stores are functional and simply fitted out. Price points offer value for money. Although targeting many of the same consumers, River Island offers larger and more vibrant stores, fitted out more expensively to provide more of a buzz than New Look. On the face of it, both New Look and River Island target many of the same consumers, but in practice some of the consumers in the intended demographic target audience prefer the vibrancy and energy of River Island, while others prefer the size, feel and pricing of New Look.

Planet, by contrast, tends to have fewer visitors to its more up-market stores and concessions in leading department stores, but once there these older and more independent-minded shoppers tend to linger, try on several outfits and are reassured by the higher price points and expensive fabrics, as they search for businesswear or a special occasion suit, coat or dress. Price points are significantly higher than in New Look or River Island, with shop ambience and displays more exclusive and staff trained to provide greater customer service.

Whether White Stuff, New Look, River Island or Planet, each company has identified a core set of consumers to target from within the overall clothes-buying population, honing their merchandise, locations, store sizes and ambience, specifying their customer service and pricing, and managing their brands accordingly. Segmentation and brand positioning drive the propositions and marketing for these well-known clothing companies.

Sources: New Look Leamington, Planet Leamington, River Island Leamington and White Stuff Stratford, March 2015.

Demographic variables Demographers study aggregate population characteristics such as the distribution of age and gender, fertility rates, migration patterns and mortality rates. Demographic characteristics that marketers commonly use in segmenting markets include age, gender, race, ethnicity, income, education, occupation, family size, family life cycle, religion and social class. Marketers rely on these demographic characteristics because they are often closely linked to customers' needs and purchasing behaviour, and can readily be measured.

Manufacturers of tea bags, such as PG and Twinings, offer their products in packages of different sizes to satisfy the needs of consumers ranging from singles to large families. Financial institutions such as banks and building societies attempt to interest children in their products by offering free gifts such as book vouchers. Meanwhile, retired customers are targeted with products designed for a leisure-oriented lifestyle. The emphasis is on tailoring the service package to suit particular needs.

Age is a commonly-used segmentation variable. Population statistics help marketers to understand and keep track of changing age profiles. As the population of western Europe continues to increase, the numbers in the 0- to 19-year-old age band is falling, while the number of those over 60 continues to rise. This has ramifications for marketers, who must increasingly cater for an ageing population. Given the relative affluence of this particular group, many companies (particularly those in leisure and service industries) have benefited from this demographic change. Marketers are also recognizing the purchasing influence of children and are targeting their marketing efforts at them. Numerous products are aimed specifically at children: toys, clothing, food, drinks, computer games and entertainment. In addition, children profoundly influence certain purchasing decisions made by their parents.[13] For example, in households with only one parent or in which both parents work, children often take on additional responsibilities such as cooking, cleaning and food shopping, and thus influence the products and brands that are purchased.

FIGURE 7.6

Many brands such as Bratz dolls develop specific marketing programmes targeting children

Gender is another demographic variable commonly used to segment markets, including the markets for clothing, alcoholic drinks, books, magazines, non-prescription drugs and even cigarettes. Lego traditionally sold its bricks to boys, but its hugely successful *Friends* range has attracted many girls to this top-selling toy brand, exactly as intended by Lego's marketers. Efforts by manufacturers of skincare products to develop lines specifically aimed at men have been highly successful in recent years, significantly expanding the category and resulting revenues.

The way in which marketers treat ethnicity varies in different parts of the world. For instance, in the USA, where a quarter of the population is made up of ethnic minorities, ethnicity is widely used as a means of segmenting markets for goods and services of all kinds. The US Hispanic population, comprising people of Mexican, Cuban, Puerto Rican, and Central and South American heritage, is growing five times faster than the general population. Consequently, it is being targeted by more and more companies. However, targeting Hispanic customers is not an easy task. For example, although marketers have long believed that Hispanic consumers are exceptionally brand loyal and prefer Spanish-language media, research does not support these assumptions. Not only do advertisers disagree about the merits of using Spanish-language media, they also question whether it is appropriate to advertise to Mexicans, Puerto Ricans and Cubans using a common Spanish language.[14] In the UK, where ethnic groups have expanded significantly, brands from Tesco to Lloyds have developed propositions tailored to specific ethnic groups' buying behaviours, languages and cultural needs.

Product and service needs also vary according to marital status, and the number and age of children. These factors are collectively taken into consideration by the 'family life cycle' concept. Some of the more obvious markets in which the impact of different life cycles is seen are tourism, housing and financial services. The family life cycle has been broken down in several different ways. Table 7.1 illustrates one such scheme.

TABLE 7.1   The Wells and Gubar life cycle stages

Bachelor stage (young single people not living with parents)
Newly married couples without children
Full nest I (youngest child under 6)
Full nest II (youngest child 6 or over)
Full nest III (older married couple with dependent children)
Empty nest I (no children living at home, family head working)
Empty nest II (family head retired)
Solitary survivor (working)
Solitary survivor (retired)

Source: Copyright © ESOMAR® 2000. Permission for using this material has been granted by ESOMAR®, Amsterdam, the Netherlands (www.esomar.ni).

The scheme presented in Table 7.1 assumes that individuals at different life cycle stages have varying product needs. Marketers can respond to this by targeting such groups with marketing mixes designed to capitalize on these differences. For example, parents whose children have grown up and left home ('empty nesters') tend to have more disposable income than those with young children, and tend to spend more on the home, holidays and new cars. Banks and financial institutions in particular are getting better at gearing their marketing efforts to life cycle changes. Critics of the life cycle concept point out that it can be difficult to decide to which categories families belong. Some households, such as single-parent families and older married couples who have never had children, do not appear to fit in at all.

Obviously, this discussion of demographic variables is not exhaustive. However, the variables described above probably represent the most widely-used demographics.

Socio-economic variables include income, occupation, education and social class. Some marketing academics and practitioners include these variables under the 'demographics' label. Income can be a very useful way of dividing markets because it strongly influences people's product needs. It affects their ability to buy (as discussed in Chapter 2) and their aspirations for a certain style of living. Obvious products in this category include housing, furniture, clothing, cars, food, certain kinds of sporting goods and leisure activities.

The occupations of the members of the household are known to have an impact on the types of products and services that are purchased. The type of housing individuals and families own or rent, is strongly linked to this variable. It is obvious, for example, that sales of products for refurbishment and decoration, such as paints, fabrics and wallpapers, will occur predominantly among those professions that have owner-occupier status. Occupation is also known to affect the types of sporting and leisure activities people prefer. For example, professionals may be active with walking, swimming, cycling and jogging, but not so involved with darts or football. Intermediate managers enjoy walking, swimming and keep fit/yoga. Unskilled manual workers are not particularly active in sports and physical activities. Other socio-economic variables that may be used to segment markets include education level and social class.

Geographic variables The needs of consumers in different geographic locations may be affected by their local climate, terrain, natural resources and population density. Markets may be divided into regions because one or more geographic variables may cause customers' needs to differ from one region to another. A company that sells products throughout the EU will, for example, need to take the different languages spoken into account when labelling its goods, and regional preferences when specifying its channel strategy.

City size can be an important segmentation variable. For example, one franchised restaurant organization will not locate in cities of fewer than 100 000 people because experience shows that a smaller population base could make the operation unprofitable. The same company may add a second, or even a third, restaurant once the city reaches a certain size. Other businesses, however, seek out opportunities in smaller towns. The major petroleum retailers, such as Esso and Shell, have traffic density thresholds, below which they perceive a local market as unviable. It is, therefore, quite common, particularly in villages and small towns in rural areas, for petroleum retailing to be dominated by independent garage owners and the smaller petroleum companies.

Market density
The number of potential customers within a unit of land area.

Market density refers to the number of potential customers within a unit of land area, such as a square kilometre. Although market density is generally related to population density, the correlation is not exact. For example, in two different geographic markets of approximately equal size and population, the market density for office supplies might be much higher in the first than in the second if the first contains a significantly greater proportion of business customers. Market density may be a useful segmentation variable because low-density markets often require different sales, advertising and distribution activities from high-density markets.

Climate can be used as a geographic segmentation variable. Companies entering new markets increasingly need to consider the impact of climate on their customer base.

For example, washing machines sold in Italy do not require such fast spin speeds as those sold in Germany because the Italian climate is much sunnier. Other markets affected by climate include air conditioning and heating equipment, clothing, gardening equipment, recreational products and building materials.

Marketers are increasingly using geodemographic segmentation. **Geodemographic segmentation** clusters people according to postcode areas. For example, ACORN (A Classification of Residential Neighbourhoods) uses information taken from the population census and many other sources, so that people may be grouped according to a number of factors, including demographic data, social factors, population and consumer behaviour. Mosaic from Experian is another popular proprietary geodemographic system. CACI's ACORN provides valuable consumer insight, helping with targeting, acquisition and developing customer relationships (http://acorn.caci.co.uk/downloads/Acorn-User-guide.pdf). All 1.9 million UK postcodes have been described using hundreds of demographic statistics and lifestyle variables. The underlying concept is that customers living in different residential neighbourhoods have different profiles in respect of these variables. Their product needs in terms of styling and features, therefore, also vary. Consumers can be classified under ACORN on the basis of the postcode of their home address and then allocated to one of the groups in Table 7.2. These categories further sub-divide to give a total of 17 groups and 62 neighbourhood types. For example, the 17 groups include *Executive Wealth*, *Career Climbers*, *Comfortable Seniors*, *Modest Means*, *Young Hardship* and *Difficult Circumstances*. The *Comfortable Seniors* group then sub-divides into two types, *older people, neat and tidy neighbourhoods* and *elderly singles in purpose-built accommodation*. Table 7.2 below describes ACORN in more detail.

> **Geodemographic segmentation**
> Clustering people according to postcode areas and census data.

Psychographic variables   Marketers sometimes use psychographic variables, such as personality characteristics, motives and lifestyles to segment markets. A psychographic dimension can be used by itself or combined with other types of segmentation variables.

TABLE 7.2   The ACORN Categorization of UK Consumers

Category 1: **Affluent Achievers**	**Lavish Lifestyle**	1	Exclusive enclaves
		2	Metropolitan money
		3	Large house luxury
	Executive Wealth	4	Asset rich families
		5	Wealthy countryside commuters
		6	Financially comfortable families
		7	Affluent professionals
		8	Prosperous suburban families
		9	Well-off edge of towners
	Mature Money	10	Better-off villagers
		11	Settled suburbia, older people
		12	Retired and empty nesters
		13	Upmarket downsizers
Category 2: **Rising Prosperity**	**City Sophisticates**	14	Townhouse cosmopolitans
		15	Younger professionals in smaller flats
		16	Metropolitan professionals
		17	Socialising young renters
	Career Climbers	18	Career driven young families
		19	First time buyers in small, modern homes
		20	Mixed metropolitan areas

(Continued)

TABLE 7.2 Continued

	Countryside Communities	21	Farms and cottages
		22	Larger families in rural areas
		23	Owner occupiers in small towns and villages
	Successful Suburbs	24	Comfortably-off families in modern housing
		25	Larger family homes, multi-ethnic areas
		26	Semi-professional families, owner occupied neighbourhoods
Category 3: Comfortable Communities	**Steady Neighbourhoods**	27	Suburban semis, conventional attitudes
		28	Owner occupied terraces, average income
		29	Established suburbs, older families
	Comfortable Seniors	30	Older people, neat and tidy neighbourhoods
		31	Elderly singles in purpose-built accommodation
	Starting Out	32	Educated families in terraces, young children
		33	Smaller houses and starter homes
	Student Life	34	Student flats and halls of residence
		35	Term-time terraces
		36	Educated young people in flats and tenements
	Modest Means	37	Low cost flats in suburban areas
		38	Semi-skilled workers in traditional neighbourhoods
		39	Fading owner occupied terraces
		40	High occupancy terraces, many Asian families
Category 4: Financially Stretched	**Striving Families**	41	Labouring semi-rural estates
		42	Struggling young families in post-war terraces
		43	Families in right-to-buy estates
		44	Post-war estates, limited means
	Poorer Pensioners	45	Pensioners in social housing, semis and terraces
		46	Elderly people in social rented flats
		47	Low income older people in smaller semis
		48	Pensioners and singles in social rented flats
	Young Hardship	49	Young families in low cost private flats
		50	Struggling younger people in mixed tenure
		51	Young people in small, low cost terraces
	Struggling Estates	52	Poorer families, many children, terraced housing
		53	Low income terraces
Category 5: Urban Adversity		54	Multi-ethnic, purpose-built estates
		55	Deprived and ethnically diverse in flats
		56	Low income large families in social rented semis
	Difficult Circumstances	57	Social rented flats, families and single parents
		58	Singles and young families, some receiving benefits
		59	Deprived areas and high-rise flats
Category 6: Not Private Households	**Not Private Households**	60	Active communal population
		61	Inactive communal population
		62	Business addresses without resident population

Source: 'The Acorn Categorization of UK Consumers', ACORN categories by CACI, reproduced by permission of CACI; CACI, March 2015.

Personality characteristics are useful when a product is similar to many competing products and when consumers' needs are not significantly affected by other segmentation variables. However, segmenting a market according to personality characteristics can be problematic. Although marketing practitioners have long believed that consumer choice and product use should vary with personality and lifestyle, marketing research has shown only weak relationships. However, the weakness of such relationships may be due to the difficulty of accurately measuring personality traits, because most existing personality tests were developed for clinical use, not for segmentation purposes. As the reliability of more recent measurement instruments increases, a greater association between personality and consumer behaviour has been demonstrated.[15] For example, it has been shown that personality sometimes influences the clothes, make-up and hairstyles that individuals adopt.

When motives are used to segment a market, it is divided on the basis of consumers' reasons for making a purchase. Product durability, value for money, concern for the environment, convenience and status are all motives affecting the types of product purchased and the choice of stores in which they are bought. For example, one consumer may be motivated to purchase recycled kitchen paper out of concern for the environment. Another may travel to a large supermarket in order to buy the most absorbent, high-quality brand of kitchen towel. Some consumers are driven by nothing more than perceived self-image and purchasing choices are steered by such views of 'self'.

Individuals are grouped by lifestyle segmentation according to how they live and spend their time, the importance of items in their surroundings (their homes or their jobs, for example), their beliefs about themselves and broad issues, and some socio-economic characteristics, such as income and education.[16] Lifestyle analysis provides a broad view of buyers because it encompasses numerous characteristics related to people's activities, interests and opinions (see Table 7.3). It can be thought of as going beyond a simple understanding of personality.

The use of lifestyle as a segmentation variable is commonplace, but not without challenges because it is so difficult to measure accurately compared with other types of segmentation variables. In addition, the relationships between psychographic variables and consumers' needs are sometimes obscure and unproven, and the segments that result from psychographic segmentation may not be reachable.[17] For example, a marketer may determine that highly compulsive individuals want a certain type of clothing. However, no specific stores or particular media appeal precisely to this group and this group alone.

TABLE 7.3   Characteristics related to activities, interests and opinions

Activities	Interests	Opinions
Work	Family	Themselves
Hobbies	Home	Social issues
Social events	Job	Politics
Holidays	Community	Business
Entertainment	Recreation	Economics
Club membership	Fashion	Education
Community	Food	Products
Shopping	Media	Future
Sports	Achievements	Culture

Source: Reprinted, adapted from Joseph Plummer, 'The concept and application of life style segmentation', *Journal of Marketing,* January 1974, p. 34. Reprinted by permission of the American Marketing Association.

Profiling and targeting customers with ACORN

Building customer relationships

Along with Experian's Mosaic system, ACORN from CACI is a leading geodemographic tool used by marketing practitioners to identify and understand the UK population and the demand for products and services. ACORN is a geodemographic segmentation of the UK's population which segments small neighbourhoods, postcodes or consumer households into 6 categories, 17 groups and 62 types, as detailed in Table 7.2. Clients of CACI use this information to improve their understanding of customers and target markets, and to determine where to locate operations. The geodemographic and lifestyle data provided by ACORN's detailed analysis of the official census statistics, supplemented with financial, purchasing and behaviour information, are an invaluable input to the market segmentation analyses of many consumer marketers.

As CACI explains, informed decisions can be made on where direct marketing and advertising campaigns will be most effective; where branches should be opened or closed; or where sites are located, including retail outlets, leisure facilities and public services. Acorn provides valuable consumer insight to help with targeting, acquiring and developing profitable customer relationships, and improving service delivery. Acorn helps clients to understand the attributes of households and postcodes, and for specialist requirements CACI has developed classifications covering health, retail and leisure activities.

ACORN categorizes all 1.9 million UK postcodes, which have been described using over 300 demographic statistics. The basic principle is that people in similar areas – postcode zones – have the same needs, behaviours and lifestyles. CACI claims the new ACORN is more accurate for targeting than previous versions, across all sectors, from finance, automotive, eCommerce, holidays, food shopping and electrical goods. As detailed on CACI's website, just some of the consumer profiling and targeting information available includes:

- mortgages
- winter snow holidays
- time left on mortgage
- weekend breaks
- company medical insurance
- classical music/opera
- private pension
- weekly food spend
- car insurance
- eating out
- child savings plan
- family income
- guaranteed income bonds
- house price
- National Savings
- 'new player' credit cards
- stocks and shares
- own a DVD player
- unit trusts
- have cable TV/phone
- buy new car
- have satellite TV
- buy car over £20 000
- own a laptop computer
- can choose company car
- use PC for finance
- car kept in garage
- use PC for education
- European holidays
- use email
- USA holidays.

Marketers may purchase reports about specific products or ACORN's consumer classifications. A popular application is to capture the postcodes of customers of a company, so as to analyze the ACORN profile of these customers. Armed with such a profile, the client company's marketers are able to locate similar consumers to target with their marketing communications.

Sources: CACI, 2004, 2007, 2011, 2015; www.caci.co.uk, March, 2015.

One of the more popular programmes studying lifestyles is conducted by the Stanford Research Institute's Value and Lifestyle Programme (VALS). This programme surveys consumers to select groups with identifiable values and lifestyles. Initially, VALS identified three broad consumer groups: Outer-directed, Inner-directed, and Need-driven consumers. The current VALS classification categorizes consumers into eight basic lifestyle groups: Innovators, Thinkers, Achievers, Experiencers,

Believers, Strivers, Makers and Survivors (www.strategicbusinessinsights.com/vals/ustypes.shtml). The VALS studies have been used to create products as well as to segment markets.

Behaviouristic variables   Marketers can also segment markets on the basis of an aspect of consumers' behaviour towards the product. This might relate to the way the particular product is used or purchased, or perhaps to the benefits consumers require. Purchase behaviour can be a useful way of distinguishing between groups of customers, giving marketers insight into the most appropriate marketing mix. For example, brand-loyal customers may require a different kind of treatment from those who switch between brands. On-pack sales promotions are often geared towards building loyalty in brand switchers.

The occasion on which customers buy a particular product may impact upon product choice because in different sets of circumstances different product selection criteria may be applied. For instance, a customer who replaces a car tyre in an emergency will probably be less concerned about price than one who is routinely maintaining his or her car. **Benefit segmentation** is the division of a market according to the benefits consumers want from the product.[18] Although most types of market segmentation are based on the assumption that there is a relationship between the variable and customers' needs, benefit segmentation is different in that the benefits the customers seek are their product needs. By determining the benefits desired, marketers may be able to divide people into groups seeking certain sets of benefits.

Benefit segmentation
The division of a market according to the benefits consumers want from the product.

The effectiveness of benefit segmentation depends on several conditions. First, the benefits people seek must be identifiable. Second, using these benefits, marketers must be able to divide people into recognizable segments. Finally, one or more of the resulting segments must be accessible to the companies' marketing efforts.

Product usage is another method marketers sometimes use to segment their customers. Individuals can be divided into users and non-users of a particular product. Users can then be classified further as heavy, moderate or light. To satisfy a specific user group, marketers sometimes create a distinctive product, set special prices or initiate special promotion and distribution activities. Thus, airlines such as British Airways and KLM offer frequent-flier programmes to reward their regular customers with free trips and discounts for car hire and hotel accommodation. Light users or non-users of products often receive little attention from companies. There is a tendency sometimes to dismiss these groups when developing a marketing programme. For example, research in the holiday industry tends to focus on feedback from current customers, often forgetting to question why non-users failed to buy.

How customers apply the product may also determine segmentation. To satisfy customers who use a product in a certain way, some feature – packaging, size, texture or colour – may have to be designed with special care to make the product easier to use, more convenient or more environmentally friendly. For instance, Unilever and Procter & Gamble are focusing more and more on the development of refill packs of detergents and other household products, to cater for increasing consumer concerns about the environment.

The varying attitude of customers towards products constitutes another set of variables that can be used to segment markets. Clothing retailers like River Island and Benetton are particularly conscious of this. While one customer seeks outfits that are practical and comfortable, another is concerned with achieving a highly fashionable image.

As this brief discussion shows, consumer markets can be divided according to numerous characteristics. Ultimately, the choices marketers make will depend on a host of market and company factors. As a generalization, most segmentation embraces a diversity of variables cutting across the categories detailed above, made easier, quicker and cheaper by today's data, analytics and computer power.

Variables for segmenting business markets

Like consumer markets, business or organizational markets are often segmented. Here the marketer's aim is to satisfy the needs of businesses for products. Marketers may segment business markets according to company demographics, operating variables, purchasing approach, situational factors or the personal characteristics of buyers.

Marketers attempting to segment business markets may face various problems.[19] The particular characteristics of the market or the distribution structure in place may restrict the types of segment bases that can be used. For example, many European car manufacturers are dependent upon the fleet car market. This market tends to be structured on the basis of car engine and vehicle size, with companies providing their more senior managers with more powerful, larger and expensive vehicles. It is likely that customers would resist a move away from this accepted structure by the car manufacturers, who are therefore not in a position to use possibly contradictory segmentation approaches. Various segmentation approaches have been developed to try to make it easier for companies to deal with these kinds of constraints.[20]

Whatever the approach adopted, just as in consumer markets, some segment bases are easier to measure and apply than others.[21] For example, it is much more straightforward to segment on the basis of company size or its sector of activity, which are measurable and visible characteristics, than on the basis of buying centre structure (see Chapter 6), which may be much more difficult to appraise but arguably is far more useful as a means for grouping together 'similar' client organizations. Table 7.4 provides an overview of the variables for segmenting business markets, and illustrates the relative ease with which they can be measured.

Company demographics or firmographics
Variables relating to the type of business or industry, geographic location, company age and size are probably the most widely used segmentation variables in business markets.

A company sometimes segments a market by the types of business within that market, perhaps on the basis of industry area or SIC code (see Chapter 6). Different types of organization often require different product features, distribution systems, price structures and selling strategies. Given these variables, a company may either concentrate on a single segment with one marketing mix (concentration strategy) or focus on several groups with multiple mixes (multi-segment strategy). A paint manufacturer such as Dulux could segment customers into several groups, such as paint wholesalers, do-it-yourself retail outlets, vehicle manufacturers, decorators and housing developers.

The demand for some consumer products can vary considerably by geographic area because of differences in climate, terrain, customer preference or similar factors. Demand for business-to-business products also varies according to geographic location. For example, the producers of certain types of timber divide their markets geographically because their customers' needs vary regionally. Geographic segmentation may be especially appropriate for reaching industries that are concentrated in certain locations; for example, textiles in West Yorkshire, information technology along the M4 corridor in England or financial services in London.

TABLE 7.4 Variables for segmenting business markets

Personal characteristics of buyers
Just as in consumer markets, the demographics, experience, personality and lifestyle of those individuals in the buying centre impact upon purchasing decisions, practices, attitudes towards risk and loyalty to suppliers

Situational factors
The urgency of purchase, perceived risk, size of order or product application can play an important role in the choices that are made

Purchasing approach
Buying centre structure (centralized/decentralized), buying policies (sealed bidding, service contracts, leasing), nature of existing relationships (focus on new or existing customers), balance of power among decision-makers and buying criteria (quality, delivery, service, price, product range, innovation) may shape an organization's purchase decisions

Operating variables
The technologies applied by an organization, the manner in which products are used or customer capabilities can fundamentally affect purchase choice

Demographics
Company age, location, industry (SIC code) and size are likely to alter product requirements

Operating variables   Customer requirements can be affected in a range of ways by different operating variables, such as the technology applied by the buying organization or the product types used. Certain products, especially raw materials such as steel, petrol, plastics and timber, are used in numerous ways. Sometimes the technology used by a company will play an important role. How a company uses products affects the types and amounts it purchases, as well as the method of making the purchase.[22] For example, computers are used for engineering purposes, design, scientific research, business operations such as word processing and book-keeping, as well as internet access and games in the home. A computer manufacturer may segment the computer market by types of use because organizations' needs for computer hardware and software depend on the purpose for which the products are purchased, as Dell has done in the previous chapter.

Purchasing approach   Although it may be difficult for a company to appraise the buying approach of its customers, this is nonetheless sometimes an appropriate way for business markets to be segmented. The characteristics of the buying centre or decision-making unit, including its structure and where the balance of buying power lies, and the nature of any buying policies, can all affect the product requirements of customers. For example, suppliers of building materials must organize their sales efforts to satisfy a wide array of customer types who organize their buying activities in vastly different ways. While dealing with large buyers, such as Carillion or Tarmac, will require an understanding of a relatively complex buying structure, small local builders may be perfectly satisfied with a much simpler supply arrangement.

Situational factors   Sometimes it is appropriate to segment a business market on the basis of situational factors, such as the urgency or size of an order. How urgently the order is required may have an impact on the importance a customer attaches to particular product features. For example, if a robot on a car production line has broken down, bringing the entire production process to a standstill, the price of replacement parts to fix it may be less important than their availability. However, if the same part is being replaced as part of a routine service, price may be the most important factor. The size and frequency of different orders can be effective segmentation variables because they have ramifications concerning the way the customer relationship is handled. For example, a university that regularly orders vast amounts of stationery would expect a different level of service to that of a small business that only infrequently buys small quantities of paper and envelopes.

Personal characteristics   Although individuals involved in business buying may not have as much control over the products and services selected as when they are making purchases for personal or family use, their individual characteristics still play a role in the preferences they demonstrate. For this reason it is sometimes appropriate to segment business markets on the basis of the characteristics of individuals within the buying centre. For example, the demographics, personality, motives and lifestyle of managers tasked with buying a selection of new office furniture will influence the preferred designs. If power in the buying centre rests with one senior manager who strongly dislikes modern designs, this will influence the final selection of products. Understanding how managers perceive risk and how this may alter their decision-making is a useful aspect to include in business segmentation.

Increasingly, business-to-business marketers recognize that business segmentation is as much about understanding the needs, characteristics and behaviours of the managers in their target customers, as analyzing the characteristics and commercial activities of these client businesses. One IT company has identified a group of client organizations which are all risk-averse and ill-disposed to innovation, so grouping these businesses together – irrespective of their sectors of operation – has helped in creating appropriate marketing programmes. A separate market segment contains the innovators prepared to trial new technology and solutions.

Profiling
The task of building up a fuller picture of the target segments.

Descriptors
Variables used to profile or build a fuller picture of target segments brand's desired stature.

Profiling market segments

Whatever the variable, or combination of variables, used to group customers, a more comprehensive understanding of the characteristics of individuals is likely to be required. For example, a company that segments the market for energy drinks on the basis of age, focusing on customers in their late teens, would do well to understand as much as possible about its particular target group in other respects. What reference groups influence them? Where do they live? Where and when do they socialize? What social background are they from? What motivates them? The more comprehensive the image developed, the better the opportunity to develop an effective marketing mix with maximum appeal.

Profiling is the task of building up a fuller picture of target segments, and the variables being used in the description are termed **descriptors**. The profiles in Figure 7.7

Talk 'n' Texters– **'I just have a mobile phone because it is practical'.**
- The conservative consumer, not immersed in technology but with a few practical needs that can be fulfilled by technical appliances. He or she relies on mobile phones for practical reasons only.
- Interested in basic functions, especially SMS, but not attracted at all by more sophisticated or fun services, be it via mobile phone or the internet.
- No interest in social media, Skype, smartphone mobile shopping or extensive web browsing.

Talkative Trendies– **'Talk around the clock'.**
- The modern fun/fashion-oriented socializer. This customer needs a mobile phone to keep in constant touch with the social scene and fulfil a strong need for communication.
- Interested in all applications and services, particularly social media.

Aspiring to be Accepted– **'Would like to have it but is not really up to it'.**
- Wants to be part of the 'in-crowd', but is not there yet, and possibly never will be! These customers have a mobile phone because they just want to show it off: they seek to have the same trendy handsets they believe are adopted by peer sets which they aspire to join.
- Show a special affinity towards social media, photo, video and mp3 applications.

Laggards– **'Torn between conservative values and the modern world'.**
- Traditionalist views, low level communication needs and basic technical usage.
- The 'don't need' or those late into the market!
- He or she holds specific aversions to mobile phones (SMS) but also views them as a practical-only device (e.g. for emergency calls only).

Gaming Youths– **'Game-oriented mobile world addict'.**
- Young and very technology-oriented people, belonging to the mobile generation, who need a mobile phone in order to maintain a fast-living fun life.
- Games, games, games! Plus music and social media.
- These customers search for images and brands that help them keep track with the modern world.

Sophisticated Careerists– **'Be successful with mobile technology'.**
- Career-oriented individualists with lots of contacts. Highly immersed in technology and very mobile.
- Demanding value for money, but customer care and respect are very important to these customers.
- They need a mobile phone to organize their life and business, but they are not emotionally attached.
- Self-choosers for work mobiles are included here.

Organization Paid– **'No choice – the corporation decides'.**
- Demanding value for money and customer care.
- Network coverage, reliability and volume tariff discounts are the focus, along with data security.
- Users have little influence on selection, so not particularly fashion or technology-led.

International Business Users– **'Frequent connected business travellers'.**
- Easy global roaming and smooth data transfer.
- Some similarities with *Sophisticated Careerists* but with much greater emphasis on functionality and flexibility of at-destination services.
- Influenced by corporate choice of network and tariff plans.

The first five are consumer segments. The last two are business user segments. The *Sophisticated Careerists* are mainly business users who have a self-select mobile network, handset and tariff option and behave as consumers rather than business users.

These were the 'macro' segments. Deep-dive analysis further divided these into micro segments for acquisition and retention marketing.

Figure 7.7
Illustration of market segmentation in the mobile phone market

help bring to life the different mobile phone segments identified in a recent segmentation study for mobile phones. The types of descriptors available to marketers are broadly the same as the variables used to segment markets in the first place; that is, demographics, socio-economics and so on. This is sometimes a cause of confusion for students, who struggle to remember whether they are dealing with base or descriptor variables. It helps to note that while base variables should discriminate between customer needs, descriptors are simply used to enrich the picture, to help summarize what else can be gleaned about the customers in a particular segment. This gives added inspiration to the creative team developing the product and promotional material, and helps to fine-tune decisions on price and distribution. Overall, profiling segments in this way ensures that the impact of the marketing mix on the customer is maximized. If segments are not properly profiled, it is unlikely sales personnel, advertising agency staff or senior managers will fully comprehend the proposed segmentation scheme. Therefore its effective implementation may be jeopardized. Today's 'big data' fuelled environment provides a wealth of customer information to assist in profiling and bringing to life segments.

Segmentation effectiveness

As Table 7.5 illustrates, segmentation analysis invariably involves several stages. Marketers must be aware that whatever the approach followed and whichever base variables are used, haphazard implementation can lead to ineffective market segmentation, missed opportunities and inappropriate investment. To avoid such difficulties marketers should take note of the following criteria. The first is that there must be real differences in the needs of consumers for the product or service. There is no value in segmenting a homogeneous market. Equally, dissimilar consumers in terms of their needs and purchasing behaviour must not be grouped together in the same market segment. In addition, the segments revealed must be:

- *measurable* easy to identify and measure; some basis must be found for effectively separating individuals into groups or segments with relatively homogeneous product or service needs
- *substantial* large enough to be sufficiently profitable to justify developing and maintaining a specific marketing mix
- *accessible* easy to reach with the marketing mix developed for example, the promotional effort should target the relevant consumers

TABLE 7.5 Stages in segmentation analysis

Objectives
Marketers must know the purpose of the exercise and have clear objectives

Data
Required information must be specified and collected. This may encompass a qualitative phase to develop a robust view of consumer or customer attitudes, motives, behaviour and perceptions, and a quantitative phase involving larger samples, 'big data' mining and statistical analysis of questionnaire responses (see Chapter 9)

Analysis
Various statistical packages, such as SPSS, can be used. Factor analysis, conjoint analysis and cluster analysis are commonly used techniques for analyzing the collected data. Multidimensional scaling (MDS) is widely used in product positioning studies. Such techniques should not be applied by those without the necessary statistical skills, if inappropriate solutions are to be avoided[23]

Interpretation
Marketers must interpret the proposed solutions to ensure any adopted segmentation scheme is statistically valid (complies with the relevant statistical significance tests) and managerially or intuitively valid, and that it presents market segments that are effective. Ultimately, the analysis should comply with statistical validity tests. Any recommendations must also be sensible in the view of managers[24]

Recommendation
The final proposed solution must first be presented internally to senior and line managers expected to approve the segments, and then actioned for the external audience of distributors and customers

Sources[25, 26, 27]

- *stable* the question of segment stability over time is not often addressed; if companies are to make strategic decisions on the basis of revealed segments, they need to be reasonably certain that those segments will be around long enough for action to be taken

- *useful* the selected segments must be meaningful to the managers tasked with operationalizing them and be likely to enable the company to better satisfy its target market.

Using market segmentation also requires a good deal of common sense. It is often difficult for companies to implement totally new segmentation schemes because they would be at odds with the existing marketing structures and ways of doing things. In such cases companies sometimes choose to make minor changes to what is already in place.

CRM

Having divided a market into segments, a company must decide which segments should be pursued as priorities in terms of its marketing programmes and budget allocation, as explored in the next chapter. Once a company has determined its target markets, it should strive to exploit relationships with its customers in these segments. Customer relationship management enables certain customers in the key segments to be handled more closely, so as to create a bond and loyalty.

Customer relationship management (CRM) is the term used to describe the processes for managing such relationships, with the aim of maintaining the interest and support of the most worthwhile and valuable customers within the most important segments. Technology enables such approaches and today most companies operate some form of a CRM system. Even smaller businesses can afford off-the-shelf systems for handling customer data, building profiles of purchasing and behaviours, and regularly communicating with selected customers.

Customer relationship management (CRM)
The identification of the most worthwhile and valuable customers within targeted segments and the development of ongoing relationships to foster loyalty and repeat purchasing.

Customer relationship management (CRM) aims to increase profitability by identifying the best customers within targeted segments, developing ongoing relationships and satisfying their needs in order to encourage these customers to remain loyal and to keep returning.[28] The aim is to enhance the life time value to a company of a particular customer.[29] CRM provides a framework for achieving coordination between marketing, customer service and quality programmes.[30]

CRM hinges on the notion that pursuing long-term relationships with customers, instead of a one-off transaction-oriented approach, is more profitable for marketers. The idea that detecting and collecting data about customers could help them acquire and retain profitable customers through learning-based and evolving relationships is key to CRM. Through interaction and ongoing dialogues with customers, marketers are able to monitor and learn about their customers' needs, enabling them to make changes both internal to the organization as well as in external communications to suit the needs of the customers. Digital marketing, notably the increased two-way interaction a brand increasingly has with individual customers, has made CRM even more important.[31] Amazon was a forerunner, building up a profile of customers' reading habits and preferences, tailoring subsequent offers and suggested reading lists accordingly. Florists and gift companies remember birthdays of relatives or friends for which a customer has previously purchased a gift, so as to be able to prompt the customer in advance of such a date next year. This 'reminder service' will be deemed helpful by the customer and may well lead to a new order and sale. Personalized and customized marketing messages to separate customers are a result of CRM.

CRM assists in tailoring customer service, in order to build strong bonds with highly valued customers. CRM also helps to ensure that a company does not waste a disproportionate amount of time, energy and budget on managing poor or non-viable individual customers or corporate business accounts.

There are two broad areas of CRM:[32] operational CRM that focuses on the IT-related processing which affects day-to-day operations and an analytical CRM that focuses on the strategic planning of how a company may build customer relationships and enhance their value base. Emphasis must

Learning relationships
Understanding better a
customer's needs and
behaviours.

be put on learning relationships – a key factor for success in CRM. Developing **learning relationships** (understanding better a customer's needs and behaviours) has many benefits for marketers, including repeat purchases, increased purchases, cross-selling opportunities, up-selling, reduced costs, free word-of-mouth communications between customers, added customer life-time value and possibly less attention to price.

Technology is essential, as without adequate data capture and analysis, CRM is not possible. Digital is increasingly integral to CRM systems, which is partly to blame for the growth of spyware monitoring customers' online behaviours and purchasing records. How often does your web browser apparently spontaneously show adverts for brands and products you happen to frequently use or view online? This is not accidental. With recent advancement in CRM applications, the communication directed towards potential buyers can now be customized at an individual level through emails and social media, such as Facebook pages and Twitter, and web fora and blogs. Such interactions between buyer and seller should be stored in a CRM database system. The marketer must track and store customer information, in order to customize and personalize offerings to suit individual customer needs and desires. Knowledge management is a key tool here. Learning-based relationships are a way for companies to evolve and modify their behaviour.

Essential requirements for effective CRM include:[33]

- a focus on customer needs
- interaction, ongoing dialogue and transparent communication
- learning relationships and customer involvement/integration
- customization, personalization, individualization, one to-one
- adoption of technological advancements and applications
- monitoring, tracking and use of data and ability to make sense of information
- use of customer databases and CRM tools
- ability to create value added through positive experiences
- understanding buyer–seller relationships which involve the psychology of trust, commitment, satisfaction, symmetry, dependence, fairness and morality.

Effective CRM requires a growth of value so that both buyer and seller are better off. However, marketers must recognize consumers' and the public's concerns linked to monitoring and managing customer data. Privacy and data security are big worries for many consumers and regulatory bodies. Inappropriate and incomplete use of CRM may jeopardize the reputation of a brand, damage trust and alienate intended customers. Marketers increasingly must be aware of alienating some of their customers, particularly if they treat customers differently and customers become aware of such differential treatment, which apparently advantages some customers but not others. Social media enables consumer-to-consumer sharing of information about brands and their varying offerings across consumers, many of whom now share instantly with large numbers on social media their displeasure. CRM enables marketers to identify their most desirable customers and to give them preferential attention more frequent communications, tailored propositions, deals and so forth, but inevitably this is at the expense of certain other customers who are not deemed quite so valuable or desirable. When these disadvantaged customers find out, they may be less than happy. Research has shown that such favouritism and differential treatment of customers may cause perceptions of unfairness.[34]

One of the real advantages of CRM is that marketers obtain other measures and information that are of strategic value, including information about customers' lifetime value or acquisition and retention costs, all of which can contribute to the value creation process. Recent developments in CRM are increasingly sophisticated, with methods to understand consumer behaviours and needs through brain scanning, the ability for machines to have 'eyes' so they can recognize customers individually and monitor their shopping patterns, targeted advertising on Facebook, intelligent billboards capable of recognizing customers, and even customized adverts based on an individual customer's appearance (e.g. age, gender, hair, style, etc.).

Summary

A *market* is defined as a group of people who, as consumers or as part of organizations, need and have the ability, willingness and authority to purchase products in a product class. A *consumer market* consists of purchasers and/or those in their households who intend to consume or benefit from the purchased products and who do not buy products for the main purpose of making a profit. A *business market* consists of people and groups who purchase a product for resale, direct use in producing other products or for general day-to-day operations. Although products are classified according to use, the same product may be classified as both a consumer product and an industrial product.

At the heart of marketing strategy are the decisions about which opportunities to pursue and which market segments to target. The varying characteristics, needs, wants and interests of customers mean that there are few markets where a single product or service is satisfactory for all.

Markets made up of individuals with different needs are called *heterogeneous markets*. The *market segmentation* approach divides the total market into smaller groups of customers who have similar product needs and buying characteristics. A *market segment* is a group of individuals, groups or organizations sharing one or more similar characteristics that cause them to have relatively similar product needs.

Segmentation and the customer understanding underlying it can make it easier for companies to identify and exploit different market opportunities. The approach offers businesses a number of advantages at the customer level, in relation to the competition or in terms of the effectiveness of resource allocation and strategic planning.

There are three stages to carrying out market segmentation: segmentation, targeting and positioning. Segmentation uses one or more base variables to group similar customers into segments. *Targeting* involves decisions about which and how many customer groups – segments – to target. *Positioning* involves deciding precisely how and where within the targeted segments to aim a product or products, brand or brands.

Marketers must decide how many segmentation variables to use. *Single variable segmentation* involves only one variable, but in the more commonplace *multivariable segmentation*, more than one characteristic is used to divide a total market. The latter is often more meaningful. One-to-one *marketing* involves developing long-term relationships with individual customers in order to understand and satisfy their needs. Although technological advances are making it easier for companies to achieve this goal, this approach involves considerable investment. One-to-one typically is focused within priority market segments.

Segmentation variables or *bases* are the dimensions or characteristics of individuals, groups or businesses that are used for dividing a total market into segments. The segmentation variable should be related to customers' needs for, uses of, or behaviour towards the product. Consumer segmentation variables can be grouped into four categories: demographics (age, gender, race, ethnicity, income, education, occupation, family size, family life cycle, religion and social class), geographic (population, *market density*, climate), psychographic (personality traits, motives, lifestyles) and behaviouristic (volume usage, end use, expected benefits, brand loyalty, price sensitivity). *Geodemographic segmentation*, which combines geographic and demographic factors, involves clustering people according to postcode areas. Variables for segmenting business markets include demographic factors or firmographics, operating variables, purchasing approach, situational factors and the personal characteristics of buyers. *Benefit segmentation* is the division of a market according to the benefits consumers want from the product.

Certain conditions must exist for market segmentation to be effective. First, consumers' needs for the product should be heterogeneous. Second, the segments of the market should be measurable so that the segments can be compared with respect to estimated sales potential, costs and profits. Third, at least one segment must be substantial enough to have the profit potential to justify developing and maintaining a special marketing mix for that segment. Fourth, the company must be able to access the chosen segment with a particular marketing mix. Fifth, the segment should be reasonably stable over time. Sixth, the resulting segmentation scheme must be managerially useful. Customers with dissimilar needs and buying behaviour must not be grouped together in the same market segment.

Profiling segments using *descriptor* variables can help the marketer build up a fuller picture and design a marketing mix (or mixes) that more precisely matches the needs of people in a selected market segment (or segments).

Once a company has determined its target markets, it should strive to exploit relationships with its customers in these segments. *Customer relationship management* (CRM) is the term used to describe the processes for managing such relationships, with the aim of maintaining the ongoing interest and support of the most worthwhile and valuable customers in the priority market segments. CRM builds up knowledge of individual customers' characteristics, purchasing and interactions, using these insights to tailor propositions and marketing to the most important customers, in order to develop loyalty and extract maximum spending from separate customers within the prioritized targeted segments.

Key links

This chapter has explained a core aspect of marketing strategy: market segmentation. It should be read in conjunction with:

- Chapter 2's overview of marketing strategy.
- Chapter 8's examination of targeting and positioning.
- The requirement to understand consumers and business customers, as described in Chapters 5 and 6.
- Chapter 11's explanation of effective branding.
- The analytical tools, notably the directional policy matrix used for choosing priority target markets, as presented in Chapter 12.

Important terms

Benefit segmentation
Business market
Consumer market
Customer relationship management
Descriptors
Geodemographic segmentation
Heterogeneous markets
Market
Market density
Market segment
Market segmentation
Multivariable segmentation
One-to-one marketing
Profiling
Segmentation variables or bases
Single variable segmentation
Undifferentiated or total market approach

Discussion and review questions

1. What is a market? What are the requirements for a market?

2. In the area where you live, is there a group of people with unsatisfied product needs who represent a market? Could this market be reached by an organization? Why or why not?

3. Identify and describe the two major types of market. Give examples of each.

4. What is the total market approach? Under what conditions is it most useful? Describe a current situation in which a company is using a total market approach. Is the business successful? Why or why not?

5. What is the market segmentation approach? Describe the basic conditions required for effective segmentation. Identify several companies that use the segmentation approach.

6. Why might social marketers find market segmentation particularly helpful?

7. Describe the basic conditions required for effective segmentation.

8. List the differences between concentration and differentiated strategies. Describe the advantages and disadvantages of each strategy.

9. Identify and describe four major categories of base variables that can be used to segment consumer markets. Give examples of product markets that are segmented by variables in each category.

10. Explain how geodemographic approaches such as ACORN or MOSAIC support marketers.

11. What dimensions are used to segment business markets?

12. How do marketers decide whether to use single variable or multivariable segmentation?

13. Give examples of product markets that are divided using multivariable segmentation.

14. What is customer relationship management?

15. In what ways does customer relationship management benefit an organization?

16. How does customer relationship management benefit from market segmentation?

Recommended readings

Baran, R.J. and Glaka, R., *Principles of Customer Relationship Management* (Routledge, 2012).

Buttle, F. and Maklan, S., *Customer Relationship Management: Concepts and Technologies* (Routledge, 2015).

Dibb, S. and Simkin, L., *Market Segmentation Success: Making It Happen!* (The Haworth Press/Routledge, 2008).

Dibb, S. and Simkin, L., *The Market Segmentation Workbook* (Thomson, 1996).

Hooley, G., Piercy, N.F. and Nicoulaud, B., *Marketing Strategy and Competitive Positioning* (FT/Prentice Hall, 2011).

Hutt, M.D. and Speh, T.W., *Business Marketing Management: B2B* (Cengage, 2013).

McDonald, M. and Dunbar, I., *Market Segmentation* (John Wiley, 2012).

Nguyen B., Simkin, L. and Canhoto, A., *The Dark Side of CRM* (Routledge, 2015).

Ries, A. and Trout, J., *Positioning: The Battle for Your Mind* (McGraw-Hill, 2001).

Tsiptsis, K. and Chorianopoulos, A., *Data Mining Techniques in CRM: Inside Customer Segmentation* (Wiley-Blackwell, 2010).

Webber, H., *Divide and Conquer: Target your Customer through Market Segmentation* (Wiley, 1998).

Weinstein, A., *Handbook of Market Segmentation: Strategic Targeting for Business and Technology Firms* (The Haworth Press/Routledge, 2004).

Internet exercise

Adventure Travel Abroad is an internet company that offers a variety of travel and adventure products: *Discovery & Culture; Activity & Adrenaline; Deserts & Wilderness; Wildlife & Nature*. Learn more about its goods, services and travel advice through its website at: www.adventureworldwide.co.uk.

1. Based on the information provided on the website, what are some of Adventure Travel Abroad's basic products?

2. What market segments does Adventure Travel Abroad appear to be targeting with its website?

3. What segmentation variables is the company using to segment these markets?

Group tasks

1. Which customer groups do car producers Kia, BMW and Porsche target? What segmentation variables have you used in order to create these segments or customer groups?

2. Consider the different target segments your business school pursues. How do the needs and expectations of these various market segments differ? What are the implications for your school's marketing strategy?

Applied mini-case

Most readers of *Marketing: Concepts and Strategies* will have a Facebook account and be used to social media networking. Business executives and professionals often are on LinkedIn, which has 347 000 000 users, 17 million of whom are in the UK. It is the largest network for professionals on the web. LinkedIn explains:

> Our mission is simple: connect the world's professionals to make them more productive and successful. When you join LinkedIn, you get access to people, jobs, news, updates, and insights that help you be great at what you do.

● Build your professional identity online and stay in touch with colleagues and classmates.

● Discover professional opportunities, business deals and new ventures.

● Get the latest news, inspiration and insights you need to be great at what you do.

Source: www.linkedin.com, March 2015.

Question

What is the brand positioning proposition at the heart of LinkedIn's proposition? Explain how this relates to the apparent target market strategy for LinkedIn.

Marriott: getting down to business with business travellers

Case study

Imagine marketing more than 4000 hotels and resorts, under 19 brands in 78 countries. This is the challenge facing Marriott, a multinational marketer that provides lodging services to millions of customers every day. The company, founded by J. Willard Marriott in 1927, started with a single root-beer stand and the 'spirit to serve'. Today, it achieves $12 billion in global sales from guest room revenue, meals, meeting and special events and other services.

Each of Marriott's hotel brands has its own positioning. See www.marriott.co.uk/hotel-brands.mi for a current summary. The flagship Marriott brand stands for full service: properties have restaurants, meeting rooms, fitness centres and other facilities. The JW Marriott brand is more up-market and the Ritz-Carlton brand is known for top quality service. BVLGARI hotels and resorts is pitched as the leading luxury hospitality collection in the world. Marriott's newest hotel brand is Edition, a chain of stylish luxury highly contemporary hotels, starting in Istanbul and London. TownePlace Suites are mid-priced suite hotels for customers who plan an extended stay away from home. Fairfield Inn & Suites are for businesspeople and vacationers seeking value-priced accommodation.

Sluggish economic conditions have only intensified rivalry within the hyper-competitive hotel industry. Major hotel companies such as Accor, Hilton, Hyatt, InterContinental and Starwood all offer a wide range of hotel and resort brands for different customers' needs and tastes. In addition, local hotels and regional chains compete on the basis of location, ambience, price, amenities and other elements. To compete effectively in this pressured environment, Marriott is relying on extensive marketing research, expert segmentation and careful targeting.

Marriott uses a variety of research techniques to find out about customer needs and behaviour, including focus groups, online surveys, and in-room questionnaires. For example, when it conducted focus groups with customers who had stayed at its Marriott and Renaissance properties, it discovered some interesting differences. Renaissance customers said they like to open the curtains and look out of the window when they first enter their rooms. In contrast, Marriott guests said they get unpacked quickly and get right to work in their rooms. 'That's when we started making connections about the individual personalities that gravitate toward the Marriott brand,' says the vice president of marketing strategy. With this research in hand, marketers for the Marriott hotel brand targeted a segment they call 'achievers'; business travellers who feel driven to get a lot done in a short time. They created an advertising campaign to communicate that Marriott is about productivity and performance. The print and online adverts featured interviews with six real customers, who discussed their drive to accomplish personal and professional goals.

When Marriott looked at visitors who prefer SpringHill Suites, one of its suite hotel brands, it found a slightly different profile. These are business people who travel often and see a suite hotel as a place to spread out, feel refreshed, and take a break from the stress of being on the road. These customers are also heavy users of technology, especially mobile communication devices such as smartphones. In reaching out to this target market, Marriott uses mobile marketing as well as traditional media to get its message across. It invites business travellers to download its iPhone app and runs adverts designed especially for viewing on smartphone screens. Customers can click on the mobile advert to check room availability online or to speak with the reservations department. The Marriott app enables check-in-free access to rooms and no-queue payment at check-out.

Marriott also targets companies that need hotel space to hold meetings and seminars. In most cases, these companies bring in attendees from outside the immediate location, which means Marriott can fill more guest rooms during meetings. Meetings usually involve additional purchases, such as snacks or meals, another profitable reason to target businesses. Sales reps at major Marriott properties are ready to help companies plan employee workshops, supplier and distributor events and other meetings, for a handful to a ballroom full of people.

Studying the needs and buying patterns of companies that hold business meetings, Marriott's marketers have found that a growing number are interested in videoconferencing and other high-tech extras. To appeal to this segment, Marriott has equipped many of its meeting rooms with the latest in recording and communications technology. It has also partnered with AT&T and Cisco to offer 'virtual meeting' capabilities in its Marriott, JW Marriott, and Renaissance Hotels. This teleconferencing technology allows a group gathered in one of Marriott's hotel meeting rooms to collaborate with colleagues, clients or others anywhere in the world.

The segment of consumers and business travellers who care about the environment is sizeable these days, and

Marriott wants its share of this growing market. The company has developed prototype green hotels for several of its brands, designing the public space and guest rooms with an eye toward conserving both water and energy. Marriott will build hundreds of these green hotels during the next decade. Thanks to the company's emphasis on saving power, 275 of its hotels already qualify for the US Environmental Protection Agency's Energy Star designation. Marriott is also going green by working with suppliers that operate in environmentally friendly ways. It provides pads made from recycled paper for attendees of business meetings held at its properties and buys key cards made from recycled plastic. Even the pillows in the guest rooms are made from recycled plastic bottles.

Marriott set up a central database to capture details such as how long customers stay and what they purchase and when they stay at any of its hotels or resorts. It also stores demographic data and tracks individual preferences so it can better serve customers. By analyzing the information in this huge database, Marriott discovered that many of its customers visit more than one of its brands. Therefore, the company created sophisticated statistical models to target customers for future marketing offers based on their history with Marriott. In one campaign, Marriott sent out three million email messages customized according to each recipient's unique history with the company. Due to its database capabilities, Marriott was able to track whether recipients returned to one of its properties after this campaign and actual sales results exceeded corporate expectations. This database technology has paid for itself many times over with improved targeting efficiency and higher response rates.

Questions for discussion

1. How is Marriott segmenting the market for hotel services?

2. Which of the targeting strategies is Marriott using? Explain your answer.

3. What specific types of data should Marriott have in its customer database for segmentation purposes?

CHAPTER 8
Targeting and positioning

"Strategy requires trade-offs ... informed compromises and agreed priorities"

Objectives

- To understand targeting decisions for emerging opportunities.

- To consider various segmentation targeting strategies.

- To discover how marketers prioritize target markets and select between market segments.

- To appreciate the importance of assessing sales potential, market share and value share in creating a target market strategy.

- To learn about strategies for positioning.

- To complete our coverage of the market segmentation process of segmenting a market, selecting which segments to target, and positioning a proposition in those chosen target market segments.

- To explore customer value propositions and their linkage with effective positioning strategy.

INTRODUCTION

As explained in Chapter 2, marketing strategy revolves around the choice of which opportunities should be pursued, the specification of an associated target market strategy and the creation of a competitive edge. Limited resources generally result in organizations being unable to serve all of the needs and different customers in an overall market or commercial sector, so marketers must make trade-off choices when creating a targeting strategy based on the relative merits of various opportunities and target markets. Having made the necessary trade-off choices, the consumers or business customers in markets and segments deemed to be priorities must be communicated with in a manner emphasizing their importance to the company and also reflecting their expectations, which is the positioning task. Positioning is particularly effective when strong customer value propositions underpin the adopted positioning.

This chapter focuses on the second and third stages of the market segmentation process – targeting and positioning – presenting a framework for selecting both opportunities and target markets to pursue with an appropriate positioning strategy.

Targeting strategies for business schools

Warwick Business School has a clear vision of what it should be doing as a leading business school:

Our vision is straightforward
What underlies everything is academic excellence and the impact it has on society

Our vision
To be the leading university-based business school in Europe

Our mission
To produce and disseminate world-class, cutting edge research that shapes the way organisations operate and businesses are led and managed
To produce world-class, socially responsible, creative leaders and managers who think on a global scale, regardless of the size of their organisation.

In the UK, Warwick Business School was one of the first major players to mark out a very clear positioning … its research-led brand proposition proved popular with aspirational MBA students desiring topical and thought-provoking thinking, while many more cerebral and less vocationally-inclined undergraduates were also attracted to this pitch. Leading MBA competitor Cranfield, meanwhile, played to its extensive links with corporate clients and its large network of former students now senior practitioners in industry, by stressing its practitioner links and the commercial relevance of its degrees. Meanwhile, Aston emphasized employability and the practical relevance of its degree programmes.

Two major global business schools also promote very clear positionings. Harvard is not shy at explaining its reach

and heritage for over a century of producing high-achieving graduates and research:

> We educate leaders who make a difference in the world. For over a century, our faculty have drawn on their passion for teaching, their experience in working with organizations worldwide, and the insights gained from their research to educate generations of leaders who have shaped the practice of business in every industry and in every country around the world.

France-based INSEAD has a long-standing reputation for attracting a multi-cultural and diverse set of aspirational students from across the globe, as a business school designed from its birth to be international in its operations:

> As a global educational institution with a pioneering multi-campus model, our mission is to create a non-dogmatic learning environment that brings together people, cultures and ideas from around the world, in order to transform individuals and organizations through business education.
>
> Through teaching, we develop responsible, thoughtful leaders and entrepreneurs who create value for their organizations and their communities.
>
> Through research, we expand the frontiers of knowledge and influence business practice.

Many of Warwick's students find little empathy with Cranfield's positioning, and vice-versa. This worries neither business school, as each has made conscious decisions about which audiences to target in their core markets of research and teaching. Similarly, Harvard recognizes some will view it as arrogant and too hard-nosed, while many aspirational CEOs and strategy consultants will be hooked by its brand positioning. INSEAD evidently also seeks the leaders of the future, but with a strong set of values around responsibility, community and diversity. Some students, potential faculty and corporate clients will be alienated by these very stark positionings, but there will be segments finding great appeal in these propositions. Each of these reputable business schools has determined to which segments to appeal, developing clear positioning strategies and marketing communications pertinent to their audiences. Differentiation and reputation are essential in this market and that requires clarity of purpose in terms of targeting and positioning.

Marketers have a responsibility to act as the eyes and ears for their organizations, identifying opportunities and emerging target markets. This is a core component of strategic marketing. Well-crafted propositions reflecting target market expectations and requirements should be developed which are intended to stand out from competitors. Whether Mini, Skoda or Mercedes in the car market; CapGemini or McKinsey in the consulting sector; Veetee, Uncle Ben's or Tilda in the rice market; or competing business schools, organizations must select their target markets and develop positioning strategies which are appropriate to such audiences' expectations and perceptions.

Building on the previous chapter's exploration of market segments, this chapter begins by considering the nature and options for segmentation targeting strategies. The review of targeting considers the strategies used to select and prioritize target markets. The associated tools are also often deployed to make the necessary trade-off decisions for identifying opportunities to pursue, as also described within this chapter. The chapter also looks at the importance of assessing sales potential in creating a target market strategy. The full segmentation process involves creating the segmentation, selecting which segments to pursue and determining a positioning strategy appropriate for the selected target market segments. Therefore, having explored the targeting stage of this segmentation process, this chapter examines the positioning phase and approaches for developing a positioning plan. The chapter concludes by looking at the concept of customer value propositions, which underpin positioning to create compelling propositions for targeted consumers and business customers.

Segmentation targeting strategies

Segmentation targeting
The decision about which market segment(s) an organization decides to prioritize for its sales and marketing efforts.

Segmentation targeting involves marketers in decisions about which market segment(s) an organization should prioritize for its sales and marketing efforts. As Figure 8.1 shows, the three basic targeting strategies are undifferentiated, concentrated and differentiated. The decision made regarding the targeting strategy to follow must be based on a clear understanding of a company's capabilities and resources, financial performance, the nature of the competition, the product or service in question, the characteristics of the market, as well as emerging threats and opportunities.

Undifferentiated strategy

Undifferentiated targeting strategy
When a company targets an entire market for a product with a single marketing mix.

An organization sometimes defines an entire market for a particular product as its target market. When a company designs a single marketing mix and directs it at the entire market for a particular product, it is using an **undifferentiated targeting strategy**. For example, a one-product soft drink business targeting all consumers in the overall market for soft drinks. This is a strategy in which an organization defines an entire market for a particular product as its target market, designs a single marketing mix, and directs it at that market. The strategy assumes that all customers in the target market for a specific kind of product have similar needs, and thus the organization can satisfy most customers with a single marketing mix. This mix consists of one type of product with little or no variation, one price, one promotional programme aimed at everybody and one distribution system to reach most customers in the total market. However, there are relatively few companies opting to follow this targeting approach, because of the risk that better honed or tailored propositions from rivals appeal much more strongly to specific sub-groups of consumers in the market … which they will. There are few situations where such an approach is viable. Although customers may have similar needs for a few products, for most products their needs are quite different. In such instances, a company should use a concentrated or a differentiated strategy.

Concentration strategy
A process by which an organization directs its marketing effort towards a single market segment through one marketing mix.

Concentrated strategy

When an organization directs its marketing efforts towards a single market segment by creating and maintaining one marketing mix, it is employing a **concentration strategy**.

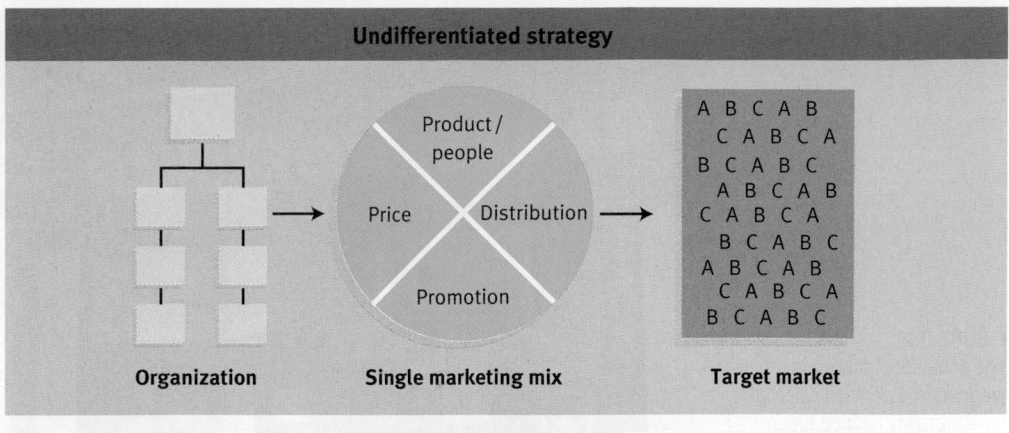

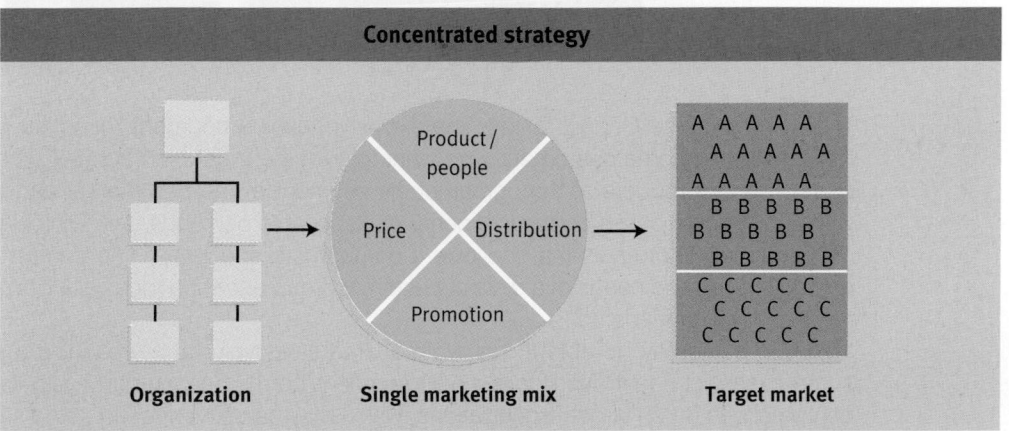

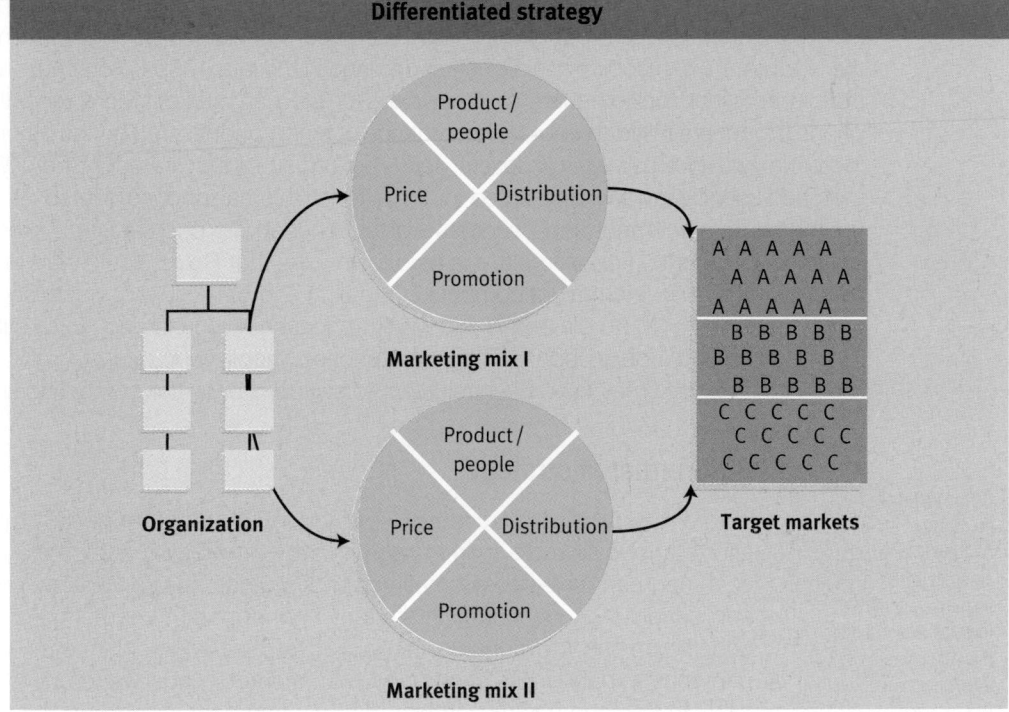

FIGURE 8.1
Targeting strategies. The letters in each target market represent portential customers. Customers with the same letters have similar characteristics and similar product needs

FIGURE 8.2
The contents of this store retailing wargames have been selected for a narrowly defined group of shoppers in a concentrated strategy

The fashion house Chanel targets the exclusive fashion segment, directing its marketing effort towards high-income customers who want to own the most chic apparel. The Cross Pen Company aims its products at the upmarket gift segment of the pen market and does not compete with Bic, which focuses on the inexpensive, disposable pen segment. The chief advantage of the concentration strategy is that it allows a company to specialize. The company can analyze the characteristics and needs of a distinct customer group and then focus all of its energies on satisfying that group's needs.

A company may be able to generate a large sales volume by reaching a single segment. In some cases, concentrating on a single segment permits a company with limited resources to compete with much larger organizations, which may have overlooked some smaller segments.

Concentrating on one segment also means that a company puts 'all its eggs in one basket', which is clearly a disadvantage. If a company's sales depend on a single segment and the segment's demand for the product declines, the company's financial strength declines as well. When the North American sports coupé market declined in the late 1980s, Porsche found itself in severe trouble as it had no exposure to other parts of the car market. More recently, several mobile phone producers failed to spot the emergence of smart phones, led by the iPhone and Samsung. Motorola and Nokia were big losers, focusing on a product category from which consumers switched user behaviours and opted for the alternative smartphones. Moreover, when a company penetrates one segment and becomes well entrenched, its popularity may keep it from moving into other segments. For example, it is hard to imagine that Rolex would start producing low-cost watches, or that Swatch might compete at the high end of the luxury watch segment. This might have been true for Motorola and Nokia initially, because Motorola and Nokia still had high-selling ranges of existing mobile phones when smartphones, mobile web browsing and messaging/social media took off, and may have been reluctant to switch over to the competing smartphones.

Differentiated strategy

Differentiated strategy
A strategy by which an organization directs its marketing efforts towards two or more market segments by developing a marketing mix for each.

With a **differentiated strategy** (see Figure 8.1), an organization directs its marketing efforts at two or more market segments by developing a separate marketing mix for each segment selected. Sometimes this is a natural progression from the successful application of a concentration strategy in one market segment. For example, Jockey underwear has traditionally been aimed at one segment, men. However, the company has expanded its efforts and now markets underwear for women and children as well. Porsche has moved into the SUV segment in addition to sports coupés. The marketing mixes used for a differentiated strategy may vary relating to product/service differences, place/distribution methods, promotion methods, prices and customer service. The majority of users of Gatwick Airport near London are package holiday travellers. A significant minority, however, are business users, so the airport now has various marketing programmes targeting different segments. Most brand-led mainstream businesses today adopt a differentiated multi-segment targeting strategy, with a portfolio of propositions and marketing programmes targeting a set of segments in order to pursue a selection of opportunities.

An organization can usually increase its sales in the aggregate market through a differentiated strategy because its marketing mixes are aimed at more people. For example, Gap, which established its retail clothes reputation by targeting people under 25, now targets several age groups, from infants to people over 60. A company with excess production capacity may find a differentiated strategy advantageous because the sale of products to additional segments may absorb this excess capacity. On the other hand, a differentiated strategy often demands a greater number of production processes, materials and people. Thus production and marketing costs may be higher than with a concentration strategy.

One-to-one marketing
Customized marketing engaging individual customers for the development of longer-term relationships.

One-to-one marketing fits with either a concentrated or differentiated strategy. The growth of customer insight and enhanced customer relationship management systems enables identification of individual customers who might warrant special attention and customized marketing in order to develop longer-term relationships. One-to-one marketing, enabled through CRM and digital marketing, has grown considerably within recent years. As illustrated in Figure 8.3, one-to-one is focused primarily on target customers within the prescribed priority target market segments.

Factors affecting choice of a segmentation targeting strategy

Irrespective of the type of targeting strategy an organization chooses to adopt when faced with the decision about whether or not to enter a new segment, it must consider a number of issues. These issues include:

1. the nature of the needs and wants of end users
2. the size, structure and future potential of the segment
3. the availability of company resources
4. the intensity of the competition
5. the size of the company's existing market share, and
6. the possibility of any production/marketing scale economies with existing activities.

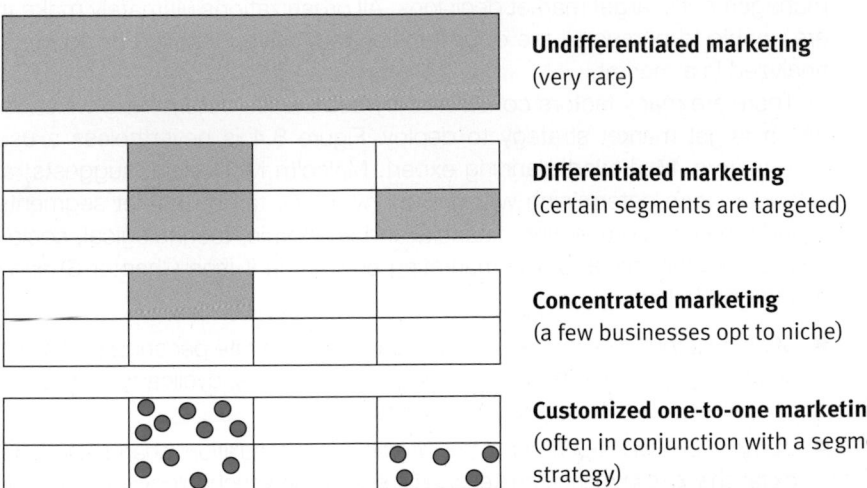

FIGURE 8.3
Targeting strategies

Undifferentiated marketing
(very rare)

Differentiated marketing
(certain segments are targeted)

Concentrated marketing
(a few businesses opt to niche)

Customized one-to-one marketing
(often in conjunction with a segment strategy)

FIGURE 8.4
Factors affecting choice of target market strategy
Source: Adapted from David W. Cravens, *Strategic Marketing* (Homewood, IL.: Irwin, 1982) 0256-026459 http://catalogs .mhhe.com/mhhe /viewProductDetails.do? isbn=0073381004

Figure 8.4 sums up the core factors affecting the choice of targeting strategy. A company may recognize that a fit between its products or capabilities and target customer needs is stronger and more 'marketable' in one market segment than in another. However, in some cases a decision may be made to expand into a new area, market or territory where the fit between customer needs and the product and marketing proposition is poor, with the intention of rectifying such shortcomings. Certain markets' size or value makes them attractive, as does a company's existing or potential sizeable market share. There may be economies of scale available in targeting a particular market segment alongside related ones, so that certain aspects of the production, sales and marketing activity may be shared. Of course, if truly homogeneous market segments have been identified, then each segment will require certain unique aspects of sales and marketing activity. If two segments really can be treated identically in terms of marketing mix programmes, then they are probably really one segment! Highly intensive and well-established competition may to some companies be something of a 'turn-off', whereas others may take such competitor activity to be indicative of extensive market growth and business opportunity. It is worth noting that even a company the size of Ford or GM does not have the time, capacity, people or financial resources to develop a marketing mix for every single segment in the vehicle market. Available resources play a significant role in management's target market decisions. All organizations ultimately make trade-off choices and are unable to pursue all the opportunities they have identified or address all of the segments analyzed in a market.

There are many factors considered by companies determining which markets to target and which target market strategy to deploy. Figure 8.4 is nevertheless a useful summary of the core factors. Marketing planning expert, Malcolm McDonald, suggests[1] a variety of issues to consider when determining which and how many target market segments to prioritize. These include market, competition, financial and economic, technological, socio-political and regulatory factors the forces of the marketing environment (see Chapter 3) and core market trends, as outlined below:

● *Market factors:* size (money, units or both); growth rate per annum; diversity of the market; sensitivity to price, service features and external factors; cyclicality; seasonality; bargaining power of upstream and downstream suppliers.

● *Competition:* types of competitor; degree of concentration; changes in type and mix; entries and exits; changes in market share; substitution by new technology; degrees and types of integration.

Innocent goes mumsy

Building customer relationships

Innocent Smoothies transformed the category of fruit-based smoothie drinks into big business for retail stockists and Innocent alike. What started as a small venture by three friends has become a brand, now part-owned by Coca-Cola. Innocent promotes the health and nutritional values of its fruit smoothie major drinks, but in a fun and 'huggy' style which proves very popular with its users. The company has diversified into Veg Pots, a children's range, and to other areas of the market. The brand has wide appeal, largely to health- and taste-conscious consumers. Few readers will be unfamiliar with its range. The launch of its Kids range was supported with advertising and sales promotions targeting children and their parents, so a link with Mumsnet is not too surprising.

Mumsnet is now the UK's biggest network for parents, generating over 70 million page views and over 14 million visits per month. Politicians and brands, including Ford and Asda, have turned regularly to the site in order to convey their messages but also to learn about their targeted audiences. According to Mumsnet, 'The idea was to create a website where parents could swap advice about holidays, pushchairs and last night's TV. Our aim is to make parents' lives easier by pooling knowledge, advice and support. We try, as far as possible to let the conversation flow and not to over-moderate. Mumsnet is a site for grown-ups.'

Mumsnet offers product reviews and advice, but has created a panel of mums which brands may use in order to glean insights into the behaviours and attitudes of parents and their children. Innocent plans to improve the appeal of its brand to children and their parents by benefiting from the feedback provided by Mumsnet's panel of expert mothers and also from the millions of users of the website. Innocent's nutritionists hold online Q&As with Mumsnet parents, supporting the brand but also learning about consumers' views, concerns and desires.

Immediately there were benefits for Innocent's team, as they explained to Mumsnet users on the website:

When we decided to make a recipe book all about healthy, tasty, no-fuss food that the whole family could enjoy (and that didn't take ages to make), we thought it'd be a good idea to get as many mums, dads and kids as possible to test the recipes first.

So thanks to a group of Mumsnetters, who very kindly took the time to test, taste and tell us what they thought of a selection of the recipes, the result is a book that's got the thumbs up from parents and kids alike.

Filled with over 100 delicious, simple, healthy recipes (from two-minute breakfasts to proper Sunday lunches) and with 85 per cent of recipes containing at least one of your five-a-day, there are also loads of tips, distractions and ways of getting everyone involved in cooking, making and eating.

We couldn't have done it without you. So thank you very much.

www.mumsnet.com

Innocent still targets adult users and households without any children, adopting different campaigns for its 'grown up' audiences. In this instance, however, the company is explicitly developing products and marketing programmes targeted at children and their parents.

Sources: 'Innocent to Fine-Tune Range with Mumsnet', Russell Parsons, *Marketing Week*, February 3 2011, p. 4; Innocent, 2011 and March 2015; www.Mumsnet .com, June 2011; www.mumsnet.com/Talk/food/a1299506-Q-A-with-Innocent -Company-Nutritionist-and-Dietitian-Vanessa-Hattersley-ANS, 17 March 2015.

- *Financial and economic:* contribution margins; leveraging factors such as economies of scale and experience; barriers to entry or exit; capacity utilization.
- *Technology:* maturity and volatility; complexity; differentiation; patents and copyrights; manufacturing process technology required.
- *Socio-political and regulatory:* social attitudes and trends; influence with pressure groups, government and regulatory bodies; laws, government and EU regulations; human factors such as unionization and community acceptance.

Target market attractiveness and opportunity selection

In practice, every organization has its own preferences for which variables to consider when assessing the relative attractiveness of markets or opportunities to serve. Unfortunately, some corporate leaders only assess profitability as their measure of attractiveness, which is too

TABLE 8.1 Market attractiveness factors adopted by UK companies

Companies' market attractiveness criteria	
First tier: • Profitability **Second tier:** • Market growth • Market size • Likely customer satisfaction • Sales volume **Third tier:** • Likelihood of a sustainable differential advantage over rivals • Ease of access for the business • Opportunities in the industry • Product differentiation • Competitive rivalry	• Market share • Relative strength/key functions • Customers' price sensitivity • Customer image of company **Fourth tier:** • Technological factors • Fit with business strategy • Stability of market • Environmental factors • Threat of substitutes • Barriers to entry • Negotiating power of buyers • Ease of profiling customers • Supplier power

Source: Sally Dibb and Lyndon Simkin

short-term and fails to reflect the evolving dynamics of a market. A survey[2] of marketing practices in the largest UK companies revealed an interesting set of variables utilized in determining target market attractiveness (see Table 8.1). This study revealed the extent to which UK businesses are overly restricted by the City analysts' short-termism, and the emphasis placed by financial journalists and pundits on performance only in terms of profitability in the most recent few months. US, German and South-east Asian financial markets tend not to be quite so short-termist in their thinking.[3] Outside the UK, organizations worry about market share and profitability, not just for today and tomorrow, but for a few years to come. Profits do matter, but it is desirable to adopt a balanced set of variables or criteria with which to judge the relative merits of possible opportunities and target markets.

A market may well be targeted because of its future potential, not just because of current sales. For-profit businesses inevitably will be driven by likely financial rewards, but often these result from other factors, such as competitor intensity, customer salience and the ability to achieve differentiation. Success should be construed in terms of both today's performance and longer-term potential. The UK survey had some good news: it is reassuring to see the ability to deliver customer satisfaction, sustainable differential/competitive advantage and likely product differentiation well up the list of factors considered in the UK. Chapter 1 explained the importance in marketing of satisfying customers, outpacing competitors and developing differentiation. It is not so good to note that the marketing environment and issues relating to non-direct competitor activity are so low down the list. Organizations really should adopt a balanced list of criteria, mixing short-term and longer-term issues and internal and external factors such as financial considerations and market characteristics.

Understanding what is worthwhile or attractive is not restricted to the selection of target markets and which segments to pursue. Marketers must also identify worthwhile opportunities for their organizations to follow. Often, the same criteria used to select between segments are used to prioritize opportunities to go after. Therefore, this section of *Marketing: Concepts and Strategies* considers the selection of opportunities, before the chapter returns to examine target market selection.

Identifying and selecting opportunities

Most businesses have a set of corporate objectives guiding their strategic thinking (see Chapter 2). Some companies may have a strategy of consolidation or survival, but even they will face trade-offs between resourcing and supporting viable or growing markets against markets facing declining fortunes. Driven by shareholders' and investors' financial desires, most leadership teams seek growth in sales. Accordingly, a marketing strategy is expected to identify parts of the market likely to generate growing sales or where the company's brand and capabilities will generate commercial opportunities. Two very frequently posed questions by senior executives are:

1. Where is big growth likely?
2. Have we assessed all possible opportunities?

Rarely posed but strategically important, a third question should be *What do we stop doing?*

Armed with topical insights from the market, knowledge of customers' expectations, and awareness of competitors' developments, marketers should be well placed to answer such questions and assist in their organizations' strategy creation. They should also address these questions in their annual marketing planning activity, as described later in Chapter 22 of *Marketing: Concepts and Strategies*.

Companies adopt different approaches for identifying such growth or new opportunity options. Away days for executives or so-termed 'off-sites' away from day-to-day disturbances, meetings and conferences are used for managerial brainstorming. Sometimes, these sessions are encouraged to reflect on emerging opportunities by either staging a 'PESTLE workshop'

Ansoff's matrix
Assessment of competitive strategies and growth opportunities based on new/current products and new/current markets, providing market penetration, market development, product development and diversification.

or an '**Ansoff** Day'. By examining the forces of the marketing environment (see Chapter 3), executives will, under each element of the popularly named PEST or PESTLE analysis, identify opportunities and threats. They will explore whether external drivers in terms of politics, legal and regulatory issues, technology, societal and environmental concerns and economic forces present any opportunities. Such factors should also be taken into account when considering which market segments to target. In an Ansoff workshop – so called because it is based on the strategic planning framework created by Ansoff – executives look to populate the four cells of his matrix (see Chapter 2), as depicted in Figure 8.5. They will base such thoughts on intuition, experience, knowledge of their markets and products, feedback from distributors, customers and suppliers, as well as research findings. Having identified possible options in the brainstorming session, individual executives or teams typically would subsequently spend some weeks researching in more detail the apparently most important issues, so that informed decisions about whether to proceed can be made.

FIGURE 8.5
Ansoff's matrix. For a particular energy company considering growth opportunities, adopting the Ansoff framework (see Chapter 2) these were leading contenders

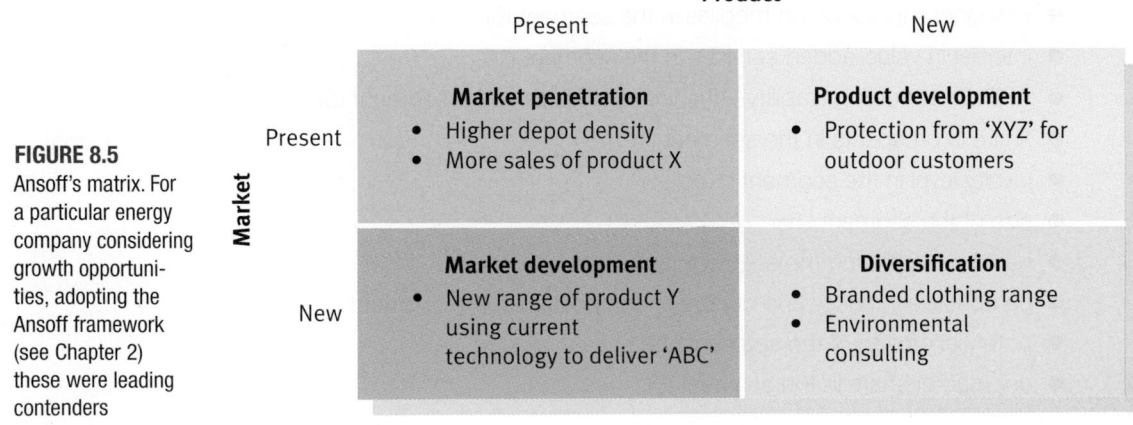

SWOT analyses, explained in Chapter 2, competitor analyses and research into customer satisfaction and expectations, will all additionally reveal possible commercial opportunities. All of these analyses also feature in marketers' annual marketing planning, but they occur *ad hoc* and routinely within the calendar of corporate activities. The result is that an organization and its marketers generate many ideas for new business opportunities or emerging target markets. Unfortunately, in practice, there are never enough time, people, focus, budget, skills or management bandwidth to be able to pursue all of the interesting opportunities that emerge … trade-offs are necessary.

Sometimes such trade-offs and prioritization are achieved by rather dictatorial direction from a senior manager. It is not unknown for a senior director or company owner to instruct colleagues to pursue a particular opportunity or market with little apparent prior analysis, which is not highly desirable behaviour. However, generally there is discussion between business functions and senior managers. There is still a danger that 'who shouts loudest for longest' wins the argument and the budget in such management meetings. It is preferable to adopt a set of criteria or variables with which to judge the relative attractiveness of emerging opportunities. This same approach can be used very effectively to identify the most attractive segments to pursue with dedicated marketing programmes. For example, one telecoms company's segmentation study identified six consumer segments, but its leadership only chose to devote marketing resources to capturing more customers in three of these, based on a set of pre-agreed criteria which included financial performance variables but also many market-led criteria.

When organizations recognize the undesirability of only judging attractiveness in terms of short-term profitability, they tend to identify a more balanced set of criteria. These factors rarely are of equal importance, so they are weighted in terms of their relative importance or power. In such situations, the directional policy matrix (DPM) – or market attractiveness business strength matrix – is often adopted by leadership teams and marketers to help with the selection of opportunities, market segments and target markets to pursue. This technique is explained in detail in Chapter 12, pages 365–368. A real-life step-by-step illustration is provided in the Marketing Tools and Techniques box in that chapter.

As explored in Chapter 12, the DPM assessment of attractiveness may be applied to selecting which brands or product groups to support, which opportunities to pursue, or which markets to target: it increasingly is used within the targeting phase of market segmentation to decide which segments to pursue. The telecoms company just referred to, selecting between its six consumer segments, adopted this technique, specifying the following variables and their weightings to sum up the views of its directors in terms of what constituted a worthwhile or attractive pursuit and target segment:

- disposable income in the segment (8)
- willingness to spend on mobiles in the segment (6)
- interest in value-added services in the segment (10)
- ARPU/revenue/profitability – the financial worth of the segment (8)
- share in prospects in the segment (10)
- loyalty level in the segment (10)
- size of the segment (16)
- barriers to entering the segment (8)
- competitive intensity and degree of competition in the segment (6)
- potential growth of the segment (12)
- our market share in the segment (6).

The figures in brackets after each variable in the list indicate the relative importance of these variables, as voted by the directors in this company's senior leadership team. They total to 100 per cent.

As explored in Chapter 12, when using the directional policy matrix to select between opportunities or market segments, there are essential steps:

1. Select a 'balanced' set of attractiveness variables, not only expected profitability. These should include financial criteria, but also market-facing criteria, such as the ability to satisfy the customers in question, the likelihood of achieving differentiation versus competitors, the longevity and growth prospects and so forth.

2. Select a set of business strength or capability variables, pertinent to the industry in question, with which it is possible to compare strengths against the strongest competitor. Each industry tends to have certain unique capabilities, appropriate for comparisons between competitors in terms of their strengths and weaknesses for achieving success with consumers or business customers in opposition to their strongest rivals.

3. For both sets of variables – market attractiveness and business strengths — the selected variables should be weighted, because some matter more than others. Typically, this involves allocating 100 points across the market attractiveness variables (as in the above list for the telecoms business) and 100 points across the business strength variables.

4. These two sets of variables and their respective weightings should be held constant over time, so that progress – quarter by quarter or year by year – of the opportunities or market segments may be observed.

5. Each opportunity or individual market segment, depending on the unit of analysis for the study, should then be judged variable by variable. If the specific opportunity or segment performs well against a selected variable it should be scored '1'; if it performs only 'so-so' it should be scored '0.5'; while if it performs poorly it should be scored '0'.

6. For each variable, the weighting (out of 100) multiplied by the score ('1', '0.5' or '0') will result in a value for the variable.

7. In both lists separately – market attractiveness and business strengths – the summation of these values will provide total values between 0 and 100: one total for the market attractiveness dimension and one total for business strengths.

Directional policy matrix
A market attractiveness and business strength/capability assessment tool ideal for trade-off analyses for identifying resourcing priorities.

8. These total values enable the relative position of each opportunity being assessed or each market segment under examination to be plotted on the **directional policy matrix**. The value – between 0 and 100 – indicates the position on the axis.

9. Those opportunities or market segments plotted upper left (NW) on the DPM are more desirable than anything plotted towards the lower right (SE). Arguably anything plotted to the bottom right should not be pursued or resourced. See Figure 8.6 for an illustration. The DPM is explained again in Chapter 12.

10. This analysis should feature in the annual marketing plan, but some businesses repeat it quarterly in order to assess progress and judge the performance of their marketing activity. Any opportunity or segment migrating from the NW to the SE on the matrix is not performing well. Reasons need exploring. Disinvestment or withdrawal might be necessary, or a revised marketing strategy and customer engagement plan specifying.

In the telecoms example, each identified market segment was judged against these variables in order to agree which segments should be the focus of the company's resources. The same approach could trade-off identified opportunities to determine which are the most attractive to pursue. While there is an element of subjectivity in this approach, the mix of variables, the balance between financial factors and external characteristics of the market, and

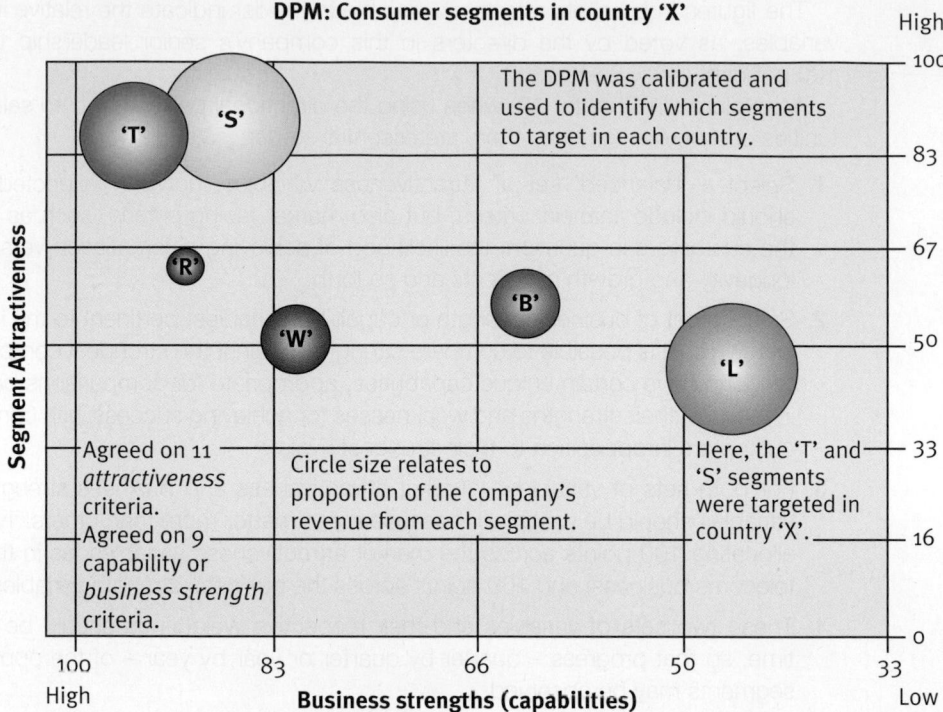

FIGURE 8.6
Illustration of the directional policy matrix's assessment of market segment prioritization

DPM: Consumer segments in country 'X'

The DPM was calibrated and used to identify which segments to target in each country.

Agreed on 11 *attractiveness* criteria.
Agreed on 9 capability or *business strength* criteria.

Circle size relates to proportion of the company's revenue from each segment.

Here, the 'T' and 'S' segments were targeted in country 'X'.

Segment Attractiveness

Business strengths (capabilities)

the cross-section of executives involved in the assessment, generally lead to a much better decision about where to spend the product development and marketing budgets than under the 'who shouts loudest' approach or if simply taking current profitability levels as the measure of desirability.

Whether assessing opportunities, market segments or target markets to prioritize, marketers must be able to determine the best ones to pursue because they will never have permission or resources to go after them all. Life is about trade-off choices, and this is very much the case when creating a target market strategy or business opportunity pursuit list. The tools originally designed to assist in resourcing decisions for brands and products, as explored in Chapter 12 – such as the market attractiveness – business capability directional policy matrix – are very useful in the targeting stage of creating a marketing strategy or market segmentation strategy. The main lesson is to adopt a balanced set of attractiveness criteria, which includes financial worth but additionally looks to more market-facing criteria. More is stated about this in Chapter 12 of *Marketing: Concepts and Strategies*. Underpinning any such assessment about investment, budget allocations and strategy priorities must be a robust set of marketing analyses. Analyses of current performance, market trends and the forces of the marketing environment, capabilities, competitors and consumer/business customer behaviour must provide a robust and topical foundation for selecting priorities and developing the marketing strategy.

Evaluating markets and forecasting sales

Whatever segmentation choices organizations make, measuring the sales potential of the chosen target market or markets is crucial. Moreover, a marketing manager must determine the portion or share of the selected market that the company can capture relative to its objectives, resources and managerial skills, as well as to those of its competitors. Unless this is assessed, financial returns cannot be calculated and no judgement is possible about the desirability of the necessary marketing spend.

Sales potential is the amount of sales possible for a particular brand or product in the context of market conditions in a specific period of time. This assessment should reflect the attributes of the brand or product, likely customer interest, the nature of competitors' propositions, and market trends. For example, in the current depressed economic climate, the sales potential for some upmarket lines has decreased. Following the terrible 2011 Japanese nuclear power station incidents, the potential for more nuclear installations globally declined but sales potential for competing energy generating technologies rose, reflecting consumer, regulator and government concerns about civil nuclear safety. Medical pandemics are good news for producers of testing kits and medical supplies, while periods of political inter-government tension provide opportunities for manufacturers of weapons.

Market share is a long-standing measure of marketing success: if market share rises in a particular time period, the view would be that a marketing strategy is achieving some of its goals. Market share is the company's brand or product share of total sales in a particular target market or market segment, versus competing brands. Arguably, were more organizations equally focused on driving up market share and profitability, as opposed to only profitability, they would be more successful and secure in the longer term. The pursuit of increased market share in priority target markets should be a key success metric for marketers, as explored in Chapter 23.

Some businesses, particularly those producing fast moving consumer goods (FMCG), such as those products retailed in supermarkets, examine **value share** as a performance metric. Value share is the proportion of total market monetary sales attracted by an individual brand or product within a particular market. Market share may be 6 per cent while value share is 9 per cent for a premium-priced brand. For longer-term security, it is important that market share rises as well as value share: it is possible for a short-term rise in value share to satisfy directors and improve necessary cash flow, but only market share will safeguard future fortunes.

Developing and maintaining a marketing mix consumes a considerable amount of a company's resources. Thus the target market or markets selected must have enough sales potential to justify the costs of developing and maintaining one or more marketing mixes. Arguably, to be an attractive target market, there must be the propensity for growing market share and value share. As part of developing an effective target market strategy, it is necessary for marketers to calculate and assess market size and sales potential, along with achievable market share and value share. Some or all of these variables often feature in companies' directional policy matrix trade-off assessments.

The potential for sales can be measured along several dimensions, including product, geographic area, time and level of competition.[4] With respect to product, potential sales can be estimated for a specific product item (for example, Diet Coke) or an entire product line (for example, Coca-Cola, Coca-Cola Classic, Diet Coke, Coke Zero, Coca-Cola Life, Diet Caffeine-Free Coke, Coca-Cola Vanilla and Cherry Coca-Cola are one product line). A manager must also determine the geographic area to be included in the estimate. In relation to time, sales potential estimates can be: short range, one year or under; medium range, one to five years; or long range, longer than five years. The competitive level specifies whether sales are being estimated for a single company or for an entire industry. Marketers measure sales potential both for the entire market and for their own companies, and then develop a sales forecast. A target market strategy is incomplete without an appraisal of the likely sales potential and expected levels of sales within the prioritized target market segments, with assessment of the implications for market share and value share.

Sales potential
The amount of sales possible for a particular brand or product in the context of market conditions in a specific period of time.

Market share
The company's brand or product share of total sales in a particular target market or market segment, versus competing brands.

Value share
The proportion of total market monetary sales attracted by an individual brand or product within a particular market.

Marketing programmes

The final stage of the marketing process is the execution of marketing programmes utilizing the ingredients of the marketing mix. These product, people, place, pricing and promotion decisions are in effect the final phase of the creation and operationalization of a target market strategy. These aspects of an effective marketing programme are covered at length in the following Part of *Marketing: Concepts and Strategies*. Before they are specified and executed, marketing analyses must have identified the opportunities to pursue, market segments to target and a compelling proposition to take to market. This analysis phase will have included customers, competitors, market trends and the forces of the marketing environment, along with internal capabilities, resources and performance.

For the selected opportunities and target markets, marketers must decide a positioning strategy. The desired positioning should be agreed before marketing programmes and their marketing mixes are created. The adopted positioning must reflect the expectations of targeted consumers or business customers, the nature of competitors' propositions, and the characteristics of the product or service in question. Positioning is the final component of the so-termed STP process of market segmentation: segmentation, targeting and positioning. Effective positioning is fundamental to the success of a marketing strategy.

Positioning

Figure 7.3 illustrated the link between market segmentation, targeting and positioning. Having identified the segments in a market and decided on which segment (or segments) to target, a company must position its product, service or idea. A product's positioning has been described as the psychological place occupied in a particular market, as perceived by the customer segment at which that product is targeted.[5] Another definition suggests that the positioning of a product is the sum of those attributes normally ascribed to it by the consumers: its standing, its quality, the type of people who use it, its strengths, its weaknesses, any other unusual or memorable characteristics it may possess, its price and the value it represents.[6]

Positioning
The process of creating an image for a product in the minds of target customers.

Positioning starts with a product, a piece of merchandise, a service, a company, an institution or even a person. **Positioning** is not what is done to the product, it is what image is created in the minds of the targeted consumers or business customers. The product is positioned in the minds of these customers and is given an image.[7] There may be a few cosmetic changes to the product, to its name, price, packaging, styling or channel of distribution, but these are to facilitate the successful promotion of the image desired by the target customers. Targeted consumers or business customers must perceive the product to have a distinct and desirable image and positioning vis-à-vis its competitors. Product differentiation is widely viewed as the key to successful marketing; the product must stand out and have a clearly defined positioning.

Determining a positioning

Positioning is based on customers' perceptions and is therefore only partly within the control of marketers. Positionings are essentially selected by customers, based on variables and within parameters that are important to them. Word-of-mouth and social media consumer-to-consumer communication are increasingly able to shape a company's brand positioning. Brand managers no longer fully control communications about their products and brands, so consumers also help shape a brand positioning, with both positive and negative observations.

Price may be the key in grocery shopping, service level and trust in selecting a bank, quality and reliability in buying computer hardware, value for money and speed of access in choosing which theme park to visit. In-depth qualitative marketing research (commonly using depth interviews or focus group discussions and possibly experimentation) is required if customer motivations and expectations in a particular market are to be fully understood. Management's intuition is not always sufficient. For example, research for a major furniture retailer revealed that consumers often have to decide between replacement living room or dining room furniture and a family holiday abroad. Managers at most leading furniture retailers perceived other furniture retailers to be their competitors, when in reality they were competing for a consumer's disposable income and attention against other product areas, such as holidays or the timing of replacing the family car. In the budget-conscious sector of the furniture buying market, retailers believed only price to be important. In-depth research proved that value for money, a concept that includes product quality and durability in addition to price, was perceived to be the main purchase consideration.

Consumers generally assign positionings to a company or a product that is the market leader and probably has the highest profile or greatest familiarity, and the limited number of competitors they can recollect are oriented to this market leader. For example, in the market for tomato ketchup, perceptions of brands are oriented towards market leader Heinz. Other smartphones are compared with the iPhone. Occasionally the brand consumers regard as the market leader may not be the genuine market leader in terms of market share, but simply the one most visible at that time, possibly because of heavy promotional exposure. Customers respond to the attributes of a product and to its promotional imagery, but the product's positioning as perceived by its target customers is affected by the reputation and image of the company, coupled with its other products, and by the activities of its competitors. For

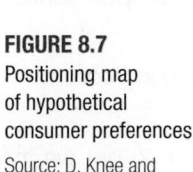

Perceptual mapping
A tool used by marketers and marketing researchers to visually depict consumer perceptions and prioritizing of brands and their perceived attributes.

example, bad publicity such as that experienced by British Airways (BA) following the opening of Terminal 5 at Heathrow damaged BA's image and transitory iPhone quality issues impacted briefly on Apple.

In-depth marketing research leads to an understanding of how consumers perceive different brands and companies, which marketing variables they believe to be most important and by what magnitude. **Perceptual mapping** is a tool commonly adopted by marketers and marketing researchers to visually depict such consumer perceptions and prioritizing of brands and their perceived attributes. Figure 8.7 illustrates an example in which consumers thought product range width and price

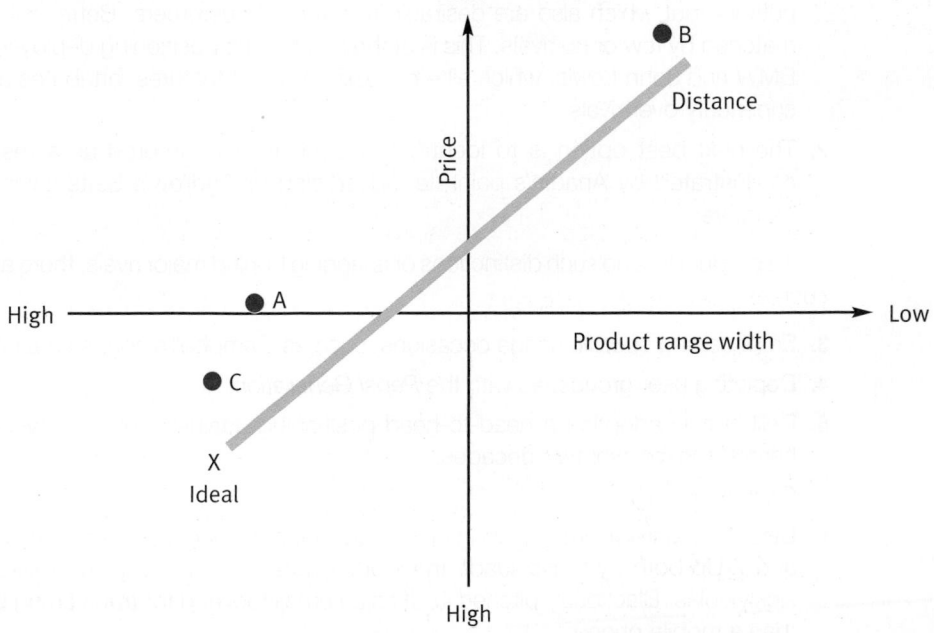

FIGURE 8.7
Positioning map of hypothetical consumer preferences

Source: D. Knee and D. Walters, *Strategy in Retailing* (St Albans, UK: Philip Allan, 1985), p. 27. Reproduced by permission of Philip Allan, a division of Prentice Hall International

mattered most, so the two axes were these key characteristics of the market. On the chart, a cross marks the ideal positioning, with high product range width and above average price. Brands A and C are perceived as being relatively close to the ideal – their pricing policy does not fully match the image required – but brand B is viewed as being too cheap, with inadequate product range width.

Although customers' perceptions play an important role in positioning, the role of marketers is also crucial. A simple step-by-step approach can be used for establishing a clear positioning plan for a product. This process commences with the identification of target market priorities, as outlined below:

1. Define the segments in a particular market.

2. Decide which segment(s) to target.

3. Understand what the target segment's consumers or business customers expect and believe to be the most important considerations when deciding on the purchase, particularly their most important wants and needs.

4. Develop a product – or products – catering specifically for these needs and expectations.

5. Evaluate the positioning and images, as perceived by the target customers, of competing products in the selected market segment or segments.

6. Select an image that sets the product – or products – apart from the competing products, thus ensuring that the chosen image matches the aspirations of the target customers.

7. Inform target consumers about the product. Although this is primarily a task for marketing communications, it is also vital that the product is made readily available at the right price, through the development of the full marketing mix.

The selected positioning and imagery must be credible: consumers would not believe Kia or Skoda if they promoted their cars in the same manner as Porsche or Aston Martin.

The Marketing Tools and Techniques box on the next page illustrates how Ford developed the positioning of the Focus to broaden its appeal to female drivers.

There are various options when determining a positioning strategy:

1. The approach most plausible in terms of the consumer and the most defensible against competitors' marketing ploys is to identify product attributes or features that are superior to competitors, but which also are desirable to targeted customers. Better still if these features are matched by few or no rivals. This is at the heart of the positioning deployed by Bang & Olufsen, BMW and John Lewis, which all emphasize product features, attributes and service providing superiority over rivals.

2. The next best option is to identify key benefits encountered as a result of consumption, as illustrated by Anadin's painkiller advertising or Andrew's Salts saving the day from *that* hangover.

If a product has no such distinctions or is lagging behind major rivals, there are other approaches, such as:

3. Emphasizing specific usage occasions, such as Campbell's soups as a cooking ingredient.

4. Depicting user groups, as with the *Pepsi Generation*.

5. Deliberately adopting a head-to-head positioning against a rival – 'Avis is No. 2, but we try harder' ran for over two decades.

Or, if all else fails:

6. Dissociating from direct rivals in order to develop a clear image and differentiation – Dr Pepper and 7 Up both try to persuade the marketplace they are fizzy and refreshing drinks, but not sickly colas. Blackberry pitched itself as an email tool and for transferring business data, rather than a mobile phone.

Practitioners' use of brand positioning theory

There are essential stages in developing a brand positioning, assuming target segments have already been decided:

1. Identify the positionings of the competitive set.

2. Determine the desired positioning for the brand in question.

3. Develop a set of actions in order to achieve the desired positioning, as it will not happen by itself!

4. Decide on an appropriate brand positioning statement to communicate the positioning.

5. Produce a marketing communications plan to promote the brand positioning to the target audience: the target market segment and key stakeholders inside the business and within the marketing channel.

Ford benchmarks itself against many competitors, but particularly VW. The Ford Focus is either market leader in its category or a leading challenger in most countries. In order to build on this success, the company had to attract greater numbers of customers, but also to stretch the brand so that not only middle-aged males purchased the Focus. A few years ago, the company wanted to attract more female purchasers, to emulate VW's Golf customer profile. This resulted from production of a perceptual map of the competing brands, featuring the age and sex of the drivers.

'Life's Better When You Take Control' was one of several working brand positioning statements developed, aimed to appeal to younger, aspirational female car buyers.

The action plan included:

- no TV campaign targeted at independent, confident females; the company could not confuse the marketplace and risk alienating the existing customer base, which included many males

- special edition models of the Focus; research with women identified the required product features and colours

- direct mail dialogue campaign, with 48-hour at-home test drive on offer

- brand liaison with relevant magazines, such as *Elle*; led to the Ford Focus Elle special edition

- targeted interactive promotional campaign, such as at Handbag.com or TotallyJewish.com

- interactive micro sites, such as public relations at the *Elle* Style Awards and associated branding, including key rings.

Subscribers to *Elle* magazine received bespoke brochures, linking Ford, *Elle* magazine and the Ford Focus Elle special edition:

Ford Focus Elle
The place to be seen this season

In colours such as Ebony, Moondust Silver and Chic, this model offered a 1.6i three-door Zetec, with alloy wheels, chrome tailpipe, remote-control CD/radio, air conditioning, ABS, side airbags and leather trim. The brochures featured a fashion shoot and the Focus Elle car, with captions such as:

Pink sheer 'Butterfly' dress, Rodeo Drive
Two-tone V-neck contoured vest, Milan
Ford Focus, the perfect accessory

Visitors to *Elle*'s website were greeted with information about the Focus Elle, plus a pop-up link directly into Ford's website. If they wanted further information, or to arrange a test drive, the Ford system dealt with such requests, not *Elle*'s.

This strategy proved to be highly effective for Ford. Every two months, a new special edition was offered, in limited numbers to maintain exclusivity. All editions sold out quickly. This success for Ford resulted from researching the target market's requirements, thinking carefully about the required brand positioning, and being smart in terms of executing the associated promotional activity.

At the heart of this marketing activity was the use of the brand positioning perceptual map, the development of a brand positioning statement deemed relevant by the target audience – aspirational young female drivers – and the specification of a detailed action plan. However, without the clearly thought-through action plan, the desired brand positioning would never have been achieved. Marketers must plan their brand positioning strategy and manage its implementation and roll-out.

© Dibb/Simkin

Sources: Ford; *Elle magazine*; 'Ford Focus Elle the place to be seen this season' (brochure), Ford GB; automotive sources.

Note: the information above, and the interpretation placed upon it, is not the official Ford view and is based on a variety of industry sources. A more extensive explanation of these brand positioning techniques is offered in either *The Market Segmentation Workbook* (Dibb and Simkin) or *The Marketing Planning Workbook* (Dibb, Simkin and Bradley), both originally published in 1996 by Thomson, London, or in the authors' newer titles *Market Segmentation Success: Making It Happen!* (The Haworth Press, 2008) and *Marketing Planning* (Cengage Learning, 2008).

Positioning statement
A plausible, memorable, image-enhancing written summation of a product's or brand's desired stature.

The final stage in developing a positioning in many instances is the determination of a suitable **positioning statement**, a plausible, memorable, image-enhancing written summation of a product's or brand's desired stature. This should strike a chord with the targeted consumers or business customers; reflect the nature of the product, its branding and attributes; plus demonstrate to targeted consumers the company's understanding of customer needs similar to a strapline in advertising. Everest double glazing's positioning statement is decades old, yet instantly recognizable: 'Fit the best, fit Everest'. 'The ultimate driving machine' can only be BMW; 'Because I'm worth it' is L'Oréal; and 'We try harder' is still used by car rental company Avis. Ultimately, a product or brand positioning must be memorable, plausible and relevant to the target market's perceptions. The intention is to develop a distinctive image for the product or service and, through a well-honed positioning statement, to establish a platform for its effective communication.

Customer Perceived Value

There are two related concepts which should be considered when developing a brand positioning strategy. The brand itself first should have been clearly articulated and managers must know for what it stands. Brand positioning focuses on ensuring that in each market segment targeted, the brand's positioning vis-à-vis competitors and consumers' expectations is appropriate. However, a brand cannot have very different meanings across various markets or market segments, as this would cause confusion for consumers, executives within the company and for suppliers. Brand positioning is more concerned with nuancing and the subtle focusing on particular market segment requirements, but within the brand's over-arching architecture and messaging. As explained in Chapter 11 of *Marketing: Concepts and Strategies*, marketers should have a clear view of their brand and its constituent components. This identification of the bigger picture brand strategy

FIGURE 8.8
Apple have branched out with their Apple Nano product, positioned to emphasize versatility and functionality

should be in place before marketers develop brand positionings for each target market. Brand positioning is the subsequent skill of positioning this brand for maximum impact within each target market segment to create differentiation versus competitors and to assist in persuading consumers that the brand is the one for them to adopt.

The second related concept builds on this theme, to ensure that marketers have a truly compelling and attractive proposition to underpin the brand positioning plan. This involves understanding what consumers or business customers[8] value and ensuring there are strong components of the offered proposition so as to attract and satisfy those targeted customers. Customer perceived value relates to the needs and wants of customers and their perception of the benefits they will receive from a product, service or brand. Some of these benefits will be tangible or actual, while others will be more emotional and relate to their self-image. Customers make an assessment of these benefits vis-à-vis the outlay they must make in order to acquire the product.[9]

Often the customer is faced with an array of options from competing suppliers, so their trade-off value assessment is undertaken against this set of competing propositions. This rating of competing propositions determines which brand is purchased, so it is important that marketers understand how customers will rate their product against competitors and on what criteria. Several frameworks have been developed to assist in this analysis and to guide marketers to specify compelling propositions which will appeal to customers and compete successfully.

Customer value proposition
Based on understanding the perceived customer values and psychological, functional and economic factors traded-off when customers select a particular product or brand to purchase, this is the compelling proposition intended to appeal to targeted customers.

The **customer value proposition**, or perceived customer value as it is sometimes known, is a concept promoted by the likes of Hollensen, Kotler and Keller. It is important not to confuse the connotations of *value* intended here … this is not suggesting the notion of value in terms of low-price or being cheap. These researchers mean value in the context of those aspects of the marketing mix which targeted customers will rate highly or value as they trade-off anticipated tangible and emotional benefits against the cost to acquire a product or service. Such value drivers include product differentiation, product quality, service, packaging, branding, price differentiation, and creating customer relationships[10]; all of which vary between those competitors seeking a customer's share of wallet. Consumers or business customers trade-off a set of desired attributes as they make their choice between competing brands.

Kotler and Keller[11] simplify this construct, explaining that, 'The buyer chooses between different offerings on the basis of which is perceived to deliver the most value. Value reflects the perceived tangible and intangible benefits and costs to the customer. Value can be seen as primarily a combination of *quality*, *service* and *price*'. More recently, a fourth element is added, that of a brand's *reputation*. When making purchasing choices, customers trade-off quality, service, price and reputation across those brands or suppliers identified as potentially being of interest.

Inevitably, there are many ways for depicting these relationships and for mapping a brand's response. One technique popular amongst marketers and which provides clarity of the compelling nature of the proposition offered to customers, is the customer value proposition triangle. This explores functional, economic and psychological elements which consumers or business customers use when trading-off their views of quality, service, price and reputation in order to rate alternative options to purchase.

It is necessary for marketers to develop a clear strategic positioning, based on a smart value proposition, which satisfies and excites customers, and which strives to remain relevant and attractive to these customers. The customer value proposition triangle helps marketers clarify what is the essence of the customer value proposition, or in some instances reveals how little they currently have to offer. It is not necessary to have all three vertices of the value triangle covered, but at least one must be addressed strongly in order to a have a viable message. If all three elements of the customer value triangle are addressed, as in the B2C and B2B examples in Figure 8.9, there is an even stronger and highly competitive proposition. A strong value proposition should underpin the positioning strategy developed in each segment targeted.

In these examples, it becomes clear why Pringles and JCB have been so successful. Pringles, developed by P&G but now owned by Kellogg's, innovated in the form of its distinctively shaped

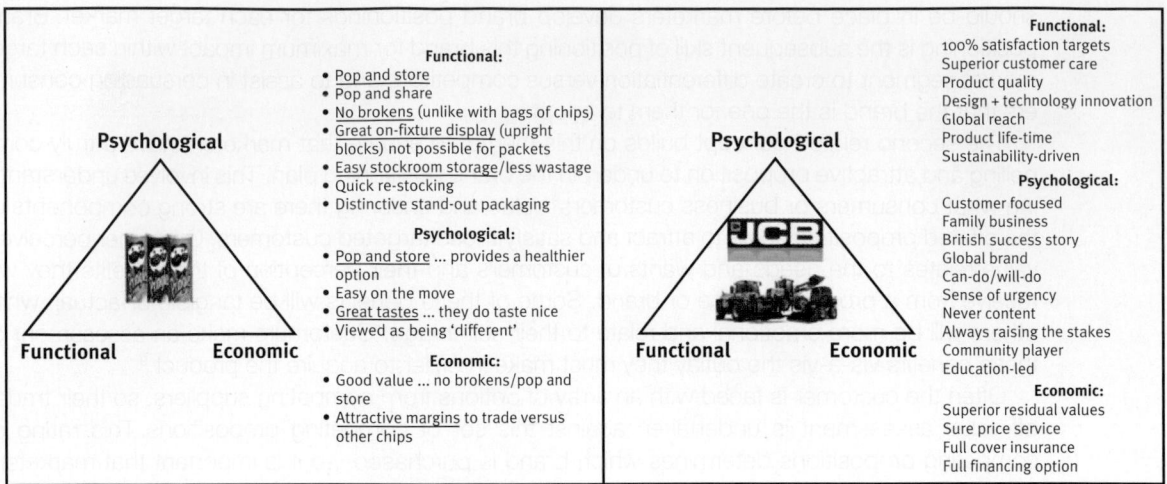

FIGURE 8.9
The customer value propositions of Pringles and JCB

product and its tube. Re-sealable, this tube allows consumers to 'pop and share', keep some for another day and transport these crisps without breakages. For retailers, the tubes enable high margin, fast-turnaround products to be displayed on the fixture's top-shelf – normally a slow and poor margin part of the supermarket fixture – with very high visibility and few breakages in the stock room. For both consumers and retail stockists, there is a very strong value proposition. JCB's construction equipment has always been known for innovation, quality engineering and the longevity of its machines. These attributes present a value proposition, but JCB has gone beyond these in providing extensive customer service and financing aspects of its value proposition, as well as emotional foundations to its very strong branding. As Pringles and JCB develop positioning plans in each market segment being targeted, their marketers seek to embrace the ingredients of their value propositions.

Many organizations struggle to have much to say about a single element of the triangle, let alone populate all three as in the cases of Pringles and JCB, which is why they fail to compete effectively. Once understood, these elements of the customer value proposition should underpin the separate brand positioning plans for individual targeted market segments. Brand positioning may focus on additional issues, but at the very least should not contradict or deflect from the over-arching customer value proposition designed to be compelling to targeted consumers or business customers.

Marketers need to develop a statement of the total set of benefits that the brand/company promises to deliver. The customer value proposition triangles assist in mapping these ingredients against the economic, functional and psychological criteria that consumers or business customers use when selecting a brand or supplier to adopt. The value proposition statement also indicates the expected customer experience that will result from interacting with the brand/company. Matching these expectations with the reality of the subsequent customer experience is achieved via the organization's value delivery when its marketers execute their marketing programmes and customer management plans.

All three inter-linked concepts – brand, customer value proposition and positioning – are designed to develop strong, differentiated and appealing messages for those customers or market segments identified as important targets, whether marketers are attracting new customers or retaining those they already have. The brand's overall standing, the customer value proposition underpinning a marketing programme, and the positioning developed as part of a market segmentation strategy are important assessments and decisions for marketers, forming an essential part of their marketing strategy.

Summary

No organization has the resources or will to pursue all possible opportunities or target markets: there must be trade-off choices. These need to be informed by topical and robust market analyses. *Targeting* is the task of prioritizing which markets and market segment(s) to address. When a company designs a single marketing mix and directs it at the entire market for a particular product, it is using an *undifferentiated (or total market)* approach as its targeting strategy. Although customers may have similar needs for a few products, for most products their needs are very different. In such instances, a company should use a concentrated or a differentiated strategy. In the *concentration strategy*, an organization directs its marketing efforts towards a single market segment through one marketing mix. In the *differentiated strategy*, an organization develops different marketing mixes for two or more market segments. The decisions about which segment or segments to enter are linked to considerations about company resources, performance, expertise and the nature of customers and competitors.

Marketers have a responsibility to identify opportunities and target markets which provide growth potential for their companies. Marketers routinely achieve this during their annual marketing planning activity, but many companies have intervening strategy requirements which benefit from insights into marketing environment trends, *SWOT* analyses, *Ansoff*-inspired assessments of new opportunities, customer-led developments and knowledge of competitors' intentions.

Inevitably, companies are faced with far many more opportunities, market segments and target market options than they have the resources, desire or aptitude to pursue. There must be informed trade-off choices which take into account more than only short-term profitability levels. Many approaches prove useful, but none more than the *directional policy matrix* or market attractiveness–business strength model. This approach identifies and weights two sets of criteria: variables with which to judge the relative attractiveness of whatever is under consideration and variables with which to evaluate business strengths against the capabilities of strong competitors. The desire is to avoid the 'who shouts loudest' solution to executive decision-making in terms of selecting priorities and budget allocation.

Measuring the sales potential of the chosen target market or markets is crucial, as a target market strategy is incomplete without an appraisal of the likely sales potential and expected levels of sales within the prioritized target market segments. This can be measured along several dimensions, including product, geographic area, time and level of competition, as well as at segment level.

Sales potential is the amount of sales possible for a particular brand or product in the context of market conditions in a specific period of time. *Market share* is a long-standing measure of marketing success. Market share is the company's brand or product share of total sales in a particular target market or market segment, versus competing brands. *Value share* is the proportion of total market income attracted by an individual brand or product within a particular market.

Developing and maintaining a marketing mix consumes a considerable amount of a company's resources. The target market or markets selected must have enough sales potential to justify the costs of developing and maintaining one or more marketing mixes. As part of developing an effective target market strategy, it is necessary for marketers to calculate and assess market size and sales potential, along with achievable market share and value share.

Having decided which segment or segments to target, the marketer must position the product in order to create a clearly defined image in the minds of its target consumers, which is the *positioning* aspect of marketing strategy and market segmentation. The product's positioning must be perceived by its consumers to be different from the positionings of competing products. *Perceptual maps* assist marketers in graphically depicting the relative positionings of the products in a particular market. Although a product's attributes and styling, along with its pricing, service levels and channel of distribution, contribute to how consumers perceive the product, a marketer uses mainly marketing communications to establish a product's positioning. The final stage in developing a positioning is the *positioning statement,* a plausible and memorable written summation of a product's or brand's desired stature.

Before creating a positioning strategy, the brand itself should be clearly articulated and managers must know for what it stands. Brand positioning focuses on ensuring that in each market segment targeted, the brand's positioning vis-à-vis competitors and consumers' expectations is appropriate. However, a brand cannot have very different meanings across various markets or market segments, as this would cause confusion for consumers. Positioning strategy must reflect brand strategy decisions.

To support the brand positioning plan, marketers need a strong *customer value proposition*. Customer value reflects the perceived tangible and intangible benefits and costs to the customer, and primarily is a combination of perceived quality, service, price and reputation. A positioning strategy should reflect customers' priorities and how, in a particular segment, they trade-off these dimensions of perceived value. The customer value proposition should underpin the positioning plan and certainly cannot be contradicted by the adopted positioning.

Key links

This chapter has explained a core aspect of marketing strategy: target market selection and the choice of opportunities to pursue. It should be read in conjunction with:

- Chapter 2's overview of marketing strategy.

- The requirement to understand consumers and business customers, as described in Chapters 5 and 6.

- Chapter 11's explanation of effective branding.

- The analytical tools, notably the directional policy matrix used for choosing priority target markets, as presented in Chapter 12.

- Chapter 7's examination of market segmentation.

Important terms

Ansoff's matrix
Concentration strategy
Customer value proposition
Differentiated strategy
Directional policy matrix
Market share
One-to-one marketing
Perceptual mapping
Positioning
Positioning statement
Sales potential
Segmentation targeting
SWOT analysis
Undifferentiated targeting strategy
Value share

Discussion and review questions

1. What are the general segmentation targeting options?

2. What are the essential ingredients for ensuring a balanced discussion about worthwhile opportunities and segments to target?

3. What criteria should be considered when selecting between opportunities or market segments to prioritize?

4. Outline an approach to assessing the relative merits of emerging opportunities or market segments.

5. Summarize the stages for producing a directional policy matrix (DPM) led assessment of the relative attractiveness of possible target market segments.

6. Why must marketers evaluate the sales potential of possible priority target market segments?

7. Why is it important to decide on the desired positioning for a product, service or brand?

8. Choose a product and discuss how it could best be positioned in the market. Determine a suitable positioning statement.

9. What are the essential stages in developing a positioning?

10. What is a customer value proposition?

11. How do the concepts of customer value propositions and positioning relate?

12. For a new hotel chain just launching, explain how the three stages – segmentation, targeting and positioning – of the market segmentation process are important.

13. For a product of your choice, explain which stage of the market segmentation process matters the most.

14. When might it not be necessary to segment a market?

Recommended readings

Dibb, S. and Simkin, L., *Market Segmentation Success: Making It Happen!* (The Haworth Press/Routledge, 2008).

Hooley, G., Piercy, N.F. and Nicoulaud, B., *Marketing Strategy and Competitive Positioning* (FT/Prentice Hall, 2011).

Hutt, M.D. and Speh, T.W., *Business Marketing Management: B2B* (Cengage, 2013).

McDonald, M. and Dunbar, I., *Market Segmentation* (John Wiley, 2012).

Ries, A. and Trout, J., *Positioning: The Battle for Your Mind* (McGraw-Hill, 2001).

Weinstein, A., *Handbook of Market Segmentation: Strategic Targeting for Business and Technology Firms* (The Haworth Press/Routledge, 2004).

Internet exercise

Hotel Chocolat operates shops, mail order and an eCommerce site, all with one thing at the heart of the proposition: luxurious, adventurous and delicious, mouth-watering chocolate! Learn more about its products and services by viewing the company's website at: www.hotelchocolat.co.uk.

1. Based on the information provided at the website, what are Hotel Chocolat's core products and for what occasions are these intended?

2. What market segments does Hotel Chocolat appear to be targeting with its website?

3. How would you describe the company's brand positioning?

Group tasks

1. Review the extensive brand portfolio of Accor Hotels (http://www.accor.com/en/brands.html). Describe the different positioning adopted for Sofitel, Pullman, Mercure, Novotel, Ibis and Hotel F1 and how the targeting strategy for each chain varies.

2. Your group has been tasked with launching an intervention designed to combat obesity. How would you decide who best to target and how would you go about creating an appropriate customer value proposition?

Applied mini-case

Banking is not generally perceived as innovative or creative. HSBC's telephone and online bank *first direct* broke the mould when it was launched in the 1980s, and it still strives to be different, as explained on its website:

> We are the unexpected bank.
>
> *first direct* is currently the most recommended bank*. We're open 24 hours a day, 7 days a week, and every time you pick up the phone, so do we, because a real person answers every single call, whatever the time, day or night. We're also available online and on your mobile and tablet, so it doesn't matter where you are or what you're doing: we're here for you.
>
> What we're about.
>
> We offer you all the usual banking services, like a current account, savings, cards, mortgages, loans and insurance, but where we're different is the way we offer them. We listen, we have a conversation and we recognize that it's your money, not ours.

www2.firstdirect.com/1/2/uncovered? 15 March 2015

Question

What is the brand positioning proposition at the heart of *first direct's* marketing strategy? To what extent does this differentiate *first direct* from the other principal banking groups?

Case study

IAMS understands people who love pets

Any company that wants to retain current customers and attract new ones must be aware of trends and be able to adapt to the changing needs of its customers, but it must first decide exactly who those customers are out of all those available in a particular market. P&G-owned IAMS, the successful producer of IAMS and Eukanuba pet products, is a good example of a company making the most of understanding consumer behaviour to successfully grow its business. IAMS recognizes the importance of psychological and social influences in pet food purchasing, and has used these insights to steer its target market strategy.

I am more than just a pet. I am an IAMS pet.

Many pet owners treat their pets as family members and want to provide them with high quality products. Procter & Gamble (P&G) and its IAMS pet food operation market premium pet products mirroring products purchased and used by humans. For example, IAMS ProActive Health™ formulas include PreBiotics, good bacteria that promote healthy digestion. The company also has a Healthy Naturals™ line that includes ingredients such as Atlantic salmon and contains no artificial colours, flavours or preservatives. The popularity of these products indicates that consumers are developing a higher level of involvement when shopping for pet food. Not all pet-owners agree, but some consumers believe that as an additional member of the family, pets are entitled to the same quality and nutrition as other family members. These are the consumers targeted by P&G.

At one time, IAMS focused primarily on pet nutrition. Now the company has expanded to products aimed at making pet owners happy by fulfilling their requests for fancy pet treats, sauces and other items that allow them to spoil their pets. The company has made this shift as a result of surveying its customers. For example, certain customers were concerned about feeding cats in multi-cat households in which one cat might be overweight while another was not. As a result, the company created a Multi-Cat formula with ingredients aimed at reducing fat in heavy cats while still providing protein for lean cats. The company's Savoury Sauce™ formulas for dogs are bottled just like human barbecue sauces or marinades. The sauces are fortified with vitamins, minerals and antioxidants, are low in calories and fat, and come in flavours such as Pot Roast or Country Style Chicken. Premium products like these reflect the changes in some consumers' attitudes towards their pets and their pets' food, and these are the consumers targeted by P&G.

Realizing the importance of consumers' relationships with their pets, IAMS is now expanding its business into the veterinary industry. The company works with insurers to provide pet health insurance. In the US, IAMS is also branching out into MRI (magnetic resonance imaging) machines, in

partnership with ProScan. IAMS Pet Imaging Centres in selected cities allow vets to investigate health problems in pets without resorting to exploratory surgery. By offering a wide variety of healthy products, IAMS is clearly paying attention to the needs of certain pet owners and making it possible for them to create healthy lifestyles for their pets.

Questions for discussion

1. What are some of the psychological influences that are most important to IAMS in understanding their buyers?

2. Which segments have P&G targeted with its IAMS range?

3. Outline the positioning strategy being pursued by IAMS.

Sources: Bill Pride and O.C. Ferrell, *Marketing*, Cengage South-Western, 2012; www.iams.co.uk, March 2015; www.pg.com, March 2015.

CHAPTER 9

Marketing research

"Marketers have a responsibility to understand and to find out … research"

Objectives

- To understand the importance of marketing research in marketing decision-making.

- To distinguish between research and intuition in solving marketing problems.

- To learn the five basic steps of the marketing research process.

- To understand the fundamental methods of gathering data for marketing research.

- To gain a sense of the relative advantages and disadvantages of marketing research tools.

- To understand how tools such as databases, decision support systems and the internet facilitate marketing research.

- To identify key ethical considerations in marketing research.

INTRODUCTION

As the preceding chapters have explained, effective marketing is contingent upon marketers having a clear understanding of customers, competitors, market trends and aspects of the marketing environment. **Marketing research** is the systematic design, collection, interpretation and reporting of information to help marketers solve particular problems or take advantage of marketing opportunities. As the word 'research' implies, it is the process of gathering information not currently available to decision-makers.

Marketing research
The process of gathering, interpreting and reporting information to help marketers solve specific marketing problems or take advantage of marketing opportunities.

The purpose of marketing research is to inform an organization about customers' needs and desires, marketing opportunities for particular goods and services, and changing attitudes and purchase patterns. Detecting shifts in buyers' behaviour and attitudes helps companies stay in touch with the ever-changing marketplace, which often necessitates marketing research.

Mobile devices generate rich consumer insights

Mobile and wearable technologies are providing new ways to gather consumer data. These data-gathering devices are linked to the idea of the 'quantified self', which involves individuals using technology to improve aspects of their behaviour. Some of this data gathering involves a 'life-logging' approach, in which technologies such as smartphones, GPS monitoring, wearable sensors and social media activity build a detailed picture of the carrier's behaviour. A number of benefits arise because these devices are involved in '... *measuring cognitive, behavioural and affective phenomena as they occur in natural settings and in, or near real-time*' (Cohn et al., 2011: 1). First, the gathered data relate to actual rather than reported consumer behaviour; second, it can be captured automatically and continuously; and, third, it gives invaluable insights into the sequence in which events occur. The description below illustrates the kind of profile that is possible using these technologies.

After walking to the bus stop on Monday morning, once onboard the bus, Sara uses her smartphone to compare her activity levels with other women in the area of a similar age, socioeconomic group and family status. Sara discovers that her activity levels are within the top 10 per cent for her group and is pleased that her efforts over recent weeks have improved her fitness. Spurred on by this positive feedback she has received, upon arriving at work in the centre of town, Sara decides to take the stairs instead of the lift and even contemplates cycling to work tomorrow. At lunchtime, she uses her smartphone to scan the quick response

(QR) code on her sandwich pack and juice bottle, capturing their nutritional and calorific values. The app instantly offers several healthy dessert options from a well-known slimming brand, showing the impact of each on Sara's daily calorie consumption. Although Sara decides to skip dessert for now, the data will be available for her to peruse on her tablet when she gets home and she can always have the pudding then.

Individuals can benefit from these profiles because they help them to change their behaviour in positive ways. They also provide opportunities for marketers, who can benefit if their marketing activities rely on a detailed understanding of certain behaviours, or if it is advantageous for them to interact with consumers while these behaviours are taking place. Commercial behaviour change apps have been developed which take advantage of these features. Some, such as *RunKeeper*, measure and contribute to improving fitness by enabling users to monitor their performance and progress over time. The app keeps track of activities including running, cycling and hiking, and sets customized goals based on the user's fitness objectives. Tracking progress towards these goals provides users with positive reinforcement which motivates them to continue with their activities. For consumers watching their weight, a range of slimming apps has also hit the market. *Diet Assistant*, which offers diet plans according to users' weight loss targets, tastes and lifestyles, is one example.

These examples are just the start; hinting at the potential for mobile, interactive technologies – apps on tablets and smartphones – to generate high quality consumer insights, and to shape the products and services of the future.

Sources: Cohn, A.M., Hunter-Reel, D. Hagman, B.T. and Mitchell, J. (2011), 'Promoting behaviour change from alcohol use through mobile technology: The future of ecological momentary assessment'; Sellen, A. and Whittaker, S. (2010), 'Beyond total capture: A constructive critique of lifelogging', *Communications of the ACM*, 53(5), 70–7; Dibb, S. (2013), 'The emergence of new domains for segmentation – the rapid rise of non-commercial applications', In L. Simkin, *To Boardrooms and Sustainability: The Changing Nature of Segmentation*, Henley White Paper, Henley Business School, p. 37. When Segmentation and Behaviour Change Collide; BBC Business News (2 August 2013), 'Weight watchers shares fall 19% on profit warning', accessed 8 August 2013 www.bbc.co.uk/news/business-23556277.

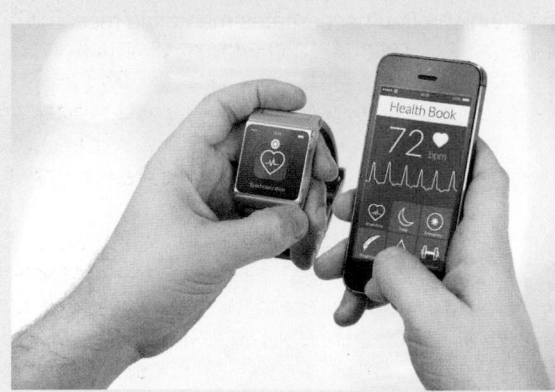

Marketing research of all kinds, whether collected from mobile devices or using other approaches, provides much needed insights into the characteristics, needs and desires of consumers and business customers. When used effectively, such information facilitates the relationship with these customers, by helping organizations focus on meeting, and even anticipating their needs.

This chapter begins by defining marketing research and examining its importance. It then analyzes the five basic steps of the marketing research process, including various methods of collecting data. This is followed by a review of how technology aids in collecting, organizing and interpreting marketing research data. Finally, the ethical aspects of marketing research are considered.

The importance of marketing research

Building an understanding of customers, competitors, market trends and the marketing environment requires that marketers have access to information and marketing intelligence.[1] Sometimes the available information will be judged as inadequate to tackle a specific decision or marketing task, in which case marketing research may provide the additional insights required. Such research is generally conducted on a project-by-project basis, with research methods being adapted to the context and problems being studied.

Marketing research involves collecting and analyzing data concerning the characteristics, attitudes, behaviour of individuals, customers or organizations. As the Market Research Society explains:

> Research evidence helps business leaders and policy makers make better decisions. More profitable decisions. More informed decisions. Evidence helps to build strategy and reduce risk. It is a support and an inspiration. It is the critical element in every decision-makers' toolkit.

https://www.mrs.org.uk/mrs/aboutmrs (accessed 9 April 2015)

Marketing intelligence
The composite of all data and ideas available within an organization, which assists in decision-making.

Quantitative research
Research aimed at producing data that can be statistically analyzed and the results of which can be expressed numerically.

Qualitative research
Research that deals with information too difficult or expensive to quantify, such as subjective opinions and value judgements, typically unearthed during interviews or discussion groups.

The purpose of marketing research is to provide information about customers' needs and desires, marketing opportunities for particular goods and services, and the changing attitudes and purchase patterns of customers. Marketing research facilitates the process of marketing planning by helping a company to better understand market opportunities, ascertain the potential for success of new products, and determine the feasibility of a particular marketing strategy. Pizza Hut, for example, conducted research to learn more about its most profitable group of customers: school and college students. The research involved asking a carefully chosen group of 350 students to refrain from eating pizza products for 30 days and record their cravings for pizza and feelings about 'going without' during the study period. One objective was to help better understand the effects of 'pizza deprivation', food cravings and food desires among this attractive market, which may lead to modifications in its marketing strategy.[2]

Marketing intelligence is the composite of all data and ideas available within an organization – for example, a company or a marketing department that assists in decision-making. Often the available information is deemed inadequate, which may lead to the commissioning of marketing research. There are, broadly, two types of marketing research: quantitative and qualitative.[3] **Quantitative research** uses techniques and sample sizes leading to the collection of data that can be statistically analyzed and whose results can be expressed numerically. These data tend to come from large surveys, sales data or market forecasts (see Figure 9.1).

Qualitative research deals with information that is too difficult or expensive to quantify: subjective opinions and value judgements that are not amenable to statistical analysis and quantification,[4] typically unearthed during in-depth interviews or discussion groups, but also now increasingly collected in online forums.

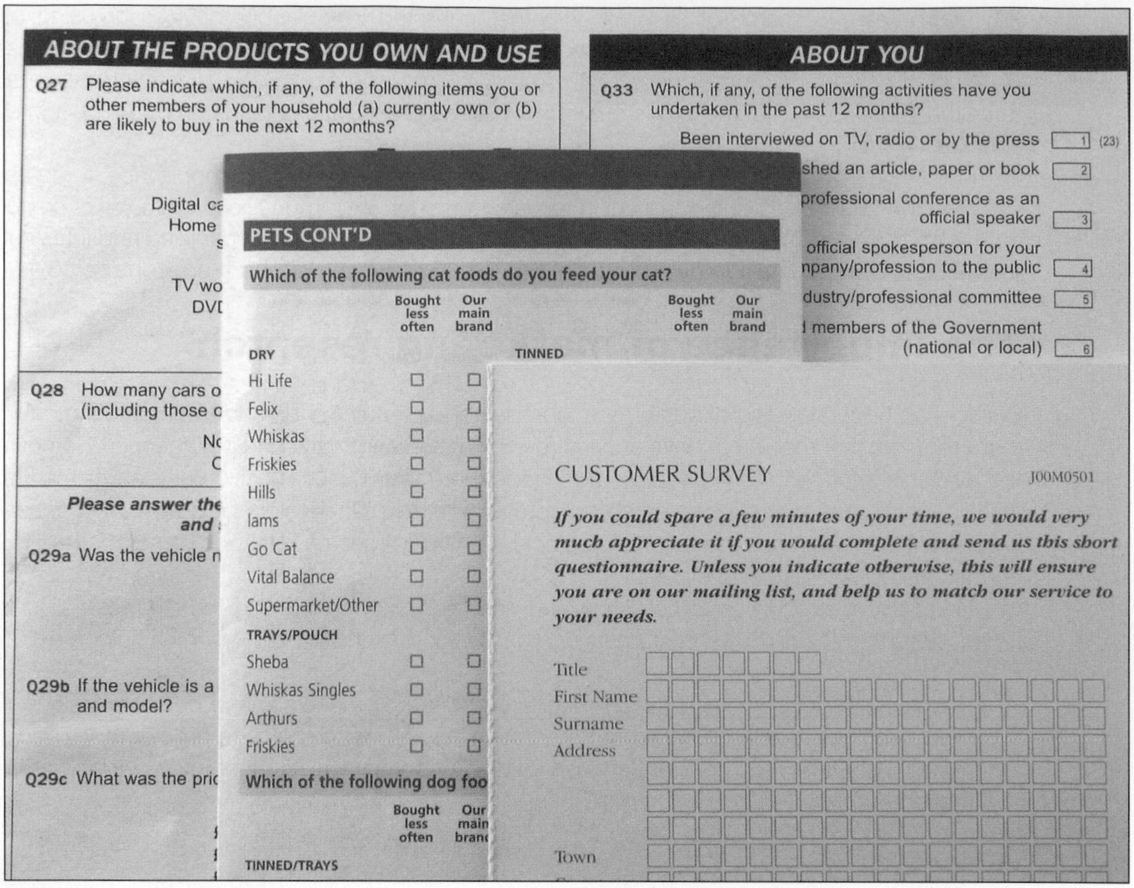

ABOUT THE PRODUCTS YOU OWN AND USE

Q27   Please indicate which, if any, of the following items you or other members of your household (a) currently own or (b) are likely to buy in the next 12 months?

Digital ca
Home
s

TV wo
DVD

Q28   How many cars o
(including those o

Nc
C

Please answer the
and

Q29a   Was the vehicle n

Q29b   If the vehicle is a
and model?

Q29c   What was the pric

ABOUT YOU

Q33   Which, if any, of the following activities have you undertaken in the past 12 months?

Been interviewed on TV, radio or by the press	1 (23)
shed an article, paper or book	2
professional conference as an official speaker	3
official spokesperson for your npany/profession to the public	4
dustry/professional committee	5
members of the Government (national or local)	6

PETS CONT'D

Which of the following cat foods do you feed your cat?

DRY	Bought less often	Our main brand	TINNED	Bought less often	Our main brand
Hi Life	☐	☐			
Felix	☐	☐			
Whiskas	☐	☐			
Friskies	☐	☐			
Hills	☐	☐			
Iams	☐	☐			
Go Cat	☐	☐			
Vital Balance	☐	☐			
Supermarket/Other	☐	☐			

TRAYS/POUCH

	Bought less often	Our main brand
Sheba	☐	☐
Whiskas Singles	☐	☐
Arthurs	☐	☐
Friskies	☐	☐

Which of the following dog foo

TINNED/TRAYS	Bought less often	Our main bran

CUSTOMER SURVEY   J00M0501

If you could spare a few minutes of your time, we would very much appreciate it if you would complete and send us this short questionnaire. Unless you indicate otherwise, this will ensure you are on our mailing list, and help us to match our service to your needs.

Title	
First Name	
Surname	
Address	
Town	

FIGURE 9.1

Questionnaires are an integral part of marketing research, often but not exclusively for quantitative studies

Source: Courtesy of Karen Beaulah

While some organizations continue to handle their own information needs, others buy in help from outside agencies that specialize in marketing research. According to ESOMAR's figures, by 2013 the total worldwide market for marketing research had reached a massive US$39 billion. North America is responsible for 34 per cent of this figure, with Europe accounting for 39 per cent.[5] Recent growth in the industry highlights marketing research's status as a management tool. Some experts suggest that this is also because the marketing research agencies have worked hard to quantify the effects of their work on business performance.[6]

Certainly, firms using marketing research need to be convinced of its benefits. For example, global business P&G used direct observation methods to gain a better understanding of how customers really use its products because these insights helped its marketers to design more suitable marketing.

All kinds of organizations use marketing research to help them develop marketing programmes that match the needs of customers or to find out more about their stakeholders' views. For example, as the following Marketing Tools and Techniques box explains, the European Commission recently supported a project using Citizen Summits to investigate how European citizens feel about different security technologies.

The CEO of a large marketing research business categorized the kinds of requests his company received for research help. For quantitative studies, these included customer satisfaction

Citizen summits give people a voice

The citizen summit method first appeared at the end of the 1990s. It was inspired by Anthony Williams, the incoming mayor of Washington DC, as a means for encouraging the public's involvement in local strategic planning. The first summit, which took place over a day, was attended by 3000 people, who sat in table groups of 10 and participated in a discussion about priorities for the city. Each table included a trained facilitator, whose role was to encourage discussion and provide light touch guidance to participants. Wireless polling keypads were available on each table, enabling the citizens to vote on questions that were posed at various points in the event. A strong feature of the method is that the results of these votes were instantly shown to participants via large projection screens.

The citizen summit method has subsequently been developed beyond a simple polling tool and can be used to assess people's views on a range of topics. The method has a number of positive features:

● Increases citizen awareness and engagement with important issues.

● Provides a forum for democratic participation.

● Enables an open debate, in which citizens can reflect on the views of others.

● Uses electronic voting technology, which can instantly display the results to citizens.

● Allows for the provision of neutral information material in a variety of formats.

● Provision can be made to gather qualitative insights from the discussions taking place at the tables.

Marketing tools and techniques

A recent series of citizen summits carried out in nine European countries, examined citizens' views about three surveillance-oriented security technologies that are being used in some countries to maintain national security:

● Smart closed-circuit television (CCTV) uses digital cameras in a linked system that can identify individuals and identify suspicious behaviour.

● Smartphone location tracking enables the movement of individuals to be tracked on the basis of the location of their mobile phones.

● Deep packet inspection (DPI) is a surveillance approach that keeps track of messages that are communicated over the internet.

Citizens were sent an information booklet about the technologies before attending the event. They were also shown information films at the summits, which introduced them to a range of views about the security and privacy issues associated with the technologies. The aim was to understand the acceptability of these technologies from the viewpoint of citizens, and also to explore the extent to which people in different countries are prepared to sacrifice their privacy in exchange for the use of security technologies. Citizens attending the summits were encouraged to discuss the issues arising with others in their table groups; after which they used hand-held electronic voting devices to respond to a series of questions displayed on a big screen. The views emerging from the summits were subsequently shared with the European Commission and made publicly available.

Sources: Moynihan, Donald P. (2003). 'Normative and instrumental perspectives on public participation: Citizen summits in Washington, DC', *The American Review of Public Administration*, 33 (2): 164–88; http://surprise-project.eu /events/citizen-summits/2015.

surveys, advertising tracking analyses, evaluations of new or modified products, brand awareness studies and customer attitude surveys. For qualitative research, the main categories were customer attitude and satisfaction studies, followed by concept testing (new products or new brand identities). After these came the testing of advertisements, packaging concepts and promotional offers.

As managers have recognized the benefits of marketing research, they have assigned it a much greater role in decision-making. For example, Japanese managers, who traditionally put greater faith in information from wholesalers and retailers, now grasp the importance of consumer surveys and scientific methods of marketing research as they seek ways to diversify their companies.[7]

TABLE 9.1   Distinctions between research and intuition in marketing decision-making

	Research	Intuition
Nature	Formal planning, predicting based on a scientific approach	Preference based on personal feelings or 'gut instinct'
Methods	Logic, systematic methods, statistical inference	Experience and demonstration
Contributions	General hypotheses for making predictions, classifying relevant variables, carrying out systematic description and classification	Minor problems solved quickly through consideration of experience, practical consequences
Situation	High-risk decision-making involving high costs, investment, strategic change or long-term effects	Low-risk problem solving and decision-making

Intuition
The personal knowledge and past experience on which marketing managers may base decisions.

Scientific decision-making
An orderly and logical approach to gathering information.

The increase in marketing research activities represents a transition from intuitive to scientific problem-solving. In relying on **intuition**, marketing managers base decisions on personal knowledge and past experience. However, in **scientific decision-making**, managers take an orderly and logical approach to gathering information. They seek facts on a systematic basis, and they apply methods other than trial and error or generalization from experience. This does not mean that intuition has no value in marketing decision-making; successful decisions blend both research and intuition. Consider an extreme example. A marketing research study conducted for Xerox Corporation in the late 1950s indicated a very limited market for an automatic photocopier. Xerox management judged that the researchers had drawn the wrong conclusions from the study, and they decided to launch the product anyway. That product, the Xerox 914 copier, was an instant success. An immediate backlog of orders developed, and the rest is history. Although the Xerox example is certainly an extreme one, by and large a proper blend of research and intuition offers the best formula for a correct decision. Table 9.1 distinguishes between the roles of research and intuition in decision-making.

Despite the obvious value of formal research, marketing decisions are often made without it. Certainly, minor, low-risk problems that must be dealt with at once can and should be handled on the basis of personal judgement and common sense. If good decisions can be made with the help of currently available information, costly formal research may be superfluous. However, as the financial, social or ethical risks increase or the possible courses of action multiply, full-scale research as a prerequisite for marketing decision-making becomes both desirable and rewarding.

Marketing research improves a marketer's ability to make decisions. Marketers should treat information in the same manner as other resources utilized by the company, and they must weigh the costs of obtaining information against the benefits derived. Information is worthwhile if it results in marketing activities that better satisfy the needs of the company's target markets, leads to increased sales and profits, or helps the company achieve some other goal.

The marketing research process

To maintain the control needed for obtaining accurate information, marketers approach marketing research in logical steps, as follows (see Figure 9.2):

1. locating and defining problems or research issues
2. designing the research
3. collecting data
4. analyzing and interpreting research findings
5. reporting research findings.

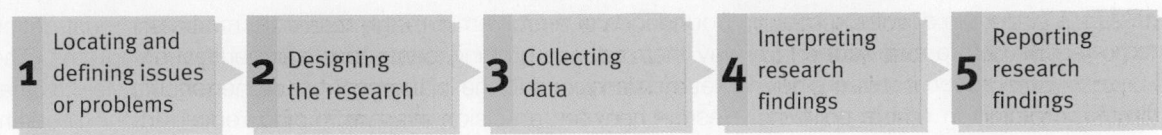

| **1** Locating and defining issues or problems | **2** Designing the research | **3** Collecting data | **4** Interpreting research findings | **5** Reporting research findings |

FIGURE 9.2
The five steps of the marketing research process

These five steps should be viewed as an overall approach to conducting research rather than a rigid set of rules to be followed in each project. In planning research projects, marketers must think about each of the steps and how they can best be adjusted for each particular problem.

Step 1: locating and defining problems or research issues

Problem definition
The process of uncovering the nature and boundaries of a situation or question.

The first step in launching a research study is **problem definition**, which focuses on uncovering the nature and boundaries of a situation or question related to marketing strategy or implementation. The first sign of a problem is usually a departure from some normal function, such as failures to attain objectives. If a company's objective is a 12 per cent return on investment and the current return is 6 per cent, this discrepancy should be analyzed to help guide future marketing strategies. Decreasing sales, increasing expenses or decreasing profits also signal problems. Conversely, when an organization experiences a dramatic rise in sales, or some other positive event, it may conduct marketing research to discover the reasons and maximize the opportunities stemming from them. Sometimes the question that needs to be addressed relates to a change the organization is anticipating in the marketing environment. For example, new EU recodesign and labelling regulations designed to improve energy efficiency, are limiting the power of electrical items such as hairdryers and vacuum cleaners. This regulatory change is having implications for manufacturers of these items, some of which will use marketing research to help them understand the implications.[8]

FIGURE 9.3
Many marketing research agencies, data analysis houses and marketing services businesses support marketers

Source: Image courtesey Metro Research.

To pin down the specific boundaries of a problem through research, marketers must define its nature and scope in a way that requires probing beneath the superficial symptoms. The interaction between the marketing manager and the marketing researcher should yield a clear definition of the problem. Researchers and decision-makers should remain in the problem definition stage until they have determined precisely what they want from the research and how they will use it. Deciding how to refine a broad, indefinite problem into a clearly defined and researchable statement is a prerequisite for the next step in planning the research: the design phase.

Step 2: designing the research

Research design
An overall plan for obtaining the information needed to address a research problem or issue.

Once the problem or issue has been defined, the next step is **research design**, an overall plan for obtaining the information needed to address it. This step requires detailed research objectives or hypotheses to be formulated, and the most appropriate type of research to be designed to ensure that the results are reliable and valid.

Developing research objectives and hypotheses

Research objective
The desired outcome from the marketing research project being undertaken.

Hypothesis
An informed guess or assumption about a certain problem or set of circumstances.

A clear statement of research objectives plays an important part in guiding a research project. A **research objective** is the desired outcome from the marketing research project being undertaken. Sometimes researchers develop hypotheses that may be drawn both from previous research and expected research findings. A **hypothesis** is an informed guess or assumption about a certain problem or set of circumstances. It is based on all the insight and knowledge available about the problem from previous research studies and other sources. As information is gathered, a researcher can test the hypothesis. For example, toy manufacturer Lego might propose the hypothesis that children today are more interested in product lines relating to characters featured in their favourite movies or television programmes than previous generations. A marketing researcher would then gather data, perhaps through surveys of children and their parents, and draw conclusions as to whether or not the hypothesis was correct.

Supermarkets worried about shoplifting would be interested in the findings of research showing that 40 per cent of supermarket managers surveyed reported cigarettes and alcohol as their most frequently shoplifted items. If a supermarket manager had hypothesized that other products, such as confectionery, were more susceptible to shoplifting, the research would lead this individual to reject that hypothesis. Sometimes several hypotheses are developed during the actual study; the hypotheses that are accepted or rejected become the study's chief conclusions.

Types of research

Exploratory research
Deliberately flexible data gathering used to discover the general nature of a problem and the factors that relate to it.

The research objectives and any hypotheses being tested determine the approach to be used for gathering data. When marketers need more information about a problem or want to make a tentative hypothesis more specific, they may conduct **exploratory research**. Exploratory studies discover the general nature of a problem and the factors that relate to it. The design is deliberately flexible.[9] For instance, this kind of research may involve reviewing the information in the company's own records or examining publicly available data. Questioning knowledgeable people inside and outside the organization may also yield new insights into the problem. Information available on the internet about industry trends or demographics may also be an excellent source for exploratory research. For example, information on the buying power of different ethnic groups is readily available through this source.

TABLE 9.2   Comparison of data-gathering approaches

Project component	Exploratory studies	Descriptive or causal studies
Purpose	Provide general insights	Confirm insights, verify hypotheses
Data sources	Ill-defined	Well-defined
Collection form	Open-ended	Structured
Sample	Small	Large
Collection procedure	Flexible	Rigid
Data analysis	Informal	Formal
Recommendations	Tentative	Conclusive

Source: from *Marketing Research*, p. 122, © 1986. Reprinted by permission by Professor A. Parasuraman.

Descriptive research
Data collection that focuses on providing an accurate description of the variables in a situation.

If marketers need to understand the characteristics of certain phenomena to solve a particular problem, **descriptive research** can aid them. Descriptive studies focus on providing an accurate description of the variables in a situation. Such studies may range from general surveys of consumers' education, occupation or age to specifics on how many pairs of sports shoes individuals purchase each year. For example, if Nike and Reebok wanted to target more young women, they might ask 15–34-year-old females how often they work out, how often they buy sports footwear and whether they wear them for casual use. Descriptive studies generally demand much prior knowledge and assume that the problem is clearly defined. The marketers' major task is to choose adequate methods of collecting and measuring data.

Causal research
Data collection that assumes that a particular variable X causes a variable Y.

Hypotheses about causal relationships call for a more complex approach than a descriptive study. In **causal research**, it is assumed that a particular variable X causes a variable Y. Marketers must plan the research so that the data collected prove or disprove that X causes Y. To do so, marketers must try to hold constant all variables except X and Y. For example, to find out whether new carpeting, curtains and ceiling fans increase the rental rate in a block of flats, marketers need to keep all variables constant except the new furnishings and the rental rate. Table 9.2 compares the features of these types of research study.

Research reliability and validity

Reliability
The quality of producing almost identical results in successive repeated trials.

In designing research, marketing researchers must ensure that their research techniques are both reliable and valid. A research technique has **reliability** if it produces almost identical results in successive repeated trials. However, a reliable technique is not necessarily valid. To have **validity**, the method must measure what it is supposed to measure, not something else. A valid research method provides data that can be used to test the hypothesis being investigated. For example, although a group of customers may express the same level of satisfaction based on a rating scale, the individuals may not exhibit the same repurchase behaviour because of different personal characteristics. This result might cause the researcher to question the validity of the satisfaction scale if the purpose of rating satisfaction was to estimate repurchase behaviour.[10]

Validity
A condition that exists when an instrument measures what it is supposed to measure.

Step 3: collecting data

The next step in the marketing research process is collecting data to satisfy research objectives and to help prove (or disprove) research hypotheses. The research design must specify what types of data to collect and how they will be collected.

Types of data

Marketing researchers have two types of data at their disposal. **Primary data** are observed and recorded or collected directly from respondents. This type of data must be gathered by observing phenomena or surveying respondents. **Secondary data** are compiled inside or outside the organization for some purpose other than the current investigation. Secondary data include general reports supplied to an enterprise by various data services. Such reports might concern market share, retail inventory levels and consumer buying behaviour. Figure 9.4 illustrates how primary and secondary sources differ. Secondary data are generally already available in private or public reports, or have been collected and stored by the organization itself. As secondary data is already available – 'second hand' – to save time and money they should be examined prior to the collection of any primary data. Clearly, primary data collection is bespoke and therefore both time-consuming and costly. For relatively straightforward problems, secondary data may prove adequate. More complex or risky situations may require specific primary data collection. Figure 9.5 reveals how marketing research companies promote their data analysis services.

In the wake of huge recent growth in the availability and volume of information, there is a radically increased capacity for using data to inform commercial decisions. This trend has led to a rethink of how the marketing research industry is conceptualized. The UK's Market Research Society (MRS) now describes all firms contributing to this market – including traditional research firms,

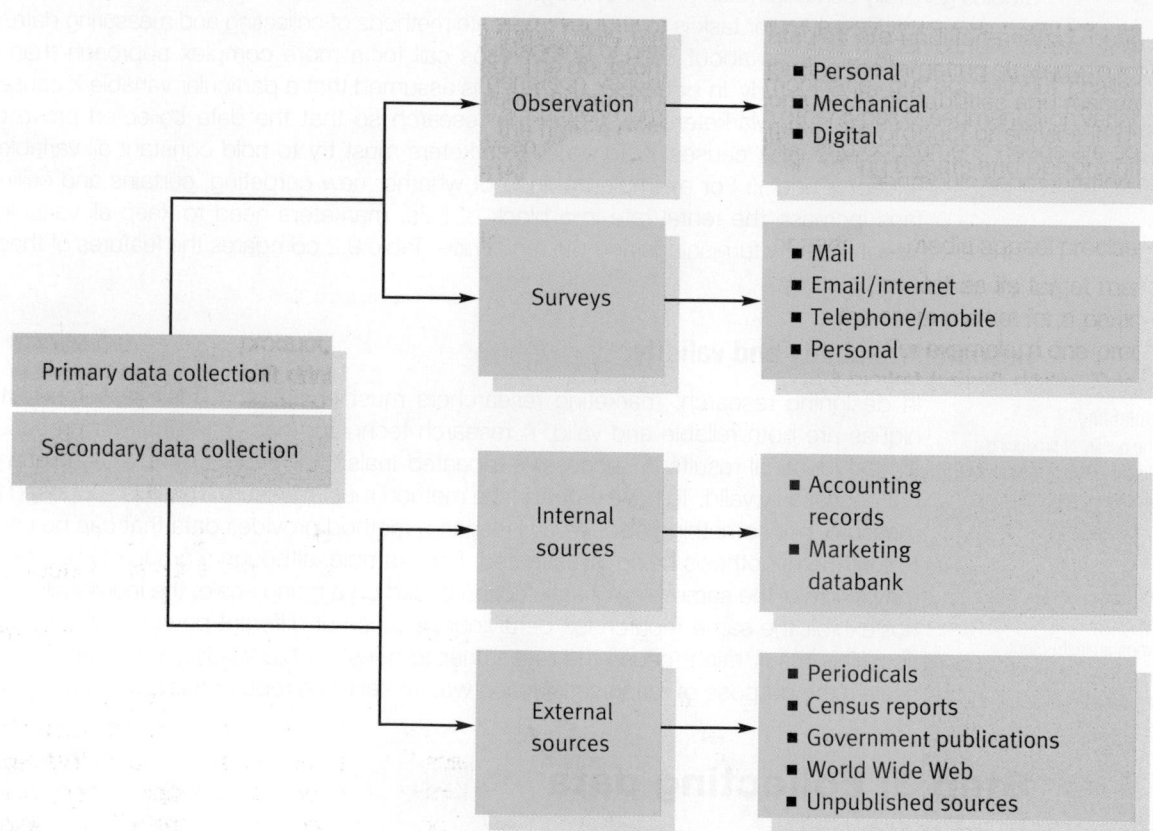

FIGURE 9.4
Approaches to collecting data

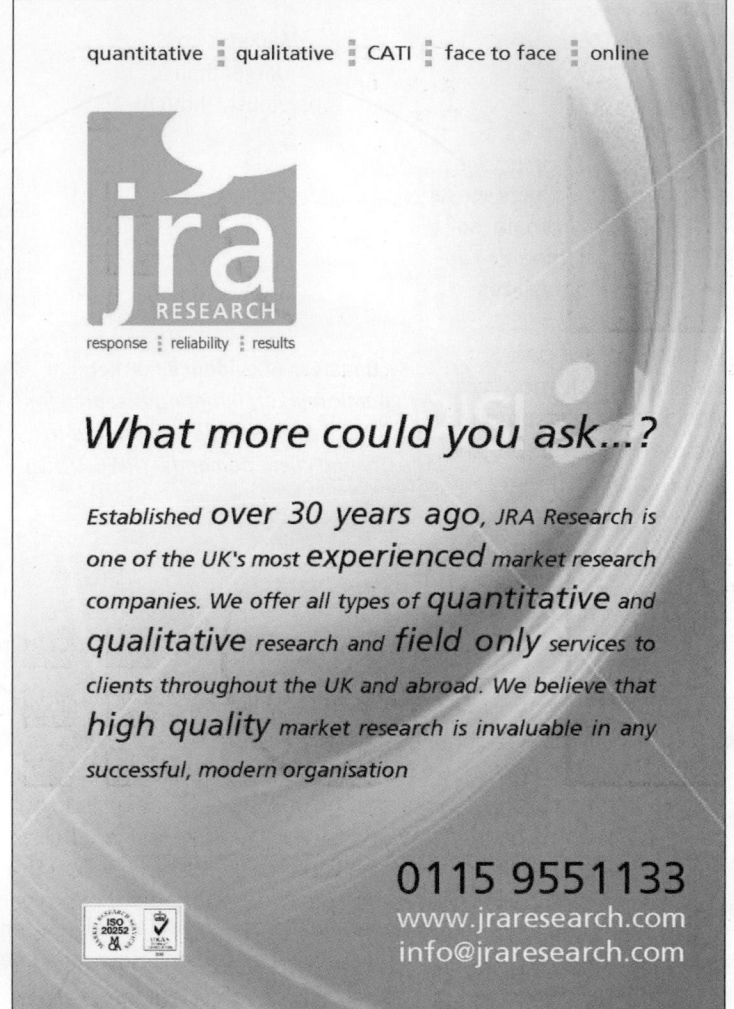

FIGURE 9.5

A business-to-business advertisement for JRA's marketing research services

Source: Image courtesy of JRA Research.

opinion researchers, data analytics experts, government, education institutes and think tanks – as being in the business of evidence. Figure 9.6 provides an overview of this market.[11]

Sources of secondary data

Marketers often begin the marketing research process by gathering secondary data. They may use available reports and other information from both internal and external sources to study a marketing problem.

Internal sources of secondary data can contribute tremendously to research, particularly given recent improvements in the customer databases that many organizations now hold. Improvements in technology coupled with changes in how customers are shopping, have contributed to better systems for recording customer data. An organization's own databases may contain information about past marketing activities, such as sales records and research reports, that can be used to test hypotheses and pinpoint problems. From sales reports, for example, a company may be able to determine not only which product sold best at certain times of the year, but also which colours and sizes were preferred and by which customers. Such information may have been gathered for management or financial purposes.[12] Table 9.3 reveals some commonly available internal company information that may be useful for marketing research purposes.

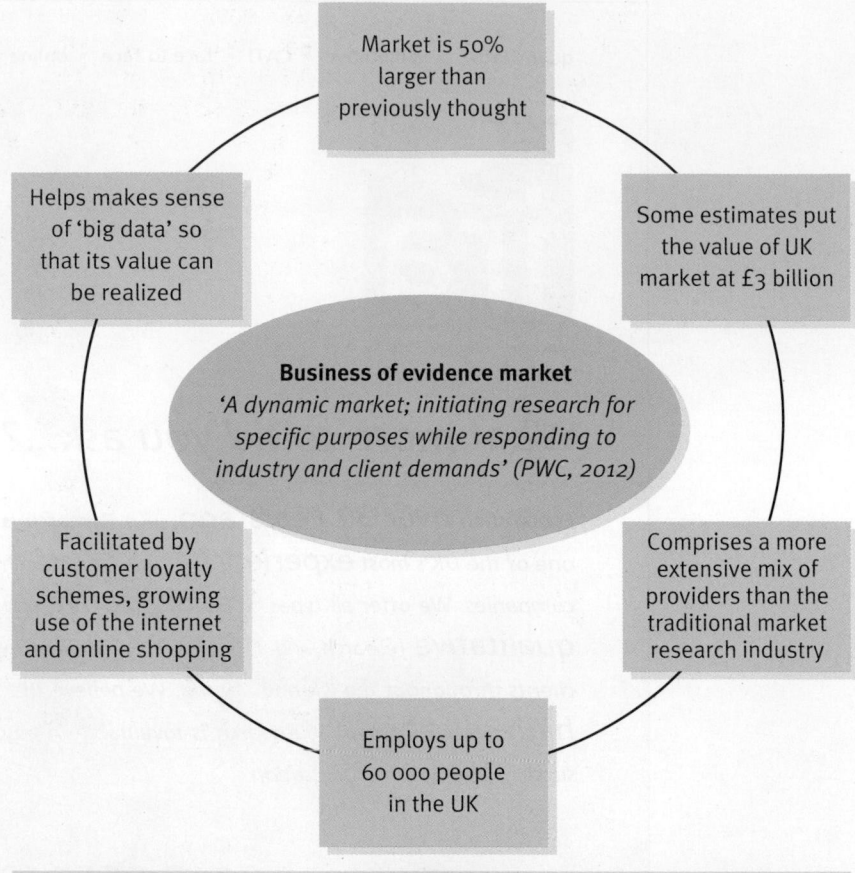

FIGURE 9.6

The business of evidence marketing

Source: Derived from PWC, The Business of Evidence: A report prepared for the Market Research Society, October 2012.

TABLE 9.3   Internal sources of secondary data

Sales data taken from periodic sales reports	The frequency with which this information is updated will vary for different organizations and industry sectors. However, the increasing use of technology to monitor sales is leading to improvements in the quality and availabiliy of such data
Customer feedback gathered by the salesforce, marketers or services functions	In addition to sales information, the salesforce is in a position to provide other data on customer views and preferences. The service functions of many organizations also have access to a range of customer feedback. Marketers capture customer views. Organizations with systems in place for capturing and managing these data are more likely to be able to take advantage of such insights
Accounting information	This can include detailed data on sales, expenses and profit levels in different product categories
Competitive information collected by the salesforce or marketers	Through contact with customers and by attending sales-related events, such as trade shows, the salesforce is often in a position to accumulate information about competitors, their product portfolios and strategies

An organization's accounting records and feedback available from any service function are excellent sources of data that are often overlooked. This is partly because the volumes of data that these departments collect may not automatically flow to the marketing area. As a result, detailed information about costs, sales, customer accounts or profits by product category may not be part of the marketing information system (MIS). This situation occurs particularly in organizations that do not store marketing information on a systematic basis.

External sources of secondary data include periodicals, census reports, government publications, the internet and unpublished sources. Periodicals available online and in hard copy, such as *Investors' Chronicle, Marketing, Campaign, Marketing Week, The Wall Street Journal* and *Fortune* print general information that is helpful for defining problems and developing hypotheses. *Business Monitor* contains sales data for major industries. Mintel publishes sector reports. Many research companies publish reports on markets, consumers, trends and products. Table 9.4 summarizes the major external sources of secondary data, excluding syndicated services.

Syndicated data services periodically collect and collate general information, from sources including census data, the elctoral roll, attitudinal and life style data and consumption data, which they sell to clients. BARB, for example, supplies television stations and media buyers with estimates of the number of viewers at specific times. You can learn more about how BARB achieves this by visiting its website.[13] Globescan furnishes monthly information that describes market shares for specific sectors. ACNielsen provides retail tracking and other data. This information includes total sales in a product category, sales of clients' own brands and sales of important competing brands.

Another type of secondary data, which is available for a fee, is demographic analysis. Companies, such as CACI or Experian, that specialize in demographic databanks, have special knowledge

> **Syndicated data services**
> Organizations that collect and collate general information and sell it to clients.

TABLE 9.4 Guide to external sources of secondary data

Trade journals	Virtually every industry or type of business has a trade journal. These journals give a feel for the industry its size, degree of competition, range of companies involved and problems. Details of trade journals are available through library databases or from online services such as *WebWire* (www.webwire.com /industrylist.asp)
Trade associations	Almost every industry, product category and profession has its own association. Many conduct research, publish journals, conduct training sessions and hold conferences
Corporate web pages	Many companies have established 'home pages' on the internet and have a presence on social media for disseminating information on their products and activities
International sources	Overseas statistics are available from sources such as the *United Nations* (http://unstats.un.org/unsd /default.htm) and the *International Labour Organization* (www.ilo.org/global/statistics-and-databases /lang—en/index.htm)
Commercial sources	Market survey/report organizations produce many sector reports and analyzes of companies or brands, for example, *Verdict, Mintel, Kompass, The Times 1000, Key British Enterprises*
Governments	Governments, through their various departments and agencies, collect, analyze and publish data on practically everything. Includes Census data, population statistics, information on business sectors, data on households and consumption. Official European statistics are available at (http://ec.europa.eu/eurostat); with UK statistics available at (www.gov.uk/government/statistics)
Books in Print (BIP)	*BIP* (www.booksinprint.com) is a several volume reference book found in most libraries. All books issued by publishers and currently in print are listed by subject, title and author
Online periodical indices and literature retrieval services	Libraries offer online access to articles in major periodicals. For example, *JSTOR* maintains an online archiving services for major periodicals (www.jstor.com); while *ABI/INFORM Complete* is a comprehensive database for business researchers available on the ProQuest platform. *Google Scholar* (https://scholar.google.co.uk) enables internet users to search and locate a wide range of sources

and sophisticated computer systems to work with the very complex census databanks. These were explored in Chapter 7. As a result, they are able to respond to specialized requests. Such information may be valuable in tracking demographic changes that have implications for consumer behaviour and the targeting of products.[14]

Primary data collection methods

The collection of primary data is a more lengthy, expensive and complex process than the collection of secondary data. To gather primary data, researchers use sampling procedures, survey methods, observation and experimentation. These efforts can be handled in-house by the company's own research personnel or contracted out to private research businesses such as Taylor Nelson Sofres, Millward Brown UK or Research International.

Sampling Since the time and resources available for research is limited, it is almost impossible to investigate all the members of a target market or other population. A **population**, or 'universe', comprises all elements, units or individuals that are of interest to researchers for a specific study. A **sample** is a limited number of units chosen to represent the characteristics of a total population. For example, if a Gallup poll is designed to predict the results of an election, all the registered voters in the country would constitute the population. A representative national sample of several thousand registered voters would be selected in the Gallup poll to project the probable voting outcome. The projection would be based on the assumption that no major political events would occur before the election. The objective of **sampling** in marketing research, therefore, is to select representative units from a total population. Sampling procedures allow marketers to predict buyer behaviour fairly accurately on the basis of responses from the representative portion of the population of interest. Most types of marketing research employ sampling techniques.

There are two basic types of sampling: probability sampling and non-probability sampling. With **probability sampling**, every element in the population being studied has a known chance of being selected for study. Random sampling is basic probability sampling. When marketers employ **random sampling**, all the units in a population have an equal chance of appearing in the sample. The various events that can occur have an equal or known chance of taking place. For example, a specific playing card in a pack has a 1/52 probability of being drawn at any one time. Sample units are ordinarily chosen by selecting from a table of random numbers which have been statistically generated so that each digit, from zero to nine, will have an equal probability of occurring in each position in the sequence. The sequentially numbered elements of a population are sampled randomly by selecting the units whose numbers appear in the table of random numbers.

Another kind of probability sampling is **stratified sampling**, in which the population of interest is divided into groups according to a common characteristic or attribute, and a probability sampling is then conducted within each group. Employing a stratified sample may reduce some of the error that could occur as a result of using a simple random sample. By ensuring that each major group or segment of the population receives its proportionate share of sample units, investigators avoid including too many or too few sample units from each stratum. Usually, samples are stratified when researchers believe that there may be variations among different types of respondent. For example, many political opinion surveys are stratified by sex, race and age.

Area sampling, a variation of stratified sampling, involves two stages:

1. selecting a probability sample of geographic areas, such as streets, census tracts or census enumeration districts

2. selecting units or individuals within the selected geographic areas for the sample.

Population
All elements, units or individuals that are of interest to researchers for a specific study.

Sample
A limited number of units chosen to represent the characteristics of a total population.

Sampling
The selection of representative units from a total population.

Probability sampling
Every element in the population has a known chance of being selected for study.

Random sampling
A sampling method in which all the units in a population have an equal chance of appearing in the sample.

Stratified sampling
A sampling method in which the population of interest is divided according to a common characteristic or attribute; a probability sampling is then conducted within each group.

Area sampling
A sampling method that involves selecting a probability sample of geographic areas and selecting units or individuals within the selected areas for the sample.

To select the units or individuals within the geographic areas, researchers may choose every nth house or unit, or they may adopt random selection procedures to pick out a given number of units or individuals from a total listing within the selected geographic areas. Area sampling may be used when a complete list of the population is not available.

Quota sampling
A sampling method in which the final choice of respondents is left to the interviewers, who base their choices on two or three variables (such as age, sex and education).

In **quota sampling**, researchers divide the population into groups and then arbitrarily choose participants from each group. A study of consumers who are diabetic for an organization seeking to market snacks to this group, for example, may be conducted by interviewing any person who has diabetes. In quota sampling, there are some controls – usually limited to two or three variables such as age, sex and education – over the selection of respondents. The controls attempt to ensure that representative categories of respondents are interviewed. As quota samples are not probability samples, not everyone has an equal chance of being selected and sampling error therefore cannot be measured statistically. Quota samples are used most often in exploratory studies, in which hypotheses are being developed. Often a small quota sample will not be projected to the total population, although the findings may provide valuable insights into a problem. A probability sample used to study people allergic to cats would be highly inefficient.

Survey methods
Interviews by mail, telephone, web and personal interviews.

Survey methods Marketing researchers often employ sampling to collect primary data through mail, telephone, online or personal interview surveys. Selection of a **survey method** depends on the nature of the problem, the data needed to satisfy the research objectives and any hypotheses, and the resources, such as funding and personnel, that are available to the researcher. Table 9.5 illustrates the current break-down of UK research spend across sectors.

Gathering information through surveys is increasingly difficult because respondent rates are declining. Many people believe that responding to surveys takes too long and have become fatigued by the frequency with which they are asked to become involved in such studies. The unethical use of 'sugging' ('selling under the guise of marketing research', i.e. sales techniques disguised as market surveys) has also contributed to decreased respondent cooperation, while internet surveys have been affected by concerns about spam (junk emails).

Mail surveys
Questionnaires sent by mail to respondents, who are encouraged to complete and return them.

In a **mail survey**, questionnaires are sent by mail to respondents, who are encouraged to complete and return them. Mail surveys are used most often when respondents are spread over a wide area and funds for the survey are limited. A mail survey can be relatively inexpensive as long as the response rate is high enough to produce reliable results. The main disadvantages of mail surveys are the possibility of a low response rate or of misleading results, if respondents are significantly different from the population being sampled. The **drop and collect** method, a variation of the mail survey, involves researchers distributing questionnaires by hand to households

Drop and collect surveys
Questionnaires distributed by hand to households, and then collected at a later date.

TABLE 9.5 Share of spend on market research by client sector

	% of total		% of total
Government & public services	17	Financial services	8
IT/telecoms & consumer tech.	12	Non-OTC pharmaceutical	6
Food & beverages	13	Business goods and services	5
Other FMCGs	10	Vehicles	4
Media	10	Retailing (incl. mail order)	4
Other consumer goods and services	9	Transport, travel and tourism	2

Source: Derived from MRS (2011) 2010 Annual Survey of the UK Market Research Industry, MRS: London.

and then returning to collect the completed version at a later date. This relatively low-cost method can work well when the data gathering is confined to a relatively restricted geographical area. It has the advantage that the researcher can encourage respondents to complete the questionnaire.[15]

Researchers can boost response rates in mail surveys by offering respondents an incentive to return the questionnaire. Incentives and follow-ups have consistently been found to increase response rates. On the other hand, promises of anonymity, special appeals for cooperation and questionnaire length have no apparent impact on the response rate. Other techniques for increasing the response rate, such as advance notification, personalization of survey materials, type of postage, corporate or university sponsorship have had mixed results.[16] Although such techniques may help increase the response rates, they can introduce sample composition bias, or non-response bias, which results when those responding to a survey differ in some important respect from those not responding to the survey. In other words, response-enhancing techniques may alienate some people in the sample and appeal to others, making the results non-representative of the population of interest.

Premiums or incentives encouraging respondents to return questionnaires have been effective in developing panels of respondents who are interviewed by mail or online on a regular basis. **Consumer panels** of respondents selected to represent a market or market segment are especially useful for evaluating new products, providing general information about consumers and providing records of consumers' purchases. Web panels are now very popular. A variant of consumer panels are **consumer purchase diaries**. These surveys are similar, but consumers keep track of purchases only. Consumer panels and consumer purchase diaries are widely used, but they do have shortcomings. Research indicates that the people who take the time to fill out a consumer purchase diary have a higher income and are better educated than the general population. If researchers include less well-educated consumers in the panel, they must risk poorer response rates.[17]

Telephone surveys, where respondents' answers to a questionnaire are recorded by interviewers on the phone, are widely used by businesses. A telephone survey has some advantages over a mail survey. The rate of response can be higher because it takes less effort to answer the telephone and talk than to fill out a questionnaire and return it. Telephone surveys can be conducted very quickly. Thus they can be used by political candidates or organizations seeking an immediate reaction to an event. This survey technique also permits interviewers to develop a rapport with respondents and ask some probing questions, although public mistrust about 'cold-calling' is negatively affecting consumers' reaction to this type of data gathering.[18]

Telephone interviews also have drawbacks, especially as a large proportion of the population is becoming increasingly unwilling to become involved. Furthermore, these interviews are limited to oral communication; visual aids or observation cannot be included. Interpreters of results must make adjustments for subjects who are not at home or who do not have telephones. Many households are excluded from the telephone directory. Others use answering machines, voicemail or caller ID to screen or block calls. Researchers seeking business respondents can also face non-response problems, particularly as secretaries frequently 'gatekeep' calls, preventing researchers from talking to their targets.

Overall, reliance on panels of various kinds is increasing. Telephone surveys, like mail and personal interview surveys, are sometimes used to develop panels of respondents who can be interviewed repeatedly to measure changes in attitudes or behaviour. Increasingly, such panels are also being run through digital media, including in the online environment. An advantage of the online setting is that it enables an ongoing dialogue with panel members to be achieved.

Consumer panels
Groups of consumers selected to represent a market or market segment, who agree to be interviewed regularly by mail or online.

Consumer purchase diaries
A marketing research tool in which consumers record their purchases.

Telephone surveys
Surveys in which respondents' answers to a questionnaire are recorded by interviewers on the phone.

Computer-assisted telephone interviewing
A survey method that integrates questionnaire, data collection and tabulations, and provides data to aid decision-makers in the shortest time possible.

Computer-assisted telephone interviewing integrates questionnaire, data collection and tabulations, and provides data to aid decision-makers in the shortest time possible. Questionnaire responses are entered on a terminal keyboard, or the interviewer can use a light-pen (a pen-shaped torch) to record a response on a light-sensitive screen. On the most advanced devices, the interviewer merely points to the appropriate response on a touch-sensitive screen with his or her finger. Open-ended responses can be typed on the keyboard or recorded with paper and pencil. This kind of interviewing saves time and facilitates monitoring the progress of interviews. Because data are available as soon as they are entered into the system, interim results can be retrieved quickly. With some systems, a mobile computer may be taken to off-site locations for use in data analysis. Some researchers believe that computer-assisted telephone interviewing is less expensive than conventional paper and pencil methods.[19]

Online survey
Questionnaires that are sent to an individual's email account or that are available over the internet or via a website.

Online surveys have evolved as an alternative to telephone surveys. In an **online survey** questionnaires can be transmitted to respondents who have agreed to be contacted and have provided their email addresses. Alternatively, links to surveys can be made available to consumers via social media or on corporate websites. In such cases, it is not necessary to have an email address in advance, although it is more difficult to control the sample because respondents are self-selecting. Because completing a survey this way is semi-interactive, recipients can ask for clarification of specific questions or pose questions of their own. The fact that the data are instantly available in electronic format also eases the process of data entry. The potential advantages of online surveys are quick response and lower costs than traditional mail and telephone surveys. However, these advantages cannot yet be fully realized because of limited access to some respondents. In general, though, the opportunities for using the internet to collect data are increasing significantly, especially as companies are pooling their e-contact lists and some are selling their e-lists to third parties. There has also been a growth in surveying by SMS and social media via people's mobile phones.

Personal interview survey
Face-to-face situation in which the researcher meets the consumer and questions him or her about a specific topic.

In a **personal interview survey**, participants respond to questions face-to-face.[20] Various audio-visual aids – pictures, products, diagrams or pre-recorded advertising copy – can be incorporated into a personal interview. Rapport gained through direct interaction usually permits more in-depth interviewing, including probes, follow-up questions or psychological tests. In addition, because personal interviews can be longer, they can yield more information. Finally, respondents can be selected more carefully, and reasons for non-response can be explored. A **depth interview** is a lengthy, one-to-one structured interview examining a consumer's views about a product in detail.

Depth interview
A lengthy, one-to-one structured interview, examining in detail a consumer's views about a product.

The object of a **focus group interview** is to observe group interaction when members are exposed to an idea or concept. Focus groups are frequently held in viewing facilities, as illustrated in Figure 9.7. Often these interviews are conducted informally, without a structured questionnaire, in small groups of eight to 12 people. Consumer attitudes, behaviour, lifestyles, needs and desires can be explored in a flexible and creative manner through this widely used technique (see Chapter 5). Questions are open-ended and stimulate consumers to answer in their own words. Researchers can ask probing questions to clarify something they do not fully understand, or something unexpected and interesting that may help to explain consumer behaviour.

Focus group interview
A survey method that aims to observe group interaction when members are exposed to an idea or concept.

When Cadbury used information obtained from focus groups to change its advertising and to test product concepts, the new advertisements and product launches pushed up sales.[21] The case study at the end of this chapter describes focus group research. Focus group discussions usually start with a general chat, which will be led by a researcher or moderator. The conversation is then narrowed during the course of the session, enabling the moderator to home in on a specific brand, product or advertisement – hence the term 'focus' group.

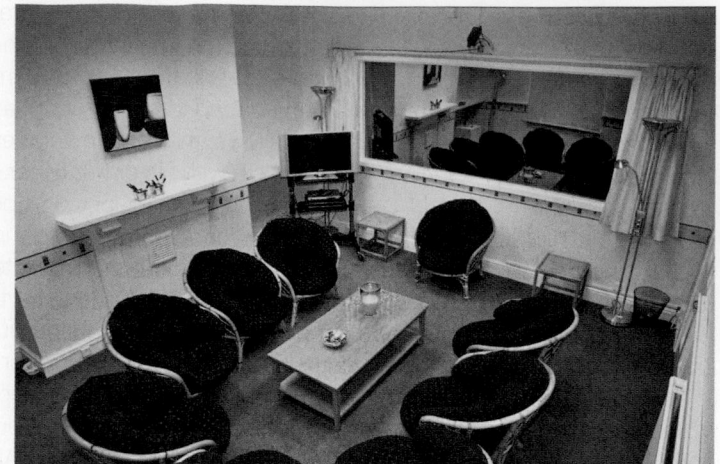

FIGURE 9.7
Viewing facilities are often used for experiments or for conducting focus group interviews

Source: Image courtesey of 3CCC.

Quali-depth interviews
25- to 30-minute intercept interviews that incorporate some of the in-depth advantages of focus group interviews with the speed and flexibility of shopping mall/pavement intercept interviews.

In-home interview
45- to 90-minute interview in which the researcher visits the respondent in his or her home.

Shopping mall/ pavement intercept interviews
Personal interviewing of a percentage of individuals who pass by certain 'intercept' points in a shopping centre or on a pavement.

Quali-depth interviews are 25- to 30-minute intercept interviews that incorporate some of the in-depth advantages of focus group interviews with the speed and flexibility of shopping mall/pavement intercept interviews (see below). Typically, intercepted consumers are taken to a nearby hall or café and asked more probing and searching questions than is possible in a three- to four-minute shopping mall/pavement intercept interview. They can also be shown a greater variety of stimulus material. This is a useful approach for sensitive issues that people might not wish to discuss in a group – gambling and drugs, for example.

Another research technique is the **in-home interview**. As it may be desirable to eliminate group influence, the in-home interview offers a clear advantage when thoroughness of self-disclosure is important. In an in-depth interview of 45 to 90 minutes, respondents can be probed to reveal their real motivations, feelings, behaviours and aspirations. In-depth interviews permit the discovery of emotional 'hot buttons' that provide psychological insights.[22] Door-to-door interviews last only a few minutes and are similar to pavement intercepts.

The nature of personal interviews has changed. In the past, most personal interviews, which were based on random sampling or pre-arranged appointments, were conducted in the respondent's home. Today, many personal interviews are conducted in shopping centres or malls, or on pavements. **Shopping mall/pavement intercept interviews** involve interviewing a percentage of people who pass by certain 'intercept' points in a shopping centre or pavement. Like any face-to-face interviewing method, shopping mall/pavement intercept interviewing has many advantages. The interviewer is in a position to recognize and react to respondents' non-verbal indications of confusion. Respondents can be shown product prototypes, videos of advertisements and the like, and reactions can be sought. The environment lets the researcher deal with complex situations. For example, in taste tests, researchers know that all the respondents are reacting to the same product, which can be prepared and monitored from the shopping centre's test kitchen or some other facility. In addition, lower cost, greater control and the ability to conduct tests requiring bulky equipment make shopping mall/pavement intercept interviews popular.

Research indicates that given a comparable sample of respondents, shopping mall/pavement intercept interviewing is a suitable substitute for telephone interviewing.[23] In addition, there seem to be no significant differences in the completeness of consumer responses between telephone interviewing and shopping mall/pavement intercept interviewing. In fact, for questions dealing with socially desirable behaviour, shopping mall/pavement intercept respondents appear to be more honest about their past behaviour.[24]

On-site computer interviewing
A survey method that requires respondents to complete a self-administered questionnaire displayed on a computer monitor.

In **on-site computer interviewing**, a variation of the shopping mall/pavement intercept interview, respondents complete a self-administered questionnaire displayed on a computer monitor. A computer software package can be used to conduct such interviews in shopping centres or transport termini. After a brief lesson on how to operate the software, respondents can go through the survey at their own pace. Questionnaires can be adapted so that respondents see only those items that may provide useful information about their attitudes.[25]

Questionnaire
Base document for research purposes, providing the questions and structure for an interview or self-completion, and providing space for respondents' answers.

Questionnaire construction A carefully constructed questionnaire is essential to the success of any survey. A **questionnaire** is a base document for research purposes that provides the questions and the structure for an interview or self-completion, and has provision for respondents' answers.[26] Questions must be designed to elicit information that meets the study's data requirements. These questions must be clear, easy to understand and directed towards a specific objective. Researchers need to define the objective before trying to develop a questionnaire because the objective determines the substance of the questions and the amount of detail. A common mistake in constructing questionnaires is to ask questions that interest the researchers but do not yield information useful in deciding whether to accept or reject a hypothesis. Finally, the most important rule in composing questions is to maintain impartiality.

The questions are usually of four kinds:

1. open-ended
2. dichotomous
3. multiple choice
4. Likert scale.

Here are some examples.

1. OPEN-ENDED QUESTION

   What is your general opinion of broadband internet access for your computer?

   _____
   _____
   _____

2. DICHOTOMOUS QUESTION

   Do you presently have broadband access at home?
   Yes _____ Provider's identity _____
   No _____

3. MULTIPLE-CHOICE QUESTION

   What age group are you in?
   Under 20   _____
   20–29   _____
   30–39   _____
   40–49   _____
   50–59   _____
   60 and over _____

4. LIKERT SCALE QUESTION

   To what extent do you expect to use the internet for buying travel products (flights, hotel accommodation) in the near future?

   Not at |___|___|___|___|___|A great
   all   1   2   3   4   5   deal

The design of questionnaires is extremely important because it affects the validity and usefulness of the results. Testing a questionnaire on a few respondents before conducting a full survey helps to eliminate such difficulties. There are also certain guidelines that should be followed when undertaking questionnaire design. The questions must relate to the research objectives. The layout of the questionnaire must not be off-putting to respondents or to the researchers conducting the work. This is particularly pertinent given that the lay-out of a questionnaire affects how quickly data from it can be analyzed by computers. This can save researchers a great deal of time. Question type is also an important factor. Open-ended questions can be the most revealing, but are time consuming – and therefore off-putting – for respondents, as well as difficult to analyze. Dichotomous questions are straightforward but not very revealing. Multiple-choice questions are popular, but care must be exercised in the choice of categories. Likert scale questions are very popular and can enable batches or strings of questions to be listed together in a space-saving style that can be time-saving for the respondent. They allow respondents to express degrees of a positive or negative response, rather than give an absolute yes or no. There is also the option to give a 'neutral' ('3') answer. Most questionnaires include a mix of question styles.

Sometimes respondent fatigue can affect the quality of questionnaire responses. This may result in answers being rushed, or the questionnaire being abandoned altogether. For example, sometimes when faced with a long list of Likert scale questions, respondents move through the questions ticking the same point in the scale, rather than taking time to reflect on their answers. The wording of questions is also critical. Researchers must ensure that personal questions, such as those about income or educational attainment, are worded in as inoffensive a manner as possible. These types of question are often placed towards the end of the questionnaire, because it is believed that they are more likely to be answered once the respondent has invested time in the research instrument.

Observation methods Methods by which researchers record respondents' overt behaviour and take note of physical conditions and events.

Ethnography observing consumers' real-world behaviours and product usage.

Observation methods In using **observation methods**, researchers record respondents' overt behaviour, taking note of physical conditions and events. Direct contact with respondents is avoided; instead, their actions are examined and noted systematically. For example, researchers might use observation methods to answer the question, 'How long do shoppers in computer game stores such as Game, typically spend browsing?' As the opener to this chapter and the marketing insight early on demonstrate, observation methods can make use of new technologies to record behaviour and also use ethnographic techniques, such as watching customers interact with a product in a real-world environment. **Ethnography** is increasingly being used by many marketing research agencies to gain greater insights into consumer lifestyles. Indeed, in a recent survey of the marketing research industry, 27 per cent of respondents giving an opinion about the most exciting developments mentioned ethnographic research.[27]

Observation may also be combined with interviews. For example, during a personal interview, the condition of a respondent's home or other possessions may be observed and recorded, and demographic information such as ethnic origin, approximate age and sex can be confirmed. Some forms of 'observation' are now common on e-shopping sites, with businesses monitoring the amount of time consumers spend browsing and even whether they complete the purchase process once they have started. Observation is also not confined to consumers; shops and service establishments can also be observed, through 'mystery shopper' research, as the Marketing Tools and Techniques box below explains.

Mechanical observation devices Cameras, recorders, counting machines and other equipment that records physiological changes in individuals.

Data gathered through observation can sometimes be biased if the respondent is aware of the observation process. An observer can be placed in a natural market environment, such as a grocery store, without biasing or influencing shoppers' actions. However, if the presence of a human observer is likely to bias the outcome or if human sensory abilities are inadequate, mechanical means may be used to record behaviour. **Mechanical observation devices** include cameras, recorders, sensors, GPS trackers, counting machines and other equipment that records physiological changes in individuals. For instance, a special camera can be used to record the eye movements of respondents looking at an advertisement, and to detect the sequence of reading and the parts of the advertisement that receive greatest attention. Electronic scanners in supermarkets can provide accurate data on sales and consumers' purchase patterns, and marketing researchers may buy such data from the supermarket company. Observation is straightforward and avoids a central problem of survey methods: motivating respondents to state their true feelings or opinions. Technological advances, such as the growth in wearable technologies like smart watches, are also increasing the opportunities to gather data in this way.

Marketing tools and techniques

The intrigues of 'mystery shopper' research programmes

Retailers and providers of services depend increasingly not only on the products they sell or deliver but also on the ability, attitude and quality of their personnel and the internal environment of their branch outlets. The regional directors and head office managers who check such standards all too often enter through the staff door at the rear of the branch, focusing primarily on operations and not on customer concerns. The branch's customers enter from the front, having first seen the exterior of the branch. They deal with all levels of personnel, not just the manager or manageress to whom the visiting director talks. These customers are not wrapped up in the company's products and operations; they seek help and advice. They expect courtesy and professionalism.

Customers buy a company's products; quite often the company's management never does, instead requesting items direct from storage at staff discount rates without ever visiting shops or showrooms. Car manufacturers give their senior management vehicles and offer all employees highly attractive deals. The result is that few senior managers ever visit a showroom or dealer – even their servicing is taken care of – so they never see the 'sharp end', their dealers, as customers do.

One car producer instigated a programme of 'mystery shopper' surveys. This programme involved visits by bogus potential car buyers to dealers to rate the upkeep and appearance of showrooms, technical knowledge and attitude of personnel, quality of displays, negotiating criteria and adherence to company policies. Dealers did not know who the bogus buyers were, or when they were to visit. Service reception staff were similarly targeted. A favourite ploy by the researchers was to book a car service by telephone and then phone again to cancel, judging the receptionist's response to the lost

business. As a result of these frequent but anonymous visits, the car producer was able to improve the standards of its dealers, the attitude of its personnel and ultimately the quality of its service and customer satisfaction.

This form of marketing research – 'mystery shopper' – is one of the fastest-growing areas in the industry. It is defined by MSPA (the Mystery Shoppers Providers' Association), is valuable because:

● Most customers who have unsatisfactory experiences will not complain … they will just never come back.

● Dissatisfied customers are likely to tell many others about their experience, who in turn probably will avoid doing business with the offending merchant.

● The use of mystery shopping to provide independent and impartial feedback reduces any perception of favoritism in incentive programmes.

● Mystery shopping helps determine whether customers' actual experiences are as intended.

● Mystery shopping programmes can identify areas of training which need improvement and can identify areas of training that are working particularly well.

(Source: www.mspa-global.org/en/aboutmysteryshop.html, accessed 24 April 2015.)

Even so, market research companies such as GfK, which offers mystery shopping services, must take care that staff are trained to a high standard and must also ensure that they behave in an ethical manner. Employees must be trained to evaluate how customers are greeted, how stores that they visit look and whether shop assistants understand the products on sale. They are also expected to be able to blend in inconspicuously in the settings they visit.

Recently concerns have been expressed about the use of mystery shopper research by organizations such as the

European Society for Opinion and Marketing Research (ESO-MAR), over worries that employees might be tricked into handling awkward customers in an inappropriate way and that this might have future consequences for those individuals' jobs. In other forms of research, those involved have the opportunity to withdraw from the process, but this opportunity is not provided to those being inspected by mystery shoppers. Another concern is that in most forms of ethical marketing research, the respondent is guaranteed anonymity, but if mystery shopper research is deployed to check up on staff or to develop 'league tables' of branch performance, it is difficult for the research findings not to identify the personnel in question.

Some marketing research firms that use mystery shopping are trying to address these concerns by ensuring that they comply with the guidelines laid down by organizations such as ESOMAR and the Market Research Society. Others have joined the MSPA, an association of organizations providing mystery shopping services. MSPA is a membership organization which aims to 'improve the acceptance, performance, reputation and use of mystery shopping services' Its members must be able to demonstrate that have at least two years' experience, have a reputation for excellence, and agree to abide by the Association's codes of professional ethics and standards (www.mspa-eu.org/en/what-is-ms.html, accessed 8 March 2011).

Sources: *Marketing Guides: Market Research*, 13 June 1996; www.mystery-shoppers.co.uk; www.gfk.com/solutions/mystery-shopping/Pages/default.aspx, April 2015.

However, observation tends to be descriptive and may not provide insights into causal relationships. Another drawback is that analyses based on observation are subject to the biases of the observer or the limitations of the mechanical device.

Experimentation
Data collection that involves maintaining certain variables as constant so that the effects of the experimental variables can be measured.

Experimentation Experimentation can be used to determine which variable or variables caused an event to occur. It involves keeping certain variables constant so that the effects of the experimental variables can be measured. For instance, if an online fashion vendor wishes to examine the effect of a price reduction on sales, all other marketing variables should be held constant except the change in price.

Independent variable
A variable not influenced by or dependent on other variables in experiments.

In experimentation, an **independent variable** (a variable not influenced by or dependent on other variables) is manipulated and the resulting changes measured in a **dependent variable** (a variable contingent on, or restricted to, one value or a set of values assumed by the independent variable). Figure 9.8 illustrates the relationship between these variables. For example, when Coca-Cola introduces a new variant of its carbonated soft drink, it may want to estimate the number of each variant that could be sold at various levels of advertising expenditure and price. The dependent variable would be sales, the independent variables would be advertising expenditure and price. Researchers would design the experiment to control other independent variables that might influence sales, such as distribution and variations of the product.

Dependent variable
A variable that is contingent on, or restricted to, one value or a set of values assumed by the independent variable.

Laboratory settings
Central locations at which participants or respondents are invited to react or respond to experimental stimuli.

Experiments may be conducted in the laboratory or in the field; each research setting has advantages and disadvantages. In **laboratory settings**, participants or respondents are invited to a central location to react or respond to experimental stimuli. In such an isolated setting it is possible to control independent variables that might influence the outcome of an experiment. The features of laboratory settings might include a taste kitchen, video equipment, projection facilities, digital recorders, internet hook-ups, one-way mirrors, central telephone banks and interview rooms. In an experiment to determine the influence of price (independent variable) on sales of a new line of microwave ready meals (dependent variable), respondents would be invited to a laboratory – a room with table, chairs and sample ready meals – before the product was available in

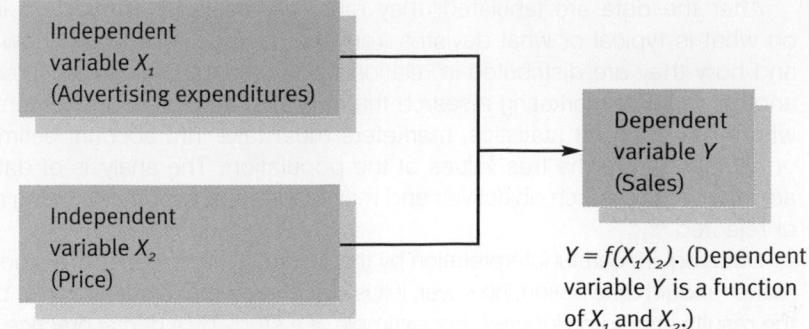

FIGURE 9.8
Relationship between independent and dependent variables

Independent variable X_1 (Advertising expenditures)

Independent variable X_2 (Price)

Dependent variable Y (Sales)

$Y = f(X_1X_2)$. (Dependent variable Y is a function of X_1 and X_2.)

Field settings
'Real world' environments in which experiments take place.

stores. The ready meal would be placed on a table with competing products. Analysts would then question respondents about their reactions to the ready meal at various prices. One problem with a laboratory setting is its isolation from the real world, making it difficult, or impossible, to duplicate all the conditions that affect choices in the marketplace.

The experimental approach can also be used in **field settings**, which are 'real world' environments. A taste test of regional cheeses conducted in a supermarket is one example of an experiment in a field setting. Field settings can allow a more direct test of marketing decisions than laboratory settings. However, these experiments also have their drawbacks. It may be difficult to encourage respondents to cooperate with the experiment, or the findings may be influenced or biased by unexpected events, such as the weather or major economic news. Sometimes the experiment itself can cause bias. For example, in **home placements** (when a product is used in the home in a real setting) or **diary tests** (when households log their weekly purchases and consumption patterns), people may become artificially involved with the product. They might sniff items they would not normally sniff, or ask for their children's opinions about a food item when, normally, they would just give their children the meal and expect them to eat it.[28]

Home placements
Experiments in which a product is used in a home setting.

Diary tests
Experiments in which households log their weekly purchases and consumption patterns.

Step 4: analyzing and interpreting research findings

After collecting data to test their hypotheses, marketers analyze and interpret the research findings. Interpretation is easier if marketers plan their data analysis methods carefully and early in the research process. All too often, when data collection has been completed, it is discovered that different wording of questions or ordering of the sections in a questionnaire could have simplified the analysis. Marketers should also allow for continual evaluation of the data during the entire collection period. They can then gain valuable insight into areas that ought to be probed during the formal interpretation.

Statistical interpretation
An analysis of data that focuses on what is typical or what deviates from the average.

The first step in drawing conclusions from most research is displaying the data in table format. If marketers intend to apply the results to individual categories of the things or people being studied, cross-tabulation may be quite useful, especially in tabulating joint occurrences. For example, a cross-tabulation of data using the two variables 'gender' and 'purchase rates of car tyres' would show differences in how men and women purchase this product.

After the data are tabulated, they must be analyzed. Statistical interpretation focuses on what is typical or what deviates from the average. It indicates how widely responses vary and how they are distributed in relation to the variable being measured. This interpretation is another facet of marketing research that relies on marketers' judgement or intuition. Moreover, when they interpret statistics, marketers must take into account estimates of expected error or deviation from the true values of the population. The analysis of data helps researchers to achieve their research objectives and may lead to the hypothesis being studied being accepted or rejected.[29]

Data require careful interpretation by the marketer. If the results of a study are valid, the decision-maker should take action; however, if it is discovered that a question has been worded incorrectly, the results should be ignored. For example, if a study by a dental practice reveals that 50 per cent of its customers believe that its dentists are caring, is that finding good, bad or indifferent? Two important benchmarks help interpret the result: how the 50 per cent figure compares with that for other dental practices and how it compares with a previous time period. To make the best use of this data, it is important to understand what the research results mean and to relate them to a context that permits effective decision-making.[30]

Step 5: reporting research findings

The final step in the marketing research process is reporting the research findings. Before preparing the report, the marketer must take a clear, objective look at the findings to see how well the gathered facts answer the research question, or support or negate the hypotheses posed in the beginning. In most cases, it is extremely doubtful that the study can provide everything needed to answer the research question. Thus, the report must highlight the deficiencies and the reasons for them, perhaps suggesting areas that require further investigation.

The report presenting the results is usually a formal, written document. Researchers must allow time for the writing task when they plan and schedule the project. Since the report is a means of communicating with the decision-makers who will use the research findings, researchers need to determine beforehand how much detail and supporting data to include. They should keep in mind that corporate executives prefer reports that are short, clear and simply expressed. Often researchers will give their summary and recommendations first, especially if decision-makers do not have time to study how the results were obtained. Such summary findings tend to be presented via a face-to-face audio-visual presentation or possibly via a virtual webinar. A technical report allows its users to analyze data and interpret recommendations because it describes the research methods/procedures and the most important data gathered. Thus, researchers must recognize the needs and expectations of the report user and adapt to them.

When marketing decision-makers have a firm grasp of research methods and procedures, they are better able to integrate reported findings and personal experience. If marketers can spot limitations in research from reading a report, their personal experience assumes additional importance in the decision-making process. Marketers who cannot understand basic statistical assumptions and data gathering procedures may misuse research findings. Consequently, report writers should be aware of the backgrounds and research abilities of those who will rely on the report in making decisions. Clear explanations presented in plain language make it easier for decision-makers to apply the findings and less likely that a report will be misused or ignored. Talking to potential research users before writing a report can help researchers supply information that will improve decision-making.

Care must be taken when writing the report to avoid bias and distortion. Marketing researchers want to find out about behaviour and opinions, and they need accurate data for making decisions. Reliable marketing research and marketing information systems provide a clearer understanding of dynamics in the marketplace and are more likely to be used by managers in decision-making.

Using technology to improve marketing information gathering and analysis

Marketing information systems

Marketing information system (MIS)
The framework for the day-to-day management and structuring of information gathered from sources both inside and outside an organization.

A **marketing information system (MIS)** is a framework for the day-to-day management and structuring of information gathered regularly from sources both inside and outside an organization. As such, an MIS provides a continuous flow of information about prices, advertising expenditure, sales, competition and distribution expenses.[31] Kraft Foods, for example, operates one of the largest marketing information systems in the food industry, maintaining, using and sharing information with others to increase the value of what the company offers customers.

The main focus of the marketing information system is on data storage and retrieval. Regular reports of sales by product or market category, data on inventory levels and records of sales people's activities are all examples of information that is useful in making marketing decisions. In the MIS, the means of gathering data receive less attention than do the procedures for expediting the flow of information. The inputs into a marketing information system include the information sources inside and outside the organization assumed to be useful for future decision-making. An effective marketing information system starts by determining the objective of the information – that is, by identifying decision needs that require certain information. The business can then specify an information system for continuous monitoring to provide regular, pertinent information on both the external and internal environment.

Databases

Most marketing information systems include internal databases. A database is a collection of information arranged for easy access and retrieval. Databases allow marketers to tap into an abundance of information useful in making marketing decisions: internal sales reports, newspaper articles, company press releases, government economic reports, bibliographies and more, often accessed through a computer system. Information technology has made it possible to develop databases to guide strategic planning and help improve customer services. Wal-Mart, for example, maintains one of the largest company databases, with data on sales and inventory levels, as well as data mined from customer receipts in its stores. These data help Wal-Mart pinpoint purchasing patterns, which helps the company manage inventory levels and determine effective product placement. Frequent-flier programmes permit airlines to ask loyal customers to participate in surveys about their needs and desires, allowing the airlines to track their best customers' flight patterns by time of day, week, month and year. Supermarkets, such as Tesco and Sainsbury's, gain a substantial amount of data through checkout scanners tied to loyalty cards.

Marketing researchers can also use commercial databases developed by information research organizations to obtain useful information for marketing decisions. Many of these commercial databases are accessible online for a fee. In most commercial databases, the user typically does a computer search by key word, topic or company, and the database service generates abstracts, articles or reports that can be printed out. Accessing multiple reports or

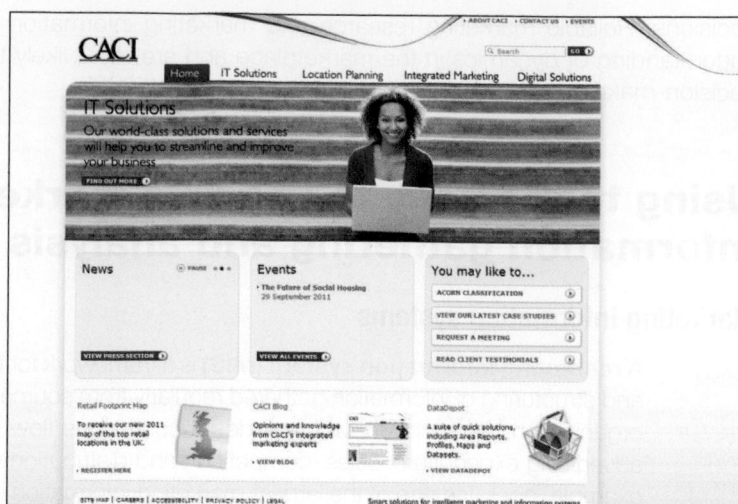

FIGURE 9.9

CACI markets itself as an unrivalled range of marketing solutions and information systems, to a number of businesses from all industry sectors

Source: Screenshot courtesy of CACI.

a complete article may cost extra. Information provided by a single company – for example, on household demographics, purchases, television viewing behaviour, and responses to promotions such as coupons or loyalty schemes – is called **single-source data**.[32] For example, CACI provides demographic and lifestyle information on people living in different UK neighbourhoods; see Figure 9.9.

Single-source data
Information provided by a single marketing research company.

Data gathering in a digitally-enabled world

The internet has evolved as a powerful communication medium, linking customers and companies around the world via computer networks with email, forums, social media, web pages and more. In this digitally-enabled world, the availability of data and the opportunities to gather market and consumer insight have dramatically increased. These trends have been fuelled by **big data**, which is data that are too large, numerous, complex and frequent for conventional data tools to capture, store, manage and analyze. Open source platforms are enabling organizations to extract real time value from the huge volumes of data being produced.

Big data
Data that are too large, numerous, complex and frequent for conventional data tools to capture, store, manage and analyze. Open source platforms enable organizations to extract real time value from the huge volumes of data being produced.

Many companies now employ market insight managers or have set up customer insight teams. **Market insight** is the process by which firms learn about consumers, competitors and market trends to identify strategic direction and improve returns. Market insight managers embrace all of the techniques that have already been discussed in this chapter, but in addition they use an array of web-enabled and social media-based techniques. These approaches offer instant and interactive means of gathering information and are much faster than distributing surveys or staging focus groups. Some brands have set up their own discussion forums or use existing ones, such as netmums to gauge opinion about their products. Brand managers also often use Twitter to tweet about their product, perhaps to comment on a new design, promote a pricing event, or test out a new service idea. These managers can monitor the reaction of other Twitter users; insight which can then be used to shape aspects of the brand's marketing. This kind of approach has been likened to throwing a stone into a pond and then monitoring the ripples as they move across the water.

Market insight
Learning about consumers, competitors and market trends to identify strategic direction and improve returns.

Companies can also mine their own websites for useful information. Amazon, for example, has built a relationship with its customers by tracking the types of books and music they purchase. Each time a customer logs on to its website, Amazon can offer recommendations based on the customer's previous purchases. Such a marketing system helps the company track the changing desires and buying habits of its most valued customers.

Growth of the internet has launched an entire industry that is working to make market information easily accessible both to marketing organizations and customers. Marketing researchers can use a range of internet sites set up to support their data collection activities. Some sites, such as SurveyMonkey (www.surveymonkey.com), provide the means to design research instruments and collect data in a format that can be readily analyzed. With millions of customers around the world, organizations ranging from charities such as the National Multiple Sclerosis Society (NMSS) to corporates such as Samsung have used this service to acquire the insights they need. Other organizations, such as Lightspeed and Populus, have created online market research panels, providing their clients with ready access to consumers around the world who can answer questions about the products and services they prefer, their purchase behaviour and lifestyles, or even their views about global events. Marketers can also subscribe to 'mailing lists' that periodically deliver electronic newsletters to their computer screens and they can participate in on-screen discussions with thousands of network users. This enhanced communication with a business's customers, suppliers and employees provides a high-speed link that boosts the capabilities of the business's marketing information system.

While most web pages are open to anyone with internet access, big organizations like Cisco Systems also maintain internal 'intranets', that allow employees to access such internal data as customer profiles and product inventory information once hidden in databases only technicians could unlock. Such sensitive company information can be protected from outside users of the internet by special security firewalls.

The importance of ethical marketing research

The increasing availability of digital data is helping to fuel the increasing use by organizations of marketing research. Marketing managers and other professionals are relying more and more on marketing insights, marketing information systems and new technologies to make better decisions. It is therefore essential that professional standards are established by which to judge the reliability of this research. Such standards are necessary because of the ethical and legal issues that develop in gathering marketing research data. In addition, the relationships between research suppliers, such as marketing research agencies, and the marketing managers who make strategy decisions, require ethical behaviour. Without such clear standards, ethical conflict can lead to mistrust and questionable research results.[33] Attempts to stamp out shoddy practices and establish generally accepted procedures for conducting research are important developments in marketing research. Other issues of great concern relate to researchers' honesty, manipulation of research techniques, data manipulation, invasion of privacy, and failure to disclose the purpose or sponsorship of a study in some situations. Too often, respondents are unfairly manipulated and research clients are not told about flaws in data. For example, one dubious practice that damages the image of marketing research is nuisance phone calls, including abandoned or silent cold calls. An abandoned call happens when a consumer answers the phone, but receives a recorded information message rather than being able to talk to the caller. A silent call is when a call is received, but the line is silent. These calls arise because call centres use automated calling systems to maximize the productivity of their agents, but may not always have enough operators on hand to take the calls. These calls have become such a problem that Ofcom, the independent regulator and competition authority for the UK communications industries, has developed a range of resources to help consumer tackle them.[34]

All kinds of organizations involved in research have developed codes of conduct and guidelines to promote ethical marketing research.[35] These include professional associations, academic research funders, as well as government bodies, commercial organizations and universities.

To be effective, such guidelines must instruct those who participate in marketing research on how to avoid misconduct. For example, the Market Research Society's Delphi Group recently published a report on consumer privacy and its implications for marketing research. Table 9.6 compares the principles driving the ethics codes of professional association[36] (www.mrs.org.uk/article/item/1918), the Market Research Society (MRS), and academic research funding body, the Economic and Social Science Research Council (ESRC).

Marketing research is essential in planning and developing marketing strategies. Information about target markets provides vital input in planning the marketing mix and in controlling marketing activities. It is no secret that companies can use information technology as a key to gaining an advantage over the competition.[37] In short, the marketing concept – the marketing philosophy of customer orientation – can be implemented better when adequate information about customers, competition and trends is available.

TABLE 9.6   The Principles of the MRS and ESRC Codes of Conduct

MRS principles	ESRC principles
1 Researchers shall ensure that participation in their activities is based on voluntary informed consent.	1 Research participants should take part voluntarily, free from any coercion or undue influence, and their rights, dignity and (when possible) autonomy should be respected and appropriately protected.
2 Researchers shall be straightforward and honest in all their professional and business relationships.	2 Research should be worthwhile and provide value that outweighs any risk or harm. Researchers should aim to maximize the benefit of the research and minimize potential risk of harm to participants and researchers. All potential risk and harm should be mitigated by robust precautions.
3 Researchers shall be transparent as to the subject and purpose of data collection.	3 Research staff and participants should be given appropriate information about the purpose, methods and intended uses of the research, what their participation in the research entails and what risks and benefits, if any, are involved.
4 Researchers shall respect the confidentiality of information collected in their professional activities.	4 Individual research participant and group preferences regarding anonymity should be respected and participant requirements concerning the confidential nature of information and personal data should be respected.
5 Researchers shall respect the rights and well-being of all individuals.	5 Research should be designed, reviewed and undertaken to ensure recognized standards of integrity are met, and quality and transparency are assured.
6 Researchers shall ensure that respondents are not harmed or adversely affected by their professional activities.	6 The independence of research should be clear, and any conflicts of interest or partiality should be explicit.
7 Researchers shall balance the needs of individuals, clients and their professional activities.	
8 Researchers shall exercise independent professional judgement in the design, conduct and reporting of their professional activities.	
9 Researchers shall ensure that their professional activities are conducted by persons with appropriate training, qualifications and experience.	
10 Researchers shall protect the reputation and integrity of the profession.	

Source: from the MRS Code of Conduct (September 2014) Annual Survey of the UK Market Research Industry, MRS: London.

Summary

Effective marketing is contingent on marketers having information about the characteristics, needs and wants of their target markets. Marketing research and information systems that furnish practical, unbiased information help companies avoid the assumptions and misunderstandings that could lead to poor marketing performance.

Marketing research is the systematic design, collection, interpretation and reporting of information to help marketers solve specific marketing problems or take advantage of marketing opportunities. Marketing research projects are adapted to the context and problems under study.

All organizations have some *marketing intelligence*, which is the composite of all data and ideas available within the organization. Often the information is inadequate, leading to the commissioning of marketing research.

Quantitative marketing research leads to findings that can be quantified and statistically analyzed. *Qualitative research* examines subjective opinions and value judgements.

The increase in marketing research activities represents a transition from intuitive to scientific problem-solving. Intuitive decisions are made on the basis of personal knowledge and past experience. *Scientific decision-making* is an orderly, logical and systematic approach to gathering information. Minor, non-recurring low-risk problems can be handled successfully by *intuition*. As the amount of risk and alternative solutions increases, the use of research becomes more desirable and rewarding.

The five basic steps of planning marketing research are: (1) locating and defining problems or research issues; (2) designing the research; (3) collecting data; (4) analyzing and interpreting research findings; (5) reporting research findings.

The first step towards finding a solution or launching a research study means uncovering the nature and boundaries of a negative, or positive, situation or question. Researchers and decision-makers should remain in the *problem definition* stage until they have determined precisely what they want from the research and how they will use it.

Careful *research design* is of vital importance as a clear statement of research objectives guides a research project. Sometimes hypotheses – or informed guesses or assumptions about a certain problem or set of circumstances – are formulated. The *research objectives* and *any hypotheses* determine the approach for gathering data: *exploratory research*, *descriptive research or causal research*. Researchers need to be concerned about issues of reliability and validity: techniques are *reliable* if they produce almost identical results in successive repeated trials; they have *validity* if they measure what they are supposed to measure and not something else.

Collecting data is the third step of the research process. *Secondary data* are compiled inside or outside the organization for some purpose other than the current investigation. Secondary data may be collected from an organization's databank and other internal sources; from periodicals, census reports, government publications, the internet and unpublished sources; and from *syndicated data services*, which collect and collate general information and sell it to clients. Secondary data 'pre-exist' and should be examined prior to the collection of any primary data.

To gather *primary data*, researchers use sampling procedures, survey methods, observation and experimentation. *Sampling* involves selecting a limited number of representative units, or a *sample*, from a total *population*. There are two basic types of sampling: probability and non-probability. In *probability sampling*, every element of the population has a known chance of being selected. In *random sampling*, all the units in a population have an equal chance of appearing in the sample. In *stratified sampling*, the population of interest is divided into groups according to a common characteristic or attribute, and then a probability sampling is conducted within each group. *Area sampling* involves selecting a probability sample of geographic areas such as streets, census tracts or census enumeration districts, and selecting units or individuals within the selected geographic areas for the sample. *Quota sampling* differs from other forms of sampling in that it is judgemental (or non-probability).

Survey methods include *mail surveys* and *mail and online panels*, email and internet surveys (*online surveys*), *consumer purchase diaries, telephone surveys, computer assisted telephone interviewing and personal interview surveys*, such as *depth interviews, shopping mall/pavement intercept interviews, on-site computer interviewing, focus group interviews, quali-depth interviews and in-home interviews. Questionnaires* are instruments used to obtain information from respondents and to record observations; they should be unbiased and objective. Observation methods including ethnographic techniques that involve researchers recording respondents' overt behaviour and taking note of physical conditions and events. Observation may be facilitated by *mechanical observation devices*.

Experimentation involves maintaining as constants those factors that are related to or may affect the variables under investigation, so that the effects of the experimental variables can be measured. Marketing experimentation is a set of rules and procedures according to which the task of data gathering is organized so as to expedite analysis and interpretation. In experimentation, an *independent variable* is manipulated and the resulting changes are measured in a *dependent variable*.

Experiments may take place in *laboratory settings*, which provide maximum control over influential factors, or in *field settings*, which are preferred when marketers want experimentation to take place in 'real world' environments, such as with *home placements* and *diary tests*.

To apply research findings to decision-making, marketers must tabulate, analyze and interpret their findings properly. *Statistical interpretation* is analysis of data that focuses on what is typical or what deviates from the average. After interpreting their research findings, researchers must prepare a report of the findings that the decision-makers can use and understand. Information provided by a single firm is called *single-source data*.

The *marketing information system (MIS)* is a framework for the day-to-day managing and structuring of information regularly gathered from sources both inside and outside an organization. The inputs into a marketing information system include the information sources inside and outside the organization considered useful for future decision-making. They may include internal databases. Processing information involves classifying it and developing categories for meaningful storage and retrieval. Marketing decision-makers then determine which information – the output – is useful for making marketing decisions. Feedback enables those who are responsible for gathering internal and external data to adjust the information inputs systematically.

Growth of the internet has launched an entire industry that is working to make market information easily accessible to both organizations and customers. Companies can also mine their own websites for useful information, subscribe to online services, and join 'mailing lists' that periodically deliver electronic newsletters to their computer screens so that they can participate in on-screen discussions with thousands of network users.

Marketing managers and other professionals are relying more and more on marketing research, marketing information systems and new technologies to make better decisions. Professional standards are needed to judge the reliability of such research. These enable ethical and legal issues associated with data gathering to be handled.

Key links

This chapter has concentrated on the marketing research tools available to capture information about markets and customers. It should be read in conjunction with:

● Chapter 2's examination of the nature of opportunity analysis and the importance of analyzing competitors.

● Chapters 5 and 6, reviewing the required insights into buying behaviour.

● Chapters 7 and 8, discussing how to create market segments from an understanding of customers, and how best to develop a brand positioning strategy.

Important terms

Area sampling
Big data
Causal research
Computer-assisted telephone interviewing
Consumer panels
Consumer purchase diaries
Dependent variable
Depth interview
Descriptive research
Diary tests
Drop and collect surveys
Ethnography
Experimentation
Exploratory research
Field settings
Focus group interview
Home placements
Hypothesis
Independent variable
In-home interviews
Intuition
Laboratory settings
Mail surveys
Market insight
Marketing information system (MIS)
Marketing intelligence
Mechanical observation devices
Observation methods
Online survey
On-site computer interviewing
Personal interview survey
Population
Primary data
Probability sampling

Problem definition
Quali-depth interviews
Qualitative research
Quantitative research
Questionnaire
Quota sampling
Random sampling
Reliability
Research design
Research objective
Sample
Sampling
Scientific decision-making
Secondary data
Shopping mall/pavement intercept interviews
Single-source data
Statistical interpretation
Stratified sampling
Survey methods
Syndicated data services
Telephone surveys
Validity

Discussion and review questions

1. What is the marketing information system (MIS) of a small organization likely to include?

2. What are the differences between quantitative and qualitative marketing research?

3. How do the benefits of decisions guided by marketing research compare with those of intuitive decision-making? How do marketing decision-makers know when it will be worthwhile to conduct research?

4. Give specific examples of situations in which intuitive decision-making would probably be more appropriate than marketing research.

5. What are the differences between exploratory, descriptive and causal research?

6. What are the major limitations of using secondary data to solve marketing problems?

7. List some of the problems of conducting a laboratory experiment on respondents' reactions to the taste of different brands of beer. How would these problems differ from those of a field study of beer taste preferences?

8. In what situation would it be best to use random sampling? Quota sampling? Stratified or area sampling?

9. Suggest some ways to encourage respondents to cooperate in mail surveys.

10. What are the benefits of the focus group technique?

11. How has the growth of the internet increased the opportunities for collecting information?

12. Give some examples of marketing problems that could be solved through information gained from observation.

13. Why is questionnaire design important? Why should questionnaires be tested?

14. What is 'sugging'? Why is it damaging to the marketing research industry?

15. Why are ethics so important in conducting marketing research?

Recommended readings

Aaker, D., Kumar, V., Leone, R. and Day, G., *Marketing Research* (John Wiley & Sons, 2012).

Bradley, N., *Marketing Research: Tools and Techniques* (Oxford University Press, 2013).

Hague, P., *Market Research in Practice: How to Get Greater Insight From Your Market* (Kogan Page, 2013).

McQuarrie, E.F., *The Market Research Toolbox: A Concise Guide for Beginners* (Sage, 2016).

Malhotra, N.K. and Birks, D.F., *Marketing Research: An Applied Approach* (Pearson, 2012).

Internet exercise

The World Association of Opinion and Marketing Research Professionals (ESOMAR, founded as the European Society for Opinion and Marketing Research in 1948) is a non-profit association for marketing research professionals. ESOMAR promotes the use of opinion and marketing research to improve marketing decisions in companies worldwide and works to protect personal privacy in the research process. Visit the association's website at: www.esomar.org/

1. How can ESOMAR help marketing professionals conduct research to guide marketing strategy?

2. How can ESOMAR help marketers protect the privacy of research subjects when conducting marketing research in other countries?

3. ESOMAR introduced the first professional code of conduct for marketing research professionals in 1948. The association continues to update this document to address new technology and other changes in the marketing environment. According to ESOMAR's code, what are the specific professional responsibilities of marketing researchers?

Group tasks

1. Your group has been asked to examine people's opinions of sugar and salt in food and drinks and their impact on health. What research process would you recommend and why?

2. Two brand managers wish to update their insights into customer preferences. One is the brand manager for a well-known cola while the other is a marketer for a leading laptop brand. What would you recommend to each in terms of marketing research?

Applied mini-case

Advances in information technology, especially in terms of data storage and processing capacity, have made available an ever-growing quantity of data about customer buying behaviour. To extract from this mound of data potentially useful information to guide marketing decisions, marketers are developing methods of mining data. Data mining refers to the discovery of patterns hidden in databases that have the potential to contribute to marketers' understanding of customers and their needs. Data mining employs computer technology to extract data from internal and external sources; translate and format the data; analyze, substantiate, and assign meaning to data; organize databases; and build and implement support systems to make data mining results accessible to decision-makers.

Question

Adopt the role of a retail analyst who is helping a large retail group to organize its databases. You have been asked to help guide the process by providing a list of the kinds of information helpful to a company when making decisions about marketing strategy.

Focus group interviewing: in-depth views from group discussions

Focus group interviews, which are generally informal group discussions about marketing ideas or concepts conducted by a marketer or marketing research company, are used by most major organizations in developing marketing or business plans. In the 1980s, focus group interviewing became one of the most widely practised types of marketing research, expanding from the packaged goods industry into financial services and industrial applications.

However, the function of focus group interviewing is expected to change. Traditionally, companies have relied on focus group interviews to define the input going into quantitative studies, but a new trend is to conduct focus group interviews after tabulating research results, to provide insight into why the results were achieved. The trend is also towards higher costs (the average today is £2500 for 90 minutes and £3000 for an extended, video-recorded group lasting two and a half hours).

Other changes pertain to moderator guides and their reports. The moderator guides will be expected to involve clients in the development process. Their reports will concentrate on providing conclusions that interpret the findings and on making recommendations for action by the client. The reports will also contain fewer actual quotations from individual focus group participants. The post-focus group debriefing techniques are also being altered. The shift is towards disciplined debriefing that asks participants their reactions to the group session. Such debriefing can provide the link between concept development and application, and can serve as a rough check on validity and reliability.

Another new development in focus group interviewing is the use of electronics to offer three-way capabilities. Computerized decision-making software can supplement research findings and consolidate opinions from three different audiences. For example, in healthcare research in a hospital setting, the three audiences would be former patients, medics and employees. The advantages of using electronics include easier scheduling of participating groups and more interaction among the three audiences.

A major UK service retailer was faced with declining sales and two new competitors. In order to re-establish itself as the dominant force in its market, it decided to undertake some in-depth qualitative marketing research

using focus groups. The retailer's new competitors were opening stores at the rate of six per month, and the company realized it had to act quickly to defend its position. However, it had not conducted any consumer research for many years and was uncertain why its customers preferred its stores, how competitors were perceived and what types of people constituted its customer profile. Before modifying its marketing mix and launching an advertising campaign to combat its new competitors, the company had to gain a better understanding of its target market. For approximately £14 000, using a specialist consumer qualitative agency, in just three weeks the company managed to get a good 'feel' for its standing in its core trading area, as perceived by customers. The table shows that the information resulted from a fairly 'standard' programme of focus groups.

Each group had eight consumers, four of whom were shoppers in the retailer's stores and four of whom shopped in competitors' stores. Each group session lasted three hours, and a free merchandise voucher and buffet meal was provided for participants. The same moderator ran all eight groups to maintain consistency. Each session was tape recorded, the tapes being transcribed later into a report and presentation to the retailer's board of directors. Two sessions were video recorded, and several were 'secretly viewed' by the company's marketing executives.

Group composition	Social class	Location
1 Male 25–39, white-collar commuters[†]	A, B	Eastcheap
2 Male 40–55, white-collar commuters	A, B	Hitchin
3 Female 25–44, executives/PAs	A, B, C1	Bristol
4 Female 25–44, semi-skilled	C2	Woking
5 Female 35–40 'housewives'[†]	A, B	Leamington
6 Female 25–34, 'housewives'	C1, C2	Sheffield
7 Male 18–29, young earners[†]	C1, C2	Ealing
8 Female 18–29, young earners	C1, C2	Telford

Note: [†]Held in branches after hours

Questions for discussion

1. What are the strengths and benefits of focus group marketing research?

2. This retailer chose to commission a programme of focus groups. Given the aims of the company's research, what other research tools might the company have used? Explain your selection.

Sources: Lynne Cunningham, 'Electronic focus groups offer 3-way capability', *Marketing News*, 8 January 1990, pp. 22, 39; Thomas L. Greenbaum, 'Focus group spurt predicted for the '90s', *Marketing News*, 8 January 1990, pp. 21, 22; Nino DeNicola, 'Debriefing sessions: the missing link in focus groups', *Marketing News*, 8 January 1990, pp. 20, 22; Peter Jackson, *Adsearch*, Richmond, 1989, 2007, 2011; www.focusgroupsuk.com/ qualitative, April 2015.

Postscript

Academics and practitioners define marketing as involving the understanding and satisfying of customers. It is not possible to accomplish these requirements without a sound understanding of buying behaviour, the processes involved and the associated influencing factors. Accordingly, Part Two of *Marketing: Concepts and Strategies* has presented a comprehensive examination of the nature of consumer buying behaviour and then business-to-business buying behaviour.

Part Two has built on understanding customers' buying behaviour by examining one of the principal elements of marketing strategy: target market selection. The concept of market segmentation is of paramount importance to effective marketing and for many organizations guides their target market strategy. Part Two has explored target market selection and the creation of a brand positioning strategy. Over time, marketers develop knowledge of their markets. Many marketing decisions are based on this experience and on the intuition of the managers concerned. However, marketers often recognize that they do not fully understand their customers, competitors or aspects of the marketing environment forces. In such instances, they conduct marketing research. The nature and use of marketing research has also been discussed in Part Two of *Marketing: Concepts and Strategies*.

Before progressing, readers should be confident that they are now able to address the following:

Describe consumer buying behaviour

- Understand the different types of consumer buying behaviour.
- Recognize the stages of the consumer buying decision process and understand how this process relates to different types of buying decisions.
- Explore how personal factors may affect the consumer buying decision process.
- Learn about the psychological factors that may affect the consumer buying decision process.
- Examine the social factors that influence the consumer buying decision process.
- Understand why it is important for marketers to attempt to understand consumer buying behaviour and the role of this behaviour in marketing strategy.

- Appreciate the growing role of consumer-to-consumer communication and the digital environment on buying behaviour.

Describe business-to-business buying behaviour

- Become familiar with the various types of business market.
- Identify the major characteristics of business buyers and transactions.
- Understand several attributes of business demand.
- Become familiar with the major components of a buying centre.
- Understand relationship marketing and exchanges between business buyers and sellers.
- Understand the stages of the business buying decision process and the factors that affect this process.
- Learn how to select and analyze business target markets.
- Appreciate some of the nuances of marketing business products.

Adopt the concept of market segmentation

- Understand the definition of a market.
- Recognize different types of market.
- Appreciate what is meant by market segmentation.
- Know the most commonly adopted bases for segmenting markets.
- Learn how companies go about segmentation.
- Understand the role and nature of customer relationship management (CRM).

Explain the process of target market selection

- Distinguish between the different segmentation targeting strategies.
- Understand targeting decisions for emerging opportunities.
- Discover how marketers prioritize target markets and select between market segments.
- Appreciate the importance of assessing sales potential, market share and value share in creating a target market strategy.
- Learn about strategies for positioning.
- Understand the role of customer value propositions in positioning.

Outline the core aspects of marketing research

- Understand the importance of marketing research in marketing decision-making.
- Distinguish between research and intuition in solving marketing problems.
- Learn the five basic steps of the marketing research process.
- Understand the fundamental methods of gathering data for marketing research.
- Gain a sense of the relative advantages and disadvantages of marketing research tools.
- Understand how tools such as databases, decision support systems and the internet facilitate marketing research.
- Learn about how digital trends, such as social media and big data, are creating opportunities for marketing research.
- Identify key ethical considerations in marketing research.

Reebok races into the urban market

Strategic case

Reebok's UK founder, Joseph Foster, produced some of the first ever running shoes with spikes, as athletes in the late 1890s wanted to run even faster. In 1924, J.W. Foster & Sons was making by hand the running shoes used in the 1924 Summer Games, as depicted in the hit film *Chariots of Fire*. In 1958, two of the founder's grandsons started a sister company called Reebok, named after a type of African gazelle. By 1979, three running shoe styles were introduced to the USA: at US$60 per pair, they were the most expensive on the market. In 1982, Reebok caught the market unawares with the launch of Freestyle, the first ever athletic shoe designed specifically for women. By the 1980s, Reebok was a publicly quoted company active in more than 170 countries. Continual product innovation and customer research gave the company leadership in most of its key target markets. But then Nike emerged.

Step Reebok followed in 1989, a totally revolutionary workout programme that led to millions of users across the globe. By 1992 the company was broadening its ranges to include footwear and clothing products linked to many sports. These moves were supported with major sponsorship deals linked with leading sports stars, teams and sporting events. Venus Williams was one of the Reebok stars. In the summer of 2008, Reebok and driving ace Lewis Hamilton announced a multi-year partnership at a spectacular 3D event in Amsterdam, home of Reebok's European Headquarters. At the event, Reebok unveiled 'The Athlete within the Driver,' giving media a rare insight into Hamilton's demanding fitness regime. Hamilton revealed how Reebok's Smoothfit training footwear and clothing range helped him to train better than ever before.

Flying JUKARI

Recently, Reebok has again transformed the way in which people train, with the creation of the JUKARI Fit to Fly workout programmes, based on Cirque du Soleil's artistry and Reebok's knowledge of fitness, as always building on the company's philosophy that it should be fun to stay in shape and that sport and life are entwined for the good of the individual. The workouts have been created on a specially-designed piece of equipment called the FlySet. The result is a workout that gives the sensation of flying while strengthening and lengthening the body through cardio, strength, balance and core training.

Reebok has also made a pledge to tone the butts and legs of women around the world with its innovative EasyTone footwear. Featuring first-of-its-kind balance pod technology, the shoe generates incredible results thanks to proprietary technology invented by a former NASA engineer.

German Adidas-owned Reebok wants to give front-runner Nike a run for its money in the race for market share in athletic footwear, clothing and equipment. Reebok, now based in Massachusetts, USA, gained speed from the 1980s into the early 1990s by marketing special aerobics shoes for women, before Nike pulled ahead with new clothing and equipment endorsed by high-profile athletes such as Michael Jordan and Tiger Woods. Nike has remained the market leader, completely out distancing all competitors to dominate the industry with a 35 per cent share of the market. In contrast, Reebok's market share is about half that of Nike's. Now Reebok is seeking to close the gap by changing its selection of target markets. In the process, Reebok is aiming to change consumers' perceptions of and attitudes towards its brand and its products, with the objective of boosting both sales and profits.

Breaking tradition with hip-hop

Traditionally, manufacturers of athletic shoes have captured market attention by signing successful or up-and-coming sports stars to promote their shoes. Reebok still likes to link its brand to popular sports and individual champions. The fierce rivalry with Nike continues on the playing field: Reebok has lucrative contracts to make branded hats for the US National Basketball Association (NBA) and to supply the US National Football League (NFL) with uniforms and equipment, while Nike has an exclusive contract to provide performance wear to all 30 Major League Baseball teams. Many other sports around the world are similarly supported by Reebok and Nike, including stadia, teams and individual players.

Looking beyond sports, Reebok's marketers investigated the urban market, where fashion, rather than performance, is the deciding factor in buying decisions. Urban teens tend to be extremely style-conscious, buying as many as ten pairs of athletic shoes a year so they can be seen in the very latest thing. In the US, many are also fans of hip-hop music and buy clothing designed by hip-hop celebrities such as Jay-Z, Sean 'P. Diddy' Combs and Russell Simmons. Reebok's marketing research confirmed this market's considerable buying power and the influence of hip-hop artists. To reach this market effectively, Reebok needed a new brand, new products and new promotional efforts: the Reebok brand did not have a suitably desirable image with this youth market in any of the company's principle countries of operation. First, the company took the focus off its mainstream Reebok brand by creating Rbk as a new brand specifically for the urban market. Next, it partnered with hip-hop artists such as Jay-Z and 50 Cent to develop special footwear collections, backed by targeted promotional efforts emphasizing style with attitude.

New street credibility

Reebok found it was tapping into a significant marketing opportunity. Soon after it introduced its soft leather, flat-soled S. Carter shoes – after Jay-Z's original name, Shawn Carter – the line sold out. Demand for the US$100 shoes quickly peaked, leading to eager buyers bidding up to US$250 for one pair on the eBay auction website. Within eight months, the company had shipped 500 000 pairs to retailers around the USA and was preparing to launch a second S. Carter shoe.

On the back of this success, Reebok introduced G-Unit footwear, named after a hit song by rapper 50 Cent, who says that 'Reebok's Rbk Collection is the real thing when it comes to connecting with the street and hip-hop culture.' Hip-hop's Eve was also asked to design a shoe. 'She is one of the first artists in the campaign who has male and female appeal, urban and suburban,' observed Reebok's director of global advertising; 'she is as much a fashion icon as a music icon'.

The company also found a way to bring sports and hip-hop together by launching the 13 Collection line of shoes by basketball star Allen Iverson. Iverson promoted the line by appearing in a series of fast-paced adverts filmed in rap video style. Although he was shown playing basketball for a second or two, the adverts focused more on his off-court style than his on-court technique.

Despite the added credibility that such celebrities bring to the Rbk brand, the strategy entails some risks. Fads in street fashion and music can come and go at a dizzying pace, which means a shoe that is 'red hot' on one day may be 'ice cold' the next. Reebok could also suffer from negative repercussions if one of its celebrities runs into trouble. Still, the company's chief marketing executive is committed to the strategy. 'With athletes, they wear the shoes for the length of a basketball season,' he comments. 'With hip-hop, the publicity is intense but short, just like movies.' The advantage, in his view, is that, 'you'll know very quickly whether you hit or miss'.

Targeting urban markets in China

In pursuit of growth, Reebok is also targeting promising global markets, with China high on its list of priorities. Interest in sports is skyrocketing in China, thanks in part to Chinese basketball star Yao Ming's move to the NBA. According to the company's research, 93 per cent of Chinese males aged 13–25, a prime market for athletic shoes, watch NBA broadcasts on a regular basis. Reebok's Asia-Pacific general manager cites one projection showing 50 per cent annual growth in footwear sales, stating that, 'it's hard to say what the [actual sales] numbers are going to be, but they are going to be huge'. China's successes at the 2004 Olympics in Athens merely fuelled market growth, which simply exploded when China then staged the 2008 Games.

To make the most of this opportunity, Reebok set up 'Yao's House' basketball courts around central Shanghai. Each features the Reebok trademark and a giant *Sports Illustrated* cover showing the basketball star. By giving teens and young adults a place to hone their slam-dunks, Reebok hopes to shape their attitudes towards its products. 'The trends [in China] are made in the urban areas and on street basketball courts, just like in the United States,' says one Reebok executive. Reebok is not the only athletic shoe manufacturer entering this market. Nike sponsors a basketball court in Beijing, New Balance is building awareness of its shoes, and Pony is selling sneakers in Beijing, Shanghai and Guandong.

Reebok's 'vector'

Nike has one of the most recognized trademarks in the world and now Reebok has its Vector, a streamlined trademark designed to communicate the brand's attributes in a fast and fun way. The idea is to make the Vector synonymous with Reebok, just as the Swoosh is synonymous with Nike. 'Our research suggests that consumers react better to logos than words, and it's a very effective marketing tool,' stresses Reebok's head of marketing.

In addition, the company is giving its brand a touch of glamour with 'showcase stores' in major cities. In New York City, for example, Reebok opened a new men's store right next to its women's store. Both feature footwear, clothing and accessories, and both share the building with the Reebok Sport Club/NY. The displays are as stylish as the products, showing a mix of cashmere sweaters, jackets, wrist-watches and sunglasses along with shoes. 'We want people to say, "I didn't know Reebok made that",' noted Reebok's director of retailing.

Questions for discussion

1. What segmentation variables is Reebok using for its products? Why are these variables appropriate?

2. Which of the three targeting strategies is Reebok applying? Explain.

3. What influences on the consumer buying decision process appear to have the most impact on Reebok's customers' purchase decisions?

Sources: http://corporate.reebok.com/en/reebok_ history/default.asp. July 2011. www.adidas-group.com/en/group/history. April 2015.

PART THREE

Marketing programmes – products and services, brands, place and channels, promotion and marketing communications, digital and pricing

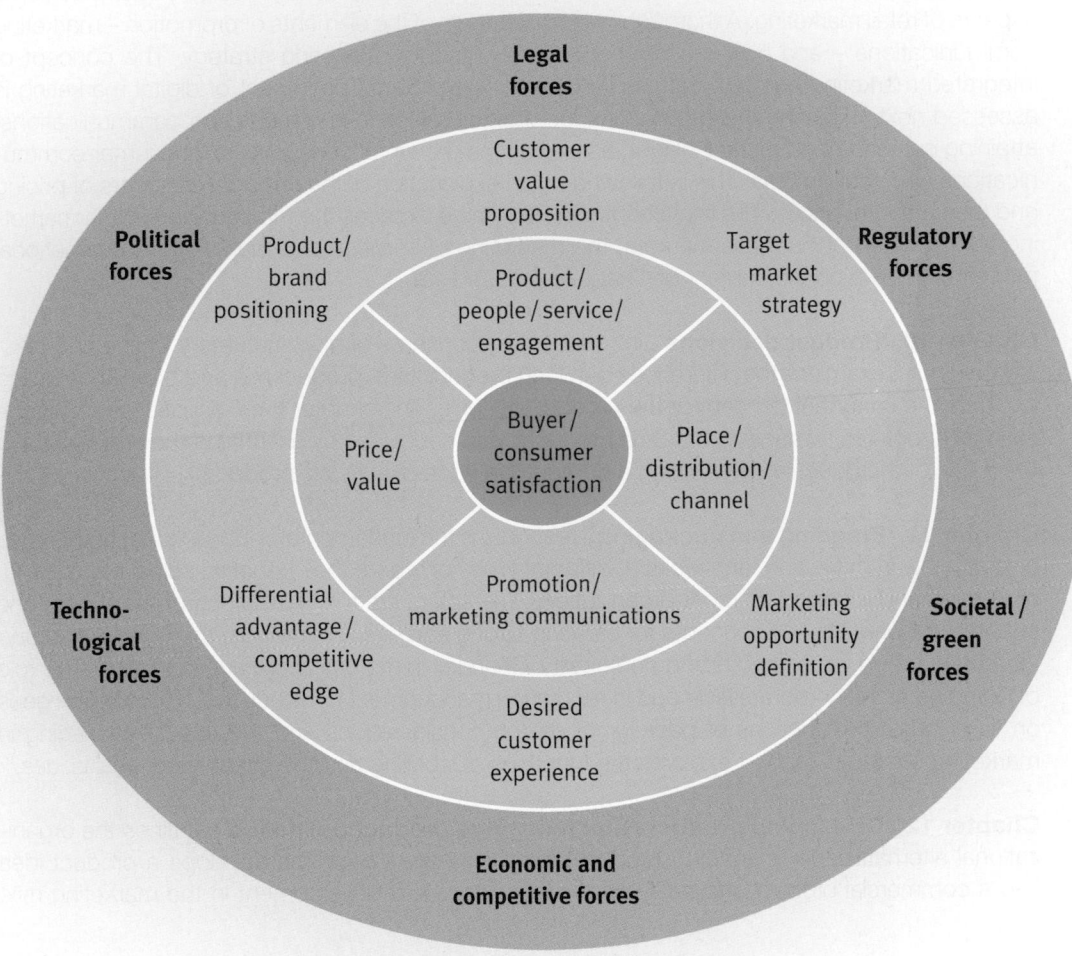

In Chapter 1, marketing was said to involve marketing opportunity analysis, target market selection and the development of a marketing mix for each target market. The marketing mix is the set of activities deployed by marketing managers in order to implement a company's agreed marketing strategy. The marketing mix centres on the '5Ps' of product, people, place/distribution, promotion and pricing decisions. The marketing mix must endeavour to match the identified needs of target consumers or business customers in order to satisfy these customers' requirements. It must also communicate the desired brand or product positioning, support the agreed customer value proposition and emphasize any differential advantage held by a business and its products over rivals. As explained in Chapters 1 and 2, marketers should first analyze the forces of the marketing environment, customer buying behaviour, competitors' strategies and their own organizational capabilities and performance before developing their marketing strategies. The marketing mix for a specific target market segment should only be specified once the marketing strategy has been formulated and agreed by senior management … analyses first, followed by strategy, and only then should marketing programmes be specified and executed.

Part Three of *Marketing: Concepts and Strategies* examines the marketing mix, commencing with the product and people ingredients of the marketing mix, the integral issues of branding, packaging and customer service, as well as the important concepts of the product life cycle and the management of product portfolios. Next, Part Three addresses the nature of marketing channels, wholesalers and distributors, the physical distribution of products and services, plus some aspects of retail marketing. A thorough overview follows of the elements of promotion – marketing communications – and how the promotional mix fits into marketing strategy. The concept of integrated marketing communications (IMC) is also explored. The impact of digital marketing is assessed next, exploring the implications for channel selection and marketing communications, attaining customer and market insight, as well as the growth of consumer-to-consumer communications and social media. This is followed by an explanation of the principal concepts of pricing and the setting of prices. The final chapter in Part Three explores the manipulation of the marketing mix to cater for business markets, the marketing of services and marketing in international markets, building on the content of Chapters 4, 6 and 13.

Chapter 10, 'Product decisions', introduces the concepts of how marketers define and classify products; examines the differences between product item, product line and product mix; and explores the important concept of the product life cycle. The chapter then discusses the organizational structures available to manage products, and concludes by examining the importance of the levels of a product in determining a competitive edge over rivals' products.

Chapter 11, 'Branding and packaging', recognizes the fundamental importance of brands and brand equity in marketing, and looks at different types of brand, their benefits, selection, naming, protection and licencing. In most organizations, marketers are the champions of the brand. The chapter presents the key concepts for creating strong and effective brands, then explores brand attributes, brand values and brand personality. Changes in the digital era are examined. The role of branding at the corporate level and in reputation management is introduced. The chapter goes on to discuss the functions of packaging, design considerations and the role of packaging in marketing strategy. Finally, it explores the functions of labelling and the associated legal issues.

Chapter 12, 'Developing products and managing product portfolios', outlines the organizational alternatives for managing products, explains how a business develops a product idea into a commercial product and analyzes the role of product development in the marketing mix.

The chapter includes a discussion of how products should be managed during the various stages of a product's life cycle. It discusses how existing products can be modified and how product deletion can sometimes benefit a marketing mix. The chapter concludes with a look at some of the related analytical tools associated with the planning of a product portfolio: the BCG product portfolio analysis, the market attractiveness-business position model or directional policy matrix (DPM) and the ABC sales: contribution analysis.

Chapter 13, 'The marketing of services', explores how services differ from tangible goods and considers the implications for marketers. The chapter begins by explaining the nature and characteristics of services, classifying services and the development of marketing strategies for services. It goes on to discuss the significant problems encountered in developing a differential advantage for a service and also addresses the crucial concept of service quality. The chapter then explores the concept of marketing in non-business or not-for-profit situations, the development of marketing strategies in non-business organizations and methods for controlling non-business marketing activities. The ways in which marketers handling services manipulate the ingredients of the marketing mix are explored further in Chapter 21.

Chapter 14, 'Marketing channels', explains the marketing channel concept, the role of supply chain management, the functions and different types of marketing channel. The chapter considers channel integration and the levels of market coverage, and then examines the selection of distribution channels, including the increasingly popular options of direct marketing and online. The impact of multi-channel management on marketing is considered. Behavioural aspects of channels, particularly the concepts of cooperation and relationship building, conflict and leadership, are then explored. The chapter concludes by examining legal issues in channel management.

Chapter 15, 'Channel players and physical distribution', presents a description of the nature of wholesaling in its broadest forms in the marketing channel, explains channel players' activities and their classification, examines agencies which facilitate wholesaling and explores some changing patterns in wholesaling and distribution. Next the nature of retailing within marketing channels is examined. The chapter then moves on to discuss physical distribution management and objectives. It explains order processing, materials handling, and different types of warehousing and their objectives. The chapter then examines inventory management. The chapter also highlights transport options for marketers.

Chapter 16, 'An overview of marketing communications', discusses the role of promotion in the marketing mix, the process of communication *per se*, the nature of marketing communications and the way in which the concept of the product adoption process relates to promotional activity. The chapter goes on to explain the aims of promotion and the elements of the promotional mix. The chapter concludes by examining the factors that influence the selection of promotional mix ingredients. Throughout the chapter, the notion of integrated marketing communications (IMC) is discussed.

Chapter 17, 'Advertising, public relations and sponsorship', takes these three aspects of the promotional mix and explores their use in more detail. The chapter commences by describing the nature and uses of advertising, and then examines the steps and personnel involved in developing an advertising campaign. The emphasis then switches to the nature of publicity and public relations. Finally, the chapter explores the rapidly evolving specialist area of sponsorship.

Chapter 18, 'Sales management, sales promotion, direct mail, the internet, digital and direct marketing', begins by examining the nature and major purposes of personal selling, along with the basic steps in the personal selling process. It identifies the types of salesforce personnel and goes on to explore the nature of sales management. Key account management is also examined. The chapter explains the uses of sales promotion and the wide range of related activities, and then focuses on the role of direct mail in the promotional mix. The expanding role of the web and digital applications are explored. The chapter concludes with an overview of direct marketing.

Chapter 19, 'Digital marketing', builds on the previous chapter to explore how digital has impacted on consumer behaviour and decision-making; the new requirements of understanding search engine management and content marketing, types of digital media and multi-screen marketing; the all-important issue of social media strategy; the exciting options provided by mobile marketing; email marketing and online public relations; the way in which digital is driving innovation like never before; turning 'big data' into meaningful insights; and, the challenges for organizations in deciding on a channel-to-market strategy, addressing multiple channels and restructuring their operations to manage these choices.

Chapter 20, 'Pricing', explains the characteristics and role of price in marketing, outlines the differences between price and non-price competition, explores the factors affecting pricing decisions and examines different pricing objectives. The chapter then discusses perceived value for money before turning to the complex aspect of pricing in business markets. The chapter analyzes the concept of economic value to the customer. The chapter explores the eight major stages in the process used to establish prices. In doing so, the chapter considers various activities that must be addressed: selecting pricing objectives; assessing the target market's evaluation of price and ability to buy; determining the demand for a product; and analyzing the relationships between demand, costs and profits.

Chapter 21, 'Modifying the marketing mix for business markets, services and in international marketing', recognizes the reality of formulating the marketing mix in a variety of complex business environments. The chapter commences by explaining why in many situations the basic marketing mix requires modification. It examines the nature of the marketing mix for business and organizational markets, and presents the complex and extended marketing mix required for services. To conclude, the chapter highlights the many additional issues considered by marketers involved with global markets and relates them to the development of the marketing mix.

By the conclusion of Part Three of *Marketing: Concepts and Strategies,* readers should understand the core product decisions that must be made in determining a marketing mix, including branding, packaging, people and service issues, as well as the management of product life cycles and portfolios of products. Readers should understand decisions concerning marketing channels and distribution in the marketing mix and they should appreciate the essential decisions concerning marketing communications, the nature of integrated marketing communications and the composition of the promotional mix within the marketing mix. The step-change brought about by the digital era should be apparent. Readers should understand the core pricing decisions required in the formulation of the marketing mix. In addition, readers should understand why in certain circumstances – notably for business-to-business markets, the marketing of services and when involved with international marketing – the standard marketing mix requires modification and manipulation.

CHAPTER 10
Product decisions

Marketers must have appropriate and desirable products in order to satisfy customers and fend off competitors

Objectives

To learn how marketers define products.

To define product levels.

To understand how to classify products.

To become familiar with the concepts of product item, product line and product mix.

To understand the concept of product life cycle.

To understand the types of organizational structure used to manage products.

To grasp the importance of the levels of a product in determining a competitive edge.

INTRODUCTION

The product is defined as everything that is received by a customer in an exchange or transaction. It is a complexity of tangible and intangible attributes, including functional, social, economic and psychological utilities or benefits.[1] A product can be a physical good, a service, an idea, or any combination of these three. This definition also covers supporting services that go with goods, such as installation, guarantees, product information and promises of repair or maintenance. In other words, the product is everything the consumer or business customer receives.

The product is a key element of the marketing mix and is central to a company's marketing proposition. Without the 'right' product, it is unlikely that marketers will be able to satisfy their customers and persuade them to become repeat buyers. As will be explored in this chapter, there is much more to the product component of the marketing mix than the actual tangible product or the service supplied to a customer.

A successful product will not remain so indefinitely. Marketers must judge when to modify their products, launch new ones and delete existing perhaps once highly successful products. While identifying a new product that will prove successful is challenging for marketers, knowing when to cut a product and walk away from it, is often harder.

Innocent product development

Hello, we're Innocent

... and we're here to make it easy for people to do themselves some good (whilst making it taste nice, too).

We started Innocent in 1999 after selling our smoothies at a music festival. We put up a big sign asking people if they thought we should give up our jobs to make smoothies, and put a bin saying 'Yes' and a bin saying 'No' in front of the stall. Then we got people to vote with their empties. At the end of the weekend, the 'Yes' bin was full, so we resigned from our jobs the next day and got cracking.

Since then we've started making veg pots, juices and kids' drinks, in our quest to make natural, delicious, healthy foods that help people live well and die old.

Now largely owned by Coca-Cola, Innocent has not lost its zany humour and health-conscious ethos, despite growing to be a £200 million business and the number one smoothie maker in Europe. Available in 15 countries, there are offices in Copenhagen, Hamburg and Salzburg as well as in the UK. Innocent was the official provider of smoothies and juices at the London Olympics.

First came its smoothies and then variations for children. Product development has been at the heart of Innocent's success. The Innocent Kids range now includes juice, fruity water, fruit tubes – a sneaky way for encouraging children claiming to dislike fruit to eat more healthily – and, of course, smoothies. Veg Pots brought Innocent out of the drinks section in supermarkets and diversified into food and vegetables. Noodle Pots have followed this success.

Juicy Water became so successful that its profits outstripped those of the Innocent brand. Innocent Bubbles is a recent innovation, bringing to consumers a lightly sparkling blend of fruit juice and spring water in cans. There is also a line of Innocent 100 per cent Coconut Water. Perhaps one of the company's most daring moves was to take on head-to-head PepsiCo's Tropicana in the juice market, with the 2011 launch of Innocent Juices, now firmly established on the fixtures of leading supermarkets.

Some ideas have been tested and dropped. Innocent's ice cream came out well in consumer trials, but was not brought to market because of production and channel complexities and a fear by the founders that ice cream would distract them from the core business's growth. A complete departure has been the opening of the Innocent café concept. The first outlet in Shoreditch (London) on day one served 5000 customers their five-a-day in great style.

So what next for Innocent? More drinks? An extension to the Kids range? Perhaps more foods? Maybe ice cream will appear in Innocent's quirky packaging and with its whacky humour? Or, as indicated by the departure into cafes, will the Innocent brand pop up somewhere very unexpected? No matter the eventual outcome, product development and a growing portfolio will be part of this marketing success story's onwards strategy.

Sources: www.innocentdrinks.co.uk/us/our-story, April 2015; Waitrose Kenilworth, April 2015.

Product
Everything, both favourable and unfavourable, tangible and intangible, received in an exchange of an idea, service or good.

Products, such as the smoothies and veg pots devised by Innocent, are among a company's most crucial and visible contacts with buyers. If a company's products do not meet its customers' desires, the company will have to adjust its offering in order to survive. Developing a successful **product** requires knowledge of fundamental marketing and product concepts. This chapter starts by introducing and defining the concepts that help clarify what a product is, and looks at how buyers view products. The next section examines the concepts of product mix and product line as an introduction to product planning. The chapter then explores the stages of the product life cycle. Each life-cycle stage generally requires a specific marketing strategy, operates within a certain competitive environment and has its own sales and profit pattern. The final section discusses the constituent elements that make up a product.

What is a product?

Good
A tangible physical entity.

A **good** is a tangible physical entity, such as a bottle of Pantene shampoo, a loaf of Hovis bread, a Muse CD or an iPad. A **service**, by contrast, is intangible; it is the result of the application of human and mechanical efforts to people or objects. Examples of services include hairdressing, tennis tuition and medical treatment. Chapter 13 provides a detailed discussion of services marketing. **Ideas** are concepts, philosophies, images or issues. They provide the psychological stimulus to solve problems. For example, Oxfam provides famine relief and attempts to improve the long-term prospects of people in hunger-stricken countries by raising awareness of these issues.

Service
The application of human and mechanical efforts to people or objects in order to provide intangible benefits to customers.

When buyers purchase a product, they are really buying the benefits and satisfaction they think the product will provide. A pair of adidas football boots, for example, is purchased for status and image, not just to protect the feet. Services, in particular, are bought on the basis of anticipated satisfaction. Promises, with the images and appearances of symbols, help consumers make judgements about tangible and intangible products.[2] Symbols and cues are often used to make intangible products more tangible to the consumer. Intel's famous Blue Men imagery personalized computer chips and differentiated Intel very effectively from rival chip producers.

Ideas
Concepts, philosophies, images or issues that provide the psychological stimulus to solve problems or adjust to the environment.

Classifying products

Products fall into one of two general categories. **Consumer products** are purchased to satisfy personal and family needs. **Industrial** or **business products** are bought for use in a company's operations or to make other products. The same item can be both a consumer product and an industrial product. For example, when consumers purchase lightbulbs for their homes, they are classified as consumer products. However, when a large company purchases lightbulbs to provide lighting in a factory or office the same goods are considered industrial products. Thus the buyer's intent, or the ultimate use of the product, determines whether an item is classified as a consumer or a business product. It is common for more people to be involved in buying a business product than in a consumer purchase. Chapters 5 and 6 explained the differences in buying and decision-making for consumer and business-to-business products.

Consumer products
Items purchased to satisfy personal or family needs.

Industrial/business products
Items bought for use in a company's operations or to make other products.

It is important to know about product classifications because different classes of product are aimed at particular target markets, and classification affects distribution, promotion and pricing decisions. Furthermore, the types of marketing activity and effort needed differ according to how a product is classified. This section examines the characteristics of consumer and business products and explores the marketing activities associated with some of them.

Consumer products

The most widely accepted approach to classifying consumer products relies on the common characteristics of consumer buying behaviour. It divides products into four categories: convenience, shopping, speciality and unsought products. However, not all buyers behave in the same way when purchasing a specific type of product. Thus, a single product can fit into more than one category. To minimize this problem, marketers think in terms of how buyers *generally* behave when purchasing a specific item. In addition, they recognize that the 'correct' classification can be determined only by considering a particular company's intended target market and the needs of customers within targeted market segments.

Convenience products

Relatively inexpensive, frequently purchased and rapidly consumed items on which buyers exert only minimal purchasing effort are called **convenience products**. They range from chocolate, magazines and chewing gum to petrol and soft drinks. The buyer spends little time planning the purchase or comparing available brands or sellers. Even a buyer who prefers a specific brand will readily choose a substitute if the preferred brand is not conveniently available. They are low-risk frequently bought items.

Convenience products
Inexpensive, frequently purchased and rapidly consumed items that demand only minimal purchasing effort.

Classifying a product as a convenience product has several implications for a company's marketing strategy. A convenience product is normally marketed through many retail outlets. As sellers experience high inventory turnover, the per unit gross margins can be relatively low. Producers of convenience products such as PG Tips tea and Domestos bleach expect little promotional effort at the retail level and so must provide their own through advertising, sales promotion and the item's packaging. The package may have an especially important role to play, because many convenience items are available only on a self-service basis at the retail level. On-pack sales promotion and point-of-sale displays are ways to maximize the impact of the package (see Figure 10.1). Such products are known as low-involvement products because, as explored in Chapter 5, consumers spend very little time considering their purchase and there is little opportunity for marketers to persuade consumers to examine alternatives ... except for price discounting and prominent point-of-sale offers.

Shopping products

Items that are chosen more carefully than convenience products are called **shopping products**. They are purchased infrequently and are expected to last a long time. Buyers are willing to expend effort in planning and purchasing these items. They allocate time for comparing stores and brands with respect to prices, credit, product features, qualities, services and perhaps guarantees. Appliances, furniture, bicycles, mp3 players, jewellery and cameras are examples of shopping products. Even though shopping products are more expensive than convenience products, few buyers of shopping products are particularly brand loyal. If they were, they would be unwilling to shop and compare brands.

Shopping products
Items chosen more carefully than convenience products; consumers will expend effort in planning and purchasing these items.

Marketers seeking to market shopping products effectively must consider that they require fewer retail outlets than convenience products. As they are purchased less frequently, inventory (stock) turnover is lower and middlemen (retailers) expect to receive higher gross margins. Although large sums of money may be required to advertise shopping products, an even larger proportion of resources is likely to be used for personal selling. Indeed, the quality of the service may be a factor in the consumer's choice of outlet. Thus, a couple that buys a new dishwasher might expect sales personnel in the chosen retail outlet to explain the advantages and features of competing brands. In many cases, the producer and the middlemen also expect some cooperation from one another with respect to providing parts and repair services, and performing promotional activities.

Speciality products

Products that possess one or more unique characteristics and which a significant group of buyers is willing to expend considerable effort to obtain are called **speciality products**. Buyers plan the purchase of a speciality product carefully; they know exactly what they want and will not accept a substitute. An example of a speciality product is a painting or a Cartier watch. When searching for speciality products, buyers do not compare alternatives; they are concerned primarily with finding an outlet that has a pre-selected product available.

Speciality products
Items that possess one or more unique characteristics; consumers of speciality products plan their purchases and will expend considerable effort to obtain them.

The marketing of a speciality product is very distinctive. The exclusivity of the product is accentuated by the fact that speciality products are often distributed through a limited number of retail outlets. Some companies go to considerable lengths to control this aspect of their distribution. Like shopping goods, speciality products are purchased infrequently, causing lower inventory turnover and thus requiring relatively high gross margins.

Unsought products Products that are purchased when a sudden problem arises, or when aggressive selling obtains a sale that otherwise would not take place, are called **unsought products**. The consumer does not usually expect to buy these products regularly. Emergency windscreen replacement services and graveyard headstones are examples of unsought products. Life insurance and pension schemes are examples of unsought products that often need aggressive personal selling.

Unsought products
Items that are purchased when a sudden problem arises or when aggressive selling is used to obtain a sale that would not otherwise take place.

Business products

Business products are usually purchased on the basis of a company's goals and objectives. The functional aspects of these products are usually more important than the psychological rewards sometimes associated with consumer products. Business products can be classified into seven categories according to their characteristics and intended uses:

1. raw materials
2. major equipment
3. accessory equipment
4. component parts
5. process materials
6. consumable supplies
7. industrial/business services.[3]

Raw materials
The basic materials that become part of physical products.

Raw materials The basic materials that become part of physical products are **raw materials**. These include minerals, chemicals, agricultural products, and materials from forests and oceans. They are usually bought and sold in relatively large quantities according to grades and specifications.

Major equipment
Large tools and machines used for production purposes.

Major equipment Large tools and machines used for production purposes, such as cranes and spray painting machinery, are types of **major equipment**. Major equipment is often expensive, may be used in a production process for a considerable length of time and is often custom-made to perform specific functions. For example, Alsthom manufactures purpose-built large gears and turbines. Other items are more standardized, performing similar tasks for many types of company. Due to major equipment

FIGURE 10.1
Confectionery brands are convenience products

being so expensive, purchase decisions are often long and complex and may be made by senior management. Marketers of major equipment are frequently called upon to provide a variety of services, including installation, training, repair, maintenance assistance and financing. This may lead to long-term relationships being developed between suppliers of major equipment and their customers.

Accessory equipment
Tools and equipment used in production or office activities that do not become part of the final physical product.

Accessory equipment   Equipment that does not become a part of the final physical product, but is used in production or office activities is referred to as **accessory equipment**. Examples include telephone systems, stationery supplies, fractional horsepower motors and tools. Compared with major equipment, accessory items are usually much cheaper, are purchased routinely with less negotiation and are treated as expenditure items rather than capital items because they are not expected to last long. More outlets are required for distributing accessory equipment than for major equipment, but sellers do not have to provide the multitude of services expected of major equipment marketers.

Component parts
Parts that become a part of the physical product and are either finished items ready for assembly or products that need little processing before assembly.

Component parts   Parts that become part of the physical product and are either finished items ready for assembly or products that need little processing before assembly are called **component parts**. Although they become part of a larger product, component parts can often be easily identified and distinguished. Tyres, spark plugs, gears, lighting units, screws and wires are all component parts of a delivery van. Buyers purchase such items according to their own specifications or industry standards. They expect the parts to be of specified quality and delivered on time so that production is not slowed or stopped. Producers that are primarily assemblers, such as most washing machine or lawnmower manufacturers, depend heavily on suppliers of component parts.

Process materials
Materials used directly in the production of other products, but not readily identifiable.

Process materials   Materials that are used directly in the production of other products are called process materials. Unlike component parts, **process materials** are not readily identifiable. For example, Reichhold Chemicals markets a treated fibre product: a phenolicresin, sheet-moulding compound used in the production of flight deck instrument panels and aircraft cabin interiors. Although the material is not identifiable in the finished aircraft, it retards burning, smoke and formation of toxic gas when subjected to fire or high temperatures.

Consumable supplies
Supplies that facilitate production and operations but do not become part of the finished product.

Consumable supplies   Supplies that facilitate production and operations, but do not become part of the finished product, are referred to as **consumable supplies**. Paper, print cartridges, pencils, oils, cleaning agents and paints are in this category. They are purchased by many different types of business. Consumable supplies are purchased routinely and sold through numerous outlets. To ensure that supplies are available when needed, buyers often deal with more than one seller. Consumable supplies can be divided into three subcategories: maintenance, repair and operating (or overhaul) supplies, and are sometimes called **MRO items**.

MRO items
Consumable supplies in the sub-categories of maintenance, repair and operating (or overhaul) supplies.

Industrial/business services
The intangible products that many organizations use in their operations, including financial, legal, marketing research, computer programming and operation, caretaking and printing services.

Industrial/business services   **Industrial/business services** are the intangible products that many organizations use in their operations. They include financial, human resource, legal, marketing research, computer programming and operation, facilities management, real estate, caretaking and printing services for business. Some companies decide to provide their own services internally, while others outsource them. This decision depends largely on the costs associated with each alternative and the frequency with which the services are needed.

The three levels of product

The product may appear obvious – a carton of fresh orange juice or a designer handbag – but generally the purchaser is buying much more than a drink or a means of carrying personal items. To be motivated to make the purchase, the product must have a perceived or real core benefit or service. This level of product, termed the **core product**, is illustrated in Figure 10.2. The **actual product** is a composite of several factors: the features and capabilities offered, quality and durability, design and product styling, packaging and – often of great importance – the brand name.

In order to make the purchase, the consumer often needs the assistance of sales personnel; there may be delivery and payment credit requirements and, for bulky or very technical products, advice regarding installation. The level of warranty back-up and after-sales support, particularly for innovative, highly technical or high value goods, will be of concern to most consumers. Increasingly, the overall level of customer service constitutes part of the purchase criteria, and in many markets it is deemed integral to the product on offer. These 'support' issues form what is termed the **augmented product** (see Figure 10.2).

When a £40 000 BMW 3 Series executive car is purchased, the vehicle's performance, specification and design may have encouraged the sale. Speed of delivery and credit payment terms may have been essential to the conclusion of the deal. The brand's image, particularly in the case of a car costing £40 000, will also have influenced the sale. Once behind the wheel of the BMW, its new owner will expect reliability and efficient, friendly, convenient service in the course of maintenance being required. The purchase might have been lost at the outset had the salesperson mishandled the initial enquiry. Repeat servicing business and the subsequent sale of another new car may be ruled out if the owner encounters incompetent, unhelpful service engineers. The core benefit may have been a car to facilitate journeys to work, transport for the family or the acquisition of a recognized status symbol. Customer satisfaction will depend on the product's actual performance and also on service aspects of the augmented product. This example is not unusual. For most consumer or business products and services, the consumer is

Core product
The level of a product that provides the perceived or real core benefit or service.

Actual product
A composite of the features and capabilities offered in a product, quality and durability, design and product styling, packaging and brand name.

Augmented product
Support aspects of a product, including customer service, warranty, delivery and credit, personnel, installation and after-sales support.

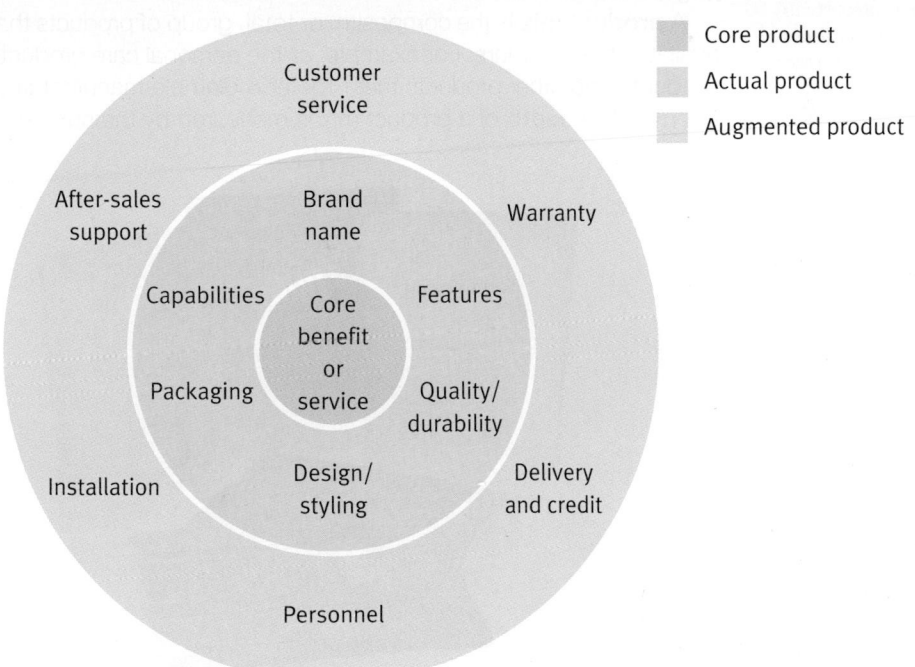

FIGURE 10.2
The three levels of product: core, actual and augmented

influenced by the three levels of the product: core, actual and augmented. Marketers need to take this into consideration when developing product offers. Careful consideration of all levels of the product can provide the basis for a competitive edge. Indeed, often it is aspects of the augmented product which make or break the relationship with the customer and can create differentiation vis-à-vis competing propositions.

Many marketers now recognize the important role that personnel play in product exchanges. People are responsible for the design, production, marketing, sale and distribution of products. As will be explained in Chapter 13, personnel are especially important in the sale and delivery of services. Thus, a financial services adviser must have considerable expertise in the sector to give good advice. Similarly, a good-quality haircut can only be delivered by a skilled hairdresser. As consumers, people make decisions and ultimately adopt products for use and consumption. When deciding which products to adopt and use, people now pay considerable attention to the skills, attitudes and motivations of personnel involved in the marketing channel. As explained in Chapter 1, personnel also constitute an essential ingredient of the marketing mix for consumer and business goods.

Product line and product mix

Marketers must understand the relationships between all their organization's products if they are to coordinate their marketing. The following concepts describe the relationships between an organization's products. A **product item** is a specific version of a product that can be designated as a distinct offering among a business's products for example, Procter & Gamble's Pantene shampoo. A **product line** includes a group of closely related product items that are considered a unit because of marketing, technical or end-use considerations. All the shampoos manufactured by Procter & Gamble constitute one of its product lines. Figure 10.3 illustrates a product line for Tilda. The Topical Insight box on page 307 explains how manufacturers of nicotine replacement products are expanding their product line to allow them to capitalize on the opportunities this market provides. To come up with the optimum product line, marketers must understand buyers' goals.[4] Specific items in a product line reflect the desires of different target markets or the different needs of consumers.

A **product mix** is the composite, or total, group of products that a company makes available to customers. For example, all the personal care products, laundry detergent products and other products that Procter & Gamble manufactures constitute its product mix. The **depth** of a product mix is measured by the number of different products

Product item
A specific version of a product that can be designated as a distinct offering among a business's products.

Product line
A group of closely-related product items that are considered a unit because of marketing, technical or end-use considerations.

Product mix
The composite group of products that a company makes available to customers.

Depth (of product mix)
The number of different products offered in each product line.

FIGURE 10.3
This advertisement for leading rice brand Tilda makes clear that the Tilda line includes a wide range of rice types

Laundry detergents	Toothpastes/ dental	Bar soaps	Deodorants	Shampoos	Tissue/towel
Ivory Snow 1930	Gleem 1952	Ivory 1879	Old Spice 1948	Head & Shoulders 1961	Charmin 1928
Dreft 1933	Crest 1955	Camay 1926	Secret 1956	Pantene Pro 1965	Puffs 1960
Tide 1946	Oral-B 2005	Zest 1952	Sure 1972	Vidal Sassoon 1974	Bounty 1965
Cheer 1950	Scope	Safeguard 1963		Pert Plus 1979	Royale 1996
Bold 1965		Olay 1993		Ivory 1983	
Gain 1966					
Era 1972					
Febreze 1998					

Product line depth (vertical axis label)

◄ Product mix width ►

FIGURE 10.4
The concepts of width of product mix and depth of product line applied to selected Procter & Gamble products

Source: Reproduced with permission from the Procter & Gamble Company.

Width (of product mix)
The number of product lines a company offers.

offered in each product line. The **width** of a product mix is measured by the number of product lines a company offers. Figure 10.4 shows the width of the product mix and the depth of each product line for selected Procter & Gamble products in the USA. Procter & Gamble is known for using distinctive technology, branding, packaging and consumer advertising to promote individual items in its detergent product line. Bold, Ariel, Daz and Dreft – all Procter & Gamble detergents – share similar distribution channels and manufacturing facilities. Yet due to variations in product formula and attributes, each is promoted as being distinct, adding depth to the product line.

Product life cycles

Product life cycle
The four major stages through which products move: introduction, growth, maturity and decline.

Just as biological cycles progress through growth and decline from birth to death, so too do **product life cycles**. A new product is introduced into the marketplace; it grows; it matures; and when it loses appeal and sales decline, it is terminated.[5] As explained in Chapter 12, different marketing strategies are appropriate at different stages in the product life cycle. Thus, packaging, branding and labelling techniques, price promotions and marketing communications can be used to help create or modify products that have reached different points in their life. Understanding a product's current position in its life cycle and modifying its strategy accordingly is a fundamental part of product management.

As Figure 10.5 shows, a product life cycle has four major stages:

1. introduction
2. growth
3. maturity
4. decline.

When a product moves through its cycle, the strategies relating to competition, promotion, place/distribution, pricing and market information must be evaluated periodically and possibly changed. Astute marketing managers use the life-cycle concept to make sure that the introduction, alteration and termination of a product are timed and executed properly. By understanding the typical life-cycle pattern, marketers are better able to maintain profitable products and drop unprofitable ones within their overall product portfolio.

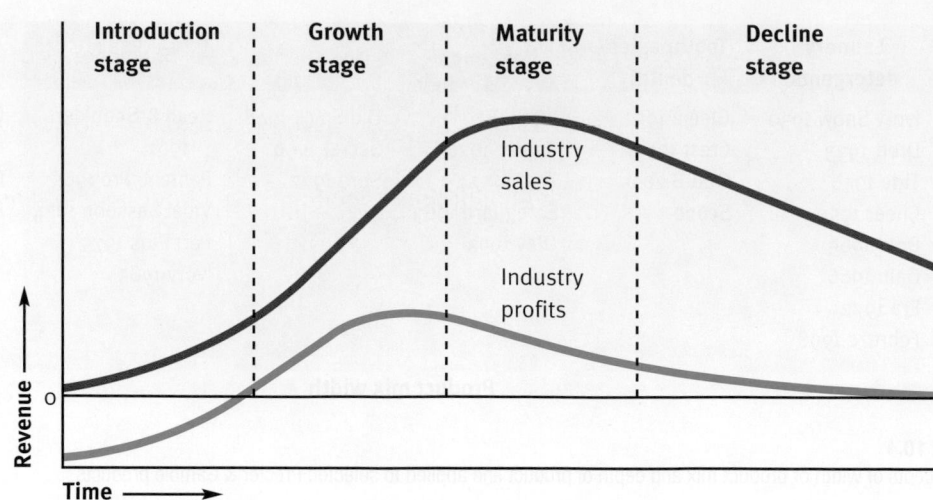

FIGURE 10.5
The four stages of
the product life cycle

Introduction

Introduction stage
A product's first
appearance in the
marketplace, before any
sales or profits have
been made.

The **introduction stage** of the life cycle begins at a product's first appearance in the marketplace, when sales are zero and profits are negative. Profits are below zero because a new product incurs development costs, initial revenues are low, and at the same time a company must generally incur the significant expenses incurred during promotion and distribution. As time passes, sales should move upwards from zero and profits should build up from the negative position (see Figure 10.5).[6]

As a result of cost, very few product introductions represent major inventions. Developing and introducing a new product can mean an outlay of many millions of pounds. The failure rate for new products is quite high, ranging from 60 to 90 per cent depending on the industry and on how product failure is defined. For example, in the food and drinks industry, 80 per cent of all new products fail. Typically, product introductions involve a new style of deodorant, a new type of vacuum cleaner or a new leisure concept rather than a major product innovation. In general, the more marketing-oriented the company, the more likely it will be to launch innovative products that are new to the market, such as Apple's never-ending stream of launches.[7]

New product ideas are more likely to be successful when senior management is involved in product development and launch. In addition, research shows that a clear, stable vision, flexibility and improvisation, information exchange and collaboration are also key ingredients in new product success.[8] Increasingly, consumers and supply chain partners are consulted in the

Co-creation
The involvement
of, or consultation
with, consumers and
supply chain partners
in the collaborative
development of new
products.

co-creation of new products, rather than only internally-led product development teams subsequently hoping consumers will be interested in their creations.

Potential buyers must be made aware of the new product's features, uses and advantages. Two difficulties may arise at this point. Only a few sellers may have the resources, technological knowledge and marketing know-how to launch the product successfully; and the initial product price may have to be high in order to recoup expensive marketing research or development costs. Given these difficulties, it is not surprising that many products never get beyond the introduction stage; indeed many are never launched commercially at all.

Growth stage
The stage at which a
product's sales rise
rapidly and profits reach
a peak, before levelling
off into maturity.

Growth

During the **growth stage**, sales rise rapidly, and profits reach a peak and then start to decline (see Figure 10.5). The growth stage is critical to a product's survival because competitive reactions to its success during this period will affect the product's life expectancy. For example, Mars successfully launched Ice Cream Mars, the first

Great things can happen when you sacrifice a cigarette

Topical insight

Patch, lozenge or gum, Nicotinell 'can double your chances of quitting compared to willpower alone', claims Novartis. Nicotine replacement therapy (NRT) fights nicotine dependence and relieves the symptoms of withdrawal in smokers who are trying to give up the habit. Leading brands include Nicotinell, NiQuitin CQ and Nicorette. Novartis, the company behind Nicotinell nicotine replacement patches has also launched food products designed to help smokers quit the habit. Many consumers are already familiar with patches, but as smoking becomes increasingly socially unacceptable, the company believes there are a variety of new product development opportunities for its brand. Novartis launched a nicotine replacement lozenge that, when sucked, provides a continual low-level boost of nicotine for relatively light smokers. Nicotinell Support Icemint Gum helps fight cravings as well as the weight gain endured by many quitting smokers. Supportive counselling services are viewed as a key part of the therapy and most of the leading players have examined how to offer services alongside their patches, gums, pills and lozenges.

It is not difficult to understand the attractions of the nicotine replacement therapy market and to appreciate why Novartis is seeking to extend its product offerings. As millions seek to leave their smoking habit behind, the market for nicotine replacement products is growing rapidly. Indications also show that 1 in 20 of those attempting to 'kick the habit' will use some form of nicotine replacement therapy. Not surprisingly, Novartis is not alone in seeking to develop its product range. Since NRT products were first launched in the UK more than two decades ago, several companies have dominated the market: Novartis, with its Nicotinell patch and gum; Pharmacia & Upjohn (P&U), with its Nicorette gum, inhalator and patches; and Boots, with its own-label patches and gum. Developments include Boots' inhalator and competing brand Nicorette's launch of its micro-tab, a kind of nicotine pill that, when placed under the tongue, takes half an hour to dissolve.

Perhaps the most aggressive challenge to the market has come from pharmaceutical giant SmithKline Beecham (SKB), which spent £12 million on the UK launch of NiQuitin CQ (CQ stands for 'committed quitters'). SKB claimed this to have been the largest ever over-the-counter launch in the UK. Clearly the company expected the brand, already the best-seller in the USA, to claim a large slice of the UK market. Company representatives suggested that this was achieved by the unique 'personalized literature pack' included with the NiQuitin CQ product. This pack featured a questionnaire for smokers to fill in, detailing the circumstances in which they are most vulnerable to lighting up. Advice was then offered tailored to match the answers provided in the questionnaire.

In such a volatile market, future trends are difficult to predict. When NRT products were first launched in the UK in 1993, they were met with considerable consumer excitement. However, following an initial growth in sales, consumer confidence in the capabilities of the products declined. Today, with the products widely available in supermarkets as well as pharmacies, and governments throughout the EU launching further anti-smoking measures, the key players are looking for innovative ways to ensure that their products play a major role in the continued fight against smoking. New product development is likely to be just part of the solution, with manufacturers also seeking a fresh and more realistic promotional stance. For Novartis, this involves repositioning the brand to stress its role in harm reduction and Nicotinell's role in supporting the quitter's willpower and resolve to stop smoking, while also making the Nicotinell product desirable.

The biggest threat to these products has not come from smokers' intransigence and a lack of interest in quitting. The last few years has seen the emergence of substitute competition in the form of e-cigarettes and vaping, with brands such as Aspire, Frenchy Fog, ProVape and Smok-e Mountain becoming increasingly familiar to smokers trying to quit or those combatting the ban on smoking indoors in bars and restaurants. Time will tell whether Novartis and the other players continue to meet the challenge from this alternative to their nicotine replacement products.

Sources: Novartis Consumer Healthcare, 2004–15;Boots, November 2007, March 2011 and April 2015; www.cloud9vaping.co.uk, April 2015; www.nicotinell.co.uk/ help-and-advice, April 2015.

ice-cream version of an established confectionery product. Today the product competes with more than a dozen other brands. Some of the competing brands failed quickly and others followed. Profits decline late in the growth stage as more competitors enter the market, driving prices down and creating the need for heavy promotional expenses. At this point a typical marketing strategy encourages strong brand loyalty, perhaps using sales promotion, and competes with aggressive emulators of the product. During the growth stage, a company tries to strengthen its market share and develop a competitive position by emphasizing the product's benefits. This is what the various smartphone providers are currently striving to achieve.

Aggressive promotional pricing, including price cuts, is typical during the growth stage. The smartphone industry is now well into its growth stage, and many competitors have entered the market. Companies like Samsung, HTC and Apple must battle hard to maintain their existing positions in this competitive arena, while the likes of Eriksson and Moto have gone and Blackberry and Sony struggle to maintain a foothold.

Maturity

Maturity stage
The stage during which a product's sales curve peaks and starts to decline, and profits continue to decline.

During the **maturity stage**, the sales curve peaks and starts to decline, and profits continue to decline (see Figure 10.5). This stage is characterized by severe competition, with many brands in the market. Competitors emphasize improvements and differences in their versions of the product. Inevitably, during the maturity stage, some weaker competitors are squeezed out or switch their attention to other products. For example, some broadband and mobile phone service providers are perishing or being acquired by rivals, now that these products are in the maturity stage.

During the maturity stage, the producers who remain in the market must make fresh promotional and distribution efforts. These efforts must focus on dealers as much as on consumers to ensure that brand visibility is maintained at the point-of-sale. Advertising and dealer-oriented promotions are typical during this stage of the product life cycle. The promoters must also take into account the fact that, as the product reaches maturity, buyers' knowledge of it attains a high level. Consumers of the product are no longer inexperienced generalists, but rather experienced specialists.

Decline

Decline stage
The last stage of a product's life cycle, during which sales fall rapidly.

During the **decline stage**, sales fall rapidly (see Figure 10.5). New technology or a new social trend may cause product sales to take a sharp downturn. For example, mp3 players and downloads have reduced CD sales, while smartphones have reduced sales of both mp3 players and cameras. When this happens, the marketer must consider pruning items from the product line to eliminate those not earning a profit. Sony surprised the market by announcing it would be pulling out of selling its well-regarded Vaio laptops and PCs. The decision came because Sony believed that technology changes are signalling a move away from these devices towards multifunctional smartphones and tablets.[9] At this time, the marketer may cut promotion efforts, eliminate marginal distributors and, finally, plan to phase out the product.

As most businesses have a product mix consisting of multiple products, a company's destiny is rarely tied to one product. A composite of life-cycle patterns is formed when various products in the mix are at different stages in the cycle. As one product is declining, other products are in the introduction, growth or maturity stage. Marketers must deal with the dual problems of prolonging the life of existing products and introducing new products to meet sales goals. More details of this kind of portfolio management activity are given in Chapter 12, which also explores the development of new products and considers how they can be managed in their various life-cycle stages.

Why some products fail and others succeed

Thousands of new products are introduced each year and many of them fail. Some estimates put the product failure rate as high as 60 to 90 per cent. Failure and success rates vary in different industries and from company to company. Figures suggest that consumer products are more likely to fail than those directed at business markets. Being one of the first brands launched in a product category is no guarantee of success. One study found that in 50 product categories, only half of the pioneers survived.[10]

Products fail for many reasons. One of the most common is the company's failure to match product offerings to customer needs. When products do not offer value and lack the features customers want, they fail in the marketplace. That is why it is important to identify what the customer value proposition will be, at the heart of a product's marketing strategy, as explained in Chapter 8. Ineffective or inconsistent branding has also been blamed for product failures. Other reasons often given for new product failure include technical or design problems, poor timing, over-estimation of market size, ineffective promotion and inefficient distribution. The problems leading to the downfall of Coca-Cola's UK launch of bottled water Dasani were widely debated in the press. Technical difficulties led to bromide contamination at the company's plant. At a time when consumers were already concerned about the purity of tap water, the withdrawal of the product was inevitable.[11] Another common reason for failure is a poor understanding of competitors and the merits of their products.

Degrees of product failure

It is important to distinguish between degrees of product failure. Absolute failure occurs when a company loses money on a new product because it is unable to recover development, production and marketing costs. Such a product is usually deleted from the product mix. Relative product failure occurs when a product returns a profit but does not meet a company's profit or market share objectives. If a relative product failure is repositioned or improved, it may become a successful member of the product line. Some products experience relative product failure after years of success. Drinks business Diageo stepped in to stem declining sales of Guinness stout. Part of this effort involved reformulating the canned version of the drink, to make its taste closer to that of draught Guinness. The cans were also redesigned to appeal to a younger segment of drinkers.

The ingredients for success

Despite this gloomy picture of product failure, some new products are very successful. Perhaps the most important ingredient for success is the product's ability to provide a significant and perceivable benefit to a sizeable number of customers. New products with an observable advantage over similar available products such as more features, ease of operation or improved technology have a greater chance of success, such as the iPhone or iPad.

Tangible and intangible product characteristics

When developing products, marketers make many decisions. Some of these involve the tangible, or physical, characteristics of the product; others focus on less tangible support services that are very much a part of the total product.

Physical characteristics and product quality

Quality
The core product's ability to achieve the basic functional requirements expected of it.

The question of how much **quality** to build into the product is crucial for marketers. In the core product, quality constitutes the product's ability to achieve the basic functional requirements expected of it. A major dimension of quality is durability. Higher quality often demands better materials and more expensive processing, which increases production costs and, ultimately, the product's price. How much the target market is prepared to pay will affect the level of quality specified. The concepts of quality and value are related. Consumers may be happy to pay a premium for a hard-wearing paint, because they perceive it as better value than competing offerings.

In general, a company should set consistent quality levels for all products with a similar brand. The quality of competing brands is also an important consideration. As explained in Chapter 9, marketing research plays an important role in determining the optimum physical features such as quality of a product.

Upgrading service for competitive advantage

Building customer relationships

Many consumers of high-tech products, such as computers and home entertainment systems, will have visited retailers only to find little more product information or advice available than is already printed in the manufacturers' brochures or in online product reviews. It is a frustrating experience to encounter a sales person with no more insight into the products on display than the naïve customer already has. A worse experience often befalls the user of a high-tech product which has failed and requires aftermarket support. Those days may be drawing to a close if retailer Dixons Stores Group has its way. Trading as PC World, Currys and Dixons, the company has a large share of the market for electrical goods, appliances and high-tech products.

Under its *Knowhow* programme, Dixons wants to be recognized by consumers for knowledge and service, rather than only the brands it stocks.

Knowhow is the new face of technology service and support – we want you to be able to enjoy your new product for years to come. From getting it home and setting it up, or helping you get the most from your technology, we are here to help with our knowhow. If your product lets you down, we can get you back up and running again.

You can find *Knowhow* at Currys and PC World, ready to offer friendly help and advice. We'll be there to deliver and install your new TV, washing machine or fridge freezer. We're at the end of the phone 24/7 or online with loads of useful hints, tips and guides. Whichever way you want to get in touch, we promise you this – we'll talk to you like a human being and won't use a lot of tech speak.

The *Knowhow Team* has experts in all areas of technology, whether it be kitchen appliances, computers, music players or gadgets. We've got:

- Our team of 500 technicians on the road visiting people at home.
- A 1400 strong team of experts in our UK Contact Centre helping people 24/7 every day of the year.
- 1000 people in our team of engineers fixing TVs, laptops and games consoles in our state of the art repair lab.
- A team of 700 installers fitting new washing machines, satellite dishes, dishwashers and cookers,

For Dixons Stores Group, the stated aim is to remove the 'wheel of uncertainty' for consumers purchasing technology products, often for large sums of money and which will be in the home for many years. Such high involvement purchases are often perceived as risky by consumers. This strategy also enables the company to fight back against online retailers by providing enhanced customer service.

DELIVER & INSTALL – we deliver the big stuff from Currys and PC World, and get you connected and plumbed in.

SET UP – don't wade through confusing manuals. We can get your gadgets set up and working in no time.

SUPPORT – the Knowhow Team is ready and waiting to give you friendly, expert advice and guidance over the phone or online. We never sleep so call us whenever you need us.

REPAIR & PROTECT – if something breaks don't panic. Our state of the art repair lab and nationwide technicians can get you back on the road.

Dixons' *Knowhow* brings much aftercare in-house and away from erratic subcontractors, consolidates the practices of the company's call centres, and boosts delivery and installation provision, and even recycling of old products no longer wanted by customers. The company has invested heavily in upgrading these service aspects of its operation so that consumers may purchase well-known brands with more certainty and confidence. The likes of Sony, HP or Whirlpool may well design and produce very attractive and reliable products, but for Dixons the expectation is that the wrap-around service component of its product offering will provide an edge over rivals and bolster consumer satisfaction.

Sources: 'Dixons upgrades service levels with a little Knowhow', Rosie Baker, *Marketing Week*, 25 November 2010, p. 11; 'Dixons sets up new technical support service Knowhow', Andrew Clark, *The Observer*, 21 November 2010; www.dixons.co.uk, March 2011; www.currys.com, April 2015; www.knowhow.com, April 2015.

Supportive product-related services

All products possess intangible features. When prospective customers are unable to experience the product in advance, they are making decisions based on promises of satisfaction.[12] A woman buying lingerie over the internet hopes that when the garments she ordered arrive, they will meet her expectations of quality, look and fit. Should she be disappointed, she will expect to be able to return the items. Arrangements for product returns are just one of many product-related services. Others include product guarantees, credit and repair facilities. Although these product features may be less tangible than the product itself, they are often a strong influence on the choices that customers make. Can you imagine buying an expensive watch with no guarantee, or a technology product that cannot be repaired? As the Building Customer Relationships box explains, Currys and PC World have turned to aspects of the augmented product in order to gain competitive advantage.

Guarantee
An agreement specifying what the producer or supplier will do if the product malfunctions.

The type of guarantee a company provides can be critical for buyers, especially when expensive, technically complex goods such as appliances are involved. A **guarantee** specifies what the producer or supplier will do if the product malfunctions. Some photographic processors offer free processing on prints not ready within 24 hours. A leading hotel group will not charge for room service meals if there is a long delay on the order being delivered to the hotel guest. Guarantors are legally required to state more simply and specifically the terms and conditions under which the company will take action. For example, changes in EU law now require electrical items to carry a two-year guarantee. Marketers are now using guarantees more aggressively as tools to give their brands a competitive advantage.

An effective guarantee should be unconditional, easy to understand and communicate, meaningful, easy to invoke and quick and easy to act on. The customer should be able to return a product and get a replacement, a refund or credit for the returned item. Such guarantees are beneficial because they generate feedback from customers and help build customer loyalty and sales.[13] Although it is more difficult to provide guarantees for services than for goods, some service marketers do guarantee customer satisfaction. For example, some opticians offering a one-hour turnaround for new lenses or frames do not charge customers who have to wait longer than this time.

Establishing a system to provide replacement parts and repair services is an essential support service for complex and expensive consumer or business products. For example, builders expect construction machinery manufacturers like Caterpillar to be able to provide replacement parts quickly and without fuss. Sometimes these services are provided directly to buyers, in other cases regional service centres or middlemen are used.

Finally, a company must sometimes provide credit services to customers. Even though credit services place a financial burden on a business, they can be beneficial. For instance, a company may acquire and maintain a stable market share. Many major oil companies, for example, have competed effectively against petrol discounters by providing credit services to distributors. The customer value proposition described for JCB in Chapter 8 reveals the importance of financing within JCB's proposition. For marketers of relatively expensive items, such as cars or soft furnishings, offering credit services enables a larger number of people to buy the product, thus enlarging the market for the item.

Summary

A *product* is everything that is received in an exchange. It is a complex set of tangible and intangible attributes, including functional, social, economic and psychological utilities or benefits. A product can be a good, a service, an idea or any combination of these three. Customers buy the benefits and satisfaction they think the product will provide.

Products can be classified on the basis of the buyer's intentions. *Consumer products* are purchased to satisfy personal and family needs. *Industrial* or *business products* are purchased for use in a company's operations or to make other products.

The same product may be classified as both a consumer product and a business product. Consumer products can be subdivided into *convenience*, *shopping*, *speciality* and *unsought products*. Business products can be divided into *raw materials*, *major equipment*, *accessory equipment*, *component parts*, *process materials*, *consumable supplies (MRO items)* and *business services*.

It is important to remember that a product has three levels: core, actual and augmented. The purchaser buys a core benefit or service (the *core product*) in addition to the product's brand name, features, capabilities, quality, packaging and design (the *actual product*). Increasingly, aspects of the *augmented product* are important considerations for purchasers of consumer goods, services and business goods. Warranties, delivery and credit, personnel, installation, after-sales support and customer service are integral to the actual product's appeal and perceived benefits. The role of personnel in particular is of fundamental concern to marketers; people and customer service now form a central part of the marketing mix.

A *product item* is a specific version of a product that can be designated as a distinct offering among a business's products. A product line is a group of closely related product items that are a unit because of marketing, technical or end-use considerations. A company's total group of products is called the *product mix*. The *depth* of a product mix is measured by the number of different products offered in each product line. The *width* of the product mix is measured by the number of product lines a company offers.

The *product life cycle* describes how product items in an industry move through four major stages: (1) *introduction stage*, (2) *growth stage*, (3) *maturity stage* and (4) *decline stage*. The life-cycle concept is used to make sure that the introduction, alteration and termination of a product are timed and executed properly. *Co-creation* is increasingly used in the development and introduction of new products. The sales curve is at zero on introduction, rises at an increasing rate during growth, peaks at maturity and then declines. Profits peak towards the end of the growth stage of the product life cycle. The life expectancy of a product is based on buyers' wants, the availability of competing products and other environmental conditions. Most businesses have a composite of life-cycle patterns for various products in their overall portfolio. It is important to manage existing products and develop new ones to keep the overall sales performance at the desired level.

Thousands of new products are introduced each year and many of them fail. Some estimates put the product failure rate as high as 60 to 90 per cent. Failure and success rates vary in different industries and from company to company. Products fail for many reasons: because of a failure to match product offerings to customer needs, ineffective or inconsistent branding, technical or design problems, poor timing, over-estimation of market size, ineffective promotion, inefficient distribution and a poor understanding of competing products' merits.

It is important to distinguish between degrees of product failure. Absolute failure occurs when a company loses money on a new product because it is unable to recover development, production and marketing costs. Relative product failure occurs when a product returns a profit but does not meet a company's profit or market share objectives.

Despite this gloomy picture of new product failure, some new products are very successful. Perhaps the most important ingredient for success is the product's ability to provide a significant and perceivable benefit to a sizeable number of customers.

When creating products, marketers must take into account other product-related considerations, such as physical characteristics and less tangible support services. Specific physical product characteristics that require attention are the level of quality and product features, such as textures, colours and sizes. Support services that may be viewed as part of the total product include guarantees, repairs/replacements and credit.

Key links

This chapter has given an overview of the product element of the marketing mix.

- It must be read in conjunction with Chapter 12, which examines how marketers manage portfolios of products.
- For those involved in marketing services, there are additional considerations, as discussed in Chapter 13.

Important terms

Accessory equipment
Actual product
Augmented product
Co-creation
Component parts
Consumable supplies
Consumer products
Convenience products
Core product
Decline stage
Depth (of product mix)
Good
Growth stage
Guarantee
Ideas
Industrial/business products
Industrial/business services
Introduction stage
Major equipment
Maturity stage
MRO items
Process materials
Product item
Product life cycle
Product line
Product mix
Quality
Raw materials
Service
Shopping products
Speciality products
Unsought products
Width (of product mix)

Discussion and review questions

1. List the tangible and intangible attributes of a tablet such as an iPad. Compare the benefits of the tablet with those of an intangible product such as life insurance.

2. A product has been referred to as a 'psychological bundle of satisfaction'. Is this a good definition of a product?

3. Is a roll of carpet in a shop a consumer product or a business product? Defend your answer.

4. How do convenience products and shopping products differ? What are the distinguishing characteristics of each type of product?

5. Would a music system that sells for £750 be a convenience, shopping or speciality product?

6. In the category of business products, how do component parts differ from process materials?

7. How does a company's product mix relate to its development of a product line?

8. When should a company add depth to its product lines rather than width to its product mix?

9. How do industry profits change as a product moves through the four stages of its life cycle?

10. What is the relationship between the concepts of product mix and product life cycle?

11. What factors must marketers consider when deciding what quality level to build in to a product? What support services can be offered to back up product quality?

12. What are aspects of the augmented product for a new car?

13. Why is the augmented product increasingly important when determining a differential advantage?

Recommended readings

Baker, M. and Hart, S., *Product Strategy and Management* (Pearson/FT, 2007).

Busuttil, J., *The Practitioner's Guide to Product Management* (Piatkus, 2015).

Crawford, C.M. and Di Benedetto, C.A., *New Products Management* (McGraw-Hill, 2014).

Haines, S., *The Product Manager's Desk Reference* (McGraw-Hill, 2014).

Lehmann, D. and Winer, R., *Product Management* (McGraw-Hill, 2004).

Loch, C. and Kavadias, S., *Handbook of Product Management* (Butterworth-Heinemann, 2008).

Wind, Y.J., *Product Policy: Concepts, Methods and Strategy* (Addison-Wesley, 1982).

Internet exercise

Goodyear Tyres

In addition to providing information about the company's products, Goodyear's website helps customers to find the exact products they want and will even direct them to the nearest Goodyear retailer. Visit the Goodyear site at: www.goodyear.eu/uk_en/

1. How does Goodyear use its website to communicate information about the quality of its tyres?

2. How does Goodyear's website demonstrate product design and features?

3. Based on what you learned at the website, describe what Goodyear has done to position its tyres.

Group tasks

1. Your team is made up of managers working for a well-known travel brand. Your new CEO wants lots of ideas for new products to launch. What is the best way to generate these ideas and how would you determine which ideas are preferable?

2. Consider a leading hotel brand such as Hilton, Marriott or Holiday Inn. To this brand's guests, what is the product? For their marketers, which facets of the product permit differentiation?

Applied mini-case

'Just when you thought our legendary hatchback couldn't get any better, along comes the stunning new Golf', stated the VW website. The Volkswagen Golf is over 40! Yet VW is celebrating the launch of the latest generation of the model, which seems to have defied middle age and maintained its status as a trendy brand. The motoring magazines commented about its advantages 'brushing the others aside' (*What Car?*) and 'quieter, plusher and completely redecorated' (*Car Magazine*). These plaudits and sales figures vindicate VW's decision to continually upgrade the Golf, rather than replace it with a different model.

Source: www.volkswagen.co.uk/#/new/golf-vi

Question

Several years from now you have secured a job as brand manager for the Golf. Assume that VW is about to make a decision about whether to launch a new generation of the Golf or replace it with a new model with a new name. Prepare a report arguing in support of one of these options. You should explore the arguments for and against each option.

Heineken's portfolio of brands

Case study

Heineken is Europe's largest brewer, having acquired part of the UK's Scottish & Newcastle. While 50 per cent of its sales are European, worldwide Heineken the company is one of the biggest beer businesses. Heineken beer is recognized around the globe. With a presence in more than 178 countries and more than 90 per cent of sales originating outside the domestic Dutch market, Heineken has been described as the most international beer brand. However, there is more to the company than the single Heineken brand. While some rivals have tackled the global market with a strategy of focusing only on international premium beer brands, Heineken has

adopted a tiered approach, with strong international premium brands such as Amstel and Desperados, alongside numerous local 'champion' or regional brands. Heineken brews and sells more than 200 international premium, regional, local and speciality beers and ciders, including Primus, Birra Moretti, Sagres, Cruzcampo, Foster's, Strongbow, Bulmers, Newcastle Brown Ale, Zywiec, Ochota, Kingfisher, Tiger, Equis, Tecate and Sol (www.heinekeninternational.com/aboutheineken.aspx).

Many acquisitions over the past decade have cemented the company's number one status in Europe. The latest is Slovenia's Pivovarna Lasko. In Europe, despite the mass appeal of the Heineken brand, to stay ahead of the competition the company has to adjust its product mix to suit the needs of different countries, fitting in with local cultures and tastes. This strategy has been adopted globally. Heineken offers a portfolio of three core brands in each country:

1. A local brand, aimed at the standard and largest market segment. In Italy this is Dreher, in France '33' and in Spain Aguila Pilsener.

2. A brand targeted at the 'upper' end of the market; sometimes this is a locally produced brand, such as the Spanish Aguila Master, in other cases Amstel is preferred.

3. The eponymous Heineken brand itself, aimed at the premium market segment; the beer offered may be manufactured locally or it may be exported from the Netherlands; either way, the Dutch head office works hard to maintain product quality and brand image.

As the company explains,

'The consistent growth of our brands requires solid creative brand management, which we coordinate centrally. By carefully balancing our brand portfolios and achieving optimal distribution and coverage, we aim to build and sustain strong positions in local markets. For the Heineken and Amstel brands, we develop and maintain central guidelines and standards for brand style, brand value and brand development.'

Currently, significant growth is evident in the company's sales in Africa and the Middle East, Asia Pacific, Mexico, India and South Africa, reflecting the company's global footprint. The company now achieves 50 per cent of revenue and 60 per cent of its profits in Africa/Middle East, Asia Pacific and the Americas.

Sales of Heineken in the premium segment are rising at around 3.4 per cent per annum. No other brewer has secured strong market positions in as many countries and no individual beer brand is as successful in as many countries as the

Heineken brand. Heineken is market leader in Austria, Romania, Hungary, Poland, Slovakia, Bulgaria and Macedonia, illustrating the company's identification some time ago of the growing commercial opportunities in eastern Europe, where there have been many acquisitions of local brewers. Low and zero alcohol brands 0.0% MAXX and Radler 0.0% also have been making inroads. More recently, significant sales growth has come from its cider business, built on UK brands Strongbow and Bulmers as well as Old Mout from New Zealand.

Sources: www.Heineken.com, 2004–2011; www.heinekeninternational.com /aboutheineken.aspx, 26 November, 2007; www.heinekeninternational.com, 5 March 2011; www.heineken.co.uk, 2010/11; www.theheinekencompany.com /investors/performance-highlights-2014.

Questions for discussion

1. Why does Heineken opt for a mix of internationally known brands marketed alongside local beers?

2. In what ways is Heineken continuously updating its product portfolio and its marketing mix?

3. What problems are likely for Heineken from trading such a large portfolio of beer brands?

CHAPTER 11

Branding and packaging

"Marketers must create and manage powerful, differentiated and compelling brands"

Objectives

- To recognize the importance of brands and brand equity.

- To understand the types and benefits of brands and how to select, name, protect and licence them.

- To explore the concepts of brand loyalty, brand advocacy and brand communities.

- To appreciate the best practice guidelines for creating strong brands.

- To examine the roles of brand attributes, brand values and brand personality in brand development.

- To explore the changing nature of branding in the digital era.

- To understand the role of branding at the corporate level and in reputation management.

- To become aware of the major packaging functions and packaging design considerations.

- To consider the ways in which packaging is used in marketing strategies.

- To examine the functions of labelling and the legal issues associated with labelling.

INTRODUCTION

Effective marketing requires product or service differentiation. Such differentiation entails product design, features and attributes, customer service, branding and the other ingredients of the marketing mix, linked to a strong customer value proposition. These need to appeal to targeted consumers or business customers more than competing brands. Branding is seen as a core activity of a company's marketing function. Inside most organizations there is little disagreement … marketers are responsible for brand strategy and brands.

Brands enable customers to readily identify their favoured products and marketers to more easily communicate their advantages. Marketers invest vast sums in persuading targeted customers to prefer their products over and above those supplied by competitors, as they strive to create brand loyalty or brand preference. Effectively creating a well-differentiated and memorable image for the brand is a core requirement for a marketing-oriented organization.

Brand equity is increasingly important in many boardrooms and results from the financial and marketing value that can be placed on a brand owing to its market position and standing. Brand awareness, brand loyalty, perceived brand quality and brand associations create brand equity. An effective brand has what is termed 'brand strength', and generally to achieve a strong brand marketers will have defined brand attributes, values and personality for their brands. These constructs are explored in this chapter of *Marketing: Concepts and Strategies*.

Packaging and labelling are also part of the marketing process. Packaging includes the immediate container (the primary packaging) and the shipping packaging (the secondary packaging). Both need to exhibit functionality in order to protect and convey the product inside, and facilitate its easy use and storage. Additionally, packaging should support the product's branding and differentiation. Many products, particularly those found in supermarkets, explicitly use their pack designs to support their brand identities.

Polos: are you a sucker? Or, are you a cruncher?

At a factory in York, each day a mountain of thumbnail-sized tyre-shaped white mints is deemed slightly imperfect: chipped, broken or improperly moulded. The sight is awe-inspiring, but gives a clue as to the volume of perfectly formed Polo mints manufactured: 20 million are produced each day in York, and Nestlé makes 5.2 billion each year. 150 mints are eaten every second. Nestlé's takeover of the UK's Rowntree – creator of the Polo – assured the world domination of Polo, 'the mint with the hole'.

Polo is the UK's top-selling mint and has established leadership in many other countries, too. It was not too long before trial flavours and strengths were tested by product developers at Nestlé. For example, in India there was a cinnamon flavoured Polo to 'spice things up, while being refreshing'. Now there are Polo Ice, Polo Smoothies and Polo Candy, supplementing the core portfolio of Polo Original, Polo Spearmint and Polo Fruits. Polo Sugar Free is even approved by the Dental Health Foundation.

Back in 1998 saw one of the most successful spin-offs from the original Polo concept: the sugar-free Polo Supermint, for 'instant refreshment'. This was not only a masterful brand extension of the Polo name but also proved to be an inspired packaging execution.

The Polo Supermint from Nestlé was even awarded Millennium Products' status by the Design Council, an accolade reserved for just a few new designs. The new mini-mints 'with the hole' weighed only a tenth of the original, yet contained four times the amount of peppermint oil in relation to their size. This super-strength mint not only appealed to traditional Polo mint buyers, but also enabled the brand to compete head-to-head with the plethora of extra-strong mints produced by rival manufacturers such as Trebor. The new size and extra-strong Polo would inevitably have caught the eye of confectionery buyers on the back of the Polo heritage and the extensive distribution network established by the mighty Nestlé.

Marketers at Nestlé wanted to ensure a successful launch and were determined to make the new item distinctive and appealing in its own right. The innovative packaging design and eye-catching styling made an immediate impact in a rather crowded marketplace. The Supermints were packed in plastic dispensers, developed by RPC Market Rasen, which were shaped as giant versions of the original and very familiar Polo mint. The pack housed a pop-up hatch that enabled it to dispense individual mini-Polos and to be resealed easily. The regular user soon developed the ability to dispense one-handed and in suitable quantities to appease friends also requiring a refreshing treat. The plastic dispenser was packaged in a cool blue, square container with eye-catching graphics, permitting easy stocking and shelf displays.

Nestlé explained that while the mini-Polos were launched to celebrate the Polo brand's 50th birthday, the new item emerged as one of the company's greatest successes ever. Nestlé believed this demonstrated that it is possible to innovate with a brand now over 60 years old. The Supermints line matched the brand values and positioning of the original Polo mint: an effective brand extension must have an affinity with existing brand values. This, and other related Polo product developments, reflected competitor moves and responded to consumer tastes. With the Polo Supermint, the combination of astute branding and clever packaging certainly created a very successful product for Nestlé and a welcome alternative for Polo fans. Few products have been able to achieve such strong branding on the basis of shape and distinctive packaging.

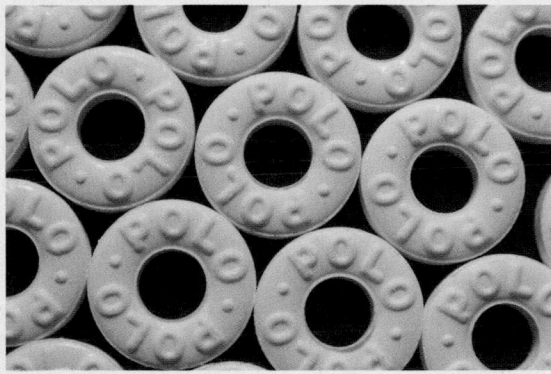

Sources: The Museum of Brands, 2011 and 2014; Nestlé Rowntree, York, 1999; One Stop, 2011; *Marketing*, 4 February 1999, p. 22; www.nestle.co.uk, May 2004 and January 2008; www.nestle.in, January, 2008; www.polomint .co.uk, 2–11 June; www.nestle.co.uk/brands/chocolate_and_confectionery, April 2015.

Brands and packages are part of a product's tangible features, the verbal and physical cues that help customers identify the products they want and influence their purchase choices. For Nestlé's Polo mints, branding and packaging have been central to the product's success. A good brand is distinctive and memorable; without one, companies could not differentiate their products and shoppers' choices may, essentially, be arbitrary. A good package design is cost effective, safe, environmentally responsible and valuable as a promotional tool.

This chapter first defines branding and explains its benefits to customers and sellers; it examines brand loyalty, the role of digital brand communities and brand advocacy; then examines the importance of brand equity, brand attributes, values and personality, strong brands and the various types of brand. The chapter should be read in conjunction with Chapter 8 of *Marketing: Concepts and Strategies*, which explored brand positioning and the creation of a suitable image for a brand. The next section of this chapter examines how companies choose brands, how they protect them, the various branding policies that companies employ and brand licencing. The changing nature of branding in the digital era is explored. The chapter goes on to discuss how organizations manage brands and how they ensure that they contribute effectively to a company's fortunes and reputation. Packaging is then the focus, as part of the product and how it is marketed: the functions of packaging, issues to consider in packaging design, packaging development and how the package can be a major element in marketing strategy. After considering criticisms of packaging, the chapter concludes with a brief discussion of labelling.

Branding

Most marketers believe a key focus for their activity is the differentiation of their product proposition vis-à-vis competing products and services. For many consumers, services or business products, such differentiation entails a mix of product design, features and attributes, along with the creation of a distinctive image. This generally involves creating a brand and brand identity for products or services. Indeed, without distinctive branding, many service products, in particular, would struggle to differentiate themselves against rivals (see Chapter 13).

In addition to making decisions about actual products, as described in Chapter 10, marketers must make many decisions associated with branding, such as brand architecture, brand

Brand
A name, term, design, symbol or any other feature that identifies one seller's good or service as distinct from those of other sellers.

names, brand marks, trademarks and tradenames, as well as the overarching guiding brand strategy. A **brand** is a name, term, design, symbol or any other feature that identifies one seller's good or service as distinct from those of other sellers. A brand may identify one item, a family of items or all items of that seller.[1] A **brand name** is that part of a brand that can be spoken and depicted – including letters, words and numbers – such as Coca-Cola or Channel Four. A brand name is often a product's only distinguishing characteristic. Without the brand name and how it is depicted, a company could not identify its products, which is one of the reasons moves to ban branded cigarette packaging are causing anguish for the tobacco industry. Note how many TV channels display their channel identifier or logo throughout a programme and how much brand building goes on with short brand inserts between programmes or either side of news bulletins. To consumers, brand names are as fundamental as the product itself. Brand names simplify shopping, guarantee a specific level of quality and allow self-expression. Table 11.1 details the world's most valuable brands. For many marketers, establishing a distinctive brand, which is easily remembered and recognized by targeted customers, is one of the primary activities of effective marketing management.

Brand name
That part of a brand that can be spoken, including letters, words and numbers.

The element of a brand that is not made up of words but is often a symbol or design is called a **brand mark**. One example is the symbol of a baby on Procter & Gamble's Fairy Liquid detergent. Occasionally, brand marks are modified for local markets.

Brand mark
The element of a brand that cannot be spoken, often a symbol or design.

TABLE 11.1 Interbrand's Most Valuable Brands By $m Value, 2014

Brand	Country of Origin	Brand Value ($m)	Brand	Country of Origin	Brand Value ($m)
Apple	USA	118 863	Oracle	USA	25 980
Google	USA	107 439	HP	USA	23 758
Coca-Cola	USA	81 563	Gillette	USA	22 845
IBM	USA	72 244	Louis Vuitton	France	22 552
Microsoft	USA	61 154	Honda	Japan	21 673
General Electric	USA	45 480	H&M	Finland	21 083
Samsung	S Korea	45 462	Nike	USA	19 875
Toyota	Japan	42 392	Amex	USA	19 510
McDonald's	USA	42 254	Pepsi	USA	19 119
Mercedes	Germany	34 338	SAP	Germany	17 340
BMW	Germany	34 214	IKEA	Sweden	15 885
Intel	USA	34 153	UPS	USA	14 470
Disney	USA	32 223	eBay	USA	14 358
Cisco	USA	30 936	Facebook	USA	14 349
Amazon	USA	29 478	Pampers	USA	14 078

Trademark
Legal designation indicating that the owner has exclusive use of a brand.

Trade name
The full and legal name of an organization.

For example, Microsoft topped its brand name with a butterfly in France, a fish in Portugal and a sun in Spain. A **trademark** is a legal designation indicating that the owner has exclusive use of a brand or a part of a brand, and that others are prohibited by law from using it. To protect a brand name or brand mark, a company must register it as a trademark with the appropriate patenting office. A **trade name** is the full and legal name of an organization, such as Ford Motor Company, rather than the name of a specific product.

Benefits of branding

Branding provides benefits for both buyers and sellers.[2] Brands help buyers identify specific products that they do and do not like, a process that in turn facilitates the purchase of items that satisfy their needs and reduces the time required to purchase the product. Without brands, product selection would be quite random, because buyers could have no assurance that they were purchasing what they preferred. Imagine the chaos in a supermarket if every shopper entered not knowing which products and brands to purchase! Research indicates that the bulk of supermarket shoppers are highly brand loyal or routinized in their selections.

A brand also helps buyers evaluate the quality of a product, especially when they are unable to judge its characteristics. In other words, a purchaser for whom a brand symbolizes a certain quality level will transfer that perception of quality to the unknown item. A brand helps to reduce a buyer's perceived risk of purchase. In addition, it may offer the psychological reward that comes from owning a brand that symbolizes status. Certain brands of watches (Rolex) and cars (Rolls-Royce) fall into this category.[3]

Sellers benefit from branding because each company's brands identify its products, which makes repeat purchasing easier for consumers. Branding helps a company introduce a new product that carries the name of one or more of its existing products, because buyers are already familiar with the company's existing brands. For example, Heinz regularly introduces new products, and the introduction of the new BMW i range of electric cars was smoother because of the credibility provided by BMW's brand reputation. As consumers are used to buying the brand and have a high regard for its quality, they are likely to try the new offerings. Branding also facilitates promotional efforts because the promotion of each branded product indirectly promotes all other products that are similarly branded.

Brand loyalty
A strongly motivated and long-standing decision to purchase a particular product or service.

Branding helps sellers by fostering brand loyalty. **Brand loyalty** is a strongly motivated and long-standing decision to purchase a particular product or service. To the extent that buyers become loyal to a specific brand, the company's market share for that product achieves a certain level of stability, allowing the company to use its resources more efficiently.[4] Loyal customers are highly desirable and much marketing activity is aimed at reassuring existing customers and canvassing their ongoing support and interest. It should be stated that some experts argue that there is not really true brand loyalty as many consumers are quite prepared to try alternatives when the mood takes or promos inspire them to do so, but there is certainly in most markets evidence of stated brand preference amongst many consumers and many buyers have highly routinized purchasing behaviours. When a company succeeds in fostering some degree of customer loyalty to a brand, it might be able to charge a premium price for the product. For example, brand loyal buyers of Anadin aspirin are willing to pay two or three times more for Anadin than for a generic brand of aspirin with the same amount of pain-relieving agent. Tilda rice commands a significant price premium over competing brands of rice, partly due to its brand reputation. For a brand to foster loyalty over time it must be able to deliver a valued and consistent experience, otherwise its customers will switch to alternatives. Consumers and business customers must be able to have trust in 'their' brand, if they are over time to continue to prefer it. Ongoing consistent customer experience is an important necessary outcome for effective brand management.

However, brand loyalty is argued to be declining, partly because of marketers' increased reliance on discounted sales, coupons and other short-term promotions, and partly because of the sometimes overwhelming array of similar new products from which consumers can choose. The emergence of increased consumer-to-consumer communication and e-word-of-mouth means so much brand communication now stems from other consumers rather than the brand's managers. There is evidence that consumers value such opinions and can be steered away from their once-preferred brands because of negative chatter online. The power of digital communication operates the other way, too. The growth of consumer-to-consumer communication, fostered by social media networking, quickly creates interest in a product or brand, prompting others to experiment or try out the much tweeted about brand. For example, if a well-known celeb tweets about a great experience with a brand, many followers will try it out. To stimulate loyalty to their brands, some marketers are stressing image advertising, mailing personalized catalogues and magazines to regular users, and creating membership clubs for brand users; for example, Tesco's Clubcard or Sainsbury's Nectar points. Many brands have created digital or virtual brand communities in order to foster interest and some degree of loyalty in their proposition. Sometimes consumers make repeat purchases of products for reasons other than brand loyalty. Spurious loyalty is not stable and may result from non-availability of alternative brands or the way in which products are displayed in retail outlets.

Brand community
A group of consumers and observers focused on a particular brand, often based on social media, centred on a set of social relations and interactions among admirers of the brand.

An interesting spin-off from increased web access and the growth of social media has been the creation of digital brand communities.[5] Designed to foster both loyalty to a particular brand and interest in its products/services, a **brand community** is a group of consumers and observers focused on a particular brand, often web-based, centred on a set of social relations and interactions amongst admirers of the brand.[6] The digital Harley Davidson Owners' Club is a typical example, and one well-adopted by fans of this brand. Brand communities generally are controlled and instigated by the brand's owner for commercial gain, but buy-in from followers of the brand creates much of the activity and dialogue. Mobile phone provider Geocell in Georgia created a separate brand targeted at its youth consumers, based on an online community. Lai-Lai offers its cellular network subscribers live music events, merchandise, special tariffs, game and music downloads and the opportunity to create their own friendship groups. In this way, Geocell has created a strongly bonded set of consumers tied in to its Lai-Lai brand, which is aimed at 15- to 25-year-olds.

Blog communities, such as the Nike blog *The Art of Speed* – which was one of the first – are an enhancement, where spokespersons for a brand share their views in blogs, permitting tailored communication with members and between members of the digital brand community. Technology in the form of digital brand communities and blogs enables so-termed **dynamic branding**, with very rapid communication and sharing of brand information and almost instant take-up by the brand's followers.[7] Companies increasingly view such digital brand community activity as core to their attempts to build loyalty and to create brand advocacy. **Brand advocacy** is where consumers are encouraged to share very positive feelings towards a brand with other consumers, whether word-of-mouth, online or in the print and broadcast media. Many people believe in the views of others who are 'like them' more than they trust the statements of companies and brands. Creating a set of brand ambassadors, advocates or evangelists is on the increase, made so much easier in the digital era.

The strategy literature has suggested that the concept of brand advocacy is more important than tracking customer satisfaction or even loyalty, as it is a business strategy built on trust. In a digital world in which rapid communication of positives and negatives is possible, often from consumer-to-consumer outside of the brand manager's control, having a set of brand 'super fans' who truly trust the brand and will both defend it and promote it, may even be a competitive advantage. A customer brand advocate differs from being a supporter, influencer, loyalist or satisfied customer. A **brand advocate** supports the brand, actively promotes the brand and is also emotionally attached to the brand. He or she will silence detractors, help build a positive customer experience, and share exemplars of the brand 'going that extra mile'. It is likely that more and more brands will develop both brand communities and a subset of super fans acting as brand advocates. One leading food brand has created a 'club' of consumers who adore its products, who are given inside information about new launches and invitations to special events, such as live sessions with well-known chefs. These enthusiasts readily share their positive views of this brand with their families, friends and colleagues, and online with other consumers, so becoming brand advocates or super fans. While communicating one-to-one with such advocates is more costly per capita than television advertising, many brand experts argue such consumer-to-consumer advocacy is very cost effective in terms of its impact and for persuading others to trial a brand. This theme is explored further in Chapter 16 of *Marketing: Concepts and Strategies*.

For most marketing managers, two long-established performance metrics are to assess the level of repeat purchasing and customer loyalty to a brand. There are three degrees of brand loyalty: recognition, preference and insistence.

Brand recognition **Brand recognition** exists when a customer is aware that a brand exists and views it as an alternative to purchase if the preferred brand is unavailable or if the other available brands are unfamiliar to the customer. This is the mildest form of brand loyalty. The word loyalty is clearly being used very loosely here. One of the initial objectives of a marketer introducing a new brand is to create widespread awareness of the brand in order to generate brand recognition. This theme is considered in Chapter 16.

Blog communities
Where spokespersons for a brand share their views in blogs, permitting one-to-one tailored communication with members and between members of the digital brand community.

Dynamic branding
Digital brand communities and blogging enable dynamic branding, with very rapid communication and sharing of brand information and almost instant take-up by the brand's followers.

Brand advocacy
When consumers are encouraged to share very positive feelings towards a brand with other consumers, whether word-of-mouth, online or in the print and broadcast media.

Brand advocate
Supporter of a brand who actively promotes the brand and is also emotionally attached to the brand. He or she will silence detractors, help build a positive customer experience, and share exemplars of the brand 'going that extra mile'.

Brand recognition
A customer's awareness that a brand exists and is an alternative to purchase.

Brand preference
The degree of brand loyalty in which a customer prefers one brand over competitive offerings.

Brand preference

Brand preference is a stronger degree of brand loyalty in which a customer definitely prefers one brand over competitive offerings and will purchase this brand if it is available. However, if the brand is not available, the customer will accept a substitute brand rather than expend additional effort finding and purchasing the preferred brand. A marketer is likely to be able to compete effectively in a market when a number of customers have developed brand preference for its specific brand.

Brand insistence
The degree of brand loyalty in which a customer strongly prefers a specific brand and will accept no substitute.

Brand insistence

Brand insistence is the degree of brand loyalty in which a customer strongly prefers a specific brand, will accept no substitute and is willing to spend a great deal of time and effort to acquire that brand. If a brand-insistent customer goes to a store and finds the brand unavailable, rather than purchasing a substitute brand, he or she will seek the brand elsewhere. Brand insistence is the strongest degree of brand loyalty. It is a marketer's dream. However, it is the least common type of brand loyalty. Customers vary considerably regarding the product categories for which they may be brand insistent.

Brand equity

Brand equity
The marketing and financial value associated with a brand's strength in a market, which is a function of the goodwill and positive brand recognition built up over time, underpinning the brand's sales volumes and financial returns.

A well-managed brand is an asset to an organization. The value of this asset is often referred to as brand equity. **Brand equity** is the marketing and financial value associated with a brand's strength in a market. Besides the actual proprietary brand assets, such as patents and trademarks, four major elements underlie brand equity. These components are brand name awareness, brand loyalty, perceived brand quality and brand associations, as shown in Figure 11.1.[8] Brand equity is a function of the goodwill and positive brand recognition built up over time, which underpin sales volumes and financial returns. Strong brand equity should equate to higher sales and margins vis-à-vis competing brands.

Being aware of a brand leads to brand familiarity, which in turn results in a level of comfort with the brand. A familiar brand is more likely to be selected than an unfamiliar brand because often the familiar brand is viewed as reliable and of acceptable quality compared to the unknown brand. The familiar brand is likely to be in a customer's evoked set (see Chapter 5), whereas the unfamiliar brand is not.

Brand loyalty is a valued component of brand equity because it reduces a brand's vulnerability to competitors' actions. Brand loyalty allows an organization to keep its existing customers and avoid having to spend enormous amounts of resources gaining new ones. Loyal customers provide brand visibility and reassurance to potential new customers. Because customers expect their brand to be available when and where they shop, retailers strive to carry the brands known for their strong customer following.

Customers associate a certain level of perceived overall quality with a brand. A brand name itself stands for a certain level of quality in a customer's mind and is used as a substitute for actual judgement of quality. In many cases, customers cannot actually judge the quality of the product for themselves and instead must rely on the brand as a quality indicator. Perceived high brand quality helps to support a premium price, allowing a marketer to avoid severe price competition. Favourable perceived brand quality can ease the introduction of brand extensions, as the high regard for the brand is likely to translate into high regard for the related products.

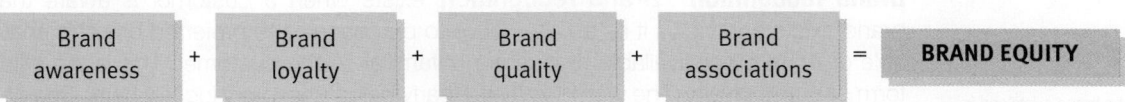

FIGURE 11.1
Major elements of brand equity

The set of associations linked to a brand is another key component of brand equity. At times a marketer works to connect a lifestyle, or in some instances a certain personality type, with a particular brand. For example, customers associate Volvo cars with protecting family members; a De Beers diamond with a loving, long-lasting relationship (a diamond is for ever); and Drambuie liqueur with a unique taste. These types of brand association contribute significantly to the brand's equity.

Although difficult to measure, brand equity represents the value of a brand to an organization. An organization may buy a brand from another company at a premium price because outright brand purchase may be less expensive and less risky than creating and developing a brand from scratch. For example, Kraft acquiring Cadbury's strong portfolio of brands. Brand equity helps to give a brand the power to capture and maintain a consistent market share, which provides stability to an organization's sales volume. The top brands with the highest economic value are shown in Table 11.1. Any company that owns a brand listed in Table 11.1, such as Nestlé with Nescafé, would agree that the economic value of that brand is likely to be the greatest single asset in the organization's possession. A brand's overall economic value rises and falls with the brand's profitability, brand awareness, brand loyalty, perceived brand quality and strength of positive brand associations.

Brand identity

Brand identity
A unique set of brand associations reflecting what a brand stands for and the intended promise to the customer as a relationship is forged.

Leading brand strategists have promoted the notion of **brand identity**, said to be a unique set of brand associations reflecting what a brand stands for and the intended promise to the customer as a relationship is forged.[9] Brand identity is composed of attributes of the product and its usage, the organization's attributes, the brand's personality and its symbols and imagery. Marketers should manage their brands' identities, ensuring they reflect target segment expectations and the nature of the competitive challenge. More recently this construct has been extended[10] to include:

- Physique: tangible characteristics which can be recognized by consumers' senses (shape, smell, colour, sound, taste, etc.).
- Personality: human characteristics associated with the brand (caring, arrogant, loving, bullying, money-grabbing, sharing, etc.).
- Culture: the underlying values and behaviours of the organization (challenging, ethical, collaborative, innovative, conservative, etc.).
- Relationship: the nature and quality of the brand-customer relationship (supportive, friendly, aggressive, authoritative, etc.).
- Reflection: the brand as a communication tool (a premium deluxe brand reflects status).
- Self-image: internal reflection (rewards, benefits, exhibited image, etc.).

Brand personality and brand attributes are important to understand and to agree. They must be aligned with the organization's values and behaviours, to avoid customer dissatisfaction when engaging with the brand.

Brand personality, values and attributes

Brand attributes
The bullet-point specific benefits to the customer from purchasing or using the brand.

Most companies have identified specific attributes that should be linked to their brands and emphasized in associated brand communication. **Brand attributes** are the bullet-point selling-type features listed in brochures or in an advertisement: the specific benefits to the customer from purchasing or using the brand. Two decades ago, it became fashionable to also identify brand values, to help differentiate a brand and

Brand values
The emotional benefits and less tangible identifiers attached to the brand inside the organization, providing reassurance and credibility for employees and, indirectly, targeted consumers or business customers.

build its appeal to target audiences, particularly those within an organization. **Brand values** are the emotional benefits and less tangible identifiers attached to the brand, creating a sense of identity and purpose within the organization, providing reassurance and credibility for employees and, indirectly, targeted consumers or business customers, and supplementing the specific brand attributes in making the brand attractive to current or potential purchasers. Brand values focus on those inside the organization, to help foster a collegiality around the brand that ultimately will manifest itself to customers and suppliers. For example, IT services company Fujitsu has many brand attributes, including its ability to manage business clients' IT infrastructure, offer the latest technology and thinking, and be cost effective and reliable. Its brand values are defined as knowledge, dependability, technical excellence, reassurance and passion, but to staff the message is that 'we tell it as it is'. These values are far more emotional than the brand attributes. It is important that the internal values and behaviours are aligned to the brand attributes and personality relayed to external audiences, otherwise the adopted brand strategy will falter.

Practitioners' use of the brand development theory: the brand personality grid

Marketing tools and techniques

Leading branding exponents, such as Prophet (David Aaker) and Interbrand, suggest that organizations identify core values that are evident in their business capabilities and behaviours and which are reflected in their brands' positioning. Specific features or attributes that can be construed as brand benefits should be defined. However in order to truly make a brand 'come alive' and be distinctive in the marketplace a *brand personality* should be specified to create emotion. Such personality traits are the emotive characteristics of the brand, whereas the brand benefits are more tangible and specific attributes, as outlined opposite. The internal brand values need to be aligned to these external brand attributes and personality traits, otherwise the company's behaviours will disappoint customers.

1. *Personality*
   What sets the company apart/describes its character and personality emotionally.

2. *Values*
   The heart of the organization's ethos and values as perceived internally within the company.

3. *Brand benefits/attributes*
   Detailed/specific features of benefit to the customer; Fujitsu's evolving branding is a good example of this.

Japanese-based Fujitsu is one of the world's biggest businesses, focusing mainly on electronics and IT services. The company had traded under different names across the world and in the UK was once familiar to business clients as ICL. Fujitsu decided to maximize its global standing under the Fujitsu name and looked to create a leading brand. Globally, Fujitsu is the world's number four IT services company. In the UK, Fujitsu handles IT outsourcing and management for major banks and retailers, central and local government, the Post Office and many manufacturers.

The old brand in the UK was somewhat staid: hardware-led, overly 'techy', 'grey' and stood for ICL's old values from when the company focused on producing mainframe computers rather than offering innovative IT solutions and management options to leading-edge businesses. The new-look Fujitsu is a dynamic, progressive, forward-thinking business, partnering other leading-edge suppliers to address clients' fast-changing IT requirements and to help clients to transform their business practices.

There are many providers of IT support and many may be able to offer the brand benefits stated on the following page, in the right-hand column. However, fewer B2B companies could claim to have a reputation for being caring, passionate, likeable, dependable and knowledgeable about clients' business issues. Certain rivals would struggle to be described by clients as caring, likeable or dependable. In IT services, interpersonal relationships between the supplier and the client are of paramount importance. Clients also perceive high risks in handing over their IT – on which the success of their operations may depend – to a third party. The brand values and brand personality suggested in this analysis would be highly attractive to many senior executives in current or potential business clients.

Having developed a brand proposition personality, values and attributes as hypothesized in the example to the right, the marketing challenges are then to ensure that both:

- all promotional activity reflects this overall message
- any interface with clients and suppliers or partners conveys these sentiments, whether in print format, e-communications, broadcast media or even with any personnel meeting and when working with clients.

In addition to developing suitable marketing communications materials, therefore, there is a core requirement to ensure that a company's workforce understands and utilizes the brand proposition developed, not only a company's marketers. There is a requirement for internal marketing.

The brand personality grid for Fujitsu could easily look like this:*

*The suggested brand personality grid for Fujitsu is an external observer's view and does not necessarily reflect the company's own analyses or intended brand strategy.

Fujitsu
The Possibilities are Infinite

Brand personality	Brand values	Brand benefits
Friendly people	**Knowledge**	**Infrastructure management**
Customer-focused	Customer's business Across sectors	**Free-up resources**
Confident	**Dependability**	**Operational efficiency**
Dynamic	Trusted to deliver 30/40-year track record	**Customers enabled to focus on** *their* **business imperatives**
Future-focused	**Technical excellence**	**Latest technology**
Passionate	At forefront of change	**Total solutions**
Likeable staff	Tap into Fujitsu's huge R&D	**Leading-edge partnerships**
Global	**Passion** Staff are passionate Deliver for customers	**Reliable**
	Collaboration Working together Networking with partners	**Cost effective**

© Dibb/Simkin

Many branding experts argue that in addition to brand attributes and brand values, an effective brand strategy should identify brand personality variables, in order to facilitate greater differentiation in relation to competitors' products and to form a stronger affinity with customers.[11]

Brand personality
The psychological cues and less tangible desirable facets of a well-presented brand.

Brand personality traits are the psychological cues and less tangible desirable facets of a well-presented brand. They provide the emotion for the brand's messaging. In Fujitsu's case, the brand personality variables include having friendly, customer-focused personnel who are confident, technically savvy and passionate about assisting clients to improve their organizations. In the market for IT services to large corporations, these are desirable traits. Many companies readily identify the brand attributes and, after a little deliberation, they are able to scope out a few brand values. However, the identification of an attractive set of brand personality traits is often more difficult. Once developed, such emotive sentiments often 'bring the brand to life' and help to establish differentiation vis-à-vis rivals. Brand personality traits and brand attributes together combine to present a compelling proposition to targeted consumers or business customers, offering both the emotion of the brand and specific attributes deemed desirable to these targeted customers. The Marketing Tools and Techniques box on page 329 illustrates this approach to effective branding.

Implicit in this discussion is the need to determine a strong and relevant brand image that is managed effectively. As explained in Chapter 8's examination of brand positioning, a management team must determine the desired brand proposition and manage its portfolio of brands in order to ensure that the target market recognizes the specified brand attributes, values and personality. Targeted customers should never be left to deduce for themselves a brand's proposition and messages. Marketers must debate and agree the basis for their branding. The role of the brand manager and the management of portfolios of brands are examined in Chapter 12.

FIGURE 11.2
There are many examples of retailer own-label brands, but Marks & Spencer deliberately created a stand-alone brand for its own, highly popular, range of Per Una clothing emulating the major manufacturer brands

Source: Image courtesy of Marks & Spencer.

Types of brand

There are three categories of brand: manufacturer brands, own label brands (also called private brands, store brands or dealer brands) and generic brands.

Manufacturer brands
Brands initiated by producers to ensure that they are identified with their products at the point of purchase.

Manufacturer brands   Manufacturer brands are initiated by producers and ensure that they are identified with their products at the point of purchase for example, Green Giant, Apple and Wall's ice cream. A manufacturer brand usually requires a producer to become involved in distribution, promotion and, to some extent, pricing decisions. Brand loyalty is encouraged by promotion, quality control and guarantees; it is a valuable asset to a manufacturer. The producer tries to stimulate demand for the product, which tends to encourage middlemen to make the product available (stock).

Own label brands
Brands initiated and owned by resellers wholesalers or retailers.

Own label brands   Own label brands are initiated and owned by resellers (wholesalers or retailers). The major characteristic of own-label brands is that the manufacturers are not identified on the products. Retailers and wholesalers use these brands to develop more efficient promotion, to generate higher gross margins and to improve store images. Own label brands give retailers or wholesalers freedom to purchase products of a specified quality at the lowest cost without disclosing the identity of the manufacturer. Wholesale brands include Intersport, Family Choice, Happy Shopper and Lifestyle. Familiar retailer brand names include Per Una (Marks & Spencer), Yessica (C&A) and George (ASDA). Many successful own label brands are distributed nationally and are as well-known as most manufacturer brands. Sometimes retailers with successful distributor brands start manufacturing their own products to gain more control over product costs, quality and design in the hope of increasing profits. While one might think that store brands appeal most strongly to lower-income shoppers or to upmarket shoppers who compare labels, studies indicate that buyers of own label brands have characteristics that match those of the overall population.[12] Indeed, many consumers now perceive the own label ranges from the likes of Tesco, Marks & Spencer or John Lewis to be superior to many 'true' brands stocked by these retailers. One reason for the growth of store brands is that retailers advertise manufacturer brands, bringing customers to their stores, but sell the store brands, especially to price-sensitive customers.[13] Another reason is that retailers with store labels negotiate better prices from producers of manufacturer brands.[14]

Generic brands   Some marketers of products that have traditionally been branded have embarked on a policy of not branding, often called generic branding. A **generic brand** indicates only the product category such as aluminum foil and does not include the company name or other identifying terms. Usually generic brands are sold at prices lower than those of comparable branded items. Although at one time generic brands may have represented as much as 10 per cent of all retail grocery sales, today they account for less than 1 per cent.[15] They are popular for pharmaceuticals and in some discount grocery stores.

> **Generic brand**
> A brand that indicates only the product category and does not include the company name or other identifying terms.

The battle of the brands   Competition between manufacturer brands and own label brands – sometimes called 'the battle of the brands' – is intensifying in several major product categories, particularly tinned foods, breakfast cereal, sugar and soft drinks. Own label brands now account for around 55 per cent of all supermarket sales. For manufacturers, developing multiple manufacturer brands and distribution systems has been an effective means of combating increased competition from own label brands. By developing a new brand name, a producer can adjust various elements of a marketing mix to appeal to a different target market. For example, Scott@Brand has developed lower-priced brands of paper towels; it has tailored its new products to a target market that tends to purchase own label brands.

Manufacturers find it hard to ignore the marketing opportunities that come from producing own label brands for resellers. If a manufacturer refuses to produce an own label brand for a reseller, a competing manufacturer will. Moreover, the production of own label brands allows the manufacturer to use excess capacity during periods when its own brands are at non-peak production. The ultimate decision whether to produce an own label or a manufacturer brand depends on a company's resources, production capabilities and goals.

Choosing a brand name

Marketers should consider a number of factors when they choose a brand name. The name should be easy for customers – including foreign buyers, if the company intends to market its products in other countries – to say, spell and recall. Short, one-syllable names such as Mars or Daz satisfy this requirement. The brand name should indicate the product's major benefits and, if possible, should suggest in a positive way the product's uses and special characteristics: negative or offensive references should be avoided. For example, a deodorant should be branded with a name that signals freshness, dryness or long-lasting protection, as do Sure, Right Guard and Arrid Extra Dry. The brand should be distinctive, to set it apart from competing brands. If a marketer intends to use a brand for an entire product line, it must be compatible with all products in the line. Finally, a brand should be designed so that it can be used and recognized in all of the various types of media.

Finding the right brand name has become a challenging task, because many obvious product names have already been used. The Marketing Tools and Techniques box on page 329 outlines the role played by brand name consultancies in the naming process.

How are brand names derived? Brand names can be created from single or multiple words; for example, Bic or Apple iPad. Initials, numbers or sometimes combinations of these are used to create brands, such as IBM. At times, words, numbers and initials are combined to yield brand names such as Mazda MX5 or Mitsubishi 3000GT. To avoid terms that have negative connotations, marketers sometimes use fabricated words that have absolutely no meaning at the time they are created; for example, Kodak and Esso. Occasionally, a brand is simply brought out of storage and used as it is or modified. Companies often maintain banks of registered brands, some of which may have been used in the past. Cadillac, for example, has a bank of many hundreds of registered trademarks. Possible brand names are sometimes tested in focus groups, on social media or in other settings, to assess customers' reactions.

Who actually creates brand names? Brand names can be created internally by the organization. Sometimes a name is suggested by individuals who are close to the development of the product. Some organizations have committees that participate in brand name creation and approval. Large companies that introduce numerous new products annually are likely to have a department that develops brand names. Increasingly, outside consultants are used in the process of developing brand names. An organization may also hire a company that specializes in brand name development.

Even though most of the important branding considerations apply to both goods and services, services branding has some additional dimensions. The brand of the service is usually the same as the company name. For example, American Express, Vidal Sassoon, ProntoPrint and Sheraton are names of companies and the services that they provide. Whereas companies that produce tangible goods (such as Procter & Gamble) can use separate brand names for separate products (such as Daz, Head & Shoulders, Flash and Camay), service providers (such as British Airways) are perceived by customers as having one brand name, even though they offer multiple products (first class, business class and economy or holiday packages). As the service brand name and company name are so closely interrelated, a service brand name must be flexible enough to encompass a variety of current services, as well as new ones that the company may offer in the future. For example, British Airways (BA) has Club World or Euro Traveller (economy) services, each separately branded, but both strongly branded as BA. Geographical references like 'western' and descriptive terms like 'trucking' limit the scope of associations that can be made with the brand name. Northwest Airlines became less of a good name as the company began to fly south and east more regularly.[16] Frequently, a service marketer will employ a symbol along with its brand name to make the brand distinctive and to communicate a certain image.

Protecting a brand

Marketers need to design brands that can be protected easily through registration. Among the most difficult to protect are generic words, such as aluminium foil, surnames and descriptive geographic or functional names.[17] Research shows that, overall, consumers prefer descriptive and suggestive brand names, and find them easier to recall than fanciful and arbitrary names.[18] As a result of their designs, some brands can be legally infringed upon more easily than others. Although registration provides trademark protection, a company should develop a system for ensuring that its trademarks will be renewed as needed. To protect its exclusive rights to a brand, the company must make certain that the selected brand is not likely to be considered an infringement on any existing brand already registered with the relevant patent office. This task may be complex because infringement is determined by the courts, which base their decisions on whether a brand causes consumers to be confused, mistaken or deceived about the source of the product. McDonald's is one company that aggressively protects its trademarks against infringement; it has brought charges against a number of companies with 'Mc' names because it fears that the use of the 'Mc' will give consumers the impression that these companies are associated with or owned by McDonald's.

If possible, marketers must guard against allowing a brand name to become a generic term used to refer to a general product category.[19] Generic terms cannot be protected as exclusive brand names. For example, names such as aspirin, escalator and shredded wheat – all brand names at one time – were eventually declared generic terms that refer to product classes; thus they could no longer be protected. To keep a brand name from becoming a generic term, the business should spell the name with a capital letter and use it as an adjective to modify the name of the general product class, as in Kellogg's Rice Krispies.[20] Including the word 'brand' just after the brand name is also helpful. An organization can deal with this problem directly by advertising that its brand is a trademark and should not be used generically. The company can also indicate that the brand is a registered trademark by using the symbol®.

Who thought of that name?!

Burger King, Coca-Cola, JCB, Nike, Sony or Virgin – no matter what the brand, someone, somewhere, sometime created the names now recognized instantly by millions of loyal customers. All too often clients focus on the physical properties of their new products – features, size, colours, quality, performance, operation – at the expense of name consideration, which is 'tacked on' to the new product development process just prior to launch. Branding consultancies believe that creating the right atmosphere and having a very clear understanding of both client culture and target market characteristics are fundamental to the creation of a suitable brand name. Very often a creative workshop is used by a branding consultancy to probe the minds of the client personnel in order to establish buzzwords or emotive trigger descriptions for the new product that may be incorporated into the brand name. Or the consultants might drop creative pebbles into the pond of social media and monitor the ripples and reaction.

The real difficulty comes not from creating a suitable name, but in registering the preferred choice. Intellectual property lawyers now specialize in trademark registration and searching. Qualitative research, such as focus groups or social media discussions, often throws up many brand names consumers believe might be appropriate. Marketing strategy workshops amongst managers in a company do the same. The result is that some organizations compile extensive lists of names with potential for their types of product, which are then registered, even though at the time there is no expectation of using these names. Companies such as Cadbury and Ford have large lists of already registered brand names which at some time they may use but that are no longer available to any other company. This is not 'sharp practice', merely a logical extension of marketers hearing good suggestions from colleagues, distributors and consumers and marking them down for possible future use.

Another consideration for branding consultancies is how the new product's name will work alongside the client's umbrella brand. For example, Per Una range is given independence from owner Marks & Spencer and Cap Colombie from Nescafé; whereas the Focus, Mondeo and Fiesta names are very much tied to the Ford umbrella brand, just as Apple's products link together. There is no right or wrong in this dilemma. Some companies, such as Nescafé with Cap Colombie, want to create sub-brands that, in the eyes of target consumers, are apparently free-standing. For Ford, the logic of cross-promotion and economies of scale in creating brand awareness, have persuaded senior marketers to always utilize the Ford brand and its blue oval alongside the individual model name.

Most brand names are, at some point in the creation process, tested out on consumers, but such tests have to be carefully constrained so as not to allow consumer suggestions to set the process back to square one. Ultimately, a good name cannot overcome product deficiencies, poor distribution, ineffectual promotion, incorrect pricing or inferior customer service, nor can it combat the superiority of a competitor's marketing strategy. A poor, inappropriate, confusing, unmemorable or misleading name can, though, do much harm to an otherwise good product offering.

Companies that try to protect a brand in a foreign country frequently encounter problems. In many countries, brand registration is not possible; the first company to use a brand in such a country has the rights to it. In some instances, a company has actually had to buy its own brand rights from a company in a foreign country because the foreign company was the first user in that country.

Marketers trying to protect their brands must also contend with brand counterfeiting. In many countries it is possible to buy fake General Motors parts, fake Rolex watches, fake Chanel perfume, fake Microsoft software, fake Walt Disney character dolls and a host of other products illegally marketed by manufacturers that do not own the brands. Many counterfeit products are manufactured overseas in South Korea, Italy, Taiwan and China, for example, but some are counterfeited in the countries in which they are sold. The International Anti-Counterfeiting Coalition estimates that roughly $600 billion in annual world trade involves counterfeit merchandise. The sale of this merchandise obviously reduces the brand owners' revenues from marketing their own legitimate products.

FIGURE 11.3
Unilever opts to develop individual brands, in this case for its range of deodrants, including the feminine Impulse and the masculine-focused Lynx

Brand counterfeiting is particularly harmful because the usually inferior counterfeit product undermines consumers' confidence in the brand and their loyalty to it. After unknowingly purchasing a counterfeit product, the buyer may blame the legitimate manufacturer if the product is of low quality or even worse if its use results in damage or injury. Since counterfeiting has become such a serious problem, many companies are taking legal action against counterfeiters. Others have adopted such measures as modifying the product or the packaging to make counterfeit items easier to detect, conducting public awareness campaigns and monitoring distributors to ensure that they stock only legitimate brands.

Branding policies

Before it establishes branding policies, a company must first decide whether to brand its products at all. If a company's product is homogeneous and similar to competitors' products, it may be difficult to brand. Raw materials such as coal, salt, sand and milk are hard to brand because of the homogeneity of such products and their physical characteristics. Marketers must also consider the degree to which consumers differentiate among brands of a product. For example, while brand may be an important factor in the purchase of coffee, snacks and frozen foods, it is not usually so important a consideration in buying lightbulbs, cheese and cling film.

If a company chooses to brand its products, it may opt for one or more of the following branding policies: individual, overall family, line family and brand extension branding.

Individual branding
A policy of naming each product differently.

Individual branding   Individual branding is a policy of naming each product differently. Procter & Gamble relies on an individual branding policy for its line of fabric washing products, which includes Ariel, Bold, Daz, Dreft and Fairy.

A major advantage of individual branding is that if an organization introduces a poor product, the negative images associated with it will not contaminate the company's other products. An individual branding policy may also facilitate market segmentation when a company wishes to enter many segments of the same market. Separate, unrelated names can be used, and each brand can be aimed at a specific segment. Such a policy also encourages internal competition for growth and success between the different brand teams.

FIGURE 11.4
Heinz uses its name on its products, along with a generic description of the item

Overall family branding
A policy of branding all of a company's products with the same name, or at least part of the name.

Overall family branding   In overall family branding, all of a company's products are branded with the same name, or at least part of the name, such as Kraft, Heinz, Microsoft or Ford. In some cases, a company's name is combined with other words to brand items. Heinz uses its name on its products along with a generic description of the item, such as Heinz Salad Cream, Heinz Baked Beans, Heinz Spaghetti and Heinz Tomato Soup. The quality image of its products increases consumer confidence in what they are buying. This brand consistency is stressed in Heinz advertisements (see Figure 11.4). Unlike individual branding, overall family branding means that the promotion of one item with the family brand promotes the company's other products.

Line family branding
A policy of using family branding only for products within a single line.

Line family branding   Sometimes an organization uses family branding only for products within a single line. This policy is called line family branding. Colgate–Palmolive, for example, produces a line of cleaning products that includes a cleanser, a powdered detergent and a liquid cleaner, all with the name Ajax. Colgate also produces several brands of toothpaste, none of which carries the Ajax brand name.

Brand extension branding
A company's use of one of its existing brand names as part of an improved or new product, usually in the same product category as the existing brand.

Brand extension branding   Brand extension branding occurs when a company uses one of its existing brand names as part of a brand for an improved or new product that is usually in the same product category as the existing brand. Unilever, the makers of Timotei shampoo, extended the name to hair conditioner and skincare products. There is one major difference between line family branding and brand extension branding. With line family branding, all products in the line carry the same name, but with brand extension branding this is not the case. The producer of Arrid deodorant, for example, also makes other brands of deodorant.

Choice of branding policy   An organization is not limited to a single branding policy. Instead, branding policy is influenced by the:

- number of products and product lines the company produces
- characteristics of its target markets
- number and type of competing products available
- size of its resources.

Anheuser–Busch, for example, uses both individual and brand extension branding. Most of the brands are individual brands; however, the Michelob Light brand is an extension of the Michelob brand. Sometimes companies must update brands so that they remain fresh and interesting.

Brand licencing

A recent trend in branding strategies involves the licencing of trademarks. By means of a licencing agreement, a company may permit approved manufacturers to use its trademark on other products for a licencing fee. Royalties may be as low as 2 per cent of wholesale revenues or higher than 10 per cent. The licensee is responsible for all manufacturing, selling and advertising functions, and bears the costs if the licenced product fails. Not long ago, only a few companies licenced their corporate trademarks, but today the licencing business is worth billions of pounds and is growing. Harley-Davidson, for example, has authorized the use of its name on non-motorcycle products such as cologne, wine coolers, gold rings and shirts. Disney also licences its brand for use on a range of products. JCB and Coca-Cola both now licence ranges of clothing sold in high-street stores.

The advantages of licencing range from extra revenues and low cost to free publicity, new images and trademark protection. For example, Coca-Cola has licenced its trademark for use on glassware, radios, trucks and clothing in the hope of protecting its trademark. However, brand licencing is not without its drawbacks. The major disadvantages are a lack of manufacturing control, which could hurt the company's name, and the undesirability of bombarding consumers with too many unrelated products bearing the same name. Licencing arrangements can also fail because of poor timing, inappropriate distribution channels or mismatching of product and name.

Managing brands

With the need for brands to create product differentiation, assist in establishing a competitive edge and encourage product awareness, marketers must manage their brands with care.[21] This involves understanding when a brand requires repositioning, modifying, deleting or simply being left alone. Most companies operate with a portfolio of separate brands and products, and must make difficult decisions in terms of which are to receive support and the bulk of an organization's marketing resource, and which are to be killed off or given only minimal support. Chapter 12 of *Marketing: Concepts and Strategies* explores these strategic choices.

As explained in Chapter 5's discussion of consumer buying behaviour, without an understanding of brand loyalty and brand switching, it is difficult to manage an organization's brands effectively. It is essential for companies to make an effort to research brand loyalty and brand perceptions, to help them make sensible decisions that accurately reflect consumers' views.

Research shows that to create **successful brands**, a company must:

> **Successful brands**
> Brands for which a company must prioritize quality, offer superior service, get there first, differentiate brands, develop a unique positioning concept, have a strong communications programme and be consistent and reliable.

- prioritize quality – the top brands are all high quality in their product fields
- offer superior service less easily copied by competitors than pure product attributes
- get there first, not necessarily technologically but, in the minds of targeted customers, by:
  - exploiting new technology (Apple, Samsung)
  - new positioning concepts (first direct bank)
  - new distribution channels (Amazon, Direct Line)
  - new market segments (Lidl, Ocado)
  - using gaps resulting from environmental change (Ecover, Toyota Prius)
- differentiate its brands so that consumers perceive the brands on offer as being different
- develop a unique positioning concept, making the brand and its differentiating characteristics stand out with a clear image and positioning message against rival brands
- support the brand and its positioning with a strong communications programme so that target consumers are aware of the brand and its positioning proposition
- deliver consistency and reliability over time keeping the brand's values trustworthy as perceived by target consumers.

Branding experts[22] state that to build effective brands, it is essential for an organization to understand that there is more to a brand than simply a catchy name and visible logo. **Brand strength** is a function of the product's attributes and functionality, its differentiation, plus any demonstrable added value to the purchaser or user. For example, Nike sports shoes are designed for serious running and are fit for this core purpose, but Nike has a reputation for innovation and progression, so the brand is perceived as a 'first mover', providing differentiation versus rival brands. For the purchaser, the reputation of the brand for being state-of-the-art and highly desirable, provides 'street cred', which is the added value to the consumer.

Brand strength
A function of the product's attributes and functionality, its differentiation, plus any demonstrable added value to the purchaser or user.

There are, in fact, four **levels of brands**: the tangible product, the 'basic' brand, the 'augmented' brand and the 'potential' of the brand. Level 1, the tangible product, is the degree of quality, performance, features and actual attributes. Level 2, the 'basic' brand, is the identity, differentiation and positioning. Level 3, the 'augmented' brand, is the aggregated impact from including supplementary products and service support. Level 4, the 'potential' of the brand, is reached when customers will not willingly accept substitutes and are unhappy to switch to rival brands; psychological benefits and barriers in the minds of target customers are important determinants of brand potential.

Levels of brands
The tangible product, the 'basic' brand, the 'augmented' brand and the 'potential' of the brand.

There are three essential acid tests for determining whether a brand is successful. Although most companies consider only the overall profit contribution to the end-of-year financial annual report and accounts, when determining a brand's success they should ask the following three fundamental questions:

1. Has the brand captured the leading share in its market segment or distribution channel?
2. Does the brand command prices sufficiently high enough to produce a large profit margin?
3. Will the brand sustain its strong share of profits when rival and generic versions of the product enter the market?

Using these core criteria, many brands are relatively unsuccessful. For marketers, managing brands must include knowing when a brand is succeeding, when it is faltering but may be saved, and when a brand is a lost cause and should be deleted from the company's range of brands. Chapter 12 examines this difficult issue in more detail.

Corporate branding

Corporate branding
The application of product branding at the corporate level, reflected visibly through the company name, logo and visual presentation and in the organization's underlying values.

Corporate branding involves applying the principles of product branding at the corporate level. Corporate branding is reflected in visible manifestations, such as the company name, logo and visual presentation, and also in the organization's underlying and guiding values. Apple, McDonald's, Wal-Mart and Manchester United Football Club each has a corporate brand that is based around the organization itself. Sometimes the terms **corporate image** and **corporate identity** are also used in relation to corporate branding. The concepts of corporate identity and corporate branding overlap: both referring to what the company transmits about itself.[23] Corporate image reflects the perceptions that external audiences hold about the organization.[24]

Corporate image
Reflects the perceptions that external audiences hold about an organization.

Corporate branding plays a role in guiding all of a company's marketing activities. The corporate brand is transmitted through tangible and intangible features. The tangible dimensions include visual features of the corporate brand, such as corporate logo and symbols, typography, colour, website design, buildings, staff uniforms, vehicles and stationery. For example, Unilever overhauled its corporate identity to fit with the company's mission: 'creating a better future for every day'. The corporate brand was reflected in a new logo and images showing the everyday contributions its products make to people's lives. Less tangible features include how the corporate brand is portrayed through what people inside and outside the organization believe and say.

Corporate identity
Overlapping with the corporate branding concept: branding at the corporate level.

To be effective, the corporate brand should be embedded in all company actions. This means that all aspects of the company's communication, including internal communication with employees and external marketing activities, ranging from the annual report through to its web pages, advertising and PR, must convey a consistent message about the corporate brand. Corporate branding is particularly important for services organizations, because customers look for help in understanding and visualizing the services product. A strong corporate brand can help buyers to overcome the intangibility of some of these products. For example, first direct bank has worked hard to build a corporate image based on service quality and easy access,[25] which reflects the company's reliability and flexible approach to meeting customer needs. This has helped to build a corporate image based around the notion of good service. The fact that this image is also reflected in research examining service in the financial services sector adds credibility to the bank's offering.

Packaging and labelling

Packaging and labelling are also part of the marketing process and are linked to brand identity. They impact on the image of the product, its functionality and, ultimately, on the customer's perception of satisfaction. At times, they create differentiation vis-à-vis rival products. For example, Coca-Cola introduced limited-edition packaging for its iconic glass bottle to appeal to more upmarket consumers. Rice company Tilda markets premium-priced rice, so ensures its packaging has a more deluxe-looking appearance than its lower-priced rivals, befitting the superiority of its carefully selected basmati rice grains.

Packaging
The development of a product's container and label, complete with graphic design.

Packaging involves the development of a container and label, complete with graphic design for a product. A package can be a vital part of a product, making it more versatile, safer or easier to use. Like a brand name, a package can influence customers' attitudes towards a product and thus affect their purchase decisions. For example, several producers of sauces, salad dressings and ketchups have packaged their products in squeezable containers to make use and storage more convenient. Package characteristics help shape buyers' impressions of a product at the time of purchase or during use. This section examines the main functions of packaging and considers several major packaging decisions. The role of the package in marketing strategy is also analyzed.

Packaging functions

Effective packaging means more than simply putting products into containers and covering them with wrappers. First of all, packaging materials serve the basic purpose of protecting the product and maintaining its functional form. Fluids such as milk, orange juice and hairspray need packages that preserve and protect them; the packaging should prevent damage that could affect the product's usefulness and increase costs. Since product tampering has become a problem for marketers of many types of goods, several packaging techniques have been developed to counter this danger. Some packages are also designed to foil shoplifters.

Another function of packaging is to offer convenience for consumers. For example, small sealed packages, individual sized boxes or plastic bags that contain liquids and do not require refrigeration, appeal strongly to children and young adults with active lifestyles. Putting McVitie's Jaffa Cakes into lunch-box-sized plastic tubs greatly boosted sales of this well-known brand by adding a level of functionality and convenience for packed lunches and school snacks. The size or shape of a package may relate to the product's storage, convenience of use or replacement rate. Small, single-serving tins of fruit, such as Del Monte's Fruitini, may prevent waste and make storage easier. Low, regular-shaped packets may be easier to stack and use cupboard space more efficiently. The tube used by Pringles facilitates easy storage at home and in-store. A third function of packaging is to promote a product by communicating its features, uses, benefits and image.

At times, a reusable package is developed to make a product more desirable. For example, some ice-cream containers can be used again as food storage containers.

Major packaging considerations

Packaging must support a product's brand image and positioning, helping develop differentiation vis-à-vis rival products. When developing packages, marketers must take many factors into account. Some of these factors relate to consumers' needs; others relate to the requirements of resellers. Retailers, wholesalers and distributors will be required to handle and stock the products, and in many instances to display and deliver them. Packaging solutions must reflect the needs of these channel members in addition to the requirements of end-user customers. Obviously, one major consideration is cost. Although a variety of packaging materials, processes and designs are available, some are rather expensive. In recent years buyers have shown a willingness to pay more for improved packaging, but there are limits. Marketers should try to determine, through research, just how much customers are willing to pay for packages.

Developing tamper-resistant packaging is very important. Although no package is totally tamper-proof, marketers can develop packages that are difficult to tamper with and that also make any tampering evident to resellers and consumers. As new, safer packaging technologies are being explored, marketers should be aware of changes in packaging technology and legislation, and be prepared to make modifications that will ensure consumer safety. One packaging innovation includes an inner pouch that displays the word 'open' when air has entered the pouch after opening. Marketers now also have an obligation to inform consumers of the possibilities and risks of product tampering by educating them to recognize possible tampering and by placing warnings on packaging.[26] For example, the tops of many sauce and condiment bottles now have plastic seals around them, so that consumers can be confident they have not been opened. Baby food manufacturers, such as Cow & Gate and Heinz, have taken this protection method one step further by using special metal jar tops with pop-up discs showing when a jar has been opened. This move followed cases of tampering in which foreign bodies were introduced into baby foods. Now the special tops expressly warn consumers to watch out for tampering. Although effective tamper-resistant packaging may be expensive to develop, when balanced against the costs of lost sales, loss of consumer confidence and a company's reputation, and potentially expensive product liability lawsuits, the costs of ensuring consumer safety are minimal.[27]

Marketers should consider how much consistency is desirable in a company's package designs. The best policy may be not to attempt consistency, especially if a company's products are unrelated or aimed at vastly different target markets. To promote an overall company image, a company may decide that all packages are to be similar or include one major element of the design. This approach is called **family packaging**. Sometimes it is used only for lines of products, as with Campbell's soups, Weight Watchers foods and Planters nuts.

Family packaging
An approach in which all of a company's packages are similar or include one major element of the design.

A package's promotional role is an important consideration. Through verbal and non-verbal symbols, the package can inform potential buyers about the product's content, features, uses, advantages and hazards. A company can create desirable images and associations by its choice of colour, design, shape and texture. Many cosmetics manufacturers, for example, design their packages to create impressions of richness, luxury and exclusiveness. Many perfumes are in packs deliberately designed to suggest sensuality and sex appeal. A package performs a promotional function when it is designed to be safer or more convenient to use, if such characteristics help stimulate demand.

To develop a package that has a definite promotional value, a designer must consider size, shape, texture, colour and graphics.[28] Beyond the obvious limitation that the package must be large enough to hold the product, a package can be designed to appear taller or shorter. For instance, thin vertical lines make a package look taller; wide horizontal stripes make it look shorter. A marketer may want a package to appear taller because many people perceive something that is taller as being larger.

Colours on packages and in branding are often chosen to attract attention. People associate specific colours with certain feelings and experiences, as outlined below:

Blue is soothing, it is also associated with wealth, trust and security.
Grey is associated with strength, exclusivity and success.
Orange can stand for low cost.
Red has connotations of excitement, stimulation and danger.
Yellow is associated with cheerfulness and joy.
Purple is linked with dignity and stateliness.
Black is associated with being strong and masterful.[29]

For example, BMW always uses the blue and grey colour palettes in its advertising and brochures, while easyJet's planes famously are adorned in orange. Uncle Ben's rice is familiar in its orange packaging as it emphasizes convenience and value for money, while more up-market competitor Tilda, focusing on premium quality and superior taste, utilizes blue in its branding and smart new packaging.

When selecting packaging colours, marketers must decide whether a particular colour will evoke positive or negative feelings when it is linked to a specific product. Rarely, for example, do processors package meat or bread in green materials, because customers may associate green with mould. However, recent concern about the state of the environment has, in general, led to an increase in the use of green-coloured packaging and neutral shades/textures. Marketers must also decide whether a specific target market will respond favourably or unfavourably to a particular colour. Cosmetics for women are more likely to be sold in pastel-coloured packaging than are personal care products for men. Packages designed to appeal to children often use primary colours and bold designs.

Packaging must also meet the needs of resellers. Wholesalers and retailers consider whether a package facilitates transportation, storage and handling. Packages must allow these resellers to make maximum use of storage space, both in transit and in the shops. Products should be packed so that sales staff can transfer them to the shelves with ease. The shape and weight of packaging are also important. Resellers may refuse to carry certain products if their packages are cumbersome. Figure 11.5 shows how these factors have been taken into consideration in developing the product's packaging.

A final consideration is whether to develop packages that are environmentally responsible. This is a major issue for marketers, with consumer pressure to cut back on packaging waste and the sustainability agendas of major retailers threatening to de-list non-compliant brands. A CNN report on the growing refuse disposal problem in the USA stated that nearly 50 per cent of all rubbish consists of discarded plastic packaging, such as polystyrene containers, plastic soft drink bottles, carrier bags and other packaging items. Plastic packaging material does not biodegrade, and using paper requires the destruction of valuable forest lands. Consequently, a number of companies are recycling more materials and exploring packaging alternatives, helped by packaging experts such as Tetra Pak. Heinz, for example, is looking for alternatives to its plastic squeezable ketchup bottles. Marketers must carefully balance society's desires to preserve the environment against consumers' desires for convenience.

Packaging development

Packaging development
A mix of aesthetic considerations and structural necessities to guarantee the functionality of the design.

Packaging development requires a mix of aesthetic considerations and structural necessities to guarantee the functionality of the design. There are cartons, bottles, tubes, cans, tubs and jars, multipacks, clamshells and blister packs, CD/DVD boxes, gift packs, plus many innovative formats for storing, displaying and dispensing products in a manner that is ahead of the competition. Material selection is an important stage in the design process, as are the specification and application of surface graphics and

FIGURE 11.5
Manufacturers, particularly of children's toys, often use brightly coloured packaging to attract youngsters to their products

typography. Decisions must be made concerning information layout and the hierarchy of messages, front-of-pack versus back-of-pack detailing, choice of language and jargon, the photography and images to be selected, illustrations and use of colour, deployment of symbols and icons, final finishes and effects. There are often practical requirements to consider, such as weights, measures, ingredients, nutritional information and barcoding to display. Legal requirements for health and safety have forced changes to packaging, while legal requirements relating to the labelling of ingredients, sourcing and health-related issues have forced producers to include more information on-pack.

Packaging and marketing strategy

Packaging can be a major component of a marketing strategy. A new cap or closure, a better box or wrapping, or a more convenient container may give a product a competitive edge. With increased home deliveries, the shipping packaging becomes both a functional concern and an intrinsic facet of the product's appeal to the receiving consumer. The right type of package for a new product can help it gain market recognition very quickly. In the case of existing brands, marketers should periodically re-evaluate packages. Particularly in the case of consumer convenience products, marketers should view packaging as a major strategic tool. It is intrinsically linked to innovation. Tilda developed innovative packaging to allow two-minute steaming of pre-cooked microwavable rice, opening up a whole new category and creating significant growth of rice sales to convenience-oriented time-pressured consumers previously unlikely to cook rice at home. This section examines ways in which packaging can be used strategically.

Altering the package   At times, a marketer changes a package because the existing design is no longer in style, especially when compared with competitive products. A package may also be redesigned because new product features need to be highlighted on the package, or because new packaging materials have become available. A company may decide to change a product's packaging to make the product more convenient or safer to use, or to reposition the product. A major redesign of a simple package costs about £50 000, and the redesign of a line of products may cost up to £500 000. Choosing the right packaging material is an important consideration when redesigning. Different materials vary in popularity at different times. For example, glass is becoming more popular, as views on the environment and the need for recyclability come to the fore.

Secondary use packaging

Secondary use package
A package that can be reused for purposes other than its initial use.

Secondary use packaging   A secondary use package is one that can be reused for purposes other than its initial one. For example, a margarine container can be reused to store leftovers, a jam jar can be used as a drinking glass and shortbread tins can be reused for storing cakes and biscuits. Secondary use packages can be viewed by customers as adding value to products. If customers value this type of packaging, then its use should stimulate unit sales.

Category-consistent packaging

Category-consistent packaging
The packaging of a product according to the packaging practices associated with a particular product category.

Category-consistent packaging   Category-consistent packaging means that the product is packaged in line with the packaging practices associated with a particular product category. Some product categories – for example, mayonnaise, mustard, ketchup and jam – have traditional package shapes. Other product categories are characterized by recognizable colour combinations – red and white for soup or black and yellow for tea. When a company introduces a brand in one of these product categories, marketers will often use traditional package shapes and colour combinations to ensure that customers will recognize the new product as being in that specific product category. Few pizza brands are not packaged in square flat boxes coloured red, yellow and black!

Innovative packaging   Sometimes, a marketer will employ a unique cap, design, applicator or other feature to make the product competitively distinctive, as illustrated in Figure 11.6. Such packaging can be effective when the innovation makes the product safer or easier to use, or when the unique package provides better protection for the product. In some instances, marketers use innovative or unique packages that are inconsistent with traditional packaging practices, to make the brand stand out relative to its competitors. Kellogg's, for example, uses an innovative, crush-proof cylinder to package its Pringles potato crisps. Innovative packaging generally requires considerable resources, not only for the package design itself but also to make customers aware of the unique package and its benefit. Sometimes, innovative packaging can change the way in which consumers use a product. The introduction of cardboard-boxed, single serving soft drinks made it easier for consumers to have a drink while travelling by car, train and plane. Even cyclists can drink with ease while on the move.

Multiple packaging

Multiple packaging
Packaging that includes more than one unit of a product, such as twin packs, tri-packs and six-packs.

Multiple packaging   Rather than packaging a single unit of a product, marketers sometimes use twin packs, tri-packs, six-packs or other forms of multiple packaging. For certain types of product, multiple packaging is used to increase demand because it increases the amount of the product available at the point of consumption in consumers' houses, for example. However, multiple packaging does not work for all types of product. Consumers would not use additional table salt simply because an extra box was in the cupboard. Multiple packaging can make products easier to handle and store, as in the case of six-packs for soft drinks; it can also facilitate special price offers, such as two-for-one sales. In addition, multiple packaging may increase consumer acceptance of the product by encouraging the buyer to try the product several times.

Handling improved packaging   Packaging of a product may be changed to make it easier to handle in the distribution channel – for example, changing the outer carton, special bundling, shrink wrapping or palletizing. In some cases the shape of the package may need to be changed.

FIGURE 11.6

Leading packaging supplier Tetra Pak promotes the functionality and applicability of its cartons

Source: Image courtesy of Tetra Pak (UK) Ltd.

For example, an ice-cream producer may switch from a cylindrical package to a rectangular one to facilitate handling. In addition, at the retail level, the ice-cream producer may be able to get more shelf facings with a rectangular package as opposed to a round one. Outer containers for products are sometimes changed so that they will proceed more easily through automated warehousing systems.

As package designs improve, it becomes harder for any one product to dominate because of packaging. However, marketers still attempt to gain a competitive edge through packaging. Skilled artists and package designers who have experience in marketing research, test out packaging to see what sells well, not just what is aesthetically appealing. Since the typical large store stocks 15 000 items or more, products that stand out are more likely to be bought.

Criticisms of packaging

The last few decades have seen a number of improvements in packaging. However, some packaging problems still need to be resolved. Some packages simply do not work well. The packaging for flour and sugar is, at best, often not much better than poor. Both grocers and consumers are very much aware that these packages leak and are easily torn. Can anyone open and close a bag of flour without spilling at least a little bit? Certain packages, such as biscuit tins, milk cartons with fold-out spouts and potato crisp bags, are frequently difficult to open. The traditional shapes of packages for products such as ketchup and salad dressing make the products inconvenient to use. Have you ever questioned, when slapping a ketchup bottle, why the producer did not put the ketchup in a mayonnaise jar?

Certain types of packaging are being questioned with regard to their recyclability and biodegradability. For example, throw-away bottles take considerably more resources to produce than do reusable glass bottles. Social concerns and regulatory pressures are bringing green issues to the fore, with significant implications for marketers and packaging designers.

Although many steps have been taken to make packaging safer, critics still focus on health and safety issues. Containers with sharp edges and easily broken glass bottles are sometimes viewed as a threat to safety. Certain types of plastic packaging and aerosol containers represent possible health hazards.

At times, packaging is viewed as being deceptive. Package shape, graphic design and certain colours may be used to make a product appear larger than it actually is. The inconsistent use of certain size designations such as 'giant', 'economy', 'family', 'king' and 'super' can certainly lead to customer confusion. Although customers have traditionally liked attractive, effective, convenient packaging, the cost of such packaging is high. For some products, such as cosmetics, the cost of the package is higher than the cost of the product itself.

Labelling

Labelling
Packaging information that can be used for a variety of promotional, informational and legal purposes.

Labelling is very closely related to packaging and can be used for a variety of promotional, informational and legal purposes. The label can be used to facilitate the identification of a product by presenting the brand and a unique graphic design. For example, Heinz's ketchup is easy to identify on a supermarket shelf because the brand name is easy to read and is coupled with a distinctive, crown-like graphic design. Labels have a descriptive function. For certain types of product, the label indicates the grade of the product, especially for tinned fruit. Labels can describe the source of the product, its contents and major features, how to use the product, how to care for the product, nutritional information, type and style of the product and size and number of servings. The label can play a promotional function through the use of graphics that attract attention. The food and drug administrations and consumer protection agencies in different countries have varying requirements concerning warnings, instructions, certifications and manufacturers' identifications. Increasingly the EU is demanding similar standards in all member countries. Despite the fact that consumers have responded favourably to the inclusion of this type of information on labels, evidence as to whether they actually use it has been mixed. Several studies indicate that consumers do not use nutritional information, whereas other studies indicate that the information is considered useful. Labels can also promote a manufacturer's other products or encourage proper use of products, resulting in greater customer satisfaction with them.

Universal product code (UPC) or barcode
A series of thick and thin lines that identifies the product, and provides inventory and pricing information readable by an electronic scanner.

The label for many products includes a **universal product code (UPC)** or **barcode** a series of thick and thin lines that identifies the product, and provides inventory and pricing information that can be read by an electronic scanner. The UPC is read electronically at the retail checkout counter. This information is used by retailers and producers for price and inventory control purposes.

Colour and eye-catching graphics on labels overcome the jumble of words known to designers as 'mouse print' that have been added to satisfy government regulations. Because so many similar products are available, an attention-getting device or 'silent salesperson' is needed to attract interest. As one of the most visible parts of a product, the label is an important element in a marketing mix.

Labelling is an integral part of packaging that can be used effectively to convey product information and benefits to customers, and to promote a brand's positioning image. There are increasing legal considerations that marketers must address, such as EU regulations in terms of food sourcing, ingredient content, nutritional information, weights and measures, as well as cooking or application instructions. Ethical marketing requires that consumers are not misled or 'over-sold' owing to the information provided on labels. Concerns about obesity and diabetes are forcing manufacturers of foods to include nutritional and healthy-eating information on their packaging. This provides a window of opportunity for healthier brands to compete with many leading brands whose domination was once viewed as impregnable. *Innocent* smoothies have stolen market share from the colas in most supermarkets, and Innocent's humorous packaging stresses its wholesome and healthy qualities.

Summary

A *brand* is a name, term, design, symbol or any other feature that identifies one seller's good or service as distinct from those of other sellers. A *brand name* is that part of a brand that can be spoken, including letters, words and numbers; the element that cannot be spoken often a symbol or design is called a *brand mark*. A *trademark* is a legal designation indicating that the owner has exclusive use of a brand or part of a brand, and that others are prohibited by law from using it. A *trade name* is the legal name of an organization.

Branding helps buyers identify and evaluate products, helps sellers facilitate repeat purchasing and product introduction, and fosters *brand loyalty* a customer's strongly motivated and long-standing decision to purchase a particular product or service.

A recent development has been marketers' use of online brand communities and blog communities. In a *brand community* a group of consumers and observers who admire a brand are encouraged to share their positive feelings, often online through social media. *Blog communities* permit one-to-one tailored communication with and between members of the digital brand community. Such developments permit *dynamic branding*, with very rapid communication and sharing of brand information. In order to nurture loyalty, brands are turning to *brand advocacy* and *brand advocates*, investing in creating brand advocates, who will share their positive feelings and experiences of a brand in return for insider knowledge and access to bespoke events. The digital era has shifted the balance of power from brand managers, who previously issued most communications about their brands, to consumers who increasingly use social media to share views with other consumers and thereby impact a brand's standing.

The three degrees of brand loyalty are recognition, preference and insistence. *Brand recognition* exists when a customer is aware that a brand exists and views it as an alternative to purchase if the preferred brand is unavailable. *Brand preference* is the degree of brand loyalty in which a customer prefers one brand over competing brands and will purchase it if it is available. *Brand insistence* is the degree of brand loyalty in which a customer will accept no substitute. *Brand equity* is the marketing and financial value associated with a brand's strength in a market. It represents the value of a brand to an organization. The four major elements underlying brand equity are brand name awareness, brand loyalty, perceived brand quality and brand associations.

Brands need to have a well-specified *brand identity*, reflecting target segment expectations and the brand strategies adopted by competitors. Brand attributes and personality underpin the brand's identity. Branding experts believe that well-managed, strong and desirable brands should identify a set of specific tangible benefits to attach to the brand, known as *brand attributes*, a set of *brand values* which help develop a unified sense of purpose among staff and align with messaging to external audiences, plus a set of appealing and desirable *brand personality* traits to create emotion and excitement. Implicit in this view is the importance of effectively creating a well-differentiated and memorable image for the brand that is carefully controlled.

A *manufacturer brand*, initiated by the producer, makes it possible to associate the company more easily with its products at the point of purchase. An *own label brand* is initiated and owned by a reseller, such as a retailer. A *generic brand* indicates only the product category and does not include the company name or other identifying terms. Manufacturers combat the growing competition from own label brands by developing multiple brands.

When selecting a brand name, a marketer should choose one that is easy to say, spell and recall, and that alludes to the product's uses, benefits or special characteristics. Brand names are created inside an organization by individuals, committees or branding departments, or by outside consultants. Brand names can be devised from words, initials, numbers, nonsense words or a combination of these. Services as well as products are branded, often with the company name and an accompanying symbol that makes the brand distinctive or conveys a desired image.

Producers protect ownership of their brands through patent and trademark offices. Marketers at a company must make certain that their selected brand name does not infringe on an already-registered brand by confusing or deceiving consumers about the source of the product. In many countries, brand registration is on a first-come, first-served basis, making protection more difficult. Brand counterfeiting, increasingly common, has potential for undermining consumer confidence in, and loyalty to, a brand.

Companies brand their products in several ways. *Individual branding* designates a unique name for each of a company's products; *overall family branding* identifies all of a company's products with the same name; *line family branding* assigns all products within a single line the same name; and *brand extension branding* applies an existing name to a new or improved product. Trademark licencing enables producers to earn extra revenue, receive low cost or free publicity, and protect their trademarks. Through a licencing agreement, and for a licencing fee, a company may permit approved manufacturers to use its trademark on other products.

Successful brands tend to prioritize quality, offer superior service, get to market or the targeted segment first, be clearly differentiated from rival brands, have a unique positioning concept supported by a strong communications programme and be consistent over time. *Brand strength* is a function of the product's attributes and functionality, its differentiation, plus any demonstrable added value to the purchaser or user. Strong brands usually create product differentiation, help establish a competitive edge, encourage product awareness and demand a significant amount of management and control. Four *levels of brands* need to be addressed: the tangible product, the 'basic' brand, the 'augmented' brand and the 'potential' of the brand. To be successful, a brand should capture the leading share in its market segment or distribution channel, command prices sufficiently high to offer high profit margins and be likely to maintain its profit position after more brands and generic versions enter the market. Many companies should be more effective in managing their brands, many of which do not live up to these success criteria.

Corporate branding involves applying the principles of product branding at the corporate level. Corporate branding is reflected in visible manifestations such as the company name, logo and visual presentation and also in the organization's underlying and guiding values. Sometimes the terms *corporate image* and *corporate identity* are also used in relation to corporate branding. Corporate branding plays a role in guiding all of a company's marketing activities. Corporate branding is transmitted through tangible and intangible features and, to be effective, should be embedded in all company actions.

Packaging involves the development of a container and label, complete with graphic design for a product. Effective packaging offers protection, economy, safety and convenience. It can influence the customer's purchase decision by promoting a product's features, uses, benefits and image. When developing a package, marketers must consider costs relative to how much the target market is willing to pay. Other considerations include how to make the package tamper-resistant; whether to use *family packaging, secondary use packaging, category-consistent packaging* or *multiple packaging*; how to design the package as an effective promotional tool; how best to accommodate resellers; and whether to develop environmentally responsible packaging.

Packaging development involves aesthetic and structural choices. Other considerations include: material selection, surface graphics, typography, information layout and hierarchies, front-of-pack versus back-of-pack detailing, language and jargon, photography and illustrations, use of colour, symbols and icons, final finishes and effects, labelling practicalities and barcoding/ tracking. There are numerous primary packaging options: cartons, bottles, tubes, cans, tubs and jars, multipacks, clamshells, blister packs, CD/DVD boxes, gift packs and a host of innovative solutions for storing, displaying and dispensing products.

Packaging can be a major component of a marketing strategy. Companies choose particular colours, designs, shapes and textures to create desirable images and associations. Producers alter packages to convey new features or to make them safer or more convenient. If a package has a secondary use, the product's value to the consumer may be increased. Category-consistent packaging makes products more easily recognized by consumers, and innovative packaging enhances a product's distinctiveness. Consumers may criticize packaging that does not work well, is not biodegradable or recyclable, poses health or safety problems, or is deceptive in some way. The sustainability agenda within the supply chain is a significant issue for marketers.

Labelling is an important aspect of packaging that can be used for promotional, informational and legal purposes. Because labels are attention-getting devices, they are significant features in the marketing mix. Various regulatory agencies can require that products be labelled or marked with warnings, instructions, certifications, nutritional information and the manufacturer's identification. Increasingly, most products even cars have a *universal product code (UPC)* or *barcode*. There are ethical considerations for marketers as customers should not be misled or mis-sold owing to the information conveyed on a product's packaging.

Key links

- This chapter, about effective branding, should be read in conjunction with the section of Chapter 8 that addresses the linked concept of brand positioning.

- The branding strategy must reflect the characteristics of the product, as explored in Chapter 10.

- Many companies operate a portfolio of brands and often must select some for priority investment and marketing spend, as described in Chapter 12.

- The implications of the digital environment must be considered when managing brands, as overviewed in Chapter 19.

Important terms

Blog communities
Brand
Brand advocacy
Brand advocate
Brand attributes
Brand community
Brand equity
Brand extension branding

Brand identity
Brand insistence
Brand loyalty
Brand mark
Brand name
Brand personality
Brand preference
Brand recognition
Brand strength
Brand values
Category-consistent packaging
Corporate branding
Corporate identity
Corporate image
Dynamic branding
Family packaging
Generic brand
Individual branding
Labelling
Levels of brands
Line family branding
Manufacturer brands
Multiple packaging
Overall family branding
Own label brands
Packaging

Packaging development
Secondary use package
Successful brands
Trade name
Trademark
Universal product code (UPC) or barcode

Discussion and review questions

1. What is the difference between a brand and a brand name? Compare and contrast the terms brand mark and trademark.

2. How does branding benefit customers and organizations?

3. What are the advantages associated with brand loyalty?

4. In what ways have social media and the web enabled brands to create communities of supporters?

5. Why are companies seeking to identify or create brand advocates amongst their customers?

6. In what ways have brand managers been forced to relinquish control over what is communicated about their brands in the digital era?

7. What are the distinguishing characteristics of own label brands?

8. Given the competition between own label brands and manufacturer brands, should manufacturers be concerned about the popularity of own label brands? How should manufacturers fight back in the brand battle?

9. Identify and explain the major considerations consumers take into account when selecting a brand.

10. The brand name JCB is sometimes used generically to refer to diggers or backhoe loaders. How can JCB protect this brand name?

11. Identify and explain the four major branding policies and give examples of each. Can a company use more than one policy at a time? Explain your answer.

12. What are the major advantages and disadvantages of licencing?

13. Why is there more to a brand than its name? Explain your response.

14. What are the most commonly found foundations for successful brands? Illustrate your response with brand examples.

15. What constitutes brand strength?

16. What are the differences between brand attributes, brand values and brand personality?

17. What is brand equity and why is this notion increasingly important?

18. What are the three core criteria for assessing the success of a brand?

19. Describe the functions that a package can perform. Which function is most important? Why?

20. When developing a package, what are the major issues that a marketer should consider?

21. In what ways can packaging be used as a strategic tool?

22. What are the major criticisms of packaging?

23. How is the sustainability drive impacting on packaging decisions?

24. What are the major functions of labelling?

Recommended readings

Aaker, D.A., *Aaker On Branding: 20 Principles That Drive Success* (Morgan James Publishing, 2014).

Aaker, D.A., *Building Strong Brands* (Pocket Books, 2010).

Ambrose, G. and Harris, P., *Packaging The Brand: The Relationship Between Packaging Design and Brand Identity* (AVA Publishing, 2011).

Calver, G., *What is Packaging Design?* (RotoVision SA, 2007).

De Chernatony, L., McDonald, M. and Wallace, E., *Creating Powerful Brands* (Butterworth-Heinemann, 2010).

Kapferer, J.-N., *The New Strategic Brand Management: New Insights and Strategic Thinking* (Kogan Page, 2012).

Keller, K.L., *Strategic Brand Management* (FT/Prentice Hall, 2011).

Kirkpatrick, J., *New Packaging Design* (Laurence King, 2009).

Klimchuk, M.R. and Krasovec, S.A., *Packaging Design: Successful Product Branding from Concept to Shelf* (John Wiley, 2013).

Ries, A. and Ries, L., *The 22 Immutable Laws of Branding: How to Build any Product or Line into a World Class Brand* (Profile Books, 2002).

Rowles, D., *Digital Branding: A Complete Step-by-Step Guide to Strategy, Tactics and Measurement* (Kogan Page, 2014).

Internet exercise

Packaging has to reflect manufacturers' requirements and also evolving consumer issues. Log on to: www.tetrapak.com. Consider the information on this leading packaging company's website, notably the information offered about the company, its ethos, core values, vision and mission, innovation and new product development.

1. To what extent and in what ways is Tetra Pak addressing changing and evolving manufacturer and consumer issues?

2. What innovative packaging solutions is Tetra Pak currently developing?

Group tasks

1. Each member of your team should nominate three 'great brands'. Select one brand that several members of the team have nominated. Explore why the brand in question is 'great'. Identify its brand personality.

2. Collect examples of packaging from your recent purchases. Explore what purposes the packaging serves. Consider the extent to which the packaging is part of the product's branding.

Applied mini-case

In the 1980s, one of Europe's retailing success stories was the creation by George Davies of fashion chain Next. Leading out-of-town grocery retailer ASDA persuaded Davies to leave Next and to rekindle the fortunes of its clothing range. The result was the *George* range of men's, women's and children's clothing, positioned as a low price, high style fashion brand. 'Styles straight off the catwalk' at affordable prices, targeted at ASDA's value-conscious shoppers, proved incredibly successful. In the highly competitive clothing market in 2004, the George range in ASDA grocery superstores overtook Debenhams to become the UK's third biggest retailer of clothing. George Davies moved on and, to the surprise of many onlookers, was approached by erstwhile arch-rival Marks & Spencer to help improve the former market leader's fortunes. The result for Marks & Spencer was the highly successful range of stylish fashion, branded *Per Una*.

Both ASDA with *George*, and Marks & Spencer with *Per Una* decided to utilize freshly created brands for their new clothing ranges. In the case of Marks & Spencer, this was even more remarkable, as previously all of its merchandise retailed under the *St Michael* retailer's own label brand, familiar to generations of shoppers. It is believed that without brand identities so deliberately far removed from the host retailers' own brands, neither *George* nor *Per Una* would have been so successful. Both brands have themselves enabled their owners to extend their operations: *George* is available by catalogue and online, and both *George* and *Per Una* have now been given fashion-only high-street branches.

Sources: George/ASDA, 2004; Marks & Spencer stores, 2003/2004 and 2015; Rachel Barnes, 'ASDA to highlight style in George repositioning', *Marketing*, 25 March 2004, p. 4: www.marksandspencer.com/peruna, June 2011 and April 2015; http://direct.asda.com/george/clothing, May 2011 and April 2015.

Question

Why did ASDA and Marks & Spencer both opt to launch clothing ranges with new brand identities that were different to the host retailers' brands?

Rebranding Macmillan

Case study

Cancer affects many families. In the UK, most cancer sufferers will be aware of the Macmillan charity's cancer specialists, nurses and counsellors. A problem for the charity was that those unaffected by cancer knew little or nothing about Macmillan. Charities are loath to devote their much-needed resources to marketing or branding, but recognize that without the public's awareness of their activities and a positive view of their brand, donations of money or time are unlikely. Around a decade ago, Macmillan decided to rebrand as Macmillan Cancer Support.

Before the new brand strategy, brand awareness was around 6 per cent. Even those who knew about the brand did not appreciate how Macmillan provides much more than its highly regarded cancer nurses. A decade later and brand awareness is now much higher, reaching 29 per cent. Macmillan's aim is to become known in everyday life and to gain the public's interest in a wide array of its activities. The charity's aims go beyond building awareness ... there are fund-raising aspirations as well. Upwards of £200 million is required. Volunteering is an important need. A brave decision, to underpin these objectives was to target youngsters and young adults.

The traditional coffee morning target audience has remained in place, now supplemented with youngsters

The Source is a digital platform for people to post their own hints and tips for those affected by cancer. Macmillan promotes the best advice posted on the discussion forum. The charity uses a host of platforms and postings, but still values its traditional brand-building campaigns and advertising. Nevertheless, Macmillan is also now harnessing social media and messaging to appeal to its target group. Macmillan integrates its activities to ensure its core target audiences do not feel to be ousted.

Sources: Sarah Bentley, Accenture; Jude Brooks, Coca-Cola; 'Brandbuilders look to online space for growth', *Marketing Week*, November 2010, pp. 42–3; Hilary Cross of Macmillan, March 2015.

who are more likely to volunteer. The World's Biggest Coffee Morning – devised to create awareness, attract volunteers and generate cash donations – still is part of Macmillan's plans, targeting the people previously deemed the core target market. Social media campaigns have been added alongside, intended to attract younger donors and volunteers. A series of challenge events has mobilized these younger targets. *Go Sober* and *A Good Night In* targeted students and young adults, leading to volunteering and donations.

Questions for discussion

1. Why might marketers wish to use the digital environment for brand building?

2. Highlight how marketers are not in control of their own destiny online.

3. What are the threats and opportunities to a brand from the growth of social media networking?

CHAPTER 12

Developing products and managing product portfolios

" Success depends on great new products but also the courage to drop products from the portfolio when the time is right "

Objectives

- To become aware of organizational alternatives for managing products.

- To understand how organizations develop a product idea into a commercial product.

- To understand the importance and role of product development in the marketing mix.

- To acquire knowledge of the management of products during the various stages of a product's life cycle.

- To become aware of how existing products can be modified.

- To learn how product deletion can be used to improve product mixes.

- To examine tools for the strategic planning of product or market portfolios.

INTRODUCTION

Companies have to create new ideas for products and turn some of these into marketable product or service propositions. Such a process is far from easy, with more new product launches failing than succeeding. As additional products are included in a company's portfolio, it becomes increasingly difficult to identify on which of them investment and sales/marketing resources should be focused. A range of tools, known as product portfolio techniques, exists to assist marketers in such decision-making. A related and important concept is that of product life-cycle management: the logic being that products are launched and if successful they grow, then mature, before going into decline and dying. Marketers must be aware of the relative standings of their respective products and brands to ensure they always have a viable portfolio overall. These are the themes of this chapter of *Marketing: Concepts and Strategies*.

Virgin Money: is innovation enough?

Richard Branson's Virgin brand is known to consumers across a range of products and services, from airlines to entertainment to mobile phones. In 1995, Virgin launched its financial services arm with Virgin Direct. At a time when major retailers such as Marks & Spencer and Tesco were entering many sectors of financial services – from banking to insurance – the entry of Virgin Direct made many of the traditional businesses in the financial services sector very anxious. Branson's reputation among consumers for 'taking on faceless corporations' gave Virgin Direct a head start.

Virgin Direct, replicating the activities of Virgin in other sectors, intended to be seen as an innovator that strove to offer a value-for-money proposition strongly benefiting the consumer. Virgin launched a tracker fund that tracked shares across the entire stock market rather than across only a limited selection. This innovation was subsequently copied by many rivals. Then Virgin lobbied the government to launch stakeholder pensions. Virgin also led the way with off-set mortgages, with the original Virgin One account. The innovations have continued from the company, now branded as Virgin Money. There is now a growing network of branches, but also *Virgin Money Lounges*:

> Our Lounges are about more than money and banking – they are designed to be places where our customers can relax and local communities come together. They are all part of our ambition to be a very different kind of bank – one that makes everyone better off.
>
> Lounge membership is completely free, and so are the refreshments, wi-fi and use of our iPads. You're welcome to bring a friend or family member in with you.

Virgin Money offers current accounts, credit cards, mortgages, savings, ISAs, investments and insurance. The philosophy is simple. Virgin Money intends to introduce more interesting propositions, rather than simply churning out new products. The company has a focus on being customer-led, rather than product-led, explaining that by focusing on small changes the experience is so much better:

> There's money. And there's Virgin Money. We are building a better kind of bank.
>
> – Making managing your money easier
> – Helping you make the right choices
> – Treating you as a person not a number
> – Helping you raise more for charity
> – Using our expertise to do some good
>
> We sweat the small stuff, because we know it makes a big difference for our customers. And sets us apart as a bank.

https://uk.virginmoney.com/virgin/about

Virgin-branded financial services products are innovative and place an emphasis on addressing consumer needs and consumer concerns about the sprawling global financial services corporations. Value for money, simplicity, ease of setting up and the Virgin brand have proved irresistible propositions for thousands of consumers who perceive Virgin and Branson to represent a desirable alternative to large and faceless corporations. As a result of this approach, Virgin Money has won countless industry awards in recent years and a growing band of customers.

Sources: Virgin Money; http://uk.virginmoney.com, March 2011; https://uk.virginmoney.com/virgin/about-lounges, April 2015.

To compete effectively and achieve their goals, companies must develop products that reflect consumer needs and preferences, while seeking to be different from competitors. They also must recognize that customer expectations, competitors and market trends do not stand still, so product portfolios must be constantly appraised and uprated. This is certainly the approach adopted by Virgin Money. A company often has to modify existing products, introduce new products or eliminate products that were successful perhaps only a few years ago. Sometimes, product alterations are required to keep pace with changing consumer demographics and new technologies. Whatever the reasons for altering products, the product mix must be managed and kept fresh, reflecting customer expectations, changing market trends and competitors' products. It may be appropriate to expand a company's product mix to take advantage of excess marketing and production capacity.

The product portfolio approach tries to create specific marketing strategies to achieve a balanced mix of products that will maximize a company's longer-term profits. This chapter begins by considering how businesses are organized to develop and manage products. Next, several ways to improve a company's product mix, including new product development – from idea generation to commercialization – are reviewed. The chapter then considers issues and decisions associated with managing a product through the growth, maturity and declining stages of its life cycle. Different types of product modification are also examined. The deletion of weak products from the product mix, often one of the hardest decisions for a marketer, is examined. The chapter concludes with a look at some of the related analytical tools associated with the planning of product portfolio: the Boston Consulting Group (BCG) product portfolio analysis, the market attractiveness – business position model or directional policy matrix (DPM) and the ABC sales: contribution analysis.

Organizing to manage products

A company must often manage a complex set of products, markets or both. Management must find an organizational approach that accomplishes the tasks necessary to develop and manage products.

Product manager
The person responsible for a product, a product line or several distinct products that make up an interrelated group within a multi-product organization.

The product or brand manager approach A **product manager** is responsible for a product, a product line or several distinct products that make up an interrelated group within a multi-product organization. A **brand manager**, on the other hand, is responsible for a single brand, for example Dove or IAMS. A product or brand manager operates cross-functionally to coordinate the activities, information and strategies involved in marketing an assigned product. Product managers and brand managers plan marketing activities to achieve objectives by coordinating a mix of place/distribution, promotion and especially sales promotion, advertising and digital, customer service and price. They must consider packaging and branding decisions, and work closely with research and development, engineering and production departments. The product manager or brand manager approach is used by many large, multi-product companies in the consumer goods sector. Increasingly it is a popular approach adopted by marketers responsible for services brands and business-to-business markets.

Brand manager
The person responsible for a single brand.

Marketing manager
The person responsible for managing the marketing activities that serve a particular group or class of customers.

The marketing manager approach A **marketing manager** is responsible for managing the marketing activities that serve a particular group or class of customers. This organizational approach is particularly effective when a company engages in different types of marketing activity to provide products to diverse customer groups. For example, a company may have one marketing manager for business markets and another for consumer markets. These broad market categories may be broken down into more limited market responsibilities. IT services company Fujitsu has identified core target market sectors, such as government customers, retail, financial services, utilities and so forth. There is a separate marketing manager responsible for each sector, all reporting to the central marketing director. Each Fujitsu marketing manager handles the implementation of marketing programmes bespoke to his or her clients in the assigned sector, but is also tasked with developing new products or services relevant to their category of clients.

The venture or project team approach   A venture or project team is designed to create entirely new products that may be aimed at new markets. Unlike a product or marketing manager, a venture team is responsible for all aspects of a product's development: research and development, production and engineering, finance and accounting, and marketing. Venture teams work outside established divisions to create inventive approaches to new products and markets. As a result of this flexibility, new products can be developed to take advantage of opportunities in highly segmented markets. Fujitsu has a separate team of marketers and new product development specialists working outside any specific client sectors, who are also striving to develop the next generation of attractive IT services but are not focused on a particular client sector, which is the role of the marketing managers. For example, their cloud computing offering has relevance to most of the company's client markets.

The members of a venture team come from different functional areas of an organization. Companies are increasingly using such cross-functional teams for product development in an effort to boost product quality. Quality may be positively related to information integration within the team, customers' influence on the product development process, and a quality orientation within the business.[1] When the commercial potential of a new product has been demonstrated, the members may return to their functional areas, or they may join a new or existing division to manage the product. The new product may be turned over to an existing division, a marketing manager or a product manager. Innovative organizational forms such as venture teams are especially important for well-established companies operating in mature markets. These companies must take a dual approach to marketing organization. They must accommodate the management of mature products and also encourage the development of new ones.[2]

New product development

Developing and introducing new products is frequently expensive and risky. The initial development of Gillette's Sensor razor took over eight years and resulted in a £150 million investment.[3] Thousands of new consumer products are introduced annually, and anywhere from 60 to 90 per cent of them fail. Lack of research, technical problems in design or production, and errors in timing the product's introduction are all causes of failure. Although developing new products is risky, so is failing to introduce new products. For example, the makers of Timex watches gained a large share of the watch market through effective marketing strategies during the 1960s and early 1970s. By 1983, Timex's market share had slipped considerably, in part because the company had failed to introduce new products. Timex has since regained market share by introducing a number of new products, but in the meantime competitors such as Swatch established their brands and stole significant market share from Timex.

The term 'new product' can have more than one meaning. It may refer to a genuinely new product, such as smart watches, offering innovative benefits. However, products that are merely different and distinctly better are also often viewed as new, such as lighter-weight wireless laptops or 4G smartphones. The following items, listed in no particular order, are product innovations of the last 30 or 40 years: Post-it notes, birth-control pills, felt-tip pens, anti-ulcer drugs, deep-fat fryers, personal computers, microwave ovens, Viagra, VCRs, DVDs, mobile phones, email, soft contact lenses, wireless data networks, SatNav, streaming, cloud computing, Skype, hybrid cars, windfarms, mobile banking, 3D printing and health monitoring apps. A new product can be an innovative variation of an existing product, as in the example shown in Figure 12.1.

A radically new product such as the Kindle and fellow eReaders involves a complex development process, including an extensive business analysis to determine the possibility of success.[4] It can also be a product that a given company has not marketed previously, although similar products may be available from other companies. The first company to introduce a DVD player was

FIGURE 12.1
Building on the popularity of crisps and savoury snacks, Ryvita launched rye-based 'Ryvita Minis', promoting the product's low calorie content

clearly launching a new product, yet if Boeing introduced its own brand of DVD player, this would also be viewed as a new product, but for Boeing, because it has not previously marketed such products. Managers in companies trying something new are often highly excited by sales prospects, yet the targeted consumers have probably been able to purchase similar products from a variety of other suppliers for some time; so to be successful the new entrant must have a visible and desirable competitive edge.

Before a product is introduced, it goes through the seven phases of **new product development** shown in Figure 12.2:

1. idea generation
2. screening ideas
3. concept testing
4. business analysis
5. product development
6. test marketing
7. commercialization.

> **New product development**
> The process a product goes through before introduction, involving seven phases: idea generation, screening ideas, concept testing, business analysis, product development, test marketing and commercialization.

A product may be dropped, and many are, at any of these stages of development. This section examines the process through which products are developed from the inception of an idea to a product offered for sale. Table 12.1 shows how companies can improve their new product success rate.

> **Idea generation**
> The process by which companies and other organizations seek product ideas that will help them achieve their objectives.

Idea generation **Idea generation** involves companies and other organizations seeking product ideas that will help them achieve their objectives. This task is difficult because only a few ideas are good enough to be commercially successful. Although some organizations get their ideas almost by chance, companies trying to manage their product mixes effectively usually develop systematic approaches for generating new product ideas. Indeed, there is a relationship between the amount of market information

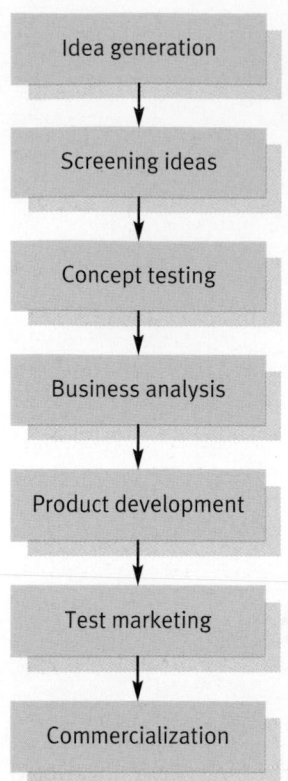

Idea generation

↓

Screening ideas

↓

Concept testing

↓

Business analysis

↓

Product development

↓

Test marketing

↓

Commercialization

FIGURE 12.2
Phases of new product
development screening ideas

Co-creation
The involvement of,
or consultation with,
consumers and supply
chain partners in the
collaborative development
of new products.

gathered and the number of ideas generated by work groups in organizations.[5] At the heart of innovation is a purposeful, focused effort to identify new ways to serve a market. Unexpected occurrences, incongruities, new needs, industry and market changes and demographic changes may all indicate new opportunities.[6] The forces of the marketing environment (see Chapter 3) often create new opportunities, as well as threats to combat.

New product ideas can come from several sources. They may come from internal sources: marketing managers, researchers, sales personnel, engineers or other organizational personnel. Brainstorming and incentives or rewards for good ideas are typical intra-organization devices for stimulating the development of ideas. The company 3M is well known for encouraging the generation of new ideas. The idea for 3M's Post-it adhesive-backed yellow notes came from an employee. As a church choir member, he used slips of paper for marking songs in his hymn book. As the pieces of paper fell out, he suggested developing an adhesive-backed note. Hewlett Packard keeps its labs open to engineers 24 hours a day to help generate ideas; it also encourages its researchers to devote 10 per cent of company time to exploring their own ideas for new products.[7] Company suggestion boxes for employees' ideas provide many of the stimuli for BMW's automotive innovations.

New product ideas may also arise from sources outside the company, for example customers, competitors, advertising agencies, management consultants and private research organizations. Johnson & Johnson, for example, acquired the technology for its clear orthodontic braces through a joint venture with Saphikon, the developer of the technology behind the braces. Developing new product alliances with other businesses has also been found to enhance the acquisition and use of information helpful for creating new product ideas.[8] Sometimes ideas come from potential buyers of a product. Asking weekend fishermen what they wanted in a sonar fish finder led Techsonic to develop its liquid crystal recorder fish finder.[9] For example, Chapter 3 outlined how companies such as Fujitsu discuss with clients their marketing environment drivers so that they can develop new products and services that reflect these client issues. In some markets, it is particularly important for new ideas to stem from customers. For example, many defence programmes take ten years to instigate, and the big defence equipment manufacturers are led by the stated buying plans and budgets of government defence departments. Increasingly popular is the process of **co-creation**, in which executives collaborate with their customers and possibly supply chain partners to dream up new concepts.[10]

TABLE 12.1 How to improve new product success

1	Talk with consumers and observe them; don't introduce a product just because you have the technology to make it.
2	Set realistic sales goals. Unrealistic goals can result in potentially successful products being terminated.
3	Make all parts of the company (research, manufacturing, marketing and distribution) work together for customer orientation.
4	At each stage of development, the product should have consumer acceptance, the ability to be manufactured at an acceptable cost and sales support.
5	Test market a product long enough to get an accurate assessment. Some products fail because consumers buy them early as a novelty only.
6	Carefully evaluate all product failures to provide information for future product introductions.
7	Monitor competitor developments: a new product must not merely replicate a rival.
8	Keep internal colleagues up-to-date and explain new developments to them.

Source: Adapted from Christopher P. Power, Kathleen Kerwin, Ronald Grover, Keith Alexander and Robert D. Hof, 'Flops: too many new products fail. Here's why – and how to do better', from Business Week, 16 August 1993, pp. 78–9.

Screening ideas
The process by which a company assesses whether product ideas match its organizational objectives and resources.

Screening ideas Screening ideas involves first assessing whether they match organizational objectives and resources, and then choosing the best ideas for further review. Next, the company's overall ability to produce and market the product is analyzed. Other aspects of an idea that should be weighed are the nature and wants of buyers, and possible marketing environment changes. More new product ideas are rejected during the idea-screening phase than during any other phase.

Sometimes a checklist of new product requirements is used to ensure that the screening process is as systematic as possible. If a critical factor on the checklist remains unclear, the type of formal marketing research described in Chapter 9 may be needed. To screen ideas properly, it may be necessary to test product concepts. A product concept and its benefits can be described or shown to consumers or business customers. Several product concepts may be tested to discover which might appeal most to a particular target market.

Concept testing
Seeking potential buyers' responses to a product idea.

Concept testing Concept testing is a phase in which a small sample of potential buyers is presented with a product idea, often in focus groups, through a written or oral description and perhaps a few drawings to determine their attitudes and initial buying intentions regarding the product. Online fora and digital brand communities often are used to tease out the views of intended customers. Many brands use Mumsnet.com for this purpose, suggesting ideas to seek reactions or providing prototypes for exploration and testing. For a single product idea, an organization can test one or several concepts of the same product. Concept testing is a low-cost procedure that lets a company determine customers' initial reactions to a product idea before it invests considerable resources in research and development. The results of concept testing can be used by product development personnel to better understand which product attributes and benefits are most important to potential customers.

Business analysis
A company's evaluation of a product idea to determine its potential contribution to the company's sales, costs and profits.

Business analysis During the business analysis phase, the product idea is evaluated to determine its potential contribution to the company's sales, costs and profits. In the course of a business analysis, evaluators ask a variety of questions:

- Does the product fit in with the company's existing product mix? Does the company have the right expertise to develop the new product?
- Is demand strong enough to justify entering the market and will the demand endure?
- What types of environmental and competitive changes can be expected, and how will these changes affect the product's future sales, costs and profits?
- Are the organization's research, development, engineering and production capabilities adequate?
- If new facilities must be constructed, how quickly can they be built and how much will they cost?
- If additional staff are required, when will they be in post?
- Is the necessary financing for development and commercialization on hand or obtainable at terms consistent with a favourable return on investment?
- Will the new product or idea benefit the company's existing portfolio of products?
- Is there any danger that existing products or services will be cannibalized?
- How soon will competitors catch up?
- Will distributors be receptive?
- How credible a supplier of this type of product is this company?
- What partnerships might be required?

In the business analysis stage, companies seek market information. The results of consumer surveys, along with secondary data, supply the specifics needed for estimating potential sales, costs and profits. At this point, a research budget should explore the financial objectives and related considerations for the new product.

Product development
The phase in which the organization determines if it is technically and financially feasible to produce a new product.

Product development

Product development is the phase in which the organization determines if it is technically feasible to produce the product and if it can be produced at costs low enough to make the final price reasonable. To test its acceptability, the idea or concept is converted into a prototype, or working model. Concept cars are used in the development of new vehicles. The prototype should reveal tangible and intangible attributes associated with the product in consumers' minds. The product's design, mechanical features and intangible aspects must be linked to wants in the marketplace. This includes the service aspects of the product, which are a vital component of many products. Failure to determine how consumers feel about the product and how they would use it may lead to the product's failure.

The development phase of a new product is frequently lengthy and expensive; thus a relatively small number of product ideas are put into development. If the product appears sufficiently successful during this phase to merit testing, then during the latter part of the development phase marketers begin to make decisions regarding branding, packaging, labelling, pricing and promotion for use in the test marketing phase.[11]

Test marketing
The limited introduction of a product in geographic areas or a channel chosen to represent the intended market.

Test marketing

The limited introduction of a product in geographic areas or a marketing channel chosen to represent the intended market is called **test marketing**. Its aim is to determine the reactions of probable buyers. For example, after McDonald's developed fried chicken products for its fast-food menu, it test marketed the idea in certain McDonald's restaurants to find out how those customers felt about eating chicken at McDonald's. The company followed a similar strategy for test marketing its range of salads and pizza. Test marketing is not an extension of the development phase. It is a sample launching of the entire marketing mix, and should be conducted only after the product has gone through development and after initial plans regarding the other marketing mix variables have been made.

Companies of all sizes use test marketing to reduce the risk of product failure. The dangers of introducing an untested product include undercutting already profitable products and, should the new product fail, loss of credibility with distributors and customers. Test marketing provides several benefits. It lets marketers expose a product to a natural marketing environment to gauge its sales performance. While the product is being marketed in a limited area, the company can seek to identify weaknesses in the product or in other parts of the marketing mix. Corrections can be made more cheaply than if the product had already been introduced nationwide. Test marketing also allows marketers to experiment with variations in advertising, price and packaging in different test areas and to measure the extent of brand awareness, brand switching and repeat purchases that result from alterations in the marketing mix. Digital fora, such as Mumsnet.com, and a company's own online digital brand ambassadors are very useful for test marketing and soliciting feedback.

The accuracy of test marketing results often hinges on where the tests are conducted. The selection of appropriate test areas is very important. The validity of test marketing results depends heavily on selecting test sites that provide an accurate representation of the intended target market. The criteria used for choosing test cities, television regions or online fora depend on the product's characteristics, the target market's characteristics and the company's objectives and resources.

Test marketing can be risky because it is expensive and a company's competitors may try to interfere. This is common in the confectionery market. A competitor may invalidate test results in an attempt to 'jam' the test programme by increasing advertising or promotions, lowering prices or offering special incentives all to combat the recognition and purchase of a new brand. Sometimes competitors copy the product in the testing stage and rush to introduce a similar product. It is therefore desirable to move quickly and commercialize as soon as possible after testing. When the product introduction is delayed to the point where the public begins to doubt its existence, such products may become known as 'vapourware', particularly in the computer software industry.[12]

To avoid these risks, companies may use alternative methods to gauge consumer preferences. One such method is simulated test marketing. Typically, consumers at shopping centres are asked to view an advertisement for a new product and are given a free sample to take home. These consumers are subsequently interviewed and asked to rate the product. The major advantages of simulated test marketing are lower costs, tighter security and, consequently, a reduction in the flow of information to competitors, and the elimination of jamming. Scanner-based test marketing is another, more sophisticated version of the traditional test marketing method. Some marketing research companies, such as ACNielsen, offer test marketing services to help provide independent assessment of products.

Commercialization

Commercialization
The process of refining and settling plans for full scale manufacturing and marketing.

Commercialization During the **commercialization** phase, plans for full-scale manufacturing and marketing must be refined and settled, and budgets for the project must be prepared. Early in the commercialization phase, marketing managers analyze the results of test marketing to find out what changes in the marketing mix are needed before the product is introduced. For example, the results of test marketing may tell the marketers to change one or more of the product's physical attributes, modify the distribution plans to include more retail outlets, alter promotional efforts or change the product's price, or modify the positioning platform. During this phase, the company also has to gear up for production and may face sizeable capital expenditure and personnel costs.

The product enters the market during the commercialization phase. One study indicates that only 8 per cent of new product projects started by major companies reach this stage.[13] When introducing a product, marketers often spend enormous sums of money on advertising, personal selling, digital and other types of promotion. These expenses, together with capital outlays, can make commercialization extremely costly; such expenditures may not be recovered for several years. For example, when Ford introduced its new Focus model, the company spent millions of pounds on advertising to communicate the new car's attributes, with payback not expected that year. Commercialization is easier when customers accept the product rapidly, which they are more likely to do if marketers can make them aware of its benefits and desirability.

Line extensions

Line extension
A product that is closely related to existing products in the line, but meets different customer needs.

A **line extension** is the development of a product that is closely related to one or more products in the existing product line, but is designed specifically to meet the somewhat different needs of customers. For example, Fairy Liquid washing-up detergent was used as a springboard for various detergent-based Fairy products including washing powder for automatic washing machines. Dove has been extended into a diversity of products, from soap and washing, deodorant, body lotions and haircare. Many of the so-called new products introduced each year by organizations are in fact line extensions. Line extensions are more common than radically new products because they are a less expensive, lower-risk alternative for increasing sales. A line extension may focus on a different market segment or may be an attempt to increase sales within the same market segment by more precisely satisfying the needs of people in that segment. For example, Nestlé launched an extra-strong variant of its Polo mints, Supermints, aimed at lovers of strong peppermints. However, one side-effect of employing a line extension is that it may result in a more negative evaluation of the core product.[14] It has been suggested that the success of line extensions is partly affected by consumer perceptions of how well the extension fits with the core brand.[15]

Product adoption process

Product adoption process
The stages buyers go through in accepting a product: awareness, interest, evaluation, trial and adoption.

The following stages of the **product adoption process** are generally recognized as those that buyers go through in accepting a product, from gaining awareness of it to buying the product:

1. *Awareness* – the buyer becomes aware of the product.
2. *Interest* – the buyer seeks information and is generally receptive to learning about the product.
3. *Evaluation* – the buyer considers the product's benefits and determines whether to try it.
4. *Trial* – the buyer examines, tests or tries the product to determine its usefulness relative to his or her needs.
5. *Adoption* – the buyer purchases the product and can be expected to use it when the need for this general type of product arises again.[16]

In the first stage, when individuals become aware that the product exists, they have little information about the product and are not concerned about obtaining more. Consumers enter the interest stage when they are motivated to obtain information about the product's features, uses, advantages, disadvantages, price or location. During the evaluation stage, individuals consider whether the product will satisfy certain criteria that are crucial for meeting their specific needs. In the trial stage, they use or experience the product for the first time, possibly by purchasing a small quantity, by taking advantage of a free sample or demonstration, or by borrowing the product from someone. Supermarkets, for instance, frequently offer special promotions to encourage consumers to taste products. During this stage, potential adopters determine the usefulness of the product under the specific conditions for which they need it.

Individuals move into the adoption stage by choosing the specific product when they need a product of that general type. However, the fact that a person enters the adoption process does not mean that she or he will eventually adopt the new product. Rejection may occur at any stage, including adoption. Both product adoption and product rejection can be temporary or permanent. Just because a consumer or business customer adopts a particular product once, does not guarantee future loyalty to the product or brand. Marketers must work hard to achieve a customer's ongoing loyalty and repeat purchasing.

This adoption process model has several implications for the commercialization phase. First, the company must promote the product to create widespread awareness of its existence and its benefits. Samples or simulated trials should be arranged to help buyers make initial purchase decisions. Marketers should also emphasize quality control and provide solid guarantees to reinforce buyer opinion during the evaluation stage. Finally, production and physical distribution must be linked to patterns of adoption and repeat purchase. The product adoption process is also discussed in Chapter 16, as marketing communications are not only important for achieving awareness, but also for informing and persuading customers right through the product adoption process. When launching a new product, companies must realize that buyers differ in the speed with which they adopt a product. Identifying buyers who are most open to new products can help expedite this process.

Consumers do not always pass through all the stages of the product adoption process as formally as this overview may have implied. A minor upgrade to a familiar brand may not cause consumers much concern, whereas an innovative product launched by an unknown supplier will give rise to much more extensive consumer decision-making. Business customers making routine re-buys or consumers making routine response purchases – see Chapters 5 and 6 – already have awareness of a particular product and are interested. Previously, they have tried and adopted the product, so their limited decision-making does not require them to pass through the product

adoption process in this manner. On the whole, marketers would do well to remember the importance of all five stages in this important concept. Consumers and business customers must be
aware of, have interest in, and be prepared to evaluate and try out a product or service if they are
to adopt it: that is, to buy and consume it. The marketing task does not end with first-time adoption, however. The ongoing requirement for marketers is to ensure customer loyalty and repeat
purchase.

Products are not usually launched nationwide overnight but are introduced through a process
called a roll-out. In a roll-out, a product is introduced in stages, starting in a set of geographic
areas and gradually expanding into adjacent areas. Thus, Cadbury's Wispa bar appeared initially in
the north-east of England. It may take several years to market a product nationally. Sometimes the
test cities are used as initial marketing areas, and the introduction becomes a natural extension of
test marketing. Gradual product introduction reduces the risks of introducing a new product. If the
product fails, the company will experience smaller losses. Furthermore, it may take some time for
a company to develop a suitable distribution network. Also, the number of units needed to satisfy
the national demand for a successful product can be enormous, and a company cannot usually
produce the required quantities in a short time.

Despite the good reasons for introducing a product gradually, marketers realize that this
approach creates some competitive problems. A gradual introduction allows competitors to
observe what a company is doing and to monitor results, just as the company's own marketers
are doing. If competitors see that the newly introduced product is successful, they may enter the
same target market quickly with similar products. Avoiding competition is critical when a company
introduces a brand into a market in which it already has one or more brands. Marketers usually
want to avoid cannibalizing sales of their existing brands, unless the new brand generates substantially larger profits. When KP introduces a new snack brand, it must take care to ensure that
sales of other KP brands do not suffer.

If a product has been planned properly, its attributes and brand image will give it the distinctive
appeal needed. Style, shape, construction, quality of work and colour help create the image and
the appeal. Of course buyers are more likely to purchase the product if they can easily identify the
benefits. When the new product does not offer some preferred attributes, there is room for another
new product or for repositioning of an existing product.[17] Methods of positioning are discussed in
the penultimate part of Chapter 8.

Product life cycle management

Most new products start off slowly and seldom generate enough sales to produce profits immediately. As buyers learn about the new product, marketers should be looking out for any weaknesses and be ready to make corrections quickly, in order to prevent the product's early demise.
Computer software companies expect to modify 'bugs' when launching new software products.
Consumers must be informed quickly and efficiently of any difficulties if damage to the brand
image is to be avoided. Marketing strategy should be designed to attract the segment that is
most interested in, and has the fewest objections to, the product. If any of these factors need
adjustment, this action, too, must be taken quickly to sustain demand. As the sales curve moves
upwards and the break-even point is reached, the growth stage begins. See Figure 10.5 in
Chapter 10 for an explanation of the product life cycle concept, which assumes a path from
introduction to growth, into maturity and then decline, mimicking the human life cycle from birth
to death.

Marketing strategy in the growth stage

As sales increase, management must support the momentum by adjusting the marketing strategy.
The goal is to establish the product's positioning and to fortify it by encouraging brand loyalty.

As profits increase, the company must brace itself for the entrance of aggressive competitors, who may make specialized appeals to selected market segments.

During the growth stage, product offerings may have to be expanded. To achieve greater penetration of an overall market, segmentation may have to be used more intensely. That would require developing product variations to satisfy the needs of customers in several different market segments. Marketers should analyze the product positioning regarding competing products, and correct weak or omitted attributes. Further quality, functional or style modifications may be required.

Gaps in the marketing channels should be filled during the growth period. Once a product has won acceptance, new distribution outlets may be easier to obtain. Sometimes marketers tend to move from **exclusive distribution** or **selective distribution** to a more **intensive distribution** of dealers to achieve greater market penetration. Marketers must also make sure that the physical distribution system is running efficiently and delivering supplies to distributors before their inventories are exhausted. Because competition increases during the growth period, good service and an effective mechanism for handling complaints are important.

Exclusive distribution
Market coverage in which only one outlet is used in a geographic area.

Advertising expenditure may be lowered slightly from the high level of the introductory stage, but still needs to be quite substantial. As sales increase, promotion costs should drop as a percentage of total sales. A falling ratio between promotion expenditure and sales should contribute significantly to increased profits. The advertising messages should aim to stress brand benefits and emphasize the product's positioning. Coupons and samples may be used to increase market share.

Selective distribution
Market coverage in which only some available outlets in an area are chosen to distribute a product.

After recovering development costs, an organization may be able to lower prices. As sales volume increases, efficiencies in production can result in lower costs. These savings may be passed on to buyers. If demand remains strong and there are few competitive threats, prices tend to remain stable. If price cuts are feasible, they can improve price competition and discourage new competitors from entering the market. For example, when compact disc players were introduced in the early 1980s, they carried an £800 price tag. Primarily because of the price, the product was positioned as a 'toy for audiophiles' a very small market segment. To generate mass-market demand, compact disc player manufacturers dropped their prices to around £150, and the cost of discs also dropped. The price was at a point where the margin was low but the turnover was high. However, with most homes having a CD player, sales volumes inevitably diminished. A similar pattern has emerged in the sale of smart phones and tablets, as unit prices have plummeted. Widescreen home entertainment systems are now following this pattern, as margins reduce but volumes increase.

Intensive distribution
Market coverage in which all available outlets are used for distributing a product.

Marketing strategy for mature products

As many products are in the maturity stage of their life cycles, marketers must always be ready to improve the product and marketing mix. During maturity, the competitive situation stabilizes and some of the weaker competitors drop out. It has been suggested that as a product matures, its customers become more experienced and their requirements more diverse, so that market segmentation opportunities increase. As customers' needs change, new marketing strategies for mature products may be called for.[18] Marketers may also need to modify the product. Symptoms of a mature product include price cutting, increased competitive action and shifting from a product orientation to a non-product orientation (price, promotion and place/distribution adaptation); in addition, market growth slows.[19]

Product modification
The alteration of one or more characteristics of a company's product.

Product modification means changing one or more characteristics of a company's product. This strategy is most likely to be used in the maturity stage of the product life cycle, to give a company's existing brand a competitive edge. Even well-established brands such as Sellotape must be modified from time to time, with innovative dispensers or versions with 'Happy Birthday' or suchlike printed along the tape. Altering a

Telebanking, TV banking, eBanking, texting and now banking apps: what next?

Topical insight

Marketers must constantly look at ways to keep their products 'fresh' and up to date, modifying existing products as appropriate or bringing out new ones. Personal banking has gone through many phases. Many readers will remember the days when high street banks were the only option for interacting with a bank, but were open only until mid-afternoon Monday to Friday, and there were no ATMs for easy cash withdrawals. Queuing at ageing tills in austere branches was the primary means of operating bank current accounts. Direct debits and standing orders helped, but the real revolution came in the late 1970s with the growth of ATMs (cash dispensers) and then in the early 1990s as most leading banks extended their opening hours and range of services aimed at private customers.

Technology has emerged as a driving force for change for banking services, in addition to ATMs. HSBC's *first direct* broke ranks by launching as a telephone-only, 365 days-a-year, 24-hour full-service personal banking provider. Rapid take-off of *first direct* encouraged its traditional high-street competitors to offer their own 24-hour telephone services such as Barclays' BarclayCall, based on heavy investment in call centres.

Another departure from the traditional high-street bank branch was the launch of TV banking. NatWest joined with Microsoft to provide an interactive banking service on Microsoft's WebTV network (which closed a few years ago as broadband took over). The service included information about mortgages, travel insurance, currency rates, plus standard current account banking, based on NatWest's PC banking package already established online.

More recently, first home-based internet banking and now mobile technology have changed the ways in which many customers interact with their banks. Now many customers prefer eBanking, anywhere they happen to be at any time. Smartphone apps, 3G and 4G, wi-fi hot spots and broadband have combined to transform the way in which many customers engage with their bank and manage their finances. For example, *first direct* now offers mobile phone users texting access to their banking details and mobile apps, no longer relying on call centres. As more people use their apps on their smartphones and tablets, there is an increase in accessing bank accounts on the go: a far cry from the queues in fuddy-duddy branches. No doubt other technological solutions will soon emerge. To banking customers, such product developments are revolutionizing their banking habits and access to financial services 24/7.

Sources: NatWest, *first direct* and Barclays' websites, 2000–15.

---

product mix in this way entails less risk than developing a new product because the product is already established in the market.

If certain conditions are met, product modification can improve a company's product mix. First, the product must be modifiable. Second, existing customers must be able to perceive that a modification has been made, assuming that the modified item is still aimed at them. Third, the modification should make the product more consistent with customers' desires so that it provides greater satisfaction. If these conditions are not met, it is unlikely that the product modification, however innovative, will be successful. The Topical Insight box above describes several successful modifications to personal banking that have been developed due to emerging technology. Product modifications fall into three major categories: quality, functional and style modifications.

Quality modifications Changes concerning a product's dependability and durability are called **quality modifications**. Usually, they are executed by altering the materials or the production process. Reducing a product's quality may allow a company to lower its price and direct the item at a larger target market.

Quality modifications
Changes that affect a product's dependability and durability.

By contrast, increasing the quality of a product may give a company an advantage over competing brands. During the last 30 years, marketers have been forced by increased global competition, technological change and more demanding customers to improve product integrity.[20] Higher quality may enable a company to charge a higher price by creating customer loyalty and by lowering customer sensitivity to price. However, higher quality may require the use of more expensive components, less standardized production processes, and other man-ufacturing and management techniques that force a company to charge higher prices.[21]

Functional modifications
Changes that affect a product's versatility, effectiveness, conveni-ence or safety.

Functional modifications   Changes that affect a product's versatility, effectiveness, convenience or safety are called functional modifications; they usually require the product to be redesigned. Typical product categories that have undergone consider-able functional modifications include home computers, audio equipment and cleaning products. Functional modifications can make a product useful to more people, thus enlarging its market, or improve the product's competitive position by providing benefits that competing items do not offer. Functional modifications can also help a company achieve and maintain a progressive image. For example, washing machine manufac-turers such as Whirlpool or AEG have developed appliances that use less heat and water. In Figure 12.3 well known brand Fairy has opted to promote additional ways of washing your clothes efficiently and easily by using dissolvable casings and cool temperatures. At times functional modi-fications are made to reduce the possibility of product liability claims.

Style modifications
Changes that alter a product's sensory appeal taste, texture, sound, smell or visual characteristics.

Style modifications   Style modifications change the sensory appeal of a product by altering its taste, texture, sound, smell or visual characteristics. Such modifications can be important, because when making a purchase decision, a buyer is swayed by how a product looks, smells, tastes, feels or sounds.

Although style modifications can be used by a company to differentiate its product from competing brands, their major drawback is that their value is highly subjective. A company may strive to improve the product's style, but customers may actually find the modified product less appealing. Some companies try to minimize these problems by altering product style in subtle ways. For example, Mattel's Barbie doll has gradually changed over the years in terms of career and lifestyle to reflect changing fashions.

During the maturity stage of the cycle, marketers actively encourage dealers to support the product, perhaps by offering promotional assistance or help in lowering their inventory costs. In general, marketers go to great lengths to serve dealers and to provide incentives for selling the manufacturer's brand, partly because own label or retailer brands are a threat at this time. Own label brands are both an opportunity and a threat to manufacturers, who may be able to sell their products through recognized own-label or retailer brand names as well as their own. However, own label or retailer brands frequently undermine manufacturers' brands.

Maintaining market share during the maturity stage requires moderate and sometimes heavy advertising expenditure. Advertising messages focus on differentiating a brand from numerous competitors, and sales promotion efforts are aimed at both consumers and resellers.

FIGURE 12.3
Fairy Liquitabs – modification focused on unique 'liquitabs' as a new laundry method

Source: Image courtesy of Fairy.

A greater mixture of pricing strategies is used during the maturity stage. In some cases, strong price competition occurs and price wars may break out. Sometimes marketers develop price flexibility to differentiate offerings in product lines. Mark-downs and price incentives are more common, but prices may rise if distribution and production costs increase. Marketers of mature products also often alter packaging and even positioning strategies. For example, in the USA, Heinz repackaged and repositioned its vinegar as an all-natural cleaning product.

Marketing strategy for declining products

As a product's sales curve turns downwards, industry profits continue to fall. A business can justify maintaining a product as long as it contributes to profits or enhances the overall effectiveness of a product mix. In this stage of the product life cycle, marketers must determine whether to eliminate the product or seek to reposition it in an attempt to extend its life. Usually, a declining product has lost its distinctiveness because similar competing products have been introduced. Competition engenders increased substitution and brand switching as buyers become insensitive to minor product differences. For these reasons, marketers do little to change a product's style, design or other attributes during its decline. New technology, product substitutes or environmental considerations may also indicate that the time has come to delete a product. Digital broadcasting has forced producers to drop analogue TVs, for example.

During a product's decline, outlets with strong sales volumes are maintained and unprofitable outlets are weeded out. An entire marketing channel may be eliminated if it does not contribute adequately to profits. Sometimes a new marketing channel, such as a factory outlet, will be used to liquidate remaining inventory of an obsolete product. Advertising expenditure is at a minimum. Advertising or special offers may slow the rate of decline. Sales promotions, such as coupons and premiums, may temporarily regain buyers' attention. Digital chatter will become less frequent and less positive. As the product continues to decline, the sales staff shifts its emphasis to more profitable products. The strategy pursued depends heavily on the nature of the portfolio. Apple has focused less on its iPod music players as sales of smartphones and MacBooks have rocketed.

To have a product return a profit may be more important to a company than to maintain a certain market share. To squeeze out all possible remaining profits, marketers may maintain the price despite declining sales and competitive pressures. Prices may even be increased as costs rise if a loyal core market still wants the product, such as those consumers still preferring turntables for vinyl to CD or mp3 players. In other situations, the price may be cut to reduce existing inventory so that the product can be deleted. Severe price reductions may be required if a new product is making an existing product obsolete.

Deleting products

Product deletion
The process of eliminating a product that no longer satisfies a sufficient number of customers.

Product deletion is the process of eliminating a product that no longer satisfies a sufficient number of customers. Products cannot usually contribute to an organization's goals indefinitely, and a declining product reduces a company's profitability, draining resources that could be used to modify other products or develop new ones. A marginal product may require shorter production runs, which can increase per unit production costs. Finally, when a dying product completely loses favour with customers, the negative feelings may transfer to some of the company's other products, as both Sony and Blackberry have found.

Most companies find it difficult to delete a product or a brand. It was probably a hard decision for Sony to cease producing Vaio laptops or for Thomas Cook to drop the long-standing Going Places chain of travel agents. Many observers felt Motorola's failure to drop its hugely successful but long-in-the-tooth Razr line of mobile phones permitted rivals to leapfrog with enhanced technology and so steal much of Motorola's market share. A decision to drop a product may be opposed by management and other employees who feel that the product is necessary in the

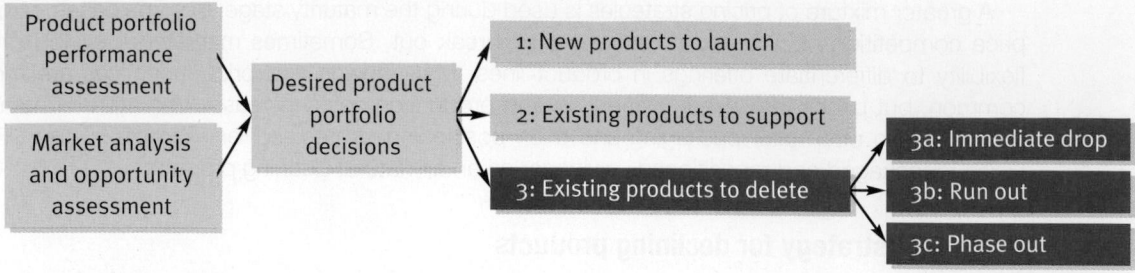

FIGURE 12.4
The product deletion process

product mix, or by sales people who still have some loyal customers. Considerable resources and effort are sometimes spent in trying to improve the product's marketing mix enough to increase sales and thus avoid having to delete it.

Some companies delete products only after they have become heavy financial burdens. A better approach is to institute some form of systematic review to evaluate each product and monitor its impact on the overall effectiveness of the company's product mix. Such a review should analyze a product's contribution to the company's sales for a given period and should include estimates of future sales, costs and profits associated with the product. It should also gauge the value of making changes in the marketing strategy to improve the product's performance. A systematic review allows a company to improve product performance and to ascertain when to delete products. Although many companies do systematically review their product mixes, one research study found that few companies have formal, written policies concerning the process of deleting products. The study also found that most companies base their decisions to delete weak products on poor sales and profit potential, low compatibility with the company's business strategies, unfavourable market outlook and historical declines in profitability.[22]

There are three ways to delete a product, either (see Figure 12.4):

1. phase it out
2. run it out
3. drop it immediately.

Phase out
An approach that lets the product decline without a change in marketing strategy.

Run out
A policy that exploits any strengths left in the product.

Immediate drop
An option that drops an unprofitable product immediately.

A **phase out** approach allows the product to decline without a change in the marketing strategy. No attempt is made to give the product new life. A **run out** policy exploits any strengths left in the product. Intensifying marketing efforts in core markets or eliminating some marketing expenditures, such as advertising, may cause a sudden profit increase. This approach is commonly taken for technologically obsolete products, such as older models of camcorders or computers, and is often accompanied by a price reduction. Some car manufacturers use a run out approach to dispose of certain models just before a new launch. The third option, an **immediate drop** of an unprofitable product, is the best strategy when losses are too great to prolong the product's life.

Tools for managing product portfolios

A number of tools have been developed to aid marketing managers in their planning efforts. Based on ideas used in the management of financial portfolios, several models that classify an organization's product portfolio have been proposed.[23]

These models allow strategic business units (SBUs) or products to be classified and visually displayed both according to the attractiveness of various markets and a business's relative market share within those markets. Three of these tools are the Boston Consulting Group (BCG) product portfolio analysis, the market attractiveness – business position model, and the ABC sales: contribution analysis. In addition, the product life cycle concept explored in Chapter 10 is an important tool often utilized in determining future strategies for brands and products. This assessment, based on the notion of the introduction, growth, maturity and decline stages in the life of a product or market, is useful in recommending a marketing strategy. As described above, the options are quite different for marketers facing growth or mature stages, and markedly so for the introduction versus the decline stages. The BCG matrix, described next, builds on this suggestion.

The Boston Consulting Group (BCG) product portfolio analysis

Product portfolio analysis
A strategic planning tool that takes a product's market growth rate and its relative market share into consideration in determining a marketing strategy.

Just as financial investors have different investments with varying risks and rates of return, businesses have a portfolio of products characterized by different market growth rates and relative market shares. **Product portfolio analysis**, the BCG approach, is based on the philosophy that a product's market growth rate and its relative market share are important considerations in determining its marketing strategy. All the company's products should be integrated into a single, overall matrix and evaluated to determine appropriate strategies for individual SBUs and the overall portfolio strategies. However, a balanced product portfolio matrix is the end result of a number of actions, not just the analysis alone. Portfolio models can be created on the basis of present and projected market growth rates and proposed market share strategies. These strategies include four options:

1. build share
2. maintain share
3. harvest share
4. divest business.

Managers can use these models to determine and classify each product's expected future cash contributions and future cash requirements.

Stars
Products with a dominant share of the market and good prospects for growth.

Generally, managers who use a portfolio model must examine the competitive position of a product or product line and the opportunities for improving that product's contribution to profitability and cash flow.[24] The BCG analytical approach is more of a diagnostic tool than a guide for making strategy prescriptions.

Figure 12.5, which is based on work by the BCG, enables the marketing manager to classify a company's products into four basic types: stars, cash cows, dogs and problem children.[25]

Cash cows
Products with a dominant share of the market but low prospects for growth.

- **Stars** are products with a dominant share of the market and good prospects for growth. However, they use more cash than they generate to finance growth, add capacity and increase market share.

- **Cash cows** have a dominant share of the market but low prospects for growth. Typically, they generate more cash than is required to maintain market share. Cash cows generate much needed funds to support the stars and problem children.

Dogs
Products that have a subordinate share of the market and low prospects for growth.

- **Dogs** have a subordinate share of the market and low prospects for growth. These are struggling products. They are frequently found in mature markets and often should be phased out or withdrawn immediately.

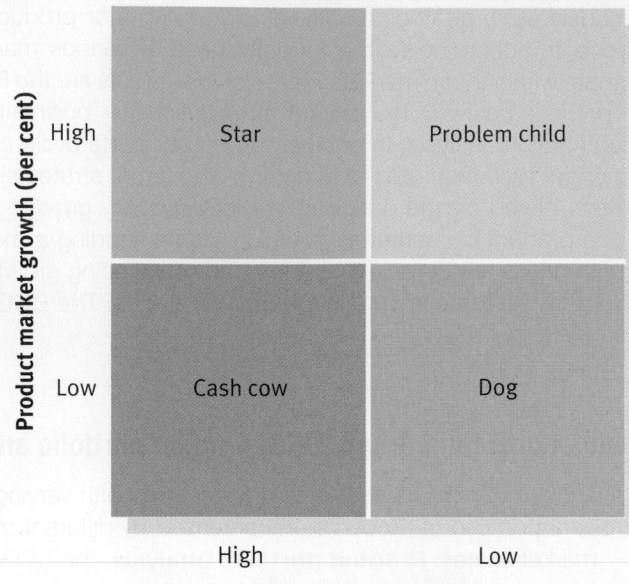

FIGURE 12.5
Illustrative growth-share matrix developed by the Boston Consulting Group

Source: Figure 12.5 'The BCG Portfolio Matrix' from the Product Portfolio Matrix, copyright © 1970, The Boston Consulting Group

Problem children
Products that have a small share of a growing market, generally requiring a large amount of cash to build share.

- **Problem children** sometimes called 'question marks', have a small share of a growing market and generally require a large amount of cash to build share. The question is, are they capable of becoming star products or are they destined to be dogs?

The product portfolio growth-share matrix in Figure 12.5 can be expanded to show a company's whole portfolio by providing for each product:

- its cash sales volume, illustrated by the size of a circle on the matrix
- its market share *relative* to competition, represented by the horizontal position of the product on the matrix
- the growth rate of the market, indicated by the position of the product in the vertical direction.

It should be noted that relative market share is a company's own market share relative to the biggest competitor's. Figure 12.6 suggests marketing strategies appropriate for cash cows, stars, dogs and problem children. By following these guiding philosophies, an organization can make strategic decisions based on the diagnosis of the BCG product portfolio growth-share matrix.

The long-term health of an organization depends on having some products that generate cash and provide acceptable profits, plus others that use cash to support growth. Among the indicators of overall health are the size and vulnerability of the cash cows, the prospects for the stars, if any, and the number of problem children and dogs. Particular attention must be paid to those products with large cash appetites. Unless the company has an abundant cash flow, it cannot afford to sponsor many such products at one time. If resources, including debt capacity, are spread too thinly, the company will end up with too many marginal products and will be unable to finance promising new product entries or acquisitions in the future.

Although a popular tool in the 1980s, the BCG growth-share matrix is not commonly deployed these days. Many marketers believe that market attractiveness equates to more than simply the growth rate of a market and a product's or brand's respective market share. As marketers have sought more complex approaches, utilizing many variables, the market attractiveness – business position model has grown in popularity.

Stars	Problem children
Characteristics ■ Market leaders ■ Fast growing ■ Substantial profits ■ Require large investment to finance growth **Strategies** ■ Protect existing share ■ Re-invest earnings in the form of price reductions, product improvements, providing better market coverage, production efficiency and so on ■ Obtain a large share of the new users	**Characteristics** ■ Rapid growth areas ■ Poor profit margins ■ Enormous demand for cash **Strategies** ■ Invest heavily to get a disproportionate share of new sales ■ Buy existing market shares by acquiring competitors ■ Divestment (see Dogs) ■ Harvesting (see Dogs) ■ Abandonment (see Dogs) ■ Focus on a definable niche where dominance can be achieved
Cash cows	**Dogs**
Characteristics ■ Profitable products ■ Generate more cash than needed to maintain market share **Strategies** ■ Maintain market dominance ■ Invest in process improvements and technological leadership ■ Maintain price leadership ■ Use excess cash to suppport research and growth elsewhere in the company	**Characteristics** ■ Greatest number of products fall in this category ■ Operate at a cost disadvantage ■ Few opportunities for growth at a reasonable cost ■ Markets are not growing; therefore, little new business **Strategies** ■ Focus on a specialized segment of the market that can be dominated and protected from competitive inroads ■ Harvesting—cut back all support costs to a minimum level; support cash flow over the product's remaining life ■ Divestment—sale of a growing concern ■ Abandonment—deletion from the product line

Vertical axis: Product market growth (per cent) — High / Low
Horizontal axis: Relative market share — High / Low

FIGURE 12.6

Characteristics and strategies for the four basic product types in the growth-share matrix

Source: Adapted and reprinted with permission from 'Diagnosing the product portfolio' by George S. Day, *Journal of Marketing*, April 1977, pp. 30–1. Published by the American Marketing Association.

Market attractiveness – business position model
A two-dimensional matrix that helps determine which SBUs have an opportunity to grow and which should be divested.

Market attractiveness – business position model

The **market attractiveness – business position model**, illustrated in Figure 12.7, is another 2D matrix, often known as the directional policy matrix or DPM. However, rather than using single measures to define the vertical and horizontal dimensions of the matrix, the model employs multiple measurements and observations. It is an increasingly popular tool, particularly in businesses producing detailed annual

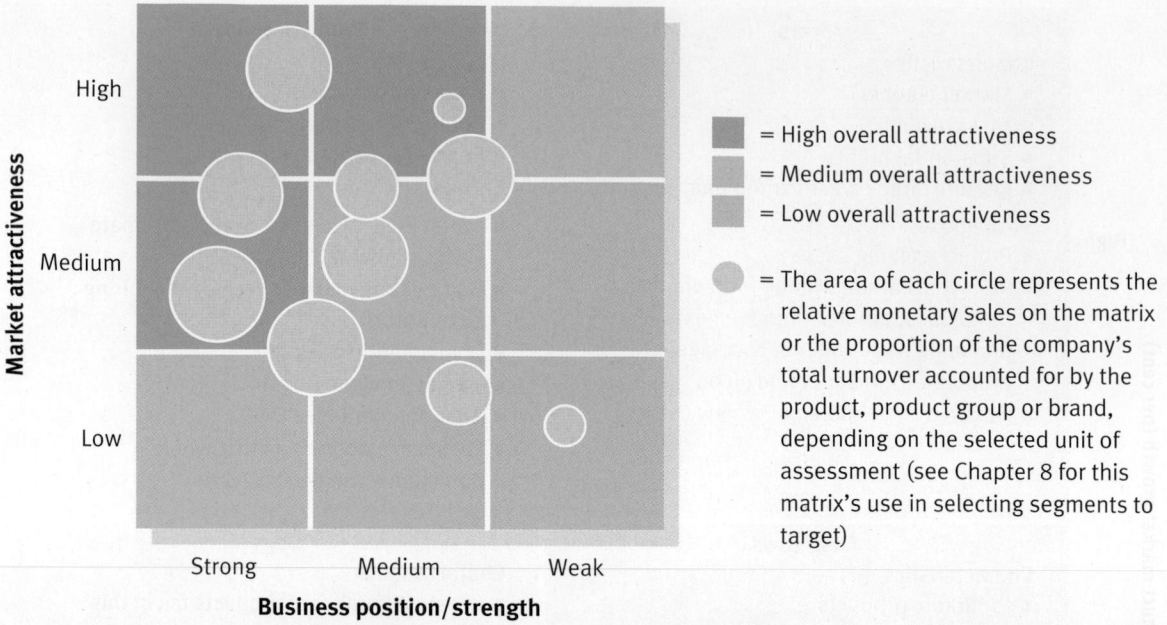

FIGURE 12.7
Market attractiveness – business position model – known as the Directional Policy Matrix (DPM)

marketing plans. The vertical dimension – market attractiveness – includes all the issues that relate to the market, for example, seasonality, economies of scale, competitive intensity, industry sales, and the overall cost and feasibility of entering the market. The horizontal axis – business position – is a composite of factors; for example, sales, relative market share, research and development, price competitiveness, product quality and market knowledge. These are only examples, because each set of marketers will select variables as they relate to the product and particular market. Each company deploying this tool selects its own criteria, but uses these same ones over time to analyze changes. A slight variation of this matrix is called General Electric's Strategic Business Planning Grid because General Electric is credited with extending the product portfolio planning tool to examine market attractiveness and business strength.

The best situation for a company is to have a strong business position in an attractive market. The upper-left area in Figure 12.7 represents the opportunity for an invest/grow strategy, but the matrix does not indicate how to implement this strategy. The purpose of the model is to serve as a diagnostic tool to highlight SBUs, products, brands or market segments – the tool can be used to assess many areas of interest – that have an opportunity to grow or that should be divested or approached selectively.[26] SBUs that occupy the invest/grow position can lose their position through faulty marketing strategies.

Decisions on allocating resources to SBUs of medium overall attractiveness should be arrived at on a basis relative to other SBUs that are either more or less attractive. The lower-right area of the matrix is a low-growth harvest/divest area. Harvesting is a gradual withdrawal of marketing resources on the assumption that sales will decline at a slow rate but profits will still be significant at a lower sales volume. Harvesting and divesting, even abandonment, or deletion from the product line, may be appropriate strategies for SBUs characterized by low overall attractiveness.

Marketers proficient in this technique often use the agreed variables and weightings to evaluate market segments in order to determine investment priorities: certain segments will be more attractive than others, while the organization's strengths will vary between segments (see Chapter 7). The matrix can also be used for mapping a company's products or brands.

Practitioners' use of the directional policy matrix (DPM)

Most organizations have more than one product and operate in several markets. This results in the need to prioritize in which markets to focus resources, particularly in terms of sales and marketing activities. Often the 'who shouts the loudest' approach to management meetings wins, or else historical successes with specific clients, products or markets colour the judgement of decision-makers irrespective of current business performance. One effective approach to ensuring that objectivity has an input into such prioritization is the directional policy matrix (DPM) or GE grid.

Along with the PEST marketing environment analysis described in Chapter 3, the directional policy matrix is a pivotal tool in strategic business planning. The DPM is useful to marketers as a means for identifying the relative merits of apparently attractive opportunities. Suggested worthwhile opportunities may be benchmarked against a company's existing activities to judge the value of supporting the new ideas. The tool can be used to evaluate the relative merits of individual products or product groups. The DPM is useful, too, in selecting between market segments (see Chapter 8). The market attractiveness criteria identified for the DPM can easily be utilized to assess the relative merits of market segments (see figure 12.7).

Marketing tools and techniques

So, how is a DPM produced? Occasionally, a strategic planner or marketing director may produce such an analysis, but often the variables to be used in order to construct the DPM are selected and weighted by a team of senior decision makers, often the directors or leadership team of a company, supplemented by marketing managers and analysts who understand the trends and dynamics of individual markets. The steps are as follows:

1. Identify a set of opportunity or market attractiveness criteria. These should be a mix of short-term variables (e.g. sales volumes and current profitability) and longer-term variables (e.g. market growth prospects or ability to sustain a differential advantage). In addition, some variables should be internal-facing (e.g. profitability) and some variables must be market-facing (e.g. customer satisfaction or intensity of competition). The aim is to have a balanced set of criteria.

2. Allocate 100 points across the selected variables in order to weight them in terms of their relative importance. If a team of managers is involved, each should 'vote' with 100 points, then the whole team's votes should be aggregated.

3. Identify business strength variables and, as with market attractiveness, allocate 100 points between these business strength variables for their weighting.

4. Then the main task. Score each major product group, market segment or marketing opportunity (whatever is

Marketing attractiveness	weighting	Business strengths	weighting
Long-term prospects with the client	14	Clarity and cohesion of message	19
Profitability	14	Thought leadership	16
Strategic fit	12	Easy to do business with/flexibility	15
Size of the opportunity	12	Right people/right support/right milieu	14
(Right) relationship	9	Perceived quality of delivery	12
Ability to deliver the necessary solution	9	Understanding of the market sector	10
How well the opportunity can be defined/realized	8	Referenceability	7
Current presence in the client	8	Price competitive	3
Nature of competition	6	Winning business/closure mindset	2
Risk	5	Breadth and depth	2
Whether the task can be replicated or referenced	3		

the specific context of the analysis). To score, a simple three-category scoring system is usually adequate: $n \times 1$ = strong/good; $n \times 0.5$ = 'so-so'/average; $n \times 0$ = low/ weak/poor (where n = the selected variable). When scoring, business strength variables are usually taken as being relative to the dominant player(s) in the market, while market attractiveness scoring is usually one product or market segment versus 'the others' in the company's portfolio.

5. Weight $\times$ score = total to be plotted. Therefore, each product group, segment or opportunity is allocated a value of between 0 and 100 for market attractiveness and separately for business strength, so its position may be plotted on the DPM grid. The Y axis represents market attractiveness (0–100), while the X axis represents business strength (0–100).

In the real B2B example, the company identified 11 market attractiveness criteria and 10 business strength criteria. Each market segment was in turn judged against all 21 variables, warranting 1, 0.5 or 0. For example, market segment 'A' scored 0.5 for 'long-term prospects with the client' ($14 \times 0.5 = 7$) and 0.5 for 'current presence in the client' ($8 \times 0.5 = 4$) and so forth. However, segment 'B' scored 1 for the first variable ($14 \times 1 = 14$). The result is depicted in the DPM chart.

Having assessed each of its many market segments, this company plotted them on a DPM. In addition, the management team predicted where the segments would head over the following three years. The circle size represents the proportion of total income to the company from each market segment.

Further details may be found in the authors' titles *Market Segmentation Success: Making It Happen!* (Routledge/The Haworth Press, 2008) and *Marketing Planning* (Cengage Learning, 2009).

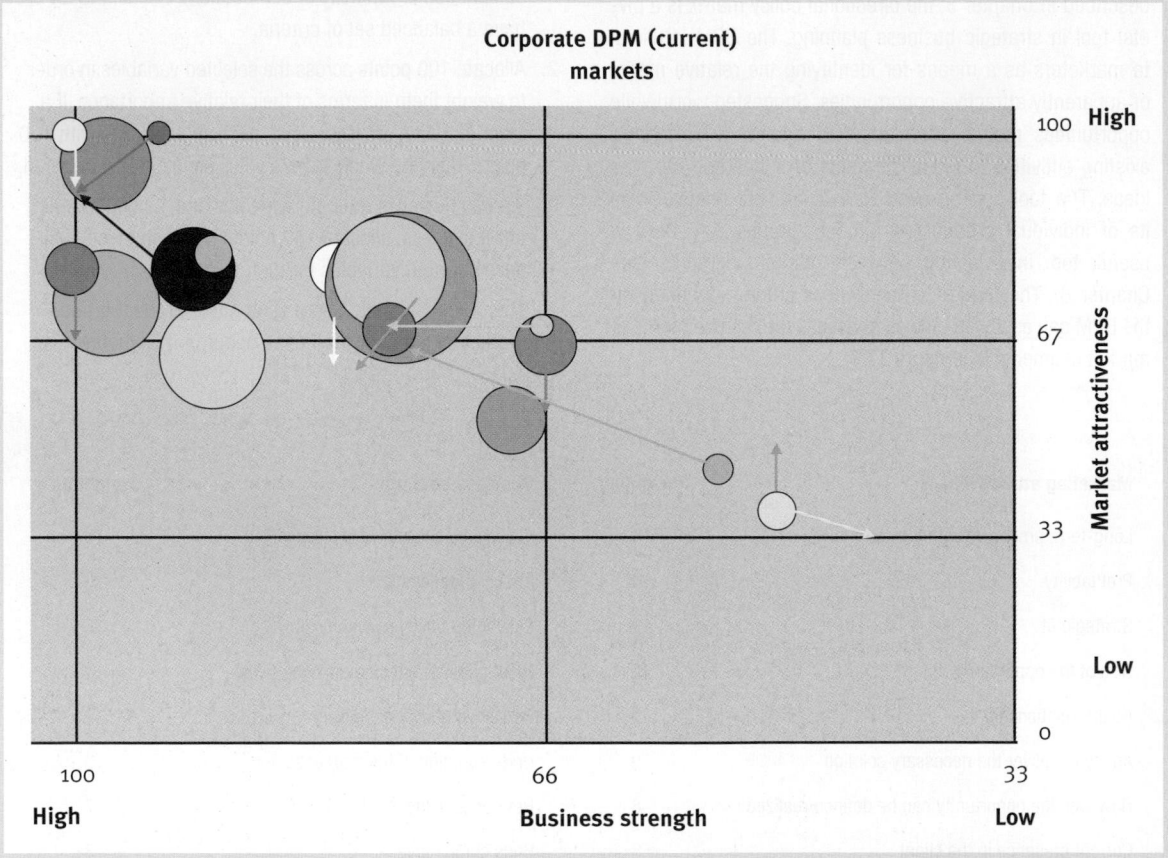

Corporate DPM (current) markets

The Marketing Tools and Techniques box on page 367 offers a step-by-step example of one company's use of the **directional policy matrix (DPM)**, in this instance examining the relative performance of different market segments. The same approach could be deployed to examine SBUs' products, rather than market segments.

Directional policy matrix (DPM)
A more commonly used name for the market attractiveness – business position model.

The ABC sales: contribution analysis

ABC sales: contribution analysis
An approach that examines the financial worth to a company of its products, product groups or customers.

The **ABC sales: contribution analysis** can be conducted at product group or product line level; for the total market, territories or sub-markets; for customer groups/market segments; or for individual customer accounts. In other words, whatever the unit of analysis, the ABC sales: contribution analysis is revealing. In the context of this chapter, individual products or product groups may be plotted. Sales managers focusing on key accounts may plot individual key customer accounts, instead of products, while marketers developing target market strategies may well plot different market segments in order to understand their relative performance better (see Chapter 8).

FIGURE 12.8
The White Company has a reputation for retailing superior products, a theme emphasized in this shop window

The aim of this analysis is to show both the amount of sales and the financial contribution from these sales that is, the financial worth to the company's fortunes. Financial success after all, is not confined to sales volume figures; a company must have an adequate level of contribution – sales revenue minus all variable costs – from its sales. This analysis helps companies to identify the relative value of different products, markets or even individual customer accounts, assisting with the allocation of resources.

An example of an ABC sales: contribution analysis chart is shown in Figure 12.9. The 45-degree diagonal line from bottom left to top right is the optimum. It is a straightforward rule, not a regression line. Ideally, the dots plotted on the chart would be located on the line – having both good sales and contribution – and be at the top right of the graph – with high sales and high contribution. These 'sell a lot, make a lot' plots to the top right, are the 'A' class. Typically, however, this is not the case: often the majority of products, customers or markets – depending on the selected unit of analysis – fall to the bottom left of the graph. Here, they are low sales and low contribution (the 'C' class) or they have average sales and average contribution (the 'B' class).

Three important conclusions can be drawn from an ABC analysis:

1. The analysis can identify highly attractive customers, markets or products (depending on the chosen unit of analysis) in terms of the associated contributions, but where sales are relatively low. For such accounts, an increase in sales, no matter how slight, with associated high prices and good financial returns, will be highly rewarding.

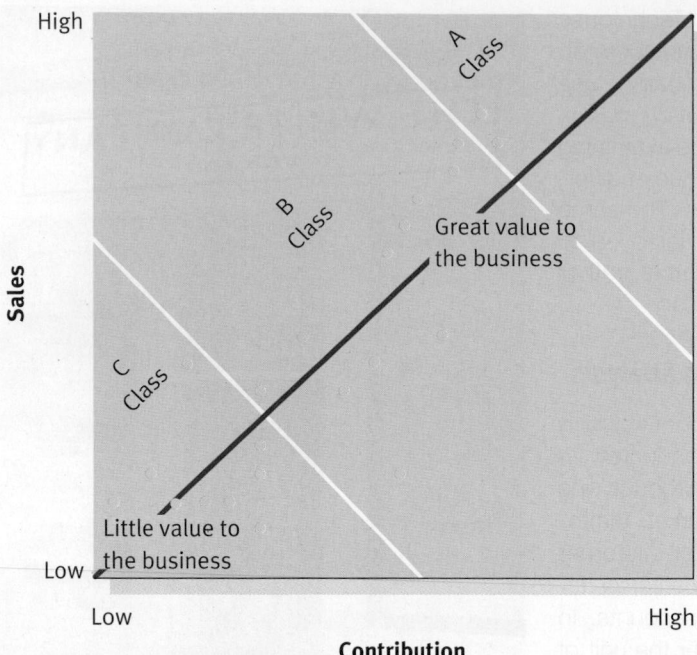

The dots could be products, product groups, market territories, segments or even individual customer accounts depending on the chosen level of analysis

FIGURE 12.9
Example of an ABC sales: contribution chart

2. The analysis can determine accounts with high sales figures but low or pitiful contributions. Cash flow may be good, but the company's profitability is not helped. Even a slight increase in contribution is most desirable and will greatly assist the company's overall fortunes.

3. The analysis can challenge the historical perspective that often clouds judgement as to what constitutes a good product, market or customer. Every organization has its historically most rewarding customers and products that in reality are no longer performing in terms of sales, contribution or both ... the tail. Often, managers still believe the historical rhetoric, rather than recognize that the situation has moved on; new priorities must benefit from the available resources and marketing effort. The ABC analysis generally unearths a few such instances and identifies the rump of unrewarding products or accounts that are not worth pursuing.

The approaches presented here provide an overview of the most popular analytical methods used in strategic market planning. This chapter has focused on the management of product portfolios, but as has been explained, techniques such as the directional policy matrix (DPM) and the ABC sales: contribution analysis are extremely helpful in evaluating the relative merits of market segments or even individual customer accounts.

The BCG's portfolio analysis, the market attractiveness – business position model, the ABC sales: contribution analysis and the product life cycle concept are used not only to diagnose problem areas or to recognize opportunities, but also to facilitate the allocation of resources among business units. They are not intended to serve as formulae for success or prescriptive guides, which lay out specific strategic action plans.[27] These approaches are supplements to, not substitutes for, the marketing manager's own judgement. The real test of each approach, or any integrated approach, is how well it helps management diagnose the company's strengths and weaknesses and prescribe strategic actions for maintaining or improving performance. The emphasis should be on making sound decisions with the aid of these analytical tools.[28]

Summary

To maximize the effectiveness of a product mix, a company usually has to alter its mix through the modification of existing products, deletion of a product or new product development. Developing and managing products is critical to a company's survival and growth. The various approaches available for organizing product management share common activities, functions and decisions necessary to guide a product through its life cycle. A *product manager* is responsible for a product, a product line or several distinct products that make up an interrelated group within a multi-product organization. A *brand manager* is responsible for a single brand. *Marketing managers* are responsible for managing the marketing activities that serve a particular group or class of customers or a market sector. A *venture or project team* is sometimes used to create and develop entirely new products that may be aimed at new markets.

A new product may be an innovation that has never been sold by any organization; or it can be a product that a given company has not marketed previously, although similar products have been available from other organizations. Before a product is introduced, it goes through the seven phases of *new product development.* (1) In the *idea generation* phase, new product ideas may come from internal or external sources. *Co-creation* is nowadays popular, involving customers and supply chain partners in the collaborative design of new products. (2) In the process of *screening ideas,* those with the greatest potential are selected for further review. (3) *Concept testing* presents a small number of potential buyers with the concept idea in order to ascertain early approval indicators. (4) During the *business analysis* stage, the product idea is evaluated to determine its potential contribution to the company's sales, costs and profits. (5) *Product development* is the phase in which the organization determines if it is technically feasible to produce the product and if it can be produced at costs low enough for the final price to be reasonable. (6) *Test marketing* is a limited introduction of a product in geographic areas or channels chosen to represent the intended market. (7) The decision to enter the *commercialization* phase means that full-scale production of the product begins and a complete marketing strategy is developed.

Not all 'new' products are genuinely new! Many product introductions are in fact a *line extension* – the development of a product that is closely related to products in the existing product line, but designed to meet different customer needs. The *product adoption process* that buyers go through in accepting a product includes awareness, interest, evaluation, trial and adoption.

As a product moves through its life cycle, marketing strategies will require continual adaptation. In the growth stage, it is important to develop brand loyalty and a market position. Marketers may move from an *exclusive distribution* or *selective distribution* to a more *intensive distribution* of dealers. In the maturity stage, a product may be modified or new market segments may be developed to rejuvenate its sales.

Product modification involves changing one or more characteristics of a company's product. This approach to altering a product mix can be effective when the product is modifiable, when customers can perceive the change and when customers want the modification. *Quality modifications* are changes that relate to a product's dependability and durability. Changes that affect a product's versatility, effectiveness, convenience or safety are called *functional modifications. Style modifications* change the sensory appeal of a product.

A product that is declining may be maintained as long as it makes a contribution to profits or enhances the product mix. Marketers must determine whether to eliminate the declining product or to reposition it to extend its life.

Product deletion is the process of eliminating a product that is unprofitable, consumes too many resources and no longer satisfies a sufficient number of customers. *Phase out, run out* and *immediate drop* are three ways to delete a product. A product mix should be systematically reviewed to determine when to delete products.

A number of tools have been developed to aid marketing managers in their portfolio planning efforts; these include the Boston Consulting Group (BCG) *product portfolio analysis,* the market attractiveness – business position model, and the ABC sales: contribution analysis. The product life cycle concept is also important in determining marketing strategies.

The BCG approach is based on the philosophy that a product's market growth rate and its relative market share are key factors influencing marketing strategy. All the company's products are integrated into a single, overall matrix including *stars, cash cows, dogs* and *problem children* and are evaluated to determine appropriate strategies for individual SBUs and the overall portfolio strategies.

The *market attractiveness – business position model* is a two-dimensional matrix, often known as the *directional policy matrix (DPM).* The market attractiveness dimension includes multiple variables that relate to the attractiveness of the market or product opportunity, such as seasonality, economies of scale, competitive intensity, industry sales and the cost of competing. The business position axis measures multiple variables that relate to a business's strengths and capabilities, such as sales levels, relative market share, research and development expertise, and other factors that support building market share for a product. Each set of marketers will select variables pertinent to the respective company and industry.

The *ABC sales: contribution analysis* examines the financial worth to a company of its products, product groups or customers. The analysis highlights areas in which to avoid or limit further investment and sales and marketing activity. It also reveals specific targets for financial contribution improvement or sales volume improvement.

Tools for portfolio planning are used only to diagnose problem areas or recognize opportunities. They are supplements to, not substitutes for, the marketing manager's own judgement. The real test of each approach, or any integrated approach, is how well it helps management diagnose the company's strengths and weaknesses, and prescribe strategic actions for maintaining or improving performance.

The portfolio planning approaches presented here provide an overview of the most popular analytical methods used in strategic market planning. This chapter has focused on the management of product portfolios, but techniques such as the market attractiveness – business position model – more commonly now known as the directional policy matrix (DPM) – and the ABC sales: contribution analysis are extremely helpful in evaluating the relative merits of market segments or even individual customer accounts.

Key links

- This chapter has examined the development of products and the first part should be read in conjunction with Chapter 10, on product decisions.

- The management of products should be considered in harmony with the material presented in Chapter 11, on branding.

- The product portfolio techniques explained in this chapter, particularly the directional policy matrix and ABC sales: contribution analysis, are often deployed by marketers making trade-off decisions between emerging opportunities or various market segments. These techniques are useful when reading about targeting in Chapter 8's discussion of market segmentation and targeting decisions.

Important terms

ABC sales: contribution analysis
Brand manager
Business analysis
Cash cows
Co-creation
Commercialization
Concept testing
Directional policy matrix (DPM)
Dogs
Exclusive distribution
Functional modifications
Idea generation
Immediate drop
Intensive distribution
Line extension
Market attractiveness – business position model
Marketing manager

New product development
Phase out
Problem children
Product adoption process
Product deletion
Product development
Product manager
Product modification
Product portfolio analysis
Quality modifications
Run out
Screening ideas
Selective distribution
Stars
Style modifications
Test marketing
Venture or project team

Discussion and review questions

1. What organizational alternatives are available to a company with two product lines, each consisting of four product items?

2. When is it more appropriate to use a product manager than a marketing manager?

3. What type of company might use a venture team to develop new products? What are the advantages and disadvantages of such a team?

4. Do small companies that manufacture one or two products need to be concerned about developing and managing products? Why or why not?

5. Why is product development a cross-functional activity within an organization? That is, why must finance, engineering, manufacturing and other functional areas be involved?

6. Develop a list of information sources for new product ideas for the car industry.

7. What are the advantages and disadvantages of test marketing?

8. Compare and contrast three ways of modifying a product.

9. What are the stages of the product adoption process, and how do they affect the commercialization phase?

10. Detail the key stages of the product life cycle.

11. How can a company prolong the life of a mature product? What actions should be taken to try to stem the product's decline?

12. Give several reasons why a company might be unable to eliminate an unprofitable product.

13. In what ways do the stages of the product life cycle impact on a company's management of its product portfolio?

14. What are the major considerations in developing the BCG product portfolio matrix? Define and explain the four basic types of product suggested by the Boston Consulting Group.

15. What are the advantages of the directional policy matrix (DPM) over the BCG product portfolio matrix?

16. What are the diagnostic capabilities of the ABC sales: contribution analysis?

Recommended readings

Baker, M. and Hart, S., *Product Strategy and Management* (Pearson/FT, 2007).

Busuttil, J., *The Practitioner's Guide To Product Management* (Piatkus, 2015).

Crawford, C.M. and Di Benedetto, C.A., *New Products Management* (McGraw-Hill, 2014).

Day, G.S., *Analysis for Strategic Marketing Decisions* (West, 1986).

Haines, S., *The Product Manager's Desk Reference* (McGraw-Hill, 2014).

Lehmann, D. and Winer, R., *Product Management* (McGraw-Hill, 2007).

Loch, C. and Kavadias, S., *Handbook of Product Management* (Butterworth-Heinemann, 2008).

Trott, P., *Innovation Management and New Product Development* (FT/Pearson, 2011).

Wind, Y.J., *Product Policy: Concepts, Methods and Strategy* (Addison-Wesley, 1982).

Internet exercise

The success of BMW's Mini has been phenomenal. Despite a limited range of cars, each one on the road appears unique, and research reveals that Mini owners feel they have the power to tailor their car to suit their specific tastes and driving styles. BMW and Mini have incorporated this individualization, of what in reality is far from a bespoke one-to-one product, in their product development process and in their commercialization of this product. Take a look at either: www.mini.co.uk or www.mini.com and in particular the section detailing accessories and *Design Your Mini*.

1. What product features and characteristics are portrayed on the Mini website?

2. To what extent does Mini's commercialization enable customers to individualize or personalize their cars?

Group tasks

1. Brainstorm ideas for new products or services which might assist students in finding suitable accommodation. Outline the process you would need to follow in order to take the best of these ideas to market.

2. Think about a product or service which has disappointed you. Why were you disappointed? How could the marketers of this product or service have avoided your disappointment? What process should they have followed?

Applied mini-case

People visit cinemas to watch a film for many reasons: to catch the latest release; because friends are going; to be entertained; to go on a date; to occupy the children; to escape from the children; to be with people; to have an emotional experience; to kill time; to have a rest, or 'just because it's somewhere to go'. The choice of which film to see may often be the first decision, but these days, with the growth of multiplexes and record cinema attendances, the choice may be which multiplex: Odeon, Cineworld, Vue, Showcase? For rival operators, the 'augmented' product is becoming increasingly important as they seek to develop a competitive edge and to encourage customer loyalty. For example, Showcase strongly emphasizes many once secondary or minor features in an attempt to add to the appeal of its cinemas:

- state-of-the-art film projection
- acres of free, illuminated car parking
- best seats in town and exclusive rocking loungers
- bargain matinees daily
- freshly-popped popcorn
- cinema hire and special group rates
- comedy nights
- on main coach/bus routes
- Dolby stereo-equipped auditoria
- Sony Digital
- air conditioning
- excellent facilities for the disabled
- autism friendly screenings
- screenings for the elderly and deaf
- late-night shows every Friday and Saturday
- efficient, courteous service
- gift certificates always available
- art gallery with prints for sale.

For many companies, not only Showcase, the augmented product is an increasingly important element in the marketing strategy and the search for customer satisfaction. The new product development process increasingly includes the required customer service attributes desired by targeted customers to accompany the purchased product.

Source: Showcase Cinema, Coventry; www.showcasecinemas.co.uk, March 2015.

Question

As a marketing manager, to what extent does inclusion of the augmented product simplify or complicate the new product development process?

Sellotape or adhesive tape? Increasing market penetration – a classic tale

Case study

Just as JCB is a generic term for backhoe diggers in the construction industry, Hoover for vacuum cleaners, Post-it for those useful sticky stationery tags, and iPad for tablets, for many decades Sellotape has been the term applied to sticky transparent tape. It is even cited in the Oxford Dictionary. However, over the years many other brands and suppliers have entered the market and eaten away Sellotape's once dominant market share. So where was Sellotape to seek growth?

At the end of 1995, following nearly two years of research and planning, Sellotape enjoyed a £2 million relaunch. This represented the 'most significant change in the brand's 60 year history', according to Neil Ashley, then executive director of the company renamed the Sellotape Company. The name Sellotape had been the company's core marketing asset for many decades, with nine out of ten consumers familiar with the brand. However, the company had for some time sold a wider range of products than its sticky tape association implies. Michael Peters of the branding specialist Identica, responsible for the Sellotape rethink, was more fervent in his view: 'While it was a very famous trademark, it was a grey one'. Qualitative marketing research revealed that, although well known, hardly any consumer asked for Sellotape by name. Worse, they readily accepted other brands because they could see no obvious product or brand features that gave Sellotape a competitive edge or differentiation over rival products.

The relaunch aimed to address the inherent weakness in becoming a generic name for a product by re-establishing a new brand identity alongside existing core brand values. Rival products not using cellulose are cheaper, so alongside its traditional tape, the Sellotape Company offered a range of tape made from other source materials. For example, Elephant Tape was a heavy-duty fabric tape that was targeted at the do-it-yourself (DIY) market.

Under the sub-brand Sellotape Office, a range of products aimed at office use was launched. Ranges were also targeted at the children's market and the home security market. The view that there were three distinct markets – retail, DIY and office – led to the development of novel product applications and totally separate ranges.

The key problem to overcome was 'the Colman's mustard dilemma'. Colman's, the market leader in mustards, had tremendously high brand awareness, and consumers perceived its mustards to be of high quality. Unfortunately these con-sumers usually bought only one type of mustard, English; and that one jar lasted for years! Colman's had to increase usage. It achieved this by both:

1. demonstrating in advertisements and cookery supplements that mustard could be used in a variety of ways, particularly as an additional ingredient in many sauces, just like a herb or spice

2. bringing out a range of different mustards, each with unique strengths, flavours and applications, French, Italian and American mustards, along with the traditional English.

Consumers were encouraged to have several jars in their cupboards and to consume greater quantities.

For Sellotape, research showed that most customers bought only one roll of sticky tape each year, often around Christmas. The launch of ranges designed for different target markets – retail, DIY and office – and for various applications – children's activities and home security uses – emulated the brand extension principles so well deployed by Colman's.

Sellotape's strong brand awareness and identity meant that the company did not need to advertise heavily. Instead, the Sellotape Company relied on direct marketing and point-of-sale promotion to create awareness of its new sub-brands and their applications. A core task for the company had been to break down the traditional views of the product and its customers held by employees, and to establish additional channels of distribution through toy shops and garden centres to reflect the extended and additional product ranges. If the Sellotape Company could, like Colman's, encourage its customers to buy two products annually instead of just one and to look for its branded products by name, the heritage of the brand and the reorganization of the company would reap significant rewards. Today, owned by global adhesives giant Henkel, this strategy is proving very successful for Sellotape. The company has maintained the targeting strategy, with ranges for everyday, gifting, crafts, home and office, as well as its dispensers.

Questions for discussion

1. At what stages in their product life cycle are the different Sellotape products, and what are the management implications?

2. Why was it necessary for the Sellotape Company to relaunch its Sellotape range?

3. How might new lines help Sellotape develop its competitive position in this market?

Sources: 'Sellotape acts to avoid getting stuck in a rut', *Independent on Sunday*, 26 November 1995, IB8; the Sellotape Company, 1996; B&Q, 1996; Sainsbury's Homebase, 1996, 2004. With grateful thanks to Meg Carter; http://sellotape .henkel-online.co.uk/home.php, January, 2008; 'Welcome to Sellotape', http://sellotape.ctisn-online.com/home.php, 5 March 2011; www.henkel.com /brands-and-solution/adhesives-sealants-surfacetreatments-12123.htm, 2011; www.sellotape.com, April 2015.

CHAPTER 13
The marketing of services

"Nebulous and difficult to differentiate, for services, consistent quality and effective delivery are paramount"

Objectives

- To understand the nature and characteristics of services.

- To classify services.

- To understand the development of marketing strategies for services.

- To understand the problems involved in developing a differential advantage in services.

- To examine the concept of service quality.

- To explore the concept of marketing in non-profit situations.

- To understand the development of marketing strategies in non-profit organizations.

- To describe methods for controlling non-profit marketing activities.

INTRODUCTION

As discussed in Chapter 10, all products, goods, services and ideas possess a certain amount of intangibility. For service products, intangibility is often all-embracing because a service is something provided to consumers or business customers which happens or takes place. A **service** is an intangible product involving a deed, a performance or an effort that cannot physically be possessed.[1]

This chapter presents concepts that apply specifically to the marketing of services. Services marketing also involves marketing in non-profit organizations such as education, healthcare, charities and government, as well as for-profit making areas such as entertainment, tourism, finance, personal services and professional services. The characteristics of services and the markets for services demand important adaptation of the marketing toolkit and warrant specific discussion of the nuances of the service 'product'. This chapter should be read in conjunction with Chapter 21.

> **Service**
> An intangible product involving a deed, a performance or an effort that cannot physically be possessed.

Marketing a solution to today's stresses

Champneys were pioneers of the concept of holistic wellbeing, the first UK health spa chain and the first purpose-built health resort, all located in the English counties of Bedfordshire, Hertfordshire, Leicestershire and Hampshire.

Our pioneering spirit continues with state of the art facilities, cutting-edge medicine and sports science, and the newest and most exotic treatments from around the world.

At our college, we train our therapists to the most exacting standards in the world. A qualification from Champneys is seen as a benchmark.

Our flagship health and wellbeing spas, with their unequalled range of treatments and offerings, attract A-listers, the sporting world, the spa cognoscenti and those who simply seek a treat.

Led by our four luxury resort spas, the Champneys experience can be shared by all through the urban Day Spas and our Champneys Spa Collection. Our distinct brand of Englishness is also growing in Europe, Asia, the Middle East and North America.

www.champneys.com/About-Champneys

Champneys is but one of dozens of spa businesses to emerge during the past few decades, responding to the stresses of modern living and hectic business lives, as consumers seek solace from the rigours of daily life, either for routine 'pick-me-ups' or special occasion pampering. There are plenty of tangible aspects to a typical spa, from treatment beds to invigorating spa pools, but for most consumers it is the experience that they seek, supplemented with an appropriate ambience and attentive staff. The marketing concept is just as relevant for such experiential and nebulous products as for the marketers of smartphones or tablets. However, the execution of the marketing process has rather important characteristics unique to experiential services, as suggested by the sentiments of Champneys' proposition, with its focus on expert staff, surroundings, proficient processes and the customer's experience.

The health and wellbeing products offered by Champneys are services rather than tangible goods and they are experiential. This chapter presents concepts that apply specifically to products that are services. The organizations that market service products include: for-profit businesses, such as those offering financial, personal and professional services; and non-profit organizations, such as educational institutions, religious groups, charities and governments. The activities of the so-termed third sector lie within these realms. The practices of social marketing, as explored in Chapter 1, are directly applicable for many non-profit services.

The chapter begins by considering the contribution of service industries to the economy. It then addresses the unique characteristics of services and the problems they present to marketers: these traits often form the basis for examination questions and they explain why marketers of services have to manipulate an extended marketing mix, devote extensive resources to branding and often struggle to create a differential advantage over rivals. Next, the chapter presents various classification schemes that can help services marketers develop marketing strategies. A variety of marketing mix considerations are discussed, along with the associated problems of creating and sustaining a differential advantage. The important concept of service quality is then explored. Finally, the chapter defines non-profit marketing and examines the development of non-profit marketing strategies and the control of non-profit marketing activities.

The nature and importance of services

Few products can be classified as a pure good or a pure service. Consider, for example, the purchase of a laptop computer. When consumers buy a laptop, they take ownership of a physical item which they might use at work and at home, but the maintenance contract linked with the purchase and providing reassurance is a service and a helpline facility offering software support is providing a service. Most products, such as computers and other high-tech goods, contain both tangible and intangible components. An airline provides a service, yet offers tangible items such as lounges and comfortable seats; hotels require tangible items such as pools, beds, tables, yet fundamentally provide a service...somewhere to stay. One component, however, will dominate, and it is this dominant component that leads to the classification of goods, services and ideas.

Figure 13.1 illustrates the tangibility concept by placing a variety of 'products' on a continuum of tangibility and intangibility. Tangible dominant products are typically classified as goods, and intangible dominant products are typically considered services. A restaurant meal or taxi cab may be tangible and physical, but the restaurant or taxi operator is providing a service: refreshment or transportation. Thus, as defined in Chapter 10, services are intangible dominant products that involve the application of human and mechanical efforts to people or objects.

Growth of services

In Europe, as in the United States, the importance of services in the economy is increasing, with nearly two-thirds of the EU workforce employed in the sector. Service industries encompass trade, communications, transport, leisure, food and accommodation, financial and medical services, education, government and technical services. There are services intended for consumers – **consumer services** – and those designed to satisfy businesses – **business services**.

Consumer services
Services such as education, healthcare, leisure, catering, tourism, financial, entertainment, home maintenance and other services to help consumers.

Economic prosperity has been a major catalyst for consumer services growth, leading to an increase in financial services, travel, entertainment and personal care. Lifestyle changes have also encouraged expansion of the service sector. Smaller families result in more free time and relatively higher disposable income. Consumers are keener than ever to 'buy in' outside services. With the growth of households in which both adults are working, many consumers want to avoid tasks such as meal preparation, house cleaning, home maintenance and preparation of tax returns, so they buy-in such service provision or assistance. Furthermore, Europeans have become more fitness and recreation oriented and, with greater leisure time, the demand for fitness and recreational facilities has escalated. In terms of demographics, the population is growing older, and this change has promoted tremendous expansion of healthcare services. Finally, the number and complexity of goods needing servicing have spurred demand for installation and repair services.

Business services
Services such as repairs and maintenance, consulting and professional advice, installation, equipment leasing, marketing research, advertising, temporary office personnel and caretaking services.

Not only have consumer services grown in the economy, business services have prospered as well. Business services include repairs and maintenance, consulting and professional advice, installation, equipment leasing, banking and legal advice, marketing

Goods (tangible)	Bananas	Jewellery	TV	Cars/ maintenance	Fast-food restaurants	Airlines	Beauty salons	Financial services	Telephone services	Education	Services (intangible)

FIGURE 13.1
A continuum of product tangibility and intangibility

research, advertising, temporary office personnel, real estate and facilities management services. Expenditures for business services have risen even faster than expenditures for consumer services. This growth has been attributed to the increasingly complex, specialized and competitive business environment and a trend for businesses to outsource to third party specialists many routine operations such as catering, IT and facilities management.[2]

There are four key reasons behind the growth of business-to-business services:

1. Specialization – the delegation of non-care tasks, such as advertising, digital and car fleet management.

2. Technology – the increase in sophistication leading to the 'buying in' of expert knowledge and skills, such as IT computing consultants or manufacturing design.

3. Outsourcing of support functions to external providers who take over a company's processes and personnel, for payroll and recruitment, catering, healthcare and insurance arrangements, facilities management and real estate, and IT services.

4. Flexibility – the need in many organizations to avoid fixed overhead costs; for example, marketing research, executive recruitment, event catering, maintenance and overhaul of systems are often brought in only on an ad hoc basis when required.

Characteristics of services

The marketing of services is distinct from goods marketing.[3] To understand the nature of services marketing, it is necessary to appreciate the particular characteristics of services. Services have for a long time been viewed in marketing circles as 'being different' to goods, because of four fundamental distinguishing characteristics:

1. intangibility
2. inseparability of production and consumption
3. perishability
4. heterogeneity.[4]

Table 13.1 summarizes these characteristics and the resulting marketing challenges.

Intangibility The characteristic of **intangibility** stems from the fact that services are performances. They cannot be seen, touched, tasted or smelled, nor can they be possessed or stock-piled. Intangibility also relates to the difficulty that consumers may have in understanding service offerings.[5] Services have a few tangible attributes, called **search qualities**, which can be viewed prior to purchase, such as the décor in a restaurant or the facilities in a care home. When consumers cannot examine a service product in advance, they may not understand exactly what is being offered. Even when consumers do gain sufficient knowledge about service offerings, they may not be able to evaluate the possible choices. On the other hand, services are rich in experience and credence qualities. **Experience qualities** are those qualities that can be assessed only after purchase and consumption (satisfaction, courtesy, pleasure). Fitness centres and holidays are examples of services that are high in experience qualities. **Credence qualities** are those qualities that cannot be assessed even after purchase and consumption.[6] A medical operation, car repairs, consulting and legal representation are examples of services high in credence qualities. How many consumers are knowledgeable enough to assess the quality of an appendectomy, even after the surgery has been performed?

A Renault car can be test-driven before being purchased. It can be viewed in the dealer's showroom and on the streets. It can to an extent be consumed (tested) prior to purchase. A new smartphone or tablet may be trialled in the store or by using a friend's

Intangibility
An inherent quality of services that are performed and therefore cannot be tasted, touched, seen, smelled or possessed.

Search qualities
Tangible attributes of a service that can be viewed prior to purchase.

Experience qualities
Attributes that can be assessed only after purchase and consumption, including satisfaction and courtesy.

Credence qualities
Attributes that cannot be assessed even after purchase and consumption.

TABLE 13.1   Service marketing challenges

Service characteristics	Resulting marketing challenges
Intangibility	Difficult for customer to evaluate Customer does not take physical possession Difficult to advertise and display Difficult to set and justify prices Service process is not usually protected by patents
Inseparability of production and consumption	Service provider cannot mass-produce services Customer must participate and comply in production Other consumers affect service outcomes Services are difficult to distribute and replicate
Perishability	Services cannot be stored Very difficult to balance supply and demand Unused capacity is lost forever Demand may be very time-sensitive
Heterogeneity	Service quality is difficult to control Difficult to standardize service delivery
Client-based relationships	Success depends on satisfying and keeping customers over the long term Generating repeat business is challenging Relationship building becomes critical
Customer contact	Service providers are critical to delivery Requires high levels of service employee training and motivation Changing a high-contact service into a low-contact service to achieve lower costs without reducing customer satisfaction

Sources: Adapted from the ideas of K. Douglas Hoffman and John E.G. Bateson, *Essentials of Services Marketing* (Fort Worth, TX: Dryden Press, 1997), pp. 25–38; Valarie A. Zeithaml, A. Parasuraman and Leonard L. Berry, *Delivering Quality Service: Balancing Customer Perceptions and Expectations* (New York: Free Press, 1990); Leonard L. Berry and A. Parasuraman, *Marketing Services: Competing through Quality* (New York: Free Press, 1991), p. 5.

device prior to purchase. The same is not true of a beauty treatment or an opera seat. The beauty treatment and the opera may fail to live up to expectations, but by the time this disappointment is recognized it is too late – the service has been partially consumed and paid for and the opportunity cost long gone.

Inseparability
In relation to production and consumption, a characteristic of services that means they are produced at the same time as they are consumed.

Inseparability   Related to intangibility is **inseparability** of production and consumption. Services are normally produced at the same time as they are consumed. A medical examination is an example of simultaneous production and consumption. In fact, the doctor cannot possibly perform the service without the patient's presence, and the consumer is actually involved in the production process. With other services, such as taking tennis lessons, consumers are simultaneously involved in production. Due to high consumer involvement in most services, standardization and control are difficult to maintain. The Building Customer Relationships box on page 389 illustrates how students may be as much to blame for a poor lecture as their tutor.

Perishability
A characteristic of services whereby unused capacity on one occasion cannot be stockpiled or inventoried for future occasions.

Perishability   As production and consumption are simultaneous, services are also characterized by **perishability**. The consumer of a service generally has to be present and directly involved in the consumption of the service at the time of its production. This means that unused capacity in one time period cannot be stockpiled or inventoried for future time periods. This is a problem that airline operators face every day. Each operator engages in an ongoing struggle to maintain seat occupancy levels. Empty seats mean lost business. Many operators offer 'last-minute' cut-price deals to reduce the numbers of empty seats. In many cases it is not possible to change the flight on

FIGURE 13.2
Many services are targeted at business customers. Here wholesalers Capital Hair and Beauty attempt to entice new clients for its services, via a wide range of products

Source: Image courtesy of Capital Hair.

which the seat is booked and monies paid are generally not refunded in the event of cancellation. This example illustrates how service perishability presents problems very different from the supply and demand problems encountered in the marketing of goods.[7] While an empty airline seat on a flight is a sale lost forever, cans of soup remaining on the supermarket shelf at the close of business will be available for sale the following day.

Heterogeneity Most services are labour intensive, so they are susceptible to **heterogeneity**. For the service to be provided and consumed, the client generally meets and deals directly with the service provider's personnel. Direct contact and interaction are distinguishing features of services. However, the people delivering services do not always perform consistently. There may be variation from one service to another within the same organization or variation in the service that a single individual provides from day to day and from customer to customer. A good branch manager is crucial for a restaurant chain such as Pizza Express or a coffee shop like Starbucks. Poor customer reaction and branch performance can often be traced back to a poor branch manager.[8] Waiting times in either outlet can vary greatly, often due to teamwork, speed and efficiency variations between branches. This may result in varying levels of customer satisfaction between one Starbucks and another. Thus, standardization and quality are extremely difficult to control. However, it is also true that the characteristics of services themselves may make it possible for marketers to customize their offerings to consumers. In such cases, services marketers often face a dilemma: how to provide efficient, standardized service at an acceptable level of quality, while simultaneously treating each customer as a unique person.

Client-based relationships The success of many services depends on creating and maintaining **client-based relationships**, interactions with customers that result in satisfied customers who use a service repeatedly over time.[9] In fact, some service providers, such as solicitors, accountants and financial advisers, call their customers 'clients' and often develop and maintain close, long-term relationships with them. Customers are generally more satisfied in relational exchanges over time than they are with exchanges based on single transactions. Indeed, research suggests that customer loyalty and re-patronage behaviour can be encouraged through this approach.[10] The building of such relationships has also been shown to be important in non-profit contexts.[11] It seems that services businesses are successful only to the degree to which they can maintain a group of clients who use their services on an ongoing basis. For example, a dentist may serve a family for many years. If the family members are confident in the dentist and think he or she offers a good service, they are likely to recommend the dentist to friends. If this positive word-of-mouth communication continues, the dentist may acquire a large number of clients through this route. To ensure that client-based relationships are created and maintained, a service provider must take action to build trust, demonstrate customer commitment, and satisfy customers so well that they become very loyal to the provider and unlikely to switch to competitors.

Customer contact Not all services require a high degree of **customer contact**, but many do. Customer contact refers to the level of interaction between the service provider and the customer that is necessary to deliver the service. High-contact services include healthcare, real estate, and hair and beauty services. Examples of low-contact services are car repairs and dry cleaning. As the following section explains, the level of customer contact is sometimes used as the basis for classifying services.

Heterogeneity
Variability in the quality of service because services are provided by people, and people perform inconsistently.

Client-based relationships
Interactions that result in satisfied customers who use a service repeatedly over time.

Customer contact
The level of interaction between the provider and customer needed to deliver the service.

Classification of services

Services are a very diverse group of products, and an organization may provide more than one kind. Examples of services include car hire, maintenance services, healthcare, hairdressing, health centres, childcare, domestic services, legal advice, banking, insurance, air travel, education, entertainment, catering, business consulting, dry cleaning and accounting. Nevertheless, services can be meaningfully analyzed using a **five-category classification** scheme:

Five-category classification
A method of analyzing services according to five criteria: type of market, degree of labour intensiveness, degree of customer contact, skill of the service provider and goal of the service provider.

1. type of market
2. degree of labour intensiveness
3. degree of customer contact
4. skill of the service provider, and
5. goal of the service provider.

Table 13.2 summarizes this scheme.

Type of market   Services can be viewed in terms of the market or type of customer they serve, consumer or business.[12] The implications of this distinction are very similar to those for all products.

Degree of labour intensiveness   A second way to classify services is by degree of labour intensiveness. Many services – such as domestic cleaning, education and medical care – rely heavily on human labour. Other services – such as telecommunications, fitness centres and public transport – are more equipment intensive.

Labour-based (that is, people-based) services are more susceptible to heterogeneity than most equipment-based services. Marketers of people-based services must recognize that the service providers are often viewed as the service itself. Therefore, strategies relating to selecting, training, motivating and controlling employees are crucial to the success of most service businesses. A bad attitude from Ryanair's ground staff would colour the customer's view not just of the employee concerned but also of the company, the brand and all of its service products. A customer who has

TABLE 13.2   Classification of services

Category	Examples
Type of market	
Consumer	Childcare, legal advice, entertainment
Business	Consulting, facilities management, installation
Degree of labour intensiveness	
Labour-based	Education, haircuts, dentistry
Equipment-based	Telecommunications, fitness centres, public transport
Degree of customer contact	
High	Healthcare, hotels, air travel
Low	Home deliveries, postal service
Skill of the service provider	
Professional	Legal advice, healthcare, accountancy
Non-professional	Domestic services, dry cleaning, public transport
Goal of the service provider	
Profit	Financial services, insurance, tourism
Non-profit	Some healthcare, education, government

flown quite happily with Ryanair for many years may, so badly treated, consider taking his or her custom to a rival company.

Degree of customer contact   The third way in which services can be classified is by degree of customer contact. High-contact services include healthcare, hotels, property agents and restaurants; low contact services include home deliveries, theatres, dry cleaning and spectator sports.[13] High contact services generally involve actions that are directed towards individuals. As these services are directed at people, the consumer must be present during production. Sometimes, for example in the case of a car valeting service, it is possible for the service provider to go to the consumer. However, high-contact services typically require that the consumer goes to the 'production' facility. Consequently, the physical appearance and ambience of the facility may be a major component of the consumer's overall evaluation of the service. The enjoyment of a visit to a health spa stems not just from the quality of the beauty treatments, or the suitability of the dietary or fitness programmes on offer, but also from the décor and furnishings, general ambience, and the abilities and attitude of the staff. Since the consumer must be present during production of a high-contact service, the process of production may be just as important as its final outcome. For example, open-plan banks, quick queue systems and ATM facilities aim to improve the transaction process and make the service more enjoyable for the consumer.

Low-contact service, in contrast, commonly involves actions directed at 'things'. Although consumers may not need to be present during service delivery, their presence may be required to initiate or terminate the service. The Post Office maintains a network of branches, sorting offices and vehicles. The process of sending a parcel from Edinburgh to Cardiff or Lille is lengthy. Yet consumers only need to be present to initiate the service. The appearance of the production facilities and the interpersonal skills of actual service providers are thus not as critical in low-contact services as they are in high-contact services.[14]

Skill of the service provider   Skill of the service provider is a fourth way to classify services. Professional services tend to be more complex and more highly regulated than non-professional services. In the case of legal advice, for example, the final product is situation-specific. As a result, consumers often do not know what the actual service will involve or how much it will cost until the service is completed.

Goal of the service provider   Finally, services can be classified according to whether they are profit or non-profit. The second half of this chapter examines non-profit (not-for-profit) marketing, such as that present in the public sector and charities. Most non-profit organizations provide services rather than goods.

Developing marketing strategies for services

Strategic considerations

In developing marketing strategies, the marketer must first understand what benefits the customer wants, how the company's service offer and brand are perceived relative to the competition and what services consumers buy.[15] In other words, the marketer must develop the right service for the right people at the right price, in the right place with the right positioning and image. The marketer must then communicate with consumers so that they are aware of the need-satisfying services available to them. The key aspects of effective target marketing as explained in Chapters 7 and 8 and of managing the implementation of the determined marketing strategy apply strongly to the marketing of services.[16]

One of the unique challenges service marketers face is matching supply and demand. Price can be used to help smooth out demand for a service. There are also other ways in which marketers can alter the marketing mix to deal with the problem of fluctuating demand. Through price incentives, advertising and other promotional efforts, marketers can remind consumers of busy times and encourage them to come for service during slack periods. Additionally, the product itself can be altered to cope with fluctuating demand. Restaurants, for example, may change their menus, vary their lighting and décor, open or close the bar, and change the entertainment on offer. A historical tourist destination may stage theatrical events and firework displays to attract customers out of season. Theme parks heavily price discount in colder and wetter months. Finally, distribution can be modified to reflect changes in demand. For example, some libraries have mobile units that travel to different locations during slack periods.[17]

The strategies that services marketers implement are contingent upon a good understanding of the pattern and determinants of demand. Does the level of demand follow a cycle? What are the causes of this cycle? Are the changes random?[18] An attempt to use price decreases to shift demand for public transport to off-peak periods would achieve only limited success because of the cause of the cyclical demand for public transport. Employees have little control over their working hours and are therefore unable to take advantage of pricing incentives.

Table 13.3 summarizes a range of marketing and non-marketing strategies that service businesses may use to deal with fluctuating demand. Non-marketing strategies essentially involve internal, employee-related actions.[19] They may be the only choices available when fluctuations in demand are random.

Creating a differential advantage in services

The aim of marketing is to satisfy customers by achieving product or brand differentiation with an advantage over competitors' products. This **differential advantage**, sometimes termed a 'competitive edge', is determined by customers' perceptions. A differential advantage is something desired by the customer that only one company can offer, as explained in Chapter 2. If the targeted customers do not perceive an advantage, in marketing terms the product offers no benefit over rival products and its financial viability is in doubt.

Differential advantage
Something desired by the customer that only one company – not its rivals – can offer.

For any product, achieving and sustaining a differential advantage is difficult, but for services the challenge is even greater. The intangibility of the service product and the central role of people in its delivery are the prime causes of this difficulty, but, as Table 13.4 shows, there are others, such as difficulties ensuring consistent service quality delivery and the fact that the interface with the customer may be difficult to control.

The difficulty encountered in creating a differential advantage in services makes it even more important that marketing activities are carried out in a systematic and appropriate manner. Thus, services marketers must ensure that the needs of targeted markets are well understood in order to bring service products and the marketing mix into line with customers' exact requirements. There must be a clear appreciation of competitors' service offerings and marketing programmes, and regular efforts are needed to research customers' satisfaction levels. Branding, supported with well-constructed promotional campaigns, is even more central to the reinforcement and communication of any differential advantage for services.

TABLE 13.3   Strategies for coping with fluctuations in demand for services

Marketing strategies	Non-marketing strategies
Use different pricing	Hire extra staff/lay off employees
Alter product	Work employees overtime/part time
Change place/distribution	Cross-train employees
Use promotional efforts	Use employees to perform non-vital tasks during slack times
Modify customer service levels	Subcontract work/seek subcontract work
Alter branding and positioning	Slow the pace of work
Focus on a niche segment	Turn away business

TABLE 13.4 Difficulties in creating a differential advantage in services

Intangibility minimizes product differentiation
No or little patent protection exists
Few barriers to entry enable competitors to set up and copy successful initiatives
The interface with customers is difficult to control
Growth is hard to achieve, particularly since key personnel can only be spread so far
Service quality is irregular
It is difficult to improve productivity and lower the cost to the consumer
Innovation leads to imitation
Restrictive regulations abound, particularly in the professions

The extended marketing mix for services

The standard marketing mix comprises the '4Ps':

- product
- promotion
- price
- place/distribution.

The discussion about the classification of services has emphasized the importance of three additional elements:

Extended marketing mix for services
In addition to the standard '4Ps' marketing mix – product, promotion, price and place/distribution – there are 3Ps: process, physical evidence (ambience) and people.

- process
- physical evidence (ambience)
- people.

Collectively, these seven elements, which are sometimes called the '7Ps', form what is termed the **extended marketing mix for services** (see Figure 13.3). It is essential for services marketers to recognize the importance of these additional '3Ps'. The implications for marketing mix activities are discussed further in Chapter 21 of *Marketing: Concepts and Strategies*.

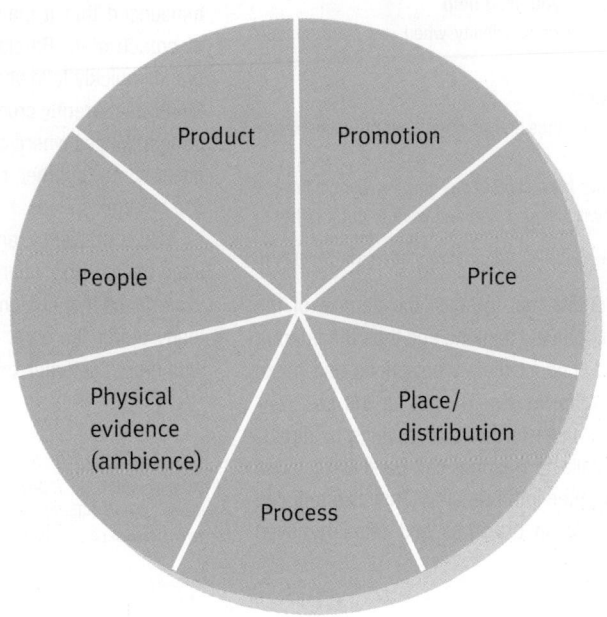

FIGURE 13.3
The extended marketing mix for services

We're committed to helping you: banks remember customer service

Building customer relationships

A trend for close to 30 years has been for banks to close rural branches and reduce the number of town-centre branches. Many Victorian banks, with their large chambers, grand facades and prime locations, have been turned into bars or restaurants. TV viewers in the UK will have seen a well-known retail bank advertising the last of its branches being turned into wine bars, stating that instead branches are to be kept open in order to benefit its customers. A separate advertisement revealed that customers would once again be able to talk directly to staff in their local branch, rather than only to anonymous personnel in a far-flung faceless call centre. In 2010, NatWest went even further, announcing its *Customer Charter* and stating that it intended to be the UK's most helpful bank, to be verified via independent research, with a focus on in-branch customer service.

It's not just words, it's a goal at our very core, guided by four promises that are outlined in our Customer Charter for all to see.

Promises we've created by speaking to customers like you. And that we plan to deliver against by always providing the best quality service, no matter how you bank with us:

We put our customers' needs first
– We will listen and then help you find solutions that meet your needs

We make banking easier
– We will help you bank with us in the simplest and most convenient way

We are there whenever you need help
– We will take personal responsibility when you need support from us

We are fair and honest
– We will explain the features and pricing of our products clearly and simply

If you think we have fallen short at any time, we want to know – you can be sure we will always listen and work to put it right.

www.natwest.com/global/customer-charter.ashx, April 2015

For some time pundits had forecast the demise of the bank branch, as first telephone banking and then the internet enabled customers to conduct their transactions and make enquiries via telecommunications. The era of the call centre permitted banks to make further cost savings by directing apparently local calls to regional call centres or those based overseas, rather than into branches. This also reduced the number of personnel in branches and often removed mortgage, investment and insurance specialists altogether. In effect, for many customers, this had the impact of further reducing or downgrading the appeal of visiting branches. Mergers and acquisitions in the banking sector have also encouraged a reduction in branch numbers, as newly merged chains close and relocate branches in order to reduce duplication and operating costs.

There is little doubt that telephone banking, e-banking and now mobile apps have become increasingly popular. Nevertheless, there is talk of an end to the culling of bank branches. This is because marketing research reveals that not all customers wish to deal with call centres or to conduct their business via a PC or smartphone. Many customers find face-to-face contact reassuring, and only the bank branch environment provides this direct interaction.

The role of the branch may be rejuvenated even further. Even customers utilizing e-banking often need to visit branches, and many customers still believe that complex enquiries or topics perceived as risky are better handled face-to-face inside a bank branch. Unfortunately, the removal of specialist staff from many branches and the downgrading of the majority of branches to simple transaction-processing points, led to a growing level of customer dissatisfaction with bank branches.

Now, in a strategy shift, the leading high-street banking brands are acknowledging that they must reinvest in their bank branches: more and better trained staff, improved IT enabling speedy processing of enquiries and creating more opportunities for the cross-selling of products, plus enhanced interior designs. As part of this shift in emphasis, staff with a greater customer orientation are required. NatWest announced that it planned to invest in additional members of branch staff. Barclays, Santander and the other leading brands quickly followed suit. To raise the stakes more, Virgin Money is currently creating lounges for the benefit of its customers; places where customers can relax and local communities come together, providing free refreshments, wi-fi and use of Virgin's iPads.

While efficiency and reducing operating costs are still important to the boards of these companies, there is an acceptance that customers expect improved service and that many prefer the bank branch as the setting for interactions with more customer-oriented personnel.

Sources: NatWest 2003–15; Barclays, 2004–15; 'Back to the branch', *Marketing*, 26 May 2004, pp. 30–2; www.natwest.com/global/customer-charter.ashx, March 2011; http://uk.virginmoney.com/virgin/about-lounges, April 2015; www.natwest.com/global/customer-charter.ashx, April 2015.

Service quality

The delivery of high-quality services is one of the most important and difficult tasks that any service organization faces. As a result of their unique characteristics, services are very difficult to evaluate. Hence customers must look closely at service quality when comparing services. Service quality

Service quality
Customers' perception of how well a service meets or exceeds their expectations.

is defined as customers' perception of how well a service meets or exceeds their expectations.[20] Service quality is judged by customers, not the organization. This distinction is critical because it forces services marketers to examine their quality from the customer's viewpoint. For example, a dental surgery may view service quality as having friendly and knowledgeable employees. However, the customers may be more concerned with waiting time, cleanliness and the effectiveness of patient pain relief. Thus, it is important for service organizations to determine what customers expect and then develop service products that meet or exceed those expectations.

Customer evaluation of service quality

The biggest obstacle for customers in evaluating service quality is the intangible nature of the service. How can customers evaluate something they cannot see, feel, taste, smell or hear? The evaluation of a good is much easier because all goods possess 'search qualities' in the form of tangible attributes, such as colour, style, size, feel or fit, that can be evaluated prior to purchase. Trying on a new coat and taking a car for a test drive are examples of how customers evaluate search qualities. Services, on the other hand, have very few search qualities; instead, they abound in experience and credence qualities. Experience qualities – such as taste, satisfaction or pleasure – are attributes that can be assessed only during the purchase and consumption of a service. Restaurants and holidays are examples of services high in experience qualities. Credence qualities are attributes that customers may be unable to evaluate even after the purchase and consumption of the service. Examples of services high in credence qualities are surgical operations, vehicle repairs, consulting, and legal representation. Most consumers lack the knowledge or skills to evaluate the quality of these types of service. Consequently they must place a great deal of faith in the integrity and competence of the service provider.

Despite the difficulties in evaluating quality, service quality may be the only way customers can choose one service over another. For this reason, service marketers live or die by understanding how consumers judge service quality. This is one reason behind many retail banks now returning staff to their branches and refocusing on their branches as a key part of their customer relationship building, as described in the Building Customer Relationships box on page 386. Table 13.5 defines five dimensions consumers use when evaluating service quality:

1. tangibles
2. reliability
3. responsiveness
4. assurance
5. empathy.

Note that all of these dimensions have links to employee performance. Of the five, reliability is the most important in determining customer evaluations of service quality.[21]

Services marketers pay a great deal of attention to the tangibles dimension of service quality. Tangible attributes, or search qualities, such as the appearance of facilities and employees, are often the only aspects of a service that can be viewed before purchases and consumption. Therefore, services marketers must ensure that these tangible elements are consistent with the overall image of the service product.

Except for the tangibles dimension, the criteria that customers use to judge service quality are intangible. For instance, how does a customer judge reliability? Since dimensions such as reliability cannot be examined with the senses, consumers must rely on other ways of judging service criteria. One of the most important factors in customer judgements of service quality is

TABLE 13.5 Dimensions of service quality

Dimension	Evaluation criteria	Examples
Tangibles Physical evidence of the service	Appearance of physical facilities Appearance of service personnel Tools or equipment used to provide the service	A clean and professional-looking doctor's office A clean and neatly dressed repair person The appearance of food in a restaurant The equipment used in a medical examination
Reliability Consistency and dependability in performing the service	Accuracy of billing or recordkeeping Performing services when promised	An accurate bank statement A confirmed hotel reservation An airline flight departing and arriving on time
Responsiveness Willingness or readiness of employees to provide the service	Returning customer phone calls Providing prompt service Handling urgent requests	A server refilling a customer's cup of tea without being asked An ambulance arriving within three minutes
Assurance Knowledge/competence of employees and ability to convey trust and confidence	Knowledge and skills of employees Company name and reputation Personal characteristics of employees	A highly trained financial adviser A known and respected service provider A doctor's bedside manner
Empathy Caring and individual attention provided by employees	Listening to customer needs Caring about customers' interests Providing personalized attention	A store employee listening to and trying to understand a customer's complaint A nurse counselling a heart patient

Sources: Adapted from Leonard L. Berry and A. Parasuraman, *Marketing Services: Competing through Quality* (New York: Free Press, 1991); Valarie A. Zeithaml, A. Parasuraman and Leonard L. Berry, *Delivering Quality Service: Balancing Customer Perceptions and Expectations* (New York: Free Press, 1990); A. Parasuraman, Leonard L. Berry and Valarie A. Zeithaml, 'An empirical examination of relationships in an extended service quality model', *Marketing Science Institute Working Paper Series*, report no. 90–112 (Cambridge, MA: Marketing Science Institute, 1990), p. 29.

Service expectations
A factor used in judging service quality involving impressions from past experiences, word-of-mouth communication and the company's advertising.

service expectations. These are influenced by past experiences with the service, word-of-mouth communication from other customers and the service company's own advertising. For example, customers are usually eager to try a new restaurant, especially when friends recommend it. These same customers may also have seen advertisements placed by the restaurant. As a result, these customers have an idea of what to expect when they visit the restaurant for the first time. When they finally dine at the restaurant, the quality they experience will change the expectations they have for their next visit and affect their own comments to friends. That is why providing consistently high service quality is important. If the quality of a restaurant, or any services marketer, begins to deteriorate, customers will alter their own expectations and word-of-mouth communication to others accordingly.

Delivering exceptional service quality

Service quality factors
Factors that increase the likelihood of providing high-quality service: understanding customer expectations, service quality specifications, employee performance, managing service expectations.

Providing high-quality service on a consistent basis is very difficult. All consumers have experienced examples of poor service: long queues at retail checkouts, trains and buses that are late, or rude cinema employees. Obviously, it is impossible for a service organization to ensure exceptional service quality 100 per cent of the time. However, there are many steps that can be taken to increase the likelihood of providing high-quality service. First, though, the service company must understand the four **service quality factors**. As shown in Table 13.5, they are:

1. analysis of customer expectations
2. service quality specifications
3. employee performance
4. managing service expectations.[22]

Building customer relationships

People's performance is inconsistent…good lecture?

How often have you seen a truly awesome lecturer perform consistently session to session without a drop in her or his performance? Just as actors have an 'off performance', so do your lecturers. It is unlikely they left home with the express intention of disappointing you, failing to provide you with value for money, or not helping you with your studies… and yet they might fail to deliver to their normally high standards.

More likely, an email rant from a colleague, an annoying tweet, a worrying situation for a student under their care, rejection from the editor of a journal for a hard-crafted research paper, or a problem at home, has distracted your tutor. Academics often deliver back-to-back lectures with identical visual aids and script to ostensibly similar cohorts of students in terms of their profiles and motivations for attending the lecture. Nevertheless, rarely are such sessions delivered in identical fashion or to similar levels of acclaim… one lecture zings while the other in the supposed matching pair falls flat. Not only because of the tutor's service delivery, but perhaps the students in the first session were more participative, upbeat and prepared, so played their parts more effectively than the 'customers' in the second session.

Universities do a great deal to maintain the consistency and quality of session delivery. Training of staff, systems for reviewing teaching materials, peer reviews, student evaluation processes seeking feedback and formal staff appraisals, are just some of the devices employed. Nevertheless, an outstandingly engaging and informative lecture may well be followed with one not so strong or well received.

You might have found a reassuring and sympathetic dentist who seems capable, courteous and attentive. Unfortunately, your next appointment occurs after your dental practitioner has been awake all night looking after a poorly toddler, or while he or she is still seething following a morning row with their spouse, or your dentist might be distracted having learned of a relative's illness. Your experience is in no way similar to your previous visit and you feel somewhat let down and possibly very annoyed. Unfortunately, service delivery often is erratic and is inextricably linked to the mood, skills, behaviour and engagement of the person delivering the service.

Occasionally, you may encounter a pleasant surprise: the car dealer's service personnel listen attentively to your concerns, locate the problem promptly, fix it soon after, and the cost is considerably less than you feared. Their attentive, smiling and engaging manner has left you with an all-round good feeling of your experience. As a result, you feel more positive about the dealership, the brand of car you are driving and your experience of customer service. The problem is that you suspect it will not be such a good experience next time you visit. The challenges for marketers are to maintain consistency in the customer's experience and to ensure the level of satisfaction is high. These desires will not be achieved by accident. They must be planned, monitored, controlled and modifications made continually.

Analysis of customer expectations Providers need to understand customer expectations when designing a service to meet or exceed those expectations. Only then can they deliver good service. Customers usually have two levels of expectations: desired and acceptable. The desired level of expectations is what the customer really wants. If this level of expectations is provided, the customer would be very satisfied. The acceptable level is viewed as a reasonable level of performance that the customer considers as being adequate. The difference between these two levels of expectations is called the **customer's zone of tolerance**.[23]

Customer's zone of tolerance
The difference between the customer's desired level of expectations and the customer's acceptable level of expectations.

Service marketers sometimes use marketing research, such as surveys and focus groups, as a means of discovering customer needs and expectations, and they monitor online chatter and discussions on social media. Some services companies, such as hotel chains, seek customer feedback using comment cards. Another approach is to ask employees. Since customer-contact employees interact daily with customers, they often know what customers want from the company. Service managers should interact regularly with their employees to ensure that they remain in touch with this useful source of information.

Service quality specifications   Once an organization understands its customers' needs, it must establish goals to help ensure good service delivery. These goals, or service specifications, are typically set in terms of employee or machine performance. For example, a bank may require its employees to conform to a dress code. The same bank may insist that all incoming phone calls are answered by the third ring. Specifications like these can be very important in providing quality service as long as they are linked to customer needs.

Service managers who are visibly committed to service quality become role models for all employees in the organization.[24] Such commitment motivates personnel at all levels in the organization, from customer-contact employees through to senior managers, to comply with service specifications.

Employee performance   Once an organization sets service quality standards and managers are committed to them, the organization must find ways to ensure that customer contact employees perform their jobs well. Contact employees in many service industries – bank tellers, flight cabin crew, waiters, sales assistants – are often the least trained and lowest-paid members of the organization. Yet these individuals represent the most important link to the customer and are the 'face of the brand', so their performance is critical to customer perceptions of service quality.[25] Well-managed recruitment and training are essential if employees are to understand properly how to do their jobs. Providing information about customers, service specifications and the organization itself, during the training promotes this understanding.[26]

The use of evaluation and remuneration systems plays a part in employee performance. Many service employees are evaluated and rewarded on the basis of output measures such as sales volume for car salespeople, or lack of errors during work for data-input administrators. Such systems may overlook certain key aspects of job performance: friendliness, teamwork, effort and customer satisfaction. As the importance of customer relationship building comes more to the fore, companies are increasingly considering that customer-oriented measures of performance may be a better basis for evaluation and reward. For example, Dun & Bradstreet has tied employee commissions to customer satisfaction surveys rather than sales volume.[27] This type of system stimulates employees to take care of customer needs rather than focus solely on sales or profits.

Managing service expectations   As expectations are so significant in customer evaluations of service quality, service companies recognize that they must set realistic expectations about the service they can provide. These expectations can be set through advertising and good internal communication. In their advertisements, service companies make promises about the kind of service they will deliver. In fact, a service company is forced to make promises since the intangibility of services prevents it from showing them in the advertisement. However, the advertiser should not promise more than it can deliver; doing otherwise may mean disappointed customers.

To deliver on promises made, a company needs to have good internal communication among its departments, especially management, advertising and operations. Assume, for example, that a supermarket's advertising guarantees that shoppers will not have to queue at the checkout for more than five minutes. In order to meet this promise, the retailer will need to ensure that its operations and staff levels can support such a guarantee. Failure to do so may result in customers' service expectations not being met, with a consequent loss of credibility for the company.

Word-of-mouth and digital communication from other customers also shape customer expectations. However, service companies cannot manage this 'advertising' directly. The best way to ensure positive word-of-mouth communication is to provide exceptional service quality. It has been estimated that customers tell four times as many people about bad service as they do about good service. Consequently, services marketers must provide four good service experiences for every bad experience just to break even. Social media in this digital area has speeded up the likelihood of consumers informing others about a specific brand, for better or for worse depending on how well they regarded their experience.

The dominance of relationships and service

Many marketers argue that services are now more important than goods, with services marketing forming 'a new dominant logic for marketing, one in which service provision rather than goods is fundamental to economic exchange'. Vargo and Lusch have popularized this notion in recent years, suggesting that marketing has moved from a goods-dominant view, in which tangible output and discrete transactions were central, to a service-dominant view, in which intangibility, exchange processes, and relationships are central to marketing, as well as an understanding of what customers value.[28] Certainly the growth of interest in maintaining ongoing relationships (see Chapter 1) with customers and building the augmented product (see Chapter 10) in order to satisfy customers support this contention. Many tangible goods are marketed together with associated services in order to provide targeted customers with added value, peace of mind, support in using the purchased product and to create differentiation vis-à-vis competitors. Department store John Lewis sells goods, but its positioning promotes its customer service, returns policy, technical support and after-sales provision. Customers value this support and peace of mind when they buy new shoes, a carpet, baby's highchair or a flatscreen TV from John Lewis.

Non-profit marketing

Marketing was broadly defined earlier as a set of individual and organizational activities aimed at facilitating and expediting satisfying exchanges in a dynamic environment through the creation, distribution, promotion and pricing of goods, services and ideas. Most of the concepts and approaches to managing marketing activities discussed above also apply to non-profit situations, such as the public sector and charities. This is largely why **social marketing** has emerged as a sub-set of the marketing discipline. Of special relevance is the material offered in the first half of this chapter, because many non-profit organizations and public bodies provide services. As a discipline, marketing is becoming increasingly important in the non-profit sector. Particularly in the context of government interventions to change people's usage and attitudes towards eating more healthily, exercising, quitting smoking, saving energy, responsibly managing personal debt, avoiding reckless gambling and viewing other ethnic groups more favourably. All of these interventions by government bodies or agencies active in each of these fields requires an appreciation of the 'consumer', identification of which 'consumers' will be receptive to change intervention, the creation of appropriate messaging, and engagement with the selected targets. Although there is no product being sold and no price charged as is the case in commercial marketing situations, this process hinges on the marketing process explained throughout this book. Social marketing uses tools and techniques from commercial marketing to encourage positive behavioural changes, such as quitting smoking, reducing alcohol consumption, minimizing anti-social behaviours, reducing carbon footprint, and to raise awareness of important social issues. The health and well-being of individuals, society and the planet are at the core of social marketing. This is an area of significant growth, employing many who apply the tools of marketing but to create interventions rather than profit from selling goods.

Social marketing
Social marketing uses tools and techniques from commercial marketing to make interventions and encourage positive behavioural changes, such as quitting smoking, reducing alcohol consumption, minimizing anti-social behaviours or reducing carbon footprint. The health and wellbeing of individuals, society and the planet are at the core of social marketing.

Non-profit marketing includes marketing activities conducted by individuals and organizations to achieve some goal other than the ordinary business goals of profit, market share or return on investment. Charities, the voluntary sector, not-for-profit organizations and NGOs form the third sector and government departments utilize the marketing concept and toolkit.[29] Although a non-profit organization has primary goals that are non-economic, it may be required to become involved in 'profit making' in order to achieve those goals.[30] Thus a charity, such as Oxfam, must raise funds to support its charitable work. Non-profit marketing can be divided into two categories: non-profit organization marketing and social marketing. Non-profit organization marketing is the application of marketing concepts and techniques to organizations such as hospitals and colleges. Social marketing is the development of programmes designed to influence the acceptability of social ideas, such

Non-profit marketing
Activities conducted by individuals and organizations to achieve some goal other than the ordinary business goals of profit, market share or return on investment.

as getting people to recycle more newspapers, plastics and aluminum, quit smoking, or promoting the regeneration of a deprived inner-city area.[31] **Cause-related marketing** is the linking of an organization's products to a particular social cause on an ongoing or short term basis, The Body Shop-style, or when certain brands link-up with telethons such as Comic Relief.

As discussed in Chapter 1, an exchange situation exists when individuals, groups or organizations possess something that they are willing to give up in an exchange. In non-profit marketing, the objects of the exchange may not be specified in financial terms. Usually, such exchanges are facilitated through **negotiation** – mutual discussion or communication of terms and methods – and **persuasion** – convincing and prevailing upon by argument. Often, negotiation and persuasion are conducted without reference to, or awareness of, marketing's role in transactions. The discussion here concerns the non-profit performance of marketing activities, whether exchange takes place or not.

The rest of this chapter first examines the concept of non-profit marketing to determine how it differs from marketing activities in commercial organizations. Next it explores the overall objectives of non-profit organizations, their marketing objectives and the development of their marketing strategies. The discussion closes by illustrating how a marketing audit can control marketing activities and promote marketing awareness in a non-profit organization.

Why is non-profit marketing different?

Traditionally and mistakenly, people have not thought of non-profit exchange activities as marketing, but consider the following example. Warwick Business School provides educational services. It used to promote its degree courses solely through the University of Warwick's prospectuses. In the early 1980s, its main programmes received small advertising budgets. As courses were improved and cohorts grew, the wider use of advertising increased awareness of the school and its programmes. The school is not commercially driven in the context of seeking profits for stakeholders or shareholders: any income from fees, training and consultancy is reinvested into its degree programmes, research and teaching facilities. A new corporate identity was developed by Coley Porter Bell of London, and each degree programme, led by the MBA, developed its own full marketing mix and more extensive promotional strategy, all in line with the school's new mission statement. Even when the corporate identity was updated, the school continued to ensure a good fit between the marketing mixes for its different programmes and its overall strategy. As the school moved into the twenty-first century, it became a budget holder within the university and managed its own budgets. This move facilitated the appointment of a marketing director, public relations manager and external affairs manager. These personnel developed target market strategies, updated the school's marketing programmes, and monitored the performance of these marketing activities, just as marketers in a for-profit company would do. Many university departments and state-maintained schools are now engaging in developing a marketing strategy and associated marketing programmes.

Many non-profit organizations strive for effective marketing activities. Charitable organizations and supporters of social causes are major non-profit marketers. Political parties, unions, religious groups and student organizations also perform marketing activities, yet they are not considered businesses. Whereas the chief beneficiary of a business enterprise is whoever owns or holds shares in it, the main beneficiaries of a non-profit organization are its clients, its members or the public at large.

Non-profit organizations have a greater opportunity for creativity than most business organizations, but trustees or board members of these organizations may find it harder to evaluate the performance of doctors, lecturers or social workers than it is for sales managers to evaluate the performance of salespeople or financial returns in a for-profit organization.

Another way in which non-profit marketing differs from for-profit marketing is that non-profit organizations are sometimes quite controversial. Amnesty International, Oxfam and Greenpeace spend lavishly on lobbying efforts to persuade government and even the courts to support their interests, in part because acceptance of their aims is not always guaranteed. Although marketing aims to provide a body of knowledge to further an organization's goals, it does not attempt to judge their appropriateness. It is for individuals to decide whether they approve of an organization's goal orientation. Most marketers would agree that profit and consumer satisfaction are appropriate goals for business enterprises, but there may be considerable disagreement about the goals of a non-profit organization, particularly a more controversial one.

Non-profit marketing objectives

The basic aim of non-profit organizations is to obtain a desired response from a target market. The use of marketing principles is directly pertinent to third sector non-profit organizations, as they seek to target and convey their messages. The response could be a change in values, a financial contribution, the donation of services or some other type of exchange. Non-profit marketing objectives are shaped by the nature of the exchange and the goals of the organization. BBC-sponsored Children in Need and Comic Relief telethons have raised millions of pounds. Telethons have three specific marketing objectives:

1. to raise funds to support programmes
2. to plead a case on behalf of disadvantaged groups
3. to inform the public about the organization's programmes and services.

Tactically, telethons have received support by choosing good causes; generating extensive grass-roots support; portraying disadvantaged people in a positive and dignified way; developing national, regional and local support; and providing quality entertainment.[32] Figure 13.4 illustrates how the exchanges and the purpose of the organization can influence marketing objectives. These objectives are used as examples and may or may not apply to specific organizations.

Non-profit marketing objectives should state the rationale for an organization's existence. An organization that defines its marketing objective merely in terms of providing a product can be

FIGURE 13.4

Examples of marketing objectives for different types of exchange

Source: Adapted from Philip D. Cooper and George E. McIlvain, 'Factors influencing marketing's ability to assist non-profit organizations', John H. Summey and Ronald D. Taylor, eds, 'Evolving Marketing Thought for 1980', *Proceedings of the Southern Marketing Association* (19–22 November 1980), p. 315. Used by permission.

Police's marketing objective: To serve the public by enforcing laws and to gain public support and cooperation

Police → Protection and security → Citizen

Citizen → Taxes, cooperation and support → Police

Church's marketing objective: To inform the public about the church's doctrine and convince people to become members

Church → Religious values and services → Member

Member → Contributions, service and acceptance of values → Church

Charity's marketing objective: To serve the needs and wants of clients and the donor public

Charity → Satisfaction from solving social problems or promoting a cause → Donor

Donor → Financial contributions, time and support → Charity

left without a purpose if the product becomes obsolete. However, serving and adapting to the perceived needs and wants of a target public or market, enhances an organization's chances of surviving and achieving its goals.

Developing non-profit marketing strategies

Non-profit organizations must also develop marketing strategies, by defining and analyzing a target market, and creating and maintaining a marketing mix that appeals to that market. They practice the techniques promoted by marketing, as described in this chapter's concluding case study, and apply many of the concepts routinely deployed by commercial marketers in for-profit businesses.

Target markets The concept of target markets needs to be revised slightly to apply to non-profit organizations. Whereas a business is supposed to have target groups that are potential purchasers of its product, a non-profit organization may attempt to serve many diverse groups.

Target public
A collective of individuals who have an interest in or concern about an organization, a product or a social cause.

A **target public** is broadly defined as a collective of individuals who have an interest in or concern about an organization, a product or a social cause. The terms target market and target public are difficult to distinguish for many non-profit organizations. The target public for campaigns promoting healthy eating is adults and teenagers of all ages. However, the target market for many of the advertisements may be individuals currently suffering from a weight problem. When an organization is concerned about changing values or obtaining a response from the public, it views the public as a market.[33]

Client publics
In non-profit organizations, direct consumers of a product.

In non-profit organizations, direct consumers of a product are called **client publics** and indirect consumers are called **general publics**.[34] For example, the client public for a university is its student body, and its general public includes parents, graduates, employers and the university senate. The client public usually receives most of the attention when an organization develops a marketing strategy. The techniques and approaches to segmenting and defining target markets discussed in Chapters 7 and 8 very much apply to non-profit target markets.

General publics
In non-profit organizations, indirect consumers of a product.

Developing a marketing mix A marketing mix strategy limits choices and directs marketing activities towards achieving organizational goals. The strategy should outline or develop a blueprint for making decisions about product, place/channel, promotion/communication, price and personnel. These decision variables should be blended to serve the target market as specified in the marketing strategy.

When considering the product variable, it is important to recognize that non-profit organizations deal more often with ideas and services than with goods. This means it is crucial for organizations to have clearly defined exactly what they are providing. For example, what products do the Women's Institute or a work's social club provide? They offer a forum for social gatherings, courses, outings and a sense of cooperation. Their products are more difficult to define than the average business product. As indicated in the first part of this chapter, the intangibility of services means that the marketing of ideas and concepts is more abstract than the marketing of tangibles, and it requires considerable effort to present benefits.

Considering most non-profit products are ideas and services, distribution decisions relate to how these ideas and services will be made available to clients and stakeholders. If the product is an idea, selecting the right media (the promotional strategy) to communicate the idea will facilitate distribution. The availability of services is closely related to product decisions. By nature, services consist of assistance, convenience and availability. Availability is part of the total service. For example, making a product such as health services or personal debt management available on the high street calls for knowledge of such retailing concepts as site location analysis, queuing and operations management.

Developing a channel of distribution to coordinate and facilitate the flow of non-profit products to clients is a necessary task, but in a non-profit setting the traditional concept of the marketing channel may need to be reviewed. The independent wholesalers available to a business enterprise do not exist in most non-profit situations. Instead, a very short channel – non-profit organization to client – is prevalent, because production and consumption of ideas and services are often simultaneous. For example, local government departments often deal directly with householders. Charities generally pitch their fundraising activities directly to their target customers/householders/donors.

Making promotional decisions may be the first sign that non-profit organizations are performing marketing activities. Non-profit organizations use advertising, publicity and the web to communicate with clients and the public. As the Case study at the end of this chapter explains, direct mail remains a means of fundraising for services such as those provided by Christian Aid and UNICEF. In addition to direct mail, organizations such as these use press advertising, public relations and sponsorship, supported by increasingly sophisticated websites and social media campaigns. Face-to-face selling is also used by non-profit organizations, although it may be called something else. Churches and charities rely on personal selling when they send volunteers to recruit new members or request donations. The armed forces use personal selling when recruiting officers and when attempting to persuade men and women to enlist. Special events to obtain funds, communicate ideas or provide services are sales promotion activities. Competitions, entertainment and prizes offered to attract donations resemble the sales promotion activities of business enterprises. Amnesty International, for example, has held worldwide concert tours, featuring artists such as Sting and Phil Collins, to raise funds and increase public awareness of political prisoners around the world.

The number of advertising agencies that are donating their time for public service announcements (PSAs) or public information films is increasing, and the quality of print PSAs is improving. Not-for-profit groups are becoming more interested in the impact of advertising on their organizations, and they realize that second-rate PSAs can cause a credibility loss.[35] For example, each year the UK government's 'Don't drink and drive' campaign, usually timed to coincide with the Christmas and New Year period, is a high-spending and hard-hitting programme of well-produced advertisements designed to attract as much attention as possible.

Although product and promotion techniques may require only slight modification when applied to non-profit organizations, the pricing structure is generally quite different and the decision-making more complex. The different pricing concepts that the non-profit organization faces include pricing in user and donor markets. There are two types of monetary pricing: fixed and variable. Membership fees, such as the amount paid to become a member of a social club, or monthly fixed sum direct debit contributions to a charity, represent a fixed approach to pricing, whereas fundraising activities that lead to donations that help with the society's running costs represent a variable pricing structure.[36]

The broadest definition of price (valuation) must be used when considering non-profit products or services. Financial price, an exact monetary value, may or may not be charged for a non-profit product. Economists recognize the giving up of alternatives as a cost. **Opportunity cost** is the value of the benefit that is given up by selecting one alternative rather than another. This traditional economic view of price means that if a non-profit organization can persuade someone to donate time to a cause, or to change his or her behaviour, the alternatives given up are a cost to or a price paid by the individual. Volunteers who answer phones for a university counselling service or suicide hotline give up the time they could have spent studying or doing other things, as well as the income they might have earned from working part-time in a bar or shop.

Opportunity cost
The value of the benefit that is given up by selecting one alternative instead of another.

For other non-profit organizations, financial price is an important part of the marketing mix. Non-profit organizations today are raising money by increasing the prices of their services or starting to charge for services if they have not done so before. For example, many museums and art galleries, which traditionally allowed free entry to their exhibits, are now charging nominal entrance fees. Organizations like these often use marketing research to determine for what kinds of product people will pay.[37] The pricing strategies of non-profit organizations often stress public and client welfare over equalization of costs and revenues. If additional funds are needed to cover costs, then donations, contributions or grants may be solicited.

The additional elements of the marketing mix for services are also important in non-profit marketing. The physical environment quite often poses problems: subscribers and donors want an organization with the appearance of business-like efficiency without any extravagance or high costs of operation. It is important that funds do not appear to have been wasted on luxuries. The process for transactions is increasingly important: regular donors are offered direct debits, automatic payment methods and regular information packs or leaflets detailing the recipient organization's activities, expenditures and plans. People, too, are important: capable administrators, sympathetic helpers, trustworthy fundraisers; they must project a caring yet efficient image to the client and general publics and promote the desired brand positioning for the charity or cause.

Controlling non-profit marketing activities

To control marketing activities in non-profit organizations, managers use information obtained in the marketing audit to make sure that goals are achieved. Table 13.6 lists several summary statistics that are useful for both planning and control. Control is designed to check that the activities outlined in the marketing strategy have taken place and to take corrective action where any deviations are found. The purpose of control is not only to point out errors but to revise organizational goals and marketing objectives as necessary. One way to measure the impact of an advertisement is to audit the number of requests for information or applications, such as those received by Amnesty International, the Army or the World Wildlife Fund (WWF). Hits on an organization's website via leading search engines are also counted (see Figure 13.5). Costs must be tightly controlled, the returns on activities understood, and often public statements of these have to be made available in order to comply with the regulatory environment.

TABLE 13.6   Examples of data useful in controlling non-business marketing requirements

Financial resources:	Size and usage:
• Types of funding	• Cash flows
• EU	• Budgets
• Government grants/loans	• Numbers of staff
• Local government grants/loans	• Seconded personnel
• Foundations and charities	• Volunteer personnel
• National Lottery funding awards	• Paid and non-paid staff
• Public appeals	• Numbers of users
• Philanthropic donations	• Types of users
• Corporate partnerships	• Dependency of users
• Sponsorships	• Frequency of use
• Fees and charges	• Sole and multi-provider usage mix
• Number/proportion using each	
• Number combining several sources	
Product/service mix:	**Facilities:**
• Nature of products or services	• Number of facilities/locations
• Number of providers	• Nature of facilities
• Strategic partners and suppliers	• Location(s) of facilities
• Channel characteristics	• Investment pattern in facilities
	• Investment priorities for facilities
	• Sponsoring partnerships

Source: Adapted from Philip D. Cooper and George E. McIlvain, 'Factors influencing marketing's ability to assist non-profit organizations', John H. Summey and Ronald D. Taylor, eds, 'Evolving Marketing Thought for 1980', *Proceedings of the Southern Marketing Association* (19–22 November 1980), p. 315. Used by permission.

FIGURE 13.5

Many non-business organizations judge the effectiveness of their marketing in terms of hits on their websites and requests for information

Source: Screenshot courtesy of NSPCC

Many potential contributors decide which charities to support based on the amount of money actually used for charitable purposes. Charities are more aggressively examining their own performance and effectiveness. For example, the Salvation Army contributes the majority of every pound (£) it receives to the needy; its employees are largely volunteers, who work for almost nothing. Charities are making internal changes to increase their effectiveness, and many are hiring professional managers and fundraisers to help with strategic planning in developing short-term and long-range goals, marketing strategies and promotional plans.

To control non-profit marketing activities, managers must make a proper inventory of activities performed, and be prepared to adjust or correct deviations from standards. Knowing where and how to look for deviations and knowing what types of deviation to expect are especially important in non-profit situations. As non-profit marketing activities may not be perceived as marketing, managers must define clearly what activity is being examined and how it should function.

It may be difficult to control non-profit marketing activities, because it is often hard to determine whether goals are being achieved. A support group for victims of childhood abuse that wants to inform community members of its services may not be able to find out whether it is communicating with those people who need assistance. Surveying to discover the percentage of the population that is aware of the assistance the group offers can show whether the awareness objective has been achieved, but it fails to indicate what percentage of victims of abuse has been assisted. The detection and correction of deviations from standards are certainly major purposes of control, but standards must support the organization's overall goals. Managers can refine goals by examining the results that are being achieved and analyzing the ramifications of those results.

Techniques for controlling overall marketing performance must be compatible with the nature of an organization's operations. Obviously, it is necessary to control the marketing budget in most non-profit organizations, but budgetary control is not tied to standards of profit and loss; responsible management of funds is the objective. Central control responsibility can facilitate orderly, efficient administration and planning. For example, most universities evaluate graduating students' progress to control and improve the quality of education provided. The audit phase typically relies on questionnaires sent to students and eventual employers. The employer completes a questionnaire to indicate the former student's progress; the graduate completes a questionnaire to indicate what additional concepts or skills were needed to perform duties. In addition, a number of faculty members may interview certain employers and former students to obtain information for control purposes. Results of the audit are used to develop corrective action if university standards have not been met. Corrective action could include an evaluation of the deficiency and a revision of the curriculum.

Summary

Services are experiential, intangible, dominant products that cannot physically be possessed, the result of applying human or mechanical efforts to people or objects. The importance of services in the economy is increasing. There are *consumer services* and *business services*.

Services have a number of distinguishing characteristics: *intangibility*, *inseparability* of production and consumption, *perishability*, *heterogeneity*, *client-based relationships* and *customer contact*. Intangibility places greater importance on *search, experience* and *credence qualities*. Services can be viewed in terms of a *five-category classification*: type of market, degree of labour intensiveness, degree of customer contact, skill of the service provider and goal of the service provider.

Fluctuating demand is a major problem for most service organizations. Marketing strategies and the marketing mix can be used to deal with the problem. Before attempting to undertake any such strategies, however, services marketers must understand the patterns and determinants of demand. The intangibility of the service product, together with the importance of the people component of the extended marketing mix for services, leads to significant difficulties in creating and sustaining a *differential advantage*.

The basic marketing mix is augmented for services through the addition of people, physical evidence (ambience) and the process of transaction in order to produce the '7Ps' or the *extended marketing mix for services*.

Service quality is the perception of how well a service meets or exceeds customers' *service expectations*. The intangibility of services makes service quality very difficult for customers to evaluate. When competing services are very similar, service quality may be the only way for customers to distinguish between them. It is crucial for marketers to comprehend the four *service quality factors*: (1) understanding customer expectations, (2) service quality specifications, (3) employee performance, and (4) managing service expectations. To achieve customer satisfaction, a service must fall within the *customer's zone of tolerance*.

Non-profit marketing includes marketing activities conducted by individuals and organizations to achieve goals other than normal business goals. The chief beneficiary of a business enterprise is whoever owns or holds shares in the business, but the beneficiary of a non-profit enterprise should be its clients, its members or its public at large. The goals of a non-profit organization reflect its unique philosophy or mission. Some non-profit organizations have very controversial goals, but many organizations exist to further generally accepted social causes. Government and agency interventions to improve society and well-being use *social marketing*, which has been a significant growth area in recent years.

The marketing objective of non-profit organizations is to obtain a desired response from a target market, often through *negotiation* or *persuasion*. Developing a non-profit marketing strategy consists of defining and analyzing a target market, and creating and maintaining a marketing mix. *Target, client* and *general publics* must all be identified. In non-profit marketing, the product is usually an idea or service.

Distribution is involved not so much with the movement of goods as with the communication of ideas and the delivery of services, which results in a very short marketing channel. Promotion is very important in non-profit marketing; personal selling, sales promotion, advertising and publicity are all used to communicate ideas and inform people about services. Digital marketing and social media campaigns are particularly important. Price is more difficult to define in non-profit marketing because of *opportunity costs* and the difficulty of quantifying the values exchanged.

It is important to control marketing strategies in non-profit situations. Control is designed to identify what activities have occurred in conformity with marketing strategy and to take corrective action where deviations are found. The standards against which performance is measured must support the non-profit organization's overall goals.

Important terms

Business services
Cause-related marketing
Client publics
Client-based relationships
Consumer services
Credence qualities
Customer contact
Customer's zone of tolerance
Differential advantage
Experience qualities
Extended marketing mix for services
Five-category classification
General publics
Heterogeneity
Inseparability
Intangibility
Negotiation
Non-profit marketing
Opportunity cost
Perishability
Persuasion
Search qualities
Service
Service expectations
Service quality
Service quality factors
Social marketing
Target public

Discussion and review questions

1. Identify and discuss the distinguishing characteristics of services. What problems do these characteristics present to marketers?

2. What is the significance of 'tangibles' in service industries?

3. Use the five-category classification scheme (page 382) to analyze a car valeting service, and discuss the implications for marketing mix development.

4. How do search, experience and credence qualities affect the way consumers view and evaluate services?

5. What additional elements must be included in the marketing mix for services? Why?

6. Why is it difficult to create and maintain a differential advantage in many service organizations?

7. Analyze the demand for the hire of sunbeds and discuss ways to cope with fluctuating demand.

8. What is the most important dimension in determining customer evaluation of service quality?

9. Compare and contrast the controversial aspects of non-profit versus business marketing.

10. Relate the concepts of product, place/distribution, promotion and price to a marketing strategy aimed at preventing drug abuse.

11. What are the differences between clients, publics and consumers? What is the difference between a target public and a target market?

12. Provide examples of social marketing interventions and consider who the target audiences are.

13. Discuss the development of a marketing strategy for a university. What marketing decisions should be made in developing this strategy?

14. Why is the concept of market segmentation relevant in the marketing of social causes?

Recommended readings

Berry, L., *On Great Service* (The Free Press, 1995).
Grönroos, C., *Service Management and Marketing* (Wiley, 2007).
Kasper, H., van Helsdingen, P. and Gabbott, M., *Services Marketing Management: A Strategic Perspective* (John Wiley, 2006).
Lovelock, C.H. and Wirtz, J., *Services Marketing* (Pearson, 2011).
Lusch, R. and Vargo, S., *Services Dominant Logic: Premises, Perspectives, Possibilities* (Cambridge University Press, 2014).
Palmer, A., *Principles of Services Marketing* (McGraw-Hill, 2014).
Zeithaml, V., Bitner, M. and Gremler, D., *Services Marketing: Integrating Customer Focus Across The Firm* (McGraw-Hill, 2012).

Internet exercise

As web usage rises, the number of people using this method to identify services and compare prices has rocketed, with numerous comparison websites providing a price and feature comparison service across many suppliers, seeking to fulfil the 'honest broker' role. This is particularly so for assisting consumers searching for the best deal for insurance policies. Take a look at: www.comparethemarket.com /insurance and its range of information across car, home, van, travel, pet and life insurance.

1. Classify comparethemarket.com's offering in terms of its position on the service continuum.

2. How does comparethemarket.com enhance customer service and foster its relationship with customers?

3. Discuss the degree to which experience and credence qualities exist in the services offered by comparethemarket.com.

Group tasks

1. Consider the services provided by the Students' Union facility on your campus. What are the principal difficulties involved with marketing and then delivering these services?

2. Select a service which members of your group consider to be 'good'. Unpick the reasons why your team perceives the selected service to be good. Consider how the marketers for this service have ensured you perceive it to be good.

Applied mini-case

Express carriers such as TNT, UPS and Federal Express do much more than provide a swift delivery service for letters and packages. As the sector has become more competitive and eShopping increases the numbers of packages delivered each day, the expectations of clients have also risen. The home delivery service for many well-known brands is subcontracted to the major carriers, which in effect impact through their reliability and service levels on their clients' brand reputation and customer satisfaction. Inventory handling, assistance with customs clearance, barcoded tracking that can be monitored over the web, and the provision of a responsive customer services function, are just some of the extra services that are now expected as part of the product offering. Some clients even require their carriers to play a role in the packing process in their pursuit of a delivery solution that eases the movement of packages from the point of dispatch to the point of receipt.

Question

Assume the role of a management consultant who has been retained by one of the express carriers to undertake an analysis of service quality. Prepare a report that outlines the key dimensions of service quality.

Case study

Marketing for charities

Marketing is not an activity that consumers automatically associate with charities. Instead they link advertising, sales promotion and digital marketing with big brands such as Coca-Cola, McDonald's, John Lewis and Virgin. In reality, while commercial organizations such as these seek high returns and profits, charities must find ways to boost awareness of their work and increase their revenues to fund their good causes. In recent years, the fundraising activities of charities have become characterized by an increasing professionalism, often involving the appointment of marketing managers, strategists, public relations executives and digital experts. This has resulted in a greater variety of fundraising methods than ever before, including the use of viral campaigns, creative affinity tie-ups, e-marketing and internet-based approaches.

Research shows that nearly 90 per cent of UK adults have participated in charitable activities in the past 12 months.

Most are involved in giving money, but a third of these have taken part in a special charity activity or event. Others have been involved in organizing events or have worked for a charity. Face-to-face fundraising remains the most popular way to give, with 67 per cent of all those donating using this approach. However, there has been a trend away from traditional tin-rattling and towards the use of 'chugging' or face-to-face recruitment, designed to encourage would-be donors to agree to regular direct debit or covenant arrangements. More than ever, charities are recognizing that fundraising activities should be targeted particularly at those in the population who are prepared to become committed donors. In some cases this means attracting a new generation of people prepared to donate regularly. A NOP survey suggested that just 15 per cent of fundraising revenue is accrued from long-term donors, with human rights charities the biggest winners, and good causes supporting the young or elderly gaining least from this means.

Even though many consumers dislike the use of direct marketing methods such as direct mail and telephone calls to solicit funds, the second most important channel for donations is by post. This approach has proved particularly popular with human rights and wildlife causes. However, relatively few supporters of children's charities and those supporting the elderly choose this method. Indeed, it seems that traditional personal approaches to collecting funds, such as the use of collecting tins in shopping malls and high streets, are declining in effectiveness. Instead, the public's imagination has been captured by a host of media-based activities. For example, specially organized events, and television appeals and programmes have been shown to be particularly effective ways of attracting funds. The use of high-profile individuals in such appeals, such as royalty, television personalities, and well-known actors or sports stars, is particularly popular. In a survey, 80 per cent of consumers questioned also supported the use of commercial and promotional schemes, such as the sale of products through gift shops and catalogues. A similar percentage stated that they like to buy products that involve the manufacturer making a contribution to charity.

Evidence of increasing professionalism in fundraising is readily apparent across the charity sector. Cancer Research overhauled its marketing strategy to focus afresh on fundraising. This followed a period when the charity concentrated on brand building, following its creation out of the merger of Imperial Cancer Research and the Cancer Research Campaign. Social marketing techniques have been embraced by most leading charities, while web-based communications have now enabled many to target and reach their audiences more effectively

than in the past. Many charities are utilizing the web to good effect. Dog's Trust focuses on dog welfare and has used its social media networks to convey messages about re-homing, neutering and microchipping. Mainstream TV commercials also regularly appear, but the social media messages arguably are harder hitting and more outspoken than the TV broadcasters or viewing public will tolerate. A recent debate on Facebook was deliberately timed to coincide with a lobbying campaign aimed at MPs regarding microchipping of pets. Bullying UK, the anti-bullying charity, used social media to foster word-of-mouth communication of its core messages. The charity's posters have a mobile download version which can then be shared easily by readers amongst their social media contacts. Children's charity Barnardo's is using the web as a means of recruiting and communicating with its younger donors. In the age of television, the internet and the smartphone, it seems that charities such as these must be ready, willing and able to use the full range of media-based approaches available as they enact their social marketing strategies.

Questions for discussion

1. Why are charities such as Barnardo's and Cancer Research UK turning more to the marketing approaches deployed by consumer goods companies?

2. To what kinds of donor must charities appeal? How might collection methods vary for these different groups?

3. How might the marketing strategy vary according to whether a charity is targeting consumers or corporate donors?

Sources: www.bullying.co.uk, March 2011 and April 2015; www.barnardos.org.uk, March 2011 and April 2015; www.wspa.org.uk; Ross McCulloch of Third Sector Lab, 'How four charities got the social marketing mix right', www.mycustomer.com, March 2011; www.dogstrust.org.uk/, March 2011 and April 2015.

CHAPTER 14

Marketing channels

"Channel selection and multi-channel management drive products to market"

Objectives

- To understand the marketing channel concept and the nature of marketing channels.

- To discuss the functions of marketing channels.

- To examine different types of channel.

- To examine channel integration and levels of market coverage.

- To consider the selection of distribution channels and the emergence of direct marketing.

- To understand the impact of multi-channel management on marketing.

- To explore the behavioural aspects of channels, especially the concepts of cooperation, relationship building, conflict and leadership.

- To examine legal issues in channel management.

INTRODUCTION

Distribution involves activities that make products available to customers when and where they want to purchase them. It is sometimes referred to as the 'place' element in the marketing mix of the 5Ps: product, place (distribution), promotion, price and people. Choosing which channels of distribution to use is a major decision in the development of marketing strategies, particularly with the advances in digital options. High customer service levels may require heavy investment in distribution and the shrewd identification of channel members with which to work. There has to be a compromise between adequate responsiveness to customers' needs and expectations and delivering to their requirements in a cost-effective manner.

This chapter focuses on the description and analysis of marketing channels, first discussing the nature of channels and their functions, and then explaining the main types of channel and their structures. These sections are followed by a review of several forms of channel integration. Consideration is given to how marketers determine the appropriate intensity of market coverage for a product and to the factors that are considered when selecting suitable channels of distribution. The chapter explores how increasingly many organizations operate through multiple channels, requiring the management of customer experience across channels. After examining behavioural patterns within marketing channels, and the relationships that develop between channel members, the chapter concludes by looking at several legal issues affecting channel management.

BA's focus on eCommerce

ot too many years ago, the bulk of BA flights were booked either via travel agents or over the telephone by passengers. In late 2003, BA made a radical decision. Its 24-hour telephone booking service ceased: night-time tele-booking or changes to travel itineraries became a thing of the past, too. Although partly driven by a cost-saving strategy, the reduction in call centres also reflected the growth in the airline's e-booking service. 'If you choose to complete your booking by phone, you will incur a £15 offline service fee per passenger', greeted customers dialling 0870 8507850 intending to book seats by phone, as BA steered customers towards its web-based operation. While passengers wishing to book at night could no longer speak over the telephone to a BA customer service agent, they could go online 24 hours a day in order to make or change a booking. Since then, BA has nudged its customers towards the web and also harnessed mobile marketing in a big way.

BA introduced e-tickets, rather than sending out traditional books of travel coupon tickets, and passengers could print off their own documentation. Soon, even such behaviour was passé, as a simple booking reference sufficed and paperless travel had arrived. Passengers either inserted their credit card into a ticket dispenser at the airport or told a customer service agent their allocated booking reference code in order for the agent to allocate a seat and boarding pass. No paper was necessary. Now, most travellers simply scan a passport or insert a credit card into self-serve kiosks in order to self-check in, or print-off boarding passes at home before leaving for the airport. Even access to a boarding card has changed, as increasing numbers of passengers simply download a booking barcode onto their smartphones to be scanned at airport security for totally paperless transactions and boarding.

Prior to the opening of Heathrow's Terminal 5, BA's new hub, marketing researchers probed consumers' buy-in to e-tickets and self-check-in. The result was the opening of a very different passenger experience, with numerous self-check kiosks, bag drop-off points and few queues at old-style check-in counters.

The BA website reflects this shift in emphasis, suggesting special offers, linking to customer support and providing web users with corporate information, but focusing on:

- *Flights and Holidays*
- *Manage My Booking*
- *Information*
- *Executive Club*
- *Company Travel.*

The primary focus on the home page, though, is on a *Find Flights* menu-driven system providing speedy access to BA's network and timetable. *Find Flights* enables users to check for routes, suitable times, prices and seat availability in seconds, or to place a confirmed booking in under a minute. The company launched a set of related mobile services, with timetables, booking, check-in and now boarding enabled digitally and remotely. The airline has fully embraced eCommerce and mobile as a channel to market.

Sources: www.BA.com, May 2004; BA, BAA, January 2008; www.ba.com, January 2008; www.britishairways.com, June 2011 and March 2015.

As in the example of BA's move to focus on eCommerce and mobile, changes in the manner in which products are distributed have a major impact on customers. For example, moves by food retailers to sell petrol from sites adjacent to their supermarkets affected the UK petrol market in a number of important ways. Reducing petrol prices and increasing promotional activity damaged margins to a point where profitability was severely threatened and many independent garages ceased trading. Declining numbers of smaller forecourts in fact limited consumer choice. The web and mobile marketing have radically altered distribution channels in many markets. In some markets, such as music sales and banking transactions, there has been a huge shift to online transactions away from music stores and bank branches. Such direct marketing and digital transactions negate the need for high-street shops and bank branches, and changes the nature of the proposition being marketed.

All products and services pass through a distribution channel or supply chain. The selection of the type most applicable to a particular target market is an important choice for marketers. This chapter focuses on the nature of marketing channels and their functions, types of channel and their structures. The factors relevant in selecting a channel of distribution are discussed, along with the nature of relationships within the marketing channel.

The nature of marketing channels and supply chain management

Channel of distribution (or marketing channel)
A group of individuals and organizations that direct the flow of products from producers to customers.

A **channel of distribution** (sometimes called a **marketing channel**) is a group of individuals and organizations that direct the flow of products from producers to customers. Providing customer satisfaction should be the driving force behind all marketing channel activities. Buyers' needs and behaviour are important concerns of channel members. Channels of distribution make products available at the right time, in the right place and in the right quantity by providing such product-enhancing functions as transport, storage and customer service.[1]

The basic premise is simple. A manufacturer of a particular product could sell directly to the intended ultimate consumers, or the manufacturer could utilize the services of wholesalers, retailers or other channel members, rather than bear the hassle and costs of dealing with many end-user consumers directly. Alternatively, the manufacturer could opt to use a mix of routes to convey its products to the ultimate consumers: some direct selling, links with wholesalers and retailers, and possibly alliances with the selling activities of other manufacturers. Multiple channels require management and are costly to operate, but expose a brand or product to more potential customers. There has to be a balance between optimizing customer satisfaction and making an adequate return on investment. These are the challenges of channel management for marketers. Challenges which are significantly complicated with the onset of digital channels and often a new set of online competitors given access to markets previously ignored or unattainable to them.

Marketing intermediary
A middleman who links producers to other middlemen or to those who ultimately use the products.

Most, but not all, channels of distribution have marketing intermediaries, although there is currently a growth in direct marketing with some suppliers interacting with consumers without the use of intermediaries. A **marketing intermediary**, or 'middleman', links producers to other middlemen or to those who ultimately use the products. Marketing intermediaries perform the activities described in Table 14.1. There are two major types of intermediary: merchants and functional middlemen – agents and brokers. **Merchants** take title to products and resell them, whereas **functional middlemen** do not take title to products. Both types facilitate the movement of goods and services from producers to consumers.

Merchants
Intermediaries who take title to products and resell them.

Both retailers and wholesalers are intermediaries. Retailers purchase products for the purpose of reselling them to users. Merchant wholesalers resell products to other wholesalers and to retailers. Functional wholesalers, such as agents and brokers, expedite exchanges among producers and resellers, and are compensated by fees or commissions. For purposes of discussion in this chapter, all wholesalers are considered merchant middlemen unless otherwise specified.

Functional middlemen
Intermediaries who do not take title to products.

Channel members share certain significant characteristics. Each member has different responsibilities within the overall structure of the distribution system, but mutual profit and success can be attained only if channel members cooperate in delivering

TABLE 14.1 Marketing channel activities performed by intermediaries

Category of marketing activities	Possible activities required
Marketing information and market insight	Collect and analyze information such as sales data; perform or commission marketing research studies
Marketing management	Establish objectives; plan activities; manage and coordinate financing, personnel and risk taking; evaluate and control channel activities
Facilitating exchange	Choose and stock product assortments that match the needs of buyers
Promotion	Set promotional objectives; coordinate advertising, personal selling, web activity, sales promotion, publicity, sponsorship, direct mail and packaging
Price	Establish pricing policies and terms of sales
Physical distribution	Manage transport, warehousing, materials handling, inventory control and communication
Customer service	Provide channels for advice, technical support, after sales back-up and warranty provision
Relationships	Facilitate communication, products and parts, financial support and credit, inventory levels, after-market needs, on-time delivery and customer service to maintain relationships with other marketing intermediaries and between suppliers and their targeted customers

products to the market. The area of relationship management has received a great deal of attention in marketing circles. This is increasingly important in delivering adequate customer service to target market customers. A supplier desires an ongoing and lucrative relationship with its customers: it recognizes the importance of the various channel members in maintaining this relationship and strives for mutually beneficial relationships with its channel intermediaries.

Although distribution decisions need not precede other marketing decisions, they do exercise a powerful influence on the rest of the marketing mix. Channel decisions are critical because they determine a product's market presence and buyers' accessibility to the product. They also affect customers' overall satisfaction with the product or service provider.[2] At a time when organizations increasingly offer their products through multiple channels, the challenges of maintaining quality of delivery and guaranteeing a customer's experience of a brand across channels irrespective of the channel used, are very much to the fore. The strategic significance of channel decisions is further heightened by the fact that they often entail long-term commitments. For example, it is much easier for a company to change prices or packaging than to change existing distribution systems.

It may be necessary for companies to use different distribution paths in different countries, for different target market segments or for the various products in its portfolio. Some companies, particularly clothing retailers, have stores and a web proposition in their home country but only an online presence overseas. The links in any channel are the merchants – including producers and agents – who oversee the movement of products through that channel. Marketing channels are commonly classified into channels for consumer products/services or channels for business-to-business products/services.

Supply chain management
Long-term partnerships among marketing channel members that reduce inefficiencies, costs and redundancies in the marketing channel and develop innovative approaches to satisfying targeted customers.

Increasingly, an important function of the marketing channel is the joint effort of all channel members to create a supply chain, which is a total distribution system that serves customers and creates a competitive advantage. **Supply chain management** refers to long-term partnerships among marketing channel members that reduce inefficiencies, costs and redundancies in the marketing channel and develop innovative approaches to satisfying targeted customers. The goal is still to provide customers with the product or service demanded, in line with their expectations, but in a more coordinated way that builds on the combined strengths of the members of the distribution channel. Key tasks in supply chain management include planning and coordination of marketing channel partnerships; sourcing necessary resources, goods and services to support the supply chain; facilitating delivery; handling customer service and the after-market; and relationship building in order to nurture ongoing customer relationships.

Functions of marketing channels

Marketing channels serve many functions. Although some of these functions may be performed by a single channel member, most are accomplished through both the independent and joint efforts of channel members. These functions include creating utility, facilitating exchange efficiencies, alleviating discrepancies, standardizing transactions and providing customer service.

Creating utility

Marketing channels create four types of utility: time, place, possession and form:

1. Time utility is having products available when the customer wants them.
2. Place utility is created by making products available in locations where customers wish to purchase them.
3. Possession utility is created by giving the customer access to the product to use or store for future use. Possession utility can occur through ownership or through arrangements such as lease or rental agreements that give the customer the right to use the product.
4. Channel members sometimes create form utility by assembling, preparing or otherwise refining the product to suit individual customer needs.

Facilitating exchange efficiencies

Marketing intermediaries can reduce the costs of exchanges by performing certain services or functions efficiently. Even if producers and buyers are located in the same city, there are costs associated with exchanges. As Figure 14.1 shows, when four buyers seek products from four producers, 16 transactions are possible. If one intermediary serves both producers and buyers, the number of transactions can be reduced to eight. Intermediaries are specialists in facilitating exchanges. They provide valuable assistance because of their access to, and control over, important resources used in the proper functioning of marketing channels.

Nevertheless, the press, consumers, public officials and other marketers freely criticize intermediaries, especially retail wholesalers, dealers and distributors. Critics accuse wholesalers of being inefficient and parasitic. Consumers often wish to make the distribution channel as short as possible, assuming that the fewer the intermediaries, the lower the price. For example, Virgin's financial services operation or Direct Line insurance aim to offer competitive prices by cutting out brokers. Because suggestions to eliminate them come from both ends of the marketing channel, wholesalers must be careful to perform only those marketing activities that are truly desired. To survive, they must be more efficient and more customer-focused than alternatives.

Critics who suggest that eliminating wholesalers would lower consumer prices do not recognize that doing so would not remove the need for services that wholesalers provide. Although wholesalers can be eliminated, in many markets the functions they perform cannot. Other channel members would have to perform those functions, and customers would still have to fund them. In addition, all producers would have to deal directly with retailers or consumers, so that every producer would have to keep voluminous records and hire enough personnel to deal with a multitude of customers. Customers might end up paying a great deal more for products because prices would reflect the costs of less efficient channel members.

Direct customer–supplier marketing is possible in some markets. For instance, telesales-led Direct Line has a successful direct relationship with its insurance-buying customers. JCB, on the other hand, would find it difficult to sell directly and depends on its dealers for parts and maintenance provision to its construction equipment customers. Heinz, Kellogg's, Sony, Ford and BA all utilize channel members, retailers, dealers or travel agents in order to sell

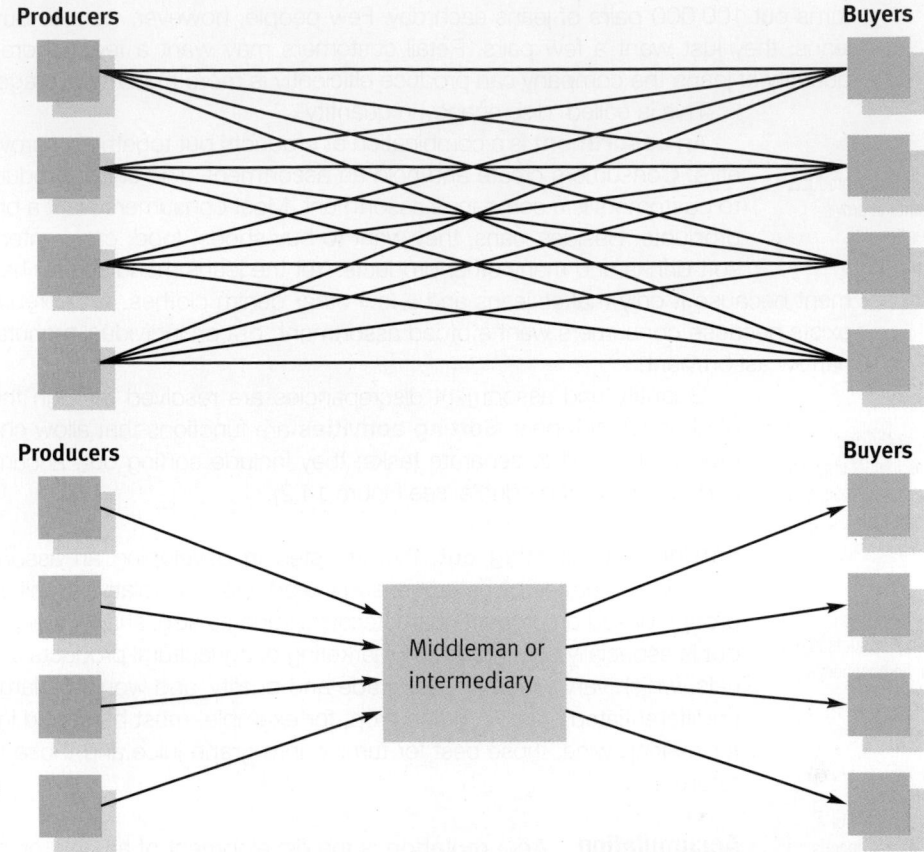

Producers   **Buyers**

Producers   **Buyers**

Middleman or intermediary

FIGURE 14.1
Efficiency in exchanges provided by an intermediary

their products and services. These companies may well use the web and other marketing communications to contact their existing or potential customers, but channel members play an important role in some of their marketing programmes. Some, such as BA, utilize multiple channels. BA sells direct online and also through third party travel agencies and ticketing operators.

To illustrate wholesalers' efficient services, assume that all wholesalers have been eliminated. As there are millions of retailers, a widely purchased consumer product such as toilet paper would require an extraordinary number of sales contacts, possibly more than a million, to maintain the current level of product exposure. For example, Kimberly-Clark would have to deliver its paper products, establish warehouses all over Europe and maintain fleets of trucks. Selling and distribution costs for Kimberly-Clark's products would rocket. Instead of a few contacts with food brokers, large retail businesses and merchant wholesalers, such manufacturers would face thousands of expensive contacts with, and shipments to, smaller retailers. Such an operation would be highly inefficient, and costs would be passed on to consumers. Wholesalers are often more efficient and less expensive.

Alleviating discrepancies

The functions performed within marketing channels help to overcome two major distribution problems: discrepancies in quantity and discrepancies in assortment. With respect to discrepancies in quantity, consider a company that manufactures jeans. The company specializes in the goods it can produce most efficiently: denim clothing. To make jeans most economically, the producer turns out 100 000 pairs of jeans each day. Few people, however, want to buy 100 000 pairs of jeans; they just want a few pairs. Retail customers may want a few hundred pairs. Thus, the quantity of jeans the company can produce efficiently is more than the average customer wants. This is called 'discrepancy in quantity'.

> **Assortment**
> A combination of products put together to provide customer benefits.

An **assortment** is a combination of products put together to provide customer benefits. Consumers create and hold an assortment. The set of products made available to customers is a company's assortment. Most consumers want a broad assortment of products. Besides jeans, they want to buy shoes, food, cars, entertainment systems, soft drinks and many other products. Yet the jeans manufacturer has a narrow assortment because it only makes jeans and a few other denim clothes. A discrepancy in assortment exists because consumers want a broad assortment, but an individual manufacturer produces a narrow assortment.

> **Sorting activities**
> Functions that let channel members divide roles and separate tasks.

Quantity and assortment discrepancies are resolved through the sorting activities of channel members. **Sorting activities** are functions that allow channel members to divide roles and to separate tasks; they include sorting out, accumulation, allocation and assorting of products (see Figure 14.2).[3]

> **Sorting out**
> Separating products into uniform, homogeneous groups.

Sorting out   **Sorting out**, the first step in developing an assortment, is separating conglomerates of heterogeneous products into relatively uniform, homogeneous groups based on product characteristics such as size, shape, weight or colour. Sorting out is especially common in the marketing of agricultural products and other raw materials, which vary widely in size, grade and quality, and would be largely unusable in an undifferentiated mass. A grape crop, for example, must be sorted into grapes suitable for making wine, those best for turning into grape juice and those to be sold by food retailers.

> **Accumulation**
> The development of a bank of homogeneous products with similar production or demand requirements.

Accumulation   **Accumulation** is the development of a bank, or inventory, of homogeneous products with similar production or demand requirements. Farmers who grow relatively small quantities of grapes, for example, transport their sorted grapes to central collection points, where they are accumulated in large lots for movement into the next level of the channel. Accumulation lets producers continually use up stocks and replenish them, thus minimizing losses from interruptions in the supply of materials.

> **Allocation**
> The breaking down of large homogeneous inventories into smaller lots.

Allocation   **Allocation** is the breaking down of large homogeneous inventories into smaller lots. This process, which addresses discrepancies in quantity, enables wholesalers to buy efficiently in lorry loads or railway car loads, and apportion products by cases to other members. A food wholesaler serves as a depot, allocating products according to market demand. The wholesaler may divide a single lorry load of Del Monte canned tomato juice among several retail food stores.

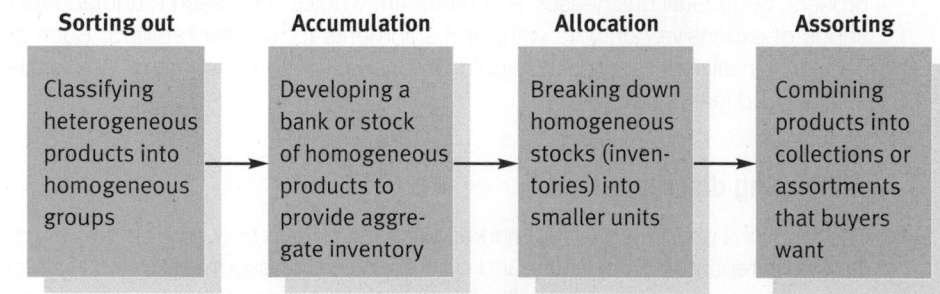

Sorting out	Accumulation	Allocation	Assorting
Classifying heterogeneous products into homogeneous groups	Developing a bank or stock of homogeneous products to provide aggregate inventory	Breaking down homogeneous stocks (inventories) into smaller units	Combining products into collections or assortments that buyers want

FIGURE 14.2
Sorting activities conducted by channel members

Tesco's multi-channel approach to market leadership

Building customer relationships

The internet has changed the way in which consumers shop. In the past, those seeking to replenish their kitchen cupboards, fridges and freezers would usually visit their local supermarket or hypermarket. Now, these same consumers can go online – from their home, place of work or while on the move – to order their groceries for direct delivery to their homes. The concept is seen to be particularly attractive to professional, high-earning, ABC1 men and women who work long hours and have limited leisure time, but many other consumers increasingly buy their groceries online. Indeed, some of the most visited websites each week are those operated by Tesco, Asda, Sainsbury's and Ocado. Tesco.com is one service that allows customers to buy their groceries direct over the internet. Consumers can access the Tesco website at Tesco.com and select their purchase items. Their orders are then compiled by a team of in-store sales assistants for delivery to consumers' homes at a time of their choosing. So large is the internet part of the grocery market that many supermarket retailers now operate fully 'dark stores', where no consumers visit and only teams of staff operate, picking online orders for home delivery. Assorting within such stores into clusters or product categories is particularly important for operations staff, just as it is within normal stores for consumers requiring similar products to be grouped together.

Initially, the Tesco.com concept was trialled in 11 stores in two major UK cities. The company's preliminary research showed that around 200 000 consumers were using the service offered by these 11 stores and that this was increasing by 10 000 every week. Before long, the obvious popularity of internet shopping prompted Tesco to roll out Tesco.com to other parts of the UK. By the end of the first year, the company offered the service from 100 Tesco stores. Careful consideration has been given to the marketing of the internet shopping service. The sight of the Tesco logo displayed by the company's delivery vans has become very familiar. In addition, the retailer is using a combination of local poster and in-store advertising, direct mail and a web campaign to promote the Tesco.com operation. Today, Tesco's is the most used website of all e-tailers.

Increasing familiarity with shopping on the internet looks set to increase the demand for services like Tesco.com. A whole generation of young adults is emerging that has grown up with the convenience and reassurance of web-based shopping. Tesco management clearly understands that retaining its market-leading position means being ready to respond to changing shopping needs. Most grocery retailers are managing multiple channels alongside each other, striving to 'own' consumers' spending wherever it occurs.

In common with many retailers, Tesco has a multi-channel operation. Tesco Extra is an edge-of-town hypermarket business offering mixed merchandise on top of groceries. Tesco Superstores are large grocery-led supermarkets, often on edge-of-town retail parks. The town centre and suburbs are not ignored in Tesco's multi-channel strategy: Tesco Express is a large chain of C-stores (convenience stores) – often mini-marts – in the suburbs and Tesco Metro is a chain of town centre supermarkets focusing on only groceries. These store-based propositions are joined by Tesco.com for groceries, the online Tesco Bank and Tesco Direct. This online shopping service provides home deliveries of everything found in a Tesco Extra hypermarket and more, from furniture, electrical goods, jewellery, entertainment and clothing to groceries. Some consumers may prefer just one of these channel options, while others will use a mix of Tesco stores depending on their whereabouts, the occasion and time of shopping, and may prefer the web and Tesco.com. Tesco's management must understand the different customer profiles that its concepts attract and engage accordingly with these consumers in order to build loyalty.

Assorting
The grouping of products that buyers want to have available in one place.

Assorting Assorting is the process of combining products into collections or assortments that buyers want to have available in one place. Assorting eliminates discrepancies in assortment by grouping products in ways that satisfy buyers. Assorting is especially important to retailers, for they strive to create assortments matching the demands of consumers who visit their stores. Although no single customer is likely to buy one of everything in the store, retailers must anticipate the probability of purchase and provide a satisfactory range of product choices. For example, the same food wholesaler that supplies local shops with Del Monte tomato products may also buy canned goods from competing food processors so that the grocery store can choose from a wide assortment of canned fruit and vegetables. The Building Customer Relationships box on page 409 outlines Tesco's multi-channel strategy and the importance of assorting.

Standardizing transactions

Marketing channels help to standardize the transactions associated with numerous products. In many purchase situations, the price is not negotiable; it is predetermined. Although there may be some variation in units of measurement, package sizes, delivery schedules and location of the exchange, marketing channel members tend to limit customer options with respect to these types of issue. When a customer goes to a supermarket to purchase a loaf of bread, it is unlikely that the individual will be able to buy half a loaf of bread, buy a loaf sliced lengthwise, negotiate the price, obtain a written warranty or return an unused portion of the loaf. Many of the details associated with the purchase of a loaf of bread are standardized.

Providing customer service

Channel members participate in providing customer service. Retailers of durable goods are expected to provide in-store advice and demonstrations, technical know-how, delivery, installation, repair services, parts and perhaps instruction or training. Channel members above the retailers are responsible for supporting retailers' efforts to provide end-user service and satisfaction, even though they may not come into direct contact with ultimate customers. To gain and maintain a differential advantage, channel members make decisions and take actions to provide excellent customer service and support.

In mature markets with relatively little product differentiation between rival brands – such as packaged holidays, audio/hi-fi systems, conference venues or replacement car exhausts/tyres – and in newly emerging markets with innovative products and inexperienced consumers, it is often the customer service provided through the distribution channel that provides marketers with an edge over their competitors. In many markets – from cars and financial services to grocery retailing and PCs – it is the service provided by channel members that maintains an ongoing, mutually satisfactory relationship between supplier and consumer, and that may be responsible for maintaining brand loyalty.

Types of channel

Because marketing channels appropriate for one product may be less suitable for others, many different distribution paths have been developed. The various marketing channels can be classified generally as channels for consumer products and services, or channels for business-to-business products and services.

Channels for consumer products or services

Figure 14.3 illustrates several channels used in the distribution of consumer products or services. Besides the channels listed, a manufacturer may use a network of its own sales branches or sales offices.

Channel A Channel A describes the direct movement of goods from producer to consumers. Customers who pick their own fruit from commercial orchards or buy cosmetics from door-to-door salespeople are acquiring products through a direct channel. A producer who sells goods directly from the factory to end-users and ultimate consumers is using a direct marketing channel; for example, Direct Line's teleselling of its own car insurance policies. Although this

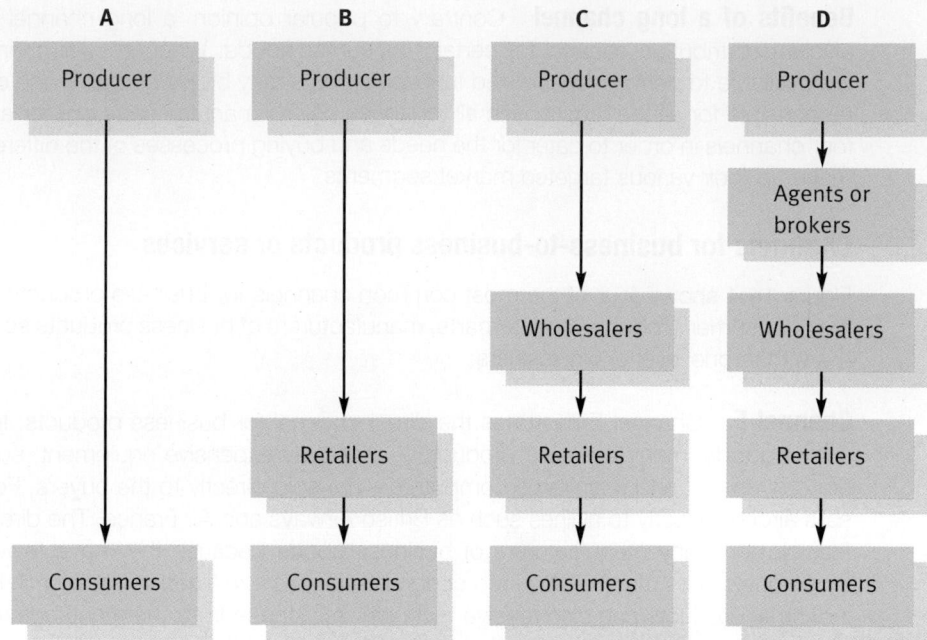

FIGURE 14.3
Typical marketing
channels for
consumer products

eCommerce
The use of the internet
for marketing com-
munications, selling and
purchasing.

channel is the simplest, it is not necessarily the cheapest or the most efficient method of distribution. **eCommerce** – the use of the internet for marketing communications, selling and purchasing – has in recent years led to a growth in direct marketing for a variety of products, notably travel tickets, music downloads and movie streaming, financial services and merchandise retailed by the traditional mail-order catalogue operators. Channel A, the direct approach, certainly is no longer the preserve of only farm shops and factory outlets. Indeed, companies have entered markets with digital channels only.

Channel B Channel B, which moves goods from producer to retailers and then to consumers, is often used by large retailers that can buy in quantity from a manufacturer. Such retailers as Marks & Spencer, Sainsbury's, Aldi and Carrefour sell clothing, food, household goods and many other items they have purchased directly from the producers. Cars are also commonly sold through this type of marketing channel.

Channel C A long-standing distribution channel, especially for consumer products, channel C takes goods from producer to wholesalers, then to retailers and finally to consumers. This option is very practical for a producer who sells to hundreds of thousands of consumers through thousands of retailers. A single producer finds it hard to do business directly with thousands of retailers. For example, consider the number of retailers that stock Coca-Cola. It would be extremely difficult, if not impossible, for Coca-Cola to deal directly with all the retailers that sell its brand of soft drink. Manufacturers of tobacco products, confectionery, some home appliances, hardware and many convenience goods sell their products to wholesalers, who then sell to retailers, who in turn do business with individual consumers.

Channel D Channel D, through which goods pass from producer to agents to wholesalers to retailers, and only then to consumers, is frequently used for products intended for mass distribution, such as processed food. For example, to place its biscuit line in specific retail outlets, a food processor may hire an agent (or a food broker) to sell the biscuits to wholesalers. The wholesalers then sell the biscuits to supermarkets, vending machine operators and other retail outlets.

Benefits of a long channel   Contrary to popular opinion, a long channel may be the most efficient distribution channel for certain consumer goods. When several channel intermediaries are available to perform specialized functions, costs may be lower than if one channel member is responsible for all the functions in all territories. Some manufacturers opt for all or most of these four channels in order to cater for the needs and buying processes of the different customers that make up their various targeted market segments.

Channels for business-to-business products or services

Figure 14.4 shows four of the most common channels for business products and services. Like their consumer products' counterparts, manufacturers of business products sometimes work with more than one level of wholesalers.

Channel E   Channel E illustrates the direct channel for business products. In contrast to consumer goods, many business products – especially expensive equipment, such as steam generators, aircraft and mainframe computers – are sold directly to the buyers. For example, Airbus sells aircraft directly to airlines such as British Airways and Air France. The direct channel is most feasible for many manufacturers of business goods because they have fewer customers, and those customers may be clustered geographically, as explained in Chapter 6. Buyers of complex industrial products can also receive technical assistance from the manufacturer more easily in a direct channel. In some cases the provision of such information may continue for the lifetime of the product. As with consumer markets, eCommerce and the desire to develop one-to-one direct relationships have led to a growth in the use of channel E.

Industrial distributor
An independent business that takes title to industrial products and carries inventories.

Channel F   If a particular line of business products is aimed at a larger number of customers, the manufacturer may use a marketing channel that includes **industrial distributors** or merchants who take title to products and carry inventory (channel F). Construction products made by Case or JCB are sold through distributors, as are building materials, operating supplies and air-conditioning equipment. Industrial distributors are carrying an increasing percentage of business products. Due to mergers and acquisitions, they have become larger and more powerful.[4] Industrial distributors can be

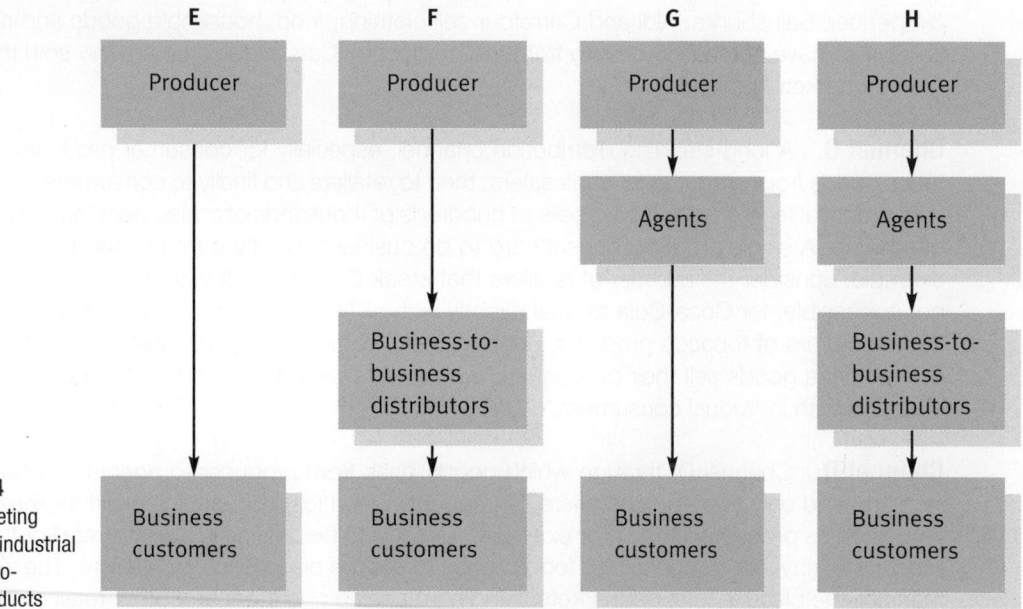

FIGURE 14.4
Typical marketing channels for industrial or business-to-business products

most effectively used when a product has broad market appeal, is easily stocked and serviced, is sold in small quantities and is needed rapidly to avoid high losses.[5]

Channel G   Channel G – from producer to agents to business buyers – may be chosen when a manufacturer without a marketing department needs market information, when a company is too small to field its own salesforce or when a company wants to introduce a new product or to enter a new market without using its own salespeople. Thus, a large soya bean producer might sell its product to animal food processors through an agent.

Channel H   Channel H is a variation of channel G: goods move from producer to agents to distributors and then to business customers. A manufacturer without a salesforce may rely on this channel if its business customers purchase products in small quantities or if they must be re-supplied frequently and therefore need access to decentralized inventories. For example, Chinese manufacturers of electronic components work through export agents who sell to distributors serving small producers or dealers overseas.

Multiple marketing channels

When aiming at diverse target markets, it may be appropriate for a manufacturer to use several marketing channels simultaneously, with each channel involving a different group of intermediaries. For example, a manufacturer turns to multiple channels when the same product is directed to both consumers and business customers. When Procter & Gamble sells cleaning products for household use, the products are sold to supermarkets through grocery wholesalers or, in some cases, directly to the larger retailers, whereas the cleaning products going to restaurants or institutions follow a different distribution channel. In some instances, a producer may prefer **dual distribution**: the use of two marketing channels for distributing the same products. Villeroy & Boch is a respected supplier of fine china and glassware to households across the world. The company also has ranges for the catering industry, sold and promoted through a separate marketing channel.

A **strategic channel alliance** exists when the products of one organization are distributed through the marketing channels of another. The products are often similar with respect to target markets or product uses, but they are not direct competitors. For example, a brand of bottled water might be distributed through a marketing channel for soft drinks, or a US cereal producer could form a strategic channel alliance with a European food processor. Alliances can provide benefits both for the organization that owns the marketing channel and for the company whose brand is being distributed through the channel.

Multi-channel marketing is the decision to reach target consumers or business customers through more than one channel. Increasingly, companies opt to serve their target markets via online channels and more traditional channels side by side. For example, Sony products are available online or in-store, while many business-to-business products and services now can be sourced online as well as from industrial distributors, brokers or other middle players. **Omni-channel marketing** is the term applied to multi-channel marketing when it involves marketers utilizing *all* available channels to offer customers a seamless brand experience across a company's channels (see Chapter 19).

Dual distribution
A channel practice whereby a producer distributes the same products through two different channels.

Strategic channel alliance
Arrangement for distributing the products of one organization through the marketing channels of another.

Multi-channel marketing
The decision to reach target consumers or business customers through more than one channel.

Omni-channel marketing
When multi-channel marketing involves marketers utilizing *all* available channels to offer customers a seamless brand experience across a company's channels.

Channel integration

Channel functions may be transferred among intermediaries, to producers and even to customers. This section examines how channel members can either combine and control most activities or pass them on to another channel member. Remember that the channel member cannot eliminate functions; unless buyers themselves perform the functions, they must pay for the labour and resources needed for the functions to be performed. Middlemen may be eliminated but not their functions.

Many marketing channels are determined by consensus. Producers and intermediaries coordinate their efforts for mutual benefit. However, some marketing channels are organized and controlled by a single leader, which can be a producer, a wholesaler or a retailer, depending on the industry and the relative power within the supply chain. The channel leader may establish channel policies and coordinate the development of the marketing mix. Marks & Spencer and IKEA, for example, are channel leaders for several of the many products they sell, exerting significant pressure on suppliers to adhere to their production, delivery and pricing standards. The various links or stages of the channel may be combined under the management of a channel leader, either horizontally or vertically. Integration may stabilize supply, reduce costs and increase coordination of channel members.

Vertical channel integration

Vertical channel integration
The combination of two or more stages of the channel under one management.

Combining two or more stages of the channel under one management is **vertical channel integration**. One member of a marketing channel may purchase the operations of another member or simply perform the functions of the other member, eliminating the need for that intermediary as a separate entity. For example, changes in the regulations controlling the UK electricity industry led to an increase in vertical channel integration, as companies controlling the generation and distribution of electricity have merged. Total vertical integration encompasses all functions from production to ultimate buyer; it is exemplified by oil companies such as BP or Shell, which own oil wells, pipelines, refineries, terminals, consumer-facing brands and service station forecourts.

Whereas members of conventional channel systems work independently and seldom cooperate, participants in vertical channel integration coordinate their efforts to reach a desired target market.[6] This more progressive approach to distribution enables channel members to regard other members as extensions of their own operations. Vertically integrated channels are often more effective against competition because they result in increased bargaining power, the ability to inhibit competitors, and the sharing of information and responsibilities.[7] At one end of an integrated channel, a manufacturer might provide advertising and training assistance, and the retailer at the other end would buy the manufacturer's products in quantity and actively promote them.

Vertical marketing system (VMS)
Marketing channel in which a single channel member coordinates or manages channel activities to achieve efficient, low-cost distribution aimed at satisfying target market customers.

In the past, integration has been successfully institutionalized in marketing channels called vertical marketing systems. A **vertical marketing system (VMS)** is a marketing channel in which a single channel member coordinates or manages channel activities to achieve efficient, low-cost distribution aimed at satisfying target market customers. As the efforts of individual channel members are combined in a VMS, marketing activities can be coordinated for maximum effectiveness and economy, without duplication of services. Vertical marketing systems are also competitive, accounting for a growing share of retail sales in consumer goods. Most vertical marketing systems today take one of three forms: corporate, administered or contractual.

The corporate VMS The corporate VMS combines all stages of the marketing channel, from producers to consumers, under a single ownership. Supermarket chains that own food-processing plants, and large retailers that purchase wholesaling and production facilities, are examples of corporate VMSs.

The administered VMS In an administered VMS, channel members are independent, but a high level of inter-organizational management is achieved by informal coordination. For example, members of an administered VMS may agree to adopt uniform accounting and ordering procedures, and to cooperate in promotional activities. Although individual channel members maintain their autonomy, as in conventional marketing channels, one channel member – such as the producer or a large retailer – dominates the administered VMS, so that distribution decisions take into account the system as a whole. Due to its size and power as a retailer, Marks & Spencer exercises a strong influence over the independent manufacturers in its marketing channels, as do Kellogg's (cereals) and BMW (cars).

The contractual VMS   Under a contractual VMS, the most popular type of vertical marketing system, inter-organizational relationships are formalized through contracts. Channel members are linked by legal agreements that spell out each member's rights and obligations. For instance, franchise organizations such as McDonald's and KFC are contractual VMSs. Other contractual VMSs include wholesaler-sponsored groups such as SPAR or Mace stores, in which independent retailers band together under the contractual leadership of a wholesaler.

Horizontal channel integration

Horizontal channel integration
The combination of institutions at the same level of channel operation under one management.

Combining institutions at the same level of channel operation under one management constitutes **horizontal channel integration**. An organization may integrate horizontally by merging with other organizations at the same level in a marketing channel. For example, the owner of a bistro chain may buy another bistro or a bar chain and then rebrand it in the same way as the existing business and merge the two chains' supply channels. Horizontal integration may enable an organization to generate sufficient sales revenue to integrate vertically as well.

Although horizontal integration permits efficiencies and economies of scale in purchasing, marketing research, advertising and specialized personnel, it is not always the most effective method of improving distribution. The increase in size may result in decreased flexibility, difficulties in coordination, and the need for additional marketing research and large-scale planning. Unless distribution functions for the various units can be performed more efficiently under unified management than under the previously separate managements, horizontal integration will not reduce costs or improve the competitive position of the integrating company.

Different levels of market coverage

The kind of coverage that is appropriate for different products is determined by the characteristics and behaviour patterns of buyers. Chapter 10 divided consumer products into three broad categories – convenience products, shopping products and speciality products – according to how the purchase is made. In considering products to buy, consumers take into account replacement rate, product adjustment, duration of consumption, time required to find the product and similar factors.[8] Three major levels of market coverage are intensive, selective and exclusive distribution.

Intensive distribution

Intensive distribution
The use of all available outlets for distributing a product.

In **intensive distribution**, all available outlets are used for distributing a product. Intensive distribution is appropriate for convenience products such as bread, chewing gum, beer and newspapers. To consumers, availability means a store located nearby and minimal time necessary to search for the product at the store. Sales may have a direct relationship to availability. The successful sale of bread and milk at service stations or of petrol at convenience grocery stores has shown that the availability of these products is more important than the nature of the outlet. Convenience products have a high replacement rate and require almost no service. To meet these demands, intensive distribution is necessary, and multiple channels may be used to sell through all possible outlets. Producers of packaged consumer items rely on intensive distribution. In fact, intensive distribution is one of L'Oréal's key strengths.

FIGURE 14.5
L'Oréal hair products
are intensively distributed

L'Oréal shampoo and its other products such as make-up, skincare, sun screen and perfume, are expected to be readily and intensively available by consumers.

Selective distribution

Selective distribution
The use of only some available outlets in an area to distribute a product.

In **selective distribution**, only some available outlets in an area are chosen to distribute a product. Selective distribution is appropriate for shopping products. Durable goods – such as electrical appliances and exclusive fragrances – usually fall into this category. Such products are more expensive than convenience goods. Consumers are willing to spend more time searching: visiting several retail outlets to compare prices, designs, styles and other features.

Selective distribution is desirable when a special effort, such as customer service, from a channel member is important. Shopping products require differentiation at the point of purchase. To motivate retailers to provide adequate pre-sale service, selective distribution and company-owned stores are often used. Many business products are sold on a selective basis to maintain a certain degree of control over the distribution process. For example, agricultural herbicides are distributed on a selective basis because dealers must offer services to buyers, such as instructions about how to apply the herbicides safely, or offer the option of having the dealer apply the herbicide.

Exclusive distribution

Exclusive distribution
The use of only one outlet in a relatively large geographic area to distribute a product.

In **exclusive distribution**, only one outlet is used in a relatively large geographic area. Exclusive distribution is suitable for speciality products that are purchased rather infrequently, consumed over a long period of time, or require service or information to fit them to buyers' needs. Exclusive distribution is not appropriate for convenience products and many shopping products. It is often used as an incentive to sellers when only a limited market is available for products. For example, cars such as the Rolls-Royce are sold on an exclusive basis. Royal Copenhagen's premium china is retailed through carefully selected, exclusive retail outlets. A producer who uses exclusive distribution generally expects a dealer to be very cooperative with respect to carrying a complete inventory, sending personnel for sales and service training, participating in promotional programmes and providing excellent customer service. Exclusive distribution gives a company tighter image control because the types of distributors and retailers that distribute the product are monitored closely.[9]

Choosing distribution channels

Choosing the most appropriate distribution channels for a product can be a complex affair. Some well-known store-based retailers still are reluctant to lose in-store impact by switching to the web. Consumers interested in IKEA or Selfridges were until relatively recently frustrated by not being able to purchase online, as these companies perceived their store-based offerings to be their core appeal. The Building Customer Relationships box on page 418 outlines the multi-channel strategy developed by Games Workshop. Producers must choose specific intermediaries carefully, evaluating their sales and profit levels, performance records, other products carried, clientele, availability and so forth. In addition, producers must examine other factors that influence distribution channel selection, including organizational objectives and resources, market characteristics, buying behaviour, product attributes and environmental forces. In some markets, such as the distribution of insurance products, these factors may indicate that multiple channels should be used.[10]

Organizational objectives and resources

Producers must consider carefully their objectives and the cost of achieving them in the marketplace. A company's objectives may be broad – such as higher profits, increased market share and greater responsiveness to customers – or narrow, such as replacing an intermediary that has left the channel or adding an additional product line. The organization may possess sufficient financial and marketing muscle to control its distribution channels, such as by engaging in direct marketing or by operating its own delivery fleet. On the other hand, an organization may have no interest in performing distribution services or may be forced by lack of resources and experience to depend on retailers or wholesalers.

Companies must also consider how effective their past distribution relationships and methods have been, and question their appropriateness with regard to current objectives. One organization might decide to maintain its basic channel structure but add members for increased coverage in new territories. Another company might alter its distribution channel so as to provide same-day delivery on all orders. The digital market has acted as a game-changer. With increasing numbers of consumers expecting 24/7 online access to their brands and favourite retailers, most companies have added an online channel of distribution to their channel strategy.

Market characteristics

Beyond the basic division between consumer markets and business markets, several market variables influence the design of distribution channels. Geography is one factor; in most cases, the greater the distance between the producer and its markets, the less expensive is distribution through intermediaries rather than through direct sales. Market density must also be considered; when customers tend to be clustered in several locations, the producer may be able to eliminate middlemen.

Transport, storage, communication and negotiation are specific functions performed more efficiently in high-density markets. Market size measured by the number of potential customers in a consumer or business market is yet another variable. Direct sales may be effective if a producer has relatively few buyers for a product, but for larger markets the services of middlemen may be required.[11] eCommerce is encouraging many suppliers to deal directly with customers, even when they are geographically spread or diverse in nature. This provides a growing role for logistics companies to facilitate deliveries on behalf of suppliers serving customers spread far and wide, increasingly expecting same-day delivery options. There is no doubt that the growing popularity

Games Workshop: the best model soldiers in the world!

Building customer relationships

As its name suggests, Games Workshop manufactures and sells games, but these are no ordinary games and this is no ordinary business. Games Workshop is 'the largest and most successful tabletop fantasy and futuristic battle-games company in the world'. With a turnover of over £126 million, now the company employs more than 2000 people. It has over 400 of its own retail outlets, plus another 4000 toy and hobby stores stock the company's products, in Australia, Canada, France, Germany, Hong Kong, Italy, Spain, the USA and the UK, with growing South American, Asian and Eastern European markets. Seventy per cent of sales now come from outside the UK. The fantasy games produced by Games Workshop take place in one of two settings:

1. a fantasy world filled with dwarves, elves, rat-like scaven, green orcs and goblins

2. the future of a war-torn universe in the forty-first millennium – a setting occupied by the enigmatic Eldar, genetically-enhanced space marines and an alien race called the Tyranids, who are all battling for survival.

In addition, the company has the franchise for a range linked to *The Lord of The Rings* movies.

> We have a simple strategy at Games Workshop. We make the best fantasy miniatures in the world and sell them globally at a profit, and we intend to do this forever.
>
> We make things. We are a manufacturer, not a retailer. We do have outlets in retail locations. We call these Games Workshop Hobby centres because they show customers how to engage with our hobby of collecting, painting and playing with our miniatures and games. They are the front end of our manufacturing business. If our Hobby centres do a great job, we will recruit lots of customers into our Hobby and they will enjoy spending their money on the products we make.
>
> The products we make for our customers are the best in the war-gaming world. This is because everyone at Games Workshop is passionate about our Hobby.

> http://investor.games-workshop.com/our-business-model,
> March 2015.

Games Workshop enthusiasts can buy from a range of boxed games, containing the rule book, charts and templates, dice and miniature figures needed to begin their battle. The basics can then be added to from the extensive range of Games Workshop troops, special squads, and fantasy and war machines. As enthusiasts develop their armies and paint them in colours of their choice, they begin to build their own personalized version of their game of choice. The success of Peter Jackson's *The Lord of the Rings* films has added a new dimension, as Games Workshop holds a global licence for games based on this award-winning trilogy.

For those unfamiliar with the fantasy game concept, the uncharted territory of the retail outlets can itself feel like alien territory. Wall space is stacked high with numerous games, figures, paints, magazines, books and T-shirts. In the centre is a gaming table, which is usually covered with the remains of an ongoing battle. At other times, the shops are full of teenagers and children, conducting a closely fought Warhammer contest. On some days the outlets resemble a crèche for big kids, with staff carefully orchestrating activities. The battles organized in-store are an important part of the weekly itinerary. The featured game varies on different days, so that enthusiasts of Warhammer, Warhammer 40 000, Necromunda and the other Games Workshop products can all get their turn. These games induct newcomers into the gaming experience, while for 'old hands' they showcase new product launches.

The shop staff, always Games Workshop enthusiasts, are vital to the success of the retail outlets. They must be able to maintain an enthusiasm for the brand, keeping up to date with all of the latest new product launches. The ability to handle customers of all ages and backgrounds from the young teenagers who regularly hang out at the stores to the uninitiated visiting the outlets for the first time is also essential. Nonplussed parents clutching 'Christmas lists' or birthday present suggestions experience a friendly welcome from staff, who will happily search among the reams of Games Workshop packaging to retrieve some bizarrely named item.

As well as its network of retail stores, Games Workshop has agencies – typically specialist modelling and hobbyist shops – distributing its figures and games, while even the likes of Toys 'R' Us has been known to stock the popular gaming sets. In total, more than 4000 independent shops retail the company's ranges. In addition, there is a mail-order operation that can be accessed through the retail stores as well as directly by telephone or the web. The online operation has grown significantly recently. This £40 million mail-order operation has 40 staff and a growing database of contacts. The aim is to provide a fast and efficient service, despatching all orders within 24 hours. This facility handles up to a thousand calls daily and can deal with enquiries in a range of languages. While the stores are an integral feature of the Games Workshop 'experience', the company has been quick to recognize the value of adopting a mix of distribution channels to support its rapid expansion plans: online sales and mail order contribute significantly to the company's sales. The company believes its destiny is in its own hands, saying, 'Games Workshop remains a vertically integrated company, retaining control over every aspect of design, manufacture, distribution, and retail of our models and rulebooks.'

Sources: Jervis Johnson and Chris Prentice of Games Workshop; James Dibb-Simkin; Sally Dibb and Lyndon Simkin, *The Marketing Casebook*, 2nd edition (London: Cengage), www.games-workshop.com, May 2004, June 2011 and March 2015; Games Workshop Leamington Spa, July 2011 and March 2015.

of direct marketing and web-based marketing is forcing marketers to reappraise their market characteristics and deployment of channel intermediaries. This results in direct customer–supplier relationships in those channels where wholesaler/retailer channel members once dominated, such as music, books, holidays, clothing and financial services. Figure 14.6 shows supermarket store Tesco's home delivery operation.

Buying behaviour

Buying behaviour is a crucial consideration in selecting distribution channels. To be able to match intermediaries with customers, the producer must have specific, current information about customers who are buying the product and how, when and where they are buying it.[12] With changing behaviours in the digital era, 24/7 mobile access to many brands and consumers who have grown up expecting to access their favoured brands online, it is important for marketers to stay abreast of their customers' behaviours and preferences, as well as to combat the channel strategies adopted by competitors as they seek to pursue their customers.

The producer must also understand how buyer specifications vary according to whether buyers perceive products as convenience, shopping or speciality items (see Chapters 5 and 10). For example, customers for magazines are likely to buy the product frequently – even impulsively – from a variety of outlets. Buyers of computers, however, carefully evaluate product features, dealers, prices and after-sales services, while seeking the views of experts and also friends on social media.

FIGURE 14.6

Leading supermarket retailer Tesco now operates a successful online catalogue operation called Tesco Direct, offering a wide range of products from furniture to cameras to home accessories

Source: Tesco for a Tesco camera and camcorder advertisement, copyright © Tesco.

Product attributes

Another variable in the selection of distribution channels is the product itself. As producers of complex business products must often provide technical services to buyers both before and after the sale, these products are usually shipped directly to buyers. Perishable or highly fashionable consumer products with short shelf lives are also marketed through short channels. In other cases, distribution patterns are influenced by the product's value; the lower the price per unit, the longer the distribution chain. Additional factors to consider are the weight, bulkiness and relative ease of handling the products. Producers may find wholesalers and retailers reluctant to carry items that create storage or display problems.[13] For example, manufacturers of breakfast cereals, such as Kellogg's, must use packaging that retailers find easy to handle and display.

Marketing environmental forces

Finally, producers making decisions about distribution channels must consider the broader forces in the total marketing environment – political, legal, regulatory, societal/green, technological, economic and competitive forces. Technology, for example, made possible electronic scanners, computerized inventory systems such as EPoS (electronic point-of-sale), electronic shopping devices and remote payment systems, making it harder for technologically unsophisticated companies to remain competitive. Mobile maketing apps, downloads of certain entertainment products, automated delivery processes, online comparison sites, are recent examples of technology impacting on channel practices. Internet access has led to a growth in home shopping and direct marketing. Changing family patterns and the emergence of important minority consumer groups are driving producers to seek new distribution methods for reaching specific market segments. Interest rates, inflation and other economic variables affect members of distribution channels at every level. Marketing environmental forces are numerous and complex, and must be taken into consideration if distribution efforts are to be appropriate, efficient and effective, as explained in Chapter 3 of *Marketing: Concepts and Strategies*.

Behaviour of channel members

The marketing channel is a social system with its own conventions and behaviour patterns. Each channel member performs a different role in the system and agrees implicitly or explicitly to accept certain rights, responsibilities, rewards and sanctions for non-conformity. Channel members have certain expectations of other channel members. For instance, retailers expect wholesalers and manufacturers to maintain adequate inventories and to deliver goods on time. For their part, wholesalers expect retailers to honour payment agreements and to keep them informed of inventory needs. This section discusses several issues related to channel member behaviour, including cooperation and relationship building, conflict and leadership. Marketers need to understand these behavioural issues in order to make effective channel decisions, and to maintain relationships with facilitating channel members and loyal customers.

Channel cooperation and relationship building

Channel cooperation is vital if each member is to gain something from other members.[14] Without cooperation, neither overall channel goals nor member goals can be realized. Policies must be developed that support all essential channel members, otherwise failure of one link in the chain could destroy the channel.

There are several ways to improve channel cooperation. A marketing channel should consider itself a unified system, competing with other systems. This way, individual members will be less likely to take actions that would create disadvantages for other members. Similarly, channel members should agree to direct their efforts towards a common target market so that channel roles can be structured for maximum marketing effectiveness, which in turn can help members achieve their individual objectives.

Heineken, for example, was having difficulty with its 450 distributors; at one point, the time between order and delivery stretched to 12 weeks. A cooperative system of supply chain management, with web-based communications, decreased the lead time from order to delivery to four weeks, and Heineken's sales increased 24 per cent.[15] It is crucial to define precisely the tasks that each member of the channel is to perform. This definition provides a basis for reviewing the intermediaries' performance and helps reduce conflicts because each channel member knows exactly what is expected. It is often in the interests of channel members to build long-term relationships. These relationships can improve channel cooperation and help individual channel members adapt better to the needs of the others.[16]

Channel conflict

Although all channel members work towards the same general goal – distributing goods and services profitably and efficiently – members may sometimes disagree about the best methods for attaining this goal.[17] Each channel member wants to maximize its own profits while maintaining as much autonomy as possible.[18] However, if this self-interest leads to misunderstanding about role expectations, the end result is frustration and conflict for the whole channel. For individual organizations to function together in a single social system, each channel member must communicate clearly and understand role expectations, especially as channel conflict often arises when a channel member does not conduct itself in the manner expected by the other channel members. Communication difficulties are a particular form of channel conflict and can lead to frustration, misunderstandings and poorly coordinated strategies.

The increased use of multiple channels of distribution, driven partly by new technology, has increased the potential for conflict between manufacturers and intermediaries. For example, Hewlett Packard (HP) makes products available directly to consumers through its website (www8.hp.com/uk), thereby directly competing with existing distributors and retailers stocking HP products.

Channel conflicts also arise when dealers over-emphasize competing products or diversify into product lines traditionally handled by other, more specialized intermediaries. In some cases, conflict develops because producers strive to increase efficiency by circumventing intermediaries, as happened in marketing channels for software and video games. Many software-only stores established direct relationships with software producers, bypassing wholesale distributors altogether. Some dishonest retailers also pirated software and made unauthorized copies, thus cheating other channel members of their due compensation. Consequently, suspicion and mistrust heightened tensions in software marketing channels.

Although there is no single method for resolving conflict, an atmosphere of cooperation can be re-established if two conditions are met. First, the role of each channel member must be specified. To minimize misunderstanding, all members must be able to expect unambiguous, agreed-on levels of performance from one another. Second, channel members must institute certain measures of channel coordination, a task that requires leadership and the benevolent exercise of control.[19] To prevent channel conflict, producers or other channel members may provide competing resellers with different brands, allocate markets among resellers, define direct sales policies to clarify potential conflict over large accounts, negotiate territorial issues between regional distributors and provide recognition to certain resellers for the importance of their role in distributing to others.

Channel leadership

The effectiveness of marketing channels hinges on channel leadership, which may be assumed by producers, retailers or wholesalers. To become a leader, a channel member must want to influence and direct overall channel performance. Furthermore, to attain desired objectives, the

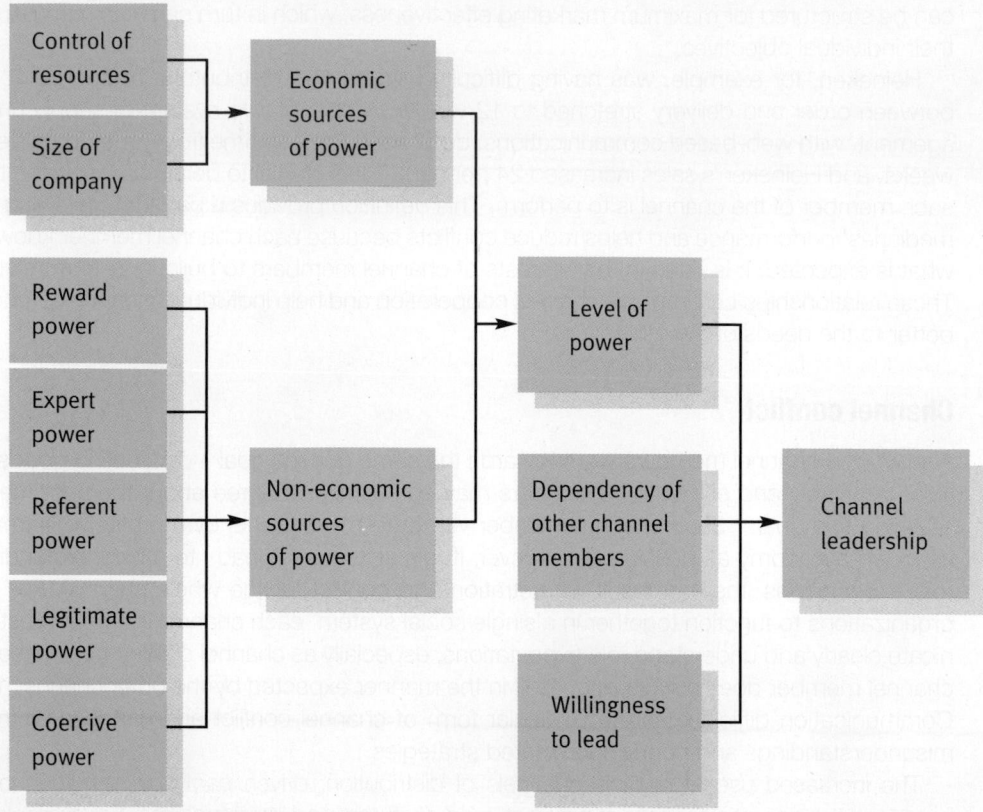

FIGURE 14.7
Determinants of channel leadership

Source: *Marketing Channels and Strategies*, 2nd edn by R.D. Michman and S.D. Sibley, Publishing Horizons, Inc., 1980, p. 413. Reproduced by permission of Dr Ronald D. Michman.

Channel power
The ability to influence another channel member's goal achievement.

leader must possess **channel power**, which is the ability to influence another channel member's goal achievement. As Figure 14.7 shows, the channel leader derives power from seven sources, two of them economic and five non-economic.

The five non-economic sources of power: reward, expert, referent, legitimate and coercive, are crucial for establishing leadership.

1. A channel leader gains *reward* power by providing financial benefits.
2. *Expert* power exists when other channel members believe that the leader provides special expertise required for the channel to function properly.
3. *Referent* power emerges when other members identify strongly with and emulate the leader.
4. *Legitimate* power is based on a superior–subordinate relationship.
5. *Coercive* power is a function of the leader's ability to punish other channel members.[20]

In many countries, producers assume the leadership role in marketing channels. A manufacturer whose large-scale production efficiency demands increasing sales volume may exercise power by giving channel members financing, business advice, ordering assistance, advertising and support materials.[21] For example, BMW and Mercedes-Benz control their dealers totally, specifying showroom design and layout, discount levels and quotas of models. Coercion, though, causes dealer dissatisfaction that is stronger than any impact from rewards, so the use of coercive power can be a major cause of channel conflict.[22]

Retailers can also function as channel leaders, and with the domination of national chains and own-label merchandise they are increasingly doing so. For example, Sainsbury's challenged Coca-Cola with its own-label cola, whose packaging bore a strong resemblance to that of the market leader. Small retailers may share in the leadership role when they command particular consumer respect and patronage in local or regional markets. Among large retailers, Carrefour, IKEA, Marks & Spencer and Tesco base their channel leadership on wide public exposure to their products. These retailers control many brands and sometimes replace uncooperative producers. IKEA exercises power by dictating manufacturing techniques, lead times, quality levels and product specifications.

Wholesalers assume channel leadership roles as well, although they were more powerful decades ago, when most manufacturers and retailers were small, under-financed and widely scattered. Today, wholesaler leaders may form voluntary chains with several retailers, which they supply with bulk buying or management services or which market their own brands. In return, the retailers shift most of their purchasing to the wholesaler leader. In Scandinavia, buying groups act as wholesalers, with bulk ordering price advantages, expert advertising and purchasing. Other wholesaler leaders, such as Intersport or SPAR, may also help retailers with store layouts, accounting and inventory control.

Legal issues in channel management

The multitude of laws governing channel management are based on the general principle that the public is best served when competition and free trade are protected. Under the authority of national legislation or EU Competition Laws and dictates, the courts and regulatory agencies determine under what circumstances channel management practices violate this underlying principle and must be restricted, and when these practices may be permitted. Although channel managers are not expected to be legal experts, they should be aware that attempts to control distribution functions may have legal repercussions. The following practices are among those frequently subject to legal restraint.

Restricted sales territories

Restricted sales territories
System by which a manufacturer tries to prohibit intermediaries from selling its products outside designated sales territories.

To tighten its control over the distribution of its products, a manufacturer may try to prohibit intermediaries from selling its products outside designated sales territories, creating **restricted sales territories**. The intermediaries themselves often favour this practice, because it lets them avoid competition for the producer's brands within their own territories. Many companies have long followed the policy of restricting sales in this fashion. In recent years, the courts have adopted conflicting positions with regard to restricted sales territories. Although they have deemed restricted sales territories a restraint of trade among intermediaries handling the same brands except for small or newly established companies, the courts have also held that exclusive territories can actually promote competition among dealers handling different brands. At present, the producer's intent in establishing restricted territories and the overall effect of doing so on the market must be evaluated for each individual case.

Tying contract

Tying contract
Arrangement whereby a supplier (usually a manufacturer or franchiser) furnishes a product to a channel member with the stipulation that the channel member must purchase other products as well.

When a supplier, usually a manufacturer or franchiser, furnishes a product to a channel member with the stipulation that the channel member must purchase other products as well, a **tying contract** exists. Suppliers, for instance, may institute tying arrangements to move weaker products along with more popular items. To use another example, a franchiser may tie the purchase of equipment and supplies to the sale of franchises, justifying the policy as necessary for quality control and protection of the franchiser's reputation. A related practice is full-line forcing. In this situation, a supplier requires that channel members purchase the supplier's entire line to obtain any of the products. Manufacturers sometimes use full-line forcing to ensure that intermediaries accept new products and that a suitable range of products is available to customers. The courts accept tying contracts when the supplier alone can provide products of a certain quality, when the intermediary is free to carry competing products as well, and when a company has just entered the market. Most other tying contracts are considered illegal.

Exclusive dealing

Exclusive dealing
System by which a manufacturer forbids an intermediary to carry the products of competing manufacturers.

When a manufacturer forbids an intermediary to carry the products of competing manufacturers, the arrangement is called **exclusive dealing**. A manufacturer receives considerable market protection in an exclusive dealing arrangement and may cut off shipments to an intermediary that violates such an agreement. An exclusive dealing contract is generally legally permitted if dealers and customers in a given market have access to similar products or if the exclusive dealing contract strengthens an otherwise weak competitor.

Refusal to deal

Refusal to deal
Situation in which suppliers will not do business with wholesalers or dealers simply because these wholesalers or dealers have resisted policies that are anti-competitive or in restraint of trade.

Producers have the right to choose the channel members with whom they will do business and the right not to choose others. Within existing distribution channels, however, suppliers may not refuse to deal with wholesalers or dealers just because these wholesalers or dealers have resisted policies that are anti-competitive or in restraint of trade. Suppliers are further prohibited from organizing some channel members in **refusal to deal** actions against other members who choose not to comply with illegal policies.

Summary

Distribution refers to activities that make products available to customers when and where they want to purchase them. A *channel of distribution* (or *marketing channel*) is a group of individuals and organizations that direct the flow of products from producers to customers. In most channels of distribution, producers and customers are linked by *marketing intermediaries* or middlemen, called *merchants* if they take title to products and *functional middlemen* if they do not take title. Channel structure reflects the division of responsibilities among members. Ongoing relationships with customers are seen as increasingly important via relationship marketing. Effective distribution channels and the deployment of channel intermediaries are central to the development of mutually satisfactory ongoing relationships between intermediaries, and between producers and their customers. Most businesses today distribute through more than one channel, with multi-channel selection and management a significant activity for marketers.

Supply chain management is the creation of long-term partnerships among marketing channel members that reduce inefficiencies, costs and redundancies in the marketing channel and develop innovative approaches to satisfying targeted customers. The goal is still to provide customers with the product or service demanded, in line with their expectations, but in a more coordinated way that builds on the combined strengths of the members of the distribution channel. Key tasks in supply chain management include planning, sourcing, facilitating delivery and relationship building to nurture ongoing customer relationships.

Marketing channels serve many functions that may be performed by a single channel member but are mostly accomplished through both the independent and joint efforts of channel members. These functions include creating utility, facilitating exchange efficiencies, alleviating discrepancies, standardizing transactions and providing customer service. Although intermediaries can be eliminated, their functions are vital and cannot be dropped; these activities must be performed by someone in the marketing channel or passed on to customers. Because intermediaries serve both producers and buyers, they reduce the total number of transactions that would otherwise be needed to move products from producer to ultimate users. Intermediaries' specialized functions also help keep down costs.

An *assortment* is a combination of products assembled to provide customer benefits. Intermediaries perform *sorting activities* essential to the development of product assortments. Sorting activities allow channel members to divide roles and separate tasks. Through the basic tasks of *sorting out*, *accumulation*, *allocation* and *assorting* products for buyers, intermediaries resolve discrepancies in quantity and assortment. The number and characteristics of intermediaries are determined by the assortments and the expertise needed to perform distribution activities.

Direct marketing, aided by *eCommerce,* has recently encouraged many marketers to cut out channel intermediaries in both consumer and business-to-business transactions.

Channels of distribution are broadly classified as channels for consumer products or channels for business products. Within these two broad categories, different marketing channels are used for different products. Although some consumer goods move directly from producer to consumers, consumer product channels that include wholesalers and retailers are often more economical and efficient. Business goods move directly from producer to end users more frequently than do consumer goods. Channels for business products may also include agents, *industrial distributors* or both. Most producers use *dual distribution* or multiple channels so that the distribution system can be adjusted for various target markets. Sometimes *strategic channel alliances* are used so that the products of one organization can be distributed through the marketing channels of another. *Multi-channel marketing* is the decision to reach target consumers or business customers through more than one channel. In the digital era with consumers expecting 24/7 access to their favourite brands, multi-channel marketing is increasingly commonplace. *Omni-channel marketing* refers to marketers utilizing all available channels. Consumer brands may be retailed in store and via websites, while business products pass through dealers and directly via web-selling.

Integration of marketing channels brings various activities under the management of one channel member. *Vertical channel integration* combines two or more stages of the channel under one management. In the *vertical marketing system (VMS)* a single channel member coordinates or manages channel activity for the mutual benefit of all channel members. Vertical marketing systems may be corporate, administered or contractual. *Horizontal channel integration* combines institutions at the same level of channel operation under a single management.

A marketing channel is managed so that products receive appropriate market coverage. In *intensive distribution*, producers distribute a product using all available outlets. In *selective distribution,* outlets are screened to use those most qualified for exposing a product properly. *Exclusive distribution* usually uses one outlet to distribute a product in a large geographic area when there is a limited market for the product.

When selecting distribution channels for products, manufacturers evaluate potential channel members carefully. Producers consider the organization's objectives and available resources; the location, density and size of a market; buying behaviour in the target market; product attributes; and external forces in the marketing environment. Technology, notably eCommerce, has recently played a major role in certain markets in the selection of distribution channels.

A marketing channel is a social system in which individuals and organizations are linked by a common goal: the profitable and efficient distribution of goods and services. The positions or roles of channel members are associated with rights, responsibilities and rewards, as well as sanctions for non-conformity. Channels function most efficiently when members cooperate; when they deviate from their roles, channel conflict can arise. Effective marketing channels are usually a result of channel leadership and of relationship building between channel members.

Channel leaders can facilitate or hinder other channel members' goal achievement, deriving this *channel power* from seven sources, two of them economic and five non-economic. Producers are in an excellent position to structure channel policy and to use technical expertise and consumer acceptance to influence other channel members. Retailers gain channel control through consumer confidence, wide product mixes and intimate knowledge of consumers. Wholesalers and buying groups become channel leaders when they have expertise that other channel members value and when they can coordinate functions to match supply with demand.

Channel management is governed by a variety of legal issues. These are based on the principle that the public is best served when competition and free trade are protected. Various practices may be subject to legal restraint. To tighten their distribution control, manufacturers may try to operate *restricted sales territories*, where intermediaries are barred from selling products outside designated areas. A *tying contract* occurs when a supplier stipulates that another channel member must purchase other products in addition to the one originally supplied. *Exclusive dealing* occurs when a manufacturer forbids an intermediary to carry the products of competing manufacturers. *Refusal to deal* means that a producer will not do business with a wholesaler or dealer that has resisted policies that are anti-competitive or in restraint of trade.

Key links

The choice of marketing channel is critical to the success of a marketing strategy, as explored in this chapter, and channel selection is very much a part of the marketing remit. This chapter should be read in conjunction with:

- Chapter 2, the overview of marketing strategy.
- Chapter 10, the explanation of the product element of the marketing mix.
- Chapter 15, which examines the players within marketing channels.

Important terms

Accumulation
Allocation
Assorting
Assortment
Channel of distribution (or marketing channel)
Channel power
Dual distribution
eCommerce
Exclusive dealing
Exclusive distribution
Functional middlemen
Horizontal channel integration
Industrial distributor
Intensive distribution
Marketing intermediary
Merchants
Multi-channel marketing
Omni-channel marketing

Refusal to deal
Restricted sales territories
Selective distribution
Sorting activities
Sorting out
Strategic channel alliance
Supply chain management
Tying contract
Vertical channel integration
Vertical marketing system (VMS)

Discussion and review questions

1. Compare and contrast the four major types of marketing channel for consumer products. Through which type of channel is each of the following products most likely to be distributed: (a) new cars, (b) cheese biscuits, (c) cut-your-own Christmas trees, (d) new textbooks, (e) sofas, (f) soft drinks?

2. 'Shorter channels are usually a more direct means of distribution and therefore are more efficient.' Comment on this statement.

3. Describe an industrial distributor. What types of product are marketed through industrial distributors?

4. Why might a producer choose to use more than one marketing channel?

5. Why do consumers often blame intermediaries for distribution inefficiencies? List several reasons.

6. How do the major functions that intermediaries perform help resolve discrepancies in assortment and in quantity?

7. How does the number of intermediaries in the channel relate to the assortments retailers need?

8. Can one channel member perform all channel functions?

9. Identify and explain the major factors that influence decision-makers' selection of marketing channels.

10. Name and describe companies that use (a) vertical integration and (b) horizontal integration in their marketing channels.

11. Explain the major characteristics of each of the three types of vertical marketing system (VMS).

12. Explain the differences among intensive, selective and exclusive methods of distribution.

13. What impact has the growing popularity of eCommerce had on marketing channels?

14. 'Channel cooperation requires that members support the overall channel goals to achieve individual goals.' Comment on this statement.

15. How do power bases within the channel influence the selection of the channel leader?

16. Why is multi-channel marketing increasingly the norm?

17. What considerations should influence multi-channel selection?

Recommended readings

Arikan, A., *Multichannel Marketing: Metrics and Methods for On and Offline Success* (Wiley, 2008).

Christopher, M., *Logistics and Supply Chain Management* (FT/Prentice-Hall, 2011).

Gattorna, J., ed., *Strategic Supply Chain Alignment: Best Practices in Supply Chain Management* (Gower, 2005).

Harrison, A., van Hoek, R. and Skipworth, H., *Logistics Management and Strategy: Competing Through the Supply Chain* (Pearson, 2014).

Rosenbloom, B., *Marketing Channels: A Management View* (Cengage, 2012).

Rushton, A., Croucher, P. and Baker, P., *The Handbook of Logistics and Distribution Management* (Kogan Page, 2014).

Internet exercise

The fortunes of many manufacturers depend on their dealer network, particularly producers of construction equipment. Take a look at two such companies' websites, and examine what they say about their dealer network and parts/service support: www.caterpillar.com and www.jcb.com

1. In the context of these websites, how important to these businesses is the chosen route to market: the dealer network?

2. In terms of delivering customer service, what is the role in the marketing channel of these dealerships?

Group tasks

1. Identify a brand your team buys online and also in-store. For each channel, does the marketing differ? To what extent is the brand experience consistent across these two channels?

2. Traditional betting shops still exist on every high street, but online there are now dozens of rivals. For a business such as William Hill, Ladbrokes or Coral – with betting shops and online gambling sites – what problems are faced in managing the customer experience for a punter (customer) who gambles both in shops and online?

Applied mini-case

Most recorded music used to be purchased by consumers from music stores or mail-order catalogues. First the internet enabled e-selling from retailers' catalogues, and now it has permitted the instant downloading of a fan's favourite tracks. Not only are bands cutting out traditional distribution channels by offering new material directly to their fans via the web, but mainstream labels have also side-tracked the music store as a response to this growing trend.

Question

How can traditional music store operators retailing vinyl, CDs and DVDs strive to maintain a strong customer base in the face of such strong competition from web-based rivals and downloads?

First direct's innovative banking channels

Case study

We are the unexpected bank.

First direct is currently the most recommended bank. We're open 24 hours a day, 7 days a week, and every time you pick up the phone, so do we, because a real person answers every single call, whatever the time, day or night. We're also available online and on your mobile and tablet, so it doesn't matter where you are or what you're doing: we're here for you.

What we're about.

We offer you all the usual banking services, like a current account, savings, cards, mortgages, loans and insurance, but where we're different is the way we offer them. We listen, we have a conversation and we recognize that it's your money, not ours.

www1.firstdirect.com, March 2015

Most consumers have a bank cheque account from which cash is drawn, bills are paid and cheques written, and into which salaries, pensions or student loan cheques are paid. For many consumers, the bank is a high-street or shopping-centre office – imposing, formal and often intimidating. Whether it's NatWest, Barclays or Lloyds TSB in the UK or ABN AMRO or Rabobank in the Netherlands, each high street bank is fairly alike, with similar products and services, personnel, branch layouts, locations and opening hours. Differentiation has been difficult to achieve and generally impossible to maintain over any length of time, as competitors have copied rivals' moves. Promotional strategy and brand image have been the focus for most banking organizations, supported with more minor tactical changes in opening hours or service charges. For many bank account holders the branch – with its restricted openings, formal ambience and congested town-centre location – has been the only point of contact for the bulk of transactions.

First direct, owned by HSBC but managed separately, broke the mould in 1989. Launched with a then massive £6 million promotional campaign, *first direct* bypassed the traditional marketing channel. *First direct* has no branches and no branch overhead and operating costs. It provides free banking, unlike its high-street competitors with their systems of bank charges. *First direct* is a telephone and online banking service that offers full banking, mortgage, loan, investment/saving, insurance, foreign currency and credit card services, plus ATM 'hole in the wall' cash cards through HSBC's international service-till network. All normal banking transactions can be completed over the telephone or online.

Initial reactions were positive, with many non-HSBC account holders switching to the innovative new style of banking. The more traditional consumer – who equates the marbled halls of the Victorian branches with heritage, security and traditional values – was less easily converted. For the targeted, more financially aware and independent income earner, *first direct* has proved to be very popular. Research shows that *first direct* is the most recommended bank with the most satisfied customers. *First direct's* services and products were not new, but the chosen marketing channels were innovative: no branches, only telephone call centres, online banking and texting. Customers no longer have to reach inaccessible, parked-up, town-centre branches with queues and restricted opening hours. The company is fast to adopt evolving technologies and opportunities to interact with its customers digitally.

First direct has introduced a service, alien to some more traditional tastes perhaps, that is more readily available and with fewer costs. Hundreds of thousands of consumers have welcomed the launch of this new option, but millions have preferred to bank the traditional way. For HSBC, this is fine: its HSBC proposition caters for those consumers preferring the more traditional banking format, while *first direct* caters for the new breed of telephone, online and texting customers.

Source: www1.firstdirect.com, March 2015.

Questions for discussion

1. Why is innovation in marketing channels generally difficult to achieve?

2. Why was *first direct* different from its rivals? What gave it differentiation when it first launched?

3. Why might some potential customers of *first direct* have reservations about the innovative nature of the service?

CHAPTER 15

Channel players and physical distribution

"Products must reach customers effectively, which depends on many players within the distribution channel"

Objectives

- To understand the nature of wholesaling in its broadest forms in the marketing channel.

- To examine channel players that facilitate wholesaling and distribution.

- To understand the purpose and function of retailing in the marketing channel.

- To describe and distinguish retail locations, major store types and non-store retailing.

- To understand how physical distribution activities are integrated into marketing channels and overall marketing strategies, and to examine physical distribution objectives.

- To learn about order processing, materials handling and different types of warehousing and their functions.

- To appreciate the importance of inventory management and the development of adequate assortments of products for target markets.

- To gain insight into different transportation methods and how they are selected and coordinated.

INTRODUCTION

This chapter examines the roles of wholesaling, retailing and physical distribution management within the marketing channel, without which products would not reach intended users appropriately. Although these areas are normally managed by specialists, marketers must appreciate their importance when developing their marketing programmes.

Wholesaling includes all transactions in which the purchaser intends to use the product for resale, for making other products or for its general business operations. Wholesaling does not include exchanges with the ultimate consumers. It is the domain of intermediaries within the marketing channel. Hence, the term wholesaling is used here in its broadest sense: inter-mediaries' activity in the marketing channel between producers and business or trade customers. The focus is on:

- merchant wholesalers and distributors
- agents and brokers
- manufacturers' own branches and offices
- the 'middlemen' in many marketing channels
- retailers, which are an important part of the marketing channel for many products.

In addition to being part of the distribution channel for a host of products, the characteristics of retailing present retail marketers with many challenges. Retailers are an influential link in the marketing channel because they are both marketers for, and customers of, producers and wholesalers. They perform many marketing activities, such as buying, selling, grading, risk-taking and developing information about consumers' requirements. Of all marketers, retailers are often the most visible to ultimate consumers. They are in a strategic position to gain feedback from consumers, and to relay ideas to producers and intermediaries in the marketing channel. Retailing is an extraordinarily dynamic area of marketing.

Physical distribution is a set of activities that moves products from producers to consumers or end users. These activities include order processing, materials handling, warehousing, inventory management and transportation. While none of these activities would normally be the responsibility of marketing managers, their smooth deployment impacts on customer service levels, customer satisfaction and also customers' perceptions of a brand or business.

The main objective of physical distribution is to decrease costs while increasing customer service. Order processing, the first stage in a physical distribution system, is the receipt and transmission of sales order information. Materials handling, or the physical handling of products, is an important element of physical distribution: packaging, loading, movement and labelling systems must be coordinated to maximize cost reduction and the meeting of customer requirements. Warehousing involves the design and operation of facilities for storing and moving goods. The objective of inventory management is to minimize inventory costs while maintaining a supply of goods adequate for customers' needs. Transportation adds time and place utility to a product by moving it from where it is made to where it is purchased and then to where it is used. Physical distribution activities should be integrated with marketing channel decisions and adjusted to meet the unique needs of a channel member customer or facilitator.

Multi-channel changes the rules

How did you purchase your last smartphone? From inside a Vodafone or O2 store? A few years ago, this is how most consumers would have selected and acquired their mobile phone upgrade. Then 'home shopping' kicked in. Teleselling and then the web enabled an increasing number of consumers to browse selections, read reviews and compare tariffs from the comfort of their homes, receiving their new phone at home in the post. Today's mobile marketing world has further broadened this freedom, so that we are able to select a brand and model while sitting on a train, waiting for friends at a bar or during the break of a sports fixture.

While for consumers, new ways of acquiring information, interacting with sellers and purchasing products have been most welcome, opening up an 'anytime/anywhere' purchasing culture, this change of buying behaviour has presented significant challenges for those businesses supplying consumers' needs and for the managers tasked with delivering our products.

In the original business model, Samsung or HTC had to ensure products were distributed in a timely fashion to the major retailers' or mobile phone companies' central warehouses, letting these companies manage distribution out to their stores and thereby to consumers. Some companies also employed rack jobbers to visit stores directly to stock shelves and store rooms with their handsets. The growth of eCommerce forced the manufacturers and big mobile phone networks to adopt multi-channel distribution, with home delivery now accounting for more than half of units shipped. Of course, the mobile phone sector is not alone in this growth of home delivery and direct distribution, which has proved good news for TNT, UPS, Royal Mail and other delivery firms. The change in consumers' buying behaviour also enabled non-store competitors to emerge, without an expensive store network and instead with single channels of distribution direct to the purchaser's selected address, be it home or workplace.

This growth of mobile commerce has not only impacted on the channels of distribution, warehousing, inventory management, delivery modes and all aspects of logistics management, but it has altered the mix of third party suppliers and partner companies rely on in order to do business. Digital selling depends on skills of content providers, social media experts, bloggers and tweeters and a whole set of opinion formers and influencers. In addition to the physical distribution management players relevant to more traditional channels of distribution, the adoption of a direct channel, digital marketing and direct distribution has necessitated the involvement of a new generation of channel members and facilitating bodies.

Multi-channel marketing is now the norm for many manufacturers, brands and retailers, with significant consequences for their channel management and use of third parties to facilitate effective delivery to end-users. Marketers may not be tasked with executing distribution of their products, but they should be aware of the consequences of their channel selection strategies and appreciate the practicalities of managing customers' experiences via the channels they select.

Chapter 15 of *Marketing: Concepts and Strategies* addresses wholesalers' and distributors' activities within a marketing channel, the nature of retailing, plus the importance of physical distribution management. Wholesaling is viewed here as *all* exchanges among organizations and individuals in marketing channels, except transactions with ultimate consumers. After examining the role of wholesaling and the major types, the chapter overviews retailing and then turns to physical distribution, its concepts, objectives and techniques: primarily order processing, materials handling, warehousing, inventory management and transportation.

The nature and importance of wholesaling

Wholesaling
Intermediaries' activity in the marketing channel between producers and business customers to facilitate the exchange – buying and selling of goods.

Wholesaling comprises all transactions in which the purchaser intends to use the product for resale, for making other products or for general business operations. It does not include exchanges with ultimate consumers. Wholesaling establishments are engaged primarily in selling products directly to industrial, reseller (such as retailers), government and institutional users. This is a broader definition than that applied by the retail trade for cash and carry wholesale suppliers.

The term **wholesaling** is used in its broadest sense: intermediaries' activity in the marketing channel between producers and business customers to facilitate the exchange – buying and selling of goods. A **wholesaler** is an individual or business engaged in facilitating and expediting exchanges that are primarily wholesale transactions. Only occasionally does a wholesaler engage in retail transactions, which are sales to ultimate consumers. A related topic is that of **supply chain management**, which is the orchestration of the channel of distribution from sourcing supplies, manufacture to delivery to the customer often with the intention of creating long-term mutually beneficial relationships. Although not part of marketing's remit, those responsible for a business's logistics often focus on the concept of supply chain management. Effective supply chain management is essential if consumer expectations are to be met.

Wholesaler
An individual or business engaged in facilitating and expediting exchanges that are primarily wholesale transactions.

Supply chain management
The orchestration of the channel of distribution from sourcing supplies, manufacture to delivery to the customer.

The activities of wholesalers

In the USA and in Europe more than 50 per cent of all products are exchanged, or their exchange is negotiated, through wholesaling institutions. The strength of wholesaling third parties varies, depending on the market, country and degree of direct commerce.

TABLE 15.1   Major wholesaling activities

Activity	Description
Supply chain management	Creating long-term partnerships among channel members
Wholesale management	Planning, organizing, staffing and controlling wholesaling operations
Negotiating with suppliers	Serving as the purchasing agent for customers by negotiating supplies
Promotion	Providing a salesforce, advertising, sales promotion, publicity and other promotional mix activity
Warehousing and product handling	Receiving, storing and stock-keeping, order processing, packaging, shipping outgoing orders and materials handling
Transport	Arranging and making local and long-distance shipments
Inventory control and data processing	Controlling physical inventory, book-keeping, recording transactions, keeping records for financial analysis
Security	Safeguarding merchandise
Pricing	Developing prices and providing price quotations
Financing and budgeting	Extending credit, borrowing, making capital investments and forecasting cash flow
Management and marketing assistance to clients	Supplying information about markets and products and providing advisory services to assist customers in their sales efforts

However, it is important to remember that the distribution of all goods requires wholesaling activities, whether or not a wholesaling institution is involved. Table 15.1 lists the major activities wholesalers perform. The activities are not mutually exclusive; individual wholesalers may perform more or fewer activities than Table 15.1 shows. Wholesalers provide marketing activities for organizations above and below them in the marketing channel.

Services for producers

Producers, above wholesalers in the marketing channel, have a distinct advantage when they use wholesalers. Wholesalers perform specialized accumulation and allocation functions for a number of products, thus allowing producers to concentrate on developing and manufacturing products that match business customers' or consumers' wants. Wholesalers provide services to producers as well. By selling a manufacturer's products to retailers and other customers, and by initiating sales contacts with the manufacturer, wholesalers serve as an extension of the producer's salesforce. Wholesalers also provide four forms of financial assistance:

1. they often pay the costs of transporting goods
2. they reduce a producer's warehousing expenses and inventory investment by holding goods in inventory
3. they extend credit and assume the losses from buyers who turn out to be poor credit risks
4. when they buy a producer's entire output and pay promptly or in cash, they are a source of working capital.

In addition, wholesalers are conduits for information and market insights within the marketing channel, keeping manufacturers up-to-date on market developments and passing along the manufacturers' promotional plans to other middlemen in the channel.

Ideally, many producers would like more direct interaction with retailers, as close contact with major retail chains may lead to greater shelf-space allocation and higher margins for a producer's goods, there being no middlemen to take a cut. Wholesalers, however, often have close contact with retailers because of their strategic position in the marketing channel. Besides, even though a producer's own salesforce is probably more effective in its selling efforts, the costs of maintaining a salesforce and performing the activities normally carried out by wholesalers are usually higher than the benefits received from better selling. Wholesalers can also spread their costs over many more products than most producers, resulting in lower costs per product unit. For these reasons, many producers have chosen to control promotion and influence the pricing of products, and have shifted transport, warehousing and financing functions to wholesalers. It must be remembered that the close relationship in the UK, Benelux, France and Germany between manufacturers and the large retail groups is not typical of all of Europe, where wholesalers tend to act as the manufacturer–retailer interface, particularly in southern, central and eastern Europe.

Services for retailers

Wholesalers help their retailer customers select inventory (stock). In industries where obtaining supplies is important, skilled buying is essential. A wholesaler that buys is a specialist in understanding market conditions and an expert at negotiating final purchases. For example, based on its understanding of local customer needs and market conditions, a building supplies wholesaler purchases inventory ahead of season so that it can provide its retail customers with the building supplies they want when they want them.[1] A retailer's buyer can thus avoid the responsibility of looking for and coordinating supply sources. Moreover, if the wholesaler makes purchases for several different buyers, expenses can be shared by all customers. A manufacturer's sales team can offer retailers only a few products at a time, but independent wholesalers or dealers have a wide range of products always available, often from a variety of producers.

By buying in large quantities and delivering to customers in smaller lots, a wholesaler can perform physical distribution activities – such as transport, materials handling, stock planning, communication and warehousing – more efficiently and can provide more service than a producer or retailer would be able to do with its own physical distribution system. Furthermore, wholesalers can provide quick and frequent delivery even when demand fluctuates. They are experienced in providing fast delivery at low cost, thus allowing the producer and the wholesalers' customers to avoid the risks associated with holding large product inventories.[2]

Since they carry products for many customers, wholesalers can maintain a wide product line at a relatively low cost. Often wholesalers can perform storage and warehousing activities more efficiently, permitting retailers to concentrate on other marketing activities. When wholesalers provide storage and warehousing, they generally take on the ownership function as well; an arrangement that frees retailers' and producers' capital for other purposes.

Wholesalers are very important in reaching global markets. Approximately 85 per cent of all prescription medicines sold in Europe go through wholesalers that are within national borders. In the future, it is anticipated that more wholesalers will operate across borders.

Classifying wholesalers

Many types of wholesaler meet the different needs of producers and retailers. In addition, new institutions and establishments develop in response to producers and retail organizations that want to take over wholesaling functions. Wholesalers adjust their activities as the forces of the marketing environment change.

Wholesalers are classified along several dimensions. Whether a wholesaler is owned by the producer – often termed a company-owned dealership – influences how it is classified. Wholesalers are also grouped according to whether they take title to (actually own) the products they handle. The range of services provided is another criterion used for classification. Finally, wholesalers

Merchant wholesalers
Wholesalers that take title to goods and assume the risks associated with ownership.

Full service wholesalers
Middlemen who offer the widest possible range of wholesaling functions.

Limited service wholesalers
Middlemen who provide only some marketing services and specialize in a few functions.

General merchandise wholesalers
Middlemen who carry a wide product mix but offer limited depth within the product lines.

are classified according to the breadth and depth of their product lines. Using these dimensions, this section discusses three general categories or types of wholesaling establishment:

1. merchant wholesalers
2. agents and brokers
3. manufacturers' sales branches and offices.

Remember that the term 'wholesaling' is used here in its broader context: intermediaries' activity in the marketing channel between producers and business-to-business customers.

Merchant wholesalers

Merchant wholesalers (see Figure 15.1) take title to goods and assume the risks associated with ownership. They are independently-owned businesses, buying and reselling products to business or retailer customers. Some are involved with packaging and developing their own-label brands for their retailer customers. Industrial product merchant wholesalers tend to be better established and earn higher profits than consumer goods wholesalers and are likely to have selective distribution arrangements with manufacturers. These wholesalers enable producers to service customers if they have inadequate resources to sell directly. Wholesalers provide the producer with market coverage, making sales contacts, storing stock, handling orders, collecting marketing intelligence and providing customer service.[3] Merchant wholesalers are referred to by various names: wholesaler, jobber, distributor, assembler, exporter and importer. They fall into two categories: full service or limited service.

Full service merchant   **Full service wholesalers** are middlemen who offer the widest possible range of wholesaling functions. Their business customers rely on them for product availability, suitable assortments, bulk breaking of larger quantities into smaller orders, financial

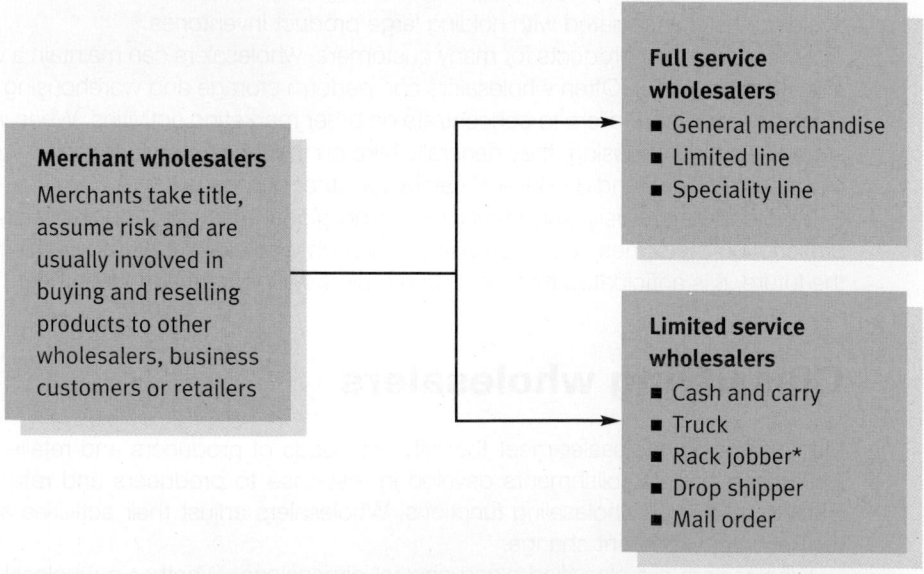

FIGURE 15.1
Types of merchant wholesaler

*Rack jobbers, in many cases, provide such a large number of services that they can be classified as full service, speciality line wholesalers

Distributors
Companies that buy and sell on their own account but tend to deal in the goods of only certain specified manufacturers.

Limited line wholesalers
Wholesalers that carry only a few product lines but offer an extensive assortment of products within those lines.

Speciality line wholesalers
Middlemen who carry the narrowest range of products, usually a single product line or a few items within a product line.

Rack jobbers
Speciality line wholesalers that own and maintain their own display racks in supermarkets and chemists.

Cash and carry wholesalers
Middlemen whose customers will pay cash and provide transport.

Truck wholesalers
Limited service wholesalers that transport products direct to customers for inspection and selection.

Drop shippers
Intermediaries who take title to goods and negotiate sales but never actually take possession of products.

assistance and credit lines, technical advice and after-sales service. Full service wholesalers often provide their immediate customers with marketing support. Grocery wholesalers help smaller retailers with store design and layout, site selection, personnel training, financing, merchandizing, advertising, coupon redemption and scanning. Gross margins are high, but so are operating expenses.

Limited service merchant wholesalers Limited service wholesalers provide only some marketing services and specialize in few functions. The other functions are provided by producers, other middlemen or even by customers. Limited service merchant wholesalers take title to merchandise, but often do not deliver the merchandise, grant credit, provide marketing intelligence, carry stocks or plan ahead for customers' future needs. They earn smaller profit margins than full service merchant wholesalers. Relatively few in number, these wholesalers are important for speciality foods, perishable items, construction supplies and fuels.

Table 15.2 summarizes the different categories of full service and limited service merchant wholesalers: **general merchandise wholesalers**, including **distributors**, **limited line wholesalers**, **speciality line wholesalers**, plus: **rack jobbers**; **cash and carry wholesalers**; **truck wholesalers**; **drop shippers**; and **mail order wholesalers**.

Agents and brokers

Agents and brokers (see Figure 15.2) negotiate purchases and expedite sales but do not take title to products. They are **functional middlemen**; intermediaries who perform a limited number of marketing activities in exchange for a commission, which is generally based on the products' selling price. Agents are middlemen who represent buyers or sellers on a permanent basis. Brokers are usually middlemen whom either buyers or sellers employ temporarily.

Although agents and brokers perform even fewer functions than limited service wholesalers, they are usually specialists in particular products or types of customer, and can provide valuable sales expertise. They know their markets well and often form long-lasting associations with customers. Agents and brokers enable manufacturers to expand sales when resources are limited, to benefit from the services of a trained sales force and to hold down personal selling costs. However, despite the advantages they offer, agents and brokers face increased competition from merchant wholesalers, manufacturers' sales branches and offices, and direct sales efforts, including the growing use of the internet.

This section concentrates on three types of agent:

1. manufacturers' agents
2. selling agents
3. commission merchants

as well as examining the brokers' role in bringing about exchanges between buyers and sellers. Table 15.3 summarizes services provided by wholesalers including limited service merchant wholesalers, agents and brokers.

Agents Manufacturers' agents – who account for over half of all agent wholesalers – are independent middlemen or distributors who represent two or more sellers and usually offer customers complete product lines. They sell and take orders year round, much as a manufacturer's sales office does. Restricted to a particular territory, a manufacturer's agent handles non-competing and complementary products. The relationship between the agent and each manufacturer is governed by written agreements explicitly outlining territories, selling price, order handling and terms of sale relating to delivery,

TABLE 15.2 Types of full and limited service merchant wholesalers

Categories of full service merchant wholesalers	Categories of limited service merchant wholesalers
1. General merchandise wholesalers Middlemen who carry a wide product mix but offer limited depth within product lines. Medicines, hardware, non-perishable foods, cosmetics, detergents, tobacco. Develop strong, mutually beneficial relationships with local retail stores, who often buy all their needs from these wholesalers. For industrial customers, these wholesalers provide all supplies and accessories and are often called *industrial distributors* or *mill supply houses*. Distributors are companies which buy and sell on their own account but tend to deal in the goods of only certain specified manufacturers.	**1. Cash and carry wholesalers** Their customers are retailers or small industrial businesses who provide their own transport and collect from wholesale depots. Some full service wholesalers also set up cash and carry depots in order to reduce their operating costs and boost margins when supplying smaller retailer or business customers. Cash and carry middlemen generally handle a limited line of products with a high turnover rate, such as groceries, building materials, electrical supplies, office supplies. For example, Booker has a network of cash and carry warehouse depots stocking fresh and frozen foods, cigarettes, wines and spirits, meats and provisions. Selling only to the trade, Booker offers bulk discounts to hotels, restaurants, the catering industry and local small shops. Cash and carry operators have little or no expenditures for outside sales staff, marketing, research, promotion, credit or delivery. Their business customers benefit from lower prices and immediate access to products.
2. Limited line wholesalers Wholesalers that carry only a few product lines, such as groceries, lighting fixtures, drilling equipment, construction equipment, but offer an extensive assortment of products within these lines. They provide similar services to general merchandise wholesalers. In business markets, they serve large geographic areas and provide technical expertise. In consumer goods markets, they often supply single or limited line retailers. Some computer limited line wholesalers provide customers with the products of only four or five manufacturers, but for only a limited number of their lines.	**2. Truck wholesalers** These wholesalers, sometimes called *truck jobbers*, transport a limited line of products directly to customers for on-the-spot inspection and selection. Often small operators who own and drive their own trucks or vans, they tend to have regular routes, calling on retailers and businesses to determine their needs. They may carry items, such as perishables, which other wholesalers do not stock. Meat, service station supplies and tobacco lines are often carried by truck jobbers. Truck jobbers sell, promote and transport goods, but tend to be classified as limited service merchant wholesalers because they do not provide credit lines. Low volume sales and relatively high levels of customer service result in high operating costs. In eastern and southern Europe, truck jobbers are common marketing channel intermediaries.
3. Speciality line wholesalers These middlemen carry the narrowest range of products, often only a single product line or a few items within a product line. Shellfish, fruit or cheese wholesalers are speciality line wholesalers. They understand the particular requirements of the ultimate buyer and offer their customers detailed product knowledge and depth of choice. To assist retailers, they may set up displays and arrange merchandise. In industrial markets, they are often better placed than the manufacturer to offer customers technical advice and service. *Rack jobbers* are speciality line wholesalers who own and maintain their display racks in supermarkets and pharmacies. They specialize in non-food items, notably branded, widely advertised products sold on a self-service basis, which retailers prefer not to order or stock themselves because of inconvenience or risk. Health and beauty aids, toys, books, magazines, games, DVDs, hardware, housewares and stationery are typical products handled by rack jobbers. They send out delivery personnel who set up displays, mark merchandise, stock shelves and keep billing records. The retailer customer only has to provide the space. Most rack jobbers operate on a pay and display basis, taking back any unsold stock from the retailer.	**3. Drop shippers** These intermediaries, also known as *desk jobbers*, take title to goods and negotiate sales, but never take actual possession of products. They forward orders from retailers, industrial buyers or other wholesalers to manufacturers and arrange for large shipments of items to be delivered directly from producers to customers. The drop shipper assumes responsibility for products during the entire transaction, including the costs of any unsold goods. Drop shippers are involved most commonly in the large volume purchases of bulky goods such as coal, coke, oil, chemicals, timber and building materials. Normally sold in wagon loads, these products are expensive to handle and ship relative to their unit value, so it is sensible to minimize unloading. One facet of drop shipping is its use by the large supermarket retailers, direct from manufacturers to the larger supermarket stores. These large supermarkets can each sell an entire lorry load of certain produce. Drop shippers incur no stockholding costs and provide only minimal customer assistance, leading to low operating costs which can be passed on to customers. They do provide planning, credit and personal selling services. **4. Mail order wholesalers** These wholesalers use catalogues/web sites instead of sales forces to sell to retail, institutional and industrial buyers. Customers use telecommunications, the internet or post to send orders which are often despatched through courier companies or the postal service. This enables customers in remote, inaccessible areas to be serviced. As explained in Chapter 18, mail order in general is growing, and is particularly important for cosmetics, speciality foods, hardware, sporting goods, business and office supplies, car parts, clothing and music. Payment is usually expected upfront by cash or credit card, but discounts may be offered for bulk orders. Mail order wholesalers hold stocks but provide little other service.

Sources: Louis W. Stern, Barton A. Weitz, 'The revolution in distribution: challenges and opportunities' (Special Issue: The Revolution in Retailing), *Long Range Planning*, December 1997, 30 (6), pp. 823–9; Leonard J. Kistner, C. Anthony Di Benedetto, Sriraman Bhoovaraghavan, 'An integrated approach to the development of channel strategy', *Industrial Marketing Management*, October 1994, 23 (4), pp. 315–22; Elizabeth Jane Moore, 'Grocery distribution in the UK: recent changes and future prospects', *International Journal of Retail & Distribution Management*, 19 July 1991, pp. 18–24; 'Drop-shipping grows to save depot costs', *Supermarket News*, 1 April 1985, pp. 1, 17.

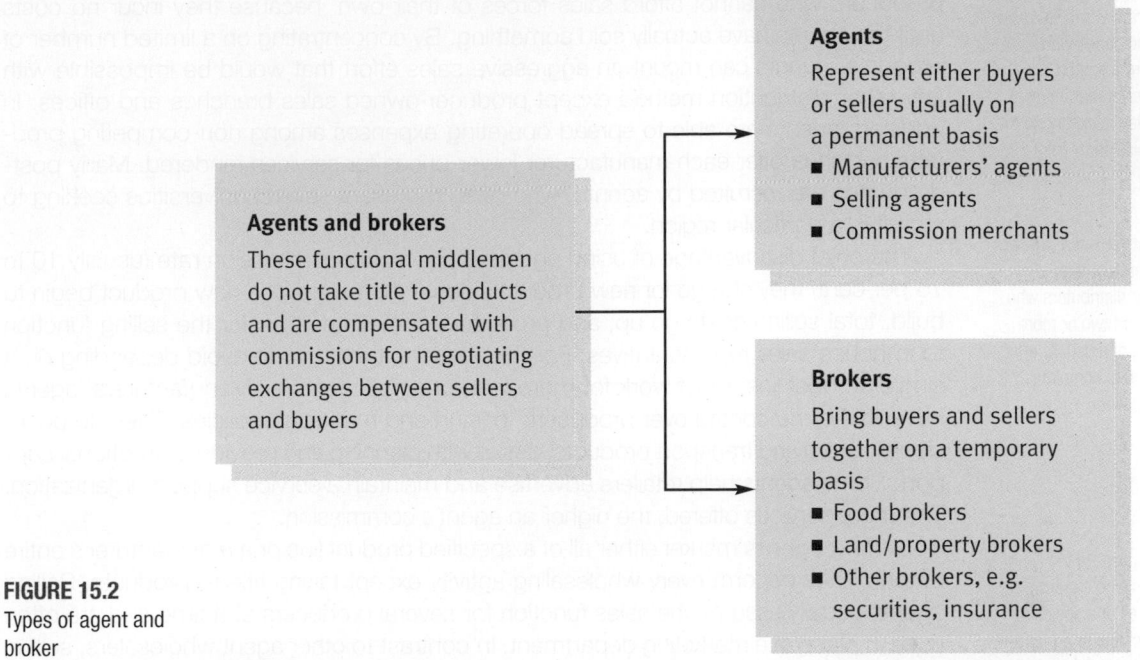

FIGURE 15.2
Types of agent and broker

TABLE 15.3   Services provided by wholesalers

a. Various services provided by limited service merchant wholesalers	Cash and carry	Truck wholesaler[a]	Drop shipper[b]	Mail order
Physical possession of merchandise	Yes	Yes	No	Yes
Personal sales calls on customers	No	Yes	No	No
Information about market conditions	No	Yes	Yes	Yes
Advice to customers	No	Yes	Yes	No
Stocking and maintenance of merchandise in customers' stores	No	Yes	No	No
Credit to customers	No	No	Yes	Some
Delivery of merchandise to customers	No	Yes	No	No

b. Various services agents and brokers provide	Brokers	Manufacturers' agents	Selling agents	Commission merchants
Physical possession of merchandise	No	Some	No	Yes
Long-term relationship with buyers or sellers	No	Yes	Yes	Yes
Representation of competing product lines	Yes	No	No	Yes
Limited geographic territory	No	Yes	No	No
Credit to customers	No	No	Yes	Some
Delivery of merchandise to customers	No	Some	Yes	Yes

[a]Also called truck jobber.
[b]Also called desk jobber.

Mail order wholesalers
Wholesalers that use catalogues instead of sales forces to sell products to retail, industrial and institutional buyers.

service and warranties. Manufacturers' agents are commonly used in the sale of clothing and accessories, machinery and equipment, iron, steel, furniture, automotive products, electrical goods and certain food items.

Although most manufacturers' agents run small enterprises, their employees are professional, highly skilled sales people. The agents' major advantages, in fact, are their wide range of contacts and strong customer relationships. These intermediaries help large producers minimize the costs of developing new sales territories and adjust sales strategies for different products in different locations. Agents are also useful to small

Functional middlemen
Intermediaries who perform a limited number of marketing activities in exchange for commission.

Manufacturers' agents
Independent middlemen or distributors who represent two or more sellers, and usually offer customers complete product lines.

Selling agents
Agents who market either all of a specified product line or a manufacturer's entire output.

Commission merchants
Agents who receive goods on consignment from local sellers and negotiate sales in large central markets.

producers who cannot afford sales forces of their own, because they incur no costs until the agents have actually sold something. By concentrating on a limited number of products, agents can mount an aggressive sales effort that would be impossible with any other distribution method except producer-owned sales branches and offices. In addition, agents are able to spread operating expenses among non-competing products and thus offer each manufacturer lower prices for services rendered. Many postgraduates are recruited by agents, who often represent several universities seeking to recruit in a particular region.

The chief disadvantage of using agents is the higher commission rate (usually 10 to 15 per cent) they charge for new product sales. When sales of a new product begin to build, total selling costs go up, and producers sometimes transfer the selling function to in-house sales representatives. For this reason, agents try to avoid depending on a single product line; most work for more than one manufacturer. Manufacturers' agents have little or no control over producers' pricing and marketing policies. They do occasionally store and transport products, assist with planning and provide promotional support. Some agents help retailers advertise and maintain a service support organization. The more services offered, the higher an agent's commission.

Selling agents market either all of a specified product line or a manufacturer's entire output. They perform every wholesaling activity except taking title to products. Selling agents usually assume the sales function for several producers at a time and are often used in place of a marketing department. In contrast to other agent wholesalers, selling agents generally have no territorial limits, and have complete authority over prices, promotion and distribution. They play a key role in the advertising, marketing research and credit policies of the sellers they represent, at times even advising on product development and packaging.

Selling agents, who account for about 1 per cent of the wholesale trade, are used most often by small producers or by manufacturers who find it difficult to maintain a marketing department because of seasonal production or other factors. A producer having financial problems may also engage a selling agent. By so doing, the producer relinquishes some control of the business but may gain working capital by avoiding immediate marketing costs. To avoid conflicts of interest, selling agents represent non-competing product lines. The agents play an important part in the distribution of textiles, and they also sometimes handle canned foods, household furnishings, clothing, timber and metal products. In these industries, competitive pressures increase the importance of marketing relative to production, and the selling agent is a source of essential marketing and financial expertise.

Commission merchants are agents who receive goods on consignment from local sellers and negotiate sales in large central markets. Most often found in agricultural marketing, commission merchants take possession of commodities in lorry loads, arrange for any necessary grading or storage, and transport the commodities to auction or markets where they are sold. When sales have been completed, an agent deducts a commission plus the expense of making the sale and then turns over the profits to the producer.

Sometimes called factor merchants, these agents may have broad powers regarding prices and terms of sale, and they specialize in obtaining the best price possible under market conditions. Commission merchants offer planning assistance and sometimes extend credit, but they do not usually provide promotional support. As commission merchants deal in large volumes, their per unit costs are usually low. Their services are most useful to small producers who must get products to buyers but choose not to field a sales force or accompany the goods to market themselves. In addition to farm products, commission merchants may handle textiles, art, furniture, or seafood products. Businesses including farms that use commission merchants have little control over pricing, although the seller can specify a minimum price. Generally, the seller is able to supervise the agent's actions through a check of the commodity prices published regularly in newspapers. Large producers, however, need to maintain closer contact with the market and so have limited need for commission merchants.

Brokers   Brokers seek out buyers or sellers and help negotiate exchanges. In other words, brokers' primary purpose is to bring buyers and sellers together. Thus, brokers perform fewer functions than other intermediaries. They are not involved in financing or physical possession, have no authority to set prices and assume almost no risks. Instead, they offer their customers specialized knowledge of a particular commodity and a network of established contacts.

Brokers are especially useful to sellers of certain types of product who market those products only occasionally. Sellers of used machinery, seasonal food products, financial securities and land/property may not know of potential buyers. A broker can furnish them with this information. The party who engages the broker's services – usually the seller – pays the broker's commission when the transaction is completed. Many consumers these days deal with insurance brokers when insuring a car or house contents, or with a mortgage broker when buying a house or moving.

Food brokers
Intermediaries who sell food and general merchandise items to retailer-owned and merchant wholesalers, grocery chains, industrial buyers and food processors.

Food brokers, the most common type of broker, are intermediaries who sell food and general merchandise items to retailer-owned and merchant wholesalers, grocery chains, industrial buyers and food processors. Food brokers enable buyers and sellers to adjust to fluctuating market conditions. They also aid in grading, negotiating and inspecting foods, and in some cases they store and deliver products. Due to the seasonal nature of food production, the association between broker and producer is temporary though many mutually beneficial broker-producer relationships are resumed year after year. As food brokers provide a range of services on a somewhat permanent basis and in specific geographic territories, they can more accurately be described as manufacturers' agents.

Manufacturers' sales branches and offices

Sales branches
Manufacturer-owned middlemen selling products and providing support services to the manufacturer's sales force, especially in locations where large customers are concentrated and demand is high.

Sometimes called manufacturers' wholesalers or dealerships, manufacturers' sales branches and offices resemble merchant wholesalers' operations. These producer-owned middlemen account for about 9 per cent of wholesale establishments and generate approximately a third (31 per cent) of all wholesale sales.[4] **Sales branches** are manufacturer-owned middlemen selling products and providing support services to the manufacturer's sales force, especially in locations where large customers are concentrated and demand is high. They offer credit, deliver goods, give promotional assistance and furnish other services. In many cases they carry inventory, although this practice often duplicates the functions of other channel members and is now declining. Customers include retailers, business buyers and other wholesalers. Branch operations are common in the electrical supplies, plumbing, timber and car parts industries.

Sales offices
Manufacturer-owned operations that provide support services normally associated with agents.

Sales offices are manufacturer-owned operations that provide support services that are normally associated with agents. Like sales branches, they are located away from manufacturing plants, but unlike branches, they carry no inventory. A manufacturer's sales offices or branches may sell products that enhance the manufacturer's own product line. For example, Hiram Walker, a distiller, imports wine from Spain to increase the number of products its sales offices can offer wholesalers. Most large manufacturers have their own networks of sales branches and sales offices.

Manufacturers may set up sales branches or sales offices so that they can reach customers more effectively by performing wholesaling functions themselves. A manufacturer may also set up these branches or offices when the required specialist wholesaling services are not available through existing middlemen. In some situations, however, a manufacturer may bypass its wholesaling organization entirely, if the producer decides to serve large retailer customers or even consumers directly. One major distiller bottles own-label spirits for a UK grocery chain and separates this operation completely from the company's sales office, which serves other retailers.

Coca-Cola seeks more control over distribution channels

Building customer relationships

Coca-Cola depends on partners, agents, stockists and the efforts of its own sales offices to achieve growth, as much as the company requires a desirable product and strong brand able to attract consumers. Can Coca-Cola double its global revenue to $200 billion by 2020? That is one major goal of the Atlanta-beverage company's long-term *Vision 2020* plan for super-charging future growth. Another goal is to be selling 3 billion servings of its soft drinks every day by 2020, counting purchases in stores, restaurants, vending machines and every other outlet where its beverages are available. Currently the company sells 1.9 billion daily servings of its beverages and has sales of $47 billion.

To achieve these ambitious targets and compete with both local brands and multinational rivals such as PepsiCo, Coca-Cola is working with bottlers, agent distributors, and retail accounts to get its 500-plus beverage brands to customers worldwide. Twenty of its brands each achieve annual sales of over a billion dollars, including Fanta, Sprite, Powerade, Schweppes, Aquarius, Minute Maid, Dasani, Fuze Tea and, of course, Coca-Cola. More than 75 per cent of its revenue comes from non-US sales, which is why the company is expanding distribution in international markets and making its brands more visible to customers when and where they want to buy.

For example, Coca-Cola has its eye on the fast-growing market in India, where ready-to-drink beverages are becoming more popular. Getting its products into more stores, restaurants, bakeries and other outlets is only the beginning. The company arranges for branded cooling units to be prominently positioned where customers can see and reach them. It also provides colourful signs to build demand at the point of purchase. These are only a few of the supports it provides to its stockists, working closely with its locally based bottlers and distributors.

In China, Coca-Cola's bright red vending machines are now commonplace in urban centres, which is one reason that the nation's average annual per capita consumption of its beverages has reached 28 bottles. To support higher sales, Coca-Cola has joint ventures with several Chinese enterprises, to build new production facilities, open more warehouses, identify more stockists, expand the delivery fleet, and computerize routes for higher efficiency. Without third party assistance, in the form of local partners, distribution agents and retail stockists, Coca-Cola could not achieve its growth projections.

Sources: Bill Pride and O.C. Ferrell, *Marketing*, Cengage South-Western, 2012; Coca-Cola, 2015; www.coca-cola.co.uk/packages/history/our-story-2000-to-now-living-positively-125-years-on, April 2015; www.coca-colacompany.com/our-company/infographic-coca-cola-at-a-glance, April 2015.

Facilitating agencies

Facilitating agencies
Organizations such as transport companies, insurance companies, advertising agencies, marketing research agencies and financial institutions that perform activities that enhance channel functions.

The total marketing channel is more than a chain linking the producer, intermediary and buyer. **Facilitating agencies** – transport companies, insurance companies, advertising agencies, marketing research agencies and financial institutions – may perform activities that enhance channel functions. Note, however, that any of the functions these facilitating agencies perform may be taken over by the regular marketing intermediaries in the marketing channel.

The basic difference between channel members and facilitating agencies is that channel members perform the negotiating functions (buying, selling and taking title), whereas facilitating agencies do not: they perform only the various tasks that are detailed below.[5] In other words, facilitating agencies assist in the operation of the channel, but they do not sell products. The channel manager may view the facilitating agency as a subcontractor to which various distribution tasks can be farmed out according to the principle of specialization and division of labour.[6]

Channel members (producers, wholesalers, distributors or retailers) may rely on facilitating agencies because they believe that these independent businesses will perform various activities more efficiently and more effectively than they themselves could. Facilitating agencies are functional specialists that perform special tasks for channel members without getting involved in directing or controlling channel decisions. Public warehouses, finance companies, transport companies, trade shows and trade markets are facilitating agencies that expedite the flow of products through marketing channels.

Public warehouses

Public warehouses
Storage facilities available for a fee.

Public warehouses are storage facilities available for a fee. Producers, wholesalers and retailers may rent space in a warehouse instead of constructing their own facilities or using a merchant wholesaler's storage services. Many warehouses also order, deliver, collect accounts and maintain display rooms where potential buyers can inspect products.

To use goods as collateral for a loan, a channel member may place products in a bonded warehouse. If it is too impractical or expensive to transfer goods physically, the channel member may arrange for a public warehouser to verify that goods are in the channel member's own facilities and then issue receipts for lenders.[7] Under this arrangement, the channel member retains possession of the products but the warehouser has control. Many field public warehousers know where their clients can borrow working capital and are sometimes able to arrange low-cost loans.

Finance companies

Wholesalers and retailers may be able to obtain financing by transferring ownership of products to a sales finance company or bank while retaining physical possession of the goods. Often called 'floor planning', this form of financing enables wholesalers and retailers – especially car and electrical appliance dealers – to offer a greater selection of products for customers and thus increase sales. Loans may be due immediately upon sale, so products financed this way are usually well known, sell relatively easily and present little risk.

Other financing functions are performed by factors – organizations that provide clients with working capital by buying their accounts receivable or by lending money, using the accounts receivable as collateral. Most factors minimize their own risks by specializing in particular industries, in order to better evaluate individual channel members within those industries. Factors usually lend money for a longer time than banks. They may help clients improve their credit and collection policies, and may also provide management expertise.

Transport companies

Rail, road, air and other carriers are facilitating agencies that help manufacturers and retailers transport products. Each form of transport has its own advantages. Railways ship large volumes of bulky goods at low cost; in fact, outside the UK, a 'unit train' is the cheapest form of overland

FIGURE 15.3
Many consumer durables and food lines depend on sea freight to reach their intended markets

transport for ore, grain or other commodities. Air transport is relatively expensive but is often preferred for shipping high-value or perishable goods. Trucks, which usually carry short-haul, high-value goods, now carry more and more products because factories are moving closer to their markets. As a result of technological advances, pipelines now transport powdered solids and fluidized solid materials, as well as petroleum and natural gas.

Transport companies sometimes take over the functions of other middlemen. Due to the ease and speed of using air transport for certain types of product, parcel express companies can eliminate the need for their clients to maintain large stocks and branch warehouses. In other cases, freight forwarders perform accumulation functions by combining less than full shipments into full loads and passing on the savings to customers perhaps charging a wagon rate rather than a less-than-wagon rate.

Trade shows and trade markets

Trade shows
Industry exhibitions that offer both selling and non-selling benefits.

Trade shows and trade markets enable manufacturers or wholesalers to exhibit products to potential buyers, and so help the selling and buying functions. **Trade shows** are industry exhibitions that offer both selling and non-selling benefits.[8] On the selling side, trade shows let vendors identify prospects; gain access to key decision-makers; disseminate facts about their products, services and personnel; and actually sell products and service current accounts through contacts at the show.[9] Trade shows also allow a company to reach potential buyers who have not been approached through regular selling efforts. In fact, many trade show visitors have not recently been contacted by a sales representative of any company within the past year. Many of these individuals are willing to travel several hundred miles to attend trade shows to learn about new goods and services. The non-selling benefits include opportunities to maintain the company image with competitors, customers and the industry; gather information about competitors' products and prices; and identify potential channel members.[10] Trade shows have a positive influence on other important marketing variables, such as maintaining or enhancing company morale, product testing and product evaluation.

Trade shows can permit direct buyer–seller interaction and may eliminate the need for agents. Companies exhibit at trade shows because of the high concentration of prospective buyers for their products. Studies show that it takes, on average, 5.1 sales calls to close an industrial business-to-business sale but less than 1 sales call (0.8) to close a trade show lead. The explanation for the latter figure is that more than half of the customers who purchase a product based on information gained at a trade show order the product by phone or email after the show. When customers use these more impersonal methods to gather information, the need for major sales calls to provide such information can be eliminated. Most manufacturers have sales and technical personnel who attend relevant trade shows in key target market territories. Birmingham's National Exhibition Centre (NEC) offers a 240-hectare (600-acre) site, with open display areas, plus 125 000 square metres (156 000 square yards) of covered exhibition space, hotels, parking

Trade markets
Relatively permanent facilities that businesses can rent to exhibit products year round.

for thousands of cars, plus rail and air links. Each year there are toy, fashion, giftware and antique trade fairs at the NEC, when trade customers can select merchandise for their next sales seasons. **Trade markets** are relatively permanent facilities that businesses can rent to exhibit products year round. At these markets, such products as furniture, home decorating supplies, toys, clothing and gift items are sold to wholesalers and retailers.

Retailing
All transactions in which the buyer intends to consume the product through personal, family or household use.

Retailing

Retailing includes all transactions in which the buyer intends to consume the product through personal, family or household use. The buyers in retail transactions are the ultimate consumers.

Retailer
A business that purchases products for the purpose of reselling them to ultimate consumers – the general public – often from a shop or store.

A **retailer** is a business that purchases products for the purpose of reselling them to the ultimate consumers – the general public – often from a shop or store, but increasingly also online, adopting a multi-channel strategy. As the link between producers and consumers, retailers occupy an important and highly demanding position in the marketing channel. It is complicated, too: retailers sell other companies' products, yet have to devise their own product/service mixes. They devise their own target market strategies and conduct analyses of marketing opportunities. The merchandise they sell derives from producers that have undertaken their own analysis of marketing opportunities and developed their own target market strategies and brand positioning. These strategies producers and retailers have to mesh in order for all channel members to make adequate financial returns, while ultimately striving to give satisfaction to the consumer. The growth of retail own-label brands has added to the complexity, with retailers now creating their own brands, products and designs of merchandise, often retailed alongside the proprietary brands of manufacturers.

By providing assortments of products to match consumers' requirements, retailers create place, time, possession and form utilities:

- *Place utility* means moving products from wholesalers or producers to a location where consumers want to buy them.
- *Time utility* involves maintaining specific business hours to make products available when consumers want them.
- *Possession utility* means facilitating the transfer of ownership or use of a product to consumers.
- In the case of services such as hairdressing, dry cleaning, restaurants and car repairs, retailers themselves develop most of the product utilities. The services of such retailers provide aspects of *form utility* associated with the production process.

Central business district (CBD)
The traditional hub of most cities and towns; the focus for shopping, banking and commerce, and hence the busiest part of the whole area.

Retailers of services usually have more direct contact with consumers and more opportunity to alter the product in the marketing mix (see Chapter 13).

Retail locations

The traditional hub of most cities and towns is the **central business district (CBD)**, the focus for shopping, banking and commerce, and hence the busiest part of the whole area for traffic, public transport and pedestrians. Examples are London's Oxford and Regent streets, the Champs Elysées in Paris and Berlin's Kurfürstendamm.[11] The CBD is subdivided into zones: generally, retailers are clustered together in a zone; banking and insurance companies locate together; legal offices occupy neighbouring premises; municipal offices and amenities are built on adjoining plots (town hall, library, law courts, art galleries). Within the shopping zone certain streets at the centre of the zone will have the main shops and the highest levels of pedestrian footfall. In this area, known as the **prime pitch**, the key traders or magnet brands will occupy prominent sites, so generating much of the footfall. Other retailers vie to be located close to these key traders so as to benefit from the customer traffic they generate. The highest rents are therefore paid for such sites. Secondary sites are suitable for speciality retailers or discounters, which have either lower margins or lower **customer thresholds** – the number of customers required to make a profit. Figure 15.4 shows the composition of a typical central business district (CBD).

Prime pitch
The area at the centre of the shopping zone with the main shops and the highest levels of pedestrian footfall.

Customer threshold
The number of customers required to make a profit.

Historically, as urban areas expanded during the early part of the twentieth century, they joined and subsequently swallowed up neighbouring towns and villages. The shopping centres of these settlements survived to become the **suburban centres** of the now larger city or town. Where the expansion of the town was planned, suburban centres were created at major road junctions to cater for local shopping needs and reduce demands and congestion in the CBD.[12] During the 1970s, as rents in the CBD rose and sites sufficient for large, open-plan stores became harder to obtain, retailers

Suburban centres
Shopping centres created at major road junctions that cater for local shopping needs.

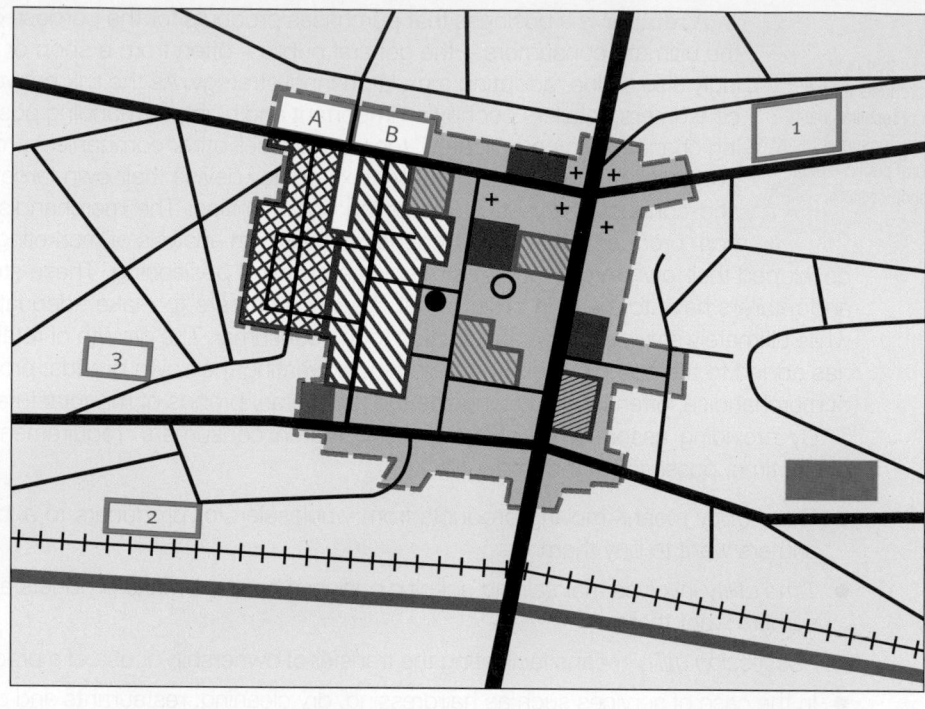

CBD legend and key below:

CBD		Banks, building societies, insurance companies		Town hall, art gallery, library (B)	
Bus station (1)		Solicitors/legal		Covered shopping centres/malls	
Railway station (2)		Central shopping area		Peak land value intersection (retail) ○	
Coach station (3)		Head Post Office		Zone in transition*	
Main road		Department stores		Peak overall land value (CBD) ●	
Minor road		Market hall		Sports stadium	
Railway +++		Law courts (A)		Cinema/theatre +	
Canal					

FIGURE 15.4

The composition of a typical central business district (CBD)

Source: Lyndon Simkin and Sally Dibb

*The zone in transition is the land use between the CBD and suburban housing areas: light manufacturing, transport termini, wholesaling, garages, medical, multi-family residences.

Edge-of-town sites
Retail locations on undeveloped land, providing purpose-built stores, parking facilities and amenities for their customers on the edge of a built-up area.

Retail parks
Groupings of freestanding superstores, forming a retail village.

looked to the green fields adjacent to outer ring roads for expansion. The superstore era had dawned, as the major grocery, carpet and furniture, electrical and DIY retailers opened free-standing retail 'sheds'. Needing more space to display stock and sell their goods than they could afford or obtain in the CBD or even suburban centre, but still requiring high traffic levels, they sought sites adjacent to major road arteries into the CBD. Relocating these stores to non-retail areas of the city, and particularly to **edge-of-town sites**, helped redistribute traffic volumes and make use of the latest infrastructure. Retailers no longer had to occupy run-down warehouses; they could acquire undeveloped land on the edge of built-up areas and provide purpose-built stores, parking facilities and amenities for their customers.[13] The progression of the out-of-town concept and relaxation of planning regulations by local authorities led to the mid-1980s initiation of **retail parks**, in which free-standing superstores, each over 2500 square metres (27 500 square feet) are grouped together to form retail villages or parks. Located close to major roads, they offer extensive free parking.

Major store types

Retail stores are often classified according to width of product mix and depth of product lines. **Department stores** are physically large – around 25 000 square metres (275 000 square feet) – and occupy prominent positions in the traditional heart of the town or city, the central shopping centre. Out-of-town shopping malls, such as Manchester's Trafford Park or Kent's Bluewater, include leading department stores as 'anchors' to attract consumers and smaller retail store tenants. Department stores are characterized by wide product mixes in considerable depth for most product lines. Within a department store, related product lines are organized into separate departments, such as cosmetics, men's and women's fashions and accessories, house wares, home furnishings, haberdashery and toys. **Variety stores** tend to be slightly smaller and are often more specialized, such as BHS, offering a reduced range of merchandise.

In a **catalogue showroom** such as Argos, one item of each product class is on display and the remaining inventory is stored out of the buyers' reach. Using catalogues that have been mailed to their homes or which are available on counters in the store, customers order the goods at their leisure. Shop assistants usually complete the order form and then collect the merchandise from the adjoining warehouse. Such showrooms tend to be in secondary town centre locations or on retail parks.

In the 1960s, grocery retailers led by Sainsbury's, Tesco and Fine Fare expanded in to 1000-square-metre (11 000-square-foot) supermarkets, either in the city centre or within suburban centres. As product ranges grew, self-service requirements called for more space; and as city centre rents rose, the age of the superstore arrived. Size requirements grew further still, and there was an exodus from the city centre. In the 1980s, the average grocery superstore grew from 2500 square metres to 5500 square metres (27 500 to 61 000 square feet) and moved away from the suburban centre either to free-standing superstore sites or out-of-town retail parks with plenty of car parking. Now they are often over 6000 square metres. **Supermarkets** and grocery **superstores** are large, self-service stores that carry a complete line of food products as well as other convenience items, such as cosmetics, non-prescription medicines and kitchenware. Some, such as ASDA or Tesco, sell clothing and electrical appliances. Grocery superstores are laid out in departments for maximum efficiency in stocking and handling products, but have central checkout facilities by the exits to the ample, free parking. **Category management** is now a core approach to merchandizing, inventory control and display in many retailers, with similar lines from several suppliers being controlled by a category manager. He or she is often an employee of one of the major suppliers to the category, giving that supplier significant power over its rivals within the particular retailer account. **Hypermarkets** take the benefits of the superstore even further, using their greater size over 9000 square metres (100 000 square feet) to give the customer a wider range and depth of products.

The move away from the city or town centre was not confined to multiple grocery retailers. Furniture, carpets and electrical appliances require large display areas, ranges with strength in depth and, if possible, one-floor shopping. The concentration of retailers in the city centre led to limited store opening opportunities – large enough sites were hard to find – and to high rents. Originally freestanding, these 2000 to 3500-square-metre (22 000 to 39 000-square-foot) stores are increasingly found in out-of-town retail parks. **Discount sheds** are cheaply constructed, one-storey retail stores with no window displays and few add-on amenities. Oriented towards car-borne shoppers, they have large, free car parks and spacious stock facilities to enable shoppers to take delivery of their purchases immediately.

Often categorized separately, **category killers** are large stores, tending to be superstore sized, that specialize in a narrow line of merchandise. They are known

Department stores
Physically large stores that occupy prominent positions in the traditional heart of the town or city, or as anchor stores in out-of-town malls.

Variety stores
Slightly smaller and more specialized stores than department stores, offering a reduced range of merchandise.

Catalogue showroom
Outlets in which one item of each product class is on display and the remaining inventory is stored out of the buyers' reach.

Supermarkets and grocery superstores
Large, self-service stores that carry a complete line of food products as well as other convenience items.

Category management
A core approach to merchandising, inventory control and display in many retailers, with similar lines from several suppliers being controlled by a category manager and managed as a discrete unit.

Hypermarkets
Stores that take the benefits of the superstore even further, using their greater size to give the customer a wider range and depth of products.

Discount sheds
Cheaply constructed, one-storey retail stores with no window displays and few add-on amenities; oriented towards car-borne shoppers.

Category killers
Large stores, tending to be superstore sized, which specialize in a narrow line of merchandise.

Warehouse clubs
Large-scale, members-only selling operations combining cash-and-carry wholesaling with discount retailing.

Speciality shops
Stores that offer self-service but a greater level of assistance from store personnel than department stores, and carry a narrow product mix with deep product lines.

Markets
Halls where fresh foods, clothing and housewares are sold, catering for budget-conscious shoppers who typically have a middle- and down-market social profile.

Convenience stores
Shops that sell essential groceries, alcoholic drinks, medicines and newspapers outside the traditional shopping hours.

as category killers – an 'Americanism' – because they have a huge selection within a narrow category of merchandise and 'kill off' the smaller stores retailing similar lines of merchandise. They require high footfall to be viable and tend to be located in large towns and cities on edge-of-town sites. The expansion of large DIY operators such as B&Q, Castorama and Homebase has led to the closure of many small, traditional hardware stores. Currys (electrical goods), Office World (office supplies) and the superstores of Sports Direct (sporting goods) are examples of category killers.

A rapidly growing form of mass merchandising, **warehouse clubs** are large-scale, members-only selling operations combining cash and carry wholesaling with discount retailing. For a nominal annual fee, small retailers can purchase products at wholesale prices for business use or for resale. Warehouse clubs also sell to ultimate consumers affiliated with credit unions, schools, hospitals and banks, but, instead of paying a membership fee, individual consumers pay about 5 per cent more on each item than do business customers.

Most shopping centres and towns have a major department store. At the other end of the spectrum is the traditional corner shop. Few small shops these days retail a variety of product groups. In suburban areas, such shops tend to specialize in retailing one convenience product category – newsagents with cigarettes and newspapers, greengrocers, chemists, hair salons and so on. In the town centre (CBD) few retailers of convenience goods, with their low margins, can afford the rents and business tax. Instead, the small store retailers – 250 square metres (2750 square feet) and under – in the CBD specialize in shopping or comparison items: clothing, footwear, computer games, CDs and DVDs, cosmetics, jewellery. **Speciality shops** offer self-service but a greater level of assistance from store personnel than department stores, and carry a narrow product mix with deep product lines. A typical 300-square-metre (3300-square-foot) footwear or clothing retail store will have window displays to entice passing pedestrians, one or two checkout points, and three or four assistants. Such stores depend on the town centre's general parking facilities and on proximity to a key trader, such as Boots or Marks & Spencer, which will generate pedestrian traffic.

In most towns there are wholesale **markets** selling meat, greengrocery, fruit, flowers and fish from which speciality retailers make their inventory purchases. Traditional, too, is the general retail market selling to the general public, either in recently refurbished Victorian market halls or in council-provided modern halls adjacent to the town centre shopping malls. Such market halls sell fresh foods, clothing and housewares, and cater for budget-conscious shoppers who typically have a middle and down-market social profile.

As the number of neighbourhood grocery stores declined in the 1960s and 1970s with the expansion of the superstore-based national grocery chains, a niche emerged in the market to be filled by **convenience stores**. These shops – also known as 'C-stores' – sell essential groceries, alcoholic drinks, medicines and newspapers outside the traditional 9.00 a.m. to 6.00 p.m. shopping hours. The major superstores extended their opening hours to 8.00 p.m. to facilitate after-work shopping, but no major retailers catered for 'emergency' or top-up shopping. There was a resurgence of the traditional corner shop located in suburban housing estates, offering limited ranges but extended opening hours. Consumers pay a slight price premium but receive convenience in terms of location and opening hours. Tesco Express is an example of retail majors targeting the growth of the C-store.

Retail villages initially sold seconds – imperfect new merchandise similar to the lines stocked in many factory shops – in converted mills or rural locations, in some instances with eight to ten shop units clustered together. Now developers are designing and building out-of-town **factory outlet villages**, such as Cheshire Oaks on Merseyside, for major manufacturers' and branded goods, with up to 20 mini-superstores grouped together. Increasingly, major manufacturers and retailers are using these stores to off-load last season's lines, excess stocks and branded seconds, or to trial new lines. These outlets are very popular for designer-label clothing, linens, crockery and homewares.

Cash and carry warehouses, such as Booker or Makro, retail extensive ranges of groceries, tobacco, alcohol, beverages and confectionery to newsagents, small supermarkets and convenience stores and the catering trade (hotels, guest houses, restaurants and cafés). By purchasing from manufacturers in bulk, cash and carry companies can offer substantial price savings to their customers, who in turn can add a retail margin without alienating their customers.

Non-store retailing

Non-store retailing is the selling of goods or services outside the confines of a retail facility. This form of retailing accounts for an increasing percentage of sales and includes personal sales methods, such as in-home retailing and telemarketing, and non-personal sales methods, such as automatic vending and mail order retailing (which includes catalogue retailing). Of course, the main source of growth for non-store sales has been the use of the internet to promote and sell goods and services; orders can be placed online using a credit card from home, office, or, increasingly, while mobile via a smartphone, as explored in Chapter 19.

Certain non-store retailing methods are in the category of **direct marketing**: the use of non-personal media, the internet or telesales to introduce products to consumers, who then purchase the products by mail, telephone or the internet. In the case of telephone orders, sales people may be required to complete the sales. Telemarketing, mail order and catalogue retailing are all examples of direct marketing, as are sales generated by coupons, direct mail and Freephone 0800 numbers and the web. This topic is revisited in Chapter 18 of *Marketing: Concepts and Strategies*.

Innovation and change

Retail technology innovations changing customer experiences

Fashion house Ted Baker has followed House of Fraser, Hawes & Curtis and Bentalls in introducing beacon-enabled mannequins. These let customers receive details about the clothes on display via their mobile. Customers using the app when in range access product information and purchase on the phone. Andy Harding, Multichannel Director at House of Fraser said, 'With such demand from mobile devices, it's important we continue to bring new technology to our stores, and believe that the *Iconeme App* provides retailers with an opportunity to really engage with their customers.'

Other changes are imminent in store. *Amelia*, which was launched at the end of 2014, is a multilingual artificial intelligence engine designed to take over about a quarter of all retail jobs within two decades. It is claimed that this new artificial intelligence will be able to consume, process and use knowledge like a human being, only without the cost of employing a human. In a scenario where a customer has a problem which *Amelia* the robot is unable to address, *Amelia* observes a human helper tackling the problem, deconstructs how the problem has been solved and next time around *Amelia* will be able to tackle the issue unaided. In retail *Amelia* could deal with phone, email or web chat queries. Computers already direct data to the right person or department and they suggest possible answers, but *Amelia* would go one step further and look to fully replace the human. Gartner has predicted that by 2017 cognitive platforms like *Amelia* will drive a 60 per cent reduction in the cost of services staff. When combined with robotics, could we see the sales assistant replaced by *Amelia* inside a robot?

In Land Rover showrooms augmented reality technology is bridging the gap between the announcement of a new model and the vehicles arriving in showrooms. The new technology delivers a life-like 3D model to showrooms. When visiting the

Land Rover retailer, customers put on the virtual reality headset and are immersed in a detailed photo-realistic 3D model of the new car. Customers will be able to walk around the vehicle to sense the size and scale of the car. When arriving at the driver's door, it will open to allow a full 360-degree view of the interior. Laura Schwab, Jaguar Land Rover UK Marketing Director said, 'This will give an exciting immersive experience, beyond that of a traditional online configurator or sales brochure.'

The challenge for retail marketers is to embrace technology which enhances customer experience, befits the brand and its personality, results in a return on investment, and which targeted consumers are ready to accept. Simply adopting new toys because they are fun, innovative, newsworthy or create excitement for the brand team must be avoided.

Sources: 'House of Fraser, Hawes & Curtis, Bentalls trial beacon-enabled mannequins', *Essential Retail*, 12 August 2014; Meet 'Amelia: the computer that's after your job', *The Telegraph*, 29 September, 2014; 'Land Rover offers augmented reality preview of new car', *Luxury Daily*, 12 December 2014; http://retail-innovation.com, April 2015.

Direct marketing
The use of non-personal media, the internet or telesales to introduce products to consumers, who then purchase the products by mail, telephone or the internet.

In-home retailing
Selling via personal contacts with consumers in their own homes.

Telemarketing
The direct selling of goods and services by telephone, based on either a cold canvass of the telephone directory or a pre-screened list of prospective clients.

Automatic vending
The use of coin- or credit-card-operated self-service machines to sell small, standardized, routinely purchased products such as chewing gum, sweets, newspapers, cigarettes, soft drinks and coffee.

In-home retailing is selling via personal contacts with consumers in their own homes. Companies such as Avon, Amway and Betterware send representatives to the homes of preselected prospects. A variation of in-home retailing is the home demonstration, or party plan, which companies such as Tupperware, Ann Summers and Mary Kay Cosmetics use successfully. One consumer acts as a host and invites a number of friends to view merchandise at his or her home, where a sales person is on hand to demonstrate the products.

Many organizations use the telephone to strengthen the effectiveness of traditional marketing methods. **Telemarketing** is the direct selling of goods and services by telephone, based on either a cold canvass of the telephone directory or a pre-screened list of prospective clients. Telemarketing can generate sales leads, improve customer service, speed up collection of overdue accounts, raise funds for not-for-profit groups and gather market data.[14] In some cases, telemarketing uses advertising to encourage consumers to initiate a call or to request information about placing an order. Such advertisements will include 'a call to action' to prompt target consumers to dial an 0800 Freephone number. This type of retailing is only a small part of total retail sales, but its use is growing. Research indicates that telemarketing is most successful when combined with other marketing strategies, such as direct mail or advertising in newspapers, radio and television.

Automatic vending makes use of coin- or credit-card-operated self-service machines and accounts for less than 1 per cent of all retail sales. However, there are approximately 1.5 million vending machines in the UK, accounting for sales of around £4 billion.

Mail order retailing involves selling by description, because buyers usually do not see the actual product until it arrives in the mail. Sellers contact buyers through direct mail, catalogues, television, radio, magazines and newspapers and increasingly via the web. A wide assortment of products, such as DVDs, books and clothing is sold to consumers through the mail. When **catalogue retailing** – a specific type of mail order retailing – is used, customers receive their catalogues by mail, or they may pick them up if the catalogue retailer has stores. The *Next Directory* is an example. Although in-store visits result in some catalogue orders, most are placed by mail, telephone or the internet.

Physical distribution

Wholesalers, in their various guises, are essential 'players' in many businesses' marketing channels. Also important is the ability to physically deliver products to customers. **Physical distribution** is a set of activities consisting of order processing, materials handling, warehousing, inventory management and transportation, used in the movement of products from producers

Mail order retailing
Selling by description because buyers usually do not see the actual product until it arrives in the mail.

Catalogue retailing
A type of mail order retailing in which customers receive their catalogues by mail, the web, or pick them up if the catalogue retailer has stores.

Physical distribution
A set of activities consisting of order processing, materials handling, warehousing, inventory management and transportation used in the movement of products from producers to consumers or end-users.

to consumers or end users. Planning an effective physical distribution system can be a significant decision in developing a marketing strategy. A company that has the right goods in the right place at the right time in the right quantity, and with the right support services, is able to sell more than competing businesses that fail to accomplish these goals. Physical distribution is an important variable in a marketing strategy because it can decrease costs and increase customer satisfaction. In fact, speed of delivery, along with service and dependability, is often as important to buyers as cost. In some situations – for example the emergency provision of a spare part for vital production-line machinery – it may even be the single most important factor. For most companies, physical distribution accounts for about a fifth of a product's retail price.

Physical distribution deals with physical movement and inventory holding – the storing and tracking of inventory or stock until it is needed – both within and among marketing channel members. Often, one channel member will arrange the movement of goods for all channel members involved in exchanges. For example, a packing company ships fresh salmon and champagne (often by air) to remote markets on a routine basis. Frequently, buyers are found while the goods are in transit.

The physical distribution system is often adjusted to meet the needs of a channel member. For example, an agricultural equipment dealer who keeps a low inventory of replacement parts requires the fastest and most dependable service when parts not in stock are needed. In this case, the distribution cost may be a minor consideration when compared with service, dependability and promptness. Grocery retailers, such as Aldi and ASDA, receive some deliveries to central and regional warehouses, whereas other deliveries from manufacturers such as Heinz or Kellogg's go directly to individual stores as required, and insisted upon, by the retail companies. Failure to deliver products to customers where, when and how they demand is likely to lose orders, diminish customer loyalty and provide opportunities for competing suppliers, and is not going to create a mutually satisfying relationship between supplier and customer.

Physical distribution objectives

Objective of physical distribution
Decreasing costs while increasing customer service.

For most companies, the main **objective of physical distribution** is to decrease costs while increasing customer service.[15] In the real world, however, few distribution systems manage to achieve these goals in equal measure. The large stock inventories and rapid transport, essential to facilitate high levels of customer service, drive up costs. On the other hand, reduced inventories and slower, cheaper shipping methods cause customer dissatisfaction because of stock-outs or late deliveries. Physical distribution managers strive for a reasonable balance of service, costs and resources. They determine what level of customer service is acceptable yet realistic, develop a 'system' outlook of calculating total distribution costs, and trade higher costs at one stage of distribution for savings in another. In this section these three performance objectives are examined more closely.

Customer service
Customer satisfaction in terms of physical distribution, based on availability, promptness and quality.

Customer service To varying degrees, all businesses attempt to satisfy customer needs and wants through a set of activities known collectively as **customer service**. Many companies claim that service to the customer is their top priority. These companies see service as being as important in attracting customers and building sales as the cost or quality of the companies' products.

Customers require a variety of services. At the most basic level, they need fair prices, acceptable product quality and dependable deliveries.[16] There are many facets of service, as described throughout this book, but in the physical distribution area, availability, promptness and quality are the most important dimensions of customer service. These are the main factors that determine how satisfied customers are likely to be with a supplier's physical distribution activities.[17] Customers seeking a higher level of customer service may also want sizeable inventories, efficient order processing, availability of emergency shipments, progress reports, post-sale services, prompt replacement of defective items and warranties. Customers' inventory requirements influence the level of physical distribution service they expect. For example, customers who want to minimize inventory storage and shipping costs may require that suppliers assume the cost of maintaining inventory in the marketing channel, or the cost of premium transport.[18] Since service needs vary from customer to customer, companies must analyze and adapt to customer preferences. Attention to customer needs and preferences is crucial to increasing sales and obtaining repeat sales. A company's failure to provide the desired level of service may mean the loss of customers. Without customers there can be no profit.

Companies must also examine the service levels offered by competitors and match those standards, at least when the costs of providing the services can be balanced by the sales generated. For example, companies may step up their efforts to identify the causes of customer complaints or institute corrective measures for billing and shipping errors. In extremely competitive businesses, such as the market for vehicle parts, businesses may concentrate on product availability. To compete effectively, manufacturers may strive for inventory levels and order processing speeds that are deemed unnecessary and too costly in other industries.[19]

Services are provided most effectively when service standards are developed and stated in terms that are specific, measurable and appropriate for the product – for example 'Guaranteed delivery within 48 hours'. Standards should be communicated clearly both to customers and employees, and rigorously enforced. In many cases, it is necessary to maintain a policy of minimum order size to ensure that transactions are profitable: special service charges are added to orders smaller than a specified quantity. A number of carrier or courier companies operate on this basis. Many service policies also spell out delivery times and provisions for back ordering, returning goods and obtaining emergency shipments. The overall objective of any service policy should be to improve customer service just to the point beyond which increased sales would be negated by increased distribution costs.

Total distribution costs   Although physical distribution managers try to minimize the costs of each element in the system – transportation, warehousing, inventory carrying, order entry/customer service and administration – decreasing costs in one area often raises them in another. Figure 15.5 shows the percentage of total costs that physical distribution functions represent. By using a total cost approach to physical distribution, managers can view the distribution system as a whole, not as a collection of unrelated activities. The emphasis shifts from lowering the separate costs of individual functions to minimizing the total cost of the entire distribution system.

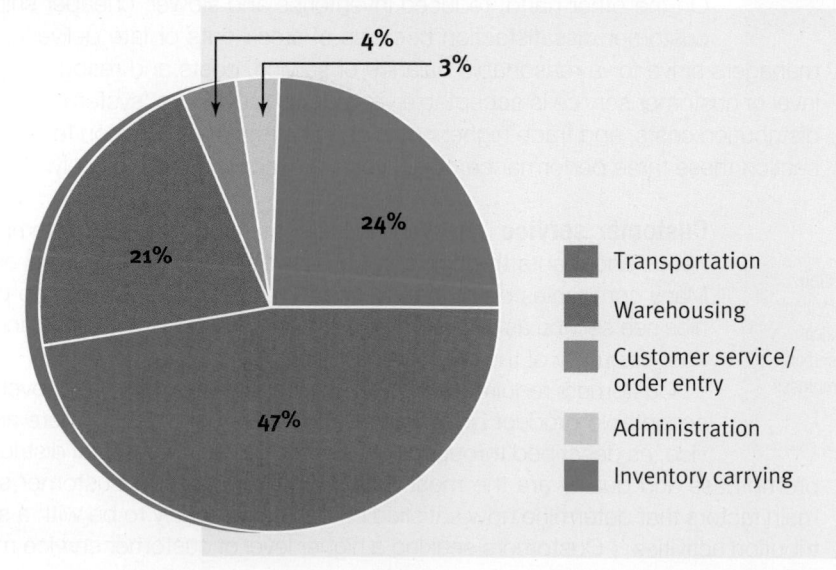

FIGURE 15.5
Proportional cost of each physical distribution function as a percentage of total distribution costs

Total cost analysis
Weighs inventory levels against warehousing expenses; and materials handling costs against various modes of transport; and all distribution costs against customer service standards.

The total cost approach calls for analyzing the costs of all possible distribution alternatives, even those considered too impractical or expensive. **Total cost analysis** weighs inventory levels against warehousing expenses; materials handling costs against various modes of transport; and all distribution costs against customer service standards. The costs of potential sales losses from lower performance levels are also considered. In many cases, accounting procedures and statistical methods can be used to calculate total costs. Where hundreds of combinations of distribution variables are possible, computer simulations may be helpful. In no case is a distribution system's lowest total cost the result of using a combination of the cheapest functions; instead, it is the lowest overall cost compatible with the company's stated service objectives.

Cost trade-offs
The off-setting of higher costs in one area of the distribution system by lower costs in another area, to keep the total system cost-effective.

Cost trade-offs   A distribution system that attempts to provide a specific level of customer service for the lowest possible total cost must use **cost trade-offs** to resolve conflicts about resource allocations. That is, higher costs in one area of the distribution system must be offset by lower costs in another area, if the total system is to remain cost-effective.

Trade-offs are strategic decisions to combine and recombine resources for greatest cost-effectiveness. When distribution managers regard the system as a network of interlocking functions, trade-offs become useful tools in a unified distribution strategy.

The furniture retailer IKEA uses a system of trade-offs. To ensure that each store carries enough inventory to satisfy customers in the area, IKEA groups its retail outlets into regions, each served by a separate distribution centre. In addition, each IKEA store carries a five-week back stock of inventory. Thus, IKEA has chosen to trade higher inventory warehousing costs for improved customer service.[20]

The remainder of this chapter focuses on order processing, materials handling, warehousing, inventory management and transportation, all of which are essential physical distribution activities. While none of these activities would normally be the responsibility of marketing managers, their smooth deployment impacts on customer service levels, customer satisfaction and also customers' perceptions of a brand or business.

Order processing

Order processing
The receipt and transmission of sales order information.

Order processing   The first stage in a physical distribution system is the receipt and transmission of sales order information. Although management sometimes overlooks the importance of these activities, efficient order processing facilitates product flow. Computerized order processing, used now by many businesses, speeds the flow of information from customer to seller.[21] Indeed, in many industries key suppliers are linked 'live' to retailers' or distributors' tills and order books: they are then able to replenish or supply exactly in line with demand and actual sales. When carried out quickly and accurately, order processing contributes to customer satisfaction, repeat orders and increased profits.

Generally, there are three main tasks in order processing:

1. order entry
2. order handling
3. order delivery.[22]

Order entry begins when customers or sales people place purchase orders by mail, telephone, text, fax or the web. In some companies, sales service representatives receive and enter orders personally and also handle complaints, prepare progress reports and forward sales order information.[23]

The next task, order handling, involves several activities. Once an order has been entered, it is transmitted to the warehouse, where the availability of the product is verified; and to the credit department, where prices, terms and the customer's credit rating are checked. If the credit department approves the purchase, the warehouse begins to fill the order. If the product requested is not in stock, a production order is sent to the factory or the customer is offered a substitute item.

Thanks to technology, these various tasks are carried out simultaneously in many businesses and in only a few seconds. When the order has been filled and packed for shipment, the warehouse schedules pick up with an appropriate carrier. If the customer is willing to pay for express service, priority transport, such as an overnight courier, is used. The customer is sent an invoice, inventory records are adjusted and the order is delivered.

Order processing can be done manually or electronically, depending on which method provides greater speed and accuracy within cost limits. Manual processing suffices for a small volume of orders and is more flexible in special situations; electronic processing is more practical for a large volume of orders and lets a company integrate order processing, production planning, inventory, accounting and transport planning into a total information system.[24] These days, most companies use **electronic data interchange (EDI)**, which uses IT to integrate order processing with production, inventory, accounting and transportation. Many leading retail groups, with products from groceries to electrical goods, have their stores networked to the head office. Suppliers are also linked electronically to the retailers' head offices, so that stock can be ordered electronically.

Electronic data interchange (EDI)
The use of IT to integrate order processing with production, inventory, accounting and transportation.

Materials handling

Materials handling, or the physical handling of products, is important for efficient warehouse operations, as well as in transport from points of production to points of consumption. The characteristics of the product itself often determine how it will be handled. For example, fresh dairy produce has unique characteristics that determine how it can be moved and stored. Materials handling procedures and techniques should increase the usable capacity of a warehouse, reduce the number of times a good is handled, improve service to customers and increase their satisfaction with the product. Packaging, loading, movement and labelling systems must be coordinated to maximize cost reduction and customer satisfaction.

Materials handling
The physical handling of products.

In Chapter 11, it was noted that the protective functions of packaging are important considerations in product development. Appropriate decisions about packaging materials and methods allow for the most efficient physical handling; most companies employ packaging consultants or specialists to accomplish this important task. Materials handling equipment is used in the design of handling systems. **Unit loading** is grouping one or more boxes on a pallet or skid; it permits movement of efficient loads by mechanical means, such as forklifts, trucks or conveyor systems. **Containerization** is the practice of consolidating many items into a single large container that is sealed at its point of origin and opened at its destination. As individual items are not handled in transit, containerization greatly increases efficiency and security in shipping.

Unit loading
Grouping one or more boxes on a pallet or skid, permitting movement of efficient loads by mechanical means.

Containerization
The practice of consolidating many items into a single large container that is sealed at its point of origin and opened at its destination, greatly increasing efficiency and security in shipping.

Warehousing

Warehousing, the design and operation of facilities for storing and moving goods, is an important physical distribution function. Warehousing provides time utility by enabling companies to compensate for dissimilar production and consumption rates. That is, when mass production creates a greater stock of goods than can be sold immediately, companies may warehouse the surplus goods until customers are ready to buy. Warehousing also helps stabilize the prices and availability of seasonal items. There follows a description of the basic functions of warehouses and the different types of warehouse available. Distribution centres, special warehouse operations designed so that goods can be moved rapidly, are also examined.

Warehousing
The design and operation of facilities for storing and moving goods.

Warehousing functions   Warehousing is not limited simply to the storage of goods. When warehouses receive goods by wagon loads or lorry loads, they break the shipments down into smaller quantities for individual customers; when goods arrive in small lots, the warehouses assemble the lots into bulk loads that can be shipped out more economically.[25] Warehouses perform the following basic distribution functions:

1. *Receiving goods.* The merchandise is accepted, and the warehouse assumes responsibility for the goods.
2. *Identifying goods.* The appropriate stock-keeping units are recorded, along with the quantity of each item received; the item may be marked with a physical code, tag or other label, or it may be identified by an item code (a code on the carrier or container) or by physical properties.
3. *Sorting goods.* The merchandise is sorted for storage in appropriate areas.
4. *Despatching goods to storage.* The merchandise is put away so that it can be retrieved when necessary.
5. *Holding goods.* The merchandise is kept in storage and properly protected until needed.
6. *Recalling and picking goods.* Items customers have ordered are retrieved efficiently from storage and prepared for the next step.
7. *Marshalling the shipment.* The items making up a single shipment are brought together and checked for completeness or explainable omissions. Order records are prepared or modified as necessary.
8. *Despatching the shipment.* The consolidated order is packaged suitably and directed to the right transport vehicle; necessary shipping and accounting documents are prepared.[26]

Types of warehouse   A company's choice of warehouse facilities is an important strategic consideration. By using the right warehouse, a company may be able to reduce transportation and inventory costs or improve its service to customers; the wrong warehouse may drain company resources. For example, a company that produces processed foods must locate its warehousing close to main transport routes to facilitate delivery to supermarkets in different parts of the country. Besides deciding how many facilities to operate and where to locate them, a company must determine which type of warehouse will be most appropriate. Warehouses fall into two general categories: private and public. In many cases, a combination of private and public facilities provides the most flexible approach to warehousing. Many companies operate their own warehousing, whereas others outsource this requirement to specialist inventory management and haulage companies.

Inventory management

Inventory management involves developing and maintaining adequate assortments of products to meet customers' needs. Since a company's investment in inventory usually represents 30 to 50 per cent of its total assets, inventory decisions have a significant impact on physical distribution costs and the level of customer service provided. When too few products are carried in inventory, the result is a **stock-out**, or shortage of products, which results in fewer sales and customers switching to alternative brands. But when too many products or too many slow-moving products are carried, costs increase, as do the risks of product obsolescence, pilferage and damage. The objective of inventory management, therefore, is to minimize inventory costs while maintaining an adequate supply of goods.

There are three types of inventory cost:

1. *Carrying costs* are holding costs; they include expenditures for storage space and materials handling, financing, insurance, taxes and losses from spoilage of goods.
2. *Replenishment costs* are related to the purchase of merchandise. The price of goods, handling charges and expenses for order processing contribute to replenishment costs.
3. *Stock-out costs* include sales lost when demand for goods exceeds supply, and the clerical and processing expenses of back ordering.

Inventory management
The development and maintenance of adequate assortments of products to meet customers' needs.

Stock-outs
Shortages of products resulting from a lack of products carried in inventory.

Reorder point
The inventory level that signals the need to order more inventory.

Order lead time
The average time lapse between placing the order and receiving it.

Usage rate
The rate at which a product's inventory is used or sold during a specific time period.

Safety stock
Inventory needed to prevent stock-outs.

Economic order quantity (EOQ)
The order size that minimizes the total cost of ordering and carrying inventory.

A company must control all the costs of obtaining and maintaining inventory in order to achieve its profit goals. Management must therefore have a clear idea of the level of each type of cost incurred. Customers' expectations of product availability and tolerable delivery lead times will vary between target market segments.

Inventory managers deal with two issues of particular importance. They must know when to reorder and how much merchandise to order. In general, to determine when to order, a marketer calculates the **reorder point**, which is the inventory level that signals that more inventory should be ordered. Three factors determine the reorder point:

1. the **order lead time**, which is the expected time between the date an order is placed and the date the goods are received and made ready for resale to customers

2. the **usage rate** or rate at which a product is sold or used up

3. the quantity of **safety stock** on hand, or inventory needed to prevent stock-outs.

The reorder point can be calculated using the following formula:

$$\text{reorder point} = (\text{order lead time} \times \text{usage rate}) + \text{safety stock}$$

Thus, if order lead time is 10 days, usage rate is 3 units per day and safety stock is 20 units, the reorder point is 50 units.

The inventory manager faces several trade-offs when reordering merchandise. Large safety stocks ensure product availability and thus improve the level of customer service; they also lower order-processing costs because orders are placed less frequently. Small safety stocks, on the other hand, cause frequent reorders and high order-processing costs but reduce the overall cost of carrying inventory. To quantify this trade-off between carrying costs and order-processing costs, a model for an **economic order quantity (EOQ)** has been developed (see Figure 15.6); it specifies the order size that minimizes the total cost of ordering and carrying inventory.[27] The fundamental relationships underlying the widely accepted EOQ model are the basis of many inventory control systems. However, the objective of minimum total inventory cost must be balanced against the customer service level necessary for maximum profits. Therefore, because increased costs of carrying inventory are usually associated with a higher level of customer service, the order quantity will often lie to the right of the optimal point in the figure, leading to a higher total cost for ordering and larger carrying inventory.

Fluctuations in demand for example, in times of economic recession mean that it is not always easy to predict changing inventory levels. When management miscalculates reorder points or order

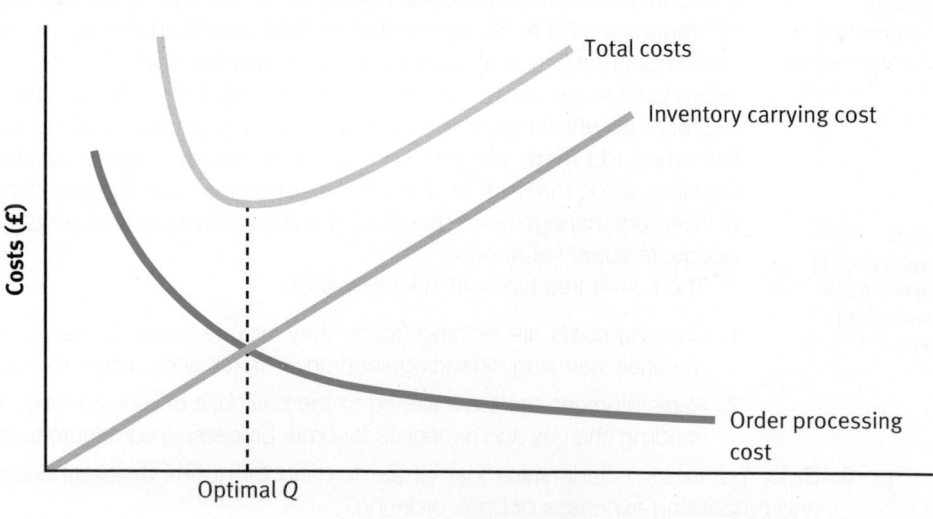

FIGURE 15.6
Economic order quantity (EOQ) model

quantities, inventory problems develop. Warning signs include an inventory that grows at a faster rate than sales, surplus or obsolete inventory, customer deliveries that are consistently late or lead times that are too long, inventory that represents a growing percentage of assets, and large inventory adjustments or write-offs. However, there are several tools for improving inventory control.

From a technical standpoint, an inventory system can be planned so that the number of products sold and the number of products in stock are determined at certain checkpoints. The control may be as simple as tearing off a code number from each product sold so that the correct sizes, colours and models can be tabulated and reordered. Many bookshops insert reorder slips of paper into each item of stock, which can be scanned and removed at the checkout. A sizeable amount of technologically advanced electronic equipment is available to assist with inventory management. In many stores, such as Tesco and Toys 'R' Us, checkout terminals connected to central computer systems instantaneously update inventory and sales records. For continuous, automatic updating of inventory records, some companies use pressure-sensitive circuits installed under ordinary industrial shelving to weigh inventory, convert the weight to units and display any inventory changes on a video screen or computer printout.

Various techniques have also been used successfully to improve inventory management. The just-in-time concept calls for companies to maintain low inventory levels and purchase products and materials in small quantities, just at the moment they are needed for production. Ford, for example, sometimes receives supply deliveries as often as every two hours.[28] Just-in-time inventory management depends on a high level of coordination between producers and suppliers, but the technique enables companies to eliminate waste and reduce inventory costs significantly. Another inventory management technique, the 80/20 rule, holds that fast-moving products should generate a higher level of customer service than slow-moving products, on the theory that 20 per cent of the items account for 80 per cent of the sales. Thus, an inventory manager attempts to keep an adequate supply of fast-selling items and a minimal supply of the slower moving products. ABC sales: contribution analysis strives to maintain inventory levels while maximizing financial returns to the business (see Figure 12.9 in Chapter 12).

Transportation

Transportation
The process of moving a product from where it is made to where it is purchased and used.

Transportation adds time and place utility to a product by moving it from where it is made to where it is purchased and used.[29] As product availability and timely deliveries are so dependent on transport functions, a company's choice of transport directly affects customer service and satisfaction. A business may even build its distribution and marketing strategy around a unique transport system if the system ensures on-time deliveries that will give the business a competitive edge. This section considers the principal modes of transport, the criteria companies use to select one mode over another, and several methods of coordinating transport services.

Transport modes
Methods of moving goods; these include railways, motor vehicles, inland waterways, airways and pipelines.

Transport modes   There are five major **transport modes**, or methods of moving goods: railways, motor vehicles, inland waterways, airways and pipelines. Each mode offers unique advantages; many companies have adopted physical handling procedures that facilitate the use of two or more modes in combination.

Criteria for selecting transport   Marketers select a transport mode on the basis of costs, transit time, reliability, capability, accessibility, security and traceability.[30] It is important to remember that these relationships are approximations and that the choice of a transport mode involves many trade-offs. These attributes all have a significant impact on a customer's perception of customer service levels.

Costs
One consideration that helps determine transportation mode, involving comparison of alternative modes to determine whether the benefits of a more expensive mode are worth the higher costs.

Costs   Marketers compare alternative means of transport to determine whether the benefits from a more expensive mode are worth the higher **costs**. Air freight carriers provide many benefits, such as high speed, reliability, security and traceability, but at higher costs relative to other transport modes. When speed is less important, marketers prefer lower costs. Recently, marketers have been able to cut expenses and increase efficiency. Railways, airlines, road hauliers, barges and pipeline companies have all become more competitive and more responsive to customers' needs. Surveys reveal that in recent years transport costs per tonne and as a percentage of sales have declined, now averaging 7.5 per cent of sales. This figure varies by industry, of course: electrical machinery, textiles and instruments have transport costs of only 3 or 4 per cent of sales, whereas timber products, chemicals and food have transport costs close to 15 per cent of sales.

Transit time

Transit time
The total time a carrier has possession of goods.

Transit time is the total time a carrier has possession of goods, including the time required for pick up and delivery, handling, and movement between the points of origin and destination. Closely related to transit time is frequency, or number of shipments per day. Transit time obviously affects a marketer's ability to provide service, but there are some less obvious implications as well. A shipper can take advantage of transit time to process orders for goods en route, a capability especially important for agricultural and raw materials shippers. Some railways also let shipments that are already in transit be redirected, for maximum flexibility in selecting markets.

Reliability

Reliability
The consistency of service provided.

The total **reliability** of a transport mode is determined by the consistency of the service provided. Marketers must be able to count on their carriers to deliver goods on time and in an acceptable condition. Along with transit time, reliability affects a marketer's inventory costs, which include sales lost when merchandise is not available. Unreliable transport necessitates maintaining higher inventory levels to avoid stock-outs. Reliable delivery service, on the other hand, enables customers to save money by reducing inventories; for example, if pharmacists know that suppliers can deliver medicines within hours of ordering, they can carry a smaller inventory.

Capability

Capability
The ability of a transport mode to provide the appropriate equipment and conditions for moving specific kinds of goods.

Capability is the ability of a transport mode to provide the appropriate equipment and conditions for moving specific kinds of goods. For example, many products must be shipped under conditions of controlled temperature and humidity. Other products, such as liquids or gases, require special equipment or facilities for their shipment.

Accessibility

Accessibility
The ability to move goods over a specific route or network.

A carrier's **accessibility** refers to its ability to move goods over a specific route or network: flights, rail lines, waterways or roads.

Security

Security
The measure of the physical condition of goods upon delivery.

A transport mode's **security** is measured by the physical condition of goods on delivery. A business does not incur costs directly when goods are lost or damaged, because the carrier is usually held liable in these cases. Nevertheless, poor service and lack of security will lead indirectly to increased costs and lower profits for the company, since damaged or lost goods are not available for immediate sale or use. In some cases, companies find it necessary to transport products using courier companies such as UPS or TNT.

Traceability

Traceability
The relative ease with which a shipment can be located and transferred.

Traceability is the relative ease with which a shipment can be located and transferred or found if it is lost. Quick traceability is a convenience that some businesses value highly. Shippers have learned that the ability to trace shipments, along with prompt invoicing and processing of claims, increases customer loyalty and improves a company's image in the marketplace.[31] Courier companies now offer clients internet tracking of goods in transit.

Physical distribution's importance to marketing

The physical distribution functions discussed in this chapter – order processing, materials handling, warehousing, inventory management and transportation – account for about a third of all marketing costs. Moreover, these functions have a significant impact on customer service and satisfaction, as well as people's perceptions of a brand's or business's image, which are of prime importance to marketers.[32] Effective marketers accept considerable responsibility for the design and control of the physical distribution system. They work to ensure that the business's overall marketing strategy is enhanced by physical distribution, with its dual objectives of decreasing costs while increasing customer service. Remember, to ensure that customers are satisfied, they must be able to obtain, within reason, the product or service when and where they want it and with a perception of 'no hassle'. The growth of multi-channel marketing has given customers greater flexibility and more options for purchasing and delivery, but places more responsibility on marketers to manage these experiences to ensure customer satisfaction. The growth of multi-channel marketing and home delivery has placed greater importance on channel management to safeguard customer experience and ensure brand experience is similar across channels. The increase in direct delivery and eCommerce has added to the facilitating agents and channel players on which marketers rely to effectively manage their customers.

The strategic importance of physical distribution is evident in all elements of the marketing mix. Product design and packaging must allow for efficient stacking, storage and transport; decisions to differentiate products by size, colour and style, must take into account the additional demands that will be placed on warehousing and shipping facilities. Competitive pricing may depend on a company's ability to provide reliable delivery or emergency shipments of replacement parts; a company trying to lower its inventory costs may offer quantity discounts to encourage large purchases. Promotional campaigns must be coordinated with distribution functions, so that advertised products are available to buyers; order processing departments should be able to handle additional sales order information efficiently. Distribution planners must consider warehousing and transportation costs, which may influence, for example, the company's policy on stock-outs or its choice to centralize or decentralize its inventory.

No single distribution system is ideal for all situations, and any system must be evaluated continually and adapted as necessary. For instance, pressures to adjust service levels or reduce costs may lead to a total restructuring of the marketing channel relationships; changes in transportation, warehousing, materials handling and inventory may affect speed of delivery, reliability and economy of service. Marketing strategists must consider customers' changing needs and preferences, and recognize that changes in any one of the major distribution functions will necessarily affect all other functions. Consumer-oriented marketers will analyze the various characteristics of their target markets and *then* design distribution systems to provide products at acceptable costs. In many instances, external logistics specialists are subcontracted to handle inventory and physical distribution requirements. The use of third parties may in fact be fully outsourced: **outsourcing** is where a third party is empowered to manage and control a particular activity such as catering, IT infrastructure management, fleet cars, human resources and recruitment or, as in this case, a company's logistics.

Outsourcing
Where a third-party organization is empowered to manage and control a particular activity, such as logistics.

Summary

Wholesaling includes all transactions in which the purchaser intends to use the product for resale, for making other products or for general business operations. It does not include exchanges with the ultimate consumers. Hence, the term *wholesaling* is used in its broadest sense: intermediaries' activity in the marketing channel between producers and business-to-business customers to facilitate the exchange buying and selling of goods. Marketers use wholesaling to mean much more than the function of retail wholesalers. *Wholesalers* are individuals or businesses that facilitate and expedite primarily wholesale transactions between producers and business-to-business customers. *Supply chain management* has become strategically important in recent years and, for marketers, this involves an improved appreciation of the role of wholesaling and marketing intermediaries.

Except in many consumer markets, where large multiple retailers dominate, more than half of all goods are exchanged through wholesalers (middlemen in the distribution channel), although the distribution of any product requires that someone must perform wholesaling activities, whether or not a wholesaling institution is involved. For producers, wholesalers perform specialized accumulation and allocation functions for a number of products, letting the producers concentrate on developing and manufacturing the products. For retailers, wholesalers provide buying expertise, wide product lines, efficient distribution, warehousing and storage services.

Various types of wholesaler serve different market segments. How a wholesaler is classified depends on whether the wholesaler is owned by a producer, whether it takes title to products, the range of services it provides and the breadth and depth of its product lines. The three general categories of wholesaler are (1) merchant wholesalers, (2) agents and brokers and (3) manufacturers' sales branches and offices.

Merchant wholesalers are independently owned businesses that take title to goods and assume risk; they account for over half of all wholesale revenues. They are either *full service wholesalers,* offering the widest possible range of wholesaling functions or *limited service wholesalers,* providing only some marketing services and specializing in a few functions. Distributors buy and sell on their own account but tend to deal in the goods of only certain manufacturers. Full service wholesalers include: (1) *general merchandise wholesalers,* which offer a wide but relatively shallow product mix; (2) *limited line wholesalers,* which offer extensive assortments in a few product lines; and (3) *speciality line wholesalers,* which offer great depth in a single product line or in a few items within a line. *Rack jobbers* are speciality line wholesalers that own and service display racks in supermarkets and chemists. There are four types of limited service wholesalers. (1) *Cash and carry wholesalers* sell to small businesses, require payment in cash and do not deliver. (2) *Truck wholesalers* transport a limited line of products directly to customers for inspection and selection. (3) *Drop shippers* own goods and negotiate sales but never take possession of products. (4) *Mail order wholesalers* sell to retail, industrial and institutional buyers through direct mail catalogues.

Agents and brokers, sometimes called *functional middlemen,* negotiate purchases and expedite sales but do not take title to products. They are usually specialists and provide valuable sales expertise. *Agents* represent buyers or sellers on a permanent basis. *Manufacturers' agents* offer customers the complete product lines of two or more sellers; *selling agents* market a complete product line or a producer's entire output, and perform every wholesaling function except taking title to products; *commission merchants* receive goods on consignment from local sellers and negotiate sales in large central markets. *Brokers,* such as *food brokers,* negotiate exchanges between buyers and sellers on a temporary basis.

Manufacturers' sales branches and offices are vertically integrated units owned by manufacturers. *Sales branches* sell products and provide support services for the manufacturer's sales force in a given location. *Sales offices* carry no inventory, and function much as agents do.

Facilitating agencies do not buy, sell or take title but perform certain activities that enhance channel functions. They include *public warehouses,* finance companies, transport companies and *trade shows* and *trade markets.* In some instances, these organizations eliminate the need for a wholesaling establishment.

Retailing includes all transactions in which the buyer intends to consume the product through personal, family or household use. *Retailers* are businesses that purchase products for the purpose of reselling them to ultimate consumers. They are important links in the marketing channel because they are customers for wholesalers and producers. Much retailing takes place inside stores or service establishments, but retail exchanges may also occur outside stores through telemarketing, vending machines, mail order catalogues and the internet. By providing assortments of products to match consumers' wants, retailers create place, time, possession and form utilities.

Retail stores locate in the *central business district (CBD)* – the traditional centre of the town – or the *prime pitch,* or in locations that provide an adequate *customer threshold* in *suburban centres,* in *edge-of-town sites* or in *retail parks.* The national chains occupy the prime pitch sites in the CBD and the edge-of-town sites. Locally based independent retailers tend to dominate in the suburbs and focus on convenience and some comparison goods.

Retail stores are often classified according to their width of product mix and depth of product lines. The major types of retail store are *department stores, variety stores, catalogue showrooms, supermarkets and superstores, hypermarkets, discount sheds, category killers, warehouse clubs, speciality shops, markets, convenience stores, discounters, factory outlet villages* and *cash and carry warehouses. Category management* is strategically important in marketing, providing a supplier with the opportunity to control a retail account's category. Department stores are characterized by wide product mixes in reasonable depth for most product lines. Their product lines are organized into separate departments that function much as self-contained businesses do. Speciality retailers offer substantial assortments in a few product lines. They include traditional speciality shops, which carry narrow product mixes with deep product lines.

Non-store retailing is the selling of goods or services outside the confines of a retail facility. *Direct marketing* is the use of non-personal media, the internet or telesales to introduce products to consumers, who then purchase the products by mail, telephone or the internet. The web is very important in direct marketing. Forms of non-store retailing include: *in-home retailing* (selling via personal contacts with consumers in their own homes); *telemarketing* (direct selling of goods and services by telephone based on either a cold canvass of the telephone directory or a pre-screened list of prospective clients); *automatic vending* (selling through machines); *mail order retailing;* the internet and *catalogue retailing* (selling by description because buyers usually do not see the actual product until it arrives in the mail).

Physical distribution is a set of activities that moves products from producers to consumers or end users. These activities include order processing, materials handling, warehousing, inventory management and transportation. While none of these activities would normally be the responsibility of marketing managers, their smooth deployment impacts on customer service levels, customer satisfaction and also customers' perceptions of a brand or business. An effective physical distribution system can be an important component of an overall marketing strategy, because it can decrease costs and lead to higher levels of customer satisfaction. Physical distribution activities should be integrated with marketing channel decisions and should be adjusted to meet the unique needs of a channel member. For most companies, physical distribution accounts for about a fifth of a product's retail price.

The main *objective of physical distribution* is to decrease costs while increasing customer service. Physical distribution managers therefore try to balance service, distribution costs and resources. Companies must adapt to customers' needs and preferences, offer service comparable to or better than that of their competitors, and develop and communicate desirable *customer service* policies. The costs of providing service are minimized most effectively through the *total cost analysis* approach, which evaluates the costs of the system as a whole rather than as a collection of separate activities. *Cost trade-offs* must often be used to offset higher costs in one area of distribution against lower costs in another area.

Order processing, the first stage in a physical distribution system, is the receipt and transmission of sales order information. Order processing consists of three main tasks: (1) order entry is the placement of purchase orders from customers or sales people by mail, telephone, fax or the web; (2) order handling involves checking customer credit, verifying product availability and preparing products for shipping; and (3) order delivery is provided by the carrier most suitable for a desired level of customer service. Order processing may be done manually or electronically, depending on which method gives greater speed and accuracy within cost limits. *Electronic data interchange (EDI)* helps facilitate order processing.

Materials handling, or the physical handling of products, is an important element of physical distribution. Packaging, loading, movement and labelling systems must be coordinated to maximize cost reduction and customer requirements. Basic handling systems include *unit loading* on pallets or skids, permitting movement by mechanical devices, and *containerization,* the practice of consolidating many items into a single large container.

Warehousing involves the design and operation of facilities for storing and moving goods. It is important for companies to select suitable warehousing conveniently located close to main transport routes.

The objective of *inventory management* is to minimize inventory costs while maintaining a supply of goods adequate for customers' needs. All inventory costs – carrying, replenishment and stock-out costs – must be controlled if profit goals are to be met. To avoid *stock-outs* without tying up too much capital in inventory, a business must have a systematic method of determining a *reorder point*, which is the inventory level at which more inventory is ordered. The *order lead time* is lapsed time between order placement and delivery. The *usage rate* is the rate at which inventory is used during a specific period of time. The trade-offs between the costs of carrying larger average *safety stocks* and the costs of frequent orders can be quantified using the *economic order quantity (EOQ)* model. Inventory problems may take the form of surplus inventory, late deliveries, write-offs and inventory that is too large in proportion to sales or assets. Methods for improving inventory management include systems that monitor stock levels continuously, techniques such as just-in-time management and the 80/20 rule.

Transportation adds time and place utility to a product by moving it from where it is made to where it is purchased and used. The five major *transport modes* are motor vehicles, railways, inland waterways, airways and pipelines. Marketers evaluate transport modes with respect to *costs*, *transit time*, *reliability*, *capability*, *accessibility*, *security* and *traceability*; the final selection of a transport mode involves many trade-offs.

Physical distribution affects every element of the marketing mix: product, price, promotion, place/distribution and personnel/customer service. To give customers products at acceptable prices, marketers consider consumers' changing needs and any shifts within the major distribution functions. They then adapt existing physical distribution systems for greater effectiveness. Physical distribution functions account for about a third of all marketing costs and have a significant impact on customer satisfaction. Therefore, effective marketers are actively involved in the design and control of physical distribution systems. Increasingly, many of the logistics activities described in this chapter are subject to *outsourcing*.

The growth of multi-channel marketing and home delivery has placed greater importance on channel management to safeguard customer experience and ensure brand experience is similar across channels. The increase in direct delivery and eCommerce has added to the facilitating agents and channel players on which marketers rely to effectively manage their customers.

Key links

Although wholesaling and logistical support are rarely controlled by the marketing function, they do impact on the customer's ability to attain a product, and on the customer's experience, buying behaviour and satisfaction.

- This chapter should be read in conjunction with Chapter 14, which examines the nature of marketing channels and key participating channel members.

- And in conjunction with Chapter 18, which looks at the growth of web-based retailing and direct marketing.

- Chapter 19 overviews digital marketing and its implications on channels and channel members.

Important terms

Accessibility
Automatic vending
Capability
Cash and carry warehouses
Cash and carry wholesalers
Catalogue retailing
Catalogue showroom
Category killers
Category management
Central business district (CBD)
Commission merchants
Containerization
Convenience stores

Cost trade-offs
Costs
Customer service
Customer threshold
Department stores
Direct marketing
Discount sheds
Distributors
Drop shippers
Economic order quantity (EOQ)
Edge-of-town sites
Electronic data interchange (EDI)
Facilitating agencies
Factory outlet villages
Food brokers
Full service wholesalers
Functional middlemen
General merchandise wholesalers
Hypermarkets
In-home retailing
Inventory management
Limited line wholesalers
Limited service wholesalers
Mail order retailing
Mail order wholesalers
Manufacturers' agents
Markets
Materials handling
Merchant wholesalers
Non-store retailing
Objective of physical distribution
Order lead time
Order processing

Outsourcing
Physical distribution
Prime pitch
Public warehouses
Rack jobbers
Reliability
Reorder point
Retail parks
Retailer
Retailing
Safety stock
Sales branches
Sales offices
Security
Selling agents
Speciality line wholesalers
Speciality shops
Stock-outs
Suburban centres
Supermarkets and grocery superstores
Supply chain management
Telemarketing
Total cost analysis
Traceability
Trade markets
Trade shows
Transit time
Transport modes
Transportation
Truck wholesalers
Unit loading
Usage rate
Variety stores
Warehouse clubs
Warehousing
Wholesaler
Wholesaling

Discussion and review questions

1. Is there a distinction between wholesalers and wholesaling? If so, what is it?

2. Generically, what services do wholesalers provide to producers and retailers?

3. Drop shippers take title to products but do not accept physical possession. Commission merchants take physical possession of products but do not accept title. Defend the logic of classifying drop shippers as wholesale merchants and agents as commission merchants.

4. What are the advantages of using agents to replace merchant wholesalers? What are the disadvantages?

5. Why are manufacturers' sales offices and branches classified as wholesalers? Which independent wholesalers are replaced by manufacturers' sales branches? Which independent wholesalers are replaced by manufacturers' sales offices?

6. Discuss the role of facilitating agencies. Identify three facilitating agencies and explain how each type performs this role.

7. What role do retailers undertake in distribution?

8. What are the principal types of retailers?

9. Describe the most common forms of non-store retailing and what is driving growth for some of these?

10. Discuss the cost and service trade-offs involved in developing a physical distribution system.

11. What factors must physical distribution managers consider when developing a customer service mix?

12. What is the advantage of using a total cost approach to distribution?

13. What are the main tasks involved in order processing?

14. How does a product's package affect materials-handling procedures and techniques?

15. Explain the major differences between private and public warehouses. What is a field public warehouse?

16. Describe the costs associated with inventory management.

17. How can managers improve inventory control? Give specific examples of techniques.

18. Compare the five major transport modes in terms of costs, transit time, reliability, capability, accessibility, security and traceability.

19. Discuss how the elements of the marketing mix affect physical distribution strategy.

Recommended readings

Arikan, A., *Multichannel Marketing: Metrics and Methods for On and Offline Success* (Wiley, 2008).

Berman, B.R. and Evans, J.R., *Retail Management* (Pearson, 2012).

Christopher, M., *Logistics and Supply Chain Management* (Pearson, 2011).

Dent, J., *Technology Distribution Channels: Understanding and Managing Channels to Market* (Kogan Page, 2014)

Gattorna, J., ed., *Strategic Supply Chain Alignment: Best Practices in Supply Chain Management* (Gower, 2005).

Harrison, A., van Hoek, R. and Skipworth, H., *Logistics Management and Strategy: Competing Through the Supply Chain* (Pearson, 2014).

Hines, T., *Supply Chain Strategies* (Routledge, 2012).

Rosenbloom, B., *Marketing Channels: A Management View* (Cengage, 2012).

Rushton, A., Croucher, P. and Baker, P., *The Handbook of Logistics and Distribution Management* (Kogan Page, 2014).

Varley, R. and Rafiq, M., *Principles of Retail Management* (Palgrave Macmillan, 2014).

Waters, D. and Rinsler, S., *Global Logistics: New Directions in Supply Chain Management* (Kogan Page, 2014).

Internet exercise

Choose a major retail brand, such as Tesco, John Lewis, Top Shop or IKEA. Ensure it is a business whose stores you visit often. Then identify its website and log on.

1. Are there any differences in the merchandise selection offered in-store versus online? Why?

2. Why has the selected retailer developed such an in-store/online strategy?

Group tasks

1. All small shops and catering establishments depend on wholesalers for the bulk of their supplies, rather than buying directly from producers. Consider why this must be the case.

2. Very few producers operate wholesalers. Even fewer retailers have reached back in the supply chain to become wholesalers. Why do other players in the distribution channel shy away from acquiring or setting up wholesale businesses?

Applied mini-case

Heathrow Airport, part-owned by Spain's Ferrovial Group, is one of the world's busiest hubs. Ninety airlines serve 170 destinations, transporting 74 million passengers each year. It is the main base for British Airways and Virgin Atlantic. Some years ago, the then CEO John Egan instigated a policy review emphasizing a commitment to quality service, on-site competition and the introduction of branded operations and concessions. All proposals followed extensive marketing research.

Caffe Nero, Café Rouge, Carluccio's, Costa, EAT, Gordon Ramsey, Oriel, Pret, Strada, Wetherspoon, Yo! Sushi and Wagamama are some of the catering businesses now operating within Heathrow, along with retailers such as Alexander McQueen, Boots, Boss, Bulgari, Burberry, Cath Kidston, Chanel, Gucci, Harrod's, Jack Wills, John Lewis, Louis Vuitton, M&S, Mac, Miu Miu, Montblanc, Paul Smith, Reiss, Rolex, Swarovski, Ted Baker, Vodafone and WH Smith. Only well-known retail brands are welcome.

Initially, the move by Heathrow was to compensate for the loss of duty-free sales when the EU phased out intra-community duty-free trade, but today retailing within the airport is viewed as the way to continue generating profits and adding to customer experience. Over 15 per cent of terminal space is devoted to retailing. Heathrow has taken restless passengers waiting for flights and put them into shops selling well-known brands and a variety of merchandise. Research from 120,000 interviews each year has shown that retail outlets are a high priority for passengers. The captive audience is appreciative of the changes, as are the retailers.

Question

Why has Heathrow devoted so much terminal space to retailing and in particular to well-known high street-branded retail businesses? What impact has the introduction of shopping malls had on the ambience of the terminals?

Case study

Today's cash and carry mega-depots depend on effective stockholding and physical distribution

The wholesale grocery trade is worth £20 billion in the UK, 47 per cent of which is delivered trade and 53 per cent cash and carry. Cash and carry businesses stock manufacturers' products and have as their customers other businesses, such as small shopkeepers or the hospitality sector, which select merchandise appropriate for their respective target consumers. In order to satisfy the demands of small retail businesses, for example, the leading grocery cash and carry operators have to stock extensive ranges, only a small part of which may be selected by an individual retailer client. Inventory control is particularly important to these cash and carry businesses, but so too are the logistical considerations of receiving deliveries from manufacturers and enabling customers to take out their orders. In the UK, Booker has 172 depots at an average of 80,000 square feet and Bestway has 63 depots. Makro has 30 depots at an average size of 150,000 square feet. For Makro, the task of replenishing such mighty cash and carry depots is a core part of its business proposition.

Although price remains a core trading proposition, service and brand image are increasingly important. Indeed, the cash and carry sector was shaken up by the entry of Holland's Makro, a self-service wholesaler. Makro then was part of Metro Group, the world's largest wholesaler, operating in over 30 countries. In the UK, 30 stores serve the country. Makro's depots have the latest computer systems, customer service points and in-store displays. Makro serves the trade as a cash and carry wholesaler of groceries, fresh foods, wines, spirits, beer and cigarettes, household goods, clothing, toys and sports equipment. The company retails a clutch of own-label brands in these categories, including Aro, Horeca Select (kitchen ware), Rioba (coffee solutions for bars, cafes and hotels), H-Line (hotels and guest houses), Fine Food (for corner shops, kiosks, forecourts) and Sigma (office goods).

In a relatively traditional sector dominated by several long-standing companies, Makro had a major impact in a short time. Its mix of merchandise is more comprehensive than that of its competitors, forcing several – such as Booker and Bestway – to rethink their merchandising strategies. As depth and breadth of stock within individual product categories are not as extensive as those of UK rivals, the industry has been prompted to rethink, and most companies have reduced the number of lines stocked. Although not the first wholesaler with own-label products, Makro's promotion of its own ranges has encouraged its competitors to divert more attention to this area.

Perhaps Makro's biggest impact has been in the sales and marketing techniques it has brought to the UK. Cash and carry warehouses used to be dowdy depots that paid little attention to layout, upkeep, design or ambience, and demonstrated even less regard for customer service and satisfaction. Price was the name of the game ... customers could buy in bulk at a discount, but were offered few additional benefits. Makro's philosophy brings to the cash and carry sector the retailing techniques of the hypermarket: carefully controlled branch designs and layouts, high levels of staff training and a significant focus on building ongoing relationships with customers. An emphasis on managing its inventory and the associated need for effective physical distribution are pivotal to Makro's ability to serve its business

customers in the retail and catering trades. Perhaps this is why long-standing competitor Booker acquired the UK business of Makro.

Makro's philosophy is encouraging other wholesalers to follow suit. Now customers are being offered better service, together with assistance in building their own company image through local press and television advertising. The leading cash and carry companies are offering marketing support to their key accounts, not just to stimulate sales but also to build up those customers' loyalty to their nearby warehouse. Depots have been uprated by the leading groups, with new equipment, better stocking systems and improved physical distribution. They have also initiated sales promotions campaigns and incentive programmes. In most of the leading businesses, branches are being rationalized, both to respond to economic downturns, and to benefit from cost economies and enhanced computer systems. Companies are either consolidating three outdated neighbouring depots into one central, spacious, service-oriented depot, or they are closing a branch while extending and refurbishing a neighbouring one.

Sources: www.igd.com, June, 2011; www.makro.co.uk, April, 2015; http://www.booker.co.uk, April 2015; http://www.bookergroup.com/about-booker/what-we-do.aspx, April 2015; http://www.bestwaygroup.co.uk/sectors/wholesale, April 2015.

Questions for discussion

1. How are the major cash and carry companies responding to changing customer needs?

2. In what ways are state-of-the-art inventory management and physical distribution systems important to companies such as Makro or Bestway?

CHAPTER 16

An overview of marketing communications

" If consumers or business customers are unaware or not seduced, they won't try, buy or return for more "

Objectives

- To understand the role of promotion in the marketing mix.

- To examine the process of communication.

- To understand the product adoption process and its implications for promotional efforts.

- To understand the aims of promotion.

- To explore the elements of the promotional mix.

- To appreciate the nature of integrated marketing communications (IMC).

- To acquire an overview of the major methods of promotion.

- To explore the factors that influence the selection of promotional mix ingredients.

- To appreciate the role of marketing communications.

INTRODUCTION

Marketers spend large sums of money and significant amounts of time developing advertising campaigns, public relations (PR) programmes, sales promotions, websites and mobile communications, to list only some of the activities grouped under promotional activity within the marketing mix. As discussed in Chapter 1 of *Marketing: Concepts and Strategies*, many members of the public consider there to be little more to the role of marketing than the management of a company's marketing communications. In fact, there is much more to strategic marketing, described in Chapters 1 and 2, as the creation, execution and control of a company's marketing communications is indeed a significant task, occupying the time of many marketers and using up their budgets.

Communication is a sharing of meaning through the transmission of information. Marketing communication is the transmission of persuasive information about a good, service or an idea, targeted at key stakeholders and consumers within the target market segment. Not only commercial products and services require effective programmes of marketing communications ... the growth of social marketing causes and messages which must be conveyed effectively by government agencies and third sector bodies to their target audiences is huge. Marketing communications centre on the promotional mix, which comprises advertising, public relations (PR), personal selling, sales promotion, direct mail, sponsorship and the internet. Until relatively recently, each of these specialist areas was handled disparately within many companies. Integrated marketing communications (IMC) emerged as a concept, to coordinate and integrate all marketing communication tools, avenues and sources within a company into a seamless programme that maximizes the impact on consumers and other end users.

The 'target audience' is the marketing communications practitioner's term for those within the target market segment intended as the principal recipients of the promotional message ... those customers and potential customers who must be enticed and whose interest must be maintained. The goal is to encourage consumers or business customers to try and then purchase a product and to return for more. The product adoption process is awareness, interest, evaluation, trial and adoption; marketing communications play a key role in enticing customers to progress from awareness to adoption consumption of a product. In this context, there are five 'communications effects': category need, brand awareness, brand attitude, brand purchase intention and purchase facilitation. Marketers must be clear about their promotional objectives, and realistic about the likely returns.

There must be synergy with the specified segmentation or target market strategy, brand positioning and brand strategy. There should be strong associations between the executed MarComms and the understanding of consumers' or customers' buying behaviour, market trends and drivers, competitors' propositions and activities and the apparent capabilities of the product or brand being promoted: marketing communications must be informed by the core marketing analysis explored in Parts One and Two of this book.

Every childhood is worth fighting for. FULL STOP.

The National Society for the Prevention of Cruelty to Children (NSPCC) exists to end cruelty to children. FULL STOP. The NSPCC wants you to join to fight to end cruelty to children. FULL STOP. 'Be the Full Stop ... Join.'

Child abuse happens in many situations: in the home, at school and sports facilities, in residential care and on vacations. The NSPCC's strategy is to protect children in all areas of their lives, through action programmes such as ChildLine, community projects, advising professionals and children, researching the issues around child abuse and of course campaigning. *Someone to turn to* has been a key part of these programmes, collectively termed the 'Full Stop' campaign.

Well at least it was *Full Stop* for over a decade. The campaign was in many ways a victim of its own success, raising awareness of child abuse, encouraging open debate about such issues and leading to many cases being prosecuted.

By placing the issue so firmly in the open, the view was that the climate had changed and therefore so must the nature of the NSPCC's campaigns. This switch was driven also by financial needs. The charity made the brave decision to re-think its branding and use of its long-standing campaign, as explained by its Director of Fundraising: 'The Full Stop campaign focused on the problem. Our new brand shifts that focus to the positive, demonstrating that, although child abuse is a huge issue, it is something we can work together to prevent.'

The charity's Full Stop campaign was extraordinarily successful in terms of creating awareness and attracting donations, raising more than any other UK fundraising appeal in history. It raised more than £250 million by its end in 2009 and had put child abuse firmly on the agenda. Since then, the charity's income has declined. Research indicated that the public was now aware of the problem of child abuse, but did not fully appreciate how the charity helped. With a new strapline – *Every childhood is worth fighting for* – the new campaign focuses on the NSPCC's activities, interventions and outcomes, to reveal how it is preventing child abuse.

Paul Farthing of the NSPCC, speaking to the *Guardian* newspaper, explained:

We have always believed that we can end abuse, and this is now cemented in our new strapline: 'Every childhood is worth fighting for'. We believe it is time to focus on what we can do to prevent child abuse in the first place, with the ultimate goal being to ensure that every child grows up free from abuse. Our new brand will allow us to move the conversation on and talk about the life-changing work we carry out every day.

We're prioritizing front-line services so we can help many more families as well as give parents, teachers and professionals information, advice and support so that they are better-equipped to keep children safe. We are increasing our work in schools to ensure that we talk to every child about what abuse is, and who they can talk to if they need help.

Effective targeting and communication of strong messages are central to the work of the NSPCC. The charity uses public relations, as revealed in the coverage given to its Director of Fundraising in the media, mainstream advertising, direct marketing, digital campaigns and social media, endorsements and events, as well as personal selling, all within a carefully coordinated and tightly budgeted programme of marketing communications.

Sources: www.nspcc.org.uk; *The Guardian*, 3 October 2014; www.civilsociety.co.uk/fundraising/news, 26 September 2014.

Organizations use various promotional approaches to communicate with target markets. Not only for-profit businesses harness the power of effective marketing communications, as evidenced with the NSPCC and its *Every childhood is worth fighting for* message and various campaigns. Practitioners generally refer to the use of the promotion ingredient of the marketing mix as 'marketing communications' or 'MarComms'. It is important not to confuse the promotion ingredient of the marketing mix with either sales promotion or price offer promotions. Promotion in the marketing mix incorporates all aspects of the promotional mix, including advertising, public relations, sponsorship, direct mail, sales promotion, personal selling and the use of the web to communicate with an organization's target audiences. Increasingly, these elements of the promotional mix are coordinated in the guise of integrated marketing communications (IMC).

This chapter looks at the general dimensions of promotion, defining it in the context of marketing and examining the roles it plays. Next, to understand how promotion works, the chapter analyzes the meaning and process of communication, as well as promotion's role within the product adoption process. The remainder of the chapter discusses the major types of promotional method and the factors that influence an organization's decision to use specific methods of promotion: advertising, personal selling, publicity and public relations, sales promotion, sponsorship, direct mail, the internet and direct marketing. The chapter includes an explanation of IMC.

The role of promotion

The nature of promotion in the marketing mix has altered radically in recent years. First, the web enabled communication to customers and potential users with virtually instant responses and follow-up possible along with tailored one-to-one messages not previously possible with mass media communications. Second, the take-off of social media networking removed the power of communication about products, services, brands, companies and those behind these, enabling easy customer-to-customer communication about products, brands and experiences, as explored in Chapters 5 and 19. Few marketers would disagree that Facebook, YouTube, Twitter and the like have presented significant challenges, opportunities and also threats. As a result, many people's views about product or brand communications have changed.

People's attitudes towards promotion anyway vary. Some hold that promotional activities, particularly advertising and personal selling, paint a distorted picture of reality because they provide the customer with only selected information.[1] Proponents of this view often suggest that promotional activities are unnecessary and wasteful, and that promotion costs are too high, resulting in higher prices. They may also argue that too much promotion has caused changes in social values, such as increased materialism. Others take a positive view. Some welcome the potential to communicate well-being and social cause messages. Others believe that advertising messages often project wholesome values, such as affection, generosity or patriotism[2] or that advertising, as a powerful economic force, can free countries from poverty by communicating information.[3] It has also been argued that the advertising of consumer products was a factor in the decline of communism and the move towards a free enterprise system in eastern Europe. However, none of these impressions is completely accurate. Here we confine the discussion to the use of the promotional mix in the execution of a marketing strategy.

Promotion
Communication with individuals, groups or organizations in order to facilitate exchanges by informing and persuading audiences to accept a company's products.

The role of **promotion** in a company is to communicate with individuals, groups or organizations, with the aim of directly or indirectly facilitating exchanges by informing and persuading one or more of the audiences to accept the company's products.[4] Marketers try to communicate with selected audiences about their company and its goods, services and ideas in order to facilitate exchanges.

Exchanges are facilitated by marketers ensuring that information is targeted at appropriate individuals and groups: potential customers, special interest groups such as environmental and consumer groups, current and potential investors and regulatory agencies. Some marketers use **cause-related marketing**, which links the purchase of their products to philanthropic efforts for a particular cause. Cause-related marketing often helps a marketer boost sales and generate goodwill through contributions to causes that members of its target markets want to support. For example, Procter & Gamble has tied promotional efforts for some of its products to a campaign to promote cleaner water for children in developing countries so as to help 300 million children, by reducing illness and saving 20 000 lives each year with purer water in these communities.

Cause-related marketing
Links the purchase of a product to philanthropic efforts for a particular 'good' cause.

Viewed from this wider perspective, promotion can play a comprehensive communications role.[5] Some promotional activities, such as publicity and public relations, can be directed towards helping a company justify its existence and maintain positive, healthy relationships between itself and various groups or stakeholders.

Although a company can direct a single type of communication – such as an advertisement – towards numerous audiences, marketers often design a communication precisely for a specific target market. A company frequently communicates several different messages concurrently, each to a different group. For example, McDonald's may direct one communication towards customers for its Big Mac, a second message about its salads towards health-concerned consumers, a third message towards investors about the company's stable growth, and a fourth communication towards society in general regarding the company's Ronald McDonald Houses, which provide support to families of children suffering from cancer.

To gain maximum benefit from promotional efforts, marketers must make every effort to properly plan, implement, coordinate and control communications. As is explained later, the concept of integrated marketing communications helps to harmonize and coordinate an organization's promotional activities. Effective promotional activities are based on information from the marketing environment (see Chapter 3) and the company's market insights. How effectively marketers can use promotion to maintain positive relationships depends largely on the quantity and quality of information an organization takes in. For example, concerns about genetically modified (GM) foods have led certain supermarkets to improve in-store labelling, so that consumers are better informed about those products affected.

The basic role of promotion is to communicate, so it is important to analyze what communication is and how the communication process works.

The communication process

Communication can be viewed as the transmission of information.[6] For communication to take place, both the sender and the receiver of the information must share some common ground. They must share an understanding of the symbols used to transmit information, usually pictures

Communication
A sharing of meaning through the transmission of information.

Marketing communication
The transmission of persuasive information about a product, service or an idea, targeted at key stakeholders and consumers within the target market segment.

Source
A person, group or organization that has an intended meaning it attempts to share with an audience.

Receiver
An individual, group or organization that decodes a coded message.

Receiving audience
Two or more receivers who decode a message.

Coding process
The process of converting meaning into a series of signs that represent ideas or concepts; also called encoding.

or words. For instance, an individual transmitting the following message may believe he or she is communicating with readers of *Marketing: Concepts and Strategies*:

在工廠吾人製造化粧品,在商店吾人銷售希望。

However, communication has not taken place, because few readers understand the intended message.[7] Thus **communication** is defined here as a sharing of meaning.[8] Implicit in this definition is the notion of transmission of information, because sharing necessitates transmission. Communication is a sharing of meaning through the transmission of information. **Marketing communication** is the transmission of persuasive information about a product, service or an idea, targeted at key stakeholders and consumers within the target market segment. Marketing communications centre on the promotional mix, which comprises advertising, public relations, personal selling, sales promotion, direct mail, sponsorship and the web.

As Figure 16.1 shows, communication begins with a source. A **source** is a person, group or organization that has an intended meaning it attempts to share with an audience. For example, a source could be a political party wishing to recruit new members or an organization that wants to send a message to thousands of consumers through an advertisement. Developing a strategy can enhance the effectiveness of the source's communication. For example, a strategy in which a sales person attempts to influence a customer's decision by eliminating competitive products from consideration has been found to be effective.[9] A **receiver** is the individual, group or organization that decodes a coded message. A **receiving audience** is two or more receivers who decode a message. The intended receivers, or audience, of an advertisement for MBA courses might be business executives wishing to broaden their managerial skills. The source may be a European business school, such as INSEAD.

To transmit meaning, a source must convert that meaning into a series of signs that represent ideas or concepts. This is called the **coding process** or encoding. When encoding meaning into a message, a source must take into account certain characteristics of the receiver or receiving audience. First, to share meaning, the source should use signs that are familiar to the receiver or receiving audience. Marketers who understand this fact realize how important it is to know their target market and to make sure that an advertisement, for example, is written in language that the target market can understand. Thus, when Unilever advertises its Persil washing powder, it makes no attempt to explain the chemical reactions involved when the product removes dirt and grease, because this would not be meaningful to consumers. There have been some notable problems in the language translation of advertisements. For example, Budweiser has been advertised in Spain as the 'Queen of Beers' and the Chinese have been encouraged to 'eat their fingers off' when receiving KFC's slogan 'Finger-Lickin' Good'.[10]

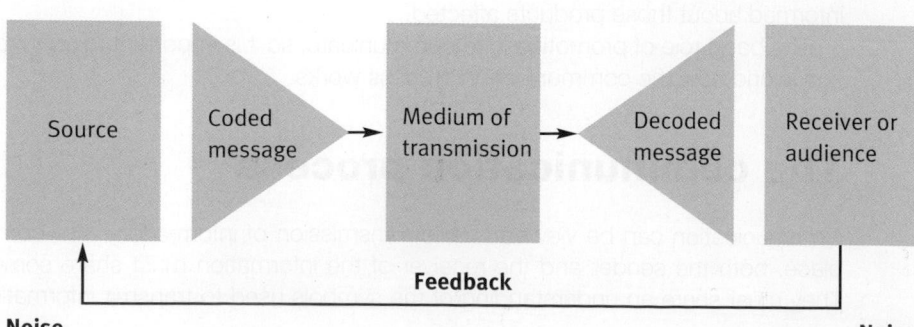

FIGURE 16.1
The communication process

Second, when encoding a meaning, a source should try to use signs that the receiver or receiving audience uses for referring to the concepts the source intends. Marketers should generally avoid signs that can have several meanings for an audience. For example, an international advertiser of soft drinks should avoid using the word soda as a general term for soft drinks. Although in some places soda is taken to mean 'soft drink', in others it may connote bicarbonate of soda, an ice-cream drink, or something to mix with Scotch whisky.

Medium of transmission
The tool used to carry the coded message from the source to the receiver or receiving audience.

To share a coded meaning with the receiver or receiving audience, a source must select and use a medium of transmission. A **medium of transmission** carries the coded message from the source to the receiver or receiving audience. Transmission media include ink on paper, vibrations of air waves produced by vocal cords, chalk marks on a chalkboard and electronically produced communication, as in radio, television, mobile phones, the internet and broadband.

Sometimes a source chooses an inappropriate medium of transmission. A coded message may reach some receivers, but not the right ones. For example, suppose a local theatre group spends most of its advertising budget on radio advertisements. If theatre-goers depend mainly on newspapers for information about local drama, then the theatre group will not reach its intended target audience via radio. Coded messages may also reach intended receivers in an incomplete form because the intensity of the transmission is weak or is not sustained/frequent enough to register.

Decoding process
The process in which signs are converted into concepts and ideas.

In the **decoding process**, signs are converted into concepts and ideas. Seldom does a receiver decode exactly the same meaning that a source encoded. When the result of decoding is different from what was encoded **noise** exists. Noise has many sources and may affect any or all parts of the communication process. When a source selects a medium of transmission through which an audience does not expect to receive a message, noise is likely to occur. Noise sometimes arises within the medium of transmission itself. Erratic broadband coverage, prolonged buffering, radio static, faulty printing processes and laryngitis are sources of noise. Interference on viewers' television sets during an advertisement is noise and reduces the impact of the message. Noise also occurs when a source uses a sign that is unfamiliar to the receiver or that has a different meaning from the one the source intended. Noise may also originate in the receiver. As Chapter 5 discussed, a receiver may be unaware of a coded message because his or her perceptual processes block it out or because the coded message is too obscure.

Noise
A condition that exists when the decoded message is different from that which was encoded.

Feedback
The receiver's response to a message.

The receiver's response to a message is **feedback** to the source. The source usually expects and normally receives feedback, although it may not be immediate. During feedback, the receiver or receiving audience is the source of a message that is directed towards the original source, which then becomes a receiver. Feedback is encoded, sent through a medium of transmission – for example, a survey questionnaire – and then decoded by the receiver, the source of the original communication. It is logical to think of communication as a circular process.

During face-to-face communication, such as in personal selling or product sampling, both verbal and non-verbal feedback can be immediate. Instant feedback enables communicators to adjust their messages quickly to improve the effectiveness of their communication. For example, when a sales person realizes through feedback that a customer does not understand a sales presentation, he or she adapts the presentation to make it more meaningful to the customer. This may be why face-to-face sales presentations create higher behavioural intentions to purchase services than do telemarketing sales contacts.[11] In interpersonal communication, feedback occurs through talking, touching, smiling, nodding, eye movements and other body movements and postures.

When mass communication such as advertising is used, feedback is often slow and difficult to recognize in terms of impact on sales or even buy-in to a brand proposition. If Disneyland Paris increased its advertising in order to raise the number of visitors, it might be 6 to 18 months before the theme park could recognize the effects of the expanded advertising. Although it is harder to recognize, feedback does exist for mass communication. Advertisers do obtain feedback in the form of changes in sales volume or in consumers' attitudes and awareness levels, monitored

FIGURE 16.2
This direct response advertisement provides an opportunity for feedback based on the coupon redemption rate

Source: Courtesy of Nestlé, Cheerios.

through tracking research. The coupon redemption rate for the advertisement in Figure 16.2 provides an opportunity for feedback. It should be noted that web-based comms provide much more instant feedback; response to web-based advertising and other online tools is much more rapidly apparent and easier to assess (see Chapter 19).

Channel capacity
The limit on the volume of information that a particular communication channel can handle effectively.

Each communication channel has a limit on the volume of information it can handle effectively. This limit, called **channel capacity**, is determined by the least efficient component of the communication process. Communications that depend on vocal speech provide a good illustration of this. An individual source can talk only so fast, and there is a limit to how much an individual receiver can take in aurally. Beyond that point, additional messages cannot be decoded; thus, meaning cannot be shared. Although a radio announcer can read several hundred words a minute, a one-minute advertising message should not exceed 150 words because most announcers cannot articulate the words into understandable messages at a rate beyond 150 words per minute. This figure is the limit for both source and receiver, and marketers should keep this in mind when developing radio advertisements. At times, a company creates a television advertisement that contains several types of visual material and several forms of audio message, all transmitted to viewers at the same time. Such communication may not be totally effective, because receivers cannot decode all the messages simultaneously.[12] Researchers believe that Generation Y consumers devote less than ten seconds to viewing a web message, TV advertisement or paragraph of a text document, so advertisers targeting younger consumers must tailor their approach accordingly, as in effect this attention span presents a capacity restraint.

Now that the basic communication process has been explored, it is worth considering more specifically how promotion is used in marketing communications to influence individuals, groups or organizations to accept or adopt a company's products. Although the product adoption process was touched upon briefly in Chapter 10, it is discussed more fully in the following section in order to provide a better understanding of the conditions under which promotion occurs.

Promotion and the product adoption process

Marketers do not promote simply to inform, educate and entertain; they communicate to facilitate exchanges of products or services for money or donations. One long-run purpose of promotion is to influence and encourage buyers to accept or adopt goods, services and ideas. At times, an advertisement may be informative or entertaining, yet it may fail to entice the audience to purchase the product. For example, some advertisements seem to be weak in communicating benefits; they focus instead on getting customers to feel good about the product. The ultimate effectiveness of promotion is determined by the degree to which it affects product adoption among potential buyers or increases the frequency of current buyers' purchases.

To establish realistic expectations about what promotion can do, product adoption should not be viewed as a one-step process. Rarely can a single promotional activity cause an individual to buy a previously unfamiliar product. The acceptance of a product involves many steps. Although there are several ways to look at the **product adoption process**, it is commonly divided into five stages, as depicted in Figure 16.3 and explored in Chapter 10:

1. awareness
2. interest
3. evaluation
4. trial
5. adoption.[13]

In the **awareness stage**, individuals become aware – are made aware by marketers and consumer-to-consumer communication – that the product exists, but they have little information about it and are not concerned about obtaining more.

Consumers enter the **interest stage** when they are motivated to obtain information about the product's features, uses, advantages, disadvantages, price or location. During the **evaluation stage**, individuals consider whether the product will satisfy certain criteria that are crucial for meeting their specific needs. In the **trial stage**, they use or experience the product for the first time, possibly by purchasing a small quantity, by taking advantage of a free sample or demonstration, or by borrowing the product from someone. Supermarkets, for example, frequently offer special promotions to encourage consumers to taste products such as cheese, cooked meats, snacks or pizza. During

Product adoption process
A series of five stages in the acceptance of a product: awareness, interest, evaluation, trial and adoption.

Awareness stage
The beginning of the product adoption process, when individuals become aware that the product exists but have little information about it.

Interest stage
The stage of the product adoption process when customers are motivated to obtain information about the product's features, uses, advantages, disadvantages, price or location.

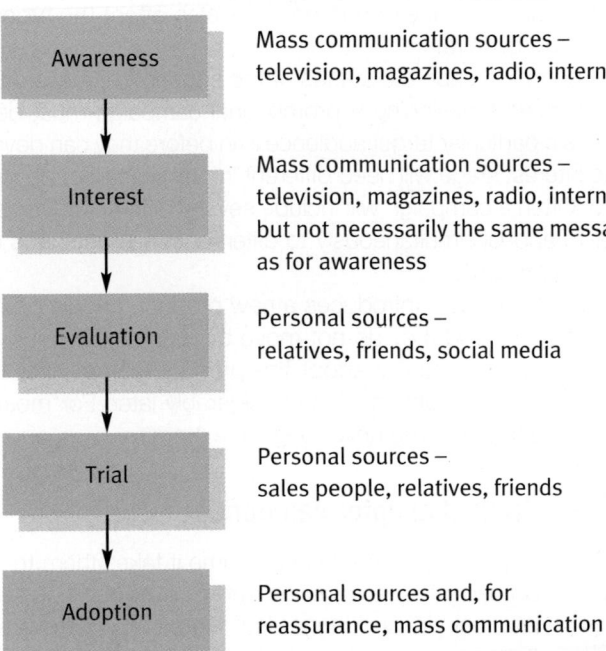

FIGURE 16.3
Effective promotional tools for reaching consumers in various stages of the product adoption process

Evaluation stage
The stage of the product adoption process when customers decide whether the product will satisfy certain criteria that are crucial for meeting their specific needs.

Trial stage
The stage of the product adoption process when individuals use or experience the product for the first time.

Adoption stage
The final stage of product acceptance, when customers choose a specific product.

this stage, potential adopters determine the usefulness or desirability of the product under the specific conditions for which they need it.

Individuals move into the **adoption stage** by choosing the specific product when they need a product of that general type. It cannot be assumed that because a person enters the adoption process he or she will eventually adopt the new product. Rejection may occur at any stage, including adoption. Both product adoption and product rejection can be temporary or permanent. Even if adoption occurs, as explored in Chapter 5, there is no guarantee of brand loyalty. Marketers must work hard to ensure repeat buying and an ongoing relationship.

For the most part, people respond to different information sources at different stages of the adoption process. Figure 16.3 illustrates the most effective sources for each stage. Mass communication sources, such as television advertising or the internet, are often effective for moving large numbers of people into the awareness stage. Producers of consumer goods commonly use massive advertising campaigns when introducing new products. They do so to create product awareness as quickly as possible within a large portion of the target market.

Mass communication sources may also be effective for people in the interest stage who want to learn more about a product. During the evaluation stage, individuals often seek information, opinions and reinforcement from personal sources – relatives, friends and associates. In the trial stage, individuals depend on sales people and postings online for information about how to use the product properly in order to gain the most out of it. Marketers must use advertising carefully when consumers are in the trial stage. If advertisements greatly exaggerate the benefits of a product, the consumer may be disappointed when the product does not meet expectations.[14] It is best to avoid creating expectations that cannot be satisfied, because rejection at this stage will prevent adoption. Friends and peers may also be important sources during the trial stage, along with groups on social media. By the time the adoption stage has been reached, both personal communication from sales personnel and mass communication through advertisements may be required. Even though the particular stage of the adoption process may influence the types of information source consumers use, marketers must remember that other factors – such as the product's characteristics, price and uses, as well as the characteristics of customers – also affect the types of information source that buyers desire and believe.

As people in separate stages of the adoption process often require different types of information, marketers designing a promotional campaign must determine what stage of the adoption process a particular target audience is in before they can develop the message. Potential adopters in the interest stage will need different information from people who have already reached the trial stage. Often a campaign will include several different advertisements and promotional mix tools in order to appeal simultaneously to different consumers who are at different stages in the product adoption process.

When a company introduces a new product, people do not all begin the adoption process at the same time and they do not move through the process at the same speed. Of those people who eventually adopt the product, some enter the adoption process rather quickly, whereas others start considerably later. For most products, there is a group of non-adopters who never begin the process.

Adopter categories
Five groups into which customers can be divided according to the length of time it takes them to adopt a product: innovators, early adopters, early majority, late majority and laggards.

Product adopter categories

Depending on the length of time it takes them to adopt a new product, people can be divided into five major **adopter categories**: innovators, early adopters, early majority, late majority and laggards.[15] Figure 16.4 shows each adopter category and indicates the percentage of total adopters that it typically represents.

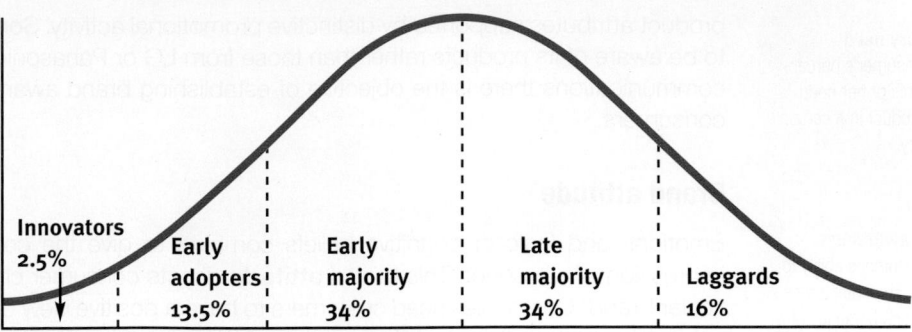

FIGURE 16.4
Distribution of product adopter categories

Innovators 2.5% | Early adopters 13.5% | Early majority 34% | Late majority 34% | Laggards 16%

Innovators
The first people to adopt a new product.

Early adopters
People who choose new products carefully and are often consulted by people from the remaining adopter categories.

Early majority
People who adopt products just prior to the average person.

Late majority
People who are quite sceptical about new products but eventually adopt them because of economic necessity or social pressure.

Laggards
The last people to adopt a new product, suspicious of new products and oriented towards the past.

Five communication effects
Communication aims that include category need, brand awareness, brand attitude, brand purchase intention and purchase facilitation.

Innovators are the first to adopt a new product. They enjoy trying new products and tend to be venturesome. **Early adopters** choose new products carefully and are viewed as 'the people to check with' by those in the remaining adopter categories. People in the **early majority** adopt just prior to the average person; they are deliberate and cautious in trying new products. **Late majority** people, who are quite sceptical about new products, eventually adopt them because of economic necessity or social pressure. **Laggards**, the last to adopt a new product, are oriented towards the past. They are suspicious of new products or unable to afford them easily, and when they finally adopt the innovation, it may already have been replaced by a newer product. When developing promotional efforts, a marketer should bear in mind that people in different adopter categories often need different forms of communication and different types of information or message.

Aims of promotion

Product adoption is a major focus for any promotional activity. In addition, there are five basic communications aims, known as the **five communication effects**. These are:[16]

1. category need
2. brand awareness
3. brand attitude
4. brand purchase intention
5. purchase facilitation.

Category need

The consumer must realize he or she wants a particular product – particularly for innovative new category product launches – and must perceive a **category need** in order to be motivated even to consider a product. Mobile phone networks have persuaded many users of the need for built-in cameras, web browsing or music downloads: eye-catching advertising communicated the benefits of these mobile attributes, creating category need. Tablets had to adopt a similar need-generating approach in their launch communications.

Brand awareness

The consumer must be able to identify – recognize or recall – a manufacturer's or retailer's brand within the category in sufficient detail to make a purchase. **Brand awareness** means that the manufacturer or retailer must make its brand stand out, initially through

Category need
The consumer's perception of his or her need for a product in a certain category.

product attributes supported by distinctive promotional activity. Sony wants consumers to be aware of its products rather than those from LG or Panasonic. In most marketing communications there is the objective of establishing brand awareness among target consumers.

Brand attitude

Brand awareness
The consumer's ability to identify a manufacturer's or retailer's brand in sufficient detail to distinguish it from other brands.

Emotions and logic or cognitive beliefs combine to give the consumer a particular impression of a product. This **brand attitude** directs consumer choice towards a particular brand. Companies need customers to have a positive view of their brands. Much promotional mix activity and the creation of the promotional message relate to developing a favourable brand attitude, but other marketing mix ingredients also impact on these perceptions, notably product design, features and performance.

Brand attitude
A consumer's particular impression of a brand, formed by emotions and logic or cognitive beliefs.

Brand purchase intention

Once a category need and brand awareness are established, if the consumer's brand attitude is favourable, he or she will decide to purchase the particular product and take steps to do so, showing **brand purchase intention**.

Purchase facilitation

Brand purchase intention
The consumer's decision and efforts to purchase the particular product.

Having decided to buy, the consumer requires the product to be readily available at a convenient location, at a suitable price and from a familiar dealer: **purchase facilitation**. A manufacturer or supplier must ensure that other marketing mix factors product, people, place (distribution) and price do not hinder the purchase. Sony customers expect wide distribution from reputable retailers, with no budget pricing. Sony produces high-quality goods, but it has several well-respected competitors and must ensure product availability and continued product improvement to prevent brand switching.

Purchase facilitation
Circumstances that make it possible for the consumer to purchase the product: availability, location, price and familiarity of vendor.

To provide a better understanding of how promotion can move people closer to the acceptance of goods, services and ideas, the next section focuses on the major promotional methods available to an organization the promotional mix and integrated marketing communications.

The promotional mix

Promotional mix
The specific combination of ingredients an organization uses to promote a product, traditionally including four ingredients: advertising, personal selling, publicity and public relations and sales promotion.

Several types of promotional methods can be used to communicate with individuals, groups and organizations. When an organization combines specific ingredients to promote a particular product, that combination constitutes the promotional mix for that product. The four traditional ingredients of a **promotional mix** are advertising, personal selling, publicity/public relations and sales promotion. Increasingly, sponsorship and direct mail are elements of the promotional mix in their own right (see Figure 16.5).[17] The internet and direct marketing are relatively recent additions to the promotional mix. For some products, organizations use all of these ingredients; for other products, two or three will suffice. Each has its pros and cons, but each must be pertinent to the product category's accepted norms, to targeted buyers' expectations and behaviours, and to the product's adopted brand positioning and tone of voice. This section analyzes the major ingredients of a promotional mix and the chief factors that influence an organization to include specific ingredients in the promotional mix for a specific product. Each ingredient is explored more thoroughly in subsequent chapters.

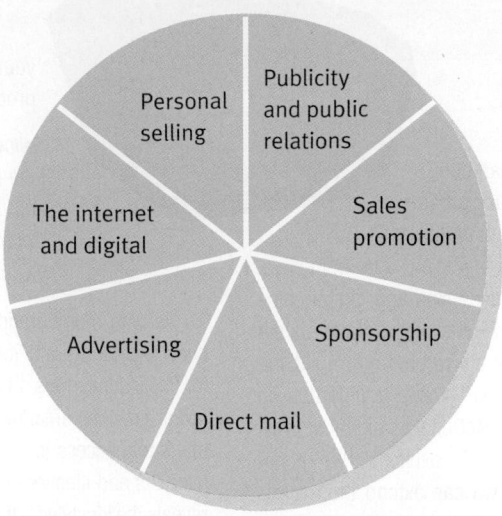

FIGURE 16.5
Possible ingredients of an organization's promotional mix

Promotional mix ingredients

At this point consideration is given to some general characteristics of advertising, personal selling, publicity and public relations, sales promotion, sponsorship, direct mail, the internet and direct marketing.

Advertising
A paid form of non-personal communication about an organization and its products that is transmitted to a target audience through a mass medium.

Advertising   **Advertising** is a paid form of non-personal communication about an organization and its products that is transmitted to a target audience through a mass medium such as television, radio, newspapers, magazines, direct mail, public transport, outdoor displays, catalogues or the web. Individuals and organizations use advertising to promote goods, services, ideas, issues and people. As it is highly flexible, advertising offers the options of reaching an extremely large target audience or focusing on a small, precisely defined segment of the population. For instance, McDonald's advertising focuses on a large audience of potential fast-food consumers, ranging from children to adults, whereas advertising for DeBeers' diamonds focuses on a much smaller and specialized target market. The main uses of advertising include the promotion of products or an organization in order to create awareness among targeted audiences, the stimulation of demand, the off-setting of competitors' advertising, to support personal selling drives, for the education of a target market about a brand and its enhanced marketing mix or product benefits and attributes, to increase consumption and the perceived uses of a product, to remind and reinforce with intended customers, and to even-out seasonal sales fluctuations or manage production cycles.

Advertising offers several benefits. It can be an extremely cost-efficient promotional method because it reaches a vast number of people at a low cost per person. For example, if the cost of an eight-colour, one-page advertisement in the *Sunday Telegraph* is £34 000, and the newspaper reaches 500 000 readers, the cost of reaching 1000 subscribers is only £68 per person. Advertising also enables the user to repeat the message a number of times. Unilever advertises many of its products – cleaning products, foods, cosmetics – on television, in magazines, via the web and through outdoor advertising. Advertising repetition has been found to be especially effective for brand name extensions beyond the original product category.[18] In addition, advertising a product in a certain way can add to its value. For example, BMW cars are advertised as having more sophistication, style and technical innovation than Honda, Toyota and other Japanese companies' vehicles. The visibility that an organization gains from advertising enhances the company's public image. There clearly is a link between a product's brand positioning and the role of marketing communications.

A web presence: now routine behaviour

Topical insight

In the early days of web-based marketing many corporate giants avoided using banners, buttons and other early forms of internet advertising, believing them to be inefficient and ineffective. Now companies embrace web advertising and digital communications. McDonald's uses its website and digital media to develop a relationship with its consumers and build the brand's profile. *McDonald's on your mobile* and *Wraps on YouTube* are just two examples of McDonald's digital activity. As the company's director for media explains, 'We're not going to sell burgers online, but we can extend the experience of the brand online and bring McDonald's to life online.'

Digital experts believe few consumer or business brands can now avoid harnessing web-based marketing communications, particularly if – as in the case of McDonald's – the target audience is young and made up of consumers who have been brought up as 'digital dream kids', used to 24-hour online access anywhere they happen to be.

Nike has many websites, some of which promote specific brands, linking into its sponsorship of entertainers and sports stars. Guerrilla moves, such as mentioning its websites or celebrity tie-ins in chat room messages, have been hugely successful for the company in attracting hundreds of thousands of visitors to its websites for specific online promotions and advertising campaigns. Sports-focused video clips, downloadable tracks, musical ePostcards suitable for personalization, and games have proved a big hit with the youth market targeted by so many Nike products.

Follow Us on Twitter
Like Us on Facebook
Join Us on Instagram
Connect With Us on Google+
Watch Us on YouTube

As with many brands, a digital presence on Twitter, Facebook, Instagram and YouTube are now routinized expectations for Pepsi consumers and the company's brand managers. Pepsi online provides entertainment, promotions, news, merchandise offers and access to a digital community of consumers sharing interests and lifestyles in which Pepsi plays a part. *Pepsi Pulse* reveals the lifestyles – the pulse – of Pepsi users, harnessing the blogs and posted photos of consumers around the world to create an entertaining and involving way for consumers to become part of a lifestyle-led online community. As *Pepsi Pulse* states, *Now is what you make of it. Show us how you #livefornow.*

The Beautiful Game site celebrates soccer, reflecting Pepsi's growing sponsorship of the sport, but in a manner which engages with Pepsi consumers in another lifestyle experience. *Beats of the Beautiful Game* linked soccer with Pepsi's long-term love of music, with the album available on iTunes. Whether sports, celeb postings, consumers' blogs and videos, Pepsi is harnessing the web to advertise its wares, build its brand and engage consumers in its online community.

Sources: McDonald's, Nike and Pepsi, with thanks to *Advertising Age* and *Campaign*.

Advertising also has several disadvantages. Even though the cost per person reached may be low, the absolute monetary outlay can be extremely high, especially for advertisements shown during popular television programmes. These high costs can limit, and sometimes prevent, the use of advertising in a promotional mix. Moreover, advertising rarely provides rapid feedback. Measuring its effect on sales is difficult, and it ordinarily has a less persuasive impact on customers than, for example, personal selling.[19] With the growth in satellite channels, the creation of ever greater numbers of consumer and trade magazines, the role of the web for advertisers and interactive television, the choice of media for advertisers is growing increasingly complex and prone to error unless handled by specialist media buyers.

As illustrated in Figure 16.6, there are eight stages in creating an advertising campaign:

1. The identification and understanding of the advertising target audience, which relates to the company's target market strategy and a deep appreciation of targeted consumers' or business customers' expectations, perceptions, requirements and buying behaviour, as explored in Chapters 5 and 6.

2. The scoping of objectives for the campaign, such as sales levels, increased awareness of the brand, a specific impact on a competitor or a change in the target audience's perceptions and attitudes.

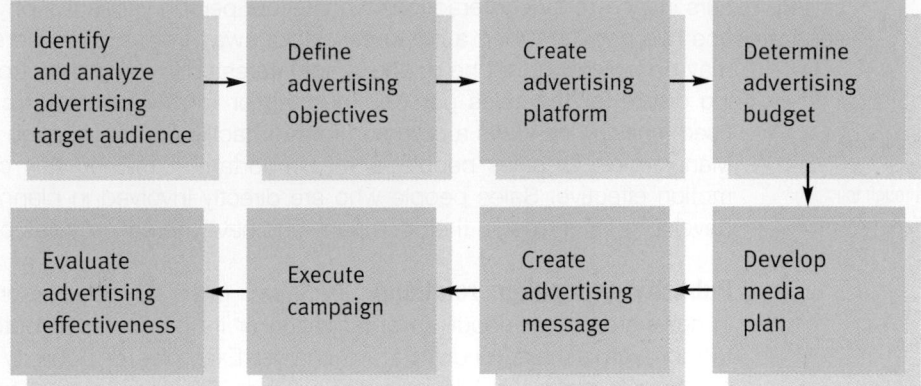

FIGURE 16.6
General steps for developing and implementing an advertising campaign

3. The creation of the advertising platform which has relevance to the target audience and seeks to differentiate the brand from rivals, such as Andrex's puppies or BMW's *The Ultimate Driving Machine*.

4. Agreement on the available advertising budget, which is often a specific project amount, the percentage of sales approach or an amount set to match a specific competitor's activity.

5. The highly specialized act of establishing a media plan, which with the proliferation of TV channels, consumer magazines, local radio stations, eChannels and viral possibilities, has become far more flexible but much more complex.

6. The creation of the specific message, such as Direct Line's triumphant red phone proposition or Asda's value-led deals.

7. The execution of the campaign using the agreed platform, message, media and associated IMC activities.

8. The evaluation of the effectiveness of the campaign and assessment of its apparent benefits.

Personal selling
The use of personal communication in an exchange situation to inform customers and persuade them to purchase products.

Personal selling   Selling that involves informing customers and persuading them to purchase products through personal communication in an exchange situation is called **personal selling**. The phrase 'to purchase products' should be interpreted broadly to encompass the acceptance of ideas and issues. **Telemarketing**, described as direct selling over the telephone, relies heavily on personal selling.

Personal selling has both advantages and limitations when compared with advertising. Advertising is general communication aimed at a relatively large target audience, whereas personal selling involves more specific communication aimed at one person or several people. Reaching one person through personal selling costs considerably more than doing so through advertising, but personal selling efforts often have a greater impact on customers. Personal selling also provides immediate feedback, which allows marketers to adjust their message to improve communication. It helps them determine and respond to customers' needs for information.

Telemarketing
Direct selling over the telephone, relying heavily on personal selling.

Kinesic communication
Body language, including winking, head nodding, hand gestures and arm movements.

Proxemic communication
A subtle form of communication used in face-to-face interactions when either person varies the physical distance that separates the two.

When a sales person and customer meet face-to-face, they use several types of interpersonal communication. Obviously, the predominant communication form is language, both speech and writing. In addition, a sales person and customer frequently use **kinesic communication** or body language by moving their heads, eyes, arms, hands, legs or torsos. Winking, head nodding, hand gestures and arm motions are forms of kinesic communication. A good sales person can often evaluate a prospect's interest in a product or presentation by watching for eye contact and head nodding. **Proxemic communication**, a less obvious form of communication used in personal selling, occurs in face-to-face interactions when either person varies the physical distance that separates the two people. When a customer backs away from a sales person, that individual may be indicating that he or she is not interested in the product or may be expressing dislike for the sales person. Touching or **tactile communication** can also be used; shaking hands is a common form of tactile communication in many countries. Management of sales people is very important in making this component of promotion effective. Sales people who are directly involved in planning sales activities develop greater trust in their company and have increased sales performance.[20]

Tactile communication
Interpersonal communication through touching, including shaking hands.

Publicity and public relations   **Publicity** refers to non-personal communication in news-story form about an organization or its products, or both, that is transmitted through a mass medium at no charge. Examples of publicity include magazine, newspaper, radio and television news stories about new retail stores, new products or personnel changes in an organization. Although both advertising and publicity are transmitted through mass communication, the sponsor does not pay the media costs for publicity and is not identified. Nevertheless, publicity should never be viewed as free communication. There are clear costs associated with preparing news releases and encouraging media personnel to broadcast or print them. A business that uses publicity regularly must have employees to perform these activities, or obtain the services of a public relations consultancy or an advertising agency. Either way, the company bears the costs of the activities.

Publicity
Non-personal communication in news-story form about an organization and/or its products that is transmitted through a mass medium at no charge.

Publicity must be planned and implemented so that it is compatible with, and supportive of, other elements in the promotional mix.[21] However, publicity cannot always be controlled to the extent that other elements of the promotional mix can be. For example, just as Toyota prepared for new model launches, major component failures led to a series of embarrassing product recalls, causing issues for the brand's reputation and credibility which suddenly had to be addressed by the company's public relations partners. The **public relations** mechanism manages and controls the process of using publicity.[22]

Marketing public relations, now so important because of information availability online and growing digital consumer-to-consumer communications via social media, promotes products or brands, while corporate public relations focuses on the company and its impact on society with all stakeholders and not just intended customers. Marketers make use of PR events, campaigns and programmes. In addition to using a company's web pages to communicate information, PR practitioners use press releases, feature articles, press conferences, interviews, visits and stunts. Third party endorsement of a product or company by trusted and respected independent authorities and personalities can prove very effective. In addition to creating product or brand awareness and generating interest, public relations is very important in handling crises and combating any negative publicity engineered by competitors or stemming from the media, regulatory bodies or public interest groups.

Public relations
Managing and controlling the process of using publicity effectively. It is the planned and sustained effort to establish and maintain goodwill and understanding between an organization and its target publics.

Sales promotion   A **sales promotion** is an activity or material that acts as a direct inducement by offering added value to, or incentive for, the product to resellers, sales people or consumers.[23] Examples of sales promotion include coupons, on-pack deals, trade shows, bonuses and contests used to enhance the sales of a product. The term sales promotion should not be confused with promotion; sales promotion is but a part of the more comprehensive area of promotion that encompasses advertising, personal selling, publicity and public relations, sponsorship, direct mail, the web and direct marketing. Some sales promotions, however, are closely associated with additional elements of the promotional mix. Currently, marketers spend about half as much on sales promotion as they do on advertising. Sales promotion appears to be growing in use more than advertising.

Sales promotion
An activity or material that acts as a direct inducement by offering added value to or incentive for the product to resellers, sales people or consumers.

Marketers frequently rely on sales promotion to improve the effectiveness of other promotional mix ingredients, especially advertising and personal selling. For example, some organizations allocate 25 per cent of their annual promotional budget to trade shows in order to introduce new products, meet key industry personnel and identify likely prospects.[24] For many business-to-business marketers, sales promotions are very important.

Marketers design sales promotion to produce immediate, short-run sales increases. For example, the major brewers, such as Heineken and Coors, use a continuous programme of sales promotion techniques to boost sales in the highly competitive beer and lager market: free drinks and prize competitions, scratch cards and trade incentives.

Generally, if a company employs advertising or personal selling, it either depends on them continuously or turns to them cyclically. However, a marketer's use of sales promotion tends to be irregular. Many products are seasonal. For example, Thomas Cook promotes summer package holidays predominantly in the winter and spring months. Flymo pushes its lawn mowers and other gardening equipment from Easter onwards. On the whole, sales promotions are infrequent, ad hoc campaigns.

Consumer sales promotions encourage consumers to patronize a specific retail store or to try a particular product, or they strive to bring forward purchases by existing customers. Techniques include coupons, free samples, demonstrations, competitions, frequent-user incentives and loyalty programmes, point-of-sale materials, money refunds, premiums, product bundling and price-off offers. Trade sales promotions encourage wholesalers, retailers or distributors to stock a product, increase display space and market the product. Popular techniques include buy-back allowances, buying allowances/temporary price reductions, count and re-count promotions, free merchandise, point-of-sales materials, merchandise allowances, cooperative advertising, dealer listings, money to incentivize sales personnel, sales competitions and dealer loaders/gifts.

Sponsorship

The financial or material support of an event, activity, person, organization or product by an unrelated organization or donor.

Sponsorship   The financial or material support of an event, activity, person organization or product by an unrelated organization or donor is called **sponsorship**. Funds are made available to the recipient of the sponsorship in return for prominent public recognition of the benefactor's generosity and display of the sponsor's name, products and brands. Sponsorship is no longer confined to the arts or the sporting world, although many galleries, theatrical companies, sports events and teams could not survive without sponsorship. Research and development, buildings, degree courses and charitable events all often benefit from sponsorship. The donor or sponsor gains the benefits of enhanced company, brand or individual reputation and awareness, as well as improved morale and employee relations. Note the number of prestigious or well-known brands sponsoring the Olympics or football's World Cup. It is important to select sponsorship partners with care, as negative publicity about one may in turn tarnish the reputation of the other.

Direct mail

A method of communication used to entice prospective customers or charitable donors to invest in products, services or worthy causes.

Direct mail   The direct mail industry takes a significant slice of the promotional budgets for many companies and organizations. Few households and companies fail to receive direct mail solicitations. **Direct mail** is used to entice prospective customers or charitable donors to invest in products, services or worthy causes. Throughout Europe, direct mail is used as a pre-sell technique prior to a sales call, to generate orders, qualify prospects for a sales call, follow up a sale, announce special or localized sales, and raise funds for charities and not-for-profit organizations. Good database management is essential, and the material must be targeted carefully to overcome the growing public aversion to 'junk mail'.

Internet

A network of computer networks stretching across the world, linking computers of different types and sharing information.

The internet   From humble beginnings as a 'talking shop' for boffins and computer buffs, the **internet** – a network of computer networks stretching across the world,

Topical insight

Facebook can be a marketer's best friend and her worst enemy

Founded in 2004, Facebook was initially created just to connect students at Harvard with other Ivy League universities; it soon expanded to include family, friends and colleagues. Since being opened to the general public, it has grown to support more than 900 million users daily. There are 1.4 billion monthly active users and two billion mobile users. Facebook users share more than 5 billion pieces of web content daily. Although it still serves its original purpose, Facebook has acquired diverse new roles, even changing how people use the web in conducting purchasing research … many people now seek recommendations from their social media networks before conducting other kinds of searches.

Marketing strategists say businesses now must worry about how to connect to consumers via social media. One of the ways is to create a fan page, of which Facebook has billions. The average user becomes a fan of four pages each month. Fan pages use widgets, which help companies keep information on who is becoming a fan of their page. Businesses can use widgets to learn about and track their customers in order to better understand and serve them. These pages are inexpensive and easy to produce, making them accessible to all businesses.

Businesses must tread carefully, however. Generally, Facebook users do not want to feel as if they are being subjected to sales pitches. In order to make fans feel connected to a company – without making them feel like they are being pressured to buy something against their will – companies must dedicate time to responding to fan posts and providing relevant information. Problems aside, fan pages and other uses of widgets are a cheap way for companies to advertise their goods and services while also garnering information about consumers. However, Facebook and other social media present challenges, too. For Example, Facebook is readily available to competitors and is vulnerable to sharing of negative messaging by unscrupulous rivals and third parties with vested interests.

linking computers of different types – is now firmly established in many office workers' daily routines, accessed in millions of households and by consumers on the move through smartphones and tablets. Marketers have been quick to identify this additional medium as an opportunity for providing existing and potential customers with company, product and brand information. Most large companies now have their own websites, while the major internet servers such as Google and Yahoo! are targeting small businesses and providing eCommerce capability at affordable prices.[25] Web-based marketing is particularly important in many business-to-business markets. Use of the internet is not uniform across all parts of society, although there is evidence to suggest that it is no longer the pastime of only the young, affluent and well educated. Scrambling of confidential information such as credit card and bank account details has enabled the recent explosion in the number of purchases made online.

Digital marketing
The use of technology-led channels of communication and selling to manage customer interaction and provide customer experience in a digitally connected environment.

As a promotional mix ingredient, the internet provides a tool that can be interactive, updated or modified quickly, and that can produce material aimed at very tightly defined target groups or even individual consumers. This is why **digital marketing** is so popular (see Chapter 19). From Interflora to Tesco to JCB, the internet is increasingly part of the promotional mix and, for direct marketers, the actual point of the sales transaction. Many television and press advertisements for services or consumer goods now direct their target audience to associated websites for additional information. Consumers can then interact with these hosts, in many instances, via email, chatrooms and interactive web page information request facilities. Websites must be tailored to match the target customer buying behaviour and expectations, and must be informative but not mesmerizing, while reflecting the existing branding and product positioning already established by an organization's marketers. They require expert design and updating, as with any ingredient in the promotional mix.

Intranets – internal in-company internet networks – have improved communications within many organizations, becoming an important facet of internal marketing.

Direct marketing   First used in the 1960s, until recently direct marketing described the most common direct marketing approaches: direct mail and mail order. Currently experiencing a surge in popularity, direct marketing now encompasses all the communications tools that enable a marketer to deal directly with targeted customers: direct mail, telemarketing, direct response television advertising, door-to-door/personal selling, the web and **mobile marketing**. **Direct marketing** is a decision by a company's marketers to both:

- select a marketing channel that avoids dependence on marketing channel intermediaries
- focus marketing communications activity on promotional mix ingredients that deal directly with targeted customers.

Direct marketing is now adopted by a host of organizations ranging from fast-moving consumer goods companies, business-to-business marketers, charities and even government departments.[26] Of all elements of the promotional mix, it is reported to be the fastest growing, but this is partly a reflection of the large number of promotional mix ingredients it includes and the role of the web.[27]

In terms of the promotional mix, there are several key implications. Direct mail is on the increase. Telemarketing has grown and will continue to do so, with more organizations turning to the direct marketing toolkit aided by advances in automated call centres. Door-to-door selling and leaflet dropping, visible forms of direct marketing encountered by most householders, are also on the increase. Direct response advertising containing a call for action within the advertisement by coupon, telephone or web now makes up close to a third of all advertising as marketers turn to direct marketing, and as the growth in satellite and cable television channels enables more direct response television advertising. The internet, too, is used by direct marketers to communicate with current and prospective customers. The deployment of any direct marketing campaign must strive to reflect targeted customer behaviour, needs and perceptions; provide a plausible proposition that is clearly differentiated from competitors' propositions; and match an organization's corporate goals and trading philosophy.

The more radical shift in recent years towards digital channels, digital marketing and mobile marketing, along with greater consumer-to-consumer communication facilitated by social media, have revolutionized how marketers manage their promotional strategies, create awareness and foster product adoption. The digital era has added significantly to marketers' fire power and provided the opportunity for more tailored, frequent and interactive communication. The core ingredients of the promotional mix are still integral to marketing communications, but the digital era has brought a new wealth of options. These are explored in Chapter 19.

Integrated marketing communications (IMC)

Currently popular is the concept of **integrated marketing communications (IMC)**. This is the coordination and integration of all marketing communication tools, avenues and sources within a company into a seamless programme of marketing communications activities. As marketers increasingly operate across multiple channels and embrace digital marketing, the principles of IMC are particularly pertinent to ensure consistent customer experience and branding across channels. The intention of IMC is to maximize the impact on consumers or business customers and other target audiences at the lowest possible cost. IMC avoids the waste and duplication inherent in some organizations in which each element of the promotional mix is controlled by separate managers and may even be executed through different external agencies. There is nothing worse than when an advertising campaign on radio created by one agency has little resemblance to a television campaign running at the same time, and created by another advertising agency. This is often compounded by digital, public relations, sponsorship, packaging

---

Mobile marketing
Marketing to encourage consumer engagement anywhere or anytime while on or using a mobile device, such as a smartphone or tablet, and heavily dependent on mobile apps which provide users with information, entertainment and location based services.

Direct marketing
A decision by a company's marketers to select a marketing channel which avoids dependence on marketing channel intermediaries and to focus marketing communications activity on promotional mix ingredients which deal directly with targeted customers.

Integrated marketing communications (IMC)
The coordination and integration of all marketing communication tools, avenues and sources within a company into a seamless programme that maximizes the impact on consumers and other end-users, at minimal cost.

and sales promotions being implemented by yet more agencies in a poorly coordinated fashion. On one occasion, five different agencies were developing marketing communications for market-leading Gordon's Gin, each using different shades of green – the brand's famous identity – and adopting various typefaces for the logo.

IMC is the integration of the whole promotional mix, but also all business-to-business, marketing channel, customer-focused and internally directed communications. IMC as a concept is focused on complete coordination and harmonized execution of various campaigns across the elements of the promotional mix. Rather than treating all aspects of the promotional mix and internal marketing separately, often utilizing many different departments and external agencies in an uncoordinated manner, the company instead opts to fully harmonize these activities. This does not have to result in only one supplying agency being commissioned: coordination ensures shared goals and common approaches to execution in a carefully scheduled manner. The benefits of IMC include greater clarity to customers, marketing channel members, employees and suppliers, as well as reduced costs, stronger impact in the marketplace and more effective branding.

Advertising, along with the rest of the promotional mix, exists to help implement a brand's target market strategy by communicating the product appeal and the brand positioning image to intended customers and other key stakeholders (see Chapter 8). Occasionally, a creative execution can be sufficiently memorable and strike a chord so well with the target audience, that an organization rethinks its whole marketing mix for a brand or product. BMW had already decided to focus its whole strategy on the driving experience, but the inception of the memorable *The Ultimate Driving Machine* positioning strapline has for over 35 years steered the strategy. While Mercedes emphasizes the comfort and luxury of its cars to all in the cabin, German rival BMW designs its vehicles around the driver, whose experience is indeed more rewarding than that of cabin passengers. The company prides itself on its engineering and technology innovation, updating new models with dozens of improvements and innovative gadgets, but all orientated primarily around the driver's position and use, along with the drivability of the vehicle. The brand's marketing communications, using all aspects of the promotional mix (just go to www.bmw.co.uk for some examples) in an integrated programme, emphasizing both the driving experience and the technical prowess of the range, under *The Ultimate Driving Machine* brand positioning.

Now that the basic components of an organization's promotional mix have been discussed, it is important to consider how that mix is created. The factors and conditions that affect the selection of the promotional methods a specific organization uses in its promotional mix for a particular product need to be examined.

Selecting promotional mix ingredients

Marketers vary the composition of promotional mixes for many reasons. Although all ingredients can be included in a promotional mix, frequently a marketer chooses not to use them all. In addition, many organizations that market multiple product lines use several promotional mixes simultaneously.

An organization's promotional mix (or mixes) is not an unchanging part of the marketing mix. Marketers can and do change the composition of their promotional mixes, often more easily and faster than adjusting the product or channel ingredients of the marketing mix. The specific promotional mix ingredients employed and the intensity with which they are used depend on a variety of factors, including the organization's promotional resources, objectives and policies; characteristics of the target market; competitors' activities; characteristics of the product; and the cost and availability of promotional methods.

Promotional resources, objectives and policies   The quality of an organization's promotional resources affects the number and relative intensity of promotional methods that can be included in a promotional mix. If a company's promotional budget is extremely limited, the business is likely to rely on personal selling because it is easier to measure a sales person's contribution to sales than to measure the effect of advertising. A company must have a sizeable promotional budget if it is to use regional or national advertising and sales promotion activities. Organizations with extensive promotional resources can usually include more ingredients in their promotional mixes. However, larger promotional budgets do not necessarily imply that the companies will use a greater number of promotional methods.

An organization's promotional objectives and policies also influence the types of promotion used. If a company's objective is to create mass awareness of a new convenience good, its promotional mix is likely to lean heavily towards advertising, the web, sales promotion and possibly publicity. If a company hopes to educate consumers about the features of durable goods, such as home electrical appliances, its promotional mix may combine a moderate amount of advertising, possibly some sales promotion efforts designed to attract customers to retail stores and a great deal of in-store personal selling, this being an excellent way to inform customers about these types of product. If a company's objective is to produce immediate sales of consumer non-durables, such as paper products and many grocery goods, the promotional mix will probably stress advertising and sales promotion efforts. Business-to-business marketers often use detailed trade advertising, personal selling through sales representatives, sales promotions – often in the guise of bulk discounts and trade show exhibits – and direct mail of brochures and price lists, as well as their websites.

Characteristics of the target market   The size, geographic distribution and socio-economic characteristics of an organization's target market also help dictate the ingredients to be included in a product's promotional mix. To some degree, market size determines the composition of the mix. If the size is quite limited, the promotional mix will probably emphasize personal selling, which can be quite effective for reaching small numbers of people. Organizations that sell to business markets, and companies that market their products through only a few wholesalers, frequently make personal selling the major component of their promotional mixes. When markets for a product consist of millions of customers, organizations use advertising and sales promotion because these methods can reach masses of people at a low cost per person.

The geographic distribution of a company's customers can affect the combination of promotional methods used. Personal selling is more feasible if a company's customers are concentrated in a small area than if they are dispersed across a vast region. When the company's customers are numerous and dispersed, advertising an online activity may be more practical.

The distribution of a target market's socio-economic characteristics, such as age, income or education, may dictate the types of promotional technique that a marketer selects. For example, personal selling may be much more successful than print advertisements for communicating with poorly educated people, because it allows meaning or product attributes to be explained face-to-face.

Activities of competitors   While in general terms, differentiation is sought by marketers, if key competitors are educating customers to expect a certain form of marketing communication, it is difficult not to follow suit. If a strong rival is promoting new product features or attractive pricing, a brand may be forced to adopt similar messaging and choices of media.

Characteristics of the product   Generally, promotional mixes for business products concentrate on personal selling and the web. In promoting consumer goods, on the other hand, advertising plays a major role. This generalization should be treated with caution, however. Industrial goods producers do use some advertising to promote their goods, particularly in the trade press and online. Advertisements for computers, road-building equipment and aircraft are not altogether uncommon, and sales promotion is deployed to promote industrial goods. Personal selling is used extensively for services and consumer durables, such as insurance, leisure and education, home appliances, cars and houses, and consumer convenience items are promoted mainly through advertising and sales promotion. Publicity appears in promotional mixes for business goods, consumer goods and services. Many organizations use direct mail, and more are now examining the growing use of corporate sponsorship. Of course most organizations have websites and now use digital marketing.

Marketers of highly seasonal products are often forced to emphasize advertising, and possibly sales promotion, because off-season sales will not support an extensive year-round salesforce. Although many toy producers have salesforces to sell to resellers (retailers), a number of these companies depend to a large extent on advertising to promote their products.

The price of a product also influences the composition of the promotional mix. High-priced products call for more personal selling because consumers associate greater risk with the purchase of such products and usually want the advice of a sales person. For example, few consumers would be willing to purchase a refrigerator or personal computer from a self-service establishment. For low-priced convenience items, marketers use advertising rather than personal selling at the retail level. The profit margins on many of these items are too low to justify the use of sales people, and most customers do not need advice from sales personnel when buying such products.

A further consideration in creating an effective promotional mix is the stage of the product life cycle (see Chapter 10). During the introduction stage, a good deal of advertising and digital marketing may be necessary for business-to-business and consumer products to make potential users aware of a new product. For many products, personal selling and sales promotion are also helpful at this stage. In the case of consumer non-durables, the growth and maturity stages call for a heavy emphasis on advertising and a strong web presence. Business products, on the other hand, often require a concentration of personal selling and some sales promotion efforts during these stages. In the decline stage, marketers usually decrease their promotional activities, especially advertising. Promotional efforts in the decline stage often centre on personal selling, sales promotion efforts and a web presence.

The intensity of market coverage is yet another factor that affects the composition of the promotional mix. When a product is marketed through intensive distribution, the organization depends strongly on advertising and sales promotion. A number of convenience products – such as lotions, cereals and coffee – are promoted through samples, coupons and cash refunds. Where marketers have opted for selective distribution, marketing mixes vary considerably in terms of amount and type of promotional method. Items handled through exclusive distribution frequently demand more personal selling and less advertising. Expensive watches and high-quality furniture are products that are typically promoted heavily through personal selling. Intensive, selective and exclusive distribution were discussed in Chapter 14.

A product's use also affects the combination of promotional methods. Manufacturers of highly personal products, such as non-prescription contraceptives, feminine hygiene products and haemorrhoid treatments, count on advertising for promotion because many users do not like to talk to sales personnel about such products.

Cost and availability of promotional methods The cost of promotional methods is a major factor to analyze when developing a promotional mix. National advertising and sales promotion efforts require large expenditures. For example, some detergent brands have annual advertising budgets of £20 to £30 million. Some retailers spend £20 million in only the few weeks leading up to Christmas. However, if the efforts are effective in reaching extremely large numbers of people, the cost per individual reached may be quite small, possibly a few pence per person. Moreover, not all forms of advertising are expensive. Many small, local businesses advertise their products through local newspapers, magazines, radio stations, outdoor signs, public transport and on the web.

Another consideration that marketers must explore when formulating a promotional mix is the availability of promotional techniques. Despite the tremendous number of media vehicles, a company may find that no available advertising medium reaches a certain market effectively. For example, a product may be banned from being advertised on television, as are cigarettes in many countries. A stockbroker may find no suitable advertising medium for investors in Manchester United Football Club – should the stockbroker use financial publications, sports magazines or general media?

The problem of media availability becomes even more pronounced when marketers try to advertise in other countries. Some media, such as television, simply may not be available to advertisers. Television advertising in Scandinavia is minimal. In the UK 12 minutes of advertising are permitted per average hour of terrestrial television. The media that are available may not be open to certain types of advertisement. For example, in Germany, advertisers are forbidden to make brand comparisons in television advertisements. Other promotional methods have limitations as well. An organization may wish to increase the size of its salesforce but be unable to find qualified personnel. In the US, some state laws prohibit the use of certain types of sales promotion activities, such as contests. Such prohibited techniques are thus 'unavailable' in those locations.

Push policy versus pull policy

Another element that marketers should consider when they plan a promotional mix is whether to use a push policy or a pull policy. With a **push policy**, the producer promotes the product only to the next institution down the marketing channel. For instance, in a marketing channel with wholesalers and retailers, the producer promotes to the wholesaler, in this case the channel member just below the producer (see Figure 16.7). Each channel member in turn promotes to the next channel member. A push policy normally stresses personal selling. Sometimes sales promotion, direct mail and advertising are used in conjunction with personal selling to push the products down through the channel.

As Figure 16.7 shows, a company using a **pull policy** promotes directly to consumers with the intention of developing a strong consumer demand for the products. It does so through advertising, sales promotion, direct mail, the web, sponsorship and packaging that helps manufacturers build and maintain market share.[28] As a result, consumers are persuaded to seek the products in retail stores, and retailers will in turn go to wholesalers or the producer to buy the products. The policy is thus intended to 'pull' the goods down through the channel by creating demand at the consumer level.

A push policy can be combined with a pull policy. Mars, for example, has a pull policy aimed at the consumer: sponsorship of events and advertising create awareness; packaging, sales promotions such as competitions or discounts and direct mail prompt product trial and adoption. Simultaneously, the company's push policy of trade advertising, sales promotions and personal selling persuades channel members to stock and retail its products.

Push policy
A promotional policy in which the producer promotes the product only to the next institution down the marketing channel.

Pull policy
A promotional policy in which an organization promotes directly to consumers in order to develop a strong consumer demand for its products.

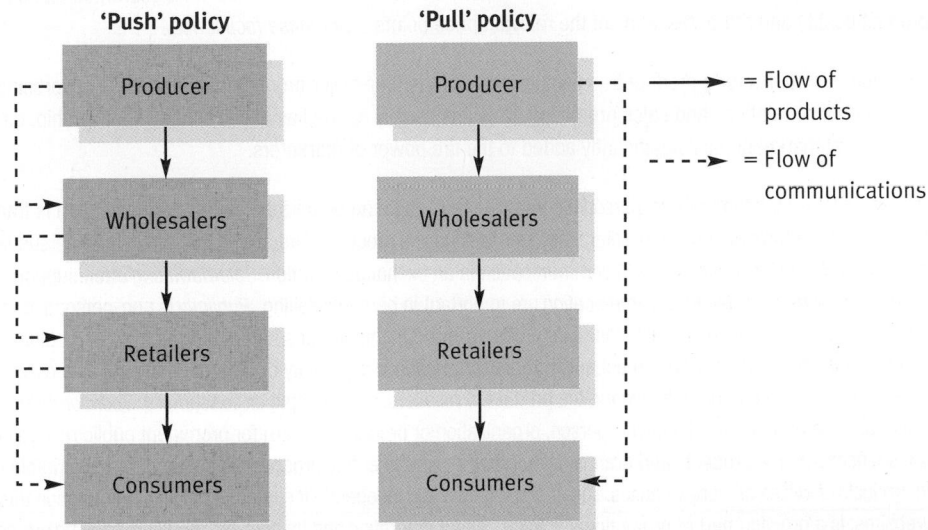

FIGURE 16.7
Comparison of push and pull promotional policies

Summary

The primary role of *promotion* is to communicate with individuals, groups or organizations with the aim of directly or indirectly facilitating exchanges. Promotion is commonly known as marketing communications. The nature of promotion in the marketing mix has altered radically in recent years owing to the web's immediacy and tailored messages, along with far more rapid consumer-to-consumer communication about brands, products and experiences via social media networks and mobile communications.

Communication is a sharing of meaning through the transmission of information. The communication process involves several steps. Using the *coding process*, the *source* first converts the meaning into a series of signs that represent concepts. The source should employ signs that are familiar to the *receiver* or receiving audience, and choose signs that the receiver or *receiving audience* uses for referring to the concepts or ideas being promoted. The coded message is sent through a *medium of transmission* to the receiver or receiving audience. The receiver or receiving audience then uses the *decoding process* to convert the signs into concepts and usually supplies *feedback* to the source. When the decoded message differs from the encoded one, a condition called noise exists. Occasionally, *channel capacity* is reached when the volume of information can no longer be handled effectively.

Marketing communication is the transmission of persuasive information about a product, service or an idea, targeted at key stakeholders and consumers within the target market segment. Marketing communications centre on the promotional mix, which comprises advertising, public relations, personal selling, sales promotion, direct mail, sponsorship and the internet. Cause-related marketing links product purchases to a 'good' cause. The recent growth of social marketing largely hinges on the effective use of appropriate communications to convey messages to relevant target audiences for well-being and sustainability causes.

One long-run purpose of promotion is to influence and encourage customers to accept or adopt goods, services and ideas. The ultimate effectiveness of promotion is determined by the degree to which it affects product adoption or increases the frequency of current buyers' purchases. The *product adoption process* consists of five stages: (1) in the *awareness stage*, individuals become aware of the product; (2) people move into the *interest stage* when they seek information about the product; (3) in the *evaluation stage*, individuals decide whether the product will meet certain criteria that are crucial for satisfying their specific needs; (4) during the *trial stage*, the consumer actually uses or experiences the product for the first time; (5) in the *adoption stage*, the consumer decides to use the product on a regular basis.

Product rejection may occur at any stage. People can be divided into five major *adopter categories innovators, early adopters, early majority, late majority* and *laggards* according to how long it takes them to start using a new product.

There are *five communication effects*. A manufacturer or retailer must establish a *category need* for a product. Consumers must have *brand awareness* and a *favourable brand attitude* towards the products. If the consumer decides to make a purchase – *brand purchase intention* – the company's overall marketing policy must guarantee distribution, suitable product quality and attributes, and set the relevant price points – *purchase facilitation*.

The *promotional mix* for a product traditionally included the four major promotional methods – advertising, personal selling, publicity/public relations and sales promotion. Now it is usually defined as also including sponsorship, direct mail and the web. Digital marketing has significantly added to the fire power of marketers.

Advertising is a paid form of non-personal communication about an organization and its products that is transmitted to a target audience through a mass medium. *Personal selling* is a process of informing customers and persuading them to purchase products through personal communication in an exchange situation. *Telemarketing* often supports personal selling. *Kinesic, proxemic* and *tactile communication* are important in personal selling. *Publicity* is non-personal communication in news-story form about an organization or its products, or both, that is transmitted through a mass medium at no charge, and controlled by the *public relations* mechanism. *Sales promotion* is an activity or material that acts as a direct inducement by offering added value to, or incentive for, the product to resellers, sales people or consumers. *Sponsorship* involves financial or material support of an event, activity, person, organization or product in return for prominent public recognition and display of the sponsor's name, products and brands. *Direct mail* is used to entice prospective customers or charitable donors to invest in products, services or worthy causes. The *internet*, networked independent computers sharing information through organizations' websites, is a growing part of promotional activity. *Digital marketing* and its spin-off *mobile marketing* are now at the forefront of most marketing communications, indeed of many companies' marketing strategies, as explored in Chapter 19.

Many businesses are turning to *direct marketing*, which is a decision to avoid the use of marketing channel intermediaries and to focus marketing communications activity on promotional mix ingredients that deal directly with targeted customers, such as personal selling, direct mail, direct response advertising, telemarketing and the internet.

Currently popular is the concept of *integrated marketing communications (IMC)*. IMC is the coordination and integration of all marketing communication tools, avenues and sources within a company into a seamless programme that maximizes the impact on consumers and other end users at the lowest possible cost. It is integration of the whole promotional mix but also all business-to-business, marketing channel, customer-focused and internally directed communications. Rather than treating all aspects of the promotional mix and internal marketing separately, often utilizing many different departments and external agencies in an uncoordinated manner, a company instead opts to fully harmonize these activities. The benefits of IMC include greater clarity, reduced costs, stronger impact in the marketplace and more effective branding. Multiple channel marketing in the digital era places greater importance on such principles of coordination, to ensure consistent consumer experience of a brand.

There are several major determinants of what promotional methods to include in a promotional mix: the organization's promotional resources, objectives and policies; the characteristics of the target market; the activities of competitors; the characteristics of the product; and the cost and availability of promotional methods. Marketers must also consider whether to use a push policy or a pull policy, or a combination of the two. With a *push policy*, the producer promotes the product only to the next institution down the marketing channel. A company that uses a pull *policy* promotes directly to consumers, with the intention of developing a strong consumer demand for the products. Once consumers are persuaded to seek the products in retail stores, retailers in turn go to wholesalers or the producer to buy the products.

Key links

This chapter overviews the role of promotion – marketing communications – within the marketing mix. It should be read in conjunction with:

- Chapter 10, which features the product adoption process in developing products.
- Chapter 8, which examines brand positioning.
- Chapter 11, which covers branding.
- Chapters 17 and 18, which examine in more detail the various ingredients of the promotional mix.
- Chapter 19, which summarizes digital marketing.

Important terms

Adopter categories
Adoption stage
Advertising
Awareness stage
Brand attitude
Brand awareness
Brand purchase intention
Category need
Cause-related marketing
Channel capacity

Coding process
Communication
Decoding process
Digital marketing
Direct mail
Direct marketing
Early adopters
Early majority
Evaluation stage
Feedback
Five communication effects
Innovators
Integrated marketing communications (IMC)
Interest stage
Internet
Kinesic communication
Laggards
Late majority
Marketing communication
Medium of transmission
Mobile marketing
Noise
Personal selling
Product adoption process
Promotion
Promotional mix
Proxemic communication
Public relations

Publicity
Pull policy
Purchase facilitation
Push policy
Receiver
Receiving audience
Sales promotion
Source
Sponsorship
Tactile communication
Telemarketing
Trial stage

Discussion and review questions

1. What is the major task of promotion?

2. What significant developments have impacted most on marketers' use of marketing communications?

3. What is communication? Describe the communication process. Is it possible to communicate without using all of the elements in the communication process? If so, which ones can be omitted?

4. Identify several causes of 'noise'. How can a source reduce noise?

5. Describe the product adoption process. In certain circumstances, is it possible for a person to omit one or more of the stages in adopting a new product? Explain your answer.

6. Describe a product that many people are in the process of adopting. Have you begun the adoption process for this product? If so, what stage have you reached?

7. What is category need? Illustrate your answer with examples.

8. Identify and briefly describe the major promotional methods that can be included in an organization's promotional mix.

9. How does publicity differ from advertising?

10. What forms of interpersonal communication in addition to language can be used in personal selling?

11. List the communications tools that direct marketing encompasses and explain the recent surge in popularity of this promotional tool.

12. What is digital marketing and how does it impact on promotional strategy?

13. How do target market characteristics determine which promotional methods to include in a promotional mix?

14. Assume that a company is planning to promote a cereal to both adults and children. Along what major dimensions would these two promotional efforts have to be different?

15. How can a product's characteristics affect the composition of its promotional mix?

16. Explain the difference between a pull policy and a push policy. Under what conditions should each be used?

17. What is integrated marketing communications (IMC) and what are the benefits of this approach?

Recommended readings

Belch, G. and Belch, M., *Advertising and Promotion: An Integrated Marketing Communications Perspective* (McGraw-Hill, 2014).

De Pelsmacker, P., Geuens, M. and van den Bergh, J., *Marketing Communications: A European Perspective* (Pearson, 2013).

Fill, C., *Marketing Communications: Brands, Experiences and Participation* (Pearson, 2013).

Pickton, D. and Broderick, A., *Integrated Marketing Communications* (FT Prentice-Hall, 2011).

Shimp, T.A. and Andrews, J.C., *Integrated Marketing Communications in Advertising and Promotion* (Cengage, 2013).

Internet exercise

Most leading brands embrace a mix of promotional techniques, including advertising, sales promotions, publicity, the web and the rest of the promotional mix. Pepsi is no exception.

Pepsi's *Pepsi World* award-winning website is an important part of the company's promotional activity, integrating advertising, sales promotions activity and publicity releases with customer involvement. Brand information, TV advertisements, music links, sports, promotions and street motion – there is much on offer on Pepsi's web pages. Log on to www.pepsi.com.

1. In what ways and with what messages is Pepsi engaging with customers through the pages of its website?

2. How do these approaches support the brand's positioning?

3. How do the web pages relate to the brand's television advertising?

Group tasks

1. Consider a major sporting event such as the Olympics or the World Cup. What forms of marketing communications are used by the organisers to maximise their revenues?

2. Brands such as Pepsi or Coca-Cola traditionally depended on broadcast advertising, in-store sales promotions and sponsorships to gain brand awareness and encourage sales. What forms of marketing communications dominate their activities today?

Applied mini-case

Whether from Nintendo, Sony, Atari or Microsoft, gamers are well used to the 'next big thing'. The Xbox, Playstation, Nintendo 64, Wii and many others all strive to create maximum impact when launching or introducing their next generation. Straightforward broadcast adverts have, over the years, been supplemented with celebrity blogs, publicity stunts, competitions, in-store displays, PR campaigns and significant social media activity. While gamers tend to look forward with relish to impending developments and launches, these companies require also much broader interest among current non-users, in order to leverage their heavy investments in these new products, grow their market shares and volumes, and dent competitors' fortunes.

Question

As marketing manager for Nintendo, Sony or Microsoft, tasked with launching the next generation of your gaming platform, how would you gain the attention of existing customers and also that of consumers not currently hooked on in-home gaming? What would be the core messages and what ways could be used to communicate these messages?

Häagen-Dazs: Secret Sensations

Case study

Häagen-Dazs makes the best-selling superpremium ice cream in North America. Its luscious ingredients include chocolate from Belgium, vanilla from Madagascar, coffee from Brazil, strawberries from Oregon and nuts from Hawaii. The packaging serenely asserts that it is the world's best ice cream. Its *Secret Sensations* reflect its adult positioning. 'Our passion for your pleasure is at the very heart of the Häagen-Dazs philosophy.'

London's Leicester Square shop served close to one million ice-cream lovers in its first year. The success of the Victor Hugo Plaza shop in Paris, now one of the company's busiest, led to the establishment of its first European factory in France. Häagen-Dazs shops have opened in Italy, Spain, Benelux, Scandinavia and many other places. The appealing flavours can now be found not only in the company's shops but also at airports, in cafés and in carefully selected delicatessens, with rapidly growing popularity.

The product's high quality has been essential in maintaining a loyal customer following, but it was promotional work that led to the successful take-off of what was previously an unheard-of brand in Europe. Sales promotion – in the guise of free tasting – was a major part of the promotional mix: over 5 million free cupfuls of ice cream were given away during the company's initial launch over in Europe. Thousands of retailers, cafés and delis were supplied with branded freezers both to display and carefully look after the new premium ice cream. As part of its European launch, Häagen-Dazs spent £30 million on advertising, stressing the deluxe ingredients, unusual flavours and novelty of its product. Europeans currently eat 25 per cent of the 3 billion gallons of ice cream each year consumed worldwide.

Innovative targeting and messaging were core to the brand's success, against well-established brands already with strong popularity. Häagen-Dazs intended to increase consumption by appealing to more than traditional ice cream-loving children. The summer afternoon stroll with an ice cream cornet, the family trip to a fun park or beach,

a snack during a film or concert, the sticky climax of a birthday party feast, had long been the core market for Wall's and Nestlé. Ice Cream Mars changed all that by creating an ice cream bar suitable for any occasion and particularly attractive to adults. Häagen-Dazs went further. Award-winning press adverts, artistically shot, often in black and white, featured lithe, semi-nude couples entwined in exotic poses while feeding each other Häagen-Dazs ice cream. The appeal of vanilla ice cream bars hand-dipped in Belgian chocolate and rolled in roasted almonds now seems hard to resist for adults everywhere. The advertising imagery promotes an adult, upmarket, glamorous positioning for this superpremium ice cream.

The Häagen-Dazs range has grown, expanding to include frozen yoghurts, sorbets and ice cream novelties, such as the ice cream sandwich made with cookies. Formats have evolved, from sharing tubs to minis, stick-bars to novelty lines. Product development and quality controls are important to Häagen-Dazs' brand positioning as an upmarket, indulgent treat for adults, but so is the company's innovative promotional mix and the messages at the heart of its advertising. Industry observers suggest that despite the exceptional quality and novel flavours, without marketing communications Häagen-Dazs would not have been so successful.

Sources: Sainsbury's, 2004–11; 'Dairy produce', *Campaign*, 15 March 1996, p. 34; 'Häagen-Dazs cinema first', *Campaign*, 26 March 1995, p. 5; 'Pillsbury's global training plan', *Crossborder Monitor*, 19 April 1995, p. 9; G. Mead, 'Sex, ice and video beer', *Financial Times*, 26 September 1992, p. 5; 'Saucy way to sell a Knicker-bocker Glory Häagen-Dazs' new ice cream campaign', *Financial Times*, 8 August 1991, p. 8; 'Häagen-Dazs is using sex to secure an up market niche in Britain's £400m ice cream market', *Observer*, 4 August 1991, p. 25; M. Carter, 'The luxury ice cream market', *Marketing Week*, 22 May 1992, p. 30; www.haagen-dazs.com, July 2004, January 2008, June 2011, April 2015; www.haagen-dazs.co.uk, June 2011 and April 2015.

Questions for discussion

1. Why did the London launch of Häagen-Dazs utilize more than just advertising?

2. Why did Häagen-Dazs target the adult market rather than families or children?

3. Was the 'adult' positioning and promotional execution risky? Why did Häagen-Dazs deploy this positioning strategy?

CHAPTER 17

Advertising, public relations and sponsorship

"Advertising still drives MarComms and most marketers' budgets"

Objectives

To explore the nature and uses of advertising.

To become aware of the major steps involved in developing an advertising campaign.

To find out who is responsible for developing advertising campaigns.

To gain an understanding of publicity and public relations.

To examine the nature and uses of sponsorship.

To develop a sound understanding of these ingredients of the promotional mix and of marketing communications.

INTRODUCTION

Ask a lay person – someone who has not read Chapters 1 or 2 of this book! – to define marketing, and the most common polite responses are 'advertising', 'selling' or 'marketing research'. While readers of this book will by now appreciate that there is much more to marketing than these activities, it is true that advertising is a major output of the marketing process and accounts for a large proportion of marketers' budgets.

This chapter overviews the importance of advertising, and discusses its core uses and the stages required in developing an advertising campaign. Digital advertising is explored in subsequent chapters. This chapter also explores public relations (PR) and a key output from a public relations programme, which is publicity. Sponsorship used to be limited and often was handled by those responsible for PR. While many PR consultancies do advise their clients about sponsorship, there are now also specialist sponsorship agencies, reflecting the growing role within the promotional mix of sponsorship, whether corporate or for individual brands. Few observers could fail to appreciate the role of sponsorship when at major cultural or sporting events, such as the Olympics.

Cancer – advertising awareness of the early signs

Not only big brands harness the weight of advertising: it is also powerful for supporting many social marketing causes. Despite UK government spending cuts in the wake of the global economic meltdown, a £9 million programme to alert people to the early signs of cancer was ring-fenced and allowed to proceed. The initial programme was made up of 59 local campaigns addressing breast, bowel and lung cancers, which are three big killers in the UK. The *Be Clear on Cancer* programme is led by Public Health England, working in partnership with the Department of Health and NHS England. Each campaign is tested locally and then regionally, with a view to rolling them out nationally if they prove to be effective.

The Department of Health appointed the agency M&C Saatchi in 2010 and together they created the *Be Clear on Cancer* brand. *Be Clear on Cancer* has been in use since January 2011 to promote awareness and early diagnosis. While it depends on the cancer type, for most activities the target audience for *Be Clear on Cancer* is primarily men and women from lower socio-economic groups who are over the age of 50. Public awareness of key symptoms of cancer is low and research shows that, for some cancers, people from lower socio-economic backgrounds or people who have lower education levels tend to delay seeing their GP. At the heart of the *Be Clear on Cancer* campaign is a centrally led awareness campaign, using PR, press, radio, TV and social media.

The early *Be Clear on Cancer* campaign plans included advertising on bus routes to encourage early presentation to clinicians by members of the public suspecting they are exhibiting early signs of lung cancer. NHS Brighton and Hove raised awareness among its catchment that a change in bowel habits might be a sign of colorectal cancer. NHS Liverpool encouraged sufferers to seek help at an earlier stage in the development of their cancers, particularly lung and bowel problems.

These, and many other initiatives within the overall *Be Clear on Cancer* awareness programme, will save the NHS significant sums of money in ongoing treatments for those detected too late, while evidently there will be significant benefits for those members of the public who respond to the programme and are able to be more effectively treated. The advertisers' toolkit has many such applications, away from the more visible advertising of McDonald's, Pepsi or Walker's, but the same fundamental principles for powerful, targeted and relevant advertising still apply.

Sources: www.dh.gov.uk, February 2011; www.cancerresearchuk.org/health -professional/early-diagnosis-activities/be-clear-on-cancer/about-be-clear-on -cancer, April 2015; www.gov.uk/government/news/be-clear-on-cancer-campaign -highlights-links-between-heartburn-and-cancer, April 2015.

This chapter explores the many dimensions of advertising, publicity, public relations and sponsorship. It should be remembered that Chapter 16 explained how companies are increasingly benefiting from a more coordinated approach to their marketing communications through integrated marketing communications (IMC). Indeed, research suggests that higher levels of integration in marketing communications leads to enhanced performance.[1] However, this chapter examines specific ingredients of the promotional mix to aid a thorough understanding of these components – the other promotional mix ingredients are addressed in the next chapters, including the growth of the web and digital marketing.

The present chapter commences by focusing on how traditional advertising is used, before examining the major steps by which an advertising campaign is developed, and describing who is responsible for developing such campaigns. After analyzing publicity and public relations, and comparing their characteristics with those of advertising, the chapter explores the different forms publicity may take. The following section considers how publicity is used and what is required for an effective public relations programme. After discussing negative publicity and some problems associated with the use of publicity, the chapter looks at the increasing use of sponsorship in the promotional mix.

The nature of advertising

Advertising permeates everyone's daily lives.[2] It may be perceived positively or as an annoyance, encouraging channel hopping during advertising breaks or fast-forwarding of programme recordings.[3] Some advertising informs, persuades or entertains; some of it bores or even offends. For example,

Innovation and change

First ambient and now 'live' advertising

When did you last spot an advertisement in a surprising place? Perhaps it was a Volkswagen promotion on the handle of a petrol pump, an advert on a bus ticket, a large building completely draped in a Ford Mondeo banner, a transfer of a brand's logo on a famous cricketer's face, or even the promotion of clean air in Wales on the back of a dirty van. The industry refers to the use of such media as ambient advertising. According to outdoor advertising agency Concord, which claims to have been the first to define the form, ambient advertising is 'non-traditional out-of-home advertising'. An early example, at the Atlanta Olympic Games, was when sprinter Linford Christie promoted Puma by wearing contact lenses featuring the sportswear brand. Finding new and creative ways of advertising using the outdoor world represents a move away from the traditional media of television, radio, cinema, press and posters. Advocates of this approach believe that ambient advertising has huge potential.

Companies commissioning promotional work involving ambient media have been pleased to discover that much free press coverage can result. Ben and Jerry's, the American ice-cream business, attracted considerable publicity when it hired cows to act as mobile advertising hoardings. The animals, which were grazing alongside a major motorway, were fitted with coats sporting an ice-cream advertisement. Meanwhile Beck's beer was promoted using an advertisement mown on a 30-acre field sited alongside a heavily used railway line.

In addition to identifying new surfaces as replacement billboards, ambient advertising makes use of existing objects as promotional sites. Elida Fabergé advertised its Vaseline Intensive Care deodorant by attaching fake roll-on containers to the hanging grabstraps on the London Underground. The aim was to draw attention to the product at a time when commuters might be particularly amenable to considering its benefits.

Views about the effectiveness of ambient advertising vary, given ambient campaigns do not always target a specific audience. The Beck's advert targeted a whole commuter train of people, only a small number of whom like to drink Beck's. Arguably the publicity associated with this stunt generated more impact and awareness among beer drinkers. Nevertheless, as advertisers seek novel executions and ways of attracting the attention of consumers, ambient advertising is a welcome addition to adland's armoury.

One of the latest forms of advertising, instigated in London by a leading South African agency, is so-called 'live' advertising. Cinema-goers are used to 15 minutes' preamble on the screen prior to the blockbuster feature, including trailers for forthcoming attractions and advertisements familiar from television. London movie-goers were surprised by an interruption to the screened advertisements when a group of actors took to the stage and re-enacted a popular television commercial live on stage. The agency argued that this form of 'in your face' advertising is necessary when consumers are assailed by so many promotional messages every day. Certainly, the London movie-goers exposed to these 'live' role-playing advertisements were distracted from shuffling in their seats, chatting and snacking! It is expected that live advertising – a variation on sales promotion stunts – will become more popular, particularly for fast-moving consumer goods but even at business conventions and trade shows for business-to-business products and services.

TABLE 17.1   Leading global advertising agencies

- Y&R (USA/UK)
- Dentsu (Japan)
- BBDO (USA – Omnicom)
- TBWA (USA – Omnicom)
- J. Walter Thompson (USA/UK – WPP)
- Havas (France – formerly Euro RSCG)
- McCann Worldwide (USA – Interpublic)
- DDB (USA – Omnicom)
- Ogilvy (UK/USA – WPP)
- Publicis (France)
- Leo Burnett (USA/France – Publicis)
- FCB (USA – Interpublic)

Source: Adbrands, 2015. Adbrands profiles all of the world's leading agencies (www.adbrands.net/top_advertising_agencies_index .htm). The table above is based on revenue estimates.

there were instances of consumer groups whitewashing billboards advertising tobacco products because they believed such advertisements encouraged children to smoke.

Advertising
A paid-for form of non-personal communication that is transmitted through mass media such as television, radio, newspapers, magazines, direct mail, public transport vehicles, outdoor displays and the internet.

Advertising is a paid-for form of non-personal communication that is transmitted through mass media such as television, radio, newspapers, magazines, direct mail, public transport vehicles, outdoor displays and now the internet. As explained in the Innovation and Change box above, advertising takes on some innovative forms. An organization can use advertising to reach a variety of audiences, ranging from small precise groups, such as the stamp collectors in the major conurbations, to large audiences, such as all the buyers of iPads in America.

When people are asked to name major advertisers, most immediately mention business organizations. However, many types of organization – including governments, churches, universities, civic groups and charities – take advantage of advertising. For example, the UK government is one of the largest advertisers: 'Heroin Screws You Up', Employment Training, road safety campaigns, drink driving and business initiatives are just a few examples. So even though advertising is analyzed here in the context of business organizations, it should be borne in mind that much of the discussion applies to all types of organization.

Marketers sometimes give advertising more credit than it deserves. This attitude causes them to use advertising when they should not. For example, manufacturers of basic products such as sugar, flour and salt often try to differentiate their products, with minimal success. Under certain conditions, advertising can work effectively for an organization. The questions in Table 17.2 raise some general points that a marketer should consider when assessing the potential value of advertising as an ingredient in a product's promotional mix. However, the list is not all-inclusive,

TABLE 17.2   Some issues to consider when deciding whether to use advertising

1. Does the product possess unique and important features?
Although homogeneous products such as cigarettes, petrol and beer have been advertised successfully, they usually require considerably more effort and expense than other products. On the other hand, products that are differentiated on physical rather than psychological dimensions are much easier to advertise. Even so, 'being different' is rarely enough. The advertisability of product features is enhanced when buyers believe that those unique features are important and useful. Shell added chemicals to its petrol, branded this formula and featured this in its advertising.

2. Are 'hidden qualities' important to buyers?
If by viewing, feeling, tasting or smelling the product buyers can learn all there is to know about the product and its benefits, advertising will have less chance of increasing demand. Conversely, if not all product benefits are apparent to consumers on inspection and use of the product, advertising has more of a story to tell, and the probability that it can be profitably used increases. The 'hidden quality' of vitamin C in oranges once helped explain why Sunkist oranges could be advertised effectively, whereas the advertising of lettuce has been a failure.

3. Is the general demand trend for the product favourable?
If the generic product category is experiencing a long-term decline, it is less likely that advertising can be used successfully for a particular brand within the category. For example, CDs virtually extinguished the demand for turntables, while downloads are killing off CDs.

4. Is the market potential for the product adequate?
Advertising can be effective only when there are sufficient actual or prospective users of the brand in the target market. Without clear segmentation and explicit targeting of certain customer types success is unlikely.

(Continued)

TABLE 17.2   Continued

5. Is the competitive environment favourable?
The size and marketing strength of competitors, and their brand shares and loyalty, will greatly affect the possible success of an advertising campaign. For example, a marketing effort to compete successfully against Apple's range, Heinz baked beans, or McDonald's restaurants would demand much more than simply advertising.

6. Are general economic conditions favourable for marketing the product?
The effects of an advertising programme and the sales of all products are influenced by the overall state of the economy and by specific business conditions. For example, it is much easier to advertise and sell luxury leisure products (home entertainment systems, sailing boats, video cameras, exotic holidays) when disposable income is high.

7. Is the organization able and willing to spend the money required to launch an advertising campaign?
As a general rule, if the organization is unable or unwilling to undertake an advertising expenditure that as a percentage of the total amount spent in the product category is at least equal to the market share it desires, advertising is not likely to be effective. A new product launch wholly dependent on hefty advertising, lacking other differentiators and appeal, is doomed to failure when inevitably the advertising budget is cut or shelved.

8. Does the company possess sufficient marketing expertise to market the product?
The successful marketing of any product involves a complex mixture of product and consumer research, product development, packaging, pricing, financial management, promotion, customer service and distribution and business acumen. Weakness in any area of marketing is an obstacle to the successful use of advertising.

Source: Updated and adapted from Charles H. Patti, 'Evaluating the role of advertising', *Journal of Advertising*, Fall 1977, pp. 32–3. Reprinted by permission of the *Journal of Advertising*.

as numerous factors have a bearing on whether advertising should be used at all and if so, to what extent.

The uses of advertising

Advertising can serve a variety of purposes. Individuals and organizations use it to promote products and organizations, to stimulate demand, to off-set competitors' advertising, to make sales personnel more effective, to educate a market's customers and dealers, to increase the uses of a product, to remind and reinforce customers, and to reduce sales fluctuations (see Figure 17.1).

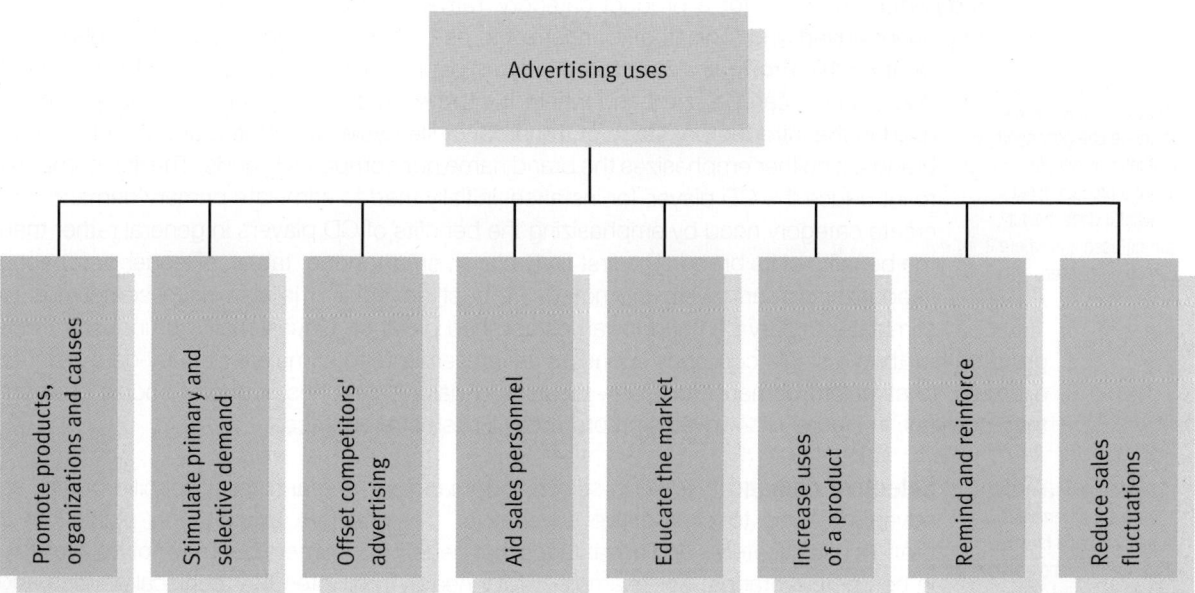

FIGURE 17.1
Major uses of advertising

Promoting products and organizations

Institutional advertising
The type of advertising that promotes organizational images, ideas or political issues.

Advertising is used to promote goods, services, ideas, images, issues, people and indeed anything that the advertiser wants to publicize or foster. Depending on what is being promoted, advertising can be classified as institutional or product advertising. **Institutional advertising** promotes organizational images, ideas or political issues. Institutional advertisements may deal with broad image issues, such as organizational strength or the friendliness of employees. They may also aim to create a more favourable view of the company in the eyes of non-customer groups – such as stakeholders, consumer advocacy groups, potential stockholders or the general public. For example, the advertising of some manufacturers of alcoholic beverages promotes the idea that drinking and driving do not mix, in order to create and develop a socially responsible image. When a company promotes its position on a public issue – for instance, a tax increase, the Euro, sustainability, well-being, abortion or international coalitions – institutional advertising is referred

Advocacy advertising
Promotes a company's position on a public issue.

to as **advocacy advertising**. Institutional advertising may be used to promote socially approved behaviour such as recycling and moderation in consuming alcohol. This type of advertising not only has societal benefits but also helps build an organization's image. As explained in Chapters 1 and 24, social marketing harnesses the marketing toolkit to create changes in behaviour for the benefit of society or for well-being, and is heavily dependent on segmentation and targeting, positioning and marketing communications.

Product advertising
The type of advertising that promotes goods and services.

Product advertising promotes goods and services. Business, government and private non-business organizations turn to it to promote the uses, features, images and benefits of their products or services. When Monsanto introduced a new pesticide to help farmers clean up weeds in post-harvest stubble, it used press advertising to tout the benefits of Sting CT, including a competition to win a trip to Italy and a coupon to mail in for further technical details of the product. It is this type of advertising that most readers of this book will be familiar with, be it in the form of advertisements for Ford cars, Kellogg's cereals or Barclays' banking services.

Stimulating primary and selective demand

Primary demand   When a specific business is the first to introduce an innovation, it tries to stimulate *primary demand* for a product category, rather than a specific brand of the product through pioneer advertising. This is often referred to as creating category need, as explained in

Pioneer advertising
The type of advertising to create category need that informs people about a product: what it is, what it does, how it can be used and where it can be purchased.

Chapter 16. **Pioneer advertising** informs people about a product: what it is, what it does, how it can be used and where it can be purchased. As pioneer advertising is used in the introductory stage of the product life cycle when there are no competitive brands, it neither emphasizes the brand name nor compares brands. The first company to introduce the CD player, for instance, initially tried to stimulate primary demand and create category need by emphasizing the benefits of CD players in general rather than the benefits of its brand. The first DVD player, smartphone, tablet, eReader or tobacco vapouriser similarly were promoted. Product advertising is also used sometimes to stimulate primary demand for an established product. Occasionally, an industry trade group rather than a single company sponsors advertisements to stimulate primary demand. For example, to stimulate demand for many meats and dairy categories, industry bodies promote their qualities. In Figure 17.2 advertising promotes British strawberries.

Competitive advertising
The type of advertising that points out a brand's uses, features and advantages, which may not be available in competing brands.

Selective demand   To build *selective demand,* or demand for a specific brand, an advertiser turns to competitive advertising. **Competitive advertising** points out a brand's uses, features and advantages that benefit consumers but may not be available in competing brands. For example, BMW heavily promotes the technical abilities and innovative features of its cars in its advertising.

Another form of competitive advertising is **comparative advertising**, in which two or more brands are compared on the basis of one or more product attributes.

FIGURE 17.2
This advertising aims to stimulate primary demand for strawberries but also stresses the particular merits of Tesco's recently-picked British strawberries

Source: Image courtesey of Tesco.

> **Comparative advertising**
> The type of advertising that compares two or more brands on the basis of one or more product attributes.

Companies must not, however, misrepresent the qualities or characteristics of the comparison product and, in certain countries, overt comparisons of rival products or brands are prohibited. The leading nappy manufacturers often name and shame their inferior rivals when their product has new attributes which out-perform competing brands. Rivals producing nappies tend to use comparative advertising.

Off-setting competitors' advertising

> **Defensive advertising**
> The type of advertising that aims to off-set or lessen the effects of a competitor's promotional programme.

When marketers advertise to off-set or lessen the effects of a competitor's promotional programme, they are using **defensive advertising**. Although defensive advertising does not necessarily increase a company's sales or market share, it may prevent a loss in these areas. For example, when McDonald's first test-marketed pizza, Pizza Hut countered with defensive advertising to protect its market share and sales. Pizza Hut advertised both on television and in newspapers in two test cities, emphasizing that its product is made from scratch, whereas McDonald's was made using frozen dough.[4] Defensive advertising is used most often by companies in extremely competitive consumer product markets, such as the fast-food industry.

Making sales personnel more effective

Business organizations that stress personal selling often use advertising to improve the effectiveness of sales personnel. Advertising created specifically to support personal selling activities tries to pre-sell a product to buyers by informing them about its uses, features and benefits, and by encouraging them to contact local dealers or sales representatives. This form of advertising helps sales people find good sales prospects. Advertising is often designed to support personal selling efforts for business products, insurance and consumer durables, such as cars and major household appliances. For example, advertising may bring a prospective buyer to a showroom, but usually a sales person plays a key role in actually closing the sale.

Educating the market

A change to a company's strategy may lead to it entering new markets or introducing innovative products. This will require an orientation programme for targeted customers and the required channel intermediaries. Part of this communications task may entail advertising. Even if a company modifies its marketing mix in existing markets – new product specifications, after-sales policies or pricing, for example – it may need to educate the market, customers and dealers regarding the changes.

Increasing the uses of a product

The absolute demand for any product is limited because people in a market will consume only so much of it. Given both this limit on demand and competitive conditions, marketers can increase sales of a specific product in a defined geographic market only to a certain point. To improve sales beyond this point, they must either enlarge the geographic market and sell to more people, or develop and promote a larger number of uses for the product. If a business's advertising convinces buyers to use its products in more ways, the sales of the products go up. For example, Shredded Wheat used advertising to inform consumers that its cereal contains no added sugar and is high in natural fibre, which is essential to a healthy and balanced diet. The aim is to position Shredded Wheat as part of a wholesome diet, as well as a popular children's cereal. When promoting new uses, an advertiser attempts to increase the demand for its own brand without driving up the demand for competing brands.

Reminding and reinforcing customers

Reminder advertising
The type of advertising that reminds customers of the uses, characteristics and benefits of an established brand.

Reinforcement advertising
The type of advertising that tries to assure current users that they have made the right choice and tells them how to get the most satisfaction from the product.

Marketers sometimes employ **reminder advertising** to let consumers know that an established brand is still around and that it has certain uses, characteristics and benefits. Procter & Gamble, for example, reminds consumers that its Crest toothpaste is still best at preventing cavities. **Reinforcement advertising**, on the other hand, tries to assure current users that they have made the right choice and tells them how to get the most satisfaction from a product.

Both reminder and reinforcement advertising aim to prevent a loss in sales or market share. Much of Ford's range-focused advertising is designed to reassure existing Ford owners that the company is forward thinking and customer oriented. The advertising for Head & Shoulders shampoo is as much concerned with reminding existing users of its virtues as it is about building awareness for potential new users.

Reducing sales fluctuations

The demand for many products varies from month to month because of such factors as climate, holidays, seasons and customs. However, a company cannot operate at peak efficiency when sales fluctuate rapidly. Changes in sales volume translate into changes in the production or inventory, personnel and financial resources it requires. To the extent that marketers can generate sales during slow periods, they can smooth out fluctuations. When advertising reduces fluctuations, a manager can use the business's resources more efficiently. Business-user-oriented hotels such as Holiday Inn or Hilton promote discounted rooms for weekend leisure breaks in order to utilize otherwise unused facilities.

Advertising is often designed to stimulate business during sales slumps. For example, advertisements promoting price reductions of lawn care equipment or summer holidays can increase sales during the winter months. On occasion, a business advertises that customers will get better service by coming in on certain days rather than others. During peak sales periods, a marketer may refrain from advertising to prevent over-stimulating sales to the point where the company cannot handle all the demand. For example, money-off coupons for the delivery of pizza are often valid only from Monday to Thursday, not Friday to Sunday, which are the peak delivery days.

A company's use of advertising depends on its objectives and resources, as well as on external environmental forces. The degree to which advertising accomplishes the marketer's goals depends to a large part on the advertising campaign.

Developing an advertising campaign

Advertising campaign
An attempt to reach a particular target market by designing a series of advertisements and placing them in various advertising media.

An **advertising campaign** involves designing a series of advertisements and placing them in various advertising media to reach a particular target market. As Figure 17.3 indicates, the general steps in developing and implementing an advertising campaign are:

1. identifying and analyzing the advertising target audience
2. defining the advertising objectives
3. creating the advertising platform
4. determining the advertising budget
5. developing the media plan
6. creating the advertising message
7. executing the campaign
8. evaluating the effectiveness of the advertising.

The number of steps and the order in which they are carried out may vary according to an organization's resources, the nature of its product, the types of target market or audience to be reached, the product's stage in its life cycle (see Chapter 10), the current sales levels and market standing of the product, the nature of competitors' promotional mix activity, and the advertising agency selected.[5] The agreed overall objectives and strategy for the marketing communications will also steer the development of the campaign, as explained in the previous chapter. However, these general guidelines for developing an advertising campaign are appropriate for all types of organization.

Identifying and analyzing the advertising target audience

Advertising target audience
The group of people at which advertisements are aimed.

The **advertising target audience** is the group of people at which advertisements are aimed. For example, the target audience for Special K and All-Bran cereals is health-conscious adults, and the *Be Clear on Cancer* programme cited in this chapter's opener targeted the over-50s in specific socio-economic groups in certain regions of the UK. Identifying and analyzing the advertising target are critical processes; the information they yield helps determine the other steps in developing the campaign. The advertising target often includes everyone in a company's target market. However, marketers may seize some opportunities to slant a campaign at only a portion of the target market. Web advertising has presented even greater opportunities for targeting separate advertisements at narrowly defined target audiences.

Advertisers analyze advertising targets, or target audiences, to establish an information base for a campaign. Information commonly needed includes the location and geographic distribution

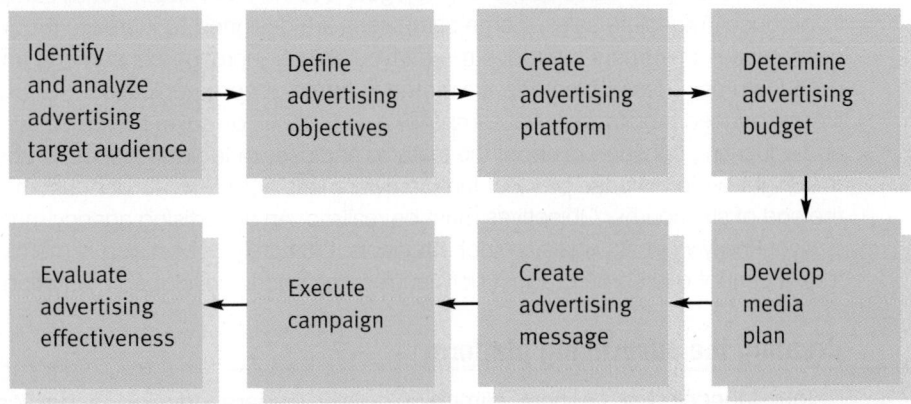

FIGURE 17.3
General steps for developing and implementing an advertising campaign

of the target group; the distribution of age, income, ethnic origin, sex and education; consumer attitudes regarding the purchase and use of both the advertiser's products and competing products; the lifestyles of these consumers, their buying behaviour, their media habits and networks. It is important to be able to profile the targeted consumers, but also to be able to understand their views likes/dislikes, uses, anxieties about, peer expectations of the product being advertised. It is crucial to know how consumers perceive the standing and brand positioning of the product vis-à-vis competitors' propositions. Qualitative marketing research is very important in this process, particularly the use of focus group discussions and social media fora, as explored in Chapter 9.[6] The exact kinds of information that an organization will find useful depend on the type of product being advertised, levels of brand awareness, the characteristics of the advertising target, and the type and amount of competition. Generally, the more advertisers know about the advertising target (those people intended to be influenced by the advertising), the more likely they are to develop an effective advertising campaign. When the advertising target is not precisely identified and properly analyzed, the campaign may not succeed.

Defining the advertising objectives

The advertiser's next step is to consider what the company hopes to accomplish with the campaign. Since advertising objectives guide campaign development, advertisers should define their objectives carefully to ensure that the campaign will achieve what they want. Advertising campaigns based on poorly defined objectives seldom succeed.

Advertising objectives should be stated clearly, precisely and in measurable terms. Precision and measurability allow advertisers to evaluate advertising success: to judge, at the campaign's end, whether the objectives have been met and if so how well. To provide precision and measurability, advertising objectives should contain benchmarks, the current condition or position of the business, and indicate how far and in what direction the advertiser wishes to move from these benchmarks. For example, the advertiser should state the current sales level (the benchmark) and the amount of sales increase that is sought through advertising. Brand awareness should be assessed prior to the campaign, during its run and at its conclusion, so as to ascertain progress. An advertising objective should also specify a timeframe, so that advertisers know exactly how long they have in order to accomplish the objective. Thus, an advertiser with average monthly sales of £450 000 (the benchmark) might set the following objective: 'Our primary advertising objective is to increase average monthly sales from £450 000 to £540 000 within 12 months.' Another company might set the following objective: 'We have 12 per cent brand awareness in our core target market. At the end of 15 months, we wish this percentage to match that of our key rival.' This also tells the advertiser when evaluation of the campaign should begin. As explained in Chapter 23, marketers must increasingly be able to assess the performance of their marketing programmes.

If an advertiser defines objectives by sales, the objectives focus on raising absolute monetary sales, increasing sales by a certain percentage or increasing the company's market share. However, even though an advertiser's long-run goal is to increase sales, not all campaigns are designed to produce immediate sales. Some campaigns are designed to increase product or brand awareness, make consumers' attitudes more favourable or increase consumers' knowledge of a product's features. These objectives are stated in terms of communication. For example, when Apple first introduced tablets, its initial campaign did not focus on sales but on creating brand awareness and educating consumers about the features and uses of tablets. A specific communication objective might be to increase product feature awareness from 0 to 40 per cent in the target market at the end of six months. Objectives must be realistic. An advertising agency must be prepared to let a client know when its goals are not attainable. Ultimately, advertising is merely a communications tool: it cannot overcome product deficiencies or a poorly developed marketing strategy.

Creating the advertising platform

Before launching a political campaign, party leaders develop a political platform, which states the major issues that will be the basis of the campaign. Like a political platform, an

Advertising platform
The basic issues or selling points that an advertiser wishes to include in the advertising campaign.

advertising platform consists of the basic issues or selling points that an advertiser wishes to include in the advertising campaign. A single advertisement in an advertising campaign may contain one or several issues in the platform. Although the platform sets forth the basic issues, it does not indicate how they should be presented.

A marketer's advertising platform should consist of issues that are important to consumers. One of the best ways to determine what those issues are is to survey consumers about what they consider most important in the selection and use of the product involved. For example, Procter & Gamble has developed refill packages for some of its cleaning products. These refill packages provide a unique benefit by not adding to solid waste disposal problems. Environmentally conscious consumers consider this a positive selling feature. McDonald's has added healthier eating options to its menu and advertised these, to reflect consumers' growing awareness of obesity problems. The selling features of a product must not only be important to consumers; if possible, they should also be features that competitive products do not have.

Although research is the most effective method for determining the issues of an advertising platform, it is expensive. As a result, the advertising platform is most commonly based on the opinions of personnel within the business and of individuals in the advertising agency, if an agency is used. As discussed in Chapter 9, qualitative research typically in the form of focus groups or online fora is often used to test the validity of these insiders' views before the campaign is produced. This trial-and-error approach generally leads to some successes and some failures.

As the advertising platform is a base on which to build the message, marketers should analyze this step carefully. A campaign can be perfect in the selection and analysis of its advertising target, the statement of its objectives, its media strategy and the form of its message. But the campaign will still fail if the advertisements communicate information that consumers do not consider important when they select and use the product.

Determining the advertising budget

Advertising budget
The total amount of money that a marketer allocates for advertising over a period of time.

The **advertising budget** is the total amount of money that a marketer allocates for advertising over a period of time. It is difficult to determine this amount because there is currently no way to measure the precise effects of spending a certain amount of money on advertising.

Many factors affect a business's decision about how much to spend on advertising. The geographic size of the market and the distribution of buyers within the market have a great bearing on this decision. Both the type of product being advertised and a business's sales volume relative to competitors' sales volumes play a part in determining what proportion of a business's revenue is spent on advertising. Advertising budgets for business products are usually quite small relative to the sales of the products. More is spent on personal selling, direct mail and trade shows, whereas consumer convenience items, such as soft drinks, soaps and cosmetics, generally have large budgets.

Objective and task approach
A technique for determining an advertising budget that involves determining campaign objectives and then attempting to list the tasks required to accomplish them.

The objective and task approach   Of the many techniques used to determine the advertising budget, intuitively one of the most logical is the **objective and task approach**. Using this approach, marketers initially determine the objectives that a campaign is to achieve and then attempt to list the tasks required to accomplish them. The costs of the tasks are then calculated and added to arrive at the amount of the total budget. This approach has one main problem: marketers usually find it hard to estimate the level of effort needed to achieve certain objectives. A coffee marketer, for example, might find it extremely difficult to determine by what amount it should increase national television advertising in order to raise a brand's market share from 8 to 12 per cent. As a result of this problem, advertisers do not often use the objective and task approach.

Percentage of sales approach
A budgeting technique that involves multiplying a company's past sales, plus a factor for planned sales growth or decline, by a standard percentage based on both what the business traditionally spends on advertising and what the industry averages.

The percentage of sales approach   In the more widely used **percentage of sales approach**, marketers simply multiply a company's past sales, plus a factor for planned sales growth or decline, by a standard percentage based on both what the business traditionally spends on advertising and what the industry averages. This approach has one major flaw: it is based on the incorrect assumption that sales create advertising, rather than the reverse. Consequently, a marketer using this approach at a time of declining sales will reduce the amount spent on advertising. However, such a reduction may further diminish sales. Though illogical, this technique has gained wide acceptance because it is easy to use and less disruptive competitively; it stabilizes a company's market share within an industry. However, in times of declining sales, many businesses do increase their contribution to advertising in the hope of reversing the decline.

Competition matching approach
A budgeting technique in which marketers either match their major competitors' budgets or allocate the same percentage of sales for advertising as their competitors.

The competition matching approach   Another way to determine the advertising budget is the **competition matching approach**. Marketers who follow this approach try either to match their major competitors' budgets or to allocate the same percentage of sales for advertising as their competitors do. Although a wise marketer should be aware of what competitors spend on advertising, this technique should not be used by itself, because a company's competitors probably have different advertising objectives and different resources available for advertising. Many companies and advertising agencies engage in quarterly competitive spending reviews, comparing competitors' expenditures in print, radio, television and digital with their own spending levels. Competitive tracking of this nature occurs at both the national and regional levels.

Arbitrary approach
A budgeting technique in which a high-level executive in the business states how much can be spent on advertising over a certain time period.

The arbitrary approach   At times, marketers use the **arbitrary approach**: a high-level executive in the business states how much can be spent on advertising for a certain time period. The arbitrary approach often leads to under-spending or over-spending. Although hardly a scientific budgeting technique, it is expedient.

Establishing the advertising budget is critically important. If it is set too low, the campaign cannot achieve its full potential for stimulating demand. When too much money is allocated for advertising, the over-spending that results wastes financial resources. An advertising agency being briefed must know the budget size in order to be able to plan the campaign effectively.

Developing the media plan

Media plan
The process of establishing the exact media vehicles to be used for advertising, and the dates and times when the advertisements will appear.

Advertisers spend tremendous amounts of money on advertising media. These amounts have grown rapidly during the past two decades. To derive the maximum results from media expenditures, a marketer must develop an effective media plan. A **media plan** sets forth the exact media vehicles to be used for advertising (specific magazines, television channels, newspapers, radio programmes, movies, billboards, websites, mobile and so forth), and the dates and times when the advertisements will appear. The effectiveness of the plan determines how many people in the advertising target will be exposed to the message. It also determines, to some degree, the effects of the message on those individuals. Media planning is a complex task that requires thorough analysis of the advertising target, as well as of any legal restrictions that might apply. For example, the EU has strict regulations pertaining to the advertising of tobacco, foods and pharmaceuticals, and to comparative advertising. More regulations are on their way too, in connection with alcohol, financial services, cars, environmental labelling and the portrayal of women.

Reach
The percentage of consumers in the advertising target actually exposed to a particular advertisement in a stated time period.

To formulate a media plan, the planner selects the media for a campaign and draws up a time schedule for each medium. The media planner's primary goal is to reach the largest possible number of people in the advertising target for the amount of money spent on media. In addition, a secondary goal is to achieve the appropriate message reach and frequency for the target audience while staying within the budget. **Reach** refers to the percentage of consumers in the advertising target audience actually exposed to a particular advertisement in a stated time period. **Frequency** is the number of times these targeted consumers are exposed to the advertisement. Some experts believe that a target consumer must be exposed more than 30 times to an advertisement for a

Frequency
The number of times targeted consumers are exposed to a particular advertisement.

TABLE 17.3   Results of tested recall of advertisements

Q: Which of the following TV commercials do you remember seeing recently?

Last Week	Brand	Agency/TV Buyer	%
1 (2)	Halifax	*Delaney Lund Knox Warren/Vizeum UK*	77
2 (1)	Asda	*Publicis/Carat*	75
3= (10)	National Lottery	*Abbott Mead Vickers BBDO/OMD UK*	74
3= (4=)	McDonald's	*Leo Burnett/OMD UK*	74
5 (4=)	Specsavers	*In-house/Mediaedge:cia*	73
6 (7)	Churchill	*EBP/MediaCom*	72
7= (3)	Tesco	*Lowe/Initiative*	70
7= (4=)	B&Q	*J Walter Thompson/ZenithOptimedia*	70
9 (–)	Walkers	*Abbott Mead Vickers BBDO/OMD UK*	68
10 (–)	Argos	*Euro RSCG London/MindShare*	66
11 (12=)	Currys	*M&C Saatchi/Walker Media*	65
12 (–)	PC World	*M&C Saatchi/Walker Media*	61
13= (–)	Abbey	*TBWA\London/MindShare*	59
13= (–)	DFS	*Phillipson Ward Longworth Camponi/Brilliant Media*	59
15= (–)	3	*WCRS/MindShare*	54
15= (–)	Norwich Union	*Abbott Mead Vickers BBDO/Brand Connection*	54
17 (–)	Pot Noodle	*HHCL Red Cell/Initiative*	51
18 (–)	Quaker Oatso Simple	*Abbott Mead Vickers BBDO/OMD UK*	50
19= (–)	Iceland	*HHCL Red Cell/MediaCom*	49
19= (16)	KFC	*Bartle Bogle Hegarty/Walker Media*	49

Source: *Adwatch of the Year, Marketing* magazine

consumer durable or fast-moving consumer good before there is acceptance and full awareness of the advertising platform. However, most consumers, unless highly stimulated by the advertising, are not prepared to read, watch or hear an advertisement so many times. The platform, creativity and media choices must be smart enough to overcome this lack of interest in advertising.

Media planners begin with rather broad decisions, but eventually they must make very specific choices. A planner must first decide which kinds of media to use: radio, television, newspapers, magazines, direct mail, outdoor displays, ambient, public transport, the web,[7] or a combination of two or more of these. After making the general media decision, the planner selects specific subclasses within each medium. For example, Estée Lauder might advertise its Clinique cosmetic line in lifestyle magazines, as well as during daytime, prime-time and late-night television.

Media planners take many factors into account as they devise a media plan. They analyze the location and demographic characteristics of people in the advertising target because the various media appeal to particular demographic groups in particular locations. For example, there are radio stations directed mainly at teenagers, magazines for men in the 18–34 age group and television programmes aimed at specific ethnic groups. Media planners should also consider the size and type of audiences that are reached by specific media. Several data services collect and periodically publish information about the circulations and audiences of various media. Most publishers and broadcasters offer prospective advertisers media packs, containing independently audited data about readership or viewing figures. For example, satirical magazine *Private Eye* states that each issue has the potential to be read by 889 000 people, who are carefully profiled for advertisers in terms of socio-economics. The cost of media is an important but troublesome consideration. Planners try to obtain the best coverage possible for the amount of money spent, yet there is no accurate way of comparing the cost and impact of a television advertisement with the cost and impact of a newspaper advertisement.

The content of the message sometimes affects the choice of media. Print media can be used more effectively than broadcast media to present many issues or numerous details. The makers of many food brands produce wordy magazine advertisements, including recipes as well as product details, to boost demand and educate consumers about the product's uses. If an advertiser wants to promote beautiful colours, patterns or textures, media that offer high-quality colour reproduction – magazines, television or digital – should be used instead of newspapers. For example, cosmetics can be far more effectively promoted in a full-colour magazine advertisement than in a black and white newspaper advertisement. The medium selected is determined by the characteristics, advantages and disadvantages of the major media available.

Given the variety of vehicles within each medium, media planners must deal with a vast number of choices. The multitude of factors that affect media rates obviously add to the complexity of media

Cost comparison indicator
A measure that allows an advertiser to compare the costs of several vehicles within a specific medium in relation to the number of people reached by each vehicle.

planning. A **cost comparison indicator** enables an advertiser to compare the costs of several vehicles within a specific medium such as two newspapers in relation to the number of people reached by each vehicle. For example, the 'milline rate' is the cost comparison indicator for newspapers; it shows the cost of exposing a million people to a space equal to one agate line (an agate line is one column wide and the height of the smallest type normally used in classified newspaper advertisements: there are 14 agate lines in one column inch).

Figure 17.4 shows how one major advertising agency links many of these stages for creating advertising and their outputs into a formal brief for both its creatives and for seeking client sign-off for the proposed course of action. This example also illustrates the importance of having a clear targeting strategy, well-articulated positioning and sensible objectives. It also demonstrates the importance of having first undertaken analysis of targeted consumers or business users, competitors and external macro drivers.

Creating the advertising message

The basic content and form of an advertising message are a function of several factors. The product's features, uses and benefits affect the content of the message. Characteristics of the people in the advertising target audience – their sex, age, education, ethnic origin, income, occupation, lifestyle, media habits and other attributes – influence both the content and form. When Procter & Gamble promotes its Crest toothpaste to children, the company emphasizes the importance of daily brushing and decay control. When it markets Crest to adults, it discusses tartar, plaque and whiteness. To communicate effectively, an advertiser must use words, symbols and illustrations that are meaningful, familiar and attractive to the people who constitute the advertising target: the target audience.

The objectives and platform of an advertising campaign also affect the content and form of its messages. For example, if a company's advertising objectives involve large sales increases, the message demands hard-hitting, high-impact language and symbols. When campaign objectives aim at increasing brand awareness, the message may use much repetition of the brand name, and words and illustrations associated with it. Thus the advertising platform is the foundation on which campaign messages are built. Agencies strive to develop platforms with longevity in order to foster long-term brand building. For example, JWT's Andrex puppies have represented the toilet tissue in close to 40 years of advertising; 'ASDA price' is the long-term strapline to the supermarket chain's value-led advertising, and 'The Ultimate Driving Machine' is BMW's famous ongoing positioning.

The choice of media obviously influences the content and form of the message. Effective outdoor displays and short broadcast spot announcements require concise simple messages. Magazine and newspaper advertisements can include more detail and long explanations. Digital advertising can use links to direct viewers to further information. As several different kinds of media offer geographic selectivity, a precise message can be tailored to a particular

```
Client:                                  Interim Review:
Account Owner:                           Final Review:
Product:                                 Presentation:
Job Number:                              Cost Group:
_____

What Is The Advertising Required To Do?

Media Budget?                            Production Budget?

Requirements?  (One-off ad, campaign, new campaign)

Format?  (TV  Cinema  Press  Radio  Poster  Outdoor  Internet  Viral)

Size/Time/Length

Any Possible Links Between Media Channel & Message?

What Is The Single Most Important Thing We Want To Say?

Why Should People Believe This?

What Tone Of Voice Should We Use?

What Are The Mandatory Requirements?  (logo, colour, web address, etc.)

Who Are We Talking To?

What Do We Want Them To Think Or Feel Having Seen The Advertising?

What Have We Said Previously?

Which Brands Are We Up Against and What Are They Saying/Claiming?

How Will We Stand Out?

When Is This Required?

What Problems Are Anticipated?

Signatures:  Client_____ Agency_____ (Legal_____)
```

FIGURE 17.4
How one agency underpins the creative brief during the advertising process

---

Regional issues
Versions of a magazine or newspaper that differ across geographic regions in their advertising and editorial content.

Copy
The verbal portion of an advertisement.

AIDA
A persuasive sequence used in advertisements: attention, interest, desire and action.

---

geographic section of the advertising target. Some magazine and national newspaper publishers produce **regional issues**: for a particular issue, the advertisements and editorial content of copies appearing in one geographic area differ from those appearing in other areas. A clothing manufacturer may decide to use one message in London and another in the rest of the UK. A company may also choose to advertise in only a few regions. Such geographic selectivity enables a business to use the same message in different regions at different times.

The messages for most print advertisements depend on the use of copy and artwork.

Copy   The verbal portion of an advertisement is **copy**. It includes headlines, sub-headlines, body copy and the signature (see Figure 17.5).

When preparing advertising copy, marketers attempt to move the target audience through a persuasive sequence called **AIDA**: attention, interest, desire and action. Consumers will not visit a store, trial a product or make a purchase of an unfamiliar product unless marketers first grab their attention, gain their interest and make the product appear desirable. Emotive and persuasive advertising plays a key role in this process. Not all copy needs be this extensive, however.

FIGURE 17.5
Copy and artwork elements of advertisements. This advertisement clearly differentiates between the basic elements of print advertising

The headline is critical because often it is the only part of the copy that people read. It should attract readers' attention and create enough interest to make them want to read the body copy. The sub-headline, if there is one, links the headline to the body copy; sometimes it helps explain the headline.

Body copy for most advertisements consists of an introductory statement or paragraph, several explanatory paragraphs and a closing paragraph. Some copy-writers have adopted a pattern or set of guidelines to develop body copy systematically:

1. identify a specific desire or problem for consumers
2. suggest the good or service as the best way to satisfy that desire or solve that problem
3. state the advantages and benefits of the product
4. indicate why the advertised product is the best for the buyer's particular situation
5. substantiate the claims and advantages
6. prompt the buyer into action.[8]

The signature identifies the sponsor of the advertisement. It may contain several elements, including the company's trademark, logo, name, address and web-links. The signature should be designed to be attractive, legible, distinctive and easy to identify in a variety of sizes.

As radio listeners are often not fully 'tuned in' mentally, radio copy should be informal and conversational to attract their attention and achieve greater impact. The radio message is highly perishable; thus radio copy should consist of short and familiar terms. Its length should not require a delivery rate exceeding approximately two-and-a-half words per second.

In television copy, the audio material must not overpower the visual material, and vice versa. However, a television message should make optimal use of the visual capabilities available. Copy for a television advertisement is initially written in parallel script form. The video is described in the left column and the audio in the right. When the parallel script is approved, the copywriter and the artist combine the copy with the visual material through use of a **storyboard**, which depicts a series of miniature television screens showing the sequence of major scenes in the advertisement. During the creative thinking phase, storyboards tend to be cartoon sketches. Once an idea is deemed worthy of production, a more polished storyboard is produced. Technical personnel use the storyboard as a blueprint when they produce the advertisement.

Artwork   **Artwork** consists of the illustration and layout of the advertisement (see Figure 17.5). Although **illustrations** are often photographs, they can also be drawings, graphs, charts or tables. Illustrations are used to attract attention, to encourage the audience to read or listen to the copy, to communicate an idea quickly or to communicate an idea that is difficult to put into words.[9] They are especially important because consumers tend to recall the visual portion of advertisements better than the verbal portions.

The **layout** of an advertisement is the physical arrangement of the illustration, headline, sub-headline, body copy and signature. The arrangement of these parts in Figure 17.6 is only one possible layout. These same elements could be arranged in

Storyboard
A series of miniature television screens or cartoons used to show the sequence of major scenes in an advertisement.

Artwork
The illustration and layout of the advertisement.

Illustrations
Photographs, drawings, graphs, charts or tables used in advertisement artwork.

Layout
The physical arrangement of the illustration, headline, sub-headline, body copy and signature of an advertisement.

FIGURE 17.6
While many advertisements are dominated by colourful and emotive images, many business-to-business advertisements contain extensive detail and illustrations of data

Source: Image courtesy of O$_2$.

many ways. The final layout is the result of several stages of preparation. As it moves through these stages, the layout helps people involved in developing the advertising campaign exchange ideas. It also provides instructions for production personnel.

Executing the campaign

The execution of an advertising campaign requires an extensive amount of planning and coordination. Regardless of whether or not an organization uses an advertising agency, many people and organizations are involved in the execution of a campaign.[10] Production companies, directors, video and lighting experts, voice-over actors, research organizations, media houses, companies providing special effects, printers, photo engravers and commercial artists are just a few of the people and organizations that contribute to a campaign.

Implementation requires detailed schedules to ensure that various phases of the work are done on time. Advertising management personnel must evaluate the quality of the work and take corrective action when necessary. In some instances, changes have to be made during the campaign so that it meets campaign objectives more effectively, better satisfies the client managers or responds to consumer research feedback.

Evaluating the effectiveness of the advertising

There are various ways to evaluate the effectiveness of advertising. They include measuring achievement of advertising objectives; gauging the effectiveness of copy, illustrations or layouts; and assessing certain media.

Pre-tests
Evaluations performed before an advertising campaign that attempt to assess the effectiveness of one or more elements of the message.

Advertising can be evaluated before, during and after the campaign. Evaluations performed before the campaign begins are called **pre-tests** and usually attempt to evaluate the effectiveness of one or more elements of the message. To pre-test advertisements, marketers sometimes use a **consumer focus group**, a semi-structured discussion, led by a moderator, involving actual or potential buyers of the advertised product. Members are asked to judge one or several dimensions of two or more advertisements. Such tests are based on the belief that consumers are more likely than advertising experts to know what will influence them. Teasing out ideas and responses to them via social media is also common.

Consumer focus group
A semi-structured discussion, led by a moderator, involving actual or potential buyers of advertised products who are asked to judge one or several dimensions of the advertisements.

To measure advertising effectiveness during a campaign, marketers usually take advantage of 'enquiries'. In the initial stages of a campaign, an advertiser may use several direct response advertisements simultaneously, each containing a coupon, an 0800 contact number, a form requesting information or a click through web-link. The advertiser records the number of coupons, calls or clicks that are returned from each type of advertisement. If an advertiser receives 78 528 coupons from advertisement A, 37 072 coupons from advertisement B and 47 932 coupons from advertisement C, then advertisement A is judged superior to advertisements B and C. For advertisements that do not demand action – clicking, coupon returning or dialling an 0800 Freefone number – enquiries are difficult to monitor.

Post-campaign test or post-test
The evaluation of advertising effectiveness after a campaign.

Evaluation of advertising effectiveness after the campaign is over is called a **post-campaign test** or **post-test**. Advertising objectives often indicate what kind of post-test will be appropriate. If an advertiser sets objectives in terms of communication – product awareness, brand awareness or attitude change – then the post-test should measure changes in one or more of these dimensions. Typically, qualitative marketing research – focus groups or depth interviews – is used before, during and after a campaign to monitor shifts in consumers' perceptions, or quantitative panels evaluate shifts in responses, often now online. It is hoped that brand awareness will have improved following the running of a particular advertising campaign. Advertisers sometimes use consumer surveys or experiments to evaluate a campaign based on communication objectives.

For campaign objectives that are stated in terms of sales, advertisers should determine the change in sales or market share that can be attributed to the campaign. Unfortunately, such changes brought about by advertising cannot be measured precisely[11] because many factors independent of advertisements affect a company's sales and market share. Competitive actions, government actions, and changes in economic conditions, consumer preferences and weather are only a few factors that might enhance or diminish a company's sales or market share. However, by using data about past and current sales and advertising expenditures, an advertiser can make gross estimates of the effects of a campaign on sales or market share.

Since consumer surveys and experiments are expensive, and because it is so difficult to determine the direct effects of advertising on sales, many advertisers evaluate print, television and web advertisements according to the degree to which consumers can remember them. The post-test methods based on memory include recognition and recall tests. Such tests are usually performed by research organizations through consumer surveys. If a **recognition test** is used, individual respondents are shown the actual advertisement and asked whether they recognize it. If they do, the interviewer asks additional questions to determine how much of the advertisement each respondent read, heard or viewed. When recall is evaluated, the respondents are not shown the actual advertisement but instead are asked about what they have seen or heard recently. Recall can be measured through either unaided or aided recall methods. In an **unaided** or **spontaneous recall test**, subjects are asked to identify advertisements that they have seen recently, but are given no clues to help them remember. A similar procedure is used in an **aided** or **prompted recall test**, except that subjects are shown a list of products, brands, company names or trademarks to jog their memory. Several research organizations, such as ACNielsen and Gallup, provide research services that test recognition and recall of advertisements.

The major justification for using recognition and recall methods is that people are more likely to buy a product if they can remember an advertisement about it than if they cannot. However, recalling an advertisement does not necessarily lead to buying the product or brand advertised. For example, most people can remember the zany meercat campaigns for the comparethemarket.com comparison site, yet not everyone uses this site. Research shows that the more 'likeable' an advertisement is, the more it will influence consumers. People who enjoy an advertisement are twice as likely to be persuaded that the advertised brand is best. Yet only a small percentage of those who are neutral about the advertisement feel more favourable towards the brand as a result of the advertisement. The type of television programme in which the product is advertised can also affect consumers' feelings about the advertisement and the product it promotes. Viewers judge advertisements placed in happy programmes as more effective and recall them somewhat better.[12]

Researchers are also using a sophisticated technique called 'single source data' to help evaluate advertisements. With this technique, individuals' behaviour is tracked from television sets to the checkout counter. Monitors are placed in pre-selected homes, and computers record when the television set is on and which channel is being viewed. At the supermarket checkout, the individual in the sample household presents an identification card or smartphone app. The cashier records the purchases by scanner, and the data are sent to the research facility. Some volunteer consumers even have bar scanners in their larders or fridges, and web cameras recording their in-home consumption patterns, cross-referenced with their media viewing habits. These techniques are offering more insight into people's buying patterns than ever before.

Recognition test
A test in which an actual advertisement is shown to individual respondents, who are then asked whether they recognize it.

Unaided or spontaneous recall test
A test in which subjects are asked to identify advertisements that they have seen recently but are given no clues to help them remember.

Aided or prompted recall test
A test in which subjects are asked to identify advertisements while being shown a list of products, brands, company names or trademarks to jog their memory.

Who develops the advertising campaign?

An advertising campaign may be handled by:

1. an individual or a few people within the company
2. an advertising department within the organization or
3. an advertising agency.

In very small businesses, one or two individuals are responsible for advertising and many other activities as well. Usually these individuals depend heavily on personnel at local newspapers and broadcasting stations for copywriting, artwork and advice about scheduling media.

In certain types of large business – especially in larger retail organizations – advertising departments create and implement advertising campaigns. Depending on the size of the advertising programme, an advertising department may consist of a few multi-skilled people or a sizeable number of specialists, such as copywriters, artists, media buyers, web creators and technical production coordinators. An advertising department sometimes obtains the services of independent research organizations and also hires freelance specialists when they are needed for a particular project.

When an organization uses an advertising agency, such as Ogilvy & Mather or JWT, the organization and the agency usually develop the advertising campaign jointly. How much each party participates in the campaign's total development depends on the working relationship between the client marketers and the agency. Ordinarily, a company relies on the agency for copywriting, artwork, technical production and formulation of the media plan.

An advertising agency can assist a business in several ways. An agency, especially a larger one, supplies the client company with the services of highly skilled specialists – not only copywriters, artists and production coordinators, but also media experts, researchers and legal advisers. Agency personnel have often had broad experience in advertising and are usually more objective than a client's employees about the organization's products. Figure 17.7 outlines the structure of a typical advertising agency. Most marketers using an external advertising agency cite agency creativity and media buying skills as the two main reasons for opting to use an agency rather than in-company expertise. When an agency is used it is important to carefully coordinate the activities of the various suppliers providing advertising, public relations, direct mail, sales promotion, web design, mobile marketing, sponsorship and so forth. All output in terms of marketing communications should reflect the desired brand positioning (see Chapter 8) and the marketing

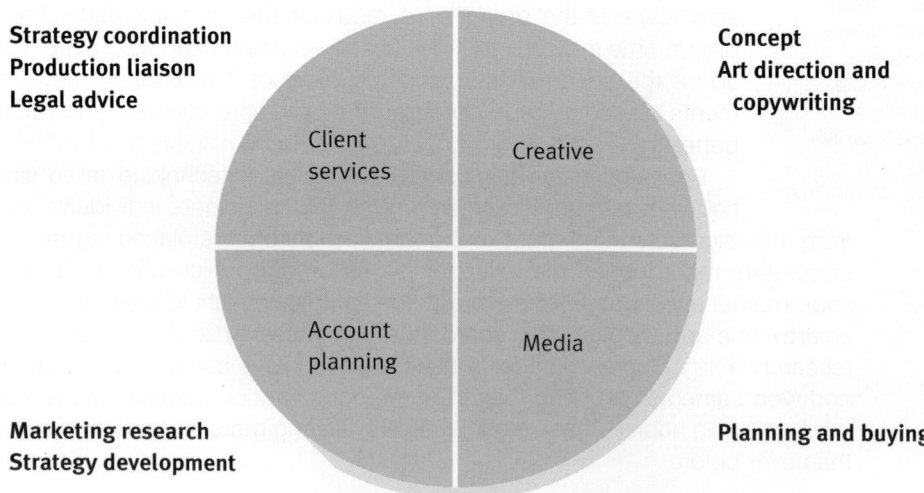

FIGURE 17.7
A typical advertising
agency structure

Strategy coordination
Production liaison
Legal advice

Concept
Art direction and
    copywriting

Client
services

Creative

Account
planning

Media

Marketing research
Strategy development

Planning and buying

strategy. Some marketers opt, therefore, to deal with multi-service agencies that offer all aspects of promotional mix support.

As an agency traditionally receives most of its income from a percentage commission on media purchases, marketers can obtain some agency services at a low or moderate cost. For example, if an agency contracts for £400 000 of television time for a client, it typically receives a commission of £60 000 from the television company. Although the traditional compensation method for agencies is changing and now includes other factors, the media commission still offsets some costs of using an agency. Some agencies have broken the mould, being paid by results. Clients pay a bonus to the agency for meeting targets or receive a payback (refund) if the advertising fails to deliver.[13] The difficulty arises when striving to agree the performance criteria and methods for assessment.

Now that advertising has been explored as a potential promotional mix ingredient, it is time to consider a related ingredient: publicity and its controlling mechanism, public relations.

Publicity and public relations

Publicity is communication in news-story form about an organization, its products or both, that is transmitted through a mass medium at no charge; although the publicity activity will incur production and personnel costs. Publicity can be presented through a variety of vehicles, several of which are examined here. Online is a key outlet, particularly the use of social media, as explored in Chapter 19.

Within an organization, publicity is sometimes viewed as part of public relations, which is a larger and more comprehensive communications function. **Public relations** is a planned and sustained effort to establish and maintain goodwill and mutual understanding between an organization and its **target publics**: customers, employees, the media, shareholders, trade bodies, suppliers, government officials and society in general.[14] Most publicity will be targeted at a single stakeholder type, whereas public relations is ongoing communication across all of an organization's key stakeholder groups. A key foundation for effective public relations is the identification of the pertinent stakeholders or target publics, which are often diverse in nature, requiring different messages and forms of communication.

For example, core publics for Barclays Bank include customers, potential customers, staff and unions, other businesses, suppliers, shareholders, the Treasury, Bank of England, EU regulators, city analysts and journalists. For the Boy Scouts' Association, publics include boys (!), the younger Cubs who are destined to become Scouts, the community, business sponsors, potential Scout leaders, parents, former members whose views will influence others, teachers, plus local press journalists.

Publicity is the result of various public relations efforts. For example, when Tesco decided to make a special effort to stock environmentally safe products and packaging, its public relations department sent out press releases to various newspapers, magazines and television contacts, as well as to its suppliers. The result was publicity in the form of magazine articles, newspaper acknowledgements and television coverage. There are three broad categories of public relations (PR):

1. The **PR event** – one-shot ad hoc affairs concerned with a specific purpose, such as an open day or VIP visit.
2. The **PR campaign** – a period of PR activity involving several events and techniques, but with definite start and end dates.
3. The **PR programme** – ongoing, lengthy-duration, awareness-building or awareness-maintaining multi-technique PR activity.

Publicity
Communication in news-story form about an organization and/or its products, which is transmitted through a mass medium at no charge.

Public relations
A planned and sustained effort to establish and maintain goodwill and mutual understanding between an organization and its target publics.

Target publics
An organization's target audiences: customers, employees, the media, shareholders, trade bodies, suppliers, government officials and society in general.

PR event
A public relations event concerned with a specific purpose such as an open day or VIP visit.

PR campaign
A period of PR activity involving several events and techniques but with definite start and end dates.

PR programme
An ongoing, lengthy-duration, awareness-building or awareness-maintaining multi-technique PR activity.

There is an important distinction between *marketing public relations* and *corporate public relations*. Most large organizations have a corporate affairs function that liaises with investors, institutional analysts and the press, using the toolkit of public relations. Most marketers turn to the same toolkit under marketing public relations, in order to promote new products or market-leading developments, maintain awareness of their brands or products, and enhance their reputation with their target customers and marketing channel members. The public relations tools may be the same, but the issues and stakeholders differ between marketing public relations and corporate public relations.

Publicity and advertising compared

Although publicity and advertising both depend on mass media, they differ in several respects. Advertising messages tend to be informative or persuasive, whereas publicity is primarily informative. Advertisements are sometimes designed to have an immediate impact on sales; publicity messages are more subdued. Publicity releases do not identify sponsors; advertisements do. The sponsor pays for media time or space for advertising, but not for publicity, and there is therefore no guarantee of inclusion. Communications through publicity are usually included as part of a television programme or a print story, but advertisements are normally separated from the broadcast programmes or editorial portions of print media so

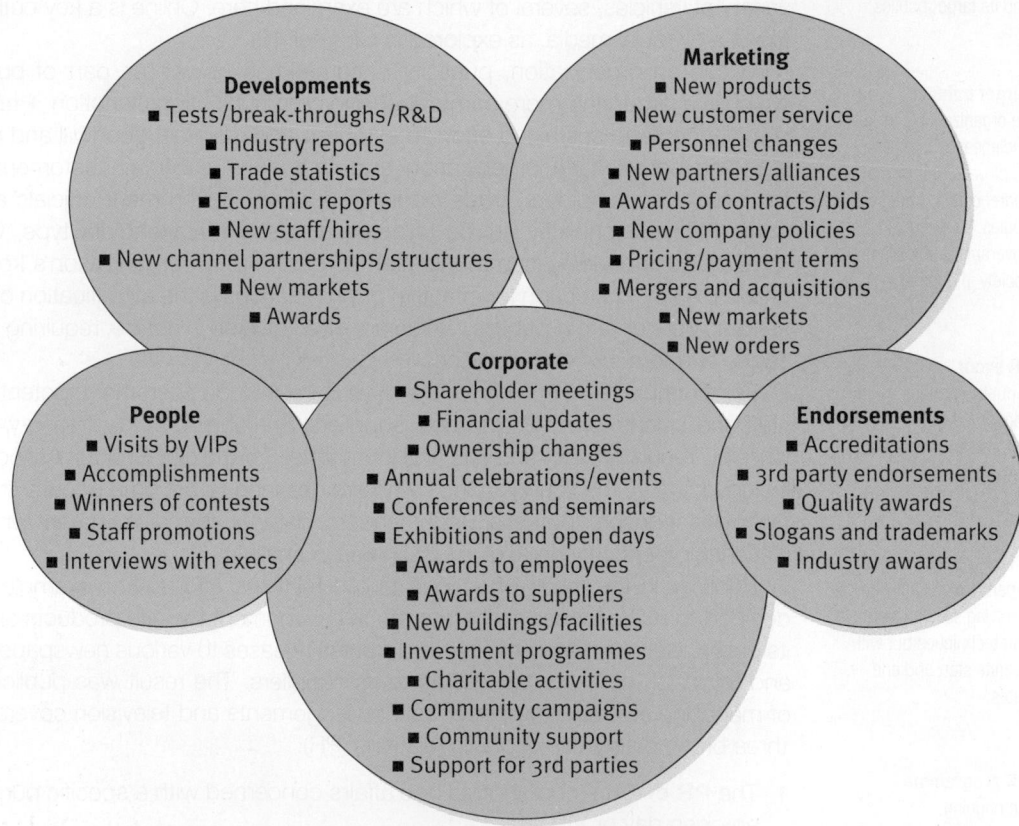

FIGURE 17.8

Possible topics for publicity releases

Source: Adapted from Albert Wesley Frey, ed., *Marketing Handbook*, 2nd Edition (New York: Ronald Press, 1965), pp. 19–35. Copyright © 1965. Reprinted by permission of John Wiley & Sons, Inc.

that the audience or readers can easily recognize or ignore them. Publicity may have greater credibility than advertising among consumers because as a news story it may appear more objective. Finally, an organization can use advertising to repeat the same messages as many times as desired; publicity is generally not subject to repetition and is rarely news-worthy more than once.

Kinds of publicity

Press (news) release
A publicity mechanism, usually consisting of a single page of typewritten copy.

Feature article
A manuscript longer than a press release (up to 3000 words) that is usually prepared for a specific publication.

Captioned photograph
A photograph with a brief description explaining its content.

Press conference
A meeting called to announce a major news event.

Digital environment
A stunt, idea or activity can become the focus of blogs and tweets, whether from client personnel or by consumers.

Third party endorsement
A recommendation from an opinion leader or respected personality used to increase the credibility of publicity and public relations.

There are several types of publicity mechanism.[15] The most common is the **press (news) release**, which is usually a single page of copy containing up to about 300 words. A press release, sometimes called a news release, also gives the company's or agency's name, its address and phone number and details of the contact person.[16] Car makers often use press releases to introduce new products. Figure 17.9 is an example of a press release. A **feature article** is a longer document (up to 3000 words) that is usually prepared for a specific publication. A **captioned photograph** is a photograph with a brief description explaining the picture's content. Captioned photographs are especially effective for illustrating a new or improved product with highly visible features.

There are several other kinds of publicity. A **press conference** is a meeting called to announce a major news event. Media personnel are invited and are usually supplied with written materials, photographs and web-links. In addition, letters to the editor and editorials are sometimes prepared and sent to newspapers and magazines. However, newspaper editors frequently allocate space on their editorial pages to local writers and national columnists. Finally, films and tapes may be distributed to broadcasting companies in the hope that they will be aired. The broader remit of public relations also includes training personnel to meet and handle the media (journalists); arranging interviews; establishing links with VIPs and influential bodies; managing visits, seminars and meetings; and maintaining information flows within the organization. To many, the most important addition to the PR toolkit has been the **digital environment** for PR, in which a stunt, idea or activity can become the focus of blogs and tweets – often going viral – whether from client personnel or by consumers. Although Facebook and Twitter enable rapid consumer-to-consumer sharing of poor experiences of a brand or product, service experience or value for money, which can become a PR nightmare for a brand manager under such scrutiny, the digital environment has presented marketers with a host of PR opportunities and a whole new channel of activity, as explored in the Innovation and Change box on page 517. The impact of digital on PR is featured in a subsequent chapter.

A marketer's choice of specific types of publicity depends on considerations that include the type of information being transmitted, the characteristics of the target audience, the receptivity of media personnel, the importance of the item to the public and the amount of information that needs to be presented. Sometimes a marketer uses a single type of publicity in a promotional mix. In other cases, a marketer may use a variety of publicity mechanisms, with publicity being the primary ingredient in the promotional mix. **Third party endorsement** – for example, from a trade body, VIP or media personality – increases the credibility and interest-value of publicity and public relations. This is a recommendation – written, verbal or visual – from an opinion leader or respected personality. The use of apparently impartial endorsement from among the general public, within social media communities, is a new yet important form of endorsement. Consumers are increasingly influenced by the visible support they read on Facebook or Twitter or see on YouTube around a brand and its activities, but are often unaware that such endorsements and rave reviews are planted by brands or agencies acting on their behalf.

Date as postmark

High Demand Leads to 2nd Edition

NEWS...NEWS...NEWS

In 2001, an innovative book concept was published: a revision guide that included thumbnail overviews of key concepts alongside 'how to pass' examination question tips for undergraduate, MBA and CIM exams.

This text has proved so successful that already a new edition has appeared, endorsed by the Chartered Institute of Marketing. *"Marketing Briefs: A Revision and Study Guide"* provides topical and insightful overviews of key strategic marketing concepts, supported by detailed illustrations and highly topical applied examples. In addition, there is guidance on revision and exam technique, plus recommended further readings.

Everything from buying behaviour, CRM, value-based marketing, one-to-one marketing, target marketing, portfolio analysis, marketing shareholder value analysis, competitive advantage and brand value.

"Marketing Briefs: A Revision and Study Guide" is authored by two of the UK's leading marketing academics, who also author many other leading texts: Sally Dibb and Lyndon Simkin of Warwick Business School.

The book is right up to date in terms of concepts, but also brings the best practice learning tools so popular in Sally and Lyndon's other market leading texts. In addition to students panicking about their exams, the book has been very popular amongst senior managers desiring a quick-learning guide to the latest strategic management tools.

ENDS

Further information:
Tel: Lyndon Simkin, 024 7652 2168, email lyndon.simkin@wbs.ac.uk
"Marketing Briefs: A Revision and Study Guide", Sally Dibb & Lyndon Simkin, Oxford: Elsevier Butterworth-Heinemann, 2nd edition July 2004, pp. 363, ISBN: 0-7506-6200-X.

Warwick Business School:
Founded in 1967, Warwick Business School is one of the most successful and highly regarded business schools in Europe. It has a turnover of £24.6 million. The current student population of 1,070 undergraduates, 170 research students and 2,824 taught masters, MPA and MBA students, come from 108 countries worldwide.

+44 (0)24 7652 4306
+44 (0)24 7652 3719
enquiries@wbs.ac.uk
www.wbs.ac.uk

THE UNIVERSITY OF
WARWICK

Warwick Business School
The University of Warwick
Coventry CV4 7AL
United Kingdom

FIGURE 17.9
An example of a press release, in this case for a student revision aid

Blogs and tweets in PR

Innovation and change

There is a growing belief that businesses embracing social media tools to convey their PR messages are able to communicate compelling content rather than spin or hype. The PR industry has for a while persuaded clients to tweet and blog, and is often behind celebrity tweets endorsing their clients' brands and products. Public relations professionals are experts in establishing a tone of voice and content supportive of a brand which will gel comfortably with intended consumers or business users. Arguably, such expertise has significant relevance in ensuring a company's digital output and presence on social media is empathetic with intended target audiences.

Unfortunately, it is reported that many brands merely post their standard press releases and product news online, without attempting to think about what messages and content will truly inspire intended readers or viewers. Electrolux was one, but recognized the error of its ways, instead customizing shorter messages truly in the style of Facebook, Flickr or YouTube. The result was that visitor numbers to the Electrolux Design Lab blog trebled, YouTube videos were viewed twice as many times and the company's Facebook following saw a hefty ten-fold increase. However, this required a new style of writing, a new approach to content, and a vision for publicity not previously in evidence. This required different people producing material and also trust from those in senior positions that these younger content providers would not damage the brand.

Rentokil, the leading pest eradicator, has harnessed Facebook to promote its services but indirectly, creating smart platforms for publicizing its brand and services in ways deemed highly relevant to certain communities and consumers. Its '#UKwaspwatch' site encourages sharing of problems connected with wasps, to identify hotspots for wasps. According to Rentokil's social media manager, the site was not promoted heavily but created much chatter. Rentokil repeated the initiative, combining it with other activities, including a 'spring cleaning Twitter party', providing advice on cleaning and pest control. Rentokil believes there is a fine line between engaging people and simply boring them with brand messages, so many tweets contain no mention whatsoever of Rentokil and any mention of the brand is very subtle. Rentokil encourages blogs from anyone in the industry or with sensible and relevant opinions, as well as comic enthusiasts in order to brighten up consumers' days.

Previously, a wasp campaign or spring cleaning initiative probably would have been the brainchild of the account team within the public relations agency. Good old fashioned press releases and a few highly visible stunts to provide photo opportunities would have caught the attention of local newspaper editors and freesheets. Occasionally, local radio and regional TV news magazine programmes would have bought-in, too. Today, the digital environment provides much more instant direct contact, controlled instead by the client company's own staff and digital team. Tweets, blogs and digital events have provided PR with a very different toolkit.

Sources: Rentokil; Innovation Update, *Marketing Week*, 24 March 2011, pp. 28–30; www.rentokil.co.uk, April 2015.

Uses of publicity

Publicity has a number of uses. It can make people aware of a company's products, brands or activities; help a company maintain a certain level of positive public visibility; and enhance a particular image, such as innovativeness or progressiveness. Companies also try to overcome negative images through publicity. Some businesses seek publicity for a single purpose and others for several purposes. It must be remembered that an organization has a number of audiences – customers, suppliers, distributors, shareholders, journalists, as well as its internal market of employees and management. Publicity needs to target all of these publics.

The requirements of a publicity programme

For maximum benefit, a business should create and maintain a systematic, continuous publicity programme. If this is achieved, there is likely to be a sustained public relations process in place. A single individual or department within the organization or from its advertising agency or public relations consultancy should be responsible for managing the programme. Relationships must be maintained with the media, particularly to facilitate crisis-management public relations. Effective public relations are impossible without well-developed ongoing contacts with newspaper, television, web and radio journalists. It is important to establish and maintain good working relationships with these media personnel. Often, personal contact with editors, reporters and other news personnel is essential; without their input a company may find it hard to design its publicity programme so as to facilitate the work of news people. Media personnel reject a great deal of publicity material because it is poorly written, badly tailored or not newsworthy. To maintain an effective publicity programme, a company must strive to avoid these flaws. Guidelines and checklists can aid in this task. Material submitted must match the particular newspaper's style – for example, in terms of length, punctuation and layout. Marketers who hire the services of a PR consultancy do so to 'buy' the consultancy's media contacts and its expertise in maintaining an ongoing flow of activity that appeals to journalists.

Finally, an organization has to evaluate its publicity efforts.[17] Usually, the effectiveness of publicity is measured by the number of press releases actually published or broadcast, or the frequency of clicks and online searches. To monitor print media and determine which releases are published and how often, an organization can hire a cuttings service – a business that cuts out, counts and sends published news releases to client companies. To measure the effectiveness of television publicity, a company can request that the television company records its name and the dates when the news item is broadcast, but companies do not always comply. Although some television and radio tracking services do exist, they are costly. Digital executions are easier to monitor and count hits or postings.

The assessment of the effectiveness of an organization's publicity or public relations is of growing importance (see Chapter 23). Many leading exponents of public relations believe there must be four facets to an effective PR programme:

1. *research* into the problem opportunity
2. *action* which includes assessment and planning
3. *communication* of key messages to the relevant publics
4. *evaluation* of the effects of these messages.

A public relations consultancy can be very helpful in achieving these four requirements.

Dealing with unfavourable publicity

Up to this point, publicity has been discussed as a planned ingredient of the promotional mix. However, companies may have to deal with unfavourable publicity regarding an unsafe product, an accident, the actions of a dishonest employee or some other negative event. For example, Toyota had rightly prided itself on the quality of its vehicles and reputation for reliability. A string of product failures and high visibility media coverage in the US during 2010 severely damaged its reputation, requiring much remedial activity by those handling the company's public relations.

Such unfavourable publicity can arise quickly and dramatically. A single negative event that produces unfavourable publicity can wipe out a company's favourable image and destroy consumer attitudes that took years to build through promotional efforts. Moreover, the mass media today can disseminate information faster and to larger audiences than ever before, and bad news generally receives a great deal of attention in both the broadcast and social media. Social media enable the rapid communication of good and bad stories about a brand. Thus, the negative publicity surrounding an unfavourable event now reaches more people. By dealing effectively with a negative situation, an organization can minimize the damage from unfavourable publicity.

To protect an organization's image, it is important to avoid unfavourable publicity or at least to lessen its effects. First and foremost, the organization can directly reduce negative incidents and events through safety programmes, inspections and effective quality control procedures. However, because organizations obviously cannot eliminate all negative occurrences, they need to establish policies and procedures for the news coverage of such events. In today's era of social media-fuelled comment by consumers and other third parties, this is particularly necessary. These policies and procedures should aim at reducing negative impact.

In most cases, organizations should expedite news coverage of negative events rather than try to discourage or block it. The expediting approach not only tends to diminish the fall-out from negative events but also fosters a positive relationship with media personnel. Such a relationship is essential if news personnel are to cooperate with a company and broadcast favourable news stories about it and its affairs. Facts are likely to be reported accurately, but if news coverage is discouraged, rumours and misinformation may be perpetuated. An unfavourable event can easily be blown up into a scandal or a tragedy. It can even cause public panic.

Crisis management involves:

Crisis management
A process in which a company responds to negative events by identifying key targets (publics) for which to provide publicity, developing a well-rehearsed contingency plan, reporting facts.

1. the identification of key target publics for which to provide material or publicity
2. the need for a well-rehearsed contingency plan and public relations exercise
3. the ability and skills of the organization to report quickly and accurately details of the crisis itself
4. the provision of immediate access by journalists to information and personnel
5. monitoring of social media chat and coverage, with appropriate interventions.

Above all, the organization must remain in control of the situation and the material being published or broadcast. See the case study on page 525 for a 'textbook' example of crisis management.

The limitations of using publicity

Free media publicity is a double-edged sword: the financial advantage comes with several draw-backs. If company's messages are to be published or broadcast, media personnel must judge them newsworthy. Consequently, messages must be timely, interesting and accurate. Many communications simply do not qualify. It may take time and effort to convince media personnel of the news value of publicity releases. Even a top public relations consultancy achieves a hit rate of only one out of every four press releases being published in the press.

Although marketers usually encourage media personnel to air a press release at a certain time, they control neither the content nor the timing of the communication. Media personnel alter the length and content of publicity releases to fit publishers' or broadcasters' requirements, and may even delete the parts of the message that the business's marketers deem most important. Furthermore, media personnel use publicity releases in time slots or positions that are most convenient for them; thus the messages often appear at times or in locations that may not reach the business's target audiences. These limitations can be frustrating. Nevertheless, properly managed publicity offers an organization substantial benefits at a relatively low cost. The commissioning of a professional public relations consultancy may come at a price, but the benefits are generally very clear as stakeholders' perceptions are managed. Compared with advertising, the costs of PR are usually trivial.

This chapter concludes with an overview of sponsorship in marketing, which is an element of the promotional mix that is increasingly apparent to many consumers and a promotional tool now used by many organizations.

Sponsorship

Sponsorship
The financial or material support of an event, activity, person, organization or product by an unrelated organization or donor.

Sponsorship is the financial or material support of an event, activity, person, organization or product by an unrelated organization or donor. Generally, funds will be made available to the recipient of the sponsorship deal in return for the prominent exposure of the sponsor's name or brands.[18] For example, SAP's logo visibly dominates McLaren's F1 racing cars and Waitrose appears on the England cricket team's shirts.

The increasing popularity of sponsorship

In the 1990s sponsorship in the arts became an established form of funding for individual performances, tours, whole seasons or exhibitions; indeed some theatrical companies and galleries came to depend on it.[19] Many orchestras, ballet, opera or theatre companies, museums and art galleries would not have survived in the face of declining government subsidies for the arts had it not been for corporate sponsorship. The recent credit crunch has again revealed the role commercial sponsorship plays in enabling many arts groups to survive. Sports were soon to follow, as numerous football teams found that gate receipts and pitch advertising revenues were no longer adequate to cover wage bills and operating costs. While the larger clubs earn eight-figure revenues from shirt sponsorship by companies such as Samsung, Standard Chartered or Emirates, deals for as little as £50 000 are not uncommon in the lower leagues; either way, this form of financial support is becoming essential to guarantee the survival of many clubs.

The popularity of corporate sponsorship has grown dramatically: few leading sports or arts events are without corporate sponsorship. Sponsors believe there are two key benefits to the company and its products. First and foremost, media coverage is unbridled. Few spectators at the Olympics or the World Cup football championships can fail to notice the identities of the leading sponsors. FIFA has two levels of prime sponsors: adidas, Coca-Cola, Hyundai/Kia, Emirates, Sony and Visa are classed as FIFA Partners, while Budweiser, Castrol, Continental, McDonald's, oi, Seara and Yingli Solar were World Cup Sponsors for 2014. To many sports enthusiasts, the leading competitions become generically known as the LV County Championship, NatWest T20 Trophy, Heineken Cup or Capital One Cup. In equestrian events, the horses' names often include the name of the sponsoring company. Visitors to the Royal Shakespeare Company's performances are clearly informed of the support given by leading sponsors. Opera singer Montserrat Caballe's performance at Birmingham's prestigious Symphony Hall was made possible largely by sponsorship from the Forward Trust Group, a fact made clear in all promotional material leaflets, advertising and publicity, and in the concert's programme.

The second benefit of corporate sponsorship is internal. Many organizations believe that their sponsorship of events helps improve the morale of their workforce. On one level, high-profile, brand-building sponsorship, such as Friends Life's involvement with cricket, reassures the workforce and reaffirms the company's leading position in its marketplace. On a more human level, sponsorship for altruistic projects, such as worthy community causes, helps give employees a 'warm', positive feeling towards their employer. The way in which McDonald's supports Ronald McDonald Houses close to children's hospitals and its sponsorship of local school events not only helps the community but also makes its employees feel more positive towards the company.

However, sponsorship is not confined to the promotion and exposure of corporate brands. Individual product brands sponsor many ITV, C5 and Sky programmes. While boards of directors may like to sponsor major sporting events or the arts, increasingly many marketing managers are looking for suitable activities to sponsor for individual brands. For example, supermarket operators and food brands vie to sponsor TV series of leading celebrity chef cookery programmes.

Applications for sponsorship

Sponsorship used to be a tool of public relations and the domain of public relations consultancies. Increasingly, it is a specialist area and a separate component of the promotional mix. Public relations consultancies still handle many sponsorship deals, but a growing number of specialist sponsorship advisers now introduce sponsors to appropriate recipients. It should not be thought that sponsorship is prominent only in the sports and arts worlds. It is an activity of growing importance in many fields. Universities and colleges seek sponsorship for students, technical equipment, buildings and even degree programmes. Hospitals receive and welcome the sponsorship of buildings, operating theatres and fundraising events. Engineering and scientific research, particularly in universities and 'research clubs', benefit from the sponsorship of research and development, often from organizations in completely unrelated fields of business.

No matter what the area, if a company believes its brand reputation will be enhanced and its brand awareness improved by its involvement with an organization or event, sponsorship becomes an important element in its promotional mix. Sponsorship can be for events or competitions, equipment or buildings, ideas or research, learning or development, animals or people, commercial or charitable causes, television programmes, products or services, single activities or ongoing programmes.

Reputable partnerships

There are 'ground rules' to be considered by the prospective sponsor. As with any promotional activity, the sponsor must ensure that the recipient organization, event or product is recognized by the sponsor's own target audience, that it is welcome and acceptable to its target audience, and that it is reputable and ethical in its dealings. The sponsor does not want to invest its promotional budget in activities not recognized by its own target market. **Reputable partnerships** are essential. The sponsor cannot risk becoming involved with an event or organization that has a 'dodgy' reputation and unprofessional management; such a situation threatens the sponsor's reputation and brands. Consider the effect on a prestigious brand if an athlete sponsored by that brand failed a dope test or was found guilty of cheating. The recipient needs to be wary of the donor's image and reputation.[20]

Reputable partnerships
Reputable and ethical dealings between a recognized, welcome and acceptable recipient organization and a sponsoring organization.

Even with careful selection of events or sports stars to sponsor, the sponsor cannot be guaranteed value for money. During the Euro 2004 football tournament in Portugal, Pepsi's millions sponsored England's David Beckham, Italy's Francesco Totti and Spanish strikers Raul and Torres. Beckham missed two penalties as England exited at the quarter-final stage, Totti's infamous spitting incident led to him making only one tournament appearance, and the two Spanish stars failed to score a goal, with none of the players' teams achieving glory. Whether or not Pepsi felt this particular sponsorship represented value for money was not reported.

Summary

Advertising is a paid-for form of non-personal communication that is transmitted to consumers through mass media, such as television, radio, newspapers, magazines, direct mail, public transport vehicles, outdoor displays, ambient advertising and now the web. Both non-business and business organizations use advertising. Advertising has many uses: to create awareness of products, organizations and causes; to stimulate primary and selective demand; to off-set competitors' advertising; to aid sales personnel; to educate the market; to increase uses of a product; to remind and reinforce; to reduce sales fluctuations.

Marketers use advertising in many ways. *Institutional advertising* promotes organizational images and ideas, as well as political issues. When a company promotes its position on a public issue, institutional advertising is referred to as *advocacy advertising.* The growth of nudge interventions in social marketing has added to the use of this form of advertising. *Product advertising* focuses on the uses, features, images and benefits of goods and services. To make people aware of a new or innovative product's existence, uses and benefits, marketers rely on *pioneer advertising* in the introductory stage to stimulate primary demand for a general product category often referred to as creating category need. Then they switch to *competitive advertising* to boost selective demand by promoting a particular brand's uses, features and advantages that may not be available in competing brands. *Comparative advertising* is a form of competitive advertising in which two or more brands are compared on the basis of one or more product attributes.

Through *defensive advertising,* a company can sometimes lessen the impact of a competitor's promotional programme. A company can also make its own salesforce more effective through advertising designed to support personal selling. A business modifying its marketing mix uses advertising to educate the market regarding the changes. To increase market penetration, an advertiser sometimes focuses a campaign on promoting a greater number of uses for the product. *Reminder advertising* for an established product enables consumers to know that the product is still around and that it has certain characteristics, benefits and uses. Marketers may use *reinforcement advertising* to assure current users of a particular brand that they have selected the best brand. Marketers also use advertising to smooth out fluctuations in sales.

Although marketers may vary in how they develop *advertising campaigns,* these should follow a general pattern. First, they must identify and analyze the *advertising target* or *audience.* Second, they should establish what they want the campaign to accomplish by defining the advertising objectives. The third step is creating the *advertising platform,* which contains the basic issues to be presented in the campaign. Fourth, advertisers must decide on the *advertising budget:* how much money will be spent on the campaign; they arrive at this decision through the *objective and task approach,* the *percentage of sales approach,* the *competition matching approach* or the *arbitrary approach.* Fifth, they must develop the *media plan* by selecting and scheduling the media to be used in the campaign, taking into account the desired *reach* and *frequency* as well as *cost comparison indicators.* In the sixth step, advertisers use *copy, artwork* and *illustrations* to create the message, with the aid of *storyboards* and careful *layouts,* bearing in mind *AIDA,* which is the persuasive sequence of attention, interest, desire and action. *Regional issues* of magazines and newspapers allow messages to be tailored to geographic areas. In the seventh step, marketers execute their advertising campaign, after extensive planning and coordination. Finally, advertisers must devise one or more methods for evaluating the effectiveness of the advertisements, including *pre-tests,* the use of *consumer focus groups,* online discussions and panels, direct-response coupons or 0800 freephone contact numbers, *post-campaign tests, recognition tests* and *unaided (or spontaneous) recall tests or aided (or prompted) recall tests.* The single source data technique uses technology to track buying behaviour and evaluate advertisements.

Advertising campaigns can be developed by personnel within the organization or in conjunction with advertising agencies. When a campaign is created by the organization's personnel, it may be developed by only a few people, or it may be the product of an advertising department within the organization. The use of an advertising agency may be advantageous to a client company because an agency can provide highly skilled, objective specialists with broad experience in the advertising field at low to moderate costs to the client company.

Publicity is communication in news-story form about an organization, its products or both, transmitted through a mass medium at no charge. Generally, publicity is part of the larger and more comprehensive communications function of *public relations.* There are three broad categories of public relations: the *PR event,* the *PR campaign* and the *PR programme.* Publicity is mainly informative and usually more subdued than advertising. There are many types of publicity, including *press (news) releases, feature articles, captioned photographs, press conferences,* editorials, films and tapes, blogs and tweets. In addition, public relations encompasses training managers to handle journalists and publicity, establishing links with influential bodies and VIPs, managing visits and seminars, and providing information to employees. *Third-party endorsement,* in which a VIP, trade body or celebrity publicly endorses a product or a brand, is particularly effective, including social media chatter.

Target publics include consumers, suppliers, distributors, journalists, trade bodies, government officials and shareholders, as well as employees and managers inside the business, and society in general. Effective public relations depends on the thorough identification of target publics. To have an effective publicity programme, someone either in the organization or in the business's agency must be responsible for creating and maintaining systematic and continuous publicity efforts.

There is an important distinction between corporate PR and marketing PR. While the toolkit is similar, corporate PR focuses on corporate affairs, while marketing PR addresses product and brand issues. Effective PR programmes require research, action and communication of key messages to relevant publics, as well as evaluation.

An organization should avoid negative publicity by reducing the number of negative events that result in unfavourable publicity, or at least lessen their effect. To diminish the impact of unfavourable publicity, an organization should institute policies and procedures for implementing *crisis management* – identifying key targets, developing a contingency plan, providing access for journalists and monitoring social media when negative events do occur. Problems that organizations confront when seeking publicity include the reluctance of broadcast media personnel to print or broadcast releases and a lack of control over the timing and content of messages.

Sponsorship is the financial or material support of an event, activity, person, organization or product by an unrelated organization or donor in return for the prominent exposure of the sponsor's name and brands. An additional benefit can be to raise the morale of employees within the donor organization. Once the domain of arts and sports, sponsorship applications are broadening. Universities, colleges, hospitals, and engineering and scientific research institutes also seek sponsorship. There are many corporate sponsors of events or facilities, but increasingly marketing managers are seeking relevant recipients and sponsorship partners for their individual brands. Sponsorship recipients and donors must be certain of each other's ethics, image and reputation. *Reputable partnerships* are essential.

Key links

The material in this chapter focuses on just some aspects of marketing communications and ingredients of the promotional mix, so should be read in conjunction with:

- Chapter 16's overview of the communications process and the requisites for effective marketing communications, including integrated marketing communications (IMC).

- Chapter 18's examination of personal selling and sales management, sales promotion, direct mail and the internet – the remaining ingredients of the promotional mix.

- Chapter 11's discussion of effective branding, which requires associated marketing communications.

- Chapter 19's summary of digital marketing.

Important terms

Advertising
Advertising budget
Advertising campaign
Advertising platform
Advertising target audience
Advocacy advertising
AIDA
Aided or prompted recall test
Arbitrary approach
Artwork
Captioned photograph
Comparative advertising
Competition matching approach
Competitive advertising
Consumer focus group
Copy
Cost comparison indicator
Crisis management

Defensive advertising
Digital environment
Feature article
Frequency
Illustrations
Institutional advertising
Layout
Media plan
Objective and task approach
Percentage of sales approach
Pioneer advertising
Post-campaign test or post-test
PR campaign
PR event
PR programme
Press (news) release
Press conference
Pre-tests
Product advertising
Public relations
Publicity
Reach
Recognition test
Regional issues
Reinforcement advertising
Reminder advertising
Reputable partnerships
Sponsorship
Storyboard
Target publics
Third party endorsement
Unaided or spontaneous recall test

Discussion and review questions

1. What is the difference between institutional and product advertising?

2. When should advertising be used to stimulate primary demand? When should advertising be used to stimulate selective demand?

3. What are the major steps in creating an advertising campaign?

4. What is an advertising target audience? How does a marketer analyze the target audience after it has been identified?

5. Why is it necessary to define advertising objectives?

6. What is an advertising platform and how is it used?

7. What factors affect the size of an advertising budget? What techniques are used to determine this budget?

8. Describe the steps required in developing a media plan.

9. What is the role of copy in an advertising message?

10. What role does an advertising agency play in developing an advertising campaign?

11. Discuss several ways to post-test the effectiveness of an advertisement.

12. What is publicity? How does it differ from advertising?

13. How do organizations use publicity? Give several examples of press releases that you have observed recently in local media.

14. What are target publics? Why must they be carefully identified and handled by a public relations department?

15. How should an organization handle negative publicity? Identify a recent example of a company that received negative publicity. Did the company deal with it effectively?

16. Define public relations and highlight its main roles.

17. Explain the problems and limitations associated with using public relations. How can some of these limitations be minimized?

18. In what ways has the arrival of social media complicated life for the PR professional?

19. How can sponsorship enhance brand awareness for a sponsoring organization?

20. What factors must an organization consider before selecting a sponsor or recipient organization?

Recommended readings

Belch, G. and Belch, M., *Advertising and Promotion: An Integrated Marketing Communications Perspective* (McGraw-Hill, 2014).

De Pelsmacker, P., Geuens, M. and van den Bergh, J., *Marketing Communications: A European Perspective* (Pearson, 2013).

Fenton, W. and Collett, P., *The Sponsorship Handbook: Essential Tools, Tips and Techniques for Sponsors and Sponsorship Seekers* (John Wiley, 2011).

Fill, C., *Marketing Communications: Interactivity, Communities and Content* (Pearson, 2013).

Scott, D.M., *The New Rules of Marketing and PR* (John Wiley, 2013).

Shimp, T.A. and Andrews, J.C., *Integrated Marketing Communications in Advertising and Promotion* (Cengage, 2013).

Tench, R. and Yeomans, L., *Exploring Public Relations* (Pearson, 2013).

Internet exercise

Log on to Pepsi.com at www.pepsi.com or Nike.com at www.nike.com.

Both sites offer a selection of advertisements to view. In addition, the website pages strive to advertise the merits of these brands and the specific attributes of these products.

1. What is the advertising platform being adopted by these two brands (Pepsi and Nike)?

2. To what extent are these advertising platforms relevant to the respective target audiences?

3. In developing the advertising for Pepsi or Nike, which stage of the campaign development process will be most important? Why?

Group tasks

1. The arrest of FIFA officials on charges of corruption and racketeering caused sponsors of the World Cup and FIFA activities to express disquiet and concern. Why? What could these sponsors have done to have avoided such a situation?

2. Think of a brand which has recently endured negative publicity. As the team tasked to manage this situation and to limit damage to the brand's reputation, explore what options are available and recommend a preferred way to proceed.

Applied mini-case

Many well-known brands vie to sign to be leading sponsors of major sporting events such as the Olympics, European Football Championships, FIFA's World Cup or the Wimbledon Lawn Tennis Championships. While the major tournaments attract leading beer and soft drinks brands, or manufacturers of sports goods, other tournaments – such as the Cricket World Cup, Rugby World Cup or Darts World Cup – attract a more varied mix of sponsors.

Question

As a marketing manager tasked with identifying sponsorship opportunities for your company and its key brands, what would be the selection criteria used for choosing events or organizations to sponsor and why?

Textbook PR: public relations and the Perrier crisis

Case study

On 10 February 1990, in North Carolina, USA, bottles of Perrier were found to be contaminated with benzene. For the best-selling brand of mineral water in the world this meant a huge crisis. 'Once a critical situation arises the most vital task is to do everything you can to reduce damage to the absolute minimum. We were fortunate that we had agreed procedures in advance and these procedures were followed absolutely,' stated Perrier spokesperson Wenche Marshall Foster. 'From the very beginning we were determined to keep everyone fully informed.'

Perrier's crisis team in the UK moved quickly; senior executives of Perrier, its PR agency at the time, Infoplan, and its then advertising agency, Leo Burnett, had been briefed before the contamination scare on the needs of crisis management.

Within hours of the contamination announcement, Perrier had set up product tests with an independent consultant, Hydrotechnica, so as to have accurate information to give out. The crisis team knew it had to be truthful throughout. Infoplan immediately set up a telephone information service, which dealt with 1700 calls each day from distributors, retailers and consumers.

Within three days of the crisis breaking, shelves worldwide had been cleared and all stocks returned to Perrier. The company achieved goodwill by moving so decisively. No press conferences were given. Instead, the five members of the crisis team individually met journalists for in-depth, head-to-head interviews to give precise and clear information and to minimize poor publicity.

Perrier risked competitors moving to take advantage of the crisis, since retailers would not leave shelves empty. Perrier was the clear brand leader with the only established image worldwide. Competitors would take time to develop such strength, and their stocks were not high. Evian and others had nothing to gain from drawing further attention to Perrier's crisis, which was damaging the industry as a whole.

Perrier's PR handled the crisis in textbook fashion. With, at the time, 85 per cent of the US and 60 per cent of the UK market, it had a great deal to lose. The company informed its publics of its difficulties, tackled the contamination problems and relaunched the product with new packaging and bottle sizes clearly to be seen as new stock with a 'Welcome Back' promotional campaign.

Within months, Perrier's market share was climbing back and shelf space had been regained. The company did not hide anything, it identified the various audiences to brief and it tackled its production to ensure that there were no repeat problems. Consumers, distributors, public health bodies and the media were made to feel part of Perrier's solution through the effective use of PR.

Perrier handled its crisis very efficiently, but never fully regained its domination of the bottled mineral water market, the fastest-expanding sector of the beverages market in the 1990s. Perrier's success had been noted by major beverage suppliers; the removal of its bottles from shelves and the contamination scare gave rivals the opportunity to move in. Despite repackaging, fresh designs and a new advertising agency – Publicis – Perrier struggled to rekindle its former glory days and was then acquired by Nestlé.

Sources: John Tylee, 'Publicis extends "eau" theme for Perrier blitz', *Campaign*, 19 May 1995, p. 7; Greg Prince, 'In hot water', *Beverage World*, March 1995, pp. 90–5; 'Perrier aims to recapture lost young drinkers', *Marketing*, 24 March 1994, p. 1; *Marketing Week*, 2 March 1990; *Personally Speaking*, 27 March 1990; *Fortune*, 23 April 1990; 'Nestlé's "world of water"', www.nestle.com, 2004 and April 2015.

Questions for discussion

1. How important is it to have an ongoing commitment to public relations in the event of a crisis?

2. Could Perrier's competitors have taken more advantage of the crisis?

3. Did the same publicity message go out to all of Perrier's publics or target audiences? Why?

CHAPTER 18

Sales management, sales promotion, direct mail, the internet, digital and direct marketing

"Selling and marketing go hand in hand"

Objectives

- To understand the nature and major purposes of personal selling.

- To learn the basic steps in the personal selling process.

- To identify the types of salesforce personnel.

- To gain insight into sales management decisions and activities.

- To appreciate the role of key account management.

- To become aware of what sales promotion activities are and how they can be used.

- To become familiar with specific sales promotion methods.

- To understand the role of direct mail in the promotional mix.

- To be aware of the importance of the internet in marketing communications.

- To comprehend the growing role of digital marketing.

- To appreciate direct marketing's use of the promotional mix.

INTRODUCTION

As indicated in Chapter 16, personal selling, sales promotion, direct mail, the internet and direct marketing are possible ingredients in the promotional mix, along with advertising, public relations and sponsorship, which were explored in the previous chapter. Together, they form the marketing communications toolkit for marketers and brand managers.

Personal selling is a very widely used ingredient of the promotional mix. Sometimes it is a company's sole promotional tool, although it is generally used in conjunction with other promotional mix ingredients. Personal selling is becoming more professional and sophisticated, with sales personnel acting more as consultants and advisers. Most organizations that have a salesforce have separate sales management staff, who are responsible for recruiting, training, allocating, motivating, rewarding and monitoring the salesforce; rarely are sales staff the direct responsibility of marketers. However, these sales personnel have to prioritize the customers identified by marketers in the target market strategy; they must communicate the agreed brand positioning and leverage any competitive advantage identified by the organization's marketers. Sales staff also learn about customer issues and market developments, so they must be linked with marketers in a company. It is essential that the activities of the salesforce do not conflict with the marketing strategy. That is why, although it is usually a different functional area from Marketing within the organization, personal selling is still deemed to be part of the promotional mix.

Sales promotion, direct mail and the internet also play an important role in the execution of marketing strategies.[1] Direct marketing, a term frequently cited by marketers these days, is a growing tool. Although, as discussed in Chapter 15, direct marketing is partly an aspect of marketing channel selection – in this case opting not to utilize some of the services of channel intermediaries – there are implications for marketers' promotional strategies, as discussed in this chapter. The growth of digital marketing is huge and alters the rules of engagement for marketers. Digital is touched on in this chapter, but warrants its own subsequent chapter.

Sampling nappies: parents' early exposure to Pampers

Many markets, such as fast food, colas and car rental, appear to be dominated by just a few major brands. The same is true for nappies. As soon as one brand innovates with a drier, more comfortable, easier to change or more disposable nappy, its rivals will quickly follow suit. Marketing research reveals that many parents do not switch brands, despite the enticing claims made by competing brands in television advertisements or on-pack. Once they have opted for a particular brand and are familiar with its benefits, parents tend to remain loyal. Therefore, the importance of persuading customers to actually trial a new nappy product is particularly important.

Most new mums receive a *Bounty Bag* either from hospital or via a health worker. These bags contain information leaflets and trial products for nappy cream, baby wipes, nappies, baby foods and much more. Generally, only one brand of each product is included, and the major manufacturers vie to be included. This might be the first ever nappy or baby wipe product tried by a first-time new parent, so if it seems to be effective and does the job, the likelihood is high of a consumer remaining loyal to the sampled brand.

Product sampling is not confined to the Bounty Bag. Long-time rival to Pampers was Huggies, now known for DryNites and Little Swimmers toddler lines. Huggies offered parents free samples of its nappies via television advertisements. A freefone number promised a pack of four Huggies free of charge. Kimberly-Clark, the manufacturer behind Huggies, offered parents the opportunity to trial its Super-Flex line by offering a free pack and money-off voucher to consumers who called the hotline or logged on to the *huggiesforfree* website. The brand's 'Look mum, no leaks' advertising strapline was amended to 'Look mum, free' in the accompanying television campaign. But the move from Huggies was not enough.

Rival Pampers, produced by Procter & Gamble, was included in the hospital Bounty Bags, so the television-led sampling drive was Huggies' attempt to compete in the all-important new-parent product sampling battle between the two leading brands. Huggies has now withdrawn from the UK and Irish nappy market in the face of severe competition from Pampers and retailer own-label brands, to instead concentrate on DryNites pull-ups for toddlers and Little Swimmers for toddlers' early experiences of swimming pools and beaches. Market leader Pampers, with 55 per cent of the nappy market, continues to sample and to be included in Bounty Bag give-aways to new parents.

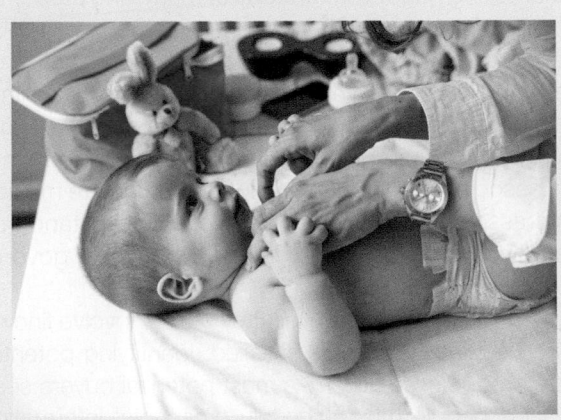

Sources: www.bounty.com/about-bounty/bounty-packs/newborn-pack; Boots; Birmingham Women's Hospital; Warwick Hospital; Kimberly-Clark.

This chapter examines the purposes of personal selling, its basic steps, the types of sales people involved in personal selling and how they are selected. It also discusses the major sales management decisions and activities, which include setting objectives for the salesforce and determining its size; recruiting, selecting, training, compensating and motivating sales people; managing sales territories; and controlling sales personnel. The discussion then goes on to explore several characteristics of sales promotion, the reasons for using sales promotion and the sales promotion methods available for use in a promotional mix, as adopted by Kimberly-Clark for its Huggies brand of nappies. Use and types of direct mail are then examined. The chapter concludes with a brief look at the role of the internet in marketing, digital marketing and the growing use of direct marketing.

The nature of personal selling and sales management

Personal selling
The process of using personal communication in an exchange situation to inform customers and persuade them to purchase products.

Personal selling is the process of informing customers and persuading them to purchase products through personal communication in an exchange situation. For example, a sales person describing the benefits of a Braun shaver to a customer in a Boots store is using personal selling. Many readers, particularly those consumers buying online, will encounter very little personal or face-to-face selling in today's digital world. However, most business-to-business transactions depend heavily on the role of personal selling, as described in Chapter 21. Personal selling gives marketers the greatest freedom to adjust a message to satisfy customers' information needs. In comparison with all other promotional methods, personal selling is the most precise, enabling marketers to focus on the most promising sales prospects. Other promotional mix ingredients are aimed at groups of people, some of whom may not be prospective customers. A major disadvantage of personal selling is its cost. Generally, it is the most expensive ingredient in the promotional mix, owing to the associated costs of salaries, cars and expenses.

Businesses spend more money on personal selling than on any other promotional mix ingredient. Millions of people earn their living through personal selling. In the UK it is estimated that 600 000 people are directly employed as sales people.[2] A selling career can offer high income, a great deal of freedom, a high level of training and a high level of job satisfaction.[3] Unfortunately, consumers often view personal selling negatively. A study of marketing students' perceptions of personal selling showed that approximately 25 per cent of the survey group associated it directly with door-to-door selling and unwelcome intrusion into households. In addition, 59 per cent of all students surveyed had a negative impression of personal selling. In the UK, there is a drive to limit the use of door-to-door selling – a form of personal selling – because of the high numbers of complaints by householders feeling overly pressured or intimidated. Major businesses, professional sales associations and academic institutions are making an effort to change the negative stereotypes associated with sales people.[4] Ethical standards of selling practice are a major part of this enhancement, prompted by EU regulations, government and consumer groups.

Personal selling goals vary from one company to another. However, they usually involve finding prospects, persuading prospects to buy, and keeping customers satisfied. Identifying potential buyers who are interested in an organization's products is critical. As most potential buyers seek information before they make a purchase, sales people must ascertain prospects' information needs and then provide the relevant information. To do so, sales personnel must be well trained, both in regard to their products and to the selling process in general.[5]

Sales people need to be aware of their competitors. They need to monitor new products being developed, and they should be aware of all competitors' sales activities in their sales territories.

They must emphasize the advantages that their products provide when their competitors' products do not offer the same advantages.[6] Sales personnel are a useful source of marketing intelligence, a fact often ignored by their marketing colleagues.

Few businesses survive solely on profits from one-sale customers. For long-run survival, most marketers depend on repeat sales. This notion is at the core of relationship marketing, as described in Chapters 1 and 23. A company has to keep its customers satisfied to obtain repeat purchases. Besides, satisfied customers help attract new ones by telling potential customers about the organization and its products. Even though the whole organization is responsible for providing customer satisfaction, much of the burden falls on sales people. The sales person is almost always closer to customers than anyone else in the company and often provides buyers with information and service after the sale. Such contact not only gives sales people an opportunity to generate additional sales but also offers them a good vantage point from which to evaluate the strengths and weaknesses of the company's products and other marketing mix ingredients. Their observations, if sought, are helpful in developing and maintaining a marketing mix that better satisfies both customers and the business.

A sales person may be involved in achieving one or more of the three general goals. In some organizations:

1. there are people whose sole job is to find prospects
2. this information is relayed to sales people, who then contact the prospects
3. after the sale, these same sales people may do the follow-up work, or a separate team of employees may have the job of maintaining customer satisfaction.

In many smaller organizations, a single person handles all of these functions: prospect list generation, prospect calling and ongoing relationship nurturing. No matter how many personnel are involved, several major sales tasks must be performed to achieve these general goals.

The literature assisting sales management is extensive and tends to focus on the sales management process:

- the importance of preparation – understanding the products and prospective customers, predicting sales and developing systems for recording sales-related data
- the techniques for introducing the sales personnel to prospective customers, either face-to-face or via telecommunications and the web
- the requisites for effective presentations or pitches and written sales proposals
- the skills required to turn a potential customer's interest into commitment
- how to negotiate
- the skills necessary to capture the order
- the ability to close the sale (win the order).

Sales personnel not only address prospective customers, they are often involved in managing ongoing client relationships, and in ensuring repeat orders are won and handled competently. There are strong links with customer relationship management (CRM) techniques, as described in Chapters 3 and 7. Personal selling involves direct customer–sales person contact, but, in addition to face-to-face interaction, personal selling now often benefits from improved telecommunications and telesales. Unlike other forms of promotional activity, personal selling can customize messages for individual customer prospects and build ongoing relationships with existing customers. However, the per capita cost of sales personnel is high; technology such as conference calls, webcasts, email and social media are also used in order to bring down costs of selling. In this digital age, there are many opportunities for networking and maintaining relationships remotely. Often, there is no substitute for face-to-face communications in selling, as explored in the Building Customer Relationships box on page 528.

Not everything is possible digitally

Building customer relationships face-to-face

Those with a vested interest in ensuring that all marketing does not eventually belong in the digital world would argue that face-to-face is still important, but they do have long – winded meetings wondering why they had committed so much time to an ineffectual occasion, or they visit a trade show that has failed to attract the industry's big hitters, or upon arriving to meet an important customer find him or her to be distracted, uncooperative or unavailable. However, all managers can point to 'light bulb' moments from particular meetings that, had they missed the session, a new opportunity would not have been spotted, an aspect of customer dissonance would have gone unnoticed, or a 'deal-breaking' customer concern could not have been explored and sorted out. Webinars, teleconferences, social media fora all have their moments, but so do face-to-face meetings, particularly for sales personnel. As one blogger on *The Economist* website stated, when discussing the role of in-person sales events, 'You can't share a beer over an email'. Sometimes only face-to-face communication permits both parties in a negotiation or transaction to really appreciate the views of all concerned and find common ground.

When the credit crunch first hit, most organizations grounded their executives, limited use of expense accounts, cancelled routine conferences and seminar attendance, and instructed executives not to travel for any 'non-essential' meetings. The sales of web conferencing kits rocketed! The problem, as research by Cornell University found, is that in-person events and meetings are better suited for capturing attendees' attention, inspiring positive emotions and building networks. Digital communications might support already established contacts and relationships or create initial interest, but in many transactions there is no substitute for face-to-face meetings, particularly in B2B. Attention is grabbed face-to-face because of the variety of stimuli surrounding a meeting or live event, compared to one-dimensional online interaction. Colleagues' positive endorsement, often through their body language, fosters satisfactory deals in meetings, while such nuances are missed online. Evidence suggests relationships are built more effectively face-to-face and that trust evolves, compared to a business relationship conducted purely digitally. Initial credibility is often very difficult to establish in only a virtual situation.

A few years ago, the European arm of a major US corporation was struggling to win manufacturing component orders from its US-based parent company's factories, even though Spanish and British plants had the track record, capabilities and products sought by the US factories. Despite the European sites being part of the US corporation, US orders were being placed with external direct competitors not part of the corporation, instead of in-house with the company's European operations. The European factories had to treat the US parent as a semi-interested prospective customer and to manage the creation of a sustainable relationship on this premise. Telecommunications, webcasts, emails and much linking with the corporation's intranet helped improve awareness among the Americans of their European colleagues, but still no orders materialized. So a regular stream of Spanish and British executives flew in to the US making sales calls. However, only when some of these executives based themselves permanently inside key factories in the American parent company were effective networks established and trust built up for doing business with the Spanish and British plants. Such sales prospecting led to these internal customers in the US being managed as key accounts. Although very resource-intensive and expensive, over a few years such activity firmly put the Europeans on the map. Today large orders routinely filter through to the European factories. Personal selling, face-to-face relationships and effective key account management all were integral to this success. Technology plays an important part in maintaining these relationships, particularly conference calls, webcasts and email, but face-to-face is essential in order to build and maintain meaningful relationships.

Sources: Margit Weisgal, 'There will always be a place for face-to-face', *B to B Magazine*, March 2011, www.btobonline.com; Erin Biba, 'The importance of in-person ', *BtoB Magazine*, March 2011, www.btobonline.com; Cornell University School of Hotel Administration, March 2011.

Elements of the personal selling process

The exact activities involved in the selling process vary from one sales person to another and differ for particular selling situations. No two sales people use exactly the same selling methods. Nonetheless, many sales people either consciously or unconsciously move through a general selling

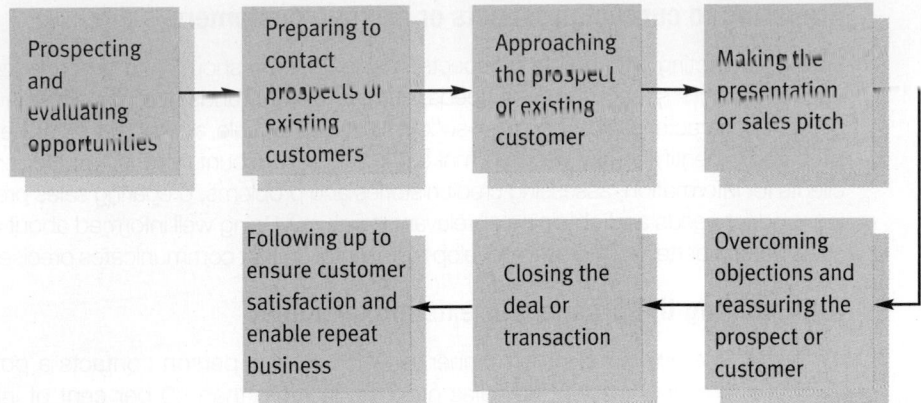

FIGURE 18.1
Elements of personal selling

process as they sell products. This process consists of seven elements, or steps, as depicted in Figure 18.1:

1. prospecting and evaluating opportunities
2. preparing to contact prospects or existing customers
3. approaching the prospect or existing customer
4. making the presentation or 'sales pitch'
5. overcoming objections and reassuring the prospect or customer
6. closing the deal or transaction
7. following up to ensure customer satisfaction and enable repeat business.

Prospecting and evaluating opportunities

Prospecting
Developing a list of potential customers.

Developing a list of potential customers is called **prospecting**. A sales person seeks the names of prospects from the company's sales records, referrals, trade shows, press announcements (of marriages, births, deaths and so on, or new contracts or product developments in business markets), public records, telephone directories, trade association directories, telemarketing lists,[7] online searches and many other sources. Online searches and bought-in telemarketing lists are the most productive. Sales personnel also use responses from advertisements that encourage interested people to send in an information request form. Trade shows, seminars and meetings may produce good leads. Seminars may be targeted at particular types of client, such as solicitors, accountants, the over-55s or specific business people.

Sales people sometimes prefer to use referrals – recommendations from customers or third parties – to find prospects. Obtaining referrals requires that the sales person has a good relationship with the current customer and so must have performed well before asking the customer for help. Research shows that one referral is as valuable as 12 cold calls. Also, 80 per cent of clients are willing to give referrals, but only 20 per cent are ever asked. Sales experts indicate that the advantages of using referrals are that the resulting sales leads are highly qualified, the sales rates are higher, initial transactions are larger and the sales cycle shorter.[8]

After developing the prospect list, a sales person evaluates whether each prospect is able, willing and authorized to buy the product. Certain prospects may have a better fit with the company's operating ethos, geographical coverage and product specification than others. On the basis of this evaluation, some prospects may be deleted, while others are deemed acceptable and ranked according to their desirability or potential.

Preparing to contact prospects or existing customers

Before contacting acceptable prospects, a sales person should find and analyze information about each prospect's specific product needs, current use of brands, feelings about available brands, and personal characteristics. The most successful sales people are thorough in their preparation. They prepare by identifying key decision-makers, reviewing account histories and reports, contacting other clients for information, assessing credit histories and problems, preparing sales presentations, identifying product needs and obtaining all relevant literature.[9] Being well informed about a prospect makes a sales person better equipped to develop a presentation that communicates precisely with the prospect.

Approaching the prospect or existing customer

Approach
The manner in which a sales person contacts a potential customer.

The **approach**, the manner in which a sales person contacts a potential customer, is a critical step in the sales process. In more than 80 per cent of initial sales calls, the purpose is to gather information about the buyer's needs and objectives. Creating a favourable impression and building rapport with the prospective client are also important tasks in the approach, because the prospect's first impression of the sales person is usually a lasting one, with long-run consequences. During the initial visit, the sales person strives to develop a relationship rather than just push a product. The sales person may have to call on a prospect several times before the product is considered.[10]

One type of approach is based on referrals. The sales person approaches the prospect and explains that an acquaintance, an associate or a relative suggested the call. The sales person who uses the cold-canvass method calls on potential customers without their prior consent. Repeat contact is another common approach; when making the contact, the sales person mentions a prior meeting. The exact type of approach depends on the sales person's preferences, the product being sold, the business's resources and the characteristics of the prospect.

Making the presentation or sales pitch

During the sales presentation, the sales person must attract and hold the prospect's attention in order to stimulate interest and stir up a desire for the product. The sales person should have the prospect touch, hold or actually use the product. If possible, the sales person should demonstrate the product and get the prospect more involved with it to stimulate greater interest. Audio-visual materials will be used to enhance the presentation.

During the presentation, the sales person must not only talk but listen. The sales presentation gives the sales person the greatest opportunity to determine the prospect's specific needs by listening to questions and comments, and observing responses. Even though the sales person has planned the presentation in advance, he or she must be able to adjust the message to meet the prospect's information needs.

Overcoming objections and reassuring the prospect or customer

An effective sales person usually seeks out a prospect's objections in order to address them. If they are not apparent, the sales person cannot deal with them, and they may keep the prospect from buying. One of the best ways to overcome a prospect's objections is to anticipate and counter them before the prospect has an opportunity to raise them. However, this approach can be risky because the sales person may mention some objections that the prospect would not have raised. If possible, the sales person should handle objections when they arise. They can also be dealt with at the end of the presentation.

Closing
The step in the selling process in which the sales person asks the prospect to buy the product or products.

Closing the deal or transaction

Closing is the step in the selling process in which the sales person asks the prospect to buy the product or products. During the presentation, the sales person may use a 'trial close' by asking questions that assume the prospect will buy the product. For example,

Innovation and change

The human face of personal selling

Japanese telecommunications retailer Softbank has introduced *Pepper*, a robot programmed to sell coffee machines. The robot is able to have two-way conversations with customers and understand 80 per cent of a conversation. Perhaps more intriguingly, it is claimed by Nestlé and Softbank that *Pepper* is able to read the emotions of consumers. The *Pepper* robot retails for around $2000 and launched in the US in 2015.

Amelia, which was launched at the end of 2014, is a multilingual artificial intelligence engine designed to take over retail jobs. Where a customer has a problem which *Amelia* the robot is unable to address, Amelia observes a human sales assistant tackling the problem, deconstructs how the problem has been solved and next time around *Amelia* will be able to tackle the issue unaided. *Amelia* can deal with phone, email or web chat queries. Computers already direct data to the right person or department and they suggest possible answers, but *Amelia* goes one step further.

Amazon launched Echo, a voice controlled device, designed to become part of the home, listening in to conversations. Consumers are able to speak instructions, such as play music, state the time, read the news and weather, as well as add items to a shopping list. The device responds to the name *Alexa* and behaves very much like Apple's Siri voice assistant, with the added benefit of being able to build a shopping order with simple voice commands.

Meanwhile the Starwood Aloft hotel in Cupertino in California introduced the world's first robot butler *A.L.O.* The robot ferries items from the front desk of the hotel to any of its 150 rooms in just three minutes or less. Using a combination of sensors to communicate with the hotel and the elevator software, the robot can get to and from the rooms without breaking anything or injuring anyone. When the robot arrives at the bedroom, the guest can enter in a rating on the robot's touchscreen, or offer a 'tip' in the form of a tweet. Brian McGuinness, SVP Specialty Select Brands at Starwood Hotels explained, 'As soon as *A.L.O.* entered the room, we knew it was what we were looking for. *A.L.O.* has the work ethic of *Wall-E*, the humour of *Rosie* from *The Jetsons* and reminds me of my favourite childhood robot *R2-D2*. We will look to roll out at our nearly 100 hotels around the world in 2015 and beyond.'

No-one is suggesting the end of personal selling and customer service in human form. Indeed, this chapter illustrates how important face-to-face interaction still is in so many transactions. Nevertheless, the nature of selling in many markets is certainly transitioning.

Sources: 'House of Fraser, Hawes & Curtis, Bentalls trial beacon-enabled mannequins', *Essential Retail*, 12 August 2014; 'Meet "Amelia": the computer that's after your job', *The Telegraph*, 29 September 2014; 'Land Rover offers augmented reality preview of new car', *Luxury Daily*, 12 December 2014; http://retail-innovation.com, April 2015; 'Nestlé employs fleet of robots to sell coffee machines in Japan', *The Guardian*, 1 December 2014; 'Amazon Echo: This is what a smart home should feel like', *MashableUK*, 10 February 2015; 'Aloft Hotel trials Botlr "robot butler" service', BBC News, 18 August 2014.

the sales person might ask the potential customer about financial terms, desired colours or sizes, delivery arrangements or the quantity to be purchased. The reactions to such questions usually indicate how close the prospect is to buying. A trial close allows prospects to indicate indirectly that they will buy the product without having to say those sometimes difficult words, 'I'll take it'.

A sales person should try to close at several points during the presentation, because the prospect may be ready to buy. One closing strategy involves asking the potential customer to take a trial order. The sales representative should either guarantee a refund if the customer is not satisfied or make the order a free offer. Often an attempt to close the sale will result in objections. Thus closing can be an important stimulus that uncovers hidden objections, which can then be addressed.

Following up to ensure customer satisfaction and enable repeat business

After a successful closing, the sales person must follow up the sale. In the follow-up stage, the sales person should determine whether the order was delivered on time and installed properly, if installation was required. He or she should contact the customer to learn what problems or questions, if any, have arisen regarding the product. The follow-up stage can also be used to determine customers' future product needs. This step provides both information and ideas that may prove helpful in selling to other likely customers, and the opportunity to cement relationships with existing customers. Many companies have specialist departments responsible for this post-sale customer service and care.

Types of sales people

To develop a salesforce, a company must decide which types of sales people will best sell and represent the business's products. Most companies deploy several types of sales people. Based on the functions they perform, sales people are generally classified as order getters, order takers or support personnel. Sometimes the same sales person performs all three sets of tasks. When recruiting sales personnel, marketers seldom focus on only one type of sales person: most businesses require a mix of selling skills. A product's uses, characteristics, competitive position, complexity, customer profile, selected marketing channel(s), promotional mix, price and margin influence the kinds and numbers of sales personnel recruited. Table 18.1 overviews these roles.

TABLE 18.1   Key roles in personal selling

Order getters

Order getters are tasked to increase a company's sales by selling to new customers and by increasing sales to existing customers. This entails a process of recognizing buyers' needs, informing prospects and persuading them to try, then buy the product. This is often termed 'creative selling' or business development.

There are two types of order getter: those dealing with current customer sales and those chasing new business sales:

1. *Current customer order getters* call on people who have already purchased a business's products. They seek to sell more to existing customers and to gain sales leads from these customers so as to contact other customers.

2. *New business order getters* are crucial for a company's longer-term survival as all businesses require additional and new customers. These sales people locate prospects and convert them into buyers. The business development function is very important in B2B marketing.

The timeshare industry uses various promotional techniques – direct mail, competitions, road shows, free trial offers – to attract potential buyers to attend seminars or open days at the timeshare site. Once on site, it is up to the new business order getters to explain the concept of timesharing, demonstrate the facilities and close the deal. Without the involvement of sales personnel, it is unlikely that prospects would sign up for a timeshare. BMW's approved used car web service attracts potential buyers, but the deals are often closed by sales people at the dealerships.

Order takers

Taking orders is a repetitive task that sales staff perform to maintain and perpetuate ongoing relationships with customers. **Order takers** seek repeat sales. A major task is to ensure that repeat customers have sufficient quantities of products when and where they are needed. This is particularly important in many business-to-business markets in which manufacturers depend on components for production of their own products. Most order takers handle repeat orders for standardized products that are purchased routinely, minimizing the selling effort.[11] IT systems increasingly link suppliers with customers, enabling the relationship to be handled remotely and automatically.

There are two types of order taker: inside order takers and field order takers:

1. *Inside order takers* are located in a business's call centre or offices, and receive orders by post, fax, email, telephone or online. They do occasionally deal face-to-face with customers; for example, sales assistants inside retail stores are classified as inside order takers.

2. *Field order takers* – the field force – are sales people who travel to customers. Customers often depend on these regular calls to maintain required inventories and keep abreast of any product modifications, while these field-based order takers rely on such ongoing relationships and customer loyalty to achieve their sales targets.

Neither inside nor field order takers should be thought of as entirely passive functionaries who simply record orders. In many businesses, order takers generate the bulk of sales.

Support personnel

Support personnel facilitate the selling function but often do more than just participate in the selling process. Particularly common in business markets, support personnel locate prospects, educate customers, build goodwill and provide after-sales service. They are very important for delivering customer service. There are three main categories of support personnel:

1. *Missionary sales people* are employed by manufacturers to assist their customers' selling efforts. For example, pharmaceutical and medical product manufacturers sell to wholesalers but employ missionary sales personnel to visit retailers to promote retailers' orders being placed with wholesalers.

2. *Trade sales people* undertake order taking as well as help trade customers promote, display and stock their products. The major manufacturers of alcoholic beverages deploy trade sales people to ensure prominent shelf displays of their products in off-licences and supermarkets. They restock shelves, obtain more shelf space, set up displays, provide in-store demonstrations, distribute samples and arrange joint promotions.

3. *Technical sales people* give technical assistance to current customers. They advise customers on product characteristics, applications, system designs and installation, as well as health and safety issues. Agrichemicals, chemicals and heavy plant are technically advanced products requiring technical sales people to support order getters and marketers. In markets with standardized products and little product differentiation, marketers may offer superior technical support and customer service as a means of developing a differential advantage over competitors.

Management of the salesforce

The salesforce is directly responsible for generating a business's primary input: sales revenue. Without adequate sales revenue, a business cannot survive for long. A company's reputation is often determined by the ethical conduct of its salesforce. On the other hand, the morale and ultimately the success of a company's salesforce are determined in large part by adequate compensation, room for advancement, sufficient training and management support – all key areas of sales management. When these elements are not satisfactory, sales staff may leave for more satisfying jobs elsewhere. It is important to evaluate the input of sales people because effective salesforce management helps to determine a company's success. This section explores nine general areas of sales management:

1. establishing salesforce objectives
2. determining salesforce size
3. recruiting and selecting sales personnel
4. training sales personnel
5. compensating sales personnel
6. motivating sales people
7. managing sales territories
8. controlling and evaluating salesforce performance
9. internal marketing.

Establishing salesforce objectives

To manage a salesforce effectively, a sales manager must develop sales objectives. Sales objectives tell sales people what they are expected to accomplish during a specified time period. These objectives give the salesforce direction and purpose, and serve as performance standards for the evaluation and control of sales personnel. In Figure 18.2, Vauxhall uses advertising to produce leads and thereby help sales people meet their sales goals. As with all types of objective, sales objectives should be stated in precise, measurable terms, and should specify the time period, customer type and geographic areas involved.

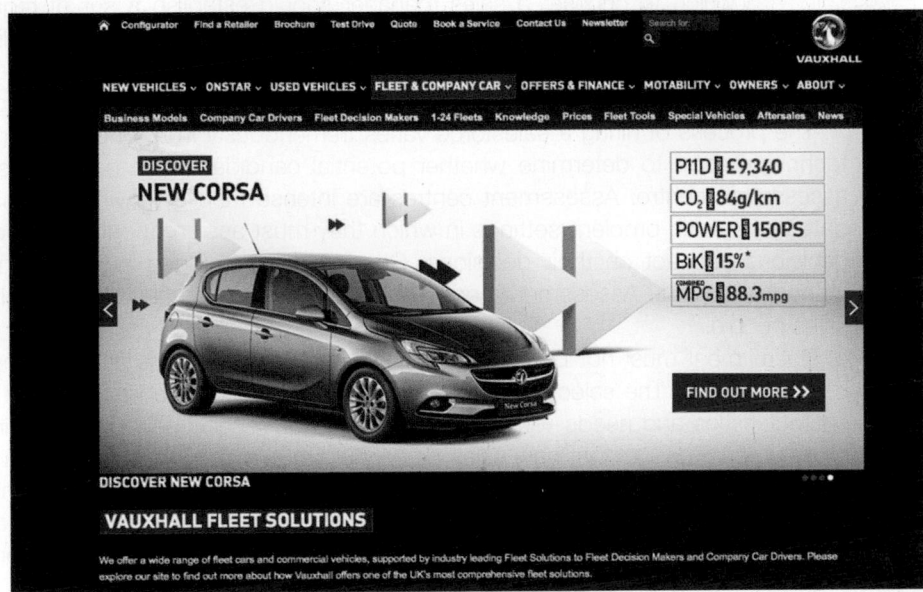

FIGURE 18.2
Vauxhall's car fleet service illustrates business-to-business selling

Source: Image courtesy of Vauxhall.

Sales objectives are usually developed for both the total salesforce and each sales person. Objectives for the entire force are normally stated in terms of sales volume, market share or profit. Volume objectives refer to a quantity of money or sales units. For example, the objective for an electric drill manufacturer's salesforce might be to sell £6 million worth of drills annually or 600 000 drills annually. When sales goals are stated in terms of market share, they usually call for an increase in the proportion of the company's sales relative to the total number of products sold by all businesses in that particular industry. When sales objectives are based on profit, they are generally stated in terms of monetary amounts or in terms of return on investment. Sales objectives, or quotas, for an individual sales person are commonly stated in terms of monetary or unit sales volume. Other bases used for individual sales objectives include average order size, average number of calls per time period and the ratio of orders to calls.

Determining salesforce size

Deciding how many sales people to use is important because the size of the salesforce influences the company's ability to generate sales and profits. Moreover, salesforce size affects the compensation methods used, sales people's morale and overall salesforce management. Salesforce size must be adjusted from time to time because a company's marketing plans change, as do markets and forces in the marketing environment. However, it is dangerous to cut back the size of the salesforce to increase profits by cutting costs. The sales organization could then lose its strength and resilience, preventing it from rebounding when growth returns or better market conditions prevail. The organization that loses capacity through cutbacks may not have the energy to accelerate.[12] There are several analytical methods for determining the optimal size of the salesforce. Although marketing managers may use one of these methods, they normally temper their decisions with a good deal of subjective judgement.[13]

Recruiting and selecting sales personnel

Recruiting
A process by which the sales manager develops a list of applicants for sales positions.

To create and maintain an effective salesforce, a sales manager must recruit the right type of sales people. **Recruiting** is a process by which the sales manager develops a list of applicants for sales positions. The cost of hiring, training and retaining a sales person is soaring; currently, costs in the UK can reach £80 000 or more.[14]

To ensure that the recruiting process results in a pool of qualified sales people from which to choose, a sales manager should establish a set of required qualifications before beginning to recruit. A sales manager generally recruits applicants from several sources: departments within the business, other companies, employment agencies, educational institutions, respondents to advertisements and individuals recommended by current employees.

The process of hiring a salesforce varies tremendously from one company to another. One technique used to determine whether potential candidates will be good sales people is an assessment centre. Assessment centres are intense training environments that place candidates in realistic problem settings in which they must assign priorities to their activities, make decisions and act on their decisions. Candidates are judged by experienced managers or trained observers. Assessment centres have proved to be valuable in helping to select good sales people.[15]

Recruitment must not be sporadic; it should be a continuous activity aimed at reaching the best applicants. The selection process should systematically and effectively match applicants' characteristics and needs with the requirements of specific selling tasks. Finally, the selection process must ensure that new sales personnel are available where and when they are needed. Recruitment and selection of sales people are not one-off decisions. The market and marketing environment change, as do an organization's objectives, resources and marketing strategies. Maintaining the proper mix of sales people thus requires the continued attention of the company's sales management.

Training sales personnel

Many businesses have formal training programmes; others depend on informal, on-the-job training. Some systematic training programmes are quite extensive; others are rather short and rudimentary. Regardless of whether the training programme is complex or simple, its developers must consider who should be trained, what should be taught and how the training should occur. A sales training programme can concentrate on the company, on products or on selling methods. Training programmes often cover all three areas. Sales training may be done in the field, at educational institutions, in company facilities or in several of these locations.

Rewarding sales personnel

To develop and maintain a highly productive salesforce, a business must formulate and administer a compensation or remuneration plan that attracts, motivates and retains the most effective individuals. The plan should give sales management the desired level of control and provide sales personnel with an acceptable level of freedom, income and incentive. It should also be flexible, equitable, easy to administer and easy to understand. Good remuneration programmes facilitate and encourage the proper treatment of customers.

Even though these requirements appear to be logical and easily satisfied, it is actually quite difficult to incorporate them all into a simple programme. Some of them will be satisfied, and others will not. Studies evaluating the impact of financial incentives on sales performance indicate four general responses, as outlined below:

1. For price-sensitive individuals, an increase in incentives will usually increase their sales efforts, and a decrease in financial rewards will diminish their efforts.

2. Unresponsive sales people will sell at the same level regardless of the incentive.

3. Leisure-sensitive sales people tend to work less when the incentive system is implemented.

4. Income satisfiers normally adjust their performance to match their income goal.

Understanding potential reactions and analyzing the personalities of the salesforce can help management evaluate whether an incentive programme might work.[16] Therefore, in formulating a compensation or remuneration plan, sales management must strive for a proper balance of freedom, income and incentives.

The developer of a compensation programme must determine the general level of compensation required and the most desirable method of calculating it. The sales manager may consider a number of factors, including the salaries of other types of personnel in the business, competitors' compensation plans, costs of salesforce turnover and the size of non-salary selling expenses and perks.

Sales compensation programmes usually reimburse sales people for their selling expenses, provide a certain number of fringe benefits such as health insurance, company car and pension scheme and deliver the required compensation level. To do that, a company may use one or more of three basic compensation methods: straight salary, straight commission or a combination of salary and commission:

Straight salary compensation/remuneration plan
A plan according to which sales people are paid a specified amount per time period.

Straight commission compensation/remuneration plan
A plan, according to which sales people are paid solely on the basis of their sales for a given time period.

- In a **straight salary compensation/remuneration plan**, sales people are paid a specified amount per time period. This sum remains the same until they receive a pay increase or decrease.

- In a **straight commission compensation/remuneration plan**, sales people's compensation is determined solely on the basis of their sales for a given time period. Commission may be based on a single percentage of sales or on a sliding scale involving several sales levels and percentage rates.

Combination compensation/ remuneration plan
A plan according to which sales people are paid a fixed salary plus a commission based on sales volume.

- In a **combination compensation/remuneration plan**, sales people are paid a fixed salary plus a commission based on sales volume. Some combination programmes require a sales person to exceed a certain sales level before earning a commission; others offer commissions for any level of sales. Car dealers pay their sales personnel small basic salaries, with sales-linked bonuses making up the bulk of earnings.

Proper administration of the salesforce compensation programme is crucial for developing high morale and productivity among sales personnel. A good sales person is highly marketable in today's workplace, and successful sales managers switch industries on a regular basis. To maintain an effective compensation programme and retain productive employees, sales management should periodically review and evaluate the plan and make necessary adjustments.

Motivating sales people

A sales manager should develop a systematic approach for motivating the salesforce to be productive. Motivating should not be viewed as a sporadic activity reserved for periods of sales decline. Effective salesforce motivation is achieved through an organized set of activities performed continuously by the company's sales management. For example, scheduled sales meetings can motivate sales people. Periodic sales meetings have four main functions:

1. recognizing and reinforcing the performance of sales people
2. sharing sales techniques that are working
3. focusing employees' efforts on matching the corporate goals and evaluating their progress towards achieving these goals
4. teaching the sales staff about new products and services.

Although financial compensation is important, a motivational programme must also satisfy non-financial needs. Sales personnel, like other people, join organizations to satisfy personal needs and achieve personal goals. A sales manager can use a variety of positive motivational incentives as well as financial compensation (see Figure 18.3). For example, enjoyable working conditions, power and authority, job security and an opportunity to excel can be effective motivators. Sales people can also be motivated by their company's efforts to make their job more productive and efficient.

Sales competitions and other incentive programmes can also be effective motivators. Sales contests can motivate sales people to focus on increasing sales or new accounts, promoting special items, achieving greater volume per sales call, covering territories better and increasing activity in new geographic areas.[17] Some companies have found such incentive programmes to be powerful motivating tools that marketing managers can use to achieve corporate goals. Some organizations also use negative motivational measures: financial penalties, demotions, even the termination of employment if targets are not met.

Managing sales territories

The effectiveness of a salesforce that must travel to its customers is influenced to some degree by sales management's decisions regarding sales territories. Sales managers deciding on territories must consider the size and shape of sales territories, and the routing and scheduling of sales people.

Controlling and evaluating salesforce performance

To control and evaluate salesforce activities properly, sales management needs information. A sales manager cannot observe the field salesforce daily and so relies on call reports, customer feedback and invoices. Call reports identify the customers called on and present detailed information about interaction with those clients. Travelling sales personnel must often file work schedules indicating where they plan to be during specific future time periods. In-field IT systems help.

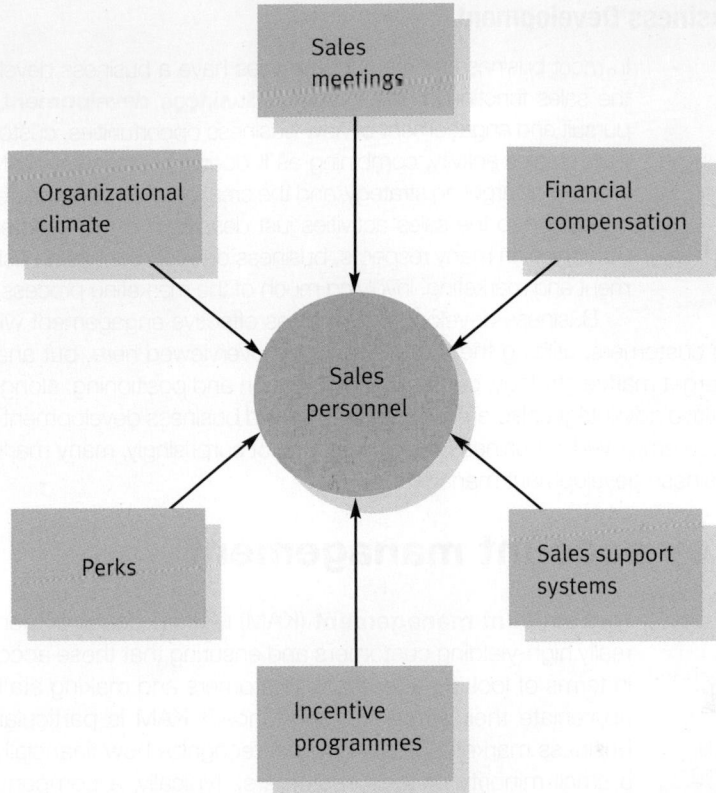

FIGURE 18.3
Motivating salesforce performance through an organized set of activities

The dimensions used to measure a sales person's performance are determined largely by sales objectives. These objectives are normally set by the sales manager. If an individual's sales objective is stated in terms of sales volume, then that person should be evaluated on the basis of sales volume generated. Even though a sales person may be assigned a major objective, he or she is ordinarily expected to achieve several related objectives as well. Sales managers evaluate many performance indicators, including average number of calls per day, average sales per customer, actual sales relative to sales potential, number of new customer orders, average cost per call and average gross profit per customer.

After evaluating their salesforce, sales managers must take any corrective action needed, because it is their job to improve the performance of the salesforce. They may have to adjust performance standards, provide additional sales training or try other motivational methods. Corrective action may demand comprehensive changes in the salesforce.

Many industries, especially technical ones, are monitoring their salesforces and increasing productivity through the use mobile broadband and mobile office capabilities. Companies that have provided their salesforces with the latest technology expect an increase in sales and productivity to result.

Internal marketing

Chapter 23 explains the importance of internal marketing: the process of ensuring that colleagues within the organization are familiar with the marketing strategy, and appreciate their roles in implementing this strategy and the associated marketing plan. The salesforce is usually pivotal to implementing marketing programmes in order to roll-out a marketing strategy, particularly in business markets. It is necessary, therefore, to have internal marketing programmes targeted at sales personnel to orientate them, explain their role, and to outline the intended marketing programmes and their expected deliverables.

Business Development

Business development
The identification, scoping, pursuit and engagement of new business opportunities, customers and accounts.

In most business markets, companies have a business development function, either within the sales function or freestanding. **Business development** is the identification, scoping, pursuit and engagement of new business opportunities, customers and accounts. It is more than a sales activity, combining as it does much market analysis and insight gathering, the shaping of targeting strategy, and the creation of an appropriate proposition to take to market, in addition to the sales activities just described in this chapter of *Marketing: Concepts and Strategies*. In many respects, business development as an activity combines sales management and marketing, involving much of the marketing process described in Chapter 1.

Business development requires effective engagement with new customers and existing customers, utilizing the sales techniques overviewed here, but analysis and the identification of a target market strategy, compelling proposition and positioning, along with a well-considered competitive advantage, also are all integral to sound business development and form part of the remit for those employed in business development. Not surprisingly, many marketing graduates find work as business development managers.

Key account management

Key account management
The process of identifying an organization's few really high-yielding customers and ensuring that these accounts are well-managed both in terms of looking after these customers and making staff within the organization fully appreciate their strategic importance.

Key account management (KAM) is the process of identifying an organization's few really high-yielding customers and ensuring that these accounts are well-managed both in terms of looking after these customers and making staff within the organization fully appreciate their strategic importance.[18] KAM is particularly common in business-to-business markets. Most suppliers recognize how financially dependent they are on just a small minority of their customers. Typically, a company will have many small customers or business clients, quite a lot of large customers, and only a few really large customers in terms of the sales volumes and gross margins earned. Losing one of the smaller customers through poor service delivery or inadequate products will not bring the business to its knees, but were it to lose one of its very large customer accounts, there would be problems.

In the UK, any brand being delisted by Tesco or Sainsbury's would notice a very large drop in its business and may have to lay off staff and reduce production. Brands heavily dependent on only a few accounts tend to allocate staff to each major account, dedicated to maintaining an appropriate relationship. These key account teams often include senior executives. Unfortunately, few companies can afford to resource all of their large accounts in this way, even though they know that such an approach tailors their activities, increases customer satisfaction, results in repeat orders and builds a barrier to competitors. Instead, they must carefully select which customers to treat as key accounts. Customers providing large chunks of business or those big accounts at risk of defecting to a rival supplier often are prioritized.

KAM involves managing key accounts to build mutually beneficial long-term relationships, but also involves identifying which accounts or customers to treat in this way. It is important to acknowledge that key accounts must be assessed from time to time. Volumes of business and relative strategic importance will vary over time, so the set of key accounts will need updating.

Key accounts exist alongside market segmentation. A company will identify market segments, as explained in Chapter 7; some will be strategically more important and attractive than others. This will inform the company's target market strategy selection. Separately, the company will manage a set of key accounts, some of which may be within priority target market segments, but a few may be outside these segments. Their level of business and cash generation may force the company to service them even though the core target market strategy and bigger marketing programmes are targeting the prioritized market segments. The dedicated key account team is still able to address the needs of such key accounts not residing in these segments.

Sales promotion

The nature of sales promotion

Sales promotion
An activity or material
that acts as a direct
inducement and offers
added value to or incen-
tive to buy the product.

As defined in Chapter 16, sales promotion is an activity or material (or both) that acts as a direct inducement and offers added value to or incentive to buy the product to resellers, sales people or consumers.[19] The sale probably would have taken place without the sales promotion activity, but not for a while; the promotion has brought the sale forward. For example, a consumer loyal to Persil washing powder may purchase a packet every four weeks. If, however, in the third week Tesco or Carrefour has Persil on offer or with an on-pack promotion, the consumer will probably buy a week early to take advantage of the deal. Sales promotion encompasses all promotional activities and materials other than personal selling, advertising, publicity and sponsorship. In competitive markets, where products are very similar, sales promotion provides additional inducements to encourage purchase.[20] Sales promotions are designed to generate short-term sales and goodwill towards the promoter.

Sales promotion has grown dramatically in the last 20 years, largely because of the focus of business on short-term profits and value, and the perceived need for promotional strategies to produce short-term sales boosts. The current recession following the Credit Crunch has increased further the role of sales promotions in many organizations' marketing communications. Estimates in the UK suggest that consumer sales promotion is worth £2 billion annually. Include price discounting and the figure could be £4 billion higher; include trade sales promotion and the total reaches £8 billion.[21] One of the most significant changes in expenditures on marketing communications in recent years has been the transfer of funds usually earmarked for advertising to sales promotion, along with the growth of digital activities. Fundamental changes in marketing, which have led to a greater emphasis on sales promotion, mean that specialist sales promotion agencies have increased and many major advertising agencies have developed sales promotion departments.

Ratchet effect
The stepped impact of
using sales promotion
and advertising together.

An organization often uses sales promotion activities in conjunction with other promotional efforts to facilitate personal selling, advertising or both.[22] Figure 18.4 depicts what is known as the **ratchet effect**, which is the stepped impact of using sales promotion (short-term sales brought forward) and advertising (longer-term build-up to generate sales) together. Sales promotion efforts are not always secondary to other promotional mix ingredients. Companies sometimes use advertising and personal selling to support sales promotion activities. For example, marketers frequently use advertising to promote competitions, free samples and special offers. Manufacturers' sales personnel occasionally administer sales contests for wholesale or retail sales people. The most effective sales promotion

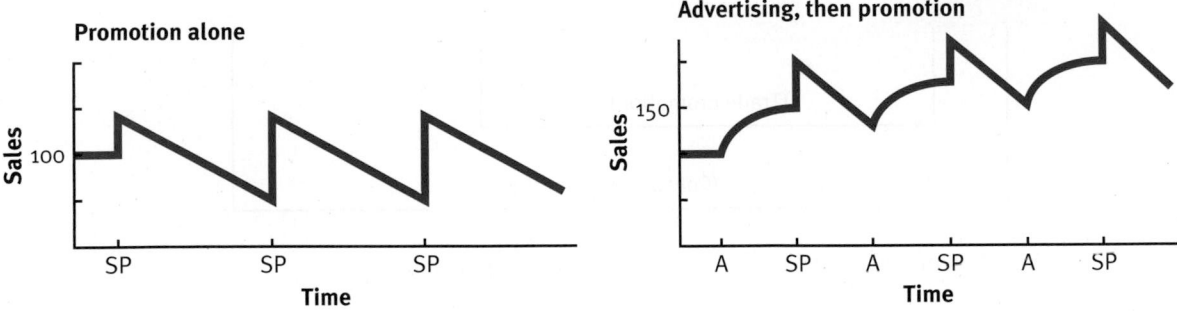

FIGURE 18.4
The 'ratchet effect'. Sales promotion (SP) brings forward sales but has an immediate effect. An advertising campaign (A) takes time to take off and to generate sales, but can switch other brand users and non-users. The ratchet effect has been identified in most consumer and service markets

Source: From 'Insights from pricing research', by W.T. Moran, in *Pricing Practices and Strategies* edited by E.B. Bailey (New York: The Conference Board, 1978), pp. 7,13. Reproduced with permission from The Conference Board, Inc. copyright © 1978 The Conference Board, Inc.

efforts are closely interrelated with other promotional activities. Therefore, decisions regarding sales promotion often affect advertising and personal selling decisions and vice versa.

Sales promotion opportunities and limitations

Sales promotion can increase sales by providing an extra incentive to purchase. There are many opportunities to motivate consumers, resellers and sales people to take a desired action. Some kinds of sales promotion are designed specifically to identify and attract new customers, to introduce a new product and to increase reseller inventories. Some are directed at increasing consumer demand; still others focus on both resellers and consumers. Regardless of the purpose, marketers need to ensure that the sales promotion objectives are consistent with the organization's overall objectives, as well as with its marketing and communications objectives.[23]

Although sales promotion can support a brand image, excessive price reduction, such as discount coupons or two-for-one pack offers, can affect it adversely. Companies must decide between short-term sales increases and the long-run need for a desired reputation and brand image.[24] Sales promotion has been catching up with advertising in total expenditure; but in the future, brand advertising may become more important relative to sales promotion. Some companies that shifted from brand advertising to sales promotion have lost market share, particularly in consumer markets, where advertising often is essential to maintain awareness and brand recognition. Advertising does not necessarily work better than sales promotion. There are trade-offs between these two forms of promotion, and the marketing manager must determine the right balance to achieve maximum promotional effectiveness.

> **Consumer sales promotion techniques**
> Techniques that encourage or stimulate consumers to patronize a specific retail store or to try a particular product.

> **Trade sales promotion methods**
> Techniques that encourage wholesalers, retailers or dealers to carry and market a producer's products.

Sales promotion methods

Most sales promotion methods can be grouped into the categories of consumer sales promotion and trade sales promotion. **Consumer sales promotion techniques** are pitched at consumers: they encourage or stimulate consumers to patronize a specific retail store or to try a particular product. **Trade sales promotion methods** are aimed at marketing channel intermediaries: they stimulate wholesalers, retailers or dealers to carry a producer's products and to market these products aggressively. Figure 18.5

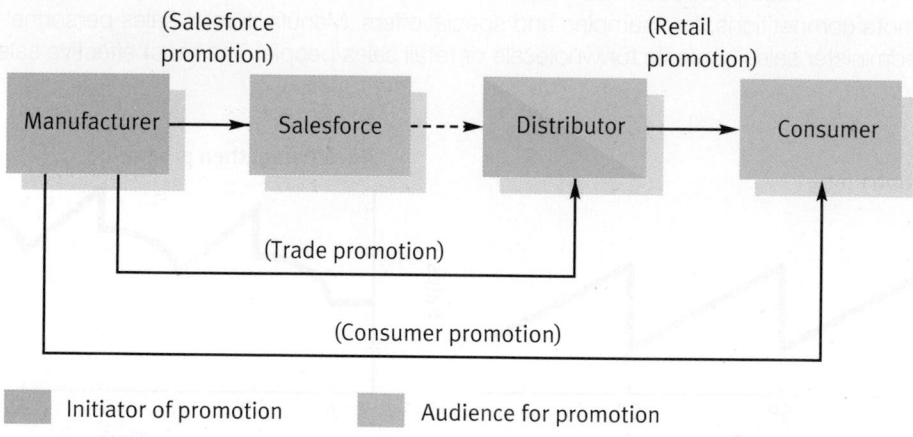

FIGURE 18.5

Uses of sales promotion in the marketing channel. Consumer: coupons, free samples, demonstrations, competitions. Trade (aimed at wholesalers, retailers, sales people): sales competitions, free merchandise, POS displays, plus trade shows and conferences

Source: From *Advertising and Promotion Management* by John R. Rossiter and Larry Percy, The McGraw-Hill Companies Inc. Copyright © 1987 by John Rossiter and Larry Percy.

shows how all members of a marketing channel can be engaged in sales promotion activities with different target audiences and techniques.

Marketers consider a number of factors before deciding which sales promotion methods to use.[25] They must take into account both product characteristics (size, weight, costs, durability, uses, features and hazards) and target market characteristics (lifestyle, age, sex, income, location, density, usage rate and shopping patterns). How the product is distributed, and the number and types of reseller, may determine the type of method used. The competitive and legal environmental forces may also influence the choice.

Consumer sales promotion techniques

The principal consumer sales promotion techniques include coupons, demonstrations, frequent-user incentives, point-of-sale (POS) materials, free samples, money refunds, premiums, price-off offers and consumer competitions.

Coupons
A promotion method that reduces the purchase price of an item in order to stimulate consumers to try a new or established product, to increase sales volume quickly, to attract repeat purchasers or to introduce new package sizes or features.

Coupons   Coupons are used to stimulate consumers to try a new or established product, to increase sales volume quickly, to attract repeat purchasers or to introduce new package sizes or features. Coupons usually reduce the purchase price of an item. The savings may be deducted from the purchase price or offered as cash. For the best results, coupons should be easy to recognize and state the offer clearly. The nature of the product – seasonality, maturity, frequency of purchase and so on – is the prime consideration in setting up a coupon promotion. Use of coupons has rocketed, prompted by the ease of emailing vouchers and using websites to distribute coupons either as incentives for new customers or CRM rewards to existing customers.

Several thousand manufacturers distribute coupons, which are used by approximately 80 per cent of all households. One study found that pride and satisfaction from obtaining savings through the use of coupons and price-consciousness were the most important determinants of coupon use.[26] Coupons are distributed through free-standing inserts (FSIs), print advertising, direct mail/leaflet drops, in stores and as web downloads. Historically, FSIs have been the dominant vehicle for coupons.[27] However, many websites provide the opportunity to download and print off coupons, which is fast becoming a preferred execution for marketers. When deciding on the proper vehicle for their coupons, marketers should consider strategies and objectives, redemption rates, availability, circulation and exclusivity. The whole coupon distribution and redemption business has become very competitive. To draw customers to their stores, grocers may double and sometimes even triple the value of the coupons they bring in.

There are several advantages to using coupons. Print advertisements with coupons are often more effective than non-promotional advertising in generating brand awareness. Generally, the larger the coupon's cash offer, the better the recognition generated. Another advantage is that coupons are a good way to reward present users of the product, win back former users and encourage purchases in larger quantities. Coupons also enable manufacturers to determine whether the coupons reached the intended target market because they get the coupons back. The advantages of using electronic coupons over paper coupons include lower cost per redemption, greater targeting ability, improved data-gathering capabilities and improved experimentation capabilities to determine optimal face values and expiration cycles.[28]

Coupons also have drawbacks. Fraud and mis-redemption are possible, and the redemption period can be quite lengthy. Table 18.2 illustrates coupon distribution and redemption rates in the UK. In addition, some experts believe that coupons are losing their value because so many manufacturers are offering them, and consumers have learned not to buy without some incentive, whether it be a coupon, a rebate or a refund. There has been a general decline in brand loyalty among heavy coupon users. In addition, many consumers redeem coupons only for products they normally buy. Studies have shown that about 75 per cent of coupons are redeemed by people

TABLE 18.2   UK coupon redemption

Media	Average Redemption Rates
Internet*	1.4
Direct mail	5.6
Door drop	3.9
Magazines	0.7
Newspapers	0.5
In/on pack	2.5
Consumer event (roadshows, outdoor events, concerts)	2.9
In store	3.5
Voucher booklet	0.9
Other (charity, postcards, parent & baby packs, coupons requested by customer application, etc.)	1.9
Number of redeemed vouchers and coupons	603 000 000 (up 35%**)
Value of vouchers and coupons redeemed	£1.7 billion

Sources: Valassis and Letterbox, 2014 and 2015.
*Web coupon redemption is the fastest growing.
**Retailer couponing is driving the overall growth; 84 per cent of supermarket shoppers use coupons.

who already use the brand on the coupon. So, as an incentive to use a new brand or product, coupons have questionable success. Another problem with coupons is that stores often do not have enough of the coupon item in stock. This situation can generate ill-will towards both the store and the product.[29]

Although the use of coupons as a sales promotion technique is expected to grow, marketers' concerns about their effectiveness could well diminish their appeal. However, coupons will probably remain a major sales promotion component for stimulating trial of new products, particularly given the ease with which they can be targeted at specific consumers via CRM systems and downloaded for ease of use. Coupons will also be used to increase the frequency of purchase for established products that show sluggish sales. On the other hand, successful, established products may be reducing their profits if 75 per cent of the coupons are redeemed by brand-loyal customers.[30] As brands seek to demonstrate value to cash-poor consumers in recession coupons are very much on the increase, supported by the growth of digital and mobile couponing.

Demonstrations   Demonstrations of products at dealers, retailers or trade shows are excellent attention-getters. Manufacturers often use them to show how a product actually works in order to encourage trial use and purchase of the product. As labour costs can be extremely high, demonstrations are not widely used. However, they can be highly effective for promoting certain types of product, such as appliances, cosmetics and cars. Cosmetics marketers, such as those for Estée Lauder, sometimes offer potential customers 'makeovers' to demonstrate their products' benefits and proper application. Food brands often undertake cooking demonstrations at major sector events or social gatherings.

Frequent user incentives   Many companies develop **frequent user incentives** to reward customers who engage in repeat purchases. For example, most major international airlines offer a frequent-flier programme through which customers who have flown a specified number of miles are rewarded with free tickets for additional travel. AirMiles takes this concept further, extending it across many products. Supermarket loyalty cards are another popular incentive; one such is Tesco's Clubcard. A **loyalty card** offers discounts or free merchandise to regular customers. Thus, frequent user incentives help foster customer loyalty to a specific company

Demonstrations
Occasions at which manufacturers show how a product actually works in order to encourage trial use and purchase of the product.

Frequent user incentives
Incentive programmes that reward customers who engage in repeat purchases.

Loyalty card
A mechanism whereby regular customers who remain loyal to a particular company are rewarded with discounts or free merchandise.

or group of cooperating companies that provides extra incentives for patronage. Frequent user incentives have also been used by service businesses, such as car hire companies, hotel chains and credit cards, as well as by marketers of consumer goods (see Figure 18.6).

An older frequent user incentive is trading stamps. **Trading stamps** are dispensed in proportion to the amount of a consumer's purchase, and can be accumulated and redeemed for goods. Retailers use trading stamps to attract consumers to specific stores. Stamps are attractive to consumers as long as they do not drive up the price of goods. They are effective for many types of retailer. Trading stamps were very popular in the 1960s, but their use as a sales promotion method declined dramatically in the 1970s.

Trading stamps
Stamps, dispensed in proportion to the amount of a consumer's purchase, that can be accumulated and redeemed for goods.

Point-of-sale (POS) materials   Point-of-sale (POS) materials include such items as outside signs, window displays, counter pieces, display racks and self-service cartons. Innovations in POS displays include sniff teasers, which give off a product's aroma in the store as consumers walk within a radius of four feet, in-store televisions, and computerized interactive displays, which ask a series of multiple-choice questions and then display information on a screen to help consumers make a product decision. IKEA stores offer interactive monitors on which room layouts and colour combinations may be tested prior to purchase. These items, which are often supplied by producers, attract attention, inform customers and encourage retailers to carry particular products. A retailer is likely to use point-of-sale materials if they are attractive, informative, well-constructed and in harmony with the store. With two-thirds of all purchases resulting from in-store decisions, POS materials can help sustain incremental sales if a brand's essential components brand name, positioning and visual image are the basis of the POS display.[31]

Point-of-sale (POS) materials
Enhancements designed to increase sales and introduce products, such as outside signs, window displays, counter pieces, display racks and self-service cartons.

A survey of retail store managers indicated that almost 90 per cent believed that POS materials sell products. The retailers surveyed also said that POS is essential for product introductions. Different forms of display materials are carried by different types of retailer. For example, convenience stores favour window banners and 'shelf talkers' (on-the-shelf displays or signs), whereas chain chemists prefer floor stands and devices that provide samples.[32]

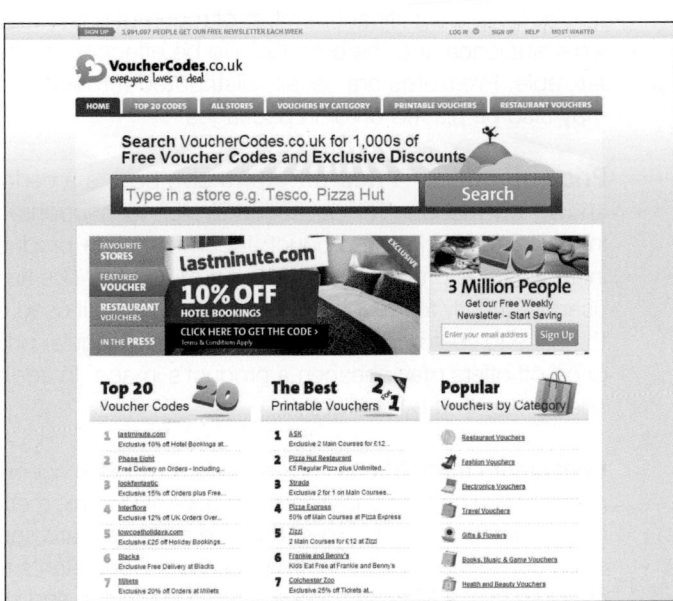

FIGURE 18.6

Example of typical online coupons

Source: Screenshot courtesy of vouchercodes.co.uk.

Free samples
Giveaways used to stimulate trial of a product, to increase sales volume in the early stages of a product's life cycle or to obtain desirable distribution.

Free samples   Free samples of merchandise are used for several reasons: to stimulate trial of a product, to increase sales volume in the early stages of a product's life cycle or to obtain desirable distribution. The sampling programme should be planned as a total event and not merely a give-away. Sampling is the most expensive of all sales promotion methods; production and distribution through such channels as mail delivery, door-to-door delivery, in-store distribution and on-package distribution entail very high costs. In designing a free sample, marketers should consider factors such as the seasonality of the product, the characteristics of the market and prior advertising. Free samples are not appropriate for mature products and products with a slow turnover.

Money refunds
A specific amount of money mailed to customers who submit proof of purchase.

Money refunds   With money refunds, consumers submit proof of purchase and are mailed a specific amount of money. Usually, manufacturers demand multiple purchases of the product before a consumer can qualify for a refund. This method, used primarily to promote trial use of a product, is relatively inexpensive. As money refunds sometimes generate a low response rate, they have tended to have limited impact on sales. The emergence of reward apps is changing this. These apps, such as QuidCo, provide cash-back or accumulated pay-back for future purchases and are becoming increasingly popular.

Reward apps
Provide cash-back rewards or accumulated pay-back for future purchases.

One of the problems with money refunds or rebates is that many people perceive the redemption process as too complicated. Consumers also have negative perceptions of manufacturers' reasons for offering rebates. They may believe that these are new, untested products or products that have not sold well. If these perceptions are not changed, rebate offers may degrade the image and desirability of the product being promoted. If the promotion objective in the rebate offer is to increase sales, an effort should be made to simplify the redemption process and proof of purchase requirements.[33]

Premiums
Items offered free or at minimum cost as a bonus for purchasing a product.

Premiums   Premiums are items offered free or at minimum cost as a bonus for purchasing a product. Vidal Sassoon offered a free, on-pack 50ml 'travel size' container of shampoo with its 200ml size of Salon Formula shampoo. Kellogg's offered easy art books with its Variety Packs. Premiums can attract competitors' customers, introduce different sizes of established products, add variety to other promotional efforts and stimulate loyalty. Inventiveness is necessary if an offer is to stand out and achieve a significant number of redemptions – the premium must be matched to both the target audience and the brand's.[34] To be effective, premiums must be easily recognizable and desirable. Premiums are usually distributed through retail outlets or the mail, but they may also be placed on or in packages.

Price-off offers
A method of encouraging customers to buy a product by offering a certain amount off the regular price shown on the label or package.

Price-off offers   Price-off offers give buyers a certain amount off the regular price shown on the label or package. Similar to coupons, this method can be a strong incentive for trying the product; it can stimulate product sales, yield short-lived sales increases and promote products out of season. It is an easy method to control and is used frequently for specific purposes. However, if used on an ongoing basis, it reduces the price to customers who would buy at the regular price anyway, and frequent use of price-off offers may cheapen a product's image. In addition, the method often requires special handling by retailers.

Consumer contests
Contests designed to generate traffic at the retail level in which consumers compete for prizes based on their analytical or creative skill.

Consumer competitions   Consumer contests encourage individuals to compete for prizes based on their analytical or creative skills. This method generates traffic at the retail level. Marriott and Hertz co-sponsored a scratchcard contest with a golf theme to boost sales during the slow winter travel season. Contestants received game cards when they checked in at a Marriott hotel or hired a Hertz car, and scratched off spots to see if they had won prizes, such as cars, holidays or golf clubs.[35] However, marketers should exercise care in setting up such competitions. Problems or errors may anger consumers or result in legal action. Contestants are usually more involved in consumer contests than they are in sweepstakes, even though total participation may be lower. Contests may be used in conjunction with other sales promotion methods, such as coupons.

Consumer sweepstakes
A method of stimulating sales in which consumers submit their names for inclusion in a draw for prizes.

The entrants in a **consumer sweepstake** submit their names for inclusion in a draw for prizes. Sweepstakes are used to stimulate sales and, as with contests, are sometimes teamed with other sales promotion methods. Sweepstakes are used more often than consumer contests and tend to attract a greater number of participants. The cost of a sweepstake is considerably less than the cost of a contest.[36] Successful sweepstakes or contests can generate widespread interest and short-term increases in sales or market share.

Trade sales promotion methods

Producers use sales promotion methods to encourage resellers, especially retailers and dealers, to carry their products and promote them effectively. The methods include buy-back allowances, buying allowances, counts and re-counts, free merchandise, merchandise allowances, cooperative advertising, dealer listings, premium or push money, sales contests and dealer loaders.

Buy-back allowance
A certain sum of money given to a purchaser for each unit bought after an initial deal is over.

Buy-back allowance A **buy-back allowance** is a certain sum of money given to a purchaser for each unit bought after an initial deal is over. This method is a secondary incentive in which the total amount of money that resellers can receive is proportional to their purchases during an initial trade deal, such as a coupon offer. Buy-back allowances foster cooperation during an initial sales promotion effort and stimulate repurchase afterwards. The main drawback of this method is its expense.

Buying allowance
A temporary price reduction given to resellers who purchase specified quantities of a product.

Buying allowance A **buying allowance** is a temporary price reduction to resellers for purchasing specified quantities of a product. For example, a soap producer might give retailers £10 for each case of soap purchased. Such offers may be an incentive to handle a new product, achieve a temporary price reduction or stimulate the purchase of an item in larger than normal quantities. The buying allowance, which takes the form of money, yields profits to resellers and is simple and straightforward to use. There are no restrictions on how resellers use the money, which increases the method's effectiveness.

Count and re-count
A promotion method based on the payment of a specific amount of money for each product unit moved from a reseller's warehouse in a given time period.

Count and re-count The **count and re-count** promotion method is based on the payment of a specific amount of money for each product unit moved from a reseller's warehouse in a given time period. Units of a product are counted at the start of the promotion and again at the end to determine how many have moved from the warehouse. This method can reduce retail stock-outs by moving inventory out of warehouses, and can also clear distribution channels of obsolete products or packages and reduce warehouse inventories. The count and re-count method might benefit a producer by decreasing resellers' inventories, making resellers more likely to place new orders. However, this method is often difficult to administer and may not appeal to resellers who have small warehouses.

Free merchandise
Giveaways sometimes offered to resellers who purchase a stated quantity of the same or different products.

Free merchandise **Free merchandise** is sometimes offered to resellers who purchase a stated quantity of the same or different products. Occasionally, free merchandise is used as payment for allowances provided through other sales promotion methods. To avoid handling and bookkeeping problems, the usual method of giving away merchandise is by reducing the invoice.

Merchandise allowance
A manufacturer's agreement to pay resellers certain amounts of money for providing special promotional efforts, such as advertising or displays.

Merchandise allowance A **merchandise allowance** is a manufacturer's agreement to pay resellers certain amounts of money for providing special promotional efforts, such as advertising or displays. This method is best suited to high-volume, high-profit, easily handled products. One major problem with using merchandise allowances is that some retailers or dealers perform their activities at a minimally acceptable level simply to obtain the allowances. Before paying retailers or dealers, manufacturers usually verify their performance. Manufacturers hope that the retailers' or dealers' additional promotional efforts will yield substantial sales increases.

Cooperative advertising
An arrangement whereby a manufacturer agrees to pay a certain amount of a retailer's or dealer's media costs for advertising the manufacturer's products.

Cooperative advertising **Cooperative advertising** is an arrangement whereby a manufacturer agrees to pay a certain amount of a retailer's or dealer's media costs for advertising the manufacturer's products. The amount allowed is usually based on the quantities purchased. Before payment is made, a retailer or dealer must show proof that advertisements did appear.

These payments give retailers or dealers additional funds for advertising. They can, however, put a severe burden on the producer's advertising budget. Some retailers or dealers exploit cooperative advertising programmes by crowding too many products into one advertisement. Some retailers or dealers cannot afford to advertise; others can afford it but do not want to advertise. Still others actually put out advertising that qualifies for an allowance but are not willing to undertake the paperwork required for reimbursement from producers.[37]

Dealer listing
An advertisement that promotes a product and identifies the names of participating retailers or dealers who sell it.

Dealer listing A **dealer listing** is an advertisement that promotes a product and identifies the names of participating retailers or dealers who sell it. Dealer listings can influence retailers or dealers to carry the product, build traffic at the retail level and encourage consumers to buy the product at participating dealers.

Premium or push money
Additional compensation/remuneration provided to sales people in order to push a line of goods.

Premium or push money **Premium or push money** is used to push a line of goods by providing additional compensation/remuneration to sales people. This promotion method is appropriate when personal selling is an important part of the marketing effort; it is not effective for promoting products that are sold through self-service. Although this method often helps a manufacturer obtain commitment from the salesforce, it can also be very expensive.

Sales competition
A way to motivate distributors, retailers and sales personnel by recognizing and rewarding outstanding achievements.

Sales competitions **Sales competitions** are designed to motivate distributors, retailers and sales personnel by recognizing and rewarding outstanding achievements. To be effective, this method must be equitable for all sales personnel involved. One advantage of the method is that it can achieve participation at all levels of distribution. However, the results are temporary and prizes are usually expensive.

Dealer loader
A gift to a retailer or dealer who purchases a specified quantity of merchandise.

Dealer loaders **Dealer loaders** are gifts to a retailer or dealer, who purchases a specified quantity of merchandise. Often dealer loaders are used to obtain special display efforts from retailers by offering essential display parts as premiums. For example, a manufacturer might design a display that includes a sterling silver tray as a major component and then give the tray to the retailer. Marketers use dealer loaders to obtain new distributors and push larger quantities of goods.

Direct mail
Printed advertising material delivered to a prospective customer's or donor's home or work address.

Direct mail

Direct mail and telephone selling are part of the direct marketing category described in Chapter 16. Direct mail is the delivery to the target's home or work address of printed advertising material to contact prospective customers or donors. The use of direct mail to contact prospective customers and to solicit interest in products or services is not new.[38] Advertising agencies, public relations consultancies and, in particular, sales promotions houses have been using mailshots for several decades. With approximately 6 per cent of all promotional budgets in consumer goods and services, its own professional bodies and trade associations, and the growing sophistication of consumer databases, the direct mail industry believes it warrants recognition as a separate element of the promotional mix alongside advertising, sales promotion, personal selling, publicity/public relations and sponsorship.[39]

The uses of direct mail

Direct mail is not confined to consumers; it is an important promotional activity in many business-to-business markets. Direct mail delivers the promotional message and sometimes the product through the postal service, private delivery businesses and the web. Direct mail is used to create brand awareness and stimulate product adoption.[40] There is even the growth of direct mail via email addresses, but the internet is addressed separately in this chapter. Throughout Europe, direct mail is widely used to generate orders, pre-sell prior to a sales call, qualify prospects for a sales call, screen out non-prospects, follow up a sale, announce special sales and localized selling initiatives, and raise funds for charities and non-profit organizations. In the UK, the average household receives 166 items of direct mail each year.

Attention-seeking flashes

Junk mail
Unwanted mail often binned unread by uninterested recipients.

Flashes
Headers printed on a direct mail package to gain the recipient's attention.

Direct mail package
A mix of mailing envelope, covering or explanatory letter, circular, response device and return device.

Direct mail packages must prompt the recipient to open them, rather than treat them as **junk mail**, which is unwanted mail often binned unread by uninterested recipients. 'Prize inside', 'Your opportunity to win', 'Not a circular', 'Important documentation enclosed' are just some of the popular headers, or **flashes**, printed prominently on the address labels to gain the recipients' attention. In some markets, these are sufficient at least to persuade the recipient to open the package. However, with the boom in direct mail and the growing adverse reaction to junk mail, persuasive phrases are often not enough. Packaging design is becoming more important in enticing recipients, through attractive or unusual shapes and designs, to examine the details and contents of the direct mailshot.

The package

The **direct mail package** is more than just the envelope. Often it is a mix of mailing envelope, covering or explanatory letter, circular, response device and return device. The mailing envelope has to overcome the recipients' inertia, often through catchy flashes and design flair. The letter needs to be personalized and clear, to appeal to the beliefs and lifestyle of the recipients, and to elicit interest in the product or service in question. The circular contains the service or product details and specifications: colour, sizes, capabilities, prices, photographs or illustrations, guarantees and endorsements from satisfied customers or personalities. The circular is the primary selling tool in the pack and often takes the form of a booklet, broadsheet, jumbo folder, brochure or flyer. The response device is typically an order form, which must be legally correct, must repeat the selling message and product benefits, must be simple to read and fill out, and comprehensive in the information requested. Alternatively, the response device can be an 0800 freefone telephone number, credit card hotline or web-link. The return device is any mechanism that enables the recipient to respond with a request for information or an order or donation. It can be an information request form, order form or payment slip, and is usually accompanied by a pre-printed and often pre-paid return envelope.

Mailing lists

Eighty per cent of direct mail is opened; 63 per cent is partially read; less still leads to an order or donation. Depending on the scale of the targeted audience, however, the costs are relatively low:

Mailing lists
Directories of suitable, relevant recipients or targets.

that is, of design, printing, postage, and the purchase or compilation of **mailing lists** – directories of suitable, relevant recipients or targets. To be effective, appropriate targeting of direct mail is essential. Mailing lists must be as up to date as possible. There is a rule of thumb in the industry that a third of addresses on a list change each year owing to deaths and relocations. Within a year or two a list can be obsolete. Internal lists are those compiled in-house from customer addresses, account details and records of enquiries. External lists are produced by list brokers or mailing houses and are bought or rented at commercial rates.

The suppliers of these external lists often undertake the complete direct mail operation for clients, from identification of recipients and compilation of lists to production of printed material, postage and even receipt of response devices. External lists can either be addresses of product category customers, including those of competing businesses if available, or general lists of targets with apparently suitable demographic profiles and lifestyles. Many of the leading geodemographic databases, such as ACORN and MOSAIC, were originally developed to assist in the targeting of direct mail. The Royal Mail is also a good data source (see Figure 18.7).

Copy writing

Copy writing
The creation and wording of the promotional message.

Targeting does not stop with the acquisition of a mailing list. The printed and product material included in the direct mail package must be written, designed and produced to appeal to the targets. The material should be prepared by people who understand the emotions and attitudes of prospective customers. **Copy writing**, the creation and wording of the promotional message, is an important skill in the promotional mix, especially in the production of direct mail. The text has to appeal to the target audience; sell the product; reassure the reader; be informative, clear and concise; and lead to a positive response.

The strengths and weaknesses of direct mail

There are many advantages associated with direct mail. The medium offers a wide variety of styles and formats – more than offered by a radio or press advertisement, for example. The package can be personalized and customized. Often it will be received and read alone, not in competition with other promotions from other products and services. Extensive and detailed information can be included – much more than with advertising – and product samples may be integral to the direct mail package. Marketing research and database management can lead to accurate targeting of direct mail. Sending material directly to people's homes and workplaces can hit targets otherwise inaccessible to promotional activity.

The primary disadvantage is the growing consumer view that direct mail is 'junk mail' that should be consigned to the dustbin without even being opened. If used on a large scale, direct

FIGURE 18.7
Direct mail is familiar to most consumers and many business customers

mail can prove costly; perhaps less so than a salesforce or television advertising, but more expensive than many public relations activities and some local or trade advertising. Direct mail packages and campaigns need to be updated to remain fresh in the fight against the junk mail image. In many countries, the paucity of up-to-date mailing lists increases the cost of direct mail, reduces response rates and adds to consumer dislike of the concept of unsolicited direct selling through the post.

For organizations as diverse as retailer Marks & Spencer, financial services group American Express, catalogue retailer Lands' End, charity Oxfam, consumer goods manufacturer Unilever, or British Airways, direct mail is an important, everyday component of the promotional mix. Whether it is on behalf of starving people in less developed countries, double glazing for windows, fast food or book clubs, direct mail is familiar to consumers in most countries. For office supplies, maintenance services, security, computing products and components, in business markets direct mail is another important promotional tool, often supporting trade advertising and personal selling campaigns.

The internet and digital marketing

Internet
A network of computer networks stretching across the world, linking computers of different types and sharing information.

Only a few years ago mainly computer buffs had accessed the **internet** – a network of computer networks stretching across the world, linking computers of different types and sharing information on a regular basis – and mostly for online discussions or searches for information. Although these are still popular activities, the information superhighway is a major focus of attention for marketers of consumer goods, services, charities, industrial products and most business marketing. As more and more businesses harness the power of the web and millions of households daily subscribe to internet services, the opportunities for interacting with prospective and current customers are immense. By the mid-1990s companies as diverse as Ford, Sony and JCB were providing product and company details on their web pages. Now, most companies and non-profit organizations – small or large – have websites and web links on their advertising, direct mail or brochures, often to facilitate much more than information sharing. eMarketing is a major revenue stream in most organizations and an important weapon in the armoury of marketing communications. As explored in Chapter 1, the growth of social media is probably the most exciting recent development in marketing per se.

Website
A coherent document readable by a web browser, containing simple text or complex hypermedia presentations.

A **website** is a coherent document readable by a web browser, containing simple text or complex hypermedia presentations. At first, these sites tended to be for information purposes rather than overtly promotional tools or selling opportunities. BMW was one of the first businesses to spot the opportunity for selling on the web, creating a directory of used cars available from its network of independent dealerships. A major hindrance to online sales and marketing of consumer goods and services was consumer concern about the security of making purchases online. Web hosts and credit card companies had to invest in technology that allowed scrambling and coding of confidential credit card or bank account information before consumers were prepared to make online purchases. Today PayPal and other secure payment systems are routine for customers of all types of products and services.

eCommerce
The use of the internet for commercial transactions.

The massive increase in **eCommerce** – the use of the internet for commercial transactions – has led to greater use of the web by marketers, as described in Chapters 3 and 19. As more and more households connect to the internet through increasing numbers of connections, worldwide confidence in using this medium for transactions has grown. This is not uniform across all consumers. Just as with any product (see Chapter 16), there are innovators, early adopters and the early majority, while others are resistant to this way of conducting business, or simply do not have the equipment, expertise or available resources to hook up. Older consumers, the less affluent and the less educated are accessing the web. As an ingredient in the promotional mix, there is no doubt that the internet is of huge importance. Due to growing global acceptance of the web, eMarketing is hugely important for exploiting global markets and international opportunities.

The internet enables frequent and customized changes of messages targeted at specific consumers. If linked to email access or social media, it also enables the consumer to have ready access to the site host, leading to an ongoing and evolving relationship between marketer and customer. Internal marketing has also befriended the web, with **intranets** – in-company internet networks – facilitating routine communications, fostering group communications, providing uniform computer applications, distributing the latest software, or informing colleagues of marketing developments and new product launches.

There is a clear process for developing a website, which includes:

1. the planning of the site's goals
2. analysis of the required content
3. examination of rival sites
4. design and build of the site
5. implementation using hypertext mark-up language (HTML)
6. ongoing development to ensure that, once up and running, the site reflects user views and is updated regularly.

> **Intranet**
> Internal, in-company internet networks for routine communications, fostering group communications, providing uniform computer applications, distributing the latest software, or informing colleagues of marketing developments and new product launches.

To be effective, a website must contain information perceived relevant and interesting by a company's targeted customers. The pages of the site need to be stylish and eye-catching but also easy to interpret. Website branding and imagery should be consistent with the brand positioning of existing products, the product's packaging and other promotional mix executions such as advertising and sales promotion materials. The website's ethos must not contradict the work of the rest of the marketing mix or the product's heritage. The information on the website should be updated regularly and accurately, and tailored carefully to reflect the buying behaviour of the targeted customer. As with any marketing activity, the website needs to be designed to be memorable and distinctive.

Far from being a minor task, marketers have realized that website design is a specialized activity that requires the skills of a qualified web master and the careful design of material to reflect the characteristics of the product, the brand and of the intended consumer. The findings presented in Table 18.3 summarize a survey of UK consumers, revealing their likes and dislikes of a selection of well-known brands' websites. The survey revealed the overriding importance to consumers of interaction, obvious and easy navigation, topical content, relationship-building tools, search

TABLE 18.3 Likes and dislikes of websites

Pros	Key issues	Cons
Clarity	Interaction	Entry page without guidance/menu
Non-fussy	Obvious and easy navigation	Confusing
Eye-catching	Topical content	Assumes product knowledge
Quick loading	Relationship building	Not user-led
Search facility	Search engine compliant	Dull
Cohesion with brand/MarComms	First time user/experienced user friendly	Out-of-date content
Motivational	Security of use/payment	Frustrating
The 'right' information	3 clicks to the desired information	No language options
'3 clicks' from everything	Links with popular social media	No search facility
Pop-up menus		Unclear navigation
Animated links		Must register to access
Rapid printing		Uncertain payment security
No registration		
Search engine compliant		
Use of key words		

engine compliance, ease of use for the first-time user, user friendliness for experienced users and security of use/payment. The web has enabled the huge growth of digital marketing, as explained in the next chapter.

An important facet of digital marketing is search engine optimization or management, whereby marketers seek to ensure that a Google search includes their brand or company in its leading selections. Agencies and consultants often provide support to marketers in this respect. **Search engine optimization (SEO)** is the process of improving the visibility of a website/web page via unpaid 'organic' or 'algorithmic' search results. This is important because the earlier or higher ranked on the search results page a brand or company appears, and the more frequently it appears in the search results list, the more visitors or potential customers it is receiving. As a web-based marketing strategy, SEO assesses how search engines work, what people search for, the actual search terms typed into search engines and which search engines are preferred by their targeted audience.

Search engine optimization (SEO)
The management of search engine behaviour so as to increase a brand's rankings in search engine organic result listings on search engine results pages (SERPS) for particular key words and phrases.

Digital marketing, mobile and social media

Digital marketing tools and techniques are used by marketers to improve their proposition to customers and overall competitiveness, with a value adding website and inter-related digital marketing techniques to drive traffic, conversion, positive experience and referrals. These techniques include website, online public relations, email, blogs/microblogs, social networks, podcasts, wikis and search engine management to ensure preferential web search.

Digital marketing
The use of technology-led channels of communication and selling to manage customer interaction and provide customer experience in a digitally connected environment: a value adding website and interrelated digital marketing techniques to drive traffic, conversion, positive experience and referrals.

To marketers, there is also a downside from the growth of digital marketing. While digital provides marketers with many new options for grabbing the attention of potential customers and maintaining relationships with existing ones, it offers consumers far greater information availability and instantly the views of fellow consumers, pundits and experts. Digital has removed much of the control marketers previously had over what is communicated about their brands and products. Nevertheless, digital is arguably one of the most exciting changes faced by marketers in decades:

1. Communicate to millions of potential and existing customers across geographies, or with only a single customer one-to-one.

2. Instantly update propositions and messages to flag new developments or reflect market challenges.

3. Respond immediately to a competitor's move and altered marketing mix.

4. Attract new interest while cementing relationships with existing customers.

5. Address multiple audiences and stakeholders rather than only one (as is often the case with other marketing communications).

6. Tap into numerous networks and influencing bodies.

Mobile marketing
Engaging users of wireless devices with time and location sensitive, personalized information that promotes goods, services and ideas, via apps, messaging, websites and social media communications.

Mobile marketing is an important and stretching development of digital marketing. A more traditional definition of mobile marketing was marketing activity in a moving manner or encountered by consumers on the move, such as moving advertising boards at sports events or stations. However, increasingly **mobile marketing** stands for marketing via a mobile device, such as a smartphone or tablet, to provide customers with time and location-sensitive, personalized information that promotes goods, services and ideas (see Chapter 3). Leading digital exponent Dave Chaffey states that it is 'engaging users of wireless devices through apps, messaging, websites and social media communications'. Many brand managers currently are launching apps and developing interactive websites suitable for smartphones and laptops on the move. Technology now permits ready and immediate access to customers wherever they are, whenever and irrespective of whatever they are doing. Search for a holiday while on a train, order a grocery delivery when sitting in a café, identify a restaurant and seek endorsements when a meeting breaks up, bet on the next horse race while listening to a seminar speaker, review peers' impressions of the new iPhone while examining one in a store, or join in a topical discussion about poor patient service at a local hospital... the possibilities provided by anywhere/anytime communication are endless and most attractive to marketers.

Social media and networks are posing perhaps the biggest challenge to marketers from the digital era. Twitter, Facebook, Digg, MySpace, LinkedIn, Bebo and YouTube are now very familiar to most consumers, but as explained in Chapter 1, they have radically shifted the boundaries for marketers and consumers. They have taken a great deal of communication about brands and products out of the hands of marketers and placed the power to create and convey such messages in the hands of consumers. These consumers may share their bad experiences and negative views with each other, not just provide positive endorsements.

Social media
The online technology and methods through which people can share content, personal opinions, swap different perspectives and insights, using text, images, audio and video, such as Facebook or YouTube.

Social media incorporates the online technology and methods through which people can share content, personal opinions, swap different perspectives and insights, using text, images, audio and video. Social networking sites such as Facebook are one form of social media; others include wikis, video sharing such as YouTube, photo sharing on sites like Flickr, news aggregators typified by Digg, social bookmarking, online gaming and micro-blogging on presence apps such as Twitter. Social media postings rarely can be controlled by a brand manager, but they should be monitored and often may be influenced.

Find out what others think about brand X, sound off about a recent in-store customer service shocker, praise a great experience, collaboratively with friends decide where to socialize that evening, co-purchase or define product options with trusted colleagues, or while at the point of purchase in a store check with network contacts whether to complete the purchase... so much is possible for consumers via social media networks. However, so much more information is available to consumers to possibly jeopardize a marketer's best laid plans. There is little doubt that social media have altered the buying behaviours of consumers (see Chapter 5). The web, digital marketing and social media impact on marketing far beyond the promotional mix, which is why they are featured throughout *Marketing: Concepts and Strategies*.

Interactive marketing
is an ongoing dialogue with a customer, harnessing CRM, the web and other direct marketing tools to develop a relationship.

Interactive marketing is a popular term within the realms of digital marketing, but it goes beyond the digital domain. Most agencies and major IT companies undertake aspects of this work. Traditional direct marketing agencies are also major players in the interactive field. The web has facilitated much of the growth of interactive marketing, but it is not only an online phenomenon. Interactive marketing engages in a dialogue with a customer, building up insight and buying behaviour knowledge over time, so that each subsequent communication can better be tailored to a buyer's requirements and behaviours. Amazon's use of its customer data to shape subsequent offers and product suggestions is an example of this. Clearly IT plays an important part in this process, requiring CRM systems and often harnessing the immediacy of the web in communications and transactions, but most of the direct marketing tools outlined in this chapter are also part of the toolkit.

Direct marketing

So far this chapter has examined personal selling, sales promotion, direct mail and the Internet. To conclude, the chapter turns to direct marketing. First used in the 1960s, until its recent rebirth and surge in popularity, direct marketing described the most common direct marketing approaches: direct mail and mail order. Now, direct marketing encompasses all the communications tools that enable a marketer to deal directly with targeted customers: direct mail, telemarketing, direct response television advertising, door-to-door/personal selling, the Internet, mobile marketing and some applications of social media. Increasingly marketers are utilizing the direct marketing toolkit to do more than simply generate sales, although sales generation remains the foremost task for direct marketers.

Direct marketing
A decision by a company's marketers to select a marketing chan nel that avoids depend- ence on marketing channel intermediaries and to focus marketing communications activity on promotional mix ingredients that deal directly with targeted customers.

Direct marketing is a decision by a company's marketers to:

1. select a marketing channel that avoids dependence on marketing channel intermediaries

2. focus marketing communications activity on promotional mix ingredients that deal directly with targeted customers.

The American Direct Marketing Association defines direct marketing as 'an inter- active system of marketing which uses one or more 'advertising' media to effect a measurable response and/or transaction at any location'. This definition raises some important aspects, as outlined below:

- Direct marketing is an interactive system. Advertising communicates via a mass medium such as television or the press. Direct marketing contacts targeted consum- ers directly, can tailor messages to the individual and solicits direct feedback. This interactive one-to-one communication is essential to the definition of direct marketing.

- The American Direct Marketing Association's definition uses the term 'advertising'; this really should be *communication*[41] in its broader sense, as direct marketing utilizes personal selling, direct mail, technology – telephone, fax and the web – plus direct response advertising contain- ing coupon response or freefone elements.

- Most ingredients of the promotional mix, particularly advertising and public relations, find it difficult to accurately measure responses and effectiveness. This is not the case with direct marketing: the interactive nature of the communication enables individual consumer responses to be tracked and counted.

- Direct marketers do not necessarily utilize retail outlets, wholesale depots or industrial distributors. They do not depend on potential customers visiting their own retail outlet or depot: they can contact consumers at home or at work via direct mail, telephone or fax, and increasingly via internet links.

Direct marketing evolved from those mail-order businesses – Littlewoods, GUS, Grattan – that developed catalogues and mailshots to customers in order to sell directly from their warehouses, negating the need for retail outlets and showrooms.[42] They were joined by a diverse mix of busi- nesses – from factory outlets to machine tool companies to specialist food producers – which wished to sell directly to consumers. In order to achieve these aims, these businesses had to devise marketing communications tools that attracted sufficient numbers of the right types of customer who would choose to deal directly with them, rather than buying from the more traditional market- ing intermediaries in the marketing channel. The agents, brokers, dealers, distributors, wholesalers and retailers were cut out of the choice of distribution channel. Although mail order sales declined in the 1980s, towards the end of that decade the major operators revitalized their fortunes and were joined by mail-order operations from major retailers such as Marks & Spencer with its home furnishings catalogue and the *Next Directory*. Ubiquitous telephone access has helped facilitate mail-order operations and the rapid growth in online access has provided a further growth spurt.

Direct marketing is now adopted by a host of businesses, ranging from fast-moving consumer goods companies and business marketers to charities and even government departments.[43] It is growing, but this is partly a reflection of the large number of promotional mix ingredients direct mar- keting includes,[44] such as direct mail, teleselling and the web. Various factors have contributed to this growth, as detailed in Figure 18.8. A desire by marketers to identify alternative media and promotional tools, the need to improve targeting of potential customers, improvements in marketing data and databases, advances in technology and systems – permitting cost-effective direct and interactive contact with certain types of consumers – all have encouraged the growth of direct marketing.

In terms of the promotional mix, direct marketing has several key implications, as follows:

- Direct mail is on the increase: 83 per cent of the largest 1500 UK companies expect to deploy more direct mail, with the bulk focusing on prospecting for sales rather than responding to direct response advertising requests for brochures or catalogues.

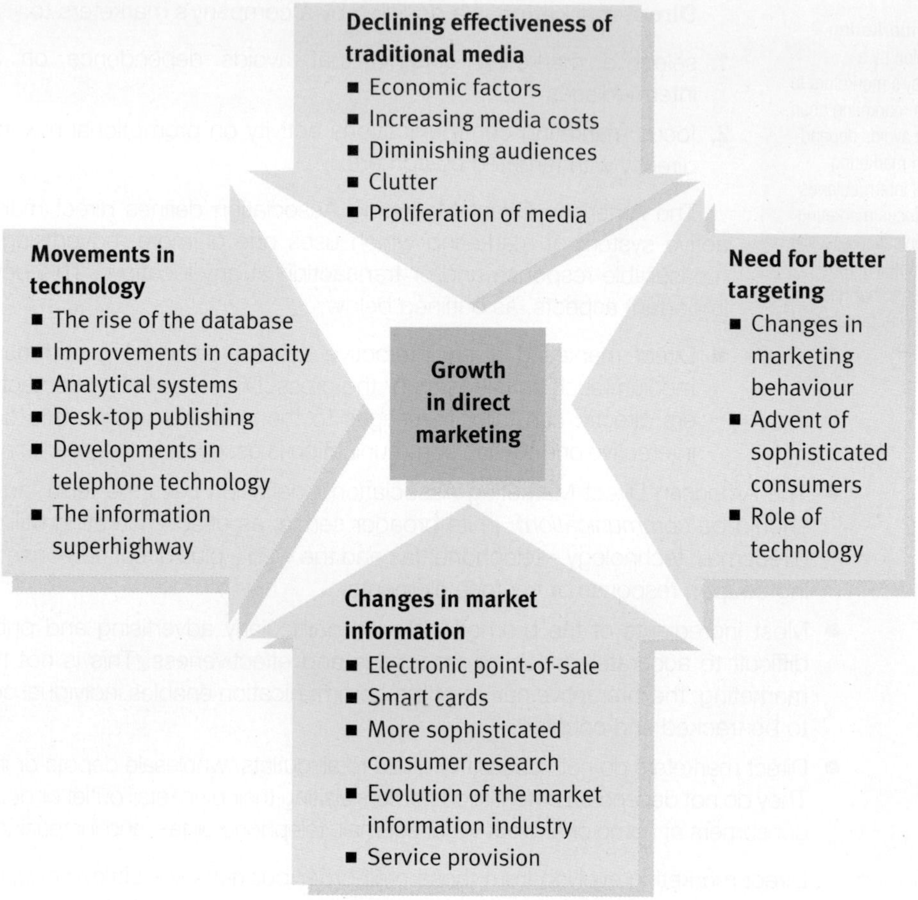

Declining effectiveness of traditional media
- Economic factors
- Increasing media costs
- Diminishing audiences
- Clutter
- Proliferation of media

Movements in technology
- The rise of the database
- Improvements in capacity
- Analytical systems
- Desk-top publishing
- Developments in telephone technology
- The information superhighway

Growth in direct marketing

Need for better targeting
- Changes in marketing behaviour
- Advent of sophisticated consumers
- Role of technology

Changes in market information
- Electronic point-of-sale
- Smart cards
- More sophisticated consumer research
- Evolution of the market information industry
- Service provision

FIGURE 18.8
Catalysts of change behind the growth of direct marketing

Source: From *Exploring Direct Marketing* by Lisa O'Malley, Maurice Patterson and Martin Evans, p. 9, copyright © 1998 Cengage Learning (EMEA) Ltd.

- Telemarketing has grown and will continue to do so as more businesses turn to the direct marketing toolkit aided by advances in automated call centres.

- Personal selling has suffered in the past from poorly identified sales targeting, but better geodemographic targeting and improved analysis of direct marketing responses are enabling more focused use of personal selling.

- Door-to-door selling and leaflet dropping are also on the increase, and are visible forms of direct marketing encountered by most householders.

- In 1989, direct response advertising containing a call for action within the advertisement either by coupon or telephone accounted for less than a fifth of advertising revenue. Now the figure is closer to a third as marketers increasingly jump on the direct marketing 'bandwagon', and as the growth in satellite and cable television channels enables more direct response television advertising.

- The most obvious implication is for use of the Internet to communicate with current and prospective customers. As more and more consumers hook up to the Internet either at home, work or particularly while on the move, the opportunity is growing for marketers to communicate directly with consumers with increasingly bespoke messages. And they are!

The highest coupon redemption came during the earlier phase of the 1990s. During this time more than 7.2 billion coupons were being redeemed in the USA. However, by 2006 only 2.5 billion coupons were redeemed. In the last couples of years, couponing has increased. The core driver of this growth has been new media, such as websites, emails, mobile phones, etc. However, online couponing represents only 1 per cent of total couponing distribution around the world. The recent rise in couponing stems also from recession, as brands seek to provide value to customers.

It is important to remember, however, that as with all marketing propositions and promotional mix executions to be welcomed by targeted customers and effective in terms of generating sales, the deployment of any direct marketing campaign must strive to reflect targeted customer behaviour, needs and perceptions; provide a plausible proposition that is clearly differentiated from competitors' propositions; and match an organization's corporate goals and trading philosophy. Direct marketing is not a substitute for marketing practice per se, nor for the traditional promotional mix. Direct marketing is an increasingly popular deployment of marketing. It stems from certain marketers' strategic choices in terms of marketing channel and the selection of which promotional mix tactics will best facilitate contact with prospective customers.

Summary

Personal selling is the process of informing customers and persuading them to purchase products through personal communication in an exchange situation. It is the most precise promotional method, but also the most expensive. The three general purposes of personal selling are finding prospects, convincing them to buy and keeping customers satisfied. It is particularly important in B2B.

The specialist area of sales management focuses on the importance of preparation, the techniques for introducing sales personnel to prospective customers, the requisites for effective presentations and written proposals, the skills required to turn a potential customer's interest into commitment, how to negotiate, the skills necessary to capture an order, and the ability to close the sale.

Many sales people either consciously or unconsciously move through a general selling process as they sell products. In *prospecting*, the sales person develops a list of potential customers. Before contacting acceptable prospects, the sales person prepares by finding and analyzing information about the prospects and their needs. The *approach* is the manner in which a sales person contacts a potential customer. During the sales presentation, the sales person must attract and hold the prospect's attention to stimulate interest and desire for the product. If possible, the sales person should handle a prospect's objections when they arise. *Closing* is the step in the selling process in which the sales person asks the prospect to buy the product or products. After a successful closing, the sales person must follow up the sale.

In developing a salesforce, a company must decide which types of sales people will sell the company's products most effectively. The three classifications of sales people are *order getters, order takers* and *support personnel.* Current customer order getters deal with people who have already purchased a business's products. New business order getters locate prospects and convert them into buyers. Order takers seek repeat sales and fall into two categories: inside order takers and field order takers. Sales support personnel facilitate the selling function, but their duties usually extend beyond making sales. The three types of support personnel are *missionary, trade* and *technical sales people.*

The effectiveness of salesforce management is an important determinant of a company's success because the salesforce is directly responsible for generating a business's sales revenue. The major decision areas and activities on which sales managers must focus are establishing salesforce objectives, determining salesforce size, recruiting and selecting sales personnel, training sales personnel, compensating/remunerating sales personnel, motivating sales people, managing sales territories, and controlling and evaluating salesforce performance.

Sales objectives should be stated in precise, measurable terms and should specify the time period, customer type and geographic areas involved. The size of the salesforce must be adjusted from time to time because a business's marketing plans change, as do markets and forces in the marketing environment.

The task of *recruiting* and selecting sales personnel involves attracting and choosing the right type of sales people to maintain an effective salesforce. When developing a training programme, managers must consider a variety of dimensions, such as who should be trained, what should be taught and how the training should occur. Rewarding sales people involves formulating and administering a compensation/remuneration plan that attracts, motivates and holds the right types of sales people for the business. Motivation of sales people should allow the company to attain high productivity. Managing sales territories, another aspect of salesforce management, focuses on such aspects as the size and shape of sales territories, and the routing and scheduling of sales people. To control and evaluate salesforce performance, the sales manager must use information obtained through sales personnel's call reports, customer feedback and invoices.

Marketers must ensure their sales colleagues are fully conversant with their strategies and marketing plans, and that sales staff appreciate their role within the execution of marketing programmes. Internal marketing is very important in this respect. Not all customers are worth the same: some matter much more than others strategically and in terms of the volume of business or financial returns likely. Very important and large customers are deemed to be key accounts, particularly in business-to-business markets. *Key account management* is the process for effectively servicing and satisfying these accounts, to ensure mutually satisfactory ongoing relationships and volumes of business.

Sales promotion is an activity or material (or both) that acts as a direct inducement and offers added value to, or incentive to, buy the product to resellers, sales people or consumers. The *ratchet effect* is the stepped impact of using sales promotion and advertising together. Marketers use sales promotion to increase sales, to identify and attract new customers, to introduce a new product and to increase reseller inventories. Sales promotion methods fall into two general categories: consumer and trade. *Consumer sales promotion techniques* encourage consumers to buy from specific retail stores or dealerships or to try a specific product. These techniques include *coupons, demonstrations, frequent user incentives* – such as *loyalty cards* or *trading stamps* – *point-of-sale (POS) materials, free samples, money refunds, rewards apps, premiums, price-off offers,* and *consumer contests and sweepstakes. Trade sales promotion methods* stimulate wholesalers, retailers or dealers to carry a producer's products and to market those products aggressively. These techniques include *buy-back allowances, buying allowances, counts and re-counts, free merchandise, merchandise allowances, cooperative advertising, dealer listings, premium or push money, sales competitions* and *dealer loaders.*

Direct mail uses the postal service to contact prospective customers or donors, and to solicit interest in products or services. The main problem facing the direct mail industry is the growing adverse reaction to it as *junk mail.* Nevertheless, direct mail is widely used for consumer goods and services, and also in business marketing. Increasingly, it is also important to non-profit organizations and charitable fundraising. Direct mail must be designed carefully, with an attention-seeking *flash,* good *copy writing* and a well-constructed *direct mail package. Mailing lists* quickly become obsolete, and good database management is essential for the effective targeting of direct mailshots.

The *Internet* is no longer just for computer buffs. Most businesses now have *websites* and recognize the potential for *eCommerce.* Scrambling and coding of credit card information have helped build consumer confidence in online purchase transactions. Websites are clearly flagged on much television and print advertising. In-company internet networks – *intranets* – are enabling the rapid dissemination of routine communications, group communications, uniform computer applications, the latest software and information about product developments, and are assisting with internal marketing. Enabling frequent updating of messages, individually targeted communications and sales ordering, the web now features in most businesses' promotional mixes.

To be popular with consumers, research reveals that websites must offer interaction, obvious and easy navigation, topical content, relationship-building tools, search engine compliance, ease of use for first-time users and user-friendliness to experienced users, and security of use/payment. They should link to social media sites.

Digital marketing tools and techniques are used by marketers to improve their proposition to customers and overall competitiveness, with a value adding website and interrelated digital marketing techniques to drive traffic, conversion, positive experience and referrals. These techniques include website, online public relations, email, blogs/microblogs, social networks, podcasts, wikis and search engine management. An important aspect of digital is *mobile marketing*, which engages users of wireless devices with time and location sensitive, personalized information promoting goods, services and ideas, via apps, messaging, websites and social media communications. For consumers, the most visible change enabled by the digital era is the emergence of *social media* such as Facebook or YouTube, which permits so much sharing of material, perspectives and insights between consumers.

Direct marketing is a decision to do without marketing channel intermediaries and to focus most promotional resources on activities that deal directly with targeted customers, such as personal selling, telemarketing and direct mail. Now adopted by consumer goods producers, services, business companies, charities and even government departments, direct marketing has recently enjoyed rapid growth. This is likely to continue, with more direct mail, automated call centres, personal selling, door-to-door selling and leaflet dropping, direct response television advertising and use of the Internet with its associated technologies to contact potential customers. Direct marketing must be tailored to suit the behaviour and expectations of the target audience, while reflecting existing branding and other promotional mix designs.

Key links

This chapter has explored various aspects of the promotional mix, but not all. It has also examined the use of the web in marketing from the perspective of marketing communications. Related chapters, therefore, include:

- Chapter 16, on the role of marketing communications and the ingredients of the promotional mix.
- Chapter 17, on the use of advertising, public relations and sponsorship in the promotional mix.
- Chapter 19, on digital marketing.

Important terms

Approach
Business development
Buy-back allowance
Buying allowance
Closing
Combination compensation/remuneration/remuneration plan
Consumer contests
Consumer sales promotion techniques
Consumer sweepstakes
Cooperative advertising
Copy writing
Count and re-count
Coupons
Dealer listing
Dealer loader
Demonstrations
Digital marketing
Direct mail
Direct mail package
Direct marketing
eCommerce
Flashes
Free merchandise
Free samples
Frequent user incentives
Interactive marketing
Internet
Intranet

Junk mail
Key account management
Loyalty card
Mailing lists
Merchandise allowance
Mobile marketing
Money refunds
Personal selling
Point-of-sale (POS) materials
Premium or push money
Premiums
Price-off offers
Prospecting
Ratchet effect
Recruiting
Reward apps
Sales competition
Sales promotion
Search engine optimization (SEO)
Social media
Straight commission compensation/remuneration plan
Straight salary compensation/remuneration plan
Trade sales promotion methods
Trading stamps
Website

Discussion and review questions

1. What is personal selling? How does personal selling differ from other types of promotional activity?

2. What are the primary purposes of personal selling?

3. Identify the elements of the personal selling process. Must a sales person include all of these elements when selling a product to a customer? Why or why not?

4. How does a sales person find and evaluate prospects? Do you find any of these methods ethically questionable?

5. Are order getters more aggressive or creative than order takers? Why or why not?

6. Identify several characteristics of effective sales objectives.

7. How should a sales manager establish criteria for selecting sales personnel? What are the general characteristics of a good sales person?

8. What major issues or questions should be considered when developing a salesforce training programme?

9. Explain the major advantages and disadvantages of the three basic methods of compensating sales people. In general, which method do you prefer? Why?

10. How does a sales manager who cannot be with each sales person in the field on a daily basis control the performance of sales personnel?

11. What is key account management?

12. How does key account management work alongside market segmentation?

13. What is sales promotion? Why is it used?

14. Does sales promotion work well in isolation from the other promotional mix elements?

15. For each of the following, identify and describe three techniques and give several examples:
    a. consumer sales promotion techniques, and
    b. trade sales promotion methods.

16. What types of sales promotion methods have you observed recently?

17. How does direct mail gain the interest of its recipients?

18. What are the problems facing users of direct mail?

19. Marketers initially viewed the Internet primarily as a means to disseminate product and manufacturer information. What technological advances had to be made before the Internet could be used for selling opportunities?

20. What are the essential requirements for a website likely to appeal to targeted consumers?

21. Why is mobile marketing exciting many brand managers?

22. Discuss the ways social media pose challenges to marketers?

23. In what ways is direct marketing an 'interactive' system? Which marketing channel intermediaries are bypassed due to the nature of this system?

Recommended readings

Belch, G. and Belch, M., *Advertising and Promotion: An Integrated Marketing Communications Perspective* (McGraw-Hill, 2014).

Bird, D., *Commonsense Direct and Digital Marketing* (Kogan Page, 2015).

Calvin, R.L., *Sales Management* (McGraw-Hill, 2007).

Chaffey, D., *Digital Business and E-Commerce Management* (Pearson, 2014).

Chaffey, D. and Ellis-Chadwick, F., *Digital Marketing: Strategy, Implementation and Practice* (Pearson, 2012).

Cummins, J. and Mullin, R., *Sales Promotion: How to Create and Implement Campaigns that Really Work* (Kogan Page, 2010).

Donaldson, W., *Sales Management: Theory & Practice* (Palgrave Macmillan, 2007).

Jobber, D. and Lancaster, G., *Selling and Sales Management* (Pearson, 2012).

Johnston, M.W. and Marshall, G.W., *Sales Force Management* (Routledge, 2013).

McNamara, R., *Personal Selling Skills: For Developing High Performance Managers* (Management Briefs, 2010).

Pickton, D. and Broderick, A., *Integrated Marketing Communications* (FT Prentice-Hall, 2011).

Rogers, B., *Rethinking Sales Management* (John Wiley, 2007).

Shimp, T.A. and Andrews, J.C., *Integrated Marketing Communications in Advertising and Promotion* (Cengage, 2013).

Tapp, A., Whitten, I. and Housden, M., *Principles of Direct, Database and Digital Marketing* (Pearson, 2013)

Internet exercise

Consider any one of your favourite brands. Log on to its website.

1. In what ways is this site finding out information about you and your product needs?

2. To what extent does the information presented help inform you of the brand's attributes and enable you to experience the brand?

3. How would you modify this website to improve its functionality? Why?

Group tasks

1. Wander around your local supermarket. Look for the 'price-offs', 'two for one' or meal deals, bundling of products wrapped together, and coupon-off promotions. Consider the pros and cons to the brands in question of these forms of sales promotion.

2. Whether via your letter box or in-box, consider how much direct marketing comes your way each week. Which types of product or service tend to dominate? How attracted to this direct marketing are you and why?

Applied mini-case

Many medium-sized business-to-business companies employ small salesforces, attend trade shows and seminars that present their category of products and attract relevant business customers, develop limited advertising, construct websites, direct mail their sales prospects and use publicity whenever they have anything worth publicising.

Question

As a new marketing manager in such a business, faced with a limited budget, how would you determine which aspects of the promotional mix should be utilized?

A marketing classic – promoting free flights and how Hoover came unstuck

Case study

Retailers and manufacturers have frequently negotiated with carriers to offer free travel or holidays to boost sales as a sales promotion. The holiday industry has welcomed the opportunity to use excess capacity and increase demand in such co-marketing initiatives. It was not too surprising when, back in 1992, consumer electronics giant Hoover joined the ranks of manufacturers offering free trips in order to stimulate demand for its white goods, first by offering free tickets to Europe with purchases of more than £100, then by extending the promotion to include free tickets to the USA. What was not predictable was the adverse publicity the scheme brought for Hoover.

The second promotion was supported by a high-profile £1 million television campaign. The offer included two free flights to either Orlando or New York for every Hoover purchase over £100, with an additional £60 towards car hire and accommodation for purchases over £300. Hoover claimed that the tickets into Europe had constituted its most successful promotion ever, putting its then top-priced £130 vacuum cleaner ahead of its £100 model and making its £380 washing machine more popular than its £300 model.

In November 1992, a *Daily Record* story, 'Hoover's flight shocker', started the trouble. This story alleged that none of the airlines Hoover claimed was involved in the US deal had any knowledge of the scheme and that Hoover had yet to reserve a single airline seat. The article also stated that the sales promotion company behind the offer was £500 000 in debt. In response, Hoover launched a major damage limitation exercise, including full-page adverts assuring people that there was no mystery, the offer was genuine and that free flights were available. Hoover's problems did not end there, however. Media attention increased, as did stories of disgruntled consumers.

From BBC consumer affairs programme *Watchdog* to the House of Commons, questions were asked about the ethics of the deal and the apparently unfair treatment of hundreds of annoyed consumers who, having purchased a Hoover product and received their vouchers, had actually attempted to claim their prizes. Many potential holidaymakers could not get first or even second choices of dates or destination. Many were refused their choices so often that Hoover's promotions company refused to permit any travel! Over 70 MPs demanded a Parliamentary investigation. Eventually, the Office of Fair Trading regulator was brought in to investigate.

Hoover, today under different ownership, had intended neither to mislead nor to disappoint its customers, but the promotion nevertheless severely affected the company's reputation. Circumstances combined in several well-publicised cases to make a deteriorating situation even worse for the company. What began as a sales-boosting, attention-getting sales promotion rapidly turned into a damaging public relations nightmare for Hoover. Key directors were dismissed and the US parent company had to shell out millions of pounds to meet travellers' demands for their prizes. Some 12 months later, disputes had still to be settled.

US parent, Maytag Corp., had bought Britain's Hoover for US$320 million in 1989. In 1995, Maytag sold its European operation to an Italian company at a loss of US$135 million. The free flights promotion was, as described in many newspapers, 'a fiasco', damaging not just this type of promotional activity but, more severely, the Hoover brand name and even the viability of the company. High-profile court cases pursued by disgruntled consumers only

made matters worse. Over two decades later, consumers and retailers still remember this disastrous marketing communications campaign.

Hoover today is a different and unrelated company and its management has no links with this classic tale of how important it is to micro-manage every aspect of a campaign, whether based on a sales promotion, digital, traditional advertising or any aspect of the promotional mix.

Sources: Clare Sambrook, 'Do free flights really build brands?', *Marketing*, 15 October 1992, p. 11; Mat Toor, 'Hoover retaliates over flights offer', *Marketing*, 3 December 1992, p. 3; Robert Dwek, 'Hoover extends its free flights deal', *Marketing*, 29 October 1992, p. 16; BBC and ITN television news broadcasts, March and April 1993; Chris Knight, 'Direct route', *Marketing Week*,

8 September 1995, pp. 58–9; Marcia Berss, 'Whirlpool's bloody nose', *Forbes*, 11 March 1996, pp. 90–2.

NB: The Hoover company today is a different business, with ownership, management, marketing campaigns and products unrelated to the Hoover described in this case.

Questions for discussion

1. How damaging to the Hoover name and reputation was this sales promotion campaign?

2. How could Hoover have avoided these problems?

3. How, in the light of this promotional disaster, should Hoover have utilized the public relations toolkit to overcome the adverse publicity?

CHAPTER 19

Digital Marketing

"Everything is now instantly accessible anytime and anywhere"

Objectives

- To explore how digital has impacted on consumer behaviour and decision-making.

- To appreciate the new requirements of understanding search engine management and content marketing, types of digital media and multi-screen marketing.

- To examine the all-important issue of social media strategy.

- To appreciate the growing role of mobile marketing.

- To recognize the change to public relations brought about with online public relations.

- To consider the way in which digital is driving innovation.

- To understand the challenges of turning 'big data' into meaningful insights.

- To explore the requirements for organizations in deciding on a multiple channel-to-market strategy.

INTRODUCTION

Not too long ago, to find out about a product a consumer had to visit a store or send off for a brochure. To compare options required many such visits and requests. Not so today, thanks to Google or Bing searches, the views of other consumers on social media, the options suggested by comparison websites, or the large number of online communities only too willing to share their views of products or services. A decade ago, to access online information or make online purchases, consumers would have been at home tethered to a PC or at work using an office-based desktop. This is no longer true, with smart TVs, tablets, smartphones, wi-fi and mobile broadband enabling consumers to compare their options, find reviews, see the opinions of friends and colleagues, make purchases and post their own reviews on the move just about anywhere a smartphone or broadband signal can be transmitted. Companies such as John Lewis have been quick to seize these opportunities, but must work hard to follow their customers across new and multiple channels.

This digital era is exciting for marketers, providing immediate two-way interaction with consumers, the opportunity for tailored offerings, data capture and much smarter management of customers. However, the digital era poses many challenges. How to ensure Google directs consumers to the marketer's brand? Whether to be online only or to juggle multiple channels? If the latter, how to manage the same consumer across channels, as their buying behaviour fluctuates during the day or week? How to encourage social media chatter to be favourably inclined? How in a digital environment to build a relationship remotely? How to make a brand relevant in a digital space? These are just some of the headaches facing a marketing manager today.

Following the shopper across channels

Twenty years ago if a John Lewis customer wanted to view products, consider alternatives or make a purchase, he or she had to travel to a store. Purchasing from the department store retailer had been this way for over a century. A decade ago, an alternative option emerged. Customers could use a desktop at home or at work to review options and make a purchase, with John Lewis's delivery vans bringing the ordered products to shoppers' homes. Now, in addition to both of these options, smartphones or tablets permit John Lewis shoppers to connect with their favourite department store brand anywhere at any time, thanks to the John Lewis app and mobile marketing. Their orders will be delivered to their selected location, or they can opt to collect their purchases in-store. Not just inside John Lewis's department stores, but also at branches of the retailer's sister business. Waitrose is letting its supermarkets be customer collection points for John Lewis merchandise. There are far more Waitrose branches across the country than there are John Lewis department stores, so this click and collect option is preferred by many customers who previously struggled to visit a distant John Lewis store.

There may be some customers of John Lewis who only ever buy in-store and some who only buy online, but many John Lewis customers interact with the company through a mix of store visits, desktop connections and while on the move via their smartphones. John Lewis is aware of this, so manages its multiple channels to provide consistent branding, a uniform customer experience and one set of core brand values across these varied customer touchpoints. John Lewis was one of the first traditional retailing giants to harness the power of the web, initially with a standalone online operation, personnel, systems and style of customer interaction. Today John Lewis strives to provide a seamlessly linked experience for its customers and has ensured its internal operations are appropriately converged to provide a consistent John Lewis brand experience.

For the first time at Christmas in 2014, click and collect sales over-took home delivery for John Lewis. Online takings grew by 19 per cent, representing 36 per cent of trade. This was a rise of 4 per cent on the previous year. The click and collect delivery option accounted for 56 per cent of these rapidly increasing online orders. This change of consumer behaviour means John Lewis must manage its multiple channels as a cohesive set, to provide the consumer with a satisfying experience across the company's operations.

However, John Lewis is also pressing ahead with plans to grow its store numbers from 42 currently to 65 large department stores, with a focus on locations such as Birmingham, Leeds and Oxford. Managing Director Andy Street explained, 'The role of the shop is absolutely critical in providing the online sales.' Establishing a physical shop presence is seen by John Lewis's MD as key to winning internet customers, so that they can browse products in-store before placing orders or use stores as locations for picking up their click and collect purchases.

The importance of online shopping is illustrated by Black Friday. John Lewis said the standout event of its whole trading year had been the success of its Black Friday promotions. Relatively new to the UK, so-called Black Friday involves significantly aggressive online price discounting by most online retailers striving to pull forward Christmas purchases and gain sales from store-based retailers. Black Friday for John Lewis resulted in record sales during that week at the end of November, including a record single trading day in the company's entire 150-year old history.

Sources: 'John Lewis: Click and collect service overtakes home delivery as online sales grow 19%', by Antonia Molloy, *The Independent*, 5 January 2015; 'Black Friday surge pushes John Lewis sales to record levels', Andrea Felsted, *ft.com*, 5 January 2015; 'John Lewis delivers "extremely strong" performance with sales up 13.3%', Tiffany Holland, *Retail Week*, 8 March 2013; www .johnlewispartnership.co.uk/financials/weekly-figures/john-lewis.html (accessed 5 March 2015).

This chapter will explore how digital has impacted on consumer behaviour and decision-making; the new requirements of understanding search engine management and content marketing, types of digital media and multi-screen marketing; the all-important issue of social media strategy; the exciting options provided by mobile marketing; email marketing and online public relations; the way in which digital is driving innovation like never before; turning 'big data' into meaningful insights; and, the challenges for organisations in deciding on a channel-to-market strategy, addressing multiple channels and restructuring their operations to manage these choices.

Digital marketing

Digital marketing
The use of technology-led channels of communication and selling to manage customer interaction and provide customer experience in a digitally-connected environment.

According to the Digital Marketing Institute, **digital marketing** is the use of **digital channels** to promote or market products and services to consumers and businesses. It makes use of computers, smartphones and tablets; websites, emails and apps; as well as some non-web-based channels such as TV, radio and SMS messaging, to engage with consumers and business customers. As will be explained, social media is a core component of the digital environment. Marketers strive to manage the **digital brand** experience across these devices and channels. Many opt for a multi-channel strategy, bringing on stream digital channels alongside their traditional channels of distribution and touchpoints with customers, but some companies are digital-only operations. Digital marketing is the use of technology-led channels of communication and selling to manage customer interaction and provide customer experience in a digitally-connected environment.

Digital channels
Different forms of digital media used for online marketing and delivery. The range of channels continues to expand requiring organizations to develop multi-channel or now omni-channel strategies.

There are five principal benefits to marketers of digital marketing. (1) Digital provides additional options for marketing communications, as internet viewing, web searches and Google become routinized behaviour; (2) digital gives marketers more direct and diverse channel possibilities, with many companies developing multi-channel strategies and some new entrants trading only online; (3) digital enables marketers to capture greater insights into consumers with immediacy and two-way interaction as never before, with extensive profiling of customer histories and behaviours; (4) digital explodes the ways in which marketers build relationships, with far more direct and frequent interactions and the bespoke tailoring of information, deals and propositions; (5) digital provides access to customers 24/7 as never before has been possible, wherever they are and whenever they want to connect.

Digital brand community
A group of consumers, observers or advocates focused on a particular brand, using social media to share admiration for their favoured brand.

Digital has provided significant opportunities and new options for marketers, but there are many downsides and complications to address. Five of the biggest are: (1) the diminishing control over a brand's messages and its perceptions, as social media facilitates greater consumer-to-consumer comment; (2) data overload, as the digital environment and online marketing capture huge amounts of often live consumer insight; (3) privacy concerns, as consumers start to realize how much is known about their whereabouts, interests, purchasing, viewership, networks and lifestyles; (4) the breakdown of trust, as a consumer quickly learns via social media chatter that her favourite brand or retailer has just offered someone else a better deal; and (5) the requirement for a whole host of new skills and agency partners. Digital is certainly exciting and offers far more options for marketers as they endeavour to attract and retain customers, but the downsides are significant, too. Worse, in some businesses, leaderships have created digital teams who are separate to the marketing function. This is a development which has the potential to reduce the impact of marketing and its ability to develop customer insight, create value propositions and manage customer relationships.

Changing consumer behaviour

The customer decision-making process – as explored in Chapters 5 and 6 of *Marketing: Concepts and Strategies* – is need recognition, information search, comparison of options, selection of the one to acquire, purchase, consumption, reflection and post-purchase evaluation. Marketers traditionally focused on the information search part of the process to ensure their messages were found, relevant and attractive, and on the purchase phase to make certain the marketing mix aided ease of purchase and satisfaction with the nature of the transaction. Marketers also tried, via marketing communications, to create or prompt a customer's need for a product or service. Certain aspects of relationship marketing and customer experience management also sought to manage post-purchase evaluation in order to nurture repeat buying and some degree of purchasing loyalty. Each stage of this buying decision-making process has been impacted by digital. Information search is often led online with web searches, posted review comments and social media gossip shaping so much of consumer decision-making. The purchase stage is no longer constrained to an in-store or direct mail interaction. Globally, one billion web-users last year made purchases online, with 40 per cent of internet users routinely buying online. In countries such as the UK and USA, the proportion is much higher. However, customer data are analyzed so that brands prompt consumers directly in order to

Online retailing continues to boom

Topical insight

According to the UK Centre for Retail Research, eCommerce is the fastest growing retail market in Europe. Sales in the UK, Germany, France, Sweden, the Netherlands, Italy, Poland and Spain were expected to grow from £132.05 billion (€156.28 billion) in 2014 to £156.67 billion (€185.39 billion) in 2015, which is a growth of +18.4 per cent, continuing to £185.44 billion (€219.44 billion) in 2016. In 2015, overall online sales were expected to grow by 18.4 per cent, as in 2014, but 13.8 per cent in the US on a much larger total. These figures relate only to *retail spending*, defined as sales of merchandise to the final consumer. In the US, online sales were expected to rise from $306.85 billion (£189.26) in 2014 to $349.20 billion (£215.39 billion) in 2015 and $398.78 billion (£245.96 billion) a year later.

These figures illustrate the significant impact of online transactions. While eCommerce is only one aspect of digital marketing, these figures reveal the increasing reach of online. According to the Centre for Retail Research, the growth of online sales at such a rate will inevitably reduce the market for traditional shops. The Centre believes that by the time online sales represent 5 per cent or more of domestic retailing then the continued growth of online retailers will occur at the expense of conventional stores. In Europe as a whole, online retailers in 2015 are expanding 14.2 times faster than conventional outlets, creating major strategic issues for store-based retailers.

Source: www.retailresearch.org/onlineretailing.php, 4 March 2015.

Online retail sales	Online sales (£bn) 2014	Growth 2014	Online sales (£bn) 2015	Growth 2015	Online sales in euros (bn) 2015
UK	£44.97	15.8%	£52.25	16.2%	€61.84
Germany	£36.23	25.0%	£44.61	23.1%	€52.79
France	£26.38	16.5%	£30.87	17.0%	€36.53
Spain	£6.87	19.6%	£8.15	18.6%	€9.64
Italy	£5.33	19.0%	£6.35	19.0%	€7.51
Netherlands	£5.09	13.5%	£5.94	16.8%	€7.03
Sweden	£3.61	15.5%	£4.17	15.5%	€4.93
Poland	£3.57	22.6%	£4.33	21.0%	€5.12
Europe	£132.05	18.4%	£156.67	18.4%	€185.39

create category need and trigger the desire to make a particular purchase. How often have you responded to a **pop-up advertisement** on your browser from a favoured supplier or been prompted when in a company's web pages to purchase offers tailored to your previous purchasing? Brands even help to manage the post-purchase evaluation, by seeking survey responses to satisfaction audits and asking directly for feedback to be posted online.

Companies traditionally viewed two occasions as 'moments of truth'. The first was at the point of purchase, when a customer committed to a specific choice of a brand. The second was subsequently when the customer used or consumed the product he or she had purchased, at which point possible verdicts on the decision were positive, negative or neutral. The web has changed this situation in three ways. First, often consumers research their options at home before arriving at the point of purchase, whether that is in-store or online. Second, even at the point of purchase, online comparisons, research and price checking take place. With the advent of smartphones, this can be in-store, too. Following use or consumption, online discussion and feedback not only influence a consumer's subsequent purchasing but share views with a multitude of other consumers and shape their thinking, too. Success for marketers now involves ensuring a positive outcome at all of these stages. Arguably the post-purchase evaluation is now hugely impactful on a brand's performance, as word-of-mouth is shared via social media. Traditional buying behaviour decision-making should be re-appraised, so that this digital pathway is included and addressed with the marketing mix. In particular, this means managers must seek to have their brand's reviews found digitally but also foster positive discussion online about their proposition. Mobile marketing, online video and social media discussion are today integral aspects of the communications mix.

> **Pop-up ads**
> Pop-ups are online advertisements which pop-up in new browser windows, designed to attract web traffic or capture contact details. Pop-under advertisements open under the active window unseen by a user until the covering window is closed.

Search engine management

Consumers surf the web for an interesting offer or to review a favoured brand. Are the websites suggested by their search engine, whether Google, Bing, Yahoo, Ask, randomly generated, in order of popularity or as a result of significant effort by brand managers and their digital partners? Inevitably, the pecking order in the browser is a result of manipulation by brand teams and a host of other parties, many of whom have discovered ways to financially benefit from providing such control of consumers' options. For some marketers, there might be the option to create a revenue stream via charging for clicks per view to see an advertisement or link. The manipulation goes beyond merely depicting such lists in a certain order. Our browsers seem to understand

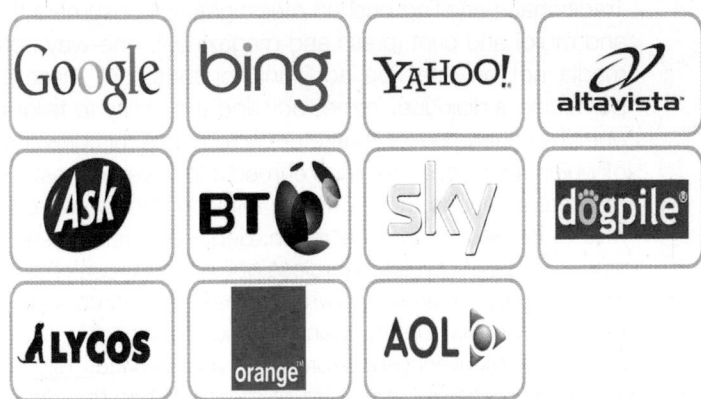

FIGURE 19.1
Search Engine Management
Web Touch Solutions Limited is one of many agencies offering help with digital marketing and search engine optimization.

our tastes and interests even before we enter a search, with banner advertisements depicting the brands we apparently favour and suggested links prompting us to look at brands with which we already have a relationship. This uncanny 'sixth sense' of our computer or smartphone is not of course by chance. Google analytics and web behaviour analysis understand each of us very well so as to provide us with tailored choices.

Google looks at many factors to determine whether a page features high up in its search lists; how many people view a site, for how long, whether they return, how long the pages take to load, the click-throughs or **pay per click** ads and sharing of comment on social media. To many consumers, this is appealing as it saves time and provides information that is pertinent. Others resent this intrusion and manipulation of their information search and short-listing of apparent options. Nevertheless, search engine optimization is the crux of digital marketing. Large companies now recruit experts in digital marketing and **search engine optimization**, while smaller businesses turn for help to the large number of digital agencies to have been established in recent years. Not to consider SEO as an important activity is risking the viability of a marketing strategy.

Content marketing

Once a Google search has directed the consumer to a particular brand's web pages, it is important the right content is quickly and easily available. The brand has a strategy, target market selection and brand positioning. This proposition has appealed to the consumer searching for it or should hook the consumer about to be directed to the brand for the first time because of the list popping up in the browser. The website should convey a tone, look and ethos reflecting the brand and its intended target market strategy. The customer insights and market segmentation outcomes already in place should inform the content of the web experience. If particular offers are available through the brand's marketing mix, particularly if they are being promoted through other advertising media, the visitor to the web page should readily find this information. Awareness of competitors should also be reflected in these pages, to ensure differentiators are well to the fore. A very important aspect of **content marketing** is to insert **keyphrases** likely to be part of a Google search on each page. Google provides a Keyword Planner tool to assist marketers in selected appropriate terms. Marketers must understand the type of content their customers wish to consume. This will vary whether they are at home, in-store, on-the-move or at work. Mobile marketing has added further complexity for marketers.

Types of media

Traditional marketing pushed messages to consumers through broadcast (TV, cinema and radio) and print (press and magazines), one-way from brand to consumer. Digital media not only provide additional options, but these channels often are two-way, permitting a dialogue, immediacy and the ability to tailor marketing messages one-to-one. The challenge for marketers is to juggle this growing mix of media options, some of which are paid, owned and earned. However, Forrester Research has suggested that marketers need to move on from thinking about paid, owned and earned digital channels to instead explore the reach, depth and relationship channels evident at different stages of the life cycle; regardless of whether those channels are digital or traditional, or whether they are earned, owned or paid. Research analyst Forrester suggests RaDaR: Reach channels, Depth channels and Relationship channels (see Figure 19.2). Most customers open to discovering new products and services rely on mass-reach channels such as TV adverts, search engines and word-of-mouth. When they want to explore products in more

Pay per click (PPC)
Text ads that are displayed on the search engine results page when specific key phrases are entered by the search user. The advertiser pays when the site visitor clicks on the ad.

Search engine optimization (SEO)
The management of search engine behaviour so as to increase a brand's rankings in search engine organic result listings on search engine results pages (SERPS) for particular key-words and phrases.

Content marketing
The creation of relevant and interesting text, audio, video and rich media content to engage specific customers in order to create brand awareness and sales.

Keyphrase
The combination of keywords used to log a query in a search engine. Keyphrase analysis is the identification and selection of relevant keywords and phrases to leverage SEO and search marketing.

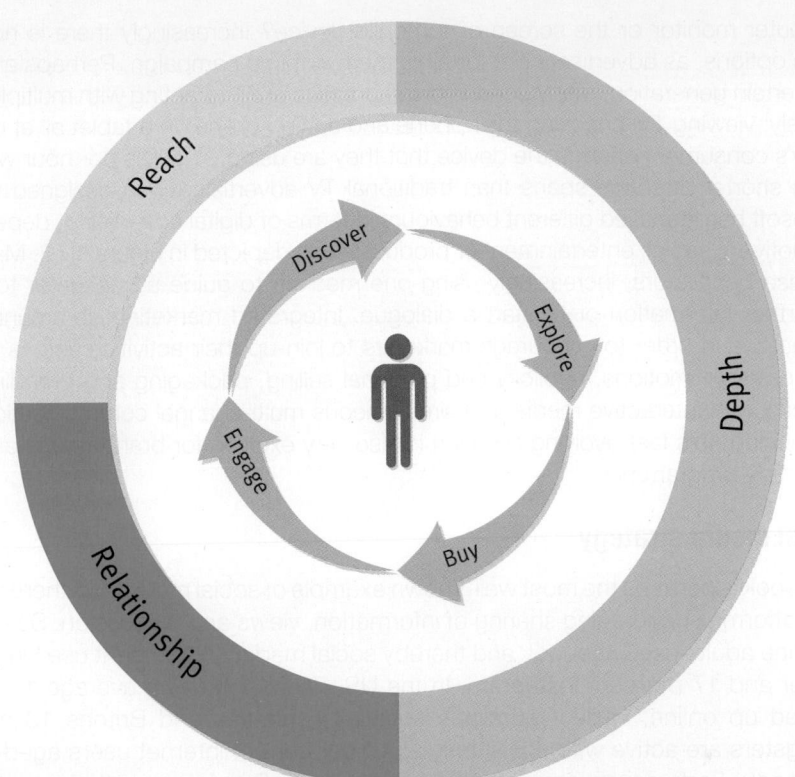

Depth channels: tell a brand's story. Its website, stores and salespeople serve a common purpose: to give customers and prospects the details they are seeking when they explore a product or brand, and to guide them to a purchase.

Relationship channels: serve existing customers. Most of the people who sign up for a brand's mailing lists or follow the brand in social media are existing and satisfied customers. These channels are not about attracting new audiences

or directly driving sales. Instead, they are about staying in touch with the brand's biggest fans and loyal users.

Reach channels: put a brand into the consideration set. Word-of-mouth and unbranded searches are the two channels customers use most to discover products, followed by traditional channels such as TV adverts and in-store displays. The reason for using these tools is to encourage customers to explore the offering in greater depth.

FIGURE 19.2
Types of media in the digital era

Source: http://blogs.forrester.com/nate_elliott/13-01-24-introducing_the_marketing_radar, June 2015.

detail, they use depth channels such as brands' websites and retail stores: the same channels they use when making eventual purchases. When they want to engage with their favourite brands, they use relationship channels, such as signing up for email lists or loyalty programmes, or 'liking' a brand on Facebook.

Multi-screen marketing

Marketing used to be rather one-dimensional and invariably one-way. Poster campaigns gave way to TV commercials, which were superseded by web banner advertisements. Most advertising media were one-direction, from a brand to a customer, but not vice-versa. In today's digital environment, brands communicate with consumers, consumers with brands and discussion groups, so that consumers share opinions with each other, too. A TV screen, cinema screen, computer monitor or the screen of a mobile device? Increasingly there is no choice between these options, as advertisers opt for all of them within a campaign. Perhaps alarmingly for those of a certain generation, many consumers in practice are interacting with multiple screens simultaneously: viewing TV, checking their phone and surfing online on a tablet all at once. On average, today's consumers change the device that they are using 21 times per hour while at home, with much shorter attention spans than traditional TV advertising was designed to accommodate. Microsoft has identified different behaviours in terms of digital advertising, depending on whether the motive is social, entertainment or productive, as depicted in Figure 19.2. Marketers are aware of these behaviours, increasingly using one medium to guide a consumer to another medium for further information or to start a dialogue. Integrated marketing communications was conceptualized in order to encourage marketers to join-up their activities across advertising, direct mail, sales promotions, publicity and personal selling, packaging and branding, but now must contend with interactive media and simultaneous multi-channel communication. While certainly challenging, this fast-evolving situation is also very exciting for brand teams as they devise their marketing programmes.

Social media strategy

Facebook is perhaps the most well-known example of social media, but there are numerous digital platforms encouraging sharing of information, views and discussion. Seventy-one per cent of online adults use Facebook and thereby social media; 22 per cent use LinkedIn, 18 per cent Twitter and 17 per cent Instagram. In the US, Facebook users average 16 minutes per hour hooked up online, while Australians spend 14 minutes and Britons 13 minutes. Not only youngsters are active with social media: 45 per cent of internet users aged over 65 now use Facebook. Forty-seven per cent of Americans cite Facebook as their number one influence on their purchasing decisions. Seventy per cent of marketers now use Facebook to gain new customers and 35 per cent use Twitter to generate leads. Ninety-three per cent of marketers turn to social media to win business. Sixty-one per cent of US consumers state they have made a purchase based on a blog posting and 81 per cent say they trust blogs. Seventy-seven per cent of internet users read blogs. Small businesses with blogs generate 126 per cent more leads than rivals failing to post blogs. Seventy per cent of consumers now learn about brands through their online articles rather than traditional forms of broadcast and print advertising. The average buyer consults 11 online reviews before purchasing. Ninety-two per cent of companies turn to social media platforms to recruit, with LinkedIn used by over 90 per cent. LinkedIn claims to power 50 per cent of world hires. Not only are these statistics mind-blowing in terms of revealing the impact of social media, they also indicate the fast-changing nature of marketing.

Social media pose a significant threat to marketers, who previously enjoyed the control of messages and opinions about their brands. Today, consumers learn more from each other and various third parties online than they do directly from brands. Leading social media sites include:

- Facebook, with over one billion users
- YouTube, the second most searched site in the world, now owned by the first, Google
- LinkedIn for business users and networks of professionals
- Google+
- Twitter
- Pinterest
- Instagram for image and video sharing via smartphones and tablets.

Social media marketing
The process of gaining website traffic or social mentions through social media sites, by creating content attracting attention of readers who will share these through their social networks.

Social media marketing enables a brand to interact with consumers on their terms, where they feel comfortable and secure. These sites are very valuable for learning about

	Content grazing	Investigative spider-webbing	Social spider-webbing	Quantum
Dominant activity	Relaxation/ entertainment	Relaxation/ entertainment, alongside shopping and tasks	Social/enjoyment	Shopping/tasks
Most common reason for multi-screening	Habit, distraction	Seeking detail and depth	Connect with others	Efficiency, location change, better user experience
Prime day-parts	Morning and evening	Evening and night	Morning, noon and evening	Morning, afternoon, evening
Work, on-the-go or home	Work, on-the-go, home	Home	Home	Work and on-the-go
Dominant need-states (by index)	Control: 'I'm in control of my moment—whether it's a task or a quick bit of fun.'	Recognition, vitality, enjoyment: 'I want to satisfy my curiosity; going deep on a topic is an enjoyable way to spend my down time.'	Enjoyment, conviviality, belonging: 'Adding a social element makes me feel like I'm part of a community.'	Power, recognition, vitality and security: 'I'm on top of things; and it feels good to use tech to get things done well.'

FIGURE 19.3
Digital advertising behaviours

Source: Cross Screen Engagement, Microsoft Advertising (2013).

their behaviours and views, for testing out new marketing ideas, and for suggesting negatives about competing brands. Sales leads are generated, product demonstrations can be shared and brand reputations managed. Digital online brand communities increasingly are important for marketers, as explained in Chapter 11 of *Marketing: Concepts and Strategies*. Effective campaigns recognize that content needs to be worth sharing through its creativity, humour or story telling. Social media channels are not sales channels and marketers must beware of antagonizing cynical consumers who will be quick to voice and share their displeasure. It is important for marketers to monitor social media chatter in case their brand is receiving negative comment or a rival brand is fairing much better or worse.

An important aspect of social media for marketers is finding out . . . learning about consumers, competitors, changing consumer behaviour and attitudes, or how their own brand or proposition is viewed. Many marketing teams now routinely monitor social media chatter or pay agencies to do so. They glean many important market, customer and competitor insights this way. Marketers may also test out their hunches, trial new product or proposition ideas, tweak pricing and suggest how a product or service plays to consumers' needs. By listening to reactions – the chat on social media – they instantly have their hunches validated or contradicted. This has meant trialling ideas, testing marketing campaigns and fine-tuning marketing mix ingredients has become much faster and two-way with consumers. Some companies also plant views about competitors in order to help validate their assumptions about a rival's strengths and weaknesses. It is important to remember that competitors may well be doing the same and that apparent consumers expressing their opinions on social media in fact might be third parties in the pay of a competitor deliberately distorting opinions in order to derail a rival brand's strategy.

Mobile marketing

Think about your own web browsing behaviour. Is it predominantly at home, in the office or on-the-move? Is it tied to a PC or more flexible and largely smartphone- or tablet-based? Or a mix? More than likely, it is a mix of behaviours, increasingly making use of mobile broadband and 4G smartphones to keep you connected to Google – and thereby to your brands – anywhere and anytime. Seventy-eight per cent of Twitter users and 41 per cent of LinkedIn users are mobile.

Mobile marketing
Marketing to encourage consumer engagement anywhere or anytime while on or using a mobile device, such as a smartphone or tablet, and heavily dependent on mobile apps which provide users with information, entertainment and location based services.

Forty per cent of mobile phone owners use social networking on their phones. There are 1.56 billion active social mobile accounts. Of a global population of 7.3 billion, there are 3.6 billion mobile users. Over a third of all internet traffic is now on a handheld mobile or tablet device.

This change of behaviour forces marketers to ensure their websites are optimized for mobile usage, yet Adobe estimates that 45 per cent of marketers have not done this. Google says that a third of searches now are from tablets and smartphones. Consumers do not only search: they make purchases on the move, too. Google Analytics enables a marketer to see visitors, their locations and the devices they are using. If a mobile visitor to a website is lingering much more briefly than a desktop-based visitor, it implies the brand's website is not set up to match the needs and expectations of the mobile user. Content and page size must be responsive and alter to reflect the consumer's device and operating system. For **mobile marketing** advertisements and headline messaging

Innovation and change

F1 on the move

Shortlisted for a mobile marketing award, digital agency Pancentric came up with a way to build interest in the Silverstone British F1 Grand Prix, to help leverage interest in the 50th anniversary of the first British Grand Prix staged at the Silverstone motor racing circuit. Each year, close to 300 000 fans enter the venue for this F1 event, with 120 000 of them having race-day tickets. The #Silverstone50 campaign invited fans to celebrate and share their favourite moments by submitting images via Instagram or Twitter. These contributions were then rated by other fans, with the winning images displayed during the event for all attendees. This tactic successfully involved many thousands of fans and enthusiasts, as well as creating increased awareness of both the event and the Silverstone brand.

Silverstone's various marketing agencies have for many years used far more than traditional advertising to build interest and sell tickets for its various events. Some of the most productive approaches have been surprisingly simple and straightforward. For example, SMS texting proved highly effective in generating last-minute take-up of unsold seats. To increase sales, Silverstone texted 45 000 on its database who had expressed an interest in attending future races but who had not bought tickets for the forthcoming race in F1's

calendar. The text was sent immediately BBC's television coverage of the previous race in Monaco had finished, making the assumption that many F1 viewers and armchair enthusiasts would be focused on the F1 calendar and the TV trailing of the next race at Silverstone. The hope was that, having just watched on TV the conclusion of an exciting race, many might be particularly receptive to the suggestion that they should attend this next race. If they did not need to move from their seats in order to then instantly book a ticket, so much the better.

The text stated, 'Enjoyed the Monaco Grand Prix? Get your tickets to the British Grand Prix at Silverstone now!' The text included a web link so that those with smartphones or tablets, whether at home or watching the race in a bar, could instantly make their ticket purchases by being quickly redirected to a ticket purchasing online site optimized for smartphones and tablets. This very simple ploy was most successful, with sales far exceeding the marketing costs involved.

Sources: http://mobilemarketingmagazine.com/most-effective-mobile-marketing-awards-social-campaign-preview#RLKVOA1lkueBzJjj.99, accessed 5 March 2015; www.tatango.com/blog/text-message-marketing-campaign-generates-680-roi/, accessed 5 March 2015; IDM Event – Silverstone: Interview with Hannah Bodley, Head of Marketing, Silverstone, www.youtube.com/watch?v=Tw_qFjoWV2c, accessed 5 March 2015; www.silverstone.co.uk.

should be simplified but no less eye-catching than for desktops. Some brands will need to specify the geographic areas they serve and ensure they are flagged by Google Places and Google Local. Marketers need to ensure they have a mobile channel that is fit for purpose.

Email marketing

Email marketing
The use of email to deliver offers, brand building messages and relationship-building information to customers, prospects and target audiences.

Instagram, Snapchat, Facebook and Flickr may have superseded email for a generation of younger or more technology-savvy consumers, but email is still an important part of the digital armoury. Email is used to deliver offers, communicate brand building messages and direct relationship-building information to customers, prospects and target audiences.

For every £1 invested in **email marketing**, the return is £40 of business. Users' SPAM protection is an issue, blocking much traffic. Dedicated email marketing service providers, such as GetResponse.com, iChamp or Mailchimp have arrangements with the major ISPs, to increase the likelihood of emails being received successfully and not blocked. Many brands encourage subscription to newsletters, but it is better to send out topical reports or white papers with links to YouTube videos cross-promoting these highlights. As with any marketing activity, the target selection should relate to the overall target segment strategy and positioning to ensure the messages are well-honed and deemed to be of interest.

Online public relations

Online public relations
Web-based communication and interaction with an organization's publics, stakeholders and target audiences in order to manage reputation, create awareness and build relationships.

The requirements for effective public relations remain as described in Chapter 17 of *Marketing: Concepts and Strategies*, but the arena has altered dramatically along with the nature of the engagement, leading to a need for **online public relations**.

FIGURE 19.4
Marketing anytime/anywhere
Connected for work, socializing or making purchases, today's consumers are targets for marketers anytime and anywhere in the era of mobile marketing.

The role of PR has not changed: audiences still require messaging with well-crafted and newsworthy stories, reputations must be managed and crises responded to. However, social media has radically altered the rules, while the web provides a first contact point of reference for many seeking information about a brand or market development. Previously brands pushed out their messages through their marketing communications, but increasingly consumers and other interested parties pull the insights they require, as and when needed, from web searches and via social media discussions. Marketers have had to adapt their use of public relations accordingly.

Driving innovation

Monetization
The ability to generate revenue through a website or blog. Monetization can be from affiliate programmes, eCommerce, premium content or advertising.

Companies' leadership teams have observed others **monetizing** digitally-collected data and making significant returns on their online operations, so have striven to encourage their organizations to innovate and try new ways of doing business online. For most companies, the challenge has been to establish multi-channel operations and to follow their customers across these various channels. However, digital has enabled start-ups to enter markets previously out of reach because of the barriers to entry in terms of establishing distribution and being accessible to intended customers. This has encouraged a spirit of innovation, as web-only businesses have come to many markets, offering greater choice to consumers, often across international boundaries.

Crowdsourcing
The task of outsourcing to a large group of people or a community via the internet for funding a task usually performed by the company itself, such as product testing.

The digital environment has encouraged businesses to collaborate with others, share insights and involve customers and partners more in product or service co-creation. The need to involve technology-savvy experts, analytics and app developers is also a driver for this new set of behaviours. Companies are recognizing that they can work globally with smart-thinkers able to bring creativity and new ideas to their businesses. Harnessing the energy and reach of social media, **crowdsourcing** and more routinized collaborations is the base of a steep learning curve for many organizations, but one deemed worthwhile by so many of today's successful, fast-moving and more innovative companies. Even long-term marketing-led corporations are seeking to harness this energy. Procter & Gamble is one such example, via its open innovation platform for collaborating with external developers (www.pgconnectdevelop.com/home/pg_open _innovation.html). No doubt the clumsily labelled **'Internet of Things'** will provide a new wave of innovation and activity for marketers, as more and more household appliances and gadgets communicate to each other and with remote third parties, sharing data and providing new insights into the behaviours of consumers.

The 'Internet of Things'
The network of physical objects or 'things' embedded with electronics, software, sensors and connectivity to enable greater value and service by exchanging data with the manufacturer, operator and/or other connected devices.

Big data

Big data
Data that are too large, numerous, complex and frequent for conventional data tools to capture, store, manage and analyze. Open source platforms enable organizations to extract real time value from the huge volumes of data being produced.

At its inception, digital brought marketers additional means for creating a marketing mix, providing additional options for channels to market and for communications with consumers or business customers. One of the biggest benefits to marketers initially was rather overlooked. Owing to the two-way dialogue permitted with consumers and the often real-time interaction facilitated by digital communication, along with the visibility of ongoing relationships with consumers which build up a history of purchasing, search behaviour and opinions expressed, arguably one of the biggest benefits for marketers from digital is the wealth of data and customer insights routinely available to an organization. Commonly referred to as **'big data'**, this wealth of topical information provides the ability to learn so much almost instantly in a way never before possible for marketers. This changing environment has required the need for analytics and experts in sifting through these huge amounts of data in order to identify genuine, directional and helpful market and customer insights. Many companies simply feel overwhelmed and are struggling to harness this potential. Digital agencies and the leading analytics consultancies have stepped into this void to provide support to marketers, while many companies have created digital insight teams, either within the traditional marketing function or as a separate resource.

The wealth of data now collected via digital marketing and social media has altered how many activities for marketers are undertaken. For example, Chapter 7 explained how much faster and cheaper market segmentation assessments are, while Chapter 9 explored some of the changes in marketing research. One of the consequences for marketers has been the growth of personnel expert in **marketing insight** and **marketing analytics** – either in-house or from external partners and agencies – in order to monitor and explore the wealth of market, consumer and competitor data to identify key marketing insights and emerging trends, and to assess the performance of the increasingly dynamic and wide-ranging set of marketing activities.

Marketing analytics and performance

According to SAS, marketing analytics comprises the processes and technologies that enable marketers to evaluate the success of their marketing initiatives by measuring performance (e.g. blogging versus social media versus channel communications), using important business metrics, such as ROI. It is a huge growth area within the field of marketing. Traditionally, marketing has struggled to measure performance and to quantify its contribution to an organization from its marketing programmes. Digital marketing and the emergence of marketing analytics are changing this situation.

Digital marketing provides a host of metrics, from counting visits to a site, time spent on a site or page, where the viewer moved to, whether a purchase or request for contact was made, and so forth. Some of the most popular metrics for online marketing include:

- **Conversion rates:** the proportion of visitors who go on to complete a defined action, such as register, complete an inquiry form or make a purchase.
- Page views: the number of pages viewed by a visitor to a website.
- Absolute unique visitors: the number of individuals who visited a site over a given time period.
- New versus returning visitors: the number of returning visitors, which is an assessment requiring cookies to be activated and good analytics.
- **Bounce rate:** the number of visitors who quickly/immediately leave without dwelling or clicking through to other content.
- **Abandonment rate:** those visitors who do not bounce straight away from a site, but who ultimately fail to convert to the hoped-for outcome.
- **Cost per conversion:** a calculation of the total cost of advertising divided by the total number of conversions generated from the campaign.

Forbes says that 37 per cent of companies lack analytics staff. Research company Gartner predicts there will be over four million big data-related analytics posts created in the next two years. *Harvard Business Review* goes as far as to say that the role of the data scientist is set to be one of the sexiest there is in corporate life.

Companies must use the wealth of intelligence emerging via digital activities and evaluate their online marketing activities alongside their more traditional marketing activities. This requires market insight analysts to sift through huge volumes of marketing data, in order to identify patterns and genuine insights with which to direct marketing strategy and align marketing programmes. To assess performance, analytics experts

---

Market insight
Learning about consumers, competitors and market trends to identify strategic direction and improve returns.

Marketing analytics
The processes and technologies that enable marketers to evaluate the success of their marketing initiatives by measuring performance across all channels and activities using important business metrics such as ROI.

Conversion rates
The proportion of visitors who go on to complete a defined action, such as register, complete an inquiry form or make a purchase.

Bounce rate
The number of visitors who quickly/immediately leave without dwelling or clicking-through to other content.

Abandonment rate
Those visitors who do not bounce straight away from a site, but who ultimately fail to convert to the hoped-for outcome.

Cost per conversion
Calculation of the total cost of advertising divided by the total number of conversions generated from the campaign.

are required, defining metrics, collecting appropriate data, creating the ability to analyze and report the implications, and encouraging leadership teams to embrace the findings.

Managing multiple channels

When asked about their biggest challenges in today's environment, leadership teams of companies cite social responsibility, sustainability and privacy concerns with data amongst their leading concerns. Invariably top of the list, however, are managing customers in the face of increasingly dominant social media-led consumer-to-consumer communication, identifying key insights from among the huge volume of big data, and managing customer experience across channels. Multi-channel management is proving to be a big challenge in many companies.

As has been explained, digital has enabled some new entrants to emerge in markets without a physical or store/depot-based presence. For many established players, digital has enabled a new channel to market to increase customer numbers and seek greater share of their spending. While this has been viewed eagerly as providing the potential for growth in sales and market share, the addition of a channel is not without its drawbacks. Marketers must manage costs prudently and be flexible enough to modify their behaviours to accommodate new business models and ways of engaging with their customers. They must seek to provide a joined-up brand strategy, market segmentation and customer experience across these channels. There is only now a growing realization that often the same customer buys online as well as in-store, so having standalone operations and separate management teams for each route to market is unlikely to provide an optimum joined-up customer experience for many of a company's customers.

Omni-channel marketing
Multi-channel marketing utilizing *all* available channels to offer customers a seamless brand experience across a company's channels.

Omni-channel marketing has emerged in the literature recently as an extension of the multi-channel concept.[1] Multi-channel refers to using many channels, while omni refers to using 'all', providing a seamless customer experience through all available channels, such as in-store, mobile internet devices, computers, television, radio, direct mail, catalogues and any other touchpoints with consumers or business customers. Customers must be tracked across all channels, with a focus on providing a joined-up brand experience. Merchandise, promotions and marketing communications are not channel-specific. The physical store often becomes an extension of the supply chain in which purchases may be collected in the store, but are researched or enacted through other channels, such as the 'click and collect' option now offered by many retailers.

Summary

This chapter has defined the nature of digital marketing and examined how digital has impacted on consumer behaviour and decision-making; the new requirements of understanding search engine management and content marketing, types of digital media and multi-screen marketing; the all-important issue of social media strategy; the exciting options provided by mobile marketing; email marketing and online public relations; the way in which digital is driving innovation like never before; turning 'big data' into meaningful insights; and, the challenges for organisations in deciding on a channel-to-market strategy, addressing multiple channels and restructuring their operations to manage these choices.

Digital marketing is the use of technology-led channels of communication and selling to manage customer interaction and provide customer experience in a digitally-connected environment. *Search engine optimization* (SEO) is the management of search engine behaviour to increase a brand's rankings in search engine organic result listings on search engine results pages (SERPS) for particular keywords and phrases. *Pay per click* (PPC) is one form of monetizing the digital journey: text ads that are displayed on the search engine results page when specific key phrases are entered by the search user result in revenue, with the advertiser paying when the site visitor clicks on the advertisement. *Keyphrases* are required in order to comply with search engine behaviours. Keyphrases are the combination of keywords used to log a query in a search engine. Keyphrase analysis is the identification and selection of relevant keywords and phrases to leverage SEO and search marketing.

Content marketing is important in digital marketing, involving the creation of relevant and interesting text, audio, video and rich media content to engage specific customers in order to create brand awareness and sales. Social media's popularity seems to have unlimited bounds. *Social media marketing* involves the process of gaining website traffic or social mentions through social media sites, by creating content attracting attention of readers who will share these through their social networks. A *digital brand community* is a group of consumers, observers or advocates focused on a particular brand, who use social media to share admiration for their favoured brand.

Mobile marketing presents so many possibilities for marketers, but also many challenges. Mobile marketing encourages consumer engagement anywhere or anytime while using a mobile device, such as a smartphone or tablet. It is heavily dependent on mobile apps, which provide users with information, entertainment and location-based services. *Email marketing* should not be overlooked. This is the use of email to deliver offers, brand building messages and relationship-building information to customers, prospects and target audiences. Web-based communication and interaction with an organization's publics, stakeholders and target audiences in order to manage reputation, create awareness and build relationships reveal that most public relations activity is undertaken digitally in *online public relations*.

Monetization is the ability to generate revenue through a website or blog. Monetization can be from affiliate programmes, eCommerce, premium content or advertising. Digital marketing has led to many innovations. *Crowdsourcing* is the task of outsourcing to a large group of people or a community via the internet for funding a task usually performed by the company itself. One of the latest breakthroughs is the *Internet of Things*, which is a network of physical objects or 'things' embedded with electronics, software, sensors and connectivity, to enable greater value and service by exchanging data with the manufacturer, operator and/or other connected devices.

Big data are too large, numerous, complex and frequent for conventional data tools to capture, store, manage and analyze. Open source platforms enable organizations to extract real time value from the huge volumes of data being produced. Big data and greater analytics power are transforming many of marketing's issues. One of the consequences for marketers has been the growth of experts in *marketing insight* and *marketing analytics* in order to monitor and explore the wealth of market, consumer and competitor data to identify key marketing insights and emerging trends, and to assess the performance of the increasingly dynamic and wide-ranging set of marketing activities with increasingly sophisticated analytics. There are many metrics deployed to examine the performance of online marketing activity, including *conversion rates*, *bounce rate*, *abandonment rate* and *cost per conversion*.

Digital channels involve different forms of digital media for online marketing and delivery. For many companies, these digital channels are additional to the traditional channels to market, such as depots or retail stores. The range of channels continues to expand, requiring organizations to develop *multi-channel* or now *omni-channel strategies*. Omni-channel marketing is multi-channel marketing utilizing *all* available channels, to offer customers a seamless brand experience across a company's channels.

The difficulty of spotting the true insights amongst the growing wealth of big data in the digital era, growing consumer-to-consumer social-media inspired interaction and managing multiple channels, are some of the biggest concerns facing companies today. These are the topics causing leadership teams sleepless nights.

There are five principal benefits of digital marketing: (1) digital provides additional options for marketing communications; (2) digital gives marketers more direct and diverse channel possibilities; (3) digital enables marketers to capture greater insights into consumers with immediacy and two-way interaction; (4) digital explodes the ways in which marketers build relationships, with far more direct and frequent interactions and the bespoke tailoring of information, deals and propositions; and (5) digital provides access to customers wherever they are and whenever they want to connect. There are many downsides and complications to address, including (1) the diminishing control over a brand's messages owing to greater consumer-to-consumer comment through social media; (2) data overload, as the digital environment provides huge amounts of consumer insight; (3) privacy concerns, as consumers start to realise how much is known about their whereabouts, interests, purchasing, viewership, networks and lifestyles; (4) the breakdown of trust, as consumers realize they are treated differently from a brand's other customers; and (5) the requirement for a whole host of new skills and agency partners.

Key links

This chapter has explored the rudiments of digital marketing. It should be read in conjunction with:

- Chapter 14's overview of marketing channels.
- Chapters 16 and 18 in Part Three's examination of marketing communications.
- Chapter 9's coverage of marketing research.
- Chapter 7's explanation of market segmentation and customer relationship management.

Important terms

Abandonment rate
Big data
Bounce rate
Content marketing
Conversion rates
Cost per conversion
Crowdsourcing
Digital brand community
Digital channels
Digital marketing
Email marketing
Keyphrase
Market insight
Marketing analytics
Mobile marketing
Monetization
Omni-channel marketing
Online public relations
Pay per click (PPC)
Pop-up ads
Search engine optimization (SEO)
Social media marketing
The 'Internet of Things'

Discussion and review questions

1. Define what is meant by the term digital marketing.
2. What are the main benefits for marketers of adopting digital marketing?
3. What are some of the biggest challenges and concerns associated with the growth of digital marketing?
4. Considering examples of your choice, outline some of the changes to the consumer buying decision-making process brought about by digital?
5. What is search engine optimization (SEO) and why is it important?
6. Explain what is meant by content marketing.
7. In what ways have media options changed with the advent of digital?
8. What is meant by multi-screen marketing?
9. What is the impact of social media on marketing?
10. In what ways do consumers embrace social media to influence their own product choices and those of others?
11. How do marketers use social media to test out ideas and research their hunches?
12. In what ways has the growth of consumer-to-consumer communication in a digital world altered the nature of marketing?
13. In what ways has mobile marketing been a game-changer?
14. Using examples of your choice, consider how well-known brands are embracing mobile marketing.
15. What is meant by email marketing? For what purposes is it most useful?
16. Why has public relations largely transferred to a digital environment?
17. What are some of the latest innovations being driven by digital and social media?
18. What is meant by the term 'big data'? In what ways are big data altering marketing practices?
19. Why are marketing analytics now so important?
20. In what ways are online marketing activities measured?
21. What is meant by omni-marketing?
22. Why is multi-channel management such an important aspect of marketing strategy?

Recommended readings

Bradley, D., *Getting Digital Right* (Kindle, Amazon, 2015).

Chaffey, D. and Ellis-Chadwick, F., *Digital Marketing Strategy, Implementation and Practice* (Pearson, 2012).

Kawasaki, G. and Fitzpatrick, P., *The Art of Social Media: Power Tips for Power Users* (Portfolio Penguin, 2014).

Pont, S., *Digital State: How The Internet Is Changing Everything* (Kogan Page, 2013).

Ryan, D., *Understanding Digital Marketing* (Kogan Page, 2014).

Smith, N., *Successful Digital Marketing in a Week* (Teach Yourself Books, 2014).

Tuten, T. and Solomon, M., *Social Media Marketing* (Sage, 2014).

Digital Minds: 12 Things Every Business Needs to Know about Digital Marketing (WSI; Friesen Press, 2013).

Internet exercise

From a desktop, log on to the website of one of your favourite retailers, whose stores you also regularly visit. Select a product category and search for product options to buy. Do not make any purchases, though! Now do the same with the selected retailer, but accessing it this time from your smartphone.

Were there any differences in terms of your browsing experience, the ease with which you found and reviewed options, and how the brand was portrayed across both modes of access? Which online browsing route did you prefer and why? In what ways are the brand experiences provided by your selected retailer in-store and online consistent?

Group tasks

1. Think about how you use your smartphone and for what purposes. What products and services interact with you via your smartphone? To what extent have these brands entered your life 24/7?

2. Iconic department store retailer Selfridges for many years resisted having an on-line selling operation, whereas rival store operator John Lewis was quick to harness the digital channel. Brainstorm the reasons behind these two retailers' initial decisions: to avoid the web and to quickly harness online selling.

Applied mini-case

The BBC is a large public service media organization broadcasting TV and radio programming, supported with extensive online material. Unlike other broadcasters and news organizations, the BBC does not force viewers or listeners to pay directly for its programming. However, its charter to operate insists that the BBC is widely accessible, politically neutral and morally responsible. The BBC has also always encouraged feedback and sought interaction with its audiences, as with its *comment and contribute* web section. There is a pattern of embracing new media channels and ways for communicating with its audiences.

Question

Spend a few minutes on www.bbc.co.uk. Consider the ways with which this predominantly TV and radio programme broadcaster is integrating its online operation and embracing the growth of digital. In what ways is this website seeking to ascertain the needs and expectations of its key audiences?

Digital and university choices

Case study

Not too many years ago, students reading *Marketing: Concepts and Strategies* would have selected their universities based on reviewing printed prospectuses and brochures, the PR-led stories in various newspapers and magazines which suggest which university is good for whatever degree, supported perhaps with the experience of a university visit or open day. Teachers, parents and friends might have voiced some opinions, based on their own limited insights, experiences of selecting universities or time spent as a student. Universities'

marketing budgets focused primarily on printed materials, some public relations and the management of open days or roadshows.

'I blogged my thoughts and soon realized I was wrong. So pleased I found out before being there!'

'My teachers were really helpful, but recent leavers already studying there gave me the real views I needed to decide. Facebook made the difference.'

'*The Times Guide* told me which universities to consider for my subject. But visiting made all the difference. Then I was down to two choices. So contacting people I knew there made my mind up.'

| Views of teachers, school careers advisors and parents to create a shortlist | → | Send for printed prospectuses for a limited number of universities and colleges | → | Visit a handful of universities for open day visits and departmental talks | → | Apply through the applications system to those shortlisted/visited |

The subsequent emergence of published guides and rankings added some degree of third party endorsement and provided reference points, but for decades the process above was how sixth formers selected their university

'Once I had decided it, I posted "my" uni online. So glad I did. I didn't go there. Came here instead. Wouldn't have done if friends hadn't steered me away.'

'I couldn't travel from my country to open days in the UK, so social media with people already in the UK really helped. And some universities don't show you much online. But others do. Some even let you talk to current students.'

'Need a job. Views of companies matter a lot. Googled these and these helped make my mind up.'

These quotes, taken from a recent student survey, reveal how much has changed from the process described above. The information sources in particular are far more diverse and, of course, accessed online. The ongoing use of peer views throughout the selection process is a departure, too. This is also enabled by social media.

Today, prospective students have so many more sources of information, many of which the individual university cannot control. There are ratings sites online suggesting which courses are well-regarded across many criteria; current students blog and post views online of their experiences; candidates can take 360-degree virtual tours of campuses, accommodation blocks, lecture theatres and entertainments; and social media allow applicants to seek the views of their peers and current students. Those from far afield who are unable to attend an open day are provided with online access to tutors and current student cohorts.

Brochures are still produced, PR is important and open days take up much of the marketing and recruitment budget for most universities, but it is the access to universities, the views of current and past students, and third party reviews made possible in a digital era which provide applicants with invaluable insight, shaping their decision-making and eventual purchasing.

The process has changed in terms of how interested sixth formers and potential post-graduates are managed. Universities are investing in complex customer relationship management (CRM) systems to manage recruitment and to develop ongoing relationships with interested applicants, so as to ensure their eventual arrival at the start of term. These systems depend on social media and online relationships.

Questions for discussion

Think about your own decision-making when selecting your degree course and institution:

1. Which were the information sources you found most useful and which you trusted?

2. How should university admissions staff utilize digital marketing to help the selection and admissions journey of interested candidates?

3. To what extent does the arrival of digital marketing help or hinder in the marketing of degree programmes?

CHAPTER 20

Pricing

"Pricing causes many arguments amongst senior management teams because it makes or breaks the business model and generally is hugely important to the customer"

Objectives

To understand the characteristics and role of price.

To be aware of the differences between price and non-price competition.

To explore key factors that affect pricing decisions.

To examine different pricing objectives.

To consider issues unique to the pricing of products for business markets.

To analyze the concept of economic value to the customer.

To understand the eight major stages of the process used to establish prices.

To learn about demand for a product and to analyze the relationships between demand, costs and profits.

To explore the selection of a pricing strategy and to understand how to determine a specific price.

INTRODUCTION

Price
The value placed on what is exchanged.

Financial price
The basis of market exchanges; the quantified value of what is exchanged.

To a buyer, **price** is the value placed on what is exchanged.[1] Something of value – usually buying power – is exchanged for satisfaction or utility. In most marketing situations, the price is very evident, and buyer and seller are aware of the amount of value each must give up to complete the exchange.[2] As described in Chapter 3, buying power depends on a buyer's income, credit and wealth. As buyers have limited resources, they must weigh up the usefulness of a product or the satisfaction derived from it against its cost to decide whether the exchange is worthwhile. **Financial price** is most usually the basis of market exchanges. This can be used to quantify almost anything of value that is exchanged, including ideas, services, rights and goods. Thus, the financial value of a Paris penthouse might be 2 million euros. Yet price does not always have to have a financial basis. Barter, the trading of products, is the oldest form of exchange. Price impacts strongly on how businesses fare competitively, so marketers need to give careful consideration to pricing issues. Price is critical to the marketing mix because it affects directly how much revenue is generated. As it can be changed very quickly, price is more flexible than other marketing mix elements. Businesses must avoid seeing price purely in terms of setting monetary price points. Due to the psychological impact of price on customers, price also has a symbolic value. A broader view of pricing is therefore needed which takes into account issues such as target customers' perceptions of value for money and requirements for easy payment terms.

There are essential stages for establishing prices, which involve taking into consideration a wide range of factors. Economic conditions, fluctuations in market growth and levels of competition all affect the price that customers are prepared to pay. Careful judgement is needed to ensure that these factors are taken into consideration when setting prices so that customers believe they are getting reasonable value for money.

What price for a great day out?

How do you price an experience? This is the challenge for Red Letter Days, a business set up in 1989 to offer customers a range of gift experiences designed to satisfy every taste. As the company's website reveals (www.redletterdays.co.uk) many different experiences and treats, offered at a range or price points, are available. Targeting consumers and business clients alike, those seeking a relaxing, exciting, indulgent experience for themselves, or for a 'different' gift for friends, family, colleagues or customers, can find an option that appeals to them.

The experiences are organized according to a number of categories, including driving, gourmet, sports, culture, animals, hobbies and pampering; and occasions, such as for Mother's Day, Valentine's Day, weddings, birthdays and holidays. Considerable variety lies behind these headings.

Perhaps your parents are tempted by the wine tasting, or your best friend has yearned to skydive or enjoy the thrills of white water rafting. Maybe arts and crafts are your passion and you fancy trying your hand at making silver jewellery, sugar-craft or pottery. All of these and many more activities are on offer.

The Gourmet gifts category gives a flavour of this diversity, including the following options: afternoon tea, London dining, food and cookery courses, celebrity chef, wine tasting and vineyard tours, cocktail making, brewery tours, short gourmet breaks, chocolate and sushi.

Those buying an experience as a gift who are unsure what their loved ones might enjoy, can buy a Flexible Experience Pack. A range of prices is available, with the pack colour determining the value and choice of experience available. Prices start at £50 for a blue and £75 for a green experience gift pack, and go right up to £500 for silver and £1000 for gold. Adventurous recipients of a blue experience gift pack, priced at £50, might enjoy a 4x4 off-road taster session, dumper truck racing or a Segway rally; while those seeking a more relaxing treat, might prefer to spend their voucher on a spa day, afternoon tea for two, or wine tasting. At the other extreme, recipients of a gold pack can choose from 780 exclusive experiences, ranging from tandem sky-driving or a river trip in Paris to spending a day as a keeper at London Zoo.

In setting the price of these gift packs and deciding for which experiences they can be swapped, Red Letter Days is making a judgement about the value that customers attach to indulging themselves or others, and spending their time in a new and interesting way.

Sources: www.redletterdays.co.uk/Experience (accessed 3 March 2015); Red Letter Days marketing materials.

All companies, irrespective of whether their products are costly or cheap, use price along with other elements to distinguish their products from competitive brands. For these companies, as for most businesses, pricing is a crucial element in the marketing mix. However, as this chapter's 'opener' clearly illustrates, a variety of factors impact upon pricing decisions. The range of factors that affect pricing are considered later in this chapter.

This chapter begins by explaining what is meant by price and considers its importance to marketing practitioners. It then explores pricing objectives and the various factors affecting pricing decisions. The notion of perceived value for money is considered next. The chapter then examines pricing in business markets and the concept of economic value to the customer, and concludes by over-viewing the essential stages for establishing prices.

The characteristics and role of price

Terms used to describe price

Price is expressed differently in various exchanges. For instance, insurance companies charge a *premium* to holidaymakers requiring protection against the cost of illness or injury. A police officer who stops a motorist for speeding writes a ticket that requires a *fine* to be paid. In London, a congestion *charge* is levied on motorists travelling in central areas. An accountant charges a *fee,* and a *fare* is charged for travelling by plane, railway or taxi. A *toll* is sometimes charged for the use of motorways or bridges. *Rent* is paid for the use of equipment or for a flat. An estate agent receives a *commission* on the sale of a property. A *deposit* is made to reserve merchandise. A *tip* helps pay waitresses or waiters for their services. *Interest* is charged for loans, and *taxes* are paid for government services. The value of many products is called *price.*

Although price may be expressed in a variety of ways, it is important to remember that the purpose of this concept is to quantify and express the value of the items in a marketing exchange.

The importance of price to marketers

As pointed out in Chapter 12, developing a product may be a lengthy process. It takes time to plan promotion and to communicate benefits. Distribution usually requires a long-term commitment to dealers who will handle the product. Often price and customer service levels are the only aspects a marketer can change quickly to respond to changes in demand or to the actions of competitors. However, as customers may be alienated by significant price changes, this does not mean that price is flexible in all situations.

Price is also a key element in the marketing mix because it relates directly to the generation of total revenue.[3] The following equation is an important one for the entire organization:

Profits = total revenues − total costs

or

Profits = (price × quantities sold) − total costs

Prices can have a dramatic impact on a company's profits. Price affects the profit equation in several ways. It directly influences the equation because it is a major component. It has an indirect impact because it can be a major determinant of the quantities sold. As will be explained, for many products an increase in price leads to a reduction of numbers sold. Even more indirectly, price influences total costs through its impact on quantities sold. Consequently, even a relatively small reduction in prices can cause profits to fall, sometimes dramatically. The relationship illustrates the difficulties faced by businesses attempting to build a differential advantage based on low prices. Marketers need to be fully aware of these stark relationships when setting prices, and the knock on ramifications for their organization's financial stability and corporate objectives.

As price has a psychological impact on customers, marketers can use it symbolically. By raising a price, they can emphasize the quality of a product and try to increase the status associated with its ownership. The declining fortunes of Chevas Royal Scotch whisky were reversed following a substantial price rise! Lowering a price can also have a dramatic impact on demand, attracting bargain-hunting customers who are prepared to spend extra time and effort to save a small amount.

Price and non-price competition

A product offering can compete on either a price or a non-price basis. The choice will affect not only pricing decisions and activities but also those associated with other marketing mix decision variables.

Price competition

Price competition
A policy whereby a marketer emphasizes price as an issue, and matches or beats the prices of competitors.

When **price competition** is used, a marketer emphasizes price as an issue, and matches or beats competitors' prices. Budget airline easyJet engages in price competition and stresses its low prices in its advertisements. To compete effectively on a price basis, a company should be the low-cost producer of the product. If all companies producing goods in an industry charge the same, the company with the lowest costs is the most profitable. Companies that stress low price as a key element in the marketing mix tend to produce standardized products. For example, suppliers of fuel oils use price competition. Sellers using this approach may be prepared and able to change prices frequently, particularly in response to competitors altering their prices. In many parts of the world, the postal service and UPS or DHL engage in direct price competition in their pricing of overnight express-delivery services.

Price competition gives a marketer flexibility. Prices can be altered to account for changes in the company's costs or in demand for the product, or when competitors cut prices. However, a major drawback of price competition is that competitors may also have the flexibility to adjust their prices to match or beat another company's price cuts. If so, a price war may result. Furthermore, if a user of price competition is forced to raise prices, competing companies may decide not to do the same. The supermarket giants sometimes seem to be locked into a spiral of price competition. Waitrose has 1000 popular lines visibly price-aligned in-store on-fixture to Tesco, often perceived to provide lower prices compared to upmarket Waitrose. Companies such as Procter & Gamble have attempted to strengthen consumer loyalty by cutting the prices of key brands permanently. The first two categories to benefit were the core markets of washing-up liquids, such as Fairy Liquid, and disposable nappies, such as Pampers.

Non-price competition

Non-price competition
A policy in which a seller elects not to focus on price but to emphasize other factors instead.

In **non-price competition**, a seller elects not to focus on price but instead emphasizes distinctive product features, service, product quality, promotion, packaging or other factors to distinguish the product from competing brands, for example Figure 20.2. Organizations that use non-price competition aim to increase unit sales in other ways. For example, Louis Vuitton stresses the exclusivity, quality and fashionability of its handbags, rather than competitive price. A company can use non-price competition to build customer loyalty towards its brand. If customers prefer a brand or store because of non-price issues, they may not easily be lured away by competing offers. Indeed, such customers might become confused or irritated if price cuts are offered. Buyers of Dior clothing, handbags or cosmetics enjoy the exclusivity associated with the high price. The implication is that price is not the most durable factor in terms of maintaining customer loyalty. However, when price is the primary reason that customers buy a particular brand, the competition can attract such customers through price cuts.

Non-price competition is workable under the right conditions. A company must be able to distinguish its brand through unique product features, higher quality, customer service, promotion, packaging and the like (see Figure 20.2). The brand's distinguishing features should be difficult, if not impossible, for a competitor to copy. Buyers must not only be able to perceive these distinguishing characteristics but must also view them as desirable. Finally, the organization must promote the distinguishing characteristics of the brand extensively in order to establish its superiority and to set it apart from competitors in the minds of buyers.

Many European companies put less emphasis on price than do their American counterparts. They look for a competitive edge by concentrating on promotion, research and development, marketing research and marketing channel considerations. In a study of pricing strategy, many companies stated specifically that they emphasize research and development and technological superiority; competition based on price was seldom a major marketing consideration.[4]

A marketer attempting to compete on a non-price basis must still consider competitors' prices. The business must be aware of competitors' prices and will probably price its brand near, or slightly above, competing brands. As an example, Sony sells flat screen televisions and Blu-ray players in a highly competitive market and charges higher prices than other manufacturers for them. Sony can achieve this because its emphasis on high product quality distinguishes it from its competitors and allows it to set higher prices.

FIGURE 20.2
Although priced to be competitive with rival brands, Olay both emotionally and functionally promotes product benefits

Factors affecting pricing decisions

Pricing decisions are affected by many factors. Often, there is considerable uncertainty about reactions to price on the part of buyers, channel members, competitors and others. Price is also an important consideration in marketing planning, market analysis and sales forecasting. It is a major issue when assessing a brand's positioning relative to competing brands. Most factors that affect pricing decisions can be grouped into one of the nine categories shown in Figure 20.3. This section explores how each of these nine groups of factors enters into price decision-making.

Organizational and marketing objectives

Marketers should set prices that are consistent with the organization's goals and mission. For example, skincare brands such as Sensai and Shiseido are positioned at the luxury end of the market, are sold through exclusive outlets and have high price tags to match. Marketers in these organizations know that discounting prices on these brands would not be in line with the overall organizational goal.

Decision-makers should also make pricing decisions that are compatible with the organization's marketing objectives. Say, for instance, that one of a producer's marketing objectives is a 12 per cent increase in unit sales by the end of the next year. Assuming that buyers are price sensitive, increasing the price or setting a price above the average market price would not be in line with the company's sales objective. A case in point: GM (Vauxhall) has introduced high-performance, well-specified model variants to the top of each of its model ranges – for example, the £19 000 Corsa 1.6 V6 VXR and the £34 000 Insignia 2.8T V6 VXR. Such prices ensure that these particular models have only limited appeal. GM's stated objective, however, is to be market leader in terms of sales volume. The company, therefore, is careful to price the great majority of its cars in line with the price expectations of the bulk of the car buying public and fleet operators – far below these £19 000 Corsa and £34 000 Insignia levels.

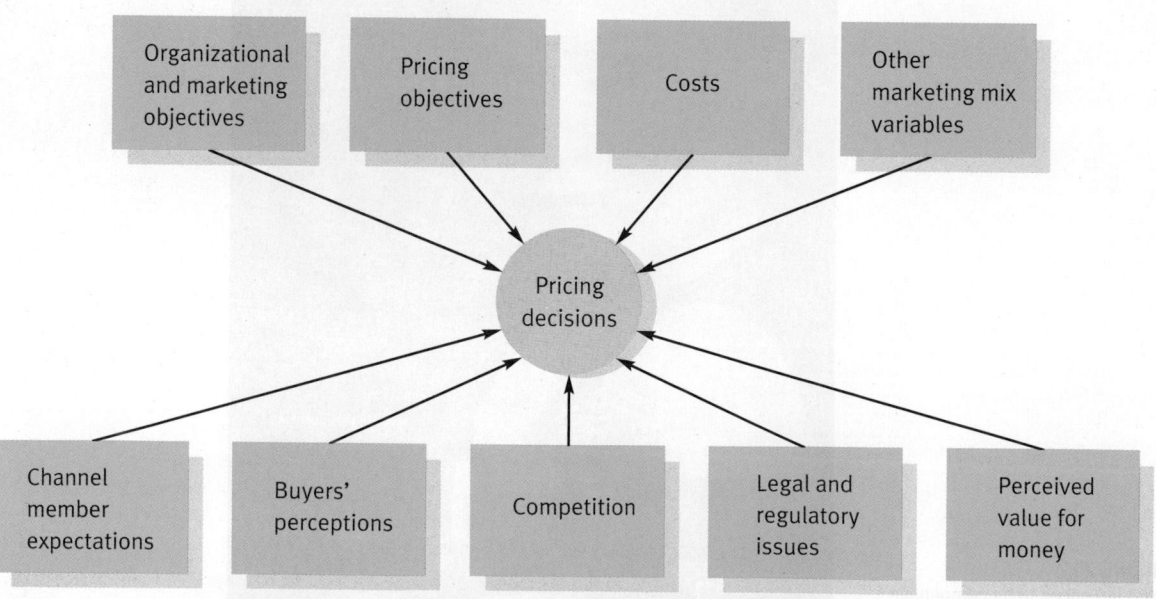

FIGURE 20.3
Factors that affect pricing decisions

Pricing objectives

Pricing objectives are overall goals that describe what a company wants to achieve through its pricing efforts. The type of pricing objective a marketer uses will have considerable bearing on the determination of prices.[5] Marketers often use multiple pricing objectives, including those that emphasize survival, profit, return on investment, market share, cash flow, status quo or product quality (see Table 20.1). Thus, a market share pricing objective usually causes a company to price a product below competing brands of similar quality to attract competitors' customers to the company's brand. This type of pricing can lead to lower profits, but may be used temporarily in the hope of gaining market share. By contrast, a cash flow pricing objective may involve setting a relatively high price, which can place the product at a competitive disadvantage. Paradoxically, a cash flow pricing objective sometimes results in a low price sustained in the long term. However, this type of objective is more likely to be addressed by using temporary price reductions, such as sales, refunds and special discounts.

As pricing objectives influence decisions in most functional areas – including finance, accounting and production – the objectives must be consistent with the company's overall mission and purpose (see Chapter 2). Insurance is an area where pricing is a major concern. As competition has intensified, insurance executives have realized that their products must be priced to meet both short-term

TABLE 20.1   Different types of pricing objectives

Survival
A fundamental pricing objective is survival. Most businesses will tolerate difficulties such as short-run losses and internal upheaval if they are necessary for survival. Because price is a flexible and convenient variable to adjust, it is sometimes used to increase sales volume to levels that match the company's expenses.

Profit
Although businesses often claim they aim to maximize profits, in practice this objective is difficult to measure. As a result, profit objectives tend to be set at satisfactory levels. Specific profit objectives may be stated in terms of actual monetary amounts or in terms of percentage change relative to previous profits.

Return on investment
Pricing to attain a specified rate of return on the company's investment is a profit-related pricing objective. Most pricing objectives based on return on investment (ROI) are achieved by trial and error, because not all cost and revenue data needed to project the return on investment are available when prices are set.

Market share
Many companies establish pricing objectives to maintain or increase a product's market share in relation to total industry sales. For example, car companies such as Volkswagen have been known to cut prices on existing models when introducing new ones, to boost share of the car market. Maintaining or increasing market share need not depend on growth in industry sales. A company can increase its market share even though sales for the total industry are decreasing. On the other hand, if the overall market is growing, a business's sales volume may actually increase as its market share decreases.

Cash flow
Some companies set prices to recover cash as fast as possible, especially when a short product life cycle (PLC) is anticipated or the capital spent to develop products needs to be recovered quickly. However, the use of cash flow and recovery as an objective oversimplifies the value of price in contributing to profits. A disadvantage of this pricing objective could be high prices, which might allow competitors with lower prices to gain a large share of the market.

Status quo
In some cases, a business may be in a favourable position and may simply wish to maintain the status quo. Such objectives can focus on maintaining a certain market share, meeting (but not beating) competitors' prices, achieving price stability or maintaining a favourable public image. Such an approach can reduce a company's risks by helping to stabilize demand for its products. The use of status quo pricing objectives sometimes leads to a climate of non-price competition in an industry.

Product quality
A company might have the objective of product quality leadership in the industry. For example, the construction equipment manufacturer JCB aims to be ranked as one of the leading companies in its industry in terms of product quality and customer satisfaction. This normally dictates a relatively high price to cover the high product quality and/or the high cost of research and development.

profit goals and long-term strategic objectives. Changes in the pricing objectives that companies use can occur for various reasons. For example, the objective of return on investment may be used less as managers and marketers in diversified companies stress the creation of shareholder value. When shareholder value is used as a performance objective, strategies – including those involving price – are evaluated according to their impact on the value investors perceive in the company.[6]

Costs

Obviously, costs must be an issue when establishing price. A business may temporarily sell products below cost to match the competition, to generate cash flow or even to increase market share; but in the long run it cannot survive by adopting this approach. A marketer should be careful to analyze all costs so that they can be included in the total costing for a product. Marketers must also take into account the costs that a particular product shares with other products in the product line, particularly the costs of research and development, production and distribution. Services are especially subject to cost sharing. For example, the costs of a bank building are spread over the costs of all services the bank offers.[7] Most marketers view a product's cost as a minimum, or floor, below which the product cannot be priced.

Other marketing mix variables

All marketing mix variables are closely interrelated. Pricing decisions can influence decisions and activities associated with product, place/distribution, promotion and customer service variables. A product's price frequently affects the demand for the item. A high price, for instance, may result in low unit sales, which in turn may lead to higher production costs per unit. Conversely, lower per-unit production costs may result from a low price. For many products, buyers associate better product quality with a high price and poorer product quality with a low price. This perceived price-quality relationship influences customers' overall image of products or brands. Thus consumers may be prepared to pay a high price for Rayban sunglasses because they believe they are a high-status item.

Pricing decisions influence the number of competing brands in a product category. When a company introduces a product, sets a relatively high price and achieves high unit sales, competitors may be attracted to this product category. If a company fixes a low price, the low profit margin may be unattractive to potential competition.

The price of a product is linked to several dimensions of its distribution. Premium-priced products are often marketed through selective or exclusive distribution; lower-priced products in the same product category may be sold through intensive distribution. For example, Montblanc pens are distributed through selective distribution and Bic pens through intensive distribution. The way in which a product is stored and transported may also be associated with its price. As Figure 20.4 shows, when deciding about a product's price, a producer must consider the profit margins of marketing channel members such as wholesalers and retailers. This way, channel members can be adequately compensated for the functions they perform.

The way a product is promoted can be affected by its price. Bargain prices are often included in advertisements, whereas premium prices are less likely to be mentioned. However, the exclusivity associated with a premium price is sometimes included in advertisements for upmarket items, such as luxury holidays or high status sound systems. Higher-priced products are more likely to require personal selling efforts than lower-priced ones. Indeed, there may be an expectation that a high price is accompanied by enhanced levels of customer service. A customer may purchase an inexpensive watch in a self-service environment but hesitate to buy an expensive watch in the same store, even if it is available there.

The price structure can affect a salesperson's relationship with customers. A complex pricing structure takes longer to explain to customers, is more likely to confuse the buyer and may cause misunderstandings that result in long-term customer dissatisfaction. For example, the pricing structure used by many hotels is complex and can confuse potential guests.

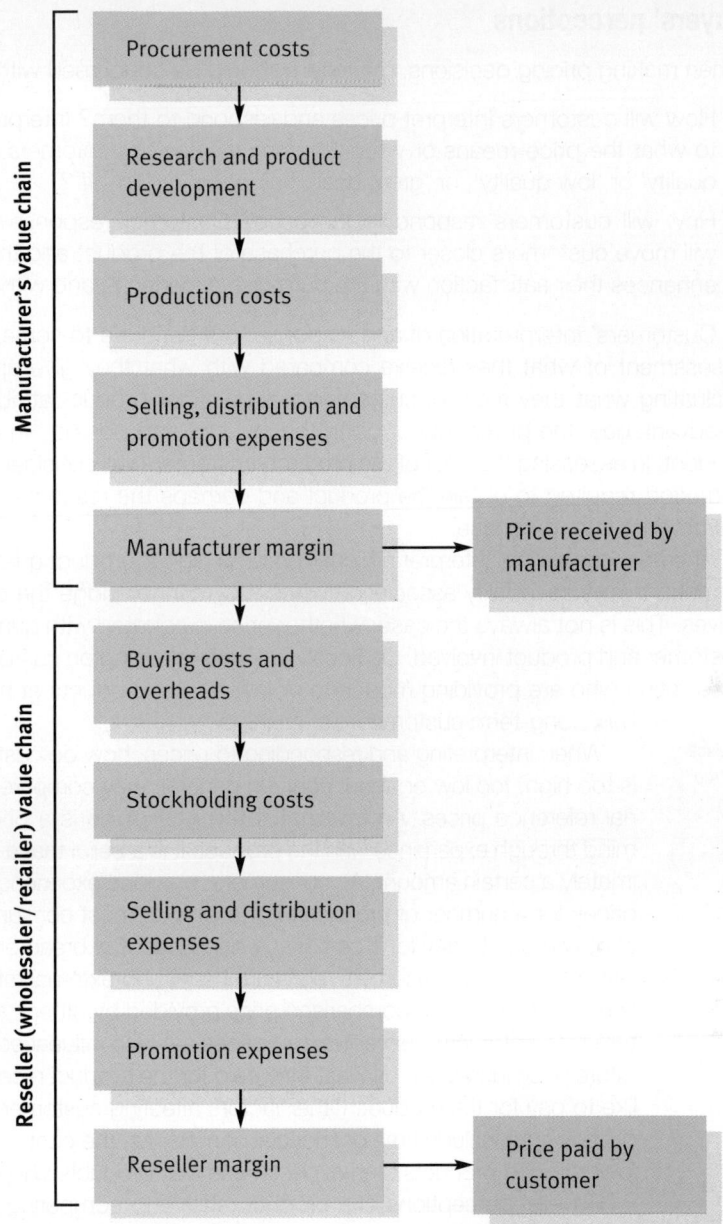

FIGURE 20.4
Wholesaler and retailer considerations when developing price

Manufacturer's value chain

- Procurement costs
- Research and product development
- Production costs
- Selling, distribution and promotion expenses
- Manufacturer margin → Price received by manufacturer

Reseller (wholesaler/retailer) value chain

- Buying costs and overheads
- Stockholding costs
- Selling and distribution expenses
- Promotion expenses
- Reseller margin → Price paid by customer

Channel member expectations

When making price decisions, a producer must consider what distribution channel members (such as wholesalers, online retailers and dealers) expect. A channel member certainly expects to receive a profit for the functions performed. The amount of profit expected depends on the amount of time and resources expended, and on an assessment of what would be gained by handling a competing product instead.

Channel members often expect producers to provide discounts for large orders and quick payment. Discounts are discussed later in this chapter. At times, resellers expect producers to provide support activities, such as sales training, online customer support, repair services, cooperative advertising, sales promotions and perhaps a programme for returning unsold merchandise to the producer. These support activities clearly incur costs, so a producer must consider these costs when determining prices.

Buyers' perceptions

When making pricing decisions, marketers should be concerned with two vital questions.

1. How will customers interpret prices and respond to them? Interpretation in this context refers to what the price means or what it communicates to customers. Does the price mean 'high quality' or 'low quality', or 'great deal', 'fair price' or 'rip-off'?

2. How will customers respond to the price? Customer response refers to whether the price will move customers closer to the purchase of the product and the degree to which the price enhances their satisfaction with the purchase experience and with the product after purchase.

Customers' interpretation of and response to a price are to some degree determined by their assessment of what they receive compared with what they give up to make the purchase. In evaluating what they receive, customers will consider product attributes, benefits, advantages, disadvantages, the probability of using the product and possibly the status associated with the product. In assessing the cost of the product, customers will consider its price, the amount of time and effort required to obtain the product and perhaps the resources required to maintain or use the product after purchase.

At times, customers interpret a higher price as higher product quality. They are especially likely to make this price–quality association when they cannot judge the quality of the product themselves. This is not always the case: whether price is equated with quality depends on the types of customer and product involved. Obviously, marketers relying on customers making a price–quality association who are providing moderate or low-quality products at high prices, will be unable to build long-term customer relationships.

Internal reference price
A price developed in the buyer's mind through experience with the product.

External reference price
A comparison price provided by others.

Value-conscious consumers
Those concerned about price and quality of a product.

Price-conscious consumers
Those striving to pay low prices.

Prestige-sensitive consumers
Individuals drawn to products that signify prominence and status.

When interpreting and responding to prices, how do customers determine if the price is too high, too low or about right? In general, they compare prices with internal or external reference prices. An **internal reference price** is a price developed in the buyer's mind through experience with the product. It is a belief that a product should cost approximately a certain amount. As consumers, previous experiences provide internal reference prices for a number of products. For example, most consumers have a reasonable idea of how much to pay for a can of soft drink, a loaf of bread or a litre of milk. When there is less experience, consumers rely more heavily on external reference prices.[8] An **external reference price** is a comparison price provided by others, such as retailers or manufacturers.[9] Customers' perceptions of prices are also influenced by their expectations about future price increases, by what they paid for the product recently, and by what they would like to pay for the product. Other factors affecting customers' perception of whether the price is right include time or financial constraints, the costs associated with searching for lower-priced products, and expectations that products will go on sale.

Buyers' perceptions of a product relative to competing products may allow a business to set a price that differs significantly from rivals' prices. If the product is deemed superior to most of the competition, a premium price may be feasible. However, even products with superior quality can be overpriced. Strong brand loyalty sometimes provides the opportunity to charge a premium price. On the other hand, if buyers view a product less than favourably – though not extremely negatively – a lower price may generate sales.

In the context of price, buyers can be characterized according to their degree of value consciousness, price consciousness and prestige-sensitivity. Marketers who understand these characteristics are better able to set pricing objectives and policies. **Value-conscious consumers** are concerned about both the price and the quality of a product. Recent economic difficulties have altered the purchasing habits of many consumers and business customers, with many more placing value-for-money high on their list of key customer values when making purchasing decisions. **Price-conscious consumers** strive to pay low prices. **Prestige-sensitive consumers** focus on purchasing products that signify prominence and status. For example, the Porsche Cayenne, one of the highest-priced sports utility vehicles ever marketed, created record sales and profits for Porsche. Only 18 per cent of Cayenne buyers had previously owned a Porsche; many of the rest were attracted to the vehicle by the prestige associated with the Porsche name. On the other hand, some consumers vary in their degree of value, price and prestige consciousness. In some segments, consumers are still 'trading up' to more status-conscious products despite the credit crunch and economic turmoil of recent years: this occurs with cars, electrical appliances, restaurants and even pet food. This trend has benefited companies such as Starbucks and BMW, which can charge premium prices for high-quality, prestige products.

Competition

A marketer needs to know competitors' prices so that a company can adjust its own prices accordingly.[10] This does not mean that a company will necessarily match competitors' prices; it may set its price above or below theirs. It is also important for marketers to assess how competitors will respond to price adjustments. Will they change their prices (some may not) and, if so, will they raise or lower them? For example, when satellite or cable entertainment providers stress their keen pricing, competitors often do the same.

Chapter 3 describes several types of competitive market structure that impact upon price setting. When a company operates as a monopoly and is unregulated, it can set whatever prices the market will bear. However, the company may avoid adopting the highest possible pricing for fear of inviting government regulation or because it wants to penetrate a market by using a lower price. If the monopoly is regulated, it normally has less pricing flexibility; the regulatory body lets it set prices that generate a reasonable, but not excessive, return. A government-owned monopoly may price products below cost to make them accessible to people who could not otherwise afford them. However, government-owned monopolies sometimes charge higher prices to control demand.

In an oligopoly, only a few sellers operate, and there are high barriers to competitive entry. A business in such an industry – for example, telecommunications, pharmaceuticals or steel – can raise its price, hoping that its competitors will do the same. Very little can be gained through price cuts because other companies are likely to follow suit when an organization cuts its price to gain a competitive edge.

A market structure characterized by monopolistic competition means numerous sellers with differentiated product offerings. The products are differentiated by physical characteristics, features, quality and brand image. The distinguishing characteristics of its product may allow a company to set a different price from its competitors. However, businesses engaged in a monopolistic competitive market structure are likely to practise non-price competition, as discussed earlier in this chapter.

Under conditions of perfect competition, there are many sellers. Buyers view all sellers' products as the same. All companies sell their products at the going market price and so there is no flexibility in setting prices.

Legal and regulatory issues

At times, government action sways marketers' pricing decisions. To curb inflation, the government may invoke price controls, 'freeze' prices at certain levels or determine the rates at which prices can be increased. Following the privatization of public utilities, the UK government set up regulatory bodies such as Ofwat for water, Ofgem for gas and electricity, and Ofcom for the communications industry, which police pricing and billing, often establishing maximum and minimum charges.

Many regulations and laws affect pricing decisions and activities. Not only must marketers refrain from fixing prices, they must also develop independent pricing policies and set prices in ways that do not involve collusion. Over the years, legislation has been established to safeguard consumers and businesses from pricing sharp practices. In the UK, the Competition and Markets Authority has taken over from the Competition Commission to prevent the creation of monopolistic situations. The consumer is protected by the Trade Descriptions Act, the Fair Trading Act, the Consumer Protection Act and many others. All countries have similar legislation, and the European Union legislates to protect consumers within the community.

Perceived value

Perceived value for money
The benefit consumers perceive to be inherent in a product or service, weighed against the price demanded.

Most discussions about pricing revolve around the actual monetary value – the price – to be charged for the good or service. However, the **perceived value for money** to consumers is also vital. This is the benefit consumers see as inherent in a product or service, weighed against the price demanded. Sometimes, particularly in consumer markets, these benefits are real and measurable, in other cases they are more psychological. For instance, interest-free credit, maintenance contracts and extended warranties are all features that may affect a consumer's perception of value for money. Consumers will not pay more than they value the benefit inherent in a product or service. Consumers balance the price demanded, typically in monetary terms, against the anticipated level of use and satisfaction to be gained from buying and using the specific product. This assessment is influenced by the consumers' previous experience of the brand and similar products, the perceived quality of the product in question, its brand image, purpose, anticipated usage, overall appeal and the nature of competing offers. These emotive issues are often difficult to quantify, but through qualitative marketing research, most businesses are able to assess their target market's views of value.

Pricing for business markets

As explored in Chapter 6, business markets consist of individuals and businesses that purchase products for resale, for use in their own operations or for producing other products. Establishing prices for this category of business-to-business buyer sometimes differs from setting prices for consumers. Differences in the size of purchases, geographic factors and transport considerations require sellers to adjust prices. This section discusses several issues unique to the pricing of industrial products and business markets including discounts, geographic pricing, transfer pricing and price discrimination. The section concludes by considering the concept of economic value to the customer (EVC).

Price discounting

Producers commonly provide intermediaries with discounts from list prices. Although there are many types of discount, they usually fall into one of five categories (see Table 20.2):

1. trade
2. quantity
3. cash discounts
4. seasonal discounts
5. allowances.

Trade or functional discount
A reduction off the list price given by a producer to an intermediary for performing certain functions.

Trade discounts   A reduction off the list price given by a producer to an intermediary for performing certain functions is called a **trade or functional discount**. The functions for which intermediaries are compensated may include selling, transporting, storing, final processing and perhaps providing credit services. The level of discount can vary considerably from one industry to another.

TABLE 20.2   Discounts used for business markets

Type	Reason for use	Practical examples
Trade (functional)	To attract and keep resellers by compensating them for certain functions, such as transportation, warehousing, selling and providing credit	Hairdressers receive a discount for shampoos, hair dyes and other hair products from manufacturers of these items
Quantity	To encourage customers to buy large quantities and, in the case of cumulative discounts, to encourage customer loyalty	Large chains of tyre and exhaust outlets purchase parts at lower prices than individually owned outlets
Cash	To reduce expenses associated with accounts receivable by encouraging prompt payment	Companies operating in business markets often offer a discount for prompt payment
Seasonal	To allow resources to be used more efficiently by stimulating sales during off-peak periods	Hotels in large cities offer companies discounted accommodation for sales and other conferences during off-peak periods
Allowance	For trade-in allowances, the buyer is assisted in making the purchase by getting money back on used equipment; for promotional allowances, dealers are able to participate in advertising and sales support programmes	Companies such as Nestlé or Masterfoods pay promotional allowances to supermarkets for setting up and maintaining end-of-aisle displays to push their products

Quantity discounts
Reductions off the list price that reflect the economies of purchasing in large quantities.

Cumulative discounts
Quantity discounts aggregated over a stated period of time.

Non-cumulative discounts
One-off quantity discounts.

Cash discount
A simple price reduction given to a buyer for prompt payment or payment in cash.

Seasonal discount
A price reduction given to buyers who purchase goods or services out of season.

Allowance
A concession in price to achieve a desired goal.

Quantity discounts   Reductions from the list price that reflect the economies of purchasing in large quantities are called quantity discounts. Cost savings usually occur in four areas. Fewer but larger orders reduce per-unit selling costs; fixed costs, such as invoicing, remain the same or go down; raw materials, costs are lower, because quantity discounts may be available; longer production runs mean no increases in holding costs.[11] In addition, a large purchase may shift some of the storage, finance and risk-taking functions to the buyer.

Quantity discounts can be either cumulative or non-cumulative. Cumulative discounts are aggregated over a stated period of time. Purchases of £10 000 (€14 000) in a three-month period, for example, might entitle the buyer to a 5 per cent, or £500 (€700), rebate. Such discounts are supposed to reflect economies in selling and encourage the buyer to purchase from one seller. Non-cumulative discounts are one-off reductions in prices based on the number of units purchased, the monetary value of the order or the product mix purchased.

Cash discounts   A cash discount, or simple price reduction, is given for prompt payment or payment in cash. A policy to encourage prompt payment is a popular practice in setting prices. For example, '2/10 net 30' means that a 2 per cent discount will be allowed if the account is paid within 10 days. However, if the buyer does not pay within the 10-day period, the entire balance is due within 30 days without a discount. If the account is not paid within 30 days, interest may be charged.

Seasonal discounts   A price reduction given to buyers who purchase goods or services out of season is a seasonal discount. These discounts let the seller maintain steadier production during the year. For example, hotels in holiday resorts offer seasonal discounts for business customers at times of year when the weather is poor.

Allowances   Another type of reduction from the list price is an allowance – a concession in price to achieve a desired goal. Trade-in allowances are price reductions granted for handing in a used item when purchasing a new one. This type of allowance is popular in the aircraft industry. Another example is promotional allowances, which are price reductions granted to dealers for participating in advertising and sales support programmes intended to increase sales.

Geographic pricing

Geographic pricing involves reductions for transport costs or other costs associated with the physical distance between the buyer and the seller. Prices may be quoted as being FOB (free-on-board) factory or destination. An **FOB factory price** indicates the price of the merchandise at the factory before it is loaded on to the carrier vehicle; it thus excludes transport costs. The buyer must pay for shipping. An **FOB destination price** means the producer absorbs the costs of shipping the merchandise to customers.

To avoid the problems involved in charging different prices to each customer, **uniform geographic pricing**, sometimes called postage stamp pricing, may be used. The same price is charged to all customers regardless of geographic location, and the price is based on average shipping costs for all customers. Petrol, paper products and office equipment are often priced on a uniform basis.

Zone prices are regional prices that take advantage of a uniform pricing system; prices are adjusted for major geographic zones as the transport costs increase. For example, the prices of a manufacturer located in the northern French town of Lille may be higher for buyers in the south of France than for buyers in Paris.

Base point pricing is a geographic pricing policy that includes the price at the factory, plus freight charges from the base point nearest the buyer. This policy, which is now rarely used, can result in all buyers paying freight charges from one location, regardless of where the product was manufactured!

When the seller absorbs all or part of the actual freight costs, **freight absorption pricing** is being used. The seller might choose this method because it wishes to do business with a particular customer or to get more business; more business will cause the average cost to fall and counter-balance the extra freight cost. This strategy is used to improve market penetration and to retain a hold in an increasingly competitive market.

Transfer pricing

When one unit in a company sells a product to another unit within the same company, **transfer pricing** occurs. The price is determined by one of the following methods.

- *Actual full cost* – calculated by dividing all fixed and variable expenses for a period into the number of units produced.
- *Standard full cost* – calculated on what it would cost to produce the goods at full plant capacity.
- *Cost plus investment* – calculated as full cost, plus the cost of a portion of the selling unit's assets used for internal needs.
- *Market based cost* – calculated at the market price less a small discount to reflect the lack of sales effort and other expenses.

The choice of transfer pricing method depends on the company's management strategy and the nature of the units' interaction. The company might initially choose to determine price by the actual full cost method but later move to an alternative method.[12]

Price discrimination

A policy of **price discrimination** results in different prices being charged to give a group of buyers a competitive edge. Some forms of price discrimination are illegal in the EU. Price differentiation is a form of market segmentation that companies use to provide a marketing mix that satisfies different segments. Since different market segments perceive the value of a particular product differently, depending on the product's importance and

Transfer pricing
The type of pricing used when one unit in a company sells a product to another unit within the same company.

value to the business buyer, marketers may charge different prices to different market segments. Price discrimination can also be used to modify demand patterns, support sales of other products, dispose of obsolete goods or excessive inventories, fill excess production capacity and respond to competitors' activities in particular markets.[13]

Various conditions must be satisfied for price discrimination to be feasible. It must be possible to segment the market and the costs associated with doing so must not exceed the additional revenue generated. The practice should not break the law or breed customer discontent. Finally, the segment that is charged the higher price should not be vulnerable to competitor attack.

Price discrimination
A policy in which different prices are charged in order to give a particular group of buyers a competitive edge.

Economic value to the customer

The relationship between price and profitability was considered briefly at the start of this chapter. It is already clear that the ability to charge a higher price can have a major impact on profitability. It is also apparent that in order to achieve higher prices, businesses must be able to offer the customer some kind of differential advantage. In business markets, this advantage must usually be measurable in economic terms because businesses are driven by the need to reduce costs and increase revenue. Thus, a manufacturer of switch gears may be prepared to change to a more expensive supplier of fork-lift trucks if the products supplied have lower running costs. The concept of economic value to the customer encapsulates this notion and is a useful aid to determining prices in business markets. The underlying principle of **economic value to the customer (EVC)** is that a premium price can be charged while still offering the customer better value than the competition.

Economic value to the customer (EVC)
The underlying principle that a premium price can be charged while still offering the customer better value than the competition.

Marketing tools and techniques

Business-to-business pricing using EVC analysis

Analyzing economic value to the customer (EVC) is a useful aid to setting prices for business-to-business organizations. This example concerns the pricing of panel presses, which are supplied to the car parts business. The analysis focuses on the market leader and two other competitors.

The analysis begins by considering a reference product against which the costs of competing products are compared.

In this case, the market leader is used as the reference product. In this example, a car parts company buying the panel press from the market leader would expect to pay the following costs. The purchase price of the press is £60 000. Start-up costs, such as installation charges, staff training and lost production during installation, are £20 000, and post-purchase costs, including operating costs such as labour, servicing/maintenance and power, are £130 000.

This means that, over its life cycle, the panel press will cost the car parts company a total of £210 000.

Companies competing with the market leader present the customer with a different profile of costs. Company A has, by incorporating a number of new design features, managed to

cut the start-up costs for a comparable panel press to £10 000 and reduced post-purchase costs to £105 000. This means that the total costs for the press are £35 000 less than those for the market leader. The result is that Company A's press offers the customer an EVC of £210 000 less £115 000, which equals £95 000. Assuming that Company A charged a purchase price of £95 000 for the panel press, the customer would face total life-cycle costs that were equivalent to the market leading product. If, however, Company A decided to offer the panel press at a purchase price of only £80 000, the lower life-cycle costs of the product would give the customer a considerable financial incentive to buy.

Consider the position of a second competitor, Company B, with similar start-up and post-purchase costs to the market leader. This company has, through certain technological advances, increased the rate at which the press can be operated, potentially increasing productivity and therefore revenue for the customer. As a result, the press has the potential to offer an additional £50 000 profit contribution over the presses of the market leader and Company A. The EVC associated with this is £110 000, because this is the highest price the customer may be expected to pay.

There are various reasons why a costly product may provide good economic value to the customer, including lower set-up or running costs, the provision of superior servicing or other after-sales support, or a better warranty deal. It is even possible that the life of the product may be longer or that its productivity may be greater than that of lower-priced alternatives. Whatever the reason behind the value on offer, if EVC is to be demonstrated, the initial high price of the product must be justified by an overall lower lifetime cost. The Marketing Tools and Techniques box above provides a worked example of how EVC works in practice.

Stages for establishing prices

When going through the stages for establishing prices, marketers must be able to grasp target customers' evaluation of price and perceived value for money, as well as understand market trends and competitors' pricing moves.[14] The 'economics' of pricing-demand curves and price elasticity, plus the relationship in the market in question between demand, costs and profits must also be addressed. The marketer must ultimately choose from a variety of pricing approaches and specific pricing strategies. The remainder of this chapter reviews the eight stages for establishing prices in greater depth. The final section explains that, in operational situations, marketers must take a broader look at pricing concerns and exercise pragmatism in determining the price element of the marketing mix.

Stage 1: Selection of pricing objectives

Pricing objectives must be stated explicitly because they form the basis for decisions about other stages of pricing.[15] The statement of pricing objectives should include the time within which the objectives are to be accomplished. Marketers must set pricing objectives that are consistent with the company's overall and marketing objectives. Inconsistent objectives cause internal conflicts and confusion, and can prevent the business from achieving its overall goals.

Businesses normally have multiple pricing objectives, some short term and others long term. For example, the pricing objective of gaining market share is normally short term in that it often requires products to be priced lower than competitors' prices. Pricing objectives are typically altered over time.

Stage 2: Assessing the target market's evaluation of price and its ability to buy

The degree to which price is a significant issue for buyers depends on the type of product, the type of target market and the purchase situation. For example, most buyers are more sensitive to

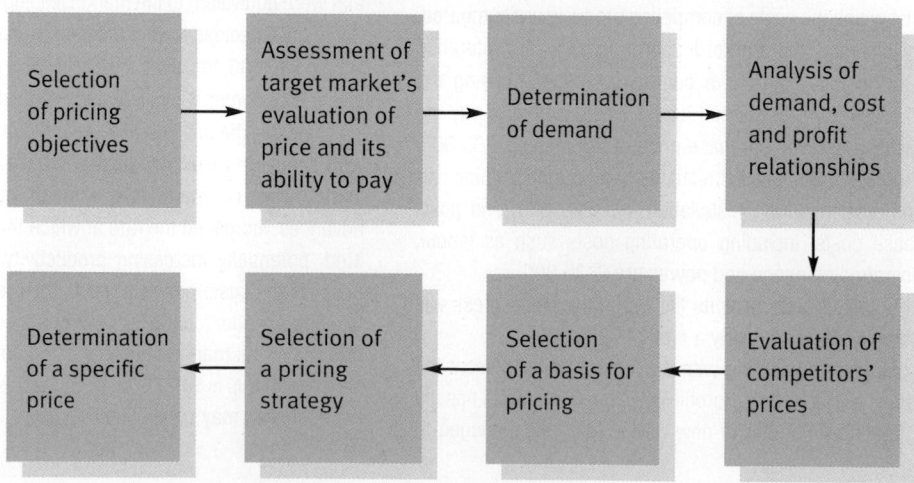

FIGURE 20.5
Stages for establishing prices

fuel prices than to the cost of a new passport. With respect to the type of target market, the price of an airline ticket is much more important to a tourist than to a business traveller. The purchase situation also has a major impact. Thus, visitors to concert venues and sporting arenas may be prepared to pay inflated prices for canned drinks and food, which is something they would not tolerate from their local supermarket. Assessing the target market's evaluation of price helps a marketer to judge how much emphasis to place on price.

Stage 3: Determining demand

Determining the demand for a product is the responsibility of marketing managers, who are aided in this task by marketing researchers and forecasters. Marketing research and forecasting techniques yield estimates of sales potential or the quantity of a product that could be sold during a specific period. Chapter 22 describes such techniques as surveys, time series analysis, correlation methods and market tests. These estimates are helpful in establishing the relationship between a product's price and the quantity demanded.

The demand curve For most products, the quantity demanded goes up as the price goes down, and goes down as the price goes up. Thus there is an inverse relationship between price and quantity demanded. Figure 20.6 illustrates the effect of one variable – price – on the quantity demanded. The classic **demand curve** (D1) is a graph of the quantity of products expected to be sold at various prices, if other factors remain constant.[16] It illustrates that as price falls, the quantity demanded usually increases. An improvement in elements of the marketing mix may cause a shift to, say, demand curve D2. In such a case, an increased quantity (Q2) will be sold at the same price (P). For example, if a manufacturer of engine oil improves the quality of its product, customers may be prepared to pay more for it because they do not need to change it as frequently.

> **Demand curve**
> A graph of the quantity of products expected to be sold at various prices, if other factors remain constant.

There are many types of demand, and not all conform to the classic demand curve. Prestige products, such as designer jewellery, fragrances and exclusive holidays seem to sell better at high prices than at low ones because their cost makes buyers feel superior.

The demand curve in Figure 20.7 shows the relationship between price and quantity for prestige products. Demand is greater, not less, at higher prices. For a certain price range – from P_1 to P_2 – the quantity demanded (Q_1) goes up to Q_2. If the price of a product goes too high, the quantity demanded goes down. When the price is raised from P_2 to P_3, quantity demanded goes back down from Q_2 to Q_1.

Demand fluctuations Changes in buyers' needs, variations in the effectiveness of other marketing mix variables, the presence of substitutes and dynamic environmental factors can influence demand. Internet search engines, restaurants and utility companies experience large fluctuations

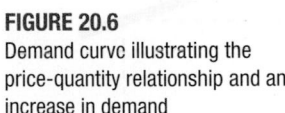

FIGURE 20.6
Demand curve illustrating the price-quantity relationship and an increase in demand

Source: Reprinted with permission from *Dictionary of Marketing Terms* by Peter D. Bennett, ed., 1988, p. 54, published by the American Marketing Association.

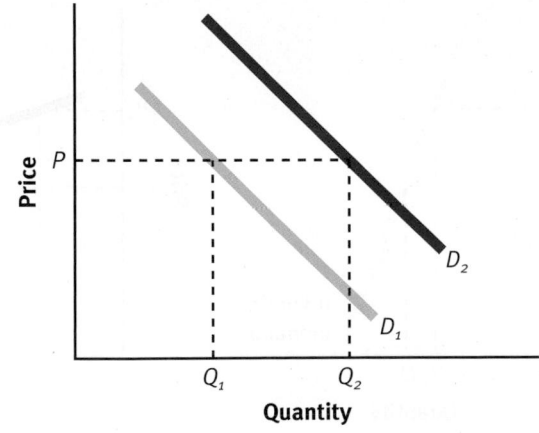

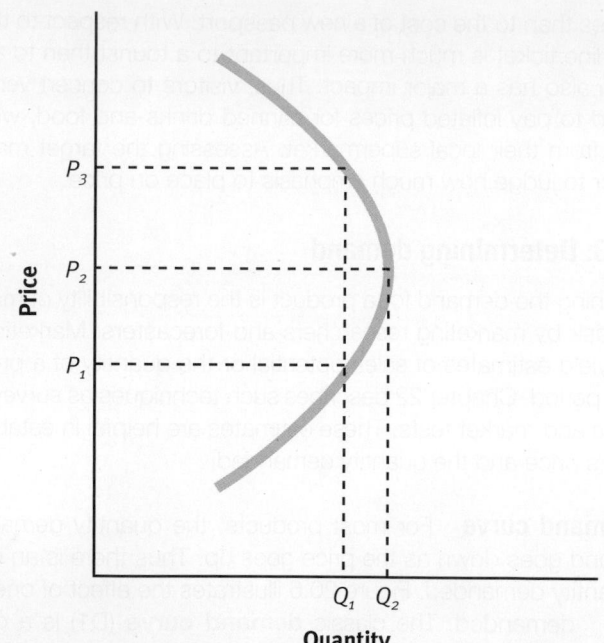

FIGURE 20.7

Demand curve illustrating the relationship between price and quantity for prestige products

in demand daily. Holiday companies, fireworks suppliers and swimming pool sellers also face demand fluctuations because of the seasonal nature of these items. The demand for smartphones, tablets and online banking services has changed significantly in recent years. In some cases, demand fluctuations are predictable and in others they are not.

Gauging price elasticity of demand   The discussion so far has considered how marketers identify the target market's evaluation of price and its ability to purchase, and how they examine whether price is related inversely or directly to quantity sold. The next stage in the process is to gauge price elasticity of demand. **Price elasticity of demand** provides a measure of the sensitivity of demand to changes in price. It is the percentage change in quantity demanded relative to a given percentage change in price (see Figure 20.8).[17] The percentage change in quantity demanded caused by a percentage change in price is much greater for elastic demand than for inelastic demand. For products such as

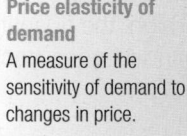

Price elasticity of demand

A measure of the sensitivity of demand to changes in price.

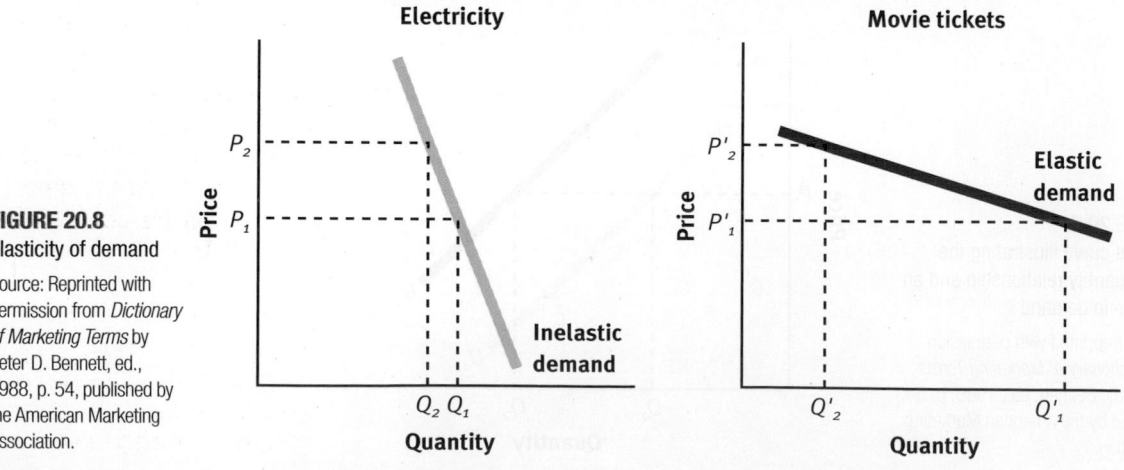

FIGURE 20.8

Elasticity of demand

Source: Reprinted with permission from *Dictionary of Marketing Terms* by Peter D. Bennett, ed., 1988, p. 54, published by the American Marketing Association.

electricity, medicines and cigarettes, demand is relatively inelastic. When price is increased, say from P_1 to P_2, quantity demanded goes down only a little, from Q_1 to Q_2. For products such as movie tickets, demand is relatively elastic. When price rises sharply, from P_1 to P_2, quantity demanded goes down a great deal, from Q_1 to Q_2.

Understanding the price elasticity of demand makes it easier for marketers to set a price. By analyzing total revenues as prices change, marketers can determine whether a product is 'price elastic'. Total revenue is price times quantity: thus 10 000 rolls of wallpaper sold in one year at a price of £10 (€14) per roll equals £100 000 (€140 000) of total revenue. If demand is *elastic,* a change in price causes an opposite change in total revenue – an increase in price will decrease total revenue, and a decrease in price will increase total revenue. An *inelastic* demand results in a change in the same direction in total revenue – an increase in price will increase total revenue, and a decrease in price will decrease total revenue. The following formula determines the price elasticity of demand:

$$\text{Price elasticity of demand} = \frac{\%\ \text{change in quantity demanded}}{\%\ \text{change in price}}$$

For example, if demand falls by 8 per cent when a seller raises the price by 2 per cent, the price elasticity of demand is −4 (the negative sign indicating the inverse relationship between price and demand). If demand falls by 2 per cent when price is increased by 4 per cent, then elasticity is half. The less elastic the demand, the more beneficial it is for the seller to raise the price. Products for which substitutes are not readily available and for which consumers have strong needs (for example, electricity or petrol) usually have inelastic demand.

Marketers cannot base prices solely on elasticity considerations. They must also examine the costs associated with different volumes and see what happens to profits.

Stage 4: Analysis of demand, cost and profit relationships

This section explores the relationships between demand, costs and profits. There are two approaches to understanding demand, cost and profit relationships: marginal analysis and break-even analysis.

Marginal analysis   Marginal analysis considers what happens to a company's costs and revenues when production (or sales volume) is changed by one unit. Both production costs and revenues must be evaluated. To determine the costs of production, it is necessary to distinguish between several types of cost. **Fixed costs** do not vary with changes in the number of units produced or sold. The cost of renting a hairdressing salon does not change if an extra hair dresser is recruited or more appointments are scheduled. **Average fixed cost**, the fixed cost per unit (or haircut) produced, is calculated by dividing fixed costs by the number of units produced.

Variable costs vary directly with changes in the number of units produced or services delivered. The wages for additional hair dressers and the cost of extra shampoos and hair dyes are extra. Variable costs are usually constant per unit – that is, twice as many hairdressers and twice as much hair products produce twice the amount of haircuts and others treatments. **Average variable cost**, the variable cost per unit produced, is calculated by dividing the variable costs by the number of units produced.

Total cost is the sum of average fixed costs and average variable costs multiplied by the quantity produced. The **average total cost** is the sum of the average fixed cost and the average variable cost. **Marginal cost (MC)** is the extra cost a company incurs when it produces one more unit of a product. Table 20.3 illustrates various costs and their relationships. Notice that the average fixed cost declines as the output increases. The average variable cost follows a U-shape, as does the average total cost.

Margin definitions (sidebar)

Fixed costs
Those costs that do not vary with changes in the number of units produced or sold.

Average fixed cost
The fixed cost per unit produced, calculated by dividing fixed costs by the number of units produced.

Variable costs
Those costs that vary directly with changes in the number of units produced or sold.

Average variable cost
The variable cost per unit produced, calculated by dividing the variable costs by the number of units produced.

Total cost
The sum of average fixed costs and average variable costs multiplied by the quantity produced.

Average total cost
The sum of the average fixed cost and the average variable cost.

Marginal cost (MC)
The extra cost a company incurs when it produces one more unit of a product.

TABLE 20.3   Costs and their relationships

1	2	3	4	5	6	7
Quantity	Fixed cost	Average fixed cost (2) ÷ (1)	Average variable cost	Average total cost (3) + (4)	Total cost (5) × (1)	Marginal cost
1	£40	£40.00	£20.00	£60.00	£60	
2	40	20.00	15.00	35.00	70	£10
3	40	13.33	11.67	25.00	75	5
4	40	10.00	12.50	22.50	90	15
5	40	8.00	14.00	22.00	110	20
6	40	6.67	16.67	23.33	140	30
7	40	5.71	20.00	25.71	180	40

Being that the average total cost continues to fall after the average variable cost begins to rise, its lowest point is at a higher level of output than that of the average variable cost. The average total cost is lowest at 5 units at a cost of £22, whereas the average variable cost is lowest at 3 units at a cost of £11.67. As shown in Figure 20.9, marginal cost equals average total cost at the latter's lowest level. In Table 20.3 this occurs between 5 and 6 units of production. Average total cost decreases as long as the marginal cost is less than the average total cost, and it increases when marginal cost rises above average total cost.

Marginal revenue (MR)
The change in total revenue that occurs when a company sells an additional unit of a product.

Marginal revenue (MR) is the change in total revenue that occurs when a company sells an additional unit of a product. Figure 20.10 depicts marginal revenue and a demand curve. Most businesses in Europe face downwards-sloping demand curves for their products. In other words, they must lower their prices to sell additional units. This situation means that each additional product sold provides the business with less revenue than the previous unit sold. MR then becomes less than average revenue, as Figure 20.10 shows. Eventually, MR reaches zero, and the sale of additional units merely hurts the company.

However, before the company can determine whether a unit makes a profit, it must know its cost, as well as its revenue, because profit equals revenue minus cost. If MR is a unit's addition to revenue and MC is a unit's addition to cost, then MR minus MC tells whether the unit is profitable or not. Table 20.4 illustrates the relationships between price, quantity sold, total revenue, marginal revenue, marginal cost and total cost. It indicates where maximum profits are possible at various combinations of price and cost.

Profit is maximized where MC = MR (see Table 20.4). In this table MC = MR at 4 units. The best price, therefore, is £33.75 and the profit is £45. Up to this point, the additional revenue

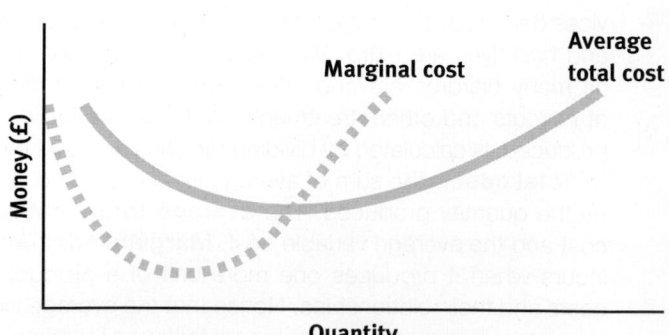

FIGURE 20.9
Typical marginal cost and average cost relationships

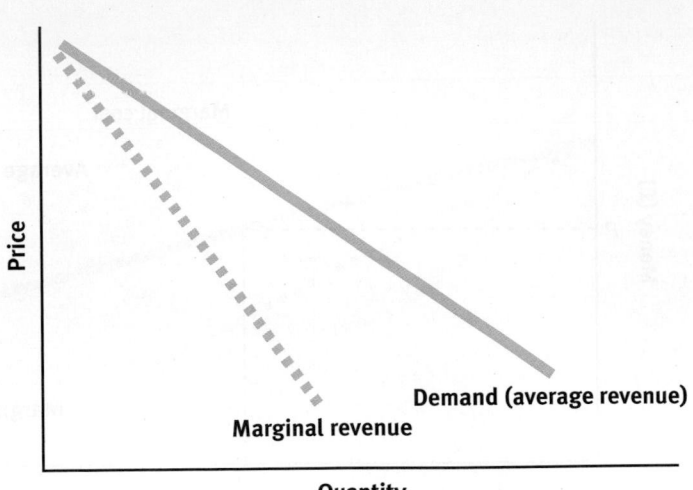

FIGURE 20.10
Typical marginal revenue and demand (average revenue) relationships

TABLE 20.4   Marginal analysis: method of obtaining maximum profit-producing price

1	2	3	4	5	6	7
Price	Quantity sold	Total revenue (1) × (2)	Marginal revenue	Marginal cost	Total cost	Profit (3) − (6)
£57.00	1	£57	£57	£–	£60	£–3
55.00	2	110	53	10	70	40
40.00	3	120	10	5	75	45
33.75*	**4**	**135**	**15**	**15**	**90**	**45**
30.00	5	150	15	20	110	40
27.00	6	162	12	30	140	22
25.00	7	175	13	40	180	−5

*Bold face indicates best price–profit combination.

generated from an extra unit of sale exceeds the additional total cost. Beyond this point, the additional cost of another unit sold exceeds the additional revenue generated, and profits decrease. If the price was based on minimum average total cost, £22 (Table 20.3), it would result in less profit: only £40 (Table 20.4) or 5 units at a price of £30 versus £45 for 4 units at a price of £33.75.

Graphically combining Figures 20.9 and 20.10 into Figure 20.11 shows that any unit for which MR exceeds MC adds to a company's profits, and any unit for which MC exceeds MR subtracts from a company's profits. The company should produce at the point where MR equals MC, because this is the most profitable level of production.

This discussion of marginal analysis may give the false impression that pricing can be highly precise. If revenue (demand) and cost (supply) remained constant, then prices could be set for maximum profits. In practice, however, cost and revenue change frequently. The competitive tactics of other companies or government action can quickly undermine a company's expectations of revenue. Thus marginal analysis is only a model from which to work. It offers little help in pricing new products before costs and revenues are established. However, when setting the prices of existing products, most marketers can benefit by understanding the relationship between marginal cost and marginal revenue.

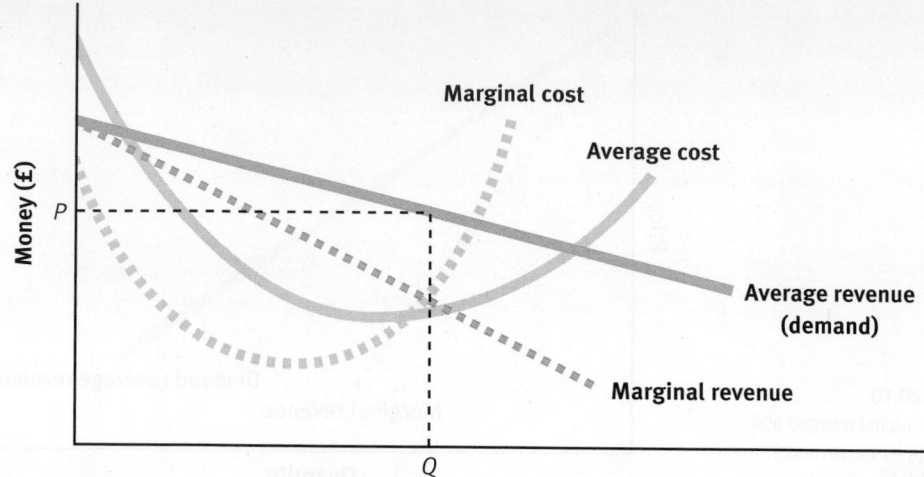

FIGURE 20.11
Combining the marginal cost and marginal revenue concepts for optimal profit

Break-even analysis   The point at which the costs of producing a product equal the revenue made from selling the product is the **break-even point**. If a hairdressing salon has total annual costs of £150 000 and in the same year sells £150 000 worth of haircuts and treatments, then the business has broken even: no profits, no losses.

Figure 20.12 illustrates the relationships of costs, revenue, profits and losses involved in determining the break-even point. Knowing the number of units necessary to break even is important in setting the price. If a product priced at £100 per unit has an average variable cost of £60 per unit, then the contribution to fixed costs is £40. If total fixed costs are £120 000, here is the way to determine the break-even point in units:

Break-even point
The point at which the costs of producing a product equal the revenue made from selling the product.

$$\text{Break-even point} = \frac{\text{fixed costs}}{\text{per unit contribution to fixed costs}}$$

$$= \frac{\text{fixed costs}}{\text{price} - \text{variable costs}}$$

$$= \frac{£120,000}{£40}$$

$$= 3\ 000 \text{ units}$$

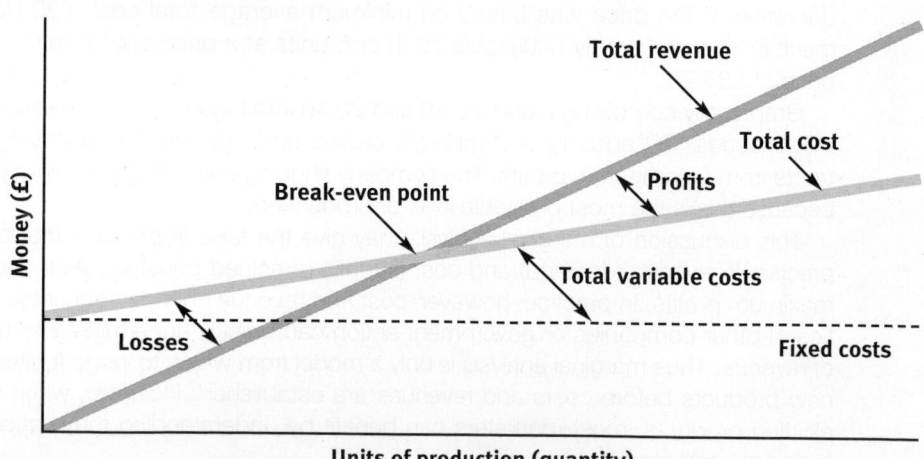

FIGURE 20.12
Determining the break-even point

To calculate the break-even point in terms of cash sales volume, multiply the break-even point in units by the price per unit. In the preceding example, the break-even point in terms of cash sales volume is 3 000 (units) times £100 or £300 000.

To use break-even analysis effectively, a marketer should determine the break-even point for each of several alternative prices. This allows the effects on total revenue, total cost and the break-even point for each price under consideration to be assessed. Although this analysis may not tell the marketer exactly what price to charge, it will identify price alternatives that should definitely be avoided.

Break-even analysis is simple and straightforward. It does assume, however, that the quantity demanded is basically fixed (inelastic) and that the major task in setting prices is to recover costs. It focuses more on how to break even than on how to achieve a pricing objective, such as percentage of market share or return on investment. Nonetheless, marketing managers can use this concept to determine whether a product will achieve at least a break-even volume. In other words, it is easier to answer the question 'Will we sell at least the minimum volume needed to break even?' than the question 'What volume of sales can we expect?'

Stage 5: Evaluation of competitors' prices

The prices marketers set will be influenced by competitors' pricing strategies. Marketers are better able to establish prices when they know the prices charged for competing brands. Learning competitors' prices is a regular function of marketing research. Many supermarkets and department stores systematically gather data on prices to support claims they make to customers about the price of their products. Price comparison websites such as www.moneysupermarket.com have also made information on prices readily accessible to customers.

Finding out what prices competitors are charging is not always easy, especially in producer and reseller markets. Even if a marketer has access to price lists, these may not reflect the actual prices at which competitive products are sold because those prices may be established through negotiation.

Marketers in an industry in which non-price competition prevails need competitive price information to ensure that their company's prices are the same as those of competitors. Sometimes a company's prices are designed to be slightly above competitors' prices to give its products an exclusive image. Alternatively, another company may use price as a competitive tool and attempt to set its prices below those of competitors. Aldi, Poundland, Kia and TK Maxx, for example, have all acquired market share through aggressive competitive prices.

Stage 6: Selecting a basis for pricing

Basis for pricing
Structures the calculation of the actual price.

After evaluating competitors' prices, a marketer must choose a **basis for pricing** to structure the calculation of the actual price. The nature of a product, its sales volume or the amount of product the company carries will determine how prices are calculated. For example, a procedure for pricing the thousands of products in a supermarket must be simpler and more direct than that for calculating the price of a limited-edition Waterford Wedgwood crystal giftware item.

Cost-based pricing
A pricing approach whereby a monetary amount or percentage is added to the cost of a product.

Cost-based pricing In **cost-based pricing**, a monetary amount or percentage is added to the cost of a product. The method thus involves calculations of desired margins or profit margins. Cost-based pricing does not necessarily take into account the economic aspects of supply and demand, nor does it necessarily relate to a specific pricing approach or ensure the attainment of pricing objectives. It is, however, simple and easy to implement. Two common cost-based approaches are cost plus pricing and mark-up pricing.

In **cost plus pricing**, the seller's costs are determined and the price is then set by adding a specified amount or percentage of the cost to the seller's costs. Cost plus pricing is appropriate when production costs are difficult to predict or production takes a long time. The government frequently uses pricing oriented to costs in granting defence contracts. The approach can be problematic, however, because some costs are difficult to determine. In periods of rapid inflation, cost plus pricing is popular, especially as the raw materials used may fluctuate in price.

Retailers commonly use **mark-up pricing**, where a price is derived by adding a predetermined percentage of the cost, called mark-up, to the cost of the product. Although the percentage mark-up in a retail store varies for different categories (35 per cent of cost for hardware items and 100 per cent of cost for a greeting card), the same percentage is often used to determine the price of items within a single product category, and may be standardized across an industry. Using a rigid percentage mark-up reduces pricing to a routine task that can be performed quickly. Mark-up can be stated as a percentage of the cost or as a percentage of the selling price.

The following example illustrates how percentage mark-ups are determined and points out the differences between the two methods. Assume that a retailer purchases a tin of mushrooms at 45p, adds 15p to the cost and then prices the mushrooms at 60p:

$$\text{Mark-up as a percentage of cost} = \frac{\text{mark-up}}{\text{cost}} = \frac{15}{45} = 33\tfrac{1}{3}\%$$

$$\text{Mark-up as a percentage of selling price} = \frac{\text{mark-up}}{\text{selling price}} = \frac{15}{60} = 25\%$$

An average percentage mark-up on cost may be as high as 100 per cent or more for jewellery or as low as 20 per cent for this textbook.

Demand-based pricing

A pricing approach based on the level of demand for a product is **demand-based pricing**. This approach results in a high price when demand for a product is strong and a low price when demand is weak. Pricing of leisure amenities often operates on this basis, with higher prices when demand is highest at weekends and during peak holiday periods. The amounts of a product that consumers will demand at different prices are estimated and the price that generates the highest total revenue is selected. Compared with cost-based pricing, demand-based pricing places a company in a better position to gain higher profits.

Competition-based pricing

In using **competition-based pricing**, an organization considers costs and revenue as secondary to competitors' prices. This approach is important if competing products are almost homogeneous and the company is servicing markets in which price is the key variable of the marketing strategy.[18] A business that uses competition-based pricing may choose to be below competitors' prices, above competitors' prices or at the same level. These firms need to be aware that online price comparison websites are making it easier than ever for consumers to compare prices, as the Topical Insight box explains. The price of domestic electricity is determined using competition-oriented pricing. Competition-based pricing should help attain a pricing objective to increase sales or market share.

Marketing-oriented pricing

More complex than cost-or competition-oriented pricing, **marketing-oriented pricing** takes account of external factors as seen by the customer and experienced by channel members, in addition to internal cost and performance drivers.

The price set must reflect the product's marketing strategy: its target market profile, brand positioning and sales targets. The price point – the actual ticket or displayed

The rise of the price comparison website

Topical insight

Shifting shopping patterns have resulted in an explosion of internet purchasing, as consumers seek the convenience of shopping at a time, place and manner of their choosing. The opportunity to compare price and choose the most cost-effective options is an attractive feature for many of these value-conscious shoppers. A rapid growth in price comparison websites, such as GoCompare.com and uswitch.co.uk, has fuelled this need.

Price comparison websites first emerged in 1999, when two sites were launched: moneysupermarket.com, which focused on mortgages and Kelkoo.fr, specializing in retailing. Since that time, the market has expanded dramatically, as reflected in the fortunes of these first entrants. While moneysupermarket.com has extended beyond financial offerings to include a wide range of products and services; Kelkoo.fr now operates in 12 countries, including recent launches in Brazil and the US.

The number of websites has grown dramatically in recent years. These include a plethora of generalist sites, such as gocompare.com, and moneysavingexpert.com; as well as more specialist ones focusing on particular product groups, such as hotelscomparison.com for hotels, pintprice.com for beer prices around the world, and mysupermarket.co.uk for the weekly food shop.

Although the main aim of price comparison websites is to identify the best deals for consumers, many go much further than reporting the basic price. In its comparison of broadband offers, moneysupermarket.com provides details of total first-year cost, line rental fees, delivery and connection charges. Hotel site Trivago, while offering the price comparisons that consumers expect, also includes customer rankings of the different booking websites and of the locations and accommodation it features. For example, hotels are rated according to location, facilities, décor, quality of the bed, bedroom, bathroom, food and staff. So while price is important, it seems that other dimensions are important in shaping perceived consumer value.

However, some sites have been criticized for misleading consumers. In 2014 the UK Financial Conduct Authority published a critical report about insurance price comparison websites which suggested that: (i) websites did not always provide product information in a clear and consistent manner; (ii) there was a lack of clarity in some cases about the role of the websites, including their involvement in distributing the products or services that they covered; and (iii) some websites were not complying with their regulatory obligations. Meanwhile, UK consumer group Which? has argued that more regulation is needed, after its research showed that consumers are not always treated fairly by these sites.

Sources: BBC Business News, 'Price comparison sites should be regulated, Which? says', 24 March 2012 (accessed March 2015): www.bbc.co.uk/news/business-17492343; Financial Conduct Authority, Thematic Review: Webcredible, 'Future comparisons: Price comparison websites in the general insurance sector', July 2014 (accessed March 2015): www.fca.org.uk/static/documents/thematic-reviews/tr14-11.pdf; 'What's next for price comparison websites?' August 2009 (accessed March 2015): www.webcredible.com/blog-reports/white-papers/price-comparison.pdf; www.marketingdonut.co.uk/marketing/marketing-strategy/pricing/a-guide-to-price-comparison-websites.

price – must also be in harmony with the other marketing mix ingredients. For example, an exclusive private dental practice will fail if its facilities are poor. Marketers must be aware of competing products' prices and their own product's value as perceived by the targeted customer. The customer has to be receptive to the determined price. This customer-focused view is also reflected in two other criteria: the price–quality relationship of the product and the explicability of the finalized prices. Just how plausible to the customer is the recommended price? If the product is part of a range, its price point will affect the other product lines on offer, and the whole range must be priced to avoid an individual product harming the achieved price and image of related lines. While a business must ensure that its costs of production, distribution and marketing are covered, it also has to recognize that its dealers and distributors must make an adequate margin on units sold and set its prices to its distribution channel partners accordingly. These channel members and the ultimate customer may expect to negotiate over price – very common in business-to-business markets – so the price must be set to permit such negotiating and discounting. Trade and government regulations may affect the flexibility a business has in establishing prices. For example, EU anti-dumping laws forbid businesses from selling products in the EU at lower than cost price.[19]

Stage 7: Selection of a pricing strategy

Pricing strategy
An approach to influencing and determining pricing decisions.

A **pricing strategy** is an approach designed to influence and determine pricing decisions. Pricing strategies help marketers to solve the practical problems of establishing prices. **Differential pricing** means charging different prices according to different buyers for the same quality and quantity of a product. New product pricing involves strategies that are geared to dealing with pricing new products. **Product line pricing** means establishing and adjusting the prices of multiple products within a product line. **Psychological pricing** aims to encourage consumers to buy based on their emotional responses to price. **Professional pricing** is used by people who have great skill or experience in a particular field or activity. In **promotional pricing**, the pricing relates to a short-term promotion of a particular product. The most common pricing strategies are described in Table 20.5.

Differential pricing
A pricing strategy involving charging different prices to different buyers for the same quality and quantity of product.

Many countries have legislation controlling the use of **misleading pricing**, which may intentionally confuse or dupe consumers. The UK Consumer Protection Act 1987,

TABLE 20.5 Common pricing strategies

Differential pricing
Involves changing different prices to different buyers for the same quality and quantity of a product. For example, red roses are more expensive on Valentine's Day than at other times.

- Negotiated pricing
  Common in some industries, occurs when the final price is established through bargaining between seller and customer. E.g.: consumers commonly negotiate prices for houses or second-hand goods.

- Secondary market pricing
  Setting one price for the primary target market and a different one for others. Price in the secondary market may be lower. E.g.: some restaurants offer 'early-bird' prices.

- Periodic discounting
  Temporary reduction of prices on a systematic basis. E.g.: fashion retailers have annual sales in January and July, while car dealers offer discounts on current models when the next year's models are introduced.

- Random discounting
  Alleviates the problems of periodic discounting by temporarily reducing prices on an unsystematic basis. Customers cannot predict when price reductions will occur. Useful way of attracting new customers.

New product pricing
Setting the right base price for a new product is critical. The base price is easily adjusted and can be set high to recover development costs quickly. When marketers set base prices, they consider how the market will develop and what the effects will be of competitors entering. Sometimes prices will be set to discourage competitive entry. Two strategies can be used.

- Price skimming
  Charging the highest possible price that buyers who most desire the product will pay. This 'pioneer approach' is the most flexible introductory base price. Demand tends to be inelastic in the introductory stage of the PLC. E.g.: tablet computers. This approach generates much needed initial cash flows to help off-set sizeable developmental costs, but can attract competitors who see the high prices as meaning the market is lucrative.

- Penetration pricing
  Setting a price below the prices of competing brands in order to penetrate a market, produce large unit sales volumes and rapidly gain market share. Penetration pricing is popular even for well-known products. This approach is less flexible than price skimming, but sometimes firms use it having first skimmed the market at a higher price. The approach is particularly appropriate when demand is highly elastic.

Product line pricing
Involves pricing a whole line of items rather than setting prices for individual items separately. The aim is to maximize profits for the entire line, rather than focusing on the profitability of a single product.

- Captive pricing
  The basic product in a line is priced low, while the price of items needed to operate or enhance it may be higher. E.g.: printers are relatively cheap, but the cartridges are often priced relatively high.

- Premium pricing
  Often used when there are several versions of the same product. The highest quality or 'best' products are given the highest prices, while others are priced to appeal to price-sensitive shoppers or to those who seek product-specific features. E.g.: beer and ice cream.

(Continued)

TABLE 20.5   Continued

- Bait pricing

  To attract customers a low price may be set on one item in the product line with the intention of selling higher priced items too. E.g.: a computer retailer might advertise its lowest price model, hoping to attract customers who may then purchase a more expensive version.

- Price lining

  A limited number of prices is set for selected groups or lines. The assumption is that demand is inelastic for some groups of products. If prices are attractive, customers will not react to slight changes in price. E.g.: a fashion retailer that has dresses priced at £30 (€42), £50 (€70) and £70 (€98) may not attract many more sales if the prices are dropped by £2 or £3. The demand curve looks like a series of steps.

Psychological pricing

Encourages purchases based on emotional rather than rational responses. Customers are influenced to perceive the price to be more attractive.

- Reference pricing

  Involves pricing a product at a moderate level and positioning it next to a more expensive brand. It is intended customers will use the higher price as an external reference price and compare the moderately priced brand favourably.

- Bundle pricing

  Involves packaging together two or more products, usually complementary ones, at a single price. The single price is usually below the combined prices for the items. E.g.: some computer manufacturers bundle together a computer, software and internet service.

- Multiple unit pricing

  Occurs when two or more identical products are packaged together and sold for a single price, usually at a lower per-unit price. Customers benefit from cost savings and convenience. E.g.: twin packs of soap, four packs of lightbulbs and six packs of beer.

- Everyday low prices (EDLP)

  Reduces the use of frequent short-term price reductions, by setting a low price on a consistent basis rather than setting higher prices and frequently discounting. Prices are set far enough below competitors' prices to make customers confident they are receiving a fair price. E.g.: Wal-Mart and Asda use this approach.

- Odd/even pricing

  Ending the price with certain numbers is assumed to influence buyers' perceptions. Odd pricing assumes that more of a product will be sold at £99.95 than at £100. The notion is that customers will think that the product is a bargain at £99, plus a few pence. Even prices are used to give a product an exclusive, high-quality or upmarket image. E.g.: a premium silk tie may retail at £50 rather than £49.95.

- Customary pricing

  Certain goods are sometimes priced on the basis of tradition. E.g.: for many years UK public telephones were geared to use 2p and 10p coins. BT initially dealt with rising costs by allowing less call time for the same money.

- Prestige pricing

  Prices are set at an artificially high level to provide prestige or a quality image. E.g.: the quality of service provided by an exclusive beauty salon is sometimes associated with price.

Promotional pricing

Price is an ingredient in the marketing mix that is often coordinated with promotion. Sometimes the two are interrelated so that the pricing approach is promotion oriented. Promotional pricing is a pricing approach whereby pricing is related to the short-term promotion of a particular product.

- Price leaders

  Products sold below usual mark-up or near cost; used most often in supermarkets and department stores to attract customers by giving low prices on just a few items. Once in store, it is hoped they will also buy higher priced items.

- Special event pricing

  Advertised 'sales' or price cutting linked to a season, event or holiday to increase sales volume. E.g.: if the pricing objective is survival, special sales may help to generate much needed operating capital.

- Comparison discounting

  Setting the price at a particular level so that it is simultaneously compared with a higher price. The higher price may be the previous product price or a manufacturer's suggested retail price. Consumers are becoming more suspicious of this approach.

Professional pricing

Used by those who have great skill or experience in a particular area. Some professionals, for example lawyers and some estate agents, who provide such products feel that their fees (prices) should not relate directly to their time and involvement, instead charging a standard fee.

which makes it illegal to mislead customers about the price at which products or services are offered for sale, is typical. This act contains a code of practice that, although not legally binding, encourages companies to offer explanations whenever price comparisons or reductions are made.

Product line pricing
Establishing and adjusting prices of multiple products within a product line.

Psychological pricing
A pricing strategy designed to encourage purchases that are based on emotional rather than rational responses.

Professional pricing
Pricing used by people who have great skill or experience in a particular field or activity.

Promotional pricing
Pricing related to the short-term promotion of a particular product.

Misleading pricing
Pricing policies that intentionally confuse or dupe consumers.

Stage 8: Determining a specific price

The basis for pricing and pricing strategies should direct and structure the selection of a final price. This means that marketers should establish pricing objectives; know something about the target market; and determine demand, price elasticity, costs and competitive factors. In addition to these economic factors, the manner in which pricing is used in the marketing mix will affect the final price.

Although a systematic approach to pricing is suggested here, in practice prices may be set by trial and error or after only limited planning. Later on, marketers determine whether the revenue minus costs yields a profit. This approach to pricing is not recommended, because unsuitable price levels are often set.

Another issue is that the external trading environment can change quickly and constantly, consumers are relatively fickle and revise their expectations, market developments alter the pattern of the market, and competitors continually modify their marketing mix – a price-cutting campaign, a new model launch, a high-profile advertising campaign or, perhaps, a customer service initiative.

In the absence of government price controls, pricing remains a flexible and convenient way to adjust the marketing mix. In most situations, prices can be adjusted quickly – in a matter of minutes or over a few days. The other components of the marketing mix do not have this flexibility or freedom.

In the context of the marketing mix, price can generally be altered relatively quickly, especially when compared with the time and resources required to launch a new product, modify a channel of distribution, improve customer service or create and run a new advertising campaign. Even in this context, however, the shrewd marketer should endeavour to minimize price cutting and discounting. In most cases the only short-term beneficiary of a price war is the consumer. Indeed, the business, its distributors, the brand or the long-term flexibility of the marketing mix may suffer as a consequence. Although marketers must never lose sight of the 'economics' of pricing, there must be a sensible trade-off, or 'pricing balance', between economic analysis and pragmatism.

Summary

Price is the value placed on what is exchanged. The buyer exchanges buying power – which depends on the buyer's income, credit and wealth – for satisfaction or utility. *Financial price* is the basis of market exchanges – the quantified value of what is exchanged. However, price does not always involve a financial exchange; barter, the trading of products, is the oldest form of exchange.

Price is a key element in the marketing mix because it relates directly to the generation of total revenue. The profit factor can be determined mathematically by first multiplying price by quantities sold to calculate total revenues and then subtracting total costs. Price is often the only variable in the marketing mix that can be adjusted quickly and easily to respond to changes in the external environment.

A product offering can compete on either a price or a non-price basis. *Price competition* emphasizes price as the product differential. Prices fluctuate frequently, and sellers must respond to competitors changing their prices. *Non-price competition* emphasizes product differentiation through distinctive product features, services, product quality or other factors. Establishing brand loyalty by using non-price competition works best when the product can be physically differentiated and these distinguishing characteristics are viewed as desirable.

Pricing objectives are overall goals that describe what a company wants to achieve through its pricing efforts. The most fundamental pricing objective is the business's survival. Price can easily be adjusted to increase sales volume to levels that match the company's expenses. Profit objectives, which are usually stated in terms of actual monetary amounts or percentage change, are normally set at a satisfactory level rather than at a level designed for profit maximization. Pricing for return on investment (ROI) sets a specified rate of return as its objective. A pricing objective to maintain or increase market share is established in relation to total industry sales. Other types of pricing objective include cash flow, status quo and product quality.

Nine factors affect pricing decisions:

(1) organizational and marketing objectives, (2) pricing objectives, (3) costs, (4) other marketing mix variables, (5) channel member expectations, (6) buyers' perceptions, (7) competition, (8) legal and regulatory issues and (9) perceived value for money. Thus, pricing decisions should be consistent with the organization's goals and mission. Pricing objectives heavily influence price-setting decisions.

When interpreting and responding to prices, customers compare prices with internal or external reference prices. An *internal reference price* is a price developed in the buyer's mind through experience with the product. When there is less experience, consumers rely more heavily on external reference prices. An *external reference price* is a comparison price provided by others, such as retailers, manufacturers or competing products. In the context of price, buyers can be characterized according to their degree of value consciousness, price consciousness and prestige-sensitivity. *Value-conscious consumers* are concerned about both the price and the quality of a product. *Price-conscious consumers* strive to pay low prices. *Prestige-sensitive consumers* focus on purchasing products that signify prominence and status.

Most marketers view a product's cost as the floor below which a product cannot be priced. Due to the interrelationship of the marketing mix variables, price can affect product, promotion, place/distribution and service-level decisions. The revenue that channel members expect for the functions they perform must also be considered when making price decisions.

Buyers' perceptions of price vary so a marketer needs to be aware of these issues when determining the price. Knowledge of the prices charged for competing brands is essential so that a company can adjust its prices relative to those of competitors. Government regulations and legislation can also influence pricing decisions through laws to enhance competition and by invoking price controls – for example, to curb inflation.

Perceived value for money is an important consideration when setting prices. Consumers do not regard price purely as the monetary value being demanded in exchange for a good or a service. The quality of the item, its brand image, purpose, usage and overall appeal – along with the consumer's previous experiences and certain tangible benefits such as interest-free credit and warranties – dictate the consumer's view of value for money.

Unlike consumers, industrial or business buyers purchase products to use in their own operations or for producing other products. When adjusting prices, business sellers take into consideration the size of the purchase, geographic factors and transport requirements. Producers commonly provide *trade* or *functional discounts* off list prices to intermediaries. The five categories of discount include (1) trade, (2) quantity, (3) cash discounts, (4) seasonal discounts and (5) allowances.

Geographic pricing involves reductions for transport costs or other costs associated with the physical distance between the buyer and the seller. An *FOB factory price* means that the buyer pays for shipping from the factory; an *FOB destination price* means that the producer pays for shipping the merchandise. When the seller charges a fixed average cost for transport, the practice is known as *uniform geographic pricing*. *Zone prices* take advantage of a uniform pricing system adjusted for major geographic zones as the transport costs increase. *Base point pricing* involves prices being adjusted for shipping expenses incurred by the seller from the base point nearest the buyer. A seller who absorbs all or part of the freight costs is using *freight absorption pricing*. *Transfer pricing* occurs when one company unit sells a product to another unit within the same company.

When a *price discrimination* policy is adopted, different prices are charged in order to give a group of buyers a competitive edge. In some countries, price differentials are legal only in circumstances where competition is not damaged.

The concept of *economic value to the customer (EVC)* is sometimes used in business markets to aid price setting. The underlying principle is that a premium price can be charged while still offering better value than the competition.

The eight stages in the process of establishing prices are: (1) selecting pricing objectives; (2) assessing the target market's evaluation of price and its ability to buy; (3) determining demand; (4) analyzing demand, cost and profit relationships; (5) evaluating competitors' prices; (6) selecting a basis for pricing; (7) developing a pricing strategy; and (8) determining a specific price.

The first stage, selecting pricing objectives, is critical because pricing objectives are the foundation on which the decisions of subsequent stages are based. The second stage in establishing prices is an assessment of the target market's evaluation of price and its ability to buy. This shows how much emphasis to place on price and may help determine how far above the competition prices can be set.

In the third stage, a business must determine the demand for its product. The classic *demand curve* is a graph of the quantity of products expected to be sold at various prices, if other factors are held constant. It illustrates that, as price falls, the quantity demanded usually increases. However, for prestige products, there is a direct positive relationship between price and quantity demanded: up to a certain point demand increases as price increases. Next, *price elasticity of demand* – the percentage change in quantity demanded relative to a given percentage change in price – must be determined.

Analysis of demand, cost and profit relationships – the fourth stage of the process – can be accomplished through marginal analysis or break-even analysis. Marginal analysis considers what happens to a company's costs and revenues when production (or sales volume) is changed by one unit. *Fixed costs* do not vary with changes in the number of units produced or sold; *average fixed cost* is the fixed cost per unit produced. *Variable costs* vary directly with changes in the number of units produced or sold. *Average variable cost* is the variable cost per unit produced. *Total cost* is the sum of average fixed costs and average variable costs multiplied by the quantity produced. *Average total cost* is the sum of the average fixed cost and average variable cost. The optimum price is the point at which *marginal cost (MC)* equals *marginal revenue (MR)*. Marginal analysis offers little help in pricing new products before costs and revenues are established. Break-even analysis involves determining the number of units necessary to break-even. The point at which the costs of producing a product equal the revenue made from selling the product is the *break-even point*.

A pricing strategy is an approach designed to achieve pricing and marketing objectives. The most common pricing strategies are differential pricing, new product pricing, product line pricing, psychological pricing, professional pricing and promotional pricing. The three major dimensions on which prices can be based are cost, demand and competition. In using *cost-based pricing,* a company determines price by adding a monetary amount or percentage to the cost of the product. Two common cost-based pricing approaches are *cost plus pricing* and *mark-up pricing*.

Demand-based pricing is based on the level of demand for a product and requires marketers to estimate the amounts of a product that buyers will demand at different prices. Demand-based pricing results in a high price when demand for a product is strong and a low price when demand is weak. In the case of *competition-based pricing,* costs and revenues are secondary to competitors' prices.

Competition-based pricing and cost approaches may be combined to arrive at the price levels necessary to generate a profit. *Marketing-oriented pricing* involves a company taking account of a wide range of factors including marketing strategy, competition, value to the customer, price-quality relationships, explicability, costs, product line pricing, negotiating margins, political factors and the effect on distributors/retailers.

A *pricing strategy* is an approach designed to influence and determine pricing decisions. Using *differential pricing* involves charging different prices for the same quality or quantity of product. *Negotiated pricing, secondary market discounting, periodic discounting* and *random discounting* are forms of differential pricing. Two strategies used in new product pricing are price skimming and penetration pricing. With *price skimming,* a company charges the highest price that buyers who most desire the product will pay. *Penetration pricing* sets a price below the prices of competing brands in order to penetrate the market and produce a larger unit sales volume.

Product line pricing establishes and adjusts the prices of multiple products within a product line. This strategy can include *captive pricing, premium pricing, bait pricing* and *price lining. Psychological pricing* encourages purchases that are based on emotional rather than rational responses. Examples of this approach include *reference pricing, bundle pricing, multiple-unit pricing, everyday low prices (EDLP), odd/even pricing.* Marketers try to influence buyers' perceptions of the prices of the product by ending the price with certain numbers. *Customary pricing* is based on traditional prices. With *prestige pricing,* prices are set at an artificially high level to project a quality image. *Professional pricing* is used by people who have great skill or experience in a particular field. *Promotional pricing* is a pricing approach in which pricing is related to the short-term promotion of a particular product. *Price leaders, special event pricing* and *comparison discounting* are examples of promotional pricing.

Misleading pricing – in which consumers are intentionally misled about the true cost or value of a product or service – is increasingly monitored and tackled through consumer protection legislation. The basis for a price and the pricing strategy should direct and structure the selection of a final price. For the most part, pricing remains a flexible and convenient way to adjust the marketing mix.

Key links

- Price impacts strongly on how businesses fare competitively. The concepts of competitive strategy and the competitive environment are explored in Chapters 2 and 3.

- Price is a key element of the marketing mix, because it directly affects how much revenue is generated. Understanding pricing concepts is critical to the development of effective marketing programmes, as discussed in Part Three.

- Pricing impacts significantly on a brand's positioning, as described in Chapter 8.

Important terms

Allowance
Average fixed cost
Average total cost
Average variable cost
Base point pricing
Basis for pricing
Break-even point
Cash discount
Competition-based pricing
Cost plus pricing
Cost-based pricing

Cumulative discounts
Demand curve
Demand-based pricing
Differential pricing
Economic value to the customer (EVC)
External reference price
Fixed costs
Financial price
FOB destination price
FOB factory price
Freight absorption pricing
Geographic pricing
Internal reference price
Marginal cost
Marginal revenue
Marketing-oriented pricing
Mark-up pricing
Misleading pricing
Non-cumulative discounts
Non-price competition
Perceived value for money
Prestige-sensitive consumers
Price
Price competition
Price discrimination
Price elasticity of demand
Price-conscious consumers
Pricing objectives
Pricing strategy

Product line pricing
Professional pricing
Promotional pricing
Psychological pricing
Quantity discounts
Seasonal discount
Total cost
Trade or functional discount
Transfer pricing
Uniform geographic pricing
Value-conscious consumers
Variable costs
Zone prices

Discussion and review questions

1. Why are pricing decisions so important to a business?

2. Compare and contrast price and non-price competition. Describe the conditions under which each form works better.

3. How does a pricing objective of return on investment (ROI) differ from a pricing objective to increase market share?

4. Why is it crucial to consider both marketing objectives and pricing objectives when making pricing decisions?

5. In what ways do other marketing mix variables affect pricing decisions?

6. What types of expectation may channel members have about producers' prices, and how do these expectations affect pricing decisions?

7. How do legal and regulatory forces influence pricing decisions?

8. Why must marketers consider consumers' perceptions of value for money when setting prices?

9. What is the difference between a price discount and price discrimination?

10. Why is the concept of EVC (economic value to the customer) important when setting prices in business-to-business markets?

11. Identify the eight stages that make up the process of establishing prices.

12. Why do most demand curves demonstrate an inverse relationship between price and quantity?

13. List the characteristics of products that have inelastic demand. Give several examples of such products.

14. Explain why optimum profits should occur when marginal cost equals marginal revenue.

15. The Chambers Company has just gathered estimates in preparation for a break-even analysis for a new product. Variable costs are £7 per unit. The additional plant will cost £48 000. The new product will be charged £18 000 a year for its share of general overheads. Advertising expenditure will be £80 000, and £55 000 will be spent on distribution.

If the product sells for £12, what is the break-even point in units? What is the break-even point in sales volume?

16. For what types of product would a pioneer price skimming approach be most appropriate? For what types of product would penetration pricing be more effective?

17. Why do consumers associate price with quality? When should prestige pricing be used?

18. What factors must be taken into consideration when adopting a marketing-oriented approach to pricing?

Recommended readings

Cram, T., *Smarter Pricing* (FT/Prentice-Hall, 2006).

Harvard Business Review, *Harvard Business Review on Pricing* (Harvard Business Press, 2008).

Hill, P., *Pricing for Profit: How to Develop a Powerful Pricing Strategy for Your Business* (Kogan Page, 2013).

Macdivitt, H. and Wilkinson, M., *Value-Based Pricing: Drive Sales and Boost Your Bottom Line by Creating, Communicating and Capturing Customer Value* (McGraw-Hill Professional, 2011).

Nagle, T., Hogan, J. and Zale, J., *The Strategy and Tactics of Pricing* (Pearson, 2014).

Smith, T., *Pricing Strategy: Setting Price Levels, Managing Price Discounts and Establishing Price Structures* (South-Western, 2011).

Internet exercise

Whether interested in buying a used or a new car, buying it outright, on credit terms or by leasing, www.buyacar.co.uk offers car buyers a comprehensive website. Take a look at this online retailer at: www.buyacar.co.uk.

1. Find the lowest-priced new Audi A1 available today and list its features.

2. If you wanted to purchase this Audi, what is the lowest monthly payment you could make and what would it cost if you were to buy this model outright?

3. Compare and contrast the relative benefits of leasing and buying this car outright.

Group tasks

1. When Apple launched its smartwatch, how would the price for this innovative product have been established?

2. Marketers drop prices with ease but struggle to raise prices. Are there examples of products or brands which have successfully achieved significant price rises? Explore what had to be put in place in order to achieve such a price rise.

Applied mini-case

Consumers can pay just 20 pence to write with a disposable biro, yet fancy fountain pens have become a common sight in the hands of influential businesspeople. Such pens have high price tags and are much more difficult to maintain than ballpoints, felt-tip pens or roller-ball pens. However, recent sales figures indicate that the semi-obsolete fountain pen is making a comeback as the writing instrument of choice for status-minded individuals. Of the premium-priced fountain pens, those produced by Montblanc are probably the most prestigious. Named after the highest mountain in Europe, these German-made fountain pens cost from about £100 to £5000 (for a solid gold one). The most popular model costs about £300. Prestige pricing has worked well for Montblanc, placing the pen in the same category as Rolex watches, BMW cars and Gucci luggage.

Question

A company competing in the same sector as Montblanc has asked you to prepare a report explaining the factors that influence the pricing decisions they should make for a new range of pens. What areas should your report include?

Order just about anything from Amazon at a reasonable price

Case study

Online retail pioneer Amazon.com has built a profitable $74.5 billion business by paying close attention to pricing details. Founded as a web-based bookstore with discount prices, Amazon has since expanded into dozens of product categories and countries. The company never stops investing in technology to upgrade its sites, systems and offerings. Although hefty high-tech costs are a drag on profit margins, they are essential to Amazon's strategy of attracting customers, and keeping them loyal by making the shopping experience easy, fast and fun.

One hallmark of Amazon's pricing is its long-running offer of free delivery. For UK shoppers, many items can be delivered free to UK addresses under the so-called Super Saver Delivery. This free of charge delivery is also available for orders that are shipped to many other locations, providing the spend is £25 or more. This gives some shoppers an incentive to keep spending until they reach the £25 threshold. Free shipping has helped Amazon build sales over the years, but it has also added to the company's costs and cut into profits. The company's Amazon Prime customers, who sign up for a range of benefits for a modest annual fee, also enjoy free delivery benefits.

Amazon is earning significant profits from serving as an online storefront for other marketers (and consumers) to sell their products. Every time a customer buys something from a seller participating in the Amazon Marketplace, Amazon collects a fee. The margins are especially attractive in this fast-growing part of the business because Amazon does not pay to buy or store any inventory, and the costs of posting items for other sellers is extremely low now that the electronic storefront is up and running.

All-digital products like electronic books, music, movies and games are lucrative because they entail no inventory or shipping costs. This is why Amazon has moved aggressively into digital content and related products. Its popular Kindle, first introduced in 2007, is an eBook reader that wirelessly connects to the internet so customers can download an electronic book, newspaper or magazine in seconds. Initially, Amazon priced the Kindle higher than the Sony Reader, its main competitor at the time. Despite the high price, demand outstripped supply for a time and Amazon struggled to increase output. As other retailers have offered their own eBook readers and sales of tablet computers have offered an alternative means to read eBooks, Amazon has lowered the price and poured on the promotion to keep up the Kindle's sales momentum.

The Kindle also created a controversy over e-book pricing. When Amazon first launched the Kindle, it priced best-selling eBooks at less than £10 each, with a few priced even lower. Publishers fumed, because the hard cover price of these books was considerably higher. The situation changed in early 2010, when Apple debuted its iPad tablet computer. Apple trumpeted the iPad's capabilities as an eBook reader and made deals with publishers to carry downloadable digital content. Under pressure from the publishers and faced with a new level of competition from Apple's much-anticipated device, Amazon

took a step back from its digital discounting. It listened to the publishers and raised the retail price of many digital best-sellers. However, today some books are available free and many others are offered at a few pounds or less via the bestseller list.

Today, Kindle customers can buy and instantly download more than 1.3 million books. 'Our vision is to have every book that has ever been in print available in less than 60 seconds,' says Amazon founder Jeff Bezos. The Kindle has become Amazon's best-selling product and dramatically increased sales of electronic books, magazines and similar products. In fact, sales of books in digital format have been outselling those in printed format since 2012, when Amazon reported it sells 114 eBook downloads for every 100 physical units. Multiply the savings in shipping costs alone, and it's easy to see why Amazon has put so much emphasis on electronic delivery of books and other content.

Looking ahead, Amazon will continue to pay close attention to the pricing of rival gadgets and the way digital content is being priced. Although it's now the undisputed leader in electronic book sales, that market share is likely to erode little by little as more customers are offered the opportunity to buy and download more books from additional sources.

Sources: www.amazon.co.uk/gp/feature.html?ie=UTF8&docId=1000351073; March 2015; www.amazon.co.uk/gp/help/customer/display.html?nodeId=201015970, March 2015.

Questions for discussion

1. Are Amazon's delivery costs variable or fixed? How is the company's profitability likely to be affected if Amazon stopped offering free delivery?

2. Why would publishers be so concerned about the difference in price between a hard cover best-seller and the digital version? Explain your answer in terms of this chapter's pricing concepts.

3. Do you think Amazon should be concerned about losing market share in e-book retailing? What are the implications for its pricing decisions?

CHAPTER 21

Modifying the marketing mix for business markets, services and in international marketing

"The fundamental principles of marketing apply to all applications, but there are important differences for business goods, the marketing of services and tackling global markets"

Objectives

- To recognize that in many situations the basic marketing mix requires modification.

- To examine the nature of the marketing mix for business markets.

- To understand the more complex and extended marketing mix required for services.

- To recognize how marketers involved with global marketing modify the marketing mix to reflect separate markets.

INTRODUCTION

The core ingredients of the marketing mix – the marketer's tactical toolkit – have been examined in detail throughout Part Three of *Marketing: Concepts and Strategies*. While these chapters have broadly covered consumer, business, service and not-for-profit markets, there inevitably has been some bias towards the marketing of consumer goods. In part this reflects the origins of marketing as a discipline and the plethora of consumer brands and their coverage in the media. It has also been deliberate ... all readers of this text, as consumers themselves, will be familiar with many of the products and services featured so far.

Marketing is marketing, and the overall approach outlined in this text and presented in Chapter 1 holds true across consumer, business, services and not-for-profit markets. However, it is important to acknowledge that the marketing of services and business products is moderately different from the marketing of consumer goods. This chapter highlights these variations in marketing practice. Those companies involved in international marketing, trading across national borders and cultures, are also faced with additional issues that have an impact on their marketing activity.

Global brands

Swiss-based Suchard had been gearing up for global markets since the late 1960s, by developing global brands, such as Milka and Toblerone, and undertaking a number of strategically important acquisitions. In taking over other European confectionery companies, such as Du Lac (Italy), Pavlides (Greece), Terry's (UK), Csemege (Hungary), Kaunas (Lithuania), Olza (Poland) and Republika (Bulgaria), Suchard became a major force in the highly competitive confectionery market. In the UK, Terry's of York was a significant brand, though relatively small next to the mighty Cadbury's and Rowntree's. While Suchard was busy acquiring Terry's, Swiss rival Nestlé purchased Rowntree's.

Through its many acquisitions, mainstream international brands such as Milka, Toblerone and Suchard were taken into these new markets by Suchard. The company also gained locally based production and the capability to supply existing national brands alongside those international 'best sellers'. This successful growth strategy did not pass unnoticed. American rival Kraft Foods desired global expansion and acquired Suchard, establishing distribution and retail channels in areas where it was not traditionally strong. This also helped Kraft to develop its own global brands alongside smaller local products. More recently, Kraft took over the large and successful UK-based Cadbury and has just merged with Heinz. By acquiring Cadbury, Kraft became the world's second largest food business with revenues close to $50 billion. Kraft Foods then split into two companies, leaving its global brands in a new company, Mondelez International. With sales of $36 billion and distribution in 80 countries, Mondelez globally markets a host of well-known food and confectionary brands, including Oreo, TUC, Peek Freans, Milka, Toblerone, Trident, Hall's, Jacobs, Kenco, Philadelphia, Nabisco and Cadbury.

Sources: www.kraftfoodsgroup.com, July 2015; Jacob Suchard archives; www.mondelezinternational.com, July 2015.

There are some differences in the characteristics of the respective markets and the use of the marketing toolkit for consumer, business and service products. These are evident in the practices of business marketers, and more so in the activities of those responsible for the marketing of services. This chapter presents a summary of some of the most important, if at times subtle, variations in marketing business products and marketing services. The chapter concludes by suggesting how international marketing requires consideration of additional issues in formulating a marketing mix, as necessary for the global brands of Mondelez. It is important that you have read Chapters 4, 6 and 13 *before* starting this chapter.

Characteristics of business marketing mixes

As with consumer marketers, business-to-business marketers must create a marketing mix that satisfies the business customers and clients in the target market. In many respects, the general concepts and methods involved in developing a business marketing mix are similar to those used in consumer product marketing. However, business customers tend to be less flexible than consumers. In this section, the focus is on the features of business marketing mixes. Each of the main components in a business marketing mix is examined: product, place/distribution, promotion, price and people.

Product

After selecting a target market (see Chapters 7 and 8), the business marketer has to decide how to compete. Production-oriented managers may fail to understand the need to develop a distinct appeal for their product to give it a differential advantage. Positioning the product (discussed in Chapters 8 and 11) is necessary to serve a market successfully, whether it is consumer or business.[1]

Compared with consumer marketing mixes, the product ingredients of business marketing mixes often include a greater emphasis on services, both before and after a sale. Business services, including on-time delivery, quality control, custom design and help in specifying product requirements, a comprehensive parts distribution system and post-delivery support, may be important components of the augmented product.

As explained in Chapter 6, in many business markets there may be only a few customers: for example, component suppliers selling to automotive producers have only a handful of key accounts. In such situations, failure to satisfy customers or to anticipate their evolving requirements is even more important than in most consumer markets, where alienation of an individual consumer is unlikely to bring a company to its knees. The ability to look after business customers is of paramount importance to business marketers. However, this might involve satisfying many different parties (see Chapter 6).

Before making a sale, business marketers provide potential customers with technical advice regarding product specifications, installation and applications. Many business marketers depend heavily on long-term customer relationships that perpetuate sizeable repeat purchases.[2] Therefore, business marketers also make a considerable effort to provide services after the sale. As business customers must have products available when needed, on-time delivery is another service included in the product component of many business marketing mixes. A business marketer unable to provide on-time delivery cannot expect the marketing mix to satisfy business customers. Availability of parts or supplies must also be included in the product mixes of many business marketers in order to prevent costly production delays. The business marketer that includes availability of parts within the product component has a competitive edge over one that fails to offer this service. Furthermore, customers whose average purchases are large often desire credit; thus some business marketers include credit services in their product mixes. When planning and developing a business product mix, a business marketer of component parts and semi-finished products must realize that a customer may decide to make the items instead of buying them.

Frequently, business products – particularly industrial products – must conform to standard technical specifications that business customers want. Thus business marketers often concentrate on functional product features rather than on marketing considerations. This has important implications for business sales people. Rather than concentrating just on selling activities, they must often assume the role of consultants, seeking to solve their customers' problems and influencing the writing of specifications.[3] For example, sales people for computer hardware often act as consultants for software as well as the basic computer kit. Most customers now expect this level of service.

Since most business products are rarely sold through self-service – there are exceptions, such as office supplies – the major consideration in package design is protection. There is less emphasis on packaging as a promotional device, unlike in consumer markets.

Research on business customer complaints indicates that such buyers usually complain when they encounter problems with product quality or delivery time. On the other hand, consumers' complaints refer to other problems, such as customer service and pricing. This type of buyer feedback allows business marketers to gauge marketing performance. It is important that business marketers respond to valid complaints because the success of most business products depends on repeat purchases. Buyer complaints serve a useful purpose; many companies facilitate this feedback by providing customer service departments and call centres for their business customers.

If a business marketer is in a mature market, growth comes from attracting market share from a competitor. Alternatively, a company can look at new applications or uses for its products. JCB dominates the backhoe digger market in Europe, but economic recession, which resulted in

FIGURE 21.1
Most computer businesses tailor computing services and packages to business users

reduced construction of buildings and infrastructure, negatively impacted on its key customers. JCB looked to stimulate its sales levels by instead targeting products currently offered by niche rivals. The company used its existing skills and facilities to design an innovative range of very safe, single-arm skid-steer machines. These nimble, compact 'mini-diggers' are now on most building sites and the hire market, proving very successful for JCB. Bringing user safety and environmental concerns to the fore, they lend themselves particularly well to buyer needs for smaller construction equipment in Germany and Scandinavia. JCB's success, managed by a well-qualified team of business marketers, stems from winning sales from its competitors, seeking new applications for its products and designing innovative products.

Place/distribution

The place/distribution ingredient in business marketing mixes differs from that for consumer products with respect to the types of channel used, the kinds of intermediaries available, and the transport, storage and inventory policies. Nonetheless, the primary objective of the physical distribution of business products, and particularly industrial products, is to ensure that the right products are available when and where needed.

Types of channel   Distribution channels tend to be shorter for business products than for consumer products. Figure 21.2 shows the four commonly used business-to-business distribution channels that were described in Chapter 14. Although **direct distribution channels**, in which products are sold directly from producers to users, are not always utilized in the distribution of many consumer products (retailers intervene), they are the most widely used for business products. More than half of all business products are sold through direct channels (channel E in Figure 21.2). Business buyers like to communicate directly with producers, especially when expensive or technically complex products are involved. For this reason, business buyers prefer to purchase expensive and highly complex mainframes and servers directly from the producers. In these circumstances, a business customer wants the technical assistance and personal assurances that only a producer can provide.

A second business distribution channel involves a business distributor to facilitate exchanges between the producer and customer (channel F in Figure 21.2). A **business distributor** is an independent business that takes title to products and carries

Direct distribution channels
Distribution channels in which products are sold directly from producers to users.

Business distributor
An independent business that takes title to products and carries inventories.

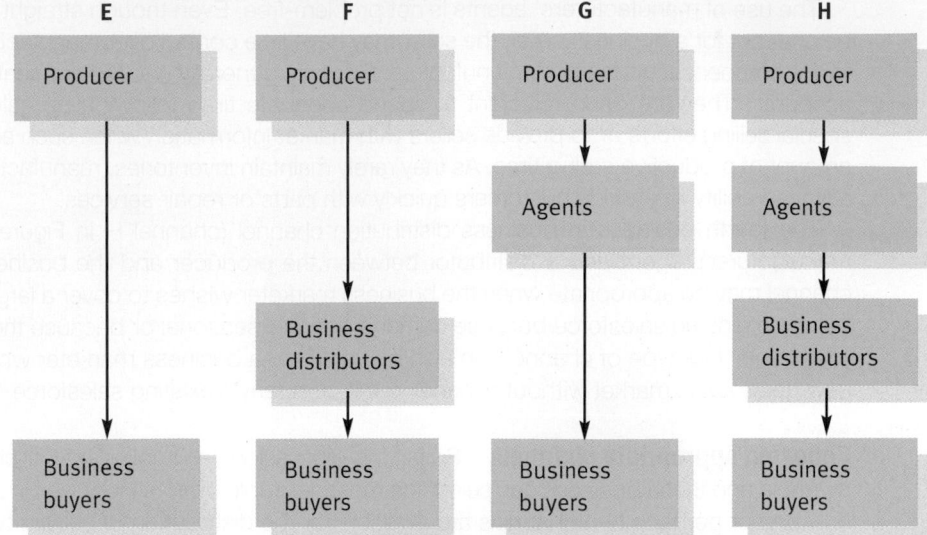

FIGURE 21.2
Typical marketing channels for business markets (see Chapter 14)

inventories. Such distributors are merchant wholesalers; they assume possession and ownership of goods, as well as the risks associated with ownership. Business distributors usually sell standardized items, such as maintenance supplies, production tools and small operating equipment. Some carry a wide variety of product lines; others specialize in one or a small number of lines. Distributors can be used most effectively when a product has broad market appeal, is easily stocked and serviced, is sold in small quantities and is needed rapidly to avoid high losses, such as a part for an assembly line machine.[4]

Business distributors or dealers offer sellers several advantages. They can perform the required selling activities in local markets at relatively low cost to a manufacturer, and they can reduce a producer's financial burden by providing their customers with credit services. As business distributors usually maintain close relationships with their customers, they are aware of local needs and can pass on market information to producers. By holding adequate inventories in their local markets, these distributors reduce the producers' capital requirements.

There are several disadvantages to using business distributors. They may be difficult to control because they are independent companies. Though they often stock competing brands, a producer cannot depend on them to sell a specific brand aggressively. Furthermore, distributors maintain inventories, for which they incur numerous expenses; consequently, they are less likely to handle bulky items or items that are slow sellers relative to profit margin, need specialized facilities or require extraordinary selling efforts. In some cases, distributors lack the technical knowledge necessary to sell and service certain business items.

In the third business distribution channel (channel G in Figure 21.2), a manufacturer's agent is employed. As described in Chapter 14, a manufacturer's agent or representative is an independent business person who sells complementary products from several producers in assigned territories and is compensated through commission. Unlike a distributor, a manufacturer's agent does not acquire title to the products and usually does not take possession. Acting as a sales person on behalf of the producers, a manufacturer's agent has no latitude, or very little, in negotiating prices or sales terms.

Using manufacturers' agents can benefit a business marketer. These agents usually possess considerable technical and market information and have an established set of customers. For a business seller with highly seasonal demand, a manufacturer's agent can be an asset because the seller does not have to support a year-round salesforce. The fact that manufacturers' agents are paid on a commission basis may also make them an economical alternative for a company that has extremely limited resources and cannot afford a full-time salesforce.

The use of manufacturers' agents is not problem-free. Even though straight commissions may be cheaper for a business seller, the seller may have little control over manufacturers' agents. Due to the compensation method, manufacturers' agents generally want to concentrate on their larger accounts. They are often reluctant to spend adequate time following up sales, to put forward special selling efforts or to provide sellers with market information when such activities reduce the amount of productive selling time. As they rarely maintain inventories, manufacturers' agents have a limited ability to provide customers quickly with parts or repair services.

The fourth business-to-business distribution channel (channel H in Figure 21.2) has both a manufacturer's agent and a distributor between the producer and the business customer. This channel may be appropriate when the business marketer wishes to cover a large geographic area but maintains no salesforce because demand is highly seasonal or because the company cannot afford one. This type of channel can also be useful for a business marketer who wants to enter a new geographic market without expanding the company's existing salesforce.

Choosing appropriate channels   So far, this discussion has implied that all channels are equally available and that a business can select the most desirable option. However, in a number of cases, only one or perhaps two channels are available for the distribution of certain types of product. In other circumstances several channels may be used simultaneously. For example, many business products that are available through traditional channels involving agents and industrial distributors can also be purchased direct via the manufacturer's website.[5] An important issue in channel selection is the manner in which particular products are normally purchased. If customers ordinarily buy certain types of product directly from producers, it is unlikely that channels with intermediaries will be effective. Other dimensions that should be considered are the product's cost and physical characteristics, the costs of using various channels, the amount of technical assistance customers need, the size of product and parts inventory needed in local markets, and the channels selected by competitors in order to be close to customers and provide a good customer experience.

Physical distribution decisions regarding transport, storage and inventory control are especially important for business marketers. Some raw materials and other industrial products may require special handling; for example, toxic chemicals used in the manufacture of some products must be shipped, stored and disposed of properly to ensure that they do not harm people or the environment. In addition, the continuity of most business-to-business buyer–seller relationships depends on the seller having the right products available when and where the customer needs them. This requirement is so important that business marketers must sometimes make a considerable investment in order processing systems, materials handling equipment, warehousing facilities and inventory control systems. For example, without high stocks and a quickly responsive distribution system, rivals may gain an edge.

Many business purchasers are moving away from traditional marketing exchange relationships in which the buyer purchases primarily on the basis of price from multiple suppliers and towards more tightly knit, relational exchanges, which are long lasting, less price-driven agreements between manufacturers and suppliers.[6] Just-in-time inventory management systems are providing the rationale that underlies these types of relationship. In order to reduce inventory costs and to eliminate waste, buyers purchase new stock just before it is needed in the manufacturing process. To make this system effective, they must share a great deal of information with their suppliers, since these relationships are collaborative. Indeed, suppliers are often treated now as strategic partners. For example, a major IT services deal won by Fujitsu will require the contributions of many big partners, whose inputs will have shaped the winning bid and without whom the customer would not have selected Fujitsu.

Promotion (MarComms)

The combination of promotional efforts used in business marketing mixes generally differs from those for consumer products, especially convenience goods. The differences are evident in the emphasis on various promotional mix ingredients (MarComms) and the activities performed in connection with each promotional mix ingredient.

Personal selling For several reasons, most business-to-business marketers rely on **personal selling**, informing and persuading customers to purchase through personal communication to a much greater extent than do consumer product marketers. Since a business seller often has fewer customers, personal contact with each customer is more feasible. Many business clients expect personalized service and come to depend on their supplier's personnel. This is one of the reasons why **key account management** is so important in many business markets. Key account management is the dedicated and close support for individual business customers whose volume of business is significant and warrants one-to-one handling. Some business products have technical features that are too numerous or too complex to explain through non-personal forms of promotion. Moreover, business purchases are frequently high in value, and must be suited to the job and available where and when needed; thus, business buyers want reinforcement and personal assurances from sales personnel. As business marketers depend on repeat purchases, sales personnel must follow-up sales to make certain that customers know how to use the purchased items effectively, as well as to ensure that the products work properly.

Sales people need to perform the role of educators, showing buyers clearly how the product fits their needs. When the purchase of a product is critical to the future profitability of the business buyer, buying decision-makers gather extensive amounts of information about all alternative products and possible suppliers. To deal with such buyers successfully, the seller must have a highly trained salesforce that is knowledgeable not only about its own company's products but also about competitors' offerings. Besides, if sales representatives offer thorough and reliable information, they can reduce the buyer's uncertainty, as well as differentiate their company's product from the competition. Finally, the gathering of information lengthens the decision-making process. Thus it is important for sales people to be patient; to avoid pressuring their clients as they make important, new and complex decisions; and to continue providing information to their prospects throughout the entire process.[7] The business development role is very important in business markets.

Telemarketing Due to the escalating costs of advertising and personal selling, telemarketing – the creative use of the telephone to enhance the sales person's function – is on the increase. Some of the activities in telemarketing include freefone 0800 phone lines, personal sales workstations, and call centres assisted by data terminals that take orders, check stock and order status, and provide shipping and invoicing information.

Although not all business sales personnel perform the same sales activities, they can generally be grouped into the following categories, as described in Chapter 18: technical, missionary and trade or inside order takers. An inside order taker could use telemarketing effectively. Regardless of how sales personnel are classified, business selling activities differ from consumer sales efforts. As business sellers are frequently asked for technical advice about product specifications and uses, they often need technical backgrounds and are more likely to have them than consumer sales personnel. Compared with typical buyer–seller relationships in consumer product sales, the interdependence that develops between business buyers and sellers is likely to be stronger. Sellers count on buyers to purchase their particular products, and buyers rely on sellers to provide information, products and related services when and where needed. Although business sales people do market their products aggressively, they almost never use 'hard sell' tactics or behave unethically because of their role as technical consultants and the interdependence between buyers and sellers. Web-based selling has supplemented call centres and personal selling, supported with good databases and CRM systems.

Advertising Advertising is emphasized less in business sales than in consumer transactions, although it is still very important and now makes good use of web-based opportunities to communicate deals and new product introductions. Some of the reasons given earlier for the importance of personal selling in business promotional mixes explain why, compared with consumer goods,

Personal selling
The task of informing and persuading customers to purchase through personal communication.

Key account management
Dedicated and close support for individual business customers whose volume of business is significant and warrants one-to-one handling.

FIGURE 21.3
Payload and capacity: B2B customers often focus on technical specifications as well as the cost to acquire and to operate products

straightforward advertising is not the dominant ingredient of the promotional mix. However, advertising often supplements personal selling efforts. Although the cost of a business-to-business sales call is high and continues to rise, advertisements that allow sales personnel to perform more efficiently and effectively are worthwhile for business marketers. Advertising can make business customers aware of new products and brands; inform buyers about general product features, representatives and organizations; and isolate promising prospects by providing enquiry forms or the addresses and phone numbers of company representatives.

As much of the demand for most business products is derived demand (for example, demand for construction equipment stems from consumer demand for more new houses, which in turn prompts building companies to require more plant and equipment), marketers can sometimes stimulate demand for their products by stimulating consumer demand. Thus a business marketer occasionally sponsors an advertisement promoting the products sold by the marketer's customers.

Print media   When selecting advertising media, business marketers primarily choose to be online, but many still often use print media, such as trade publications and direct mail. They seldom use the traditional broadcast medium of TV, but many businesses utilize radio spots. Trade publications and direct mail reach precise groups of business customers and avoid wasted circulation. In addition, they are best suited to advertising messages that present numerous details and complex product information, which are frequently the types of message that business advertisers wish to convey. Many such publications can now be delivered online and may be more interactive with potential clients than previously.

Compared with consumer product advertisements, business and particularly industrial advertisements are usually less persuasive and more likely to contain a large amount of copy and detail. In contrast, marketers that advertise to reach ultimate consumers sometimes avoid extensive advertising copy because consumers are reluctant to read it. Whereas consumers desire emotional, attention-grabbing messages in advertising, business advertisers believe that purchasers with any interest in their products will search for information and read long messages.

Sales promotion   Sales promotion activities often play a significant role in business-to-business promotional mixes. They encompass such efforts as catalogues, trade shows and trade sales promotion methods, including merchandise allowances, buy-back allowances, displays, sales contests and the other methods discussed in Chapter 18. Business marketers go to great lengths and considerable expense to provide catalogues that describe their products to customers. Customers refer to various sellers' catalogues to determine specifications, terms of sale, delivery times and other information about products. Catalogues, now often available online, help buyers to decide which suppliers to contact.

Trade shows   Trade shows can be effective vehicles for making many customer contacts in a short time. One study found that business marketers allocate 25 per cent of their annual promotional budgets to trade shows in order to communicate with their current and potential customers, promote their corporate image, introduce new products, meet key account executives, develop mailing lists, identify sales prospects and find out what their competitors are doing. Although trade shows take second place to personal selling, they rank for many sectors above print advertising in influencing business purchases, particularly as the business buyers reach the stages in the buying process of need recognition and supplier evaluation (see Chapter 6). Most organizations have key trade shows, conferences or seminars in which they participate each year.

Other types of promotion   The way in which business marketers use publicity in their promotional mixes may not be much different from the way in which marketers of consumer products use it. As described in Chapter 17, more companies are incorporating public relations automatically into their promotional mixes, particularly with the growth of online discussions and social media. There has been significant use made in recent years of the internet by business marketers, both to promote a company's products and services, and also to help manage ongoing relationships with business customers. Indeed, in many markets, companies failing to develop effective websites and digital marketing capability are now at a significant competitive disadvantage. The use of social media to engage with business customers and to build ongoing relationships is a big growth area.

Price

Compared with consumer product marketers, business marketers face many more price constraints from legal and economic forces. With respect to economic forces, an individual business-to-business company's demand is often highly elastic, requiring the company to approximate competitors' prices. This condition often results in non-price competition and a considerable amount of price stability (see Chapter 20).

Today's route to sustainable competitive advantage lies in offering customers something that the competition does not offer – something that helps them increase their productivity and profitability or which helps them build stronger relationships with their customers. Most companies achieve high market share not by offering low prices but by offering their customers superior value, product quality and customer service. Many customers are willing to pay higher prices for quality products.[8] Companies such as Caterpillar, IBM and 3M have shown that a value-added-based strategy can win a commanding lead over competition. Such companies emphasize the highest quality products at slightly higher prices. Value is a trade-off between price and quality, so a value-based proposition is often not a low-price proposition. Of course, some companies do focus on offering low prices and undercutting their rivals, particularly in commodity-like markets in which product differentiation is difficult to achieve. Best practice, though, would indicate that marketers should avoid emphasizing low prices in their market mixes unless either the target market in question contains customers who mainly buy on the basis of low price alone, or marketers' attempts to achieve product or service differentiation have failed.

Many business-to-business companies are devoting increased resources to training, so that their personnel are better qualified and more willing to provide full customer service. Corporate image, reliability and flexibility in production and delivery, technical innovation and well-executed promotional activity also present opportunities to create a differential advantage. Price used to be the basis for differentiation in many business markets, notably in numerous industrial markets, but price can be reduced only so far if companies are to remain viable. Although the cost to acquire a product is still important, in most markets companies have attempted to move away from a selling proposition based purely on low price. They have realized that value is not necessarily equal to a low price. Service, reliability, payment terms, image and design are just a few factors in addition to price that influence many sales. Value and not low price is often the deciding factor for many business customers.

Although there are various ways to determine the prices of business products, the three most common are administered pricing, bid pricing and negotiated pricing.

Administered pricing
A pricing method
in which the seller
determines the price
for a product and the
customer pays the
specified price.

Administered pricing   With **administered pricing**, the seller determines the price or series of prices for a product and the customer pays that specified price. Marketers who use this approach may employ a one-price policy in which all buyers pay the same price, or they may set a series of prices that are determined by one or more discounts. In some cases, list prices are posted on a price sheet or in a catalogue. The list price is a beginning point from which trade, quantity and cash discounts are deducted. Thus the actual (net) price a business customer pays is the list price less the discount(s). When a list price is used, the business marketer sometimes specifies the price in terms of list price times a multiplier. For example, the price of an item might be quoted as 'list price x .78', which means the buyer can purchase the product at 78 per cent of the list price. Simply changing the multiplier lets the seller revise prices without having to issue new catalogues or price sheets.

Bid pricing
Determination of prices
through sealed or open
bids submitted by the
seller to the buyer.

Bid pricing   With **bid pricing**, prices are determined through sealed or open bids. When a buyer uses sealed bids, selected sellers are notified that they are to submit their bids by a certain date. Normally, the lowest bidder is awarded the contract, as long as the buyer believes that the company is able to supply the specified products when and where needed. In an open bidding approach, several, but not all, sellers are asked to submit bids. In contrast to sealed bidding, the amounts of the bids are made public. Finally, a business purchaser sometimes uses negotiated bids. Under this arrangement, the customer seeks bids from a number of sellers and screens the bids. Then the customer negotiates the price and terms of sale with the most favourable bidders, until either a final transaction is consummated or negotiations are terminated with all sellers.

Sometimes a buyer will either be seeking component parts to be used in production for several years or custom-built equipment to be purchased currently and through future contracts. In such instances, a business seller may submit an initial, less profitable bid to win follow-on (subsequent) contracts. The seller that wins the initial contract is often substantially favoured in the competition for follow-on contracts. In such a bidding situation, a business marketer must determine how low the initial bid should be, the probability of winning a follow-on contract and what combination of bid prices on both the initial and the follow-on contract will yield an acceptable profit.[9]

Negotiated pricing
Determination of prices
through negotiations
between the seller and
the buyer.

Negotiated pricing   For certain types of business market, a seller's pricing component may have to allow for **negotiated pricing**. That is, even when there are stated list prices and discount structures, negotiations may determine the actual price a business customer pays. Negotiated pricing can benefit both seller and buyer because price negotiations frequently lead to discussions of product specifications, applications and perhaps product substitutions. Such negotiations may give the seller an opportunity to provide the customer with technical assistance and perhaps sell a product that better fits the customer's requirements; the final product choice might also be more profitable for the seller. The buyer benefits by gaining more information about the array of products and terms of sale available, and may acquire a more suitable product at a lower price.

Some business marketers sell in markets in which only one of these general pricing approaches prevails. Such marketers can simplify the price components of their marketing mixes. However, a number of business marketers sell to a wide variety of business customers and must maintain considerable flexibility in pricing.

People

This chapter has already emphasized the importance of people in the marketing of business products. The role of personal selling is especially important in many business markets, particularly those in which the purchase is deemed risky because of its size, value or complexity. For many technologically advanced products, the need to have face-to-face explanation and guidance is fundamental to the customers' perceived level of satisfaction. The development of long-term

Relationships
Regular, ongoing
contacts between
businesses and their
customers.

relationships – regular, interactive, ongoing contacts with business customers – is increasingly a driving factor in the development of marketing mixes for businesses supplying other businesses. This links with the practice of key account management. Where products are high value or complex, customers often expect such relationships. Even in commodity markets – for example, basic components, computer consumables or the provision of energy – relationships are seen as a means of maintaining contact with customers, ensuring reorders and enabling a supplying business to differentiate itself through customer service rather than price alone. More attention is being given to the effective recruitment, training and motivation of personnel who are often in regular contact with a business's immediate customers, typically other businesses in the marketing channel.

Amending the marketing mix for services

The original marketing mix defined by McCarthy and popularized by Kotler included the now well-known '4Ps' of product, promotion (MarComms), price and place (distribution/channels). Most authors now mention an additional ingredient of the marketing mix: people. Originally suggested by services marketers who acknowledged that consumers often view the personnel providing a service as part and parcel of the service 'product' being offered, the *people* aspect of the marketing mix has become an accepted part of most businesses' marketing programmes, and not only for organizations marketing services. However, the nature of services, as described in Chapter 13, has led marketers to further adapt the marketing mix.[10] The intangibility of service products, inseparability of production and consumption, perishability and heterogeneity – which are the key characteristics of services – force the marketing mix to be amended in two ways:

Extended marketing mix for services
Besides the traditional '4Ps' of product, promotion, price and place/distribution, the additional '3Ps' of people, physical evidence and process.

1. the traditional 4Ps of product, promotion, price and place/distribution have some important extra dimensions unique to the marketing of services.

2. the marketing mix is itself modified to include the additional core ingredients of process, physical evidence (ambience) and people, thereby creating the '7Ps' of what is termed the **extended marketing mix for services.**[11]

Delivering executive training and change management consultancy

Marketing tools and techniques

A major logistics company decided to invest in middle and senior management training in order to enhance their capabilities, create an exciting opportunity for career development amongst its executives, improve the company's reputation as an employer of choice, but also to add to the small number of senior executives currently able to create a strategy and plan out its execution. In order to achieve this mix of goals, the logistics company needed a supplier of training which not only understood how to train managers in various skills, but which could also enthuse participants and motivate them to want to alter the culture within the business. The Strategy and Human

Resource Directors jointly identified a short-list of potential providers. This list was based on their own previous experiences, the evidence from online searches of providers of these services, the views of certain colleagues within their company and the endorsements within their professional networks of executives from other companies. The selected four potential providers each received an invitation to tender, had the opportunity to meet the company's executives for a fact-finding half-day, and then had to submit a proposal. Two candidate suppliers were then invited to make formal pitch presentations to the logistics company's leadership.

For the suppliers receiving the invitation to tender, the welcome opportunity also posed many headaches. Was the work already lined up for a preferred candidate? Had the logistics company properly thought about its requirements? Was the required budget in place or still to be sought by the Strategy and HR Directors? Who would make the decision about final content of the training and change management programme, its budget and the selected executives to participate? What would be the expectations of these participants? Who and what would influence the decision? Did they have preferred suppliers in mind? What would be required to deliver an effective programme? Did the supplier have these capabilities and personnel in place? Were they more financially viable allocated to other projects? Which competitors had been asked to tender? What would their merits and deficiencies be? How would they be perceived by the logistics company? Who did the supplier know in other organizations and inside the potential client company who could shed light on these issues? What resource would need to be allocated to creating the response to the bid and making the presentation? Would

the outlay be worthwhile? What would be the odds for successfully winning the contract?

The strategic marketing process deployed had to help assess these issues and determine the way forward. The resulting proposition had to reflect the logistics company's needs, expectations and buying behaviour. The supplier's proposed marketing mix had to address the client's invitation to tender, the programme's needs and decision-making criteria within the client. This B2B proposal would involve much more than the traditional '4Ps' of the marketing mix, requiring people, process and physical evidence components, too. Central to a successful bid would be the supplier's brand reputation, service delivery record and perceived quality. Far more nebulous than a high-tech gadget for consumers, new model of car or branded insurance policy, the marketers of this training and consulting service had to add significantly to the toolkit applied in many B2C product markets.

Figure 21.4 presents this revised marketing mix for services, as highlighted in the Marketing Tools and Techniques example above. This section examines in more detail the amendments required when determining a marketing mix for services, commencing with the traditional 4Ps, before reviewing the additional ingredients of the extended marketing mix.[12]

Intangibility
A characteristic of services, which lack physical attributes and cannot be perceived by the senses.

Product

Goods can be defined in terms of their physical attributes, but services, because of their intangibility – that is, their inability to be perceived by the senses or be stockpiled in

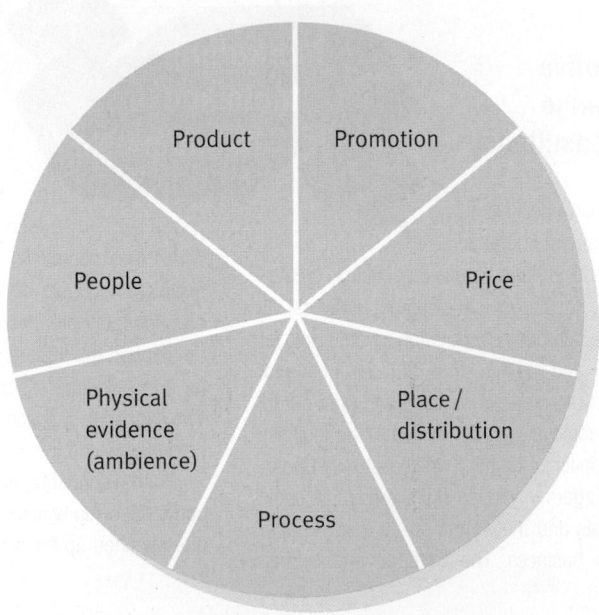

FIGURE 21.4
The extended marketing mix for services

advance of consumption – cannot. It is often difficult for consumers to understand service offerings and to evaluate possible service alternatives. Gas and electricity companies, for example, offer schemes to spread bill payments and to assist the financially disadvantaged, plus several methods for making payments. These services are explained in the companies' advertisements. What is the utility or satisfaction consumers gain from energy providers? There are many, but they are more ambiguous or subjective than the benefits consumers gain from a Kindle eReader or a Sony PlayStation.

There may also be tangibles, such as facilities, employees or communications, associated with a service. These tangible elements help form a part of the product and are often the only aspects of a service that can be viewed prior to purchase. Consequently, marketers must pay close attention to associated tangibles and make sure that they are consistent with the selected image of the service product.[13] For example, consumers perceive public transport at night as plagued by crime and therefore hesitate to use it. Improvements in the physical appearance of tube stations and reductions in the time between trains are tangible cues that consumers can use to judge public transport services.

Service provider
A person who offers a service, such as a bank clerk or hairdresser.

The service product is often equated with the **service provider**. For example, the bank clerk or the hairdresser becomes synonymous with the service a bank or a beauty salon provides and with their brands. As consumers tend to view services in terms of service personnel and because personnel are inconsistent in their behaviour, it is imperative that service providers are effective in selecting, training, motivating and controlling those staff members that come into contact with customers.

After testing many variables, the Strategic Planning Institute (SPI) in the USA developed an extensive database on the impact of various business strategies on profits. The Institute found that 'relative perceived product *quality*' is the single most important factor in determining long-term profitability. In fact, because there are generally no objective measures to evaluate the quality of professional services (medical care, legal services and so forth), the customer is actually purchasing confidence in the service provider.[14] The strength or weakness of the service provided

Service product quality
The consumer's perception of the quality of service he or she receives.

often affects consumers' perceptions of **service product quality**. The consumer's perception of the quality of service he or she receives is a fundamental driver of both customer satisfaction and marketing performance, as explained in Chapter 13. Service quality delivery is viewed as being of paramount importance to marketers of services and failure to execute such delivery to customers' satisfaction can permit competitors to make significant inroads.

Since services are performances rather than tangible goods, the concept of service quality is difficult to grasp. Price, quality and value are important considerations of consumer choice and buying behaviour for both goods and services.[15] It should be noted that it is not objective quality that matters, but the consumer's subjective perceptions. Instead of quality meaning conformity to a set of specifications – which frequently determine levels of product quality – service quality is defined by customers.[16] Moreover, quality is frequently determined through a comparison: in the case of services, by contrasting what the consumer expected of a service with his or her actual experience.[17]

Service providers and service consumers may have quite different views of what constitutes service quality. Consumers frequently enter service exchanges with a set of predetermined expectations. Whether a consumer's actual experiences exceed, match or fall below these expectations will have a great effect on future relationships between the consumer and the service provider. To improve service quality, a service provider must adjust its own behaviour to be consistent with consumers' expectations or to re-educate consumers so that their expectations will parallel the service levels that can be achieved.[18]

A study of doctor–patient relationships proposed that when professional service exceeds client expectations, a true person-to-person bonding relationship develops. However, the research also revealed that what doctors viewed as being quality service was not necessarily what patients perceived as quality service. Although interaction with the doctor was the primary determinant of the overall service evaluation, patients made judgements about the entire service experience, including factors such as the appearance and behaviour of receptionists, nurses and technicians; the décor; and even the appearance of the building.[19]

Other product concepts discussed in Chapters 10–12 are also relevant here. Management must make decisions regarding the product mix, positioning, branding and new product development of services. It can make better decisions if it analyzes the organization's service products in terms of **complexity** and **variability**. Complexity is determined by the number of steps required to perform a service. Variability reflects the amount of diversity allowed in each step of service provision. In a highly variable service, every step in performing the service may be unique, whereas in cases of low variability, every performance of the service is standardized.[20] For example, services provided by doctors are both complex and variable. Patient treatment may involve many steps, and the doctor has considerable discretion in shaping treatment for each individual patient. In general, to decrease costs and widen the potential market, and to better control quality, service providers seek to limit both complexity and variability.

Complexity
In services marketing, the number of steps required to perform a service.

Variability
The amount of diversity allowed in each step of service provision.

An examination of the complete service delivery process, including the number of steps and decisions, enables marketers to plot their service products on a complexity/variability grid, such as the one in Figure 21.5. The position of a service on the grid has implications for its positioning in the market. Furthermore, any alterations in the service delivery process that shift the position of the service on the complexity/variability grid have an impact on the positioning of the service in the marketplace. Table 21.1 details the effects of such changes. When structuring the service delivery system, marketers should consider the organization's marketing goals and target market.

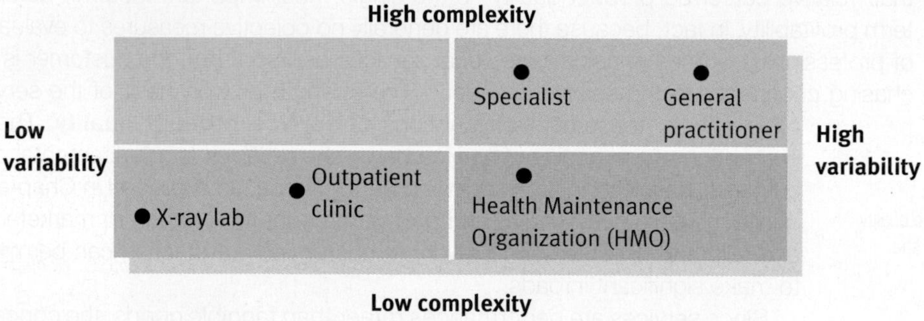

FIGURE 21.5
Complexity/variability grid for medical services

Source: Adapted and reprinted with permission from American Marketing Association Faculty Consortium on Services Marketing by Lynn Shostack, Texas A&M University, 7–11 July 1985, published by the American Marketing Association.

TABLE 21.1   Effects of shifting positions on the complexity/variability grid

Downgrading complexity/variability	Upgrading complexity/variability
Standardizes the service	Increases costs
Requires strict operating controls	Indicates higher margin/lower volume strategy
Generally widens potential market	Personalizes the service
Lowers costs	Generally narrows potential market
Indicates lower margin/higher volume strategy	Makes quality more difficult to control
Can alienate existing markets	Creates differentiation

Source: Adapted and reprinted with permission from American Marketing Association Faculty Consortium on Services Marketing by Lynn Shostack, Texas A&M University, 7–11 July 1985, published by the American Marketing Association.

Promotion (marketing communications)

As intangible-dominant products, services are not easily promoted. The intangible is difficult to depict in advertising, whether the medium is print or broadcast. Service advertising should thus emphasize tangible cues that will help consumers understand and evaluate the service. The cues may be the physical facilities in which the service is performed or some relevant tangible object that symbolizes the service itself.[21] For example, restaurants may emphasize their physical facilities: clean, elegant, casual and so on, to provide clues as to the quality or nature of the service. Service providers may also focus their advertising on the characteristics they believe customers want from their services; such as speed of service, state-of-the-art systems, or – as in the case of bank *first direct* – the opportunity to talk to a person rather than deal with an automated call centre. The symbols, catch lines and imagery common to most financial organizations reflect the increasing importance of branding in services.[22] Differentiation between rival services is difficult, as is effective promotion. Branding is helping to distinguish competing services and to provide a platform for promotional activity.[23]

To be successful, organizations must not only maximize the difference between the value of the service to the customer and the cost of providing it; they must also design the service with employees in mind. Contact personnel are critical to the perception of quality service. They must be provided with sufficient tools and knowledge to furnish the type of service the customer desires. As service industries are information driven, they can often substitute knowledgeable and highly trained personnel for the capital assets used in more product-oriented businesses.[24]

Thus employees in a service organization are an important secondary audience for service advertising. Variability in service quality, which arises from the labour-intensive nature of many services, is a problem for service marketers, because consumers often associate the service with the service-providing personnel. Advertising and strong branding can have a positive effect on customer-contact personnel, shaping employees' perceptions of the company, their jobs and how management expects them to perform.[25] For example, British Airways' famous strapline on its advertising throughout the 1980s and 1990s, 'The world's favourite airline', was designed not just to remind air travellers that more people flew with BA than with any other airline but also to develop a sense of pride among BA's flight and ground personnel. Bank *first direct* reminds employees that it is the most recommended bank peer-to-peer by consumers, so that they desire to provide great service and recognize the risks to the brand's reputation of not doing so.

Personal selling is potentially powerful in services because this form of promotion lets consumers and sales people interact. When consumers enter into a service transaction, they must as a general rule interact with the service organization's employees. Customer contact personnel can be trained to use this opportunity to reduce customer uncertainty, give reassurance, reduce dissonance and promote the reputation of the organization.[26] Once again, the proper management of customer-contact personnel is important.

Although consumer service organizations have the opportunity to interact with actual customers and those potential customers who contact them, they have little opportunity to go out into the field and solicit business from all potential consumers. The very large number of potential customers and the high cost per sales call rule out such efforts. On the other hand, marketers of business services, like the marketers of business goods, are dealing with a much more limited target market and may find personal selling the most effective way of reaching their customers.

Sales promotions, such as competitions, are feasible for service providers, but other types of promotion are more difficult to implement. How does an organization display a service? How does it provide a free sample without giving away the whole service? A complimentary visit to a health club or a free skiing lesson could possibly be considered a free sample to entice a consumer into purchasing a membership or taking lessons. Although the role of publicity and the implementation of a public relations campaign do not differ significantly in the goods and service sectors, service marketers appear to rely on publicity much more than goods marketers do.[27] Customers are receptive to stories of good and bad service, and public relations is highly cost effective (see Chapter 16). The role of social media is therefore of growing significance.

Consumers tend to value word-of-mouth communications more than company-sponsored communications. This preference is probably true for all products, but especially for services, because they are experiential in nature. For this reason, service organizations should attempt to stimulate word-of-mouth communications.[28] They can do so by encouraging consumers to tell their friends about satisfactory performance. Many businesses, for instance, display prominent signs urging customers to tell their friends if they like the service and to tell the business if they do not. Some service providers, such as hairdressers, give their regular customers discounts or free services for encouraging friends to come in for a haircut. Word-of-mouth can be simulated through communications messages that feature a testimonial – for example, television advertisements showing consumers who vouch for the benefits of a service a particular organization offers. Famous personalities tweeting about a meal or health spa, medical treatment or trip away, will have tremendous impact on their Twitter followers, just as your Facebook comments about a night out or holiday will help shape the reputations of the brands whose services you consumed and have now reported on. Or, as illustrated in the Topical Insight example below for NHS Choices, humour or hard-hitting self-interest messages might achieve buy-in. Social media discussions, comparison websites and online ratings have impacted significantly on the perceptions of quality and relevance for many service providers. Consider whose opinions you value when selecting a holiday destination and choosing a hotel or airline.

Targeting self-centred teenagers

Topical insight

Many smokers know the health consequences of their decision to smoke. However, the desire to chill-out, feel the buzz, look cool, fit in with friends, relieve boredom, enjoy the taste or whatever is their motivation outweighs the health risks. Those responsible for combatting smoking and persuading users to quit have limited resources and recognize increasingly that many hardened smokers will continue to puff away irrespective of health warnings, changes to how products are packaged and displayed, limits imposed on where smoking is permitted and tax-led price rises. So attention has been given to 'catching them young', either to encourage teenagers and students already smoking to stop or to pre-empt teens from ever starting. This target market has been identified as having significant potential for success. As a result, the National Health Service in the UK has tailored a set of messages towards this target audience through its NHS Choices website.

The younger you start smoking, the more damage your body will suffer when you get older. Here are seven reasons to quit:

1. You'll be healthier and less out of breath because smoking decreases your lung capacity.

2. You'll save yourself a packet. The average smoker spends an astonishing £27.54 a week and £90 000 over their lifetime on cigarettes. Use this tool [an NHS iPhone app] to work out how much money you are saving by quitting smoking.

3. You'll look better. Chemicals in cigarettes restrict blood flow to your skin. Smokers have more wrinkled and saggy faces by the time they're in their mid-20s.

4. Quitting helps save the planet. Deforestation due to tobacco production accounts for nearly 5 per cent of overall deforestation in the developing world.

5. Someone who starts smoking at 15 is three times more likely to die from cancer than someone who starts smoking in their mid-20s.

6. The younger you start smoking, the more damage there will be to your body as an adult.

7. Not smoking will make you instantly more attractive. Most people prefer kissing non-smokers.

There are some powerful reasons for not smoking included in the above campaign message, which are carefully conceived to touch emotions driving teenagers. Way beyond 'smoking causes cancer', which to many teenagers seems a long shot and way off being a threat. Perhaps flagging sex appeal, damage to the planet and financial ruin will nudge a behavioural change in some teenage smokers.

Source: www.nhs.uk/Livewell/smoking/Pages/Teensmokersquit, April 2015.

It is important to point out that the promotional activities of most professional service providers, such as doctors, lawyers and accountants, are severely limited. Until recently, all these professionals were prohibited by law from advertising. Although these restrictions have now been lifted in many countries, there are still many obstacles to be overcome. Professionals need to become familiar with developing advertising appropriate to their services, while consumers also need to adjust to seeing such service providers advertise. In many countries, lawyers are being forced to consider advertising, both because many potential clients do not know that they need legal services and because there is an over-supply of lawyers. Consumers want more information about legal services, and lawyers have a very poor public image.[29] On the other hand, doctors and dentists are more sceptical about the impact of advertising on their image and business. Despite the trend towards professional services advertising, the professions themselves exert pressure on their members to advertise or promote only in a limited way because such activities are still viewed as somewhat risqué.

Price

Price plays both an economic and a psychological role in the service sector, just as it does with physical goods. However, the psychological role of price in respect to services is magnified; after all, consumers must rely on price as the sole indicator of service quality when other quality indicators are absent. In its economic role, price determines revenue and influences profits. Knowing the real costs of each service provided is vital to sound pricing decisions (see Chapter 20).

Services may also be bundled together and then sold for a single price. For example, a hotel may offer a room-only rate, but will also offer meal-inclusive or spa-inclusive rates, whereby the combined price of room + meals or room + spa is much less than were consumers to purchase these services/amenities separately, so they seem to be better value. Service bundling is a practical strategy, because in many types of services there is a high ratio of fixed to variable costs and high cost sharing among service offerings. Moreover, the demand for certain services is often interdependent. For example, banks offer packages of banking services – current and savings accounts and credit lines that become active when customers overdraw their other accounts. Price bundling may help service marketers cross-sell to their current customers or acquire new customers. The policy of price leaders may also be used by discounting the price of one service product when the customer purchases another service at full price.[30] Visitors to a safari park may be offered discounted entry to the adjacent fairground and amusements or for their next visit.

Service intangibility may also complicate the setting of prices. When pricing physical goods, management can look to the cost of production as an indicator of price, but it is often difficult to determine the cost of service provision and thus identify a minimum price. Price competition is severe in many service areas characterized by standardization. Once market segmentation and specialized services are directed to specific markets, specialized prices are set. Next comes comparative pricing as the service becomes fairly standardized. Price competition is quite common in the hotel and leisure sectors, banking and insurance.

Many services, especially professional services, are situation-specific. Neither the service provider nor the consumer may know the extent of the service prior to production and consumption. As the cost is not known beforehand, price is difficult to set. Even so, many service providers attempt to use cost-plus pricing. Others set prices according to the competition or market demand.

Pricing of services can also help smooth out fluctuations in demand. Given the perishability of service products, this is an important function. A higher price may be used to deter or offset demand during peak periods, and a lower price may be used to stimulate demand during slack periods. Railways offer cheap day returns and savers to minimize sales declines in slack periods. Airlines rely heavily on price to help smooth out demand, as do many other operations, such as pubs and entertainment clubs, cinemas, resorts and hotels.

Place/distribution

In the service context, distribution is making services available to prospective users. Marketing intermediaries are the entities between the actual service provider and the consumer that make the service more available and more convenient to use.[31] For example, insurance brokers provide the direct customer contact on behalf of the large insurance companies whose products they broker. Indirect distribution of services may be made possible by a tangible representation or a facilitating good, for example, a bank credit card.[32] However, almost by definition, many services are limited to direct channels of distribution, being produced and consumed simultaneously. In high-contact services in particular, service providers and consumers cannot be separated. In low-contact services, however, service providers may be separated from customers by intermediaries. Dry cleaners, for example, generally maintain strategically located retail stores as drop-off centres, and these stores may be independent or company-owned. Consumers go to the branch to initiate and terminate service, but the actual service may be performed at a different location. The separation is possible because the service is directed towards the consumer's physical possessions, and the consumer is not required to be present during delivery.

Other service industries are developing unique ways to distribute their services. To make it more convenient for consumers to obtain their services, hotels and car hire companies have long been using intermediaries in the form of travel agencies and now online bookings services such as Bookings.com or Superbreak. In financial services marketing, electronic product delivery channels such as automatic cash dispensers and electronic funds transfer systems provide customers with financial services in a more widespread and convenient manner. Consumers no longer have to go to their bank for routine transactions; they can now receive service from the nearest cash dispenser in a shopping centre or transport terminus, or conduct transactions via smartphone apps, telebanking, text or at home on a computer. Indeed, HSBC's *first direct* banking operation is managed entirely through telecommunications – phone or web – as there is no bank branch network.

Process

The acts of purchasing and consumption are important in all markets – consumer, business-to-business or service. The direct involvement of consumers in the production of most services and the perishability of these services, place greater emphasis on the process of the transaction for services. Most services, be they health, tourism, education, financial or public sector, require the client to be present when ordering and consuming the service. Compared with the consumption of consumer goods, such as a camera or coat which may be used many times with similar results, a service experience is very transitory. Often, this sharpens the consumer's awareness of the service product, the staff providing the service and the associated service quality delivery experience. The manner in which the service is processed becomes part of the customer's experience. Marketers must treat process as part of the marketing mix, and ensure that they adequately specify, control and manage the process.

Friendliness of staff, their effectiveness and flows of information affect the customer's perception of the service product offer. Appointment or queuing systems become part of the service. Customers must comprehend how to order and then consume the service. The required process and the consumer's role should be 'transparently obvious' and readily understood. Ease or difficulty of payment can enhance or spoil the consumption of a service. The operationalization of the service must be proficient and discernible. In addition to tasty food, diners in a TGI Friday's or Pizza Express expect prompt service, informative menus, no waiting and no delays in paying their bills at the conclusion of their meals. These are operational issues that directly affect customer perceptions and satisfaction – they are important aspects of the marketing of services.[33]

Physical evidence (ambience)

The environment in which a service is offered and consumed is central to the consumer's understanding of the service, and to the enjoyment or satisfaction. Certain services, such as weighty financial matters or health consultations, may need to be delivered in a suitably respectful setting, whereas a children's birthday treat would be better in a relaxed and informal facility designed to put children and their parents at their ease. The 'feel' of the service product is very much part of the service offer. The physical evidence, ambience or setting must be designed to reflect target customer expectations, reflect the branding and selected brand positioning (see Chapter 8), and facilitate the smooth delivery of the service. Whether in a restaurant, hospital, sports club or bank, the appearance and ambience matter. Layout, décor, upkeep, noise and aroma, general ease of access and use all become part of the service product. Even tyre depots have recognized this aspect of the extended marketing mix for services, providing comfortable customer waiting areas with seating, drinks machines, TV and newspapers. In services, marketers devote much attention to creating distinctive brand positionings and to delivering customer satisfaction. The physical evidence linked to a particular service can play a major role in establishing the service's branding and in delivering customer satisfaction. Inappropriate selection of the physical evidence for a service may ruin the intended experience for the targeted customers.

People

The nature of most services requires direct interaction between the consumer and personnel representing the service provider's organization. In many services, customers interact with one another, and the organization's staff also interact with one another. This level of human involvement must be given maximum attention if customers are to maximize their use of the service and ultimately their satisfaction.[34]

Employee selection, training and motivation are central considerations. A restaurant may have a superb operation, but if the chef or waiters become demoralized and unmotivated, they will begin to deliver low-quality meals and inefficient service, possibly with a lousy attitude, resulting in a poor product from the consumer's point of view. Operational staff often help 'produce' the service product, sell it and assist in its consumption. Many service businesses are totally dependent on their personnel, as Leo Burnett, founder of the international advertising agency that bears his name, summed up: 'Every evening all our assets go down the elevator' – without the agency's creative people and media experts, the business has few marketing assets and nothing particularly tangible.

Most well-run services businesses devote as much time and resources to managing their customer contact personnel as to creating the service product being offered to customers. Without them, service quality delivery will be perceived as poor by dissatisfied customers. This requires formal audits of customers' perceptions of the abilities, attitudes and appropriateness of service delivery personnel, comparative benchmarking against competitors, plus evaluations of staff attitudes towards their ability to deliver the services. Without this attention to maintaining service delivery levels, the remainder of the marketing mix ingredients are unlikely to guarantee customer satisfaction. Marketers must devote some of their time to managing service delivery personnel. Ultimately, they are the face of the brand.

Strategic adaptation of marketing mixes for international markets

As explained in Chapter 4, marketing in non-domestic markets requires an understanding of the marketing environment, culture and local business practices, along with a specifically devised strategy. Once a company determines overseas market potential and understands the foreign environment, it develops and adapts its marketing mix(es). Creating and maintaining the marketing mix are the final steps in developing the international marketing strategy. Only if foreign marketing opportunities justify the risk will a company go to the expense of adapting the marketing mix. Of course, in some situations new products are developed for a specific country. In these cases, there is no existing marketing mix, so new marketing programmes must be designed, with significant budgetary implications.

Product and promotion (MarComms)

As Figure 21.6 shows, there are five possible strategies for adapting product and promotion across national boundaries:

1. keep product and promotion the same worldwide
2. adapt promotion only
3. adapt product only
4. adapt both product and promotion
5. invent new products.[35]

Keep product and promotion (MarComms) the same worldwide   This strategy attempts to use in the foreign country the product and promotion developed for the home market. This is an approach that seems desirable wherever possible because it eliminates the expenses of marketing research and product redevelopment. American companies PepsiCo and Coca-Cola use this approach in marketing their soft drinks. Although both translate promotional messages into the language of a particular country, they market the same products and promotional messages around the world. Despite certain inherent risks that stem from cultural differences in interpretation, exporting branding and advertising does provide the efficiency of international standardization or globalization. As the following examples imply, however, not all brands/products are suitable for export in their existing forms:

- Zit fizzy drink (Greece)
- Bum's biscuits (Sweden)
- Krapp toilet paper (Sweden)
- Grand Dick red wine (France)
- Sor Bits mints (Denmark).[36]

Global advertising embraces the same concept as global marketing, discussed in Chapter 4. An advertiser can reduce costs significantly by running the same advertisement worldwide.

Adapt promotion (MarComms) only   This strategy leaves the product basically unchanged but modifies its promotion. For example, McDonald's provides relatively similar core products throughout the world but may modify the media for its advertising messages. This approach may be necessary because of language, legal or cultural differences associated with the advertising copy.

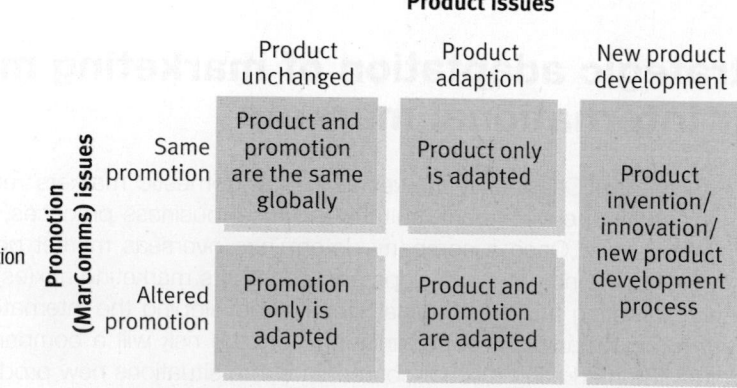

FIGURE 21.6
International product and promotion strategies

Source: Updated and adapted from Warren Keegan's work on global marketing management.

If a well-known local TV personality or sports star is used to represent a brand in one country, the same person and advertisement may have little applicability elsewhere. Many big global brands have used the face of cricket legend Sachin Tendulkar in India, but could not utilize his images in countries such as Germany, Sweden or Russia, where cricket is not followed. Promotional adaptation is a low-cost modification compared with the costs of redeveloping engineering and production, and physically changing products.

Generally, the strategy of adapting only promotion infuses advertising with the culture of the people who will be exposed to the marketing communications activity (see Figure 21.7). Often, promotion combines thinking globally and acting locally. At company headquarters, a basic global marketing strategy is developed, but promotion is modified to fit each market's needs, often using locally-based advertising agencies.

Adapt product only   The basic assumption in modifying a product without changing its promotion is that the product will serve the same function under different conditions of use. Soap and washing powder manufacturers have adapted their products to local water conditions and washing equipment without changing their promotions. Household appliances have also been altered to use different power voltages.

A product may have to be adjusted for legal reasons. Japan, for example, has some of the most stringent vehicle emissions requirements in the world. Cars produced elsewhere that do not meet set emissions standards cannot be marketed in Japan. Sometimes, products must be adjusted to overcome social and cultural obstacles. American Jell-O introduced a powdered jelly mix that failed in Britain because consumers were used to buying jelly in cube form. Resistance to a product is frequently based on attitudes and ignorance about the nature of new technology. It is often easier to change the product than to overcome technological, social or cultural bias.

Adapt both product and promotion (MarComms)   When a product serves a new function or is used differently in a foreign market, then both the product and its promotion need to be altered. For example, when Procter & Gamble marketed its Cheer washing powder in Japan, it promoted the product as being effective in all temperatures. However, most Japanese wash clothes in cold water and do not care about all-temperature washing. Moreover, the Japanese often add a lot of fabric softener to the wash, and Cheer did not produce many suds under such conditions. Procter & Gamble thus reformulated Cheer so that it would not be affected by the addition of fabric softener and changed the promotion to emphasize 'superior' cleaning in cold water. Cheer then became one of Procter & Gamble's most successful products in Japan. Adaptation of both product and promotion is the most expensive strategy discussed so far, but it should be considered if the foreign market appears large enough and competitively attractive.

Invent new products   This strategy is selected when existing products cannot meet the needs of a non-domestic market. General Motors developed an all-purpose jeep-like motor vehicle that can be assembled in developing nations by mechanics with no special training. The vehicle was designed to operate under varied conditions; it had standardized parts and was inexpensive. Colgate-Palmolive developed an inexpensive, all-plastic, hand-powered washing machine that had the tumbling action of a modern automatic machine. The product, marketed in less developed countries, was invented for households without electricity. Strategies that involve the invention of products are often the most costly, but the pay-back can be great. The clockwork radio was designed as a low-cost but effective educational medium for poor regions of southern Africa. It proved a success in this context, but surprisingly also in the US and developed economies, where it took on cult status and sold for a high price as an upmarket and trendy status symbol.

Place/distribution and pricing

Decisions about the distribution system and pricing policies are important in developing an international marketing mix. Figure 21.8 illustrates different approaches to these decisions.

TREAUPHÄE

Treauphy.

EIGENLEAUB

Bleau your own trumpet.

PREAUPAGANDE

Preaupaganda.

FEAUREVER

FIGURE 21.7
Adapting promotion across national boundaries

Source: The Trademark PERRIER is reproduced with the kind permission of the trademark owner, Nestlé waters.

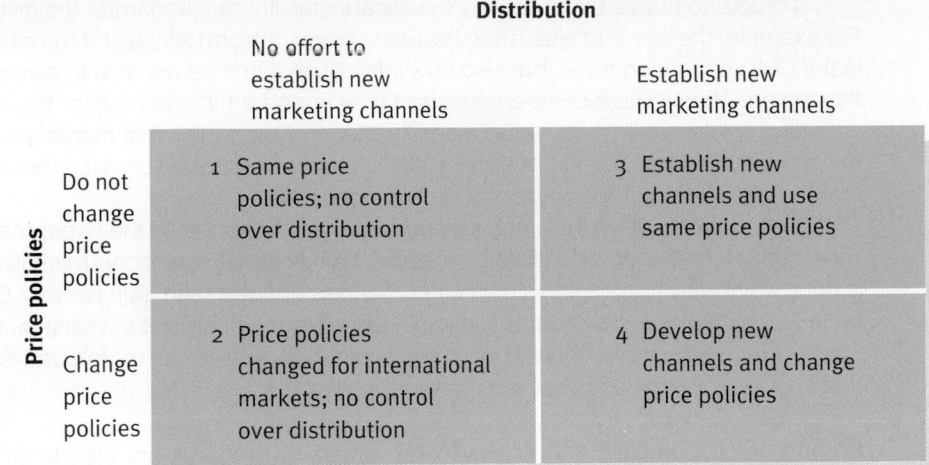

FIGURE 21.8
Strategies for international distribution and pricing

Distribution A company can sell its product to an intermediary, or it can develop new international marketing channels. Some service companies, such as DHL or Barclays, need to develop their own distribution systems owing to the nature of their products and operations. However, many products – such as hotel bookings, package holidays or insurance products – are distributed through intermediaries and brokers. A company must consider distribution both between countries and within the foreign country. The chapter's opener reveals how confectionery giants Suchard and Kraft acquired local companies in order to gain both ready-made production facilities and the acquired companies' distribution networks.

In determining distribution alternatives, the existence of retailers and wholesalers that can perform marketing functions between and within countries is one major factor. If a country has a segmented retail structure consisting primarily of one-person shops or street sellers, it may be difficult to develop new marketing channels for products such as packaged goods and prepared foods. Quite often in less developed countries, certain channels of distribution are characterized by ethnodomination. **Ethnodomination** occurs when an ethnic group occupies a majority position within a marketing channel. Indians, for example, own approximately 90 per cent of the cotton gins in Uganda; the Hausa tribe in Nigeria dominates the trade in kola nuts, cattle and housing; and Chinese merchants dominate the rice economy in Thailand. Marketers must be sensitive to ethnodomination, and must recognize that the ethnic groups operate in sub-cultures with a unique social and economic organization.[37]

Ethnodomination
This occurs when an ethnic group occupies a majority position within a marketing channel.

If the product being sold across national boundaries requires service and information, then control of the distribution process is desirable. Caterpillar, for example, sells more than half its construction and earthmoving equipment outside its native USA. Because it must provide services and replacement parts, Caterpillar has established its own dealers in foreign markets. Regional sales offices and technical experts are also available to support local dealers. A manufacturer of paint brushes, on the other hand, would be more concerned about agents, wholesalers or manufacturers of paint that would facilitate the product's exposure in a foreign market. Control over the distribution process would not be so important for that product because services and replacement parts are not needed.

Research suggests that international companies use independently-owned marketing channels when they market in countries perceived to be highly dissimilar to their home markets. However, when they market complex products, they develop vertically integrated marketing channels to gain control of distribution. To manage the distribution process from manufacturer to customer contact requires an expert salesforce that must be trained specifically to sell the company's products. When products are unique or highly differentiated from those of current competitors, international companies also tend to design and establish vertically integrated channels.[38]

It is crucial to realize that a country's political instability can jeopardize the distribution of goods. For example, the move to alter ruling bodies in much of North Africa and the oil producing nations in the Gulf impacts on trade, but also how international brands are able to service their markets in this region. Thus it must be re-emphasized how important it is to monitor the environment when engaging in international marketing (see Chapter 4). Companies that market products in unstable regions may need to develop alternative plans to allow for sudden unrest or hostility, and to ensure that the distribution of their products is not jeopardized.

It is important to have the 'right' product or service to appeal to the target market in an international market. However, a significant impediment to effective international marketing is distribution. It is not always easy to grasp how marketing channels operate in an alien territory. Companies setting up in Russia find the channels, bureaucracy and corruption difficult to manage. It is never easy to identify the most suitable channel members and players with which to do business, or to find those that should be permitted to sell a company's products.

Pricing   The domestic and non-domestic prices of products are usually different. For example, the prices charged for Disney DVDs in the UK, Germany and Spain will all vary, as well as being different from US prices. The increased costs of transport, supplies, taxes, tariffs and other expenses necessary to adjust a company's operations to international marketing can raise prices. A key decision is whether the basic pricing policy will change (as discussed in Chapter 20). If it is a company's policy not to allocate fixed costs to non-domestic sales, then lower foreign prices could result.

Dumping
The sale of products in non-domestic markets at lower prices than those charged in domestic markets, when all costs are not allocated or when surplus products are sold.

It has been common practice for EU countries to sell off foodstuffs and pharmaceuticals at knock-down prices to eastern European and African states respectively. This kind of sale of products in non-domestic markets or vice versa at lower prices than those charged in domestic markets (when all the costs have not been allocated or when surplus products are sold) is called **dumping**. Dumping is illegal in some countries if it damages domestic companies and workers.

A cost-plus approach to international pricing is probably the most common method used because of the compounding number of costs necessary to move products from their country of origin. Of course, as the discussion of pricing policies in Chapter 20 points out, understanding consumer demand and the competitive environment is a necessary step in selecting a price … witness recent issues for the euro.

Transfer pricing
The price charged between profit centres. for example between a manufacturing company and its foreign subsidiary.

The price charged in other countries is also a function of foreign currency exchange rates. Fluctuations in the international monetary market can change the prices charged across national boundaries on a daily basis. There has been a trend towards greater fluctuation (or float) in world money markets. For example, a sudden variation in the exchange rate, which occurs when a nation devalues its currency, can have wide-ranging effects on consumer prices.

Parallel imports
Goods that are imported through 'non-official' channels from low-price to high-price countries.

There are also pricing issues that stem from transfer pricing practices and the problems of parallel imports. **Transfer pricing** is the price charged between profit centres, for example a manufacturing company and its foreign subsidiary. Company policies can force subsidiaries to sell products at higher prices than the local competition, even though the true costs of their manufacture may be no different. The manufacturer tries to make a profit even from its 'internal' customer – its own subsidiary.[39] **Parallel imports** – that is, goods exported from low-price to high-price countries – are an increasing problem. For example, French and Belgian beer producers export to the UK at set price levels, but consumers and small independent retailers cross by car ferry to Calais and stock up with similar brands at much lower prices than those the manufacturers 'officially' offer to UK customers. Many well-known fmcg brands are available in other countries at lower prices, encouraging a **grey market** of unofficial export/import by third parties able to source lower priced merchandise on behalf of their clients and take a percentage of the saving in return.

Grey market
Unofficial export/import by third parties able to source lower priced merchandise on behalf of their clients and take a percentage of the saving in return.

There are also important price ramifications to consider, stemming from product or brand positioning and any differences between countries. For example, in the UK Stella Artois beer was marketed as 'reassuringly expensive', whereas in its native Belgium it was more of a commodity, mass-market brand competing against brands such as Duval or the specialist Trappist monk beers. Pricing, in any market, must reflect the brand positioning adopted.[40]

People

Great importance is now attached to the *people* ingredient of the marketing mix. The nature of many business-to-business markets and the form of most service products often lead businesses to determine formally the role of people within their marketing mixes. In the context of international marketing, the people ingredient is also very important. Chapter 4 highlighted how marketers performing across national boundaries must be aware of often striking differences, country by country or region by region, in the marketing environment. Often, cultural and social forces are the most varied and also the most difficult for marketers based in another country and culture to understand. Without people – partners, agents, advisors, staff – well-versed in the localized practices of marketing channels, consumers, competitors and regulators, it is unlikely that a marketing strategy will be executed successfully.

Companies must deploy people with the 'right' skills to address such issues from their own ranks or from third parties in the territories under scrutiny; it is common to recruit consultants, agents or advisers to help in building up an understanding of cultural and interpersonal considerations in a non-domestic market or to hire a sales manager with local experience. Channel members are very important in supplying localized knowledge of such issues. Having personnel who understand the nuances of an international market is a fundamental requirement for effective marketing, but so is the need for those personnel with the cultural and local knowledge to be able to implement a marketing mix, which itself may well have been modified to reflect the nuances of the relevant marketing environment.

Summary

This chapter explains why and how the marketing mix must be manipulated differently for business markets, services marketing and international markets.

Business marketing is a set of activities directed at facilitating and expediting exchanges of business products and services with customers in business-to-business markets. Like marketers of consumer products, business marketers must develop a marketing mix that satisfies the needs of customers in the business target market. The product component frequently emphasizes services, which are often of primary interest to business customers. Business products must meet certain standard specifications that business users require and there tends to be less flexibility than in consumer markets.

The distribution of business products differs from that of consumer products in the types of channel used, the kinds of intermediary available, and the transport, storage and inventory policies. A *direct distribution channel*, in which products are sold directly from producers to users, is common in business marketing. Also used are channels containing manufacturers' agents, *business distributors,* or both agents and distributors. Channels are chosen on the basis of several variables, including availability and the typical mode of purchase for a product.

Personal selling is a primary ingredient of the promotional component in business marketing mixes. *Key account management* is often deployed. Sales personnel may act as technical advisers both before and after a sale. Advertising is sometimes used to supplement personal selling efforts, but it is not generally as emotive in nature as in consumer marketing. Business marketers generally use print and online advertisements containing more information but less persuasive content than consumer advertisements. Other promotional activities include catalogues, trade shows and the web. Effective CRM systems and online selling are important for many business marketers.

The price component for business marketing mixes is influenced by legal and economic forces to a greater extent than it is for consumer marketing mixes. *Administered, bid* and *negotiated pricing* are additional possibilities in many business markets. Pricing may be affected by competitors' prices, as well as by the type of customer who buys the product. Increasingly, though price is still important, many companies are seeking new ways of creating a differential advantage. Value for money is important in most markets, but low price is not usually an effective competitive advantage except in the very short term. Flexibility and reliability in production and delivery can be differentiating factors, as can technical innovation, personnel and customer service, promotional activity and even payment terms. People, important in the context of personal selling, are also often required to establish ongoing long-term *relationships* with key customers.

The basic marketing mix is augmented for services through the addition of people, physical evidence (ambience) and the process of transaction in order to produce the '7Ps' or the *extended marketing mix for services.* When developing a marketing mix for services, several aspects deserve special consideration. Regarding product, service offerings are often difficult for customers to understand and evaluate. The tangibles associated with a service may be the only visible aspect of the service, and marketers must manage these scarce tangibles with care. Because services are often viewed in terms of the *service providers,* service providers must select, train, motivate and control employees carefully, particularly to guarantee *service product quality* and service delivery. Consumers determine the quality of services subjectively, often by contrasting what was expected of a service with the actual experience. Service providers need to meet these expectations or re-educate consumers. Service quality delivery is very important for marketers of services to manage effectively. Service marketers are selling long-term relationships as well as performance. It is important to understand the *complexity* of the service product and to seek to limit its *variability.*

Promoting services is problematic because of their *intangibility.* Advertising may stress the tangibles associated with the service or use some relevant tangible object. Branding is used to distinguish competing services. Personnel in direct contact with customers should be considered an important secondary audience for advertising and brand messaging. Personal selling is very powerful in service organizations because customers must interact with personnel. The publicity component of the promotional mix is vital to many service organizations. Because customers value word-of-mouth communications, messages should attempt to stimulate or simulate word-of-mouth. Social media and endorsement by consumers are particularly important for service reputation. Many professional service providers are severely restricted in their use of promotional activities by their regulators.

Price plays three major roles in the service sector. It plays a psychological role by indicating quality, and an economic role by determining revenues; price is also a way to help smooth out fluctuations in demand.

Service distribution channels are typically direct because of simultaneous production and consumption. However, innovative approaches such as drop-off points, intermediaries and electronic distribution/eBusiness are developed.

International marketing requires careful planning. Marketing activities performed across national boundaries are usually significantly different from domestic marketing activities. International marketers must have a profound awareness of the foreign environment, of social and cultural differences, and of different business practices. The international marketing strategy is ordinarily adjusted to meet the needs and desires of markets across national boundaries.

After a country's environment has been analyzed, opportunities identified and an entry strategy determined, marketers must develop a marketing mix and decide whether to adapt product or promotion. There are five possible strategies for adapting product and promotion across national boundaries: (1) keep product and promotion the same worldwide; (2) adapt promotion only; (3) adapt product only; (4) adapt both product and promotion; (5) invent new products. Foreign distribution channels are nearly always different from domestic ones. Identifying and understanding channels in foreign markets are not easy tasks. Distribution channels can become a major impediment in international marketing. The allocation of costs, transport considerations or the costs of doing business in foreign markets will affect pricing. *Transfer pricing, parallel imports* and the *grey market* are important considerations, as are the regulations pertaining to *dumping.* It is also necessary to set pricing levels that reflect the nuances of a product's brand positioning in a particular market: the same brand may occupy distinctly different positionings in separate territories.

Important terms

Administered pricing
Bid pricing
Business distributor
Complexity
Direct distribution channels
Dumping
Ethnodomination
Extended marketing mix for services
Grey market
Intangibility
Key account management
Negotiated pricing
Parallel imports
Personal selling
Relationships
Service product quality
Service provider
Transfer pricing
Variability

Discussion and review questions

1. How do business-to-business marketing mixes differ from those of consumer products?

2. What are the major advantages and disadvantages of using distributors?

3. Why do business marketers rely on personal selling more than consumer products' marketers?

4. Why would a business marketer spend resources on advertising aimed at stimulating consumer demand?

5. Compare three methods of determining the price of business products.

6. Why must a competitive advantage be based on more than just low prices?

7. Discuss the role of promotion (MarComms) in services marketing.

8. Why are social media and consumer-to-consumer communications so important in the success of services?

9. What additional elements must be included in the marketing mix for services? Why?

10. Why is it difficult to create and maintain a differential advantage in many service businesses?

11. Why do the marketers of services place so much emphasis on the *people* ingredient of the marketing mix?

12. What are the principal choices a company can make when manipulating the marketing mix for international markets?

13. How and why can the place/distribution ingredient of the marketing mix cause problems for international marketers?

14. What additional factors determine a company's pricing policy in foreign markets?

Recommended readings

Brennan, R., Canning, L. and McDowell, R., *Business-to-Business Marketing* (Sage, 2014).

Doole, I. and Lowe, R., *International Marketing Strategy* (Cengage, 2012).

Ellis, N., *Business-to-Business Marketing: Relationships, Networks and Strategies* (OUP, 2010).

Ghauri, P. and Cateora, P., *International Marketing* (McGraw-Hill, 2014).

Hakansson, H., Ford, D., Gadd, L.-E., Snehota, I. and Waluszewski, A., *Business in Networks* (Wiley, 2009).

Hutt, M.D. and Speh, T.W., *Business Marketing Management: B2B* (Cengage, 2013).

Keegan, W.J., *Global Marketing Management* (Pearson, 2013).

Kotabe, M., *International Marketing Management* (John Wiley, 2010).

Lovelock, C.H. and Wirtz, J., *Services Marketing* (Pearson, 2011).

Palmer, A., *Principles of Services Marketing* (McGraw-Hill, 2014).

Zeithaml, V., Bitner, M. and Gremler, D., *Services Marketing* (McGraw-Hill, 2012).

Internet exercise

Log on to BUPA's website. This provider of healthcare and health insurance targets both consumers and business clients. Look at the information BUPA provides for *Individuals* (consumers), for *Business* (corporate clients) and for *Healthcare Professionals* (service providers): www.bupa.co.uk.

1. What are the key BUPA service products offered to private consumers and to business clients?

2. How are BUPA's messages about its products tailored to reflect the different needs and buying behaviour of its consumers, business clients and healthcare professionals?

Group tasks

1. In Switzerland McDonald's retails wines and beers, in Portugal ice-creams, and in Hong Kong platters for sharing. Consider why an apparently uniform global brand such as McDonald's encourages such localised variations.

2. Consider how and why the marketing varies for BMW cars and BMW car servicing.

Applied mini-case

Volvo Trucks is part of Volvo Group, which produces buses and coaches, marine engines and trucks. It is the division that handles the importing, manufacturing, sales and marketing, and after-sales support for all Volvo heavy goods vehicles. The company's website states:

> Transportation solutions for the trucking industry . . .
> Volvo Trucks is the second largest producer of heavy trucks and transport solutions within the entire truck industry. We supply the haulage industry with complete transportation solutions and our customers are supported by over 2300 dealerships and workshops in more than 140 countries.

We are also a company that is dedicated to safety, quality and care for the environment.

www.volvotrucks.com/trucks/global/en-gb/Pages/home.aspx

For most of the major players in the European truck market, two major trends are dictating current marketing strategies. The decline in new vehicle sales is leading to an increased focus on the aftermarket. The market for replacement parts, tyres, fuels and lubricants is more stable and offers some degree of cushioning against the more extreme fluctuations in demand for new vehicles. The second trend has been a move by hauliers and large companies with their own transport fleets away from purchasing new vehicles outright. There has been a switch to leasing and contract hire, whereby the truck manufacturer ultimately retains ownership of the vehicle and has to offload the vehicles when they are returned by the haulier.

Source: Volvo Trucks.

Question

As sales of new trucks fluctuate and marketers increasingly focus on offering financing packages and aftermarket care, what are the key skills marketers must deploy in this evolving sector?

HP's *i-Community* targets the developing economies

Case study

In the USA and Europe – mature markets for computers and IT – Hewlett Packard (HP) markets its computing products and IT services with its own field force, advertising, direct marketing, publicity and sales promotions. Many of its products are retailed through leading computer dealers and high-street retailers. For its computers and imaging solutions, the style of marketing emulates the approaches of leading rivals such as IBM, Apple, Toshiba and Lenovo. The marketing programmes in terms of their style could be for hi-fi, photographic equipment or home entertainment systems.

Elsewhere in the world, HP is something of a mould-breaker. Where others may see low incomes and low-tech infrastructure, HP anticipates long term business opportunities.

India, Senegal, Bangladesh and other developing countries have been targeted by the US computer and printer giant as it seeks first-mover advantage ahead of its rivals. HP created a programme called *World e-Inclusion* to reach out and influence entrepreneurs and businesses in developing countries to join the online business boom. The concept aimed to foster future business development while advancing a social agenda of bringing technology resources to under-served regions of the world.

e-Inclusion is HP's vision of empowering and enabling all the world's people to access the social and economic opportunities of the digital age:

1. To establish HP as a leader in an exciting new technology growth area that also demonstrates our character and commitment to social contribution.

2. To create significant revenue and profit growth over time through the creation of new markets, products and services.

3. To provide a showcase to the world of our capabilities in terms of devices, infrastructure and services.

4. To enhance current HP business opportunities in emerging markets.

World e-Inclusion has brought together public sector, not-for-profit, government departments and local development groups to lease, buy or receive donated HP products and services. These partners in turn put the IT products in the hands of farmers, manufacturers and small business owners. Some receive off-the-shelf standard HP computers while, owing to their circumstances, other users are provided with solar-powered machines capable of wireless or satellite communication. All users are trained and shown how to make connections with local suppliers and buyers.

To support this initiative, HP opened research labs in India to investigate IT use and probable solutions in developing economies. These labs create IT products that are economically and culturally sustainable as well as technically advanced. In addition, HP has boosted its service, sales and operations in these countries. The company is also working with lenders to provide loans to budding entrepreneurs. HP joined forces with AOL to donate computers, printers, modems and Internet access to peace group volunteers in 15 countries to further encourage IT use and broaden the benefits of technology in these societies. It is not by accident that the Ethisphere Institute selected HP as one of the world's most ethical companies.

The latest initiative is a three-year alliance between Hewlett-Packard and the state of Andhra Pradesh to build an HP i-Community in Kuppam, a community of 320,000 people in four rural villages. An HP i-Community is a major initiative of HP's e-Inclusion vision. It is a concept in which information and communications technology is strategically deployed to help improve job creation, income opportunity, access to government, education and healthcare services. The goal of the i-Community is to turn the region into a thriving, self-sustaining economic community where technology helps improve literacy, job creation, income, access to government, education, and healthcare services.

www.hp.com/e-inclusion/en/project

While there is a social mission associated with HP's *World e-Inclusion* programme, the company is quite clear about its commercial motives. The long-term purpose of the strategy is business development rather than charity. In the UK, France and Portugal, HP uses a more traditional set of marketing communications to support its more conventional marketing strategy. In the developing economies, such an approach is unworkable until the point is reached when the take-up of IT products is far more advanced and routinized in the business community. As a result, HP has enjoyed significant growth around the world, notably in many developing economies.

Sources: Hewlett Packard; www.hp.com/hpinfo/globalcitenship, March 2011; www.hp.com/e-inclusion/en/project, April 2015.

Questions for discussion

1. In what ways does HP's marketing strategy in India differ from the strategy deployed in Europe?

2. What is the proposition being offered to business customers in these developing countries?

3. What are the problems and potential risks associated with operating such contrasting marketing programmes globally for a company such as Hewlett Packard?

Postscript

Having identified marketing opportunities to pursue, a business should recommend a marketing strategy that involves selecting the target market, determining the required positioning and developing a competitive advantage. For the recommended target market strategy to be implemented, a marketing mix must be developed. The marketing mix centres on the '5Ps' of product, people, place/distribution, promotion and pricing decisions.

Part Three of *Marketing: Concepts and Strategies* has examined the marketing mix, commencing with the product and people ingredients of the marketing mix, the integral issues of branding, packaging and customer service, as well as the important concepts of the product life cycle and the management of product portfolios. Part Three has addressed the nature of marketing channels, wholesalers and distributors, the physical distribution of products and services, plus some aspects of retail marketing. A thorough overview followed of the elements of promotion – marketing communications – and how the promotional mix fits into marketing strategy. The concept of integrated marketing communications (IMC) has also been explored. The impact of digital marketing was assessed next, exploring the implications for channel selection and marketing communications, attaining customer and market insight, as well as the growth of consumer-to-consumer communications and social media. This was followed by an explanation of the principal concepts of pricing and the setting of prices. The final chapter in Part Three explored the manipulation of the marketing mix to cater for business markets, the marketing of services and marketing in international markets.

Before progressing, readers should be confident that they are now able to do the following.

Describe the basic product decisions

- Learn how marketers define products
- Define product levels
- Understand how to classify products
- Become familiar with the concepts of product item, product line and product mix
- Understand the concept of product life cycle
- Understand the types of organizational structure used to manage products
- Grasp the importance of the levels of a product in determining a competitive edge

Explain the importance of branding and packaging

- Recognize the importance of brands and brand equity
- Understand the types and benefits of brands and how to select, name, protect and licence them
- Explore the concepts of brand loyalty, brand advocacy and brand communities
- Appreciate the best practice guidelines for creating strong brands
- Examine the roles of brand attributes, brand values and brand personality in brand development
- Explore the changing nature of branding in the digital era
- Understand the role of branding at the corporate level and in reputation management
- Become aware of the major packaging functions and packaging design considerations
- Consider the ways in which packaging is used in marketing strategies
- Examine the functions of labelling and the legal issues associated with labelling

Outline the requirements for developing products and managing product portfolios

- Become aware of organizational alternatives for managing products
- Understand how organizations develop a product idea into a commercial product
- Understand the importance and role of product development in the marketing mix
- Acquire knowledge of the management of products during the various stages of a product's life cycle
- Become aware of how existing products can be modified
- Learn how product deletion can be used to improve product mixes
- Examine tools for the strategic planning of product or market portfolios

Understand the special requirements for the marketing of services

- Understand the nature and characteristics of services
- Classify services

- Understand the development of marketing strategies for services
- Understand the problems involved in developing a differential advantage in services
- Examine the concept of service quality
- Explore the concept of marketing in non-profit situations
- Understand the development of marketing strategies in non-profit organizations
- Describe methods for controlling non-profit marketing activities

Explain the concept of the marketing channel

- Understand the marketing channel concept and the nature of marketing channels
- Discuss the functions of marketing channels
- Examine different types of channel
- Examine channel integration and levels of market coverage
- Consider the selection of distribution channels and the emergence of direct marketing
- Understand the impact of multi-channel management
- Explore the behavioural aspects of channels, especially the concepts of cooperation, relationship building, conflict and leadership
- Examine legal issues in channel management

Describe the functions of channel players and physical distribution management

- Understand the nature of wholesaling in its broadest forms in the marketing channel
- Examine channel members that facilitate wholesaling and distribution
- Understand the purpose and function of retailing in the marketing channel
- Describe and distinguish retail locations, major store types and non-store retailing
- Understand how physical distribution activities are integrated into marketing channels and overall marketing strategies, and to examine physical distribution objectives
- Learn about order processing, materials handling and different types of warehousing and their functions

- Appreciate the importance of inventory management and the development of adequate assortments of products for target markets
- Gain insight into different transportation methods and how they are selected and coordinated

Explain the role of promotion and marketing communications

- Understand the role of promotion in the marketing mix
- Examine the process of communication
- Understand the product adoption process and its implications for promotional efforts
- Understand the aims of promotion
- Explore the elements of the promotional mix
- Appreciate the nature of integrated marketing communications (IMC)
- Acquire an overview of the major methods of promotion
- Explore the factors that influence the selection of promotional mix ingredients
- Appreciate the role of marketing communications

Describe the use of advertising, publicity and sponsorship

- Explore the nature and uses of advertising
- Be aware of the major steps involved in developing an advertising campaign
- Find out who is responsible for developing advertising campaigns
- Gain an understanding of publicity and public relations
- Examine the nature and uses of sponsorship

Describe the use of personal selling, sales promotion, direct mail, the Internet, digital and direct marketing

- Understand the nature and major purposes of personal selling
- Learn the basic steps in the personal selling process
- Identify the types of salesforce personnel
- Gain insight into sales management decisions and activities

- Appreciate the role of key account management
- Become aware of what sales promotion activities are and how they can be used
- Become familiar with specific sales promotion methods
- Understand the role of direct mail in the promotional mix
- Be aware of the importance of the Internet in marketing communications
- Comprehend the growing role of digital marketing
- Appreciate direct marketing's use of the promotional mix

Understand the nature of digital marketing

- Explore how digital has impacted on consumer behaviour and decision-making
- Appreciate the new requirements of understanding search engine management and content marketing, types of digital media and multi-screen marketing
- Examine the all-important issue of social media strategy
- Appreciate the growing role of mobile marketing
- Recognise the change to public relations brought about with online public relations
- Consider the way in which digital is driving innovation
- Understand the challenges of turning 'big data' into meaningful insights
- Explore the requirements for organisations in deciding on a multiple channel-to-market strategy

Outline the central concepts of pricing

- Understand the characteristics and role of price
- Be aware of the differences between price and non-price competition
- Explore key factors that affect pricing decisions
- Examine different pricing objectives
- Consider issues unique to the pricing of products for business markets
- Analyze the concept of economic value to the customer
- Understand the eight major stages of the process used to establish prices
- Learn about demand for a product and analyze the relationships between demand, costs and profits
- Explore the selection of a pricing strategy and understand how to determine a specific price

Explain why, when and how the basic marketing mix requires additional manipulation

- Recognize that in many situations the basic marketing mix requires modification
- Examine the nature of the marketing mix for business markets
- Understand the more complex and extended marketing mix required for services
- Recognize that for marketers involved with global marketing, the marketing mix requires consideration of additional issues

Tata's Nano steers into low pricing

Strategic case

How can a car sell for less than $3 000? That's the price Tata Motors set for its Nano, a four-door and four-seat sub-compact designed specifically for India, where it was introduced in 2009. Launches in Sri Lanka and Nepal followed in 2011. With a rear-mounted motor, this tiny car initially included absolutely no extras – no radio, no reclining seats, certainly no aircon or electric windows. What the Nano does have, however, is an ultra-low price tag. And that is what makes it very attractive to millions of potential buyers in India. Now 'someone who never even dreamed of a car finds it within reach', says Tata's CEO. The model range today is more extensive, with various engine options and specifications, but still retails between 140 000 to 210 000 Indian rupees (£2 000 or $3 300 to £2 900 or $4 700).

Racing to develop and market the world's cheapest car has been a challenge, even for a car manufacturer with as much experience as Mumbai-based Tata, which is India's largest automaker and owner of Jaguar and Land Rover in the UK. The company began working on the Nano in 2003, with the goal of creating a functional yet eye-pleasing design that would fit buyers' lifestyles and tight budgets and at the same time be profitable to manufacture and sell. The most essential ingredient was keeping costs in line to keep the car ultra-affordable.

Low price, low costs

The first step in developing the Nano was to establish an upper level for the car's price: roughly one lakh (100 000 Indian rupees), the equivalent of less than £1 400. To sell a car at this price, 'you have to cut costs on everything – seats, materials, components, the whole package', says a Tata official. That's exactly what Tata did, using expertise gained from its years of marketing trucks, cars and buses for markets in India, Europe, South America, Southeast Asia and the Middle East. For instance, Tata sells its Indica compact car for $8 500 in Eastern Europe. The 330 horsepower engine of the Nano may not win any races, but it can get the car to a top speed of about 80 miles per hour. Thanks to low cost parts and manufacturing, the cost of each engine is only about $700. In contrast, an engine made in the West can be twice as much. By shaving the cost of each part and component, streamlining assembly methods, and offering only a stripped-down basic model, Tata has been able to achieve its low price goal.

What's driving the market?

India's healthy economy is propelling millions of consumers into the middle class and accelerating demand for affordable transportation. As many as 65 million people currently drive small motor scooters in India, often carrying family members on the back. Some of these drivers will be able to trade up to a new car if the price is right.

In fact, sales of small cars are projected to be 1 million units in 2016. Small wonder that Tata designed its Nano with four doors to appeal to buyers who often have family members and friends riding along. Finally, India's population skews young, with a median age under 25. If Tata can attract young first-time buyers with a low priced model and maintain their loyalty as they trade up to higher priced cars in the years ahead, the company will profit in the long term.

Competition on the roads of India

Competition is fierce at the low end of the car market. Maruti Suzuki India, which sells small cars starting at about $3 300,

is the market leader. With its nationwide service network, high brand recognition and new production facilities in the works, Maruti Suzuki is a formidable competitor.

Other rivals are also expanding to take advantage of this fast-growing segment of the market. Hyundai India, for instance, is opening a global centre for small car manufacturing and adding manufacturing space. Its Santro, which offers both air conditioning and power steering as standard features, sells for about 320 000 rupees ($5 200). Volkswagen's Skoda division offers the low priced Fabia model, among others, in India.

Toyota is designing a no-frills car that will sell in India and other emerging nations for under $7 500. In the process, the company expects to develop new technology that will help it cut costs on other vehicles in its global product mix. Honda has a plant in India and is opening a second plant to support its marketing initiatives in the area. Meanwhile, US carmakers are looking at how they might address the market in India.

Recent development efforts by Indian motorcycle manufacturer Bajaj to boost its sales have resulted in the development of the first offering in a new quadricycle class. Bajaj claims the RE60 is a more comfortable option than the three wheel auto-rickshaws commonly seen across India. Although at first glance this vehicle has the appearance of a small car, its top speed and other features mean it cannot be classified as such. With prices expected of around 130 000 rupees ($2 000) competition looks set to intensify.

To shave costs, Renault-Nissan limited the number of parts that go into the Logan and avoided expensive electronics. To speed development and eliminate the high costs of building prototypes, the company proceeded from digital design directly to production. This alone saved $40 million and is one reason for the CEO's confidence that Renault-Nissan can succeed in the worldwide ultra-low-price segment. 'With the Logan, we have the product and we have the lead', he says.

Environmental and safety concerns

As enthusiastic as Tata and other car manufacturers may be about marketing millions of tiny cars with tiny price tags, the car has generated both environmental and safety concerns. Some critics fear that broadening the base of car ownership will only add to the pollution problems in India's largest cities. Where national and local regulations do not require anti-pollution devices, manufacturers are unlikely to install them because of the added costs.

Safety is an issue because more cars on the road mean more traffic congestion and more opportunity for accidents.

Cars made by Tata and its competitors comply with all of India's safety standards, but those standards do not require equipment such as air bags and antilock brakes. Safety advocates worry that people travelling in the smallest and lightest cars will be more vulnerable to serious injury if involved in a traffic accident. For now, the automakers are moving ahead as they monitor the issues and stay alert for possible changes in government regulations.

Getting in gear

Buyers have responded to the Nano's low price tag. Tata received more than 200 000 orders during the 12 months after the car's introduction. Because of limited production capabilities, it used a lottery system to select the first 100 000 buyers. Recently, Tata opened a second factory that can produce 250 000 Nanos per year, in an effort to keep up with the expected surge in demand as the Indian economy grows and consumers continue to trade up from motorcycles to cars.

Tata has a long history of good marketing management and above-average profitability. Being based in India gives Tata the advantage of being close to its customers and understanding their needs. Tata's engineers and designers have found creative ways of containing costs to keep the new car ultra-affordable. However, with increased competition in the super-budget segment, Tata will have to get in gear to keep the Nano ahead of the pack.

Questions for discussion

1. Explain which factors seem to have the greatest influence on Tata's decision about pricing its Nano.

2. Assess the level of competition in India's car industry. What are the implications for Tata's marketing?

3. Why must Tata pay close attention to legal and regulatory changes when planning and pricing future models of the Nano?

Sources: http://tatanano.inservices.tatamotors.com/tatamotors/, July 2011; http://www.tatamotors.com/about-us/company-profile.php, March 2015; http://www.rediff.com/business/slide-show/slide-show-1-auto-7-awesome-small-cars-coming-soon-to-india/20140318.htm#3, March 2015.

PART FOUR
Marketing management

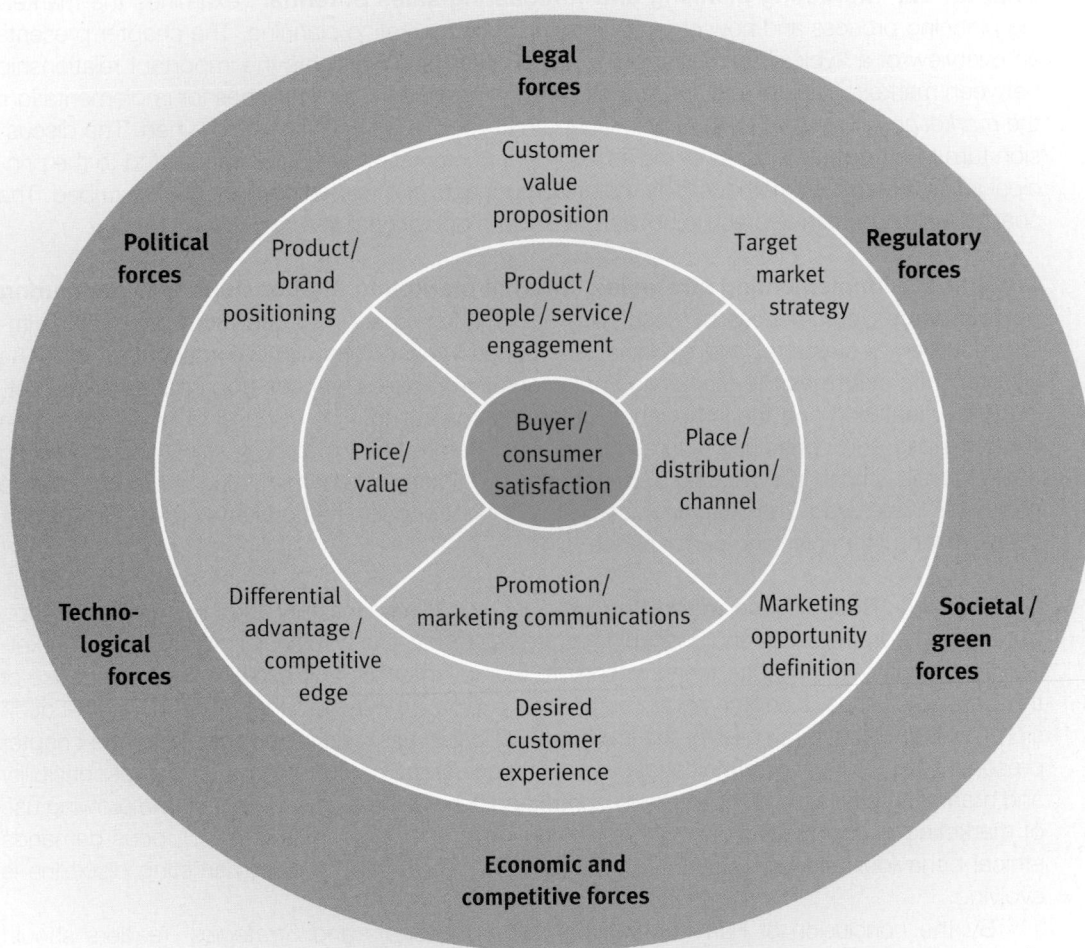

In Figure 1.4, the generic tasks of marketing strategy were identified as marketing opportunity analysis, target market strategy, marketing mix development and marketing management. Parts One to Three of *Marketing: Concepts and Strategies* examined the first three of these generic tasks. Chapter 2 discussed marketing strategy in detail, and target market selection was explored in Chapters 7 and 8. The focus of Part Four is on the core aspects of marketing management: implementation and control of marketing strategy and marketing activity, in particular the popular and important technique of marketing planning. Control of performance is very important. Of growing concern to marketers and consumers are the topics of ethics and social responsibility in marketing. These issues must be of central concern to marketers when they determine marketing strategies and then strive to implement these strategies.

Part Four of *Marketing: Concepts and Strategies* explores the central issues of marketing management: marketing planning and forecasting sales potential; implementing strategies, internal marketing relationships and measuring performance; and the role of ethics and social responsibility in responsible marketing. The growth of social marketing is also further explored.

Chapter 22, 'Marketing planning and forecasting sales potential', examines the marketing planning process and how organizations practice marketing planning. The chapter presents an overview of a 'typical' marketing plan. The chapter then highlights the important relationship between marketing analysis, marketing strategy and marketing programmes for implementation: the *marketing process* as described in Chapter 1. The SWOT analysis is explained. The discussion turns to the related issues of the assessment of market and sales potential, and to the principal sales forecasting methods. The major components of a marketing audit are described. The chapter helps readers appreciate how organizations operationalize a marketing strategy.

Chapter 23, 'Implementing strategies, internal marketing relationships and measuring performance', commences by describing how marketing activities are often organized within a company's structure, and explains the various ways of organizing a marketing unit. The chapter then examines the marketing implementation process, various approaches to marketing implementation and the importance of internal marketing. The discussion next focuses on implementing and controlling marketing activities, before looking at how sales and marketing cost analysis is used in evaluating performance. The emergence of marketing shareholder value analysis is introduced. The chapter closes with a look at popular methods and criteria for evaluating marketing strategies and performance.

Chapter 24, 'Responsible marketing', defines social responsibility, explaining the concept, exploring important issues and describing strategies for dealing with social dilemmas for marketers. The focus of the chapter then switches to marketing ethics and explains the importance of this concept in today's environment. The chapter explores the factors that influence ethical decision-making, discussing some of the important ethical issues marketers face. Next, the chapter presents ways of improving ethical decisions in marketing. The concepts of social responsibility and marketing ethics are compared and contrasted. Finally, the chapter explores the growing use of marketing in applications of social marketing, which because of its areas of focus demands ethical behaviour and high standards. This leads to a view of how the marketing discipline is evolving.

By the conclusion of Part Four of *Marketing: Concepts and Strategies,* readers should understand more about the complexities of managing marketing strategies and marketing programmes, the role of marketing planning, forecasting sales potential, evaluating marketing performance, ways of implementing marketing strategy and the significant influence of ethics and social responsibility in today's marketing, together with the broader reach of marketing in society through social marketing applications.

CHAPTER 22

Marketing planning and forecasting sales potential

"Planning identifies opportunities and creates engagement programmes, but also aligns the organization to these priorities and establishes controls"

Objectives

- To understand the marketing planning process.

- To gain an overview of the marketing plan.

- To examine the relationship between marketing analysis, marketing strategy and marketing programmes in marketing planning.

- To examine the role of the SWOT analysis in marketing planning.

- To become familiar with market and sales potential, and sales forecasting methods.

- To analyze the major components of a marketing audit.

- To appreciate how organizations operationalize a marketing strategy.

INTRODUCTION

Manipulation of the marketing mix to match target market needs and expectations constitutes a daily activity for most marketing personnel. However, as explained in the first two chapters of *Marketing: Concepts and Strategies*, fundamental strategic decisions need to be made *before* the marketing mix(es) are formulated and marketing programmes are executed. To expedite this process and link the strategic decision-making to the development of actionable marketing programmes, many organizations – small and large – turn to marketing planning. This chapter examines the nature of marketing planning. Like all business activities, marketing needs to have goals; often these are sales targets and market share objectives (see Chapter 23 for a full discussion of marketing performance metrics). To set the right goals, marketers must be able to forecast future sales and market size trends, as explained in this chapter.

Marketing planning is a systematic process involving the assessment of marketing opportunities and resources, the determination of marketing objectives, and the development of a plan for implementation and control. It is an annual activity in most organizations, helping to direct and control the activities of marketers, and guide the activities of the other functions within a company.

A sales forecast is an estimation of the amount of a service or product that an organization expects to sell during a specific period at a specified level of marketing activity. Market potential is a prediction of industry-wide market size, everything else being equal, over a specified time period. Marketers often spend large sums on executing marketing programmes, so it is necessary to assess first whether the probable levels of sales warrant such expenditure and commitment of managerial resource. The marketing audit, promoted by many

649

US academics, is a systematic examination of the objectives, strategies, organization and performance of a company's marketing unit. Although its use is far from commonplace, the marketing audit has many purposes, one of which is to help develop an organization's appreciation of its capabilities and market challenges as a prelude to marketing planning. Some companies conduct a marketing audit as a preliminary analysis to gain a realistic understanding of the organization, its personnel and its market.

Planning for growth

When US defence, space and electronics giant, Lockheed Martin, embarked on a new round of marketing planning in its European operations, the company wanted to re-think its priority activities and opportunities, re-aligning its operations accordingly. The MD recognized that this would prove a demanding task, diverting many executives from their daily business and requiring careful management. A central team was created to explore emerging commercial opportunities, diversification possibilities, mergers and acquisitions. Separately, the core planning process focused on each business unit, with their leadership teams instructed to produce updated plans and budgets for their markets and product groups.

An external advisor was appointed to help structure this process and guide the various directors involved with undertaking the planning process. The central business development function was strengthened, recruiting more analysts and networking with those knowledgeable of the company's markets. The two senior business development executives were given the remit of controlling and mentoring the whole process.

The planning process was broken into distinctive phases. For each, guidance was provided to those inputting,

and templates for capturing their outputs were created. These reflected accepted best practice and the tools explained in *Marketing: Concepts and Strategies*. They were constructed so as to steer the subsequent phase of the planning process. In this way, phase I's market analyses and opportunity assessment – which involved financial performance, marketing environment, trend, customer, competitor and capability analyses – informed the company's strategic decisions in phase II. Here, trade-offs were made between existing activities and freshly identified opportunities to pursue, identifying the most attractive realistically attainable set of pursuits and target markets. Phase III explored the required positioning in order to attract the selected customers and how best to establish competitive advantages. Having made certain that the company had compelling propositions to take to growing and highly attractive markets, the next phase considered how best to engage with intended customers and the creation of appropriate sales and marketing programmes. Finally, phase IV provided budgetary and operational frameworks to facilitate roll-out of the plan.

The process required four months of intensive activity. While a few managers were dedicated to this task, most executives were juggling inputting to the planning process alongside their existing daily activities and line management responsibilities. The result was a well-considered strategy with a fully specified marketing plan to guide execution of the strategy. Those involved in the process bought in to the outputs and soon other colleagues shared in the intended direction and detailed implementation programmes. Commercially, significant growth resulted from the re-alignment of resources and re-thought target market priorities. Marketing planning of this sort is essential to provide topical direction informed by market circumstances and developments.

Marketing planning
A systematic process of assessing marketing opportunities and resources, determining marketing objectives and developing a thorough plan for implementation and control.

Marketing plan
A document or blueprint detailing requirements for a company's marketing activity.

Marketing planning cycle
A circular process that runs in two directions, with planning running one way and feedback the other.

This chapter begins with a discussion of the marketing planning process and an overview of the marketing plan. The chapter then discusses the relationship between marketing analysis – including the popular SWOT analysis – marketing strategy and marketing programmes for implementation. The chapter proceeds to examine market and sales potential, and forecasting techniques for predicting sales, before concluding with a discussion of the major components of a marketing audit. Readers should be aware of the importance of forecasting to marketers and of the role of marketing planning, which features in most marketers' calendars.

Marketing planning

Marketing planning is a systematic process that involves assessing marketing opportunities and resources, determining marketing objectives and developing a thorough plan for implementation and control. Research shows that good-quality marketing planning can lead to a positive impact on business performance.[1] A core output of marketing planning is the **marketing plan**, a document or blueprint that details requirements for a company's marketing activity. The marketing planning process involves analyzing the marketplace, modifying or updating the recommended marketing strategy accordingly and developing detailed marketing programmes designed to implement the specified marketing strategy.[2]

Figure 22.1 illustrates the **marketing planning cycle**. Note that marketing planning is a cyclical process. As the dotted feedback lines in the figure indicate, planning is not

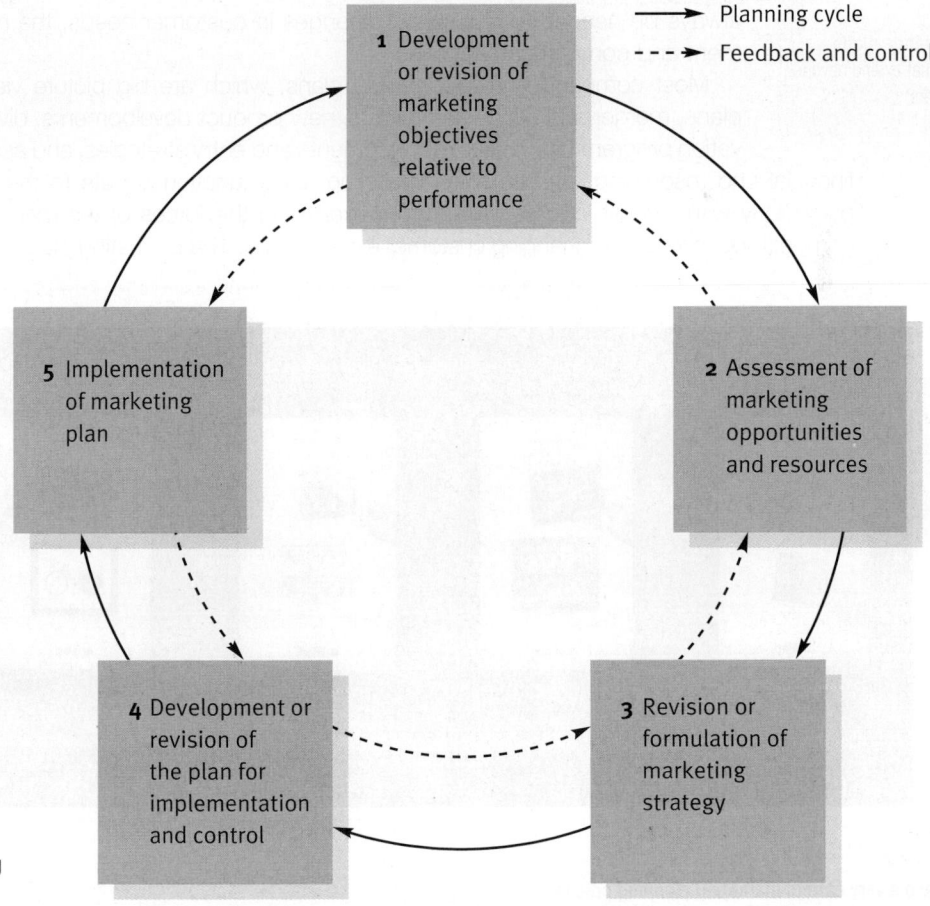

FIGURE 22.1
The marketing planning cycle

one way. Feedback is used to coordinate and synchronize all the stages of the planning cycle, to update market insights, re-think target market strategy and opportunity selection and to re-orientate marketing programmes. Markets are dynamic and endure promiscuous buyers, pesky competitors and poor operation of marketing programmes, so inevitably marketing plans must be modified and re-engineered during their life. Most businesses produce marketing plans annually, typically with a three-year perspective. The immediate 12 months' marketing activity is presented in detail, with overviews provided for years two and three in the three years featured. Once up and running, this process involves revising the previous year's plan by updating the essential marketing analyses, revising the recommended strategy accordingly, before determining detailed marketing mix action plans. Once an organization has gone through the demanding, intensive and resource-hungry process of developing a marketing plan for the first time, subsequent annual revisions are much less taxing. The resulting plan is normally presented to the board or leadership team for approval and budget before becoming a documented set of actions for sales and marketing personnel to follow.

The duration of marketing plans varies. Plans that cover a period of up to a year are called **short-range plans**. **Medium-range plans** are usually for two to four years. Marketing plans that extend beyond five years are generally viewed as **long-range plans**. Marketing managers may have short-, medium- and long-range plans all at the same time. Long-range plans are relatively rare for good reason, given the volatility evident in many markets. Most marketing plans are revised annually, and usually at the same point in an organization's annual calandar.[3] Organizations choose to update fully and revise their marketing plans, modifying their marketing programmes and changing the detail of their marketing mix(es) as a result. Corporate strategic plans, as described in Chapter 2, are unlikely to face annual changes of such magnitude, although strategy modifications will always be needed to respond to changes in customer needs, the marketing environment and competitors' activities.

Most companies have corporate plans, which are big picture views of investment plans, merger and acquisition targets, new product developments, diversifications, innovation programmes, market developments and entry strategies, and associated structure, financial and resourcing requirements. Marketing, as a function, inputs to these strategic plans, particularly with market insights gained from examining the forces of the marketing environment, competitors' moves and changing customer expectations. The marketing plan should be aligned to

Short-range plans
Plans that cover a period of up to a year.

Medium-range plans
Plans that usually cover two to four years.

Long-range plans
Plans that extend beyond five years.

FIGURE 22.2
Apple have a very careful marketing planning process

the over-arching corporate strategy and not head-off into contradictory directions. If marketers find this happening, based on their market analysis, there may be the need for the organization's leadership to re-think its overall corporate strategy.

The extent to which marketing managers develop and use plans varies. Although marketing planning provides numerous benefits, some managers do not use formal marketing plans because they spend almost all their time dealing with daily problems, many of which would be eliminated by adequate planning. However, planning is becoming more important to marketing managers, who realize that planning is necessary to develop, coordinate and control marketing activities effectively and efficiently.[4]

In the authors' *Marketing Planning,* a practitioner text, the benefit of marketing planning is stated as being to provide the basis for an organization:

- serving the 'best' target customers
- beating the competition
- keeping abreast of market developments
- maximizing returns for the organization
- using resources to best advantage
- minimizing threats
- recognizing the organization's strengths and weaknesses.

Malcolm McDonald, a leading authority on marketing planning, argues that marketing planning facilitates:

- coordination of the activities of many individuals whose actions are interrelated over time
- identification of expected developments
- preparedness to meet changes when they occur
- minimization of non-rational responses to the unexpected
- better communication among executives
- minimization of conflicts among individuals that would result in a subordination of the goals of the company to those of the individual.

When formulating a marketing plan, a new enterprise or a company with a new product does not have current performance to evaluate or an existing plan to revise. Therefore, its marketing planning focuses on assessing opportunities and analyzing capabilities appropriate for these emerging opportunities. Managers can then develop a marketing strategy and specify marketing objectives. Research suggests that companies that increase the level of resources put into planning out-perform those that reduce their allocation to these activities.

Marketing plans should do the following:

1. Execute the agreed marketing strategy by detailing appropriate marketing programmes.
2. Specify expected results so that the organization can anticipate what its situation will be at the end of the current planning period.
3. Identify the resources needed to carry out the planned activities so that a budget can be developed.
4. Describe in sufficient detail the activities that are to take place so that responsibilities for implementation can be assigned and schedules determined.
5. Provide for the monitoring of activities and the results so that control can be exerted.[5]
6. Reflect changing customer needs and evolving market developments.
7. Emphasize any differential advantages or strengths over rivals.
8. Provide clarity of purpose within an organization.

There is a logical and relatively straightforward approach to marketing planning:

1. Analysis of markets, the marketing environment, customer expectations, competitors and trends.
2. Analysis of current performance, successes and failures and the underlying reasons.
3. Identification and selection of opportunities to pursue and existing business to support.
4. Determination of core target markets relevant to these new-look priorities.
5. Identification of a basis for competing and a customer value proposition for each opportunity pursued.
6. Statement of specific goals and desired product or service positioning.
7. Development of marketing mixes to create marketing programmes to implement plans.
8. Determination of required budgets and resourcing.
9. Specification of schedules and the allocation of marketing tasks to those responsible for their execution and control.
10. Monitoring of performance and evolving market conditions, taking remedial action as is necessary to execute effectively the plan.

Table 22.1 illustrates these aspects of the marketing planning process in more detail. A good marketing plan addresses each of these aspects thoroughly and objectively, ensuring it is truly customer-focused. To succeed, a company must have a plan that is followed closely yet is flexible enough to allow for adjustments to reflect changes in the marketing environment.[6] Obviously, the

TABLE 22.1   The core steps of the marketing planning process

Analysis

Financial performance
The marketing environment and trends
Company's strengths, weaknesses, opportunities and threats (SWOT)
Customers' needs, buying behaviour and perceptions
Market segmentation and brand positioning
Competition and competitors' strategies
Marketing opportunities
The balance of the product portfolio and ABC sales: contribution analysis

Strategy

Selection of opportunities to pursue and existing business to continue to support
Determination of associated core target markets; basis for competing/differential advantage; customer value propositions; desired product/brand positioning
Agreement on marketing objectives and goals
Specification of sales targets and expected results

Programmes for implementation

Specification of plans for marketing mix programmes:

- products
- promotion
- place/distribution
- people (service) levels
- pricing

Allocation of tasks/responsibilities; timing; costs; budgets
Internal marketing of the plan's goals, strategy, key programmes, metrics, timelines and responsibilities
Ongoing work:

- Monitoring progress and benchmarking performance
- Filling gaps in market insight

Sources: Sally Dibb and Lyndon Simkin, *Marketing Planning* and *The Marketing Planning Workbook* (Cengage: 2008 and 1996). Reprinted with permission.

marketing plan document needs to be written carefully in order to satisfy these objectives. The next section of this chapter takes a closer look at the marketing plan itself.

The marketing plan

The marketing plan is the written document, or blueprint, governing all of an organization's marketing activities, including the implementation and control of those activities.[7] A marketing plan serves a number of purposes:

- offers a 'road map' for implementing a company's strategies and achieving its objectives
- assists in management control and monitoring of the implementation of a strategy
- informs new participants in the plan of their role and function
- specifies how resources are to be allocated
- stimulates thinking and makes better use of resources
- assigns responsibilities, tasks and timing
- makes participants aware of problems, opportunities and threats
- assists in ensuring that an organization is customer focused, aware of market and competitive movements, realistic in its expectations, and prudent in its use of resources
- enables the marketing team to be the 'eyes and ears' or 'radar' for the organization.

A company should have a plan for each marketing opportunity that it pursues and each target market. As such plans must be modified as company circumstances and forces in the marketing environment change, marketing planning is a continuous process. Many companies have separate marketing managers or teams addressing separate regions, different product groups, markets or market segments. Each team would typically have its own marketing plan relevant to its marketplace. In such cases, the Marketing Director or CMO would produce an over-arching all-inclusive marketing plan summarizing the key aspects of each team's plan. Organizations use many different formats when devising marketing plans. Plans may be written for strategic business units, product lines, individual products or brands, or specific markets.

Most plans share some common ground by including an executive summary; a statement of objectives; background to the market in question; headlines from market analysis and examination of realistic marketing opportunities (a description of environmental forces, customers' needs, market segments and internal capabilities); competitor activity; an outline of marketing strategy, target market priorities, differential advantage, brand and product positioning; a statement of expected sales patterns; the detail of marketing mixes required to implement the marketing plan; financial requirements and budgets; controls and performance expectations; and, any operational considerations that arise from the marketing plan (see Table 22.2).

A leading defence conglomerate wanted to use its technological expertise in non-defence markets to generate business opportunities. For example, certain sensors developed for missiles have applications in ocean drilling, fire protection systems and even baby monitors in hospital. Marketing planning enabled this defence company to task its marketers to identify possible opportunities for the company to use its expertise in the oil, alarm, automotive and rail sectors. These opportunities were checked out fully, narrowed down and then addressed with appropriate marketing programmes, through the marketing planning process. The resulting marketing plan was able to articulate the nature of the set of opportunities in non-defence markets and persuade the company's leadership team to sanction the resources required to enter these new markets.

The following sections consider the major parts of a typical marketing plan, as well as the purpose that each part serves.

Management or executive summary   The management summary, or executive summary (often only one or two pages), should be a concise overview of the entire report, including key aims,

TABLE 22.2 Parts of a typical marketing plan

1	Management or executive summary
2	Marketing objectives
	a Detailed company objectives
	b Target market priorities
	c Product group goals
3	Product/market background
	a Product range and explanation
	b Market overview and sales summary
	c Directional policy matrix and evaluation of the product portfolio
4	Marketing analyses
	a Overview of current performance drivers
	b Marketing environment and trends
	c Customers' needs and segments
	d Competition and competitors' strategies
	e Strengths, weaknesses, opportunities, threats (SWOT) analysis
5	Marketing strategies
	a Selected opportunities to pursue and current activities to support
	b Core target markets (segments) related to the priority pursuits
	c Basis for competing/differential advantage
	d Desired product/brand positioning
6	Statement of expected outcomes, sales forecasts and results
7	Marketing programmes for implementation
	a Marketing mixes
	b Tasks, responsibilities and timelines
8	Controls and evaluation: monitoring of performance
9	Financial implications/required budgets
	a Delineation of costs and budgets
	b Expected returns on investment for implementing the marketing plan
10	Operational considerations
	a Personnel issues/requirements
	b Internal marketing relationships, reporting and communications
	c Research and development/production needs
	d Marketing information needs and ongoing market insight work
11	Appendices
	a SWOT analysis details
	b Background data and information
	c Marketing research findings

Sources: Sally Dibb and Lyndon Simkin, *The Marketing Casebook* (Routledge, 1994). Reprinted with permission. Updated from Sally Dibb and Lyndon Simkin, *Marketing Planning* (Cengage, 2008).

overall strategies, fundamental conclusions and salient points regarding the suggested marketing mix programmes. Not many people – especially CEOs – read an entire report, tending to 'dip in' here and there, so the management summary should be comprehensive and clear.

Marketing objective
A statement of what is to be accomplished through marketing activities – the results expected from marketing efforts.

Marketing objectives Objectives are for the benefit of the reader, such as senior executives or new recruits, to give perspective to the report. Aims and objectives should be stated briefly but should include reference to the organization's mission statement and corporate goals, objectives and any fundamental desires for core product groups or brands. This section describes the objectives underlying the plan. A **marketing objective** is a statement of what is to be accomplished through marketing activities.

It specifies the results expected from marketing efforts. A marketing objective should be expressed in clear, simple terms, so that all marketing personnel and other colleagues understand exactly what they are trying to achieve. The marketing objective should be written in such a way that its accomplishment can be measured accurately. If a company has an objective of increasing its market share by 12 per cent, the company should be able to measure changes in its market share accurately. A marketing objective should also indicate the timeframe for accomplishing the objective. For example, a company that sets an objective of introducing three new products should state the time period in which this is to be done, as well as anticipated sales targets.

Objectives may be stated in terms of the degree of product introduction or innovation, sales volume, profitability per unit, gains in market share, heightened dealer interest, media endorsement and digital impact, or improvements in customer satisfaction or awareness of the company's products and brands. They must also be consistent with the company's overall organizational goals. Progress against these metrics should be formally monitored as part of the planning process and cycle.

Product/market background   Product/market background is a necessary section. Not everyone reading the plan will be fully familiar with the products and their markets. Senior managers may be unfamiliar with specific aspects of the product or market. This section 'scene sets', helping the readers for example, a chief executive or advertising manager to understand the context for the marketing plan and its agreed priorities.

Marketing analysis   The analysis section is the heart of the marketing planning exercise: if incomplete or highly subjective, the recommendations are likely to be based on an inaccurate view of the market and the company's potential. This section of the plan provides a sound foundation to the recommendations and marketing programmes. It includes headlines from the analyses of the marketing environment, market trends, customers, competitors, competitive positions and competitors' strategies, the suitability of the business's product portfolio and the financial performance of products, market segments and even certain customers. As this lengthy list of subjects implies, effective marketing planning is about much more than just being customer focused.[8] Marketers therefore need to be careful to include all of these areas in their analyses. However, while the analysis stage is a huge part of the marketing planning process, non-marketing colleagues do not want to read too much detail, so only headlines and highlights should be included in the actual plan, to help explain the strategy choices and underpin the required actions.

The market attractiveness – business strength matrix and the ABC sales: contribution analysis – detailed in Chapter 12 – are popular tools employed by marketers to assess portfolio performance.

The marketing environment section of the marketing plan describes the current state of the marketing environment, including the legal, political, regulatory, technological, societal/green, economic and competitive forces, as well as ethical considerations. It also makes predictions about future directions of those forces. As discussed in Chapter 3, environmental forces can hamper an organization in achieving its objectives, but also reveal opportunities for growth. This section of the marketing plan also describes the possible impact of these forces on the implementation of the marketing plan. Most marketing planning processes include extensive analyses of competitive, technological, legal and regulatory forces, perhaps even creating separate sections in the plan for these influential forces of the marketing environment. It is important that because the forces of the marketing environment are dynamic, marketing plans should be reviewed and modified periodically to adjust to change.

Marketing exists to enable an organization to meet customers' needs properly. This is particularly true in the marketing planning process. The views, needs and expectations of current and potential customers are important as a basis for formal marketing planning. Without such an understanding and analysis of likely changes in customer requirements, it is impossible to safely target those markets of most benefit to the organization's fortunes. It is also impossible to specify a correct marketing mix (or mixes).

The analysis of the market includes competitive forces and trends. As explained in Chapter 2, a meaningful marketing plan and associated programmes for implementation necessitate a prior comprehensive analysis of an organization's competitive position in its markets and territories, together with an understanding of rival organizations' marketing strategies and direction. The failure to understand or anticipate competitors' likely actions is a major weakness in most businesses.[9] Marketers should consider how key competitors will react to their proposed plans, incorporating follow-up programmes prepared to combat hostile reaction from such rivals. In practice, too few companies properly understand their competitors' strategies or capabilities, so fail to realistically appreciate how competitors will react and impact on their plans. This should not be the case: marketers have a responsibility to glean competitor insights and to share these with senior colleagues.

SWOT analysis
Analysis that determines a company's situation by examining four factors: strengths, weaknesses, opportunities and threats.

The **SWOT analysis** is an important foundation for any marketing plan, helping to produce realistic and meaningful recommendations. The section in the main body of the report should be kept to a concise overview, with detailed market-by-market or country-by-country SWOTs and their full explanations kept to the appendices. Most marketers and senior management teams conduct SWOT analyses (the letters SWOT stand for strengths, weaknesses, opportunities and threats). The first half of this analysis – strengths and weaknesses – examines the company's position and capabilities, or that of its product, vis-à-vis customers, competitor activity, environmental trends and company resources. The second half of the SWOT takes this review further to examine the opportunities and threats identified, and to make recommendations that feed into marketing strategy and the marketing mix actions. The marketing environment analysis often reveals potential opportunities and threats. Understanding and then responding to these opportunities and threats enables a business to make the most of the environmental context in which it operates. Even a potential threat can be transformed into an opportunity if appropriate action is taken.[10] The result of the SWOT analysis should be a thorough understanding of the organization's status and its standing in its markets. A SWOT analysis must be objective, with evidence provided to support the points cited. The focus should be on issues likely to concern customers. As explained in Chapter 2, which offers illustrative SWOT analyses, the checklist-style SWOT analysis is popular with marketers, particularly as part of a marketing plan; few marketing plans are without one.

Marketing strategies   Strategies should be self-evident, if the analyses have been objective and thorough: the opportunities to pursue, the target markets most beneficial to the company, the basis for competing and the desired product or brand positioning. This strategy statement must be realistic and detailed enough to act upon, providing clear direction throughout the organization and for the leadership team.

This section of the marketing plan provides a broad overview of the plan for achieving the marketing objectives and, ultimately, the organizational goals. Marketing strategy focuses on identifying opportunities to be pursued, defining a target market and developing a marketing mix to gain long-run competitive and customer advantages. There is a degree of overlap between corporate strategy and marketing strategy. Marketing strategy is unique in that it has the responsibility to assess buyer needs and the company's potential for gaining competitive advantage, both of which, ultimately, must guide the corporate mission.[11] In other words, marketing strategy guides the company's direction in relationships between customers and competitors. The bottom line is that a marketing strategy must be consistent with consumer needs, perceptions and beliefs. Thus this section should describe the company's intended target market(s) and how product, people, promotion, place/distribution and price will be used to develop a compelling proposition and product or brand positioning that will satisfy the needs of members of the target market(s).

Expected results   Having highlighted the strategic direction and intention, it is important to explain the expected results, RoI and sales volumes, to show why the strategies should be followed. These forecasts should be quantified. This stage is important if the required marketing mix budgets are to be approved by senior managers.

Marketing programmes for implementation Marketing programme recommendations are the culmination of the various analyses and statements of strategies: exactly what needs to be done, how and why. This is the detailed presentation of the proposed marketing mixes to achieve the goals and implement the strategies. In poor marketing plans, there is a lack of analysis and strategy, with the focus falling fully on the tactical marketing mix recommendations. Robust planning requires the recommendation of detailed marketing mixes, but only after time has been taken to thoroughly address the core marketing analyses and determine a detailed marketing strategy.

Each market or market segment to be targeted may require its own, tailor-made marketing mix. This section of the marketing plan is of paramount importance, as it gives the specific details of the marketing activity required to implement the marketing plan and to achieve the organization's strategic goals. Each element of the marketing mix should be discussed in turn, with specific recommendations explained in sufficient detail to enable managers to put them into action. Product, people (service), pricing, place/distribution and promotion (marketing communications) must all be addressed. Associated tasks should be allocated to personnel and responsibilities for action clearly identified. This is the core output of marketing planning: the detailed plan of action for the business's marketing programmes. Organizations must also be prepared to adapt their implementation plans if unexpected events arise that were not predicted by the plan. Research shows that in smaller businesses, marketing and business success are linked to how good they are at improvising if the unexpected happens.[12]

Controls and evaluation It is essential that controls be established along with measures to assess the ongoing implementation of the marketing plan. This section of the plan details how the results of the plan will be measured. For example, the results of an advertising campaign designed to increase market share may be measured in terms of increases in sales volume or improved brand recognition and acceptance by consumers. Next, a schedule for comparing the results achieved with the objectives set forth in the marketing plan is developed. Finally, guidelines may be offered outlining who is responsible for monitoring the programme and taking remedial action. Financial measures such as sales volumes, profitability and market shares will be included. 'Softer' issues, such as brand awareness and customer satisfaction, should also be monitored.[13] The next chapter of *Marketing: Concepts and Strategies* explains in more detail implementation controls and performance measures.

Financial implications/required budgets The full picture may not be known, but an indication of required resources and the financial implications must be given. The financial projections and budgets section outlines the returns expected through implementation of the plan. The costs incurred will be weighed against expected revenues. A budget must be prepared to allocate resources in order to accomplish specific marketing objectives. It should contain estimates of the costs of implementing the plan, including the costs of advertising, digital activity, brand building, salesforce training and remuneration, development of distribution channels and marketing research.

Operational considerations These strategies and marketing programmes may have ramifications for other product groups, sectors or territories, for research and development, for engineering or production, and so on. The operational implications must be highlighted, but too much detail may be inappropriate and politically sensitive within the organization.

Appendices The main body of the report should be as concise as possible. However, the document must tell the full story and include evidence and statistics that support the strategies and marketing programmes being recommended. The use of appendices – as long as they are fully cross-referenced in the main body of the report – helps to keep the report concise and well-focused.

Conducting marketing planning

Experienced marketers produce their own marketing plans, often with the involvement of colleagues from other functional areas within the organization and particularly the members of the sales team, who have knowledge of market trends and customer issues. Most companies set a point in the year when each business unit is expected to submit a detailed marketing plan, with fully costed marketing programmes set against detailed sales expectations and market share targets. Most marketing teams will spend at least the month before the deadline updating their marketing analyses and strategic thinking, before detailing revised marketing mix programmes.

In organizations embarking on marketing planning for the first time, there is often a significant learning curve to address, with the first round of marketing analyses requiring a long lead time and much resourcing. The managers involved have to learn new skills and accommodate the planning tasks alongside their normal tasks.[14] By year three, the marketing planning process has generally become part of the organization's fabric and the required analyses are being updated routinely throughout the year by marketers well versed in the planning process's requirements.[15] Initially, though, 'naive' organizations – those not experienced in the marketing planning process – often seek the help of external experts and facilitators, as outlined in the Marketing Tools and Techniques box below.

Marketing tools and techniques

JCB's adoption of marketing planning

Some time ago, the then incumbent Marketing Director of construction equipment leader JCB went to study strategic marketing at INSEAD in France. On his return to the UK headquarters of JCB he introduced a formal marketing planning process to the company. Recognizing the cultural diversity and complexity of a global business, the Marketing Director opted to focus initially on the UK. At the time the company had four core product groups, including backhoe loaders and telehandlers, plus some quickly emerging new product categories, such as skid steers and mini-excavators. Each product group had its own set of marketers, thus each team produced a marketing plan.

As the marketing planning process was new to the company, external trainers were brought in to establish a stage-by-stage sequence of activities, and to provide the company's sales and marketing staff with the required analytical toolkit. Stage one included the core marketing analyses: financial performance of the company's products and sales analysis; the marketing environment forces active in each product group's target markets; the buying behaviour characteristics and evolving customer needs; competitors' products, strengths, weaknesses and projected plans; the company's brand positioning vis-à-vis leading rivals; plus, JCB's capabilities. These tasks proved time-consuming for already busy personnel, so some external support was commissioned in order to research customers and competitors. Small teams from within the marketing function were allocated to the different forces of the marketing environment: technological developments, regulatory pressures, economic trends and so forth. These teams reviewed secondary sources for information, networked with JCB and dealer personnel, met with subject experts to solicit their views, and created a dialogue with industry observers. To examine competitors, the JCB marketers visited trade shows, talked with customers and dealers, analyzed rivals' products and marketing programmes, reviewed financial performance and engaged with industry-watchers. Marketing research in the form of one-to-one depth interviews and focus groups gleaned customers' views of JCB, its products and customer service, changing customer needs and the customers' views of competitors. Some of these analyses were undertaken by teams of marketers working across JCB's product groups and target markets, while much research was specific to the separate marketing teams handling each product group in the company.

Within six weeks, a significant amount of marketing intelligence had been derived, updated, collated and analyzed. Stage two, externally moderated by consultants, involved brainstorming workshops with sales and marketing personnel reflecting on current strategies in the light of the various marketing analyses conducted. As a result, the target market priorities were modified, new products commissioned, revised marketing communications created, modified pricing considered, dealer plans revisited and customer service improved. An important aspect of stage two was the sharing of marketing intelligence particularly about competitors, opportunities and threats between the separate marketing teams. The final stage of the process involved the formalization of appropriate marketing programmes to operationalize the revised marketing strategy, coordination of the separate teams' proposed marketing programmes, plus the allocation of budgets, personnel, schedules and responsibilities to these emerging tasks.

In year two, when the summer marketing planning period was reached, JCB's subsidiary companies overseas were also included, producing top-line marketing plans. Managers overseas were able to learn from their UK colleagues and emulate the format of their resulting marketing plans. For the UK marketers in their second season, there was the opportunity to address outstanding marketing analysis gaps from the previous year and to focus on utilizing the marketing planning toolkit rather than learning about its scope and tools.

By year three, the rest of JCB's non-UK operation had become involved, while in the UK the growing understanding of the marketplace facilitated by two years' marketing planning and marketing intelligence gathering led to the creation of new target market segments. The marketing plans by year three were segment-specific, ignoring the product groups created by JCB for operational convenience. This led to the formation of the company's Compact Division, recognizing that customers of mini-excavators or mini-skid steers had different purchasing behaviour to customers buying the larger-scale versions of such products.

After three years, one manager described the marketing planning process thus:

In the first year it was really hard – hell: learning new skills; realizing we had inadequate or incomplete knowledge of market trends, competitors and even customers; adjusting to undertaking the planning work alongside our 'day jobs' . . . just finding the time. The process now is routine: we never miss the opportunity to find out about customer views, examine competitors or discuss market developments with 'those in the know'. We're also much quicker in producing and delivering the marketing plan. The big difference is that now the company's strategic planning and budgeting are guided by the analyses and market understanding provided by the marketing plan. More to the point, we're selling more machines, in a larger number of segments to more satisfied customers. Even better, whether in our French subsidiary, Indian plant or American sales office, we're all addressing the market in a coordinated manner and everyone is aware of the requirements for effective marketing planning. But it has taken three years. Finding the time was hard to start with. It did 'hurt' in the first year!

Having examined marketing planning, this chapter now focuses on an important aspect of planning but one also necessary for any marketing strategy: forecasting sales and evaluating market potential. Forecasting is integral to marketing planning, in order to justify the use of resources as recommended in the marketing plan. Without some notion of likely sales and financial reward, it is difficult to sign off any new marketing strategy or commit a budget to executing suggested marketing programmes.

Market and sales potential and sales forecasting

Unfortunately, many organizations' sales and marketing activities are reactions to changes in the marketplace, particularly the actions of competitors, rather than planned and carefully orchestrated activities that anticipate consumer needs and expectations. In such reactive organizations, predictions of future changes in market size and potential tend to be rudimentary or non-existent. Estimations of their own likely sales are often based only on the hunches of managers or on the *status quo* of current performance. The forecasting of market potential and expected sales is problematic, but must be undertaken thoroughly and with as much objectivity as marketing intelligence and market insight permit. Forecasts are integral to robust marketing planning. They are also pivotal to shrewd budgeting and the allocation of promotional mix budgets. As explored in Chapter 23, monitoring performance is an essential part of the marketing process. Without an assessment of likely sales, it is difficult to evaluate performance. This section focuses on market and sales potential, and on sales forecasting techniques.

Market and sales potential

Market potential
The total amount of a product that customers will purchase within a specified period of time at a specific level of industry-wide marketing activity.

Market potential is the total amount of a product that customers will purchase within a specified period of time at a specific level of industry-wide marketing activity. Market potential can be stated in terms of monetary value or units, and can refer to a total market or to a market segment. As shown in Figure 22.3, market potential depends on economic, social and other marketing environment factors. When analyzing market potential, it is important to specify a timeframe and to indicate the relevant level of industry marketing activities. One airline determined that in one year 3 300 000 customers travelled to Europe on its aircraft, and had estimates for those travelling with competitors. The airline also had information suggesting the sizes of rivals' marketing budgets and the allocation of this funding across various activities. Based on this information, its marketers were able to estimate the market potential for European travel on its flights in the following year, taking into account other environmental factors and market trends.

Marketers have to assume a certain general level of marketing effort in the industry when they estimate market potential. The specific level of marketing effort certainly varies from one company to another, but the sum of all companies' marketing activities equals industry marketing efforts. A marketing manager must also consider whether, and to what extent, industry marketing efforts will change. For instance, in estimating the market potential for Microsoft Office, Microsoft must consider changes in marketing efforts by other software producers.

If marketing managers at Microsoft know that a rival is planning to introduce a new version of its spreadsheet product with a new advertising campaign, this fact will contribute to Microsoft's estimate of the market potential for this computer software.

Sales potential
The maximum percentage of market potential that an individual company can obtain for a specific product or service.

Sales potential is the maximum percentage of market potential that an individual company within an industry can expect to obtain for a specific product or service (see Figure 22.3). Several general factors influence a company's sales potential. First, the

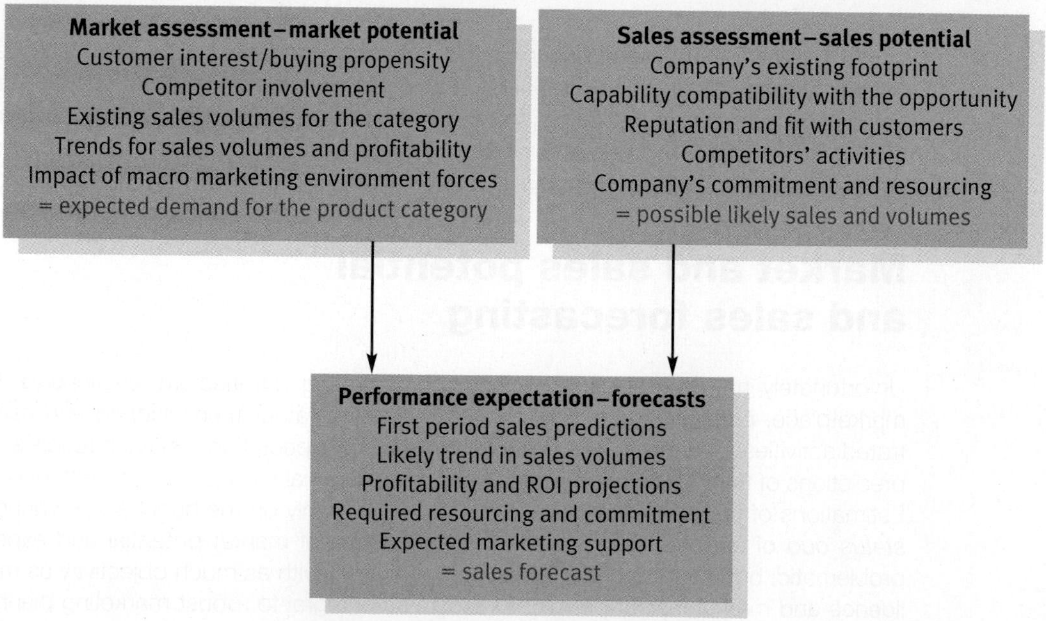

Market assessment – market potential
Customer interest/buying propensity
Competitor involvement
Existing sales volumes for the category
Trends for sales volumes and profitability
Impact of macro marketing environment forces
= expected demand for the product category

Sales assessment – sales potential
Company's existing footprint
Capability compatibility with the opportunity
Reputation and fit with customers
Competitors' activities
Company's commitment and resourcing
= possible likely sales and volumes

Performance expectation – forecasts
First period sales predictions
Likely trend in sales volumes
Profitability and ROI projections
Required resourcing and commitment
Expected marketing support
= sales forecast

FIGURE 22.3
Forecasting market potential and sales

market potential places absolute limits on the size of the company's sales potential. Second, the magnitude of industry-wide marketing activities has an indirect but definite impact on the company's sales potential. Those activities have a direct bearing on the size of the market potential. When Pizza Hut advertises home-delivered pizza, for example, it indirectly promotes pizza in general; its advertisements may, in fact, also help sell competitors' home-delivered pizza. Third, the intensity and effectiveness of a company's marketing activities relative to those of its competitors affect the size of the company's sales potential. If a company is spending twice as much as any of its competitors on marketing efforts and if every unit of currency spent is more effective in generating sales, the company's sales potential will be quite high compared with that of its competitors.

Break-down approach
An approach that derives a company's sales potential from the general economic forecast and the estimate of market potential.

There are two general approaches to measuring sales potential: break-down and build-up. In the **break-down approach**, the marketing manager first develops a general economic forecast for a specific time period. Next, market potential is estimated on the basis of this economic forecast. The company's sales potential is then derived from the general economic forecast and the estimate of market potential.

Build-up approach
An approach that measures the sales potential for a product by first calculating its market potential and then estimating what proportion of that potential the company can expect to obtain.

In the **build-up approach**, an analyst begins by estimating how much of a product a potential buyer in a specific geographic area, such as a sales territory, will purchase in a given period. Then the analyst multiplies that amount by the total number of potential buyers in that area. The analyst performs the same calculation for each geographic area in which the company sells products, and then adds the totals for each area to calculate the market potential. To determine the sales potential, the analyst must estimate, by specific levels of marketing activities, the proportion of the total market potential that the company can obtain.

For example, the marketing manager of a regional paper company with three competitors could estimate the company's sales potential for bulk gift wrapping paper using the build-up approach. The manager may determine that each of the 66 retailer business customers in a single sales territory purchases an average of 10 rolls annually. For that sales territory, the market potential is 660 rolls annually. The analyst follows the same procedure for each of the business's other nine sales territories and then totals the market potential for each sales territory (see Table 22.3). Assuming that this total market potential is 6000 rolls of paper (the quantity expected to be sold by all four paper companies), the marketing manager would estimate the company's sales potential by ascertaining that it could sell about 33 per cent of the estimated 6000 rolls at a certain level of marketing effort

TABLE 22.3   The market potential calculations for bulk wrapping paper

Territory	Number of potential customers	Estimated purchases	Total
1	66	10 rolls	660 rolls
2	62	10	620
3	55	5	275
4	28	25	700
5	119	5	595
6	50	20	1,000
7	46	10	460
8	34	15	510
9	63	10	630
10	55	10	550
		Total market potential	6000 rolls

(2000 rolls). The marketing manager may then develop several sales potentials, based on several levels of marketing effort.

Whether marketers use the break-down or the build-up approach, they depend heavily on sales estimates. To gain a clearer idea of how these estimates are derived, it is essential to understand sales forecasting.

Developing sales forecasts

Sales forecast
The amount of a product that the company actually expects to sell during a specific period of time at a specific level of marketing activity.

A **sales forecast** is the amount of a product that the company actually expects to sell during a specific period of time at a specified level of marketing activity (see Figure 22.3). The sales forecast differs from the sales potential: it concentrates on what the actual sales will be at a certain level of marketing effort, whereas the sales potential assesses what sales are possible at various levels of marketing activities, based on certain environmental conditions. Companies use the sales forecast for planning, organizing, implementing and controlling their activities. The success of numerous activities depends on the accuracy of this forecast. Forecasts help to estimate market attractiveness, monitor performances, acquire and allocate resources effectively and efficiently, and gear up production to meet demand. Excess stocks are wasteful and cost money; but production set too low leads to missed sales, and perhaps customer or distributor unease.[16] As described in the Topical Insight box on the following page, Harley-Davidson has required shrewd forecasting and planning to guide its entry into India.

A sales forecast must be time-specific. Sales projections can be short (up to a year), medium (one to four years) or long (longer than five years). The length of time chosen for the sales forecast depends on the purpose and uses of the forecast, the stability of the market, and the company's objectives and resources. Many companies set their marketers quarterly targets for the year ahead, limited to an annual projection.

To forecast sales, a marketer can choose from a number of forecasting methods. Some of these are arbitrary; others are more scientific, complex and time consuming. A business's choice of method or methods depends on the costs involved, the type of product, the characteristics of the market, the time span of the forecast, the purposes of the forecast, the stability of the historical sales data, the availability of required information, and the forecasters' expertise and experience.[17] The common forecasting techniques fall into five categories: executive judgement, surveys, time series analysis, correlation methods and market tests.[18]

Executive judgement
A way of forecasting sales based on the intuition of one or more executives.

Executive judgement
At times, a company forecasts sales chiefly on the basis of **executive judgement**, which is the intuition of one or more executives. This approach is highly unscientific but expedient and inexpensive. Executive judgement may work reasonably well when product demand is relatively stable and the forecaster has years of market-related experience. However, because intuition is swayed most heavily by recent experience, the forecast may be overly optimistic or overly pessimistic. Another drawback to intuition is that the forecaster has only past experience as a guide when deciding where to go in the future.

Surveys
A method of questioning customers, sales personnel or experts regarding their expectations about future purchases.

Surveys
A second way to forecast sales is to use **surveys**, questioning customers, sales personnel or experts regarding their expectations about future purchases.

Customer forecasting survey
A method of asking customers what types and quantities of products they intend to buy during a specific period of time.

Through a **customer forecasting survey**, marketers can ask customers what types and quantities of products they intend to buy during a specific period of time. This approach may be useful to a business that has relatively few customers. For example, a computer chip producer that markets to fewer than a hundred computer manufacturers could conduct a customer survey. PepsiCo, though, has millions of consumers and cannot feasibly use a customer survey to forecast future sales, unless its sampling

Harley rides into India

Hitting the open road on a Harley has been an American dream since 1903 and one pursued by consumers across many countries. The brand is synonymous with Hollywood movies, US road trips, freedom, fun, excitement and looking cool. Now consumers in India can share the dream. Harley-Davidson had wanted to enter the India market for several years, but government restrictions and high tariffs held it back. In 2007, a deal involving the USA and India changed Indian emissions restrictions and opened the door for Harley's entry.

Harley began selling 12 models in India in 2010, the least expensive priced at $15 000, almost twice the price US customers pay. Although India is the second-largest motorcycle market worldwide, most Indians favour cheaper motorcycles and scooters priced under $1000. However, because of India's growing economy, expanding middle class and new highway construction, Harley was not worried about selling to Indian consumers. The company believed the affluent middle classes and brand appeal of a Harley would combine to create surging sales growth, particularly in light of India's rapidly growing luxury market and the sales successes of many international brands established in India.

Harley's CEO, Keith Wandell, explained that the company was committed to making its entrance into India a long-term success. Harley initially imported its bikes into India fully assembled, avoiding the need for factories and other overheads. However, this approach resulted in high tariffs (roughly 90 per cent) as well as Indian taxes. Therefore, the company set up a production facility at Bawal in 2011, its only one outside the USA, to assemble the Sportster line, then from 2012 the Dyna line, the Softail from 2013 and the Street 750 and 500 in 2014. The Street platform is jointly manufactured at Harley-Davidson's US and India plants. The Street 750 is now exported to European and other Asian markets from the Indian plant.

Harley had to pay special attention to strategic planning, taking into account the social, cultural, economic, political and ethical forces within India, all of which differed significantly to conditions in its domestic US marketplace. These characteristics initially placed demands on Harley's planners when producing forecasts against a backdrop of incomplete knowledge of consumer demand, unfamiliar competitors and their uncertain reactions to Harley's market entry, as well as the impact of the forces of the marketing environment. Nevertheless, forecasts were necessary in order to manage production and budget for the entry into India.

Harley has come a long way in just a few years of trading in India. A dealer network of fifteen main showrooms now supplements its manufacturing base. Harley-Davidson India also sponsors the country's Harley Owners' Group (HOG). The company organizes five big rides across the north, south, east and west zones along with the *India HOG Rally* that takes place every year in Goa. Harley-Davidson India has also established *Harley Rock Riders*, its annual rock music tour. Harley is optimistic about its possibilities in India, while many Indian consumers are looking forward to owning Harley bikes and living the highway dream.

is known to reflect the entire market, which is hard to verify, or it is polling the views of its main distributors.

Customer surveys have several drawbacks. Customers must be able and willing to make accurate estimates of future product requirements. Although business-to-business buyers can sometimes estimate their anticipated purchases accurately from historical buying data and their own sales forecasts, many cannot make such estimates. In addition, for a variety of reasons, customers may not want to take part in a survey. Occasionally, a few respondents give answers that they know are incorrect, making survey results inaccurate. Moreover, customer surveys reflect buying intentions, not actual purchases. Customers' intentions may not be well formulated, and even when potential purchasers have definite buying intentions, they do not necessarily follow through with them. A common marketing research problem is probing consumers about their actual purchasing and consumption behaviour, as opposed to their perceptions or anticipated behaviour. Finally, customer surveys consume much time and money.

In a **salesforce forecasting survey**, members of the company's salesforce are asked to estimate the anticipated sales in their territories for a specified period

Salesforce forecasting survey
A method of asking members of a company's salesforce to estimate the anticipated sales in their territories for a specified period of time.

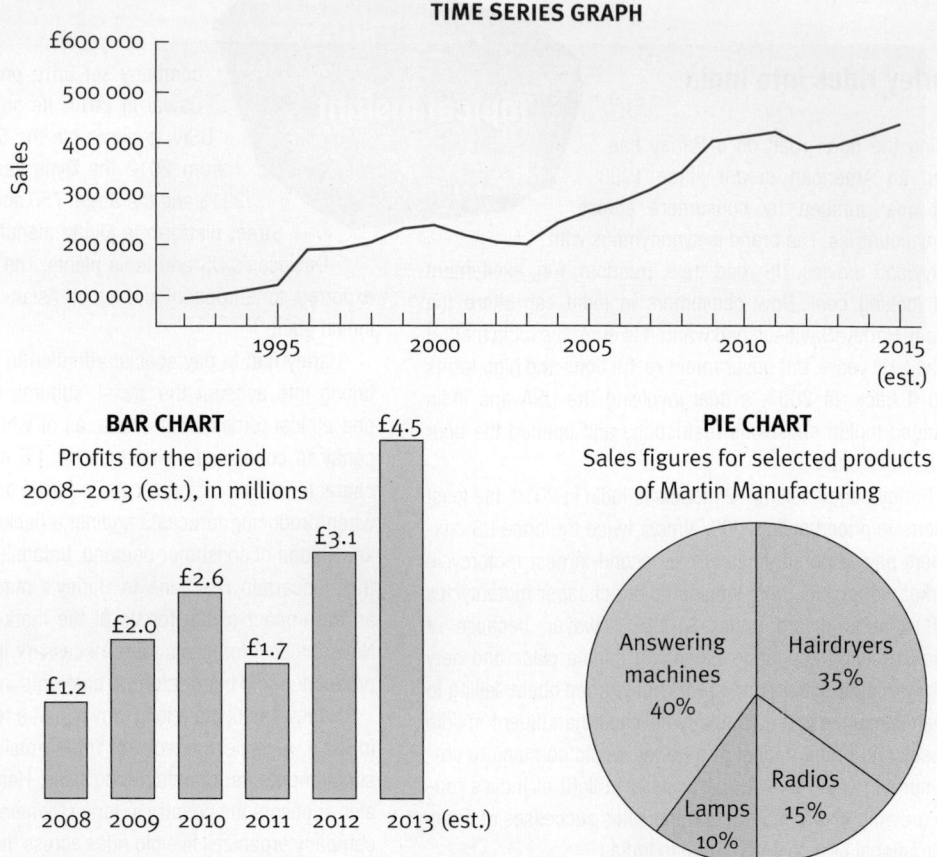

TIME SERIES GRAPH

BAR CHART
Profits for the period
2008–2013 (est.), in millions

PIE CHART
Sales figures for selected products
of Martin Manufacturing

FIGURE 22.4
Graphical presentations of forecasts and sales; visual depictions of sales and profits are popular in marketing plan documents

of time. The forecaster combines these territorial estimates to arrive at a tentative forecast (see Figure 22.3).

A marketer may survey the sales staff for several reasons. The most important one is that the sales staff are closer to customers on a daily basis than other company personnel; therefore they should know more about customers' future product needs and the intensity of competitors' activities. Moreover, when sales representatives assist in developing the forecast, they are more likely to work towards its achievement. Another advantage of this method is that forecasts can be prepared for single territories, for divisions consisting of several territories, for regions made up of multiple divisions and then for the total geographic market. Thus the method readily provides sales forecasts from the smallest geographic sales unit to the largest.

Despite these benefits, a salesforce survey has certain limitations. Sales people can be too optimistic or pessimistic because of recent experiences. In addition, they tend to underestimate the sales potential in their territories when they believe that their sales goals will be determined by their forecasts. They also dislike 'paperwork' because it takes up the time that could be spent selling. If the preparation of a territorial sales forecast is time consuming, the sales staff may not do the job adequately.

Nonetheless, salesforce surveys can be effective under certain conditions. If, for instance, the sales people as a group are accurate or at least consistent estimators, the over-estimates and under-estimates should balance each other out. If the aggregate forecast is consistently over or under actual sales, then the marketer who develops the final forecast can make the necessary adjustments. Assuming that the survey is administered well, the salesforce can have the satisfaction of helping to establish reasonable sales goals. It can also be assured that its forecasts are not being used to set sales quotas.

Delphi method
A centralized forecasting method that takes into account the views of managers, sales personnel and individual participants; aggregates them; and modifies them.

Expert forecasting survey
A survey prepared by outside experts such as economists, management consultants, advertising executives or academics.

Time series analysis
A forecasting technique that uses a company's historical sales data to discover a pattern or patterns in the company's sales over time.

Trend analysis
Analysis that focuses on aggregate sales data over a period of many years to determine whether annual sales are generally rising, falling or constant.

Cycle analysis
A forecasting technique that analyses a company's sales figures over a period of three to five years to ascertain whether sales fluctuate in a consistent, periodic manner.

Seasonal analysis
The study of daily, weekly or monthly sales figures to evaluate the degree to which seasonal factors influence the company's sales.

The **Delphi method** is very popular: managers' and sales personnel's views are validated centrally, and the resulting forecasts are returned to those involved for further comment. Participants such as field managers make separate, individual forecasts. A central analyst independently aggregates and modifies their forecasts. This revised forecast is returned to the separate participants, who can then amend their forecasts in the context of the consolidated picture. The central analyst then collates the updated forecasts to produce the company's overall final forecast. The Delphi technique avoids many weighting and judgemental problems; the median of the group's overall response will tend to be more accurate; and the approach is useful for short-, medium- and long-term forecasts, as well as for new product development, for which there is no historical information on which to base a forecast.

When a company wants an **expert forecasting survey**, it hires experts to help prepare the sales forecast. These experts are usually economists, management consultants, advertising executives, academics or other people outside the company who have solid experience in a specific market. Drawing on this experience and their analyses of available information about the company and the market, the experts prepare and present their forecasts or answer questions regarding a forecast. Using experts is expedient and relatively inexpensive. However, because they work outside the company, experts may not be as motivated as company personnel to do an effective job.

Time series analysis   The technique by which the forecaster, using the company's historical sales data, tries to discover a pattern or patterns in the company's sales over time is called **time series analysis**. If a pattern is found, it can be used to forecast sales. This forecasting method assumes that the past sales pattern will continue in the future. The accuracy, and thus the usefulness, of time series analysis hinges on the validity of this assumption.

In a time series analysis, a forecaster usually performs four types of analysis: trend, cycle, seasonal and random factor.[19] **Trend analysis** focuses on aggregate sales data, such as a company's annual sales figures, over a period of many years, to determine whether annual sales are generally rising, falling or staying about the same. Through **cycle analysis**, a forecaster analyzes sales figures – often monthly sales data – over a period of three to five years, to ascertain whether sales fluctuate in a consistent, periodic manner. When performing **seasonal analysis**, the analyst studies daily, weekly or monthly sales figures to evaluate the degree to which seasonal factors, such as climate and holiday activities, influence the company's sales. **Random factor analysis** is an attempt to attribute erratic sales variations to random, non-recurring events, such as a regional power failure, a natural disaster or political unrest in a foreign market. After performing each of these analyses, the forecaster combines the results to develop the sales forecast.

Time series analysis is an effective forecasting method for products with reasonably stable demand, but it is not useful for products with highly erratic demand. Diageo, the importer and producer of spirits and wines, uses several types of time series analysis for forecasting and has found them quite accurate.

Correlation methods   Like time series analysis, correlation methods are based on historical sales data. When using **correlation methods**,[20] the forecaster attempts to find a relationship between past sales and one or more variables, such as population, per capita income, gross national product, weather events or supply chain constraints. To determine whether a correlation exists, the forecaster analyzes the statistical relationship between changes in past sales and changes in one or more variables – a technique known as regression analysis.[21] The object of regression analysis is a mathematical formula that accurately describes a relationship between the company's sales and one or more variables; however, the formula indicates only an association, not a causal relationship. Once an accurate formula has been established, the analyst plugs the necessary information into the formula to derive the sales forecast.

Correlation methods are useful when a precise relationship can be established. However, a forecaster seldom finds a perfect correlation. Furthermore, this method can be used only when the available historical sales data are extensive and reliable. Ordinarily, correlation techniques are useless for forecasting the sales of new products, or in markets where changes are frequent and extensive.

Market tests Conducting a **market test** involves making a product available to buyers in one or more test areas, and measuring purchases and consumer responses to distribution, promotion and price. Even though test areas are often cities with populations of 200 000 to 500 000, test sites can be larger metropolitan areas or towns with populations of 50 000 to 200 000, or ITV regions. A market test provides information about consumers' actual purchases rather than about their intended purchases. In addition, purchase volume can be evaluated in relation to the intensity of other marketing activities advertising, in-store promotions, pricing, packaging, distribution and so forth. On the basis of customer response in test areas, forecasters can estimate product sales for larger geographic units. For example, Cadbury's Wispa first appeared in the north-east of England. Sales showed management that the company had to build more production capacity to cope with a national roll-out of the brand and full launch.

As it does not require historical sales data, a market test is an effective tool for forecasting the sales of new products or the sales of existing products in new geographic areas. The test gives the forecaster information about customers' real actions rather than their intended or estimated behaviour. A market test also gives a marketer an opportunity to try out various elements of the marketing mix. These tests are, however, often time consuming and expensive. In addition, a marketer cannot be certain that the consumer response during a market test represents the total market response or that such a response will continue in the future.

Using multiple forecasting methods

Although some businesses depend on a single sales forecasting method, most use several techniques. A company is sometimes forced to use several methods when it markets diverse product lines, but even for a single product line several forecasts may be needed, especially when the product is sold in different market segments. Thus, a producer of car tyres may rely on one technique to forecast tyre sales for new cars and on another to forecast the sales of replacement tyres. Variation in the length of the forecasts required may call for several forecast methods. A company that employs one method for a short-range forecast may find it inappropriate for long-range forecasting. Sometimes a marketer verifies the results of one method by using one or several other methods and comparing results.[22] No matter which technique or mix of approaches is deployed, it is essential that marketers produce accurate and useful sales forecasts and assessments of market potential.

The marketing audit

A **marketing audit** is a systematic examination of the marketing function's objectives, strategies, programmes, organization and performance. Its primary purpose is to identify weaknesses in ongoing marketing operations and plan the necessary improvements to correct these weaknesses. The marketing audit does not concern itself with the company's marketing position; that is the purpose of the company's marketing plan. Rather, the marketing audit evaluates how effectively the marketing function or department performed its assigned functions. Not all companies conduct a marketing audit, but when one is used such an assessment generally diagnoses areas requiring improvement and different working practices.

Like an accounting or financial audit, a marketing audit should be conducted regularly instead of just when performance control mechanisms show that the system is out of control. The marketing audit is not a control process to be used only during a crisis, although a business in trouble may use it to isolate problems and generate solutions. It is a useful diagnostic tool for correcting marketing activity. The marketing audit is a useful precursor to undertaking marketing planning, providing an insight into the strengths of the company's marketing function and its activities.

A marketing audit may be specific and focus on one or a few marketing activities, or it may be comprehensive and encompass all of a company's marketing activities. Table 22.4 lists many possible dimensions of a marketing audit. An audit may deal with only a few of these areas, or it may include them all. Its scope depends on the costs involved, the target markets served, the structure of the marketing mix and environmental conditions. The results of the audit can be used to re-allocate marketing effort and to re-examine marketing opportunities.

TABLE 22.4 Dimensions of a marketing audit

Part One The marketing environment audit

Marketing environment forces

A. Economic

1. What does the company expect in the way of inflation, material shortages, unemployment and credit availability in the short run, medium run and long run?
2. What effect will forecast trends in the size, age distribution and regional distribution of population have on the business?

B. Technological

1. What major changes are occurring in product technology?
2. In process technology?
3. What are the major generic substitutes that might replace this product?

C. Political/legal/regulatory

1. What laws are being proposed that may affect marketing strategy and tactics?
2. What national and local government actions should be watched? What is happening with pollution control, health and safety, equal opportunity employment, product safety, advertising, price controls and so on that is relevant to marketing planning?

D. Societal/green

1. What attitude is the public taking towards business and the types of products produced by the company?
2. What changes in consumer lifestyles and values have a bearing on the company's target markets and marketing methods?
3. Will the cost and availability of natural resources directly affect the company?
4. Are there public concerns about the company's role in pollution and conservation? If so, what is the company's reaction?

E. Digital economy

1. What is the impact of digital on the company's customers?
2. How is digital impacting on the supply chain?

3. Is digital altering channel strategy requirements?
4. Is social media creating brand reputation problems?

Markets

A. Market trends

1. What is happening to market size, growth, geographic distribution and profits?
2. What are the major market segments and their expected rates of growth?
3. Which are high opportunity and low opportunity segments?

B. Customers

1. How do current customers and prospects judge the company and its competitors on reputation, product quality, service, salesforce and price?
2. How do different classes of customers make their buying decisions?
3. What evolving needs and satisfactions are the buyers in this market seeking?
4. How will multiple marketing channels relate to these customers?

C. Competitors

1. Who are the major competitors? What are the objectives and strategy of each major competitor? What are their strengths and weaknesses? What are the sizes and trends in market shares?
2. Are new competitors emerging online?
3. What trends can be foreseen in future competition and substitutes for this product?

D. Distribution and dealers

1. What are the main trade channels bringing products to customers?
2. What are the efficiency levels and growth potentials of the different trade channels?
3. To what extent are multi-channels appropriate?
4. Is the customer experience properly managed across channels?

(*Continued*)

TABLE 22.4 Continued

E. Suppliers

1. What is the outlook for the availability of key resources used in production?
2. What trends are occurring among suppliers in their patterns of selling?

F. Facilitators and marketing organizations

1. What is the outlook for the cost and availability of transport services?
2. What is the outlook for the cost and availability of warehousing facilities?
3. What is the outlook for the cost and availability of financial resources?
4. How effectively is the advertising agency performing? What trends are occurring in advertising agency services?
5. To what extent have digital partners been harnessed?

G. Publics

1. Where are the opportunity areas or problems for the company?
2. How effectively is the company dealing with publics?
3. Is it addressing the role of social media?

Part Two Marketing strategy audit

A. Business mission

1. Is the business mission clearly focused with marketing terms and is it attainable?
2. Is the mission followed and part of the company's true ethos?

B. Marketing objectives and goals

1. Are the corporate goals clearly stated? Do they lead logically to the marketing objectives?
2. Are the marketing objectives stated clearly enough to guide marketing planning and subsequent performance measurement?
3. Are the marketing objectives appropriate, given the company's competitive position, resources and opportunities? Is the appropriate strategic objective to build, hold, harvest, divest or terminate this business?

C. Strategy

1. What is the core marketing strategy for achieving the objectives? Is it sound?
2. Are the resources budgeted to accomplish the marketing objectives inadequate, adequate or excessive?
3. Are the marketing resources allocated optimally to prime market segments, territories and products?
4. Are the marketing resources allocated optimally to the major elements of the marketing mix; i.e. product quality, service, salesforce, advertising, promotion, distribution and digital?

Part Three Marketing organization audit

A. Formal structure

1. Is there a high-level marketing manager with adequate authority and responsibility over those company activities that affect customer satisfaction?

2. Are the marketing responsibilities optimally structured along functional, product, end use and territorial lines?

B. Functional efficiency

1. Are there good communications and working relations between marketing and sales?
2. Is the product management system working effectively? Are the product managers able to plan profits or only sales volume?
3. Are there any groups in marketing that need more training, motivation, supervision or evaluation?

C. Interface efficiency

1. Are there any problems between marketing and manufacturing, research and development, purchasing, finance, accounting, legal departments, insight and digital that need attention?
2. Is there clarity and efficiency in communicating and sharing with suppliers and partners?

Part Four Marketing systems audit

A. Market insight

1. Is the marketing intelligence system producing accurate, sufficient and timely information about developments in the marketplace?
2. Is market insight being adequately used by company decision-makers?
3. Is available marketing intelligence properly shared/accessed by managers?

B. Marketing planning system

1. Is the marketing planning system well-conceived and effective?
2. Are sales forecasting and measurement of market potential soundly carried out?
3. Are sales quotas set on a proper basis?

C. Marketing control system

1. Are the control procedures (monthly, quarterly, etc.) adequate to ensure that the annual plan's objectives are being achieved?
2. Is provision made to analyze periodically the profitability and financial worth of different products, markets, territories and channels of distribution?
3. Is provision made to examine and validate periodically various marketing costs?

D. New product development system

1. Is the company well organized to gather, generate and screen new product ideas?
2. Does the company do adequate concept research and business analysis before investing heavily in a new idea?
3. Does the company carry out adequate product and market testing before launching a new product?

Part Five Marketing-productivity audit

A. Profitability analysis

1. What is the profitability of the company's different products, served markets, territories and channels of distribution?

(Continued)

TABLE 22.4 Continued

2. Should the company enter, expand, contract or withdraw from any business segments, and what would be the short- and long-run profit consequences?

B. Cost-effective analysis

1. Do any marketing activities seem to have excessive costs? Are these costs valid?
2. Are cost-reducing steps routinely sought and taken?

Part Six Marketing function audits

A. Products and service

1. What are the product line objectives? Are these objectives sound? Is the current product line meeting these objectives?
2. Are there particular products that should be phased out?
3. Are there new products that are worth adding?
4. Are any products able to benefit from quality, feature or style improvements?
5. Is adequate customer service provided?
6. Is there an aftermarket support package-warranty, parts and servicing, dealer network?

B. Price

1. What are the pricing objectives, policies, strategies and procedures? Are prices set on sound cost, demand and competitive criteria?
2. Do the customers see the company's prices as being in or out of line with the perceived value of its products?
3. Does the company use price promotions effectively?
4. Is there an adequate value proposition?

C. Distribution

1. What are the distribution objectives and strategies?
2. Is there adequate market coverage and service?
3. How effective are the following channel members: distributors, manufacturers' reps, brokers, agents and so on?
4. Should the company consider changing its distribution channels?
5. Does the company manage multiple channels effectively?

D. Promotional mix

1. What are the organization's advertising objectives? Are they sound?
2. Is the right amount being spent on advertising? How is the budget determined?
3. Are the ad themes and copy effective? What do customers and the public think about the advertising?
4. Are the advertising media well chosen?
5. Are the internal advertising staff adequate?
6. Is the sales promotion budget adequate? Is there effective and sufficient use of sales promotion tools, such as samples, coupons, displays and sales contests?
7. Is the publicity budget adequate? Is the public relations staff competent and creative?
8. Is use of the internet appropriate? If so, is the web site well designed?
9. Does the company effectively embrace digital communications?
10. Are social media activities fully executed?
11. Are there well-developed brand communities?
12. Is there an attempt to instil brand advocacy?
13. What of sponsorship? Is it relevant? Are associated third parties appropriate and reputable?
14. Is direct marketing possible? Through what media and with what proposition?

E. Salesforce

1. What are the organization's salesforce objectives?
2. Is the salesforce large enough to accomplish the company's objectives?
3. Is the salesforce organized along the proper principle(s) of specialization (territory, market, product)? Are there enough (or too many) sales managers to guide the field sales reps?
4. Does the sales compensation level and structure provide adequate incentive and reward?
5. Does the salesforce show high morale, ability and effort?
6. Are the procedures for setting quotas and evaluating performance adequate?
7. How does the company's salesforce compare with the salesforces of competitors?

Source: Adapted from Philip Kotler, *Marketing Management: Analysis, Planning, and Control*, 6th edn (Englewood Cliffs, NJ: Prentice Hall, 1988), pp. 748–51. Used by permission.

The marketing audit should aid evaluation by:

1. describing current activities and results in relation to sales, costs, prices, profits and other performance feedback (see Chapter 23)
2. gathering information about customers, competition and marketing environment developments that may affect the marketing strategy and the effective implementation of marketing mix programmes
3. exploring opportunities and alternatives for improving the marketing strategy
4. providing an overall database to be used in evaluating the attainment of organizational goals and marketing objectives
5. diagnosing reasons for the successes and failures experienced by a company's marketers, and their analyses, strategies and tactical marketing mix programmes.

Marketing audits can be performed internally or externally. An internal auditor may be a top-level marketing executive, a company-wide auditing committee or a manager from another office or of another function. Although it is more expensive, an audit by outside consultants is usually more effective; external auditors have more objectivity, more time for the audit and greater experience.

There is no single set of procedures for all marketing audits. However, companies should adhere to several general guidelines. Audits are often based on a series of questionnaires administered to the company's personnel. These questionnaires should be developed carefully to ensure that the audit focuses on the right issues. Auditors should develop and follow a step-by-step plan to guarantee that the audit is systematic. When interviewing company personnel, the auditors should strive to talk to a diverse group of people from many parts of the company. The auditor should become familiar with the product line, meet staff from headquarters, visit field organizations, interview customers, review competitors and analyze information for a report on the marketing environment. The audit framework and associated questionnaires should remain consistent over time, so that improvements and problems can be noted between audits.

To achieve adequate support, the auditors normally focus first on the company's top management and then move down through the organizational hierarchy. The auditor looks for different points of view within various departments of the organization or a mismatch between the customers' and the company's perception of the product as signs of trouble in an organization. The results of the audit should be reported in a comprehensive written document, which should include recommendations that will increase marketing productivity and determine the company's general direction. The marketing audit enables an organization to change tactics or alter day-to-day activities as problems arise. For example, marketing auditors often wonder whether a change in budgeted sales activity is caused by general market conditions or is due to a change in the company's market share.

Although the concept of auditing implies an 'official' examination of marketing activities, many organizations audit their marketing activities informally. Any attempt to verify operating results and to compare them with standards can be considered an auditing activity. Many smaller businesses probably would not use the word audit, but they do perform auditing activities. Several problems may arise in an audit of marketing activities. Marketing audits can be expensive in terms of both time and money. Selecting the auditors may be difficult because objective, qualified personnel may not be available. Marketing audits can also be extremely disruptive because employees sometimes fear comprehensive evaluations, especially by outsiders. The benefits, though, are significant. The audit reveals successes and also problem areas that need to be addressed. Many companies do not deploy a marketing audit. It is not necessary to conduct a marketing audit in order to have a marketing orientation (see Chapter 1). However, many organizations benefit significantly from routine auditing of their marketing practices, identifying good practices to replicate and share, or poor practices against which to take remedial action. As a precursor for marketing planning, a marketing audit can help rectify deficiencies and poor practices in the marketing function, so enhancing the likelihood of effective deployment of a more meaningful marketing plan. While many companies do not practice marketing auditing, most companies do produce marketing plans to steer their marketing.

FIGURE 22.5
No matter the product or the market, marketers should audit their standing and performance and make adjustments accordingly, such as when growing health/obesity concerns prompted McDonald's to promote a healthy eating campaign

Summary

In order to manipulate the marketing mix, to create marketing programmes matching target market needs and achieve organizational goals, a company must address fundamental strategic decisions. To expedite this process and to set appropriate goals, many companies use marketing planning.

Marketing planning is a systematic process that involves assessing marketing opportunities and resources, determining marketing objectives and developing a full plan for implementation and control. A core output of marketing planning is the *marketing plan,* a document or blueprint containing the requirements for a company's marketing activity. The marketing planning process involves (1) analyzing the marketplace, (2) understanding current performance, (3) modifying the recommended marketing strategy accordingly, and (4) developing detailed marketing programmes designed to implement the specified marketing strategy. The *marketing planning cycle* is a cyclical process of planning and feedback that allows for revision. Most companies update their plans annually, typically with a three-year focus. However, *short-, medium-* and *long-range plans* are available.

A key part of the marketing plan is the *marketing objective,* a statement of what is to be accomplished through marketing activities. Objectives should be measurable, indicate a timeframe and be consistent with a company's overall organizational goals.

The heart of the marketing plan is the analysis section. The elements analyzed include current performance, the marketing environment and market trends, customers, competitive positions and competitors' strategies, plus the company's capabilities to respond to marketing opportunities, and the appropriateness of its product and brand portfolio. A *SWOT analysis,* which identifies strengths, weaknesses, opportunities and threats, helps to produce realistic and meaningful marketing recommendations.

The strategy recommendations within the marketing plan examine the opportunities to be pursued and existing activities to be supported, associated target market priorities, the basis for competing, differential advantage and desired brand or product positioning. Marketing strategy guides the company's direction in relationships between customers and competitors. Marketing programmes implement the recommended marketing strategy. They discuss each element of the marketing mix in detail and the allocation of schedules and tasks, personnel, budgets, responsibilities and monitoring of ongoing performance. Without such details of the operationalization of the marketing plan, it is unlikely the plan's recommendations would be implemented.

Marketers produce marketing plans for each business unit, product group or target market, and a synthesized overview plan for the board of the company. Usually, cross-functional teams are involved. In companies embarking on marketing planning for the first time, there is a steep learning curve and the required marketing analyses are very invasive. After three years, the planning process becomes routinized. External consultants are often brought in to support a senior management team's initial attempts to develop a marketing plan.

Sales and marketing activities should be carefully planned activities that anticipate consumer needs and expectations. Whether using a total market or a market segmentation approach, a marketer must be able to measure the sales potential of the target market or markets. *Market potential* is the total amount of a product that customers will purchase within a specified period of time at a specific level of industry-wide marketing activity. *Sales potential* is the maximum percentage of market potential that an individual company within an industry can expect to obtain for a specific product or service. There are two general approaches to measuring sales potential: the *break-down approach* and the *build-up approach.*

A *sales forecast* is the amount of a product that the company actually expects to sell during a specific period of time and at a specified level of marketing activity. Several methods are used to forecast sales: *executive judgement, surveys (customers, salesforce* and *expert forecasting surveys,* including the *Delphi method), time series analysis (trend analysis, cycle analysis, seasonal analysis, random factor analysis), correlation methods* and *market tests.* Although some businesses may rely on a single sales forecasting method, most companies employ several different techniques. It is an essential part of the marketing process to develop objective and reliable sales forecasts and assessments of market potential.

To identify weaknesses in ongoing marketing operations and plan the necessary improvements to correct these weaknesses, it is sometimes necessary to audit marketing activities. A *marketing audit* is a systematic examination of the marketing group's objectives, strategies, programmes, organization and performance. A marketing audit attempts to identify what a marketing unit is doing, to evaluate the effectiveness of these activities and to recommend future marketing activities. It is a useful diagnostic tool for correcting marketing activity and some companies conduct the audit as a prelude to marketing planning. Although an insightful technique, the use of the marketing audit is far from routine.

Key links

This chapter, examining marketing planning and sales forecasting, should be read in conjunction with:

- Chapter 1, on scoping out the marketing process.
- Chapter 2, which deals with exploring the role of marketing planning within marketing strategy.
- Chapter 23, explaining the latest views about marketing performance and managing the implementation of marketing recommendations.

Important terms

Break-down approach
Build-up approach
Correlation methods
Customer forecasting survey
Cycle analysis
Delphi method
Executive judgement
Expert forecasting
Long-range plans
Market potential
Market test
Marketing audit
Marketing objective
Marketing plan
Marketing planning
Marketing planning cycle
Medium-range plans
Random factor analysis
Sales forecast
Sales potential
Salesforce forecasting survey
Seasonal analysis
Short-range plans
Surveys
SWOT analysis
Time series analysis
Trend analysis

Discussion and review questions

1. What is marketing planning? How does it help companies address their marketplaces better?
2. What is the difference between a marketing plan and a corporate plan?
3. What is the timespan for a marketing plan?
4. What are the main tasks involved with producing a marketing plan?
5. Were you asked to direct the production of a marketing plan what would be your game plan and approach?
6. In what ways do marketing environment forces affect marketing planning? Give some examples.
7. What is a SWOT analysis? How does it lead to an understanding of realistic marketing opportunities?
8. What issues *must* be analyzed thoroughly during marketing planning prior to the formulation of a marketing programme?
9. Why is it important to seek a differential advantage?
10. Why does it take three years before the use of marketing planning typically is routinized in a company?
11. In what ways does marketing planning help with establishing controls for a marketing function?
12. Why is a marketer concerned about sales potential when trying to find a target market?
13. What is a sales forecast, and why is it important?
14. What is the Delphi method of forecasting? Why is it a popular tool?
15. Why would a company use a marketing audit?

Recommended readings

Blythe, J. and Megicks, P., *Marketing Planning: Strategy, Environment and Context* (FT/Prentice Hall, 2010).
Dibb, S. and Simkin, L., *Marketing Planning* (Cengage, 2008).
Dibb, S., Simkin, L. and Bradley, J., *The Marketing Planning Workbook: Effective Marketing for Marketing Managers* (Thomson Learning, 1998).
Gilligan, C. and Wilson, R.M.S., *Strategic Marketing Planning* (Oxford: Butterworth-Heinemann, 2009).

McDonald, M.H. and Wilson, H., *Marketing Plans: How To Prepare Them, How To Use Them* (John Wiley, 2011).

Wood, M.B., *Essential Guide to Marketing Planning* (Pearson, 2013).

Internet exercise

A core task in developing a strong marketing plan is the analysis of competitors. There are many ways of finding information about competitors, as described in Chapters 2 and 9. One useful source of intelligence about rivals is to review their websites. Marketers look for the strengths cited by brands and for products on their websites. Additionally, by examining a range of competitors' websites, it is possible to infer their deficiencies. This is achieved by identifying themes popular on many rivals' websites but ignored on only one or two.

Take the example of food processors, mixers and blenders. Look at the websites for a selection of leading brands, such as Breville, Dualit, Kenwood, KitchenAid, Magimix, Morphy Richards, Moulinex and Philips. What are the respective apparent strengths and weaknesses of these brands and products?

Group tasks

1. As the new marketing team for Red Bull you have been asked to produce an updated marketing plan. What would be involved in this task and what activities would be required?

2. A long-term category leader such as Heinz is prevalent in some slumbering parts of the supermarket, such as soups and sauces. In developing a marketing plan for growth what would be the most important aspects of marketing planning and why?

Applied mini-case

Despite various economic blips and global troubles, many consumers still seek adventure and escapism, which is good news for theme park operators such as Disney or Alton Towers. In the UK, Alton Towers aims to maintain its market leadership, and invests continually in new rides and facilities. It opened a £20 million holiday village next to the park for the leisure market and the growing business conference market, to create the *Alton Towers Resort*, spent £10 million on the leading white-knuckle *Oblivion* ride and £18 million on *The Smiler* roller-coaster, as well as creating *CBeebies Land* for younger visitors along with its *Octonauts* roller-coaster. It now promotes its rides, waterpark, spa and hotels as a resort destination. The strategy is to attract new visitors to the park, from the UK and from continental Europe, while encouraging repeat visits from current users. Key target customers are young adults aged 15 to 24, families with children, school parties and, increasingly, the corporate sector. Business clients use Alton Towers for sales incentive schemes and corporate events, such as AGMs, product launches or salesforce parties. The corporate sector was a leading reason for developing good-quality on-site hotel accommodation.

Originally conceived as a day-tripper, family-oriented park, Alton Towers has monitored demographic changes and competitor activity, and has continually modified its rides, amenities and services to reflect the requirements of its evolving target market segments. The growth of corporate clients for conferences and away-days reflects this constant updating of the theme park's marketing strategy and associated marketing planning.

Question

In producing a marketing plan for a theme park such as Alton Towers, what would be the most important elements of the marketing planning process? Explain why.

Case study

Dell has to plan for a new future

Dell originally made its name selling personal computers directly to customers through its catalogues, phone orders and more recently websites. Over the years, it has expanded into related product lines while battling aggressive rivals such as Hewlett Packard and Apple. A few years ago, Dell decided to enter the world of consumer electronics, hoping to drive a large portion of revenues and profits from a wider mix of products for use beyond the home office. Flat screen television was one consumer electronics market the company targeted aggressively, seeking to take on Philips, Panasonic and Sony.

With a long history of marketing technology-based products, Dell had become a well-known US brand. Management saw the brand as a strength and set out to exploit it by marketing flat-screen televisions and tiny digital music players into then quickly growing markets, along with other non-computer based products. 'We've come out of nowhere to be the number three consumer brand in the United States in less than five years, while Coca-Cola has been doing it for 100 years', said Dell's then general manager of consumer business for the US. 'We're not in this to be number three. Number one is the only target around here.'

However, despite considerable research and marketing investment, Dell's consumer electronics strategy did not succeed. In fact, it was not long before the company reversed course, pulling back from diversifications to refocus on its core computer expertise. Indeed, many computer sector observers perceived that the diversification had deflected Dell from its core market, enabling computer competitors such as Acer and Lenovo to make inroads.

Unfortunately for Dell, it had launched its consumer electronics items just as major technological developments were changing how consumers bought and used such products. Dell's affordable handheld computers initially sparked a flurry of customer interest, but instigated a price war with Hewlett Packard as the two fought for market share. However, when Apple, Samsung, Nokia and others began marketing new generation smartphones with built-in computer capabilities and multiple entertainment functions, customers found those offerings more appealing than the kind of stand-alone handhelds that Dell was offering.

In addition, Dell was caught in the crossfire of intense competition. At the start of its consumer electronics initiative, the company introduced the *Dell Digital Jukebox*, and the *Dell Music Store*, putting it on a competitive collision course with Apple's popular iPods and iTunes store. Apple had so much momentum that Dell discontinued its own brand of music players and instead resold products made by Samsung and other manufacturers. This enabled Dell to satisfy customer demand for certain consumer electronics items but without the expense of researching, developing, manufacturing and marketing the products under the Dell name. Dell formed a mobile device division to create products such as mobile phones and other portable devices. After two years of research, Dell entered into an agreement with AT&T to carry its Mini 3 Smart Phone that used Google's Android software, to provide an entry into the growing smartphone market.

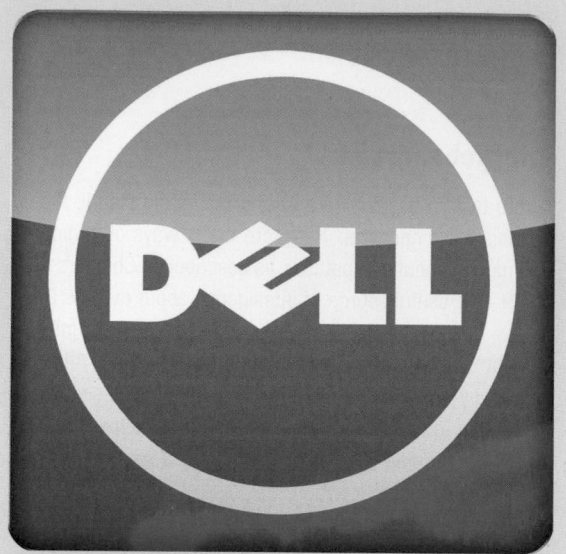

Meanwhile, Dell continued to be a major player in the computer industry. Moving away from its traditional policy of only selling directly to customers, Dell began distributing its brand of computers, monitors, printers, and accessories through WalMart, PC World, Staples office supply stores and other retailers around the world. The company also 'polished its brand' by improving customer service, an especially important step as PC sales grew more slowly throughout the industry and competitors dug in to defend market share. Dell's relentless cost cutting had damaged its ability to handle technical questions and complaints, which in turn reduced customer satisfaction scores. Dell had to rebuild relationships by increasing its service budget and encouraging customers to have their say.

An examination of Dell's current portfolio of products (www.dell.co.uk) reveals how many of these departures into consumer durables have failed to deliver success, leaving Dell to focus on its original core computing business and customers.

Questions for discussion

1. To what extent should marketing planning have helped Dell to avoid the problems encountered when it first diversified into consumer electronics?

2. In what stage of the product life cycle are personal computers? What are the implications for marketing planning in Dell?

3. Explain how marketing planning might underpin Dell's ongoing selection of opportunities and target markets.

CHAPTER 23

Implementing strategies, internal marketing relationships and measuring performance

The job does not end with a target market strategy or marketing plan . . . they have to be put into operation and executed flawlessly

Objectives

- To understand how marketing activities are organized within a company's structure.

- To examine the marketing implementation process.

- To learn about impediments to marketing implementation.

- To grasp the importance of internal marketing.

- To explore implementing and controlling marketing activities.

- To learn how sales and marketing cost analysis can be used as methods of evaluating performance.

- To describe marketing shareholder value analysis.

- To discuss the popular criteria for measuring marketing performance.

INTRODUCTION

Whether an organization creates a standalone marketing function similar to a finance unit, human resource function or production unit, or empowers specific managers in a variety of other roles to also handle the marketing process, decisions about how best to manage marketing must be made.

There is plenty of evidence to suggest that many organizations create marketing strategies and marketing plans without too many problems, but that the implementation stage is where they encounter crises. With the result that so much great analysis, strategic thinking and planning goes to waste, owing to the failure to execute the strategy or plan. Most of these impediments to the roll-out of strategies and plans are avoidable or controllable, as long as implementation is itself planned and managed. Or, if unavoidable, they can often be remedied relatively easily, if only these difficulties are spotted.

Marketers spend significant sums of money on specifying and executing their marketing programmes. Therefore, it is necessary to assess the expected returns for the organization and to examine whether there are better ways of achieving the desired results. Performance measures should be in place, but these need to reflect the full set of core activities for which marketers are responsible.

This chapter examines some popular ways for organizing marketing activity within a company, the essential 'rules' for facilitating implementation of marketing strategies and marketing plans, and the best practice approaches to evaluating marketing performance.

'I'm lovin' it': McDonald's keeps tight control

Mighty McDonald's, famous for its golden arches, was established in 1940 when Dick and Mac McDonald opened up in San Bernadino, California. Ray Kroc, credited with the chain's global ambitions, bought the rights to develop the brand in 1955 and created McDonald's Corporation. Every day, from Moscow to Hong Kong, McDonald's serves over 69 million people, including over three million each day in the UK, where the company enjoys a 70 per cent share of the quick-serve market and has 1200 sites employing 97 000 staff. There are 36 000 McDonald's restaurants and 1.9 million staff in over 100 countries. Strongest growth is currently in Europe, where the 'I'm lovin' it' positioning and healthier eating menus have resonated. Leading branding consultancy Interbrand ranks McDonald's as one of the most recognized brands in the world.

Whether in Lisbon, Chicago or Manchester, a McDonald's restaurant is instantly evident, with a homogeneous layout, ambience, design and ethos that are the envy of most services marketers. The menus change slightly to reflect local tastes, but for the most part there is consistency in the product the world over. Alcohol is available in Lausanne, while incredible ice-cream concoctions are on offer in Porto, but everywhere the core dishes are the same – the *Big Mac*, *Chicken McNuggets*, *Egg McMuffin* and *Filet-O-Fish* to eat in or – at many locations –

available as a drive-thru take-away. Single adults snacking, business reps lunching, children partying or teenagers dining before taking in a movie, McDonald's caters for a wide range of customers.

When McDonald 's first came to Europe, it had to educate its customers to expect unbuttered rolls, no knives or forks and no table service. Despite being in Lisbon, Portugal, for years, when McDonald's opened in Porto in northern Portugal, it advertised the concept of the hamburger and explained that it could be eaten for lunch or dinner and even as a snack at any time of the day. This may seem strange to a generation that has grown up with fast-food restaurants, but it was a major marketing task. Staff also had to be trained and managed to perform their duties effectively. The training and orientation of staff are still central to the success of the company. Behind the scenes, internal marketing programmes ensure that staff comprehend the fundamentals of the McDonald's trading concept and ideals.

Controls are central to the trading practices of the company. Every customer ordering a Big Mac must receive a similar meal every time: cooked identically, with similar relish, wrapping, pricing and a smile. Any complaints must be handled quickly, courteously and with no damage to the well-known branding. With 80 per cent of McDonald's restaurants franchised to independently owned companies and operators, such uniformity does not occur by accident. Country managers are allowed to source locally but must conform to well-established ingredients and standards. While Burger King emphasizes its food, McDonald's promotes the whole-restaurant experience and establishes performance standards to maintain a consistent customer offer. As the company continues to grow, with innovative outlets on ferries, at football grounds and even in London's Guy's Hospital, internal operational controls are just as important to its success as is the extensive promotional activity designed to keep the brand in the target audience's mind. McDonald's understands the importance of maintaining high standards and of integrating the brand, people, design, ambience, technology and food to create a winning experience. Not everyone is a McDonald's fan, but millions daily are happy to return to the trusted golden arches, safe in the knowledge that their anticipated experience is likely to be the reality of their experience, owing to the company's focus on operational effectiveness.

Sources: McDonald's stores UK, 2011 and 2015; www.mcdonalds.com/corp July 2004, May 2011 and April 2015; www.McDonalds.co.uk, July 2011 and May 2015.

This chapter focuses first on the marketing unit's position in the organization and the ways the unit itself can be organized. The chapter goes on to examine several issues regarding the implementation of marketing strategies, particularly the links with relationship marketing, internal marketing – so important to the success of McDonald's – and total quality management. The most frequently encountered impediments hindering implementation are discussed. The chapter then discusses the use of cost and sales analyses to evaluate the effectiveness of marketing strategies and to measure the company's performance, the emergence of marketing shareholder value analysis (MSVA), before concluding with an examination of popular marketing performance measures and metrics.

Organizing marketing activities

Some companies do not have a free-standing specialist marketing function. For them, marketing's remit is allocated between managers in other functions or is the responsibility of either the sales function or the business development team. So long as the marketing process outlined in Chapter 1 is enacted and those involved in executing the various stages in the process – marketing analyses, marketing strategy development, the creation of marketing programmes and the execution of these programmes – are coordinated and well managed, this approach to undertaking marketing may achieve adequate results. However, in general most companies have specialist marketing personnel, operating either together as a marketing unit or allocated to separate business units, product teams or market groups in order to manage the marketing activity required to support that specific part of the organization's activities. These days, most medium and large companies do have a marketing function and specialist marketing personnel.

The organization of a marketing function involves the development of an internal structure for the marketing unit, including relationships and lines of authority and responsibility that connect and coordinate individuals. Individual marketing managers, brand managers or marketing assistants must understand their roles and reporting structures. Within a business unit typically comprising planning personnel, sales and marketing staff, managers handling operations and administrative staff, non-marketers also need to understand the remit for marketing and the specific roles of those responsible for marketing activities. It should be obvious to all concerned who is tasked with analyzing customers' views; assessing competitors; monitoring the forces of the marketing environment; creating a marketing strategy; developing the brand positioning; specifying the marketing mix; creating the advertising proposition and marketing communications programme; handling customer service; managing customers; conducting marketing research; liaising with agencies and trade partners and tracking the effectiveness of the marketing programme deployed.

This section starts by looking at the place of marketing within an organization, and examines some of the major alternatives available for organizing a marketing unit. It then goes on to show how marketing activities can be structured to fit into an organization so as to contribute to the accomplishment of overall objectives.

The place of marketing in an organization

As the marketing environment is so dynamic, the importance of the marketing unit within the organization has increased during the past 30 years. As explored in Chapter 1 of *Marketing: Concepts and Strategies*, companies that truly adopt the marketing concept often develop a distinct organizational culture – a culture based on a shared set of beliefs, which makes the customers' needs the pivotal point of a company's decisions about strategy and operations.[1] When this philosophy permeates the whole organization, there is a genuine *marketing orientation* to that company's behaviour and actions. Instead of developing products in a vacuum and then trying to persuade consumers to buy them, companies using the marketing concept begin with an orientation towards their customers' needs and desires. If the marketing concept serves as a guiding philosophy, the marketing unit will be coordinated closely with other functional areas, such as production, finance and personnel. Figure 23.1 shows the organization of a marketing unit by types

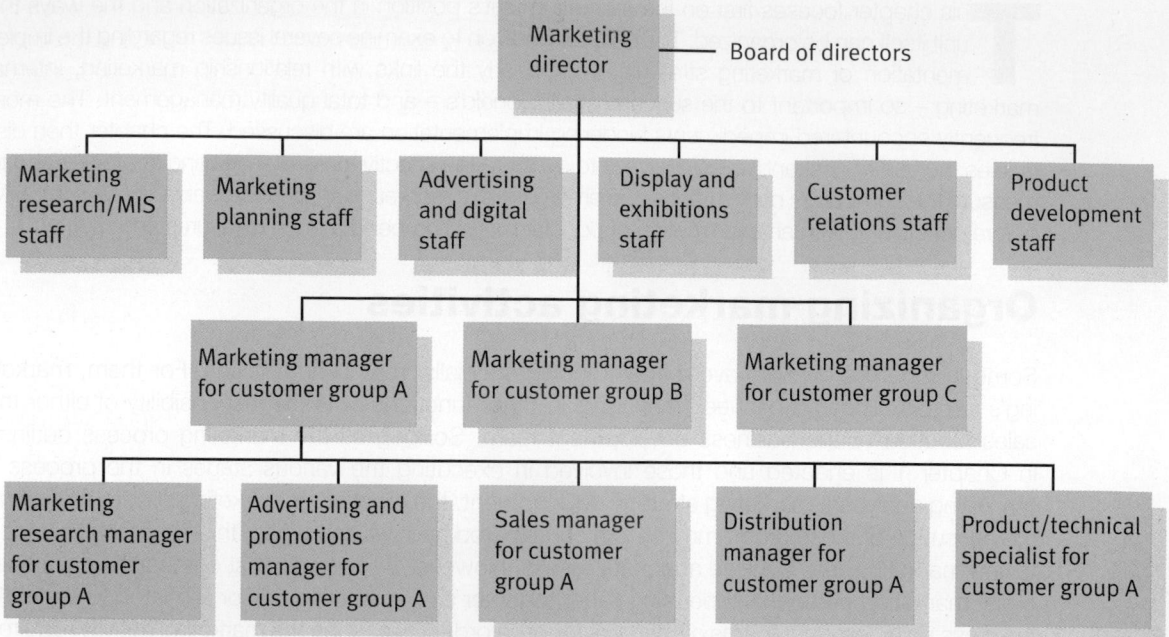

Note: In some organizations, each marketing manager would have responsibility for a product group rather than a customer group, and would be termed a product manager

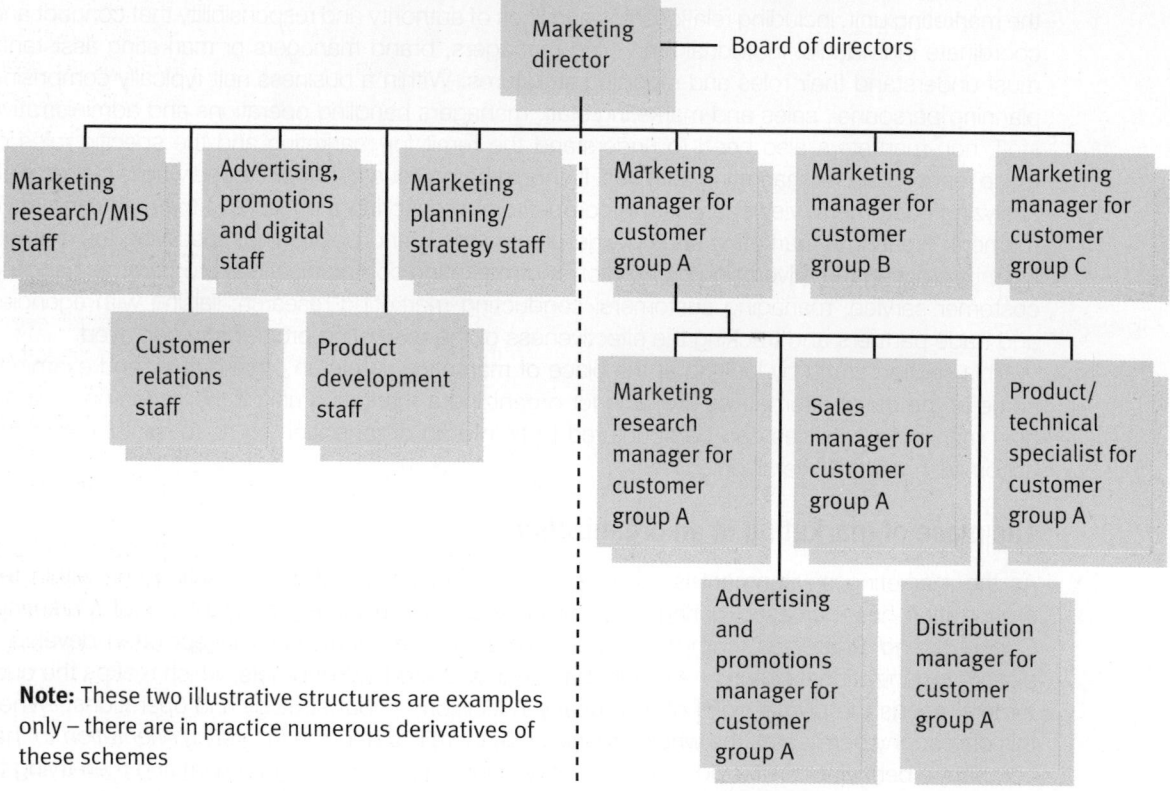

Note: These two illustrative structures are examples only – there are in practice numerous derivatives of these schemes

FIGURE 23.1
Organizing the marketing unit

of customer. This form of internal organization works well for organizations having several groups of customers whose needs differ significantly. The version in the lower part of the figure is particularly prevalent among many business-to-business organizations, such as component suppliers serving several market sectors, an IT services company active across many markets or a firm of financial advisers specializing in more than one business sector.

Marketing must interact with other functional departments in a number of key areas. It needs to work with manufacturing in determining the volume and variety of the company's products. Those in charge of production often rely on marketers for accurate sales forecasts. Research and development departments depend heavily on information gathered by marketers about product features and benefits desired by consumers, the new products launched by competitors, the implications of marketing environment trends, as well as details of complaints concerning current products. Decisions made by the physical distribution department – logistical support – hinge on information about the urgency of delivery schedules and cost/service trade-offs.[2] In many organizations there are specialist customer service departments, whose activities must reflect the marketing strategies developed by the marketers in the company, but whose knowledge of customer issues should be fed back to the marketers tasked with developing marketing and brand strategies. Similarly, sales personnel must prioritize the key target markets selected by the marketing strategy, reflect the desired brand positioning and maximize use of any differential advantage identified by the marketers, while having links with marketing colleagues in order to share their knowledge of customer issues and market developments. Whether manufacturing, services, public sector or consumer marketing, those tasked with managing the organization's marketing activities must have involvement with colleagues across the organization.

Marketing oriented
A company that concentrates on discovering what buyers want and providing it in a way that lets the company achieve its objectives.

As discussed in Chapter 1, a **marketing oriented** organization concentrates on discovering what buyers want and providing it in a way that lets the company achieve its objectives. Such a company has an organizational culture that effectively and efficiently produces a sustainable differential advantage.[3] The whole business focuses on customer analysis, competitor analysis and the integration of the business's resources to provide customer value and satisfaction, as well as long-term profits. Senior managers expect to be well informed about market developments and align their strategies to these circumstances.

As Figure 23.2 shows, the Marketing Director's position is often at the same level as those of the Finance, Production and Human Resource Directors. Thus, the Marketing Director takes part in top-level decision-making. The Marketing Director is also responsible for a variety of activities. Some of them – sales forecasting and product planning – would be under the jurisdiction of other functional managers in production or sales-oriented organizations. Some organizations do not have a Marketing Director: the head of marketing in such companies is often at the same level as the senior managers responsible for IT, logistics, purchasing and channel management. In these cases, there is usually a director responsible for Sales and Marketing or perhaps Business Development, to whom specialist marketing managers report.

To be successful, a company does not have to employ a Marketing Director. However, the core activities of marketing must be undertaken and the forward thinking enabled by the marketing process must be deployed by someone. Few other business functions are interested in external market developments, competitor moves, changing customer expectations or the likely shape of target market priorities in three years' time. Finance, Production, Human Resources and Logistics have other priorities, often although not exclusively focused on short-term performance improvement and the effective utilization of corporate resources. It is the case that marketers spend much of their time rolling-out marketing programmes, but when developing marketing strategies and undertaking marketing planning they do take a longer-term view of the company's fortunes and required strategy realignment. In addressing the core marketing analyses – customers, competitors, marketing environment trends, capabilities – and making marketing strategy recommendations about opportunities to pursue, target markets to prioritize, brand positioning and possible competitive advantage,

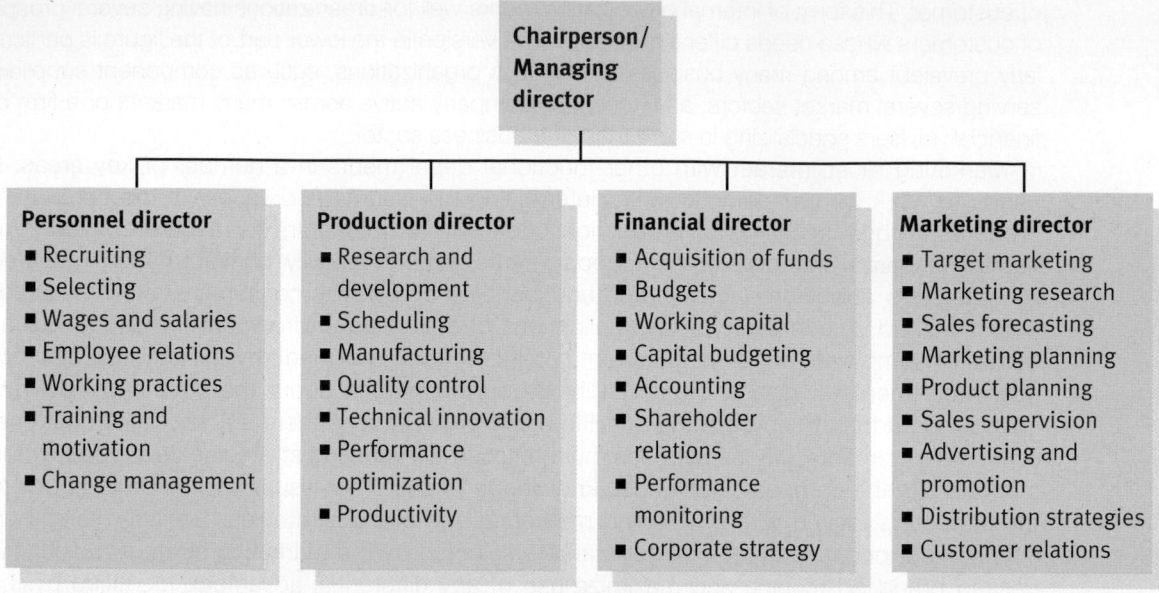

FIGURE 23.2
Organizational chart of a marketing-oriented company

marketers are well placed to warn a business about impending threats and guide their colleagues in aligning resources to emerging opportunities. There is much to be commended in having a marketing function that is viewed by the organization as offering a longer-term perspective on market developments and how markets will evolve, acting as the company's 'radar' or 'eyes and ears'.

Marketing has a limited impact when the company views the role of marketing as simply selling the products that it makes. For organizations – and there are these – in which senior managers view the role of marketing as simply 'creating advertisements', 'conducting customer surveys', 'dealing with customer complaints' or 'keeping dealers and distributors happy', the contribution of marketing is very limited. Such organizations are failing to benefit from the insights and direction provided from the marketing process. However, a marketing orientation is not achieved simply by redrawing the organizational chart: management must also adopt the marketing orientation as a management philosophy, using and connecting the stages of the marketing process – marketing analyses, marketing strategy formulation, marketing programme creation and implementation controls.

Centralized organization
A company in which top-level managers delegate very little authority to the lower levels of the organization.

Centralization versus decentralization

The organizational structure that a company uses to connect and coordinate various activities affects its success. Basic decisions relate to how various participants in the company will work together to make important decisions, as well as to coordinate, implement and control activities.

Decentralized organization
A company in which decision-making authority is delegated as far down the chain of command as possible.

Top managers create corporate strategies and coordinate lower levels. A **centralized organization** is one in which the top-level managers delegate very little authority to lower levels of the organization. In a **decentralized organization**, decision-making authority is delegated as far down the chain of command as possible. The decision to centralize or decentralize directly affects marketing in the organization.

In a centralized organization, major marketing decisions originate with top management and are transmitted to lower levels of management. A decentralized structure gives marketing managers more opportunity for making key strategic decisions. Although decentralizing may foster innovation and a greater responsiveness to customers, a decentralized company may be inefficient or appear to have a blurred marketing strategy when dealing with larger customers. A centralized organization avoids confusion among the marketing staff, vagueness in marketing strategy and autonomous decision-makers who are out of control. Of course, overly centralized companies often become dependent on top management and respond too slowly to be able to solve problems or seize new opportunities. Obviously, finding the right degree of centralization for a particular company is a difficult balancing act.

While many highly centralized organizations are quite successful, the overall trend is for companies to decentralize. This trend is partly caused by the need for organizations to remain very flexible, given the ever-changing marketing environment. For some companies, the need to adapt to changing customer needs is of critical importance. These organizations often use an extreme form of decentralization: **empowerment**. This involves giving front-line employees the authority and responsibility to make marketing decisions without seeking the approval of their supervisors.[4] In practice, for many organizations the solution is something of a hybrid: marketing activity is decentralized within business units that are responsible for individual market segments or product groups, but the marketing personnel in the organization also work collectively in order to manage tasks that cut across the activities of separate business units, such as brand development and communication, new product concept development, the assessment of the marketing environment forces, analysis of new territories for expansion or the creation of customer-handling programmes. For example, IT giant Fujitsu has specialist marketers supporting each of its business units, but these personnel also work together on aspects of the marketing process.

> **Empowerment**
> Giving front-line employees the authority and responsibility to make marketing decisions without seeking the approval of their supervisors.

The concept of empowerment is increasingly important as organizations strive to become faster moving and more customer-responsive. The following examples illustrate empowerment:

- A car sales person is allowed to negotiate the price or financing arrangement with a customer without speaking with the sales manager.
- A retail sales assistant decides, without seeking the approval of a manager, whether to refund customers' money on products they return.
- A receptionist at a hotel gives one night's free accommodation to a dissatisfied guest who complains about poor service.
- A retail store manager is permitted to lower prices on merchandise without asking the regional manager, in order to match a competitor.

Although employees at any level in an organization can be empowered to make decisions, empowerment is used most often at the front line, where employees interact daily with customers. Service and retail marketers practice empowerment quite extensively because of the interactive nature of these businesses. However, empowerment can work in a manufacturing organization as well.

One of the characteristics of empowerment is that employees can perform their jobs the way they see fit, as long as their methods and outcomes are consistent with the mission of the organization.[5] However, the effectiveness of empowerment is tied to the organization's culture. Empowerment works best when the corporate culture is guided by a sense of shared direction, which ensures that employees make the right decisions.[6] Obviously, creating this type of culture does not happen overnight. The corporate vision must be communicated to employees so that they understand how their job affects the vision. Employees must also be trained and persuaded to accept the corporate vision and to become part of the organization's culture.[7] Leading IT services company Fujitsu adopted a new brand reputation model based on honesty, straight talking and integrity. If a client's wishes could not be actioned or a project complexity was likely to cause time or cost over-runs, unlike some rival providers Fujitsu would tell a client's executives. Therefore, if staff failed to behave with openness and honesty, the whole brand proposition would crash, so an

18-month programme of staff orientation and training was launched in order to explain the new values and the importance of adhering to them.

Major alternatives for organizing the marketing unit

How effectively a company's marketing management can plan and implement marketing strategies depends on how the marketing unit is organized. Effective organizational planning can give the company a competitive edge. The organizational structure of a marketing department establishes the authority relationships between marketing personnel, and specifies who is responsible for making certain decisions and performing particular activities. This internal structure is the vehicle for directing marketing activities.

In organizing a marketing unit, managers divide the work into specific activities and delegate responsibility and authority for those activities to people in various positions within the unit. These positions include the channel manager, the segment manager, the customer service manager, the digital insight manager and the advertising manager.

No single approach to organizing a marketing unit works equally well in all businesses. A marketing unit can be organized according to:

- functions
- products
- regions, or
- types of customer (segments).

The best approach or approaches depend on the number and diversity of the company's products, the characteristics and needs of the people in the target market, and many other factors, including the expected norms amongst suppliers and customers in a particular commercial sector.

Businesses often use some combination of organization by functions, products, regions or customer types. Product features may dictate that the marketing unit be structured by products, whereas customers' characteristics require that it be organized by geographic region or by type of customer. Construction equipment manufacturers organize by product type (crawler excavators, backhoe diggers, compact equipment and so forth), but many financial institutions organize by customer type, because personal banking needs differ from commercial ones. By using more than one type of organization, a flexible marketing unit can develop and implement marketing plans to match customers' needs precisely. To develop organizational plans that give a company a differential advantage, four issues should be considered:

1. Which jobs or levels of jobs need to be added, deleted or modified? For example, if new products are important to the success of the business, marketers with strong product development skills and the ability to think innovatively should be added to the organization, or if digital marketing is deemed key managers with such expertise must be recruited.

2. How should reporting relationships be structured to create a competitive edge? This question is discussed further in the following descriptions of organizational structure.

3. To whom should the primary responsibility for accomplishing work be assigned? Identifying primary responsibility explicitly is critical for effective performance appraisal and reward systems, as without clear accountability progress is unlikely.

4. Should any committees or task forces be organized?[8]

Organizing by function
A way of structuring a marketing department in which personnel directing marketing research, product development, distribution, sales, advertising, digital and customer relations report to the top-level marketing executive.

Organizing by function   Some marketing departments adopt a structure known as **organizing by function**, such as marketing research, product development, distribution, sales, branding, advertising, digital and customer relations. The personnel who direct these functions report directly to the top-level marketing executive. This structure is fairly common because it works well for some businesses with centralized marketing operations, such as Ford and General Motors. In more decentralized companies, such as some retailers or fast-moving consumer goods giants like Procter & Gamble and Unilever, functional organization can give rise to severe coordination problems. The functional approach may suit a large, centralized company, whose products and customers are neither numerous nor diverse.

Organizing by product   A business that produces and markets diverse products may find the functional approach inadequate. The decisions and problems related to a single marketing function for one product may be quite different from those related to the same marketing function for another. As a result, businesses that produce diverse products sometimes organize their marketing units according to product groups. **Organizing by product** gives a company the flexibility to develop special marketing mixes for different products.

The product management system, which was introduced by Procter & Gamble, operates in about 85 per cent of companies in the consumer packaged goods industry or fast-moving consumer goods (FMCG), as they are often known. In this structure, the product manager oversees all activities related to his or her assigned product. He or she develops product plans, sees that they are implemented, monitors the results and takes corrective action as necessary. The product manager is also responsible for acting as a liaison point between the company and its marketing environment, transmitting essential information about the environment to the company.[9] The product manager may also draw on the resources of specialized staff in the company. **Category management**, currently popular in supermarkets, off-licences, CTNs and forecourt shops, takes this notion further, with marketers – 'category captains' – becoming responsible in-store for categories of product lines, such as fresh foods, tobacco products or all alcoholic beverages in supermarkets or off-licences. Category management is explored in more detail in Chapter 15.

Organizing by region   A large company that markets products nationally or internationally may adopt a structure for its marketing activities known as **organizing by region**. Managers of marketing functions for each region report to their regional marketing manager; all the regional marketing managers report directly to the executive marketing manager. This form of organization is especially effective for a business whose customers' characteristics and needs vary greatly from one region to another. A company with marketing managers for each separate region often has a complete marketing staff at its headquarters to provide assistance and guidance to regional marketing managers.

Organizing by type of customer   Sometimes the marketing unit opts for **organizing by type of customer**. This form of internal organization works well for a business that has several groups of customers whose needs and problems differ significantly. For example, Bic may sell pens to large retail stores, wholesalers and institutions such as schools, and disposable razors to a mix of wholesaling, retail and hotel business customers. Retailers may want more rapid delivery of small shipments and more personal selling by the producer than do wholesalers or institutional buyers. As the marketing decisions and activities required for these groups of customers differ considerably, the company may find it efficient to organize its marketing unit by type of customer.

In an organization with a marketing department broken down by customer group, the marketing manager for each group reports to the top-level marketing executive and directs most marketing activities for that group. A marketing manager controls all activities needed to market products to a specific customer group or target market segment.

The planning and organizing functions provide purpose, direction and structure for marketing activities. However, until marketing managers implement the marketing plan, exchanges

---

Organizing by product
A way of structuring a marketing department so that the company has the flexibility to develop special marketing mixes for different products.

Category management
A variation of organizing by product, whereby marketers are responsible for categories of product lines in-store.

Organizing by region
A way of structuring a marketing department, used by large national or international companies, that requires managers of marketing functions for each region to report to their regional marketing manager.

Organizing by type of customer
A way of structuring a marketing department, suitable for a business that has several groups of customers with very different needs and problems.

cannot occur. In fact, organizers of marketing activities can become excessively concerned with planning strategy while neglecting implementation. Obviously, implementation of plans is important to the success of any organization. Proper implementation of a marketing plan depends on internal marketing to employees, the motivation of personnel who perform marketing activities, effective communication within the marketing organization and the coordination of marketing activities. Whichever option is adopted, marketing must be able to effectively create and implement a successful marketing strategy.

Marketing implementation

Marketing implementation
Processes and activities deployed to action the marketing strategy or roll out the marketing plan.

Marketing implementation is the 'how?', 'what?', 'when?', 'by whom?' of marketing strategy; it involves processes and activities directed at actioning marketing strategies or rolling out the marketing plan's recommendations. The implementation process can determine whether a marketing strategy is successful. Increasingly marketers are recognizing the importance of managing implementation and planning for the execution of marketing programmes.[10] For example, the output of marketing planning – see Chapter 22 – used to be the specification of the marketing mix. Now, a robust marketing plan is not deemed complete until the 'how', 'by whom', 'when' and 'how much' issues are addressed: allocation of budgets, personnel, schedules and performance measures to the specific marketing mix recommendations. Often managers question what could go wrong . . . having created a strategy or plan, they seek to identify the likely blockers to progress, so that they might pre-empt these problems. In providing these details, marketers identify deficiencies and inadequacies in their capabilities and resources that they must address in order to implement their marketing plans effectively. These impediments often relate to operational and managerial issues. In short, good marketing strategy combined with bad marketing implementation is a recipe for certain failure. Marketing has to be made to happen!

The exponents of marketing planning have for many years realized that internal organizational barriers are likely to impede or restrict the implementation of marketing plans and marketing strategies.[11] They propose that senior managers address the people and cultural concerns detailed in Figure 23.4, before embarking on developing marketing plans, new market segmentation schemes or marketing strategies.[12] These issues reflect the importance of addressing the internal market in effectively pursuing the implementation of marketing strategies and the deployment of recommended marketing mix programmes. Failure to control internal audiences and develop suitable control strategies will reduce the viability of the marketing function's recommended strategies and marketing plan recommendations in the external marketplace.

Already-busy managers developing marketing plans or involved with revising market segmentation schemes need to be managed, cajoled, motivated and rewarded. Any planning process requires access to marketing intelligence and market insight; and the involvement of personnel

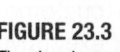
FIGURE 23.3
The development of a new car model may take six years, but its success in terms of sales volume depends as much on the implementation of the target market strategy as on the design and features of the car

Operational considerations	Level of command	Communications
■ Disruption by planning? ■ Non-marketers/directors? ■ Buy-in from functions? ■ Accessibility of personnel/information? ■ Communication of plan?	■ Who? ■ When? ■ Involvement? ■ Channels/approaches? ■ Communication?	■ Within marketing? ■ Across functions? ■ Through hierarchies? ■ Mechanisms? ■ Channels? ■ Support?

Involvement

■ Who?
■ When?
■ Levels?
■ Functions?
■ Support?

Time frames and formats		Participants' expectations
■ How long? ■ When? ■ Action learning or externally supported? ■ Hands-on/hands-off? ■ Communications?		■ What expectations? ■ Working priorities? ■ Worries/concerns? ■ 'Political' cliques? ■ Office politics?

Additional resources

■ Intelligence/information?
■ People?
■ IT/communications?
■ Time?

FIGURE 23.4

People and culture prerequisites to effective marketing and marketing planning programmes

Source: Adapted from: Sally Dibb, Lyndon Simkin and John Bradley, *The Marketing Planning Workbook* (London: Thomson, 1998).

Requisites for implementation
Process, skill, leadership, empowerment, communication, timing, information, resource and participation decisions.

Intended strategy
The strategy on which the company decides during the planning phase.

Realized strategy
The strategy that actually takes place.

with knowledge of the marketplace, customers, competitors, trends and new developments. Those directly involved must have access to their colleagues and be empowered to conduct the necessary analyses and develop appropriate strategies. 'Buy-in' from managers and colleagues, whose remit may change as a result of the planning, warrants facilitation. The necessary analytical skills and time to strategize must be provided. Senior management should be aware of the invasive nature of marketing planning or creating an updated marketing strategy, and schedule other activities accordingly. The **requisites for implementation** include process, skill, leadership, empowerment, communication, timing, information, resource and participation decisions. The learning point is straightforward: appreciation of the checklist issues outlined in Figure 23.4 *prior* to embarking on marketing planning – or the creation of a new marketing strategy – will significantly enhance the likelihood of a successful outcome. Unfortunately, many organizations only realize the importance of planning and facilitating the strategizing activity *after* problems have emerged, progress has been baulked and key stakeholders within the organization are failing to cooperate.[13]

An important aspect of the implementation process is understanding that marketing strategies almost always turn out differently from expected. In essence, all organizations have two types of strategy: intended strategy and realized strategy.[14] The **intended strategy** is the strategy that the organization decided on during the planning phase and wants to use. The **realized strategy**, on the other hand, is the strategy that actually takes place; it comes about during the process of implementing the intended strategy. The realized strategy is not necessarily any better than the intended strategy, though it is often worse.

Problems in implementing marketing activities

Why do marketing strategies sometimes turn out differently from that expected? The most common reason is that managers fail to realize that the marketing implementation is just as important as marketing strategy.[15] Both strategy and implementation are important to strategic planning. The relationship between strategic planning and implementation creates a number of problems for managers when they plan implementation activities. Three of the most important problems are described below:[16]

Marketing strategy and implementation are related   Companies that experience this problem typically assume that strategic planning always comes first, followed by implementation. In reality, marketing strategies and implementation activities should be developed simultaneously. The content of the marketing strategy determines how it will be implemented. Likewise, implementation activities may require that changes be made in the marketing strategy. Thus it is important for marketing managers to understand that strategy and implementation are highly entwined and iterative processes.

Marketing strategy and implementation are constantly evolving   This second problem refers to how strategy and implementation are both affected by the marketing environment. Since the environment and market circumstances are constantly changing, both marketing strategy and implementation must remain flexible enough to adapt. The relationship between strategy and implementation is never fixed; it is always evolving to accommodate changes in customer needs, government regulation or competition.

The responsibilities for marketing strategy and implementation are separated   This problem is often the biggest obstacle in implementing marketing strategies. Typically, marketing strategies are developed by the top managers in an organization. However, the responsibility for implementing those strategies rests at the front line of the organization. This separation can impair implementation in two ways (see Figure 23.5). First, because top managers are separated from the front line, where the company interacts daily with customers, they may not grasp the unique problems associated with implementing marketing activities. Second, people – not organizations – implement strategies. Front-line managers and employees are often responsible for implementing strategies, even though they had no voice in developing them. Consequently, these frontline employees may lack motivation and commitment.[17]

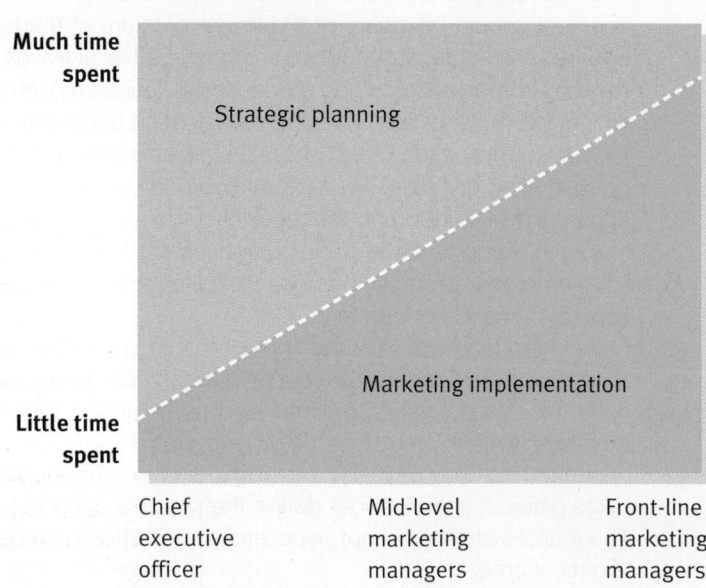

FIGURE 23.5
The separation of strategic planning and marketing implementation

Source: From *Strategic Marketing Management: Text and Cases* by O. C. Ferrell, George H. Lucas and David J. Luck. Copyright © 1994, p. 183. Reprinted with permission of the authors.

Components of marketing implementation

The marketing implementation process has several components, all of which must be synchronized if the implementation is to succeed. These components are shown in Figure 23.6. The systems component refers to work processes, procedures and the way in which information is structured – elements ensuring that the organization's day-to-day activities are carried out. Typical organizational systems include marketing information systems, strategic planning systems, marketing planning processes, budgeting and accounting systems, manufacturing and quality control systems and performance measurement systems.

The people component in Figure 23.6 refers to the importance of employees in the implementation process. It includes such factors as the quality, diversity and skills of the workforce within the organization, and also covers the human resources function. Issues like employee recruitment, selection and training have great bearing on the implementation of marketing activities.[18] Closely linked to the people component is leadership, or the art of managing people. It involves such issues as employee motivation, communication and reward policies.

At the centre of marketing implementation are shared goals, which draw the entire organization together into a single, functioning unit. These goals may be simple statements of the company's objectives. On the other hand, the goals may be detailed mission statements, outlining corporate philosophy and direction. Shared goals appear in the centre of Figure 23.6 because they hold all the other components together to ensure successful marketing implementation.[19] Without shared goals, different parts of the organization might work towards different goals or objectives, thus limiting the success of the entire organization. These ideas have been embraced within the related concepts of *internal marketing* and *relationship marketing,* as discussed later in this chapter.

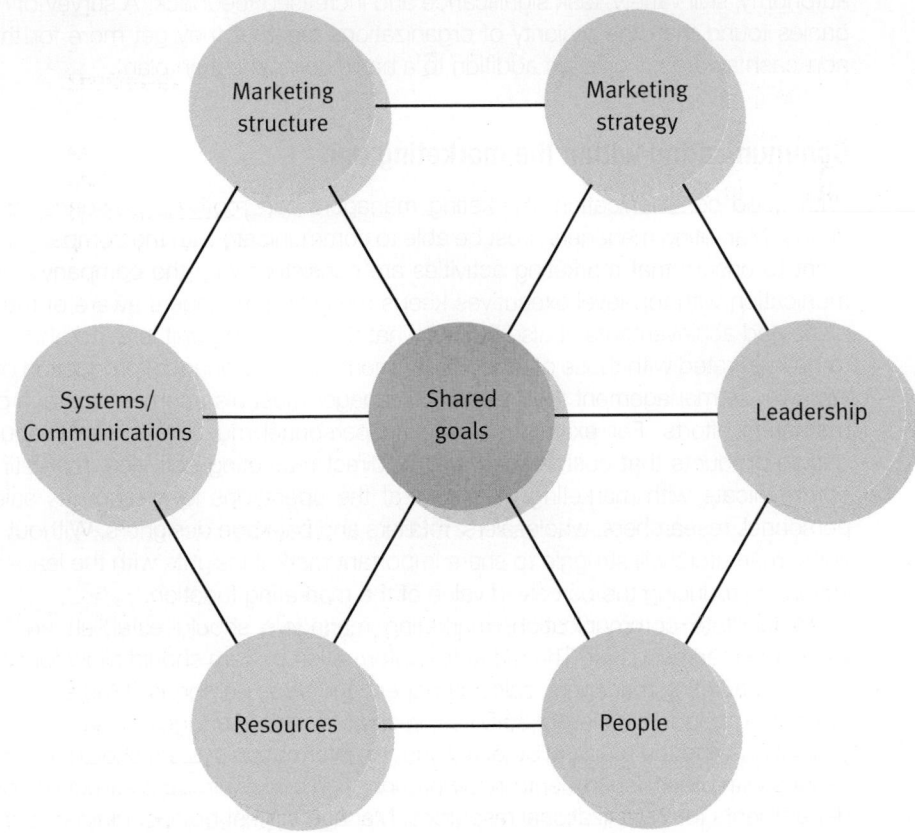

FIGURE 23.6
Elements of marketing
implementation

Motivating marketing personnel

An important element in implementing a marketing strategy or the marketing plan is motivating marketing personnel to perform effectively. People work to satisfy physical, psychological and social needs. To motivate marketing personnel, managers must discover their employees' needs and then develop motivational methods that help them satisfy those needs. It is crucial that the plan for motivating employees be fair, ethical and well understood by them. Additionally, rewards to employees must be tied to organizational goals. In general, to improve employee motivation, companies need to find out what workers think, how they feel and what they want. Some of this information can be obtained from an employee attitude survey. A business can motivate its workers by directly linking pay with performance, by informing workers how their performance affects department and corporate results, by following through with appropriate compensation, by promoting or implementing a flexible benefits programme and by adopting a participative management approach.[20]

Consider the following example. Suppose a sales person can sell product A or B to a particular customer, but not both products. Product A sells for £200 000 and contributes £20 000 to the company's profit margin. Product B sells for £60 000 and has a contribution margin of £40 000. If the sales person receives a commission of 3 per cent of sales, he or she would obviously prefer to sell product A, even though the sale of product B contributes more to the company's profits. If the sales person's commission was based on contribution margin instead of sales, and the company's goal was to maximize profits, both the company and the sales person would benefit more from the sale of product B.[21] By tying rewards to organizational goals, the company encourages behaviour that meets organizational goals.

Besides tying rewards to organizational goals, managers must motivate individuals by using different motivational tools, based on each individual's value system. For example, some employees value recognition more than a slight pay increase. Managers can reward employees with money, plus additional fringe benefits, prestige or recognition, or even non-financial rewards such as job autonomy, skill variety, task significance and increased feedback. A survey of *Fortune 1000* companies found that 'the majority of organizations feel that they get more for their money through non-cash awards, if given in addition to a basic compensation plan'.

Communicating within the marketing unit

With good communication, marketing managers can motivate personnel and coordinate their efforts. Marketing managers must be able to communicate with the company's high level management to ensure that marketing activities are consistent with the company's overall goals. Communication with top-level executives keeps marketing managers aware of the company's overall plans and achievements. It also guides what the marketing unit is to do and how its activities are to be integrated with those of other departments such as finance, production or human resources with whose management the marketing manager must also communicate in order to coordinate marketing efforts. For example, marketing personnel must work with production staff to help design products that customers want. To direct marketing activities, marketing managers must communicate with marketing personnel at the operations level, such as sales and advertising personnel, researchers, wholesalers, retailers and package designers. Without good communications, marketers will struggle to share important market insights with the leadership in the organization, so reducing the perceived value of the marketing function.

To facilitate communication, marketing managers should establish an information system within the marketing unit. The marketing information system should allow for easy communication among marketing managers, sales managers and sales personnel. Marketers need an information system to support a variety of activities, such as planning, budgeting, sales analyses, performance evaluations and the preparation of reports. An information system should also expedite communications with other departments in the organization and minimize destructive competition between departments for organizational resources. Managers must be encouraged to communicate freely, sharing ideas, insights, marketing intelligence, strategies and tactical recommendations. Such channels of communication should be across business functions and hierarchies. Stone-walling, gatekeeping, ring-fencing and deliberate misinformation – all facets of petty 'office politics' – offer no benefits.

Coordinating marketing activities

As a result of job specialization and differences related to marketing activities, marketing managers must synchronize individuals' actions to achieve marketing objectives. In addition, they must work closely with managers in research and development, production, finance and human resources to see that marketing activities mesh with other functions of the company.

Marketing tools and techniques

Practitioners' implementation management of marketing planning: the Dibb/Simkin checklists

When a company commences marketing planning for the first time, already-busy sales and marketing personnel are going to be expected to find time to produce the marketing plan. Hardly any companies employ specialist marketing planners. The organization must recognize the time pressures and resourcing issues associated with asking staff to become involved in marketing planning. Senior managers must be seen to be appreciative, but they must also create channels of communication between functions in the business so that marketing intelligence may be gathered, ideas generated and the resulting plan disseminated across the company. Rather than await problems of information availability, time pressure, poor internal communications, ineffective leadership and so forth, it is better to be aware of these issues from the outset.

The Dibb/Simkin checklist below was developed for a global B2B services company that examined how to improve its annual marketing planning activity. Such a checklist should be considered by those instigating marketing planning – senior managers and the marketing function – before the launch of a marketing planning programme.

- Who to involve, what to tell them, how to control them, how to free up their time.
- Who to put in charge, their level of hands-on involvement, their liaison with other functional areas and senior managers.
- The expected timeframe for completion of the marketing plan and the timing of the planning activity given other commitments in the business.

- Resources required in terms of people, marketing information, IT and administrative support.
- Facilitation of communications within the marketing planning team, across business functions, through the hierarchies of the company.
- Coordination of the inputs from non-marketers, the buy-in to the process by managers, and the roll-out of emerging actions.
- The marketing planning process to utilize, its stages/activities and core requirements.
- The implementation of the resulting marketing plan, its launch, internal communication, external execution, required roll-out resourcing.
- A sequence of ongoing reviews to ensure effective implementation of the marketing plan occurs and any required remedial action is taken.

As explored in Chapter 22, it is also necessary to adhere to a robust marketing planning process. This should involve:

- Marketing analysis so that the business is properly informed about current market dynamics and the reality of its standing.
- A period of strategy development to ensure that the target market strategy and defined basis for competing reflect the realities of the marketplace.
- The creation of marketing mix programmes designed to execute the devised marketing strategy.
- A process of controls and reviews to facilitate the rollout and execution of the marketing plan.

Once the marketing strategy or the plan has been developed, it must be implemented. This partly involves ensuring that specific actions from the plan have been allocated to individual managers, with clearly defined timeframes, budgets and performance measures. The facilitation of implementation also requires reviews and monitoring of progress.

'Review days' are often utilized. These generally take one of two forms:

1. Business unit teams present to senior managers and explain their progress in rolling-out their part of the company's marketing plan.

2. Cross-functional workshops are held in order to more fully review progress, explore emerging issues and determine appropriate remedial actions.

The B2B company cited above introduces its review workshops thus:

Review Workshop Agenda

● Review the current strategy.
Focus on the plan's product/service propositions and how effectively they are being taken to the specified target market segments.

● Examine what is working and what is not!
Lessons to emulate and problems to fix.

● Determine appropriate actions.
Specify tasks and responsibilities as a result of the discussion.

Generally, such a discussion revolves around:

● the product/service propositions developed to take to market, and their fine-tuning

● the message – clarity of the propositions – and their communication to target markets

● marketing communications campaign development and execution

● communication across the company of the plan and its imperatives

● orientation of channel partners/members to the revised direction of the plan

● specialist skills required to help roll out the plan

● strategy for establishing/managing channel and customer relationships

● controls and incentives required to change colleagues' behaviours in order to enact the new-look marketing strategy and marketing plan.

Often, a marketing plan changes a company's thinking and direction, so a programme of change management is required in order to realign managers, budgets, the sales force and so forth. Without the detailed planning of how best to align an organization's resources around a marketing plan, successful implementation is unlikely.

While the sentiments above have focused on marketing planning, the same procedures and tips apply to the implementation of a marketing strategy or revised target market strategy.

Sources: © Dibb/Simkin. This process is adapted from and based on material from Sally Dibb, Lyndon Simkin and John Bradley, *The Marketing Planning Workbook* (London: Cengage) and Sally Dibb and Lyndon Simkin, *The Market Segmentation Workbook* (London: Cengage); Sally Dibb and Lyndon Simkin, *Marketing Planning* (Cengage); and, Sally Dibb and Lyndon Simkin, *Market Segmentation Success: Making It Happen!* (Routledge).

Marketing managers must coordinate the activities of marketing staff within the business and integrate those activities with the marketing efforts of external organizations – advertising and digital agencies, resellers (wholesalers, retailers and dealers), researchers and shippers, among others. Marketing managers can improve coordination by using internal marketing activities to

FIGURE 23.7
The Apple iPod had been carefully researched and developed to appeal to the intended target market: the creative execution is part of the operationalization of the designed marketing strategy

make each employee aware of how his or her job relates to others, and how his or her actions contribute to the achievement of marketing plans. The Marketing Tools and Techniques box on pages 691–692 presents one particularly well-executed process for facilitating the implementation of marketing plans.

Concepts related to marketing implementation

This section discusses three concepts that exist for their own purposes, but that also relate to marketing implementation: relationship marketing, internal marketing and total quality management. These approaches, which represent mindsets that marketing managers can adopt when organizing and planning marketing activities, are not mutually exclusive. Indeed, many companies adopt a combination of these approaches when designing marketing activities.

Relationship marketing

Relationship marketing
Places emphasis on the interaction between buyers and sellers, and is concerned with winning and keeping customers by maintaining links between marketing, quality and customer service.

As outlined in Chapter 1, relationship marketing has attracted considerable attention in the marketing literature.[22] It focuses on the interaction between buyers and sellers, and is concerned with winning but *also* keeping customers by maintaining links between marketing, quality and customer service.[23] The term *relationship marketing* has been defined as attracting, maintaining and enhancing customer relationships.[24] The notion hinges on selling organizations taking a longer-term view of customer relationships, to ensure that those customers converted are also retained. Rather than focusing on the worth of an individual transaction, the relationship marketing concept is concerned with the lifetime value of the customer relationship and in winning a larger share of a customer's spending over a prolonged period. There has been a shift from transaction-based marketing towards a relationship focus, as explained by a leading exponent: 'Transaction marketing of the 1980s placed the emphasis on the individual sale. Relationship marketing of the 1990s placed the emphasis on individual customers and seeks to establish a long term relationship between customer and company.'[25]

The fundamental message is that ongoing, longer-term relationships are essential for a business's viability and market performance. While marketers are encouraged to devote greater resources to developing such customer relationships, the relationship marketing literature explains that such long-term commitment stems not only from treating customers differently, but also from addressing other audiences. As detailed in the five markets model of relationship marketing in Figure 23.8, these audiences include:

Five markets model of relationship marketing
In addition to customer markets, the core audiences of influencers, referrals, employee recruitment, suppliers and internal markets.

- referral markets, such as insurance brokers and advisers
- suppliers
- employee recruitment markets
- influencer markets, such as government bodies, EU officials and the central bank
- internal markets.

In highlighting this final 'market' or domain of the five markets model, relationship marketers are acknowledging the damage that can be done if employees do not understand their role in ensuring that marketing recommendations are adequately actioned. In order to exploit this internal market effectively, thought must be devoted to the establishment of communication channels; leadership qualities and people skills; associated resources; information content, access and sharing; IT support systems; management controls; clear internally focused propositions and messages; as well as priorities for which employees are primary targets.

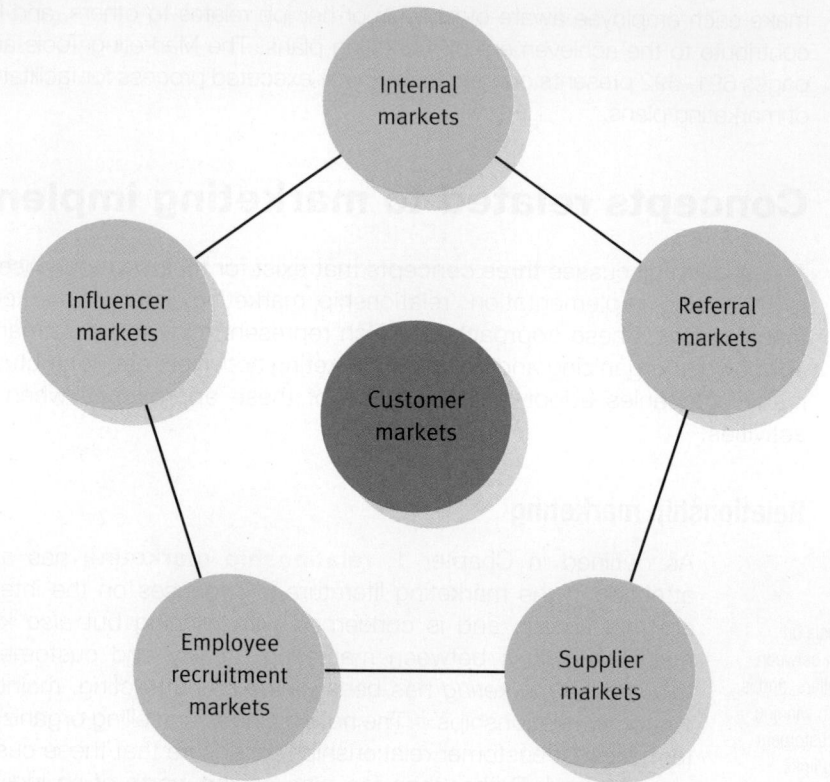

FIGURE 23.8
The five markets model of
relationship marketing

Source: From *Relationship
Marketing: Creating
Stakeholder Value*, 2nd edition
by Christopher, M., Payne,
A. and Ballantyne, D. 2002:
Butterworth-Heinemann.
Reproduced with kind
permission of the authors.

Internal marketing

Internal marketing
The application of
marketing internally
within the company, with
programmes of com-
munication and guidance
targeted at internal
audiences to develop
responsiveness and a
unified sense of purpose
among employees.

Much appears to depend on **internal marketing**, which is the application of marketing internally within the company, with programmes of communication and guidance targeted at internal audiences. For example, it has been shown that there is a relationship between satisfied employees, marketing orientation and organizational performance.[26] Internal marketing plays a vital role in developing a customer-focused organization and helps ensure coherent relationship marketing.[27] Internal marketing is based on communication, the development of responsiveness and a unified sense of purpose among employees. It aims to develop internal and external customer awareness, and to remove functional or human barriers to organizational effectiveness. Internal marketing centres on the notion that every member of the organization has a 'supplier' and a 'customer'.

Long-term, ongoing relationships require improved customer service. High levels of service depend on individuals ensuring that their suppliers and customers are happy. The concept also requires that all members of staff work together, in tune with the organization's mission, strategy and goals. The aim is to ensure that all staff represent the business in the best possible way in all transactions they have with suppliers, customers and other staff.[28] A new marketing strategy or modified marketing plan will not be implemented if personnel within the organization do not understand the direction being recommended, fail to appreciate their role in executing the strategy or refuse to comply. Internal marketing is a philosophy for managing human resources with a marketing perspective.[29]

In order to achieve this internal cohesiveness, internal marketers propose six steps:[30]

1. the creation of internal awareness
2. identification of internal 'customers' and 'suppliers'
3. determination of internal customers' expectations

4. communication of these expectations to internal suppliers
5. internal suppliers' modifications to their activities to reflect internal customers' views
6. a measure of internal service quality and feedback to ensure a satisfactory exchange between internal customers and suppliers.

Marketing activities cannot be implemented effectively without the cooperation of employees. Employees are the essential ingredient in increasing productivity, providing customer service and beating the competition. Thus, in addition to marketing activities targeted at external customers, companies use internal marketing to attract, motivate and retain qualified internal customers (employees) by designing internal products (jobs, roles, strategies and plans) to satisfy employees' wants and needs. Generally speaking, internal marketing refers to the managerial actions necessary to make all members of the marketing organization understand and accept their respective roles in implementing the marketing strategy. This means that all of them, from the CEO of the company to the hourly workers on the shop floor, must understand the role they play in carrying out their jobs and implementing the marketing strategy.[31] Everyone must do his or her part to ensure that customers are satisfied. All personnel within the company, both marketers and those who perform other functions, should recognize the tenet of customer orientation and service that underlies the marketing concept.

As with external marketing activities, internal marketing may involve market segmentation, product development, research, distribution, websites and even public relations and sales promotion. The internal marketing framework is shown in Figure 23.9. As in external marketing, the marketing mix is used in the internal marketing approach to satisfy the needs of employees. For example, an organization may sponsor sales competitions to encourage sales personnel to boost their selling efforts. Some companies encourage employees to work for their companies' customers for a period of time, often while continuing to receive their regular salaries. This helps the employees, and ultimately the company, to better understand

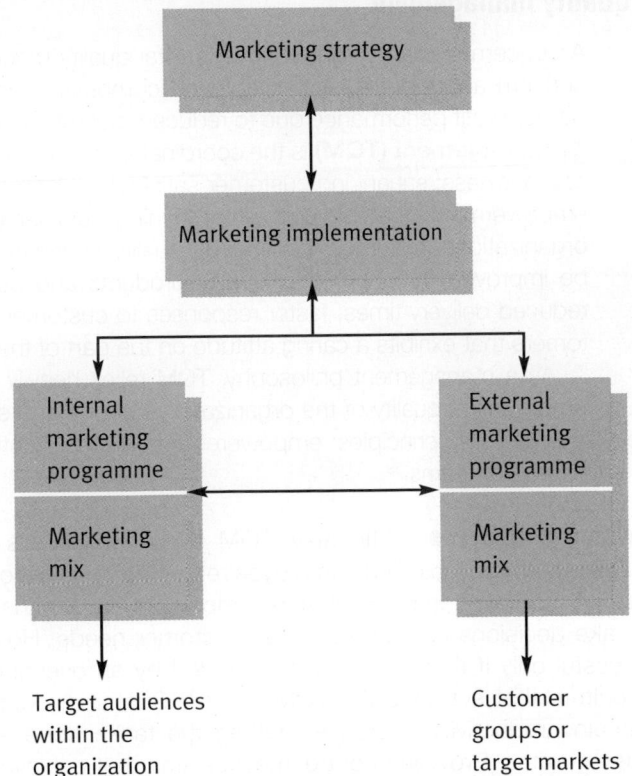

FIGURE 23.9
The internal marketing framework

Source: From *Market-Led Strategic Change* 4th edition by Nigel F. Piercy, Butterworth-Heinemann. Copyright © 2009 Nigel F. Piercy.

customers' needs and problems, enables them to learn valuable new skills and heightens their enthusiasm for their regular jobs. In addition, many companies use planning sessions, workshops, letters/emails, formal reports and personal conversations as tools of internal distribution to ensure that employees understand the corporate mission, the organization's goals and the marketing strategy. The end result is more satisfied employees, and improved customer relations.

Internal marketing requires the acceptance of the need for improved internal communication, information sharing and liaison across business functions and managerial hierarchies.[32] The core requirements are:

- information sharing of marketing intelligence/market insight
- orientation sessions to familiarize staff with marketing strategies and marketing plans
- multi-functional team interaction
- formalized internal marketing communications campaigns
- debrief and feedback sessions
- incentivized staff motivation
- empowerment of line management to take ownership of problems
- the encouragement of 'success stories' to champion
- identification of colleagues not 'buying-in' and appropriate remedial actions.

In order to exploit the internal market effectively, thought must be devoted to establishing communication channels, leadership qualities, associated resources, information, and clear internally focused propositions and messages. All of this would routinely be undertaken for an external customer or target market, so why not within the business to ensure staff understanding and cooperation?

Total quality management

Total quality management (TQM)
Coordinated efforts directed at improving all aspects of a business from product and service quality to customer and employee satisfaction.

A concern in many organizations is total quality management. Major reasons for this concern about quality are heightened competition, more demanding customers and poorer profit performance due to reduced market shares and higher costs. **Total quality management (TQM)** is the coordination of efforts directed at improving all aspects of a business: enhancing customer satisfaction, increasing employee participation and empowerment, forming and strengthening supplier partnerships, and facilitating an organizational culture of continuous quality improvement. Customer satisfaction can be improved through higher-quality products and better customer service, such as reduced delivery times, faster responses to customer enquiries and treatment of customers that exhibits a caring attitude on the part of the company.

As a management philosophy, TQM relies heavily on the talents of employees to continually improve the quality of the organization's goods and services. The TQM philosophy is founded on three basic principles: empowered employees, continuous quality improvement and quality improvement teams.[33]

Empowered employees   Ultimately, TQM succeeds or fails because of the efforts of the organization's employees. Thus employee recruitment, selection and training are critical to the success of marketing implementation. Empowerment means giving employees the authority to make decisions in order to satisfy customer needs. However, empowering employees is successful only if the organization is guided by an overall corporate vision, shared goals and a culture that supports the TQM effort.[34] Customer-contact employees often continue to maintain productivity levels (i.e. getting the tasks done) even while the quality of their work deteriorates. Providing control mechanisms that achieve desired quality standards can maintain productivity and quality.[35] Such a system cannot spring up overnight. A great deal of time, effort and patience is needed to develop and sustain a quality oriented culture in an organization. Three years of training workshops and evolution were required at JCB before TQM became firmly established as a managerial philosophy.

Continuous quality improvement   The continuous improvement of an organization's products and services is built around the notion that quality is free: not having high-quality goods and services can be very expensive, especially in terms of dissatisfied customers.[36] The continuous improvement of quality also means more than simple quality control, or the screening out of bad products during production. Rather, continuous improvement means building in quality from the very beginning, totally redesigning the product if necessary. Continuous improvement is a slow, long-term process of creating small improvements in quality. Companies that adopt TQM realize that the major advancements in quality occur because of an accumulation of these small improvements over time.

A primary tool of the continuous quality improvement process is benchmarking, or the measurement and evaluation of the quality of an organization's goods, services or processes as compared with the best-performing companies in the industry.[37] Benchmarking enables an organization to know where it stands competitively in its industry, thus giving it a goal to aim for over time. This goal is usually to be the best in the industry.

Benchmarking
The process of comparing the quality of an organization's goods, services or processes with those of its best-performing competitors.

Quality improvement teams   The idea behind the team approach is to get the best and brightest people from a wide variety of perspectives working on a quality improvement issue simultaneously. Team members are usually selected from a cross-section of jobs within the organization, as well as from among suppliers and customers. Customers are included in the quality improvement team because they are in the best position to know what they and other customers want from the company. Suppliers, too, understand the market.

Total quality management can provide several benefits. Overall financial benefits include lower operating costs, a higher return on sales and investment, and an improved ability to use premium pricing rather than competitive pricing. Additional benefits include faster development of innovations, improved access to global markets, higher levels of customer retention and an enhanced reputation.[38] Despite these advantages, not all companies use the TQM approach, although the numbers are growing. The reason is that putting the TQM philosophy into practice requires a great deal of organizational resources: time, effort, money and patience on the part of the organization. However, companies with the resources necessary to implement TQM gain an effective means of achieving major competitive advantages in their respective industries.

Although many factors can influence the effectiveness of the internal marketing and total quality management approaches, two issues are crucial. First, top management must be totally committed to internal marketing or TQM, and must make either one or both of the approaches their top priority. Committed top managers serve as role models for other managers and employees.[39] It is naive for managers to expect employees to be committed to an approach when top managers are not. Second, management must coordinate the specific elements of these approaches to ensure that they work in harmony with each other. Over-emphasizing one aspect of relationship marketing, internal marketing or TQM can be detrimental to the other components, thus limiting the success of the overall programme.

Marketing control process
One that establishes performance standards, evaluates actual performance and reduces the differences between desired and actual performance.

Controlling marketing activities

To achieve marketing objectives as well as general organizational goals, marketing managers must control marketing efforts effectively. The marketing control process consists of establishing performance standards, evaluating actual performance by comparing it with established standards, and reducing the differences between desired and actual performance, taking corrective action if necessary. Dunkin' Donuts has developed a programme to ensure consistency throughout its franchises. Dunkin' Donuts controls the quality of operations in its franchised units by having franchisees attend Dunkin' Donuts University. Owners and managers of Dunkin' Donuts outlets are required to take a six-week training course, covering everything from customer relations and marketing to production, including a test of making 140 dozen doughnuts in eight hours. As part of the test, an instructor selects six of the 1680 doughnuts made at random, to ascertain that they weigh around 350 grams (12 ounces) and measure just under 20 centimetres (8 inches) when stacked. The Dunkin' Donuts University was opened to guarantee uniformity in all aspects of the company's operations throughout the 1700 franchise units.[40]

Although the control function is a fundamental management activity, it has until recently received little attention in marketing. There are both formal and informal control systems in organizations. The formal marketing control process involves performance standards and metrics, evaluation of actual performance and corrective action to remedy shortfalls (see Figure 23.10). The informal control process, however, involves self-control, social or group control, and cultural control through acceptance of a company's value system. Which type of control system dominates depends on the environmental context of the business.[41]

Most well-run organizations monitor the roll-out of their marketing strategies and marketing plans. For example, Raytheon's senior managers hold quarterly review meetings with the business unit managers tasked with implementing the annually agreed marketing plans. At each meeting, problems in effectively actioning the plan or barriers impeding progress are highlighted and appropriate steps specified to remedy the problems. This may result in senior managers forcing

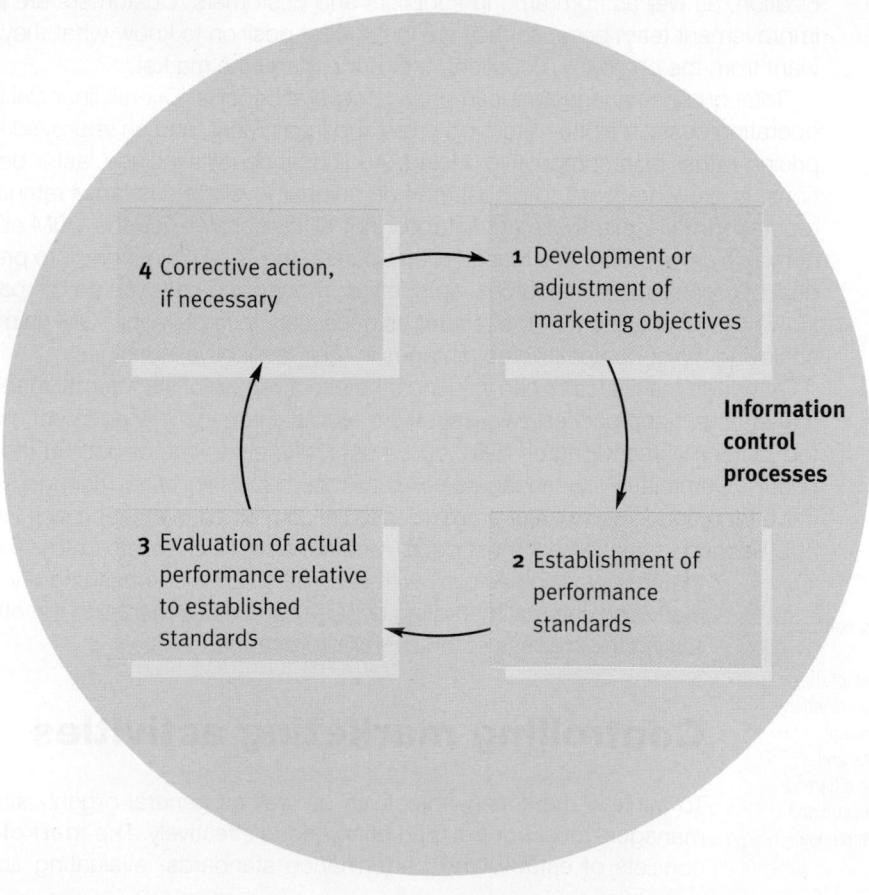

FIGURE 23.10
The marketing control process

others in the organization to comply with the plan's recommendations or reallocating resources as required. Often, the review meeting itself is sufficient motivation for the business unit managers to increase momentum. Implicit in this approach is the need to specify deliverables from the marketing strategy, marketing plan or marketing programme that may be assessed in order to determine the extent of successful implementation and the effectiveness of the marketing activity in the marketplace.

Establishing performance standards

Planning and controlling are closely linked because plans include statements about what is to be accomplished. For purposes of control, these statements function as performance stan-

Performance standard
An expected level of performance against which actual performance can be compared.

dards. A **performance standard** is an expected level of performance against which actual performance can be compared. Examples of performance standards might be the reduction of customers' complaints by 20 per cent, a monthly sales quota of £150 000, a 10 per cent increase per month in new customer accounts, or an increase in a measure of brand awareness. Performance standards are also given in the form of budget accounts – marketers are expected to achieve a certain objective without spending more than a given amount of resources.

Performance standards can relate to product quality and should be tied to organizational goals. Table 23.1 details the most frequently used performance standards adopted among the professional members of the UK's Chartered Institute of Marketing. A more recent addition to performance standards is that of marketing shareholder value.

TABLE 23.1 Currently popular performance standards

Key marketing financial performance standards include:

- revenue growth
- return on investment (ROI)
- product profitability
- customer profitability
- earnings before interest, taxes, depreciation and amortization (EBITDA)
- return on sales
- total return to shareholders
- return on capital employed
- sales per square metre (for retailers).

Leading non-financial marketing performance standards include:

- customer satisfaction
- delivery performance
- new customers gained
- market share
- customer loyalty
- customer dissatisfaction brand awareness
- lost customers
- price level achieved
- customer brand attitudes.

Source: Adapted from Sally Dibb and Lyndon Simkin, *Marketing Briefs: A Revision and Study Guide* (Oxford: Elsevier, 2004); plus a survey of UK Chartered Institute of Marketing members' views.

Digital marketing metrics are detailed in Chapter 19.

Evaluating actual performance

To compare actual performance with performance standards, marketing managers must know what marketers within the company are doing and must have information about the activities of external organizations that provide the business with marketing assistance. Records of actual performance are compared with performance standards to determine whether a discrepancy exists and if so, how much of one. For example, a sales person's actual sales are compared with his or her sales quota. If there is a significant negative discrepancy, the sales manager takes corrective action. A marketing research company may be contracted to produce quarterly surveys, providing the analyzed results within ten days of each survey's completion. If the report is late and the sampling or analysis inaccurate, the marketer will probably switch to an alternative supplier.

Taking corrective action

Marketing managers have several options for reducing a discrepancy between established performance standards and actual performance. They can take steps to improve actual performance, or they may review the performance standard and possibly redefine it. Changes in actual performance may require the marketing manager to use better methods of motivating marketing personnel or to find more effective techniques for coordinating marketing efforts. In order to prescribe corrective action, it is necessary to diagnose problems and investigate the challenges facing a company's marketers. The Marketing Tools and Techniques box on pages 701–703 presents the *market status audit,* as developed for a leading business-to-business company's marketing department. This is a comprehensive examination of trends in a market linked to the assessment of reasons for under-performance. Certain performance standards (see below) are included in this company's audit process, which is loosely related to the marketing audit described in Chapter 22. The audit featured in the Marketing Tools and Techniques box was administered via an email questionnaire to managers across the company's many business units, supported by plenary discussions.

Requirements for an effective control process

A marketing manager should consider several requirements in creating and maintaining effective marketing control processes.[42] Effective control hinges on the quantity and quality of information available to the marketing manager and the speed at which it is received. The control process should be designed so that the flow of information is rapid enough to allow the marketing manager to quickly detect differences between actual and planned levels of performance. A single control procedure is not suitable for all types of marketing activity, and internal and environmental changes affect an organization's activities. Therefore, control procedures should be flexible enough to adjust to both varied activities and changes in the organization's situation. For the control process to be usable, its costs must be low relative to the costs that would arise if controls were lacking. Finally, the control process should be designed so that both managers and subordinates can understand it and its requirements.

Problems in controlling marketing activities

When marketing managers attempt to control marketing activities, they frequently run into several problems. Often, the information required to control marketing activities is unavailable or available only at a high cost. Even though marketing controls should be flexible enough to allow for environmental changes, the frequency, intensity and unpredictability of such changes may hamper effective control. In addition, the time lag between marketing activities and their effects limits a marketing manager's ability to measure the effectiveness of marketing activities.

As marketing and other business activities overlap, marketing managers cannot determine the precise cost of marketing activities. Without an accurate measure of marketing costs, it is difficult

The Dibb/Simkin market status audit as applied to a B2B company

Marketing tools and techniques

The aims of this brief questionnaire are to identify the key issues in your sector, to unearth opportunities, threats, challenges and ultimately to agree key actions. The intention is also to identify under-performance and possible reasons for this. In addition, the hope is to reveal some common themes across the sectors in our business and ensure our planned activities reflect market conditions.

Sector: _____

Currently, which are our leading clients? For what products/services?
For each one listed, also state how much money has been brought in during the last 12 months. Also, state how much income is anticipated in the next 12 months.

Client	For what?	Income current year	Income expected next year

---

Who are the current key target prospects for new business?
For each one listed, say for what type of work and how much income is realistically likely. Also, say how the lead came about and why each prospect is worthwhile / relevant for XXXXXXXX.

Prospect	Type of work/ relevance to us	Likely income/period	How lead came about

---

For XXXXXXXX in this sector, what are the key market drivers?
List the key issues, but then identify which are threats or opportunities and why.

Political:

Regulatory:

Legal:

Economic:

Social:

Technological:

Overall, from this list which are the key threats and opportunities?

Leading threats	Leading opportunities

Who are our key competitors in this sector?
For each one listed, detail their approach/standing in the sector, their strengths and apparent weaknesses.

Competitors	Approach in sector/standing	Strengths	Weaknesses

Which are the ones hurting us right now? Why?

Which rivals are the fast movers? On what basis?

In each key client, identify the main personnel with whom we have a relationship (name and job description).

For the clients in this sector, not XXXXXXXX, identify the key market trends and drivers of most concern to them right now.

Political:

Regulatory:

Legal:

Economic:

Social:

Technological:

Customer:

Competitor:

Supplier:

Of these many issues, which are the priority ones for clients right now?

For this sector, what are our leading capabilities?

Are there currently any glaring gaps and deficiencies in our capability?

Right now, how would clients in this sector describe XXXXXXXX?

How would you sum up the key challenges in this sector?

What is required to address these challenges?

In which areas of our operations, marketing activity and customer delivery are we underperforming?

In what respect and why?

Thank you for completing this audit.

© Dibb and Simkin

Note: XXXXXXXX = the identity of the organization conducting the Dibb/Simkin market status audit. The proforma – when used for real – contains larger boxes for responses.

Sources: This audit and review process is based on material from Sally Dibb, Lyndon Simkin and John Bradley, *The Marketing Planning Workbook* (Cengage); Sally Dibb and Lyndon Simkin, *The Market Segmentation Workbook* (Cengage); Sally Dibb and Lyndon Simkin, *Marketing Planning* (Cengage); and, Sally Dibb and Lyndon Simkin, *Market Segmentation Success: Making It Happen!* (Routledge).

to know if the effects of marketing activities are worth their expense. Marketing control may be difficult because it is very hard to develop exact performance standards for certain marketing personnel.

Methods of evaluating performance

There are specific methods for assessing and improving the effectiveness of a marketing strategy. A marketer should state in the marketing plan what a marketing strategy is supposed to accomplish. These statements should set forth performance standards, which are usually stated in terms of ROI, profits, sales, market share, brand awareness, customer satisfaction levels or the variables detailed in Table 23.1. Actual performance must be measured in similar terms so that comparisons are possible. This section describes sales analysis and marketing cost analysis, two general ways of evaluating the actual performance of marketing strategies. 'Softer' measures, such as brand awareness and customer satisfaction levels, are also important and feature in the performance standards adopted by marketing-led businesses. An emerging tool for assessing performance is also described in this section: marketing shareholder value analysis.

Sales analysis

Sales analysis
The use of sales figures to evaluate a business's current performance.

Sales analysis uses sales figures to evaluate a company's current performance. It is probably the most common method of evaluation, because sales data partially reflect the target market's reactions to a marketing mix and are often readily available, at least in aggregate form.

Marketers use current sales data to monitor the impact of current marketing efforts. However, that information alone is not enough. To provide useful analyses, current sales data must be compared with forecast sales, industry sales, specific competitors' sales or the costs incurred to achieve the sales volume. For example, knowing that a store attained a £600 000 sales volume this year does not tell management whether its marketing strategy has been successful. However, if managers know that expected sales were £550 000, they are then in a better position to determine the effectiveness of the company's marketing efforts. In addition, if they know that the marketing costs needed to achieve the £600 000 volume were 12 per cent less than budgeted, they are in an even better position to analyze their marketing strategy precisely.

Sales measurements
Data regarding sales transactions that are used to analyze performance, usually in terms of cash volume or market share.

Market share
The company's sales of a product stated as a percentage of industry sales of that product.

Sales measurements   Although there are several types of **sales measurement**, the basic unit of measurement is the sales transaction. A sales transaction results in a customer order for a specified quantity of an organization's product sold under specified terms by a particular sales person or sales group on a certain date. Many organizations record these bits of information about their transactions. With such a record, a company can analyse sales in terms of cash or sales volume, or market share.

Companies frequently use cash volume sales analysis because currency is a common denominator of sales, costs and profits. However, price increases and decreases affect total sales figures. A marketing manager who uses cash volume analysis should factor out the effects of price changes.

A company's **market share** is the company's sales of a product stated as a percentage of industry sales of that product. For example, KP, Golden Wonder and Walkers account for around 70 per cent of the UK savoury snacks market. In the carbonated drinks sector, Coca-Cola has a leading share by volume.[43] Market share analysis permits a company to compare its marketing strategy with competitors' strategies. The primary reason for using market share analysis is to estimate whether sales changes have resulted from the company's marketing strategy or from uncontrollable environmental forces. When a company's sales volume declines but its share of the market stays the same, the marketer can assume that industry sales declined because of some uncontrollable factors and that this decline was reflected in the company's sales. However, if a company experiences a decline in both sales and market share, it should consider the possibility that its marketing strategy is not effective. The *competitive positions proforma* analysis described in Chapter 2 of *Marketing: Concepts and Strategies* incorporates market share analysis to infer the relative performance of the competitive set within a market segment.

Even though market share analysis can be helpful in evaluating the performance of a marketing strategy, the user must interpret results cautiously. When attributing a sales decline to uncontrollable factors, a marketer must keep in mind that such factors do not affect all companies in the industry equally. Not all companies in an industry have the same objectives, and some change their objectives from one year to the next. Changes in the objectives of one company can affect the market shares of one or all companies in that industry. For example, if a competitor increases promotional efforts significantly or drastically reduces prices to increase market share, a company could lose market share despite a well-designed marketing strategy. Within an industry, the entrance of new companies or the demise of established ones also affects a specific business's market share, and market share analysts should attempt to account for these effects. KFC, for example, probably re-evaluated its marketing strategies when McDonald's introduced its own chicken products. Most fast-food companies revised their strategies and performance expectations in the light of media attention about obesity problems and drives for healthier eating.

Whether based on sales volume or market share, sales analysis can be performed on aggregate sales figures or on disaggregated data. Aggregate sales analysis provides an overview of current sales. Although helpful, aggregate sales analysis is often insufficient, because it does not bring to light sales variations within the aggregate. It is not uncommon for a marketer to find that a large proportion of aggregate sales comes from a small number of products, geographic areas or customers. This is sometimes called the 'iceberg principle', because only a small part of an iceberg is visible above the water. To find such disparities, total sales figures are usually broken down by geographic unit, channel, sales person, product, customer type, segment or a combination of these categories.

In sales analysis by geographic unit, sales data can be classified by city, county, region, country or any other geographic designation for which a marketer collects sales information. Actual sales in a geographic unit can be compared with sales in a similar geographic unit, with last year's sales or with an estimated market potential for the area. For example, if a company finds that 18 per cent of its sales are coming from an area that represents only 8 per cent of the potential sales for the product, then it can be assumed that the marketing strategy is successful in that geographic unit.

As a result of the cost associated with hiring and maintaining a salesforce, businesses commonly analyze sales by sales person to determine the contribution each member of the salesforce makes. Performance standards for each sales person are often set in terms of sales quotas for a given time period. Evaluation of actual performance is accomplished by comparing a sales person's current sales with a pre-established quota or some other standard, such as the previous period's sales. If actual sales meet or exceed the standard, and the sales representative has not incurred costs above those budgeted, that person's efforts are acceptable.

Sales analysis is often performed according to product group or specific product item. Marketers break down their aggregate sales figures by product to determine the proportion that each contributed to total sales. Disney, for example, might break down its total sales figures by box office figures for each film produced. A company usually sets a sales volume objective and sometimes a market share objective for each product item or product group, and sales analysis by product is the only way to measure such objectives. A marketer can compare the breakdown of current sales by product with those of previous years. In addition, within industries for which sales data by product are available, a company's sales by product type can be compared with industry averages. To gain an accurate picture of where sales of specific products are occurring, marketers sometimes combine sales analysis by product with sales analysis by geographic area or sales person.

Analyses based on customers are usually broken down by type of customer. Customers can be classified by the way they use a company's products, their distribution level, producer, wholesaler, retailer size, the size of orders, or other characteristics. Sales analysis by customer type enables a company to ascertain whether its marketing resources are allocated in a way that achieves the greatest productivity. For example, sales analysis by type of customer may reveal that 60 per cent of the salesforce is serving a group that accounts for only 15 per cent of total sales. When market segments have been identified, sales per segment are compared against forecasts.

A considerable amount of information is needed for sales analyses, especially if disaggregated analyses are desired. The marketer must develop an operational system for collecting sales information; obviously, the effectiveness of the system for collecting sales information largely determines the ability of a company to develop useful sales analyses. As outlined in Chapter 18, control of a salesforce is part of effective sales management, and most organizations routinely scrutinize the performance of their salesforces.

Marketing cost analysis

Although sales analysis is critical for evaluating the effectiveness of a marketing strategy, it gives only part of the picture. A marketing strategy that successfully generates sales may also be extremely costly. To obtain a complete picture, a company must know the marketing costs associated with using a given strategy to achieve a certain sales level. **Marketing cost analysis** breaks down and classifies costs to determine which are associated with specific marketing activities. By comparing the costs of previous marketing activities with results generated, a marketer can better allocate the business's marketing resources in the future. Marketing cost analysis lets a company evaluate the effectiveness of an ongoing or recent marketing strategy by comparing sales achieved and costs incurred. By pinpointing exactly where a company is experiencing high costs, this form of analysis can help isolate profitable or unprofitable customer segments, products or geographic areas.

Marketing cost analysis
The breakdown and classification of costs to determine which are associated with specific marketing activities.

In some organizations, personnel in other functional areas such as production or accounting perceive marketers as primarily concerned with generating sales, regardless of the costs incurred. Marketers often do commit a large proportion of resources to launching products, achieving distribution or creating promotional campaigns. By conducting cost analyses, marketers can counter this criticism and put themselves in a better position to demonstrate how marketing activities contribute to generating profits. Even though hiring a sports figure such as David Beckham is costly, in many sectors sales goals cannot be reached without large expenditures for promotion. Many advertisers believe that using celebrities helps to increase sales. Research shows that the public are good at identifying which personalities are linked to advertised brands. Ultimately, cost analysis should show if promotion costs are effective in increasing sales.

A robust marketing plan – see Chapter 22 – is not complete without a detailed budget which, when balanced with the sales forecast, marketing analyses, strategic thinking and detailed marketing mix programmes, explains the required marketing spend. In effect, a sound marketing plan should offer a cost–benefit analysis in terms of setting the anticipated costs of rolling out the proposed marketing programmes against the expected sales levels and revenue gains. Marketing cost analysis is a necessary facet for managing a well run marketing department.

The task of determining marketing costs is often complex and difficult. Simply ascertaining the costs associated with marketing a product is rarely adequate. Marketers must usually determine the marketing costs of serving specific geographic areas, market segments or even specific customers. The ABC sales: contribution analysis outlined in Chapter 12 is a useful tool in this endeavour.

Natural accounts
The classification of costs based on how money was actually spent.

A first step in determining the costs is to examine accounting records. Most accounting systems classify costs into **natural accounts** – such as rent, salaries, office supplies and utilities – which are based on how the money was actually spent. Unfortunately, many natural accounts do not help explain what marketing functions were performed through the expenditure of those funds. It does little good, for example, to know that £80 000 is spent for rent each year. The analyst has no way of knowing whether the money is spent for the rental of production, storage, marketing or sales facilities. Therefore, marketing cost analysis usually requires some of the costs in natural accounts to be reclassified into **marketing function accounts**, which indicate the function performed through the expenditure of funds. Common marketing function accounts are transport, storage, order processing, sales, advertising, sales promotion, marketing research, insight, consultancy and customer credit. Most companies allocate out-goings to cost codes for auditing purposes.

Marketing function accounts
A method of indicating the function performed through the expenditure of funds.

Natural accounts can be reclassified into marketing function accounts, as shown in the simplified example in Table 23.2. Note that a few natural accounts, such as advertising, can be reclassified easily into functional accounts because they do not have to

TABLE 23.2 Reclassification of natural accounts into functional accounts

Profit and loss statement

		Functional accounts					
Sales	£250 000						
Cost of goods sold	45 000						
Gross profit	205 000	Advertising	Personal selling	Transport	Storage	Marketing research	Non-marketing
Expenses (natural accounts)							
Rent	£ 14 000		£ 7 000		£6 000		£ 1 000
Salaries	72 000	£ 12 000	32 000	£7 000		£1 000	20 000
Supplies	4 000	1 500	1 000			1 000	500
Advertising	16 000	16 000					
Freight	4 000			2 000			2 000
Taxes	2 000				200		1 800
Insurance	1 000				600		400
Interest	3 000						3 000
Bad debts	6 000						6 000
Total	£ 122 000	£29 500	£40 000	£9 000	£6 800	£2 000	£34 700
Net profit	£ 83 000						

Direct costs
Costs directly attributable to the performance of marketing functions.

Traceable common costs
Costs that can be allocated indirectly, using one or several criteria, to the functions they support.

Non-traceable common costs
Costs that cannot be assigned according to any logical criteria.

Full cost approach
An approach in which cost analysis includes direct costs, traceable common costs and non-traceable common costs.

Direct cost approach
An approach that includes only direct costs and traceable common costs.

Value-based marketing
The inclusion of the value of a marketing strategy and marketing activity in an organization's financial analysis of shareholder value.

Marketing shareholder value analysis (MSVA)
Divides the estimation of the value to the organization created by a marketing strategy into two components: (1) the present value of cash flows during the strategizing and planning phases (2) the continuing value after implementation of the strategy.

be split across several accounts. For most of the natural accounts, however, marketers must develop criteria for assigning them to the various functional accounts. For example, the number of square metres of floor space used was the criterion for dividing the rental costs in Table 23.2 into functional accounts. In some instances, a specific marketing cost is incurred to perform several functions. A packaging cost, for example, could be considered a production function, a distribution function, a promotional function, brand marketing or all four. The marketing cost analyst must reclassify such costs across multiple functions.

Three broad categories are used in marketing cost analysis: direct costs, traceable common costs and non-traceable common costs. **Direct costs** are directly attributable to the performance of marketing functions. For example, web managers' salaries might be allocated to the cost of selling a specific product item, selling in a specific geographic area or selling to a particular customer. **Traceable common costs** can be allocated indirectly, using one or several criteria, to the functions that they support. For example, if the company spends £80 000 annually to rent space for production, storage and selling, the rental costs of storage could be determined on the basis of cost per square metre used for storage. **Non-traceable common costs** cannot be assigned according to any logical criteria and thus are assignable only on an arbitrary basis. Interest, taxes and the salaries of top management are non-traceable common costs.

The manner of dealing with these three categories of costs depends on whether the analyst uses a full cost or a direct cost approach. When a **full cost approach** is used, cost analysis includes direct costs, traceable common costs and non-traceable common costs. Proponents of this approach claim that if an accurate profit picture is desired, all costs must be included in the analysis. However, opponents point out that full costing does not yield actual costs, because non-traceable common costs are determined by arbitrary criteria. With different criteria, the full costing approach yields different results. A cost-conscious operating unit can be discouraged if numerous costs are assigned to it arbitrarily. To eliminate such problems, the **direct cost approach** is used, which includes direct costs and traceable common costs but not non-traceable common costs. Opponents say that this approach is not accurate, because it omits one cost category.

Marketing shareholder value analysis

Building on the rationale for marketing cost analysis, the concept of value-based marketing has emerged in recent years. **Value-based marketing** is the inclusion of the value of a marketing strategy and programme in an organization's financial analysis of shareholder value. To achieve this, **marketing shareholder value analysis (MSVA)** divides the estimation of the value to the business created by a marketing strategy into two components:

1. the present value of cash flows during the strategizing and planning phases
2. the continuing value following implementation of the strategy.

MSVA provides a means of demonstrating the contribution of marketing to the organization's financial performance. This also enables marketing assets – such as marketing knowledge, brands, customer loyalty and strategic relationships – to be included in the shareholder value analysis (SVA), as each can be shown to have quantifiable financial value to the business. MSVA enables marketers to communicate the expected results of their marketing strategies in terms comprehended by top management and investors. The analysis supports marketers' requests for budgets, notably those traditionally most at risk of cost cutting in times of reduced demand, such as advertising and marketing research.

TABLE 23.3 Functional accounts divided into product group costs

Functional accounts		Product groups		
		A	B	C
Advertising	£29 500	£14 000	£ 8 000	£7 500
Personal selling	40 000	18 000	10 000	12 000
Transport	9 000	5 000	2 000	2 000
Storage	6 800	1 800	2 000	3 000
Marketing research	2 000	—	1 000	1 000
Total	87 300	38 800	23 000	25 500

Marketing performance
The assessment of the effectiveness of marketing programmes to implement recommended marketing strategies, fulfil corporate financial expectations and achieve the required levels of customer satisfaction.

Marketing metrics
Specific measurable and quantifiable criteria used to evaluate the effectiveness of a marketing strategy and assess marketing performance.

Sales per square metre
A financial measure retailers might use to assess marketing performance.

EBITDA
The acronym for earnings before interest, taxes, depreciation and amortization.

Customer satisfaction
A qualitative measure of marketing performance that involves surveying customers over time.

In many organizations, the lack of a true marketing orientation has allowed the finance function to take over the notion of shareholder value analysis (SVA).[44] According to leading marketing strategist Peter Doyle, by focusing on short-term profits and ignoring intangible assets such as brand awareness and customer satisfaction, traditional accounting practices have marginalized marketing activity. However, SVA can in fact bring the core strategic drivers of marketing to the fore in the form of MSVA. Marketing has struggled to quantify results in order to demonstrate its value. By adopting MSVA, marketers can reverse this state of affairs. MSVA can help justify marketing actions in terms of their propensity to bring financial value to the business. MSVA offers marketing a greater theoretical base and encourages profitable marketing investment. MSVA also penalizes arbitrary cuts to the marketing budget, something encountered regularly by marketers when a company's fortunes decline suddenly.

Performance measures

The evaluation of **marketing performance** – the assessment of the effectiveness of marketing programmes to implement recommended marketing strategies, fulfil corporate financial expectations and achieve the required levels of customer satisfaction – is a necessary control mechanism in the marketing process. Marketing must agree **marketing metrics** and be judged against these. Table 23.1 presented some popular performance measures adopted by marketers to assess overall markets, specific segments or product lines. Most UK companies are notoriously short term in their thinking, focusing on profitability as their overriding measure. Other financial measures include return on investment, return on capital employed and, for retailers, **sales per square metre** of selling space. In businesses generating a lot of cash, **EBITDA** is important: earnings before interest, taxes, depreciation and amortization. Units produced and units sold are included as measures by most manufacturers, leading to an assessment of production capacity utilization. Market share is a vital criterion for judging performance.

While it is, unquestionably, important for businesses to be financially viable, making adequate profits to be able to fund future investments in production, people, new products, new target markets and so forth, increasingly marketers have accepted the need to evaluate performance on additional, more customer oriented measures. Marketing aims to satisfy customers, so it is sensible to monitor customer satisfaction and retention. A qualitative measure of marketing performance, assessing **customer satisfaction** involves surveying customers' perceptions and expectations over time in order to determine the effectiveness of the marketing programme in servicing their needs. Over time, such surveys should reveal an improvement in customer satisfaction levels, otherwise it could be argued that the marketing strategy and programme are failing to fully address target customer needs and expectations. Most hotel companies operate room card surveys of guest satisfaction in order to monitor customers' experiences and improve the performance of their staff, services and facilities. A measure of **brand awareness** is also monitored by a growing number of marketers, usually through qualitative marketing research surveys, to ensure that their marketing programmes are effectively bringing their brands and products to their target market's attention. While such tracking involves qualitative marketing research, measures of customer satisfaction and brand awareness should be integral to a business's assessment of performance, alongside the important traditional financial performance measures.

> **Brand awareness**
> A qualitative measure of marketing performance that determines whether a company's brands capture the attention of their target markets.

Marketing communications is a major part of marketers' activity and accounts for a significant proportion of the marketing budget. Performance in the promotional mix, however, has taxed experts for decades and there remain few proven objective solutions to determining the value of promotional spend to the business's overall fortunes. It is possible in public relations to use a social media monitoring service to count the frequency of mentions of a specific brand or company in selected media, but this approach fails to assess the positive/negative mix of mentions and cannot extrapolate to draw conclusions relating to sales gains resulting specifically from this PR activity. Sponsorship agencies monitor the awareness of clients' brands when linked to sporting events or the performing arts, but cannot prove that such awareness leads directly to increased sales of products, better profitability or rising market share.

'Hits' on a company's website are counted, but do these lead to sales or an enhanced corporate reputation? If an order is placed via the internet a link can be shown, but if not it is difficult to demonstrate a causal relationship between the website and sales. Even if an order is placed via the web, it is possible that the customer was in fact responding primarily to a press or TV advertisement or to an earlier in-store demonstration. It is possible to track YouTube hits or Twitter follower numbers, but again, it is still not evident whether such digital activity led to an actual sale or order. Nevertheless, digital marketing activities arguably are easier to measure than many traditional marketing activities, as explored in Chapter 19.

Salesforce managers assess individual sales personnel in terms of the ratio of calls to orders. In addition, the salesforce is directly involved in the selling process and instantly judges its own performance. What stands for a good ratio of orders to calls is still a subjective assessment. Sales promotions are perhaps the safest to measure as they generally require customers to redeem coupons and vouchers or submit competition applications, all of which may be counted. However, subjective judgement is still used in determining what constitutes a 'good' redemption rate. Most problematic is the assessment of advertising effectiveness. This is unfortunate as advertising often accounts for the largest individual proportion of the marketing budget. It is possible, as described in Chapter 17, to monitor target audience awareness of advertising, but not to prove that exposure to a specific advertisement has led to a specific sale. At the moment, there are no easy solutions to this dilemma, yet marketers must attempt to assess the performance of their activities, seeking to validate their promotional mix spending. The tools described here are far from perfect but they demonstrate a willingness to assess promotional effectiveness. Many businesses, unfortunately, fail to utilize even these simplistic tools.[45]

Ultimately, a well-managed, customer-oriented company should use a mix of financial and qualitative measures, such as those listed in Table 23.1, to judge its performance and the effectiveness of its marketing. A company should adopt a balanced set of performance measures, mixing the short-term view of profitability with the often longer-term perspective of market share gains. It often requires considerable resources to increase market share at the expense of rivals, which may reduce short-term profitability. However, market share increases are likely to bring longer-term security and rewards. In addition to the financial performance measures, marketers should insist on being assessed on dimensions such as customer retention, customer satisfaction and brand awareness. If marketing programmes are effective, these three customer-oriented criteria should all show signs of improvement. Whatever the selected criteria for assessing marketing performance, it is essential that marketers incorporate performance monitoring within their control and management processes.

Summary

The organization of marketing activities involves allocating responsibilities for the marketing process and the development of an internal structure for the marketing unit, including relationships and lines of authority and responsibility that connect and coordinate individuals. The internal structure is the key to directing marketing activities. In a *marketing oriented organization*, the focus is on finding out what customers want and providing it in a way that enables the company to achieve its objectives, with the organization and leadership fully aligned to market developments and circumstances. A *centralized organization* is one in which the top-level managers delegate very little authority to lower levels of the business. In a *decentralized organization*, decision-making authority is delegated as far down the chain of command as possible. An extreme form of decentralization is *empowerment*, in which frontline employees are given the authority and responsibility to make marketing decisions without seeking the approval of their supervisors.

The marketing unit can be *organized by* (1) *functions*, (2) *products*, (3) *regions*, or (4) *types of customer. Category management* is an in-vogue variation of organizing by products in fmcg markets. An organization may use only one approach or a combination.

Marketing implementation, a process that involves activities to put marketing strategies into action, is an important part of the marketing management process. The *requisites for implementation* include process, skill, leadership, empowerment, communication, timing, information, resource and participation decisions. Failure to address these issues prior to embarking on marketing strategy formulation or the development of a marketing plan may result in the failure to produce recommendations that are implemented.

To help ensure effective implementation, marketing managers must consider why the intended marketing strategies do not always turn out as expected. The *intended strategies* often differ from the *realized strategies* because of the three problems of implementation: marketing strategy and implementation are related; they are constantly evolving; the responsibility for them is separated. Marketing managers must also consider other vital components of implementation resources, systems, people, leadership and shared goals to ensure the proper implementation of marketing strategies.

Implementation is an important part of the marketing management process. Proper implementation of a marketing plan depends on internal marketing to motivate personnel who perform marketing activities, effective communication within the marketing unit and the coordination of marketing activities. Managers can motivate personnel by linking rewards, both financial and non-financial, to organizational goals. A company's communication system must allow the marketing manager to communicate with high-level management, with managers of other functional areas in the company and with personnel involved in marketing activities both inside and outside the organization. Finally, marketing managers must coordinate the activities of marketing personnel, and integrate these activities with those in other areas of the company and with the marketing efforts of personnel in external organizations.

Related approaches that organizations may use to help facilitate marketing implementation include *relationship marketing, internal marketing* and *total quality management (TQM)*. In relationship marketing, the focus is on winning and keeping customers by maintaining links between marketing, quality and customer service. This requires a company to satisfy not only customers but also those audiences in the *five markets model of relationship marketing*: referral, supplier, employee recruitment markets, influencer and internal markets. *Internal marketing* is the application of marketing internally within the company, with programmes of communication and guidance targeted at internal audiences to develop responsiveness and a unified sense of purpose among employees. It is a philosophy for managing human resources with a marketing perspective so that all members of the organization understand and accept their respective roles in implementing the marketing strategy.

The TQM approach relies heavily on the talents of employees to continually improve the quality of the organization's goods and services. The three essentials of the TQM philosophy are empowered employees, continuous quality improvement and the use of quality improvement teams. One of TQM's primary tools is *benchmarking*, or measuring and evaluating the quality of an organization's goods, services or processes in relation to the best performing companies in the industry. Putting the TQM philosophy into practice requires a great deal of organizational resources. For relationship marketing, internal marketing or TQM to be successful, top management must be totally committed and the specific elements of these programmes must be coordinated to ensure that they work in harmony with each other.

The *marketing control process* consists of establishing performance standards, evaluating actual performance by comparing it with established standards, and reducing the difference between desired and actual performance. *Performance standards*, which are established in the planning process, are expected levels of performance against which actual performance can be compared. In evaluating actual performance, marketing managers must know what marketers within the business are doing and must have information about the activities of external organizations that provide the company with marketing assistance. Then actual performance is compared with performance standards. Marketers must determine whether a discrepancy exists and, if so, whether it requires corrective action, such as changing the performance standards or improving actual performance.

Effective marketing control hinges on the quantity and quality of information and the speed at which it is received. The control of marketing activities is not a simple task. Problems encountered include environmental changes, time lags between marketing activities and their effects, and difficulty in determining the costs of marketing activities. In addition to these, it may be hard to develop exact performance standards for marketing personnel.

Control of marketing strategy can be achieved through *sales* and *marketing cost analyses*. *Sales measurements* are usually analyzed in terms of either cash volume or *market share*. For a sales analysis to be effective, it must compare current sales performance with either forecast company sales, industry sales, specific competitors' sales or the costs incurred to generate the current sales volume. A sales analysis can be performed on the company's total sales, or the total sales can be disaggregated and analyzed by product, geographic area, sales person or customer type and market segment.

Marketing cost analysis involves an examination of accounting records and, frequently, a reclassification of *natural accounts* into *marketing function accounts*. Three broad categories are used in marketing cost analysis: *direct costs*, *traceable common costs* and *non-traceable common costs*. Such an analysis is often difficult, because there may be no logical, clear-cut way to allocate natural accounts into functional accounts. The analyst may choose either a *full cost approach* or *direct cost approach*. Cost analysis can focus on (1) an aggregate cost analysis of natural accounts or functional accounts, or (2) an analysis of functional accounts for products, geographic areas or customer groups.

Value-based marketing is the inclusion of the value of a marketing strategy and marketing activity in an organization's financial analysis of shareholder value. *Marketing shareholder value analysis (MSVA)* enables marketing strategies and programmes to be incorporated within this financial appraisal of shareholder value. The value to the business of a marketing strategy is estimated, based on (1) the present value of the business during the strategizing and planning stage, and (2) the continuing value of the business after the plans have been implemented and actioned.

Performance measures popular in evaluating *marketing performance* include assessing overall markets, specific segments or product lines in terms of financial profitability, contribution or return on investment; market share; *customer satisfaction* levels; and qualitative measures of customer *brand awareness*. Retail marketers additionally favour a measure of *sales per square metre* of store selling space. *EBITDA* is important in businesses generating a lot of cash.

Key links

The implementation of marketing strategy and programmes, controls and the assessment of performance go hand-in-hand with the creation of marketing strategies and marketing plans. With this in mind, read this chapter in conjunction with:

- Chapter 1, on the evolution of marketing towards the relationship marketing era.
- Chapter 2, on marketing strategy development and competitor assessment.
- Chapter 22, on marketing planning and associated processes.

Important terms

Benchmarking
Brand awareness
Category management
Centralized organization
Customer satisfaction
Decentralized organization
Direct cost approach
Direct costs
EBITDA
Empowerment
Five markets model of relationship marketing
Full cost approach
Intended strategy

Internal marketing
Market share
Marketing control process
Marketing cost analysis
Marketing function accounts
Marketing implementation
Marketing metrics
Marketing oriented
Marketing performance
Marketing shareholder value analysis (MSVA)
Natural accounts
Non-traceable common costs
Organizing by function
Organizing by product
Organizing by region
Organizing by type of customer
Performance standard
Realized strategy
Relationship marketing
Requisites for implementation
Sales analysis
Sales measurements
Sales per square metre
Total quality management (TQM)
Traceable common costs
Value-based marketing

Discussion and review questions

1. What determines the place of marketing within an organization? Which type of organization is best suited to the marketing concept? Why?

2. What marketing activities must be undertaken by an organization striving to establish the marketing concept at its heart?

3. What factors can be used to organize the internal aspects of a marketing unit? Discuss the benefits of each type of organization.

4. Why might an organization use multiple bases for organizing its marketing unit?

5. What are the implementation requisites for marketing strategies and plans?

6. Why is motivation of marketing personnel important in implementing marketing plans?

7. How does communication help in implementing marketing plans?

8. What attributes distinguish relationship marketing from transaction-based marketing?

9. What is internal marketing? Why is it important in implementing marketing strategies?

10. Total quality management is a growing force in many businesses. What is TQM? How can it help to implement marketing strategies effectively?

11. What are the major steps of the marketing control process?

12. List and discuss the five requirements for an effective control process.

13. Discuss the major problems in controlling marketing activities.

14. What is a sales analysis? What makes it an effective control tool?

15. Identify and describe three cost analysis methods. Compare and contrast direct costing and full costing.

16. What is marketing shareholder value analysis? What are its strengths?

17. What performance measures are favoured by marketers?

18. Why should more than one performance metric be adopted by an organization to assess its marketing outcomes?

Recommended readings

Aaker, D.A., *Managing Brand Equity* (Free Press, 2009).
Aaker, D.A. and McLoughlin, D., *Strategic Marketing Management* (Wiley, 2010).
Blythe, J. and Megicks, P., *Marketing Planning: Strategy, Environment and Context* (FT/Prentice-Hall, 2010).
Dibb, S. and Simkin, L., *Marketing Planning* (Cengage, 2008).
Doyle, P., *Value-Based Marketing* (Wiley, 2000).
McDonald, M.H. and Wilson, H., *Marketing Plans: How to Prepare Them, How to Use Them* (John Wiley, 2011).
Nikbin, D., *Internal Marketing and Strategy Implementation* (Lambert Academic Publishing, 2010).
Piercy, N., *Market-Led Strategic Change* (Routledge, 2012).

Internet exercise

If you are working, look at your organization's website or intranet. If you are studying, look at the intranet of your academic institution.

1. What elements of internal marketing are evident in the website's sections?

2. In what ways is the content attempting to control, coordinate and share information with employees or people within the organization?

3. How else could the organization communicate its marketing strategy and marketing plan intentions to internal stakeholders?

Group tasks

1. As a syndicate group you have probably endured many heated discussions and some disagreements, so you will recognize the difficulties of achieving consensus and buy-in to an idea. What steps should a team of marketers take to engender the support for their marketing strategy of colleagues in other functions of the business?

2. Consider the controls required to ensure effective implementation and worthwhile performance for a new marketing plan.

Applied mini-case

A leading IT services company had been marketing its IT outsourcing solutions to manufacturers, financial services companies, retailers, health providers, government departments and other sectors. The new head of its business unit, charged with marketing IT solutions to the manufacturing sector (automotive, pharmaceuticals, electrical components, domestic appliances and so on) decided that, rather than market to the businesses involved with manufacturing, the company should identify the providers of facilities, such as offices and factories, purchased by these manufacturers in order to produce their products. The plan was to promote the IT business to the big construction companies so that when a new-build factory was commissioned, the IT business would already be the agreed supplier to the building contractor. There are far fewer major construction companies than manufacturers, so this novel approach to achieving sales was accepted by the IT business's board. However, the new strategy required a major change of behaviour, as sales and marketing resources were moved from selling to manufacturers to building relationships with construction companies.

Question

Suggest the problems likely to be encountered inside the IT company as it attempts to realign its operations around this new target market strategy. What steps would the company need to take to pre-empt such obstacles?

Case study

Timex stands the test of time

During the 1970s, watches took a technological leap forward, from wind-up spring mechanisms to quartz crystals, batteries and digital displays. The Timex Corporation lagged behind other manufacturers in making such changes. When the Swiss-made Swatch watch invaded department stores and convinced customers that their watches were not just time-telling devices but fashion statements, Timex was not ready to offer any competition. At Timex, reliability and value had always been the priorities, certainly not style and fashion. For years, Timex's sales suffered because of its drab image, especially in contrast with the colourful Swatch. Then came the 1990s and the decade of value. As value came to take precedence over status, more price-conscious consumers were attracted by quality at moderate prices than by designer labels. Timex took advantage of this trend to revive its brand, the old reliable Timex watch . . .

True Value Since 1854. By blending its 'value pricing' message with some trendy new designs and diversifying its product for specific niche markets, Timex made a comeback. *Wear It Well* today focuses on the fashion-conscious consumer. Timex regularly features in surveys of the leading trendy fashion brands. The credit crunch just encountered has once more focused consumers on value, to the pleasure of Timex executives, although the growth of high-tech app-led smartwatches as health monitors, comms devices and web browsers poses interesting challenges for all traditional watch producers.

Consumers can still buy an unadorned Timex watch for under £20, and analysts say that these simple styles with easy-to-read faces are the company's best-sellers. However, to compete in a crowded market, Timex developed stylish special collections for adults: dress watches, sports watches, technology watches and outdoor watches. Timex set up studios in France and the United States to design Timex's own versions of colourful creative watches. There are many ranges, such as *Expedition* rugged watches, *Weekender* fashion and *IronMan* sports, fitness and monitoring watches.

Timex's advertising strategy is to appeal to niche markets by reviving its traditional 'durable yet inexpensive' positioning, and revitalizing its powerful brand identity. The famous Timex theme, 'It Takes a Licking and Keeps On Ticking', has taken a humorous bent in television spots, where sumo wrestlers wear the watches strapped to their middles as they grapple on the mat, and rock musicians use Timex watches to strum their guitars. In a print advertising campaign, the company featured real people who, like the Timex watches they wear, have been through rough experiences but survived to tell the tale.

With traditional watch sales in most countries declining, most watchmakers are concerned. However, at Timex executives are celebrating sales and market share increases. The company now controls a larger proportion of the market than its four biggest competitors combined. Timex is happy to be shedding its dowdy and boring image. Rising young professional people do not have to put their wrists behind their backs to hide a Timex any more, or announce loudly to colleagues that they are only wearing a Timex while their Rolex is being repaired.

Ruthless controls and continual performance monitoring are intended to avoid a repeat of the 1980s doldrums period. Marketing executives have monitored the marketing strategy carefully in order to:

1. ensure that signs of success or failure can be acted upon, and

2. modify marketing programmes continually in order to enhance the impact of Timex's new approach.

Sales and financial performance are evaluated regularly. Changing fashions and aggressive competitors – such as Swatch – caught Timex out once before. The company does not intend to be left behind again. With 5000 employees in four continents, manufacturing and distribution in 20 countries, growing sales in over 100 countries through 35 000 retail outlets, and a successful defence against the likes of Swatch, the future looks bright for Timex.

Sources: Sylvester's 2015 and www.timex.co.uk, 2015.

Questions for discussion

1. Which environmental forces are likely to be of greatest interest to marketing managers at Timex?

2. Identify the target markets towards which Timex is aiming its products.

3. Why must Timex continually assess its performance and the impact of its marketing?

CHAPTER 24

Responsible marketing

"Ethics and CSR increasingly matter to consumers . . . they should to marketers, too."

Objectives

- To understand the concept of social responsibility and to consider the importance of marketers behaving responsibly.

- To define and describe the importance of marketing ethics.

- To become familiar with ways to improve ethical decisions in marketing.

- To understand the role of social responsibility and ethics in improving marketing performance.

- To revisit the concept of social marketing and consider how it is used.

- To appreciate how the marketing discipline is evolving.

INTRODUCTION

There is a growing expectation among people and those who govern them that businesses will behave in a responsible manner. The banking crisis brought into sharp focus how poor corporate behaviour and low standards have significant consequences. This expectation of responsibility also extends to marketers and the way in which they practice. Social responsibility and ethics are two issues that can have a profound impact on the success of marketing strategies.

This chapter gives an overview of how social responsibility and ethics must be considered in marketing decision-making. Most marketers operate responsibly and within the limits of the law. However, some companies engage in activities that customers, other marketers and society in general deem unacceptable. Such activities include questionable selling practices, bribery, price discrimination, deceptive advertising, misleading packaging, spying on competitors, planting lies about rivals on social media, and marketing defective products. For example, 37 per cent of the software programmes used by businesses worldwide are illegally pirated copies.[1] Practices of this kind raise questions about marketers' obligations to society. Inherent in these questions are the issues of social responsibility and marketing ethics. Even if laws are not broken, there are growing obligations on marketers to handle customer data ethically and responsibly, question information sources and their appropriateness, and worry about collaborations and the monetization of big data via third parties.

There is also growing interest in how marketing as a discipline can overtly contribute to the well-being of society and of individuals. One way in which this can be achieved is through social marketing activities, which use commercial marketing tools and techniques for the good of communities and those who live within them.

Kit Kat shifts to Fairtrade

Fair trade promotes equal, fair and sustainable trade partnerships and aims to combat poverty by helping individuals in developing countries to compete in the global market. Many organizations support fair trade and certify fair trade products. The most well-known is the World Fair Trade Organization (WFTO), which represents more than 350 organizations committed to fair trade. However, according to the WFTO, advocating fair trade is not enough; in order for it to succeed, there must be a demand for fair trade products. This is where mainstream brands can help.

Nestlé is one mainstream brand becoming more involved in fair trade. In the past, Nestlé faced criticism for its business practices in the developing world. In order to improve its reputation, Nestlé searched for ways to establish itself as a socially responsible company and decided to focus on its use of cocoa beans. The company announced its Cocoa Plan, an investment programme designed to address economic and social issues in cocoa farming communities (www.nestlecocoaplan.com). Through its Cocoa Plan, Nestlé provides cocoa farmers with fair compensation for their cocoa beans, additional training and disease-resistant cocoa plants. Nestlé also agreed to fight child labour and to provide better healthcare to cocoa suppliers. In the UK and Ireland, the Cocoa Plan is brought to life through Fairtrade certification of four-finger and two-finger Kit-Kats, supporting 7000 farmers and their families.

Critics of Nestlé accuse the company of using fair trade merely to generate good publicity. Whether or not this is true, the company's Kit Kat bar is the second most popular chocolate bar in the UK. Nestlé needs to purchase large amounts of fair trade cocoa, which will have a huge impact on the market. Nestlé's transition into fair trade may help motivate other companies to pursue fair trade, possibly supplying the demand that the WFTO says the fair trade movement so desperately needs.

Marketers in all sectors are increasingly aware of expectations that companies will behave in a responsible and ethical manner. Having been previously criticized for some of its business activities, Nestlé has decided that turning to fair trade ingredients for its Kit Kat will help the company to be seen as more socially responsible and hopefully will also be well received by customers. Nestlé also supports the values of the fair trade initiative. The implications of decisions such as this one are considered in more detail throughout this chapter.

This chapter begins by defining social responsibility and exploring its dimensions. Various social responsibility issues are then discussed, such as the natural environment and the marketer's role as a member of the community. Next, the definition and role of ethics in marketing decisions are explored. Ethical issues in marketing, the ethical decision-making process and ways to improve ethical conduct in marketing are all considered. Next, the ways in which social responsibility and ethics can be incorporated into marketing decisions are examined. Finally, the chapter explains the concept of social marketing and considers how marketing tools and techniques can be used to improve societal well-being.

Social responsibility

Social responsibility
An organization's obligation to maximize its positive impact and minimize its negative impact on society.

The nature of social responsibility

In marketing, **social responsibility** refers to an organization's obligation to maximize its positive impact and minimize its negative impact on society. Social responsibility deals with the total effect of all marketing decisions on society. Ample evidence demonstrates that ignoring society's demands for responsible business practices and marketing activity can destroy customers' trust and even prompt government regulations, with reputational damage to then redress. This was the case when corporate tax avoidance became a dominant news story in the UK.

Irresponsible actions that anger customers, employees or competitors may not only jeopardize a marketer's financial standing but could have other repercussions as well. For example, following a report into misleading claims on food packaging, the UK's Food Standards Agency (FSA) instigated a campaign to 'name and shame' food manufacturers selling unhealthy products, including those with high sugar, salt or fat content.[2]

In contrast, socially responsible activities can generate positive publicity and boost sales. In 2007, Marks & Spencer launched its sustainability programme – Plan A – making 100 commitments on

Marketing in society

Tax shaming damages reputation

Google, Amazon, Starbucks: The rise of 'tax shaming'

- Multinationals such as Google, Amazon and Starbucks have been criticized by the Public Accounts Committee over tax avoidance.

- Stung, Starbucks plans to change its arrangements and pay UK corporation tax.

Global firms such as Starbucks, Google and Amazon have come under fire for avoiding paying tax on their British sales. There seems to be a growing culture of naming and shaming companies. But what impact does it have?

Companies have long had complicated tax structures, but a recent spate of stories has highlighted a number of tax-avoiding firms that are not seen to be playing their part.

Starbucks, for example, had sales of £400 million in the UK last year, but paid no corporation tax. It transferred some money to a Dutch sister company in royalty payments, bought coffee beans from Switzerland and paid high interest rates to borrow from other parts of the business.

Amazon, which had sales in the UK of £3.35 billion in 2011, only reported a 'tax expense' of £1.8 million.

And Google's UK unit paid just £6 million to the Treasury in 2011 on UK turnover of £395 million.

Everything these companies are doing is legal. It's avoidance and not evasion.

But the tide of public opinion is visibly turning. Even ten years ago news of a company minimizing its corporation tax would have been more likely to be inside the business pages than on the front page.

What changed? And is 'shaming' of companies justifiable and effective?

Momentum has been growing for the last few years.

In September 2009, the *Observer* ran with the headline: 'Avoiding tax robs our public services, declares minister.' The paper reported that the government was planning to say tax is a 'moral issue' and that it was 'determined to end avoidance and evasion'.

October 2010 – and the Vodafone case – saw the *Daily Mail* report: 'Vodafone closes Oxford Street store at £6bn tax protest.'

A few months later and the focus moved to Sir Philip Green's business empire. 'Crisis? What crisis?' reported the *Mail*, which said the TopShop boss was 'enjoying' a Barbados holiday while thousands of campaigners laid siege to his UK stores.

Barclays Bank was the next target – in February 2011 the *Daily Express* reported on the 'raid' by tax protesters, who shouted: 'Dave and George do your sums.' Later that same month, the *Guardian* ran with the headline 'UK Uncut: "People are starting to listen to us".'

www.bbc.co.uk/news/magazine-20560359

The above piece was splashed across BBC News in May 2013 and featured in the *BBC News Magazine*'s online pages. In an era of rolling 24-hours news, social media sharing of such stories and the ease with which interested parties can gather support to protest, companies increasingly must balance their shareholders' short-term financial interests against reputational damage and a backlash from consumers, suppliers and regulators. The digital era seemingly creates the need for greater transparency and corporate responsibility. Certainly the headlines reported in the BBC's piece above caused those brands' marketers and communications agencies significant aggravation and disruption.

Source: 'Google, Amazon, Starbucks: The rise of "tax shaming",' Vanessa Barford and Gerry Holt, *BBC News Magazine*, 21 May 2013 (accessed 1 May 2015).

ethical, environmental and social issues facing the company. The list of commitments grew to 180, divided between seven pillars of activity ranging from climate change and handling waste, to the protection of natural resources and how the company does business (marksandspencer.com/plana). 'We're all in it together' is how Plan A positions its sustainability drive. Marks & Spencer explains that it supports this initiative with a view to inspiring young people to make sustainability the new normal.

Socially responsible efforts have a positive impact on local communities; at the same time, they indirectly help the sponsoring organization by attracting goodwill, publicity and potential customers and employees. Thus, while social responsibility is certainly a positive concept in itself, most organizations embrace it in the expectation of indirect long-term benefits. Proctor & Gamble, Unilever, PepsiCo, Santander and McDonald's are just a few of the companies that have social responsibility commitments. Research suggests that an organizational culture that is conducive to social responsibility engenders greater employee commitment and improved business performance.

The dimensions of social responsibility

Marketing citizenship
The adoption of a strategic focus for fulfilling the economic, legal, ethical and philanthropic social responsibilities expected by stakeholders.

Socially responsible organizations strive for **marketing citizenship** by adopting a strategic focus for fulfilling the economic, legal, ethical and philanthropic social responsibilities that their stakeholders expect of them. **Stakeholders** include those constituents who have a 'stake', or claim, in some aspect of the company's products, operations, markets, industry and outcomes; these include customers, employees, investors and shareholders, suppliers, governments, communities and many others. Companies that consider the diverse perspectives of stakeholders in their daily operations and strategic planning are said to have a 'stakeholder orientation', an important element of social responsibility.[3] For example, DIY retailer B&Q secured stakeholder input on issues ranging from child labour, fair wages and equal opportunity to environmental impact. The company has a vision to be the first choice for sustainable home improvement and has developed a series of principles to support this goal. These include responsible forestry, promoting eco homes and living, and supporting charities involved with sustainability.[4] As Figure 24.1 shows, social responsibility dimensions can be viewed as a pyramid.[5] The economic and legal aspects have long been acknowledged, whereas philanthropic and ethical issues have gained recognition more recently.

Stakeholders
Constituents who have a 'stake', or claim, in some aspect of a company's products, operations, markets, industry and outcomes.

At the most basic level, all companies have an economic responsibility to be profitable so that they can provide a return on investment to their owners and investors, create jobs for the community, and contribute goods and services to the economy. How organizations relate to stockholders, employees, competitors, customers, the community and the natural environment affects the economy. When economic downturns or poor decisions lead companies to lay off employees, communities often suffer as they attempt to absorb the displaced employees. Customers may experience diminished levels of service as a result of fewer experienced employees. Share prices often decline when lay-offs are announced, affecting the value of stockholders' investment portfolios. Moreover, stressed-out employees facing demands to reduce expenses may make poor decisions that affect the natural environment, product quality, employee rights and customer service. An organization's sense of economic responsibility is especially significant for employees, raising such issues as equal job opportunities, workplace diversity, job safety, health and employee privacy. Economic responsibilities require finding a balance between society's demand for social responsibility and investors' desire for profits.

Marketers also have an economic responsibility to compete fairly. Size frequently gives companies an advantage over rivals. Large companies can often generate economies of scale that allow them to put smaller companies out of business. Consequently, small companies and even whole communities may resist the efforts of businesses such as Wal-Mart, Tesco and McDonald's to open outlets in their neighbourhood. These companies are able to operate at such low costs that small, local businesses cannot compete. Though consumers appreciate lower prices, the failure

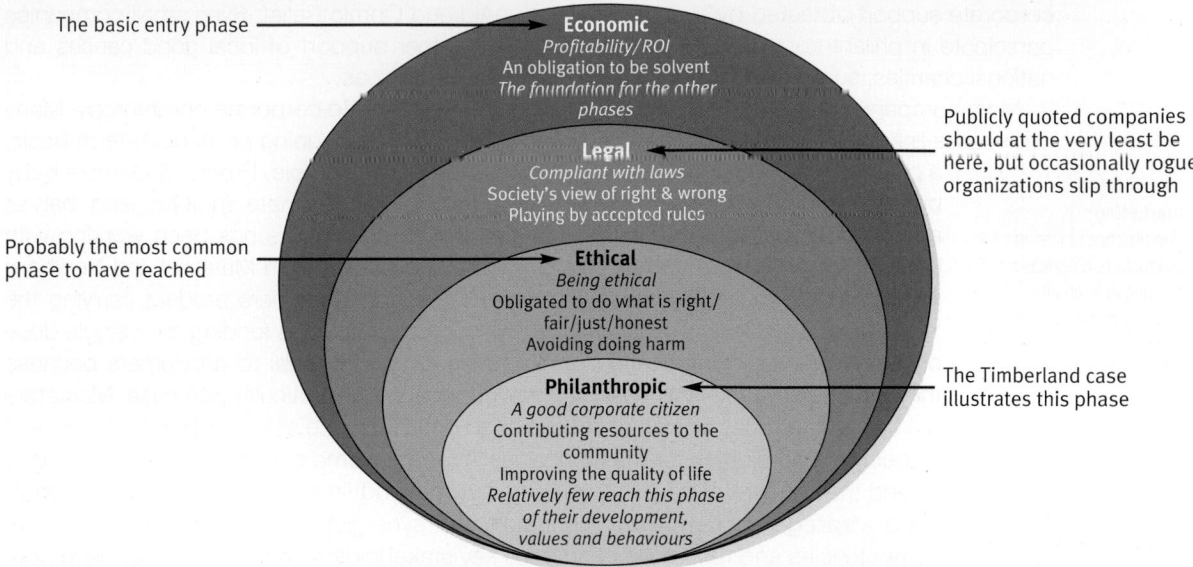

FIGURE 24.1
The phases of CSR

Source: Adapted from the work of Archie Carroll, published in *Business Horizons*, July–August, 1991, p. 42.

of small businesses creates unemployment for some members of the community. Such issues create concerns about social responsibility for organizations, communities and consumers.

Marketers are also expected to obey laws and regulations. The efforts of elected representatives and special interest groups to promote responsible corporate behaviour have resulted in laws and regulations designed to keep European companies' actions within the range of acceptable conduct. When customers, interest groups or businesses become outraged over what they perceive as irresponsibility on the part of a marketing organization, they may urge the government to draft new legislation to regulate the behaviour or engage in litigation. For example, following a record number of complaints about the practices of door-to-door sales people, the UK government looked at legislative action to control this kind of selling.

Marketing ethics
Principles and standards that define acceptable marketing conduct as determined by various stakeholders, including the public, government, regulators, private interest groups, consumers, industry and the organization itself.

Economic and legal responsibilities are the most basic levels of social responsibility for a good reason: failure to consider them may mean that a marketer is not around long enough to engage in ethical or philanthropic activities. Beyond these dimensions is **marketing ethics**, principles and standards that define acceptable conduct in marketing as determined by various stakeholders, including the public, government, regulators, private interest groups, consumers, industry and the organization itself. Some companies, including The Body Shop and The Co-operative supermarket chain, have built their businesses around ethical ideas. The most ethical principles have been codified as laws and regulations to encourage marketers to conform to society's expectations about conduct. However, marketing ethics goes beyond legal issues. Ethical marketing decisions foster trust, which helps build long-term marketing relationships. There is a more detailed look at the ethical dimension of social responsibility later in this chapter.

Philanthropic responsibilities
Not required of a company, but they promote human welfare or goodwill.

Philanthropic responsibilities At the top of the corporate responsibility tree (see Figure 24.1) are **philanthropic responsibilities**. These responsibilities, which go beyond marketing ethics, are not required of a company, but they promote human welfare or goodwill, as do the economic, legal and ethical dimensions of social responsibility. The philanthropic responsibility that companies demonstrate is shown in the level of corporate support attracted by events such as LiveAid and Comic Relief. Even small companies participate in philanthropy through donations and volunteer support of local good causes and national charities, such as the NSPCC, Oxfam and the Red Cross.

More companies than ever are adopting a strategic approach to corporate philanthropy. Many businesses link their products to a particular social cause on an ongoing or medium-term basis, a practice known as **cause-related marketing**. For example, Procter & Gamble baby brand Pampers supports UNICEF's programme to vaccinate mothers and babies against tetanus. 'With the help of parents like you, Pampers has been working with UNICEF for nine years to help protect mums and babies from Maternal and Newborn Tetanus in 15 countries around the world.'[6] For each Pampers product carrying the '1 Pack = 1 Life-Saving Vaccine' logo, the company provides funding for a single dose of vaccine. Such cause-related programmes tend to appeal to consumers because they provide an additional reason to 'feel good' about a particular purchase. Marketers like the programmes because well designed ones increase sales and create feelings of respect and admiration for the companies involved. Some companies are beginning to extend the concept of corporate philanthropy beyond financial contributions by adopting a **strategic philanthropy** approach, the synergistic use of organizational core competencies and resources to address key stakeholders' interests, and achieve both organizational and social benefits. Strategic philanthropy involves employees, organizational resources and expertise, and the ability to link these assets to the concerns of key stakeholders, including employees, customers, suppliers and social needs. Strategic philanthropy involves both financial and non-financial contributions to stakeholders (employee time, goods and services, and company technology and equipment, as well as facilities), but it also benefits the company.[7]

Cause-related marketing
The practice of linking products to a particular social cause on an ongoing or medium-term basis.

Strategic philanthropy
The synergistic use of organizational core competencies and resources to address key stakeholders' interests, and achieve both organizational and social benefits.

Social responsibility issues

Although social responsibility may seem to be an abstract ideal, managers make decisions related to social responsibility every day. To be successful, a business must determine what customers, government regulators and competitors, as well as society in general, want or expect in terms of social responsibility. The success of international retailer The Body Shop has been attributed to the company's awareness of the Green movement and demonstration of social responsibility. Table 24.1 summarizes three major categories of social responsibility issues: the natural environment, consumerism and community relations.

TABLE 24.1 Social responsibility issues

Issue	Description	Major social concerns
Natural environment	Consumers insisting not only on a good quality of life but on a healthful environment so they can maintain a high standard of living during their lifetimes	Conservation Water pollution Air pollution Land pollution
Consumerism	Activities undertaken by independent individuals, groups and organizations to protect their rights as consumers	The right to safety The right to be informed The right to choose The right to be heard
Community relations	Society eager to have marketers contribute to its well-being, wishing to know what marketers do to help solve social problems	Equality issues Disadvantaged members of society Safety and health Education and general welfare

Sustainability

One way in which marketers are increasingly demonstrating their social responsibility is through programmes designed to protect and preserve the natural environment. **Sustainability** is the potential for the long-term well-being of the natural environment, including all biological entities, as well as the interaction among nature and individuals, organizations and business strategies. Sustainability includes the assessment and improvement of business strategies, economic sectors, work practices, technologies and lifestyles all while maintaining the natural environment.

Many companies are making contributions to environmental protection organizations, supporting clean-up events, promoting recycling, re-tooling manufacturing processes to minimize waste and pollution, changing packaging, modifying logistics and generally re-evaluating the effects of their products on the natural environment. Many supermarkets, for example, provide on-site recycling for customers and encourage their suppliers to reduce wasteful packaging.

Procter & Gamble uses recycled materials in some of its packaging and markets refills for some products, which reduces packaging waste. Such efforts generate positive publicity and often increase sales for the companies involved. The Food and Drink Federation (FDF) – whose membership includes PepsiCo, Coca-Cola and Kraft – is encouraging sustainable practice by establishing strict environmental targets. These include a reduction in CO_2 emissions by 2020, zero food and packaging waste going to landfill sites, and a 20 per cent reduction in water use within the supply chain.[8]

Green marketing   **Green marketing** is the specific development, pricing, promotion and distribution of products that do not harm the natural environment. Toyota and Nissan have succeeded in marketing 'hybrid' cars that use electric motors to augment their internal-combustion engines, improving the vehicles' fuel economy without reducing their power. The UK government is now supporting these alternative fuel technologies by funding the installation of electric vehicle points in certain locations. Figure 24.2 illustrates a category in many supermarkets in response to some consumers' growing awareness of green issues: organic fruit and vegetables. Meanwhile, Hewlett Packard (HP) has taken a leadership role in the recycling of electronic waste by creating drop-off locations for rechargeable batteries and recycling programmes for printer cartridges and other electronic items.

An independent coalition of environmentalists, scientists and marketers is one group involved in evaluating products to assess their environmental impact, determining marketers' commitment to the environment. Described as 'The directory for planet-friendly living', *The Green Guide,* which was first published in 1984, offers online and print guidance on green products and ethical living.[9] Such information sources have an important role to play during what is a confusing time for many

FIGURE 24.2

Many consumers are increasingly aware of 'green' issues and some businesses are responding accordingly: here a retailer is offering organically produced fruit and vegetables to its shoppers

FIGURE 24.3
The European Ecolabel

Source: www.europa.eu.int/comm/environment/ecolabel; www.eco-label.com.

consumers, who are increasingly faced with an array of products making a variety of environmental claims. For example, most Chiquita bananas are certified through the Rainforest Alliance's Better Banana Project as having been grown using more environmentally and labour-friendly practices.[10] In Europe, companies can apply for the EU Ecolabel to indicate that their products are less harmful to the environment than competing products, based on scientifically determined criteria (see Figure 24.3).

Although demand for economic, legal and ethical solutions to environmental problems is widespread, the environmental movement in marketing includes many different groups, whose values and goals often conflict. Some environmentalists and marketers believe companies should work to protect and preserve the natural environment by implementing the following goals:

1. *Eliminate the concept of waste.* Recognizing that pollution and waste usually stem from inefficiency, the question is not what to do with waste but how to make things without waste.

2. *Reinvent the concept of a product.* Products should be reduced to only three types and eventually just two. The first type is consumables, which are eaten or, when placed in the ground, turn into soil with few harmful side-effects. The second type is durable goods such as cars, televisions, computers and refrigerators which should be made, used and returned to the manufacturer within a closed-loop system. Such products should be designed for disassembly and recycling. The third category is unsaleables and includes such products as radioactive materials, heavy metals and toxins. These products should always belong to the original makers, who should be responsible for the products and their full life-cycle effects. Reclassifying products in this way encourages manufacturers to design products more efficiently.

3. *Make prices reflect the cost.* Every product should reflect, or at least approximate, its actual cost, not only the direct cost of its effect on production but also the cost of its effect on air, water and soil.

4. *Make environmentalism profitable.* Consumers are beginning to recognize that competition in the marketplace should not occur between companies harming the environment and those trying to save it.[11]

Greenwash
Misleading claims about a brand's green credentials, resulting in loss of trust and a consumer backlash.

It is important that marketers' claims are true and can be substantiated. Consumers are cynical and are quickly alienated by **greenwash**. It might be better to say nothing than to make claims which raise suspicion or cause a backlash of negative chatter on social media. Trust is easily lost, with dire consequences for a brand's reputation and sales.

Consumerism
The efforts of independent individuals, groups and organizations to protect the rights of consumers.

Consumerism   A significant aspect in socially responsible marketing is **consumerism**, which is the efforts of independent individuals, groups and organizations to protect the rights of consumers. The underlying assumption is that consumers have a range of rights, including the right to privacy, the right to safety, the right to choose, the right to be charged fairly, the right to be properly informed and the right to fair treatment when they complain. For example, the right to safety means that marketers are obligated not to market a product that they know could harm consumers. This right can be extended to imply that all products must be safe for their intended use, include thorough and explicit instructions for proper and safe use, and have been tested to ensure reliability and quality.

Interest groups play an important role in helping to protect consumers' rights by taking action against companies they consider irresponsible, by lobbying government officials and agencies, engaging in letter-writing and social media campaigns and boycotts and making public service announcements. A number of high-profile consumer activists have also crusaded for consumer rights. Consumer activism has resulted in legislation requiring various safety features in cars: seat belts, padded dashboards, stronger door catches, headrests, baby and toddler seats, shatterproof windscreens and collapsible steering columns. Activists' efforts have furthered the passage of several consumer protection laws.

The power of angry consumers should not be underestimated. Indeed, research suggests that such individuals not only fail to make repeat purchases but may retaliate against the source of their dissatisfaction.[12] Negative reaction from the public was partly the reason why News International took the decision to close the *News of the World* newspaper following damaging publicity that journalists working there had hacked the mobile phones of celebrities and members of the public involved in tragedies. The consumer movement has been helped by news format television programmes, such as the BBC's *Watchdog*. There has also been a growth of consumer sites on the web offering advice and reviews for consumers. For instance, mumsnet.com provides product ratings and reviews, and lobbies for better practices. Financial journalist and consumer rights activist Martin Lewis's *Money Saving Expert* website promotes better financial and debt management, providing consumers with much-needed advice and links (www.moneysavingexpert.com).

Community relations
Marketers' roles as community members and their contributions to civic projects and institutions.

Community relations   Social responsibility also extends to **community relations** and marketers' roles as community members. Individual communities expect marketers to make philanthropic contributions to civic projects and institutions, and to be 'good corporate citizens'. While most charitable donations come from individuals, corporate philanthropy is on the rise, with contributions of resources (money, product, time) to community causes such as education, the arts, recreation, disadvantaged members of the community and others. British Airways' 'Change for Good' partnership with UNICEF encourages donations of foreign currency from passengers, which can then be used to fund a range of health and educational projects aimed at children around the world. Over 15 years, £27 million has been raised. McDonald's, Shell, Ogilvy & Mather and Hewlett Packard all have programmes that contribute funds, equipment and personnel to educational reform. Similarly, Sainsbury's has a scheme that allows shoppers to collect vouchers enabling their local schools to obtain sports equipment.

Actions such as these can significantly improve a community's quality of life through employment opportunities, economic development, and financial contributions to educational, health, cultural and recreational causes.[13] These efforts also indirectly help the organizations in the form of goodwill, publicity and exposure to potential future customers. Although social responsibility is certainly a positive concept, most organizations do not embrace it without the expectation of some indirect long-term benefit.

The manner in which organizations deal with equality is also a key social responsibility issue. Diversity in the work environment has focused attention on the need to integrate and utilize an increasingly diverse workforce. Companies that are successful in achieving this are finding increases in creativity and motivation, and reductions in staff turnover.

Marketing ethics

Marketing ethics is a dimension of social responsibility involving principles and standards that define acceptable conduct in marketing. Acceptable standards of conduct in making individual and group decisions in marketing are determined by various stakeholders and by an organization's ethical climate. Marketers should also use their own values and ethical standards to act responsibly and provide ethical leadership for others.

Marketers should be aware of ethical standards for acceptable conduct from several viewpoints: company, industry, government, customers, special interest groups and society at large. When marketing activities deviate from accepted standards, the exchange process can break down, resulting in customer dissatisfaction, lack of trust, damaged brand reputation and legal action. In recent years, a number of ethical scandals have resulted in a massive loss of confidence in the integrity of businesses.[14] The recent global financial crisis led to sharp criticism of the financial services sector and growing distrust among consumers. Once trust has been broken, it can take a considerable time to rebuild. In fact, some research suggests that 76 per cent of consumers would boycott the products of a socially irresponsible company, and 91 per cent would consider switching to a competitor's products.[15]

When managers engage in activities that deviate from accepted principles, continued marketing exchanges become difficult, if not impossible. The best time to deal with such problems is during the marketing strategy process, not after major problems have materialized.

Marketing ethics goes beyond legal issues. Marketing decisions based on ethical considerations foster mutual trust in marketing relationships and foster internal collegiality. Although attempts are often made to draw a boundary between legal and ethical issues, the distinction between the two is frequently blurred in decision-making. Marketers operate in an environment in which overlapping legal and ethical issues often colour decisions. To separate legal and ethical decisions requires an assumption that marketing managers can instinctively differentiate legal and ethical issues. However, while the legal ramifications of some issues and problems may be obvious others are not. Questionable decisions and actions often result in disputes that must be resolved through litigation. The legal system therefore provides a formal venue for marketers to resolve ethical disputes as well as legal ones.

Hasbro, for example, filed a lawsuit against a man who marketed a board game called Ghettopoly. Hasbro's suit accused David Chang's game of unlawfully copying the packaging and logo of Hasbro's long-selling Monopoly board game and causing 'irreparable injury' to Hasbro's reputation and goodwill. After minority-rights groups complained that Ghettopoly promoted negative stereotypes of some minorities, some retailers stopped selling the game.[16] Indeed, most ethical disputes reported in the media involve the legal system at some level. In many cases, however, settlements are reached without requiring the decision of a judge or jury.

It is not the aim of this chapter to question individuals' ethical beliefs or personal convictions. Nor is it the purpose to examine the conduct of consumers, although some do behave unethically (engaging for instance in shoplifting, returning clothing after wearing it, sharing untrue information, and other abuses). Instead, the goal here is to highlight the importance of understanding and resolving ethical issues in marketing and to help readers learn about marketing ethics.

Ethical issues in marketing

Ethical issue
An identifiable problem, situation or opportunity requiring a choice between several actions that must be evaluated as right or wrong, ethical or unethical.

An **ethical issue** is an identifiable problem, situation or opportunity requiring an individual or organization to choose between actions that must be evaluated as right or wrong . . . ethical or unethical. Any time an activity causes marketing managers or customers in their target market to feel manipulated or cheated, a marketing ethical issue exists, regardless of the legality of that activity.

Regardless of the reasons behind specific ethical issues, marketers must be able to identify these issues and decide how to resolve them.[17] To do so requires familiarity

TABLE 24.2 Typical ethical issues related to the marketing mix

Product issue Product information	Covering up defects in products that could cause harm to a consumer; withholding critical performance information that could affect a purchase decision.
Place/distribution issue Counterfeiting	Counterfeit products are widespread, especially in the areas of computer software, clothing and audio and video products; the internet has facilitated the distribution of counterfeit products.
People issue Customer service	Promising or promoting aftermarket care with no intention of honouring the promise or warranty.
Promotion issue Advertising	Deceptive advertising or withholding important product information in a personal selling situation.
Pricing issue Pricing	Indicating that an advertised sale price is a reduction below the regular list price when, in fact, that is not the case.

with the many kinds of ethical issue that may arise in marketing. Some examples of ethical issues related to product, people, promotion, price and place/distribution (the marketing mix) appear in Table 24.2.

Product-related ethical issues generally arise when marketers fail to disclose the risks associated with a product, or information regarding the function, value or use of a product. Most car companies have experienced negative publicity associated with design or safety issues that resulted in a government-required recall of specific models. Pressures can build to substitute inferior materials or product components to reduce costs. Ethical issues also arise when marketers fail to inform customers about existing conditions or changes in product quality. Consider the introduction of a new size of confectionery bar, labelled with a banner touting its 'new larger size'. However, when placed in vending machines alongside older confectionery bars of the same brand, it became apparent that the product was actually slightly *smaller* than the bar it had replaced. Although this could have been a mistake, the company still has to defend and deal with the consequences of its actions. In today's digital environment, such poor behaviours quickly are discussed on social media, with e-word-of-mouth causing damage to a brand.

Promotion can create ethical issues in a variety of ways, among them false or misleading advertising and manipulative or deceptive sales promotions, tactics and publicity. A major ethical issue in promotion pertains to the marketing of video games that allegedly promote violence and weapons to children. Many other ethical issues are linked to promotion, including the use of bribery in personal selling situations. Even bribes that might benefit the organization can be unethical, because they jeopardize trust and fairness and can damage the organization in the long run.

In pricing, common ethical issues are price fixing, predatory pricing and failure to disclose the full price of a purchase. The emotional and subjective nature of price creates many situations in which misunderstandings between the seller and buyer cause ethical problems. Marketers have the right to price their products to earn a reasonable profit, but ethical issues may crop up when a company seeks to earn high profits at the expense of its customers. Some pharmaceutical companies, for example, have been accused of pricing products at exorbitant levels and taking advantage of customers who must purchase the medicine to survive or to maintain their quality of life. Another issue relates to the quantity surcharges that occur when consumers are effectively overcharged for buying a larger package size of the same grocery product.[18]

Ethical issues in distribution involve relationships among producers and marketing middlemen. Marketing middlemen, or intermediaries (wholesalers and retailers), facilitate the flow of products from the producer to the ultimate customer. Each intermediary performs a different role and agrees to certain rights, responsibilities and rewards associated with that role. For example, producers expect wholesalers and retailers to honour agreements and keep them informed of

GAP uses behaviour change to promote sustainable living

Topical insight

Behaviour change approaches such as nudge are central to the way that environmental charity Global Action Plan (GAP) fulfils its mission. The charity works with organizations, communities and young people to deliver behaviour change projects that promote more sustainable living. These activities involve GAP in a wide range of programmes targeting a variety of different groups. For example, GAP supported Tata Consultancy Services in establishing its internal sustainability strategy, helping to recruit and train sustainability champions who delivered a range of behaviour change initiatives. The campaign spearheaded a range of changes, including swapping paper cups for ceramic mugs, removing desk bins, improving recycling signage, providing more eco-friendly travel information, reduced the amount of recyclable rubbish in waste bins by 26 per cent, and achieved a 25 per cent reduction in the numbers of appliances that were left switched on.

Meanwhile GAP's online *Water Explorer* programme engages 8–14-year-olds in learning about saving water and reducing pollution. Education is used to encourage children to think about the issues and then change their behaviour in ways which will protect this precious resource. Schools that sign up take part in a challenge to rescue a virtual reservoir and to implement practical water saving practices in school and at home. Teams can compete with other schools and prizes are available to those that perform well.

As with the Tata programme, the *Water Explorer* activities are underpinned by research evidence on behaviour change, some of which is gleaned from GAP's own studies. Included in their research are studies on the information that consumers need in order to make more sustainable choices when buying household appliances, the business case for employee engagement in sustainability initiatives, and a compilation of evidence about sustainable business travel.

GAP's research also underpins a range of tools that are used to support its programmes. Among these tools is a pack of behaviour change cards which describe simple approaches to improving sustainability. Using scientifically grounded ideas and examples, the cards are designed to inspire those working in organizations to make positive changes. For example, the 'Not the Environment' card explains that it is easier to bring about change that fits our own self-interest. Using the statement 'We all value the environment. Just not enough to change our habits', the card describes how the charity used this principle in an intervention to encourage people to wash their clothes at lower temperatures:

Wash cooler to save polar bears?

Ideally, we'd all turn the dial to a tepid 30 degrees to benefit the planet and our pockets. In reality, the polars or even pennies saved just don't do it for the public. So we ran a 'Love your clothes' trial for the Welsh Government, with people willing to drop the degrees to stop that favourite jumper fading.

www.globalactionplan.org.uk/behaviour-change-card-deck (accessed May 2015).

The impact of the charity's work is evident through the many initiatives in which it has been involved. Using behaviour change approaches as the basis, by working in partnership with business and community audiences, GAP estimates that since 1993 it has shaped the behaviour of three quarters of a million people and communicated with an additional four million.

Sources: www.globalactionplan.org.uk/behaviour-change-card-deck (accessed 1 May 2015); www.waterexplorer.org; S. McIver and S. Hyson, 'Starting at square one: Building a business case for involving employees in sustainability', Global Action Plan, www.globalactionplan.org.uk/News /starting-at-square-one (accessed 1 May 2015); www.theguardian.com /teacher-network/teacher-blog/2014/jul/08/how-to-pull-plug-water -waste-in-schools?utm_content=buffer05547&utm_medium=social&utm _source=twitter.com&utm_campaign=buffer (accessed 1 May 2015).

inventory needs. Serious ethical issues relating to distribution include manipulating a product's availability for purposes of exploitation and using coercion to force intermediaries to behave in a specific way. Some retailers have attracted criticism for driving down the price paid to producers of milk to an extent where many farmers have gone out of business. When companies outsource production and other functions, managing the supply chain become increasingly difficult. For instance, melamine-tainted milk from China founds its way into thousands of products around the world, making 300 000 people ill and killing six infants. The same issue resurfaced just over a year later. Companies that source their milk from China suffered reputational and financial damage as a result of these scandals.[19]

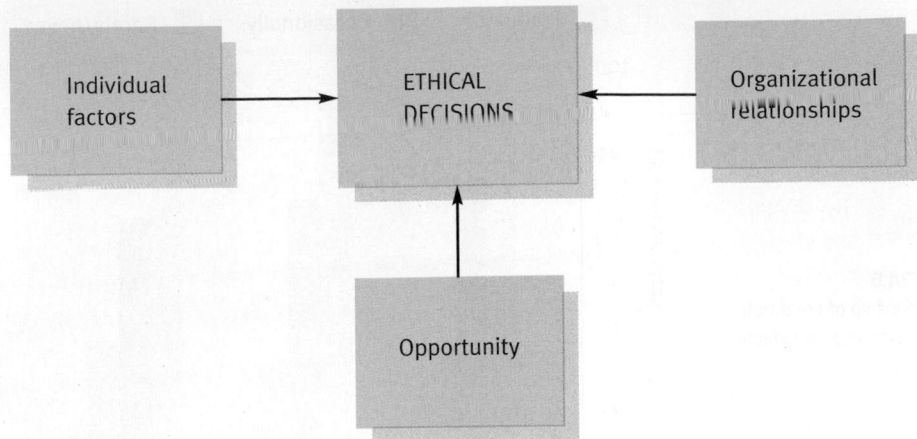

FIGURE 24.4
Factors that influence the ethical decision-making process

The nature of marketing ethics

To grasp the significance of ethics in marketing decision-making, it is helpful to examine the factors that influence the ethical decision-making process. As Figure 24.4 shows, individual factors, organizational relationships and opportunity interact to determine ethical decisions in marketing.

Individual factors
Individuals' own values and principles of right and wrong.

Individual factors   When people need to resolve ethical conflicts in their lives, they often base their decisions on their own values and principles – individual factors – of right or wrong. For example, a study by the Josephson Institute of Ethics reported that seven out of ten students admitted to cheating in a test at least once in the past year, and 92 per cent admitted to lying to their parents in the past year. One out of six students confessed to showing up for class drunk in the same period.[20] People learn values and principles through socialization by family members, social groups, religion and formal education. In the workplace, however, research has established that an organization's values often have more influence on marketing decisions than do a person's own values.[21]

Organizational relationships
Work groups, committees, conversations and discussions with colleagues.

Organizational relationships   Although people can, and do, make ethical choices relating to marketing decisions, no one operates in a vacuum.[22] Ethical choices in marketing are most often made jointly, in work groups and committees, or in conversations and discussions with colleagues. Marketing employees resolve ethical issues based not only on what they have learned from their own backgrounds but also on what they learn from others in the organization. The outcome of this learning process depends on the strength of each individual's personal values, opportunities for unethical behaviour, and exposure to others who behave ethically or unethically. Superiors, peers and subordinates in the organization influence the ethical decision-making process. Although people outside the organization, such as family members and friends, also influence decision-makers, organizational culture and structure operate through organizational relationships to influence ethical decisions.

Corporate culture
A set of values, beliefs, goals, norms and rituals that members of an organization share.

Corporate culture is a set of values, beliefs, goals, norms and rituals that members of an organization share. These values also help shape employees' satisfaction with their employer, which may affect the quality of the service they provide to customers. Figure 24.5 indicates that at least 92 per cent of surveyed employees who see trust, respect and honesty applied frequently in their organizations express satisfaction with their employers.[23] A company's culture may be expressed formally through codes of conduct, memos, manuals, dress codes and ceremonies, but it is also conveyed informally through work habits, extracurricular activities and anecdotes. An organization's culture gives its members meaning, and suggests rules for how to behave and deal with problems within the organization.

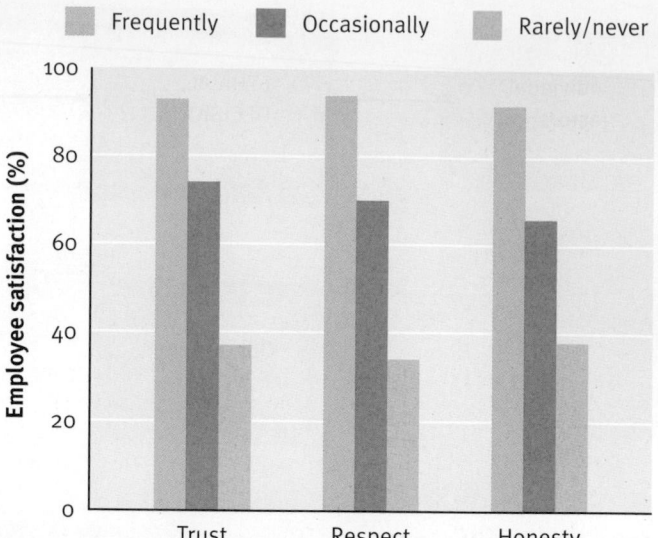

FIGURE 24.5

The relationship of organizational values to employee satisfaction

Source: Ethics Resource Center, The Ethics Resource Center's 2000 National Business Ethics Survey: *How Employees Perceive Ethics at Work* (Washington, DC: Ethics Resource Center, 2000), p. 85. Reprinted with permission.

Most experts agree that the chief executive, managing director or marketing director sets the ethical tone for the entire organization. Lower level managers take their cue from top managers, but they too impose some of their personal values on the company. This interaction between corporate culture and executive leadership helps determine the company's ethical value system.

Colleagues' influence on an individual's ethical choices depends on the person's exposure to unethical behaviour. Especially in grey areas, the more a person is exposed to unethical activity by others in the organizational environment, the more likely he or she is to behave unethically. Most marketing employees take a lead from colleagues in learning how to solve problems, including ethical problems.[24] Indeed, research suggests that marketing employees who perceive their work environment as ethical, experience less role conflict and ambiguity, are more satisfied with their jobs, and are more committed to their employer.[25]

Organizational pressure plays a key role in creating ethical issues. For example, because of pressure to meet a deadline, a superior may ask a sales person to lie to a customer over the phone about a late product shipment. Similarly, pressure to meet a sales quota may result in overly aggressive sales tactics. Research in this area indicates that superiors and colleagues can generate organizational pressure, which plays a key role in creating ethical issues. In a study by the Ethics Resource Centre, 60 per cent of respondents said they had experienced pressure from superiors or colleagues to compromise ethical standards to achieve business objectives.[26] Nearly all marketers face difficult issues whose solutions are not obvious or that present conflicts between organizational objectives and personal ethics.

Opportunity Opportunity provides another pressure that may shape ethical decisions in marketing. **Opportunity** is a favourable set of conditions that limit barriers or provide rewards. A marketing employee who takes advantage of an opportunity to act unethically and is rewarded or suffers no penalty may repeat such acts as other opportunities arise. For example, a sales person who receives a bonus after using a deceptive sales presentation to increase sales is being rewarded and thus will probably continue the behaviour. Indeed, the opportunity to engage in unethical conduct is often a better predictor of unethical activities than are personal values.[27] Beyond rewards and the absence of punishment, other elements in the business environment may create opportunities. Professional codes of conduct and ethics-related corporate policy also influence opportunity by prescribing what behaviours are acceptable, as will be explained later. The larger the rewards and the milder the punishment for unethical conduct, the greater the likelihood that unethical behaviour will occur.

Opportunity
A favourable set of conditions that limit barriers or provide rewards.

However, just as the majority of people who go into retail stores do not try to shoplift at each opportunity, most marketers do not try to take advantage of every opportunity for unethical behaviour in their organizations. Although marketing managers often perceive many opportunities to engage in unethical conduct in their companies and industries, research suggests that most refrain from taking advantage of such opportunities. Moreover, most marketing managers do not believe unethical conduct in general results in success.[28] Individual factors as well as organizational culture may influence whether an individual becomes opportunistic and tries to take advantage of situations unethically.

Improving ethical conduct in marketing

It is possible to improve ethical conduct in an organization by taking on ethical employees and eliminating unethical ones, and by improving the organization's ethical standards. One way to approach improvement of an organization's ethical standards is to use a 'bad apple/bad barrel' analogy. Some people always do things in their own self-interest, regardless of organizational goals or accepted moral standards; such people are sometimes referred to as 'bad apples'. To eliminate unethical conduct, an organization must rid itself of bad apples through screening techniques and enforcement of the company's ethical standards. However, organizations sometimes become 'bad barrels' themselves, not because the individuals within them are unethical but because the pressures to survive and succeed create conditions (opportunities) that reward unethical behaviour. One way to resolve the problem of the bad barrel is to redesign the organization's image and culture so that it conforms to industry and societal norms of ethical conduct.[29]

If senior management develops and enforces ethics and legal compliance programmes to encourage ethical decision-making, it becomes a force to help individuals make better decisions. A recent National Business Ethics Survey in the USA found that ethics programmes that include written standards of conduct, ethics training, ethics advice lines or offices and systems for anonymous reporting increase the likelihood that employees will report misconduct observed in the workplace.[30] Thus, a well implemented formal ethics and compliance programme and a strong corporate culture result in the greatest reduction of future misconduct. Companies that wish to improve their ethics, need to implement a strong ethics and compliance programme and encourage commitment to it. When marketers understand the policies and requirements for ethical conduct, they can more easily resolve ethical conflicts. However, marketers can never fully abdicate their personal ethical responsibility in making decisions. Claiming to be an agent of the business ('the company told me to do it') is unacceptable as a legal excuse and is even less defensible from an ethical perspective.[31]

Codes of conduct   Without compliance programmes, and uniform standards and policies regarding conduct, it is hard for employees to determine what conduct is acceptable within the company. In the absence of such programmes and standards, employees will generally make decisions based on their observations of how co-workers and superiors behave. To improve ethics, many organizations have developed **codes of conduct** (also called codes of ethics) consisting of formalized rules and standards that describe what the company expects of its employees. Most large businesses have formal codes of conduct. Codes of conduct promote ethical behaviour by reducing opportunities for unethical behaviour; employees know both what is expected of them and what kind of punishment they face if they violate the rules. Codes help marketers deal with ethical issues or dilemmas that develop in daily operations by prescribing or limiting specific activities. Codes of conduct have also made companies that subcontract manufacturing operations abroad more aware of the ethical issues associated with supporting facilities that underpay and even abuse their workforce.

Codes of conduct
Formalized rules and standards that describe what the company expects of its employees.

Codes of conduct do not have to take every situation into account, but they should provide guidelines that enable employees to achieve organizational objectives in an ethical and acceptable manner. The Ethical Trading Initiative (ETI) works in partnership with its membership of companies, trade unions and voluntary organizations to improve the quality of life of workers around the world. Among its members are Mothercare, The Body Shop, Superdry, The White Company, Next, M&S, Tesco, Sainsbury's, The Co-Operative, Eileen Fisher and Asos. The alliance's vision is for people to work in freedom, equity and security and to be free from discrimination and exploitation. Table 24.3 summarizes ETI's base ethical trade code.

TABLE 24.3 The ethical trade initiative base code

ETI base code
The ETI base code is founded on the conventions of the International Labour Organization (ILO) and is an internationally recognized code of labour practice.

1. Employment is freely chosen

   1.1 There is no forced, bonded or involuntary prison labour.

   1.2 Workers are not required to lodge 'deposits' or their identity papers with their employer and are free to leave their employer after reasonable notice.

2. Freedom of association and the right to collective bargaining are respected

   2.1 Workers, without distinction, have the right to join or form trade unions of their own choosing and to bargain collectively.

   2.2 The employer adopts an open attitude towards the activities of trade unions and their organizational activities.

   2.3 Workers' representatives are not discriminated against and have access to carry out their representative functions in the workplace.

   2.4 Where the right to freedom of association and collective bargaining is restricted under law, the employer facilitates, and does not hinder, the development of parallel means for independent and free association and bargaining.

3. Working conditions are safe and hygienic

   3.1 A safe and hygienic working environment shall be provided, bearing in mind the prevailing knowledge of the industry and of any specific hazards. Adequate steps shall be taken to prevent accidents and injury to health arising out of, associated with, or occurring in the course of work, by minimizing, so far as is reasonably practicable, the causes of hazards inherent in the working environment.

   3.2 Workers shall receive regular and recorded health and safety training, and such training shall be repeated for new or reassigned workers.

   3.3 Access to clean toilet facilities and to potable water, and, if appropriate, sanitary facilities for food storage shall be provided.

   3.4 Accommodation, where provided, shall be clean, safe, and meet the basic needs of the workers.

   3.5 The company observing the code shall assign responsibility for health and safety to a senior management representative.

4. Child labour shall not be used

   4.1 There shall be no new recruitment of child labour.

   4.2 Companies shall develop or participate in and contribute to policies and programmes which provide for the transition of any child found to be performing child labour to enable her or him to attend and remain in quality education until no longer a child; "child" and "child labour" being defined in the appendices.

   4.3 Children and young persons under 18 shall not be employed at night or in hazardous conditions.

   4.4 These policies and procedures shall conform to the provisions of the relevant ILO standards.

5. Living wages are paid

   5.1 Wages and benefits paid for a standard working week meet, at a minimum, national legal standards or industry benchmark standards, whichever is higher. In any event wages should always be enough to meet basic needs and to provide some discretionary income.

   5.2 All workers shall be provided with written and understandable Information about their employment conditions in respect to wages before they enter employment and about the particulars of their wages for the pay period concerned each time that they are paid.

   5.3 Deductions from wages as a disciplinary measure shall not be permitted nor shall any deductions from wages not provided for by national law be permitted without the expressed permission of the worker concerned. All disciplinary measures should be recorded.

6. Working hours are not excessive

   6.1 Working hours must comply with national laws, collective agreements, and the provisions of 6.2 to 6.6 below, whichever affords the greater protection for workers. Sub-clauses 6.2 to 6.6 are based on international labour standards.

   6.2 Working hours, excluding overtime, shall be defined by contract, and shall not exceed 48 hours per week.*

(Continued)

TABLE 24.3   Continued

6.3 All overtime shall be voluntary. Overtime shall be used responsibly, taking into account all the following: the extent, frequency and hours worked by individual workers and the workforce as a whole. It shall not be used to replace regular employment. Overtime shall always be compensated at a premium rate, which is recommended to be not less than 125 per cent of the regular rate of pay.

6.4 The total hours worked in any seven day period shall not exceed 60 hours, except where covered by clause 6.5 below.

6.5 Working hours may exceed 60 hours in any seven day period only in exceptional circumstances where all of the following are met:
- this is allowed by national law;
- this is allowed by a collective agreement freely negotiated with a workers' organization representing a significant portion of the workforce;
- appropriate safeguards are taken to protect the workers' health and safety; and
- the employer can demonstrate that exceptional circumstances apply such as unexpected production peaks, accidents or emergencies.

6.6 Workers shall be provided with at least one day off in every seven day period or, where allowed by national law, two days off in every 14 day period.

NB: This base code clause was revised with effect from 1 April 2014.

7. No discrimination is practiced

7.1 There is no discrimination in hiring, compensation, access to training, promotion, termination or retirement based on race, caste, national origin, religion, age, disability, gender, marital status, sexual orientation, union membership or political affiliation.

8. Regular employment is provided

8.1 To every extent possible work performed must be on the basis of recognized employment relationship established through national law and practice.

8.2 Obligations to employees under labour or social security laws and regulations arising from the regular employment relationship shall not be avoided through the use of labour-only contracting, sub-contracting, or home-working arrangements, or through apprenticeship schemes where there is no real intent to impart skills or provide regular employment, nor shall any such obligations be avoided through the excessive use of fixed-term contracts of employment.

9. No harsh or inhumane treatment is allowed

9.1 Physical abuse or discipline, the threat of physical abuse, sexual or other harassment and verbal abuse or other forms of intimidation shall be prohibited.

* International standards recommend the progressive reduction of normal hours of work, when appropriate, to 40 hours per week, without any reduction in workers' wages as hours are reduced.

Source: www.ethicaltrade.org/eti-base-code.

Ethics officer
Responsible for creating, distributing, enforcing and advising on a code of conduct.

Ethics officers   Organizational compliance programmes must be overseen by high-ranking members of the company, who are known to respect legal and ethical standards. Many companies, including Starbucks and Wal-mart, have **ethics officers**. They are typically responsible for creating and distributing a code of conduct, enforcing the code, and meeting with colleagues to discuss or provide advice about ethical issues. They may also set up telephone 'hotlines' to provide advice to employees faced with an ethical issue.

Implementing ethics and legal compliance programmes   To nurture ethical conduct in marketing, open communication and coaching on ethical issues are essential. This involves providing employees with ethics training, clear channels of communication and follow-up support throughout the organization. Companies need to consistently enforce standards and impose penalties on those who violate codes of conduct. In addition, businesses must take reasonable steps in response to violations of standards and, as appropriate, revise their compliance programmes to diminish the likelihood of future misconduct.

To succeed, a compliance programme must be viewed as part of the overall marketing strategy implementation. If ethics officers and other executives are not committed to the principles and initiatives of marketing ethics and social responsibility, the programme's effectiveness will be compromised. Although the virtues of honesty, fairness and openness are often assumed to be self-evident and universally accepted, marketing strategy decisions involve complex and detailed matters in which correctness may not be so clear-cut. A high level of personal morality may not be sufficient to prevent an individual from violating the law in an organizational context in which even experienced lawyers debate the exact meaning of the law.

As it is impossible to train all members of an organization as lawyers, the identification of ethical issues and the implementation of compliance programmes and codes of conduct that incorporate both legal and ethical concerns, constitute the best approach to preventing violations and avoiding litigation. Codifying ethical standards into meaningful policies that spell out what is and is not acceptable gives marketers an opportunity to reduce the probability of behaviour that could create legal problems. Without proper ethical training and guidance, it is impossible for the average marketing manager to understand the exact boundaries of illegality in the areas of price fixing, copyright violations, fraud, export/import violations and so on. A corporate focus on ethics helps create a buffer zone around issues that could trigger serious legal considerations for a company.

Incorporating social responsibility and ethics into marketing decisions

Although the concepts of marketing ethics and social responsibility are often used interchangeably, it is important to distinguish between them. *Ethics* relates to individual and group decisions: judgments about what is right or wrong in a particular decision-making situation. *Social responsibility,* on the other hand, deals with the total effect of marketing decisions on society. The two concepts are interrelated because a company that supports socially responsible decisions and adheres to a code of conduct is likely to have a positive effect on society. Figure 24.6 illustrates how the Fair Trade Movement is dedicated to working with companies in the grocery industry to benefit supplying communities. Although ethics and social responsibility programmes can be profitable as well, an increasing number of companies are incorporating them into their overall marketing ethos.

As has been emphasized throughout this chapter, ethics is just one dimension of social responsibility. Being socially responsible relates to doing what is economically sound, legal, ethical and socially conscious. One way to evaluate whether a specific activity is ethical and socially responsible is to ask other members of the organization if they approve. Contact with concerned consumer groups and industry or government regulatory groups may be helpful. A check to see whether there is a specific company policy about an activity may help resolve ethical questions. If other organization members approve of the activity and it is legal and customary within the industry, the chances are the activity is acceptable from both an ethical and a social responsibility perspective. Table 24.4 provides an audit of mechanisms to help control ethics and social responsibility in marketing.

FIGURE 24.6
The Fairtrade movement is growing, but depends on the ethical behaviour of producers and marketers in order to ensure identified products conform to the movement's standards

TABLE 24.4   Corporate audit of social responsibility and ethics control mechanisms

Answer 'True' (T) or 'False' (F) for each statement		
1. No mechanism exists for top management to detect social responsibility and ethical issues relating to employees, customers, the community and society.	T	F
2. There is no formal or informal communication within the organization about procedures and activities that are considered acceptable behaviour.	T	F
3. The organization fails to communicate its ethical standards to suppliers, customers and groups that have a relationship with the organization.	T	F
4. There is an environment of deception, repression and cover-ups concerning events that could be embarrassing to the company.	T	F
5. Reward systems are totally dependent on economic performance.	T	F
6. The only concerns about environmental impact are those that are legally required.	T	F
7. Concern for the ethical value systems of the community with regard to the company's activities is absent.	T	F
8. Products are described in a misleading manner, with no information on negative impact or limitations communicated to customers.	T	F

True answers indicate a lack of control mechanisms, which, if implemented, could improve ethics and social responsibility.

A rule of thumb for resolving ethical and social responsibility issues is that if an issue can withstand open discussion that results in agreement or limited debate, an acceptable solution may exist. Nevertheless, even after a final decision has been reached, different viewpoints on the issue may remain. Openness is not a complete solution to the ethics problem, but it creates trust and facilitates learning relationships.[32]

Being socially responsible and ethical is challenging

To promote socially responsible and ethical behaviour while achieving organizational goals, marketers must monitor changes and trends in society's values. In response to increasing concerns about sustainability, more firms are making commitments to behave responsibly in this regard. PepsiCo UK is one example, having committed to making all of its packaging renewable, biodegradable or recyclable by 2018. Although implementing the programme will not be without difficulty, the president of PepsiCo UK explains that, 'The business case is clear. Building sustainability into our corporate DNA cuts costs, drives innovation, reduces risk and motivates employees'.[33]

Likewise, when consumers began to demand greater transparency or openness from companies in the wake of a number of ethics scandals, transparency became a factor in most marketing and management decisions.[34] An organization's senior management must assume some responsibility for employees' conduct by establishing and enforcing policies that address society's desires.

After determining what society wants, marketers try to predict the long-term effects of decisions relating to those wants. Specialists outside the company, such as doctors, lawyers and scientists, are often consulted, but sometimes there is a lack of agreement within a discipline as to what is an acceptable marketing decision. Today, not all scientists agree about the causes or likely impact of global warming or whether GM foods are good. Fifty years ago, tobacco marketers promoted cigarettes as being good for people's health, yet today it is recognized that cigarette smoking is linked to cancer and other medical problems. Consequently, society's attitude towards smoking has changed, and some governments have passed legislation banning smoking in public places. This has implications for marketers, such as those in hotels and leisure sites, who must implement this change and consider whether they wish to provide smoking areas away from the rest of their customers. The change in attitude towards cigarettes will, no doubt, be mimicked in the future for many products which today are consumed without hesitation, so marketers must be vigilant.

Many of society's demands impose costs. For example, society wants a cleaner environment and the preservation of wildlife and its habitats, but it also wants low-priced products. This means that companies must carefully balance the costs of providing low-priced products against the costs of manufacturing, packaging and distributing their products in an environmentally responsible manner.

In trying to satisfy the desires of one group, marketers may dissatisfy others. Regarding the smoking debate, for example, marketers must balance non-smokers' desire for a smoke-free environment against smokers' desire or need to continue to smoke. Some anti-smoking campaigners call for the complete elimination of tobacco products to ensure a smoke-free world. However, this attitude fails to consider the difficulty smokers have in quitting. Thus, this issue, like most ethical and social responsibility issues, cannot be viewed in black and white terms.

Satisfying the demands of all members of society is difficult, if not impossible. Marketers must evaluate the extent to which members of society are willing to pay for what they want. For instance, customers may want more information about a product but be unwilling to pay the costs the business incurs in providing the data. Marketers who want to make socially responsible decisions may find the task a challenge because, ultimately, they must ensure their economic survival.

Social responsibility and ethics improve marketing performance

Increasing evidence indicates that being socially responsible and ethical pays off. Research suggests that a relationship exists between a marketing orientation and an organizational climate that supports marketing ethics and social responsibility. This relationship implies that being ethically and socially concerned is consistent with meeting the demands of customers and other stakeholders. By encouraging employees to understand their markets, companies can help them respond to stakeholders' demands.[35]

A survey of marketing managers found a direct association between corporate social responsibility and profits.[36] In a survey of consumers, around three-quarters indicated that they would pay more for a product that came from a socially responsible company. Almost half of young adults aged 18 to 25 said they would take a pay cut to work for a socially responsible company.[37]

Recognition is therefore growing that the long-term value of conducting business in a socially responsible manner far outweighs short-term costs. Companies that fail to develop strategies and programmes to incorporate ethics and social responsibility into their organizational culture may pay the price, with poor marketing performance and the potential costs of legal violations, civil litigation and damaging publicity, when questionable activities are made public.

As marketing ethics and social responsibility are not always viewed as organizational performance issues, many managers do not believe they need to consider them in the strategic planning process. Individuals also have different ideas as to what is ethical or unethical, leading them to confuse the need for workplace ethics and the right to maintain their own personal values and ethics. While the concepts are undoubtedly controversial, it is possible and desirable to incorporate ethics and social responsibility into the planning process.

Social marketing
Uses tools and techniques from commercial marketing to encourage positive behavioural changes, such as quitting smoking, reducing alcohol consumption, minimizing anti-social behaviours or reducing carbon footprint. The health and well-being of individuals, society and the planet are at the core of social marketing.

Social marketing

The use of marketing in commercial settings is well established. Social marketers use the same tools and techniques to achieve social, rather than commercial, objectives. As explained in Chapter 1, social marketing involves using commercial marketing ideas and tools to change behaviour in ways that will improve the well-being of individuals and society. For example, research evidence shows that images of smoking in movies can strongly influence young people to start smoking. The SmokeFree Liverpool youth group is using a campaign called 'SmokeFree Movies' to put pressure on the film industry to remove images of smoking from movies which are rated as suitable for young people. The group is critical of what it describes as a long history of close relationships

TABLE 24.5 Difference in approach between commercial and social marketers

	Commercial marketing	Social marketing
Product	The marketing process revolves primarily around the development and sale of goods and services	The marketing process is used to change or maintain behaviour
Primary aim	Financial gain	Individual or societal gain
Primary competition	Other organizations offering similar goods or services	The current or preferred behaviour of the target segment

Source: National Social Marketing Centre (www.thensmc.com/sites/default/files/Big_pocket_guide_2011.pdf).

between the studios and the tobacco industry.[38] Table 24.5 explains the differences in priorities and approach for commercial and social marketers.

As Figure 24.7 shows, many social marketing programmes seek to achieve changes in health behaviour[39], such as encouraging individuals to quit smoking, exercise more often, eat more healthily or drink less alcohol. However, this is not always the case. Encouraging more sustainable behaviour by increasing recycling rates, getting drivers to reduce their speed or drive more safely, managing personal debt more responsibly, and even encouraging people to pay their taxes, are some of the other situations in which social marketing has been applied. The common thread in all of these campaigns is the link between achieving behaviour change and enhancing social good, using planned interventions to nudge or encourage new attitudes and changed behaviours.

The kinds of social marketing initiatives that target individuals whose behaviour needs to be changed are sometimes referred to as downstream social marketing. Often these downstream efforts need to be combined with upstream activities targeting influential stakeholders, such as governments, regulators, health professionals and industries. For example, while health professionals in the UK have for many years targeted individual smokers with programmes designed to encourage them to quit (downstream initiatives), the introduction of legislation to ban smoking in public places (an upstream initiative) has had a profound effect on levels of quitting and smoking take-up.

Social marketers need to make sure that those who are targeted with social marketing programmes are actively involved in the process. The improvements to individual and social well-being at the heart of social marketing can only be achieved if voluntary behaviour change takes place. Just as in commercial marketing, social marketing involves an exchange between organizations

FIGURE 24.7
Social and responsibility marketing is becoming increasingly important, such as in the Change4Life marketing campaign

Source: Image courtesy of Change4Life.

or individuals responsible for a particular programme and the consumers who are on the receiving end. For example, the central exchange in a vaccination programme involves individuals who agree to be vaccinated being offered protection against future illness. Similarly, those who sign up to a programme to help them cut down on their calorie intake and increase their life expectancy as per the 'Change4Life' campaign, are hoping to improve their health and reduce their financial outlay on drink in exchange for altering their behaviour. Social marketing hinges on understanding 'consumers' and identifying which segment is best to target with a well-defined intervention and campaign.

One of the challenges faced by social marketing programmes is that the benefits on offer can be quite intangible. For instance, although the problems associated with global warming and sustainability are well recognized, many consumers struggle to change their behaviour in ways that will protect the environment. Cutting down on leisure travel, improving recycling behaviour and reducing energy use can seem like a major sacrifice for consumers. Sometimes people also find it difficult to accept that behaviour change made at the individual level can make a real difference to the global picture. For these reasons social marketers have to work hard to ensure that they are genuinely consumer orientated and must often use innovative approaches to encourage people to modify their behaviour. The Topical Insight considers how GAP has intervened regarding water consumption. Nevertheless social marketing applications have broadened the scope for marketing practice, employing many marketing graduates and applying the marketing process across a diversity of non-commercial areas.

Current hot topics in the marketing discipline

This chapter of *Marketing: Concepts and Strategies* has explored some of the hottest topics currently taxing the minds of marketers. A recent poll of senior practitioners in the discipline identified these pressures and drivers:

Big data	The wealth of up-to-the-minute insights in the digital era – enabled by improved data capture, analytics and heuristics – provides exciting opportunities for being more informed (understanding customers and mapping competitors, testing out hunches and tracking the marketing environment) as well as for developing relationships, but only if companies can avoid being swamped and if they and their partners are able to identify the real nuggets of important insight amongst the huge volume of data now incessantly being produced.
Social media and C2C	As explored in Chapters 1, 5 and 19, social media and the growth in consumer-to-consumer communications have removed the power of brand messaging from marketers – with so much product, brand, usage and attitude information now emanating from other consumers and various third parties on the web – presenting challenges for marketers, as consumers radically alter their buying behaviour, information search, decision-making, purchasing activities and relationships.
Privacy concerns	Most apps use location data, websites' cookies track behaviours and CRM systems capture and explore significant amounts of consumption, lifestyle, behavioural and financial data about consumers, raising data protection challenges, presenting ethical dilemmas for marketers and leading to growing concerns for consumers and watchdogs.
Ethics	In a rolling-news and social media-driven society misbehaviour by brands is far more evident and open to debate, with consequences for consumers' trust, loyalty, word-of-mouth support or annoyance and their spending, at a time when increasingly companies' leadership teams are striving to avoid litigation and to behave ethically . . . many marketers do have a conscience, but are let down by the unscrupulous behaviours of a damaging minority in their profession.
Sustainability	Many observers thought the trend over the past two decades towards greater responsibility socially by companies, particularly around energy use and wasteful consumption, would tone down during the recent global financial crisis, but in practice the reverse is true; so marketers must ensure their behaviours, their brands' credentials and their channel activities reflect the ongoing sustainability agenda.
Regulation	All of the above drivers lead to an increasingly regulated environment in which non-compliance is more visible – with often damaging reputational and financial consequences – so marketers' understanding of these forces from the marketing environment and their ability to act as the 'eyes and ears' for their organizations become even more important.

(Continued)

| Recruitment of talent | The digital era, big data, thirst for insight and changing managerial behaviours – driven by the issues above – require new skills and capabilities, but at a time when the growth of social marketing in non-profit fields is attracting growing numbers of marketing graduates, creating significant recruitment and staff development challenges for marketers and their human resource partners. |
| When is it wrong to encourage consumption? | While not as dominant a theme as many of the other points described here, the recent recession and pressures on household expenditures have caused some marketers to question their promotion of their brands as they strive to encourage more consumption and thereby consumer spending; resulting in some brands re-engineering their propositions in order to offer value and to reduce pressures on consumers. |

Summary

Social responsibility refers to an organization's obligation to maximize its positive impact and minimize its negative impact on society. Although social responsibility is a positive concept, most organizations embrace it in the expectation of indirect long-term benefits.

Marketing citizenship involves adopting a strategic focus for fulfilling the economic, legal, ethical and philanthropic social responsibilities expected of organizations by their *stakeholders,* those constituents who have a stake, or claim, in some aspect of the company's products, operations, markets, industry and outcomes.

At the most basic level, companies have an economic responsibility to be profitable so that they can provide a return on investment to their stockholders, create jobs for the community and contribute goods and services to the economy. Marketers are also expected to obey laws and regulations. *Marketing ethics* refers to principles and standards that define acceptable conduct in marketing as determined by various stakeholders, including the public, government regulators, private interest groups, industry and the organization itself. *Philanthropic responsibilities*, which encompass *cause-related marketing,* go beyond marketing ethics; they are not required of a company, but they promote human welfare or goodwill, known as *strategic philanthropy*.

Three major categories of *social responsibility* issues are the natural environment, consumerism and community relations. A common way in which marketers demonstrate social responsibility is through programmes designed to protect and preserve the natural environment. *Green marketing* refers to the specific development, pricing, promotion and distribution of products that do not harm the environment. Marketers must avoid ill-judged *greenwash*, which is rarely well received and risks the alienation of consumers and target audiences. *Consumerism* consists of the efforts of independent individuals, groups and organizations to protect the rights of consumers.

Whereas social responsibility is achieved by balancing the interests of all stakeholders in the organization, ethics relates to acceptable standards of conduct in making individual and group decisions. Marketing ethics goes beyond legal issues, fostering mutual trust in marketing relationships.

An *ethical issue* is an identifiable problem, situation or opportunity requiring an individual or organization to choose between actions that must be evaluated as right or wrong, ethical or unethical. A number of ethical issues relate to the marketing mix (product, people, promotion, price and place/distribution).

Individual factors, *organizational relationships* and *opportunity* interact to determine ethical decisions in marketing. Individuals often base their decisions on their own values and principles of right or wrong. However, ethical choices in marketing are often made jointly, in work groups or with colleagues, and are shaped by *corporate culture* and structure.

The more someone is exposed to unethical activity in the organizational environment, the more likely he or she is to behave unethically. Organizational pressure and *opportunity* play a key role in creating ethical issues. Improving ethical behaviour in an organization can be achieved by developing and enforcing ethics and legal compliance programmes, establishing *codes of conduct,* formalized rules and standards that describe what the company expects of its employees, and having an ethics officer.

To nurture ethical conduct in marketing, open communication and coaching on ethical issues are essential. This requires providing employees with ethics training, clear channels of communication and follow-up support throughout the organization. Companies must consistently enforce standards and impose penalties on those who violate codes of conduct, via appointed *ethics officers*.

Companies are increasingly incorporating ethics and social responsibility programmes into their marketing decisions. Increasing evidence indicates that being socially responsible and ethical results in valuable benefits: an enhanced public reputation, which can increase market share, costs savings and profits.

Social marketing uses tools and techniques from commercial marketing to encourage positive behavioural changes, such as quitting smoking, reducing alcohol consumption, more responsible personal financial management, minimizing anti-social behaviours or reducing carbon footprint. The health and well-being of individuals, society and the planet are at the core of social marketing. Whereas the main aim of commercial marketing is to generate sales, profit and shareholder value, social marketers are concerned with achieving social good and behaviour change. Downstream social marketing activities targeting behaviour change are often combined with upstream initiatives aimed at influential stakeholders, such as governments, regulators, health professionals and industries.

This chapter has explored some of the biggest challenges facing marketers today. Recent research identifies ethics, privacy concerns, driving consumption, sustainability and responsible behaviours as key drivers now steering the onwards development of marketing, along with the big date era, social media and greater consumer-to-consumer communication, regulation, the growth of social marketing and talent recruitment to help address these issues, as explored amongst the chapters of *Marketing: Concepts and Strategies*.

Key links

This chapter should be read in conjunction with:

- Chapter 2's explanation of developing marketing strategies.
- Chapter 3's description of the forces of the marketing environment, which include the increased emphasis on ethics and social responsibility.
- Chapter 23's discussion of implementing marketing strategies and marketing programmes.

Important terms

Cause-related marketing
Codes of conduct
Community relations
Corporate culture
Ethical issue
Ethics officer
Green marketing
Greenwash
Individual factors
Marketing citizenship
Marketing ethics
Opportunity
Organizational relationships
Philanthropic responsibilities

Social marketing
Social responsibility
Stakeholders
Strategic philanthropy
Sustainability

Discussion and review questions

1. What is social responsibility and why is it important?
2. What are stakeholders? What role do they play in strategic marketing decisions?
3. List four dimensions of social responsibility.
4. What are some major social responsibility issues? Give an example of each.
5. What is the difference between ethics and social responsibility?
6. Why are ethics an important consideration in marketing decisions?
7. How do the factors that influence ethical or unethical decisions interact?
8. What ethical conflicts could arise if a company's employees chose to fly only on certain airlines in order to accrue personal frequent-flier miles?
9. Give an example of how each component of the marketing mix can be affected by ethical issues.
10. How can ethical decisions in marketing be improved?
11. How can people with different personal values work together to make ethical decisions in organizations?

12. What evidence exists that being socially responsible and ethical is worthwhile?

13. What is social marketing and how does it use commercial marketing tools to change behaviour?

14. In what ways has the emergence of social marketing broadened the scope of marketing?

Recommended readings

Arnold, C., *Ethical Marketing and the New Consumer: Marketing in the New Ethical Economy* (Wiley, 2009).

Ball, K., Canhoto, A., Daniel, E., Dibb, S., Meadows, M. and Spiller, K., *The Private Security State?* (CBS Press, 2015).

Brenkert, G.G., *Marketing Ethics* (Wiley-Blackwell, 2008).

Crane, A. and Matten, B., *Business Ethics: Managing Corporate Citizenship and Sustainability in the Age of Globalization* (Oxford University Press, 2010).

Eagle, L., Dahl, S., Hill, S., Bird, S., Spotswood, F. and Tapp, A., *Social Marketing* (Pearson, 2012).

Eagle, L. and Dahl, S., *Marketing Ethics and Society* (Sage, 2015).

Ferrell, L., Fraedrich, J. and Ferrell, O.C., *Business Ethics: Ethical Decision Making and Cases,* (Cengage, 2014).

Grant, J., *The Green Marketing Manifesto* (Wiley, 2009).

Hastings, G., *Social Marketing: Why Should the Devil Have All the Best Tunes?* (Routledge, 2013).

Hastings, G. and Domegan, C., *Social Marketing* (Routledge, 2012).

Kotler, P. and Lee, N.R., *Social Marketing: Influencing Behaviours for Good* (Sage, 2011).

Martin, D. and Schouten, J., *Sustainable Marketing* (Pearson, 2013).

Nguyen B., Simkin, L. and Canhoto, A., *The Dark Side of CRM* (Routledge, 2015).

Ottman, J.A., *The New Rules of Green Marketing: Strategies, Tools, and Inspiration for Sustainable Branding* (Greenleaf Publishing, 2010).

Paetzold, K., *Corporate Social Responsibility (CSR): An International Marketing Approach* (Diplomica Verlag, 2010).

Sage Publications, *Sage Brief Guide to Marketing Ethics* (Sage, 2011).

Velasquez, M.G., *Business Ethics: Concepts and Cases* (Pearson, 2013).

Internet exercise

The Institute of Business Ethics offers guidance to organizations on doing business ethically. Its website provides advice on developing codes of business ethics and presents some simple tests on ethical decisions. Visit the Institute's website at: www.ibe.org.uk

1. What role do codes of business ethics play?

2. What steps might a business take to implement a code of conduct?

3. Using the links to sample codes of conduct on the IBE website, list the kinds of area that businesses might cover in such a code (www.ibe.org.uk).

Group tasks

1. Many businesses now publish their CSR and ethics policies. Can you identify examples of brands' marketing deviating away from the stated overarching CSR and ethics codes? Consider how this might have been possible.

2. For social marketing interventions seeking to encourage behaviour changes relating to smoking or unhealthy eating, which aspects of the strategic marketing process are most useful?

Applied mini-case

Is it possible for a retailer to become too large and powerful? This is a question some people have been asking about Wal-Mart, the world's largest retail company, and about Tesco in the UK. Wal-Mart has aggressively pursued its low-price mantra, bringing better value to consumers and forcing suppliers to innovate. A possible concern is that Wal-Mart has become so big that it can do virtually anything it wants in some areas. Obviously this kind of power has enormous ethical and social implications. Some suppliers suggest that Wal-Mart is able to dictate every aspect of its operations, from product design to pricing, in its efforts to maximize savings for customers. Some suppliers claim they have been forced to reduce staff numbers and even locate to lower-cost regions, in order to meet the biggest retailer's margin demands. Their fear is that if they hesitate to comply, they risk losing their most lucrative outlet and will find their products quickly replaced by a competitor's on Wal-Mart's shelves. For the customer, seeking keen prices and great choice, there are obvious benefits to Wal-Mart's approach, but perhaps there is also a cost.

Questions

1. What are some of the ethical and social implications of the power Wal-Mart and other huge retailers are able to exert?

2. What action can a company like Wal-Mart take to manage these issues?

Recession piles on the pressure

A large holiday travel agency business had a strong reputation for providing value for money packaged holidays to a loyal customer group which regularly returned to plan and book future holidays. Customer satisfaction levels were high and the carefully selected value-based holiday packages provided reliable experiences to customers who felt that they could depend on the company and its travel agency staff to provide guidance and suggest destinations.

However, the recession had reduced customer numbers and some previous holiday-makers were deferring booking new holidays because of reduced incomes and their rising costs of everyday living. At first, the company squeezed its operating costs and margins, in order to maintain service levels and the range of holidays it marketed. This proved insufficient and in order to remain solvent, the company made some long-term staff redundant – often those with the best knowledge of destinations and individual customer's preferences – and it started to source its holiday packages from less familiar, cheaper and overseas operators, with which it had no track record and about which it had little knowledge of reliability, honesty or customer service provision.

The company's customers knew none of this: they were not told about changing suppliers, the lack of knowledge by travel agency staff of the new destinations and hotels, or the financial uncertainty of using cheaper suppliers in less regulated regions of the world. The risks to the company's brand reputation were evident to staff and senior management, but the view was that these steps were necessary to remain in business and to safeguard employees' jobs and incomes. The potential for customers to arrive at less than satisfactory destinations and hotels was also discussed. Staff used web searches to review destinations, hotels and any information about the supplying companies, while the company's executives used their long-established corporate networks to seek reassurances from fellow travel businesses about the newly offered destinations, hotels and suppliers. Nevertheless, staff in the company's travel agencies still voiced concerns about the lack of first-hand experience and knowledge of the products they were now promoting and whether the supplying companies would service customers as well as the company's former long-term suppliers.

In effect, economic uncertainty and target customers' declining incomes were forcing the company to de-specify its products and service offering. Many companies, not just this travel business, have been forced to do this in many markets because of the global economic downturn, weakening consumer spending and consumer uncertainty about spending on higher value items, such as holidays. Some companies have opted to make such commercial decisions, in order to remain in business, without providing any information to customers about such reductions in product and service levels. By contrast, other companies have opted to communicate to their customers such changes, to explain their reasons, and offer safeguards and guarantees. Other companies have de-specified their products and services, but turned them into new launches of explicitly value-led propositions, visibly labelled as value propositions, so as to be seen to be on the side of their customers and to be supportive of the pressures their customers are under. This particular travel company did not inform customers of its changed sourcing strategy, reduction of service levels and poorer knowledge of the places to which it was sending its holidaying customers. No attempt was made to re-brand, re-position or re-state its proposition. Customers only found out when they arrived at their holiday destination.

Questions for discussion

1. What were the options available to the travel agency company as it sought to remain in business?

2. Consider the advantages and disadvantages of 'coming clean' to customers or remaining secretive? Suggest which route you would take and why.

3. How could this holiday company have turned its commercial necessity to re-think its business model into a new customer-facing proposition and launch?

Postscript

Part Four has focused on marketing management issues necessary for the operationalization of the specified marketing strategy, namely marketing planning, implementation processes and control measures. Performance had been examined. In addition, the important issues of ethics and social responsibility in marketing management have been highlighted.

Readers should be confident that they are now able to do the following:

Explain the process of marketing planning and forecasting sales potential

- Understand the marketing planning process.
- Gain an overview of the marketing plan.
- Examine the relationship between marketing analysis, marketing strategy and marketing programmes in marketing planning.
- Examine the role of the SWOT analysis in marketing planning.
- Become familiar with market and sales potential, and sales forecasting methods.
- Analyze the major components of a marketing audit.
- Appreciate how organizations operationalize a marketing strategy.

Understand the issues relating to implementing strategies, internal marketing relationships and measuring performance

- Understand how marketing activities are organized within a company's structure.

- Examine the marketing implementation process.
- Learn about impediments to marketing implementation.
- Grasp the importance of internal marketing.
- Explore implementing and controlling marketing activities.
- Learn how sales and marketing cost analysis can be used as methods of evaluating performance.
- Describe marketing shareholder value analysis.
- Discuss the popular criteria for measuring marketing performance.

Discuss the relevance of ethics and social responsibility in marketing

- Understand the concept of social responsibility and consider the importance of marketers behaving responsibly.
- Define and describe the importance of marketing ethics.
- Become familiar with ways to improve ethical decisions in marketing.
- Understand the role of social responsibility and ethics in improving marketing performance.
- Revisit the concept of social marketing and consider how it is used.
- Appreciate how the marketing concept is evolving.

At Timberland, doing well and doing good are laced together

Strategic case

Our unique culture and product designs are inspired by the rich New England heritage of our company. Everything we make, every store we open, every aspect of our business has been founded upon the outdoor lifestyle – whether that involves wooded trails or city streets – and a Timberland community that thrives on giving back.

Timberland's well-known name and tree logo are good clues as to how much this multinational company cares about

sustainability. The company, headquartered in New Hampshire in the USA, started out manufacturing shoes and boots and later expanded into clothing and accessories. Today Timberland, now part of US-based VF Corporation, known for its Wrangler, North Face and Lee brands, sells through its own network of stores as well as through thousands of department and speciality stores worldwide. Timberland also operates websites in the UK, France, Japan and the US.

Nearly half of Timberland's revenue comes from North America; Europe accounts for 40 per cent and Asia accounts for 11 per cent of its sales. To stay on top of quickly changing trends in the world of fashion, Timberland maintains an international design centre in London. Its mission is, 'to equip people to make a difference in their world. We do this by creating outstanding products and by trying to make a difference in the communities where we live and work while doing it.' As a result, the company's long-term strategy for success combines a comprehensive social responsibility agenda with careful planning for the ever-changing marketing environment.

Four pillars of social responsibility

Timberland's social responsibility agenda rests on the four 'pillars' of climate (protecting the outdoors), product (innovating responsibly), factories (improving workers' lives) and service (engaging communities). Each pillar is associated with specific short- and long-term targets that Timberland has established with the input of its stakeholders. Under the first pillar – climate – the company has reduced energy consumption, slashed harmful greenhouse gas emissions and increased its use of virtual meetings to cut down on employee travel, which saves energy as well as time and money.

The second pillar, earth-friendly products, is a key element in Timberland's social responsibility agenda. *Saved from the landfill – put in our footwear* . . . More than one-third of its shoes contain some recycled material. Its *Earthkeepers* shoes have been specially designed to incorporate a combination of organic, renewable and recyclable materials. Some *Earthkeepers* are not only made from old plastic bottles and other recycled content, they can be completely disassembled and the components can be reworked into new Timberland shoes. Soon, all Timberland products will be labelled to show their impact on the planet. For details go to http://community.timberland.com/Earthkeeping.

The third pillar relates to the workplace and the company's factories. Timberland sets tough standards for fair and safe working conditions at all the factories and facilities that make its shoes and clothing products. Although it owns and operates a factory in the Dominican Republic, the company buys most of its products from a global network of suppliers that employs 175 000 workers in 290 factories spread across 35 countries. Suppliers are required to comply with Timberland's detailed code of conduct, which forbids discrimination, child labour and unsafe practices. Factories are audited regularly and when violations are found, Timberland follows up to be sure that the necessary workplace improvements are made. Timberland employees are encouraged to call the *Integrity Line*, a 24-hour hotline answered by a third party, whenever they want to report workplace concerns, submit ideas, or ask questions.

The fourth pillar – service – has long been part of Timberland's cultural fabric. Every full-time Timberland employee can take up to 40 hours with pay to volunteer in his or her community. In addition, Timberland's CEO began the tradition of Serv-a-palooza in 1998 when he set aside one work day for global volunteerism. Today, employees are encouraged (but not required) to devote this annual day of service to volunteering in their communities. Some employees use the day to clear nature trails, some pick up trash from riverbanks and others grab their tool belts to build arts facilities or repair neighbourhood schools. Last spring, in celebration of *Earth Day*, approximately 1800 Timberland employees, business partners and consumers from around the world served close to 13 000 hours at more than 60 community service projects in 20 countries.

The changing marketing environment

As Timberland has a diverse product portfolio and is active in retailing and wholesaling, as well as manufacturing, it has to keep an eye on competitors in several industries. The outdoor retailer L.L. Bean, headquartered in Maine, is a powerful competitor, with its wide variety of private-branded footwear and clothing products. Another strong US-based rival is Wolverine World Wide, which manufactures Hush Puppies, Sebago, Merrell, Patagonia Footwear and other brands of casual and work shoes. Like Timberland, Wolverine operates company stores in the US and the UK. The UK-based R. Griggs Group (now owned by Permira), maker of Dr Martens boots, shoes and sandals, is a key competitor. In addition, particular Timberland shoe styles compete directly with footwear marketed by the world's largest athletic shoe companies.

Economic conditions can also affect Timberland's marketing situation. During the recent recession, while many consumers held back on discretionary purchases, the company's overall revenue fell. However, sales of its work boots remained constant, even as some competitors saw their sales drop. Timberland's marketing executives realized that the brand was holding its own among construction workers and other buyers who need tough, reliable footwear to use day in and day out.

Timberland's marketers have also noticed that the challenging global economic situation is influencing the way consumers think and feel about buying products such as shoes and clothing. When unemployment was low and buying power was high, consumers often used such purchases as a way to display their wealth. However, as the economy moved into recession, many cash-strapped consumers cut back on purchases of showy and expensive items, in favour of products that conveyed a more subtle message about cultural values, such as concern for the environment. Today, 'self-worth is tied to thoughtful purchases as a way to impress peers, instead of conspicuous consumption', states Timberland's senior director of merchandizing.

In addition to its international marketing initiatives in China and Europe, Timberland anticipates promising opportunities for growth in India. The company signed a strategic alliance with Reliance Industries, a local company known for marketing international brands. Reliance distributes shoes, boots and clothing through Timberland-branded stores and through selected department stores in major Indian cities. Timberland's CEO says that Reliance has, 'a clear understanding of the Timberland brand and consumer' and just as important it is 'as committed as we are to our ideology and passion for the outdoors'.

High-tech shoes and communications

Timberland is applying technological advances to improve its footwear products and to reach out to customers through digital media. For example, to satisfy customers' needs for comfort, the company has introduced patented 'Smart Comfort' footbeds in its shoes. As part of its commitment to sustainability, Timberland makes Green Rubber soles from recycled rubber and is designing its new footwear products for easy disassembly and recycling at the end of their useful lives.

Moving into digital media has helped Timberland bring its marketing messages to the attention of consumers who use the web. Through brand-specific sites, Facebook fan pages, blog entries, a Twitter feed, YouTube videos and online games, Timberland supplements its traditional marketing activities and engages consumers who seek a deeper level of involvement with their favourite brands.

Questions for discussion

1. How does Timberland's reputation for social responsibility serve as a strength, at a time when consumers are turning away from showy and expensive products?

2. Over time, Timberland plans to add labels to state how eco-friendly each of its products really is. What are the marketing advantages and disadvantages of this move?

3. To what extent should Timberland simply get on with being socially responsible, rather than communicating so explicitly about its corporate responsibility and impact?

Sources: www.timberland.com/category/, July 2011; http://responsibility .timberland.com/service, April 2015.

Notes

Chapter 1

1 Kohli, A. and Jaworski, B. J. (1990) 'Market orientation: the construct, research propositions and managerial potential', *Journal of Marketing* 54(2):1–18.

2 Lynch, J. (1994) 'What is Marketing?', in Norman Hart (ed.) *Effective Industrial Marketing*, London: Kogan Page.

3 Dibb, S., Simkin, L. and Bradley, J. (1996) *The Marketing Planning Workbook*, London: International Thomson Business Publishing.

4 Munro, H. J., Brodie, R. J. and Coviello, N. E. (1997) 'Understanding contemporary marketing: development of a classification scheme', *Journal of Marketing Management* 13(6):501–22.

5 Kotler, P. (1988) *Marketing Management: Analysis, Planning, Implementation and Control*, 6th ed., Englewood Cliffs, NJ: Prentice Hall, p. 6.

6 Ferrell, O. C. and Lucas, G. (1987) 'An evaluation of progress in the development of a definition of marketing', *Journal of the Academy of Marketing Science* 15(3):12–23.

7 Grönroos, G. (1989) 'Defining marketing: a market oriented approach', *European Journal of Marketing* 23(1):52; Srivastava, R. K., Shervani, T. and Fahey, L. (1998) 'Market-based assets and shareholder value: a framework for analysis', *Journal of Marketing* 62(1):2–18.

8 Wood, L. M. (1996) 'Added value: marketing basics?' *Journal of Marketing Management* 12(8):735–55; Robertson, T. (1994) 'New developments in marketing: a European perspective', *European Management Journal* 12(4):362–65.

9 Sheth, J. N. and Sisodia, R. (1995) 'More than ever before, marketing is under fire to account for what it spends', *Marketing Management* 4(2):13–14.

10 Grönroos, G. (1994) 'From marketing mix to relationship marketing: towards a paradigm shift in marketing', *Management Decision* 32(2):4–20; Payne, A., Christopher, M., Clark, M. and Peck, H. (1998) *Relationship Marketing for Competitive Advantage*, Oxford: Butterworth-Heinemann.

11 Saren, M., et al. (2007) *Critical Marketing: Defining the Field,* Oxford: Routledge; Tadajewski, M. and Brownlie, D. (2009) *Critical Marketing: Issues in Contemporary Marketing*, Chichester: John Wiley & Sons Ltd.

12 Polonsky, M. J., et al. (2003) 'The Harm Chain', *Marketing Theory*, 3(3):345–64; Smith, C., et al. (2010) 'Marketing's consequences', *Business Ethics Quarterly* 20(4):617–41.

13 Laczniak, G. R. and Lusch, R. F. (1986) 'Environment and strategy in 1995: a survey of high-level executives', *Journal of Consumer Marketing* 3(2):5–23.

14 Dibb, S. and Simkin, L. (1996) *The Marketing Segmentation Workbook*, London: Thomson.

Chapter 2

1 Baker, M. (2008) *The Strategic Marketing Plan Audit*, Axminster: Cambridge Strategy Publications.

2 Homburg, C., Kuester, S. and Krohmer, H. (2009) *Marketing Management – A Contemporary Perspective*, London: McGraw-Hill.

3 Johnson, G. and Scholes, K. (2008) *Exploring Corporate Strategy*, Essex: Financial Times.

4 Weitz, B. A. and Wensley, R. (1988) *Readings in Strategic Marketing*, Chicago, IL: Dryden.

5 Varadarajan, P. R. (1999) 'Strategy content and process perspectives revisited', *Journal of the Academy of Marketing Science* 27(1):88–100.

6 Homas, G., Hult, M., Cravens, D. W. and Sheth, J. (2001) 'Competitive advantage in the global marketplace: a focus on marketing strategy', *Journal of Business Research* 51(1):1–3.

7 Dibb, S., Simkin, L. and Bradley, J. (1996) *The Marketing Planning Workbook*, London: Thomson.

8 Abell, D. F. and Hammond, J. S. (1979) *Strategic Market Planning*, Englewood Cliffs, NJ: Prentice Hall, p. 10.

9 Varadarajan, P. R., Clark, T. and Pride, W. (1990) 'Determining your company's destiny', working paper, Texas A&M University.

10 Peter, J. P. and Donnelly, J. H., Jr (1991) *A Preface to Marketing Management*, 5th ed., Homewood, IL: Irwin, p. 9.

11 Adapted from Peter and Donnelly, (see note 10), pp. 8–12.

12 Abell, D. F. (1978) 'Strategic windows', *Journal of Marketing* 42(3):21–6.

13 Abell and Hammond (see note 8), p. 213.

14 Fahey, L., King, W. K. and Naraganan, V. K. (1981) 'Environmental scanning and forecasting in strategic planning – the state of the art', *Long Range Planning* 14(1):32–9.

15 Georgaff, D. M. and Mundick, R. G. (1986) 'Managers' guide to forecasting', *Harvard Business Review*, January–February, 120.

16 Kotler, P. (1980) 'Strategic planning and the marketing process', *Business*, May–June, 6–7.

17 Piercy, N. (1992) *Market-Led Strategic Change*, Oxford: Butterworth-Heinemann Ltd.

18 Di Benedetto, C. A. (2003) 'The relationship between strategic type and firm capabilities in Chinese firms', *International Marketing Review* 20(5):514–34.

19 Kerin, R. A., Majahan, V. and Varadarajan, P. R. (1990) *Contemporary Perspectives on Strategic Marketing Planning*, Boston, MA: Allyn & Bacon.

20 Grover, R. (1989) 'When Columbia met Sony … a love story', *Business Week*, 9 October, 44–5.

21 Hooley, G. and Saunders, J. (1993) *Competitive Positioning: The Key to Market Success*, London: Prentice Hall.

22 Varadarajan, P. R. (2002) 'Marketing strategy and the Internet: an organizing framework', *Journal of the Academy of Marketing Science* 30(4):296–313.

23 Ries, A. and Trout, J. (1986) *Marketing Warfare*, New York: McGraw-Hill; Saunders, J. (1987) 'Marketing and competitive success', in M. Baker (ed.) *The Marketing Book*, London: Heinemann.

24 Takada, H. (1998) 'Multiple time series analysis of competitive marketing behaviour', *Journal of Business Research* 43(2):97–107.

25 Doyle, P. (1994) *Marketing Management and Strategy*, London: Prentice Hall.

26 Aaker, D. A. (1988) *Strategic Market Management*, 2nd ed., New York: Wiley, p. 35.

27 Saunders, J. (1987) 'Marketing and competitive success', in M. J. Baker (ed.) *The Marketing Book*, London: Heinemann, pp. 10–28.

Chapter 3

1   Becherer, R. C. and Maurer, J. G. (1997) 'The moderating effect of environmental variables on the entrepreneurial and marketing orientation of entrepreneur-led firms', *Entrepreneurship Theory and Practice* 22(1):47–58; Achrol, R. S. (1997) 'Changes in the theory of interorganizational relations in marketing: toward a network paradigm', *Journal of the Academy of Marketing Science* 25(1):56–71.

2   Kotler, P. (1986) 'Megamarketing', *Harvard Business Review*, March–April, 117–24.

3   Ashton, J. K. and Pressey, A. D. (2011) 'The regulatory challenge to branding: an interpretation of UK competition authority investigations 1950–2007', *Journal of Marketing Management*, 27(9–10):1027–58.

4   *Britain 1990: An Official Handbook* (1990) London: Central Office of Information.

5   Plummer, J. (1974) 'The concept of application of life style segmentation', *Journal of Marketing* 38(1):33–7.

6   *The IBA Code of Advertising Standards and Practice* (1977) London: Independent Broadcasting Authority, December, p. 3. (The IBA is now the ITC.)

7   Bremner, B. (1989) 'A new sales pitch: the environment', *Business Week*, 24 July, 50.

8   Knight, R. and Dimmler, E. (1989) 'The greening of Europe's industries', *U.S. News & World Report*, 5 June, 45–6.

9   Reprinted by permission from Herbert Simon (1973) 'Technology and environment', *Management Science* 19(10):1110–21. Copyright 1973, The Institute of Management Sciences.

10 Business Link, http://www.businesslink.gov.uk /bdotg/action/detail?itemId=1075422931&type =RESOURCES, 1 March 2011.

11 Accenture Interactive, https://microsite.accenture .com/Accenture_Interactive/Pages/AI_PaidSearch _Digital_Marketing.aspx?c=mul_gdailfelpsgs _0610&n=g_Accenture_Digital_Marketing/a_0_k /digital_marketing&KW=4770b756-7b9c-2868 -c21b-0000459ae40b, 1 March 2011.

12 Mobile Marketing Association, www.mmaglobal .com, 1 March 2011.

13 Bradley, A., www.gartnerinsight.com, 1 March 2011.

14 Alderson, W. (1965) *Dynamic Marketing Behavior*, Homewood, IL: Irwin, pp. 195–97.

15 Porter, M. (1980) *Competitive Strategy*, New York: Free Press.

16 Kotler, P., Armstrong, G., Saunders, J. and Wong, V. (1999) *Principles of Marketing*, Hemel Hempstead: Prentice Hall.

17 Abell, D. (1980) *Defining the Business: The Starting Point of Strategic Planning*, Englewood Cliffs, NJ: Prentice Hall.

18 Doyle, P. (1998) *Marketing Management and Strategy*, Hemel Hempstead: Prentice Hall.

19 Ansoff, H. I. and McDonell, E. (1990) *Implementing Strategic Change*, Englewood Cliffs, NJ: Prentice Hall.

20 Brownlie, D. (1987) 'Environmental analysis', in M. Baker (ed.), *The Marketing Book*, Oxford: Butterworth-Heinemann.

21 Dibb, S., Simkin, L. and Bradley, J. (1996) *The Marketing Planning Workbook*, London: Thomson.

22 Diffenbach, J. (1983) 'Corporate environmental analysis in large US corporations', *Long Range Planning* 16(3):107–16.

Chapter 4

1   Terpstra, V. (1987) *International Marketing*, 4th ed., Hinsdale, IL: Dryden Press, p. 4.

2   Lascu, D.-N. (1996) 'International marketing planning and practice', *Journal of Global Marketing* 9(3): 97–9; Leeflang, P. S. H. and de Mortanges, C. P. (1993)

'The internal European market and strategic marketing planning: implications and expectations', *Journal of International Consumer Marketing* 6(2):7–23.

3 Levitt, T. (1983) 'The globalisation of markets', *Harvard Business Review* May–June, 92.

4 Ibid.

5 Jain, S. C. (1989) 'Standardisation of international marketing strategy: some research hypotheses', *Journal of Marketing* 53(1):70–9.

6 Batra, R. (1997) 'Executive insights: marketing issues and challenges in transitional economies', *Journal of International Marketing* 5(4):95–114; Wang, C. C. L. (1999) 'Issues and advances in international consumer research: a review and assessment', *Journal of International Marketing and Marketing Research* 24(1):3–21.

7 Fletcher, M., Harris, S. and Richey, R. G. (2013) 'Internationalization knowledge: what, why, where and when?', *Journal of International Marketing*, 21(3): 47–71.

8 Terpstra, V. (1983) 'Critical mass and international marketing strategy', *Journal of the Academy of Marketing Science* 11(3):269–82.

9 Ono, Y. (1992) 'Land of rising fun', *Wall Street Journal*, 2 October, A1, A10; Hanson, G. (1992) 'Japan at play', *Insight*, 27 April, 6–13, 34–37.

10 Bowman, D. and Lele-Pingle, S. (1997) 'Buyer behavior in business-to-business services: the case of foreign exchange', *International Journal of Research in Marketing* 14(5):499–508.

11 Bremner, B. and Updike, E. H. (1995) 'Made in America isn't the kiss of death anymore', *Business Week*, 13 November, 62.

12 Campbell, N. G. G., Graham, J. L., Jolibert, A. and Meissner, H. G. (1988) 'Marketing negotiations in France, Germany, the United Kingdom, and the United States', *Journal of Marketing* 52(2):49–62.

13 Wentz, L. (1985) 'Local laws keep international marketers hopping', *Advertising Age*, 11 July, 20.

14 Smith, L. (1985) 'Japan wants to make friends', *Fortune*, 2 September, 84.

15 Jeannet, J.-P. and Hennessey, H. D. (1995) *Global Marketing Strategies*, Boston, MA: Houghton Mifflin, p. 60.

16 'Timeline: BAE corruption probes', http://news.bbc.co.uk/1/hi/business/8501655.stm, 2 March 2011.

17 Leeflang, P. S. H. and de Mortanges, C. P. (1993) 'The internal European market and strategic marketing planning: implications and expectations', *Journal of International Consumer Marketing* 6(2):7–23.

18 *Europe in Figures*, 4th ed. (1995) Brussels: Eurostat.

19 Mazur, L. (1998) 'Failing the Euro test', *Marketing*, 3 December, 26–7.

20 Vandermerwe, S. and L'Huillier, M.-A. (1989) 'Euro-consumers in 1992', *Business Horizons*, January–February, 34–40.

21 Friberg, E. G. (1989) '1992: moves Europeans are making', *Harvard Business Review*, May–June, 89.

22 Keegan, W. J. (1995) *Global Marketing Management*, Englewood Cliffs, NJ: Prentice Hall, pp. 285–6.

23 Rapaport, C. (1991) 'Why Japan keeps on winning', *Fortune*, 15 July, 76.

24 Helm, L., Nakarmi, L., Soo, J. J., Holstein, W. J. and Terry, E. (1985) 'The Koreans are coming', *Business Week*, 25 December, 46–52.

25 Yang, D. J., Bennett, D. and Javerski, B. (1989) 'The other China is starting to soar', *Business Weekly*, 6 November, 60–2.

26 Kraar, L. (1989) 'Asia's rising export powers', *Fortune*, Special Pacific Rim issue, 43–50.

27 Jeannet, J.-P. and Hennessey, H. D. (1995) *Global Marketing Strategies*, Boston, MA: Houghton Mifflin, p. 173.

28 Reddy, A. C. (1991) 'The role of marketing in the economic development of eastern European countries', *Journal of Applied Business Research* 7(3):106–7.

29 Quelch, J. A., Joachimsthaler, E. and Nueno, J. L. (1991) 'After the wall: marketing guidelines for eastern Europe', *Sloan Management Review*, Winter, 90–1.

30 www.cisstat.com, August 2004.

31 'Rising in Russia' (1996) *Fortune*, 24 January, 93, 95.

32 Jeannet, J.-P. and Hennessey, H. D. (1995) *Global Marketing Strategies*, Boston, MA: Houghton Mifflin, p. 170.

33 Lapidus, R. S. (1997) 'Global marketing strategies', *Journal of Global Marketing* 10(3): 91–7.

34 Quelch, J. A. (1985) 'How to build a product licensing program', *Harvard Business Review*, May–June, 186–7.

35 Bradley, F. (1995) *International Marketing Strategy*, London: Prentice Hall, p. 393.

36 Adams, J. and Mendelsohn, M. (1986) 'Recent developments in franchising', *Journal of Business Law*, 206–19.

37 Stern, P. and Stanworth, J. (1988) 'The development of franchising in Britain', *National Westminster Quarterly Review*, May, 38–48; Ayling, D. (1987) 'Franchising has its dark side', *Accountancy* 99:113–17.

38 Kupfer, A. (1988) 'How to be a global manager', *Fortune*, 14 March, 52–8.

39 Harrigan, K. R. (1988) 'Joint ventures and competitive advantage', *Strategic Management Journal*, May, 141–58.

40 Killing, J. (1982) 'How to make a global joint venture work', *Harvard Business Review* 60:120–7.

41 Harrigan, K. R. (1988) 'Joint ventures and competitive strategy', *Strategic Management Journal*, May, 141–58.

42 Jain, S. C. (1987) 'Some perspectives on international strategic alliances', in *Advances in International Marketing*, New York: JAI Press, pp. 103–20.

43 'More companies prefer liaisons to marriage' (1988) *Wall Street Journal*, 12 April, 35.

44 Gross, T. and Neuman, J. (1989) 'Strategic alliances vital in global marketing', *Marketing News*, June, 1–2.

45 Cunningham, M. H. (1990) 'Marketing's new frontier: international strategic alliances', working paper, Queens University, Ontario.

46 Coeurderoy, R. and Murray, G. (2008) 'Regulatory environments and the location decision: evidence from the early foreign market entries of new technology-based firms', *Journal of International Business Studies* 39: 670–87.

Chapter 5

1   Engel, J. F., Blackwell, R. D. and Miniard, P. W. (1993) *Consumer Behavior*, 7th ed., Hinsdale, IL: Dryden Press, p. 4.

2   Howard, J. A. and Sheth, J. N. (1969) *The Theory of Buyer Behavior*, New York: Wiley, pp. 27–8.

3   Baumeister, R. F. and Mick, D. G. (2002) 'Yielding to temptation: self-control failure, impulsive purchasing, and consumer behavior', *Journal of Consumer Research* 28(4):670–7.

4   Foxall, G. (1995) 'Consumer decision-making', in M. Baker (ed.) *The Marketing Book*, 3rd ed., London: Heinemann/Chartered Institute of Marketing.

5   Keller, K. L. and Staelin, R. (1987) 'Effects of quality and quantity of information on decision effectiveness', *Journal of Consumer Research*, September, 200–13.

6   Biehal, G. and Chakravarti, D. (1986) 'Consumers' use of memory and external information in choice: macro and micro perspectives', *Journal of Consumer Research* 12(4):382–405.

7   Calder, B. J. and Sternthal, B. (1980) 'Television commercial wearout: an information processing view', *Journal of Marketing Research* 17(2):173–86.

8   Houston, M. J., Childers, T. L. and Heckler, S. E. (1987) 'Picture-word consistency and the elaborative processing of advertisements', *Journal of Marketing Research* 24(4):359–69.

9   Westbrook, R. A. (1987). 'Product/consumption-based affective responses and postpurchase processes', *Journal of Marketing Research* 24(3):258–70.

10 Capraro, A. J., Broniarczyk, S. and Srivastava, R. K. (2003) 'Factors influencing the likelihood of customer defection: the role of consumer knowledge', *Journal of the Academy of Marketing Science* 31(2):164–75.

11 Denny, N. (1998) 'Why complaining is our new hobby', *Marketing*, 26 November, 16.

12 Chen, Yubo, Yong Liu, and Jurui Zhang (2012), 'When do third-party product reviews affect firm value and what can firms do? The case of media critics and professional movie reviews', *Journal of Marketing* 76(March):116–34.

13 Sellers, P. (1989) 'The ABC's of marketing to kids', *Fortune*, 8 May, 115.

14 Waldrop, J. (1989) 'Inside America's households', *American Demographics* March, 20–7.

15 Houston, Childers and Heckler (see note 8), pp. 359–69.

16 Robertson, T. S. and Gatignon, H. (1986) 'Competitive effects on technology diffusion', *Journal of Marketing* 50(3):1–12.

17 Ibid., pp. 1–12.

18 Ries, A. and Trout, J. (1986) *Positioning the Battle for Your Mind*, New York: McGraw-Hill Book Co.

19 Bettman, J. R. (1979) *An Information Processing Theory of Consumer Choice*, Reading, MA: Addison-Wesley, pp. 18–24.

20 Aaker, D. and Stayman, D. (1992) 'Implementing the concept of transformational advertising', *Psychology and Marketing* May and June: 237–53.

21 Myers, J. H. (1997) 'Determinant buying attitudes: meaning and measurement', *Marketing Management* 6(2): 50–6, Summer.

22 Alba, J. W. and Hutchinson, J. W. (1987) 'Dimensions of consumer expertise', *Journal of Consumer Research* 13(4):411–54.

23 Rao, A. R. and Monroe, K. B. (1988) 'The moderating effect of prior knowledge on cue utilization in product evaluations', *Journal of Consumer Research* 15(2):253–64.

24 Ibid.

25 www.prmoment.com/2858/worst-pr-disasters-of-2014.aspx, accessed 31 March 2015.

26 Baumgartner, H. (2002) 'Towards a personology of the consumer', *Journal of Consumer Research* 29(2):286–93.

27 Lastovika, J. L. and Joachimsthaler, E. A. (1988) 'Improving the detection of personality–behavior, relationships in consumer research', *Journal of Consumer Research* 14(4):583–7.

28 Moore, M. T. (1989) 'Spring break: brand names chase sales', *USA Today*, 17 March, B1.

29 Donkin, A., Lee, Y. H. and Toson, B. (2002) 'Implications of changes in the UK social and occupational classifications in 2001 for vital statistics', *National Statistics* Spring: 23–9.

30 Rogers, E. (2004) 'Adland takes up fat challenge', *Marketing*, 11 March, 19.

31   De Mooij, M. (2003) 'Convergence and divergence in consumer behavior: implications for global advertising', *International Journal of Advertising* 22(2):183–203.

32   Berry, L. L. (1979) 'The time-sharing consumer', *Journal of Retailing*, Winter, 69.

33   Kahneman, D. (2002) *Maps of Bounded Rationality,* http://nobelprize.org/noble_prizes/economics/laureates/2002/kahneman-lecture.html.

34   Barden, P. (2014) *Decoded: The Science Behind Why We Buy*, John Wiley & Sons.

35   Szmigin, I. and Piacentini, M. (2015) *Consumer Behaviour*. Oxford University Press.

36   Srinivasan, R., *Online Social Media and Networks: Impact on Marketing Practice*, The AMA Journal Reader, https://www.ama.org/publications/E-publications/Pages/ama-journal-july-14-social-media.aspx (accessed 30 March 2015).

37   Bucklin, R. E. (1998) 'Determining segmentation in sales response across consumer purchase behaviours', *Journal of Marketing Research* 35(2):189–97.

Chapter 6

1   Jarillo, J. C. and Stevenson, H. H. (1991) 'Cooperative strategies: the payoffs and the pitfalls', *Long Range Planning* 24(1):64–70.

2   Coppett, J. I. (1988) 'Auditing your customer service activities', *Industrial Marketing Management* 17:277–84; Powers, T. L. (1988) 'Identify and fulfill customer service expectations', *Industrial Marketing Management* 17:273–76.

3   Bitner, M. J., Booms, B. H. and Tetreault, M. S. (1990) 'The service encounter: diagnosing favorable and unfavorable incidents', *Journal of Marketing* 54:71–84.

4   Royal, W. F. (1995) 'Cashing in on complaints', *Sales & Marketing Management*, May, 88–89.

5   Uddin, M. (2001) 'Loyalty programmes: the ultimate gift', *DSN Retailing Today* 40(5):12.

6   Shaw, J., Giglierano, J. and Kallis, J. (1989) 'Marketing complex technical products: the importance of intangible attributes', *Industrial Marketing Management* 18:45–53.

7   Webster, F. E. and Wind, Y. (1996) 'A general model for understanding organizational buyer behaviour', *Marketing Management* Winter/Spring: 52–7.

8   Gummesson, E. (1987) 'The new marketing: developing long-term interactive relationships', *Long Range Planning* 20(3):10–20.

9   Hakansson, H. (1982) *International Marketing and Purchasing of Industrial Goods*, Chichester: Wiley.

10   Christopher, M., Payne, A. and Ballantyne, D. (1991) *Relationship Marketing*, Oxford: Butterworth-Heinemann.

11   Ford, D. (1982) *Understanding Business Marketing and Purchasing*, London: Thomson Learning.

12   McKenna, R. (1991) *Relationship Marketing*, Reading, MA: Addison-Wesley.

13   Campbell, N. C. G., Graham, J. L., Jolibert, A. and Meissner, H. G. (1988) 'Marketing negotiations in France, Germany, the United Kingdom and the United States', *Journal of Marketing* 52(2):49–62.

14   Jarillo, J. C. and Stevenson, H. H. (1991) 'Cooperative strategies: the payoffs and the pitfalls', *Long Range Planning* February:64–70.

15   Doyle, P. and Saunders, J. (1985) 'Market segmentation and positioning in specialized industrial markets', *Journal of Marketing* 49(2):25.

16   Leek, S. and Christodoulides, G. (2011) 'A literature review and future agenda for B2B branding: challenges of branding in a B2B context', *Industrial Marketing Management* 40:830–7.

Chapter 7

1   Muhamad, R., Melewar, T. C. and Alwi, S. F. S. (2012) 'Segmenting and brand positioning for Islamic financial services', *European Journal of Marketing* 46(7/8):900–21.

2   Chau, V. S. and Ngai, L. W. L. C. (2011) 'The you market for internet banking services: perceptions, attitude and behaviour', *Journal of Services Marketing* 24(1):42–60.

3   Weinstein, A. (2004) *Handbook of Market Segmentation: Strategic Targeting for Business and Technology Firms*, New York: Haworth Press.

4   Stewart, D. W. (1998) 'Segmentation and positioning for strategic marketing decisions', *Journal of Marketing Research* 35(1):128–9.

5   Frank, R. and Wind, Y. (1972) *Market Segmentation*, Englewood Cliffs, NJ: Prentice Hall; Wind, Y. (1978) 'Issues and advances in segmentation research', *Journal of Marketing Research* 15(3):317–27.

6   Schaffer, C. M. and Green, P. E. (1998) 'Cluster-based market segmentation: some further comparisons of alternative approaches', *Journal of the Market Research Society* 40(2):155–63.

7   Wedel, M. and Kamakura, W. (2000) *Market Segmentation: Conceptual and Methodological Foundations*, Boston, MA: Kluwer Academic Publications.

8   Peppers, D. and Rogers, M. (1999) *The One-to-One Manager*, New York: Currency Doubleday.

9   Postma, P. (1998) *The New Marketing Era: Marketing to the Imagination of a Technology-Driven World*, New York: McGraw-Hill.

10   Sheth, J. H., Sisodia, R. S. and Sharma, A. (2000) 'Customer-centric marketing', *Journal of the Academy of Marketing Science* 28(1):55–66.

11   Peppers, D. and Rogers, M. (1999) *The One-to-One Manager*, New York: Currency Doubleday.

12 Chaffey, D., Mayer, R., Johnston, K. and Ellis-Chadwick, F. (2000) *Internet Marketing*, Harlow: Pearson Education.

13 McNeal, J. U. (1999) *Kids Marketing: Myths and Realities*, Ithaca, NY: Paramount Market Publishing.

14 Albonetti, J. G. and Dominguez, L. V. (1989) 'Major influences on consumer goods marketers' decision to target US Hispanics', *Journal of Advertising Research* February–March:9–11.

15 Lastovicka, J. L. and Joachimsthaler, E. A. (1988) 'Improving the detection of personality–behavior relationships in consumer research', *Journal of Consumer Research* March:583–7.

16 Plummer, J. T. (1974) 'The concept and application of life style segmentation', *Journal of Marketing* January:33–37.

17 Engel, J. F., Blackwell, R. D. and Miniard, P. W. (1990) *Consumer Behavior*, Orlando, FL: Dryden Press, pp. 348–9.

18 Haley, R. I. (1968) 'Benefit segmentation: a decision-oriented research tool', *Journal of Marketing* 32(3):30–5.

19 Wind, Y. and Cardoza, R. (1974) 'Industrial market segmentation', *Industrial Marketing Management* 3:153–66.

20 Beane, T. P. and Ennis, D. M. (1987) 'Market segmentation: a review', *European Journal of Marketing* 21(5):20–42.

21 Bonoma, T. and Shapiro, B. P. (1983) *Segmenting the Industrial Market*, Lexington, MA: Lexington Books.

22 Blumberg, D. F. (1987) 'Developing service as a line of business', *Management Review* 76:61.

23 Diamantopoulos, A. and Schlegelmilch, B. (1997) *Taking the Fear out of Data Analysis*, London: Dryden Press; Saunders, J. (1994) 'Cluster analysis', *Journal of Marketing Management* 10:13–28; and Saunders, J. (1980) 'Cluster analysis for market segmentation', *European Journal of Marketing* 14:422–35.

24 Lilien, G. L. and Kotler, P. (1983) *Marketing Decision-Making: A Model Building Approach*, New York: Harper & Row; Naert, P. and Leeflang, P. (1978) *Building Implementable Marketing Models*, Leiden: Martinus Nijhoff.

25 Maier, J. and Saunders, J. (1990) 'The implementation of segmentation in sales management', *Journal of Personal Selling and Sales Management* 10(1):39–48.

26 Saunders, J. (1994) 'Cluster analysis', *Journal of Marketing Management* 10:13–28; Saunders, J. (1980) 'Cluster analysis for market segmentation', *European Journal of Marketing* 14:422–35.

27 Diamantopoulos, A. and Schlegelmilch, B. *Taking the Fear out of Data Analysis*, London: Dryden Press, 1997; Saunders, J. (1994) 'Cluster analysis', *Journal of Marketing Management*

10:13–28; and Saunders, J. (1980) 'Cluster analysis for market segmentation', *European Journal of Marketing* 14:422–35.

28 Thomas, J. S. and Sullivan, U. Y. (2005) 'Managing marketing communications with multichannel customers', *Journal of Marketing* 69(4):239–51.

29 Boulding, W., Staelin, R., Ehret, M. and Johnston, W. J. (2005) 'A customer relationship management roadmap: what is known, potential pitfalls, and where to go', *Journal of Marketing* 69(4):155–66.

30 King, S. F. and Burgess, T. F. (2008) 'Understanding success and failure in customer relationship management', *Industrial Marketing Management* 37:421–31.

31 Harrigan, P., Ramsey, E. and Ibbotson, P. (2011) 'Critical factors underpinning the eCRM activities of SMEs', *Journal of Marketing Management* 27(5/6):503–29.

32 Peppers, D. and Rogers, M. (2004) *Managing Customer Relationships – A Strategic Framework*, New Jersey: John Wiley and Sons.

33 Nguyen, B. and Simkin, L. (2011) 'Effects of firm customization on the severity of unfairness perceptions and (mis)behaviour: the moderating role of trust', paper presented at The Academy of Marketing Conference, Liverpool, UK, July.

34 Ibid.

Chapter 8

1 McDonald, M. (1995) *Marketing Plans*, Oxford: Butterworth-Heinemann.

2 Dibb, S. and Simkin, L. (1997) *Marketing and Marketing Planning: Still Barriers to Overcome*, EMAC, Warwick, May.

3 Doyle, P., Saunders, J. and Wong, V. (1986) 'A comparative study of Japanese marketing strategies in the British market', *Journal of International Business Studies* 17(1):27–46.

4 Kotler, P. (1988) *Marketing Management: Analysis, Planning, and Control*, 6th ed., Englewood Cliffs, NJ: Prentice Hall, p. 257.

5 Wind, Y. (1980) 'Going to market: new twist for some old tricks', *Wharton Magazine*, 4.

6 Harrison, T. (1987) *A Handbook of Advertising Techniques*, London: Kogan Page, p. 7.

7 Ries, A. and Trout, J. (1981) *Positioning: The Battle for Your Mind*, New York: McGraw-Hill; Trout, J. and Rivkin, S. (1996) *The New Positioning: The Latest on the World's #1 Business Strategy*, New York: McGraw-Hill.

8 Hollensen, S. (2005) *Marketing Planning: A Global Perspective*, p. 32. Maidenhead: McGraw-Hill.

9 Kotler, P., Keller, K. L., Brady, M., Goodman, M. and Hanson, T. (2012) 'Understanding marketing management'. In *Marketing Management*, p. 15. Harlow: Pearson Education.

10 Lindgreen, A., Hingley, M. K., Grant, D. B. and Morgan, R. E. (2012) 'Value in business and industrial marketing: past, present and future', *Industrial Marketing Management* 41:07–14; Parry, S., Rowley, J., Jones, R. and Kupiec-Teahan, B. (2012) 'Customer-perceived value in business-to-business relationships', *Journal of Marketing Management* 28(7/8):887–911.

11 Hilton, T., Hughes, T. and Chalcraft, D. (2012) 'Service co-creation and value realization', *Journal of Marketing Management* 28(13–14):1504–19.

Chapter 9

1 Birks, D. (1994) Chapter 10, in M. Baker (ed.) *The Marketing Book*, Oxford: Butterworth-Heinemann.

2 'Pizza Hut studies effects of "pizza deprivation" on college and high school students' (2001) *PRNewswire*, via AmericaOnline, 30 May.

3 Wind, J. (1997) 'Marketing research forum: state of the art in quantitative research', *Marketing Research*, 9(4), p. 2.

4 Dibb, S. and Simkin, L. (2004) *The Marketing Casebook*, London: Routledge.

5 https://www.esomar.org/uploads/industry/reports/global-market-research-2014/ESOMAR-GMR2014-Preview.pdf, accessed April 27th 2015.

6 'Research league tables top 65' (2004) *Marketing*, 14 July, 37–46.

7 Johansson, J. K. and Nonaha, I. (1987) 'Market research the Japanese way', *Harvard Business Review* May–June:16–22.

8 http://www.telegraph.co.uk/news/worldnews/europe/eu/11047127/EU-rules-against-powerful-vacuum-cleaners-ban-best-models-Which-warns.html.

9 Tull, D. and Hawkins, D. (1990) *Marketing Research*, New York: Macmillan.

10 Mittal, V. and Kamakura, W. A. (2001) 'Satisfaction, repurchase intent, and repurchase behavior: investigating the moderating effects of customer characteristics', *Journal of Marketing Research* 38(1):131–42.

11 Society PWC, The Business of Evidence: A report prepared for the Market Research Society, October 2012, available at: www.mrs.org.uk/pdf/The_Business_of_Evidence_Final_08102012.pdf.

12 'Internal secondary market research' (2001) *Small Business Owner's Toolkit*, www.lycos.com/business/cch/guide-book.html?lpv=1&docNumber= P03_3020, 23 June.

13 http://www.barb.co.uk/resources/barb-facts/how-we-do-what-we-do?_s=4

14 Vaughn, R. L. (1984) 'Demographic data banks: a new management resource', *Business Horizons* November–December:38–42. See also Chapter 5.

15 Jennifer Steele, Lisa Bourke, A. E. Luloff, P. S. Liao, Gene L. Theodori, and R. S. Krannich (2001) 'The drop-off/pick-up method for household survey research', *Journal of the Community Development Society* 32(2):238–50.

16 Conant, J. S., Smart, D. T. and Walker, B. J. (1990) 'Main survey facilitation techniques: an assessment and proposal regarding reporting practices', working paper, Texas A&M University.

17 Riche, p. 8.

18 http://www.dailymail.co.uk/news/article-2540500/9-10-people-not-trust-cold-calling-companies-DO-phoning.html, accessed 25th April 2015.

19 Billing, S. M. (1982) 'Go slow, be wary when considering switch to computer assisted interviewing system', *Marketing News*, 26 November, sec. 2, p. 2.

20 Tull and Hawkins, 1990 (see note 9).

21 Yorkshire Television's *The Marketing Mix* series.

22 Sokolow, H. (1985) 'In-depth interviews increasing in importance', *Marketing News*, 13 September, 26.

23 Bush, A. J. and Parasuraman, A. (1985) 'Mall intercept versus telephone interviewing environment', *Journal of Advertising Research* 25(2):36–43.

24 Bush, A. J. and Hair, J. F., Jr (1985) 'An assessment of the mall intercept as a data collecting method', *Journal of Marketing Research* 22(2):158–167.

25 Singh, J., Howell, R. D. and Rhoads, G. K. (1990) 'Adaptive designs for Likert-type data: an approach for implementing marketing surveys', *Journal of Marketing Research* 27(3):304–21.

26 Hart, N. and Stapleton, J. (1981) *Glossary of Marketing Terms*, Oxford: Butterworth-Heinemann.

27 'Closer encounters' (2004) *Marketing*, 14 July, 48–49.

28 Jackson, P., Adsearch, Richmond.

29 Diamantopoulos, A. and Schlegelmilch, B. (1997) *Taking the Fear out of Data Analysis*, London: Dryden Press.

30 Olivette, M. J. (1987) 'Marketing research in the electric utility industry', *Marketing News*, 2 January, 13.

31 Utter, D. (1998) 'Information-driven marketing decisions: development of strategic information systems', *Journal of the Academy of Marketing Science*, Spring.

32 Goal, L. N. (1992) 'High technology data collection for measurement and testing', *Marketing Research*, March, 29–38.

33 Ferrell, O. C. and Skinner, S. J. (1988) 'Ethical behavior and bureaucratic structure in marketing research organizations', *Journal of Marketing Research* 25(1):103–4.

34 Kavanaugh, M. (1998) 'Masked brawl', *Marketing Week*, 15 October, 65.

35 http://consumers.ofcom.org.uk/phone/tackling-nuisance-calls-and-messages.

36 https://www.mrs.org.uk/article/item/1918.

37 Allen, B. (1987) 'Make information services pay its way', *Harvard Business Review*, January–February, 57.

Chapter 10

1   Part of this definition is adapted from Scott, J. D., Warshaw, M. R. and Taylor, J. R. (1985) *Introduction to Marketing Management*, 5th ed., Homewood, IL: Irwin, p. 215.

2   Levitt, T. (1981) 'Marketing intangible products and product intangibles', *Harvard Business Review*, May–June, 94–102.

3   Haas, R. W. (1986) *Industrial Marketing Management*, 3rd ed., Boston, MA: Kent Publishing, pp. 15–25.

4   Putsis, W. P., Jr and Bayus, B. L. (2001) 'An empirical analysis of firms' product line decisions', *Journal of Marketing Research* 38(1):110–18.

5   Thomas, M. J. (1987) 'Product development management', in M. Baker (ed.) *The Marketing Book*, London: Heinemann/The Chartered Institute of Marketing.

6   Radas, S. and Shugan, S. M. (1998) 'Seasonal marketing and timing new product introductions', *Journal of Marketing Research* 35(3):296–315; Adams, M. E. (1998) 'Enhancing new product development performance: an organizational learning perspective', *The Journal of Product Innovation Management* 15(5):403–22.

7   Lukas, B. A. and Ferrell, O. C. (2000) 'The effect of market orientation on product innovation', *Journal of the Academy of Marketing Science* 28(2):39–47.

8   Lynn, G. and Reilly, R. (2002) 'How to build a block-buster', *Harvard Business Review* 80(10):18–20.

9   Benady, D. (2004) 'Chopping brands', *Marketing Week* 10:22–25.

10 Tellis, G. and Golder, P. (1996) 'First to market, first to fail? Real causes of enduring market leadership', *Sloan Management Review*, Winter:65–75.

11 'Guinness in facelift as volume dips' (2004) *Marketing Week*, 20 May, 8.

12 Levitt, T. (1981) 'Marketing intangible products and product intangibles', *Harvard Business Review*, May–June, 96.

13 Hart, C. W. L. (1988) 'The power of unconditional service guarantees', *Harvard Business Review*, July–August:54–62.

Chapter 11

1   Bennett, P. D. (ed.) (1988) *Dictionary of Marketing Terms*, Chicago, IL: American Marketing Association, p. 18.

2   Doyle, P. (1993) 'Building successful brands: the strategic options', *The Journal of Consumer Marketing* 7(2):5–20.

3   Bell, J. (1998) 'Brand management for the next millennium', *The Journal of Business Strategy* 19 (2):7–10; Rooney, J. A. (1995) 'Branding: a trend for today and tomorrow', *The Journal of Product and Brand Management* 4(4):48–56.

4   Assael, H. (1992) *Consumer Behaviour and Marketing Action*, 4th ed., Boston, MA: PWS-Kent.

5   Gensler, S., Volckner, F., Liu-Thompkins, F. and Wiertz, C. (2013) 'Managing brands in the social media environment', *Journal of Interactive Marketing*, http://dx.doi.org/10.1016/j.intmar2013.09.004; Schau, H. J., Muniz, A. M. and Arnould, E. J., 'How brand community practices create value', *Journal of Marketing* 73(September):30–51.

6   Schau, H. J., Muniz, A. M. and Arnould, E. J. (2009) 'How brand community practices create value', *Journal of Marketing* 73:30–51.

7   Gensler, S., Volckner, F., Liu-Thompkins, Y. and Wiertz, C. (2013) 'Managing brands in the social media environment', *Journal of Interactive Marketing*, 27(4): 242–256.

8   Aaker, D. A. (1991) *Managing Brand Equity: Capitalizing on the Value of a Brand Name*, New York: Free Press, pp. 16–17.

9   Aaker, D. (1996) *Building Strong Brands*, New York: Free Press.

10 Kapferer, J. N. (2008) *Strategic Brand Management*, London: Kogan Page.

11 Jeanes, E. L. (2013) 'The construction and controlling effect of a moral brand', *Scandinavian Journal of Management* 29: 163–72.

12 Walker, C. (1991) 'What's in a name?' *American Demographics*, February, 54–7.

13 'British retailing: chemistry upset' (2001) *The Economist*, 24 February, 68.

14 Corstjens, M. and Lal, R. (2000) 'Building store loyalty through store brands', *Journal of Marketing Research* 37(3):281–91.

15 Nelson, T. (1999) 'Sofres superpanel'.

16 Berry, L. L., Lefkowith, E. E. and Clark, T. (1988) 'In services, what's in a name?' *Harvard Business Review* September–October:2–4.

17 Cohen, D. (1986) 'Trademark strategy', *Journal of Marketing* 50(1):61–74.

18 Kohli, C. and Suri, R. (2000) 'Brand names that work: a study of the effectiveness of different brand names', *Marketing Management Journal* 10(2):112–20.

19 Gurhan-Canli, Z. and Maheswaran, D. (1998) 'The effects of extensions on brand name dilution and enhancement', *Journal of Marketing Research* 35 (4):464–73.

20 'Trademark stylesheet', US Trademark Association, no. 1A.

21 Hurrell, G. (1997) 'Solpadol – a successful case of brand positioning', *Journal of the Market Research Society* 39(3):463–80.

22 Doyle, P. (1994) *Marketing Management and Strategy*, London: Prentice Hall; M. Baker (ed.) (1995) *The Marketing Book*, Oxford: Butterworth-Heinemann, Chapter 20.

23 de Chernatony, L. (1999) 'Brand management through narrowing the gap between identity and brand reputation', *Journal of Marketing Management* 15(1–3):157–79.

24 Simoes, C. and Dibb, S. (2001) 'Rethinking the brand concept: new brand orientation', *Corporate Communications: An International Journal* 6(4):217–24.

25 www2.firstdirect.com/1/2/uncovered.

26 Morgan, F. W. (1988) 'Tampered goods: legal developments and marketing guidelines', *Journal of Marketing* 52(2):86–96.

27 Ibid.

28 Wansink, B. (1996) 'Can package size accelerate usage volume?' *Journal of Marketing* 60(3):1–14.

29 Madden, T. J., Hewett, K. and Roth, M. S. (2000) 'Managing images in different cultures: a cross national study of color meanings and preferences', *Journal of International Marketing* 8(4):90.

Chapter 12

1 Sethi, R. (2000) 'New product quality and product development', *Journal of Marketing* 64:1–14.

2 Bennet, R. C. and Cooper, R. G. (1984) 'The product life cycle trap', *Business Horizons* 27(5):7–16.

3 Phillips, D. F. (1990) 'Product development: where planning and marketing meet', *Journal of Business Strategy* 11(5):13–16.

4 Cooper, L. G. (2000) 'Strategic marketing planning for radically new products', *Journal of Marketing* 64(1):1–16.

5 Troy, L. C., Szymanski, D. M. and Varadarajan, P. R. (2001) 'Generating new product ideas: an initial investigation of the role of market information and organizational characteristics', *Journal of the Academy of Marketing Science* 29(1):89–101.

6 Drucker, P. F. (1985) 'The discipline of innovation', *Harvard Business Review*, May–June:67–8; Couchen, W. (1999) 'A proposed method for the design of consumer products', *Journal of International Marketing and Marketing Research*, 24(1):23–33.

7 Levine, J. B. (1989) 'Keeping new ideas kicking around', *Business Week*, 128.

8 Rindfleisch, A. and Moorman, C. (2001) 'The acquisition and utilization of information in new product alliances: a strength-of-ties perspective', *Journal of Marketing* 65(2):1–18.

9 Hyatt, J. (1989) 'Ask and you shall receive', *Inc.*, Sepember, 90–101.

10 Hilton, T., Hughes, T. and Chalcraft, D. (2012) 'Service co-creation and value realization', *Journal of Marketing Management* 28(13–14):1504–19;

Gamble, J. and Gilmore, A. (2013) 'A new era of co-creational marketing in the music industry', *European Journal of Marketing,* 47(11/12):1859–88.

11 Moorman, C. and Miner, A. S. (1998) 'The convergence of planning and execution: improvisation in new product development', *Journal of Marketing* 62(3):1–20; Padmanabhan, V., Rajiv, S. and Srinivasan, K. (1997) 'New products, upgrades, and new releases: a rationale for sequential product introduction', *Journal of Marketing Research* 34(4):456–72.

12 Bayus, B. L., Jain, S. and Rao, A. G. (2001) 'Truth or consequences: an analysis of vaporware and new product announcements', *Journal of Marketing Research* February:3–13.

13 Miller, C. (1993) 'Little relief seen for new product failure rate', *Marketing News*, 21 June, 5.

14 Kim, C. K., Lavack, A. M. and Smith, M. (2001) 'Consumer evaluation of vertical brand extensions and core brands', *Journal of Business Research* 52(3):211–22.

15 Grime, I., Diamantopoulos, A. and Smith, G. (2002) 'Consumer evaluations of extensions and their effects on the core brand: key issues and research propositions', *European Journal of Marketing* 36(11, 12):1415–38.

16 Adapted from Everett M. Rogers (1962) *Diffusion of Innovations*, New York: Macmillan, pp. 81–6.

17 Hooley, G. J. and Saunders, J. (1993) *Competitive Positioning: The Key to Market Success*, Englewood Cliffs, NJ: Prentice Hall.

18 DeBruicker, F. S. and Summe, G. L. (1985) 'Make sure your customers keep coming back', *Harvard Business Review* January–February:92–8.

19 Gordon, G. L., Calantone, R. J. and di Benedetto, A. (1991) 'Mature markets and revitalization strategies: an American fable', *Business Horizons* 34(3):42.

20 Clark, K. B. and Fujimoto, T. (1990) 'The power of product integrity', *Harvard Business Review* November–December:108–18.

21 Phillips, L. W., Chang, D. R. and Buzzell, R. D. (1983) 'Product quality, cost position and business performance: a test of some key hypotheses', *Journal of Marketing* 47(2):26–43.

22 Lambert, D. M. and Sterling, J. U. (1988) 'Identifying and eliminating weak products', *Business* 38:3–10.

23 Morgan, N. A. and Rego, L. L. (2009) Brand portfolio strategy and firm performance, *Journal of Marketing* 73:59–74.

24 Guiltinan, J. P. and Paul, G. W. (1982) *Marketing Management: Strategies and Programmes*, New York: McGraw-Hill, p. 31.

25 Day, G. S. (1977) 'Diagnosing the product portfolio', *Journal of Marketing* 41(2):30–1.

26 Dibb, S. and Simkin, L. (1996) *The Market Segmentation Workbook*, London: Thomson.

27 Day, G.S. (1985) *Analysis for Strategic Market Decisions*, p. 10.

28 Cravens, D. W. (1983) 'Strategic marketing's new challenge', *Business Horizons*, March–April, p. 19.

Chapter 13

1 Berry, L. L. and Parasuraman, A. (1991) *Marketing Services: Competing Through Quality*, New York: Free Press, p. 5.

2 Voss, G. B., Parasuraman, A. and Grewal, D. (1998) 'The roles of price, performance, and expectations in determining satisfaction in service exchanges', *Journal of Marketing* 64(4):46–61; Wirtz, J. and Bateson, J. E. G. (1999) 'Consumer satisfaction with services: integrating the environment perspective in services marketing into the traditional disconfirmation paradigm', *Journal of Business Research* 44(1):55–66.

3 Cowell, D. (1984) *The Marketing of Services*, London: Heinemann.

4 Based on Hoffman, K. D. and Bateson, J. E. G. (1997) *Essentials of Services Marketing*, Fort Worth, TX: Dryden Press, pp. 25–8; and Zeithaml, V. A., Parasuraman, A. and Berry, L. L. (1990) *Delivery Quality Service: Balancing Customer Perceptions and Expectations*, New York: Free Press.

5 Bateson, J. E. G. (1979) 'Why we need service marketing', in O. C. Ferrell, S. W. Brown and C. W. Lamb, Jr (eds) *Conceptual and Theoretical Development in Marketing*, Chicago, IL: American Marketing Association, pp. 131–46.

6 Zeithaml, V. A. (1981) 'How consumer evaluation processes differ between goods and services', in J. H. Donnelly and W. R. George (eds) *Marketing of Services*, Chicago, IL: American Marketing Association, pp. 186–90.

7 Berry, L. L., Zeithaml, V. A. and Parasuraman, A. (1984) 'Responding to demand fluctuations: key challenge for service businesses', in R. Belk et al. (eds) *AMA Educators' Proceedings*, Chicago, IL: American Marketing Association, pp. 231–4.

8 Moores, B. (1986) *Are They Being Served?* Oxford: Philip Allan.

9 Peter, J. P. and Donnelly, J. H. (2000) *A Preface to Marketing Management*, Burr Ridge, IL: McGraw-Hill/Irwin, p. 203.

10 Priluck, R. 'Relationship marketing can mitigate product and service failures', *Journal of Services Marketing* 17(3):37–52.

11 Arnett, D. B., German, S. D. and Hunt, S. D. (2003) 'The identity salience model of relationship marketing success: the case of nonprofit marketing', *Journal of Marketing* 67(2):89–106.

12 Reardon, J., Miller, C., Hasty, R. and Waguespack, B. J. (1996) 'A comparison of alternative theories of services marketing', *Journal of Marketing Theory and Practice* 4(4):61–71.

13 Lovelock, C. H. (1983) 'Classifying services to gain strategic marketing insights', *Journal of Marketing*, Summer, 15 pp. 9–20.

14 Lovelock, C. H. (1984) *Services Marketing*, Englewood Cliffs, NJ: Prentice Hall, pp. 46–64.

15 Wind, Y. (1987) 'Financial services: increasing your marketing productivity and profitability', *Journal of Services Marketing* 1(2):5–18.

16 Goodwin, C. (1997) 'Marketing strategies for services: globalization, client-orientation, deregulation', *International Journal of Research in Marketing*, 14(3):291–293.

17 Lovelock (see note 14), pp. 279–89.

18 Ibid.

19 Berry, Zeithaml and Parasuraman, (see note 7).

20 Zeithaml, V. A., Parasuraman, A. and Berry, L. L. (1990) *Delivering Quality Service: Balancing Customer Perceptions and Expectations*, New York: Free Press.

21 Parasuraman, A., Berry, L. L. and Zeithaml, V. A. (1990) 'An empirical examination of relationships in an extended service quality model', *Marketing Science Institute Working Paper Series,* Report no. 90–122, Cambridge, MA: Marketing Science Institute, p. 29.

22 Zeithaml, V. A., Berry, L. L. and Parasuraman, A. (1988) 'Communication and control processes in the delivery of service quality', *Journal of Marketing* 52(2):35–48.

23 Zeithaml, V. A., Berry, L. L. and Parasuraman, A. (1993) 'The nature and determinants of customer expectations of service', *Journal of the Academy of Marketing Science* 21(1):1–12.

24 Hartline, M. D. and Ferrell, O. C. (1993) 'Service quality implementation: the effects of organizational socialization and managerial actions on the behaviors of customer-contact employees', Marketing Science Institute working paper series, Report no. 92–122, Cambridge, MA: Marketing Science Institute, pp. 36.

25 Bitner, M. J. (1990) 'Evaluating service encounters: the effects of physical surroundings and employee responses', *Journal of Marketing* 54(2):70.

26 Hartline and Ferrell, (see note 24) pp. 17–19.

27 Glassman, M. and McAfee, B. (1992) 'Integrating the personnel and marketing functions: the challenge of the 1990s', *Business Horizons* 35(3):52–9.

28 Hilton, T., Hughes, T. and Chalcraft, D. (2012) 'Service co-creation and value realization', *Journal of Marketing Management* 28(13–14):1504–19.

29 Modi, P. (2012) 'Measuring market orientation in non-profit organizations', *Journal of Strategic Marketing* 20(5):447–60.

30 Blois, K. J. (1994) 'Marketing for non-profit organisations', in M. J. Baker (ed.) *The Marketing Book*, London: Heinemann, p. 405.

31 Whyte, J. (1985) 'Organisation, person and idea marketing as exchange', *Quarterly Review of Marketing* January:25–30.

32 Garrison, J. (1987) 'Telethons – the positive story', *Fund Raising Management* November:48–52.

33 Kotler, P. (1982) *Marketing for Non-profit Organisations*, 2nd ed., Englewood Cliffs, NJ: Prentice Hall, p. 37.

34 Ibid.

35 Davids, M. (1987) 'Doing well by doing good', *Public Relations Journal* July:17–21.

36 Pitt, L. F. and Abratt, R. (1987) 'Pricing in nonprofit organisations – a framework and conceptual overview', *Quarterly Review of Marketing*, Spring–Summer, 13–15.

37 Walker, K. (1984) 'Not-for-profit profits', *Forbes*, 10 September, 165.

Chapter 14

1 Anderson, E., Day, G. S. and Rangan, V. K. (1997) 'Strategic channel design', *Sloan Management Review* 38(4):59–69.

2 Montoya-Weiss, M. M., Ross, G. B. and Grewal, D. (2003) 'Determinant of online channel use and overall satisfaction with a relational, multichannel service provider', *Journal of the Academy of Marketing Science* 31(4):448–59.

3 Alderson, W. (1957) *Marketing Behavior and Executive Action*, Homewood, IL: Irwin, pp. 201–11.

4 Goodman, L. E and Dion, P. A. (2001) 'The determinants of commitment in the distributor–manufacturer relationship', *Industrial Marketing Management* 30(3):287–300.

5 Hlavacek, J. D. and McCuistion, T. J. (1983) 'Industrial distributors: when, who, and how?' *Harvard Business Review* March–April:97.

6 Erdem, S. A. and Harrison-Walker, L. J. (1997) 'Managing channel relationships: toward an identification of effective promotional strategies in vertical marketing systems', *Journal of Marketing Theory and Practice* 5(2):80–7.

7 Lewis, J. D. (1990) 'Using alliances to build market power', *Planning Review* 18(5):4–38.

8 Aspinwall, L. (1961) 'The marketing characteristics of goods', in *Four Marketing Theories*, Boulder: University of Colorado Press, pp. 27–32.

9 Magrath, A. J. (1991) 'Differentiating yourself via distribution', *Sales & Marketing Management* March:50–7.

10 Cravens, D. W., Ingram, T. N. and LaForge, R. W. (1991) 'Evaluating multiple sales channel strategies', *Journal of Business and Industrial Marketing* 6(3):3–4.

11 Rosenbloom, B. (1987) *Marketing Channels: A Management View*, Hinsdale, IL: Dryden, p. 160.

12 Ibid., p. 161.

13 Bowersox, D. J. and Cooper, M. B. (1992) *Strategic Marketing Channel Management*, New York: McGraw-Hill, pp. 177–8.

14 Alderson, W. (1965) *Dynamic Marketing Behavior*, Homewood, IL: Irwin, p. 239.

15 Seideman, T. (1998) 'Get with the program', *Inbound Logistics* September:29.

16 Skinner, S. J., Gassenheimer, J. B. and Kelley, S. W. (1992) 'Cooperation in supplier–dealer relations', *Journal of Retailing* 68(2):174–93; Hakansson, H. (1982) *International Marketing and Purchasing of Industrial Goods*, Chichester: Wiley.

17 Cronin, J. J., Jr, Baker, T. L. and Hawes, J. M. (1994) 'An assessment of the role performance measurement of power-dependency in marketing channels', *Journal of Business Research* 30(3):201–10.

18 Kumar, N., Scheer, L. K. and Steenkamp, J.-B. (1998) 'Interdependence, punitive capability, and the reciprocation of punitive actions in channel relationships', *Journal of Marketing Research* 35(2):225–35; Lusch, R. F. (1996) 'Interdependency, contracting, and relational behavior in marketing channels', *Journal of Marketing* 60(4):19–38.

19 El-Ansary, A. I. (1979) 'Perspectives on channel system performance', in R. F. Lusch and P. H. Zinszer (eds) *Contemporary Issues in Marketing Channels*, Norman, OK: University of Oklahoma Press, p. 50.

20 Michman, R. D. and Sibley, S. D. (1980) *Marketing Channels and Strategies*, Columbus, OH: Grid Publishing, pp. 412–17.

21 Keith, J. E., Jackson, D. W. and Crosby, L. A. (1990) 'Effect of alternative types of influence strategies under different dependence structures', *Journal of Marketing* 54(3):30–41.

22 Gaski, J. F. and Nevin, J. R. (1985) 'The differential effects of exercised and unexercised power sources in a marketing channel', *Journal of Marketing Research* 22(2):130–142.

Chapter 15

1 Casson, C. (1988) '1988 wholesaler giants; making all the right moves', *Building Supply Home Centers*, September, p. 56.

2 Tyagi, R. and Das, C. (1995) 'Manufacturer and warehouse selection for stable relationships in dynamic wholesaling and location problems', *International Journal of Physical Distribution and Logistics Management* 25(6):54–72.

3 Rosenbloom, B. (1987) *Marketing Channels: A Management View*, Hinsdale, IL: Dryden Press, p. 63.

4   *US Census of Wholesale Trade*, May 1985, p. 207.
5   Rosenbloom (see note 3), p. 61.
6   Ibid.
7   Ibid., p. 62.
8   Bonoma, T. V. (1983) 'Get more out of your trade shows', *Harvard Business Review*, January–February, 75–83.
9   Rosenbloom (see note 3), p. 185.
10 Rosenbloom (see note 3), p. 185.
11 Carter, H. (1972) *The Study of Urban Geography*, London: Edward Arnold, pp. 205–47.
12 Dawson, J. A. (1983) *Shopping Centre Development*, Harlow: Longman, Chapter 2.
13 Schiller, R. (1987) 'Out of town exodus', in *The Changing Face of British Retailing*, London: Newman Books, pp. 64–73.
14 Schneider, K. C. (1985) 'Telemarketing as a promotional tool – its effects and side effects', *Journal of Consumer Marketing* 2(1):29–39.
15 Bienstock, C. C. (1997) 'Measuring physical distribution service quality', *Journal of the Academy of Marketing Science* 25(1):31–44.
16 Guelzo, C. M. (1986) *Introduction to Logistics Management*, Englewood Cliffs, NJ: Prentice Hall, p. 32.
17 Mentzer, J. T., Gomes, R. and Krapfel, R. E., Jr (1989) 'Physical distribution service: a fundamental marketing concept?' *Journal of the Academy of Marketing Science* 17(1):59.
18 Rinehart, L. M., Cooper, M. B. and Wagenheim, G. D. (1989) 'Furthering the integration of marketing and logistics through customer service in the channel', *Journal of the Academy of Marketing Science* 17(1):63–71.
19 Taff, C. A. (1984) *Management of Physical Distribution and Transportation*, Homewood, IL: Irwin, p. 250.
20 Graham, J. (1989) 'IKEA furnishing its US identity', *Advertising Age* 14:79; Reynolds, J. (1988) 'IKEA: a competitive company with style', *Retail & Distribution Management (UK)* May/June:32–4.
21 Rinehart, Cooper and Wagenheim (see note 18), p. 67.
22 Guelzo (see note 16), pp. 35–36.
23 Taff (see note 19), p. 240.
24 Doherty, C., Maier, J. and Simkin, L. (1992) 'DPP modelling in retail marketing: an application', *OMEGA* 20(3):25–33.
25 Guelzo (see note 16), p. 102.
26 Adapted from Magee, J. F. (1967) *Physical Distribution Systems*, New York: McGraw-Hill, Inc. Reprinted by permission of the author.
27 The EOQ formula for the optimal order quantity is EOQ = 2DR/I, where EOQ = optimum average order size, D = total demand, R = cost of processing an order and I = cost of maintaining one unit of inventory per year. For a more complete description of EOQ methods and terminology, see McLaughlin, F. S. and Pickardt, R. C. (1978) *Quantitative Techniques for Management Decisions*, Boston, MA: Houghton Mifflin, pp. 104–19.
28 Burt, D. N. (1989) 'Managing suppliers up to speed', *Harvard Business Review* July–August:128.
29 Bennett, P. D. (ed.) (1988) *Dictionary of Marketing Terms*, Chicago, IL: American Marketing Association, p. 204.
30 Coyle, J. J., Bardi, E. and Langley, C. J., Jr (1988) *The Management of Business Logistics*, St Paul, MN: West, pp. 327–9.
31 Foster, T. A. and Barks, J. V. (1984) 'Here comes the best', *Distribution* September:25.
32 Gentry, J. J. (1996) 'Using logistics alliances to gain a strategic advantage in the marketplace', *Journal of Marketing Theory and Practice* 4(2): 37–44; Whipple, J. S. (1996) 'Logistical alliance formation motives: similarities and differences within the channel', *Journal of Marketing Theory and Practice* 4(2):26–36.

Chapter 16

1   Pollay, R. W. (1987) 'On the value of reflections on the values in "The distorted mirror"', *Journal of Marketing* 51(3):104–9.
2   Holbrook, M. B. (1987) 'Mirror, mirror, on the wall, what's unfair in the reflections on advertising?', *Journal of Marketing* 51(3):95–103.
3   Farmer, R. N. (1987) 'Would you want your granddaughter to marry a Taiwanese marketing man?' *Journal of Marketing* 51(4):111–16.
4   Coulson-Thomas, C. (1986) *Marketing Communications*, London: Heinemann; Ailawadi, K. L. and Neslin, S. A. (1998) 'The effect of promotion on consumption: buying more and consuming it faster', *Journal of Marketing Research* 35(3):390–8.
5   Engel, J., Warshaw, M. and Kinnear, T. (1994) *Promotional Strategy: Managing the Marketing Communications Process*, Boston, MA: Irwin.
6   Rossiter, J. and Percy, L. (1987) *Advertising and Promotion Management*, New York: McGraw-Hill.
7   In case you do not read Chinese, this says, 'In the factory we make cosmetics, and in the store we sell hope'. Prepared by Chih Kang Wang.
8   Shimp, T. A. and Delozier, M. W. (1986) *Promotion Management and Marketing Communication*, Hinsdale, IL: Dryden Press, pp. 25–6.
9   Wagner, J. A., Klein, N. M. and Keith, J. E. (2001) 'Selling strategies: the effects of suggesting a decision structure to novice and expert buyers', *Journal of the Academy of Marketing Science* 29(3):289–306.
10 McClenahen, J. S. (1995) 'How can you possibly say that?' *Industry Week* 17:17–19.
11 Szymanski, D. M. (2001) 'Modality and offering effects in sales presentations for a good versus a service', *Journal of the Academy of Marketing Science* 29(2):179–89.

12 Jones, D. (1994) 'Setting promotional goals: a communications' relationship model', *Journal of Consumer Marketing* 11(1):38–49.

13 Adapted from Rogers, E. M. (1962) *Diffusion of Innovations*, New York: Free Press, pp. 81–6, 98–102.

14 Marks, L. J. and Kamins, M. A. (1988) 'Product sampling and advertising sequence, belief strength, confidence and attitudes', *Journal of Marketing Research* 25(3):266–81.

15 Rogers (see note 13), pp. 247–50.

16 Rossiter, J. and Percy, L. (1987) *Advertising and Promotion Management*, New York: McGraw-Hill.

17 Shannon, J. R. (1996) 'The new promotions mix: a proposed paradigm, process, and application', *Journal of Marketing Theory and Practice* 4(1):56–69.

18 Lane, V. R. (2000) 'The impact of ad repetition and ad content on consumer perceptions of incongruent extensions', *Journal of Marketing* 64(2):80–91.

19 Flandin, M., Martin, E. and Simkin, L. (1992) 'Advertising effectiveness research: a survey of agencies, clients and conflicts', *International Journal of Advertising* 11(3):203–14.

20 MacKenzie, S. B., Podsakoff, P. M. and Rich, G. A. (2001) 'Transformational and transactional leadership and sales person performance', *Journal of the Academy of Marketing Science* 29(2):115–34.

21 Hunt, T. and Grunig, J. (1994) *Public Relations Techniques*, Fort Worth, TX: Harcourt Brace.

22 Dibb, S., Simkin, L. and Vancini, A. (1996) 'Competition, strategy, technology and people: the challenges facing PR', *International Journal of Advertising* 15(2):116–27.

23 This definition is adapted from Luick, J. F. and Ziegler, W. L. (1968) *Sales Promotion and Modern Merchandising*, New York: McGraw-Hill, p. 4.

24 Kerin, R. A. and Cron, W. L. (1987) 'Assessing trade show functions and performance: an exploratory study', *Journal of Marketing* 51(3):87–94.

25 Kavanagh, M. (1999) 'Free ISPs spur net market growth', *Marketing Week*, 11 March, pp. 30–1.

26 Evans, M. J., O'Malley, L. and Patterson, M. (1996) 'Direct marketing communications in the UK: a study of growth, past, present and future', *Journal of Marketing Communications* 2(1):51–65.

27 *Marketing Week*, 5 July, 1996, p. 13.

28 Achenbaum, A. A. and Mitchel, F. K. (1987) 'Pulling away from push marketing', *Harvard Business Review* May–June:38.

Chapter 17

1 Reid, M. (2003) 'IMC – performance relationship: further insight and evidence from the Australian marketplace', *International Journal of Advertising* 22(2):227–49.

2 Dibb, S., Simkin, L. and Yuen, R. (1994) 'Pan-European advertising: think Europe – act local', *International Journal of Advertising* 13(2):125–36.

3 *Students' Briefs* (1988) London: The Advertising Association.

4 Hume, S. (1989) 'Pizza Hut is frosted; new ad takes slap at McDonald's test product', *Advertising Age*, 18 September, 4.

5 Douglas, T. (1985) *The Complete Guide to Advertising*, London: Macmillan.

6 Jackson, P., Adsearch, Richmond-upon-Thames.

7 Bickerton, P., Bickerton, M. and Pardesi, U. (1996) *Cybermarketing*, Oxford: Butterworth-Heinemann.

8 Littlefield, J. E. and Kirkpatrick, C. A. (1970) *Advertising Mass Communication in Marketing*, Boston, MA: Houghton Mifflin, p. 178.

9 Dunn, S. W. and Barban, A. M. (1986) *Advertising: Its Role in Modern Marketing*, 6th ed., Hinsdale, IL: Dryden Press, p. 493.

10 Quinn, P. (1988) *Low Budget Advertising*, London: Heinemann.

11 Flandin, M., Martin, E. and Simkin, L. (1992) 'Advertising effectiveness research: a survey of agencies, clients and conflicts', *International Journal of Advertising* 11(3):203–14.

12 Goldberg, M. E. and Gorn, G. J. (1987) 'Happy and sad TV programmes: how they affect reactions to commercials', *Journal of Consumer Research* 14(3):387–403.

13 *Marketing*, 24 May 1990, p. 5.

14 *Public Relations Practice – Its Role and Parameters* (1984) London: The Institute of Public Relations.

15 Wragg, D., (1987) *Public Relations for Sales and Marketing Management*, London: Kogan Page.

16 White, J. (1991) *How to Understand and Manage Public Relations*, London: Business Books.

17 Dibb, S., Simkin, L. and Vancini, A. (1996) 'Competition, strategy, technology and people: the challenges facing PR', *International Journal of Advertising* 15(2):116–27.

18 Sleight, S. (1989) *Sponsorship: What It Is and How to Use It*, Maidenhead: McGraw-Hill.

19 Crowley, M. G. (1991) 'Prioritising the sponsorship audience', *European Journal of Marketing* 25(11): 11–21.

20 Thwaites, D., Lowe, B., Monkhouse, L.L. and Barnes, B. R. (2012) 'The impact of negative publicity on celebrity ad endorsement', *Psychology and Marketing* 29(9):663–73.

Chapter 18

1 *Marketing*, 28 June 1990, p. 13.

2 Cummins, J. (1989) *Sales Promotion*, London: Kogan Page.

3 Gable, M. and Reed, B. J. (1987) 'The current status of women in professional selling', *Journal of Personal Selling & Sales Management* 7(1):33–9.

4   Weeks, W. A. and Muehing, D. D. (1987) 'Students' perceptions of personal selling', *Industrial Marketing Management* 16(2):145–51.

5   Lancaster, G. and Jobber, D. (1994) *Selling and Sales Management*, London: Pitman.

6   'Getting ahead and staying ahead as the competition heats up' (1987) *Agency Sales Magazine*, June, 38–42.

7   De Winter, C. (1988) *Telephone Selling*, London: Heinemann.

8   Lorge, S. (1998) 'The best ways to prospect', *Sales and Marketing Management*, January, 80.

9   Leigh, T. W. and McGraw, P. F. (1989) 'Mapping the procedural knowledge of industrial sales personnel: a script-theoretic investigation', *Journal of Marketing* 53(1):16–34.

10 Ibid.

11 Moncrief, W. C. (1988) 'Five types of industrial sales jobs', *Industrial Marketing Management* 17(2):161–167.

12 Magrath, J. (1988) 'Are you overdoing "lean and mean"?' *Sales & Marketing Management* January: 46–53.

13 Adams, T. (1988) *Successful Sales Management*, London: Heinemann.

14 Coleman, p. 6, 21.

15 Fleenor, P. C. (1987) 'Selling and sales management in action: assessment centre selection of sales representatives', *Journal of Personal Selling & Sales Management* 7(1):57–9.

16 Darmon, R. Y. (1987) 'The impact of incentive compensation on the salesperson's work habits: an economic model', *Journal of Personal Selling & Sales Management* 7(1):21–32.

17 Hart, S. H., Moncrief, W. C. and Parasuraman, A. (1989) 'An empirical investigation of salespeople's performance, effort and selling method during a sales contest', *Journal of the Academy of Marketing Science* 17(1):29–39.

18 Tzempelikos, N. and Gounaris, S. (2013) 'Approaching key account management for a long-term perspective', *Journal of Strategic Marketing* 21(2):179–98.

19 Luick, J. F. and Ziegler, W. L. (1968) *Sales Promotion and Modern Merchandising*, New York: McGraw-Hill; Schultz, D. E. and Robinson, W. A. (1982) *Sales Promotion Management*, Chicago, IL: Crain Books.

20 Boland, W. A., Connell, P. M. and Erickson, L. – M. (2012) 'Children's response to sales promotions and their impact on purchase behaviour', *Journal of Consumer Psychology* 22:272–9.

21 Cummins, J. (1989) *Sales Promotion*, London: Kogan Page.

22 Smith, P. R. (1993) *Marketing Communication: An Integrated Approach*, London: Kogan Page.

23 Peattie, K. and Peattie, S. (1993) 'Sales promotion: playing to win?' *Journal of Marketing Management* 9(3):225–69.

24 Phillips, W. E. and Robinson, B. (1989) 'Continued sales (price) promotion destroys brands: yes; no', *Marketing News*, 16 January, 4, 8.

25 Cummins, J. (1989) *Sales Promotion*, London: Kogan Page.

26 Babakus, E., Tat, P. and Cunningham, W. (1988) 'Coupon redemption: a motivational perspective', *Journal of Consumer Marketing* 5(2):37–43.

27 Campanella, D. (1987) 'Sales promotion: coupon-mania', *Marketing and Media Decisions*, June, 118–22.

28 Porter, A. L. (2000) 'Direct mail's lessons for electronic couponers', *Marketing Management Journal*, Spring/Summer, 107–15.

29 Campanella (see note 27), pp. 118–22.

30 Ibid.

31 Agnew, J. (1987) 'P-O-P [P-O-S] displays are becoming a matter of consumer convenience', *Marketing News*, 9 October, 16.

32 Fahey, A. (1989) 'Study shows retailers rely on P-O-P [P-O-S]', *Advertising Age*, 27 November, 83.

33 Tat, P., Cunningham, W. A. and Babakus, E. (1988) 'Consumer perceptions of rebates', *Journal of Advertising Research* 28(4):48.

34 Anthea, G. (1987) 'Sales promotion putting up the premium', *Marketing*, 16 April.

35 Colford, S. W. (1989) 'Marriott sets largest promo', *Advertising Age*, 2 October, 58.

36 Norris, E. (1983) 'Everyone will grab at a chance to win', *Advertising Age*, 22 August, M10.

37 Crimmins, E. (1983) 'A co-op myth: it is a tragedy that stores don't spend all their accruals', *Sales & Marketing Management*, 7 February, 72–3.

38 Bird, D. (1989) *Commonsense Direct Marketing*, London: Kogan Page.

39 Duncan, T. (1998) 'A communication-based marketing model for managing relationships', *Journal of Marketing* 62(2):1–13; Peltier, J. W. (1997) 'The use of need-based segmentation for developing segment-specific direct marketing strategies', *Journal of Direct Marketing* 11(4): 53–62.

40 North, B. (1993) 'Consumer companies take direct stance', *Marketing*, 20 May, 24–5.

41 Schofield, A. (1995) 'The definition of direct marketing: a rejoinder to Bauer and Miglautsch', *Journal of Direct Marketing* 9(2):37–8.

42 McGoldrick, P. (1997) *Retail Marketing*, Maidenhead: McGraw-Hill.

43 Evans, M. J., O'Malley, L. and Patterson, M. (1996) 'Direct marketing communications in the UK: a study of growth, past, present and future', *Journal of Marketing Communications* 2(1):51–65.

44 O'Malley, L. (1999) *Maurice Patterson and Martin Evans, Exploring Direct Marketing*, London: ITBP, p. 9.

Chapter 19

1 Rigby, D. (2011) 'The Future of Shopping', *Harvard Business Review*, December.

Chapter 20

1 Gourville, J. and Soman, D. (2002) 'Pricing and the psychology of consumption', *Harvard Business Review* 80(9):91–6.
2 Lichtenstein, D., Ridgway, N. M. and Netemeyer, R. G. (1993) 'Price perceptions and consumer shopping behavior: a field study', *Journal of Marketing Research* 30(2):234–45.
3 Desiraju, R. (1999) 'Strategic service pricing and yield management', *Journal of Marketing* 63(1):44–56.
4 Samier, S. (1987) 'Pricing in marketing strategies of US and foreign based companies', *Journal of Business Research* 15(1):15–23.
5 Winkler, J. (1987) 'Pricing', in M. Baker (ed.) *The Marketing Book*, London: Heinemann.
6 JCB company literature, 1992.
7 Guiltinan, J. P. (1987) 'The price-bundling of services: a normative framework', *Journal of Marketing* 51(2):74–85.
8 Zeithaml, V. A. (1988) 'Consumer perceptions of price, quality and value: a means-end model and synthesis of evidence', *Journal of Marketing* 52:2–22.
9 Anderson, E. and Simester, D. (2003) 'Mind your pricing cues', *Harvard Business Review* September:97–103.
10 Griffith, D. E. (1997) 'The price of competitiveness in competitive pricing', *Journal of the Academy of Marketing Science* 25(2): 109–116; Sivakumar, K. (1997) 'Quality tier competition: how price change influences brand choice and category choice', *Journal of Marketing* 61(3):71–84.
11 Wilcox, J. B., Howell, R. D., Kuzdrall, P. and Britney, R. (1987) 'Price quantity discounts: some implications for buyers and sellers', *Journal of Marketing* 51(3):60–1.
12 Eccles, R. G. (1983) 'Control with fairness in transfer pricing', *Harvard Business Review* November–December:149–61.
13 Morris, M. H. (1987) 'Separate prices as a marketing tool', *Industrial Marketing Management* 16(2):79–86.
14 Trout, J. (1998) 'Prices: simple guidelines to get them right', *The Journal of Business Strategy* 19(6):13–16.
15 Ansari, A., Siddarth, S. and Weinberg, C. B. (1996) 'Pricing a bundle of products or services: the case of nonprofits', *Journal of Marketing Research* 33(1):86–93.

16 Reprinted from Bennett, P. D. (ed.) (1988) *Dictionary of Marketing Terms*, Chicago, IL: American Marketing Association, p. 54. Used by permission.
17 Ibid., p. 150. Used by permission.
18 Griffith, D. E. (1997) 'The price of competitiveness in competitive pricing', *Journal of the Academy of Marketing Science* 25(2):109–16.
19 http://ec.europa.eu/trade/policy/accessing-markets/trade-defence/actions-against-imports-into-the-eu/anti-dumping/index_en.htm

Chapter 21

1 Doyle, P. and Saunders, J. (1985) 'Market segmentation and positioning in specialised industrial markets', *Journal of Marketing* 49(2):24–32.
2 Hultink, E. J. (1997) 'Industrial new product launch strategies and product development performance', *The Journal of Product Innovation Management* 14(4):243–57.
3 Anderson, E. and Coughlan, A. T. (1987) 'International market entry and expansion via independent or integrated channels of distribution', *Journal of Marketing* 51(1):71–82.
4 Hlavacek, J. D. and McCuiston, T. J. (1983) 'Industrial distributors: when, who, and how?' *Harvard Business Review* March–April:97.
5 Wise, R. and Morrison, D. (2000) 'Beyond the exchange: the future of B2B', *Harvard Business Review* 78(6):86–99.
6 Frazier, G. L., Spekman, R. E. and O'Neal, C. R. (1988) 'Just-in-time exchange relationships in industrial markets', *Journal of Marketing* 52(4):52–67.
7 McQuiston, D. H. (1989) 'Novelty, complexity and importance as casual determinants of industrial buyer behavior', *Journal of Marketing* 53(2):66–79.
8 Jacobson, R. and Aaker, D. A. (1987) 'The strategic role of product quality', *Journal of Marketing* 51(4):31–44.
9 Brooks, D. G. (1978) 'Bidding for the sake of follow-on contracts', *Journal of Marketing* 42(1):35.
10 Cowell, D. (1994) *The Marketing of Services*, Oxford: Butterworth-Heinemann.
11 Lovelock, C. (1992) *Managing Services*, Englewood Cliffs, NJ: Prentice Hall.
12 Van Waterschoot, W. and Van den Bulte, C. (1992) 'The 4P classification of the marketing mix revisited', *Journal of Marketing* 56(4):83–93.
13 Shostack, G. L. (1977) 'Breaking free from product marketing', *Journal of Marketing* 41(2):73–80.
14 Onkvisit, S. and Shaw, J. J. (1989) 'Service marketing: image, branding, and competition', *Business Horizons* 32(1):16.
15 Zeithaml, V. A. (1988) 'Consumer perceptions of price, quality, and value: a means-end model and synthesis of evidence', *Journal of Marketing* 52(3):2–22.

16 Berry, L. L. (1987) '8 keys to top service at financial institutions', *American Banker*, August.

17 Parasuraman, A., Zeithaml, V. A. and Berry, L. L. (1988) 'SERVQUAL: a multiple item scale for measuring consumer perceptions of service quality', *Journal of Retailing* 64(1):12–37.

18 Brown, S. W. and Swartz, T. A. (1989) 'A gap analysis of professional service quality', *Journal of Marketing* 53(2):92–8.

19 Ibid.

20 Shostack, G. L. (1987) 'Service positioning through structural change', *Journal of Marketing* 51(1): 34–43.

21 George, W. R. and Berry, L. L. (1981) 'Guidelines for the advertising of services', *Business Horizons* 24(4):52–6.

22 Dibb, S. and Simkin, L. (1993) 'The strength of branding and positioning in services', *International Journal of Service Industry Management* 4(1): 25–33.

23 Dibb, S. and Simkin, L. (1993) 'Strategy and tactics: marketing leisure facilities', *The Service Industries Journal* 13(3):110–24; Dibb and Simkin (see note 22) pp. 25–35.

24 Heskett, J. L. (1987) 'Lessons in the service sector', *Harvard Business Review* 65(2):118–26.

25 George and Berry (see note 21), pp. 55–70.

26 George, W. R. and Kelly, J. P. (1983) 'The promotion and selling of services', *Business* 33(3):14–20.

27 Rathmell, J. M. (1974) *Marketing in the Services Sector*, Cambridge, MA: Winthrop, p. 100.

28 George and Kelly (see note 26), pp. 14–20; George and Berry (see note 21) pp. 55–70.

29 Van Doren, D. C. and Smith, L. W. (1987) 'Marketing in the restructured professional services field', *Journal of Services Marketing* 1(1):69–70.

30 Guiltinan, J. R. (1987) 'The price bundling of services: a normative framework', *Journal of Marketing* 51(2):74–85.

31 Donnelly, J. H., Jr (1976) 'Marketing intermediaries in channels of distribution for services', *Journal of Marketing* 40(1):55–70.

32 Ibid.

33 Dibb and Simkin (see note 22), pp. 110–24.

34 Payne, A. (1993) *The Essence of Services Marketing*, Hemel Hempstead: Prentice Hall.

35 Keegan, W. J. (1989) *Global Marketing Management*, 4th ed., Englewood Cliffs, NJ: Prentice Hall, pp. 378–82.

36 Egan,C., De Montfort University.

37 Norvell, D. G. and Morey, R. (1983) 'Ethno-domination in the channels of distribution of Third World nations', *Journal of the Academy of Marketing Science* 11(3):204–35.

38 Anderson, E. and Coughlan, A. T. (1987) 'International market entry and expansion via independent or integrated channels of distribution', *Journal of Marketing* 51(1):71–82.

39 Jobber, D. (1995) *Principles and Practice of Marketing*, London: McGraw-Hill.

40 Dibb, S., Simkin, L. and Bradley, J. (1996) *The Marketing Planning Workbook*, London: Routledge.

Chapter 22

1 Pulendran, S., Speed, R. and Widing, R. E., II (2003) 'Marketing planning, orientation and business performance', *European Journal of Marketing* 37(3,4):476–501.

2 Leeflang, P. S. H. and de Mortanges, C. P. (1996) 'An empirical investigation of marketing planning', *Journal of Euro-Marketing* 6(1):77–101.

3 Dibb, S., Simkin, L. and Bradley, J. (1996) *The Marketing Planning Workbook*, London: Thomson.

4 Simkin, L. (1996) 'People and processes in marketing planning: the benefits of controlling implementation in marketing planning', *Journal of Marketing Management* 12(5):375–90; Simkin, L. (2000) 'Delivering effective marketing planning', *Targeting, Measurement and Analysis for Marketing* 8(4):335–50; and Simkin, L. (2002) 'Barriers impeding effective implementation of marketing plans – a new research and training agenda', *Journal of Business and Industrial Marketing* 17(1):8–22.

5 Luck, D. J., Ferrell, O. C. and Lucas, G (1989) *Marketing Strategy and Plans*, 3rd ed., Englewood Cliffs, NJ: Prentice Hall, p. 328.

6 Sashittal, H. C. and Jassawalla, A. R. (2001) 'Marketing implementation in smaller organisations: definition, framework, and propositional inventory', *Journal of the Academy of Marketing Science* 29(1):50–69.

7 McDonald, M. (1989) *Marketing Plans: How to Prepare Them, How to Use Them*, Oxford: Butterworth-Heinemann.

8 Bowman, D. and Gatignon, H. (1995) 'Determinants of competitor response time to a new product introduction', *Journal of Marketing Research* 32(1):42–53.

9 Simkin, L. and Chang, A. (1997) 'Understanding competitors' strategies', *Marketing Intelligence & Planning* 15(3):124–34.

10 Wind, Y. and Robertson, T. S. (1983) 'Marketing strategy: new directions for theory and research', *Journal of Marketing* 47:12–25.

11 Sashittal and Jassawalla (see note 6).

12 Simkin, L. (1996) 'Addressing organisational prerequisites in marketing planning programmes', *Marketing Intelligence and Planning* 14(5):39–46.

13 Simkin, L. (2002) 'Barriers impeding effective implementation of marketing plans: a new research

and training agenda', *Journal of Business and Industrial Marketing* 17(1):8–22.

14 Simkin, L. (2000) 'Delivering effective marketing planning', *Targeting, Measurement and Analysis for Marketing* 8(4):335–50.

15 Dibb, S. and Simkin, L. (1994) *The Marketing Casebook*, London: Routledge.

16 Hurwood, D., Grossman, E. S. and Bailey, E. (1978) *Sales Forecasting*, New York: Conference Board, p. 2.

17 Tull, D. S. and Hawkins, D. I. (1990) *Marketing Research*, New York: Macmillan.

18 Marino, K. E. (1986) *Forecasting Sales and Planning Profits*, Chicago, IL: Probus Publishing, p. 155.

19 Hurwood, Grossman and Bailey (see note 16), p. 61.

20 Naert, P. and Leeflang, P. (1978) *Building Implementable Marketing Models*, Leiden: Martinus Nijhoff.

21 Accurate Business Forecasting (Boston's Harvard Business Review Booklet, 1991).

22 Band, W. A. (1984) 'A marketing audit provides an opportunity for improvement', *Sales & Marketing Management in Canada* March:24–6.

Chapter 23

1 Despande, R. and Webster, F. E., Jr (1989) 'Organisational culture and marketing: defining the research agenda', *Journal of Marketing* 53(1):3–15.

2 Hutt, M. D. and Speh, T. W. (1984) 'The marketing strategy centre: diagnosing the industrial marketer's inter-disciplinary role', *Journal of Marketing* 48(4):16–53.

3 Piercy, N. F. (1998) 'Marketing implementation: the implications of marketing paradigm weakness for the strategy execution process', *Journal of the Academy of Marketing Science* 26(3):222–36.

4 Thomas, K. W. and Velthouse, B. A. (1990) 'Cognitive elements of empowerment: an "interpretive" model of intrinsic task motivation', *Academy of Management Review* 15(4):666–81.

5 Ferrell, O. C., Lucas, G. H. and Luck, D. J. (1994) *Strategic Marketing Management: Text and Cases*, Cincinnati, OH: South-Western Publishing, pp. 193–4.

6 Hartline, M. D. and Ferrell, O. C. (1993) 'Service quality implementation: the effects of organizational socialization and managerial actions on the behaviors of customer-contact employees', Marketing Science Institute working paper series, Report no. 93–122, Cambridge, MA: Marketing Science Institute, pp. 36–48.

7 Ibid., pp. 36–40.

8 Ulrich, D. (1987) 'Strategic human resources planning: why and how?' *Human Resources Planning* 10(1):25–57.

9 Lysonski, S. (1985) 'A boundary theory investigation of the product manager's role', *Journal of Marketing* 49(1):26–40.

10 Simkin, L. (2000) 'Delivering effective marketing planning', *Targeting, Measurement and Analysis for Marketing* 8(4):335–50.

11 McDonald, M. (1992) 'Ten barriers to marketing planning', *Journal of Business & Industrial Marketing* 7(1):5–18; McDonald, M. (1992) 'Strategic marketing planning: a state-of-the-art review', *Marketing Intelligence & Planning* 10(4):4–22; Simkin, L. (1996) 'People and processes in marketing planning: the benefits of controlling implementation', *Journal of Marketing Management* 12:375–90; and Simkin, L. (1996) 'Addressing organisational pre-requisites in marketing planning programmes', *Marketing Intelligence & Planning* 14 (5):39–46.

12 Dibb, S. and Simkin, L. (2001) 'Overcoming segmentation barriers: four case studies', *Industrial Marketing Management* 30(8):609–25.

13 Simkin, L. (2002) 'Barriers impeding effective implementation of marketing plans – a new research and training agenda', *Journal of Business and Industrial Marketing* 17(1):8–22.

14 Based on Walker, O. C., Jr and Ruekert, R. W. (1987) 'Marketing's role in the implementation of business strategies: a critical review and conceptual framework', *Journal of Marketing* 51(3):15–33.

15 Piercy, N. F. (1998) 'Marketing implementation: the implications of marketing paradigm weakness for the strategy execution process', *Journal of the Academy of Marketing Science* 26(3):222–36; Strutton, D. (1997) 'Marketing strategies: new approaches, new techniques', *Journal of the Academy of Marketing Science*, Summer: 261.

16 Howard, R. (1990) 'Values make the company: an interview with Robert Haas', *Harvard Business Review*, September–October, 132–44.

17 Ferrell, O. C., Lucas, G. H. and Luck, D. (1994) *Strategic Marketing Management*, pp. 190–200.

18 Glassman, M. and McAfee, B. (1992) 'Integrating the personnel and marketing functions: the challenge of the 1990s', *Business Horizons* May–June:52–9.

19 Ferrell, Lucas and Luck (see note 17), pp. 190–200.

20 Jones, D. C. (1987) 'Motivation the catalyst in profit formula', *National Underwriter*, 13 July, 10–13.

21 McAdams, J. (1987) 'Rewarding sales and marketing performance', *Management Review*, April, 36.

22 Kotler, P., Armstrong, G., Saunders, J. and Wong, V. (1998) *Principles of Marketing*, Hemel Hempstead: Prentice Hall.

23 Christopher, M., Payne, A. and Ballantyne, D. (1991) *Relationship Marketing*, Oxford:

Butterworth-Heinemann; Grönroos, C. (1994) 'From marketing mix to relationship marketing: towards a paradigm shift in marketing', *Management Decision* 32(2):4–20.

24 Berry, L. L. (1983) 'Relationship marketing', in L. L. Berry, G. L. Shostack and G. Upah (eds) *Emerging Perspectives on Services*, Chicago, IL: American Marketing Association, pp. 25–8.

25 Payne, A. (1994) 'Relationship marketing – making the customer count', *Managing Service Quality* 4(6):29–31.

26 Harris, L. C. and Ogbonna, E. (2001) 'Strategic human resource management, market orientation and organizational performance', *Journal of Business Research* 51(2):157–66.

27 George, W. R. (1990) 'Internal marketing and organizational behaviour: a partnership in developing customer conscious employees at every level', *Journal of Business Research* 20:63–70; Lings, I. and Brooks, F. (1998) 'Implementing and measuring the effectiveness of internal marketing', *Journal of Marketing Management* 14(4):325–51.

28 Maxwell, R. and Knox, S. (2009) 'Motivating employees to "live the brand": a comparative case study of employer brand attractiveness within the firm', *Journal of Marketing Management* 25(9–10): 893–907.

29 Gummesson, E. (1987) 'Using internal marketing to develop a new culture', *Journal of Business and Industrial Marketing* 2(3):23–8.

30 Reynoso, J. and Moores, B. (1996) 'Internal relationships', in F. Buttle (ed.) *Relationship Marketing: Theory and Practice*, London: Chapman.

31 Wieseke, J., Ahearne, M., Lam, S. K. and van Dick, R. (2009) 'The role of leaders in internal marketing', *Journal of Marketing*, 73:123–45.

32 Dibb, S. and Simkin, L. (2004) *Marketing Briefs*, Oxford: Elsevier Butterworth-Heinemann.

33 Adapted from Jablonski, J. R. (1990) *Implementing Total Quality Management*, Albuquerque, NM: Technical Management Consortium.

34 Hartline and Ferrell (see note 6) pp. 36–40.

35 Singh, J. (2000) 'Performance productivity and quality of frontline employees in service organizations', *Journal of Marketing* 64(2):15–34.

36 Crosby, P. B. (1979) *Quality is Free – The Art of Making Quality Certain*, New York: McGraw-Hill, pp. 9–10.

37 Piercy, N. (1992) *Market-Led Strategic Change*, Oxford: Butterworth-Heinemann.

38 Steingraber, F. (1990) 'Total quality management: a new look at a basic issue', *Vital Speeches of the Day*, May, 415–16.

39 Hartline and Ferrell (see note 6) pp. 36–48.

40 'Higher education in doughnuts' (1988), *Ann Arbor News*, 9 March, B7.

41 Jaworski, B. J. (1988) 'Toward a theory of marketing control: environmental context, control types, and consequences', *Journal of Marketing* 52(3):23–39.

42 See Haimann, T., Scott, W. G. and Connor, P. E. (1985) *Management*, 5th ed., Boston, MA: Houghton Mifflin, pp. 478–92.

43 'Carbonates and concentrates' (1990), *Marketing Intelligence*, January, 2.10–2.17.

44 Kelly, K. and Gross, N. (1988) 'A weakened Komatsu tries to come back swinging', *Business Week*, 22 February, 48.

45 Doyle, P. (2000) *Value-Based Marketing*, Chichester: Wiley.

46 Flack, J.-A. (1999) 'Measure of success', *Marketing Week*, 4 March, 45–49.

Chapter 24

1 'Growth in piracy reverses trend' (2001) *Star Tribune*, 28 May, D7.

2 'FSA to spotlight health offenders' (2004) *Marketing*, 26 May, 4.

3 Thorne, D., Ferrell, L. and Ferrell, O. C. (2003) *Business and Society: A Strategic Approach to Corporate Citizenship*, Boston, MA: Houghton Mifflin.

4 B&Q, www.diy.com/one-planet-home, 16 April 2001.

5 Carroll, A. (1991) 'The pyramid of corporate social responsibility: toward the moral management of organisational stakeholders', *Business Horizons* 34(4):42.

6 www.pampers.co.uk.

7 Thorne, Ferrell, and Ferrell (see note 3).

8 www.fdf.org.uk/priorities.

9 www.greenguide.co.uk/thegreenguide.

10 'Yes, we have no bananas: Rainforest Alliance certifies Chiquita bananas' (2003), *Ag Journal*, 16 December, www.agjournal.com/story.cfm?story_id=1047.

11 Hawken, P. and McDonough, W. (1993) 'Seven steps to doing good business', *Inc.*, November, 79–90.

12 Bougie, R., Pieters, R. and Zeelenberg, M. (2003) 'Angry customers don't come back, they get back: the experience and behavioral implications of anger and dissatisfaction in services', *Journal of the Academy of Marketing Science* 31(4):377–93.

13 Thorne, Ferrell and Ferrell (see note 3).

14 Carson, T. L. (2003) 'Self-interest and business ethics: some lessons of the recent corporate scandals', *Journal of Business Ethics* 43(4):389–94.

15 '2002 Cone Corporate Citizenship Study' (2002) Cone, Inc., press release, 22 October, www.coneinc.com/Pages/pr_13.html.

16 'Hasbro: do not pass go, Ghettopoly' (2003) *USA Today*, 23 October, www.usatoday.com.

17   Leonidou, L. C., Leonidou, C. N. and Kvasova, O. (2013) 'Cultural drivers and trust outcomes of consumer perceptions of organizational unethical marketing behaviour', *European Journal of Marketing*, 47 (3/4):25–6.

18   Sprott, D. E., Manning, K. C. and Miyazaki, A. D. (2003) 'Grocery price setting and quantity surcharges', *Journal of Marketing* 67(3):34–46.

19   Bottemiller, H. (2010) 'China launches food safety commission', *Food Safety News*, 11 February.

20   Durham, G. (2000) 'Study finds lying, cheating in teens', *AOL News*, 16 October.

21   Cunningham, P. H. and Ferrell, O. C. (1998) 'The influence of role stress on unethical behavior by personnel involved in the marketing research process', working paper, Queens University, Ontario, p. 35.

22   Weiss, J. W. (1994) *Business Ethics: A Managerial, Stakeholder Approach*, Belmont, CA: Wadsworth, p. 13.

23   Ethics Resource Center (2000) *The Ethics Resource Center's 2000 National Business Ethics Survey: How Employees Perceive Ethics at Work*, Washington, DC: Ethics Resource Center, p. 85.

24   Ferrell, O. C., Gresham, L. G. and Fraedrich, J. (1989) 'A synthesis of ethical decision models for marketing', *Journal of Macromarketing* Fall:58–9.

25   Babin, B. J., Boles, J. S. and Robin, D. P. (2000) 'Representing the perceived ethical work climate among marketing employees', *Journal of the Academy of Marketing Science* 28(3):345–58.

26   Ethics Resource Center (2000) *National Business Ethics Survey*, p. 38.

27   Ferrell, Gresham and Fraedrich (see note 22).

28   Chonko, L. B. and Hunt, S. D. (2000) 'Ethics and marketing management: a retrospective and prospective commentary', *Journal of Business Research* 50(3):235–44.

29   Trevino, L. K. and Youngblood, S. (1990) 'Bad apples in bad barrels: a causal analysis of ethical decision-making behavior', *Journal of Applied Psychology* 75(4):378–85.

30   Clark, M. M. (2003) 'Corporate ethics programs make a difference, but not the only difference', *HR News*, 23 May, www.shrm.org/hrnews_published /archives/CMS_004611.asp.

31   Laczniak, G. R. and Murphy, P. E. (1993) *Ethical Marketing Decisions: The Higher Road*, Boston, MA: Allyn & Bacon, p. 14.

32   Sir Cadbury, A. (1987) 'Ethical managers make their own rules', *Harvard Business Review*, September/October, 33.

33   Baker, R. 'Pepsi makes sustainability commitment', *Marketing Week*, 20 January, 9.

34   Tapscott, D. and Ticoll, D. (2003) 'The naked corporation', *Wall Street Journal*, 14 October, http://online.wsj.com/.

35   Ferrell, O. C., Fraedrich, J. and Ferrell, L. (2002) *Business Ethics*, pp. 27–30.

36   Maignan, I. (1997) 'Antecedents and benefits of corporate citizenship: a comparison of US and French businesses', PhD dissertation, University of Memphis.

37   www.smokefreeliverpool.com.

38   'Corporate Citizenship Study' (2009) *Burson -Marsteller*, www.burson-marsteller.com /Innovation_ and_insights/blogs_and_podcasts /BM_Blog/Documents/Corporate%20 Citizenship%20 Execurtive%20Summary.pdf, accessed 10 February 2010, pp. 3–7.

39   Lohie-MacIver, L. and Piacentini, M. G. (2010) 'Towards a richer understanding of consumers in social marketing contexts: revisiting the stage of change model', *Journal of Marketing Management* 27(1–2): 60–76.

Glossary

Abandonment rate Those visitors who do not bounce straight away from a site, but who ultimately fail to convert to the hoped-for outcome.

ABC sales: contribution analysis An approach that examines the financial worth to a company of its products, product groups or customers.

Accessibility The ability to move goods over a specific route or network.

Accessory equipment Tools and equipment used in production or office activities that do not become part of the final physical product.

Accumulation The development of a bank of homogeneous products with similar production or demand requirements.

Actual product A composite of the features and capabilities offered in a product, quality and durability, design and product styling, packaging and brand name.

Administered pricing A pricing method in which the seller determines the price for a product and the customer pays the specified price.

Adopter categories Five groups into which customers can be divided according to the length of time it takes them to adopt a product: innovators, early adopters, early majority, late majority and laggards.

Adoption stage The final stage of product acceptance, when customers choose a specific product.

Advertising A paid-for form of non-personal communication that is transmitted through mass media such as television, radio, newspapers, magazines, direct mail, public transport vehicles, outdoor displays and the internet.

Advertising budget The total amount of money that a marketer allocates for advertising over a period of time.

Advertising campaign An attempt to reach a particular target market by designing a series of advertisements and placing them in various advertising media.

Advertising platform The basic issues or selling points that an advertiser wishes to include in the advertising campaign.

Advertising target audience The group of people at which advertisements are aimed.

Advocacy advertising Promotes a company's position on a public issue.

AIDA A persuasive sequence used in advertisements: attention, interest, desire and action.

Aided or prompted recall test A test in which subjects are asked to identify advertisements while being shown a list of products, brands, company names or trademarks to jog their memory.

Allocation The breaking down of large homogeneous inventories into smaller lots.

Allowance A concession in price to achieve a desired goal.

Ansoff matrix Ansoff's product–market matrix for determining competitive strategies: market penetration, market development, product development or diversification.

Approach The manner in which a sales person contacts a potential customer.

Arbitrary approach A budgeting technique in which a high-level executive in the business states how much can be spent on advertising over a certain time period.

Area sampling A sampling method that involves selecting a probability sample of geographic areas and selecting units or individuals within the selected areas for the sample.

Artwork The illustration and layout of the advertisement.

Asia-Pacific Economic Cooperative (APEC) Aims to promote trade between its members: the six ASEAN members plus the United States, Australia, Canada, New Zealand, Japan, China, South Korea, Hong Kong and Taiwan.

Association of South East Asian Nations (ASEAN) Formed in 1967 with the intention of building trade and other links among its six members: Brunei, Indonesia, Malaysia, the Philippines, Singapore and Thailand.

Assorting The grouping of products that buyers want to have available in one place.

Assortment A combination of products put together to provide customer benefits.

Attitude An individual's enduring evaluation, feelings and behavioural tendencies towards an object or activity.

Attitude scale A series of adjectives, phrases or sentences about an object used by a subject to indicate his or her feelings towards that object.

Augmented product Support aspects of a product, including customer service, warranty, delivery and credit, personnel, installation and after-sales support.

Automatic vending The use of coin- or credit-card-operated self-service machines to sell small, standardized, routinely purchased products such as chewing gum, sweets, newspapers, cigarettes, soft drinks and coffee.

Average fixed cost The fixed cost per unit produced, calculated by dividing fixed costs by the number of units produced.

Average total cost The sum of the average fixed cost and the average variable cost.

Average variable cost The variable cost per unit produced, calculated by dividing the variable costs by the number of units produced.

Awareness stage The beginning of the product adoption process, when individuals become aware that the product exists but have little information about it.

Base point pricing A geographic pricing policy that includes the price at the factory, plus freight charges from the base point nearest the buyer.

Basis for competing A company's combined strengths as identified in a SWOT analysis and any differential advantage, which should form the leading edge of the company's marketing strategy.

Basis for pricing Structures the calculation of the actual price.

Benchmarking The process of comparing the quality of an organization's goods, services or processes with those of its best-performing competitors.

Benefit segmentation The division of a market according to the benefits consumers want from the product.

Bid pricing Determination of prices through sealed or open bids submitted by the seller to the buyer.

Big data Data that are too large, numerous, complex and frequent for conventional data tools to capture, store, manage and analyze. Open source platforms enable organizations to extract real time value from the huge volumes of data being produced.

Blog communities Where spokespersons for a brand share their views in blogs, permitting one-to-one tailored communication with members and between members of the digital brand community.

Bounce rate The number of visitors who quickly/ immediately leave without dwelling or clicking-through to other content.

Brand A name, term, design, symbol or any other feature that identifies one seller's good or service as distinct from those of other sellers.

Brand advocacy When consumers are encouraged to share very positive feelings towards a brand with other consumers, whether word-of-mouth, online or in the print and broadcast media.

Brand advocate Supporter of a brand who actively promotes the brand and is also emotionally attached to the brand. He or she will silence detractors, help build a positive customer experience, and share exemplars of the brand 'going that extra mile'.

Brand attitude A consumer's particular impression of a brand, formed by emotions and logic or cognitive beliefs.

Brand attributes The bullet-point specific benefits to the customer from purchasing or using the brand.

Brand awareness The consumer's ability to identify a manufacturer's or retailer's brand in sufficient detail to distinguish it from other brands.

Brand community A group of consumers and observers focused on a particular brand, often based on social media, centred on a set of social relations and interactions among admirers of the brand.

Brand equity The marketing and financial value associated with a brand's strength in a market, which is a function of the goodwill and positive brand recognition built up over time, underpinning the brand's sales volumes and financial returns.

Brand extension branding A company's use of one of its existing brand names as part of an improved or new product, usually in the same product category as the existing brand.

Brand identity A unique set of brand associations reflecting what a brand stands for and the intended promise to the customer as a relationship is forged.

Brand insistence The degree of brand loyalty in which a customer strongly prefers a specific brand and will accept no substitute.

Brand loyalty A strongly motivated and long-standing decision to purchase a particular product or service.

Brand manager The person responsible for a single brand.

Brand mark The element of a brand that cannot be spoken, often a symbol or design.

Brand name That part of a brand that can be spoken, including letters, words and numbers.

Brand personality The psychological cues and less tangible desirable facets of a well-presented brand.

Brand positioning The creation of a desirable, distinctive and plausible image for a brand in the minds of targeted customers.

Brand preference The degree of brand loyalty in which a customer prefers one brand over competitive offerings.

Brand purchase intention The consumer's decision and efforts to purchase the particular product.

Brand recognition A customer's awareness that a brand exists and is an alternative to purchase.

Brand strength A function of the product's attributes and functionality, its differentiation, plus any demonstrable added value to the purchaser or user.

Brand values The emotional benefits and less tangible identifiers attached to the brand inside the organization, providing reassurance and credibility for employees and, indirectly, targeted consumers or business customers.

Break-down approach An approach that derives a company's sales potential from the general economic forecast and the estimate of market potential.

Break-even point The point at which the costs of producing a product equal the revenue made from selling the product.

Build-up approach An approach that measures the sales potential for a product by first calculating its market potential and then estimating what proportion of that potential the company can expect to obtain.

Business (or business-to-business) buying behaviour The purchase behaviour of producers, resellers, the public sector, government units and institutions.

Business analysis A company's evaluation of a product idea to determine its potential contribution to the company's sales, costs and profits.

Business cycle Fluctuations in the economy that follow the general pattern of prosperity, recession, depression and recovery.

Business development identification, scoping, pursuit and engagement of new business opportunities, customers and accounts.

Business distributor An independent business that takes title to products and carries inventories.

Business market The customers are not consumers, private individuals or households: instead the target customers are other businesses and organizations that purchase a specific type of product or service for resale, for use in making other products, or for use in their daily operations.

Business marketing Activities directed towards facilitating and expediting exchanges between businesses.

Business services Services such as repairs and maintenance, consulting and professional advice, installation, equipment leasing, marketing research, advertising, temporary office personnel and caretaking services.

Buy-back allowance A certain sum of money given to a purchaser for each unit bought after an initial deal is over.

Buying allowance A temporary price reduction given to resellers who purchase specified quantities of a product.

Buying behaviour The decision processes and actions of people involved in buying and using products.

Buying centre The group of people within an organization who are involved in making business-to-business purchase decisions.

Buying power Resources such as goods, services and financial holdings that can be traded in an exchange situation.

Capabilities A company's distinctive competencies to do something well and efficiently.

Capability The ability of a transport mode to provide the appropriate equipment and conditions for moving specific kinds of goods.

Captioned photograph A photograph with a brief description explaining its content.

Cash and carry warehouses Outlets that retail extensive ranges of groceries, tobacco, alcohol, beverages and confectionery to newsagents, small supermarkets and convenience stores, and the catering trade.

Cash and carry wholesalers Middlemen whose customers will pay cash and provide transport.

Cash cows Products with a dominant share of the market but low prospects for growth.

Cash discount A simple price reduction given to a buyer for prompt payment or payment in cash.

Catalogue retailing A type of mail order retailing in which customers receive their catalogues by mail, the web, or pick them up if the catalogue retailer has stores.

Catalogue showroom Outlets in which one item of each product class is on display and the remaining inventory is stored out of the buyers' reach.

Category killers Large stores, tending to be superstore sized, which specialize in a narrow line of merchandise.

Category management A core approach to merchandising, inventory control and display in many retailers, with similar lines from several suppliers being controlled by a category manager and managed as a discrete unit.

Category need The consumer's perception of his or her need for a product in a certain category.

Category-consistent packaging The packaging of a product according to the packaging practices associated with a particular product category.

Causal research Data collection that assumes that a particular variable X causes a variable Y.

Cause-related marketing The linking of an organization's products to a particular social cause on a short-term or ongoing basis.

Central and Eastern Europe (CEE) Encompasses the Commonwealth of Independent States (formerly the Soviet Union), the Czech and Slovak Republics, Hungary, Poland, Slovenia, Croatia, Bosnia Herzegovina, Serbia, Montenegro, Bulgaria, FYR Macedonia and Albania.

Central business district (CBD) The traditional hub of most cities and towns; the focus for shopping, banking and commerce, and hence the busiest part of the whole area.

Centralized organization A company in which top-level managers delegate very little authority to the lower levels of the organization.

Channel capacity The limit on the volume of information that a particular communication channel can handle effectively.

Channel of distribution (or marketing channel) A group of individuals and organizations that direct the flow of products from producers to customers.

Channel power The ability to influence another channel member's goal achievement.

Client publics In non-profit organizations, direct consumers of a product.

Client-based relationships Interactions that result in satisfied customers who use a service repeatedly over time.

Closing The step in the selling process in which the sales person asks the prospect to buy the product or products.

Co-creation The involvement of, or consultation with, consumers and supply chain partners in the collaborative development of new products.

Codes of conduct Formalized rules and standards that describe what the company expects of its employees.

Coding process The process of converting meaning into a series of signs that represent ideas or concepts; also called encoding.

Cognitive dissonance Doubts that occur as the buyer questions whether she or he made the right decision in purchasing the product or service.

Combination compensation/remuneration plan A plan according to which sales people are paid a fixed salary plus a commission based on sales volume.

Commercialization The process of refining and settling plans for full scale manufacturing and marketing.

Commission merchants Agents who receive goods on consignment from local sellers and negotiate sales in large central markets.

Commonwealth of Independent States (CIS) The CIS unites Azerbaijan, Armenia, Belarus, Georgia, Kazakhstan, Kyrgyzstan, Moldova, Russia, Tajikistan, Turkmenistan, Ukraine and Uzbekistan in a trading bloc.

Communication A sharing of meaning through the transmission of information.

Community relations Marketers' roles as community members and their contributions to civic projects and institutions.

Comparative advertising The type of advertising that compares two or more brands on the basis of one or more product attributes.

Competition Those companies marketing products that are similar to, or can be substituted for, a given business's products in the same geographic area or marketing channel.

Competition and Markets Authority An independent body in the UK that investigates monopolies to determine whether they operate against the public interest.

Competition matching approach A budgeting technique in which marketers either match their major competitors' budgets or allocate the same percentage of sales for advertising as their competitors.

Competition-based pricing A pricing approach whereby a business considers costs and revenue to be secondary to competitors' prices.

Competitive advantage The achievement of superior performance vis-à-vis rivals, through differentiation to create distinctive product appeal or brand identity; through providing customer value and achieving the lowest delivered cost; or by focusing on narrowly scoped product categories or market niches so as to be viewed as a leading specialist.

Competitive advertising The type of advertising that points out a brand's uses, features and advantages, which may not be available in competing brands.

Competitive positions Competitors' roles in the marketplace, which influence their marketing strategies and programmes.

Competitive positions proforma A tool for scoping the competitive set, helping a company to understand the competitive positions in its target markets and diagnosing the effectiveness of a marketing strategy.

Competitive set All competing organizations and brands, irrespective of size and history, including substitutable solutions to customers' needs, as defined by the target market customers.

Competitor monitoring The process by which a company studies the actions of its major competitors in order to determine what specific strategies they are following and how those strategies affect its own; also used by marketers as they try to develop competitive advantages, adjust current marketing strategies and plan new ones.

Competitor scanning The monitoring of competitive positions and competitors' strategies.

Competitors Organizations viewed as marketing products similar to, or substitutable for, a company's products, when targeted at the same customers.

Complexity In services marketing, the number of steps required to perform a service.

Component parts Parts that become a part of the physical product and are either finished items ready for assembly or products that need little processing before assembly.

Comprehensive spending patterns The percentages of family income allotted to annual expenditures for general classes of goods and services.

Computer-assisted telephone interviewing A survey method that integrates questionnaire, data collection and tabulations, and provides data to aid decision-makers in the shortest time possible.

Concentration strategy A process by which an organization directs its marketing effort towards a single market segment through one marketing mix.

Concentric diversification A process that occurs when new products related to current products are introduced into new markets.

Concept testing Seeking potential buyers' responses to a product idea.

Conglomerate diversification A process that occurs when new products unrelated to current technology, products or markets are introduced into new markets.

Consumable supplies Supplies that facilitate production and operations but do not become part of the finished product.

Consumer buying behaviour The buying behaviour of ultimate consumers – those who purchase products for personal or household use.

Consumer buying decision process A five-stage process that includes problem recognition, information search, evaluation of alternatives, purchase and post-purchase evaluation.

Consumer contests Contests designed to generate traffic at the retail level in which consumers compete for prizes based on their analytical or creative skill.

Consumer focus group A semi-structured discussion, led by a moderator, involving actual or potential buyers of advertised products who are asked to judge one or several dimensions of the advertisements.

Consumer market Purchasers or individuals in their households who personally consume or benefit from the purchased products and do not buy products primarily to make a profit.

Consumer movement A diverse collection of independent individuals, groups and organizations seeking to protect the rights of consumers.

Consumer panels Groups of consumers selected to represent a market or market segment, who agree to be interviewed regularly by mail or online.

Consumer products Items purchased to satisfy personal or family needs.

Consumer purchase diaries A marketing research tool in which consumers record their purchases.

Consumer sales promotion techniques Techniques that encourage or stimulate consumers to patronize a specific retail store or to try a particular product.

Consumer services Services such as education, healthcare, leisure, catering, tourism, financial, entertainment, home maintenance and other services to help consumers.

Consumer spending patterns Information indicating the relative proportions of annual family expenditures or the actual amount of money spent on certain kinds of goods and services.

Consumer sweepstakes A method of stimulating sales in which consumers submit their names for inclusion in a draw for prizes.

Consumer-to-consumer (C2C) communication Consumer-to-consumer (C2C) communication is now routine, enabled by the digital era and social media in particular. Consumers readily and rapidly share views, experiences and information with each other. A positive or negative customer experience is tweeted instantly, blogged or shared on Facebook with potentially very many fellow consumers.

Consumerism The efforts of independent individuals, groups and organizations to protect the rights of consumers.

Consumers' Association A private organization funded by members' subscriptions, that works to further consumer interests.

Containerization The practice of consolidating many items into a single large container that is sealed at its point of origin and opened at its destination, greatly increasing efficiency and security in shipping.

Content marketing The creation of relevant and interesting text, audio, video and rich media content to engage specific customers in order to create brand awareness and sales.

Contract manufacturing The practice of hiring a foreign company to produce a designated volume of product to a set specification.

Convenience products Inexpensive, frequently purchased and rapidly consumed items that demand only minimal purchasing effort.

Convenience stores Shops that sell essential groceries, alcoholic drinks, medicines and newspapers outside the traditional shopping hours.

Conversion rates The proportion of visitors who go on to complete a defined action, such as register, complete an inquiry form or make a purchase.

Cooperative advertising An arrangement whereby a manufacturer agrees to pay a certain amount of a retailer's or dealer's media costs for advertising the manufacturer's products.

Copy The verbal portion of an advertisement.

Copy writing The creation and wording of the promotional message.

Core product The level of a product that provides the perceived or real core benefit or service.

Corporate branding The application of product branding at the corporate level, reflected visibly through the company name, logo and visual presentation and in the organization's underlying values.

Corporate culture A set of values, beliefs, goals, norms and rituals that members of an organization share.

Corporate identity Overlapping with the corporate branding concept: branding at the corporate level.

Corporate image Reflects the perceptions that external audiences hold about an organization.

Corporate strategy A strategy that determines the organization's vision and goals, and how they are to be addressed, in which markets, with what advantages over competitors, and so aligning resources in key functions accordingly across the business.

Correlation methods Attempts to find a relationship between past sales and one or more variables such as population, per capita income or gross national product.

Cost comparison indicator A measure that allows an advertiser to compare the costs of several vehicles within a specific medium in relation to the number of people reached by each vehicle.

Cost per conversion Calculation of the total cost of advertising divided by the total number of conversions generated from the campaign.

Cost plus pricing A pricing approach based on adding a specified amount or percentage to the seller's cost after that cost is determined.

Cost trade-offs The off-setting of higher costs in one area of the distribution system by lower costs in another area, to keep the total system cost-effective.

Cost-based pricing A pricing approach whereby a monetary amount or percentage is added to the cost of a product.

Costs One consideration that helps determine transportation mode, involving comparison of alternative modes to determine whether the benefits of a more expensive mode are worth the higher costs.

Count and re-count A promotion method based on the payment of a specific amount of money for each product unit moved from a reseller's warehouse in a given time period.

Coupons A promotion method that reduces the purchase price of an item in order to stimulate consumers to try a new or established product, to increase sales volume quickly, to attract repeat purchasers or to introduce new package sizes or features.

Credence qualities Attributes that cannot be assessed even after purchase and consumption.

Crisis management A process in which a company responds to negative events by identifying key targets (publics) for which to provide publicity, developing a well-rehearsed contingency plan, reporting facts.

Critical marketing Critical marketing involves challenging orthodox views that are central to the core principles of the discipline. Sometimes this involves promoting radical philosophies and theories in relation to the understanding of economies, society, markets and consumers, which may have implications for the practice of marketing. Critical marketing is connected with the growing area of critical management.

CRM Data capture about customers and their buying habits, analysis and profiling of such behaviours, so that tailored propositions and communications may be created in order to maintain an ongoing relationship and continue to interest customers in the company's brand, products and activities.

Crowdsourcing The task of outsourcing to a large group of people or a community via the internet for funding a task usually performed by the company itself, such as product testing.

Culture All the things around us that are made by human beings: tangible items, such as food, furniture, buildings, clothing and tools; and intangible concepts, such as education, the legal system, healthcare and religion; plus values and behaviours.

Cumulative discounts Quantity discounts aggregated over a stated period of time.

Customer contact The level of interaction between the provider and customer needed to deliver the service.

Customer forecasting survey A method of asking customers what types and quantities of products they intend to buy during a specific period of time.

Customer relationship management (CRM) The identification of the most worthwhile and valuable customers within targeted segments and the development of ongoing relationships to foster loyalty and repeat purchasing.

Customer satisfaction A state that results when an exchange meets the needs and expectations of the buyer.

Customer service Customer satisfaction in terms of physical distribution, based on availability, promptness and quality.

Customer threshold The number of customers required to make a profit.

Customer value proposition Based on understanding the perceived customer values and psychological, functional and economic factors traded-off when customers select a particular product or brand to purchase.

Customer's zone of tolerance The difference between the customer's desired level of expectations and the customer's acceptable level of expectations.

Cycle analysis A forecasting technique that analyzes a company's sales figures over a period of three to five years to ascertain whether sales fluctuate in a consistent, periodic manner.

Dealer listing An advertisement that promotes a product and identifies the names of participating retailers or dealers who sell it.

Dealer loader A gift to a retailer or dealer who purchases a specified quantity of merchandise.

Decentralized organization A company in which decision-making authority is delegated as far down the chain of command as possible.

Decline stage The last stage of a product's life cycle, during which sales fall rapidly.

Decoding process The process in which signs are converted into concepts and ideas.

Defensive advertising The type of advertising that aims to off-set or lessen the effects of a competitor's promotional programme.

Defensive warfare A policy of striking a balance between waiting for market developments or competitor activity and proactively parrying competitors' actions.

Delphi method A centralized forecasting method that takes into account the views of managers, sales personnel and individual participants; aggregates them; and modifies them.

Demand curve A graph of the quantity of products expected to be sold at various prices, if other factors remain constant.

Demand-based pricing A pricing approach based on the level of demand for a product, resulting in a high price when demand is strong and a low price when demand is weak.

Demographic factors Individual characteristics such as age, sex, race, ethnic origin, income, family life cycle and occupation.

Demonstrations Occasions at which manufacturers show how a product actually works in order to encourage trial use and purchase of the product.

Department stores Physically large stores that occupy prominent positions in the traditional heart of the town or city, or as anchor stores in out-of-town malls.

Dependent variable A variable that is contingent on, or restricted to, one value or a set of values assumed by the independent variable.

Depression A period during which unemployment is extremely high, wages are very low, total disposable income is at a minimum and consumers lack confidence in the economy.

Depth (of product mix) The number of different products offered in each product line.

Depth interview A lengthy, one-to-one structured interview, examining in detail a consumer's views about a product.

Derived demand Demand for business products that arises from the demand for consumer products.

Descriptive research Data collection that focuses on providing an accurate description of the variables in a situation.

Descriptors Variables used to profile or build a fuller picture of target segments brand's desired stature.

Diary tests Experiments in which households log their weekly purchases and consumption patterns.

Differential advantage An attribute of a brand, product, service or marketing mix that is desired by the targeted customer and provided by only one supplier.

Differential pricing A pricing strategy involving charging different prices to different buyers for the same quality and quantity of product.

Differentiated strategy A strategy by which an organization directs its marketing efforts towards two or more market segments by developing a marketing mix for each.

Digital brand community A group of consumers, observers or advocates focused on a particular brand, using social media to share admiration for their favoured brand.

Digital channels Different forms of digital media used for online marketing and delivery. The range of channels continues to expand requiring organizations to develop multi-channel or now omni-channel strategies.

Digital environment A stunt, idea or activity can become the focus of blogs and tweets, whether from client personnel or by consumers.

Digital marketing The use of the web, computers and smartphones, as well as radio, TV and any other forms of digital media, to attract, engage and build relationships with customers and other target audiences; the use of technology-led channels of communication and selling to manage customer interaction and provide customer experience in a digitally -connected environment.

Direct cost approach An approach that includes only direct costs and traceable common costs.

Direct costs Costs directly attributable to the performance of marketing functions.

Direct distribution channels Distribution channels in which products are sold directly from producers to users.

Direct mail Printed advertising material delivered to a prospective customer's or donor's home or work address.

Direct mail package A mix of mailing envelope, covering or explanatory letter, circular, response device and return device.

Direct marketing The use of non-personal media, the internet or telesales to introduce products to consumers, who then purchase the products by mail, telephone or the internet.

Directional policy matrix A market attractiveness and business strength/capability assessment tool ideal for trade-off analyses for identifying resourcing priorities.

Discount sheds Cheaply constructed, one-storey retail stores with no window displays and few add-on amenities; oriented towards car-borne shoppers.

Discretionary income Disposable income that is available for spending and saving after an individual has purchased the basic necessities of food, clothing and shelter.

Disposable income After-tax income, which is used for spending or saving.

Distributors Companies that buy and sell on their own account but tend to deal in the goods of only certain specified manufacturers.

Diversified growth Growth that occurs when new products are developed to be sold in new markets.

Dogs Products that have a subordinate share of the market and low prospects for growth.

Domestic marketing Marketing activities directed exclusively to business's home market.

Drop and collect surveys Questionnaires distributed by hand to households, and then collected at a later date.

Drop shippers Intermediaries who take title to goods and negotiate sales but never actually take possession of products.

Dual distribution A channel practice whereby a producer distributes the same products through two different channels.

Dumping The sale of products in non-domestic markets at lower prices than those charged in domestic markets, when all costs are not allocated or when surplus products are sold.

Dynamic branding Digital brand communities and blogging enable dynamic branding, with very rapid communication and sharing of brand information and almost instant take-up by the brand's followers.

Early adopters People who choose new products carefully and are often consulted by people from the remaining adopter categories.

Early majority People who adopt products just prior to the average person.

EBITDA The acronym for earnings before interest, taxes, depreciation and amortization.

eCommerce The use of the internet for marketing communications, selling and purchasing.

Economic and competitive forces Factors in the marketing environment such as the effects of general economic conditions; buying power; willingness to spend; spending patterns; types of competitive structure, competitive tools and competitive behaviour that influence both marketers' and consumers' decisions and activities.

Economic order quantity (EOQ) The order size that minimizes the total cost of ordering and carrying inventory.

Economic value to the customer (EVC) The underlying principle that a premium price can be charged while still offering the customer better value than the competition.

Edge-of-town sites Retail locations on undeveloped land, providing purpose-built stores, parking facilities and amenities for their customers on the edge of a built-up area.

Electronic data interchange (EDI) The use of IT to integrate order processing with production, inventory, accounting and transportation.

Email marketing The use of email to deliver offers, brand building messages and relationship-building information to customers, prospects and target audiences.

Empowerment Giving front-line employees the authority and responsibility to make marketing decisions without seeking the approval of their supervisors.

Environmental analysis The process of assessing and interpreting the information gathered through environmental scanning.

Environmental factors Uncontrollable forces such as politics, competitive and economic factors, legal and regulatory issues, technological changes and socio-cultural issues.

Environmental scanning The process of collecting information about the forces in the marketing environment.

Ethical issue An identifiable problem, situation or opportunity requiring a choice between several actions that must be evaluated as right or wrong, ethical or unethical.

Ethics officer Responsible for creating, distributing, enforcing and advising on a code of conduct.

Ethnodomination This occurs when an ethnic group occupies a majority position within a marketing channel.

Ethnography Observing consumers' real-world behaviours and product usage.

European Union (EU) The major grouping in western Europe, the EU has 27 members: Austria, Belgium, Denmark, Finland, France, Germany, Greece, Ireland, Italy, Luxembourg, the Netherlands, Portugal, Spain, Sweden and the UK have been joined by Bulgaria, Cyprus, the Czech Republic, Estonia, Hungary, Latvia, Lithuania, Malta, Poland, Romania, Slovakia and Slovenia.

Evaluation stage The stage of the product adoption process when customers decide whether the product will satisfy certain criteria that are crucial for meeting their specific needs.

Evoked set The group of products that a buyer views as possible alternatives after conducting an information search.

Exchange The provision or transfer of goods, services and ideas in return for something of value.

Exclusive dealing System by which a manufacturer forbids an intermediary to carry the products of competing manufacturers.

Exclusive distribution The use of only one outlet in a relatively large geographic area to distribute a product.

Executive judgement A way of forecasting sales based on the intuition of one or more executives.

Experience qualities Attributes that can be assessed only after purchase and consumption, including satisfaction and courtesy.

Experimentation Data collection that involves maintaining certain variables as constant so that the effects of the experimental variables can be measured.

Expert forecasting survey A survey prepared by outside experts such as economists, management consultants, advertising executives or academics.

Exploratory research Deliberately flexible data gathering used to discover the general nature of a problem and the factors that relate to it.

Export marketing Marketing activities through which a business takes advantage of opportunities outside its home market but continues production in the home country.

Exporting Use of an intermediary that performs most marketing functions associated with selling to other countries; entails the minimum effort, cost and risk involved in international marketing.

Extended marketing mix for services In addition to the standard '4Ps' marketing mix: product, promotion, price and place/distribution, there are 3Ps: process, physical evidence (ambience) and people.

Extensive decision-making Behaviour that occurs when a purchase involves unfamiliar, expensive, high-risk or infrequently bought products for which the buyer spends much time seeking information and comparing brands before deciding on the purchase.

External reference price A comparison price provided by others.

External search One that focuses on information not available from the consumer's memory.

Facilitating agencies Organizations such as transport companies, insurance companies, advertising agencies, marketing research agencies and financial institutions that perform activities that enhance channel functions.

Factory outlet villages Converted rural buildings or purpose-built out-of-town retail parks for manufacturers' outlets retailing branded seconds, excess stocks and last season's lines, or trialling new lines.

Family packaging An approach in which all of a company's packages are similar or include one major element of the design.

Fast movers Smaller rival companies not yet destined to be major challengers, but growing rapidly on a smaller scale.

Feature article A manuscript longer than a press release (up to 3000 words) that is usually prepared for a specific publication.

Feedback The receiver's response to a message.

Field settings 'Real world' environments in which experiments take place.

Financial Conduct Authority The regulatory authority for financial services in the UK.

Financial price The basis of market exchanges; the quantified value of what is exchanged.

Five communication effects Communication aims that include category need, brand awareness, brand attitude, brand purchase intention and purchase facilitation.

Five competitive forces Together these determine competition in an industry or market: rivalry amongst existing like-for-like players; the threat of new entrants; the threat of substitute solutions; the bargaining power of buyers; and the bargaining power of suppliers.

Five markets model of relationship marketing In addition to customer markets, the core audiences of influencers, referrals, employee recruitment, suppliers and internal markets.

Five-category classification A method of analyzing services according to five criteria: type of market, degree of labour intensiveness, degree of customer contact, skill of the service provider and goal of the service provider.

Fixed costs Those costs that do not vary with changes in the number of units produced or sold.

Flashes Headers printed on a direct mail package to gain the recipient's attention.

FOB destination price A price quotation indicating that the producer absorbs the costs of shipping the merchandise.

FOB factory price The price of the merchandise at the factory before it is loaded on to the carrier vehicle, which must be paid by the buyer.

Focus group A semi-structured discussion involving six to 12 people, led by a moderator.

Focus group interview A survey method that aims to observe group interaction when members are exposed to an idea or concept.

Food brokers Intermediaries who sell food and general merchandise items to retailer-owned and merchant wholesalers, grocery chains, industrial buyers and food processors.

Foreign direct investment (FDI) A long-term commitment to marketing in a foreign nation through direct ownership of a foreign subsidiary or division.

Franchising A form of licencing granting the right to use certain intellectual property rights, such as trade names, brand names, designs, patents and copyrights.

Free merchandise Giveaways sometimes offered to resellers who purchase a stated quantity of the same or different products.

Free samples Giveaways used to stimulate trial of a product, to increase sales volume in the early stages of a product's life cycle or to obtain desirable distribution.

Freight absorption pricing A pricing policy in which the seller absorbs all or part of the actual freight costs.

Frequency The number of times targeted consumers are exposed to a particular advertisement.

Frequent user incentives Incentive programmes that reward customers who engage in repeat purchases.

Full cost approach An approach in which cost analysis includes direct costs, traceable common costs and non-traceable common costs.

Full service wholesalers Middlemen who offer the widest possible range of wholesaling functions.

Functional middlemen Intermediaries who perform a limited number of marketing activities in exchange for commission and do not take title to products.

Functional modifications Changes that affect a product's versatility, effectiveness, convenience or safety.

General Agreement on Tariffs and Trade (GATT) An agreement between countries to reduce worldwide tariffs and increase international trade.

General merchandise wholesalers Middlemen who carry a wide product mix but offer limited depth within the product lines.

General publics In non-profit organizations, indirect consumers of a product.

Generic brand A brand that indicates only the product category and does not include the company name or other identifying terms.

Generic routes to competitive advantage Cost leadership, differentiation and focus; not mutually exclusive.

Geodemographic segmentation Clustering people according to postcode areas and census data.

Geographic pricing Pricing that involves reductions for transport costs or other costs associated with the physical distance between the buyer and the seller.

Global marketing A total commitment to international marketing, in which a company applies its assets, experience and products to develop and maintain marketing strategies on a global scale.

Global strategic partnerships Link-ups between companies from two or more regions which jointly decide to pursue a marketing opportunity, share resources and combine ideas, retaining independence, but pooling many activities and sharing rewards.

Globalization The development of marketing strategies that treat the entire world, or its major regions, as a single entity.

Good A tangible physical entity.

Government markets Departments that buy goods and services to support their internal operations, and to provide the public with education, water, energy, national defence, road systems and healthcare.

Green marketing The specific development, pricing, promotion and distribution of products that do not harm the natural environment.

Green movement The trend arising from society's concern about pollution, waste disposal, manufacturing processes and the greenhouse effect.

Greenwash Misleading claims about a brand's green credentials, resulting in loss of trust and a consumer backlash.

Grey market Unofficial export/import by third parties able to source lower priced merchandise on behalf of their clients and take a percentage of the saving in return.

Gross domestic product (GDP) The total value of all goods and services produced by a country in one year.

Growth stage The stage at which a product's sales rise rapidly and profits reach a peak, before levelling off into maturity.

Guarantee An agreement specifying what the producer or supplier will do if the product malfunctions.

Heterogeneity Variability in the quality of service because services are provided by people, and people perform inconsistently.

Heterogeneous markets Markets in which all customers have different requirements.

Home placements Experiments in which a product is used in a home setting.

Horizontal channel integration The combination of institutions at the same level of channel operation under one management.

Horizontal diversification A process that occurs when new products not technologically related to current products are introduced into current markets.

Hypermarkets Stores that take the benefits of the superstore even further, using their greater size to give the customer a wider range and depth of products.

Hypothesis An informed guess or assumption about a certain problem or set of circumstances.

Idea A concept, philosophy, image or issue.

Idea generation The process by which companies and other organizations seek product ideas that will help them achieve their objectives.

Ideas Concepts, philosophies, images or issues that provide the psychological stimulus to solve problems or adjust to the environment.

Illustrations Photographs, drawings, graphs, charts or tables used in advertisement artwork.

Immediate drop An option that drops an unprofitable product immediately.

Impulse buying Behaviour that involves no conscious planning but results from a powerful, persistent urge to buy something immediately.

In-depth interview The collection of data from an individual by interview.

In-home interview 45- to 90-minute interview in which the researcher visits the respondent in his or her home.

In-home retailing Selling via personal contacts with consumers in their own homes.

Income The amount of money received through wages, rents, investments, pensions and subsidy payments for a given period.

Independent variable A variable not influenced by or dependent on other variables in experiments.

Individual branding A policy of naming each product differently.

Individual factors The personal characteristics of individuals in the buying centre, such as age, education, personality, position in the organization and income level.

Industrial distributor An independent business that takes title to industrial products and carries inventories.

Industrial, organizational or business-to-business marketing See business market

Industrial/business products Items bought for use in a company's operations or to make other products.

Industrial/business services The intangible products that many organizations use in their operations, including financial, legal, marketing research, computer programming and operation, caretaking and printing services.

Inelastic demand Demand that is not significantly affected by a price increase or decrease.

Information inputs The sensations received through sight, taste, hearing, smell and touch.

Innovators The first people to adopt a new product.

Input–output data Information on what types of industries purchase the products of a particular industry.

Inseparability In relation to production and consumption, a characteristic of services that means they are produced at the same time as they are consumed.

Institutional advertising The type of advertising that promotes organizational images, ideas or political issues.

Institutional markets Organizations with charitable, educational, community or other non-business goals.

Intangibility An inherent quality of services that are performed and therefore cannot be tasted, touched, seen, smelled or possessed.

Integrated growth Growth that occurs in three possible directions: forwards, backwards or horizontally.

Integrated marketing communications (IMC) The coordination and integration of all marketing communication tools, avenues and sources within a company into a seamless programme that maximizes the impact on consumers and other end-users, at minimal cost.

Intended strategy The strategy on which the company decides during the planning phase.

Intense growth Growth that occurs when current products and current markets have the potential for increasing sales.

Intensive distribution The use of all available outlets for distributing a product.

Interactive marketing is an ongoing dialogue with a customer, harnessing CRM, the web and other direct marketing tools to develop a relationship.

Interest stage The stage of the product adoption process when customers are motivated to obtain information about the product's features, uses, advantages, disadvantages, price or location.

Internal marketing The application of marketing internally within the company, with programmes of communication and guidance targeted at internal audiences to develop responsiveness and a unified sense of purpose among employees.

Internal reference price A price developed in the buyer's mind through experience with the product.

Internal search One in which the buyer searches his or her memory for information about products.

International marketing Marketing activities in which a business reduces reliance on intermediaries and establishes direct involvement in the countries in which trade takes place.

Internet A network of computer networks stretching across the world, linking computers of different types and sharing information.

Internet A network of computer networks stretching across the world, linking computers of different types and sharing information.

Interpersonal factors The relationships among people in the buying centre and with suppliers' personnel.

Intranet Internal, in-company internet networks for routine communications, fostering group communications, providing uniform computer applications, distributing the latest software, or informing colleagues of marketing developments and new product launches.

Introduction stage A product's first appearance in the marketplace, before any sales or profits have been made.

Intuition The personal knowledge and past experience on which marketing managers may base decisions.

Inventory management The development and maintenance of adequate assortments of products to meet customers' needs.

Involvement The level of interest, emotion and activity the consumer is prepared to expend on a particular purchase.

Joint demand Demand that occurs when two or more products are used in combination to produce another product.

Joint venture A partnership between a domestic company and a foreign company or government.

Junk mail Unwanted mail often binned unread by uninterested recipients.

Key account management Dedicated and close support for individual business customers whose volume of business is significant and warrants one-to-one handling.

Key account management The process of identifying an organization's few really high-yielding customers and ensuring that these accounts are well-managed both in terms of looking after these customers and making staff within the organization fully appreciate their strategic importance.

Keyphrase The combination of keywords used to log a query in a search engine. Keyphrase analysis is the identification and selection of relevant keywords and phrases to leverage SEO and search marketing.

Kinesic communication Body language, including winking, head nodding, hand gestures and arm movements.

Knowledge Familiarity with the product and expertise – the ability to apply the product.

Labelling Packaging information that can be used for a variety of promotional, informational and legal purposes.

Laboratory settings Central locations at which participants or respondents are invited to react or respond to experimental stimuli.

Laggards The last people to adopt a new product, suspicious of new products and oriented towards the past.

Late majority People who are quite sceptical about new products but eventually adopt them because of economic necessity or social pressure.

Layout The physical arrangement of the illustration, headline, sub-headline, body copy and signature of an advertisement.

Learning Changes in a person's behaviour caused by information and experience.

Learning relationships Understanding better a customer's needs and behaviours.

Level of involvement The level of interest, emotional commitment and time spent searching for a product in a particular situation.

Levels of brands The tangible product, the 'basic' brand, the 'augmented' brand and the 'potential' of the brand.

Licencing System in which a licensee pays commissions or royalties on sales or supplies used in manufacturing.

Limited decision-making Behaviour that occurs when buying products purchased only occasionally, for which a moderate amount of information gathering and deliberation is needed.

Limited line wholesalers Wholesalers that carry only a few product lines but offer an extensive assortment of products within those lines.

Limited service wholesalers Middlemen who provide only some marketing services and specialize in a few functions.

Line extension A product that is closely related to existing products in the line, but meets different customer needs.

Line family branding A policy of using family branding only for products within a single line.

Long-range plans Plans that extend beyond five years.

Loyalty card A mechanism whereby regular customers who remain loyal to a particular company are rewarded with discounts or free merchandise.

Maastricht Treaty The treaty, signed in 1992, that established the European Union.

Macro marketing environment The broader forces affecting all organizations in a market: political, legal, regulatory, societal/green, technological and economic/competitive.

Mail surveys Questionnaires sent by mail to respondents, who are encouraged to complete and return them.

Mail order retailing Selling by description because buyers usually do not see the actual product until it arrives in the mail.

Mail order wholesalers Wholesalers that use catalogues instead of sales forces to sell products to retail, industrial and institutional buyers.

Mailing lists Directories of suitable, relevant recipients or targets.

Major equipment Large tools and machines used for production purposes.

Manufacturer brands Brands initiated by producers to ensure that they are identified with their products at the point of purchase.

Manufacturers' agents Independent middlemen or distributors who represent two or more sellers, and usually offer customers complete product lines.

Marginal cost (MC) The extra cost a company incurs when it produces one more unit of a product.

Marginal revenue (MR) The change in total revenue that occurs when a company sells an additional unit of a product.

Mark-up pricing A pricing approach whereby a product's price is derived by adding a predetermined percentage of the cost, called mark-up, to the cost of the product.

Market An aggregate of people who, as individuals or within organizations, have a need for certain products and the ability, willingness and authority to purchase such products.

Market attractiveness – business position model A two-dimensional matrix that helps determine which SBUs have an opportunity to grow and which should be divested.

Market challengers Non-market leaders that aggressively try to capture market share from their rivals.

Market density The number of potential customers within a unit of land area.

Market development A strategy of increasing sales of current products in new markets.

Market followers Low-share competitors without the resources, market position, research and development, or the commitment to challenge for extra sales and market share.

Market insight Learning about consumers, competitors and market trends to identify strategic direction and improve returns.

Market insight Learning about consumers, competitors and market trends to identify strategic direction and improve returns.

Market leader The single player enjoying the largest individual share in the market.

Market nichers Companies that specialize by focusing on only a very narrow range of products or on a select band of consumers.

Market penetration A strategy of increasing sales of current products in current markets.

Market potential The total amount of a product that customers will purchase within a specified period of time at a specific level of industry-wide marketing activity.

Market requirements Requirements that relate to customers' needs or desired benefits.

Market segment A group of individuals, groups or organizations sharing one or more similar characteristics that cause them to have relatively similar product needs and buying characteristics.

Market segmentation The process of grouping customers in markets with some heterogeneity into smaller, more similar or homogeneous segments. The identification of target customer groups in which customers are aggregated into groups with similar requirements and buying characteristics.

Market share The company's sales of a product stated as a percentage of industry sales of that product.

Market test An experiment in which a product is made available to buyers in one or more test areas, after which purchases and consumer responses to its distribution, promotion and price are measured.

Marketing Activities that facilitate and expedite satisfying exchange relationships in a dynamic environment, through the creation, distribution, promotion and pricing of goods, services and ideas. Marketing is a function and a set of processes for creating, communicating and delivering value to customers and for managing customer relationships in ways that benefit the organization and its stakeholders.

Marketing analytics The processes and technologies that enable marketers to evaluate the success of their marketing initiatives by measuring performance across all channels and activities using important business metrics such as ROI.

Marketing assets Customer, distribution and internal capabilities that managers and the marketplace view as beneficially strong.

Marketing audit A systematic examination of the marketing function's objectives, strategies, programmes, organization and performance.

Marketing citizenship The adoption of a strategic focus for fulfilling the economic, legal, ethical and philanthropic social responsibilities expected by stakeholders.

Marketing communication The transmission of persuasive information about a product, service or an idea, targeted at key stakeholders and consumers within the target market segment.

Marketing concept The philosophy that an organization should try to provide products that satisfy customers' needs through a coordinated set of activities that also allows the organization to achieve its goals.

Marketing control process One that establishes performance standards, evaluates actual performance and reduces the differences between desired and actual performance.

Marketing cost analysis The breakdown and classification of costs to determine which are associated with specific marketing activities.

Marketing environment The external forces that directly or indirectly influence an organization's acquisition of inputs and generation of outputs, comprising six categories of forces: political, legal, regulatory, societal, technological and economic/competitive.

Marketing era The period in which product and aggressive selling were no longer seen to suffice if customers either did not desire a product or preferred a rival brand, and in which customer needs were identified and satisfied.

Marketing ethics Principles and standards that define acceptable marketing conduct as determined by various stakeholders, including the public, government, regulators, private interest groups, consumers, industry and the organization itself.

Marketing function accounts A method of indicating the function performed through the expenditure of funds.

Marketing implementation Processes and activities deployed to action the marketing strategy or roll out the marketing plan.

Marketing information system (MIS) The framework for the day-to-day management and structuring of information gathered from sources both inside and outside an organization.

Marketing intelligence The composite of all data and ideas available within an organization, which assists in decision-making.

Marketing intermediary A middleman who links producers to other middlemen or to those who ultimately use the products.

Marketing management A process of planning, organizing, implementing and controlling marketing activities to facilitate and expedite exchanges effectively and efficiently.

Marketing manager The person responsible for managing the marketing activities that serve a particular group or class of customers.

Marketing metrics Specific measurable and quantifiable criteria used to evaluate the effectiveness of a marketing strategy and assess marketing performance.

Marketing mix The tactical 'toolkit' of the marketing programme; product, place/ distribution, promotion, price and people variables that an organization can control in order to appeal to the target market and facilitate satisfying exchange.

Marketing objective A statement of what is to be accomplished through marketing activities – the results expected from marketing efforts.

Marketing opportunities Circumstances and timing that allow an organization to take action towards reaching a target market.

Marketing opportunity One that exists when circumstances allow an organization to take action towards reaching a particular group of consumer or business customers in order to develop relationships and achieve commercial goals.

Marketing orientation A marketing-oriented organization devotes resources to understanding the needs and buying behaviour of customers, competitors' activities and strategies, and of market trends and external forces – now and as they may shape up in the future; inter-functional coordination ensures that the organization's activities and capabilities are aligned to this marketing intelligence.

Marketing oriented A company that concentrates on discovering what buyers want and providing it in a way that lets the company achieve its objectives.

Marketing performance The assessment of the effectiveness of marketing programmes to implement recommended marketing strategies, fulfil corporate financial expectations and achieve the required levels of customer satisfaction.

Marketing plan The written document or blueprint for specifying, implementing and controlling an organization's marketing activities and marketing mixes.

Marketing planning A systematic process of assessing marketing opportunities and resources, determining marketing objectives and developing a thorough plan for implementation and control.

Marketing planning cycle A circular process that runs in two directions, with planning running one way and feedback the other.

Marketing process Analysis of market conditions, the creation of an appropriate marketing strategy, the development of marketing programmes designed to action the agreed strategy and, finally, the implementation and control of the marketing strategy and its associated marketing programmes.

Marketing programme A marketer's marketing mix activities and implementation processes designed to operationalize the marketing strategy.

Marketing research The process of gathering, interpreting and reporting information to help marketers solve specific marketing problems or take advantage of marketing opportunities.

Marketing shareholder value analysis (MSVA) Divides the estimation of the value to the organization created by a marketing strategy into two components: (1) the present value of cash flows during the strategizing and planning phases (2) the continuing value after implementation of the strategy.

Marketing strategy The selection of new opportunities to pursue and current activities to support, identification of associated target markets and competitive positioning, and the creation of appropriate value propositions and customer engagement plans, in order to deliver the specified performance goals in the corporate strategy.

Marketing-oriented pricing A pricing approach whereby a company takes into account a wide range of factors including marketing strategy, competition, value to the customer, price–quality relationships, explicability, costs, product line pricing, negotiating margins, political factors and effect on distributors/retailers.

Markets Halls where fresh foods, clothing and housewares are sold, catering for budget-conscious shoppers who typically have a middle- and down-market social profile.

Materials handling The physical handling of products.

Maturity stage The stage during which a product's sales curve peaks and starts to decline, and profits continue to decline.

Mechanical observation devices Cameras, recorders, counting machines and other equipment that records physiological changes in individuals.

Media plan The process of establishing the exact media vehicles to be used for advertising, and the dates and times when the advertisements will appear.

Medium of transmission The tool used to carry the coded message from the source to the receiver or receiving audience.

Medium-range plans Plans that usually cover two to four years.

Merchandise allowance A manufacturer's agreement to pay resellers certain amounts of money for providing special promotional efforts, such as advertising or displays.

Merchant wholesalers Wholesalers that take title to goods and assume the risks associated with ownership.

Merchants Intermediaries who take title to products and resell them.

Micro marketing environment The more company-specific forces reflecting the nature of the business, its suppliers, marketing intermediaries, buyers, all types of competitors: direct, substitute and new entrant and its publics.

Misleading pricing Pricing policies that intentionally confuse or dupe consumers.

Mobile marketing Encourages consumer engagement anywhere or anytime while on or using a mobile device, such as a smartphone or tablet, and heavily dependent on mobile apps which provide users with information, entertainment and location-based services.

Mobile marketing Engaging users of wireless devices with time and location sensitive, personalized information that promotes goods, services and ideas, via apps, messaging, websites and social media communications.

Mobile marketing Marketing to encourage consumer engagement anywhere or anytime while on or using a mobile device, such as a smartphone or tablet, and heavily dependent on mobile apps which provide users with information, entertainment and location based services.

Modified re-buy purchase A new task purchase that is changed when it is re-ordered or when the requirements associated with a straight re-buy purchase are modified.

Monetization The ability to generate revenue through a website or blog. Monetization can be from affiliate programmes, eCommerce, premium content or advertising.

Money refunds A specific amount of money mailed to customers who submit proof of purchase.

Monopolistic competition A market structure that exists when a business with many potential competitors attempts to develop a differential marketing strategy to establish its own market share.

Monopoly A market structure that exists when a company turns out a product that has no close substitutes or rivals.

Motive An internal, energy-giving force that directs a person's activities towards satisfying a need or achieving a goal.

MRO items Consumable supplies in the sub-categories of maintenance, repair and operating (or overhaul) supplies.

Multi-channel marketing The decision to reach target consumers or business customers through more than one channel.

Multinational companies Companies that behave in their foreign markets as if they were local companies.

Multinational enterprise A company with operations or subsidiaries in many countries.

Multinational marketing Adaptation of some of a company's marketing activities to appeal to local culture and differences in taste.

Multiple packaging Packaging that includes more than one unit of a product, such as twin packs, tri-packs and six-packs.

Multiple sourcing A business's decision to use several suppliers.

Multivariable segmentation Segmentation using more than one characteristic to divide a total market.

Natural accounts The classification of costs based on how money was actually spent.

Negotiated pricing Determination of prices through negotiations between the seller and the buyer.

Negotiation Mutual discussion or communication of terms and methods in an exchange situation.

Neuromarketing is the study of consumers' brain patterns to reveal responses to marketing stimuli.

New product development The process a product goes through before introduction, involving seven phases: idea generation, screening ideas, concept testing, business analysis, product development, test marketing and commercialization.

New task purchase An organization's initial purchase of an item to be used to perform a new job or to solve a new problem.

Noise A condition that exists when the decoded message is different from that which was encoded.

Non-cumulative discounts One-off quantity discounts.

Non-price competition A policy in which a seller elects not to focus on price but to emphasize other factors instead.

Non-profit marketing Activities conducted by individuals and organizations to achieve some goal other than the ordinary business goals of profit, market share or return on investment.

Non-store retailing The selling of goods or services outside the confines of a retail facility.

Non-tariff barriers A wide range of rules, regulations and taxes that have an impact on trade.

Non-traceable common costs Costs that cannot be assigned according to any logical criteria.

North American Free Trade Agreement (NAFTA) Implemented in 1994, and designed to eliminate all tariffs on goods produced and traded between Canada, Mexico and the US, providing for a totally free trade area by 2009.

Objective and task approach A technique for determining an advertising budget that involves determining campaign objectives and then attempting to list the tasks required to accomplish them.

Objective of physical distribution Decreasing costs while increasing customer service.

Observation methods Methods by which researchers record respondents' overt behaviour and take note of physical conditions and events.

Offensive warfare A policy whereby challengers aggressively seek market share by identifying any weaknesses in the leader's and other challengers' marketing mixes and developing a genuine corresponding strength.

Oligopoly A market structure that exists when a few sellers control the supply of a large proportion of a product.

Omni-channel marketing When multi-channel marketing involves marketers utilizing *all* available channels to offer customers a seamless brand experience across a company's channels.

On-site computer interviewing A survey method that requires respondents to complete a self-administered questionnaire displayed on a computer monitor.

One-to-one marketing Customized marketing engaging individual customers for the development of longer-term relationships.

Online public relations Web-based communication and interaction with an organization's publics, stakeholders and target audiences in order to manage reputation, create awareness and build relationships.

Online survey Questionnaires that are sent to an individual's email account or that are available over the internet or via a website.

Opinion leader The member of a reference group who provides information about a specific sphere of interest to reference group participants seeking information.

Opportunity A favourable set of conditions that limit barriers or provide rewards.

Opportunity cost The value of the benefit that is given up by selecting one alternative instead of another.

Order lead time The average time lapse between placing the order and receiving it.

Order processing The receipt and transmission of sales order information.

Organizational factors Include the buyer's objectives, purchasing policies and resources, as well as the size and composition of its buying centre.

Organizational relationships Work groups, committees, conversations and discussions with colleagues.

Organizing by function A way of structuring a marketing department in which personnel directing marketing research, product development, distribution, sales, advertising, digital and customer relations report to the top-level marketing executive.

Organizing by product A way of structuring a marketing department so that the company has the flexibility to develop special marketing mixes for different products.

Organizing by region A way of structuring a marketing department, used by large national or international companies, that requires managers of marketing functions for each region to report to their regional marketing manager.

Organizing by type of customer A way of structuring a marketing department, suitable for a business that has several groups of customers with very different needs and problems.

Outsourcing Where a third-party organization is empowered to manage and control a particular activity, such as logistics.

Overall family branding A policy of branding all of a company's products with the same name, or at least part of the name.

Own label brands Brands initiated and owned by resellers wholesalers or retailers.

Packaging The development of a product's container and label, complete with graphic design.

Packaging development A mix of aesthetic considerations and structural necessities to guarantee the functionality of the design.

Parallel imports Goods that are imported through 'non-official' channels from low-price to high-price countries.

Patronage motives Those motives that influence where a person purchases products on a regular basis.

Pay per click (PPC) Text ads that are displayed on the search engine results page when specific key phrases are entered by the search user. The advertiser pays when the site visitor clicks on the ad.

People variable The aspect of the marketing mix that reflects the level of customer service, advice, sales support and after-sales back-up required, involving recruitment policies, training, retention and motivation of key personnel.

Perceived value for money The benefit consumers perceive to be inherent in a product or service, weighed against the price demanded.

Percentage of sales approach A budgeting technique that involves multiplying a company's past sales, plus a factor for planned sales growth or decline, by a standard percentage based on both what the business traditionally spends on advertising and what the industry averages.

Perception The process of selecting, organizing and interpreting information inputs to produce meaning.

Perceptual mapping A tool used by marketers and marketing researchers to visually depict consumer perceptions and prioritizing of brands and their perceived attributes.

Perfect competition A market structure that entails a large number of sellers, not one of which could significantly influence price or supply.

Performance standard An expected level of performance against which actual performance can be compared.

Perishability A characteristic of services whereby unused capacity on one occasion cannot be stockpiled or inventoried for future occasions.

Personal influencing factors Demographic, situational and level of involvement factors unique to a particular individual.

Personal interview survey Face-to-face situation in which the researcher meets the consumer and questions him or her about a specific topic.

Personal selling The use of personal communication in an exchange situation to inform customers and persuade them to purchase products.

Personality All the internal traits and behaviours that make a person unique.

Persuasion The act of prevailing upon someone by argument to facilitate an exchange.

PEST analysis/PESTLE analysis PEST is a popular name for an evaluation of the marketing environment, looking at political, including legal and regulatory issues, economic, social and technological developments, and assessing the implications of such issues. Another term used by marketers is PESTLE: political, economic, societal, technological, legal and environmental forces.

Phase out An approach that lets the product decline without a change in marketing strategy.

Philanthropic responsibilities Not required of a company, but they promote human welfare or goodwill.

Physical distribution A set of activities consisting of order processing, materials handling, warehousing, inventory management and transportation used in the movement of products from producers to consumers or end-users.

Pioneer advertising The type of advertising to create category need that informs people about a product: what it is, what it does, how it can be used and where it can be purchased.

Place/distribution variable The aspect of the marketing mix that deals with making products available, perhaps through multiple channels, in the quantities desired, to as many customers as possible, while keeping the total inventory, transport and storage costs as low as possible.

Point-of-sale (POS) materials Enhancements designed to increase sales and introduce products, such as outside signs, window displays, counter pieces, display racks and self-service cartons.

Pop-up ads Pop-ups are online advertisements which pop-up in new browser windows, designed to attract web traffic or capture contact details. Pop-under advertisements open under the active window unseen by a user until the covering window is closed.

Population All elements, units or individuals that are of interest to researchers for a specific study.

Positioning The process of creating an image for a product in the minds of target customers.

Positioning statement A plausible, memorable, image-enhancing written summation of a product's or brand's desired stature.

Post-campaign test or post-test The evaluation of advertising effectiveness after a campaign.

PR campaign A period of PR activity involving several events and techniques but with definite start and end dates.

PR event A public relations event concerned with a specific purpose such as an open day or VIP visit.

PR programme An ongoing, lengthy-duration, awareness-building or awareness-maintaining multi technique PR activity.

Pre-tests Evaluations performed before an advertising campaign that attempt to assess the effectiveness of one or more elements of the message.

Premium or push money Additional compensation/ remuneration provided to sales people in order to push a line of goods.

Premiums Items offered free or at minimum cost as a bonus for purchasing a product.

Press (news) release A publicity mechanism, usually consisting of a single page of typewritten copy.

Press conference A meeting called to announce a major news event.

Prestige-sensitive consumers Individuals drawn to products that signify prominence and status.

Price The value placed on what is exchanged.

Price competition A policy whereby a marketer emphasizes price as an issue, and matches or beats the prices of competitors.

Price discrimination A policy in which different prices are charged in order to give a particular group of buyers a competitive edge.

Price elasticity of demand A measure of the sensitivity of demand to changes in price.

Price variable The aspect of the marketing mix that relates to activities associated with establishing pricing policies and determining product prices.

Price-conscious consumers Those striving to pay low prices.

Price-off offers A method of encouraging customers to buy a product by offering a certain amount off the regular price shown on the label or package.

Pricing objectives Overall goals that describe what a company wants to achieve through its pricing efforts.

Pricing strategy An approach to influencing and determining pricing decisions.

Primary data Information gathered by observing phenomena or surveying respondents.

Prime pitch The area at the centre of the shopping zone with the main shops and the highest levels of pedestrian footfall.

Probability sampling Every element in the population has a known chance of being selected for study.

Problem children Products that have a small share of a growing market, generally requiring a large amount of cash to build share.

Problem definition The process of uncovering the nature and boundaries of a situation or question.

Process materials Materials used directly in the production of other products, but not readily identifiable.

Procompetitive legislation Laws enacted to preserve competition and to end various practices deemed unacceptable by society.

Producer markets Buyers of raw materials and semi-finished and finished items used to produce other products or in their own operations.

Product A good, service or idea.

Product adoption process A series of five stages in the acceptance of a product: awareness, interest, evaluation, trial and adoption.

Product adoption process The stages buyers go through in accepting a product: awareness, interest, evaluation, trial and adoption.

Product advertising The type of advertising that promotes goods and services.

Product deletion The process of eliminating a product that no longer satisfies a sufficient number of customers.

Product development The phase in which the organization determines if it is technically and financially feasible to produce a new product.

Product Everything, both favourable and unfavourable, tangible and intangible, received in an exchange of an idea, service or good.

Product item A specific version of a product that can be designated as a distinct offering among a business's products.

Product life cycle The four major stages through which products move: introduction, growth, maturity and decline.

Product line A group of closely-related product items that are considered a unit because of marketing, technical or end-use considerations.

Product line pricing Establishing and adjusting prices of multiple products within a product line.

Product manager The person responsible for a product, a product line or several distinct products that make up an interrelated group within a multi-product organization.

Product mix The composite group of products that a company makes available to customers.

Product modification The alteration of one or more characteristics of a company's product.

Product portfolio analysis A strategic planning tool that takes a product's market growth rate and its relative market share into consideration in determining a marketing strategy.

Product variable The aspect of the marketing mix that deals with researching consumers' product wants and designing a product with the desired characteristics.

Product-specific spending patterns The annual monetary amounts families spend for specific products within a general product class.

Production era The period of mass production following industrialization.

Professional pricing Pricing used by people who have great skill or experience in a particular field or activity.

Profiling The task of building up a fuller picture of the target segments.

Projective techniques Tests in which subjects are asked to perform specific tasks for particular reasons, while actually being evaluated for other purposes.

Promotion Communication with individuals, groups or organizations in order to facilitate exchanges by informing and persuading audiences to accept a company's products.

Promotion variable The aspect of the marketing mix that relates to marketing communications used to inform one or more groups of people about an organization and its products and to maintain an ongoing relationship.

Promotional mix The specific combination of ingredients an organization uses to promote a product, traditionally including four ingredients: advertising, personal selling, publicity and public relations and sales promotion.

Promotional pricing Pricing related to the short-term promotion of a particular product.

Prospecting Developing a list of potential customers.

Prosperity A period during which unemployment is low and total income is relatively high.

Proxemic communication A subtle form of communication used in face-to-face interactions when either person varies the physical distance that separates the two.

Psychological factors Factors that influence consumer behaviour, including perception, motives, learning, attitudes and personality.

Psychological pricing A pricing strategy designed to encourage purchases that are based on emotional rather than rational responses.

Public relations Managing and controlling the process of using publicity effectively. It is the planned and sustained effort to establish and maintain goodwill and understanding between an organization and its target publics.

Public sector markets Government and institutional not-for-profit customers and stakeholder groups.

Public warehouses Storage facilities available for a fee.

Publicity Non-personal communication in news-story form about an organization and/or its products that is transmitted through a mass medium at no charge.

Pull policy A promotional policy in which an organization promotes directly to consumers in order to develop a strong consumer demand for its products.

Purchase facilitation Circumstances that make it possible for the consumer to purchase the product: availability, location, price and familiarity of vendor.

Push policy A promotional policy in which the producer promotes the product only to the next institution down the marketing channel.

Quali-depth interviews 25- to 30-minute intercept interviews that incorporate some of the in-depth advantages of focus group interviews with the speed and flexibility of shopping mall/pavement intercept interviews.

Qualitative research Research that deals with information too difficult or expensive to quantify, such as subjective opinions and value judgements, typically unearthed during interviews or discussion groups.

Quality The core product's ability to achieve the basic functional requirements expected of it.

Quality modifications Changes that affect a product's dependability and durability.

Quantitative research Research aimed at producing data that can be statistically analyzed and the results of which can be expressed numerically.

Quantity discounts Reductions off the list price that reflect the economies of purchasing in large quantities.

Questionnaire Base document for research purposes, providing the questions and structure for an interview or self-completion, and providing space for respondents' answers.

Quota sampling A sampling method in which the final choice of respondents is left to the interviewers, who base their choices on two or three variables (such as age, sex and education).

Quotas Physical restrictions on the amount of goods that can be imported into a particular country or region.

Rack jobbers Speciality line wholesalers that own and maintain their own display racks in supermarkets and chemists.

Random factor analysis An attempt to attribute erratic sales variations to random, non-recurring events.

Random sampling A sampling method in which all the units in a population have an equal chance of appearing in the sample.

Ratchet effect The stepped impact of using sales promotion and advertising together.

Raw materials The basic materials that become part of physical products.

Reach The percentage of consumers in the advertising target actually exposed to a particular advertisement in a stated time period.

Realized strategy The strategy that actually takes place.

Receiver An individual, group or organization that decodes a coded message.

Receiving audience Two or more receivers who decode a message.

Recession A period during which unemployment rises and total buying power declines.

Reciprocity An arrangement unique to business-to-business marketing in which two organizations agree to buy from each other.

Recognition test A test in which an actual advertisement is shown to individual respondents, who are then asked whether they recognize it.

Recovery The stage of the business cycle in which the economy moves from depression or recession to prosperity.

Recruiting A process by which the sales manager develops a list of applicants for sales positions.

Reference group A group with which an individual identifies so much that he or she takes on many of the values, attitudes or behaviour of group members.

Refusal to deal Situation in which suppliers will not do business with wholesalers or dealers simply because these wholesalers or dealers have resisted policies that are anti-competitive or in restraint of trade.

Regional issues Versions of a magazine or newspaper that differ across geographic regions in their advertising and editorial content.

Reinforcement advertising The type of advertising that tries to assure current users that they have made the right choice and tells them how to get the most satisfaction from the product.

Relationship management The process of encouraging a match between the seller's competitive advantage and the buyer's requirements over an item's life cycle.

Relationship marketing Places emphasis on the interaction between buyers and sellers, and is concerned with winning and keeping customers by maintaining links between marketing, quality and customer service.

Relationship marketing era In which the focus is not only on expediting the single transaction but on developing ongoing relationships with customers to maintain lifetime share of wallet.

Relationships Regular, ongoing contacts between businesses and their customers.

Reliability The quality of producing almost identical results in successive repeated trials.

Reminder advertising The type of advertising that reminds customers of the uses, characteristics and benefits of an established brand.

Reorder point The inventory level that signals the need to order more inventory.

Reputable partnerships Reputable and ethical dealings between a recognized, welcome and acceptable recipient organization and a sponsoring organization.

Requisites for implementation Process, skill, leadership, empowerment, communication, timing, information, resource and participation decisions.

Research design An overall plan for obtaining the information needed to address a research problem or issue.

Research objective The desired outcome from the marketing research project being undertaken.

Reseller markets Intermediaries, such as wholesalers and retailers, who buy finished goods and resell them to make a profit.

Restricted sales territories System by which a manufacturer tries to prohibit intermediaries from selling its products outside designated sales territories.

Retail parks Groupings of freestanding superstores, forming a retail village.

Retailers Intermediaries that purchase products and resell them to final consumers.

Retailing All transactions in which the buyer intends to consume the product through personal, family or household use.

Reward apps Provide cash-back rewards or accumulated pay-back for future purchases.

Role A set of actions and activities that a person in a particular position is supposed to perform, based on the expectations of both the individual and surrounding people.

Routine response behaviour Behaviour that occurs when buying frequently purchased, low-cost, low-risk items that need little search and decision effort.

Run out A policy that exploits any strengths left in the product.

Safety stock Inventory needed to prevent stock-outs.

Sales analysis The use of sales figures to evaluate a business's current performance.

Sales branches Manufacturer-owned middlemen selling products and providing support services to the manufacturer's sales force, especially in locations where large customers are concentrated and demand is high.

Sales competition A way to motivate distributors, retailers and sales personnel by recognizing and rewarding outstanding achievements.

Sales era The period from the mid-1920s to the early 1950s when competitive forces and the desire for high sales volume led a company to emphasize selling and the sales person in its business strategy.

Sales forecast The amount of a product that the company actually expects to sell during a specific period of time at a specific level of marketing activity.

Sales measurements Data regarding sales transactions that are used to analyze performance, usually in terms of cash volume or market share.

Sales offices Manufacturer-owned operations that provide support services normally associated with agents.

Sales per square metre A financial measure retailers might use to assess marketing performance.

Sales potential The maximum percentage of market potential that an individual company can obtain for a specific product or service.

Sales promotion An activity or material that acts as a direct inducement and offers added value to or incentive to buy the product.

Salesforce forecasting survey A method of asking members of a company's salesforce to estimate the anticipated sales in their territories for a specified period of time.

Salience The level of importance a buyer assigns to each criterion for comparing products.

Sample A limited number of units chosen to represent the characteristics of a total population.

Sampling The selection of representative units from a total population.

Scientific decision-making An orderly and logical approach to gathering information.

Screening ideas The process by which a company assesses whether product ideas match its organizational objectives and resources.

Search engine optimization (SEO) The management of search engine behaviour so as to increase a brand's rankings in search engine organic result listings on search engine results pages (SERPS) for particular key-words and phrases.

Search qualities Tangible attributes of a service that can be viewed prior to purchase.

Seasonal analysis The study of daily, weekly or monthly sales figures to evaluate the degree to which seasonal factors influence the company's sales.

Seasonal discount A price reduction given to buyers who purchase goods or services out of season.

Secondary data Information compiled inside or outside the organization for some purpose other than the current investigation.

Secondary use package A package that can be reused for purposes other than its initial use.

Security The measure of the physical condition of goods upon delivery.

Segmentation targeting The decision about which market segment(s) an organization decides to prioritize for its sales and marketing efforts.

Segmentation variables or bases The dimensions or characteristics of individuals, groups or businesses that are used for dividing a total market into segments.

Selective distortion The changing or twisting of currently received information.

Selective distribution The use of only some available outlets in an area to distribute a product.

Selective exposure The selection of inputs that people expose to their awareness.

Selective retention The process of remembering information inputs that support personal feelings and beliefs, and of forgetting those that do not.

Self-concept A person's perception of him or herself; self-image.

Selling agents Agents who market either all of a specified product line or a manufacturer's entire output.

Service An intangible product involving a deed, a performance or an effort that cannot physically be possessed.

Service expectations A factor used in judging service quality involving impressions from past experiences, word-of-mouth communication and the company's advertising.

Service product quality The consumer's perception of the quality of service he or she receives.

Service provider A person who offers a service, such as a bank clerk or hairdresser.

Service quality Customers' perception of how well a service meets or exceeds their expectations.

Service quality factors Factors that increase the likelihood of providing high-quality service: understanding customer expectations, service quality specifications, employee performance, managing service expectations.

Service The application of human and mechanical efforts to people or objects in order to provide intangible benefits to customers.

Shopping mall/ pavement intercept interviews Personal interviewing of a percentage of individuals who pass by certain 'intercept' points in a shopping centre or on a pavement.

Shopping products Items chosen more carefully than convenience products; consumers will expend effort in planning and purchasing these items.

Short-range plans Plans that cover a period of up to a year.

Single variable segmentation Segmentation achieved by using only one variable, the simplest type of segmentation to perform.

Single-source data Information provided by a single marketing research company.

Situational factors External circumstances or conditions that exist when a consumer is making a purchase decision.

Social class An open group of individuals who have similar social rank.

Social factors The forces that other people exert on buying behaviour.

Social marketing Uses tools and techniques from commercial marketing to encourage positive behavioural changes, such as quitting smoking, reducing alcohol consumption, minimizing anti-social behaviours or reducing carbon footprint. The health and well-being of individuals, society and the planet are at the core of social marketing.

Social media Social media incorporate the online technology and methods through which people can share content, personal opinions, different perspectives and insights, using text, images, audio and video, via social networks, video and photo sharing, microblogs, wikis and news aggregators.

Social media marketing The process of gaining website traffic or social mentions through social media sites, by creating content attracting attention of readers who will share these through their social networks.

Social responsibility An organization's obligation to maximize its positive impact and minimize its negative impact on society.

Societal forces Individuals and groups, and the issues engaging them, that pressure marketers to provide high living standards and enjoyable lifestyles through socially responsible decisions and activities.

Sole sourcing A buying process that involves the selection of only one supplier.

Sorting activities Functions that let channel members divide roles and separate tasks.

Sorting out Separating products into uniform, homogeneous groups.

Source A person, group or organization that has an intended meaning it attempts to share with an audience.

Speciality line wholesalers Middlemen who carry the narrowest range of products, usually a single product line or a few items within a product line.

Speciality products Items that possess one or more unique characteristics; consumers of speciality products plan their purchases and will expend considerable effort to obtain them.

Speciality shops Stores that offer self-service but a greater level of assistance from store personnel than department stores, and carry a narrow product mix with deep product lines.

Sponsorship The financial or material support of an event, activity, person, organization or product by an unrelated organization or donor.

Stakeholders Constituents who have a 'stake', or claim, in some aspect of a company's products, operations, markets, industry and outcomes.

Standard Industrial Classification (SIC) system A system that provides information on different industries and products, and classifies economic characteristics of industrial, commercial, financial and service organizations.

Stars Products with a dominant share of the market and good prospects for growth.

Statistical interpretation An analysis of data that focuses on what is typical or what deviates from the average.

Stock-outs Shortages of products resulting from a lack of products carried in inventory.

Storyboard A series of miniature television screens or cartoons used to show the sequence of major scenes in an advertisement.

Straight commission compensation/remuneration plan A plan, according to which, sales people are paid solely on the basis of their sales for a given time period.

Straight re-buy purchase A routine re-purchase of the same products under approximately the same terms of sale.

Straight salary compensation/remuneration plan A plan according to which sales people are paid a specified amount per time period.

Strategic alliances Partnerships formed to create a competitive advantage on a worldwide basis.

Strategic business unit (SBU) A division, product line or other profit centre within a parent company.

Strategic channel alliance Arrangement for distributing the products of one organization through the marketing channels of another.

Strategic market plan An outline of the methods and resources required to achieve an organization's goals within a specific target market.

Strategic objectives Includes intense growth, diversified growth or integrated growth.

Strategic philanthropy The synergistic use of organizational core competencies and resources to address key stakeholders' interests, and achieve both organizational and social benefits.

Strategic window A temporary period of optimum fit between the key requirements of a market and the particular capabilities of a company competing in that market.

Strategic windows Major developments or opportunities triggered by changes in the marketing environment.

Strategy The direction and scope of an organization over the longer-term, which achieves advantage for the organization through its configuration of resources within a challenging environment, to meet the needs of markets and to fulfil stakeholder expectations.

Stratified sampling A sampling method in which the population of interest is divided according to a common characteristic or attribute; a probability sampling is then conducted within each group.

Style modifications Changes that alter a product's sensory appeal taste, texture, sound, smell or visual characteristics.

Sub-cultures Sub-divisions of culture according to geographic regions or human characteristics, such as age or ethnic background.

Suburban centres Shopping centres created at major road junctions that cater for local shopping needs.

Successful brands Brands for which a company must prioritize quality, offer superior service, get there first, differentiate brands, develop a unique positioning concept, have a strong communications programme and be consistent and reliable.

Supermarkets and grocery superstores Large, self-service stores that carry a complete line of food products as well as other convenience items.

Supplier analysis A formal and systematic evaluation of current and potential suppliers.

Supply chain management The orchestration of the channel of distribution from sourcing supplies, manufacture to delivery to the customer.

Survey methods Interviews by mail, telephone, web and personal interviews.

Surveys A method of questioning customers, sales personnel or experts regarding their expectations about future purchases.

Sustainability The potential for the long-term well-being of the natural environment, including all biological entities, as well as the interaction among nature and individuals, organizations and business strategies.

SWOT analysis The examination of an organization's strengths and weaknesses, opportunities and threats, usually depicted in a four-cell chart.

Syndicated data services Organizations that collect and collate general information and sell it to clients.

Tactile communication Interpersonal communication through touching, including shaking hands.

Target market A group of people or organizations for whom a company creates and maintains a marketing mix that specifically fits the needs and preferences of that group.

Target market strategy The choice for which market segment(s) an organization decides to develop marketing programmes.

Target public A collective of individuals who have an interest in or concern about an organization, a product or a social cause.

Target publics An organization's target audiences: customers, employees, the media, shareholders, trade bodies, suppliers, government officials and society in general.

Tariffs Taxes that affect the movement of goods across economic or political boundaries, and that can also affect imports, exports or goods in transit.

Technology The application of knowledge and tools to solve problems and perform tasks more efficiently.

Technology assessment A procedure by which managers try to foresee the effects of new products and processes on their company's operation, on other commercial organizations and on society in general.

Telemarketing The direct selling of goods and services by telephone, based on either a cold canvass of the telephone directory or a pre-screened list of prospective clients.

Telephone surveys Surveys in which respondents' answers to a questionnaire are recorded by interviewers on the phone.

Test marketing The limited introduction of a product in geographic areas or a channel chosen to represent the intended market.

The 'Internet of Things' The network of physical objects or 'things' embedded with electronics, software, sensors and connectivity to enable greater value and service by exchanging data with the manufacturer, operator and/or other connected devices.

Third party endorsement A recommendation from an opinion leader or respected personality used to increase the credibility of publicity and public relations.

Third sector Includes charities, the voluntary sector, not-for-profit organizations and NGOs.

Time series analysis A forecasting technique that uses a company's historical sales data to discover a pattern or patterns in the company's sales over time.

Total cost The sum of average fixed costs and average variable costs multiplied by the quantity produced.

Total cost analysis Weighs inventory levels against warehousing expenses; and materials handling costs against various modes of transport; and all distribution costs against customer service standards.

Total quality management (TQM) Coordinated efforts directed at improving all aspects of a business from product and service quality to customer and employee satisfaction.

Traceability The relative ease with which a shipment can be located and transferred.

Traceable common costs Costs that can be allocated indirectly, using one or several criteria, to the functions they support.

Trade markets Relatively permanent facilities that businesses can rent to exhibit products year round.

Trade name The full and legal name of an organization.

Trade or functional discount A reduction off the list price given by a producer to an intermediary for performing certain functions.

Trade sales promotion methods Techniques that encourage wholesalers, retailers or dealers to carry and market a producer's products.

Trade shows Industry exhibitions that offer both selling and non-selling benefits.

Trademark Legal designation indicating that the owner has exclusive use of a brand.

Trading company A company that provides a link between buyers and sellers in different countries.

Trading stamps Stamps, dispensed in proportion to the amount of a consumer's purchase, that can be accumulated and redeemed for goods.

Transfer pricing The type of pricing used when one unit in a company sells a product to another unit within the same company.

Transit time The total time a carrier has possession of goods.

Transport modes Methods of moving goods; these include railways, motor vehicles, inland waterways, airways and pipelines.

Transportation The process of moving a product from where it is made to where it is purchased and used.

Trend analysis Analysis that focuses on aggregate sales data over a period of many years to determine whether annual sales are generally rising, falling or constant.

Trial stage The stage of the product adoption process when individuals use or experience the product for the first time.

Truck wholesalers Limited service wholesalers that transport products direct to customers for inspection and selection.

Tying contract Arrangement whereby a supplier (usually a manufacturer or franchiser) furnishes a product to a channel member with the stipulation that the channel member must purchase other products as well.

Unaided or spontaneous recall test A test in which subjects are asked to identify advertisements that they have seen recently but are given no clues to help them remember.

Undifferentiated (or total market) approach An approach which assumes that all customers have similar needs and wants, and can be served with a single marketing mix.

Undifferentiated targeting strategy When a company targets an entire market for a product with a single marketing mix.

Uniform geographic pricing Pricing in which the same price is charged to all customers regardless of geographic location.

Unit loading Grouping one or more boxes on a pallet or skid, permitting movement of efficient loads by mechanical means.

Universal product code (UPC) or barcode A series of thick and thin lines that identifies the product, and provides inventory and pricing information readable by an electronic scanner.

Unsought products Items that are purchased when a sudden problem arises or when aggressive selling is used to obtain a sale that would not otherwise take place.

Usage rate The rate at which a product's inventory is used or sold during a specific time period.

Validity A condition that exists when an instrument measures what it is supposed to measure.

Value analysis An evaluation of each component of a potential purchase.

Value share The proportion of total market monetary sales attracted by an individual brand or product within a particular market.

Value-based marketing The inclusion of the value of a marketing strategy and marketing activity in an organization's financial analysis of shareholder value.

Value-conscious consumers Those concerned about price and quality of a product.

Variability The amount of diversity allowed in each step of service provision.

Variable costs Those costs that vary directly with changes in the number of units produced or sold.

Variety stores Slightly smaller and more specialized stores than department stores, offering a reduced range of merchandise.

Venture or project team The group that creates entirely new products, perhaps aimed at new markets, and is responsible for all aspects of the products' development.

Vertical channel integration The combination of two or more stages of the channel under one management.

Vertical marketing system (VMS) Marketing channel in which a single channel member coordinates or manages channel activities to achieve efficient, low-cost distribution aimed at satisfying target market customers.

Virtual corporation A pop-up global strategic partnership to exploit specific opportunities.

Warehouse clubs Large-scale, members-only selling operations combining cash-and-carry wholesaling with discount retailing.

Warehousing The design and operation of facilities for storing and moving goods.

Wealth The accumulation of past income, natural resources and financial resources.

Website A coherent document readable by a web browser, containing simple text or complex hypermedia presentations.

Wholesaler An individual or business engaged in facilitating and expediting exchanges that are primarily wholesale transactions.

Wholesalers Intermediaries who purchase products for resale to retailers, other wholesalers and producers, governments and institutions.

Wholesaling Intermediaries' activity in the marketing channel between producers and business customers to facilitate the exchange – buying and selling of goods.

Width (of product mix) The number of product lines a company offers.

Willingness to spend A disposition towards using buying power, influenced by the ability to buy, expected satisfaction from a product and numerous psychological and social forces.

World Trade Organization (WTO) An entity that promotes and facilitates free trade between member states.

Zone prices Regional prices that take advantage of a uniform pricing system.

Index